INSIDE THE FED

BOXES

The

ECONOMICS

of

MONEY,

BANKING,

and

FINANCIAL

MARKETS

THE ADDISON-WESLEY SERIES IN ECONOMICS

The
ECONOMICS
of
MONEY,
BANKING,
and
FINANCIAL
MARKETS

Fifth Edition

Frederic S. Mishkin
Columbia University

 **ADDISON-WESLEY**

An Imprint of Addison Wesley Longman, Inc.

Reading, Massachusetts • Menlo Park, California • New York • Harlow, England
Don Mills, Ontario • Sydney • Mexico City • Madrid • Amsterdam

Senior Editor: Denise Clinton

Senior Development Manager: Sylvia Mallory

Development Editor: Jane Tufts

Supplements Editor: Joan Twining

Production Supervisors: Loren Hilgenhurst Stevens,
    Mary Sanger

Art Editor: Dale Horn

Illustrator: Interactive Composition Corporation;
    Typo-Graphics, Inc.

Text and Cover Design: Barbara Atkinson

Prepress Services Manager: Sarah McCracken

Manufacturing Supervisor: Hugh Crawford

Marketing Manager: Quinn Perkson

Cover images: PhotoDisc, Inc. © 1997 and
    © Jeffrey Sylvester/FPG International Corp.

Library of Congress Cataloguing-in-Publication Data

Mishkin, Frederic S.
    The economics of money, banking, and financial markets / Frederic
S. Mishkin.—5th ed.
        p.   cm.
    Includes bibliographical references and index.
    ISBN 0-321-01440-5
    1. Finance.   2. Money.   3. Banks and banking.   I. Title.
HG173.M632   1997
332—dc21   97-19567
                                                                                  CIP

1 2 3 4 5 6 7 8 9 10—RNT—0100999897

TO SALLY

CONTENTS IN BRIEF

CONTENTS

PART III Financial Institutions 193

PART IV Central Banking and the Conduct of Monetary Policy 387

PREFACE

This edition of *The Economics of Money, Banking, and Financial Markets* is the most significant revision of the textbook to date because it has been greatly affected by my time spent in the Federal Reserve System. I have been surprised by the extent to which my understanding of four key aspects of the money and banking field has deepened. I had expected to gain a better understanding of the monetary policy process and the operation of the Federal Reserve. But I have also learned much about two other key areas: the nature of the regulation and supervision of the financial system, including the challenges posed by derivatives; and the growing impact of international considerations on our financial system.

This edition therefore has many new insights on the monetary policy process, the regulation and supervision of the financial system, and the internationalization of financial markets. However, it retains the basic hallmarks that have made it the best-selling textbook on money and banking in the past four editions, including:

- A unifying, analytic framework that uses a few basic economic principles to organize students' thinking about the structure of financial markets, the foreign exchange markets, financial institution management, and the role of monetary policy in the economy
- A careful, step-by-step development of models, an approach found in the best principles of economics textbooks, that makes it easier for students to learn
- An applications-oriented perspective that increases students' interest because it lets them apply theory to real-world examples
- A thoroughly up-to-date treatment of the latest developments in monetary theory
- Integration of an international perspective
- A high degree of flexibility that allows professors to teach the course however they want

What's New in the Fifth Edition

In addition to the expected updating of all data, there is substantial new material in every part of the text.

THE MONETARY POLICY PROCESS AND THE FEDERAL RESERVE SYSTEM

Having participated in the monetary policy process at the Federal Reserve, I have learned a great deal about central banking and the subtleties of how monetary policy is conducted and how a central bank operates. My new knowledge is reflected in this edition in substantial new material and a rewrite of Part IV on central banking and the conduct of monetary policy (Chapters 15–20). For example, in recent years, the Federal Reserve and central banks of many other countries have deemphasized the use of monetary aggregates and now focus on setting interest-rate operating targets in the pursuit of price stability. In keeping with the deemphasis of monetary aggregates in policymaking circles, this edition substantially reduces coverage of the money supply while expanding discussion of monetary policy strategy. I also share my knowledge about how the Federal Reserve operates with new material on such topics as the political genius of setting up the Federal Reserve in such a way as to preserve its independence, the special role of the Federal Reserve Bank of New York and the research staff in the Federal Reserve System, the role of member banks, the conduct of a typical Federal Open Market Committee (FOMC) meeting, and the operation of the foreign exchange and open market desks at the Federal Reserve Bank of New York. To highlight this new material, I have included some of it in a new set of special-interest boxes, titled "Inside the Fed," that provide insights on how the Federal Reserve System operates, although they are based on information that is entirely in the public domain.

MONETARY THEORY AND THE TRANSMISSION MECHANISMS OF MONETARY POLICY This text has always striven to provide the most up-to-date treatment of monetary theory of any textbook on the market. One of the most exciting contemporary areas of research in monetary economics is the transmission mechanisms of monetary policy. In pursuing the goal of keeping the textbook as up-to-date as possible, I have substantially rewritten the chapter on money and economic activity (now Chapter 25) and renamed it "Transmission Mechanisms of Monetary Policy: The Evidence." This chapter features extensive new material on the so-called credit view, which is currently receiving much research attention. In addition, Chapter 25 has an increased policy focus because it links the material on the monetary transmission mechanisms with resulting lessons for policymaking.

Another area of exciting new research has examined the validity of rational expectations and efficient markets. Recent work has uncovered fascinating anomalies that cast doubt on these theories. The chapter on the theory of rational expectations and efficient capital markets (now Chapter 27) has therefore been substantially rewritten to reflect this latest research and to give a more balanced view of these theories.

COMPLETE INTEGRATION OF AN INTERNATIONAL PERSPECTIVE In the course of my work at the Federal Reserve Bank of New York, I have been continually exposed to international issues, have written many research papers with an international orientation, and have traveled widely to foreign countries. Although users of the text in the United States and abroad were happy with the increased international focus of the last edition, my work experience and comments by users of the book have led me to take the next logical step in the internationalization of the text: I have completely integrated international material throughout the book, incorporating it into the body of the text rather than relegating such material to separate boxes as in the previous edition. Furthermore, I have altered the focus of some chapters to make them more internationally oriented. For example, the chapter on the structure of the Federal Reserve System is now more internationally focused as reflected in its new title, "Structure of Central Banks and the Federal Reserve System."

I have also included substantial additional international material in new sections on financial development and economic growth (Chapter 9), the Mexican foreign exchange and financial crisis of 1994 (Chapters 9 and 20), banking crises throughout the world (Chapter 10), the globalization of financial futures markets (Chapter 12), hedging foreign exchange rate risk (Chapter 12), separation of the banking and securities industries in other countries (Chapter 13), the decline of traditional banking throughout the world (Chapter 13), the structure and independence of foreign central banks (Chapter 15), and monetary and inflation targeting in other countries (Chapter 19). A global icon is used to designate text sections, applications, and boxes that have an international focus.

REGULATION AND SUPERVISION OF THE FINANCIAL SYSTEM My experience at the New York Fed has also exposed me to the dramatic changes that are occurring in the regulation and supervision of the financial system, particularly banks. In earlier editions, I stressed the role of capital requirements in banking regulation. With the dramatic collapse of banks such as Barings (whose capital was dissipated extremely rapidly), however, bank regulators have been seeking a new approach to bank supervision. This edition emphasizes the new trend in banking regulation and supervision in Part III, "Financial Institutions" (Chapters 9 to 14), which focuses much greater attention on risk management and disclosure requirements. New material on consumer protection legislation such as the Community Reinvestment Act (CRA) examines its effects on bank regulation and supervision.

DERIVATIVES Media reports of late have featured more and more about derivatives, especially because their use has led to major losses at both corporations and banks, such as Sumitomo and Barings. Because of their major role in the sometimes swift dissipation of capital in these and other cases, many instructors have asked for a more extensive treatment of this subject. In this edition, I have therefore added an entire new chapter (Chapter 14) on financial derivatives—forwards, futures, swaps, and options. In keeping with the basic hallmarks of the book, the treatment differs from other money and banking textbooks in that it goes well beyond the descriptive to develop analytic concepts for understanding how financial derivatives can be used by financial institutions to hedge risks. Also in keeping with the text's emphasis on flexibility, the material on derivatives can be skipped with little loss of continuity.

AN INCREASED APPLICATIONS ORIENTATION In teaching money, banking, and financial markets over the past 20 years, I have found that students get more out of an applications-oriented course. Applications help convince students that the material in the course is relevant to real-world issues, and engage them in active learning, which increases the probability that they will retain knowledge after the final exam. This is why my previous edition had over 25 special applications sections, including "Reading the *Wall Street Journal*" and "Following the Financial News" boxes, and over 400 end-of-chapter problems (half of them answered at the back of the book), including ones designed to demonstrate the use of economic analysis to predict the future.

More convinced than ever that an applications-oriented textbook is a most effective teaching tool, I have thoroughly integrated applications into the body of the text and increased their number to more than 50. Entirely new applications consider whether the low savings rate in the United States has contributed to higher interest rates (Chapter 6), the impact on interest rates of Treasury securities if they were no longer default-free (Chapter 7), financial development and economic growth (Chapter 9), financial crises in developing countries (Chapter 9), hedging with interest-rate forward contracts, financial futures, futures options, and interest-rate swaps (Chapter 14), hedging foreign exchange risk (Chapter 14), the dangers of a meltdown from financial derivatives (Chapter 14), and the Mexican peso crisis of 1994 (Chapter 20).

STREAMLINED ORGANIZATION Helpful comments from reviewers have also encouraged me to reorganize the book to improve the flow and streamline the organization. I have eliminated three chapters. The financial innovation chapter in the previous edition has been deleted, and its material has been integrated into other chapters. Because of the decreased emphasis on monetary aggregates in the monetary policy process in the United States and other countries, I have reduced the number of chapters on the money supply process from three to two. Also, I have deleted the chapter on understanding movements in the monetary base, while moving the most important material from this chapter to Chapters 16 and 26.

I also changed the chapter order to improve the flow in Part IV, on central banking and the conduct of monetary policy. The first chapter focuses on the structure of central banks and the Federal Reserve System; the next two chapters feature the money supply process; the next two examine the tools, goals, and targets of monetary policy; and the final one considers the international financial system and monetary policy.

OTHER CHANGES AND NEW MATERIAL

- Chapter 3 contains substantial new material on electronic money.
- Chapter 10 offers extensive new coverage of electronic banking.
- Chapter 11, on the banking industry, has been substantially rewritten to include new treatments of banking consolidation and the Riegle-Neal Interstate Banking and Branching Efficiency Act of 1994.
- Chapter 12 on banking regulation has a somewhat different focus from the previous edition and has thus been renamed "Economic Analysis of Banking Regulation."
- Chapter 21, on the demand for money, has been modified to include material on empirical evidence.
- Boxes, discussions of empirical evidence, and all the figures and data have been thoroughly updated—through the end of 1996 wherever possible.

Flexibility

In using previous editions, adopters, reviewers, and survey respondents have continually praised this text's flexibility. There are as many ways to teach money, banking, and financial markets as there are instructors. To satisfy the diverse needs of instructors, the text achieves flexibility as follows:

- Core chapters provide the basic analysis used throughout the book, and other chapters or sections of chapters can be used or omitted according to instructor preferences. For example, Chapter 2 introduces the financial system and basic concepts such as transaction costs, adverse selection, and moral hazard. After covering Chapter 2, the instructor may decide to give more detailed coverage of financial structure by assigning Chapter 9, or may choose to skip Chapter 9 and take any of a number of different paths through the book.

- The text also allows instructors to cover the most important issues in monetary theory and policy without having to use the *ISLM* model in Chapters 22 and 23, while more complete treatments of monetary theory make use of the *ISLM* chapters.
- The internationalization of the text through marked international sections within chapters as well as through complete separate chapters on the foreign exchange market and the international monetary system is comprehensive yet flexible. Although many instructors will teach all the international material, others will not. Instructors who want less emphasis on international topics can easily skip Chapter 8, on the foreign exchange market, and Chapter 20, on the international financial system and monetary policy. The international sections within chapters are self-contained and can be omitted with little loss of continuity. Instructors who would like to teach material on the foreign exchange market later in the course can teach Chapter 8 just before Chapter 20.

To illustrate how this book can be used for courses with varying emphases, several course outlines are suggested for a semester teaching schedule. More detailed information about how the text can be used flexibly in your course is available in the Instructor's Manual.

General Money and Banking Course: Chapters 1–6, 10–12, 15, 18, 19, 24, 26, with a choice of 6 of the remaining 14 chapters.

General Money and Banking Course with an International Emphasis: Chapters 1–6, 8, 10–12, 15, 18–20, 24, with a choice of 4 of the remaining 12 chapters.

Financial Markets and Institutions Course: Chapters 1–7, 9–14, 27, with a choice of 6 of the remaining 14 chapters.

Monetary Theory and Policy Course: Chapters 1–6, 15–19, 21, 24–26, with a choice of 5 of the remaining 13 chapters.

An Easier Way to Teach Money, Banking, and Financial Markets

The demands for good teaching have increased dramatically in recent years. To meet these demands, for the previous edition and this edition alike, I have provided the instructor with new supplementary materials, unavailable with any competing text, that should make teaching this course substantially easier.

This edition of the book comes not only with full-color PowerPoint electronic transparencies of all the figures and tables in the book but also with full-color overhead transparencies. Furthermore, the Instructor's Manual has been thoroughly reorganized for greater ease of use and contains transparency masters of the lecture notes, perforated so that they can easily be detached for use in class.

The lecture notes are comprehensive and outline all the major points covered in the text. They have been class-tested successfully—they are in fact the notes that I use in class—and they should help other instructors prepare their lectures as they have aided me. Some instructors might use these lecture notes as their own class notes and prefer to teach with a blackboard. But for those who prefer to teach with visual aids, the PowerPoint presentation and the full-color transparencies of the figures and tables afford the flexibility to take this approach.

I am also aware that many instructors want to make variations in their lectures that depart somewhat from material covered in the text. For their convenience, the entire set of lecture notes has been put on diskette using Word and the WordPerfect word processing languages, and the diskette is included with the Instructor's Manual. Instructors can modify the lecture notes as they see fit for their own use, for class handouts, or for transparencies to be used with an overhead projector.

The diskette also offers the entire contents of the Instructor's Manual, which includes chapter outlines, overviews, and teaching tips; answers to the end-of-chapter problems that are not included in the text; and discussion questions. Using this handy feature, instructors can prepare student handouts such as solutions to problem sets made up of end-of-chapter problems, the outline of the lecture that day, or essay discussion questions for homework. I have used handouts of this type in my teaching and have found them to be very effective. Instructors have my permission and are encouraged to photocopy all of the materials on the diskette and use them as they see fit in class.

Supplements Program to Accompany the Fifth Edition

The Economics of Money, Banking, and Financial Markets, Fifth Edition, includes the most comprehensive program of supplements of any money, banking, and financial markets textbook. These items are available to qualified domestic adopters but in some cases may not be available to international adopters.

FOR THE PROFESSOR

1. **Instructor's Resource Manual,** prepared by me and offering conventional elements such as sample course outlines, chapter outlines, and answers to questions and problems in the text. In addition, it has two unique features:
   - **Lecture Notes,** numbering over 300 in transparency master format, that comprehensively outline the major points covered in the text.
   - **Diskette with Entire Contents of the Instructor's Manual** (including the Lecture Notes), which contains WordPerfect and Word files that can be modified to fit any particular course.
2. **Full-Color Transparencies,** numbering over 150, for *all* of the figures, tables, and summary tables.
3. **PowerPoint Electronic Transparencies,** numbering over 300, which include all the book's figures and tables in full color, plus the lecture notes.
4. **Printed Test Bank,** which comprises over 2,500 multiple-choice test items, many with graphs.

5. **Computerized Test Bank,** allowing the instructor to produce exams efficiently. This product consists of the 2,500 multiple-choice items in the print test bank and offers editing capabilities. Free to adopters, this supplement is available in Macintosh and Windows versions.

6. **MacNeil-Lehrer/Addison-Wesley Video Library,** in which noted reporter Paul Solman presents news stories relevant to the money and banking course. Free to adopters, these videos can be obtained through the local Addison-Wesley sales representative.

7. **Mishkin Website** located at: (http://hepg.awl.com/mishkin/money &banking/) which features audio clips, teaching tips, links to relevant data sources and Federal Reserve websites, and other resources for the instructor.

FOR THE STUDENT

1. **Study Guide and Workbook,** prepared by John McArthur of Wofford College and me, which includes chapter synopses and completions, exercises, self-tests, and answers to the exercises and self-tests.

2. **Readings in Money, Banking, and Financial Markets,** edited by James W. Eaton of Bridgewater College and me, updated annually, with over half the articles new each year to enable instructors to keep the content of their course current throughout the life of an edition of the text. The reader is sold with the text at a very affordable price.

3. **Money Game Computer Software,** prepared for IBM-compatible PCs by Richard Alston and Wan Fu Chi of Weber State College, offering students hands-on experience with the analytic concepts in the text.

Pedagogical Aids

In teaching theory or its applications, a textbook must be a solid motivational tool. To this end, I have incorporated a wide variety of pedagogical features to make the material easy to learn.

1. **Previews** at the beginning of each chapter tell students where the chapter is heading, why specific topics are important, and how they relate to other topics in the book.

2. **Applications,** numbering over 50, demonstrate how the analysis in the book can be used to explain many important real-world situations. A special set of applications, called "Reading the *Wall Street Journal*," shows students how to read daily columns in this leading financial newspaper.

3. **"Following the Financial News" boxes** introduce students to relevant news articles and data that are reported daily in the press, and explain how to read them.

4. **"Inside the Fed" boxes** give students a feel for what is important in the operation and structure of the Federal Reserve System.

5. **Special-interest boxes** highlight dramatic historical episodes, interesting ideas, and intriguing facts related to the subject matter.

6. **Study Guides** are highlighted statements scattered throughout the text that provide hints on how to think about or approach a topic as students work their way through it.

7. **Summary tables** provide a useful study aid in reviewing material.

8. **Key statements** are important points that are also set in italic type so that students can easily find them for later reference.

9. **Graphs** with captions, numbering over 150, help students clearly understand the interrelationship of the variables plotted and the principles of analysis.

10. **Summary** at the end of each chapter lists the main points.

11. **Key terms** are important words or phrases, boldfaced when they are defined for the first time and listed at the end of the chapter.

12. **End-of-chapter questions and problems**, numbering over 400, help students learn the subject matter by applying economic concepts, including a special class of problems that students find particularly relevant, under the heading "Using Economic Analysis to Predict the Future."

13. **Glossary** at the back of the book provides the definitions for all the key terms.

14. **Answers section** at the back of the book, provides solutions to half of the questions and problems (marked by *).

Acknowledgments

As always in so large a project, there are many people to thank. My special gratitude goes to Bruce Kaplan, former economics editor at HarperCollins, who has been particularly valuable for both this and the two previous editions; Denise Clinton, economics editor at Addison Wesley Longman; and Jane Tufts, the best development editor in the business. I also have been assisted by comments from my colleagues at Columbia and from my students.

In addition, I have been guided by the thoughtful commentary of outside reviewers and correspondents. Their feedback has made this a better book. In particular, I thank the following:

Burton Abrams, University of Delaware
Francis W. Ahking, University of Connecticut
Stacie Beck, University of Delaware
Daniel Blake, California State University, Northridge
William Walter Brown, California State University, Northridge
Colleen M. Callahan, Lehigh University
Sergio Castello, University of Mobile
Donald H. Dutkowsky, Syracuse University
Richard Eichhorn, Colorado State University
L. S. Fan, Colorado State University
Stuart M. Glosser, University of Wisconsin, Whitewater
Fred C. Graham, American University
David Gulley, Bentley College
Daniel Haak, Stanford University
Larbi Hammami, McGill University

J. C. Hartline, Rutgers University

Dar-Yeh Hwang, National Taiwan University

Magda Kandil, University of Wisconsin, Milwaukee

Richard H. Keehn, University of Wisconsin, Parkside

Robert Leeson, University of Western Ontario

James McCown, Ohio State University

W. Douglas McMillin, Louisiana State University

William Merrill, Iowa State University

Stephen M. Miller, University of Connecticut

Thomas S. Mondschean, DePaul University

Clair Morris, U.S. Naval Academy

Chung Pham, University of New Mexico

Marvin M. Phaup, George Washington University

Ronald A. Ratti, University of Missouri, Columbia

Hans Rau, Ball State University

Larry Taylor, Lehigh University

Frederick D. Thum, University of Texas, Austin

Christopher J. Waller, Indiana University

Maurice Weinrobe, Clark University

Philip R. Wiest, George Mason University

Laura Wolff, Southern Illinois University, Edwardsville

Jeffrey Zimmerman, Methodist College

Finally, I want to thank my wife, Sally; my son, Matthew; and my daughter, Laura, who provide me with a warm and happy environment that enables me to do my work, and my father, Sydney, now deceased, who a long time ago put me on the path that led to this book.

Frederic S. Mishkin

About the Author

*F*rederic S. Mishkin is the A. Barton Hepburn Professor of Economics at the Graduate School of Business, Columbia University. He is also a research associate at the National Bureau of Economic Research. Since receiving his Ph.D. from the Massachusetts Institute of Technology in 1976, he has taught at the University of Chicago, Northwestern University, Princeton University, and Columbia. From 1994 until 1997 he was executive vice president and director of research at the Federal Reserve Bank of New York and was an associate economist to the Federal Open Market Committee of the Federal Reserve System.

Professor Mishkin's research focuses on monetary policy and its impact on financial markets and the aggregate economy. He is the author of *A Rational Expectations Approach to Macroeconometrics: Testing Policy Ineffectiveness and Efficient Markets Models* (Chicago: University of Chicago Press, 1983); *Money, Interest Rates, and Inflation* (London: Edward Elgar, 1993); and *Financial Markets and Institutions* (Reading, Mass.: Addison Wesley Longman, 1998). In addition, he has published nearly one hundred articles in such journals as the *American Economic Review,* the *Journal of Political Economy, Econometrica,* the *Quarterly Journal of Economics,* the *Journal of Finance,* and the *Journal of Monetary Economics.*

Professor Mishkin has served on the editorial board of the *American Economic Review,* has been an associate editor at the *Journal of Business and Economic Statistics,* and was the editor of the Federal Reserve Bank of New York's *Economic Policy Review.* He is currently an associate editor at the *Journal of Applied Econometrics,* the *Journal of International Money and Finance,* the *Journal of Money, Credit and Banking,* and the *Journal of Economic Perspectives.* He has been an academic consultant to the Board of Governors of the Federal Reserve System, on the Academic Advisory Panel of the Federal Reserve Bank of New York, and a visiting scholar at the Ministry of Finance in Japan and the Reserve Bank of Australia.

INTRODUCTION

Chapter 1

WHY STUDY MONEY, BANKING, AND FINANCIAL MARKETS?

PREVIEW   On the evening news you have just heard that the Federal Reserve is raising the federal funds rate by $\frac{1}{2}$ of a percentage point. What effect might this have on the interest rate of an automobile loan when you finance your purchase of a sleek new sports car? Does it mean that a house will be more or less affordable in the future? Will it make it easier or harder for you to get a job next year?

This book provides answers to these questions by examining how financial markets (such as those for bonds, stocks, and foreign exchange) and financial institutions (banks, insurance companies, mutual funds, and so on) work and by exploring the role of money in the economy. Financial markets and institutions not only affect your everyday life but also involve huge flows of funds (trillions of dollars) throughout our economy, which in turn affect business profits, the production of goods and services, and even the economic well-being of countries other than the United States. What happens to financial markets, financial institutions, and money is of great concern to our politicians and can even have a major impact on our elections. The study of money, banking, and financial markets will reward you with an understanding of many exciting issues. In this chapter we provide a road map of the book by outlining these exciting issues and exploring why they are worth studying.

WHY STUDY FINANCIAL MARKETS?

Part II of this book focuses on **financial markets,** markets in which funds are transferred from people who have an excess of available funds to people who have a shortage. Financial markets such as the bond and stock markets are important in channeling funds from people who do not have a productive use for them to those who do, a process that results in greater economic efficiency. Activities in financial markets also have direct effects on personal wealth, the behavior of businesses and consumers, and the overall performance of the economy.

The Bond Market and Interest Rates

A **security** (also called a *financial instrument*) is a claim on the issuer's future income or **assets** (any financial claim or piece of property that is subject to ownership). A **bond** is a debt security that promises to make payments periodically for a specified period of time.[1] The bond market is especially important to economic activity because it enables corporations or governments to borrow to finance their activities and because it is where interest rates are determined. An **interest rate** is the cost of borrowing or the price paid for the rental of funds (usually expressed as a percentage of the rental of $100 per year). There are many interest rates in the economy—mortgage interest rates, car loan rates, and interest rates on many different types of bonds.

Interest rates are important on a number of levels. On a personal level, high interest rates could deter you from buying a house or a car because the cost of financing it would be high. Conversely, high interest rates could encourage you to save because you can earn more interest income by putting aside some of your earnings as savings. On a more general level, interest rates have an impact on the overall health of the economy because they affect not only consumers' willingness to spend or save but also businesses' investment decisions. High interest rates, for example, may cause a corporation to postpone building a new plant that would ensure more jobs.

Because changes in interest rates have important effects on individuals, financial institutions, businesses, and the overall economy, it is important to explain fluctuations in interest rates, which have been substantial in the past 30 years. As a matter of fact, in no other 30-year period of United States history have interest-rate fluctuations been as great. For example, the interest rate on long-term U.S. Treasury bonds was about 5 percent in 1963, rose to close to 15 percent in 1981, and was below 6 percent for a short time in 1996. In the preceding 30-year period, from 1936 to 1966, the rate fluctuated between 2 and 5 percent.

Because different interest rates have a tendency to move in unison, economists frequently lump interest rates together and refer to "the" interest rate. As Figure 1 shows, however, interest rates on several types of bonds can differ substantially. The interest rate on three-month Treasury bills, for example, fluctuates more than the other interest rates and is lower, on average. The interest rate on Baa (medium-quality) corporate bonds is higher, on average, than the other interest rates, and the spread between it and the other rates became larger in the 1970s.

In Chapter 2 we study the role of bond markets in the economy, and in Chapters 4 through 7 we examine what an interest rate is, how the common movements in interest rates come about, and why the interest rates on different bonds vary.

The Stock Market

A **stock** is a security that is a claim on the earnings and assets of a corporation. Issuing stock and selling it to the public is a way for corporations to raise funds to finance their activities. The stock market, in which claims on the earnings of

---

[1] The definition of *bond* used throughout this book is the broad one in common use by academics, which covers short- as well as long-term debt instruments. However, some practitioners in financial markets use the word *bond* only to describe specific long-term debt instruments such as corporate bonds or U.S. Treasury bonds.

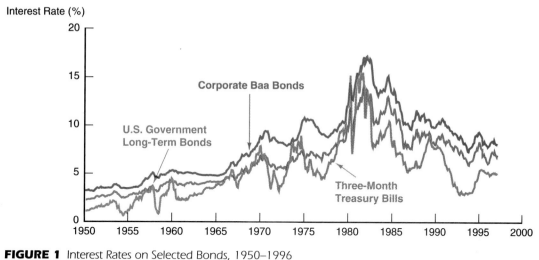

FIGURE 1 Interest Rates on Selected Bonds, 1950–1996

Sources: Federal Reserve *Bulletin*; Citibase databank.

corporations (shares of stock) are traded, is the most widely followed financial market in America (that's why it is often called simply "the market"). A big swing in the prices of shares in the stock market is always a big story on the evening news. People often express their opinion on where the market is heading and will frequently tell you about their latest "big killing" (although you seldom hear about their latest "big loss"!). The attention that the market receives can probably be best explained by one simple fact: It is a place where people can get rich quickly.

As Figure 2 indicates, stock prices have been extremely volatile. They climbed steadily in the 1950s, reached a peak in 1966, and then fluctuated up and down until 1973, when they fell sharply. Stock prices had recovered substantially by the early 1980s when a major stock market boom began, sending the Dow Jones Industrial Average (DJIA) to a peak of 2722 on August 25, 1987. After a 17 percent decline over the next month and a half, the stock market experienced the worst one-day drop in its entire history on "Black Monday," October 19, 1987, when the DJIA fell by more than 500 points, a 22 percent decline. The stock market then recovered, climbing to above the 7000 level in 1997. These considerable fluctuations in stock prices affect the size of people's wealth and as a result may affect their willingness to spend.

The stock market is also an important factor in business investment decisions because the price of shares affects the amount of funds that can be raised by selling newly issued stock to finance investment spending. A higher price for a firm's shares means that it can raise a larger amount of funds, which can be used to buy production facilities and equipment.

In Chapter 2 we examine the role that the stock market plays in the financial system, and we return to the issue of how stock prices behave and respond to information in the marketplace in Chapter 27.

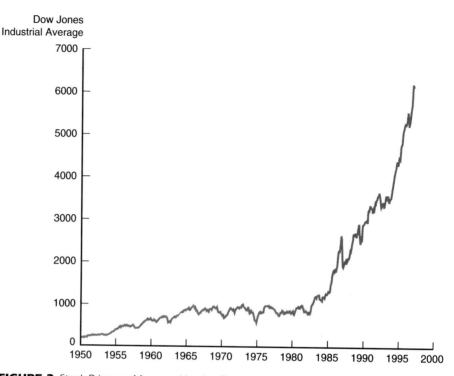

FIGURE 2 Stock Prices as Measured by the Dow Jones Industrial Average, 1950–1996

Source: Citibase databank.

The Foreign Exchange Market

For funds to be transferred from one country to another, they have to be converted from the currency in the country of origin (say, dollars) into the currency of the country they are going to (say, francs). The **foreign exchange market** is where this conversion takes place, and so it is instrumental in moving funds between countries. It is also important because it is where the **foreign exchange rate,** the price of one country's currency in terms of another's, is determined.

Figure 3 shows the exchange rate for the U.S. dollar from 1970 to 1996 (measured as the value of the American dollar in terms of a basket of foreign currencies). The fluctuations in prices in this market have also been substantial: The dollar weakened considerably from 1971 to 1973, rose slightly in value until 1976, and then reached a low point in the 1978–1980 period. From 1980 to early 1985, the dollar appreciated dramatically in value, but since then it has fallen substantially.

What have these fluctuations in the exchange rate meant to the American public and businesses? A change in the exchange rate has a direct effect on American consumers because it affects the cost of foreign goods. In 1985, when the British currency, the pound sterling, cost approximately $1.30, £100 of British goods (say, Shetland sweaters) would cost $130. When a weaker dollar raised the cost of a pound to $1.60 in 1997, the same £100 of Shetland sweaters cost $160. Thus a weaker dollar leads to more expensive foreign goods, makes vacationing

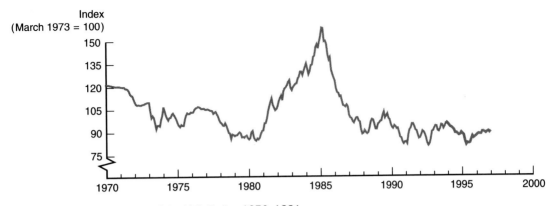

FIGURE 3 Exchange Rate of the U.S. Dollar, 1970–1996

Sources: Federal Reserve *Bulletin*; Citibase databank.

abroad more expensive, and raises the cost of indulging your yen for imported delicacies. When the value of the dollar drops, Americans will decrease their purchases of foreign goods and increase their consumption of domestic goods (such as travel in the United States or American-made sweaters).

Conversely, a strong dollar means that U.S. goods exported abroad will cost more in foreign countries, and hence foreigners will buy fewer of them. Exports of steel, for example, declined sharply when the dollar strengthened in the 1980–1985 period. A strong dollar benefited American consumers by making foreign goods cheaper but hurt American businesses and eliminated some jobs by cutting both domestic and foreign sales of their products. The decline in the value of the dollar since 1985 has had the opposite effect: It has made foreign goods more expensive but has made American businesses more competitive. Fluctuations in the foreign exchange markets have major consequences for the American economy.

In Chapter 8 we study how exchange rates are determined in the foreign exchange market in which dollars are bought and sold for foreign currencies.

WHY STUDY BANKING AND FINANCIAL INSTITUTIONS?

Part III of this book focuses on financial institutions and the business of banking. Banks and other financial institutions are what make financial markets work. Without them, financial markets would not be able to move funds from people who save to people who have productive investment opportunities. They thus also have important effects on the performance of the economy as a whole.

Structure of the Financial System

The financial system is complex and comprises many different types of financial institutions, including banks, insurance companies, mutual funds, finance companies, and investment banks, all of which are heavily regulated by the government. If you wanted to make a loan to IBM or General Motors, for example, you would not go directly to the president of the company and offer a loan. Instead, you would lend to such companies indirectly through **financial**

intermediaries, institutions that borrow funds from people who have saved and in turn make loans to others.

Why are financial intermediaries so crucial to well-functioning financial markets? Why do they give credit to one party but not to another? Why do they usually write complicated legal documents when they extend loans? Why are they the most heavily regulated businesses in the economy?

We answer these questions in Chapter 9 by developing a coherent framework for analyzing financial structure in the United States and in the rest of the world.

Banks and Other Financial Institutions

Banks are financial institutions that accept deposits and make loans. Included under the term *banks* are firms such as commercial banks, savings and loan associations, mutual savings banks, and credit unions. Banks are the financial intermediaries that the average person interacts with most frequently. A person who needs a loan to buy a house or a car usually obtains it from a local bank. Most Americans keep a large proportion of their financial wealth in banks in the form of checking accounts, savings accounts, or other types of bank deposits. Because banks are the largest financial intermediaries in our economy, they deserve the most careful study. However, banks are not the only important financial institutions. Indeed, in recent years, other financial institutions such as insurance companies, finance companies, pension funds, mutual funds, and investment banks have been growing at the expense of banks, and so we need to study them as well.

In Chapter 10 we examine how banks and other financial institutions manage their assets and liabilities to make profits. In Chapter 11 we extend the economic analysis in Chapter 9 to understand why bank regulation takes the form it does and what can go wrong in the regulatory process. In Chapters 12 and 13 we look at the banking industry and at nonbank financial institutions; we examine how the competitive environment has changed in these industries and learn why some financial institutions have been growing at the expense of others. Because the economic environment for banks and other financial institutions has become increasingly risky, these institutions must find ways to manage risk. How they manage risk with financial derivatives is the topic of Chapter 14.

Financial Innovation

In the good old days, when you took cash out of the bank or wanted to check your account balance, you got to say hello to the friendly teller. Nowadays you are more likely to interact with an automatic teller machine when withdrawing cash and can get your account balance from your home computer. To see why these options have been developed, we study why and how financial innovation takes place in Chapters 10, 11, and 14. We also study financial innovation because it shows us how creative thinking on the part of financial institutions can lead to higher profits. By seeing how and why financial institutions have been creative in the past, we obtain a better grasp of how they may be creative in the future. This knowledge provides us with useful clues about how the financial system may change over time and will help keep our knowledge about banks and other financial institutions from becoming obsolete.

WHY STUDY MONEY AND MONETARY POLICY?

Money, also referred to as the **money supply,** is defined as anything that is generally accepted in payment for goods or services or in the repayment of debts. Money is linked to changes in economic variables that affect all of us and are important to the health of the economy. The final two parts of the book examine the role of money in the economy.

Money and Business Cycles

In 1981–1982, total production of goods and services (called **aggregate output**) in the economy fell, the number of people out of work rose to more than 10 million (over 10 percent of the labor force), and more than 25,000 businesses failed. After 1982, the economy began to expand rapidly, and by 1989, the **unemployment rate** (the percentage of the available labor force unemployed) had declined from over 10 to 5 percent. In 1990, the eight-year expansion came to an end, and the economy began to decline again, with unemployment rising above the 7 percent level. The economy bottomed out in 1991, and the subsequent recovery has been a long one with unemployment rates falling well below 6 percent.

Why did the economy contract in 1981–1982, boom thereafter, and begin to contract again in 1990? Evidence suggests that money plays an important role in generating **business cycles,** the upward and downward movement of aggregate output produced in the economy. Business cycles affect all of us in immediate and important ways. When output is rising, for example, it is easier to find a good job; when output is falling, finding a good job might be difficult. Figure 4 shows

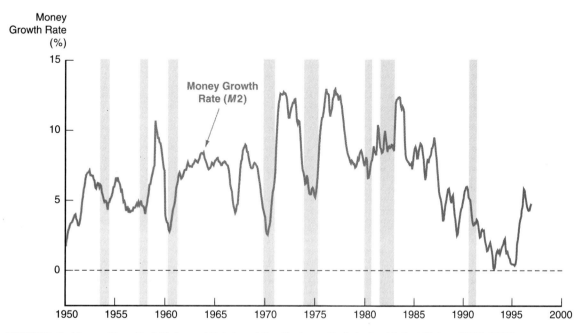

FIGURE 4 Money Growth (M2 Annual Rate) and the Business Cycle in the United States, 1950–1996

Note: Shaded areas represent recessions. *Sources:* Federal Reserve *Bulletin;* Citibase databank.

the movements of the rate of money growth over the 1950–1996 period, with the shaded areas representing **recessions,** periods when aggregate output is declining. What we see is that the rate of money growth has declined before every recession. Indeed, every recession in the twentieth century has been preceded by a decline in the rate of money growth, indicating that changes in money might also be a driving force behind business cycle fluctuations. However, not every decline in the rate of money growth is followed by a recession.

We explore how money might affect aggregate output in Chapters 21 through 28, where we study **monetary theory,** the theory that relates changes in the quantity of money to changes in aggregate economic activity and the price level.

Money and Inflation

Thirty years ago, the $7 movie you might have seen last week would have set you back only a dollar or two. In fact, for $7 you could probably have had dinner, seen the movie, and bought yourself a big bucket of hot buttered popcorn. As seen in Figure 5, which illustrates the movement of average prices in the U.S. economy from 1950 to 1996, the prices of most items are quite a bit higher now than they were then. The average price of goods and services in an economy is called the **aggregate price level** or, more simply, the *price level* (a more precise definition is found in the appendix to this chapter). From 1950 to 1996, the price level more than quintupled. **Inflation,** a continual increase in the price level, affects individuals, businesses, and the government. Inflation is generally regarded as an important problem to be solved and has often been a primary

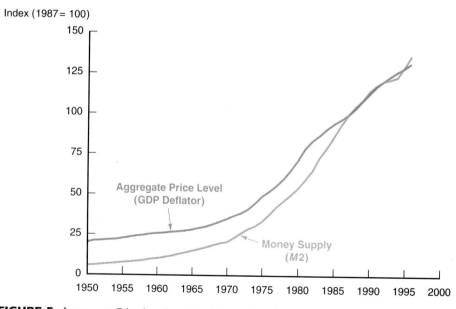

FIGURE 5 Aggregate Price Level and the Money Supply in the United States, 1950–1996

Source: Economic Report of the President.

concern of politicians and policymakers. To solve the inflation problem, we need to know something about its causes.

What explains inflation? One clue to answering this question is found in Figure 5, which plots the money supply and the price level. As we can see, the price level and the money supply generally move closely together. These data seem to indicate that a continuing increase in the money supply might be an important factor in causing the continuing increase in the price level that we call inflation.

Further evidence that inflation may be tied to continuing increases in the money supply is found in Figure 6. For a number of countries, it plots the average **inflation rate** (the rate of change of the price level, usually measured as a percentage change per year) over the ten-year period 1986–1996 against the average rate of money growth over the same period.[2] As you can see, there is a positive association between inflation and the growth rate of the money supply: The countries with the highest inflation rates are also the ones with the highest money growth rates. Argentina and Peru, for example, experienced very high inflation

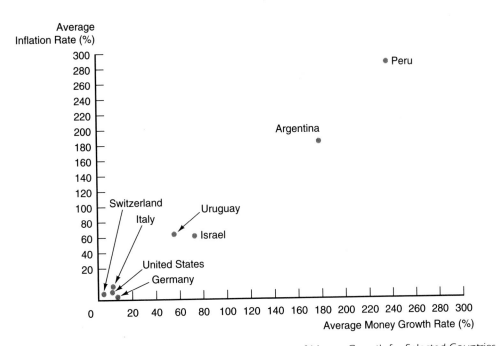

FIGURE 6   Average Inflation Rate Versus Average Rate of Money Growth for Selected Countries, 1986–1996

Source: International Financial Statistics.

---

[2]If the aggregate price level at time t is denoted by P_t, the inflation rate from time $t-1$ to t, denoted as π_t, is defined as

$$\pi_t = \frac{P_t - P_{t-1}}{P_{t-1}}$$

and their rates of money growth were high. By contrast, Switzerland and Germany have had very low inflation rates over the same period, and their rates of money growth have been low. Such evidence led Milton Friedman, a Nobel laureate in economics, to make the famous statement "Inflation is always and everywhere a monetary phenomenon."[3] We look at money's role in creating inflation by studying in detail the relationship between changes in the quantity of money and changes in the price level in Chapter 26.

Money and Interest Rates

In addition to other factors, money plays an important role in interest-rate fluctuations. Figure 7 shows the changes in the interest rate on long-term Treasury bonds and the rate of money growth. As the money growth rate rose in the 1960s and 1970s, the long-term bond rate rose with it. However, the relationship between money growth and interest rates has been less clear-cut in the 1980s and 1990s. We analyze the relationship between money and interest rates when we examine the behavior of interest rates in Chapter 6.

Conduct of Monetary Policy

Because money can affect many economic variables that are important to the well-being of our economy, politicians and policymakers throughout the world care about the conduct of **monetary policy,** the management of money and

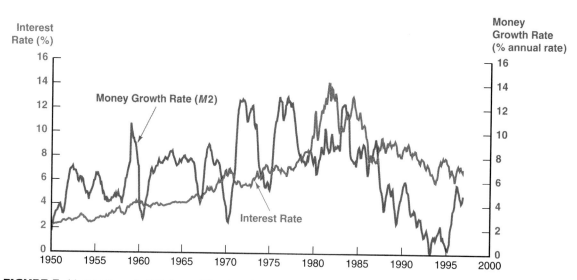

FIGURE 7   Money Growth (M2 Annual Rate) and Interest Rates (Long-Term U.S. Treasury Bonds), 1950–1996
Sources: Federal Reserve *Bulletin*; Citibase databank.

[3]Milton Friedman, *Dollars and Deficits* (Upper Saddle River, N.J.: Prentice Hall, 1968), p. 39.

interest rates. The organization responsible for the conduct of a nation's monetary policy is the **central bank.** The United States' central bank is the **Federal Reserve System** (also called **the Fed).** In Chapters 15 through 20 we study how central banks like the Federal Reserve System can affect the quantity of money in the economy and then look at how monetary policy is actually conducted in the United States and elsewhere.

Budget Deficits and Monetary Policy

The **budget deficit** is the excess of government expenditures over tax revenues for a particular time period, typically a year. The government must finance any deficit by borrowing. As Figure 8 shows, the budget deficit, relative to the size of our economy, peaked in 1983 at 6 percent of national output (as calculated by the *gross domestic product,* or *GDP,* a measure of aggregate output described in the appendix to this chapter). Since then, the budget deficit at first declined to less than 3 percent of GDP, rose again to over the 5 percent level by 1989, and has subsequently fallen to below 2 percent of GDP. Budget deficits have been the subject of legislation and bitter battles between the president and Congress in recent years. Indeed, a bruising budget battle between Democratic President Bill Clinton and a Republican-dominated Congress resulted in a brief shutdown of the federal government in late 1995.

You may have seen or heard statements in newspapers or on TV that budget deficits are undesirable. We explore the accuracy of such statements in Chapter 26 by examining why deficits might lead to a higher rate of money growth, a higher rate of inflation, and higher interest rates.

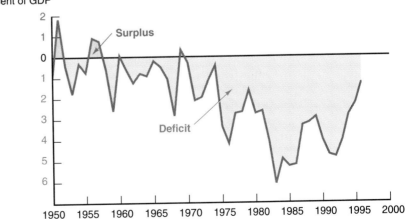

FIGURE 8 Government Budget Surplus or Deficit as a Percentage of Gross Domestic Product, 1950–1996

Source: Economic Report of the President.

HOW WE WILL STUDY MONEY, BANKING, AND FINANCIAL MARKETS

Instead of focusing on a mass of dull facts that will soon become obsolete, this textbook stresses the economic way of thinking by developing a unifying framework to study money, banking, and financial markets. This analytic framework uses a few basic economic concepts to organize your thinking about the determination of asset prices, the structure of financial markets, bank management, and the role of money in the economy. It encompasses the following basic concepts:

- A simplified approach to the demand for assets (portfolio choice)
- The concept of equilibrium
- Basic supply and demand to explain behavior in financial markets
- The search for profits
- An approach to financial structure based on transaction costs and asymmetric information
- Aggregate supply and demand analysis

The unifying framework used in this book will keep your knowledge from becoming obsolete and make the material more interesting. It will enable you to learn what *really* matters without having to memorize a mass of facts you will forget soon after the final exam. This framework will also provide you with the tools to understand trends in the financial marketplace and in variables such as interest rates, exchange rates, inflation, and aggregate output.

To help you understand and apply the unifying analytic framework, simple models are constructed in which the variables held constant are carefully delineated, each step in the derivation of the model is clearly and carefully laid out, and the models are then used to explain various phenomena by focusing on changes in one variable at a time, holding all other variables constant.

To reinforce the models' usefulness, this text uses case studies, applications, and special-interest boxes to present evidence that supports or casts doubts on the theories being discussed. This exposure to real-life events and data should dissuade you from thinking that all economists make abstract assumptions and develop theories that have little to do with actual behavior.

To function better in the real world outside the classroom, you must have the tools to follow the financial news that appears in leading financial publications such as the *Wall Street Journal*. These tools are presented in two formats. The first is a set of special boxed inserts titled "Following the Financial News" that contain actual columns and data from the *Wall Street Journal* that appear daily or periodically. These boxes give you the detailed information and definitions you need to evaluate the data being presented. The second feature is a set of special applications titled "Reading the *Wall Street Journal*" that expand on the "Following the Financial News" boxes. These applications show you how the analytic framework in the book can be used directly to make sense of the daily columns in the United States' leading financial newspaper.

CONCLUDING REMARKS

Money, banking, and financial markets is an exciting field that directly affects your life—interest rates influence earnings on your savings and the payments on loans you may seek on a car or a house, and monetary policy may affect your job prospects and the prices of goods in the future. Your study of money, banking, and financial markets will introduce you to many of the controversies about the conduct of economic policy that are currently the subject of hot debate in the political arena and will help you gain a clearer understanding of economic phenomena you frequently hear about in the news media. The knowledge you gain will stay with you long after the course is done.

SUMMARY

1. Activities in financial markets have direct effects on individuals' wealth, the behavior of businesses, and the efficiency of our economy. Three financial markets deserve particular attention: the bond market (where interest rates are determined), the stock market (which has a major effect on people's wealth and on firms' investment decisions), and the foreign exchange market (because fluctuations in the foreign exchange rate have major consequences for the American economy).

2. Banks and other financial institutions channel funds from people who might not put them to productive use to people who can do so and thus play a crucial role in improving the efficiency of the economy.

3. Money appears to be a major influence on inflation, business cycles, and interest rates. Because these economic variables are so important to the health of the economy, we need to understand how monetary policy is and should be conducted. We also need to study government budget deficits because they can be an influential factor in the conduct of monetary policy.

4. This textbook stresses the economic way of thinking by developing a unifying analytic framework for the study of money, banking, and financial markets using a few basic economic principles. This textbook also emphasizes the interaction of theoretical analysis and empirical data.

KEY TERMS

aggregate output, p. 9

aggregate price level, p. 10

asset, p. 4

banks, p. 8

bond, p. 4

budget deficit, p. 13

business cycles, p. 9

central bank, p. 13

Federal Reserve System (the
  Fed), p. 13

financial intermediaries, p. 7

financial markets, p. 3

foreign exchange market,
  p. 6

foreign exchange rate, p. 6

inflation, p. 10

inflation rate, p. 11

interest rate, p. 4

monetary policy, p. 12

monetary theory, p. 10

money (money supply), p. 9

recession, p. 9

security, p. 4

stock, p. 4

unemployment rate, p. 9

QUESTIONS AND PROBLEMS

Questions marked with an asterisk are answered at the end of the book in an appendix, "Answers to Selected Questions and Problems."

1. Has the inflation rate in the United States increased or decreased in the past few years? What about interest rates?

*2. If history repeats itself and we see a decline in the rate of money growth, what might you expect to happen to
   a. real output
   b. the inflation rate, and
   c. interest rates?

3. When was the most recent recession?

*4. When interest rates fall, how might you change your economic behavior?

5. Can you think of any financial innovation in the past ten years that has affected you personally? Has it made you better off or worse off? Why?

*6. Is everybody worse off when interest rates rise?

7. What is the basic activity of banks?

*8. Why are financial markets important to the health of the economy?

9. What is the typical relationship between interest rates on three-month Treasury bills, long-term Treasury bonds, and Baa corporate bonds?

*10. What effect might a fall in stock prices have on business investment?

11. What effect might a rise in stock prices have on consumers' decisions to spend?

*12. How does a fall in the value of the pound sterling affect British consumers?

13. How does an increase in the value of the pound sterling affect American businesses?

*14. Looking at Figure 3, in what years would you have chosen to visit the Grand Canyon in Arizona rather than the Tower of London?

15. When the dollar is worth more in relation to currencies of other countries, are you more likely to buy American-made or foreign-made jeans? Are U.S. companies that make jeans happier when the dollar is strong or when it is weak? What about an American company that is in the business of importing jeans into the United States?

DEFINING AGGREGATE OUTPUT, INCOME, AND THE PRICE LEVEL

Because these terms are used so frequently throughout the text, we need to have a clear understanding of the definitions of *aggregate output*, *income*, and the *price level*.

AGGREGATE OUTPUT AND INCOME

The most commonly reported measure of aggregate output, the **gross domestic product (GDP),** is the value of all final goods and services produced in a country during the course of the year.[1] This measure excludes two sets of items that at first glance you might think would be included. Purchases of goods that have been produced in the past, whether a Rembrandt painting or a house built 20 years ago, are not counted as part of GDP, nor are purchases of stocks or bonds. None of these enter into GDP because they are not goods and services produced during the course of the year. Intermediate goods, which are used up in producing final goods and services, such as the sugar in a candy bar or the energy used to produce steel, are also not counted separately as part of GDP. They are not counted separately because to do so would be to count them twice, as the value of the final goods already includes the value of the intermediate goods.

Aggregate income, the total income of *factors of production* (land, labor, and capital) from producing goods and services in the economy during the course of the year, is best thought of as being equal to aggregate output. Because the

---

[1]Another measure of aggregate output is *gross national product (GNP)*, the value of all final goods and services produced by domestically owned factors of production during a year. It differs from GDP in that part of U.S. GNP is earned abroad by American individuals and corporations. Also, earnings by foreign companies in the United States are excluded from U.S. GNP but are included in GDP.

payments for final goods and services must eventually flow back to the owners of the factors of production as income, income payments must equal payments for final goods and services. For example, if the economy has an aggregate output of $5 trillion, total income payments in the economy (aggregate income) are also $5 trillion.

REAL VERSUS NOMINAL MAGNITUDES

When the total value of final goods and services is calculated using current prices, the resulting GDP measure is referred to as *nominal GDP*. The word *nominal* indicates that values are measured using current prices. If all prices doubled but actual production of goods and services remained the same, nominal GDP would double even though people do not enjoy the benefits of twice as many goods and services. As a result, nominal variables can be misleading measures of economic well-being.

A more reliable measure of economic well-being expresses values in terms of prices for an arbitrary base year, currently 1992. GDP measured with constant prices is referred to as *real GDP*, the word *real* indicating that values are measured in terms of fixed prices. Real variables thus measure the quantities of goods and services and do not change because prices have changed but rather only if actual quantities have changed.

A brief example will make the distinction clearer. Suppose that you have a nominal income of $30,000 in 1998 and that your nominal income was $15,000 in 1992. If all prices doubled between 1992 and 1998, are you better off? The answer is no: Although your income has doubled, your $30,000 buys you only the same amount of goods because prices have also doubled. A real income measure indicates that your income in terms of the goods it can buy is the same. Measured in 1992 prices, the $30,000 of nominal income in 1998 turns out to be only $15,000 of real income. Because your real income is actually the same in the two years, you are no better or worse off in 1998 than you were in 1992.

Because real variables measure quantities in terms of real goods and services, they are typically of more interest than nominal variables. In this text, discussion of aggregate output or aggregate income always refers to real measures (such as real GDP).

AGGREGATE PRICE LEVEL

In the chapter we defined the aggregate price level as a measure of average prices in the economy. Two measures of the aggregate price level are commonly encountered in economic data. The first is the *GDP deflator*, which is defined as nominal GDP divided by real GDP. Thus if 1998 nominal GDP is $6 trillion but 1998 real GDP in 1992 prices is $4 trillion,

$$\text{GDP delfator} = \frac{\$6 \text{ trillion}}{\$4 \text{ trillion}} = 1.50$$

The GDP deflator indicates that, on average, prices have risen 50 percent since 1992. Typically, measures of the price level are presented in the form of a price index, which expresses the price level for the base year (in our example, 1992) as 100. Thus the GDP deflator for 1998 would be 150.

Another popular measure of the aggregate price level (and the one that is most frequently reported in the press) is the *consumer price index (CPI)*. The CPI is measured by pricing a "basket" list of goods and services bought by a typical urban household over a given period, say, one month. If over the course of the year the cost of this basket of goods and services rises from $500 to $600, the CPI has risen by 20 percent. The CPI is also expressed as a price index with the base year equal to 100.

Both the CPI and GDP deflator measures of the price level can be used to convert or deflate a nominal magnitude into a real magnitude. This is accomplished by dividing the nominal magnitude by the price index. In our example, in which the GDP deflator for 1998 is 1.50 (expressed as an index value of 150), real GDP for 1998 equals

$$\frac{\$6 \text{ trillion}}{1.50} = \$4 \text{ trillion in 1992 prices}$$

which corresponds to the real GDP figure for 1998 mentioned earlier.

Chapter 2

AN OVERVIEW OF THE FINANCIAL SYSTEM

PREVIEW   Inez the Inventor has designed a low-cost robot that cleans house (even does windows), mows the lawn, and washes the car, but she has no funds to put her wonderful invention into production. Walter the Widower has plenty of savings, which he and his wife accumulated over the years. If we could get Inez and Walter together so that Walter could provide funds to Inez, Inez's robot would see the light of day, and the economy would be better off: We would have cleaner houses, shinier cars, and more beautiful lawns.

Financial markets (bond and stock markets) and financial intermediaries (banks, insurance companies, pension funds) have the basic function of getting people like Inez and Walter together by moving funds from those who have a surplus of funds (Walter) to those who have a shortage of funds (Inez). More realistically, when IBM invents a better computer, it may need funds to bring it to market. Similarly when a local government needs to build a road or a school, it may need more funds than local property taxes provide. Well-functioning financial markets and financial intermediaries are needed to improve economic well-being and efficiency and are crucial to economic health.

To study the effects of financial markets and financial intermediaries on the economy, we must first acquire an understanding of their general structure and operation. In this chapter we learn about the major financial intermediaries and the instruments that are traded in financial markets as well as how these markets are regulated.

This chapter presents an overview of the fascinating study of financial markets and institutions. We return to a more detailed treatment of the regulation, structure, and evolution of financial markets in Chapters 9 through 14.

FUNCTION OF FINANCIAL MARKETS

Financial markets perform the essential economic function of channeling funds from people who have saved surplus funds by spending less than their income to people who have a shortage of funds because they wish to spend more than their income. This function is shown schematically in Figure 1. Those who have saved and are lending funds, the lender-savers, are at the left, and those who must borrow funds to finance their spending, the borrower-spenders, are at the right. The principal lender-savers are households, but business enterprises and the government (particularly state and local government), as well as foreigners and their governments, sometimes also find themselves with excess funds and so lend them out. The most important borrower-spenders are businesses and the government (particularly the federal government), but households and foreigners also borrow to finance their purchases of cars, furniture, and houses. The arrows show that funds flow from lender-savers to borrower-spenders via two routes.

In *direct finance* (the route at the bottom of Figure 1), borrowers borrow funds directly from lenders in financial markets by selling them *securities* (also called *financial instruments*), which are claims on the borrower's future income or assets. Securities are assets for the person who buys them but **liabilities** (IOUs or debts) for the individual or firm that sells (issues) them. For example, if General Motors needs to borrow funds to pay for a new factory to manufacture

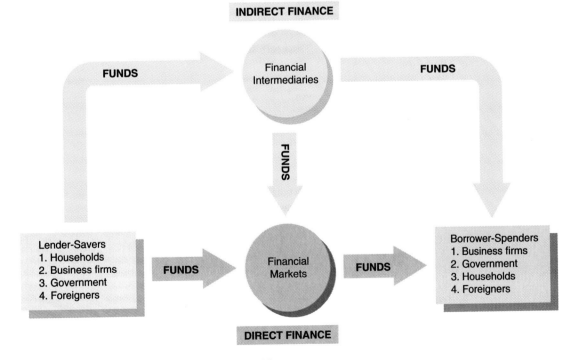

FIGURE 1 Flows of Funds Through the Financial System

computerized cars, it might borrow the funds from a saver by selling the saver a *bond*, a debt security that promises to make payments periodically for a specified period of time.

Why is this channeling of funds from savers to spenders so important to the economy? The answer is that the people who save are frequently not the same people who have profitable investment opportunities available to them, the entrepreneurs. Let's first think about this on a personal level. Suppose that you have saved $1000 this year, but no borrowing or lending is possible because there are no financial markets. If you do not have an investment opportunity that will permit you to earn income with your savings, you will just hold on to the $1000 and will earn no interest. However, Carl the Carpenter has a productive use for your $1000: He can use it to purchase a new tool that will shorten the time it takes him to build a house, thereby earning an extra $200 per year. If you could get in touch with Carl, you could lend him the $1000 at a rental fee (interest) of $100 per year, and both of you would be better off. You would earn $100 per year on your $1000, instead of the zero amount that you would earn otherwise, while Carl would earn $100 more income per year (the $200 extra earnings per year minus the $100 rental fee for the use of the funds).

In the absence of financial markets, you and Carl the Carpenter might never get together. Without financial markets, it is hard to transfer funds from a person who has no investment opportunities to one who has them; you would both be stuck with the status quo, and both of you would be worse off. Financial markets are thus essential to promoting economic efficiency.

The existence of financial markets is also beneficial even if someone borrows for a purpose other than increasing production in a business. Say that you are recently married, have a good job, and want to buy a house. You earn a good salary, but because you have just started to work, you have not yet saved much. Over time you would have no problem saving enough to buy the house of your dreams, but by then you would be too old to get full enjoyment from it. Without financial markets, you are stuck; you cannot buy the house and will continue to live in your tiny apartment.

If a financial market were set up so that people who had built up savings could lend you the money to buy the house, you would be more than happy to pay them some interest in order to own a home while you are still young enough to enjoy it. Then, when you had saved up enough funds, you would pay back your loan. The overall outcome would be such that you would be better off, as would the persons who made you the loan. They would now earn some interest, whereas they would not if the financial market did not exist.

Now we can see why financial markets have such an important function in the economy. They allow funds to move from people who lack productive investment opportunities to people who have such opportunities. By so doing, financial markets contribute to higher production and efficiency in the overall economy. They also directly improve the well-being of consumers by allowing them to time their purchases better. They provide funds to young people to buy what they need and can eventually afford without forcing them to wait until they have saved up the entire purchase price. Financial markets that are operating efficiently improve the economic welfare of everyone in the society.

STRUCTURE OF FINANCIAL MARKETS

Now that we understand the basic function of financial markets, let's look at their structure. The following descriptions of several categorizations of financial markets illustrate essential features of these markets.

Debt and Equity Markets

A firm or an individual can obtain funds in a financial market in two ways. The most common method is to issue a debt instrument, such as a bond or a mortgage, which is a contractual agreement by the borrower to pay the holder of the instrument fixed dollar amounts at regular intervals (interest and principal payments) until a specified date (the maturity date), when a final payment is made. The **maturity** of a debt instrument is the time (term) to that instrument's expiration date. A debt instrument is **short-term** if its maturity is less than a year and **long-term** if its maturity is ten years or longer. Debt instruments with a maturity between one and ten years are said to be **intermediate-term.**

The second method of raising funds is by issuing **equities,** such as common stock, which are claims to share in the net income (income after expenses and taxes) and the assets of a business. If you own one share of common stock in a company that has issued one million shares, you are entitled to 1 one-millionth of the firm's net income and 1 one-millionth of the firm's assets. Equities usually make periodic payments **(dividends)** to their holders and are considered long-term securities because they have no maturity date.

The main disadvantage of owning a corporation's equities rather than its debt is that an equity holder is a *residual claimant;* that is, the corporation must pay all its debt holders before it pays its equity holders. The advantage of holding equities is that equity holders benefit directly from any increases in the corporation's profitability or asset value because equities confer ownership rights on the equity holders. Debt holders do not share in this benefit because their dollar payments are fixed. We examine the pros and cons of debt versus equity instruments in more detail in Chapter 9, which provides an economic analysis of financial structure.

The total value of equities in the United States has typically fluctuated between $1 and $10 trillion since the early 1970s, depending on the prices of shares. Although the average person is more aware of the stock market than any other financial market, the size of the debt market greatly exceeds that of the equities market: The value of debt instruments ($15 trillion at the end of 1996) is more than 50 percent larger than the value of equities ($10 trillion at the end of 1996).

Primary and Secondary Markets

A **primary market** is a financial market in which new issues of a security, such as a bond or a stock, are sold to initial buyers by the corporation or government agency borrowing the funds. A **secondary market** is a financial market in which securities that have been previously issued (and are thus secondhand) can be resold.

The primary markets for securities are not well known to the public because the selling of securities to initial buyers takes place behind closed doors. An important financial institution that assists in the initial sale of securities in the primary market is the **investment bank.** It does this by **underwriting** securities: It guarantees a price for a corporation's securities and then sells them to the public.

The New York and American stock exchanges, in which previously issued stocks are traded, are the best-known examples of secondary markets, although the bond markets, in which previously issued bonds of major corporations and the U.S. government are bought and sold, actually have a larger trading volume. Other examples of secondary markets are foreign exchange markets, futures markets, and options markets. Securities brokers and dealers are crucial to a well-functioning secondary market. **Brokers** are agents of investors who match buyers with sellers of securities; **dealers** link buyers and sellers by buying and selling securities at stated prices.

When an individual buys a security in the secondary market, the person who has sold the security receives money in exchange for the security, but the corporation that issued the security acquires no new funds. A corporation acquires new funds only when its securities are first sold in the primary market. Nonetheless, secondary markets serve two important functions. First, they make it easier to sell these financial instruments to raise cash; that is, they make the financial instruments more **liquid.** The increased liquidity of these instruments then makes them more desirable and thus easier for the issuing firm to sell in the primary market. Second, they determine the price of the security that the issuing firm sells in the primary market. The firms that buy securities in the primary market will pay the issuing corporation no more than the price that they think the secondary market will set for this security. The higher the security's price in the secondary market, the higher will be the price that the issuing firm will receive for a new security in the primary market and hence the greater the amount of capital it can raise. Conditions in the secondary market are therefore the most relevant to corporations issuing securities. It is for this reason that books like this one, which deal with financial markets, focus on the behavior of secondary markets rather than primary markets.

Exchanges and Over-the-Counter Markets

Secondary markets can be organized in two ways. One is to organize **exchanges,** where buyers and sellers of securities (or their agents or brokers) meet in one central location to conduct trades. The New York and American stock exchanges for stocks and the Chicago Board of Trade for commodities (wheat, corn, silver, and other raw materials) are examples of organized exchanges.

The other method of organizing a secondary market is to have an **over-the-counter (OTC) market,** in which dealers at different locations who have an inventory of securities stand ready to buy and sell securities "over the counter" to anyone who comes to them and is willing to accept their prices. Because over-the-counter dealers are in computer contact and know the prices set by one another, the OTC market is very competitive and not very different from a market with an organized exchange.

Many common stocks are traded over-the-counter, although the largest corporations have their shares traded at organized stock exchanges such as the New

York Stock Exchange. The U.S. government bond market, with a larger trading volume than the New York Stock Exchange, is set up as an over-the-counter market. Forty or so dealers establish a "market" in these securities by standing ready to buy and sell U.S. government bonds. Other over-the-counter markets include those that trade other types of financial instruments such as negotiable certificates of deposit, federal funds, banker's acceptances, and foreign exchange.

Money and Capital Markets

Another way of distinguishing between markets is on the basis of the maturity of the securities traded in each market. The **money market** is a financial market in which only short-term debt instruments (maturity of less than one year) are traded; the **capital market** is the market in which longer-term debt (maturity of one year or greater) and equity instruments are traded. Money market securities are usually more widely traded than longer-term securities and so tend to be more liquid. In addition, as we will see in Chapter 4, short-term securities have smaller fluctuations in prices than long-term securities, making them safer investments. As a result, corporations and banks actively use this market to earn interest on surplus funds that they expect to have only temporarily. Capital market securities, such as stocks and long-term bonds, are often held by financial intermediaries such as insurance companies and pension funds, which have little uncertainty about the amount of funds they will have available in the future.

FINANCIAL MARKET INSTRUMENTS

To complete our understanding of how financial markets perform the important role of channeling funds from lender-savers to borrower-spenders, we need to examine the securities (instruments) traded in financial markets. We first focus on the instruments traded in the money market and then turn to those traded in the capital market.

Money Market Instruments

Because of their short terms to maturity, the debt instruments traded in the money market undergo the least price fluctuations and so are the least risky investments. The money market has undergone great changes in the past three decades, with the amount of some financial instruments growing at a far more rapid rate than others.

The principal money market instruments are listed in Table 1 along with the amount outstanding at the end of 1970, 1980, 1990, and 1996.

UNITED STATES TREASURY BILLS These short-term debt instruments of the U.S. government are issued in 3-, 6-, and 12-month maturities to finance the deficits of the federal government. They pay a set amount at maturity and have no interest payments, but they effectively pay interest by initially selling at a discount, that is, at a price lower than the set amount paid at maturity. For instance, you might buy in May 1998 for $9000 a one-year Treasury Bill that can be redeemed in May 1999 for $10,000.

U.S. Treasury bills are the most liquid of all the money market instruments because they are the most actively traded. They are also the safest of all money

TABLE 1 **Principal Money Market Instruments**

Type of Instrument	Amount Outstanding ($ billions, end of year)			
	1970	**1980**	**1990**	**1996**
U.S. Treasury bills	81	216	527	777
Negotiable bank certificates of deposit (large denominations)	55	317	543	494
Commercial paper	33	122	557	779
Banker's acceptances	7	42	52	24
Repurchase agreements	3	57	144	191
Federal funds*	16	18	61	92
Eurodollars	2	55	92	110

*Figures after 1970 are for large banks only.

Sources: Federal Reserve Flow of Funds Accounts; Federal Reserve *Bulletin; Banking and Monetary Statistics, 1945–1970; Annual Statistical Digest, 1971–1975; Economic Report of the President.*

market instruments because there is no possibility of **default,** a situation in which the party issuing the debt instrument (the federal government in this case) is unable to make interest payments or pay off the amount owed when the instrument matures. The federal government is always able to meet its debt obligations because it can raise taxes or issue **currency** (paper money or coins) to pay off its debts. Treasury bills are held mainly by banks, although small amounts are held by households, corporations, and other financial intermediaries.

NEGOTIABLE BANK CERTIFICATES OF DEPOSIT A *certificate of deposit (CD)* is a debt instrument sold by a bank to depositors that pays annual interest of a given amount and at maturity pays back the original purchase price. Before 1961, CDs were nonnegotiable; that is, they could not be sold to someone else and could not be redeemed from the bank before maturity without paying a substantial penalty. In 1961, to make CDs more liquid and more attractive to investors, Citibank introduced the first negotiable CD in large denominations (over $100,000) that could be resold in a secondary market. This instrument is now issued by almost all the major commercial banks and has been extremely successful, with the amount outstanding currently around $500 billion. CDs are an extremely important source of funds for commercial banks, from corporations, money market mutual funds, charitable institutions, and government agencies.

COMMERCIAL PAPER *Commercial paper* is a short-term debt instrument issued by large banks and well-known corporations, such as General Motors or AT&T. Before the 1960s, corporations usually borrowed their short-term funds from banks, but since then they have come to rely more heavily on selling commercial

Following the Financial News

Money Market Rates

The *Wall Street Journal* publishes daily a listing of interest rates on many different financial instruments in its "Money Rates" column. (See "Today's Contents" on page 1 of the *Journal* for the location.)

The four interest rates in the "Money Rates" column that are discussed most frequently in the media are these:

Prime rate: The base interest rate on corporate bank loans, an indicator of the cost of business borrowing from banks

Federal funds rate: The interest rate charged on overnight loans in the federal funds market, a sensitive indicator of the cost to banks of borrowing funds from other banks and the stance of monetary policy

Treasury bill rate: The interest rate on U.S. Treasury bills, an indicator of general interest-rate movements

Federal Home Loan Mortgage Corporation rates: Interest rates on "Freddie Mac"–guaranteed mortgages, an indicator of the cost of financing residential housing purchases

Source: Wall Street Journal, January 31, 1997, p. C17.

MONEY RATES

Thursday, January 30, 1997

The key U.S. and foreign annual interest rates below are a guide to general levels but don't always represent actual transactions.

PRIME RATE: 8.25% (effective 2/01/96). The base rate on corporate loans posted by at least 75% of the nation's 30 largest banks.

DISCOUNT RATE: 5%. The charge on loans to depository institutions by the Federal Reserve Banks.

FEDERAL FUNDS: 5 1/2% high, 4 3/4% low, 5% near closing bid, 5 1/4% offered. Reserves traded among commercial banks for overnight use in amounts of $1 million or more. Source: Prebon Yamane (U.S.A.) Inc.

CALL MONEY: 7%. The charge on loans to brokers on stock exchange collateral. Source: Dow Jones Telerate Inc.

COMMERCIAL PAPER placed directly by General Electric Capital Corp.: 5.30% 30 to 44 days; 5.31% 45 to 89 days; 5.33% 90 to 179 days; 5.35% 180 to 239 days; 5.36% 240 to 270 days.

COMMERCIAL PAPER: High-grade unsecured notes sold through dealers by major corporations: 5.45% 30 days; 5.45% 60 days; 5.46% 90 days.

CERTIFICATES OF DEPOSIT: 4.84% one month; 4.90% two months; 4.96% three months; 5.19% six months; 5.42% one year. Average of top rates paid by major New York banks on primary new issues of negotiable C.D.s, usually on amounts of $1 million and more. The minimum unit is $100,000. Typical rates in the secondary market: 5.32% one month; 5.40% three months; 5.50% six months.

BANKERS ACCEPTANCES: 5.25% 30 days; 5.25% 60 days; 5.28% 90 days; 5.29% 120 days; 5.30% 150 days; 5.30% 180 days. Offered rates of negotiable, bank-backed business credit instruments typically financing an import order.

LONDON LATE EURODOLLARS: 5 7/16%-5 5/16% one month; 5 1/2%-5 3/8% two months; 5 9/16%-5 7/16% three months; 5 19/32%-5 15/32 four months; 5 5/8%-5 1/2% five months; 5 11/16%-5 9/16% six months.

LONDON INTERBANK OFFERED RATES (LIBOR): 5 15/32% one month; 5 9/16% three months; 5 11/16% six months; 5 15/16% one year. The average of interbank offered rates for dollar deposits in the London market based on quotations at five major banks. Effective rate for contracts entered into two days from date appearing at top of this column.

FOREIGN PRIME RATES: Canada 4.75%; Germany 3.15%; Japan 1.625%; Switzerland 3.875%; Britain 6.00%. These rate indications aren't directly comparable; lending practices vary widely by location.

TREASURY BILLS: Results of the Monday, January 27, 1997, auction of short-term U.S. government bills, sold at a discount from face value in units of $10,000 to $1 million: 5.06% 13 weeks; 5.12% 26 weeks.

OVERNIGHT REPURCHASE RATE: 5.33%. Dealer financing rate for overnight sale and repurchase of Treasury securities. Source: Dow Jones Telerate Inc.

FEDERAL HOME LOAN MORTGAGE CORP. (Freddie Mac): Posted yields on 30-year mortgage commitments. Delivery within 30 days 7.97%, 60 days 8.03%, standard conventional fixed-rate mortgages; 5.625%, 2% rate capped one-year adjustable rate mortgages. Source: Dow Jones Telerate Inc.

FEDERAL NATIONAL MORTGAGE ASSOCIATION (Fannie Mae): Posted yields on 30 year mortgage commitments (priced at par) for delivery within 30 days 7.93%, 60 days 8.00%, standard conventional fixed rate-mortgages; 6.70%, 6/2 rate capped one-year adjustable rate mortgages. Source: Dow Jones Telerate Inc.

MERRILL LYNCH READY ASSETS TRUST: 4.91%. Annualized average rate of return after expenses for the past 30 days; not a forecast of future returns.

paper to other financial intermediaries and corporations for their immediate borrowing needs; in other words, they engage in direct finance. Growth of the commercial paper market has been substantial: The amount of commercial paper outstanding has increased by over 2000 percent (from $33 billion to $779 billion) in the period 1970–1996. We will discuss why the commercial paper market has had such tremendous growth in Chapter 11.

BANKER'S ACCEPTANCES These money market instruments are created in the course of carrying out international trade and have been in use for hundreds of years. A *banker's acceptance* is a bank draft (a promise of payment similar to a check) issued by a firm, payable at some future date, and guaranteed for a fee by the bank that stamps it "accepted." The firm issuing the instrument is required to deposit the required funds into its account to cover the draft. If the firm fails to do so, the bank's guarantee means that it is obligated to make good on the draft. The advantage to the firm is that the draft is more likely to be accepted when purchasing goods abroad because the foreign exporter knows that even if the company purchasing the goods goes bankrupt, the bank draft will still be paid off. These "accepted" drafts are often resold in a secondary market at a discount and so are similar in function to Treasury bills. Typically, they are held by many of the same parties that hold Treasury bills, and the amount outstanding has also experienced growth, rising by 250 percent ($7 billion to $24 billion) from 1970 to 1996.

REPURCHASE AGREEMENTS *Repurchase agreements (repos)* are effectively short-term loans (usually with a maturity of less than two weeks) in which Treasury bills serve as *collateral,* an asset that the lender receives if the borrower does not pay back the loan. Repos are made as follows: A large corporation, such as General Motors, may have some idle funds in its bank account, say, $1 million, which it would like to lend for a week. GM uses this excess $1 million to buy Treasury bills from a bank, which agrees to repurchase them the next week at a price slightly above GM's purchase price. The effect of this agreement is that GM makes a loan of $1 million to the bank and holds $1 million of the bank's Treasury bills until the bank repurchases the bills to pay off the loan. Repurchase agreements are a fairly recent innovation in financial markets, having been introduced in 1969. They are now an important source of bank funds (near $200 billion), and the most important lenders in this market are large corporations.

FEDERAL (FED) FUNDS These are typically overnight loans between banks of their deposits at the Federal Reserve. The *federal funds* designation is somewhat confusing because these loans are not made by the federal government or by the Federal Reserve but rather by banks to other banks. One reason why a bank might borrow in the federal funds market is that it might find that it does not have enough deposits at the Fed to meet the amount required by regulators. It can then borrow these deposits from another bank, which transfers them to the borrowing bank using the Fed's wire transfer system. This market is very sensitive to the credit needs of the banks, so the interest rate on these loans, called the **federal funds rate,** is a closely watched barometer of the tightness of credit market conditions in the banking system and the stance of monetary policy; when it is high, it indicates that the banks are strapped for funds, whereas when it is low, banks' credit needs are low.

EURODOLLARS U.S. dollars deposited in foreign banks outside the United States or in foreign branches of U.S. banks are called **Eurodollars.** American banks can borrow these deposits from other banks or from their own foreign branches when they need funds. Eurodollars have become an important source of funds for banks (over $100 billion).

Capital Market Instruments

Capital market instruments are debt and equity instruments with maturities of greater than one year. They have far wider price fluctuations than money market instruments and are considered to be fairly risky investments. The principal capital market instruments are listed in Table 2, which shows the amount outstanding at the end of 1970, 1980, 1990, and 1996.

STOCKS *Stocks* are equity claims on the net income and assets of a corporation. Their value of over $10 trillion at the end of 1996 exceeds that of any other type of security in the capital market. The amount of new stock issues in any given year is typically quite small, less than 1 percent of the total value of shares outstanding. Individuals hold around half of the value of stocks; the rest are held by pension funds, mutual funds, and insurance companies.

TABLE 2 Principal Capital Market Instruments

Type of Instrument	Amount Outstanding ($ billions, end of year)			
	1970	1980	1990	1996
Corporate stocks (market value)	906	1,601	4,146	10,090
Residential mortgages	355	1,106	2,886	4,221
Corporate bonds	167	366	1,008	1,399
U.S. government securities (marketable long-term)	160	407	1,653	2,667
State and local government bonds	146	310	870	1,087
U.S. government agency securities	51	193	435	924
Bank commercial loans	152	459	818	789
Consumer loans	134	355	813	1,226
Commercial and farm mortgages	116	352	829	833

Sources: Federal Reserve Flow of Funds Accounts; Federal Reserve *Bulletin*; *Banking and Monetary Statistics, 1941–1970.*

[handwritten margin note: Borrow over 30 years / House of Colateral]

MORTGAGES *Mortgages* are loans to households or firms to purchase housing, land, or other real structures, where the structure or land itself serves as collateral for the loans. The mortgage market is the largest debt market in the United States, with the amount of residential mortgages (used to purchase residential housing) outstanding more than quadruple the amount of commercial and farm mortgages. Savings and loan associations and mutual savings banks have been the primary lenders in the residential mortgage market, although commercial banks have started to enter this market more aggressively. The majority of commercial and farm mortgages are made by commercial banks and life insurance companies. The federal government plays an active role in the mortgage market via the three government agencies—the Federal National Mortgage Association (FNMA, "Fannie Mae"), the Government National Mortgage Association (GNMA, "Ginnie Mae"), and the Federal Home Loan Mortgage Corporation (FHLMC, "Freddie Mac")—that provide funds to the mortgage market by selling bonds and using the proceeds to buy mortgages. An important development in the residential mortgage market in recent years is the mortgage-backed security (see Box 1).

CORPORATE BONDS These are long-term bonds issued by corporations with very strong credit ratings. The typical *corporate bond* sends the holder an interest payment twice a year and pays off the face value when the bond matures. Some corporate bonds, called *convertible bonds,* have the additional feature of allowing the holder to convert them into a specified number of shares of stock at any time up to the maturity date. This feature makes these convertible bonds more desirable to prospective purchasers than bonds without it and allows the corporation to reduce its interest payments because these bonds can increase in value if the price of the stock appreciates sufficiently. Because the outstanding amount of both convertible and nonconvertible bonds for any given corporation is small, they are not nearly as liquid as other securities such as U.S. government bonds.

Although the size of the corporate bond market is substantially smaller than that of the stock market, with the amount of corporate bonds outstanding less than one-fifth that of stocks, the volume of new corporate bonds issued each year is substantially greater than the volume of new stock issues. Thus the behavior of the corporate bond market is probably far more important to a firm's financing decisions than the behavior of the stock market. The principal buyers of corporate bonds are life insurance companies; pension funds and households are other large holders.

U.S. GOVERNMENT SECURITIES These long-term debt instruments are issued by the U.S. Treasury to finance the deficits of the federal government. Because they are the most widely traded bonds in the United States (the volume of transactions on average exceeds $100 billion daily), they are the most liquid security traded in the capital market. They are held by the Federal Reserve, banks, households, and foreigners.

U.S. GOVERNMENT AGENCY SECURITIES These are long-term bonds issued by various government agencies such as Ginnie Mae, the Federal Farm Credit Bank,

Mortgage-Backed Securities

A major change in the residential mortgage market in recent years has been the creation of an active secondary market for mortgages. Because mortgages have different terms and interest rates, they were not sufficiently liquid to trade as securities on secondary markets. To stimulate mortgage lending, in 1970 the Government National Mortgage Association (GNMA, called "Ginnie Mae") developed the concept of a pass-through *mortgage-backed security* when it began a program in which it guaranteed interest and principal payments on bundles of standardized mortgages. Under this program, private financial institutions such as savings and loans and commercial banks were now able to gather a group of GNMA-guaranteed mortgages into a bundle of, say, $1 million and then sell this bundle as a security to a third party (usually a large institutional investor such as a pension fund). When individuals make their mortgage payments on the GNMA-guaranteed mortgage to the financial institution, the financial institution passes the payments through to the owner of the security by sending a check for the total of all the payments. Because GNMA guarantees the payments, these pass-through securities have a very low default risk and are very popular, with amounts outstanding exceeding $500 billion.

Mortgage-backed securities are issued not only by the government agencies but also by private financial institutions. Indeed, mortgage-backed securities have been so successful that they have completely transformed the residential mortgage market. Throughout the 1970s, over 80 percent of residential mortgages were owned outright by savings and loans, mutual savings banks, and commercial banks. Now only one-third are owned outright by these institutions, with two-thirds held as mortgage-backed securities.

or the Tennessee Valley Authority in order to finance such items as mortgages, farm loans, or power-generating equipment. Many of these securities are guaranteed by the federal government. They function much like U.S. government bonds and are held by similar parties.

STATE AND LOCAL GOVERNMENT BONDS State and local bonds, also called *municipal bonds,* are long-term debt instruments issued by state and local governments to finance expenditures on schools, roads, and other large programs. An important feature of these bonds is that their interest payments are exempt from federal income tax and generally from state taxes in the issuing state. Commercial banks, with their high income tax rate, are the biggest buyers of these securities, owning over half the total amount outstanding. The next biggest group of holders consists of wealthy individuals in high income brackets, followed by insurance companies.

CONSUMER AND BANK COMMERCIAL LOANS These are loans to consumers and businesses made principally by banks but, in the case of consumer loans, also by finance companies. There are often no secondary markets in these loans, which makes them the least liquid of the capital market instruments listed in Table 2. However, secondary markets are developing.

INTERNATIONALIZATION OF FINANCIAL MARKETS

The growing internationalization of financial markets has become an important trend. Before the 1980s, U.S. financial markets were much larger than financial markets outside the United States, but in recent years the dominance of U.S. markets has been disappearing. The extraordinary growth of foreign financial markets has been the result of both large increases in the pool of savings in foreign countries such as Japan and the deregulation of foreign financial markets, which has enabled them to expand their activities. American corporations and banks are now more likely to tap international capital markets to raise needed funds, and American investors often seek investment opportunities abroad. Similarly, foreign corporations and banks raise funds from Americans, and foreigners are becoming important investors in the United States. A look at international bond markets and world stock markets will give us a picture of how this globalization of financial markets is taking place.

International Bond Market and Eurobonds

The traditional instruments in the international bond market are known as **foreign bonds.** Foreign bonds are sold in a foreign country and are denominated in that country's currency. For example, if the Swedish automaker Volvo sells a bond in the United States denominated in U.S. dollars, it is classified as a foreign bond. Foreign bonds have been an important instrument in the international capital market for centuries. In fact, a large percentage of U.S. railroads built in the nineteenth century were financed by sales of foreign bonds in Britain.

A more recent innovation in the international bond market is the **Eurobond,** a bond denominated in a currency other than that of the country in which it is sold—for example, a bond denominated in U.S. dollars sold in London. Currently, over 80 percent of the new issues in the international bond market are Eurobonds, and the market for these securities has grown very rapidly. As a result, the Eurobond market has passed the U.S. corporate bond market as a source of new funds.

World Stock Markets

Until recently, the U.S. stock market was by far the largest in the world, but foreign stock markets have been growing in importance. Now the United States is not always number one: Since the mid-1980s, the value of stocks traded in Japan has at times exceeded the value of stocks traded in the United States. The increased interest in foreign stocks has prompted the development in the United States of mutual funds specializing in trading in foreign stock markets. American investors now pay attention not only to the Dow Jones Industrial Average but also to stock price indexes for foreign stock markets such as the Nikkei 225 Average (Tokyo) and the Financial Times–Stock Exchange 100-Share Index (London).

The internationalization of financial markets is having profound effects on the United States. Foreigners, particularly the Japanese, are not only providing funds to corporations in the United States but are also helping finance a significant fraction of the federal government's huge budget deficit. Without these foreign funds,

Following the Financial News

Foreign Stock Market Indexes

Foreign stock market indexes are published daily in the *Wall Street Journal* next to the "World Markets" column, which reports developments in foreign stock markets.

The first column identifies the foreign stock exchange and the market index; for example, the circled entry is for the Nikkei 225 Average for the Tokyo Stock Exchange. The second column, "CLOSE," gives the closing value of the index, which was 17,864.04 for the Nikkei 225 Average on January 30, 1997. The "NET CHG" column indicates the change in the index from the previous trading day, −471.26, and the "PCT CHG" column indicates the percentage change in the index, −2.57%.

Source: Wall Street Journal, January 31, 1997, p. C12.

STOCK MARKET INDEXES

Exchange	01/30/97 Close	Net Chg	Pct Chg
Amsterdam AEX Index	675.09 +	2.46 +	0.37
Argentina Merval Index	689.21 +	12.32 +	1.82
Australia All Ordinaries	2417.7 +	3.5 +	0.14
Bombay Sensex	3511.08 −	11.5 −	0.33
Brazil Sao Paulo Bovespa	77888 +	519 +	0.67
Brussels Bel-20 Index	2045.87 +	14.2 +	0.70
Dow Jones China 88	122.47 +	0.47 +	0.39
Dow Jones Shanghai	121.73 −	0.12 −	0.10
Dow Jones Shenzhen	146.28 +	1.14 +	0.79
Euro, Aust, Far East MSCI-p	1128.2 +	0 +	0.00
Frankfurt DAX	3017.32 +	18.12 +	0.60
Frankfurt IBIS DAX	3018.58 +	20.63 +	0.69
Hong Kong Hang Seng	13288.4 +	2.97 +	0.02
Johannesburg J'burg Gold	1365 −	20 −	1.44
London FT 100-share	4228.4 +	20.9 +	0.50
London FT 250-share	4572.6 +	6.1 +	0.13
Madrid General Index	459.49 −	1.51 −	0.33
Mexico I.P.C.	3672.92 +	41.30 +	1.14
Milan Mibtel Index	12246 +	47 +	0.39
Paris CAC 40	2503.06 +	38.05 +	1.54
Singapore Straits Times	2216.71 −	3.41 −	0.15
S. Korea Composite	676.52 +	12.96 +	1.95
Stockholm Affaersvaerlden	2544.32 +	14.76 +	0.58
Taiwan Weighted	7221.98 +	72.44 +	1.01
Tokyo Nikkei 225 Average	17864.04 −	471.26 −	2.57
Tokyo Nikkei 300 Index	255.85 −	3.94 −	1.52
Tokyo Topix Index	1345.70 −	20.74 −	1.52
Toronto 300 Composite	6085.1 +	13.82 +	0.23
Zurich Swiss Market	4109.1 +	39.4 +	0.94

p-Preliminary
na-Not available

the U.S. economy would have grown far less rapidly in the 1980s and 1990s. The internationalization of financial markets is also leading the way to a more integrated world economy in which flows of goods and technology between countries are more commonplace. In later chapters we will encounter many examples of the important roles that international factors play in our economy.

FUNCTION OF FINANCIAL INTERMEDIARIES

As shown in Figure 1, funds can move from lenders to borrowers by a second route, called *indirect finance* because it involves a financial intermediary that stands between the lender-savers and the borrower-spenders and helps transfer funds from one to the other. A financial intermediary does this by borrowing funds from the lender-savers and then uses these funds to make loans to borrower-spenders. For example, a bank might acquire funds by issuing a liability to the public in the form of savings deposits. It might then use the funds to acquire an asset by making a loan to General Motors or by buying a GM bond in the financial market. The ultimate result is that funds have been transferred from the public (the lender-savers) to GM (the borrower-spender) with the help of the financial intermediary (the bank).

BOX 2

The Importance of Financial Intermediaries to Securities Markets: An International Comparison

Patterns of financing corporations differ across countries, but one key fact emerges. Studies of the major developed countries, including the United States, Canada, Great Britain, Japan, Italy, Germany, and France, show that when businesses go looking for funds to finance their activities, they usually obtain them indirectly through financial intermediaries and not directly from securities markets.* Even in the United States and Canada, which have the most developed securities markets in the world, loans from financial intermediaries are far more important for corporate finance than securities markets are. The countries that have made the least use of securities markets are Germany and Japan; in these two countries, financing from financial intermediaries has been almost ten times greater than that from securities markets. However, with the deregulation of Japanese securities markets in recent years,

the share of corporate financing by financial intermediaries has been declining relative to the use of securities markets.

Although the dominance of financial intermediaries over securities markets is clear in all countries, the relative importance of bond versus stock markets differs widely across countries. In the United States, the bond market is far more important as a source of corporate finance: On average, the amount of new financing raised using bonds is ten times the amount using stocks. By contrast, countries such as France and Italy make use of equities markets more than the bond market to raise capital.

*See, for example, Colin Mayer, "Financial Systems, Corporate Finance, and Economic Development," in *Asymmetric Information, Corporate Finance, and Investment*, ed. R. Glenn Hubbard (Chicago: University of Chicago Press, 1990), pp. 307–332.

The process of indirect finance using financial intermediaries, called **financial intermediation,** is the primary route for moving funds from lenders to borrowers. Indeed, although the media focus much of their attention on securities markets, particularly the stock market, financial intermediaries are a far more important source of financing for corporations than securities markets are. This is true not only for the United States but for other industrialized countries as well (see Box 2). Why are financial intermediaries and indirect finance so important in financial markets? To answer this question, we need to understand the role of transaction costs and information costs in financial markets.

Transaction Costs

Transaction costs, the time and money spent in carrying out financial transactions, are a major problem for people who have excess funds to lend. As we have seen, Carl the Carpenter needs $1000 for his new tool, and you know that it is an excellent investment opportunity. You have the cash and would like to lend him the money, but to protect your investment, you have to hire a lawyer to write up the loan contract that specifies how much interest Carl will pay you, when he will make these interest payments, and when he will repay you the

$1000. Obtaining the contract will cost you $500. When you figure in this transaction cost for making the loan, you realize that you can't earn enough from the deal (you spend $500 to make perhaps $100) and reluctantly tell Carl that he will have to look elsewhere.

This example illustrates that small savers like you or potential borrowers like Carl might be frozen out of financial markets and thus be unable to benefit from them. Can anyone come to the rescue? Financial intermediaries can.

Financial intermediaries can substantially reduce transaction costs because they have developed expertise in lowering them and because their large size allows them to take advantage of **economies of scale,** the reduction in transaction costs per dollar of transactions as the size (scale) of transactions increases. For example, a bank knows how to find a good lawyer to produce an airtight loan contract, and this contract can be used over and over again in its loan transactions, thus lowering the legal cost per transaction. Instead of a loan contract (which may not be all that well written) costing $500, a bank can hire a topflight lawyer for $5000 to draw up an airtight loan contract that can be used for 2000 loans at a cost of $2.50 per loan. At a cost of $2.50 per loan, it now becomes profitable for the financial intermediary to loan Carl the $1000.

Because financial intermediaries are able to reduce transaction costs substantially, they make it possible for you to provide funds indirectly to people with productive investment opportunities like Carl. In addition, a financial intermediary's low transaction costs mean that it can provide its customers with liquidity services, services that make it easier for customers to conduct transactions. For example, banks provide depositors with checking accounts that enable them to pay their bills easily. In addition, depositors can earn interest on checking and savings accounts and yet still convert them into goods and services whenever necessary.

Asymmetric Information: Adverse Selection and Moral Hazard

The presence of transaction costs in financial markets explains, in part, why financial intermediaries and indirect finance play such an important role in financial markets. An additional reason is that in financial markets, one party often does not know enough about the other party to make accurate decisions. This inequality is called **asymmetric information.** For example, a borrower who takes out a loan usually has better information about the potential returns and risk associated with the investment projects for which the funds are earmarked than the lender does. Lack of information creates problems in the financial system on two fronts: before the transaction is entered into and after.

Adverse selection is the problem created by asymmetric information *before* the transaction occurs. Adverse selection in financial markets occurs when the potential borrowers who are the most likely to produce an undesirable *(adverse)* outcome—the bad credit risks—are the ones who most actively seek out a loan and are thus most likely to be selected. Because adverse selection makes it more likely that loans might be made to bad credit risks, lenders may decide not to make any loans even though there are good credit risks in the marketplace.

To understand why adverse selection occurs, suppose that you have two aunts to whom you might make a loan—Aunt Sheila and Aunt Louise. Aunt Louise is a conservative type who borrows only when she has an investment that she is quite sure will pay off. Aunt Sheila, by contrast, is an inveterate gambler who has just come across a get-rich-quick scheme that will make her a millionaire if she can just borrow $1000 to invest in it. Unfortunately, as with most get-rich-quick schemes, there is a high probability that the investment won't pay off and that Aunt Sheila will lose the $1000.

Which of your aunts is more likely to call you to ask for a loan? Aunt Sheila, of course, because she has so much to gain if the investment pays off. You, however, would not want to make a loan to her because there is a high probability that her investment will turn sour and she will be unable to pay you back.

If you knew both your aunts very well—that is, if information was not asymmetric—you wouldn't have a problem because you would know that Aunt Sheila is a bad risk and so you would not lend to her. Suppose, though, that you don't know your aunts well. You are more likely to lend to Aunt Sheila than to Aunt Louise because Aunt Sheila would be hounding you for the loan. Because of the possibility of adverse selection, you might decide not to lend to either of your aunts, even though there are times when Aunt Louise, who is an excellent credit risk, might need a loan for a worthwhile investment.

Moral hazard is the problem created by asymmetric information *after* the transaction occurs. Moral hazard in financial markets is the risk *(hazard)* that the borrower might engage in activities that are undesirable *(immoral)* from the lender's point of view because they make it less likely that the loan will be paid back. Because moral hazard lowers the probability that the loan will be repaid, lenders may decide that they would rather not make a loan.

As an example of moral hazard, suppose that you made a $1000 loan to another relative, Uncle Melvin, who needs the money to purchase a word processor so that he can set up a business typing students' term papers. Once you have made the loan, however, Uncle Melvin is more likely to slip off to the track and play the horses. If he bets on a 20-to-1 long shot and wins with your money, he is able to pay you back your $1000 and live high on the hog with the remaining $19,000. But if he loses, as is likely, you don't get paid back, and all he has lost is his reputation as a reliable, upstanding uncle. Uncle Melvin therefore has an incentive to go to the track because his gains ($19,000) if he bets correctly may be much greater than the cost to him (his reputation) if he bets incorrectly. If you knew what Uncle Melvin was up to, you would prevent him from going to the track, and he would not be able to increase the moral hazard. However, because it is hard for you to keep informed about his whereabouts—that is, because information is asymmetric—there is a good chance that Uncle Melvin will go to the track and you will not get paid back. The risk of moral hazard might therefore discourage you from making the $1000 loan to Uncle Melvin, even if you were sure that you would be paid back if he used it to set up his business.

Study Guide   Because the concepts of adverse selection and moral hazard are extremely useful in understanding the behavior we examine in this and many of the later chapters (and in life in general), you must understand them fully. One way to distinguish between them is to remember that adverse selection is a problem of asymmetric information before entering into a transaction, whereas moral hazard is a problem of asymmetric information after the transaction has occurred. A helpful way to nail down these concepts is to think of other examples, for financial or other types of transactions, in which adverse selection or moral hazard plays a role. Several problems at the end of the chapter provide additional examples of situations involving adverse selection and moral hazard.

The problems created by adverse selection and moral hazard are an important impediment to well-functioning financial markets. Again, financial intermediaries can alleviate these problems.

With financial intermediaries in the economy, small savers can provide their funds to the financial markets by lending these funds to a trustworthy intermediary, say, the Honest John Bank, which in turn lends the funds out either by making loans or by buying securities such as stocks or bonds. Successful financial intermediaries have higher earnings on their investments because they are better equipped than individuals to screen out good from bad credit risks, thereby reducing losses due to adverse selection. In addition, financial intermediaries have high earnings because they develop expertise in monitoring the parties they lend to, thus reducing losses due to moral hazard. The result is that financial intermediaries can afford to pay lender-savers interest or provide substantial services and still earn a profit.

The success of financial intermediaries is evidenced by the fact that most Americans invest their savings with them and also obtain their loans from them. Financial intermediaries play a key role in improving economic efficiency because they help financial markets channel funds from lender-savers to people with productive investment opportunities. Without a well-functioning set of financial intermediaries, it is very hard for an economy to reach its full potential. We will explore further the role of financial intermediaries in the economy in Part III.

FINANCIAL INTERMEDIARIES

We have seen why financial intermediaries play such an important role in the economy. Now we look at the principal financial intermediaries and how they perform the intermediation function. They fall into three categories: depository institutions (banks), contractual savings institutions, and investment intermediaries. Table 3 provides a guide to the discussion of the financial intermediaries that fit into these three categories by describing their primary liabilities (sources of funds) and assets (uses of funds). The relative size of these intermediaries in the United States is indicated in Table 4, which lists the amount of their assets at the end of 1970, 1980, 1990, and 1996.

Depository Institutions

Depository institutions (which for simplicity we refer to as *banks* throughout this text) are financial intermediaries that accept deposits from individuals and institutions and make loans. The study of money and banking focuses special attention on this group of financial institutions because they are involved in the creation of deposits, an important component of the money supply. These institutions include commercial banks and the so-called **thrift institutions (thrifts):** savings and loan associations, mutual savings banks, and credit unions. Their behavior plays an important role in determining the money supply.

TABLE 3   Primary Assets and Liabilities of Financial Intermediaries

Type of Intermediary	Primary Liabilities (Sources of Funds)	Primary Assets (Uses of Funds)
Depository institutions (banks)		
Commercial banks	Deposits	Business and consumer loans, mortgages, U.S. government securities and municipal bonds
Savings and loan associations	Deposits	Mortgages
Mutual savings banks	Deposits	Mortgages
Credit unions	Deposits	Consumer loans
Contractual savings institutions		
Life insurance companies	Premiums from policies	Corporate bonds and mortgages
Fire and casualty insurance companies	Premiums from policies	Municipal bonds, corporate bonds and stock, U.S. government securities
Pension funds, government retirement funds	Employer and employee contributions	Corporate bonds and stock
Investment intermediaries		
Finance companies	Commercial paper, stocks, bonds	Consumer and business loans
Mutual funds	Shares	Stocks, bonds
Money market mutual funds	Shares	Money market instruments

COMMERCIAL BANKS These financial intermediaries raise funds primarily by issuing checkable deposits (deposits on which checks can be written), savings deposits (deposits that are payable on demand but do not allow their owner to write checks), and time deposits (deposits with fixed terms to maturity). They then use these funds to make commercial, consumer, and mortgage loans and to buy U.S. government securities and municipal bonds. There are approximately 10,000 commercial banks in the United States, and as a group, they are the largest financial intermediary and have the most diversified portfolios (collections) of assets.

SAVINGS AND LOAN ASSOCIATIONS Savings and loan associations (S&Ls) obtain funds primarily through savings deposits (often called shares) and time and checkable deposits. The acquired funds have traditionally been used to make

TABLE 4 Principal Financial Int

Type of Intermediary	Va ($ billio 1970	1980		
Depository institutions (banks)				
Commercial banks	517	1481		10
Savings and loan associations and mutual savings banks	250	792	1365	1035
Credit unions +conFine to that union	18	67	215	327
Contractual savings institutions				
Life insurance companies	201	464	1367	2239
Fire and casualty insurance companies	50	182	533	804
Pension funds (private)	112	504	1629	3031
State and local government retirement funds	60	197	737	1735
Investment intermediaries				
Finance companies	64	205	610	897
Mutual funds	47	70	654	2349
Money market mutual funds	0	76	498	891

Source: Federal Reserve Flow of Funds Accounts.

mortgage loans. S&Ls are the second-largest group of financial intermediaries, numbering around 1500. In the 1950s and 1960s, S&Ls grew much more rapidly than commercial banks, but when interest rates climbed sharply from the late 1960s to the early 1980s, S&Ls encountered difficulties that slowed their rapid growth. Because most mortgages are long-term loans, with maturities in excess of 25 years, many were made years earlier when interest rates were substantially lower. When interest rates rose, S&Ls frequently found that the income from their mortgages was well below the cost of acquiring funds. Many of them suffered large losses, and many went out of business.

Until 1980, savings and loans were restricted to making mortgage loans and could not establish checking accounts. Their troubles encouraged Congress to pass legislation in the early 1980s allowing them to offer checking accounts, make consumer loans, and pursue many activities previously restricted to commercial banks. In addition, they are now subject to the same requirements as the commercial banks regarding deposits with the Federal Reserve. The net result of this legislation is that the distinction between savings and loans and commercial banks has blurred, and these intermediaries have become more alike and much more competitive with each other.

MUTUAL SAVINGS BANKS Mutual savings banks are very similar to savings and loans. They raise funds by accepting deposits (often called shares) and use them primarily to make mortgage loans. Their corporate structure is somewhat different from that of S&Ls in that they are always structured as "mutuals," or cooperatives: The depositors own the bank. There are around 500 of these institutions, located primarily in the Northeast. Like savings and loans, until 1980 they were restricted to making mortgage loans, and they suffered similar problems when interest rates rose from the late 1960s to the early 1980s. They were similarly affected by the banking legislation in the 1980s and can now issue checkable deposits and make loans other than mortgages.

CREDIT UNIONS These financial institutions, numbering about 12,000, are very small cooperative lending institutions organized around a particular group: union members, employees of a particular firm, and so forth. They acquire funds from deposits called shares and primarily make consumer loans. Thanks to the banking legislation in the 1980s, credit unions are also allowed to issue checkable deposits and can make mortgage loans in addition to consumer loans.

Contractual Savings Institutions

Contractual savings institutions, such as insurance companies and pension funds, are financial intermediaries that acquire funds at periodic intervals on a contractual basis. Because they can predict with reasonable accuracy how much they will have to pay out in benefits in the coming years, they do not have to worry as much as depository institutions about losing funds. As a result, the liquidity of assets is not as important a consideration for them as it is for depository institutions, and they tend to invest their funds primarily in long-term securities such as corporate bonds, stocks, and mortgages.

LIFE INSURANCE COMPANIES Life insurance companies insure people against financial hazards following a death and sell annuities (annual income payments upon retirement). They acquire funds from the premiums that people pay to keep their policies in force and use them mainly to buy corporate bonds and mortgages. They also purchase stocks but are restricted in the amount that they can hold. Currently, with $2.2 trillion in assets, they are among the largest of the contractual savings institutions.

FIRE AND CASUALTY INSURANCE COMPANIES These companies insure their policyholders against loss from theft, fire, and accidents. They are very much like life insurance companies, receiving funds through premiums for their policies, but they have a greater possibility of loss of funds if major disasters occur. For this reason, they use their funds to buy more liquid assets than life insurance companies do. Their largest holding of assets is municipal bonds; they also hold corporate bonds and stocks and U.S. government securities.

PENSION FUNDS AND GOVERNMENT RETIREMENT FUNDS Private pension funds and state and local retirement funds provide retirement income in the form of annuities to employees who are covered by a pension plan. Funds are acquired by contributions from employers or from employees, who either have a contribution automatically deducted from their paychecks or contribute voluntarily. The largest asset holdings of pension funds are corporate bonds and stocks. The establishment of pension funds has been actively encouraged by the federal government both through legislation requiring pension plans and through tax incentives to encourage contributions.

Investment Intermediaries

This category of financial intermediaries includes finance companies, mutual funds, and money market mutual funds.

FINANCE COMPANIES Finance companies raise funds by selling commercial paper (a short-term debt instrument) and by issuing stocks and bonds. They lend these funds to consumers, who make purchases of such items as furniture, automobiles, and home improvements, and to small businesses. Some finance companies are organized by a parent corporation to help sell its product. For example, Ford Motor Credit Company makes loans to consumers who purchase Ford automobiles.

MUTUAL FUNDS These financial intermediaries acquire funds by selling shares to many individuals and use the proceeds to purchase diversified portfolios of stocks and bonds. Mutual funds allow shareholders to pool their resources so that they can take advantage of lower transaction costs when buying large blocks of stocks or bonds. In addition, mutual funds allow shareholders to hold more diversified portfolios than they otherwise would. Shareholders can sell (redeem) shares at any time, but the value of these shares will be determined by the value of the mutual fund's holdings of securities. Because these fluctuate greatly, the value of mutual fund shares will too; therefore, investments in mutual funds can be risky.

MONEY MARKET MUTUAL FUNDS These relatively new financial institutions have the characteristics of a mutual fund but also function to some extent as a depository institution because they offer deposit-type accounts. Like most mutual funds, they sell shares to acquire funds that are then used to buy money market instruments that are both safe and very liquid. The interest on these assets is then paid out to the shareholders.

A key feature of these funds is that shareholders can write checks against the value of their shareholdings. There are generally restrictions on the use of the check-writing privilege, however; checks frequently cannot be written for amounts less than a set minimum, such as $500, and a substantial amount of money is required initially to open an account. In effect, shares in a money market mutual fund function like checking account deposits that pay interest, but with some restrictions on the check-writing privilege. Money market mutual funds have experienced extraordinary growth since 1971, when they first appeared. By 1996, their assets had climbed to nearly $900 billion.

REGULATION OF THE FINANCIAL SYSTEM

The financial system is among the most heavily regulated sectors of the American economy. The government regulates financial markets for three main reasons: to increase the information available to investors, to ensure the soundness of the financial system, and to improve control of monetary policy. We will examine how these three reasons have led to the present regulatory environment. As a study aid, the principal regulatory agencies of the U.S. financial system are listed in Table 5.

Increasing Information Available to Investors

Asymmetric information in financial markets means that investors may be subject to adverse selection and moral hazard problems that may hinder the efficient operation of financial markets. Risky firms or outright crooks may be the most eager to sell securities to unwary investors, and the resulting adverse selection problem may keep investors out of financial markets. Furthermore, once an investor has bought a security, thereby lending money to a firm, the borrower may have incentives to engage in risky activities or to commit outright fraud. The presence of this moral hazard problem may also keep investors away from financial markets. Government regulation can reduce adverse selection and moral hazard problems in financial markets and increase their efficiency by increasing the amount of information available to investors.

As a result of the stock market crash in 1929 and revelations of widespread fraud in the aftermath, political demands for regulation culminated in the Securities Act of 1933 and the establishment of the Securities and Exchange Commission (SEC). The SEC requires corporations issuing securities to disclose certain information about their sales, assets, and earnings to the public and restricts trading by the largest stockholders (known as insiders) in the corporation. By requiring disclosure of this information and by discouraging insider trading, which could be used to manipulate security prices, the SEC hopes that investors will be better informed and be protected from some of the abuses in financial markets that occurred before 1933. Indeed, in recent years, the SEC has been particularly active in prosecuting people involved in insider trading.

Ensuring the Soundness of Financial Intermediaries

Asymmetric information can also lead to widespread collapse of financial intermediaries, referred to as a **financial panic.** Because providers of funds to financial intermediaries may not be able to assess whether the institutions holding their funds are sound or not, if they have doubts about the overall health of financial intermediaries, they may want to pull their funds out of both sound and unsound institutions. The possible outcome is a financial panic that produces large losses for the public and causes serious damage to the economy. To protect the public and the economy from financial panics, the government has implemented six types of regulations.

1. State banking and insurance commissions, as well as the Office of the Comptroller of the Currency (an agency of the federal government), have created very tight regulations as to who is allowed to set up a financial intermediary. Individuals or groups that want to establish a financial intermediary, such as a

TABLE 5 Principal Regulatory Agencies of the U.S. Financial System

Regulatory Agency	Subject of Regulation	Nature of Regulations
Securities and Exchange Commission (SEC)	Organized exchanges and financial markets	Requires disclosure of information, restricts insider trading
Commodities Futures Trading Commission (CFTC)	Futures market exchanges	Regulates procedures for trading in futures markets
Office of the Comptroller of the Currency	Federally-chartered commercial banks	Charters and examines the books of federally chartered commercial banks and imposes restrictions on assets they can hold
National Credit Union Administration (NCUA)	Federally-chartered credit unions	Charters and examines the books of federally chartered credit unions and imposes restrictions on assets they can hold
State banking and insurance commissions	State-chartered depository institutions	Charter and examine the books of state-chartered banks and insurance companies, impose restrictions on assets they can hold, and impose restrictions on branching
Federal Deposit Insurance Corporation (FDIC)	Commercial banks, mutual savings banks, savings and loan associations	Provides insurance of up to $100,000 for each depositor at a bank, examines the books of insured banks, and imposes restrictions on assets they can hold
Federal Reserve System	All depository institutions	Examines the books of commercial banks that are members of the system, sets reserve requirements for all banks
Office of Thrift Supervision	Savings and loan associations	Examines the books of savings and loan associations, imposes restrictions on assets they can hold

bank or an insurance company, must obtain a charter from the state or the federal government. Only if they are upstanding citizens with impeccable credentials and a large amount of initial funds will they be given a charter.

2. There are stringent reporting requirements for financial intermediaries. Their bookkeeping must follow certain strict principles, their books are subject to periodic inspection, and they must make certain information available to the public.

3. There are restrictions on what financial intermediaries are allowed to do and what assets they can hold. Before you put your funds into a bank or some other such institution, you would want to know that your funds are safe and that the bank or other financial intermediary will be able to meet its obligations to you. One way of doing this is to restrict the financial intermediary from engaging in certain risky activities. Legislation passed in 1933 separates commercial banking from the securities industry so that banks do not engage in risky ventures associated with this industry. Another way is to restrict financial intermediaries from holding certain risky assets, or at least from holding a greater quantity of these risky assets than is prudent. For example, commercial banks and other depository institutions are not allowed to hold common stock because stock prices experience substantial fluctuations. Insurance companies are allowed to hold common stock, but their holdings cannot exceed a certain fraction of their total assets.

4. The government can insure people providing funds to a financial intermediary from any financial loss if the financial intermediary should fail. The most important government agency that provides this type of insurance is the Federal Deposit Insurance Corporation (FDIC), which insures each depositor at a commercial bank or mutual savings bank up to a loss of $100,000 per account. All commercial and mutual savings banks, with a few minor exceptions, make contributions into the FDIC's Bank Insurance Fund, which are used to pay off depositors in the case of a bank's failure. The FDIC was created in 1934 after the massive bank failures of 1930–1933 in which the savings of many depositors at commercial banks were wiped out. Similar government agencies exist for other depository institutions: The Savings Association Insurance Fund (part of the FDIC) provides deposit insurance for savings and loan associations, and the National Credit Union Share Insurance Fund (NCUSIF) does the same for credit unions.

5. Politicians have often declared that unbridled competition among financial intermediaries promotes failures that will harm the public. Although the evidence that competition does this is extremely weak, it has not stopped the state and federal governments from imposing many restrictive regulations. These regulations have taken two forms. First are the restrictions on the opening of additional locations (branches). In the past, banks were not allowed to open up branches in other states, and in some states banks were restricted from opening additional locations.

6. Competition has also been inhibited by regulations that impose restrictions on interest rates that can be paid on deposits. For decades after 1933, banks were prohibited from paying interest on checking accounts. In addition, until 1986, the Federal Reserve System had the power under **Regulation Q** to set maximum interest rates that banks could pay on savings deposits. These regulations were instituted because of the widespread belief that unrestricted interest-rate competition helped encourage bank failures during the Great Depression. Later evidence does not seem to support this view, and restrictions like Regulation Q have been abolished.

Improving Control of Monetary Policy

Because banks play a very important role in determining the supply of money (which in turn affects many aspects of the economy), much regulation of these financial intermediaries is intended to improve control over the money supply. One such regulation is **reserve requirements,** which make it obligatory for all depository institutions to keep a certain fraction of their deposits in accounts with the Federal Reserve System (the Fed), the central bank in the United States. Reserve requirements help the Fed exercise more precise control over the money supply. Deposit insurance regulation can also be rationalized along these lines: The FDIC gives depositors confidence in the banking system and eliminates widespread bank failures, which can in turn cause large, uncontrollable fluctuations in the quantity of money.

In later chapters we will look more closely at government regulation of financial markets and will see whether it has improved the functioning of financial markets.

Financial Regulation Abroad

Not surprisingly, given the similarity of the economic system here and in Japan, Canada, and the nations of Western Europe, financial regulation in these countries is similar to financial regulation in the United States. The provision of information is improved by requiring corporations issuing securities to report details about assets and liabilities, earnings, and sales of stock, and by prohibiting insider trading. The soundness of intermediaries is ensured by licensing, periodic inspection of financial intermediaries' books, and the provision of deposit insurance (although its coverage is smaller and its existence is often intentionally not advertised).

The major differences between financial regulation in the United States and abroad relate to bank regulation. In the past, the United States was the only industrialized country to subject banks to restrictions on branching, which limited banks' size and restricted them to certain geographic regions. U.S. banks are also the most restricted in the range of financial services they may provide and the assets they may hold. Banks abroad frequently hold shares in commercial firms; in Japan and Germany, those stakes can be sizable.

S U M M A R Y

1. The basic function of financial markets is to channel funds from savers who have an excess of funds to spenders who have a shortage of funds. Financial markets can do this either through direct finance, in which borrowers borrow funds directly from lenders by selling them securities, or through indirect finance, which involves a financial intermediary who stands between the lender-savers and the borrower-spenders and helps transfer funds from one to the other. This channeling of funds improves the economic welfare of everyone in the society because it allows funds to move from people who have no productive investment opportunities to those who have such opportunities, thereby contributing to increased efficiency in the economy. In addition, channeling of funds directly benefits consumers by allowing them to make purchases when they need them most.

2. Financial markets can be classified as debt and equity markets, primary and secondary markets, exchanges and over-the-counter markets, and money and capital markets.

3. The principal money market instruments (debt instruments with maturities of less than one year) are U.S. Treasury bills, negotiable bank certificates of deposit, commercial paper, banker's acceptances, repurchase agreements, federal funds, and Eurodollars. The principal capital market instruments (debt and equity instruments with maturities greater than one year) are stocks, mortgages, corporate bonds, U.S. government securities, U.S. government agency securities, state and local government bonds, and consumer and bank commercial loans.

4. An important trend in recent years is the growing internationalization of financial markets. Eurobonds, which are denominated in a currency other than that of the country in which they are sold, are now the dominant security in the international bond market and have surpassed U.S. corporate bonds as a source of new funds.

5. Financial intermediaries are financial institutions that acquire funds by issuing liabilities and in turn use those funds to acquire assets by purchasing securities or making loans. Financial intermediaries play such an important role in the financial system because they reduce transaction costs and solve problems created by adverse selection and moral hazard. As a result, financial intermediaries allow small savers and borrowers to benefit from the existence of financial markets, thereby increasing the efficiency of the economy.

6. The principal financial intermediaries fall into three categories: (a) banks—commercial banks, savings and loan associations, mutual savings banks, and credit unions; (b) contractual savings institutions—life insurance companies, fire and casualty insurance companies, and pension funds; and (c) investment intermediaries—finance companies, mutual funds, and money market mutual funds.

7. The government regulates financial markets and financial intermediaries for three main reasons: to increase the information available to investors, to ensure the soundness of the financial system, and to improve control of monetary policy. Regulations include requiring disclosure of information to the public, restrictions on who can set up a financial intermediary, restrictions on what assets financial intermediaries can hold, the provision of deposit insurance, reserve requirements, and the setting of maximum interest rates that can be paid on checking accounts and savings deposits.

KEY TERMS

adverse selection, p. 35

asymmetric information, p. 35

brokers, p. 24

capital market, p. 25

currency, p. 26

dealers, p. 24

default, p. 26

dividends, p. 23

economies of scale, p. 35

equities, p. 23

Eurobonds, p. 32

Eurodollars, p. 29

exchanges, p. 24

federal funds rate, p. 28

financial intermediation, p. 34

financial panic, p. 42

foreign bonds, p. 32

intermediate-term, p. 23

investment banks, p. 24

liabilities, p. 21

liquid, p. 24

long-term, p. 23

maturity, p. 23

money market, p. 25

moral hazard, p. 36

over-the-counter (OTC) market, p. 24

primary market, p. 23

Regulation Q, p. 44

reserve requirements, p. 45

secondary market, p. 23

short-term, p. 23

thrift institutions (thrifts), p. 37

transaction costs, p. 34

underwriting, p. 24

QUESTIONS AND PROBLEMS

*1. Why is a share of IBM common stock an asset for its owner and a liability for IBM?

2. If I can buy a car today for $5000 and it is worth $10,000 in extra income next year to me because it enables me to get a job as a traveling anvil seller, should I take out a loan from Larry the Loan Shark at a 90 percent interest rate if no one else will give me a loan? Will I be better or worse off as a result of taking out this loan? Can you make a case for legalizing loan-sharking?

*3. Some economists suspect that one of the reasons that economies in developing countries grow so slowly is that they do not have well-developed financial markets. Does this argument make sense?

4. The U.S. economy borrowed heavily from the British in the nineteenth century to build a railroad system. What was the principal debt instrument used? Why did this make both countries better off?

*5. "Because corporations do not actually raise any funds in secondary markets, they are less important to the economy than primary markets." Comment.

6. If you suspect that a company will go bankrupt next year, which would you rather hold, bonds issued by the company or equities issued by the company? Why?

*7. How can the adverse selection problem explain why you are more likely to make a loan to a family member than to a stranger?

8. Think of one example in which you have had to deal with the adverse selection problem.

*9. Why do loan sharks worry less about moral hazard in connection with their borrowers than some other lenders do?

10. If you are an employer, what kinds of moral hazard problems might you worry about with your employees?

*11. If there were no asymmetry in the information that a borrower and a lender had, could there still be a moral hazard problem?

12. "In a world without information and transaction costs, financial intermediaries would not exist." Is this statement true, false, or uncertain? Explain your answer.

*13. Why might you be willing to make a loan to your neighbor by putting funds in a savings account earning a 5 percent interest rate at the bank and having the bank loan her the funds at a 10 percent interest rate rather than loan her the funds yourself?

14. In two lists, rank the following money market instruments in terms of their liquidity and their safety:
a. U.S. Treasury bills
b. Negotiable CDs
c. Repurchase agreements
d. Commercial paper

*15. Discuss some of the manifestations of the globalization of world capital markets.

Chapter 3

WHAT IS MONEY?

P R E V I E W   If you had lived in America before the Revolutionary War, your money might have primarily consisted of Spanish doubloons (silver coins that were also called *pieces of eight*). Before the Civil War, the principal forms of money in the United States were not only gold and silver coins but also paper notes, called *banknotes*, issued by private banks. Today you use not only coins and dollar bills issued by the government as money but also checks written on accounts held at banks. Money has been different things at different times; however, it has *always* been important to people and to the economy.

To understand the effects of money on the economy, we must understand exactly what money is. In this chapter we develop precise definitions by exploring the functions of money, looking at why and how it promotes economic efficiency, tracing how its forms have evolved over time, and examining how money is currently measured.

MEANING OF MONEY

As the word *money* is used in everyday conversation, it can mean many things, but to economists it has a very specific meaning. To avoid confusion, we must clarify how economists' use of the word *money* differs from conventional usage.

Economists define *money* (also referred to as the *money supply*) as anything that is generally accepted in payment for goods or services or in the repayment of debts. Currency, consisting of dollar bills and coins, clearly fits this definition and is one type of money. When most people talk about money, they're talking about currency. If, for example, someone comes up to you and says, "Your money or your life," you should quickly hand over all your currency rather than ask, "What exactly do you mean by 'money'?"

To define money merely as currency is much too narrow for economists. Because checks are also accepted as payment for purchases, checking account deposits are considered money as well. An even broader definition of money is often needed because other items such as savings deposits can in effect function as money if they can be quickly and easily converted into currency or checking account deposits. As you can see, there is no single, precise definition of money or the money supply, even for economists.

To complicate matters further, the word *money* is frequently used synonymously with *wealth.* When people say, "Joe is rich—he has an awful lot of money," they probably mean that Joe not only has a lot of currency and a high balance in his checking account but also has stocks, bonds, four cars, three houses, and a yacht. Thus while "currency" is too narrow a definition of money, this other popular usage is much too broad. Economists make a distinction between money in the form of currency, demand deposits, and other items that are used to make purchases and **wealth,** the total collection of pieces of property that serve to store value. Wealth includes not only money but also other assets such as bonds, common stock, art, land, furniture, cars, and houses.

People also use the word *money* to describe what economists call *income,* as in the sentence "Sheila would be a wonderful catch; she has a good job and earns a lot of money." **Income** is a *flow* of earnings per unit of time. Money, by contrast, is a *stock:* It is a certain amount at a given point in time. If someone tells you that he has an income of $1000, you cannot tell whether he earned a lot or a little without knowing whether this $1000 is earned per year, per month, or even per day. But if someone tells you that she has $1000 in her pocket, you know exactly how much this is.

Keep in mind that the money discussed in this book refers to anything that is generally accepted in payment for goods and services or in the repayment of debts and is distinct from income and wealth.

FUNCTIONS OF MONEY

Whether money is shells or rocks or gold or paper, it has three primary functions in any economy: as a medium of exchange, a unit of account, and a store of value. Of the three functions, its function as a medium of exchange is what distinguishes money from other assets such as stocks, bonds, and houses.

Medium of Exchange

In almost all market transactions in our economy, money in the form of currency or checks is a **medium of exchange;** it is used to pay for goods and services. The use of money as a medium of exchange promotes economic efficiency by eliminating much of the time spent in exchanging goods and services. To see why, let's look at a barter economy, one without money, in which goods and services are exchanged directly for other goods and services.

Take the case of Ellen the Economics Professor, who can do just one thing well: give brilliant economics lectures. In a barter economy, if Ellen wants to eat, she must find a farmer who not only produces the food she likes but also wants to learn economics. As you might expect, this search will be difficult and time-consuming, and Ellen may spend more time looking for such an economics-hungry farmer than she will teaching. It is even possible that she will have to quit lecturing and go into farming herself. Even so, she may still starve to death.

The time spent trying to exchange goods or services is called a *transaction cost.* In a barter economy, transaction costs are high because people have to satisfy a "double coincidence of wants"—they have to find someone who has a good or service they want and who also wants the good or service they have to offer.

Let's see what happens if we introduce money into Ellen the Economics Professor's world. Ellen can teach anyone who is willing to pay money to hear her lecture. She can then go to any farmer (or his representative at the supermarket) and buy the food she needs with the money she has been paid. The problem of the double coincidence of wants is avoided, and Ellen saves a lot of time, which she may spend doing what she does best: teaching.

As this example shows, money promotes economic efficiency by eliminating much of the time spent exchanging goods and services. It also promotes efficiency by allowing people to specialize in what they do best. Money is therefore essential in an economy: It is a lubricant that allows the economy to run more smoothly by lowering transaction costs, thereby encouraging specialization and the division of labor.

The need for money is so strong that almost every society beyond the most primitive invents it. For a commodity to function effectively as money, it has to meet several criteria: (1) It must be easily standardized, making it simple to ascertain its value; (2) it must be widely accepted; (3) it must be divisible so that it is easy to "make change"; (4) it must be easy to carry; and (5) it must not deteriorate quickly. Forms of money that have satisfied these criteria have taken many unusual forms throughout human history, ranging from wampum (strings of beads) used by Native Americans, to tobacco and whiskey, used by the early American colonists, to cigarettes, used in prisoner-of-war camps during World War II.[1] The diversity of forms of money that have been developed over the years is as much a testament to the inventiveness of the human race as the development of tools and language.

Unit of Account

The second role of money is to provide a **unit of account;** that is, it is used to measure value in the economy. We measure the value of goods and services in terms of money, just as we measure weight in terms of pounds or distance in terms of miles. To see why this function is important, let's look again at a barter economy where money does not perform this function. If the economy has only three goods, say, peaches, economics lectures, and movies, then we need to know only three prices to tell us how to exchange one for another: the price of peaches in terms of economics lectures (that is, how many economics lectures you have to pay for a peach), the price of peaches in terms of movies, and the price of economics lectures in terms of movies. If there were ten goods, we would

---

[1] An extremely entertaining article on the development of money in a prisoner-of-war camp during World War II is R. A. Radford, "The Economic Organization of a P.O.W. Camp," *Economica* 12 (November 1945): 189–201.

need to know 45 prices in order to exchange one good for another; with 100 goods, we would need 4950 prices; and with 1000 goods, 499,500 prices.[2] Imagine how hard it would be to shop in a supermarket with 1000 different items on its shelves; deciding whether chicken or fish is cheaper would be difficult if the price of a pound of chicken were quoted as 4 pounds of butter and the price of a pound of fish were quoted as 8 pounds of tomatoes. To make sure that you can compare the prices of all items, the price tags of each item would have to list up to 999 different prices, and the time spent reading them would result in very high transaction costs.

The solution to the problem is to introduce money into the economy and have all prices quoted in terms of units of that money, enabling us to quote the price of economics lectures, peaches, and movies in terms of, say, dollars. If there were only three goods in the economy, this would not be a great advantage over the barter system because we would still need three prices to conduct transactions. But for ten goods we now need only ten prices; for 100 goods, 100 prices; and so on. At the 1000-good supermarket, there are now only 1000 prices to look at, not 499,500!

We can see that using money as a unit of account reduces transaction costs in an economy by reducing the number of prices that need to be considered. The benefits of this function of money grow as the economy becomes more complex.

Store of Value

Money also functions as a **store of value;** it is a repository of purchasing power over time. A store of value is used to save purchasing power from the time income is received until the time it is spent. This function of money is useful because most of us do not want to spend our income immediately upon receiving it but rather prefer to wait until we have the time or the desire to shop.

Money is not unique as a store of value; any asset, be it money, stocks, bonds, land, houses, art, or jewelry, can be used to store wealth. Many such assets have advantages over money as a store of value: They often pay the owner a higher interest rate than money, experience price appreciation, and deliver services such as providing a roof over one's head. If these assets are a more desirable store of value than money, why do people hold money at all?

The answer to this question relates to the important economic concept of **liquidity,** the relative ease and speed with which an asset can be converted into a medium of exchange. Liquidity is highly desirable. Money is the most liquid asset of all because it is the medium of exchange; it does not have to be converted

---

[2] The formula for telling us the number of prices we need when we have N goods is the same formula that tells us the number of pairs when there are N items. It is

$$\frac{N(N-1)}{2}$$

In the case of ten goods, for example, we would need

$$\frac{10(10-1)}{2} = \frac{90}{2} = 45$$

into anything else in order to make purchases. Other assets involve transaction costs when they are converted into money. When you sell your house, for example, you have to pay a brokerage commission (usually 5 percent to 7 percent of the sales price), and if you need cash immediately to pay some pressing bills, you might have to settle for a lower price in order to sell the house quickly. The fact that money is the most liquid asset, then, explains why people are willing to hold it even if it is not the most attractive store of value.

How good a store of value money is depends on the price level because its value is fixed in terms of the price level. A doubling of all prices, for example, means that the value of money has dropped by half; conversely, a halving of all prices means that the value of money has doubled. In an inflation, when the price level is increasing rapidly, money loses value rapidly, and people will be more reluctant to hold their wealth in this form. This is especially true during periods of extreme inflation, known as **hyperinflation,** in which the inflation rate exceeds 50 percent per month.

Hyperinflation occurred in Germany after World War I, with inflation rates sometimes exceeding 1000 percent per month. By the end of the hyperinflation in 1923, the price level had risen to more than 30 billion times what it had been just two years before. The quantity of money needed to purchase even the most basic items became excessive. There are stories, for example, that near the end of the hyperinflation, a wheelbarrow of cash would be required to pay for a loaf of bread. Money was losing its value so rapidly that workers were paid and given time off several times during the day to spend their wages before the money became worthless. No one wanted to hold on to money, and so the use of money to carry out transactions declined and barter became more and more dominant. Transaction costs skyrocketed, and as we would expect, output in the economy fell sharply.

EVOLUTION OF THE PAYMENTS SYSTEM

We can obtain a better picture of the functions of money and the forms it has taken over time by looking at the evolution of the **payments system,** the method of conducting transactions in the economy. The payments system has been evolving over centuries, and with it the form of money. At one point, precious metals such as gold were used as the principal means of payment and were the main form of money. Later, paper assets such as checks and currency began to be used in the payments system and viewed as money. Where the payments system is heading has an important bearing on how money will be defined in the future.

To obtain perspective on where the payments system is heading, it is worth exploring how it has evolved. For any object to function as money, it must be universally acceptable; everyone must be willing to take it in payment for goods and services. An object that clearly has value to everyone is a likely candidate to serve as money, and a natural choice is a precious metal such as gold or silver. Money made up of precious metals or another valuable commodity is called **commodity money,** and from ancient times until several hundred years ago, commodity money functioned as the medium of exchange in all but the most primitive societies. The problem with a payments system based exclusively on precious metals is that such a form of money is very heavy and is hard to transport from one place to another. Imagine the holes you'd wear in your pockets if you had to buy things only with coins! Indeed, for large purchases such as a house, you'd have to rent a truck to transport the money payment.

The next development in the payments system was paper currency (pieces of paper that function as a medium of exchange). Initially, paper currency embodied a promise that it was convertible into coins or into a quantity of precious metal. In most countries, however, currency has evolved into **fiat money,** paper currency decreed by governments as legal tender (meaning that legally it must be accepted as payment for debts) but not convertible into coins or precious metal. Paper currency has the advantage of being much lighter than coins or precious metal, but it can be accepted as a medium of exchange only if there is some trust in the authorities who issue it and printing has reached a sufficiently advanced stage that counterfeiting is extremely difficult. Because paper currency has evolved into a legal arrangement, countries can change the currency that they use at will. Indeed, this is currently a hot topic of debate in Europe, which is contemplating a unified currency (see Box 1).

Major drawbacks of paper currency and coins are that they are easily stolen and can be expensive to transport because of their bulk if there are large amounts. To combat this problem, another step in the evolution of the payments system occurred with the development of modern banking: the invention of checks. Checks are a type of IOU payable on demand that allows transactions to take place without the need to carry around large amounts of currency. The introduction of checks was a major innovation that improved the efficiency of the payments system. Frequently, payments made back and forth cancel each other; without checks, this would involve the movement of a lot of currency. With checks, payments that cancel each other can be settled by canceling the checks, and no currency need be moved. The use of checks thus reduces the transportation costs associated with the payments system and improves economic efficiency. Another advantage of checks is that they can be written for any amount up to the balance in the account, making transactions for large amounts much easier. Checks are advantageous in that loss from theft is greatly reduced, and they provide convenient receipts for purchases.

There are, however, two problems with a payments system based on checks. First, it takes time to get checks from one place to another, a particularly serious problem if you are paying someone in a different location who needs to be paid quickly. In addition, if you have a checking account, you know that it takes several business days before a bank will allow you to make use of the funds from a check that you have deposited. If your need for cash is urgent, this feature of paying by check can be frustrating. Second, all the paper shuffling required to process checks is costly; it is estimated that it currently costs over $5 billion per year to process all the checks written in the United States.

With the development of the computer and advanced telecommunications technology, there would seem to be a better way to organize our payments system. All paperwork could be eliminated by converting completely to what is known as an electronic means of payment (EMOP) in which all payments are made using electronic telecommunications.

Although not widely recognized, electronic means of payment has been around for many years. The Federal Reserve has a telecommunications system,

Birth of a New European Currency: The Euro?

As part of the December 1991 Maastricht Treaty of European Union, the European Economic Commission (EEC) outlined a plan to achieve the creation of a single European currency based on the ECU, the European currency unit. Advocates of monetary union point to the advantages that a single currency has in eliminating the transaction costs involved in having to exchange the currency of one country for the currency of another. However, the motive behind monetary union is not just gains in efficiency resulting from lower transaction costs; it is also the push that such a monetary union gives toward the integration of Europe's various economies.

Despite concerns about the feasibility and desirability of a single currency, in December 1995 the heads of the government of the fifteen European Union members agreed to introduce a common currency, called the Euro, in 1999. The timetable involves a decision in early 1998 to decide which countries qualify to be members of a monetary union and the creation of a new European Central Bank. Then on January 1, 1999, the exchange rates of qualifying countries will be fixed permanently,

the European Central Bank will take over monetary policy, and the governments of member countries will issue debt in Euros. By early 2002, Euro notes and coins will begin to circulate and stores will quote prices in Euros, and by June 2002, the old national currencies will be phased out completely and only Euros will be used in the member countries.

While the road to a single currency in Europe sounds smooth in theory, it may be a bumpy one. To qualify for membership in the monetary union, countries are required to satisfy the so-called Maastricht criteria of having a government budget deficit of no more than 3 percent of GDP and total government debt less than 60 percent of GDP. At the current time, only Luxembourg clearly meets these criteria, with Germany on the borderline. However, France, the Netherlands, Austria, Belgium, Ireland, and Finland are also expected to become initial members of the currency union. Whether the debt criteria may have to be relaxed—or whether the monetary union will occur at all— is still an open question. Whatever the outcome, for the first time in history, a serious plan for a single European currency is now on the table.

called Fedwire, that allows all financial institutions that maintain accounts with the Federal Reserve to wire (transfer) funds to each other without having to send checks. In addition, CHIPS (Clearing House Interbank Payment System) and SWIFT (Society for Worldwide Intertelecommunications Financial Transfers), private EMOP systems, are used to wire funds among banks internationally. Banks, money market mutual funds, securities dealers, and corporations make extensive use of these systems to wire funds. Wire transfers using these systems are typically for amounts greater than $1 million, so even though fewer than 1 percent of the number of transactions use an electronic means of payment, over 80 percent of the dollar value of transactions is conducted electronically. Indeed, when we say that a corporation is paying for something with a check, it is frequently paying with an electronic wire transfer.

Smaller wire transfers are carried out with automatic clearing houses (ACHs). It is becoming increasingly common for companies to pay their employees electronically by direct deposit of employees' pay into their bank accounts using an ACH system. Households are also now able to make bill payments by telephone using ACHs or to preauthorize regularly recurring bill payments such as mortgage payments, insurance premiums, and utility bills.

Electronic Money: A Coming Global Phenomenon

The development of cheap computer technology has meant that we are beginning to enter a new stage of a worldwide evolution of the payments system with the advent of electronic money. **Electronic money** (also known as **e-money**) is money that is stored electronically, and it takes several forms.

DEBIT CARDS Debit cards, which look like credit cards, enable consumers to purchase goods by electronically transferring funds directly from their bank accounts to a merchant's account. Debit cards are used in many of the same places that accept credit cards and are now often becoming faster to use than cash. For example, when you buy groceries at many supermarkets, you can swipe your debit card through the card reader at the checkout station and press a button, and the amount of your purchases is immediately deducted from your bank account. Most banks and companies such as Visa and MasterCard issue debit cards, and your ATM card typically can function as a debit card.

STORED-VALUE CARD Stored-value cards also look like debit and credit cards but differ in that they contain a fixed amount of digital cash. The simplest form of stored-value cards is purchased for a preset dollar amount that the consumer spends down. The more sophisticated stored-value card is known as a *smart card*. It contains its own computer chip so that it can be loaded with digital cash from its owner's bank account whenever needed. Smart cards can be loaded either from ATM machines, personal computers, or specially equipped telephones.

Stored-value cards are currently more common outside the United States, with major programs implemented or planned in Australia, Canada, Chile, Colombia, Denmark, France, Italy, Portugal, Singapore, Spain, Taiwan, and the United Kingdom. One of the most ambitious programs has been developed by London-based Mondex Corporation, which started running a test in Swindon, England, in July 1995. Not only can the Mondex smart card be used to transfer funds between consumers and retailers or between the consumer and the bank, but it also allows electronic money transfers between individuals. Funds can be transferred from one person's card to another's by using a handheld wireless device that has been dubbed an electronic wallet because it can carry out all the functions of a standard wallet, including storing phone numbers and other bits and pieces of information as well as holding money. Stored-value cards are making inroads in the United States. Large banks such as Citibank and Chemical Bank have announced trials of stored-value card programs, and a major test was conducted at the 1996 Olympics in Atlanta when First Union Bank, Wachovia, and NationsBank teamed up with Visa to issue around a million stored-value cards.

ELECTRONIC CASH *Electronic cash,* or *e-cash,* is a form of electronic money that can be used on the Internet to purchase goods or services. A consumer gets e-cash by setting up an account with a bank that has links to the Internet and then has the e-cash transferred to her PC. When a consumer wants to buy something with e-cash, she surfs to an Internet store and selects the buy option for a particular item, whereupon the e-cash is automatically transferred from her computer to the merchant's computer. The merchant can then have the funds transferred from the consumer's bank account to his before the goods are shipped. E-cash was pioneered by a Dutch company called DigiCash. In October 1995, Mark Twain Bancshares announced that it would become the first U.S. issuer of e-cash for personal computers.

ELECTRONIC CHECKS Electronic checks allow users of the Internet to pay their bills directly over the Internet without having to send a paper check. The user has his PC write the equivalent of a check and then sends the electronic check to the other party, who in turn sends it to her bank. Once the recipient's bank verifies that the electronic check is valid, it transfers money from the originator's bank account to the recipient's. Because this whole process is done electronically, it is far cheaper and more convenient than using paper checks. Experts estimate that the cost of using an electronic check is less than one-third the cost of conducting a transaction with a paper check. These cost advantages have led some organizations to begin paying bills with electronic checks. For example, in May 1994, the Department of Accounts of the Commonwealth of Virginia began using e-checks to pay some of the state's bills.

Are We Moving to a Cashless Society?

Given the advantages of electronic money, you might think that we would move quickly to the cashless society in which all payments are made electronically. However, a true cashless society is probably not around the corner. Indeed, predictions of such a society have been around for two decades but have not yet come to fruition. For example, *Business Week* predicted in 1975 that electronic means of payment would soon "revolutionize the very concept of money itself," only to reverse itself several years later. Why has the movement to a cashless society been so slow in coming?

Although electronic means of payment may be more efficient than a payments system based on paper, several factors work against the disappearance of the paper system. First, it is very expensive to set up the computer, card reader, and telecommunications networks necessary to make electronic money the dominant form of payment. Second, paper checks have the advantage that they provide receipts, something that many consumers are unwilling to give up. Third, the use of paper checks gives consumers several days of "float"—it takes several days before a check is cashed and funds are withdrawn from the issuer's account, which means that the writer of the check can earn interest on the funds in the meantime. Because electronic payments are immediate, they eliminate the float for the consumer.

Fourth, electronic means of payment may raise security and privacy concerns. We often hear media reports that an unauthorized hacker has been able to access a computer database and to alter information stored there. The fact that this is not an uncommon occurrence means that unscrupulous persons might be able to access bank accounts in electronic payments systems and steal funds by moving them from someone else's accounts into their own. Indeed, this happened in

1995, when a Russian computer programmer got access to Citibank's computers and moved funds electronically into his and his conspirators' accounts. The prevention of this type of fraud is no easy task, and a whole new field of computer science is developing to cope with security issues. A further concern is that the use of electronic means of payment leaves an electronic trail that contains a large amount of personal data on buying habits. There are concerns that government, employers, and marketers might be able to access these data, thereby encroaching on our privacy.

The conclusion from this discussion seems to be that we are moving more rapidly to a payments system in which the use of paper will diminish, although it is likely to be a gradual process that may not reach fruition for 10 to 20 years.

MEASURING MONEY

The definition of money as anything that is generally accepted in payment for goods and services tells us that money is defined by people's behavior. What makes an asset money is that people believe it will be accepted by others when making payment. As we have seen, many different assets have performed this role over the centuries, ranging from gold to paper currency to checking accounts. For that reason, this behavioral definition does not tell us exactly what assets in our economy should be considered money.

To measure money, we need a precise definition that tells us exactly what assets should be included. There are two ways of obtaining a precise definition of money: the theoretical approach and the empirical approach.

Theoretical and Empirical Definitions of Money

The theoretical approach defines money by using economic theory to decide which assets should be included in its measure. As we have seen, the key feature of money is that it is used as a medium of exchange. Therefore, the theoretical approach focuses on this aspect and suggests that only assets that clearly serve as a medium of exchange belong in a measure of the money supply. Currency, checking account deposits, and traveler's checks can all be used to pay for goods and services and clearly function as a medium of exchange. The theoretical approach suggests that a measure of the money supply should include only these assets.

Unfortunately, the theoretical approach is not as clear-cut as we would like. Other assets function like a medium of exchange but are not quite as liquid as currency and checking account deposits. Customers of brokerage firms, for example, can write checks against the value of the securities held for them by the firm. (Because there are often restrictions on the check-writing privilege—for example, a minimum amount for which you can write a check—it is not clear whether these accounts really function as a medium of exchange.) Other assets (such as savings accounts at banks) can similarly be turned quickly into cash without incurring appreciable costs.

The ambiguities inherent in the theoretical approach in determining which assets should be included in a measure of money have led many economists to suggest that money should be defined with a more empirical approach; that is, the decision about what to call money should be based on which measure of money works best in predicting movements of variables that money is supposed to explain. For example, we might look at which measure of money does the best job of predicting the inflation rate or the business cycle and then officially designate it as the preferred measure of the money supply. Unfortunately, the empirical evidence on which measure of money is best is mixed; a measure that predicts well in one period may not predict well in another, and a measure that predicts inflation may not be the best predictor of the business cycle.

As you can see, neither approach to choosing an exact definition of money is entirely satisfactory. The theoretical approach is not specific enough to tell us which assets should be included in or excluded from the appropriate measure of money. The empirical approach encounters difficulties because the evidence on which is the preferred measure of money is mixed, and even if it weren't, we could not be sure that a measure that has worked well in the past would work well in the future. The ambiguity about the precise definition of money is not a very satisfactory state of affairs because policymakers who are responsible for managing the economy need to know exactly what the components of the money supply are if they are to conduct policy by trying to control it.

The Federal Reserve's Monetary Aggregates

The Federal Reserve System (the Fed), the central banking authority responsible for monetary policy in the United States, has conducted many studies on how to define money. The problem of defining money has become especially crucial because extensive financial innovation has produced new types of assets that might properly belong in a measure of money. Since 1980, the Fed has modified its definitions of money several times and has settled on the following measures of the money supply, which are also referred to as **monetary aggregates** (see Table 1).

The narrowest definition of money that the Fed reports is **M1**, which corresponds to the definition proposed by the theoretical approach and includes currency, checking account deposits, and traveler's checks. These assets are clearly money because they can be used directly as a medium of exchange. Until the mid-1970s, only commercial banks were permitted to establish checking accounts, and they were not allowed to pay interest on them. With the financial innovation that has occurred (discussed more extensively in Chapter 10), regulations have changed so that other types of banks, such as savings and loan associations, mutual savings banks, and credit unions, can also offer checking accounts. In addition, banking institutions can offer other checkable deposits, such as NOW (negotiated order of withdrawal) accounts and ATS (automatic transfer from savings) accounts, that do pay interest on their balances. Table 1 lists the assets included in the measures of the monetary aggregates; both demand deposits (checking accounts that pay no interest) and these other checkable deposits are included in the M1 measure.

The **M2** monetary aggregate adds to M1 other assets that have check-writing features (money market deposit accounts and money market mutual fund shares) and other assets (small-denomination time deposits, savings deposits, overnight

TABLE 1 Measures of the Monetary Aggregates	Value as of December 1996 ($billions)
$M1$ = Currency	395.2
+ Traveler's checks	8.6
+ Demand deposits	402.5
+ Other checkable deposits	274.8
Total $M1$	1081.0
$M2$ = $M1$	
+ Small-denomination time deposits	944.4
+ Savings deposits and money market deposit accounts	1271.1
+ Money market mutual fund shares (noninstitutional)	536.6
Total $M2$	3833.1
$M3$ = $M2$	
+ Large-denomination time deposits	489.6
+ Money market mutual fund shares (institutional)	299.3
+ Term repurchase agreements	192.7
+ Term Eurodollars	112.6
Total $M3$	4927.3
L = $M3$	
+ Short-term Treasury securities	435.7
+ Commercial paper	495.5
+ Savings bonds	187.0
+ Banker's acceptances	11.8
Total L	6057.2

Source: Board of Governors of the Federal Reserve System, Statistical Release H.6, April 3, 1997.

repurchase agreements, and overnight Eurodollars) that are extremely liquid because they can be turned into cash quickly at very little cost.

The **M3** monetary aggregate adds to M2 somewhat less liquid assets such as large-denomination time deposits, term repurchase agreements, term Eurodollars, and institutional money market mutual fund shares.

The final measure, **L,** which is really not a measure of money at all but rather a measure of highly liquid assets, adds to M3 several types of securities that are

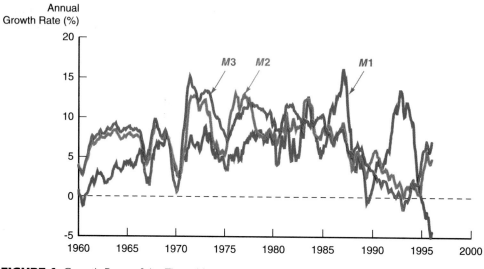

FIGURE 1 Growth Rates of the Three Money Aggregates, 1960–1996

Sources: Federal Reserve *Bulletin;* Citibase databank.

essentially highly liquid bonds, such as short-term Treasury securities, commercial paper, savings bonds, and banker's acceptances.

Because we cannot be sure which of the monetary aggregates is the true measure of money, it is logical to wonder if their movements closely parallel one another. If they do, then using one monetary aggregate to conduct policy will be the same as using another, and the fact that we are not sure of the appropriate definition of money for a given policy decision is not too costly. However, if the monetary aggregates do not move together, then what one monetary aggregate tells us is happening to the money supply might be quite different from what another monetary aggregate would tell us. The conflicting stories might present a confusing picture that would make it hard for policymakers to decide on the right course of action.

Figure 1 plots the growth rates M1, M2, and M3 from 1960 to 1996. The growth rates of these three monetary aggregates do tend to move together; the timing of their rise and fall is roughly similar until the 1990s, and they all show a higher growth rate on average in the 1970s than in the 1960s.

Yet some glaring discrepancies exist in the movements of these aggregates. According to M1, the growth rate of money did not accelerate between 1968, when it was in the 6 to 7 percent range, and 1971, when it was at a similar level. In the same period, the M2 and M3 measures tell a different story; they show a marked acceleration from the 8 to 10 percent range to the 12 to 15 percent range. Similarly, while the growth rate of M1 actually increased from 1989 to 1992, the growth rates of M2 and M3 in this same period instead showed a downward trend. Furthermore, from 1992 to 1996, the growth rate of M1 decelerated sharply, while the growth rates of M2 and M3 increased. Thus, the different measures of money tell a very different story about the course of monetary policy in the 1990s.

Following the Financial News

The Monetary Aggregates

Data for the Federal Reserve's monetary aggregates (M1, M2, and M3) are published every Friday. In the *Wall Street Journal*, the data are found in the "Federal Reserve Data" column, an example of which is presented here.

The third entry indicates that the money supply (M2) averaged $3857.3 billion for the week ending January 20, 1997. The notation "sa" for this entry indicates that the data are seasonally adjusted; that is, seasonal movements, such as those associated with Christmas shopping, have been removed from the data. The notation "nsa" indicates that the data have not been seasonally adjusted.

Source: Wall Street Journal, January 31, 1997, p. C12.

FEDERAL RESERVE DATA

MONETARY AGGREGATES
(daily average in billions)

	One week ended:	
	Jan. 20	Jan. 13
Money supply (M1) sa	1075.7	1067.7
Money supply (M1) nsa	1078.6	1090.7
Money supply (M2) sa	3857.3	3850.7
Money supply (M2) nsa	3854.9	3872.8
Money supply (M3) sa	4940.6	4935.4
Money supply (M3) nsa	4944.3	4961.9
	Four weeks ended:	
	Jan. 20	Dec. 23
Money supply (M1) sa	1074.4	1077.7
Money supply (M1) nsa	1100.3	1097.1
Money supply (M2) sa	3848.4	3832.2
Money supply (M2) nsa	3865.8	3847.8
Money supply (M3) sa	4926.2	4896.5
Money supply (M3) nsa	4943.9	4915.4
	Month	
	Dec.	Nov.
Money supply (M1) sa	1076.9	1075.8
Money supply (M2) sa	3835.3	3807.1
Money supply (M3) sa	4904.1	4854.6

nsa-Not seasonally adjusted. sa-Seasonally adjusted.

From the data in Figure 1, you can see that obtaining a single precise, correct definition of money does seem to matter and that it does make a difference which monetary aggregate policymakers and economists choose as the true measure of money.

Money as a Weighted Aggregate

The measures of the money supply listed in Table 1 make black-and-white decisions about whether a given asset is money by including it or excluding it. This distinction, however, is not always so clear-cut. Because all assets have some degree of "moneyness" or liquidity, we might want to say that some fraction of any asset functions as money. For example, a share in a money market fund that allows you to write checks with some restrictions against your shares might be viewed as being 60 percent like money, while a savings account deposit is viewed as 40 percent like money. Then you might want to define the money supply to include not only the items in M1 but also 60 percent of money market fund shares and 40 percent of savings deposits:

M1 + 0.60 (money market fund shares) + 0.40 (savings deposits)

A measure of the money supply using this approach is called a *weighted monetary aggregate* because each asset receives a different weight (for example, 1.00 for M1, 0.60 for the money market fund shares, and 0.40 for savings deposits) when added together. Research along these lines has produced measures of money that seem to predict inflation and business cycles somewhat better than more conventional measures.[3] How successful the monetary aggregates created by this approach will be in the future, only time will tell.

HOW RELIABLE ARE THE MONEY DATA?

The difficulties of measuring money arise not only because it is hard to decide what is the best definition of money but also because the Fed frequently revises earlier estimates of the monetary aggregates by large amounts later on. There are two reasons why the Fed revises its figures. First, because small depository institutions need to report the amounts of their deposits only infrequently, the Fed has to estimate these amounts until the small depository institutions provide the actual figures at some future date. Second, the adjustment of the data for seasonal variation is revised substantially as more data become available. To see why this happens, let's look at an example of the seasonal variation of the money data around Christmastime. The monetary aggregates always rise around Christmas because of increased spending during the holiday season; the rise is greater in some years than in others. This means that the factor that adjusts the data for the seasonal variation due to Christmas must be estimated from several years of data, and the estimates of this seasonal factor become more precise only as more data become available. When the data on the monetary aggregates are revised, it often means that the seasonal adjustments change dramatically from the initial calculation.

Table 2 shows how severe a problem data revisions can be. It provides the rates of money growth from one-month periods calculated from initial estimates of the M2 monetary aggregate, along with the rates of money growth calculated from a major revision of the M2 numbers published in April 1997. As the table shows, for one-month periods the initial versus the revised data can give a different picture of what is happening to monetary policy. For March 1996, for example, the initial data indicated that the growth rate of M2 at an annual rate was 11.2 percent, whereas the revised data indicate a much lower growth rate of 9.4 percent.

A distinctive characteristic shown in Table 2 is that the differences between the initial and revised M2 series tend to cancel out. You can see this by looking at the last row of the table, which shows the average rate of M2 growth for the two series and the average difference between them. The average M2 growth for the initial calculation of M2 is 4.7 percent, and the revised number is 4.7 percent, a difference of 0.0 percent. The conclusion that we can draw is that the initial data on the monetary aggregates reported by the Fed are not a reliable guide to what is happening to short-run movements in the money supply, such as the one-month growth rates. However, the initial money data are reasonably reliable for longer periods, such as a year. The moral is that ***we probably should not pay much attention to short-run movements in the money supply numbers but should be concerned only with longer-run movements.***

---

[3] For example, see William Barnett, Edward Offenbacher, and Paul Spindt, "New Concepts of Aggregate Money," *Journal of Finance* 36 (1981): 487–505, and K. Alec Chrystal and Ronald McDonald, "Empirical Evidence on the Recent Behavior and Usefulness of Simple Sum and Weighted Measures of the Money Stock," *Federal Reserve Bank of St. Louis Review* 76 (March-April 1994): 73–109.

	TABLE 2	**Growth Rate of M2: Initial and Revised Series, 1996 (percent, compounded annual rate)**		
Period	**Initial Rate**	**Revised Rate**	**Difference (Revised Rate − Initial Rate)**
January	5.2	4.9	−0.3
February	5.0	4.9	−0.1
March	11.2	9.4	−1.8
April	2.0	3.4	+1.4
May	−1.6	0.0	+1.6
June	5.6	5.2	−0.4
July	2.3	2.6	+0.3
August	3.7	4.1	+0.4
September	3.4	4.0	+0.6
October	3.6	4.0	+0.4
November	7.1	6.8	−0.3
December	8.8	7.4	−1.4
Average	4.7	4.7	0.0

Sources: Federal Reserve *Bulletin*, various issues; Board of Governors of the Federal Reserve System, Statistical Release H.6, April 3 1997.

SUMMARY

1. To economists, the word *money* has a different meaning from *income* or *wealth*. Money is anything that is generally accepted as payment for goods or services or in the repayment of debts.

2. Money serves three primary functions: as a medium of exchange, as a unit of account, and as a store of value. Money as a medium of exchange avoids the problem of double coincidence of wants that arises in a barter economy by lowering transaction costs and encouraging specialization and the division of labor. Money as a unit of account reduces the number of prices needed in the economy, which also reduces transaction costs. Money also functions as a store of value but performs this role poorly if it is rapidly losing value due to inflation.

3. The payments system has evolved over time. Until several hundred years ago, the payments system in all but the most primitive societies was based primarily on precious metals. The introduction of paper currency lowered the cost of transporting money. The next major advance was the introduction of checks, which lowered transaction costs still

further. We are currently moving toward an electronic payments system in which paper is eliminated and all transactions are handled by computers. Despite the potential efficiency of such a system, obstacles are slowing the movement to the checkless society and the development of new forms of electronic money.

4. There are two approaches to the measurement of money: theoretical and empirical. The theoretical approach defines the money supply by using economic reasoning, whereas the empirical approach decides on the best measure of money by seeing which measure best predicts inflation and business cycles. Neither approach is completely adequate: The theoretical is not specific enough, and the empirical suffers from the problem that a measure that predicts well in one period will not necessarily continue to predict well in the future. So the Federal Reserve System has defined three different measures of the money supply—M1, M2, and M3—and a measure of liquid assets, L. These measures are not equivalent and do not always move together, so they

cannot be used interchangeably by policymakers. Obtaining the precise, correct definition of money does seem to matter and has implications for the conduct of monetary policy.

5. Another problem in the measurement of money is that the data are not always as accurate as we would like. Substantial revisions in the data do occur; they indicate that initially released money data are not a reliable guide to short-run (say, month-to-month) movements in the money supply, although they are more reliable over longer periods of time, such as a year.

KEY TERMS

commodity money, p. 52

electronic money (e-money), p. 55

fiat money, p. 53

hyperinflation, p. 52

income, p. 49

liquidity, p. 51

medium of exchange, p. 49

monetary aggregates, p. 58

M1, p. 58

M2, p. 58

M3, p. 59

L, p. 59

payments system, p. 52

store of value, p. 51

unit of account, p. 50

wealth, p. 49

QUESTIONS AND PROBLEMS

1. Which of the following three expressions uses the economists' definition of money?
   a. "How much money did you earn last week?"
   b. "When I go to the store, I always make sure that I have enough money."
   c. "The love of money is the root of all evil."

*2. There are three goods produced in an economy by three individuals:

Good	Producer
Apples	Orchard owner
Bananas	Banana grower
Chocolate	Chocolatier

   If the orchard owner likes only bananas, the banana grower likes only chocolate, and the chocolatier likes only apples, will any trade between these three persons take place in a barter economy? How will introducing money into the economy benefit these three producers?

3. Why did cavemen not need money?

*4. Why were people in the United States in the nineteenth century sometimes willing to be paid by check rather than with gold, even though they knew that there was a possibility that the check might bounce?

5. In ancient Greece, why was gold a more likely candidate for use as money than wine was?

*6. Was money a better store of value in the United States in the 1950s than it was in the 1970s? Why or why not? In which period would you have been more willing to hold money?

7. Would you be willing to give up your checkbook and instead use an electronic means of payment if it were made available? Why or why not?

8. Rank the following assets from most liquid to least liquid:
   a. Checking account deposits
   b. Houses
   c. Currency
   d. Washing machines
   e. Savings deposits
   f. Common stock

*9. Why have some economists described money during a hyperinflation as a "hot potato" that is quickly passed from one person to another?

10. In Brazil, a country that was undergoing a rapid inflation, many transactions were conducted in dollars rather than in reals, the domestic currency. Why?

*11. Suppose that a researcher discovers that a measure of the total amount of debt in the U.S. economy over the past 20 years was a better predictor of inflation and the business cycle than M1, M2, or M3. Does this discovery mean that we should define money as equal to the total amount of debt in the economy?

12. Look up the M1, M2, and M3 numbers in the Federal Reserve *Bulletin* for the most recent one-year period. Have their growth rates been similar?

What implications do their growth rates have for the conduct of monetary policy?

*13. Which of the Federal Reserve's measures of the monetary aggregates, M1, M2, or M3, is composed of the most liquid assets? Which is the largest measure?

14. In a weighted monetary aggregate, which of the following assets would probably receive the highest weights? Which would receive the lowest weights?

a. Currency
b. Savings account deposits
c. NOW accounts
d. U.S. savings bonds
e. Houses
f. Furniture

*15. Why are revisions of monetary aggregates less of a problem for measuring long-run movements of the money supply than they are for measuring short-run movements?

PART II

FINANCIAL MARKETS

Chapter 4

UNDERSTANDING INTEREST RATES

P R E V I E W   Interest rates are among the most closely watched variables in the economy. Their movements are reported almost daily by the news media because they directly affect our everyday lives and have important consequences for the health of the economy. They affect personal decisions such as whether to consume or save, whether to buy a house, and whether to purchase bonds or put funds into a savings account. Interest rates also affect the economic decisions of businesses and households, such as whether to use their funds to invest in new equipment for factories or to save their money in a bank.

Before we can go on with the study of money, banking, and financial markets, we must understand exactly what the phrase *interest rates* means. In this chapter we see that a concept known as the *yield to maturity* is the most accurate measure of interest rates; the yield to maturity is what economists mean when they use the term *interest rate*. We discuss how the yield to maturity is measured on many of the credit market instruments mentioned in Chapter 2 and examine alternative (but less accurate) ways in which interest rates are quoted. We also see that a bond's interest rate does not necessarily indicate how good an investment the bond is because what it earns (its rate of return) can differ from its interest rate. Finally, we explore the distinction between real interest rates, which are adjusted for changes in the price level, and nominal interest rates, which are not.

Although learning definitions is not always the most exciting of pursuits, it is important to read carefully and understand the concepts presented in this chapter. Not only are they continually used throughout the remainder of this text, but a firm grasp of these terms will give you a clearer understanding of the role that interest rates play in your life as well as in the general economy.

MEASURING INTEREST RATES

In Chapter 2 you were introduced to a number of credit market instruments, which fall into four types:

1. A **simple loan** provides the borrower with an amount of funds (principal) that must be repaid to the lender at the maturity date along with an additional amount known as an *interest* payment. For example, if a bank made you a simple loan of $100 for one year, you would have to repay the principal of $100 in one year's time along with an additional interest payment of, say, $10. Commercial loans to businesses are often of this type.

2. A **fixed-payment loan** provides a borrower with an amount of funds that is to be repaid by making the same payment every month, consisting of part of the principal and interest for a set number of years. For example, if you borrowed $1000, a fixed-payment loan might require you to pay $126 every year for 25 years. Installment loans (such as auto loans) and mortgages are frequently of the fixed-payment type.

3. A **coupon bond** pays the owner of the bond a fixed interest payment (coupon payment) every year until the maturity date, when a specified final amount **(face value** or **par value)** is repaid. The coupon payment is so named because the bond-holder used to obtain payment by clipping a coupon off the bond and sending it to the bond issuer, who then sent the payment to the holder. Nowadays, for most coupon bonds it is no longer necessary to send in coupons to receive these payments. A coupon bond with $1000 face value, for example, might pay you a coupon payment of $100 per year for ten years and at the maturity date repay you the face value amount of $1000. (The face value of a bond is usually in $1000 increments.)

A coupon bond is identified by three pieces of information. First is the corporation or government agency that issues the bond. Second is the maturity date of the bond. Third is the bond's **coupon rate,** the dollar amount of the yearly coupon payment expressed as a percentage of the face value of the bond. In our example, the coupon bond has a yearly coupon payment of $100 and a face value of $1000. The coupon rate is then $100/$1000 = 0.10, or 10 percent. Treasury bonds and notes and corporate bonds are examples of coupon bonds.

4. A **discount bond** (also called a **zero-coupon bond**) is bought at a price below its face value (at a discount), and the face value is repaid at the maturity date. Unlike a coupon bond, a discount bond does not make any interest payments; it just pays off the face value. For example, a discount bond with a face value of $1000 might be bought for $900 and in a year's time the owner would be repaid the face value of $1000. U.S. Treasury bills, U.S. savings bonds, and long-term zero-coupon bonds are examples of discount bonds.

These four types of instruments require payments at different times: Simple loans and discount bonds make payment only at their maturity dates, whereas fixed-payment loans and coupon bonds have payments periodically until maturity. How would you decide which of these instruments provides you with more income? They all seem so different because they make payments at different times. To solve this problem, we use the concept of *present value* to provide us with a procedure for measuring interest rates on these different types of instruments.

Present Value   The concept of **present value** is based on the commonsense notion that a dollar paid to you one year from now is less valuable to you than a dollar paid to you today; this notion is true because you can deposit the dollar in a savings account that earns interest and have more than a dollar in one year. We will now define this concept more formally.

In the case of a simple loan, the interest payment divided by the amount of the loan is a natural and sensible way to measure the cost of borrowing funds: The measure of the cost is the *simple interest rate*. In the example we used to describe the simple loan, a loan of $100 today requires the borrower to repay the $100 a year from now and to make an additional interest payment of $10. Hence, using the definition just given, the simple interest rate i is

$$i = \frac{\$10}{\$100} = 0.10 = 10\%$$

If you make this $100 loan, at the end of the year you would receive $110, which can be rewritten as

$$\$100 \times (1 + 0.10) = \$110$$

If you then loaned out the $110, at the end of the second year you would receive

$$\$110 \times (1 + 0.10) = \$121$$

or, equivalently,

$$\$100 \times (1 + 0.10) \times (1 + 0.10) = \$100 \times (1 + 0.10)^2 = \$121$$

Continuing with the loan again, you would receive at the end of the third year

$$\$121 \times (1 + 0.10) = \$100 \times (1 + 0.10)^3 = \$133.10$$

These calculations of the proceeds from a simple loan can be generalized as follows: If the simple interest rate i is expressed as a decimal fraction (such as 0.10 for the 10 percent interest rate in our example), then after making these loans for n years, you will receive a total payment of

$$\$100 \times (1 + i)^n$$

We can also work these calculations backward. Because $100 today will turn into $110 next year when the simple interest rate is 10 percent, we could say that $110 next year is worth only $100 today. Or we could say that no one would pay more than $100 to get $110 next year. Similarly, we could say that $121 two years from now or $133.10 three years from now is worth $100 today. This process of calculating what dollars received in the future are worth today is called *discounting the future*. We have been implicitly solving our forward-looking equations for today's value of a future dollar amount. For example, in the case of the $133.10 received three years from now, when $i = 0.10$,

Current	Future
$\$100 \times (1 + i)^3$	$= \$133.10$

so that

$$\$100 = \frac{\$133.10}{(1 + i)^3}$$

More generally, we can solve this equation to tell us the present value *(PV)*, or **present discounted value,** of the future $1, that is, today's value of a $1 payment received *n* years from now when the simple interest rate is *i:*

$$PV \text{ of future } \$1 = \frac{\$1}{(1 + i)^n} \tag{1}$$

Intuitively, what Equation 1 tells us is that if you are promised $1 for certain ten years from now, this dollar would not be as valuable to you as $1 is today because you can earn interest on the dollar.

The concept of present value is extremely useful because it allows us to figure out today's value of a credit market instrument at a given simple interest rate *i* by just adding up the present value of all the future payments received. This information allows us to compare the value of two instruments with very different timing of their payments, such as a discount bond and a coupon bond. As we will see, this concept also allows us to obtain an equivalent measure of the interest rate on all four types of credit market instruments discussed here.

The Cost of the S&L Bailout: Was It Really $500 Billion?

The government bailout of the savings and loan industry in 1989 was one of the major news stories of the past decade. Statements frequently appeared in the press that the cost of the bailout to taxpayers would exceed $500 billion—more than $2000 for every man, woman, and child in the United States. The $500 billion–plus figure made for wonderful political rhetoric, but was the cost really this high?

The answer is no, and the concept of present value tells us why. The $500 billion figure includes bond payments over the next 40 years. The present value concept tells us that to figure out the cost of these payments in today's dollars, we have to discount them back to the present. When we do this, the present value of these payments is on the order of $150 billion, not $500 billion. It is still true that a present value of the bailout of $150 billion is nothing to sneeze at, but it is not quite as scary as a figure more than three times that size. (Chapter 12 contains an extensive discussion of the S&L crisis and bailout.) Ⓐ

Yield to Maturity

Of the several common ways of calculating interest rates, the most important is the **yield to maturity,** the interest rate that equates the present value of payments received from a debt instrument with its value today. Because the concept behind the calculation of the yield to maturity makes good economic sense, economists consider it the most accurate measure of interest rates.

To understand the yield to maturity better, we now look at how it is calculated for the four types of credit market instruments.

SIMPLE LOAN   Using the concept of present value, the yield to maturity on a simple loan is easy to calculate. For the one-year loan we discussed, today's value is $100, and the payments in one year's time would be $110 (the repayment of $100 plus the interest payment of $10). We can use this information to solve for the yield to maturity *i* by recognizing that the present value of the future payments must equal today's value of a loan. Making today's value of the loan ($100) equal to the present value of the $110 payment in a year (using Equation 1) gives us

$$\$100 = \frac{\$110}{1 + i}$$

Solving for *i,*

$$i = \frac{\$110 - \$100}{\$100} = \frac{\$10}{\$100} = 0.10 = 10\%$$

This calculation of the yield to maturity should look familiar because it equals the interest payment of $10 divided by the loan amount of $100; that is, it equals the simple interest rate on the loan. An important point to recognize is that *for simple loans, the simple interest rate equals the yield to maturity.* Hence the same term *i* is used to denote both the yield to maturity and the simple interest rate.

Study Guide   The key to understanding the calculation of the yield to maturity is equating today's value of the debt instrument with the present value of all of its future payments. The best way to learn this principle is to apply it to other specific examples of the four types of credit market instruments in addition to those we discuss here. See if you can develop the equations that would allow you to solve for the yield to maturity in each case.

FIXED-PAYMENT LOAN   Recall that this type of loan has the same payment every year throughout the life of the loan. On a fixed-rate mortgage, for example, the borrower makes the same payment to the bank every month until the maturity date, when the loan will be completely paid off. To calculate the yield to maturity for a fixed-payment loan, we follow the same strategy we used for the simple loan—we equate today's value of the loan with its present value. Because the fixed-payment loan involves more than one payment, the present value of the fixed-payment loan is calculated as the sum of the present values of all payments (using Equation 1).

In the case of our earlier example, the loan is $1000 and the yearly payment is $126 for the next 25 years. The present value is calculated as follows: At the end of one year, there is a $126 payment with a *PV* of $126/(1 + *i*); at the end of two years, there is another $126 payment with a *PV* of $126/(1 + *i*)^2; and so on until at the end of the twenty-fifth year, the last payment of $126 with a *PV* of $126/(1 + *i*)^{25} is made. Making today's value of the loan ($1000) equal to the sum of the present values of all the yearly payments gives us

$$\$1000 = \frac{\$126}{1 + i} + \frac{\$126}{(1 + i)^2} + \frac{\$126}{(1 + i)^3} + \cdots + \frac{\$126}{(1 + i)^{25}}$$

More generally, for any fixed-payment loan,

$$LV = \frac{FP}{1 + i} + \frac{FP}{(1 + i)^2} + \frac{FP}{(1 + i)^3} + \cdots + \frac{FP}{(1 + i)^N} \qquad (2)$$

where
$$LV = \text{loan value}$$
$$FP = \text{fixed yearly payment}$$
$$N = \text{number of years until maturity}$$

For a fixed-payment loan amount, the fixed yearly payment and the number of years until maturity are known quantities, and only the yield to maturity is not. So we can solve this equation for the yield to maturity i. Because this calculation is not easy, tables have been created that allow you to find i given the loan's numbers for LV, FP, and N. For example, in the case of the 25-year loan with yearly payments of $126, the yield to maturity taken from the table that solves Equation 2 is 12 percent. Real estate brokers always have such a table handy (or a pocket calculator that can solve such equations) so that they can immediately tell the prospective house buyer exactly what the yearly (or monthly) payments will be if the house purchase is financed by taking out a mortgage (see Figure 1).[1]

COUPON BOND To calculate the yield to maturity for a coupon bond, follow the same strategy used for the fixed-payment loan: Equate today's value of the bond with its present value. Because coupon bonds also have more than one payment, the present value of the bond is calculated as the sum of the present values of all the coupon payments plus the present value of the final payment of the face value of the bond.

The present value of a $1000-face-value bond with ten years to maturity and yearly coupon payments of $100 (a 10 percent coupon rate) can be calculated as follows: At the end of one year, there is a $100 coupon payment with a PV of $\$100/(1 + i)$; at the end of the second year, there is another $100 coupon payment with a PV of $\$100/(1 + i)^2$; and so on until at maturity, there is a $100 coupon payment with a PV of $\$100/(1 + i)^{10}$ plus the repayment of the $1000 face value with a PV of $\$1000/(1 + i)^{10}$. Setting today's value of the bond (its current price, denoted by P_b) equal to the sum of the present values of all the payments for this bond gives

$$P_b = \frac{\$100}{1 + i} + \frac{\$100}{(1 + i)^2} + \frac{\$100}{(1 + i)^3} + \cdots + \frac{\$100}{(1 + i)^{10}} + \frac{\$1000}{(1 + i)^{10}}$$

More generally, for any coupon bond,[2]

$$P_b = \frac{C}{1 + i} + \frac{C}{(1 + i)^2} + \frac{C}{(1 + i)^3} + \cdots + \frac{C}{(1 + i)^N} + \frac{F}{(1 + i)^N} \qquad (3)$$

---

[1]The calculation with a pocket calculator programmed for this purpose requires simply that you enter the value of the loan LV, the number of years to maturity N, and the interest rate i and then run the program.

[2]Most coupon bonds actually make coupon payments on a semiannual basis rather than once a year as assumed here. The effect on the calculations is only very slight and will be ignored here.

12%   **Monthly Payment Necessary to Amortize a Loan**

			Term (years)				
Amount($)	**19**	**20**	**21**	**22**	**23**	**24**	**25**
25	.28	.28	.28	.27	.27	.27	.27
50	.56	.56	.55	.54	.54	.54	.53
75	.84	.83	.82	.81	.81	.80	.79
100	1.12	1.11	1.09	1.08	1.07	1.07	1.06
200	2.24	2.21	2.18	2.16	2.14	2.13	2.11
300	3.35	3.31	3.27	3.24	3.21	3.19	3.16
400	4.47	4.41	4.36	4.32	4.28	4.25	4.22
500	5.58	5.51	5.45	5.39	5.35	5.31	5.27
600	6.70	6.61	6.54	6.47	6.42	6.37	6.32
700	7.81	7.71	7.63	7.55	7.48	7.43	7.38
800	8.93	8.81	8.71	8.63	8.55	8.49	8.43
900	10.04	9.91	9.80	9.71	9.62	9.55	9.48
1000	11.16	11.02	10.89	10.78	10.69	10.61	10.54
2000	22.31	22.03	21.78	21.56	21.38	21.21	21.07
3000	33.47	33.04	32.67	32.34	32.06	31.82	31.60
4000	44.62	44.05	43.55	43.12	42.75	42.42	42.13
5000	55.77	55.06	54.44	53.90	53.43	53.02	52.67

FIGURE 1 A Mortgage Payment Table

This table is for loans with a 12 percent interest rate. To find the monthly payment for the loan, pick out the amount of the loan in the first column and then follow that row across to the entry in the column with the number of years to maturity of the loan. For a $1000, 25-year fixed-payment loan with a 12 percent interest rate, following this procedure indicates that the monthly payment is $10.54 ($126 per year).

where

P_b = price of coupon bond
C = yearly coupon payment
F = face value of the bond
N = years to maturity date

In Equation 3, the coupon payment, the face value, the years to maturity, and the price of the bond are known quantities, and only the yield to maturity is not. Hence we can solve this equation for the yield to maturity i.[3] Just as in the case of the fixed-payment loan, this calculation is not easy, so bond tables (see Figure 2) have been created that allow you to read off the yield to maturity for a bond given its coupon rate, its years to maturity, and its price. Some business-oriented pocket calculators have built-in programs that solve this equation for you.[4]

---

[3]In other contexts, it is also called the *internal rate of return.*

[4]The calculation of a bond's yield to maturity with the programmed pocket calculator requires simply that you enter the amount of the yearly coupon payment C, the face value F, the number of years to maturity N, and the price of the bond P_b and then run the program.

10.00%   **Bond Values per $100 of Face Value**

Yield (%)	1	2	3	4	5	6	7	8	9	10
					Years to Maturity					
10.00	100.00	100.00	100.00	100.00	100.00	100.00	100.00	100.00	100.00	100.00
10.25	99.77	99.56	99.37	99.20	99.04	98.90	98.77	98.66	98.55	98.46
10.50	99.54	99.12	98.74	98.40	98.09	97.82	97.56	97.34	97.13	96.95
10.75	99.31	98.68	98.12	97.61	97.16	96.75	96.38	96.04	95.74	95.47
11.00	99.08	98.25	97.50	96.83	96.23	95.69	95.21	94.77	94.38	94.02
11.25	98.85	97.82	96.89	96.06	95.32	94.65	94.05	93.52	93.04	92.61
11.50	98.62	97.39	96.28	95.30	94.41	93.63	92.92	92.29	91.72	91.22
11.75	98.39	96.96	95.68	94.54	93.52	92.61	91.80	91.08	90.44	89.86
12.00	98.17	96.53	95.08	93.79	92.64	91.62	90.71	89.89	89.17	88.53
12.25	97.94	96.11	94.49	93.05	91.77	90.63	89.62	88.73	87.93	87.23
12.50	97.72	95.69	93.90	92.31	90.91	89.66	88.56	87.58	86.72	85.95
12.75	97.49	95.28	93.32	91.59	90.06	88.71	87.51	86.46	85.52	84.70

FIGURE 2 A Bond Table
This table is for bonds with a 10 percent coupon rate. To find the price of the bond, pick out its yield to maturity in the first column and then follow that row across to the entry in the column with the number of years to maturity for the bond. For a ten-year, 10 percent coupon rate bond with a yield to maturity of 11.75 percent, following this procedure indicates that the price of the bond is $89.86 per $100 of face value (which means that a $1000-face-value bond sells for approximately $900).

Let's look at some examples of the solution for the yield to maturity on our 10 percent-coupon-rate bond that matures in ten years. If the purchase price of the bond is $1000, then either using a pocket calculator with the built-in program or looking at a bond table, we will find that the yield to maturity is 10 percent. If the price is $900, we find that the yield to maturity is 11.75 percent. Table 1 shows the yields to maturity calculated for several bond prices.

Three interesting facts are illustrated by Table 1:

1. When the coupon bond is priced at its face value, the yield to maturity equals the coupon rate.
2. The price of a coupon bond and the yield to maturity are negatively related; that is, as the yield to maturity rises, the price of the bond falls. If the yield to maturity falls, the price of the bond rises.
3. The yield to maturity is greater than the coupon rate when the bond price is below its face value.

These three facts are true for any coupon bond and are really not surprising if you think about the reasoning behind the calculation of the yield to maturity. When you put $1000 in a bank account with an interest rate of 10 percent, you can take out $100 every year and you will be left with the $1000 at the end of ten years. This is similar to buying the $1000 bond with a 10 percent coupon rate analyzed in Table 1, which pays a $100 coupon payment every year and then repays $1000 at the end of ten years. If the bond is purchased at the par value of $1000, its yield to maturity must equal the interest rate of 10 percent, which is also equal

TABLE 1 **Yields to Maturity on a 10 percent Coupon Rate Bond Maturing in Ten Years (Face Value = $1000)**

Price of Bond ($)	Yield to Maturity (%)
1200	7.13
1100	8.48
1000	10.00
900	11.75
800	13.81

to the coupon rate of 10 percent. The same reasoning applied to any coupon bond demonstrates that if the coupon bond is purchased at its par value, the yield to maturity and the coupon rate must be equal.

It is straightforward to show that the bond price and the yield to maturity are negatively related. As i, the yield to maturity, rises, all denominators in the bond price formula must necessarily rise. Hence a rise in the interest rate as measured by the yield to maturity means that the price of the bond must fall. Another way to explain why the bond price falls when the interest rises is that a higher interest rate implies that the future coupon payments and final payment are worth less when discounted back to the present; hence the price of the bond must be lower.

There is one special case of a coupon bond that is worth discussing because its yield to maturity is particularly easy to calculate. This bond is called a **consol;** it is a perpetual bond with no maturity date and no repayment of principal that makes fixed coupon payments of C forever. Consols were first sold by the British Treasury during the Napoleonic Wars and are still traded today; however, they are quite rare in American capital markets. The formula in Equation 3 for the price of the consol P_c simplifies to the following:[5]

$$P_c = \frac{C}{i}$$
(4)

---

[5]The bond price formula for a consol is

$$P_c = \frac{C}{1 + i} + \frac{C}{(1 + i)^2} + \frac{C}{(1 + i)^3} + \cdots$$

which can be written as

$$P_c = C\,(x + x^2 + x^3 + \cdots)$$

in which $x = 1/(1 + i)$. From your high school algebra you might remember the formula for an infinite sum:

$$1 + x + x^2 + x^3 + \cdots = \frac{1}{1 - x} \quad \text{for} \quad x < 1$$

and so

$$P_c = C\left(\frac{1}{1 - x} - 1\right) = C\left[\frac{1}{1 - 1/(1 + i)} - 1\right]$$

which by suitable algebraic manipulation becomes

$$P_c = C\left(\frac{1 + i}{i} - \frac{i}{i}\right) = \frac{C}{i}$$

One nice feature of consols is that you can immediately see that as i goes up, the price of the bond falls. For example, if a consol pays $100 per year forever and the interest rate is 10 percent, its price will be $1000 = $100/0.10. If the interest rate rises to 20 percent, its price will fall to $500 = $100/0.20. We can also rewrite this formula as

$$i = \frac{C}{P_c} \tag{5}$$

We see then that it is also easy to calculate the yield to maturity for the consol (despite the fact that it never matures). For example, with a consol that pays $100 yearly and has a price of $2000, the yield to maturity is easily calculated to be 5% percent (=$100/$2000).

DISCOUNT BOND The yield-to-maturity calculation for a discount bond is similar to that for the simple loan. Let us consider a discount bond such as a one-year U.S. Treasury bill, which pays off a face value of $1000 in one year's time. If the current purchase price of this bill is $900, then equating this price to the present value of the $1000 received in one year, using Equation 1, gives

$$\$900 = \frac{\$1000}{1 + i}$$

and solving for i,

$$i = \frac{\$1000 - \$900}{\$900} = 0.111 = 11.1\%$$

More generally, for any one-year discount bond, the yield to maturity can be written as

$$i = \frac{F - P_d}{P_d} \tag{6}$$

where
$$F = \text{face value of the discount bond}$$
$$P_d = \text{current price of the discount bond}$$

In other words, the yield to maturity equals the increase in price over the year $F - P_d$ divided by the initial price P_d.

An important feature of this equation is that it indicates that for a discount bond, the yield to maturity is negatively related to the current bond price. This is the same conclusion that we reached for a coupon bond. For example, Equation 6 shows that a rise in the bond price from $900 to $950 means that the bond will have a smaller increase in its price over its lifetime, and the yield to maturity falls from 11.1 to 5.3 percent. Similarly, a fall in the yield to maturity means that the price of the discount bond has risen.

SUMMARY The concept of present value tells you that a dollar in the future is not as valuable to you as a dollar today because you can earn interest on this dollar. Specifically, a dollar received n years from now is worth only $\$1/(1 + i)^n$ today. The present value of a set of future payments on a debt instrument equals the sum of the present values of each of the future payments. The yield to maturity for an instrument is the interest rate that equates the present value of the future payments on that instrument to its value today. Because the procedure for calculating the yield to maturity is based on sound economic principles, this is the measure that economists think most accurately describes the interest rate.

Our calculations of the yield to maturity for a variety of bonds reveal the important fact that ***current bond prices and interest rates are negatively related: When the interest rate rises, the price of the bond falls, and vice versa.***

OTHER MEASURES OF INTEREST RATES

The yield to maturity is the most accurate measure of interest rates and is what economists mean when they use the term *interest rate*. Unless otherwise specified, the terms *interest rate* and *yield to maturity* are used synonymously in this book. However, because the yield to maturity is sometimes difficult to calculate, other, less accurate measures of interest rates have come into common use in bond markets. You will frequently encounter two of these measures, the *current yield* and the *yield on a discount basis*, when reading the newspaper, and it is important for you to understand what they mean and how they differ from the more accurate measure of interest rates, the yield to maturity.

Current Yield   The **current yield** is an approximation of the yield to maturity on coupon bonds that is often reported because in contrast to the yield to maturity, it is easily calculated. It is defined as the yearly coupon payment divided by the price of the security,

$$i_c = \frac{C}{P_b} \tag{7}$$

where

i_c = current yield
P_b = price of the coupon bond
C = yearly coupon payment

This formula is identical to the formula in Equation 5, which describes the calculation of the yield to maturity for a consol. Hence, for a consol, the current yield is an exact measure of the yield to maturity. When a coupon bond has a long term to maturity (say, 20 years or more), it is very much like a consol, which pays coupon payments forever. Thus you would expect the current yield to be a rather close approximation of the yield to maturity for a long-term coupon bond, and you can safely use the current-yield calculation instead of looking up the yield to maturity in a bond table. However, as the time to maturity of the coupon bond shortens (say, it becomes less than five years), it behaves less and less like a consol and so the approximation afforded by the current yield becomes worse and worse.

We have also seen that when the bond price equals the par value of the bond, the yield to maturity is equal to the coupon rate (the coupon payment divided by the par value of the bond). Because the current yield equals the coupon payment divided by the bond price, the current yield is also equal to the coupon rate when the bond price is at par. This logic leads us to the conclusion that when the bond price is at par, the current yield equals the yield to maturity. This means that the nearer the bond price is to the bond's par value, the better the current yield will approximate the yield to maturity.

The current yield is negatively related to the price of the bond. In the case of our 10 percent-coupon-rate bond, when the price rises from $1000 to $1100, the current yield falls from 10 percent (= $100/$1000) to 9.09 percent (= $100/$1100). As Table 1 indicates, the yield to maturity is also negatively related to the price of the bond; when the price rises from $1000 to $1100, the yield to maturity falls from 10 to 8.48 percent. In this we see an important fact: The current yield and the yield to maturity always move together; a rise in the current yield always signals that the yield to maturity has also risen.

The general characteristics of the current yield (the yearly coupon payment divided by the bond price) can be summarized as follows: The current yield better approximates the yield to maturity when the bond's price is nearer to the bond's par value and the maturity of the bond is longer. It becomes a worse approximation when the bond's price is further from the bond's par value and the bond's maturity is shorter. Regardless of whether the current yield is a good approximation of the yield to maturity, a change in the current yield *always* signals a change in the same direction of the yield to maturity.

Yield on a Discount Basis

Before the advent of calculators and computers, dealers in U.S. Treasury bills found it difficult to calculate interest rates as a yield to maturity. Instead, they quoted the interest rate on bills as a **yield on a discount basis** (or **discount yield**), and they still do so today. Formally, the yield on a discount basis is defined by the following formula:

$$i_{db} = \frac{F - P_d}{F} \times \frac{360}{\text{days to maturity}} \qquad (8)$$

where

i_{db} = yield on a discount basis
F = face value of the discount bond
P_d = purchase price of the discount bond

This method for calculating interest rates has two peculiarities. First, it uses the percentage gain on the face value of the bill $(F - P_d)/F$ rather than the percentage gain on the purchase price of the bill $(F - P_d)/P_d$ used in calculating the yield to maturity. Second, it puts the yield on an annual basis by taking the year to be 360 days long rather than 365 days.

Because of these peculiarities, the discount yield understates the interest rate on bills as measured by the yield to maturity. On our one-year bill, which is selling for $900 and has a face value of $1000, the yield on a discount basis would be as follows:

$$i_{db} = \frac{\$1000 - \$900}{\$1000} \times \frac{360}{365} = 0.099 = 9.9\%$$

whereas the yield to maturity for this bill, which we calculated before, is 11.1 percent. The discount yield understates the yield to maturity by a factor of over 10 percent. A little more than 1 percent can be attributed to the understatement of the length of the year: When the bill has one year to maturity, the second term on the right-hand side of the formula is 360/365 = 0.986 rather than 1.0, as it should be.

The more serious source of the understatement, however, is the use of the percentage gain on the face value rather than on the purchase price. Because, by definition, the purchase price of a discount bond is always less than the face value, the percentage gain on the face value is necessarily smaller than the percentage gain on the purchase price. The greater the difference between the purchase price and the face value of the discount bond, the more the discount yield understates the yield to maturity. Because the difference between the purchase price and the face value gets larger as maturity gets longer, we can draw the following conclusion about the relationship of the yield on a discount basis to the yield to maturity: The yield on a discount basis always understates the yield to maturity, and this understatement becomes more severe the longer the maturity of the discount bond.

Another important feature of the discount yield is that, like the yield to maturity, it is negatively related to the price of the bond. For example, when the price of the bond rises from $900 to $950, the formula indicates that the yield on a discount basis declines from 9.9 to 4.9 percent. At the same time, the yield to maturity declines from 11.1 to 5.3 percent. Here we see another important factor about the relationship of yield on a discount basis to yield to maturity: They always move together; that is, a rise in the discount yield always means that the yield to maturity has risen, and a decline in the discount yield means that the yield to maturity has declined as well.

The characteristics of the yield on a discount basis can be summarized as follows: Yield on a discount basis understates the more accurate measure of the interest rate, the yield to maturity; and the longer the maturity of the discount bond, the greater this understatement becomes. Even though the discount yield is a somewhat misleading measure of the interest rates, however, a change in the discount yield always indicates a change in the same direction for the yield to maturity.

Reading the WALL STREET JOURNAL
The Bond Page

Now that we understand the different interest-rate definitions, let's apply our knowledge and take a look at what kind of information appears on the bond page of a typical newspaper, in this case the *Wall Street Journal*. The "Following the Financial News" box contains the *Journal*'s listing for three different types of bonds on Monday, October 7, 1996. Panel (a) contains the information on U.S. Treasury bonds and notes. Both are coupon bonds, the only difference being their time to maturity from when they were originally issued: Notes have a time to maturity of less than ten years; bonds have a time to maturity of more than ten years.

The information found in the "Rate" and "Maturity" columns identifies the bond by coupon rate and maturity date. For example, T-bond 1 has a coupon rate of $4\frac{3}{8}$ percent, indicating that it pays out $43.75 per year on a $1000-face-value bond and matures in November 1996. In bond market parlance, it is referred to

Following the Financial News

Bond Prices and Interest Rates

Bond prices and interest rates are published daily. In the *Wall Street Journal* they can be found in the "NYSE/AMEX Bonds" and "Treasury/Agency Issues" section of the paper. Three basic formats for quoting bond prices and yields are illustrated here.

Monday, October 7, 1996

Representative Over-the-Counter quotations based on transactions of $1 million or more.

Treasury bond, note and bill quotes are as of mid-afternoon. Colons in bid-and-asked quotes represent 32nds; 101:01 means $101\frac{1}{32}$. Net changes in 32nds. n-Treasury note. Treasury bill quotes in hundredths, quoted on terms of a rate of discount. Days to maturity calculated from settlement date. All yields are to maturity and based on the asked quote. Latest 13-week and 26-week bills are boldfaced. For bonds callable prior to maturity, yields are computed to the earliest call date for issues quoted above par and to the maturity date for issues below par.

*-When issued.

Source: Federal Reserve Bank of New York.

U.S. Treasury strips as of 3 p.m. Eastern time, also based on transactions of $1 million or more. Colons in bid-and-asked quotes represent 32nds; 99:01 means $99\frac{1}{32}$. Net changes in 32nds. Yields calculated on the asked quotation. ci-stripped coupon interest. bp-Treasury bond, stripped principal. np-Treasury note, stripped principal. For bonds callable prior to maturity, yields are computed to the earliest call date for issues quoted above par and to the maturity date for issues below par.

Source: Beer, Stearns & Co. via Street Software Technology, Inc.

(a) Treasury bonds and notes

GOVT. BONDS & NOTES

	Rate	Maturity Mo/Yr	Bid	Asked	Chg.	Ask Yld.	
T-bond 1	$4\frac{3}{8}$	Nov 96n	99:29	99:31	....	4.61	— Current Yield = 4.38%
	$7\frac{1}{4}$	Nov 96n	100:07	100:09	....	4.32	
	$6\frac{1}{2}$	Nov 96n	100:06	100:08	....	4.62	
T-bond 2	$7\frac{1}{4}$	Nov 96n	100:08	100:10	— 1	4.91	— Current Yield = 7.22%
T-bond 3	$7\frac{5}{8}$	Feb 25	109:16	109:18	—19	6.86	— Current Yield = 6.96%
	$6\frac{7}{8}$	Aug 25	100:16	100:18	—17	6.83	
	6	Feb 26	89:22	89:24	—17	6.81	
T-bond 4	$6\frac{3}{4}$	Aug 26	99:18	99:20	—19	6.78	— Current Yield = 6.78%

(b) Treasury Bills

TREASURY BILLS

Maturity	Days to Mat.	Bid	Asked	Chg.	Ask Yld.	Maturity	Days to Mat.	Bid	Asked	Chg.	Ask Yld.
Oct 10 '96	0	5.04	4.94	−0.01	0.00	Feb 06 '97	119	5.04	5.02	+0.02	5.19
Oct 17 '96	7	4.89	4.79	+0.06	4.87	Feb 13 '97	126	5.04	5.02	+0.01	5.18
Oct 24 '96	14	4.85	4.75	....	4.82	Feb 20 '97	133	5.04	5.02	+0.02	5.19
Oct 31 '96	21	4.83	4.73	....	4.81	Feb 27 '97	140	5.05	5.03	+0.01	5.20
Nov 07 '96	28	4.79	4.69	+0.01	4.77	Mar 06 '97	147	5.05	5.03	....	5.21
Nov 14 '96	35	4.85	4.81	−0.02	4.91	Mar 13 '97	154	5.06	5.04	+0.01	5.22
Nov 21 '96	42	4.84	4.80	....	4.89	Mar 20 '97	161	5.05	5.03	+0.01	5.22
Nov 29 '96	50	4.81	4.77	−0.03	4.87	Mar 27 '97	168	4.99	4.97	+0.01	5.16
Dec 05 '96	56	4.84	4.80	....	4.90	Apr 03 '97	175	5.09	5.07	....	5.27
Dec 12 '96	63	4.89	4.87	−0.01	4.99	Apr 10 '97	182	5.09	5.07	+0.02	5.28
Dec 19 '96	70	4.87	4.85	....	4.96	May 01 '97	203	5.12	5.10	....	5.31
Dec 26 '96	77	4.84	4.82	−0.01	4.94	May 29 '97	231	5.16	5.14	−0.01	5.36
Jan 02 '97	84	4.92	4.90	−0.01	5.03	Jun 26 '97	259	5.17	5.15	....	5.38
Jan 09 '97	91	4.99	4.97	+0.01	5.12	Jul 24 '97	287	5.21	5.19	....	5.44
Jan 16 '97	98	4.99	4.97	+0.01	5.11	Aug 21 '97	315	5.23	5.21	+0.01	5.47
Jan 23 '97	105	4.99	4.97	+0.01	5.11	Sep 18 '97	343	5.23	5.21	....	5.49
Jan 30 '97	112	4.98	4.96	....	5.11						

(c) New York Stock Exchange bonds

CORPORATION BONDS

Volume, $18,261,000

	Bonds	Cur Yld	Vol	Close	Net Chg.	
Bond 1	ATT $4\frac{3}{4}$ 98	4.8	27	$98\frac{1}{8}$	$+\frac{1}{4}$	— Yield to Maturity = 5.76%
	ATT 6s00	6.1	154	$98\frac{1}{2}$	$+\frac{1}{8}$	
	ATT $5\frac{1}{8}$ 01	5.4	3	$94\frac{3}{8}$	$-\frac{3}{8}$	
	ATT $7\frac{1}{8}$ 02	7.0	90	$102\frac{1}{2}$	$+\frac{1}{2}$	
	ATT $6\frac{3}{4}$ 04	6.8	22	100	$+\frac{3}{8}$	
	ATT 7s05	6.9	25	$100\frac{7}{8}$	$+\frac{3}{4}$	
	ATT $7\frac{1}{2}$ 06	7.2	15	104	$+\frac{1}{8}$	
	ATT $8\frac{1}{8}$ 22	7.8	158	$103\frac{5}{8}$	....	
	ATT $8\frac{1}{8}$ 24	7.9	4	$103\frac{1}{8}$	$+\frac{1}{8}$	
Bond 2	ATT $8\frac{5}{8}$ 31	8.2	15	$105\frac{1}{8}$	$-1\frac{7}{8}$	— Yield to Maturity = 8.18%

as the Treasury's $4\frac{3}{8}$s of 1996. The next three columns tell us about the bond's price. By convention, all prices in the bond market are quoted per $100 of face value. Furthermore, the numbers after the colon represent thirty-seconds. In the case of T-bond 1, the first price of 99:29 represents $99\frac{29}{32} = 99.906$, or an actual price of $999.06 for a $1000-face-value bond. The bid price tells you what price you will receive if you sell the bond, and the asked price tells you what you must pay for the bond. (You might want to think of the bid price as the "wholesale" price and the asked price as the "retail" price.) The "Chg." column indicates how much the bid price has changed in 32nds (in this case, no change) from the previous trading day.

Notice that for all the bonds and notes, the asked price is more than the bid price. Can you guess why this is so? The difference between the two (the *spread*) provides the bond dealer who trades these securities with a profit. For T-bond 1, the dealer who buys it at $99\frac{29}{32}$, and sells it for $99\frac{31}{32}$, makes a profit of $\frac{2}{32}$. This profit is what enables the dealer to make a living and provide the service of allowing you to buy and sell bonds at will.

The "Ask Yld." column provides the yield to maturity, which is 4.61 percent for T-bond 1. It is calculated with the method described earlier in this chapter using the asked price as the price of the bond. The asked price is used in the calculation because the yield to maturity is most relevant to a person who is going to buy and hold the security and thus earn the yield. The person selling the security is not going to be holding it and hence is less concerned with the yield.

The figure for the current yield is not usually included in the newspaper's quotations for Treasury securities, but it has been added in panel (a) to give you some real-world examples of how well the current yield approximates the yield to maturity. Our previous discussion provided us with some rules for deciding when the current yield is likely to be a good approximation and when it is not.

T-bonds 3 and 4 mature in more than 20 years, meaning that their characteristics are like those of a consol. The current yields should then be a good approximation of the yields to maturity, and they are: The current yields are within two-tenths of a percentage point of the values for the yields to maturity. This approximation is reasonable even for T-bond 3, which has a price nearly 10 percent above its face value.

Now let's take a look at T-bonds 1 and 2, which have a much shorter time to maturity. The current yield is a good approximation when the price is very near the par price of 100, as it is for T-bond 1. However, the price of T-bond 2 differs by less than 1 percent from the par value, and look how poor an approximation the current yield is for the yield to maturity; it overstates the yield to maturity by more than 2 percentage points. This bears out what we learned earlier about the current yield: It can be a very misleading guide to the value of the yield to maturity for a short-term bond if the bond price is not very close to par.

Two other categories of bonds are reported much like the Treasury bonds and notes in the newspaper. Government agency and miscellaneous securities include securities issued by U.S. government agencies such as the Government National Mortgage Association, which makes loans to savings and loan institutions, and international agencies such as the World Bank. Tax-exempt bonds are the other category reported in a manner similar to panel (a), except that yield-to-maturity calculations are not usually provided. Tax-exempt bonds include bonds issued by local government and public authorities whose interest payments are exempt from federal income taxes.

Panel (b) quotes yields on U.S. Treasury bills, which, as we have seen, are discount bonds. Since there is no coupon, these securities are identified solely by their maturity dates, which you can see in the first column. The next column, "Days to Mat.," provides the number of days to maturity of the bill. Dealers in these markets always refer to prices by quoting the yield on a discount basis. The "Bid" column gives the discount yield for people selling the bills to dealers, and the "Asked" column gives the discount yield for people buying the bills from dealers. As with bonds and notes, the dealers' profits are made by the asked price being higher than the bid price, leading to the asked discount yield being lower than the bid discount yield.

The "Chg." column indicates how much the asked discount yield changed from the previous day. When financial analysts talk about changes in the yield, they frequently describe the changes in terms of **basis points,** which are hundredths of a percentage point. For example, a financial analyst would describe the +0.06 change in the asked discount yield for the October 17, 1996, T-bill by saying that it had risen by 6 basis points.

As we learned earlier, the yield on a discount basis understates the yield to maturity, which is reported in the column of panel (b) headed "Ask Yld." This is evident from a comparison of the "Ask Yld." and "Asked" columns. As we would also expect from our discussion of the calculation of yields on a discount basis, the understatement grows as the maturity of the bill lengthens.

Panel (c) has quotations for corporate bonds traded on the New York Stock Exchange. Corporate bonds traded on the American Stock Exchange are reported in like manner. The first column identifies the bond by indicating the corporation that issued it. The bonds we are looking at have all been issued by American Telephone and Telegraph (AT&T). The next column tells the coupon rate and the maturity date ($4\frac{3}{4}$ and 1998 for Bond 1). The "Cur. Yld." column reports the current yield (4.8), and "Vol." gives the volume of trading in that bond (27 bonds of $1000 face value traded that day). The "Close" price is the last traded price that day per $100 of face value. The price of $98\frac{1}{8}$ represents $981.25 for a $1000-face-value bond. The "Net Chg." is the change in the closing price from the previous trading day.

The yield to maturity is also given for two bonds. This information is not usually provided in the newspaper, but it is included here because it shows how misleading the current yield can be for a bond with a short maturity such as the $4\frac{3}{4}$s, of 1998. The current yield of 4.8 percent is a misleading measure of the interest rate because the yield to maturity is actually 5.76 percent. By contrast, for the $8\frac{5}{8}$s, of 2031, with over 30 years to maturity, the current yield and the yield to maturity are almost exactly equal.

THE DISTINCTION BETWEEN INTEREST RATES AND RETURNS

Many people think that the interest rate on a bond tells them all they need to know about how well off they are as a result of owning it. If Irving the Investor thinks he is better off when he owns a long-term bond yielding a 10 percent interest rate and the interest rate rises to 20 percent, he will have a rude awakening: As we will shortly see, Irving has lost his shirt! How well a person does by holding a bond or any other security over a particular time period is accurately measured by the **return** or, in more precise terminology, the **rate of return.** For any security, the rate of return is defined as the payments to the owner plus the change in its value, expressed as a fraction of its purchase price. To make this definition clearer, let us see what the return would look like for a $1000-face-value coupon bond with a coupon rate of 10 percent that is bought for $1000, held for one year, and then sold for $1200. The payments to the owner are the yearly coupon payments of $100, and the change in its value is $1200 − $1000 = $200. Adding these together and expressing them as a fraction of the purchase price of $1000 gives us the one-year holding-period return for this bond:

$$\frac{\$100 + \$200}{\$1000} = \frac{\$300}{\$1000} = 0.30 = 30\%$$

You may have noticed something quite surprising about the return that we have just calculated: It equals 30 percent, yet as Table 1 indicates, initially the yield to maturity was only 10 percent. This demonstrates that ***the return on a bond will not necessarily equal the interest rate on that bond.*** We now see that the distinction between interest rate and return can be important, although for many securities the two may be closely related.

Study Guide   The concept of return discussed here is extremely important because it is used continually throughout the book. Make sure that you understand how a return is calculated and why it can differ from the interest rate. This understanding will make the material presented later in the book easier to follow.

More generally, the return on a bond held from time t to time $t + 1$ can be written as

$$RET = \frac{C + P_{t+1} - P_t}{P_t} \tag{9}$$

where RET = return from holding the bond from time t to time $t + 1$
P_t = price of the bond at time t
P_{t+1} = price of the bond at time $t + 1$
C = coupon payment

A convenient way to rewrite the return formula in Equation 9 is to recognize that it can be split up into two separate terms. The first is the current yield i_c (the coupon payment over the purchase price):

$$\frac{C}{P_t} = i_c$$

The second term is the **rate of capital gain,** or the change in the bond's price relative to the initial purchase price:

$$\frac{P_{t+1} - P_t}{P_t} = g$$

where g = rate of capital gain. Equation 9 can then be rewritten as

$$RET = i_c + g \tag{10}$$

which shows that the return on a bond is the current yield i_c plus the rate of capital gain g. This rewritten formula illustrates the point we just discovered. Even for a bond for which the current yield i_c is an accurate measure of the yield to maturity, the return can differ substantially from the interest rate. Returns will differ from the interest rate especially if there are sizable fluctuations in the price of the bond that produce substantial capital gains or losses.

To explore this point even further, let's look at what happens to the returns on bonds of different maturities when interest rates rise. Table 2 calculates the one-year return on several 10 percent-coupon-rate bonds all purchased at par when interest rates on all these bonds rise from 10 to 20 percent. Several key findings in this table are generally true of all bonds:

- The only bond whose return equals the initial yield to maturity is one whose time to maturity is the same as the holding period (see the last bond in Table 2).
- A rise in interest rates is associated with a fall in bond prices, resulting in capital losses on bonds whose terms to maturity are longer than the holding period.
- The more distant a bond's maturity, the greater the size of the price change associated with an interest-rate change.

TABLE 2 One-Year Returns on Different-Maturity 10 percent Coupon Rate Bonds When Interest Rates Rise

(1) Years to Maturity When Bond Is Purchased	(2) Initial Yield to Maturity (%)	(3) Initial Price ($)	(4) Yield to Maturity Next Year (%)	(5) Price Next Year* ($)	(6) Initial Current Yield (%)	(7) Rate of Capital Gain (%)	(8) Rate of Return (6 + 7) (%)
30	10	1000	20	503	10	−49.7	−39.7
20	10	1000	20	516	10	−48.4	−38.4
10	10	1000	20	597	10	−40.3	−30.3
5	10	1000	20	741	10	−25.9	−15.9
2	10	1000	20	917	10	− 8.3	+1.7
1	10	1000	20	1000	10	0.0	+10.0

*Calculated using Equation 3.

- The more distant a bond's maturity, the lower the rate of return that occurs as a result of the increase in the interest rate.
- Even though a bond has a substantial initial interest rate, its return can turn out to be negative if interest rates rise.

At first it frequently puzzles students that a rise in interest rates can mean that a bond has been a poor investment (as it puzzles poor Irving the Investor). The trick to understanding this is to recognize that a rise in the interest rate means that the price of a bond has fallen. A rise in interest rates therefore means that a capital loss has occurred, and if this loss is large enough, the bond can be a poor investment indeed.[6] For example, we see in Table 2 that the bond that has 30 years to maturity when purchased has a capital loss of 49.7 percent when the interest rate rises from 10 to 20 percent. This loss is so large that it exceeds the current yield of 10 percent, resulting in a negative return (loss) of −39.7 percent.

Maturity and the Volatility of Bond Returns: Interest-Rate Risk

The finding that the prices of longer-maturity bonds respond more dramatically to changes in interest rates helps explain an important fact about the behavior of bond markets: *Prices and returns for long-term bonds are more volatile than those for shorter-term bonds.* Price changes of +20 percent and −20 percent within a year, with corresponding variations in returns, are common for bonds more than 20 years away from maturity.

We now see that changes in interest rates make investments in long-term bonds quite risky. Indeed, the riskiness of an asset's return that results from interest-rate changes is so important that it has been given a special name, **interest-rate risk.** Dealing with interest-rate risk is a major concern of managers of financial institutions, as we will see in later chapters.

Although long-term debt instruments have substantial interest-rate risk, short-term debt instruments do not. Indeed, bonds with a maturity that is as short as the holding period have no interest-rate risk.[7] We see this for the coupon bond at the bottom of Table 2, which has no uncertainty about the rate of return because it equals the yield to maturity, which is known at the time the bond is purchased. The key to understanding why there is no interest-rate risk for *any* bond whose time to maturity matches the holding period is to recognize that (in this case) the price at the end of the holding period is already fixed at the face value. The change in interest rates can then have no effect on the price at the end of the

---

[6]If Irving does not sell the bond, his capital loss is often referred to as a "paper loss." This is a loss nonetheless because if he had not bought this bond and had instead put his money in the bank, he would now be able to buy more bonds at their lower price than he presently owns.

[7]The statement that there is no interest-rate risk for any bond whose time to maturity matches the holding period is literally true only for discount bonds and zero-coupon bonds that make no intermediate cash payments before the holding period is over. A coupon bond that makes an intermediate cash payment before the holding period is over requires that this payment be reinvested at some future date. Because the interest rate at which this payment can be reinvested is uncertain, there is some uncertainty about the return on this coupon bond even when the time to maturity equals the holding period. However, the riskiness of the return on a coupon bond from reinvesting the coupon payments is typically quite small, and so the basic point that a coupon bond with a time to maturity equaling the holding period has very little risk still holds true.

holding period for these bonds, and the return will therefore be equal to the yield to maturity known at the time the bond is purchased.[8]

Summary

The return on a bond, which tells you how good an investment it has been over the holding period, is equal to the yield to maturity in only one special case: when the holding period and the maturity of the bond are identical. Bonds whose term to maturity is longer than the holding period are subject to interest-rate risk: Changes in interest rates lead to capital gains and losses that produce substantial differences between the return and the yield to maturity known at the time the bond is purchased. Interest-rate risk is especially important for long-term bonds, where the capital gains and losses can be substantial. This is why long-term bonds are not considered to be safe assets with a sure return over short holding periods.

Should Retirees Invest in "Gilt-Edged" Long-Term Bonds?

A common bit of conventional wisdom is that retirees should invest their money in "gilt-edged" securities like long-term U.S Treasury bonds because this will provide them with a safe return. Is this good advice given today's financial markets?

The concept of interest-rate risk indicates that the answer is no because long-term bonds have very volatile returns. To see this, let's examine the returns on a long-term Treasury bond such as the Treasury $11\frac{1}{4}$s, of 2015 (a coupon bond with a coupon rate of $11\frac{1}{4}$ percent, maturing in 2015). Table 3 provides the prices and one-year returns for this bond from 1985 to 1996. (To make sure you understand the concepts of a return and a coupon bond, you might try to calculate these returns yourself using the formula in Equation 9.)

---

[8]In the text, we are assuming that all holding periods are as short as the maturity on short-term bonds and are thus not subject to interest-rate risk. However, if an investor's holding period is longer than the term to maturity of the bond, the investor is exposed to a type of interest-rate risk called *reinvestment risk*. Reinvestment risk occurs because the proceeds from the short-term bond need to be reinvested at a future interest rate that is uncertain.

To understand reinvestment risk, suppose that Irving the Investor has a holding period of two years and decides to purchase a $1000 one-year bond at face value and will then purchase another one at the end of the first year. If the initial interest rate is 10 percent, Irving will have $1100 at the end of the year. If the interest rate rises to 20 percent, as in Table 2, Irving will find that buying $1100 worth of another one-year bond will leave him at the end of the second year with $1100 × (1 + 0.20) = $1320. Thus Irving's two-year return will be ($1320 − $1000)/1000 = 0.32 = 32 percent, which equals 14.9 percent at an annual rate. In this case, Irving has earned more by buying the one-year bonds than if he had initially purchased the two-year bond with an interest rate of 10 percent. Thus when Irving has a holding period that is longer than the term to maturity of the bonds he purchases, he benefits from a rise in interest rates. Conversely, if interest rates fall to 5 percent, Irving will have only $1155 at the end of two years: $1100 × (1 + 0.05). Thus his two-year return will be ($1155 − $1000)/1000 = 0.155 = 15.5 percent, which is 7.2 percent at an annual rate. With a holding period greater than the term to maturity of the bond, Irving now loses from a fall in interest rates.

We have thus seen that when the holding period is longer than the term to maturity of a bond, the return is uncertain because the future interest rate when reinvestment occurs is also uncertain—in short, there is reinvestment risk. We also see that if the holding period is longer than the term to maturity of the bond, the investor benefits from a rise in interest rates and is hurt by a fall in interest rates.

As you can see, there have been big swings in the returns on this supposedly safe investment, with low returns and even losses occurring in some years. If retirees at times need to sell bonds to pay bills so that they might only hold bonds for periods as short as a year, they may find themselves in financial difficulties when the bonds decline in value. Conclusion: Retirees beware!   Ⓐ

THE DISTINCTION BETWEEN REAL AND NOMINAL INTEREST RATES

So far in our discussion of interest rates, we have ignored the effects of inflation on the cost of borrowing. What we have up to now been calling the interest rate makes no allowance for inflation, and it is more precisely referred to as the **nominal interest rate,** which is to distinguish it from the **real interest rate,** the interest rate that is adjusted for expected changes in the price level so that it more accurately reflects the true cost of borrowing.[9] The real interest rate is more accurately defined by the *Fisher equation,* named for Irving Fisher, one of the great monetary economists of the twentieth century. The Fisher equation states that the nominal interest rate i equals the real interest rate i_r plus the expected rate of inflation π^e:[10]

$$i = i_r + \pi^e \tag{11}$$

Rearranging terms, we find that the real interest rate equals the nominal interest rate minus the expected inflation rate:

$$i_r = i - \pi^e \tag{12}$$

To see why this definition makes sense, let us first consider a situation in which you have made a one-year simple loan with a 5 percent interest rate ($i = 5$ percent) and you expect the price level to rise by 3 percent over the course of the year ($\pi^e = 3$ percent). As a result of making the loan, at the end of the year you will have 2 percent more in **real terms,** that is, in terms of real goods and services you can buy. In this case, the interest rate you have earned in terms of real goods and services is 2 percent; that is,

$$i_r = 5\% - 3\% = 2\%$$

as indicated by the Fisher definition.

Now what if the interest rate rises to 8 percent, but you expect the inflation rate to be 10 percent over the course of the year? Although you will have 8

---

[9]The real interest rate defined in the text is more precisely referred to as the *ex ante real interest rate* because it is adjusted for *expected* changes in the price level. This is the real interest rate that is most important to economic decisions, and typically it is what economists mean when they make reference to the "real" interest rate. The interest rate that is adjusted for *actual* changes in the price level is called the *ex post real interest rate.* It describes how well a lender has done in real terms *after the fact.*

[10]A more precise formulation of the Fisher equation is

$$i = i_r + \pi^e + (i_r \times \pi^e)$$

because

$$1 + i = (1 + i_r)(1 + \pi^e) = 1 + i_r + \pi^e + (i_r \times \pi^e)$$

and subtracting 1 from both sides gives us the first equation. For small values of i_r and π^e, the term $i_r \times \pi^e$ is so small that we ignore it, as in the text.

TABLE 3	Prices and One-Year Returns on U.S. Treasury $11\frac{1}{4}$s of 2015, 1985–1996	
Year	Price at End of Year	Return (%)
1985	117 $^{29}/_{32}$	
1986	138 $^{4}/_{32}$	+26.7
1987	121 $^{31}/_{32}$	−3.6
1988	121 $^{31}/_{32}$	+9.2
1989	133 $^{26}/_{32}$	+18.9
1990	129 $^{24}/_{32}$	+5.4
1991	141 $^{27}/_{32}$	+18.0
1992	141 $^{14}/_{32}$	+7.6
1993	154 $^{6}/_{32}$	+17.0
1994	132 $^{3}/_{32}$	−7.0
1995	160	+29.6
1996	149 $^{12}/_{32}$	+0.5

percent more dollars at the end of the year, you will be paying 10 percent more for goods; the result is that you will be able to buy 2 percent fewer goods at the end of the year and you are 2 percent worse off *in real terms.* This is also exactly what the Fisher definition tells us because

$$i_r = 8\% - 10\% = -2\%$$

As a lender, you are clearly less eager to make a loan in this case because in terms of real goods and services you have actually earned a negative interest rate of 2 percent. By contrast, as the borrower, you fare quite well because at the end of the year, the amounts you will have to pay back will be worth 2 percent less in terms of goods and services—you as the borrower will be ahead by 2 percent in real terms. ***When the real interest rate is low, there are greater incentives to borrow and fewer incentives to lend.***

A similar distinction can be made between nominal returns and real returns. Nominal returns, which do not allow for inflation, are what we have been referring to as simply "returns." When inflation is subtracted from a nominal return, we have the real return, which indicates the amount of extra goods and services that can be purchased as a result of holding the security.

The distinction between real and nominal interest rates is important because the real interest rate, which reflects the real cost of borrowing, is likely to be a better indicator of the incentives to borrow and lend. It appears to be a better guide to how people will be affected by what is happening in credit markets. Figure 3, which presents estimates from 1953 to 1996 of the real and nominal interest rates on three-month U.S. Treasury bills, shows us that nominal and real rates often do not move together. (This is also true for nominal and real interest rates in the rest of the world.) In particular, when nominal rates in the United States were high in the 1970s, real rates were actually extremely low, often negative. By the standard of nominal interest rates, you would have thought that

Interest Rate (%)

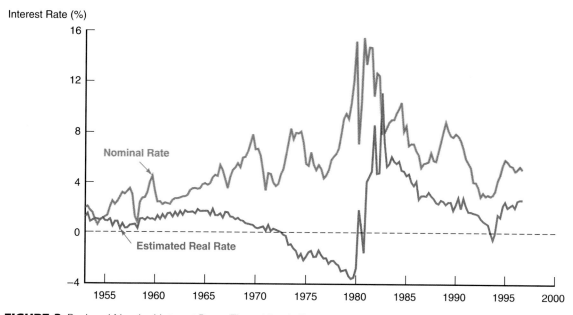

FIGURE 3 Real and Nominal Interest Rates (Three-Month Treasury Bill), 1953–1996

Sources: Nominal rates from the Citibase databank. The real rate is constructed using the procedure outlined in Frederic S. Mishkin, "The Real Interest Rate: An Empirical Investigation," *Carnegie-Rochester Conference Series on Public Policy* 15 (1981): 151–200. This involves estimating expected inflation as a function of past interest rates, inflation, and time trends and then subtracting the expected inflation measure from the nominal interest rate.

credit market conditions were tight in this period because it was expensive to borrow. However, the estimates of the real rates indicate that you would have been mistaken. In real terms, the cost of borrowing was actually quite low.[11]

---

[11]Because most interest income in the United States is subject to federal income taxes, the true earnings in real terms from holding a debt instrument are not reflected by the real interest rate defined by the Fisher equation but rather by the *after-tax real interest rate,* which equals the nominal interest rate *after income tax payments have been subtracted,* minus the expected inflation rate. For a person facing a 30 percent tax rate, the after-tax interest rate earned on a bond yielding 10 percent is only 7 percent because 30 percent of the interest income must be paid to the Internal Revenue Service. Thus the after-tax real interest rate on this bond when expected inflation is 20 percent equals −13% (= 7% − 20%). More generally, the after-tax real interest rate can be expressed as

$$i(1 - \tau) - \pi^e$$

where τ = the income tax rate.

This formula for the after-tax real interest rate also provides a better measure of the effective cost of borrowing for many corporations and individuals in the United States because in calculating income taxes, they can deduct interest payments on loans from their income. Thus if you face a 30 percent tax rate and take out a mortgage loan with a 10 percent interest rate, you are able to deduct the 10 percent interest payment and thus lower your taxes by 30 percent of this amount. Your after-tax nominal cost of borrowing is then 7 percent (10 percent minus 30 percent of the 10 percent interest payment), and when the expected inflation rate is 20 percent, the effective cost of borrowing in real terms is again −13% (= 7% − 20%).

As the example (and the formula) indicates, after-tax real interest rates are always below the real interest rate defined by the Fisher equation. For a further discussion of measures of after-tax real interest rates, see Frederic S. Mishkin, "The Real Interest Rate: An Empirical Investigation," *Carnegie-Rochester Conference Series on Public Policy* 15 (1981): 151–200.

In future years, we will have more direct measures of real interest rates in the United States. In January 1997, the U.S. Treasury began to issue **indexed bonds,** bonds whose interest and principal payments are adjusted for changes in the price level and whose interest rate thus provides a direct measure of a real interest rate. Indexed bonds have been issued by the governments of countries such as the United Kingdom, Canada, Australia, and Sweden. Not only have they acquired a successful niche in the bond market in these countries, but they are also useful to policymakers, especially monetary policymakers, because by subtracting their interest rate from a nominal interest rate, they generate more direct information on expected inflation, a valuable piece of information.

S U M M A R Y

1. The yield to maturity, which is the measure that most accurately reflects the interest rate, is the interest rate that equates the present value of future payments of a debt instrument with its value today. Application of this principle reveals that bond prices and interest rates are negatively related: When the interest rate rises, the price of the bond must fall, and vice versa.

2. Two less accurate measures of interest rates are commonly used to quote interest rates on coupon and discount bonds. The current yield, which equals the coupon payment divided by the price of a coupon bond, is a less accurate measure of the yield to maturity the shorter the maturity of the bond and the greater the gap between the price and the par value. The yield on a discount basis (also called the discount yield) understates the yield to maturity on a discount bond, and the understatement worsens the more distant the maturity of the discount secu-

rity. Even though these measures are misleading guides to the size of the interest rate, a change in them always signals a change in the same direction for the yield to maturity.

3. The return on a security, which tells you how well you have done by holding this security over a stated period of time, can differ substantially from the interest rate as measured by the yield to maturity. Long-term bond prices have substantial fluctuations when interest rates change and thus bear interest-rate risk. The resulting capital gains and losses can be large, which is why long-term bonds are not considered to be safe assets with a sure return.

4. The real interest rate is defined as the nominal interest rate minus the expected rate of inflation. It is a better measure of the incentives to borrow and lend than the nominal interest rate, and it is a more accurate indicator of the tightness of credit market conditions than the nominal interest rate.

K E Y   T E R M S

basis point, p. 84

consol, p. 77

coupon bond, p. 70

coupon rate, p. 70

current yield, p. 79

discount bond (zero-coupon

   bond), p. 70

face value (par value), p. 70

fixed-payment loan, p. 70

indexed bond, p. 92

interest-rate risk, p. 87

nominal interest rate, p. 89

present discounted value,

   p. 72

present value, p. 71

rate of capital gain, p. 86

real interest rate, p. 89

real terms, p. 89

return (rate of return), p. 85

simple loan, p. 70

yield on a discount basis

   (discount yield), p. 80

yield to maturity, p. 72

QUESTIONS AND PROBLEMS

*1. Would a dollar tomorrow be worth more or less to you today when the interest rate is 20 percent or when it is 10 percent?

2. You have just won $20 million in the state lottery, which promises to pay you $1 million (tax free) every year for the next 20 years. Have you really won $20 million?

*3. If the interest rate is 10 percent, what is the present value of a security that pays you $1100 next year, $1210 the year after, and $1331 the year after that?

4. If the security in Problem 3 sold for $4000, is the yield to maturity greater or less than 10 percent? Why?

*5. Write down the formula that is used to calculate the yield to maturity on a 20-year 10 percent coupon bond with $1000 face value that sells for $2000.

6. What is the yield to maturity on a $1000-face-value discount bond maturing in one year that sells for $800?

*7. What is the yield to maturity on a simple loan for $1 million that requires a repayment of $2 million in five years' time?

8. To pay for college, you have just taken out a $1000 government loan that makes you pay $126 per year for 25 years. However, you don't have to start making these payments until you graduate from college two years from now. Why is the yield to maturity necessarily less than 12 percent, the yield to maturity on a normal $1000 fixed-payment loan in which you pay $126 per year for 25 years?

*9. Which $1000 bond has the higher yield to maturity, a 20-year bond selling for $800 with a current yield of 15 percent or a one-year bond selling for $800 with a current yield of 5 percent?

10. Pick five U.S. Treasury bonds from the bond page of the newspaper, and calculate the current yield. Note when the current yield is a good approximation of the yield to maturity.

*11. You are offered two bonds, a one-year U.S. Treasury bond with a yield to maturity of 9 percent and a one-year U.S. Treasury bill with a yield on a discount basis of 8.9 percent. Which would you rather own?

12. If there is a decline in interest rates, which would you rather be holding, long-term bonds or short-term bonds? Why? Which type of bond has the greater interest-rate risk?

*13. Francine the Financial Adviser has just given you the following advice: "Long-term bonds are a great investment because their interest rate is over 20 percent." Is Francine necessarily right?

14. If mortgage rates rise from 5 percent to 10 percent but the expected rate of increase in housing prices rises from 2 percent to 9 percent, are people more or less likely to buy houses?

*15. Interest rates were lower in the mid-1980s than they were in the late 1970s, yet many economists have commented that real interest rates were actually much higher in the mid-1980s than in the late 1970s. Does this make sense? Do you think that these economists are right?

Chapter **5**

PORTFOLIO CHOICE

PREVIEW   Suppose you suddenly struck it rich. Maybe you've just won $25 million in the lottery and your first payment of $600,000 has arrived. Or your dear departed Aunt Thelma has remembered you with a $200,000 bequest. There are a lot of things you might want to do with this windfall: put a down payment on a mansion, buy a Ferrari, or invest in gold coins, land, Treasury bills, or AT&T stock. How will you decide what portfolio of assets you should hold to store your newfound wealth? What criteria should you use to decide among these various stores of wealth? Should you buy only one type of asset or several different types?

This chapter helps answer these questions by developing an economic theory known as the *theory of portfolio choice*. This theory outlines criteria that are important when deciding which assets are worth buying. In addition, it gives us an idea why it is good to diversify and not to put all our eggs in one basket.

The theory of portfolio choice plays a pivotal role in the study of money, banking, and financial markets and is a building block for much of the analysis in the remainder of the text. In later chapters, for example, we use the theory of portfolio choice to examine the behavior of interest rates, bank asset and liability management, financial innovation, the evolution of banking, the money supply process, the demand for money, and theories of financial market behavior.

DETERMINANTS OF ASSET DEMAND

An **asset** is a piece of property that is a store of value. Items such as money, bonds, stocks, art, land, houses, farm equipment, and manufacturing machinery are all assets. Facing the question of whether to buy and hold an asset or whether to buy one asset rather than another, an individual must consider the following factors:

1. **Wealth,** the total resources owned by the individual, including all assets
2. **Expected return** (the return expected over the next period) on one asset relative to alternative assets
3. **Risk** (the degree of uncertainty associated with the return) on one asset relative to alternative assets
4. **Liquidity** (the ease and speed with which an asset can be turned into cash) relative to alternative assets

Study Guide   As we discuss each factor that influences asset demand, remember that we are always holding all the other factors constant. Also, think of additional examples of how changes in each factor would influence your decision to purchase a particular asset, say, a house or a share of common stock. This intuitive approach will help you understand how the theory works in practice.

Wealth

When we find that our wealth has increased, we have more resources available with which to purchase assets, and so, not surprisingly, the quantity of assets we demand increases.[1] The demand for different assets responds differently to changes in wealth, however; the quantity demanded of some assets grows more rapidly with a rise in wealth than the quantity demanded of others. The degree of this response is measured by a concept known as the **wealth elasticity of demand** (which is similar to the concept of income elasticity of demand, which you might have learned in an earlier economics course). The wealth elasticity of demand measures how much, with everything else unchanged, the quantity demanded of an asset changes in percentage terms in response to a percentage change in wealth:

$$\frac{\% \text{ change in quantity demanded}}{\% \text{ change in wealth}} = \text{wealth elasticity of demand}$$

If, for example, the quantity of currency demanded increases only by 50 percent when wealth increases by 100 percent, we say that currency has a wealth elasticity of demand of $\frac{1}{2}$. If, for a common stock, the quantity demanded increases by 200 percent when wealth increases by 100 percent, the wealth elasticity of demand equals 2.

Assets can be sorted into two categories, depending on the value of their wealth elasticity of demand. An asset is a **necessity** if there is only so much that people want to hold, so that as wealth grows, the percentage increase in the quantity demanded of the asset is less than the percentage increase in wealth—in other words, its wealth elasticity is less than 1. Because the quantity demanded of a necessity does not grow proportionally with wealth, the amount of this asset

---

[1]Although it is possible that some assets (called *inferior assets*) might have the property that the quantity demanded does not increase as wealth increases, such assets are rare. Hence we will always assume that demand for an asset increases as wealth increases.

that people want to hold relative to their wealth falls as wealth grows. An asset is a **luxury** if its wealth elasticity is greater than 1; and as wealth grows, the quantity demanded of this asset grows more than proportionally, and the amount that people hold relative to their wealth grows. Common stocks and municipal bonds are examples of luxury assets, and currency and checking account deposits are necessities.

The effect of changes in wealth on the quantity demanded of an asset can be summarized in this way: ***Holding everything else constant, an increase in wealth raises the quantity demanded of an asset, and the increase in the quantity demanded is greater if the asset is a luxury than if it is a necessity.***

Expected Returns

In Chapter 4 we saw that the return on an asset (such as a bond) measures how much we gain from holding that asset. When we make a decision to buy an asset, we are influenced by what we expect the return on that asset to be. If a Mobil Oil Corporation bond, for example, has a return of 15 percent half of the time and 5 percent the other half of the time, its expected return (which you can think of as the average return) is 10 percent.[2] If the expected return on the Mobil Oil bond rises relative to expected returns on alternative assets, holding everything else constant, then it becomes more desirable to purchase it, and the quantity demanded increases. This can occur in either of two ways: (1) when the expected return on the Mobil Oil bond rises while the return on an alternative asset—say, stock in IBM—remains unchanged or (2) when the return on the alternative asset, the IBM stock, falls while the return on the Mobil Oil bond remains unchanged. To summarize, ***an increase in an asset's expected return relative to that of an alternative asset, holding everything else unchanged, raises the quantity demanded of the asset.***

Risk

The degree of risk or uncertainty of an asset's returns also affects the demand for the asset. Consider two assets, stock in Fly-by-Night Airlines and stock in Feet-on-the-Ground Bus Company. Suppose that Fly-by-Night stock has a return of 15 percent half the time and 5 percent the other half of the time, making its expected return 10 percent, while stock in Feet-on-the-Ground has a fixed return of 10

---

[2]More generally, the expected return equals a weighted sum of each possible realized return multiplied by the probability of its occurring:

$$RET^e = \Sigma \, p_i \times RET_i$$

where RET^e = expected return
$\quad p_i$ = probability of getting the realization RET_i
$\quad RET_i$ = realization of the return

For a Mobil Oil bond,

$$RET^e = \left(\frac{1}{2} \times 15\%\right) + \left(\frac{1}{2} \times 5\%\right) = 10\%$$

percent. Fly-by-Night stock has uncertainty associated with its returns and so has greater risk than stock in Feet-on-the-Ground, whose return is a sure thing.[3]

A *risk-averse* person prefers stock in Feet-on-the-Ground (the sure thing) to Fly-by-Night stock (the riskier asset), even though the stocks have the same expected return, 10 percent. By contrast, a person who prefers risk is a *risk preferrer* or *risk lover.* Most people are risk-averse: Everything else being equal, they prefer to hold the less risky asset. Hence, **holding everything else constant, if an asset's risk rises relative to that of alternative assets, its quantity demanded will fall.**

Liquidity

Another factor that affects the demand for an asset is how quickly it can be converted into cash without incurring large costs—its liquidity. An asset is liquid if the market in which it is traded has depth and breadth, that is, if the market has many buyers and sellers. A house is not a very liquid asset because it may be hard to find a buyer quickly; if a house must be sold to pay off bills, it might have to be sold for a much lower price. And the transaction costs in selling a house (broker's commissions, lawyer's fees, and so on) are substantial. A U.S. Treasury bill, by contrast, is a highly liquid asset. It can be sold in a well-organized market where there are many buyers, so it can be sold quickly at low cost. **The more liquid an asset is relative to alternative assets, holding everything else unchanged, the more desirable it is, and the greater will be the quantity demanded.**

Theory of Portfolio Choice

All the determining factors we have just discussed can be assembled into the **theory of portfolio choice,** which states that, holding all of the other factors constant:

1. The quantity demanded of an asset is usually positively related to wealth, with the response being greater if the asset is a luxury than if it is a necessity.
2. The quantity demanded of an asset is positively related to its expected return relative to alternative assets.
3. The quantity demanded of an asset is negatively related to the risk of its returns relative to alternative assets.
4. The quantity demanded of an asset is positively related to its liquidity relative to alternative assets.

These results are summarized in Table 1.

---

[3]One frequently used formal measure of risk is the standard deviation, σ:

$$\sigma = \sqrt{\Sigma p_i \times (RET_i - RET^e)^2}$$

where all the variables are as defined in footnote 2. For Fly-by-Night Airlines stock it equals $\sqrt{0.5 \times (15\% - 10\%)^2 + 0.5 \times (5\% - 10\%)^2} = 5\%$, while for stock in Feet-on-the-Ground Bus Company it is $\sqrt{1 \times (10\% - 10\%)^2} = 0\%$. As you would expect, Fly-by-Night stock, the riskier asset, has a higher standard deviation of its returns. If there is another asset, such as High Flyer, Inc., stock with a return of 0 percent half of the time and 20 percent the other half of the time, its expected return is also 10 percent. This asset is riskier than either of the other two assets, as the standard deviation of its returns shows. For High Flyer stock, the standard deviation is $\sqrt{0.5 \times (0\% - 10\%)^2 + 0.5 \times (20\% - 10\%)^2} = 10\%$, which is higher than the standard deviations for stock in Fly-by-Night or Feet-on-the-Ground.

─────── **S U M M A R Y** ───────

TABLE 1 **Response of the Quantity of an Asset Demanded to Changes in Income or Wealth, Expected Returns, Risk, and Liquidity**

Variable	Change in Variable	Change in Quantity Demanded
Income or wealth	↑	↑
Expected return relative to other assets	↑	↑
Risk relative to other assets	↑	↓
Liquidity relative to other assets	↑	↑

Note: Only increases (↑) in the variables are shown. The effect of decreases in the variables on the change in demand would be the opposite of those indicated in the rightmost column.

BENEFITS OF DIVERSIFICATION

Our discussion of the theory of portfolio choice indicates that most people like to avoid risk; that is, they are risk-averse. Why, then, do many investors hold many risky assets rather than just one? Doesn't holding many risky assets expose the investor to more risk?

The old warning about not putting all your eggs in one basket holds the key to the answer: Because holding many risky assets (called **diversification**) reduces the overall risk an investor faces, diversification is beneficial. To see why this is so, let's look at some specific examples of how an investor fares when holding two risky securities.

Consider two assets, common stock of Frivolous Luxuries, Inc., and common stock of Bad Times Products, Unlimited. When the economy is strong, which we'll assume is half of the time, Frivolous Luxuries has high sales and the return on the stock is 15 percent; when the economy is weak, the other half of the time, sales are low and the return on the stock is 5 percent. In contrast, suppose that Bad Times Products thrives when the economy is weak so that its stock has a return of 15 percent, but it earns less when the economy is strong and has a return on the stock of 5 percent. Both stocks have a return of 15 percent half of the time and 5 percent the other half of the time, and both have an expected return of 10 percent. However, both stocks carry a fair amount of risk because there is uncertainty about their actual returns.

Suppose now that instead of buying one stock or the other, Irving the Investor puts half his savings in Frivolous Luxuries stock and the other half in Bad Times Products stock. When the economy is strong, Frivolous Luxuries stock has a return of 15 percent and Bad Times Products has a return of 5 percent. The result is that Irving earns a return of 10 percent (the average of 5 percent and 15 percent) on his holdings of the two stocks. When the economy is weak, Frivolous Luxuries has a return of only 5 percent and Bad Times Products has a return of 15 percent, so Irving still earns a return of 10 percent. If Irving diversifies by buying both stocks, he earns a return of 10 percent regardless of whether the economy is strong or weak. Irving is better off from this strategy of diversification because his expected return is 10 percent, the same as from holding either Frivolous Luxuries or Bad Times Products alone, yet he is not exposed to *any* risk.

Although the case we have described demonstrates the benefits of diversification, it is somewhat unrealistic. It is hard to find two securities with the characteristic that when the return of one is low, the return of the other is always high.[4] In the real world, we are more likely to find at best returns on securities that are independent of each other; that is, when one is low, the other is just as likely to be high as to be low.

Suppose that both securities have an expected return of 10 percent, with a return of 5 percent half of the time and 15 percent the other half of the time. Sometimes both securities will earn the higher return, and sometimes both will earn the lower return. In this case, if Irving holds equal amounts of each security, he will on average earn the same return as if he had just put all his savings into one of the securities. However, because the returns on these two securities are independent, it is just as likely that when one earns the high 15 percent return, the other earns the low 5 percent return, and vice versa, giving Irving a return of 10 percent (equal to the expected return). Because Irving is more likely to earn what he expected to earn when he holds both securities instead of just one, we can see that Irving has again reduced his risk through diversification.[5]

The one case in which Irving will not benefit from diversifying occurs when the returns on the two securities move perfectly together. In this case, when the first security has a return of 15 percent, the other also has a return of 15 percent, and holding both securities results in a return of 15 percent. When the first security has a return of 5 percent, the other has a return of 5 percent, and holding both results in a return of 5 percent. The result of diversifying by holding both securities is a return of 15 percent half of the time and 5 percent the other half of the time, which is exactly the same returns that are earned by holding only one of the securities. Consequently, diversification in this case does not lead to any reduction of risk.

The examples we have just examined illustrate the following important points about diversification:

1. Diversification is almost always beneficial to the risk-averse investor because it reduces risk except in the extremely rare case where returns on securities move perfectly together.

---

[4]Such a case is described by saying that the returns on the two securities are perfectly *negatively* correlated.

[5]We can also see that diversification in our example leads to lower risk by examining the standard deviation of returns when Irving diversifies and when he doesn't. The standard deviation of returns if Irving holds only one of the two securities is $\sqrt{0.5 \times (15\% - 10\%)^2 + 0.5 \times (5\% - 10\%)^2} = 5\%$. When Irving holds equal amounts of each security, there is a probability of $\frac{1}{4}$ that he will earn 5 percent on both (for a total return of 5 percent), a probability of $\frac{1}{4}$ that he will earn 15 percent on both (for a total return of 15 percent), and a probability of $\frac{1}{2}$ that he will earn 15 percent on one security and 5 percent on the other security (for a total return of 10 percent). The standard deviation of returns when Irving diversifies is thus $\sqrt{0.25 \times (15\% - 10\%)^2 + 0.25 \times (5\% - 10\%)^2 + 0.5 \times (10\% - 10\%)^2} = 3.5\%$. Since the standard deviation of returns when Irving diversifies is lower than when he holds only one security, we can see that diversification has reduced risk.

2. The less the returns on two securities move together, the more benefit (risk reduction) there is from diversification.

SYSTEMATIC RISK

Given the benefits of diversification, you might think that by holding enough different securities in a portfolio, you could eliminate risk entirely. Unfortunately, this is not possible because securities have **systematic risk,** risk that cannot be eliminated through diversification. In other words, no matter how many different securities you hold in your portfolio, you will still be stuck with some unavoidable risk, and this is the systematic risk. To understand systematic risk better, we need to recognize that we can divide the risk of an asset into two components, systematic risk and **nonsystematic risk,** the risk unique to an asset that can be diversified away by holding enough different securities in your portfolio:

Asset risk = systematic risk + nonsystematic risk

Nonsystematic risk is unique to an asset because it is related to the part of an asset's return that does not vary with returns on other assets. With many assets in a portfolio, nonsystematic risk becomes less important because when the nonsystematic part of one asset's return goes up, it is likely that the nonsystematic part of another asset's return has gone down, movements that cancel each other out. Hence with enough diversification as a result of a portfolio containing a large number of different assets, the nonsystematic risk contributes nothing to the total risk of the portfolio. In other words, *the risk of a well-diversified portfolio is due solely to the systematic risk of assets in the portfolio.*

This fact is very important because it tells us that if we diversify sufficiently, the only component of an asset's risk that we have to worry about is its systematic risk. Systematic risk of an asset is measured by a concept called **beta,** a measure of the sensitivity of an asset's return to changes in the value of the entire market of assets. When on average a 1 percent rise in the value of the market portfolio leads to a 2 percent rise in the value of an asset, the beta for this asset is calculated to be 2.0. If, conversely, the value of the asset on average rises by only 0.5 percent when the market rises by 1 percent, the asset's beta is 0.5.

The first asset, with a beta of 2.0, has much more systematic risk than the asset with a beta of 0.5. To see this, we first recognize that the portfolio made up of the entire market is a completely diversified portfolio and hence has only systematic risk. When the value of the market fluctuates by a certain amount, the asset with a beta of 2.0 fluctuates twice as much. Therefore, its return has twice as much systematic risk. By contrast, the asset with a beta of 0.5 fluctuates less than the market and so has less systematic risk. Because an asset with a higher beta has more systematic risk, this asset is less desirable because the systematic risk cannot be diversified away. Thus, holding everything else constant, an asset with a higher beta has a lower quantity demanded. We have reached the following conclusion, which is of great importance to participants in financial markets: *The greater an asset's beta, the greater the asset's systematic risk and the less desirable the asset is to hold in one's portfolio.*

RISK PREMIUMS: CAPITAL ASSET PRICING MODEL AND ARBITRAGE PRICING THEORY

Our recognition that greater systematic risk makes an asset less desirable can be used to understand the *capital asset pricing model (CAPM),* a widely used theory developed by William Sharpe, John Litner, and Jack Treynor. The CAPM is useful because it provides an explanation for the magnitude of an asset's *risk premium,* the difference between the asset's expected return and the risk-free interest rate (the interest rate on a security that has no possibility of default).

We have seen that an asset contributes risk to a well-diversified portfolio in the amount of its systematic risk as measured by beta. When an asset has a high beta, meaning that it has a large amount of systematic risk and is therefore less desirable, we would expect that investors would be willing to hold this asset only if it yielded a higher expected return. This is exactly what the CAPM tells us in the equation

$$\text{Risk premium} = RET^e - RET_f = \beta(RET^e_m - RET_f) \tag{1}$$

where
$$RET^e = \text{expected return for the asset}$$
$$RET_f = \text{risk-free interest rate}$$
$$\beta = \text{beta of the asset}$$
$$RET^e_m = \text{expected return for the market portfolio}$$

The CAPM equation provides the commonsense result that when an asset's beta is zero, meaning that it has no systematic risk, its risk premium will be zero. If its beta is 1.0, meaning that it has the same systematic risk as the entire market, it will have the same risk premium as the market, $RET^e_m - RET_f$. If the asset has an even higher beta, say, 2.0, its risk premium will be greater than that of the market. For example, if the expected return on the market is 8 percent and the risk-free rate is 2 percent, the risk premium for the market is 6 percent. The asset with the beta of 2.0 would then be expected to have a risk premium of 12 percent ($= 2 \times 6$ percent).

Although the capital asset pricing model has proved useful in real-world applications, it assumes that there is only one source of systematic risk, that found in the market portfolio. However, an alternative theory, the *arbitrage pricing theory (APT),* developed by Stephen Ross of Yale University, takes the view that there are several sources of risk in the economy that cannot be eliminated by diversification. These sources of risk can be thought of as related to economywide factors such as inflation and changes in aggregate output. Instead of calculating a single beta, like the CAPM, arbitrage pricing theory calculates many betas by estimating the sensitivity of an asset's return to changes in each factor. The arbitrage pricing theory equation is

$$\begin{aligned}
\text{Risk premium} = RET^e - RET_f \\
= \beta_1 (RET^e_{\text{factor 1}} - RET_f) + \beta_2 (RET^e_{\text{factor 2}} - RET_f) \\
+ \cdots + \beta_k (RET^e_{\text{factor } k} - RET_f)
\end{aligned} \tag{2}$$

Arbitrage pricing theory thus indicates that the risk premium for an asset is related to the risk premium for each factor and that as the asset's sensitivity to each factor increases, its risk premium will increase as well.

Which of these theories provides a better explanation of risk premiums is still uncertain. Both agree that an asset has a higher risk premium when it has higher systematic risk, and both are considered valuable tools for explaining risk premiums.

With our understanding of the factors that influence investors' decisions to buy and hold different assets, we are ready to explore in the next chapter how the price of a particular asset, bonds, is determined.

SUMMARY

1. The theory of portfolio choice tells us that the quantity demanded of an asset is (a) positively related to wealth, (b) positively related to the expected return on the asset relative to alternative assets, (c) negatively related to the riskiness of the asset relative to alternative assets, and (d) positively related to the liquidity of the asset relative to alternative assets.

2. Diversification (the holding of more than one asset) benefits investors because it reduces the risk they face, and the benefits are greater the less returns on securities move together.

3. An asset's risk is made up of two components: systematic risk, which cannot be diversified away, and nonsystematic risk, which can. An asset's systematic

risk is measured by beta, and the higher an asset's beta and hence its systematic risk, the less desirable the asset.

4. Both the capital asset pricing model and arbitrage pricing theory provide an explanation for an asset's risk premium, the difference between the asset's expected return and the risk-free interest rate. The capital asset pricing model indicates that an asset's risk premium is positively related to the asset's beta, the sensitivity to the market return; arbitrage pricing theory indicates that an asset's risk premium is positively related to the asset's sensitivity to many factors that represent sources of nondiversifiable risk in the economy.

KEY TERMS

asset, p. 94

beta, p. 100

diversification, p. 98

expected return, p. 95

liquidity, p. 95

luxury, p. 96

necessity, p. 95

nonsystematic risk, p. 100

risk, p. 95

systematic risk, p. 100

theory of portfolio choice, p. 97

wealth, p. 95

wealth elasticity of demand, p. 95

QUESTIONS AND PROBLEMS

1. In terms of the theory of portfolio choice, explain why you would be more or less willing to buy a share of Polaroid stock in the following situations:
   a. Your wealth falls.
   b. You expect it to appreciate in value.
   c. The bond market becomes more liquid.
   d. You expect gold to appreciate in value.
   e. Prices in the bond market become more volatile.

*2. In terms of the theory of portfolio choice, explain why you would be more or less willing to buy a house under the following circumstances:

   a. You just inherited $100,000.
   b. Real estate commissions fall from 6 percent of the sales price to 4 percent of the sales price.
   c. You expect Polaroid stock to double in value next year.
   d. Prices in the stock market become more volatile.
   e. You expect housing prices to fall.

3. In terms of the theory of portfolio choice, explain why you would be more or less willing to buy gold under the following circumstances:
   a. Gold again becomes acceptable as a medium of exchange.

b. Prices in the gold market become more volatile.

c. You expect inflation to rise, and gold prices tend to move with the aggregate price level.

d. You expect interest rates to rise.

*4. In terms of the theory of portfolio choice, explain why you would be more or less willing to buy AT&T bonds under the following circumstances:

a. Trading in these bonds increases, making them easier to sell.

b. You expect a bear market in stocks (stock prices are expected to decline).

c. Brokerage commissions on stocks fall.

d. You expect interest rates to rise.

e. Brokerage commissions on bonds fall.

5. What would happen to the demand for Rembrandts if the stock market undergoes a boom? Why?

*6. If stocks are suddenly expected to yield a higher return, would this affect the demand for bonds? Explain your answer.

7. "The more risk-averse a person is, the more likely that person is to diversify." Is this statement true, false, or uncertain? Explain your answer.

*8. I own a professional football team, and I plan to diversify by purchasing shares in either a company that owns a pro basketball team or a pharmaceutical company. Which of these two investments is more likely to reduce the overall risk I face? Why?

9. "No one who is risk-averse will ever buy a security that has a lower expected return, more risk, and less liquidity than another security." Is this statement true, false, or uncertain? Explain your answer.

*10. "The demand for an asset will be lower, everything else being equal, if its beta is higher." Is this statement true, false, or uncertain? Explain your answer.

11. If on average a stock falls by 3 percent when the market rises by 2 percent, what is its beta?

*12. Which stock would you prefer to hold, everything else being equal: a stock that on average rises by 0.5 percent when the market rises by 1 percent or a stock that on average rises by 1 percent when the market rises by 2 percent?

13. "The higher a security's beta, the lower its risk premium." Is this statement true, false or uncertain? Explain your answer.

*14. If the expected return for the market portfolio is 8 percent and the risk-free rate is 5 percent, what does the capital asset pricing model predict the expected return on a security with a beta of 3.0 to be?

15. What is the basic difference between arbitrage pricing theory and the capital asset pricing model?

Chapter **6**

THE BEHAVIOR OF
INTEREST RATES

PREVIEW   In the early 1950s, nominal interest rates on three-month Treasury bills were about 1 percent at an annual rate; by 1981, they had reached over 15 percent, then fell to 3 percent in 1993 and rose to above 5 percent by the mid 1990s. What explains these substantial fluctuations in interest rates? One reason why we study money, banking, and financial markets is to provide some answers to this question.

In this chapter we examine how the overall level of *nominal* interest rates (which we refer to as simply "interest rates") is determined and the factors that influence their behavior. We learned in Chapter 4 that interest rates are negatively related to the price of bonds, so if we can explain why bond prices change, we can also explain why interest rates fluctuate. Here we will apply supply and demand analysis to examine how bond prices and interest rates change.

LOANABLE FUNDS FRAMEWORK: SUPPLY AND DEMAND IN THE BOND MARKET

We first approach the analysis of interest-rate determination by studying the supply of and demand for bonds. Because interest rates on different securities tend to move together, in this chapter we will act as if there is only one type of security and a single interest rate in the entire economy. In the following chapter, we will expand our analysis to look at why interest rates on different securities differ.

The first step in the analysis is to use the theory of portfolio choice discussed in Chapter 5 to obtain a **demand curve,** which shows the relationship between the quantity demanded and the price when all other economic variables are held constant (that is, values of other variables are taken as given). You may recall from previous economics courses that the assumption that all other economic variables are held constant is called *ceteris paribus,* which means "other things being equal" in Latin.

Demand Curve   To clarify our analysis, let us consider the demand for one-year discount bonds, which make no coupon payments but pay the owner the $1000 face value in a year. If the holding period is one year, then as we have seen in Chapter 4, the return on the bonds is known absolutely and is equal to the interest rate as measured by the yield to maturity. This means that the expected return on this bond is equal to the interest rate i, which, using Equation 6 in Chapter 4, is

$$i = RET^e = \frac{F - P_d}{P_d}$$

where
$$i = \text{interest rate} = \text{yield to maturity}$$
$$RET^e = \text{expected return}$$
$$F = \text{face value of the discount bond}$$
$$P_d = \text{initial purchase price of the discount bond}$$

This formula shows that a particular value of the interest rate corresponds to each bond price. If the bond sells for $950, the interest rate and expected return is

$$\frac{\$1000 - \$950}{\$950} = 0.053 = 5.3\%$$

At this 5.3 percent interest rate and expected return corresponding to a bond price of $950, let us assume that the quantity of bonds demanded is $100 billion, which is plotted as point A in Figure 1. To display both the bond price and the corresponding interest rate, Figure 1 has two vertical axes. The left vertical axis shows the bond price, with the price of bonds increasing from $750 near the bottom of the axis toward $1000 at the top. The right vertical axis shows the interest rate, which increases in the *opposite* direction from 0 percent at the top of the axis to 33 percent near the bottom. The right and left vertical axes run in opposite directions because, as we learned in Chapter 4, bond price and interest rate are always negatively related: As the price of the bond rises, the interest rate on the bond necessarily falls.

At a price of $900, the interest rate and expected return equals

$$\frac{\$1000 - \$900}{\$900} = 0.111 = 11.1\%$$

Because the expected return on these bonds is higher, with all other economic variables (such as income, expected returns on other assets, risk, and liquidity) held constant, the quantity demanded of bonds will be higher as predicted by the theory of portfolio choice. Point B in Figure 1 shows that the quantity of bonds demanded at the price of $900 has risen to $200 billion. Continuing with this reasoning, if the bond price is $850 (interest rate and expected return = 17.6 percent), the quantity of bonds demanded (point C) will be greater than at point B. Similarly, at the lower prices of $800 (interest rate = 25 percent) and $750 (interest rate = 33.3 percent), the quantity of bonds demanded will be even higher (points D and E). The curve B^d, which connects these points, is the demand curve for bonds. It has the usual downward slope, indicating that at lower prices of the bond (everything else being equal), the quantity demanded is higher.[1]

---

[1]Note that although our analysis indicates that the demand curve is downward-sloping, it does not imply that the curve is a straight line. For ease of exposition, however, we will draw demand curves and supply curves as straight lines.

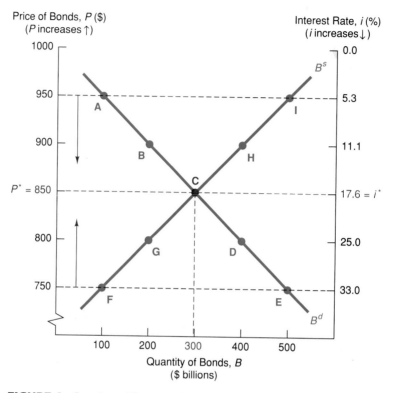

FIGURE 1   Supply and Demand for Bonds

Equilibrium in the bond market occurs at point C, the intersection of the demand curve B^d and the bond supply curve B^s. The equilibrium price is $P^* = \$850$, and the equilibrium interest rate is $i^* = 17.6\%$. (Note: *P* and *i* increase in opposite directions. *P* on the left vertical axis increases as we go up the axis from $750 near the bottom to $1000 at the top, while *i* on the right vertical axis increases as we go down the axis from 0 percent at the top to 33 percent near the bottom.)

Supply Curve

An important assumption behind the demand curve for bonds in Figure 1 is that all other economic variables besides the bond's price and interest rate are held constant. We use the same assumption in deriving a **supply curve,** which shows the relationship between the quantity supplied and the price when all other economic variables are held constant.

When the price of the bonds is $750 (interest rate = 33.3 percent), point F shows that the quantity of bonds supplied is $100 billion for the example we are considering. If the price is $800, the interest rate is the lower rate of 25 percent. Because at this interest rate it is now less costly to borrow by issuing bonds, firms will be willing to borrow more through bond issues, and the quantity of bonds supplied is at the higher level of $200 billion (point G). An even higher price of $850, corresponding to a lower interest rate of 17.6 percent, results in a larger quantity of bonds supplied of $300 billion (point C). Higher prices of $900 and $950 result in even greater quantities of bonds supplied (points H and I). The B^s curve, which connects these points, is the supply curve for bonds. It has the usual upward slope found in supply curves, indicating that as the price increases (everything else being equal), the quantity supplied increases.

Market Equilibrium

In economics, **market equilibrium** occurs when the amount that people are willing to buy (*demand*) equals the amount that people are willing to sell (*supply*) at a given price. In the bond market, this is achieved when the quantity of bonds demanded equals the quantity of bonds supplied:

$$B^d = B^s \tag{1}$$

In Figure 1, equilibrium occurs at point C, where the demand and supply curves intersect at a bond price of $850 (interest rate of 17.6 percent) and a quantity of bonds of $300 billion. The price of $P^* = 850$, where the quantity demanded equals the quantity supplied, is called the *equilibrium* or *market-clearing* price. Similarly, the interest rate of $i^* = 17.6$ percent that corresponds to this price is called the equilibrium or market-clearing interest rate.

The concepts of market equilibrium and equilibrium price or interest rate are useful because there is a tendency for the market to head toward them. We can see that it does in Figure 1 by first looking at what happens when we have a bond price that is above the equilibrium price. When the price of bonds is set too high, at, say, $950, the quantity of bonds supplied at point I is greater than the quantity of bonds demanded at point A. A situation like this, in which the quantity of bonds supplied exceeds the quantity of bonds demanded, is called a condition of **excess supply.** Because people want to sell more bonds than others want to buy, the price of the bonds will fall, and this is why the downward arrow is drawn in the figure at the bond price of $950. As long as the bond price remains above the equilibrium price, there will continue to be an excess supply of bonds, and the price will continue to fall. This will stop only when the price has reached the equilibrium price of $850, where the excess supply of bonds has been eliminated.

Now let's look at what happens when the price of bonds is below the equilibrium price. If the price of the bonds is set too low, at, say, $750, the quantity demanded at point E is greater than the quantity supplied at point F. This is called a condition of **excess demand.** People now want to buy more bonds than others are willing to sell, and so the price of bonds will be driven up. This is illustrated by the upward arrow drawn in the figure at the bond price of $750. Only when the excess demand for bonds is eliminated by the price rising to the equilibrium level of $850 is there no further tendency for the price to rise.

We can see that the concept of equilibrium price is a useful one because it indicates where the market will settle. Because each price on the left vertical axis of Figure 1 corresponds to a value of the interest rate on the right vertical axis, the same diagram also shows that the interest rate will head toward the equilibrium interest rate of 17.6 percent. When the interest rate is below the equilibrium interest rate, as it is when it is at 5.3 percent, the price of the bond is above the equilibrium price, and there will be an excess supply of bonds. The price of the bond then falls, leading to a rise in the interest rate toward the equilibrium level. Similarly, when the interest rate is above the equilibrium level, as it is when it is at 33.3 percent, there is excess demand for bonds, and the bond price will rise, driving the interest rate back down to the equilibrium level of 17.6 percent.

Supply and Demand Analysis

Our Figure 1 is a conventional supply and demand diagram with price on the left vertical axis and quantity on the horizontal axis. Because the interest rate that corresponds to each bond price is also marked on the right vertical axis, this diagram allows us to read the equilibrium interest rate, giving us a model that describes the determination of interest rates. It is important to recognize that a supply and demand diagram like Figure 1 can be drawn for *any* type of bond because the interest rate and price of a bond are *always* negatively related for any type of bond, be it a discount bond or a coupon bond.

One disadvantage of the diagram in Figure 1 is that interest rates run in an unusual direction on the right vertical axis: As we go up the right axis, interest rates fall. Because economists are typically more concerned with the value of interest rates rather than the price of bonds, we could plot the supply of and demand for bonds on a diagram that has only a left vertical axis that provides the values of the interest rates running in the usual direction, rising as we go up the axis. Figure 2 is such a diagram, in which points A through I match the corresponding points in Figure 1.

However, making interest rates run the "usual" direction on the vertical axis presents us with a problem. Our demand curve for bonds, points A through E, now looks peculiar because it has an upward slope. This upward slope is, however, completely consistent with our usual demand analysis, which produces a negative relationship between price and quantity. The inverse relationship between bond prices and interest rates means that in moving from point A to point B to point C, bond prices are falling and, consistent with usual demand analysis, the quantity demanded is rising. Similarly, our supply curve for bonds, points F through I, has an unusual-looking downward slope but is completely consistent with the usual view that price and the quantity supplied are positively related.

One way to give the demand curve the usual downward slope and the supply curve the usual upward slope is to rename the horizontal axis and the demand and supply curves. Because a firm supplying bonds is in fact taking out a loan from a person buying a bond, "supplying a bond" is equivalent to "demanding a loan." Thus the supply curve for bonds can be reinterpreted as indicating the *quantity of loans demanded* for each value of the interest rate. If we rename the horizontal axis **loanable funds,** defined as the quantity of loans, the supply of bonds can be reinterpreted as the *demand for loanable funds*. Similarly, the demand curve for bonds can be reidentified as the *supply of loanable funds* because buying (demanding) a bond is equivalent to supplying a loan. Figure 2 relabels the curves and the horizontal axis using the loanable funds terminology in parentheses, and now the renamed loanable funds demand curve has the usual downward slope and the renamed loanable funds supply curve the usual upward slope.

Because supply and demand diagrams that explain how interest rates are determined in the bond market most commonly use the loanable funds terminology, this analysis is frequently referred to as the **loanable funds framework.** However, because in later chapters describing the conduct of monetary policy we focus on how the demand for and supply of bonds is affected, we will continue to conduct supply and demand analysis in terms of bonds, as in Figure 1, rather

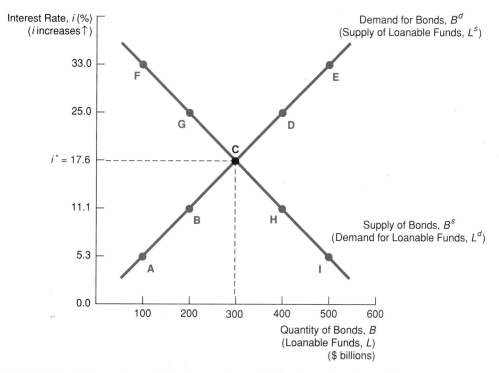

FIGURE 2 A Comparison of Terminology: Loanable Funds and Supply and Demand for Bonds
The demand for bonds is equivalent to the supply of loanable funds, and the supply of bonds is equivalent to the demand for loanable funds. (**Note:** *i* increases as we go up the vertical axis, in contrast to Figure 1, in which the opposite occurs.)

than loanable funds. Whether the analysis is done in terms of loanable funds or in terms of the demand for and supply of bonds, the results are the same; the two ways of analyzing the determination of interest rates are equivalent.

An important feature of the analysis here is that supply and demand are always in terms of *stocks* (amounts at a given point in time) of assets, not in terms of *flows*. This approach is somewhat different from certain loanable funds analyses, which are conducted in terms of flows (loans per year). The **asset market approach** for understanding behavior in financial markets—which emphasizes stocks of assets rather than flows in determining asset prices—is now the dominant methodology used by economists because correctly conducting analyses in terms of flows is very tricky, especially when we encounter inflation. (See the appendix to this chapter for an application of the asset market approach to another market.)

CHANGES IN EQUILIBRIUM INTEREST RATES

We will now use the supply and demand framework for bonds to analyze why interest rates change. To avoid confusion, it is important to make the distinction between *movements along* a demand (or supply) curve and *shifts in* a demand (or supply) curve. When quantity demanded (or supplied) changes as a result of a change in the price of the bond (or, equivalently, a change in the interest rate), we have a *movement along* the demand (or supply) curve. The change in the quantity demanded when we move from point A to B to C in Figure 1 or Figure 2, for example, is a movement along a demand curve. A *shift in* the demand (or supply) curve, by contrast, occurs when the quantity demanded (or supplied) changes *at each given price (or interest rate)* of the bond in response to a change in some other factor besides the bond's price or interest rate. When one of these factors changes, causing a shift in the demand or supply curve, there will be a new equilibrium value for the interest rate.

In the following pages we will look at how the supply and demand curves shift in response to changes in variables, such as expected inflation and wealth, and what effects these changes have on the equilibrium value of interest rates.

Shifts in the Demand for Bonds

The theory of portfolio choice developed in Chapter 5 provides a framework for deciding what factors cause the demand curve for bonds to shift. These factors include changes in four parameters:

1. Wealth
2. Expected returns on bonds relative to alternative assets
3. Risk of bonds relative to alternative assets
4. Liquidity of bonds relative to alternative assets

To see how a change in each of these factors (holding all other factors constant) can shift the demand curve, let us look at some examples. (As a study aid, Table 1 summarizes the effects of changes in these factors on the bond demand curve.)

WEALTH When the economy is growing rapidly in a business cycle expansion and wealth is increasing, the quantity of bonds demanded at each bond price (or interest rate) increases as shown in Figure 3. To see how this works, consider point B on the initial demand curve for bonds B_1^d. It tells us that at a bond price of $900 and an interest rate of 11.1 percent, the quantity of bonds demanded is $200 billion. With higher wealth, the quantity of bonds demanded at the same interest rate must rise, say, to $400 billion (point B'). Similarly, the higher wealth causes the quantity demanded at a bond price of $800 and an interest rate of 25 percent to rise from $400 billion to $600 billion (point D to D'). Continuing with this reasoning for every point on the initial demand curve B_1^d, we can see that the demand curve shifts to the right from B_1^d to B_2^d as is indicated by the arrows.

The conclusion we have reached is that *in a business cycle expansion with growing wealth, the demand for bonds rises and the demand curve for bonds shifts to the right.* However, how much demand will shift (increase) will depend on the extent to which bonds are luxuries rather than necessities. Using the same reasoning, *in a recession, when income and wealth are falling, the demand for bonds falls, and the demand curve shifts to the left.*

Another factor that affects wealth is the public's propensity to save. If households save more, wealth increases and, as we have seen, the demand for bonds rises and the demand curve for bonds shifts to the right. Conversely, if people save less, wealth and the demand for bonds will fall and the demand curve shifts to the left.

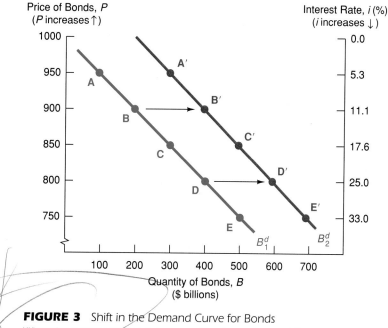

FIGURE 3 Shift in the Demand Curve for Bonds
When the demand for bonds increases, the demand curve shifts to the right as shown. (**Note:** *P* and *i* increase in opposite directions. *P* on the left vertical axis increases as we go up the axis, while *i* on the right vertical axis increases as we go down the axis.)

EXPECTED RETURNS For a one-year discount bond and a one-year holding period, the expected return and the interest rate are identical. No component of the expected return is unrelated to the bond price or the interest rate.

For bonds with maturities of greater than one year, the expected return may differ from the interest rate. For example, we saw in Chapter 4, Table 2, that a rise in the interest rate on a long-term bond from 10 to 20 percent would lead to a sharp decline in price and a very negative return. Hence if people begin to think that interest rates will be higher next year than they had originally anticipated, the expected return today on long-term bonds would fall, and the quantity demanded would fall at each interest rate. **Higher expected interest rates in the future lower the expected return for long-term bonds, decrease the demand, and shift the demand curve to the left.**

By contrast, a revision downward of expectations of future interest rates would mean that long-term bond prices would be expected to rise more than originally anticipated, and the resulting higher expected return today would raise the quantity demanded at each bond price and interest rate. **Lower expected interest rates in the future increase the demand for long-term bonds and shift the demand curve to the right** (as in Figure 3).

Changes in expected returns on other assets can also shift the demand curve for bonds. If people suddenly became more optimistic about the stock market and began to expect higher stock prices in the future, both expected capital gains and expected returns on stocks would rise. With the expected return on bonds held

—— S U M M A R Y ——

TABLE 1   Factors That Shift the Demand Curve for Bonds

Variable	Change in Variable	Change in Quantity Demanded	Shift in Demand Curve
Wealth	↑	↑	
Expected interest rate	↑	↓	
Expected inflation	↑	↓	
Riskiness of bonds relative to other assets	↑	↓	
Liquidity of bonds relative to other assets	↑	↑	

Note: Only increases (↑) in the variables are shown. The effect of decreases in the variables on the change in demand would be the opposite of those indicated in the remaining columns.

constant, the expected return on bonds today relative to stocks would fall, lowering the demand for bonds and shifting the demand curve to the left.

A change in expected inflation is likely to alter expected returns on physical assets (also called *real assets*) such as automobiles and houses, which affect the demand for bonds. An increase in expected inflation, say, from 5 to 10 percent, will lead to higher prices on cars and houses in the future and hence higher nominal capital gains. The resulting rise in the expected returns today on these real assets will lead to a fall in the expected return on bonds relative to the expected return on real assets today and thus cause the demand for bonds to fall. Alternatively, we can think of the rise in expected inflation as lowering the real interest rate on bonds, and the resulting decline in the relative expected return on bonds causes the demand for bonds to fall. ***An increase in the expected rate of inflation lowers the expected return for bonds, causes their demand to decline and the demand curve to shift to the left.***

RISK If prices in the bond market become more volatile, the risk associated with bonds increases, and bonds become a less attractive asset. ***An increase in the riskiness of bonds causes the demand for bonds to fall and the demand curve to shift to the left.***

Conversely, an increase in the volatility of prices in another asset market, such as the stock market, would make bonds more attractive. ***An increase in the riskiness of alternative assets causes the demand for bonds to rise and the demand curve to shift to the right*** (as in Figure 3).

LIQUIDITY If more people started trading in the bond market and as a result it became easier to sell bonds quickly, the increase in their liquidity would cause the quantity of bonds demanded at each interest rate to rise. ***Increased liquidity of bonds results in an increased demand for bonds, and the demand curve shifts to the right*** (see Figure 3). ***Similarly, increased liquidity of alternative assets lowers the demand for bonds and shifts the demand curve to the left.*** The reduction of brokerage commissions for trading common stocks that occurred when the fixed-rate commission structure was abolished in 1975, for example, increased the liquidity of stocks relative to bonds, and the resulting lower demand for bonds shifted the demand curve to the left.

Shifts in the Supply of Bonds

Certain factors can cause the supply curve for bonds to shift, among them these:

1. Expected profitability of investment opportunities
2. Expected inflation
3. Government activities

We will look at how the supply curve shifts when each of these factors changes (when all others remain constant). (As a study aid, Table 2 summarizes the effects of changes in these factors on the bond supply curve.)

EXPECTED PROFITABILITY OF INVESTMENT OPPORTUNITIES The more profitable investments that a firm expects it can make, the more willing it will be to borrow and increase the amount of its outstanding debt in order to finance these

——— S U M M A R Y ———

TABLE 2	Factors That Shift the Supply of Bonds		

Variable	Change in Variable	Change in Quantity Supplied	Shift in Supply Curve
Profitability of investments	↑	↑	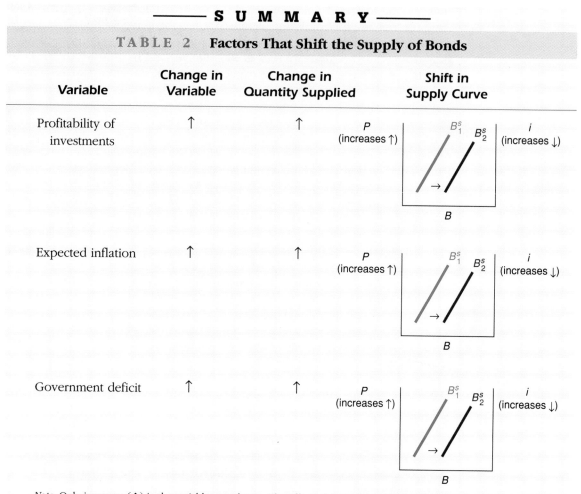
Expected inflation	↑	↑	
Government deficit	↑	↑	

Note: Only increases (↑) in the variables are shown. The effect of decreases in the variables on the change in supply would be the opposite of those indicated in the remaining columns.

investments. When the economy is growing rapidly, as in a business cycle expansion, investment opportunities that are expected to be profitable abound, and the quantity of bonds supplied at any given bond price and interest rate will increase (see Figure 4). ***Therefore, in a business cycle expansion, the supply of bonds increases, and the supply curve shifts to the right. Likewise, in a recession, when there are far fewer expected profitable investment opportunities, the supply of bonds falls, and the supply curve shifts to the left.***

EXPECTED INFLATION As we saw in Chapter 4, the real cost of borrowing is more accurately measured by the real interest rate, which equals the (nominal) interest rate minus the expected inflation rate. For a given interest rate, when expected inflation increases, the real cost of borrowing falls; hence the quantity of bonds supplied increases at any given bond price and interest rate. ***An***

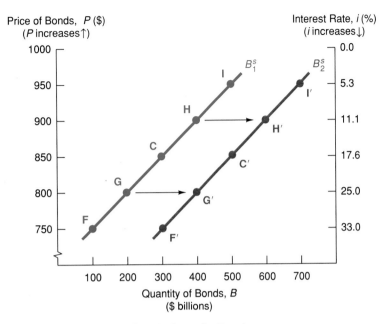

FIGURE 4   Shift in the Supply Curve for Bonds

When the supply of bonds increases, the supply curve shifts to the right. (**Note:** *P* and *i* increase in opposite directions. *P* on the left vertical axis increases as we go up the axis, while *i* on the right vertical axis increases as we go down the axis.)

increase in expected inflation causes the supply of bonds to increase and the supply curve to shift to the right (see Figure 4).

GOVERNMENT ACTIVITIES   The activities of the government can influence the supply of bonds in several ways. The U.S. Treasury issues bonds to finance government deficits, the gap between the government's expenditures and its revenues. When these deficits are large, as they have been recently, the Treasury sells more bonds, and the quantity of bonds supplied at each bond price and interest rate increases. ***Higher government deficits increase the supply of bonds and shift the supply curve to the right*** (see Figure 4).

State and local governments and other government agencies also issue bonds to finance their expenditures, and this can also affect the supply of bonds. We will see in later chapters that the conduct of monetary policy involves the purchase and sale of bonds, which in turn influences the supply of bonds.

Changes in the Equilibrium Interest Rate Due to Expected Inflation or Business Cycle Expansions

We now can use our knowledge of how supply and demand curves shift to analyze how the equilibrium interest rate can change. The best way to do this is to pursue several applications that are particularly relevant to our understanding of how monetary policy affects interest rates.

Study Guide   Supply and demand analysis for the bond market is best learned by practicing applications. When there is an application in the text and we look at how the interest rate changes because some economic variable increases, see if you can draw the appropriate shifts in the supply and demand curves when this same economic variable decreases. While you are practicing applications, keep two things in mind:

1. When you examine the effect of a variable change, remember that we are assuming that all other variables are unchanged; that is, we are making use of the ceteris paribus assumption.

2. Remember that the interest rate is negatively related to the bond price, so when the equilibrium bond price rises, the equilibrium interest rate falls. Conversely, if the equilibrium bond price moves downward, the equilibrium interest rate rises.

Changes in Expected Inflation: The Fisher Effect

We have already done most of the work to evaluate how a change in expected inflation affects the nominal interest rate in that we have already analyzed how a change in expected inflation shifts the supply and demand curves. Figure 5 shows the effect on the equilibrium interest rate of an increase in expected inflation.

Suppose that expected inflation is initially 5 percent and the initial supply and demand curves B_1^s and B_1^d intersect at point 1, where the equilibrium bond price is P_1 and the equilibrium interest rate is i_1. If expected inflation rises to 10 percent, the expected return on bonds relative to real assets falls for any given bond price and interest rate. As a result, the demand for bonds falls, and the demand curve shifts to the left from B_1^d to B_2^d. The rise in expected inflation also shifts the supply curve. At any given bond price and interest rate, the real cost of borrow-

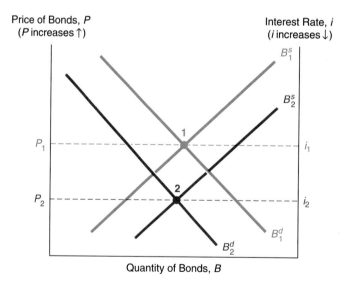

FIGURE 5   Response to a Change in Expected Inflation

When expected inflation rises, the supply curve shifts from B_1^s to B_2^s, and the demand curve shifts from B_1^d to B_2^d. The equilibrium moves from point 1 to point 2, with the result that the equilibrium bond price (left axis) falls from P_1 to P_2 and the equilibrium interest rate (right axis) rises from i_1 to i_2. (**Note:** *P* and *i* increase in opposite directions. *P* on the left vertical axis increases as we go up the axis, while *i* on the right vertical axis increases as we go down the axis.)

ing has declined, causing the quantity of bonds supplied to increase, and the supply curve shifts to the right from B_1^s to B_2^s.

When the demand and supply curves shift in response to the change in expected inflation, the equilibrium moves from point 1 to point 2, which is the intersection of B_2^d and B_2^s. The equilibrium bond price has fallen from P_1 to P_2, and because the bond price is negatively related to the interest rate (as is indicated by the interest rate rising as we go down the right vertical axis), this means that the interest rate has risen from i_1 to i_2. Note that Figure 5 has been drawn so that the equilibrium quantity of bonds remains the same for both point 1 and point 2. However, depending on the size of the shifts in the supply and demand curves, the equilibrium quantity of bonds could either rise or fall when expected inflation rises.

Our supply and demand analysis has led us to an important observation: ***When expected inflation rises, interest rates will rise.*** This result has been named the **Fisher effect,** after Irving Fisher, the economist who first pointed out the relationship of expected inflation to interest rates. The accuracy of this prediction is shown in Figure 6. The interest rate on three-month Treasury bills has usually moved along with the expected inflation rate. Consequently, it is understandable that many economists recommend that the fight against inflation must be won if we want to lower interest rates.

Business Cycle Expansion

Figure 7 analyzes the effects of a business cycle expansion on interest rates. In a business cycle expansion, the amount of goods and services being produced in the economy rises, so national income increases. When this occurs, businesses will be more willing to borrow because they are likely to have many profitable investment opportunities for which they need financing. Hence at a given bond price and interest rate, the quantity of bonds that firms want to sell (that is, the supply of bonds) will increase. This means that in a business cycle expansion, the supply curve for bonds shifts to the right (see Figure 7) from B_1^s to B_2^s.

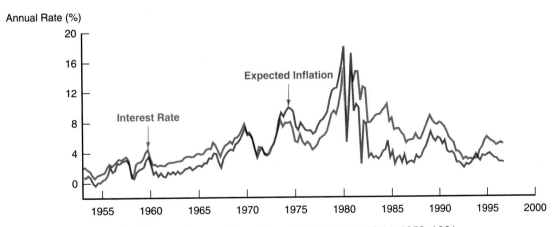

FIGURE 6   Expected Inflation and Interest Rates (Three-Month Treasury Bills), 1953–1996

Source: Expected inflation calculated using procedures outlined in Frederic S. Mishkin, "The Real Interest Rate: An Empirical Investigation," *Carnegie-Rochester Conference Series on Public Policy* 15 (1981): 151–200. This involves estimating expected inflation as a function of past interest rates, inflation, and time trends.

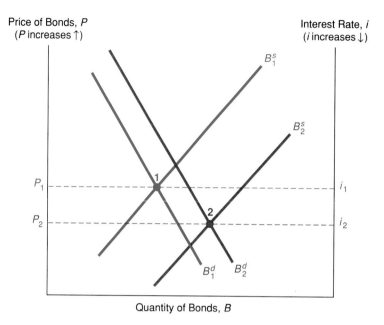

FIGURE 7 Response to a Business Cycle Expansion

In a business cycle expansion, when income and wealth are rising, the demand curve shifts rightward from B_1^d to B_2^d, and the supply curve shifts rightward from B_1^s to B_2^s. If the supply curve shifts to the right more than the demand curve, as in this figure, the equilibrium bond price (left axis) moves down from P_1 to P_2, and the equilibrium interest rate (right axis) rises from i_1 to i_2. (**Note:** P and i increase in opposite directions. P on the left vertical axis increases as we go up the axis, while i on the right vertical axis increases as we go down the axis.)

The expanding economy will also affect the demand for bonds. The theory of portfolio choice tells us that as the business cycle expands and wealth increases, the demand for bonds will rise as well. We see this in Figure 7, where the demand curve has shifted to the right from B_1^d to B_2^d.

Given that both the supply and demand curves have shifted to the right, we know that the new equilibrium reached at the intersection of B_2^d and B_2^s must also move to the right. However, depending on whether the supply curve shifts more than the demand curve or vice versa, the new equilibrium interest rate can either rise or fall.

The supply and demand analysis used here gives us an ambiguous answer to the question of what will happen to interest rates in a business cycle expansion. The figure has been drawn so that the shift in the supply curve is greater than the shift in the demand curve, causing the equilibrium bond price to fall to P_2, leading to a rise in the equilibrium interest rate to i_2. The reason the figure has been drawn so that a business cycle expansion and a rise in income lead to a higher interest rate is that this is the outcome we actually see in the data. Figure 8 plots the movement of the interest rate on three-month U.S. Treasury bills from 1951 to 1996 and indicates when the business cycle is undergoing recessions (shaded areas). As you can see, the interest rate rises during business cycle expansions and falls during recessions, which is what the supply and demand diagram indicates.

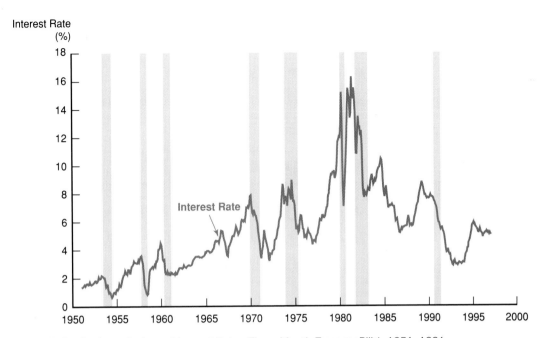

FIGURE 8   Business Cycle and Interest Rates (Three-Month Treasury Bills), 1951–1996

Shaded areas indicate periods of recession. The figure shows that interest rates rise during business cycle expansions and fall during contractions, which is what Figure 7 suggests would happen.

Sources: Federal Reserve *Bulletin;* Citibase databank.

Reading the WALL STREET JOURNAL
The "Credit Markets" Column

Now that we have an understanding of how supply and demand determines prices and interest rates in the bond market, we can use our analysis to understand discussions about bond prices and interest rates appearing in the financial press. Every day, the *Wall Street Journal* reports on developments in the bond market on the previous business day in its "Credit Markets" column, an example of which is found in the "Following the Financial News" box. Let's see how statements in the "Credit Markets" column can be explained using our supply and demand framework.

The column opens by stating that bond prices jumped on signs that the manufacturing sector grew moderately last month and on remarks by Federal Reserve Chairman Alan Greenspan suggesting that he was optimistic about the inflation outlook. This is exactly what our supply and demand analysis predicts would happen.

The National Association of Purchasing Managers composite index, a gauge of manufacturing activity, which came in lower than forecast, suggests a downward revision in the strength of the economy. As we have seen in the text, this

Following the Financial News

The "Credit Markets" Column

The "Credit Markets" column appears daily in the *Wall Street Journal;* an example is presented here. It is found in the third section, "Money and Investing."

CREDIT MARKETS

Bond Prices Are Lifted by Manufacturing Data, Remarks on Inflation Attributed to Greenspan

By CHARLENE LEE
AND VICTORIA M. ZUNITCH
Dow Jones News Services

NEW YORK—Bond prices jumped on signs that the manufacturing sector grew moderately last month. The market also drew support from remarks attributed to Federal Reserve Chairman Alan Greenspan suggesting that he is optimistic about the U.S. inflation outlook.

A business publication, the Australian Financial Review, reported that Mr. Greenspan made the comments Monday during a meeting in Washington with Australian Treasurer Peter Costello. A Fed spokesman confirmed that the two had

met, but declined to say whether the report was accurate.

But later, when read a portion of the report, Mr. Costello said the account was "fanciful." He was reluctant to address specifics of the report, adding, "I don't comment on U.S. interest rates."

Late yesterday, the benchmark 30-year Treasury bond was up 21/32 point in price, or $6.56 for a bond with $1,000 face value, at 98 13/32. Its yield, which moves in the opposite direction as prices, fell to 6.87% from 6.92% late Monday.

Bonds got an early boost when the National Association of Purchasing Management said its composite index

stood at 51.7 in September. The index, a closely monitored gauge of manufacturing activity, had been forecast by economists to be higher. "It failed to live up to the market's worst fears," said Kevin Flanagan, an economist at Dean Witter Reynolds Inc.

The Australian official was in Washington for meetings of the International Monetary Fund and the World Bank.

Traders, noting that technical factors also aided the bond market's rise, said many traders seized upon the report as an excuse to take the market higher.

Source: Wall Street Journal October 2, 1996, p. C21.

would indicate that investment opportunities are shrinking and so businesses are less likely to issue bonds, with the result that the quantity of bonds supplied decreases at each interest rate and the supply curve shifts to the left. Meanwhile, the weaker economy suggests that wealth is decreasing and hence the quantity of bonds demanded at each interest rate falls, shifting the demand curve to the left. Because, as discussed earlier, the leftward shift in the supply curve is likely to be greater than the leftward shift in the demand curve, equilibrium bond prices rise and their interest rates fall.

Greenspan's reported remarks that he is optimistic about the inflation outlook caused bond investors to lower their assessment of expected inflation. As we have seen in this chapter, the decline in expected inflation causes the expected return on bonds relative to real assets to rise, which shifts the demand curve to the right. In addition, the lower expected inflation raises the real cost of borrowing at any given interest rate, which decreases the quantity of bonds supplied at each interest rate and shifts the supply curve to the left. The outcome is a rise in bond prices

and a drop in interest rates. Our analysis thus shows why both Greenspan's inflation optimism and the weaker than expected manufacturing activity both contributed to the upward jump in bond prices.

Have Low Savings Rates in the United States Led to Higher Interest Rates?

Since 1980, the United States has experienced a sharp drop in personal savings
rates, falling from 8 percent of personal income to around the 5 percent level
today. Many commentators, including high officials of the Federal Reserve System,
have blamed the profligate behavior of the American public for high interest rates.
Are they right?

Our supply and demand analysis of the bond market indicates that they could
be. The decline in savings means that the wealth of American households is lower
than would otherwise be the case. This smaller amount of wealth decreases the
demand for bonds and shifts the demand curve to the left from B_1^d to B_2^d in Figure
9. The result is that the equilibrium bond price drops from P_1 to P_2 and the interest rate rises from i_1 to i_2. Low savings can thus raise interest rates, and the higher
rates may retard investment in capital goods. The profligacy of Americans may
therefore lead to a less productive economy and is of serious concern to both
economists and policymakers. Suggested remedies for the problem range from
changing the tax code to encourage saving to forcing Americans to save more by
mandating increased contributions into retirement plans.

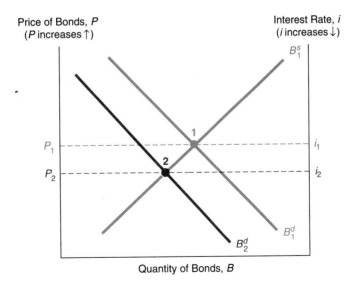

FIGURE 9   Response to a Lower Savings Rate

With a lower savings rate, wealth decreases, and the demand curve shifts in from B_1^d to B_2^d. The equilibrium moves from point 1 to point 2, with the result that the equilibrium bond price (left axis) drops
from P_1 to P_2 and the equilibrium interest rate (right axis) rises from i_1 to i_2. (**Note:** *P* and *i* increase in
opposite directions. *P* on the left vertical axis increases as we go up the axis, while *i* on the right vertical axis increases as we go down the axis.)

LIQUIDITY PREFERENCE FRAMEWORK: SUPPLY AND DEMAND IN THE MARKET FOR MONEY

Whereas the loanable funds framework determines the equilibrium interest rate using the supply of and demand for bonds, an alternative model developed by John Maynard Keynes, known as the **liquidity preference framework,** determines the equilibrium interest rate in terms of the supply of and demand for money. Although the two frameworks look different, the liquidity preference analysis of the market for money is closely related to the loanable funds framework of the bond market.[2]

The starting point of Keynes's analysis is his assumption that there are two main categories of assets that people use to store their wealth: money and bonds. Therefore, total wealth in the economy must equal the total quantity of bonds plus money in the economy, which equals the quantity of bonds supplied B^s plus the quantity of money supplied M^s. The quantity of bonds B^d and money M^d that people want to hold and thus demand must also equal the total amount of wealth because people cannot purchase more assets than their available resources allow. The conclusion is that the quantity of bonds and money supplied must equal the quantity of bonds and money demanded:

$$B^s + M^s = B^d + M^d \tag{2}$$

Collecting the bond terms on one side of the equation and the money terms on the other, this equation can be rewritten as

$$B^s - B^d = M^d - M^s \tag{3}$$

The rewritten equation tells us that if the market for money is in equilibrium ($M^s = M^d$), the right-hand side of Equation 3 equals zero, implying that $B^s = B^d$, meaning that the bond market is also in equilibrium.

Thus it is the same to think about determining the equilibrium interest rate by equating the supply and demand for bonds or by equating the supply and demand for money. In this sense, the liquidity preference framework, which analyzes the market for money, is equivalent to the loanable funds framework, which analyzes the bond market. In practice, the approaches differ because by assuming that there are only two kinds of assets, money and bonds, the liquidity preference approach implicitly ignores any effects on interest rates that arise from changes in the expected returns on real assets such as automobiles and houses. In most instances, both frameworks yield the same predictions.

The reason that we approach the determination of interest rates with both frameworks is that the loanable funds framework is easier to use when analyzing the effects from changes in expected inflation, whereas the liquidity preference framework provides a simpler analysis of the effects from changes in income, the price level, and the supply of money.

---

[2]Note that the term *market for money* refers to the market for the medium of exchange, money. This market differs from the *money market* referred to by finance practitioners, which is the financial market in which short-term debt instruments are traded.

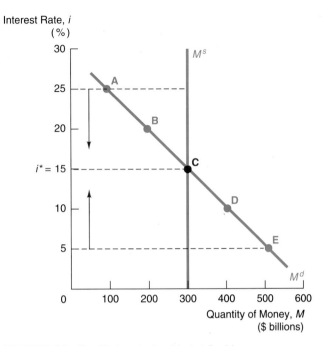

Interest Rate, i (%)

FIGURE 10   Equilibrium in the Market for Money

Because the definition of money that Keynes used includes currency (which earns no interest) and checking account deposits (which in his time typically earned little or no interest), he assumed that money has a zero rate of return. Bonds, the only alternative asset to money in Keynes's framework, have an expected return equal to the interest rate i.[3] As this interest rate rises (holding everything else unchanged), the expected return on money falls relative to the expected return on bonds, and as the theory of portfolio choice tells us, this causes the demand for money to fall.

We can also see that the demand for money and the interest rate should be negatively related by using the concept of **opportunity cost,** the amount of interest (expected return) sacrificed by not holding the alternative asset—in this case, a bond. As the interest rate on bonds i rises, the opportunity cost of holding money rises, and so money is less desirable and the quantity of money demanded must fall.

Figure 10 shows the quantity of money demanded at a number of interest rates, with all other economic variables, such as income and the price level, held constant. At an interest rate of 25 percent, point A shows that the quantity of money demanded is $100 billion. If the interest rate is at the lower rate of 20 percent, the opportunity cost of money is lower, and the quantity of money demanded rises to $200 billion, as indicated by the move from point A to point B. If the interest rate is even lower, the quantity of money demanded is even

---

[3]Keynes did not actually assume that the expected returns on bonds equaled the interest rate but rather argued that they were closely related (see Chapter 23). This distinction makes no appreciable difference in our analysis.

higher, as is indicated by points C, D, and E. The curve M^d connecting these points is the demand curve for money, and it slopes downward.

At this point in our analysis, we will assume that a central bank controls the amount of money supplied at a fixed quantity of $300 billion, so the supply curve for money M^s in the figure is a vertical line at $300 billion. The equilibrium where the quantity of money demanded equals the quantity of money supplied occurs at the intersection of the supply and demand curves at point C, where

$$M^d = M^s \tag{4}$$

The resulting equilibrium interest rate is at $i^* = 15$ percent.

We can again see that there is a tendency to approach this equilibrium by first looking at the relationship of money demand and supply when the interest rate is above the equilibrium interest rate. When the interest rate is 25 percent, the quantity of money demanded at point A is $100 billion, yet the quantity of money supplied is $300 billion. The excess supply of money means that people are holding more money than they desire, so they will try to get rid of their excess money balances by trying to buy bonds. Accordingly, they will bid up the price of bonds, and as the bond price rises, the interest rate will fall toward the equilibrium interest rate of 15 percent. This tendency is shown by the downward arrow drawn at the interest rate of 25 percent.

Likewise, if the interest rate is 5 percent, the quantity of money demanded at point E is $500 billion, but the quantity of money supplied is only $300 billion. There is now an excess demand for money because people want to hold more money than they currently have. To try to get the money, they will sell their only other asset—bonds—and the price will fall. As the price of bonds falls, the interest rate will rise toward the equilibrium rate of 15 percent. Only when the interest rate is at its equilibrium value will there be no tendency for it to move further, and the interest rate will settle to its equilibrium value.

CHANGES IN EQUILIBRIUM INTEREST RATES

Analyzing how the equilibrium interest rate changes using the liquidity preference framework requires that we understand what causes the demand and supply curves for money to shift.

Study Guide   Learning the liquidity preference framework also requires practicing applications. When there is an application in the text to examine how the interest rate changes because some economic variable increases, see if you can draw the appropriate shifts in the supply and demand curves when this same economic variable decreases. And remember to use the ceteris paribus assumption: When examining the effect of a change in one variable, hold all other variables constant.

Shifts in the Demand for Money

In Keynes's liquidity preference analysis, two factors cause the demand curve for money to shift: income and the price level.

INCOME EFFECT   In Keynes's view, there were two reasons why income would affect the demand for money. First, as an economy expands and income rises, wealth increases and people will want to hold more money as a store of value. Second, as the economy expands and income rises, people will want to carry out more transactions using money, with the result that they will also want to hold more money. The conclusion is that *a higher level of income causes the demand for money to increase and the demand curve to shift to the right.*

PRICE-LEVEL EFFECT   Keynes took the view that people care about the amount of money they hold in real terms, that is, in terms of the goods and services that it can buy. When the price level rises, the same nominal quantity of money is no longer as valuable; it cannot be used to purchase as many real goods or services. To restore their holdings of money in real terms to its former level, people will want to hold a greater nominal quantity of money, so *a rise in the price level causes the demand for money to increase and the demand curve to shift to the right.*

Shifts in the Supply of Money

We will assume that the supply of money is completely controlled by the central bank, which in the United States is the Federal Reserve. (Actually, the process that determines the money supply is substantially more complicated and involves banks, depositors, and borrowers from banks. We will study it in more detail later in the book.) For now, all we need to know is that *an increase in the money supply engineered by the Federal Reserve will shift the supply curve for money to the right.*

Changes in the Equilibrium Interest Rate Due to Changes in Income, the Price Level, or the Money Supply

To see how the liquidity preference framework can be used to analyze the movement of interest rates, we will again look at several applications that will be useful in evaluating the effect of monetary policy on interest rates. (As a study aid, Table 3 summarizes the shifts in the demand and supply curves for money.)

Changes in Income

When income is rising during a business cycle expansion, we have seen that the demand for money will rise. It is shown in Figure 11 by the shift rightward in the demand curve from M_1^d to M_2^d. The new equilibrium is reached at point 2 at the intersection of the M_2^d curve with the money supply curve M^s. As you can see, the equilibrium interest rate rises from i_1 to i_2. The liquidity preference framework thus generates the conclusion that *when income is rising during a business cycle expansion (holding other economic variables constant), interest rates will rise.* This conclusion is unambiguous when contrasted to the conclusion reached about the effects of a change in income on interest rates using the loanable funds framework.

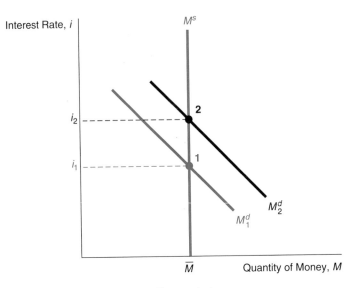

FIGURE 11 Response to a Change in Income

In a business cycle expansion, when income is rising, the demand curve shifts from M_1^d to M_2^d. The supply curve is fixed at $M^s = \overline{M}$. The equilibrium interest rate rises from i_1 to i_2.

Changes in the Price Level

When the price level rises, the value of money in terms of what it can purchase is lower. To restore their purchasing power in real terms to its former level, people will want to hold a greater nominal quantity of money. A higher price level shifts the demand curve for money to the right from M_1^d to M_2^d (see Figure 12). The equilibrium moves from point 1 to point 2, where the equilibrium interest rate has risen from i_1 to i_2, illustrating that **when the price level increases, with the**

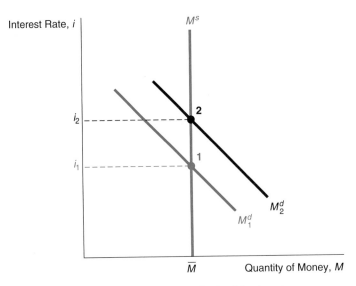

FIGURE 12 Response to a Change in the Price Level

An increase in price level shifts the money demand curve from M_1^d to M_2^d, and the equilibrium interest rate rises from i_1 to i_2.

SUMMARY

TABLE 3   Factors That Shift the Demand for and Supply of Money

Variable	Change in Variable	Change in Money Demand (Md) or Supply (Ms)	Change in Interest Rate	
Income	↑	M^d ↑	↑	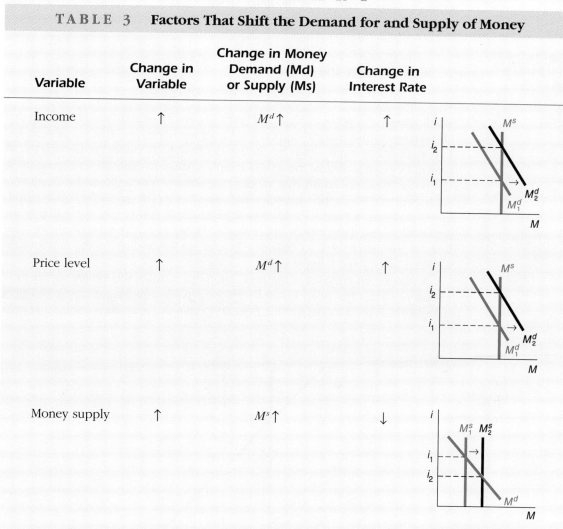
Price level	↑	M^d ↑	↑	
Money supply	↑	M^s ↑	↓	

Note: Only increases (↑) in the variables are shown. The effect of decreases in the variables on the change in demand would be the opposite of those indicated in the remaining columns.

supply of money and other economic variables held constant, interest rates will rise.

Changes in the Money Supply   An increase in the money supply due to expansionary monetary policy by the Federal Reserve implies that the supply curve for money shifts to the right. As is shown in Figure 13 by the movement of the supply curve from M^s_1 to M^s_2, the equilibrium moves from point 1 down to point 2, where the M^s_2 supply curve intersects with the demand curve M^d and the equilibrium interest rate has fallen from i_1 to i_2. ***When the money supply increases (everything else remaining equal), interest rates will decline.***[4]

Money and Interest Rates

The liquidity preference analysis in Figure 13 seems to lead to the conclusion that an increase in the money supply will lower interest rates. This conclusion has important policy implications because it has frequently caused politicians to call for a more rapid growth of the money supply in order to drive down interest rates.

But is this conclusion that money and interest rates should be negatively related correct? Might there be other important factors left out of the liquidity preference analysis in Figure 13 that would reverse this conclusion? We will provide answers to these questions by applying the supply and demand analysis we have learned in this chapter to obtain a deeper understanding of the relationship between money and interest rates.

An important criticism of the conclusion that a rise in the money supply lowers interest rates has been raised by Milton Friedman, a Nobel laureate in economics. He acknowledges that the liquidity preference analysis is correct and calls

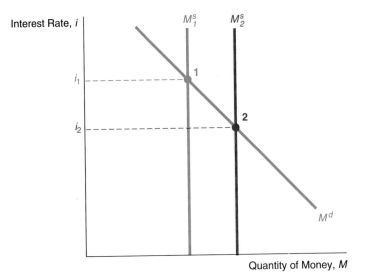

FIGURE 13 Response to a Change in the Money Supply
When the money supply increases, the supply curve shifts from M_1^s to M_2^s, and the equilibrium interest rate falls from i_1 to i_2.

---

[4]This same result can be generated using the loanable funds framework. As we will see in Chapters 16 and 17, the primary way that a central bank produces an increase in the money supply is by buying bonds and thereby decreasing the supply of bonds to the public. The resulting shift to the left of the supply curve for bonds will lead to a decline in the equilibrium interest rate.

the result—that an increase in the money supply (*everything else remaining equal*) lowers interest rates—the *liquidity effect*. However, he views the liquidity effect as merely part of the story: An increase in the money supply might not leave "everything else equal" and will have other effects on the economy that may make interest rates rise. If these effects are substantial, it is entirely possible that when the money supply rises, interest rates too may rise.

We have already laid the groundwork to discuss these other effects because we have shown how changes in income, the price level, and expected inflation affect the equilibrium interest rate.

Study Guide   To get further practice with the loanable funds and liquidity preference frameworks, show how the effects discussed here work by drawing the supply and demand diagrams that explain each effect. This exercise will also improve your understanding of the effect of money on interest rates.

1. Income Effect. Because an increasing money supply is an expansionary influence on the economy, it should raise national income and wealth. Both the liquidity preference and loanable funds frameworks indicate that interest rates will then rise (see Figures 7 and 11). Thus **the income effect of an increase in the money supply is a rise in interest rates in response to the higher level of income.**

2. Price-Level Effect. An increase in the money supply can also cause the overall price level in the economy to rise. The liquidity preference framework predicts that this will lead to a rise in interest rates. So **the price-level effect from an increase in the money supply is a rise in interest rates in response to the rise in the price level.**

3. Expected-Inflation Effect. The rising price level (the higher inflation rate) that results from an increase in the money supply also affects interest rates by affecting the expected inflation rate. Specifically, an increase in the money supply may lead people to expect a higher price level in the future—hence the expected inflation rate will be higher. The loanable funds framework has shown us that this increase in expected inflation will lead to a higher level of interest rates. Therefore, **the expected-inflation effect of an increase in the money supply is a rise in interest rates in response to the rise in the expected inflation rate.**

At first glance it might appear that the price-level effect and the expected-inflation effect are the same thing. They both indicate that increases in the price level induced by an increase in the money supply will raise interest rates. However, there is a subtle difference between the two, and this is why they are discussed as two separate effects.

Suppose that there is a onetime increase in the money supply today that leads to a rise in prices to a permanently higher level by next year. As the price level rises over the course of this year, the interest rate will rise via the price-level effect. Only at the end of the year, when the price level has risen to its peak, will the price-level effect be at a maximum.

The rising price level will also raise interest rates via the expected-inflation effect because people will expect that inflation will be higher over the course of the year. However, when the price level stops rising next year, inflation and the expected inflation rate will fall back down to zero. Any rise in interest rates as a result of the earlier rise in expected inflation will then be reversed. We thus see that in contrast to the price-level effect, which reaches its greatest impact next year, the expected-inflation effect will have its smallest impact (zero impact) next year. The basic difference between the two effects, then, is that the price-level effect remains even after prices have stopped rising, whereas the expected-inflation effect disappears.

An important point is that the expected-inflation effect will persist only as long as the price level continues to rise. As we will see in our discussion of monetary theory in subsequent chapters, a onetime increase in the money supply will not produce a continually rising price level; only a higher rate of money supply growth will. Thus a higher rate of money supply growth is needed if the expected-inflation effect is to persist.

Does a Higher Rate of Growth of the Money Supply Lower Interest Rates?

We can now put together all the effects we have discussed to help us decide whether our analysis supports the politicians who advocate a greater rate of growth of the money supply when they feel that interest rates are too high. Of all the effects, only the liquidity effect indicates that a higher rate of money growth will cause a decline in interest rates. In contrast, the income, price-level, and expected-inflation effects indicate that interest rates will rise when money growth is higher. Which of these effects are largest, and how quickly do they take effect? The answers are critical in determining whether interest rates will rise or fall when money supply growth is increased.

Generally, the liquidity effect from the greater money growth takes effect immediately because the rising money supply leads to an immediate decline in the equilibrium interest rate. The income and price-level effects take time to work because the increasing money supply takes time to raise the price level and income, which in turn raise interest rates. The expected-inflation effect, which also raises interest rates, can be slow or fast, depending on whether people adjust their expectations of inflation slowly or quickly when the money growth rate is increased.

Three possibilities are outlined in Figure 14; each shows how interest rates respond over time to an increased rate of money supply growth starting at time T. Panel (a) shows a case in which the liquidity effect dominates the other effects so that the interest rate falls from i_1 at time T to a final level of i_2. The liquidity effect operates quickly to lower the interest rate, but as time goes by, the other effects start to reverse some of the decline. Because the liquidity effect is larger than the others, however, the interest rate never rises back to its initial level.

Panel (b) has a smaller liquidity effect than the other effects, with the expected-inflation effect operating slowly because expectations of inflation are slow to adjust upward. Initially, the liquidity effect drives down the interest rate. Then the income, price-level, and expected-inflation effects begin to raise it. Because these effects are dominant, the interest rate eventually rises above its

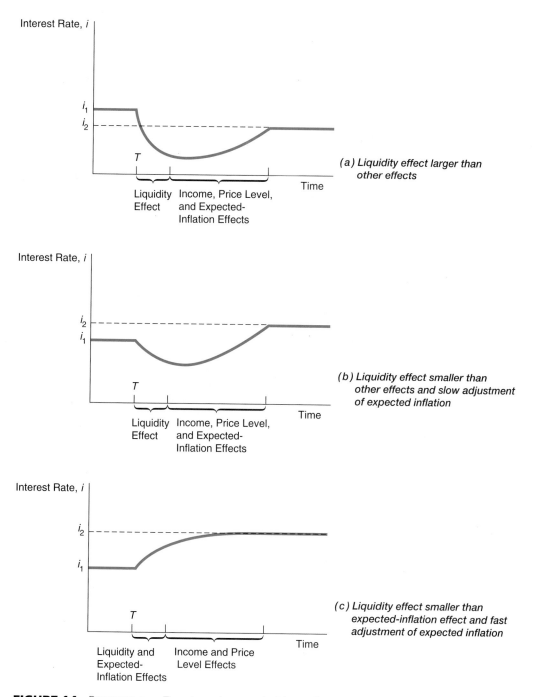

FIGURE 14   *Response over Time to an Increase in Money Supply Growth*

Following the Financial News

Forecasting Interest Rates

Forecasting interest rates is a time-honored profession. Economists are hired (sometimes at very high salaries) to forecast interest rates because businesses need to know what the rates will be in order to plan their future spending, and banks and investors require interest-rate forecasts in order to decide which assets to buy. Interest-rate forecasters predict what will happen to the factors that affect the supply and demand for bonds and for money—factors such as the strength of the economy, the profitability of investment opportunities, the expected inflation rate, and the size of government budget deficits and borrowing. They then use the supply and demand analysis we have outlined in this chapter to come up with their interest-rate forecasts.

The *Wall Street Journal* reports interest-rate forecasts by leading prognosticators twice a year (early January and July) in its "Economy" column or in its "Credit Markets" column, which surveys developments in the bond market daily. Forecasting interest rates is a perilous business. To their embarrassment, even the top experts are frequently far off in their forecasts.

A SAMPLING OF INTEREST-RATE, ECONOMIC AND CURRENCY FORECASTS

In percent except for dollar vs. yen

GDP	JUNE 1996 SURVEY 3-MO. TREASURY BILLS-a 12/31	30-YR. BONDS 12/31	GDP-b 2nd HALF 1996	CPI-c NOV. 1996	DLR. vs. YEN 12/96	NEW FORECASTS FOR 1997 3-MO. TREASURY BILLS-a 6/30	3-MO. TREASURY BILLS-a 12/31	30-YR. TREASURY BONDS 6/30	30-YR. TREASURY BONDS 12/31	GDP-b 1st HALF 1997	GDP-b 2nd HALF 1997	CPI-c MAY	CPI-c NOV.	DOLLAR vs. YEN 6/30	DOLLAR vs. YEN 12/31
Maureen Allyn, Scudder Stevens & Clark	5.00	7.10	1.5	3.1	112	4.80	4.25	6.00	6.00	0.0	0.4	2.6	2.8	116	119
Wayne Angell, Bear Stearns	5.75	7.40	2.7	3.0	110	5.30	5.30	6.70	6.50	2.5	2.4	3.3	3.2	113	113
Richard B. Berner, Mellon Bank	5.85	7.10	2.8	2.9	110	5.60	6.00	7.20	6.50	3.1	1.7	2.7	3.0	112	105
David Berson, Fannie Mae	5.30	7.00	2.3	2.9	110	5.10	5.10	6.50	6.40	2.2	1.9	2.6	2.9	114	117
David Blitzer, S&P	5.65	7.55	2.7	3.0	110	5.25	5.45	6.65	6.75	2.6	1.8	3.1	2.8	115	110
Paul W. Boltz, T. Rowe Price	5.70	7.20	2.7	3.2	107	5.50	5.88	7.00	7.25	2.3	2.5	3.3	3.5	110	105
David Bostian, Herzog, Heine, Geduld	4.75	6.25	1.2	2.9	112	4.75	4.25	6.00	5.75	-0.9	-0.4	2.4	1.6	116	114
Phillip Braverman, DKB Securities	5.00	6.50	2.0	3.0	110	4.75	4.50	6.00	5.75	1.5	2.0	3.0	3.0	115	117
William Brown, J.P. Morgan	5.75	7.35	3.1	3.3	108	5.60	5.85	7.10	7.20	3.0	2.3	2.8	2.9	113	105
Rosanne Cahn, CS First Boston	5.06	6.25	2.3	3.1	110	5.75	5.75	7.25	6.25	3.0	1.6	2.8	2.7	110	115
James Coons, Huntington Natl Bank	5.10	6.75	1.7	3.2	112	4.77	4.54	6.69	6.64	1.6	2.0	3.0	2.9	117	121
Michael Cosgrove, The Econoclast	5.60	6.70	2.2	3.2	110	5.40	4.80	6.90	6.00	2.6	1.0	3.3	3.0	110	100
Robert Crow, Bechtel Group	N.A.	N.A.	N.A.	N.A.	N.A.	4.80	4.80	6.30	6.10	2.0	2.2	2.8	2.7	114	116
Dewey Daane, Vanderbilt Univ.	5.75	7.50	2.7	3.4	110	5.25	5.45	7.00	7.25	2.1	2.1	3.1	3.3	114	112
William Dudley, Goldman Sachs	6.30	7.40	3.1	3.4	116	5.60	6.20	7.20	7.40	3.2	2.3	3.0	3.4	106	105
Michael Englund, MMS Int'l.	5.60	6.75	2.7	3.2	110	5.40	5.00	6.50	6.00	2.9	2.1	3.3	3.4	110	108
Gail Fosler, Conference Board	5.50	7.65	3.2	3.5	98	5.70	5.80	7.60	7.00	3.0	1.6	3.3	3.9	100	96
Maury Harris, PaineWebber	5.25	6.50	1.75	2.75	110	5.00	5.00	6.50	6.10	2.4	1.7	2.9	2.8	115	115
Mitchell J. Held, Smith Barney	N.A.	N.A.	N.A.	N.A.	N.A.	5.35	6.50	6.50	6.25	2.3	2.6	2.9	2.8	115	115
Tracy Herrick, Jefferies	5.30	7.10	3.1	3.2	110	6.00	7.00	6.60	6.70	3.5	2.3	3.4	3.9	115	200
Stuart Hoffman, PNC Bank	5.60	6.95	2.3	3.1	113	5.10	4.80	6.60	6.40	2.0	1.0	3.1	2.8	115	108
William B. Hummer, Wayne Hummer	5.56	7.25	3.0	2.9	112	5.30	5.50	7.12	7.25	2.4	2.3	3.1	3.0	110	108
Edward Hyman, ISI Group	4.90	6.20	2.2	2.8	112	4.40	4.40	5.70	5.90	1.0	2.7	2.5	2.5	115	117
Saul Hymans, Univ. of Michigan	5.24	6.85	2.3	2.7	N.A.	5.12	5.14	6.47	6.46	2.5	2.5	2.1	1.9	110	108
Mieczyslaw Karczmar, Deutsche Bank AG	5.25	7.50	2.7	2.8	105	5.20	5.20	7.00	7.20	2.3	1.9	3.3	3.5	110	102
Kurt Karl, WEFA Group	4.90	6.20	1.9	2.6	108	4.90	4.80	6.40	6.30	1.8	2.2	2.5	2.5	114	113
Irwin L. Kellner, Chase Regional Bank	5.25	7.10	1.0	2.6	110	5.00	4.95	6.20	6.00	2.3	3.0	2.2	2.1	115	120
Daniel Laufenberg, Amer. Exp. Finl. Adv.	5.10	6.50	2.1	3.2	115	5.50	6.00	6.90	7.20	2.3	2.7	3.1	3.4	110	105
Carol A. Leisenring, CoreStates Finl.	5.00	6.80	2.5	2.7	105	4.90	4.60	6.20	5.90	2.0	2.5	2.7	2.6	118	121
Mickey D. Levy, NationsBank	5.20	6.90	2.4	2.6	110	5.00	4.80	6.30	6.20	2.0	2.8	2.5	2.4	114	114
David L. Littmann, Comerica	5.20	6.90	2.6	3.1	112	5.15	5.15	6.50	6.50	2.2	2.1	3.0	3.0	115	118
John Lonski, Moody's Investors Svc	5.70	7.00	2.8	3.3	110	5.60	5.30	7.00	6.60	2.5	2.2	3.5	3.2	110	110
Paul McCulley, UBS Securities	5.20	6.90	1.3	3.0	114	4.70	4.50	6.30	6.30	1.5	2.2	2.7	2.7	120	116
John McDevitt, 3M	5.00	6.20	2.0	2.6	105	5.10	5.00	6.30	6.20	2.1	2.0	2.7	2.8	112	109
Arnold Moskowitz, Moskowitz Capital	5.60	7.28	2.7	3.1	113	5.40	6.20	6.50	6.50	2.7		3.0	3.1	110	115
John Mueller, LBMC	4.50	6.25	-1.6	3.2	98	4.50	3.50	6.25	5.90	-1.3	0.3	3.0	2.8	110	105
David Munro, High Frequency Econ.	5.40	6.75	2.5	3.0	115	5.10	5.20	6.30	6.50	1.9	2.5	2.8	2.6	N.A.	N.A
Carl Palash, MCM Money Watch	5.50	7.00	2.5	3.2	108	6.00	5.75	7.25	6.50	3.0	2.0	3.5	3.5	120	115

--- *Following the Financial News* ---

Forecasting Interest Rates (cont.)

Name															
Nicholas S. Perna, Fleet Finl. Group	5.19	6.83	2.3	3.3	108	5.30	5.20	6.60	6.50	2.2	2.1	3.1	3.3	116	118
Elliott Platt, Donaldson Lufkin & Jenrette	5.10	6.00	1.5	2.8	110	4.45	3.94	5.75	5.50	1.3	0.9	2.8	2.3	108	108
Maria F. Ramirez, MF Ramirez	5.40	7.00	2.3	3.0	104	5.10	5.25	6.40	6.50	1.8	2.0	2.9	2.5	115	108
Donald Ratajczak, George State Univ.	5.63	7.11	2.8	3.0	108.5	5.05	5.12	6.55	6.30	2.6	2.1	3.2	3.3	113	110
David Rester, Nomura Securities Int'l.	4.95	6.67	1.6	2.9	112	5.00	4.75	6.25	6.10	2.1	2.4	2.7	2.7	115	115
Allan Reynolds, Hudson Institute	4.80	6.80	1.4	3.3	107	4.80	5.20	6.30	6.90	1.6	1.2	3.1	3.6	108	104
Richard D. Rippe, Prudential Securities	5.65	7.25	2.0	3.1	110	5.30	5.15	6.30	6.00	2.3	1.2	3.0	3.2	112	105
A. Gary Shilling, Shilling & Co.	5.00	6.50	2.8	3.0	115	6.50	6.00	7.50	7.00	2.0	1.5	2.5	2.5	119	125
Allen Sinai, Lehman Brothers	5.71	7.28	2.5	3.2	115.3	5.37	5.10	6.98	6.33	2.6	2.3	3.3	3.1	120	118
James F. Smith, Univ. Of N.C.	4.18	5.45	2.4	2.1	119	4.55	3.95	5.65	4.75	2.6	2.8	2.4	2.2	122	125
Susan M. Sterne, Economic Analysis Assoc.	4.50	6.00	1.0	2.5	N.A.	4.75	4.75	5.00	6.00	0.0	3.0	2.8	3.0	N.A.	N.A
Donald Straszheim, Merrill Lynch	5.10	6.40	2.0	2.7	108	5.00	5.25	6.50	6.90	1.8	2.2	2.7	2.9	118	120
Thomas Synott 3rd, U.S. Trust	4.90	6.50	2.3	3.3	116	4.70	4.90	6.00	6.25	0.8	2.5	3.3	3.0	115	115
John Walter, Dow Corning	N.A.	N.A.	N.A.	N.A.	N.A.	4.60	4.20	5.50	5.00	1.3	2.6	2.8	2.4	114	112
John Williams, Bankers Trust	5.60	6.80	2.0	3.0	120	5.45	5.60	7.05	6.80	2.4	2.2	3.2	3.3	120	118
Raymond Worseck, A.G. Edwards	5.40	7.70	1.5	3.6	104	5.25	5.25	6.80	7.20	1.3	1.8	3.3	3.5	107	102
David Wyss, DRI/McGraw-Hill	5.50	7.10	2.2	3.0	110	5.20	5.00	6.70	6.70	2.1	2.4	2.8	2.9	110	105
Edward Yardeni, Deutsche Morgan Grenfell	5.00	6.25	1.5	2.2	112	4.75	4.75	5.50	5.00	1.7	2.5	3.0	2.2	120	128
Mark Zandi, Regional Finl. Associates	5.78	7.29	2.7	3.0	105.4	5.50	5.50	7.10	6.70	2.7	2.0	3.0	3.2	108	104
AVERAGE-d	5.31	6.86	2.3	3.0	110	5.16	5.10	6.52	6.39	2.0	2.0	2.9	2.9	113	112
CLOSING RATES as of 12/31/96	5.19	6.64	N.A.	3.2	116										

N.A. Not Available; a Treasury bill rates are on a bond-equivalent basis; b Real gross domestic product, annualized rate vs. prior six months; c Year-to-Year change in the consumer price index; d Averages for the June survey are for the analysts polled at that time.

Source: Wall Street Journal, January 2, 1997, p. C2.

initial level to i_2. In the short run, lower interest rates result from increased money growth, but eventually they end up climbing above the initial level.

Panel (c) has the expected-inflation effect dominating as well as operating rapidly because people quickly raise their expectation of inflation when the rate of money growth increases. The expected-inflation effect begins immediately to overpower the liquidity effect, and the interest rate immediately starts to climb. Over time, as the income and price-level effects start to take hold, the interest rate rises even higher, and the eventual outcome is an interest rate that is substantially above the initial interest rate. The result shows clearly that increasing money supply growth is not the answer to reducing interest rates but rather that money growth should be reduced in order to lower interest rates!

An important issue for economic policymakers is which of these three scenarios is closest to reality. If a decline in interest rates is desired, then an increase in money supply growth is called for when the liquidity effect dominates the other effects, as in panel (a). A decrease in money growth is appropriate if the other effects dominate the liquidity effect and expectations of inflation adjust rapidly, as in panel (c). If the other effects dominate the liquidity effect but expectations of inflation adjust only slowly, as in panel (b), then whether you want to increase or decrease money growth depends on whether you care more about what happens in the short run or the long run.

Which scenario is supported by the evidence? The relationship of interest rates and money growth from 1951 to 1996 is plotted in Figure 15. When the rate of money supply growth began to climb in the mid-1960s, interest rates rose, indi-

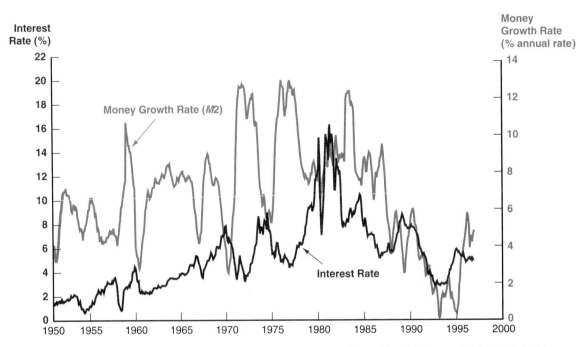

FIGURE 15 Money Growth (M2, Annual Rate) and Interest Rates (Three-Month Treasury Bills), 1950–1996

Sources: Federal Reserve *Bulletin;* Citibase databank.

cating that the liquidity effect was dominated by the price-level, income, and expected-inflation effects. By the 1970s, interest rates reached levels unprecedented in the period after World War II, as did the rate of money supply growth.

The scenario depicted in panel (a) of Figure 14 seems doubtful, and the case for lowering interest rates by raising the rate of money growth is much weakened. Looking back at Figure 6, which shows the relationship between interest rates and expected inflation, you should not find this too surprising. The rise in the rate of money supply growth in the 1960s and 1970s is matched by a large rise in expected inflation, which would lead us to predict that the expected-inflation effect would be dominant. It is the most plausible explanation for why interest rates rose in the face of higher money growth. However, Figure 15 does not really tell us which one of the two scenarios, panel (b) or panel (c) of Figure 14, is more accurate. It depends critically on how fast people's expectations about inflation adjust. However, recent research using more sophisticated methods than just looking at a graph like Figure 15 do indicate that increased money growth temporarily lowers short-term interest rates.[5]

---

[5]See Lawrence J. Christiano and Martin Eichenbaum, "Identification and the Liquidity Effect of a Monetary Policy Shock," in *Business Cycles, Growth, and Political Economy,* ed. Alex Cukierman, Zvi Hercowitz, and Leonardo Leiderman (Cambridge, Mass.: MIT Press, 1992), pp. 335–370; Eric M. Leeper and David B. Gordon, "In Search of the Liquidity Effect," *Journal of Monetary Economics* 29 (1992): 341–370; Steven Strongin, "The Identification of Monetary Policy Disturbances: Explaining the Liquidity Puzzle," *Journal of Monetary Economics* 35 (1995): 463–497; and Adrian Pagan and John C. Robertson. "Resolving the Liquidity Effect," *Federal Reserve Bank of St. Louis Review* 77 (May-June 1995): 33–54.

SUMMARY

1. The supply and demand analysis for bonds, known as the loanable funds framework, provides one theory of how interest rates are determined. It predicts that interest rates will change when there is a change in demand because of changes in income (or wealth), expected returns, risk, or liquidity or when there is a change in supply because of changes in the attractiveness of investment opportunities, the real cost of borrowing, or government activities.

2. An alternative theory of how interest rates are determined is provided by the liquidity preference framework, which analyzes the supply of and demand for money. It shows that interest rates will change when there is a change in the demand for money because of changes in income or the price level or when there is a change in the supply of money.

3. There are four possible effects of an increase in the money supply on interest rates: the liquidity effect, the income effect, the price-level effect, and the expected-inflation effect. The liquidity effect indicates that a rise in money supply growth will lead to a decline in interest rates; the other effects work in the opposite direction. The evidence seems to indicate that the income, price-level, and expected-inflation effects dominate the liquidity effect such that an increase in money supply growth leads to higher rather than lower interest rates.

KEY TERMS

asset market approach, p. 109

demand curve, p. 104

excess demand, p. 107

excess supply, p. 107

Fisher effect, p. 117

liquidity preference framework, p. 122

loanable funds, p. 108

loanable funds framework, p. 108

market equilibrium, p. 107

opportunity cost, p. 123

supply curve, p. 106

QUESTIONS AND PROBLEMS

Answer each question by drawing the appropriate supply and demand diagrams.

*1. As we will see in Chapter 16, an important way in which the Federal Reserve decreases the money supply is by selling bonds to the public. Using the loanable funds framework, show what effect this action has on interest rates. Is your answer consistent with what you would expect to find with the liquidity preference framework?

2. Using both the liquidity preference and loanable funds frameworks, show why interest rates are procyclical (rising when the economy is expanding and falling during recessions).

*3. Why should a rise in the price level (but not in expected inflation) cause interest rates to rise when the nominal money supply is fixed?

4. Find the "Credit Markets" column in the *Wall Street Journal.* Underline the statements in the column that explain bond price movements, and draw the appropriate supply and demand diagrams that support these statements.

5. What effect will a sudden increase in the volatility of gold prices have on interest rates?

*6. How might a sudden increase in people's expectations of future real estate prices affect interest rates?

7. Explain what effect a large federal deficit might have on interest rates.

*8. Using both the loanable funds and liquidity preference frameworks, show what the effect is on interest rates when the riskiness of bonds rises. Are the results the same in the two frameworks?

9. If the price level falls next year, remaining fixed thereafter, and the money supply is fixed, what is likely to happen to interest rates over the next two years? (*Hint:* Take account of both the price-level effect and the expected-inflation effect.)

*10. Will there be an effect on interest rates if brokerage commissions on stocks fall? Explain your answer.

USING ECONOMIC ANALYSIS TO PREDICT THE FUTURE

11. The president of the United States announces in a press conference that he will fight the higher inflation rate with a new anti-inflation program. Predict what will happen to interest rates if the public believes him.

*12. The chairman of the Fed announces that interest rates will rise sharply next year, and the market believes him. What will happen to today's interest rate on AT&T bonds, such as the $8\frac{1}{8}$s of 2022?

13. Predict what will happen to interest rates if the public suddenly expects a large increase in stock prices.

*14. Predict what will happen to interest rates if prices in the bond market become more volatile.

15. If the next chair of the Federal Reserve Board has a reputation for advocating an even slower rate of money growth than the current chair, what will happen to interest rates? Discuss the possible resulting situations.

APPLYING THE ASSET MARKET APPROACH TO A COMMODITY MARKET: THE CASE OF GOLD

Both models of interest-rate determination in Chapter 6 make use of an asset market approach in which supply and demand are always considered in terms of stocks of assets (amounts at a given point in time). The asset market approach is useful in understanding not only why interest rates fluctuate but also how any asset's price is determined.

One asset that has fascinated people for thousands of years is gold. It has been a driving force in history: The conquest of the Americas by Europeans was to a great extent the result of the quest for gold, to cite just one example. The fascination with gold continues to the present day, and developments in the gold market are followed closely by financial analysts and the media. This appendix shows how the asset market approach can be applied to understanding the behavior of commodity markets, in particular the gold market. (The analysis in this appendix can also be used to understand behavior in many other asset markets.)

SUPPLY AND DEMAND IN THE GOLD MARKET

The analysis of a commodity market, such as the gold market, proceeds in a similar fashion to the analysis of the bond market by examining the supply of and demand for the commodity. We again use the theory of portfolio choice to obtain a demand curve for gold, which shows the relationship between the quantity of gold demanded and the price when all other economic variables are held constant.

Demand Curve

To derive the relationship between the quantity of gold demanded and its price, we again recognize that an important determinant of the quantity demanded is its expected return:

$$RET^e = \frac{P^e_{t+1} - P_t}{P_t} = g^e$$

where

RET^e = expected return
P_t = price of gold today
P^e_{t+1} = expected price of gold next year
g^e = expected capital gain

In deriving the demand curve, we hold all other variables constant, particularly the expected price of gold next year P^e_{t+1}. With a given value of the expected price of gold next year P^e_{t+1}, a lower price of gold today P_t means that there will be a greater appreciation in the price of gold over the coming year. The result is that a lower price of gold today implies a higher expected capital gain over the coming year and hence a higher expected return: $RET^e = (P^e_{t+1} - P_t)/P_t$. Thus because the price of gold today (which for simplicity we will denote as P) is lower, the expected return on gold is higher, and the quantity demanded is higher. Consequently, the demand curve G^d_1 slopes downward in Figure A1.

Supply Curve

To derive the supply curve, expressing the relationship between the quantity supplied and the price, we again assume that all other economic variables are held constant. A higher price of gold will induce producers to mine for extra gold and also possibly induce governments to sell some of their gold stocks to the public, thus increasing the quantity supplied. Hence the supply curve G^s_1 in Figure A1 slopes upward. Notice that the supply curve in the figure is drawn to be very steep. The reason for this is that the actual amount of gold produced in any year is only a tiny fraction of the outstanding stock of gold that has been accumulated over hundreds of years. Thus the increase in the quantity of gold supplied in response to a higher price is only a small fraction of the stock of gold, resulting in a very steep supply curve.

Market Equilibrium

Market equilibrium in the gold market occurs when the quantity of gold demanded equals the quantity of gold supplied:

$$G^d = G^s$$

With the initial demand and supply curves of G^d_1 and G^s_1, equilibrium occurs at point 1, where these curves intersect at a gold price of P_1. At a price above this equilibrium, the amount of gold supplied exceeds the amount demanded, and this condition of excess supply leads to a decline in the gold price until it reaches P_1, the equilibrium price. Similarly, if the price is below P_1, there is excess demand for gold, which drives the price upward until it settles at the equilibrium price P_1.

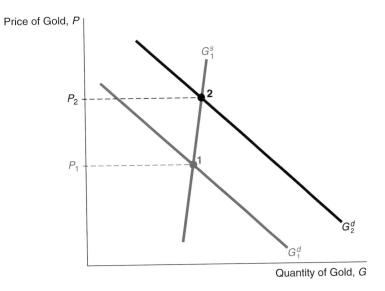

FIGURE A1   A Change in the Equilibrium Price of Gold

When the demand curve shifts rightward from G^d_1 to G^d_2, say, because expected inflation rises, equilibrium moves from point 1 to point 2, and the equilibrium price of gold rises from P_1 to P_2.

CHANGES IN THE EQUILIBRIUM PRICE OF GOLD

Changes in the equilibrium price of gold occur when there is a shift in either the supply curve or the demand curve, that is, when the quantity demanded or supplied changes at each given price of gold in response to a change in some factor other than today's gold price.

Shift in the Demand Curve for Gold

The theory of portfolio choice provides the factors that shift the demand curve for gold: wealth, expected return on gold relative to alternative assets, riskiness of gold relative to alternative assets, and liquidity of gold relative to alternative assets. The analysis of how changes in each of these factors shift the demand curve for gold is the same as that found in the chapter

When wealth rises, at a given price of gold, the quantity demanded increases, and the demand curve shifts to the right, as in Figure A1. When the expected return on gold relative to other assets rises—either because speculators think that the future price of gold will be higher or because the expected return on other assets declines—gold becomes more desirable; the quantity demanded therefore increases at any given price of gold, and the demand curve shifts to the right, as in Figure A1. When the relative riskiness of gold declines, either because gold prices become less volatile or because returns on other assets become more volatile, gold becomes more desirable, the quantity demanded at every given price rises, and the demand curve again shifts to the right. When the gold market becomes relatively more liquid and gold therefore becomes more desirable, the quantity demanded at any given price rises, and the demand curve also shifts to the right, as in Figure A1.

Shifts in the Supply Curve for Gold

The supply curve for gold shifts when there are changes in technology that make gold mining more efficient or when governments at any given price of gold decide to increase sales of their holdings of gold. In these cases, the quantity of gold supplied at any given price increases, and the supply curve shifts to the right.

Changes in the Equilibrium Price of Gold Due to a Rise in Expected Inflation

To illustrate how changes in the equilibrium price of gold occur when supply and demand curves shift, let's look at what happens when there is a change in expected inflation.

Suppose that expected inflation is 5 percent and the initial supply and demand curves are at G_1^s and G_1^d so that the equilibrium price of gold is at P_1 in Fig. A1. If expected inflation now rises to 10 percent, prices of goods and commodities next year will be expected to be higher than they otherwise would have been, and the price of gold next year P_{t+1}^e will also be expected to be higher than otherwise. Now at any given price of gold today, gold is expected to have a greater rate of appreciation over the coming year and hence a higher expected capital gain and return. The greater expected return means that the quantity of gold demanded increases at any given price, thus shifting the demand curve from G_1^d to G_2^d. Equilibrium therefore moves from point 1 to point 2, and the price of gold rises from P_1 to P_2.

By using a supply and demand diagram like that in Figure A1, you should be able to see that if the expected rate of inflation falls, the price of gold today will also fall. We thus reach the following conclusion: ***The price of gold should be positively related to the expected inflation rate.***

Because the gold market responds immediately to any changes in expected inflation, it is considered a good barometer of the trend of inflation in the future. Indeed, Alan Greenspan, the chairman of the Board of Governors of the Federal Reserve System, has advocated using the price of gold as an indicator of inflationary pressures in the economy. Not surprisingly, then, the gold market is followed closely by financial analysts and monetary policymakers. Ⓐ

Study Guide   To give yourself practice with supply and demand analysis in the gold market, see if you can analyze what happens to the price of gold for the following situations, remembering that all other things are held constant: (1) Interest rates rise, (2) the gold market becomes more liquid, (3) the volatility of gold prices increases, (4) the stock market is expected to turn bullish in the near future, (5) investors suddenly become fearful that there will be a collapse in real estate prices, and (6) Russia sells a lot of gold in the open market to raise hard currency such as U.S. dollars to feed its people.

The analysis in this appendix can also be applied to many other asset markets. See if you can apply the analysis here to understand fluctuations in the prices of classic comic books, old baseball cards, oil, Rembrandt paintings, or the other commodities mentioned in the following application.

Following the Financial News

The "Commodities" Column

The "Commodities" column appears daily in the *Wall Street Journal*; an example is presented here.

It is typically found in the third section, "Money and Investing."

COMMODITIES

Crude Oil Prices Plunge Amid Rumors U.S. Urged Saudis to Boost Production

Dow Jones News Services

Crude oil futures plunged on reports that the Clinton administration has asked Saudi Arabia to boost its oil output in case U.S.-Iraqi tensions cause disruptions in oil deliveries from the Persian Gulf region.

Saudi Arabian officials denied the report after trading had ended, and Clinton administration officials weren't immediately available to comment.

But that didn't change the reaction on the New York Mercantile Exchange, where crude oil for October delivery fell $1.32 to $23.19 a barrel; October heating oil fell 2.65 cents to 65.29 cents a gallon and October unleaded gasoline fell 1.73 cents to 62.87 cents a gallon.

Crude and crude products faced heavy selling pressure throughout the day. The concern among traders is that Saudi Arabia will increase its production but that the flow of oil from Iraq won't be affected.

The result, traders fear, will be a glut, albeit a temporary one, of oil on the world market.

"The market is nervous enough about Iraq right now to react to any rumor that could be legitimate," said Tim Evans, an analyst at Pegasus Econometric Group. Saudi Arabia is the largest exporter of the Organization of Petroleum Exporting Countries. While many nations in the oil cartel exceed their quotas, Saudi Arabia has the best reputation for staying below its output ceiling despite ample capacity to export more.

Iraqi leader Saddam Hussein late last week said his military will stop firing on U.S. warplanes in American-enforced no-fly zones in the north and south of his country. Mr. Clinton said yesterday that the deployment of at

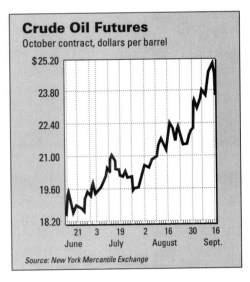

Crude Oil Futures
October contract, dollars per barrel

Source: New York Mercantile Exchange

least 3,000 troops to Kuwait doesn't indicate the U.S. is seeking a military confrontation with Iraq.

In other commodity markets:

GRAINS: Corn and soybean futures prices fell on the Chicago Board of Trade on forecasts calling for moderate temperatures through the end of the month. Moderate temperatures—as distinct from those that are below freezing—will help ensure a good fall harvest.

Source: Wall Street Journal, September 17, 1996, p. C19.

Reading the WALL STREET JOURNAL
The "Commodities" Column

The supply and demand analysis in this appendix can help you evaluate events in commodity markets that are reported in the media. Every day, the *Wall Street Journal* reports on developments in the commodities markets on the previous business day in its "Commodities" column, an example of which is found in the "Following the Financial News" box.

The column focuses on the fall in crude oil prices because of rumors that the U.S. government asked Saudi Arabia to increase its oil production. Our supply and demand analysis explains why this development would cause the price of oil to fall.

Increased oil production in the future would lead to a shift in the supply curve to the right, producing a future fall in oil prices. The lower future oil prices therefore imply that P_{t+1}^e has fallen, so that the expected return on holding oil has declined. Thus the quantity demanded of oil today also declines, shifting the demand curve today to the left, and causing oil prices to decline today. The decline in corn and soybean prices because of the prospect of a good fall harvest can be explained with a similar argument. Ⓐ

Chapter 7

THE RISK AND TERM STRUCTURE OF INTEREST RATES

PREVIEW   In our supply and demand analysis of interest-rate behavior in Chapter 6, we examined the determination of just one interest rate. Yet we saw earlier that there are enormous numbers of bonds on which the interest rates can and do differ. In this chapter we complete the interest-rate picture by examining the relationship of the various interest rates to one another. Understanding why they differ from bond to bond can help businesses, banks, insurance companies, and private investors decide which bonds to purchase as investments or which ones to sell.

We first look at why bonds with the same term to maturity have different interest rates. The relationship among these interest rates is called the **risk structure of interest rates,** although risk, liquidity, and income tax rules all play a role in determining the risk structure. A bond's term to maturity also affects its interest rate, and the relationship among interest rates on bonds with different terms to maturity is called the **term structure of interest rates.** In this chapter we examine the sources and causes of fluctuations in interest rates relative to one another and look at a number of theories that explain these fluctuations.

RISK STRUCTURE OF INTEREST RATES

Figure 1 shows the yields to maturity for several categories of long-term bonds from 1919 to 1996. It shows us two important features of interest-rate behavior for bonds of the same maturity: Interest rates on different categories of bonds differ from one another in any given year, and the spread (or difference) between the interest rates varies over time. The interest rates on municipal bonds, for example, are above those on U.S. government (Treasury) bonds in the late 1930s but lower thereafter. In addition, the spread between the interest rates on Baa corpo-

Annual Yield (%)

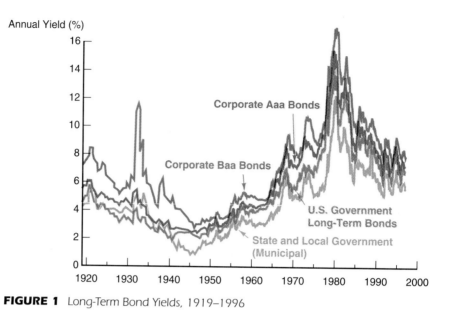

FIGURE 1 Long-Term Bond Yields, 1919–1996

Sources: Board of Governors of the Federal Reserve System, *Banking and Monetary Statistics, 1941–1970*; Federal Reserve *Bulletin*.

rate bonds (riskier than Aaa corporate bonds) and U.S. government bonds is very large during the Great Depression years 1930–1933, is smaller during the 1940s–1960s, and then widens again in the 1970s–1990s. What factors are responsible for these phenomena?

Default Risk

One attribute of a bond that influences its interest rate is its **default risk,** the chance that the issuer of the bond will default, that is, be unable to make interest payments or pay off the face value when the bond matures. A corporation suffering big losses, such as Chrysler Corporation did in the 1970s, might be more likely to suspend interest payments on its bonds.[1] The default risk on its bonds would therefore be quite high. By contrast, U.S. Treasury bonds have usually been considered to have no default risk because the federal government can always increase taxes or even print money to pay off its obligations. Bonds like these with no default risk are called **default-free bonds.** (However, during the budget negotiations in Congress in 1995 and 1996, the Republicans threatened to let Treasury bonds default, and this had an impact on the bond market, as one application following this section indicates.) The spread between the interest rates on bonds with default risk and default-free bonds, called the **risk premium,** indicates how much additional interest people must earn in order to be willing to hold a risky bond. Our supply and demand analysis of the bond market in Chapter 6 can be

---

[1]Chrysler did not default on its loans in this period, but it would have were it not for a government bailout plan intended to preserve jobs that in effect provided Chrysler with funds that were used to pay off creditors.

used to explain why a bond with default risk always has a positive risk premium and why the higher the default risk is, the larger the risk premium will be.

To examine the effect of default risk on interest rates, let us look at the supply and demand diagrams for the default-free (U.S. Treasury) and corporate long-term bond markets in Figure 2. To make the diagrams somewhat easier to read, let's assume that initially there is no possibility of default on the corporate bonds, so they are default-free like U.S. Treasury bonds. In this case, these two bonds have the same attributes (identical risk and maturity); their equilibrium prices and interest rates will initially be equal ($P_1^c = P_1^T$ and $i_1^c = i_1^T$), and the risk premium on corporate bonds ($i_1^c - i_1^T$) will be zero.

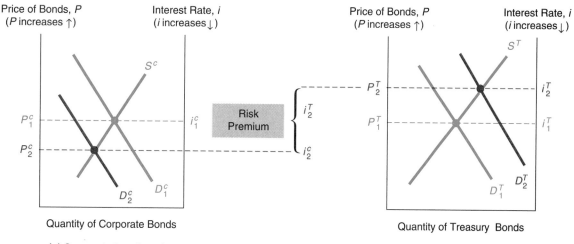

FIGURE 2 Response to an Increase in Default Risk on Corporate Bonds

An increase in default risk on corporate bonds shifts the demand curve from D_1^c to D_2^c. Simultaneously, it shifts the demand curve for Treasury bonds from D_1^T to D_2^T. The equilibrium price for corporate bonds (left axis) falls from P_1^c to P_2^c, and the equilibrium interest rate on corporate bonds (right axis) rises from i_1^c to i_2^c. In the Treasury market, the equilibrium bond price rises from P_1^T to P_2^T, and the equilibrium interest rate falls from i_1^T to i_2^T. The brace indicates the difference between i_2^c and i_2^T, the risk premium on corporate bonds. (**Note:** *P* and *i* increase in opposite directions. *P* on the left vertical axis increases as we go up the axis, while *i* on the right vertical axis increases as we go down the axis.)

If the possibility of a default increases because a corporation begins to suffer large losses, the default risk on corporate bonds will increase, and the expected return on these bonds will decrease. In addition, the corporate bond's return will be more uncertain as well. The theory of portfolio choice predicts that because the expected return on the corporate bond falls relative to the expected return on the default-free Treasury bond while its relative riskiness rises, the corporate bond is less desirable (holding everything else equal), and demand for it will fall. The demand curve for corporate bonds in panel (a) of Figure 2 then shifts to the left from D_1^c to D_2^c.

At the same time, the expected return on default-free Treasury bonds increases relative to the expected return on corporate bonds while their relative riskiness declines. The Treasury bonds thus become more desirable, and demand rises, as shown in panel (b) by the rightward shift in the demand curve for these bonds from D_1^T to D_2^T.

As we can see in Figure 2, the equilibrium price for corporate bonds (left axis) falls from P_1^c to P_2^c, and since the bond price is negatively related to the interest rate, the equilibrium interest rate on corporate bonds (right axis) rises from i_1^c to i_2^c. At the same time, however, the equilibrium price for the Treasury bonds rises from P_1^T to P_2^T, and the equilibrium interest rate falls from i_1^T to i_2^T. The spread between the interest rates on corporate and default-free bonds—that is, the risk premium on corporate bonds—has risen from zero to $i_2^c - i_2^T$. We can now conclude that ***a bond with default risk will always have a positive risk premium, and an increase in its default risk will raise the risk premium.***

Because default risk is so important to the size of the risk premium, purchasers of bonds need to know whether a corporation is likely to default on its bonds. Two major investment advisory firms, Moody's Investors Service and Standard and Poor's Corporation, provide default risk information by rating the quality of corporate and municipal bonds in terms of the probability of default. The ratings and their description are contained in Table 1. Bonds with relatively low risk of default are called *investment-grade* securities and have a rating of Baa (or BBB) and above. Bonds with ratings below Baa (or BBB) have higher default risk and have been aptly dubbed **junk bonds.**

Next let's look back at Figure 1 and see if we can explain the relationship between interest rates on corporate and U.S. Treasury bonds. Corporate bonds always have higher interest rates than U.S. Treasury bonds because they always have some risk of default, whereas U.S. Treasury bonds do not. Because Baa-rated corporate bonds have a greater default risk than the higher-rated Aaa bonds, their risk premium is greater, and the Baa rate therefore always exceeds the Aaa rate. We can use the same analysis to explain the huge jump in the risk premium on Baa corporate bond rates during the Great Depression years 1930–1933 and the rise in the risk premium in the 1970s, 1980s, and 1990s (see Figure 1). The depression period saw a very high rate of business failures and defaults. As we would expect, these factors led to a substantial increase in default risk for bonds issued by vulnerable corporations, and the risk premium for Baa bonds reached unprecedentedly high levels. The 1970s, 1980s, and 1990s again saw higher levels of business failures and defaults, although they were still well below Great Depression levels. Again, as expected, default risks and risk premiums for corpo-

TABLE 1	Bond Ratings by Moody's and Standard and Poor's		
Rating			
Moody's	**Standard and Poor's**	**Descriptions**	**Examples of Corporations with Bonds Outstanding in 1997**
Aaa	AAA	Highest quality (lowest default risk)	General Electric, Johnson and Johnson, Wisconsin Bell
Aa	AA	High quality	McDonalds, Mobil Oil, Wal-Mart
A	A	Upper medium grade	Anheuser-Busch, Ford Motor, Xerox
Baa	BBB	Medium grade	Chrysler, General Motors, Wendy's
Ba	BB	Lower medium grade	McDonnell Douglas, RJR-Nabisco, Time-Warner
B	B	Speculative	Marriott, Revlon, Turner Broadcasting
Caa	CCC, CC	Poor (high default risk)	
Ca	C	Highly speculative	
C	D	Lowest grade	

rate bonds rose, widening the spread between interest rates on corporate bonds and Treasury bonds.

The Stock Market Crash of 1987 and the Junk Bond–Treasury Spread

The stock market crash on "Black Monday," October 19, 1987, when the Dow Jones Industrial Average fell more than 500 points, had a major impact not only on prices of stocks but on the bond market as well. Let's see how our supply and demand analysis explains the behavior of the spread between interest rates on junk bonds and Treasury securities in the aftermath of the crash using Figure 2.

As a consequence of the Black Monday crash, many investors began to doubt the financial health of corporations with lower credit ratings that had issued junk bonds. The increase in default risk for junk bonds made them less desirable at any given interest rate, decreased the quantity demanded, and shifted the demand curve for junk bonds to the left. As shown in panel (a) of Figure 2, the interest rate on junk bonds should have risen, which is indeed what happened: Interest rates on junk bonds shot up by about one percentage point. But the increase in the perceived default risk for junk bonds after the crash made default-free U.S. Treasury bonds relatively more attractive and shifted the demand curve for these securities to the right—an outcome described by some analysts as a "flight to quality." Just as our analysis predicts in Figure 2, interest rates on Treasury securities fell by about one percentage point. The overall outcome was that the spread between interest rates on junk bonds and government bonds rose by two percentage points, from 4 percent before the crash to 6 percent immediately after. Ⓐ

What If Treasury Securities Were No Longer Default-Free?

Throughout our history, the U.S. Treasury has never defaulted on its securities. However, in late 1995 and early 1996, the budget battle between congressional Republicans and President Clinton almost led to an unprecedented default. In an attempt to get their way in the budget negotiations, the Republicans threatened to refuse to raise the federal government debt ceiling. If the threat had been carried out, the Treasury would have missed interest payments on its debt because it would not have been able to issue new debt to cover its interest outlays and other expenditures when the debt ceiling was reached. Default was averted when a budget compromise was finally reached and the debt ceiling was raised after several shutdowns of the federal government in which "nonessential" government workers were sent home. What would have been the impact of a Treasury default?

Our analysis in Figure 2 provides the answer. Default on Treasury bonds would mean that they would no longer be considered default-free and would now have the attributes of corporate bonds in panel (a) of Figure 2. The increase in default risk would decrease the quantity of Treasury bonds demanded at any given interest rate and would thus cause their demand curve to shift to the left. As we see in panel (a), this would result in a fall in their bond price and a rise in their interest rate. Indeed, just as our analysis predicts, when budget talks stalled on December 18, 1995, and fear of a possible government default rose, the Treasury bond market slumped: Bond prices fell, and the interest rate on 30-year Treasury bonds rose by 11/100s of a percentage point, the largest one-day rise in more than six months. Ⓐ

Liquidity

Another attribute of a bond that influences its interest rate is its liquidity. As we learned in Chapter 5, a liquid asset is one that can be quickly and cheaply converted into cash if the need arises. The more liquid an asset is, the more desirable it is (holding everything else constant). U.S. Treasury bonds are the most liquid of all long-term bonds because they are so widely traded that they are the easiest to sell quickly and the cost of selling them is low. Corporate bonds are not as liquid because fewer bonds for any one corporation are traded; thus it can be costly to sell these bonds in an emergency because it may be hard to find buyers quickly.

How does the reduced liquidity of the corporate bonds affect their interest rates relative to the interest rate on Treasury bonds? We can use supply and demand analysis with the same figure that was used to analyze the effect of default risk, Figure 2, to show that the lower liquidity of corporate bonds relative to Treasury bonds increases the spread between the interest rates on these two bonds. Let us start the analysis by assuming that initially corporate and Treasury bonds are equally liquid and all their other attributes are the same. As shown in Figure 2, their equilibrium prices and interest rates will initially be equal: $P^c_1 = P^T_1$ and $i^c_1 = i^T_1$. If the corporate bond becomes less liquid than the Treasury bond because it is less widely traded, then as the theory of portfolio choice indicates, its demand will fall, shifting its demand curve from D^c_1 to D^c_2 as in panel (a). The Treasury bond now becomes relatively more liquid in comparison with the corporate bond, so its demand curve shifts rightward from D^T_1 to D^T_2 as in panel (b). The shifts in the curves in Figure 2 show that the price of the less liquid corporate bond falls and its interest rate rises, while the price of the more liquid Treasury bond rises and its interest rate falls.

The result is that the spread between the interest rates on the two bond types has risen. Therefore, the differences between interest rates on corporate bonds and Treasury bonds (that is, the risk premiums) reflect not only the corporate bond's default risk but its liquidity too. This is why a risk premium is sometimes called a *liquidity premium*. Most accurately, it should be called a "risk and liquidity premium," but convention dictates that it be called a *risk premium*.

Income Tax Considerations

Returning to Figure 1, we are still left with one puzzle—the behavior of municipal bond rates. Municipal bonds are certainly not default-free: State and local governments have defaulted on the municipal bonds they have issued in the past, particularly during the Great Depression and even more recently in the case of Orange County, California, in 1994 (more on this in Chapter 14). Also, municipal bonds are not as liquid as U.S. Treasury bonds.

Why is it, then, that these bonds have had lower interest rates than U.S. Treasury bonds for at least 40 years, as indicated in Figure 1? The explanation lies in the fact that interest payments on municipal bonds are exempt from federal income taxes, a factor that has the same effect on the demand for municipal bonds as an increase in their expected return.

Let us imagine that you have a high enough income to put you in the 40 percent income tax bracket, where for every extra dollar of income you have to pay 40 cents to the government. If you own a $1000-face-value U.S. Treasury bond that sells for $1000 and has a coupon payment of $100, you get to keep only $60 of the payment after taxes. Although the bond has a 10 percent interest rate, you actually earn only 6 percent after taxes.

Suppose, however, that you put your savings into a $1000-face-value municipal bond that sells for $1000 and pays only $80 in coupon payments. Its interest rate is only 8 percent, but because it is a tax-exempt security, you pay no taxes on the $80 coupon payment, so you earn 8 percent after taxes. Clearly, you earn more on the municipal bond after taxes, so you are willing to hold the riskier and less liquid municipal bond even though it has a lower interest rate than the U.S. Treasury bond. (This was not true before World War II, when the tax-exempt status of municipal bonds did not convey much of an advantage because income tax rates were extremely low.)

Another way of understanding why municipal bonds have lower interest rates than Treasury bonds is to use the supply and demand analysis displayed in Figure 3. To begin with, we assume that municipal and Treasury bonds have identical attributes and so have the same bond prices and interest rates as drawn in the figure: $P_1^m = P_1^T$ and $i_1^m = i_1^T$. Once the municipal bonds are given a tax advantage that raises their after-tax expected return relative to Treasury bonds and makes them more desirable, demand for them rises, and their demand curve shifts to the right from D_1^m to D_2^m. The result is that their equilibrium bond price rises from P_1^m to P_2^m, and their equilibrium interest rate falls from i_1^m to i_2^m. By contrast, Treasury bonds have now become less desirable relative to municipal bonds, demand for Treasury bonds decreases, and D_1^T shifts to D_2^T. The Treasury bond price falls from P_1^T to P_2^T, and the interest rate rises from i_1^T to i_2^T. The resulting lower interest rates for municipal bonds and higher interest rates for Treasury bonds explains why municipal bonds can have interest rates below those of Treasury bonds.[2]

Summary

The risk structure of interest rates (the relationship among interest rates on bonds with the same maturity) is explained by three factors: default risk, liquidity, and the income tax treatment of the bond's interest payments. As a bond's default risk increases, the risk premium on that bond (the spread between its interest rate and the interest rate on a default-free Treasury bond) rises. The greater liquidity of Treasury bonds also explains why their interest rates are lower than interest rates on less liquid bonds. If a bond has a favorable tax treatment, as do municipal bonds, whose interest payments are exempt from federal income taxes, its interest rate will be lower.

Effects of the Clinton Tax Increase on Bond Interest Rates

As part of the Clinton administration's 1993 deficit reduction plan, the top income tax bracket was raised from 31 to 40 percent and the corporate income tax rate was raised from 34 to 35 percent. What was the effect of this income tax increase on interest rates in the municipal bond market relative to those in the Treasury bond market?

---

[2]In contrast to corporate bonds, Treasury bonds are exempt from state and local income taxes. Using the analysis in the text, you should be able to show that this feature of Treasury bonds provides an additional reason why interest rates on corporate bonds are higher than those on Treasury bonds.

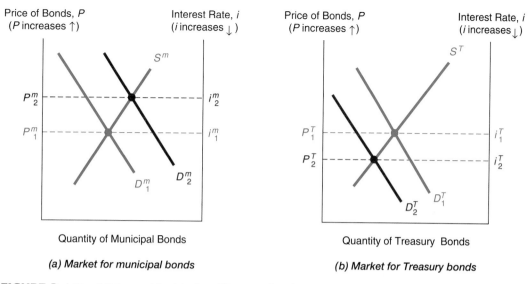

FIGURE 3 Interest Rates on Municipal and Treasury Bonds

When the municipal bond is given tax-free status, demand for the municipal bond shifts rightward from D_1^m to D_2^m and demand for the Treasury bond shifts leftward from D_1^T to D_2^T. The equilibrium price of the municipal bond (left axis) rises from P_1^m to P_2^m, so its interest rate (right axis) falls from i_1^m to i_2^m, while the equilibrium price of the Treasury bond falls from P_1^T to P_2^T and its interest rate rises from i_1^T to i_2^T. The result is that municipal bonds end up with lower interest rates than those on Treasury bonds. (**Note:** P and i increase in opposite directions. P on the left vertical axis increases as we go up the axis, while i on the right vertical axis increases as we go down the axis.)

The supply and demand analysis in Figure 3 provides the answer. An increased income tax rate for rich people and corporations means that the tax-free status of municipal bonds raises their after-tax expected return relative to that on Treasury bonds because the interest on Treasury bonds is now taxed at a higher rate. Because municipal bonds now become more desirable, their demand increases, shifting the demand curve to the right as in Figure 3, which raises their price and lowers their interest rate. Conversely, the higher income tax rate makes Treasury bonds less desirable; that shifts their demand curve to the left, lowers their price, and raises their interest rates, as in Figure 3.

Our analysis thus shows that the Clinton tax increase lowered the interest rates on municipal bonds relative to interest rates on Treasury bonds. Ⓐ

TERM STRUCTURE OF INTEREST RATES

We have seen how risk, liquidity, and tax considerations (collectively embedded in the risk structure) can influence interest rates. Another factor that influences the interest rate on a bond is its term to maturity: Bonds with identical risk, liquidity, and tax characteristics may have different interest rates because the time remaining to maturity is different. A plot of the yields on bonds with differing terms to maturity but the same risk, liquidity, and tax considerations is called a **yield curve,** and it describes the term structure of interest rates for particular types of bonds, such as government bonds. The "Following the Financial News" box shows several yield curves for Treasury securities that were published in the *Wall*

Street Journal. Yield curves can be classified as upward-sloping, flat, and downward-sloping (the last sort is often referred to as an **inverted yield curve**). When yield curves slope upward, as in the "Following the Financial News" box, the long-term interest rates are above the short-term interest rates; when yield curves are flat, short- and long-term interest rates are the same; and when yield curves are inverted, long-term interest rates are below short-term interest rates. Yield curves can also have more complicated shapes in which they first slope up and then down, or vice versa. Why do we usually see upward slopes of the yield curve as in the "Following the Financial News" box but sometimes other shapes?

Besides explaining why yield curves take on different shapes at different times, a good theory of the term structure of interest rates must explain the following three important empirical facts.

1. As we see in Figure 4, interest rates on bonds of different maturities move together over time.
2. When short-term interest rates are low, yield curves are more likely to have an upward slope; when short-term interest rates are high, yield curves are more likely to slope downward and be inverted.
3. Yield curves almost always slope upward, as in the "Following the Financial News" box.

Three theories have been put forward to explain the term structure of interest rates, that is, the relationship among interest rates on bonds of different maturities reflected in yield curve patterns: (1) the expectations hypothesis, (2) the segmented markets theory, and (3) the preferred habitat theory (which is closely

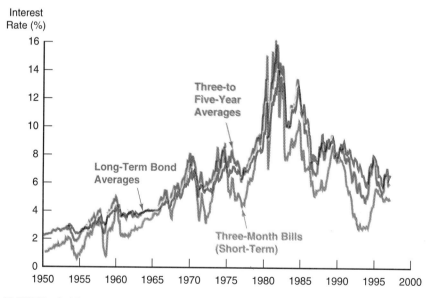

FIGURE 4 *Movements over Time of Interest Rates on U.S. Government Bonds with Different Maturities*

Sources: Board of Governors of the Federal Reserve System, *Banking and Monetary Statistics, 1941–1970;* Federal Reserve *Bulletin;* Citibase databank.

Following the Financial News

Yield Curves

The *Wall Street Journal* publishes a daily plot of the yield curves for Treasury securities, an example of which is presented here. It is typically found next to the "Credit Markets" column.

The numbers on the vertical axis indicate the interest rate for the Treasury security, with the maturity given by the numbers on the horizontal axis. For example, the yield curve marked "Yesterday" indicates that the interest rate on the three-month Treasury bill yesterday was 5.20% percent, while the one-year bill had an interest rate of 5.55 percent and the ten-year bond had an interest rate of 6.60 percent. As you can see, the yield curves in the plot have the typical upward slope.

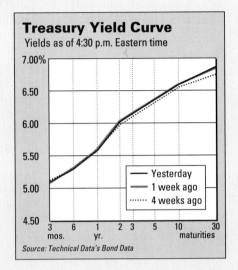

Treasury Yield Curve
Yields as of 4:30 p.m. Eastern time

— Yesterday
— 1 week ago
······ 4 weeks ago

Source: Technical Data's Bond Data

Source: Wall Street Journal, January 31, 1997, p. C17.

related to the liquidity premium theory). The expectations hypothesis does a good job of explaining the first two facts on our list but not the third. The segmented markets theory can explain fact 3 but not the other two facts, which are well explained by the expectations hypothesis. Because each theory explains facts that the other cannot, a natural way to seek a better understanding of the term structure is to combine features of both theories, which leads us to the preferred habitat theory and the closely related liquidity premium theory, which can explain all three facts.

If the preferred habitat and liquidity premium theories do a better job of explaining the facts and are hence the most widely accepted theories, why do we spend time discussing the other two theories? There are two reasons. First, the ideas in these two theories provide the groundwork for the preferred habitat and liquidity premium theories. Second, it is important to see how economists modify theories to improve them when they find that the predicted results are inconsistent with the empirical evidence.

Expectations Hypothesis

The **expectations hypothesis** of the term structure states the following commonsense proposition: The interest rate on a long-term bond will equal an average of short-term interest rates that people expect to occur over the life of the long-term bond. For example, if people expect that short-term interest rates will be 10 percent on average over the coming five years, the expectations hypothesis predicts that the interest rate on bonds with five years to maturity will be 10 percent too. If short-term interest rates were expected to rise even higher after this five-year period so that the average short-term interest rate over the coming 20 years is 11 percent, then the interest rate on 20-year bonds would equal 11 percent and would be higher than the interest rate on five-year bonds. We can see that the explanation provided by the expectations hypothesis for why interest rates on bonds of different maturities differ is that short-term interest rates are expected to have different values at future dates.

The key assumption behind this theory is that buyers of bonds do not prefer bonds of one maturity over another, so they will not hold any quantity of a bond if its expected return is less than that of another bond with a different maturity. Bonds that have this characteristic are said to be *perfect substitutes*. What this means in practice is that if bonds with different maturities are perfect substitutes, the expected return on these bonds must be equal.

To see how the assumption that bonds with different maturities are perfect substitutes leads to the expectations hypothesis, let us consider the following two investment strategies:

1. Purchase a one-year bond, and when it matures in one year, purchase another one-year bond.
2. Purchase a two-year bond and hold it until maturity.

Because both strategies must have the same expected return if people are holding both one- and two-year bonds, the interest rate on the two-year bond must equal the average of the two one-year interest rates. For example, let's say that the current interest rate on the one-year bond is 9 percent and you expect the interest rate on the one-year bond next year to be 11 percent. If you pursue the first strategy of buying the two one-year bonds, the expected return over the two years will average out to be (9% + 11%)/2 = 10% per year. You will be willing to hold both the one- and two-year bonds only if the expected return per year of the two-year bond equals this. Therefore, the interest rate on the two-year bond must equal 10 percent, the average interest rate on the two one-year bonds.

We can make this argument more general. For an investment of $1, consider the choice of holding, for two periods, a two-period bond or two one-period bonds. Using the definitions

i_t = today's (time t) interest rate on a one-period bond
i^e_{t+1} = interest rate on a one-period bond expected for next period (time $t + 1$)
i_{2t} = today's (time t) interest rate on the two-period bond

the expected return over the two periods from investing $1 in the two-period bond and holding it for the two periods can be calculated as

$$(1 + i_{2t})(1 + i_{2t}) - 1 = 1 + 2i_{2t} + (i_{2t})^2 - 1$$

After the second period, the $1 investment is worth $(1 + i_{2t})(1 + i_{2t})$. Subtracting the $1 initial investment from this amount and dividing by the initial $1 investment gives the rate of return calculated in the above equation. Because $(i_{2t})^2$ is extremely small—if $i_{2t} = 10\% = 0.10$, then $(i_{2t})^2 = 0.01$—we can simplify the expected return for holding the two-period bond for the two periods to

$$2i_{2t}$$

With the other strategy, in which one-period b154onds are bought, the expected return on the $1 investment over the two periods is

$$(1 + i_t)(1 + i^e_{t+1}) - 1$$

After the first period, the $1 investment becomes $1 + i_t$, and this is reinvested in the one-period bond for the next period, yielding an amount $(1 + i_t)(1 + i^e_{t+1})$. Subtracting the $1 initial investment from this amount and dividing by the initial investment of $1 gives the expected return for the strategy of holding one-period bonds for the two periods. Because $i_t(i^e_{t+1})$ is also extremely small—if $i_t = i^e_{t+1} = 0.10$, then $i_t(i^e_{t+1}) = 0.01$—we can simplify this to

$$i_t + i^e_{t+1}$$

Both bonds will be held only if these expected returns are equal, that is, when

$$2i_{2t} = i_t + i^e_{t+1}$$

Solving for i_{2t} in terms of the one-period rates, we have

$$i_{2t} = \frac{i_t + i^e_{t+1}}{2} \tag{1}$$

which tells us that the two-period rate must equal the average of the two one-period rates. We can conduct the same steps for bonds with a longer maturity so that we can examine the whole term structure of interest rates. Doing so, we will find that the interest rate of i_{nt} on an n-period bond must equal

$$i_{nt} = \frac{i_t + i^e_{t+1} + i^e_{t+2} + \ldots + i^e_{t+(n-1)}}{n} \tag{2}$$

Equation 2 states that the n-period interest rate equals the average of the one-period interest rates expected to occur over the n-period life of the bond. This is a restatement of the expectations hypothesis in more precise terms.[3]

A simple numerical example might clarify what the expectations theory in Equation 2 is saying. If the one-year interest rate over the next five years is expected to be 5, 6, 7, 8, and 9 percent, Equation 2 indicates that the interest rate on the two-year bond would be

$$\frac{5\% + 6\%}{2} = 5.5\%$$

while for the five-year bond it would be

$$\frac{5\% + 6\% + 7\% + 8\% + 9\%}{5} = 7\%$$

Doing a similar calculation for the one-, three-, and four-year interest rates, you should be able to verify that the one- to five-year interest rates are 5.0, 5.5, 6.0, 6.5, and 7.0 percent, respectively. Thus we see that the rising trend in

---

[3]The analysis here has been conducted for discount bonds. Formulas for interest rates on coupon bonds would differ slightly from those used here but would convey the same principle.

expected short-term interest rates produces an upward-sloping yield curve along which interest rates rise as maturity lengthens.

The expectations hypothesis is an elegant theory that provides an explanation of why the term structure of interest rates (as represented by yield curves) changes at different times. When the yield curve is upward-sloping, the expectations hypothesis suggests that short-term interest rates are expected to rise in the future, as we have seen in our numerical example. In this situation, in which the long-term rate is currently above the short-term rate, the average of future short-term rates is expected to be higher than the current short-term rate, which can occur only if short-term interest rates are expected to rise. This is what we see in our numerical example. When the yield curve slopes downward and is inverted, the average of future short-term interest rates is expected to be below the current short-term rate, implying that short-term interest rates are expected to fall, on average, in the future. Only when the yield curve is flat does the expectations hypothesis suggest that short-term interest rates are not expected to change, on average, in the future.

The expectations hypothesis also explains fact 1 that interest rates on bonds with different maturities move together over time. Historically, short-term interest rates have had the characteristic that if they increase today, they will tend to be higher in the future. Hence a rise in short-term rates will raise people's expectations of future short-term rates. Because long-term rates are the average of expected future short-term rates, a rise in short-term rates will also raise long-term rates, causing short- and long-term rates to move together.

The expectations hypothesis also explains fact 2 that yield curves tend to have an upward slope when short-term interest rates are low and are inverted when short-term rates are high. When short-term rates are low, people generally expect them to rise to some normal level in the future, and the average of future expected short-term rates is high relative to the current short-term rate. Therefore, long-term interest rates will be substantially above current short-term rates, and the yield curve would then have an upward slope. Conversely, if short-term rates are high, people usually expect them to come back down. Long-term rates would then drop below short-term rates because the average of expected future short-term rates would be below current short-term rates and the yield curve would slope downward and become inverted.[4]

The expectations hypothesis is an attractive theory because it provides a simple explanation of the behavior of the term structure, but unfortunately it has a major shortcoming: It cannot explain fact 3 that yield curves usually slope upward. The typical upward slope of yield curves implies that short-term interest rates are usually expected to rise in the future. In practice, short-term interest rates

---

[4]The expectations hypothesis explains another important fact about the relationship between short-term and long-term interest rates. As you can see looking back at Figure 4, short-term interest rates are more volatile than long-term rates. If interest rates are mean-reverting—that is, if they tend to head back down after they are at unusually high levels or go back up when they are at unusually low levels—then an average of these short-term rates must necessarily have lower volatility than the short-term rates themselves. Because the expectations hypothesis suggests that the long-term rate will be an average of future short-term rates, it implies that the long-term rate will have lower volatility than short-term rates.

are just as likely to fall as they are to rise, and so the expectations hypothesis suggests that the typical yield curve should be flat rather than upward-sloping.

Segmented Markets Theory

As the name suggests, the **segmented markets theory** of the term structure sees markets for different-maturity bonds as completely separate and segmented. The interest rate for each bond with a different maturity is then determined by the supply of and demand for that bond with no effects from expected returns on other bonds with other maturities.

The key assumption in the segmented markets theory is that bonds of different maturities are not substitutes at all, so the expected return from holding a bond of one maturity has no effect on the demand for a bond of another maturity. This theory of the term structure is at the opposite extreme to the expectations hypothesis, which assumes that bonds of different maturities are perfect substitutes.

The argument for why bonds of different maturities are not substitutes is that investors have strong preferences for bonds of one maturity but not for another, so they will be concerned with the expected returns only for bonds of the maturity they prefer. This might occur because they have a particular holding period in mind, and if they match the maturity of the bond to the desired holding period, they can obtain a certain return with no risk at all.[5] (We have seen in Chapter 4 that if the term to maturity equals the holding period, the return is known for certain because it equals the yield exactly, and there is no interest-rate risk.) For example, people who have a short holding period would prefer to hold short-term bonds. Conversely, if you were putting funds away for your young child to go to college, your desired holding period might be much longer, and you would want to hold longer-term bonds.

In the segmented markets theory, differing yield curve patterns are accounted for by supply and demand differences associated with bonds of different maturities. If, as seems sensible, investors have short desired holding periods and generally prefer bonds with shorter maturities that have less interest-rate risk, the segmented markets theory can explain fact 3 that yield curves typically slope upward. Because the demand for long-term bonds is relatively lower than that for short-term bonds in the typical situation, long-term bonds will have lower prices and higher interest rates, and hence the yield curve will typically slope upward.

Although the segmented markets theory can explain why yield curves usually tend to slope upward, it has a major flaw in that it cannot explain facts 1 and 2. Because it views the market for bonds of different maturities as completely segmented, there is no reason for a rise in interest rates on a bond of one maturity to affect the interest rate on a bond of another maturity. Therefore, it cannot explain why interest rates on bonds of different maturities tend to move together

---

[5]The statement that there is no uncertainty about the return if the term to maturity equals the holding period is literally true only for a discount bond. For a coupon bond with a long holding period, there is some risk because coupon payments must be reinvested before the bond matures. Our analysis here is thus being conducted for discount bonds. However, the gist of the analysis remains the same for coupon bonds because the amount of this risk from reinvestment is small when coupon bonds have the same term to maturity as the holding period.

(fact 1). Second, because it is not clear how demand and supply for short- versus long-term bonds changes with the level of short-term interest rates, the theory cannot explain why yield curves tend to slope upward when short-term interest rates are low and to be inverted when short-term interest rates are high (fact 2).

Because each of our two theories explains empirical facts that the other cannot, a logical step is to combine the theories, which leads us to the preferred habitat theory and closely related liquidity premium theory.

Preferred Habitat and Liquidity Premium Theories

The **preferred habitat theory** of term structure states that the interest rate on a long-term bond will equal an average of short-term interest rates expected to occur over the life of the long-term bond plus a term (liquidity) premium that responds to supply and demand conditions for that bond.

The preferred habitat theory's key assumption is that bonds of different maturities are substitutes, which means that the expected return on one bond *does* influence the expected return on a bond of a different maturity, but it allows investors to prefer one bond maturity over another. In other words, bonds of different maturities are assumed to be substitutes but not perfect substitutes. We might think of investors as having a preference for bonds of one maturity over another, a particular bond maturity where they are most comfortable to stay; we might then say that they have a preferred habitat. Investors still care about the expected returns on bonds with a maturity other than their preferred maturity, and so they will not allow expected returns on one bond to get too far out of line with that on another bond with a different maturity. Because they prefer bonds of one maturity over another, they will be willing to buy bonds that do not have the preferred maturity only if they earn a somewhat higher expected return. If investors prefer the habitat of short-term bonds over longer-term bonds, for example, they might be willing to hold short-term bonds even though they have a lower expected return. This means that investors would have to be paid a positive term premium to be willing to hold a long-term bond. Such an outcome would modify the expectations hypothesis by adding a positive term premium to the equation that describes the relationship between long- and short-term interest rates. The preferred habitat theory is thus written as

$$i_{nt} = \frac{i_t + i^e_{t+1} + i^e_{t+2} + \cdots + i^e_{t+(n-1)}}{n} + k_{nt} \tag{3}$$

where k_{nt} = the term premium for the n-period bond at time t.

Closely related to the preferred habitat theory is the **liquidity premium theory,** which takes a somewhat more direct approach to modifying the expectations hypothesis. It reasons that a positive term (liquidity) premium must be offered to buyers of longer-term bonds to compensate them for their increased interest-rate risk. This reasoning leads to the same Equation 3 implied by the preferred habitat theory, with the proviso that the term premium k_{nt} is always positive and rises with the term to maturity of the bond.

A simple numerical example similar to the one we used for the expectations hypothesis further clarifies what the preferred habitat and liquidity premium theories in Equation 3 are saying. Again suppose that the one-year interest rate over the next five years is expected to be 5, 6, 7, 8, and 9 percent, while investors' preferences for holding short-term bonds means that the term premiums for one- to five-year bonds are 0, 0.25, 0.5, 0.75, and 1.0 percent, respectively. Equation 3 then indicates that the interest rate on the two-year bond would be

$$\frac{5\% + 6\%}{2} + 0.25\% = 5.75\%$$

while for the five-year bond it would be

$$\frac{5\% + 6\% + 7\% + 8\% + 9\%}{5} + 1\% = 8\%$$

Doing a similar calculation for the one-, three-, and four-year interest rates, you should be able to verify that the one- to five-year interest rates are 5.0, 5.75, 6.5, 7.25, and 8.0 percent, respectively. Comparing these findings with those for the expectations hypothesis, we see that the preferred habitat and liquidity premium theories produce yield curves that slope more steeply upward because of investors' preferences for short-term bonds.

Let's see if the preferred habitat and liquidity premium theories are consistent with all three empirical facts we have discussed. They explain fact 1 that interest rates on different-maturity bonds move together over time: A rise in short-term interest rates indicates that short-term interest rates will, on average, be higher in the future, and the first term in Equation 3 then implies that long-term interest rates will rise along with them.

They also explain why yield curves tend to have an especially steep upward slope when short-term interest rates are low and to be inverted when short-term rates are high (fact 2). Because investors generally expect short-term interest rates to rise to some normal level when they are low, the average of future expected short-term rates will be high relative to the current short-term rate. With the additional boost of a positive term premium, long-term interest rates will be substantially above current short-term rates, and the yield curve would then have a steep upward slope. Conversely, if short-term rates are high, people usually expect them to come back down. Long-term rates would then drop below short-term rates because the average of expected future short-term rates would be so far below current short-term rates that despite positive term premiums, the yield curve would slope downward.

The preferred habitat and liquidity premium theories explain fact 3 that yield curves typically slope upward by recognizing that the term premium rises with a bond's maturity because of investors' preferences for short-term bonds. Even if short-term interest rates are expected to stay the same on average in the future, long-term interest rates will be above short-term interest rates, and yield curves will typically slope upward.

How can the preferred habitat and liquidity premium theories explain the occasional appearance of inverted yield curves if the term premium is positive? It must be that at times short-term interest rates are expected to fall so much in the future that the average of the expected short-term rates is well below the current short-term rate. Even when the positive term premium is added to this average, the resulting long-term rate will still be below the current short-term interest rate.

As our discussion indicates, a particularly attractive feature of the preferred habitat and liquidity premium theories is that they tell you what the market is predicting about future short-term interest rates just by looking at the slope of the yield curve. A steeply rising yield curve, as in panel (a) of Figure 5, indicates that short-term interest rates are expected to rise in the future. A moderately steep yield curve, as in panel (b), indicates that short-term interest rates are not expected to rise or fall much in the future. A flat yield curve, as in panel (c), indicates that short-term rates are expected to fall moderately in the future. Finally, an inverted yield curve, as in panel (d), indicates that short-term interest rates are expected to fall sharply in the future.

Recent Evidence on the Term Structure

In the 1980s, researchers examining the term structure of interest rates questioned whether the slope of the yield curve provides information about movements of future short-term interest rates.[6] They found that the spread between long- and short-term interest rates does not always help predict future short-term interest rates, a finding that may stem from substantial fluctuations in the term premium for long-term bonds. More recent research using more discriminating tests now favors a different view. It shows that the term structure contains quite a bit of information for the very short run, over the next several months, and the long run, over several years, but is unreliable at predicting movements in interest rates over the intermediate term, the time in between.[7]

Summary

The preferred habitat and liquidity premium theories are the most widely accepted theories of the term structure of interest rates because they explain the major empirical facts about the term structure so well. They combine the features of both the expectations hypothesis and the segmented markets theory by asserting that a long-term interest rate will be the sum of a term (liquidity) premium and the average of the short-term interest rates that are expected to occur over the life of the bond.

The preferred habitat and liquidity premium theories explain the following facts: (1) Interest rates on bonds of different maturities tend to move together over time, (2) yield curves usually slope upward, and (3) when short-term interest rates are low, yield curves are more likely to have a steep upward slope, whereas when short-term interest rates are high, yield curves are more likely to be inverted.

The theories also help us predict the movement of short-term interest rates in the future. A steep upward slope of the yield curve means that short-term rates are expected to rise, a mild upward slope means that short-term rates are expected to remain the same, a flat slope means that short-term rates are expected

---

[6]Robert J. Shiller, John Y. Campbell, and Kermit L. Schoenholtz, "Forward Rates and Future Policy: Interpreting the Term Structure of Interest Rates," *Brookings Papers on Economic Activity* 1 (1983): 173–217; N. Gregory Mankiw and Lawrence H. Summers, "Do Long-Term Interest Rates Overreact to Short-Term Interest Rates?" *Brookings Papers on Economic Activity* 1 (1984): 243–247.

[7]Eugene Fama, "The Information in the Term Structure," *Journal of Financial Economics* 13 (1984): 509–528; Eugene Fama and Robert Bliss, "The Information in Long-Maturity Forward Rates," *American Economic Review* 77 (1987): 680–692; John Y. Campbell and Robert J. Shiller, "Cointegration and Tests of the Present Value Models," *Journal of Political Economy* 95 (1987): 1062–1088; John Y. Campbell and Robert J. Shiller, "Yield Spreads and Interest Rate Movements: A Bird's Eye View," *Review of Economic Studies* 58 (1991): 495–514.

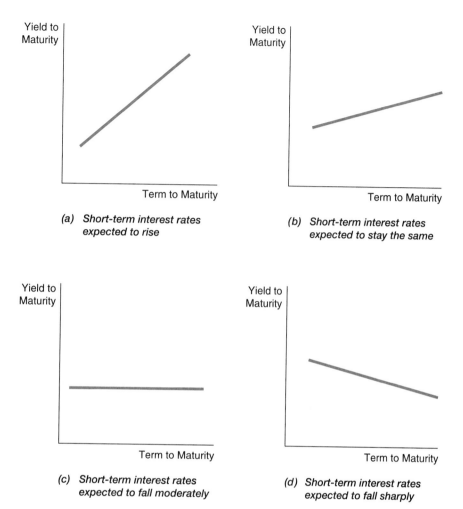

FIGURE 5   Yield Curves and the Market's Expectations of Future Short-Term Interest Rates

to fall moderately, and an inverted yield curve means that short-term rates are expected to fall sharply.

Interpreting Yield Curves, 1980–1997

Figure 6 illustrates several yield curves that have appeared for U.S. government bonds in recent years. What do these yield curves tell us about the public's expectations of future movements of short-term interest rates?

Study Guide   Try to answer the preceding question before reading further in the text. If you have trouble answering it with the preferred habitat and liquidity premium theories, first try answering it with the expectations hypothesis (which is simpler because you don't have to worry about the term premium). When you understand what the expectations of future interest rates are in this case, modify your analysis by taking the term premium into account.

The steep inverted yield curve that occurred on January 15, 1981, indicated that short-term interest rates were expected to decline sharply in the future. In order for longer-term interest rates with their positive term premium to be well below the short-term interest rate, short-term interest rates must be expected to decline so sharply that their average is far below the current short-term rate. Indeed, the public's expectations of sharply lower short-term interest rates evident in the yield curve were realized soon after January 15; by March, three-month Treasury bill rates had declined from the 16 percent level to 13 percent.

The steep upward-sloping yield curves on March 28, 1985, indicated that short-term interest rates would climb in the future. The long-term interest rate is above the short-term interest rate when short-term interest rates are expected to rise because their average plus the term premium will be above the current short-term rate. The moderately upward-sloping yield curves on May 16, 1980, and

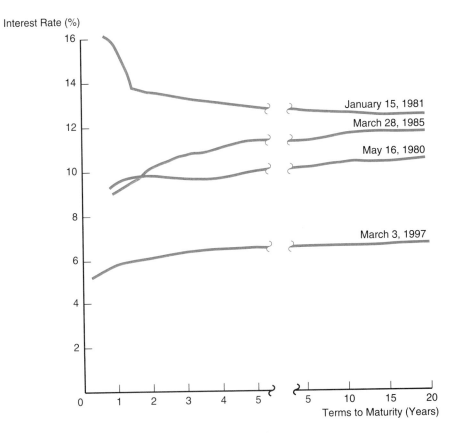

FIGURE 6 Yield Curves for U.S. Government Bonds

Sources: Federal Reserve Bank of St. Louis; *U.S. Financial Data,* various issues; *Wall Street Journal,* various dates.

March 3, 1997, indicated that short-term interest rates were expected neither to rise nor to fall in the near future. In this case, their average remains the same as the current short-term rate, and the positive term premium for longer-term bonds explains the moderate upward slope of the yield curve.

SUMMARY

1. Bonds with the same maturity will have different interest rates because of three factors: default risk, liquidity, and tax considerations. The greater a bond's default risk, the higher its interest rate relative to other bonds; the greater a bond's liquidity, the lower its interest rate; and bonds with tax-exempt status will have lower interest rates than they otherwise would. The relationship among interest rates on bonds with the same maturity that arise because of these three factors is known as the risk structure of interest rates.

2. Four theories of the term structure provide explanations of how interest rates on bonds with different terms to maturity are related. The expectations hypothesis views long-term interest rates as equaling the average of future short-term interest rates expected to occur over the life of the bond; by contrast, the segmented markets theory treats the determination of interest rates for each bond's maturity as the outcome of supply and demand in that market only. Neither of these theories by itself can explain both the fact that interest rates on bonds of different maturities move together over time and that yield curves usually slope upward.

3. The preferred habitat and liquidity premium theories combine the features of the other two theories and by so doing are able to explain the facts just mentioned. They view long-term interest rates as equaling the average of future short-term interest rates expected to occur over the life of the bond plus a term premium that reflects the supply of and demand for bonds of different maturities. These theories allow us to infer the market's expectations about the movement of future short-term interest rates from the yield curve. A steeply upward-sloping curve indicates that future short-term rates are expected to rise, a mildly upward-sloping curve indicates that short-term rates are expected to stay the same, a flat curve indicates that short-term rates are expected to decline slightly, and an inverted yield curve indicates that a substantial decline in short-term rates is expected in the future.

KEY TERMS

default-free bonds, p. 144

default risk, p. 144

expectations hypothesis, p. 153

inverted yield curve, p. 152

junk bonds, p. 146

liquidity premium theory,
   p. 158

preferred habitat theory, p. 158

risk premium, p. 144

risk structure of interest rates,
   p. 143

segmented markets theory,
   p. 157

term structure of interest rates,
   p. 143

yield curve, p. 151

QUESTIONS AND PROBLEMS

1. Which should have the higher risk premium on its interest rates, a corporate bond with a Moody's Baa rating or a corporate bond with a C rating? Why?

*2. Why do U.S. Treasury bills have lower interest rates than large-denomination negotiable bank CDs?

3. Risk premiums on corporate bonds are usually anticyclical; that is, they decrease during business cycle expansions and increase during recessions. Why is this so?

*4. "If bonds of different maturities are close substitutes, their interest rates are more likely to move together." Is this statement true, false, or uncertain? Explain your answer.

5. If yield curves, on average, were flat, what would this say about the term premiums in the term structure? Would you be more or less willing to accept the expectations hypothesis?

*6. Assuming that the expectations hypothesis is the correct theory of the term structure, calculate the interest rates in the term structure for maturities of one to five years, and plot the resulting yield curves for the following series of one-year interest rates over the next five years:
   (a) 5%, 7%, 7%, 7%, 7%
   (b) 5%, 4%, 4%, 4%, 4%
   How would your yield curves change if people preferred shorter-term bonds over longer-term bonds?

7. Assuming that the expectations hypothesis is the correct theory of the term structure, calculate the interest rates in the term structure for maturities of one to five years, and plot the resulting yield curves for the following path of one-year interest rates over the next five years:
   (a) 5%, 6%, 7%, 6%, 5%
   (b) 5%, 4%, 3%, 4%, 5%
   How would your yield curves change if people preferred shorter-term bonds over longer-term bonds?

*8. If a yield curve looks like the one shown in (a), what is the market predicting about the movement of future short-term interest rates? What might the yield curve indicate about the market's predictions about the inflation rate in the future?

9. If a yield curve looks like the one shown in (b), what is the market predicting about the movement of future short-term interest rates? What might the

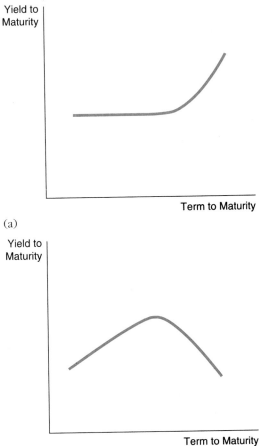

(a)

(b)

yield curve indicate about the market's predictions about the inflation rate in the future?

*10. What effect would reducing income tax rates have on the interest rates of municipal bonds? Would interest rates of Treasury securities be affected, and if so, how?

USING ECONOMIC ANALYSIS TO PREDICT THE FUTURE

11. Predict what will happen to interest rates on a corporation's bonds if the federal government guarantees today that it will pay creditors if the corporation goes bankrupt in the future. What will happen to the interest rates on Treasury securities?

*12. Predict what would happen to the risk premiums on corporate bonds if brokerage commissions were lowered in the corporate bond market.

13. If the income tax exemption on municipal bonds were abolished, what would happen to the interest rates on these bonds? What effect would it have on interest rates on U.S. Treasury securities?

*14. If the yield curve suddenly becomes steeper, how would you revise your predictions of interest rates in the future?

15. If expectations of future short-term interest rates suddenly fall, what would happen to the slope of the yield curve?

Chapter 8

THE FOREIGN EXCHANGE MARKET

PREVIEW More foreigners are traveling to the United States now than in the early 1980s. The increase in foreigners traveling to the United States did not occur because foreigners suddenly increased their taste for adventure. The increase occurred because U.S. dollars had become cheaper in terms of foreign currencies—a change that made it less expensive for foreigners to travel here.

The price of one currency in terms of another (say francs per dollar) is called the **exchange rate.** It affects the economy and our daily lives because when the U.S. dollar becomes less valuable relative to foreign currencies, foreign goods and travel become more expensive. When the U.S. dollar rises in value, foreign goods and travel become cheaper. We begin our study of international finance by examining the **foreign exchange market,** the financial market where exchange rates are determined.

In the 1980s, exchange rates were highly volatile. As shown in Figure 1, from the beginning of 1980 to early 1985, the dollar strengthened, and its value relative to many other currencies climbed sharply—100 percent against the pound sterling, 90 percent against the German mark, and 75 percent against the Swiss franc. From early 1985 to the end of 1996, the dollar weakened and fell in value relative to other currencies—over 50 percent against the Japanese yen, 50 percent against the German mark and the Swiss franc, and 15 percent against the pound sterling. What factors explain the former strength and later weakness of the dollar that has caused foreign goods to be more expensive since 1985 and has made overseas travel less of a bargain? Why are exchange rates so volatile from day to day?

To answer these questions, we develop a modern view of exchange rate determination that explains recent behavior in the foreign exchange market.

FOREIGN EXCHANGE MARKET

Most countries of the world have their own currencies: The United States has its dollar; France, its franc; Brazil, its real; and India, its rupee. Trade between coun-

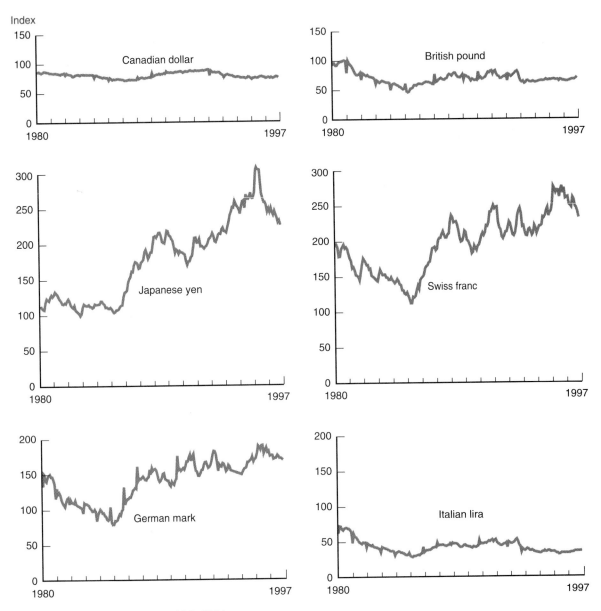

FIGURE 1 Exchange Rates, 1980–1996

Dollar prices of selected foreign currencies (monthly averages; index: March 1973 = 100). Note that a decline in these plots means a strengthening of the dollar, and an increase indicates a weakening of the dollar.

Sources: International Financial Statistics; Citibase databank.

tries involves the mutual exchange of different currencies (or, more usually, bank deposits denominated in different currencies). When an American firm buys foreign goods, services, or financial assets, for example, U.S. dollars (typically, bank deposits denominated in U.S. dollars) must be exchanged for foreign currency (bank deposits denominated in the foreign currency).

The trading of currency and bank deposits denominated in particular currencies takes place in the foreign exchange market. The volume of these transactions worldwide averages over $1 trillion daily. Transactions conducted in the foreign exchange market determine the rates at which currencies are exchanged, which in turn determine the cost of purchasing foreign goods and financial assets.

What Are Foreign Exchange Rates?

There are two kinds of exchange rate transactions. The predominant ones, called **spot transactions,** involve the immediate (two-day) exchange of bank deposits. **Forward transactions** involve the exchange of bank deposits at some specified future date. The **spot exchange rate** is the exchange rate for the spot transaction, and the **forward exchange rate** is the exchange rate for the forward transaction.

When a currency increases in value, it experiences **appreciation;** when it falls in value and is worth fewer U.S. dollars, it undergoes **depreciation.** At the beginning of 1980, for example, the French franc was valued at 24 cents, and as indicated in the "Following the Financial News" box, on October 8, 1996, it was valued at 19.36 cents. The franc *depreciated* by 19 percent: $(19.36 - 24)/24 = -0.19 = -19\%$. Conversely, we could say that the U.S. dollar, which went from a value of 4.23 francs per dollar in 1980 to a value of 5.17 francs per dollar in October 1996, appreciated by 22 percent: $(5.17 - 4.23)/4.23 = 0.22 = 22\%$.

Why Are Exchange Rates Important?

Exchange rates are important because they affect the relative price of domestic and foreign goods. The dollar price of French goods to an American is determined by the interaction of two factors: the price of French goods in francs and the franc/dollar exchange rate.

Suppose that Wanda the Winetaster, an American, decides to buy a bottle of 1961 (a very good year) Château Lafite Rothschild to complete her wine cellar. If the price of the wine in France is 2000 francs and the exchange rate is $0.1936 to the franc, the wine will cost Wanda $387 (= 2000 francs × $0.1936/franc). Now suppose that Wanda delays her purchase by two months, at which time the French franc has appreciated to $0.20 per franc. If the domestic price of the bottle of Lafite Rothschild remains 2000 francs, its dollar cost will have risen from $387 to $400.

The same currency appreciation, however, makes the price of foreign goods in that country less expensive. At an exchange rate of $0.1936 per franc, a Compaq computer priced at $2000 costs Claude the Programmer 10,331 francs; if the exchange rate increases to $0.20 per franc, the computer will cost only 10,000 francs.

A depreciation of the franc lowers the cost of French goods in America but raises the cost of American goods in France. If the franc drops in value to $0.10, Wanda's bottle of Lafite Rothschild will cost her only $200 instead of $387, and the Compaq computer will cost Claude 20,000 francs rather than 10,331.

Following the Financial News

Foreign Exchange Rates

Foreign exchange rates are published daily and appear in the "Currency Trading" column of the *Wall Street Journal*. The entries from one such column, shown here, are explained in the text.

The first entry for the French franc lists the exchange rate for the spot transaction (the spot exchange rate) on October 8, 1996, and is quoted in two ways: $0.1936 per franc and 5.1655 francs per dollar. Americans generally regard the exchange rate with France as $0.1936 per franc, while the French think of it as 5.1655 francs per dollar. The three entries immediately below the spot exchange rates give the rates for forward transactions (the forward exchange rates) that will take place 30, 90, and 180 days in the future. For example, Tuesday's 180-day forward rate for the French franc is $0.1956 per franc or, equivalently, 5.1131 francs per dollar.

CURRENCY TRADING

EXCHANGE RATES

Tuesday, October 8, 1996

The New York foreign exchange selling rates below apply to trading among banks in amounts of $1 million and more, as quoted at 3 p.m. Eastern time by Dow Jones Telerate Inc. and other sources. Retail transactions provide fewer units of foreign currency per dollar.

Country	U.S. $ equiv. Tue	U.S. $ equiv. Mon	Currency Per U.S. $ Tue	Currency Per U.S. $ Mon
Argentina (Peso)	1.0012	1.0012	.9988	.9988
Australia (Dollar)	.7911	.7878	1.2641	1.2694
Austria (Schilling)	.09319	.09289	10.731	10.766
Bahrain (Dinar)	2.6490	2.6490	.3775	.3775
Belgium (Franc)	.03176	.03173	31.485	31.520
Brazil (Real)	.9737	.9737	1.0270	1.0270
Britain (Pound)	1.5625	1.5630	.6400	.6398
30-Day Forward . . .	1.5618	1.5623	.6403	.6401
90-Day Forward . . .	1.5611	1.5615	.6406	.6404
180-Day Forward . . .	1.5601	1.5604	.6410	.6409
Canada (Dollar)	.7386	.7390	1.3539	1.3532
30-Day Forward . . .	.7398	.7401	1.3518	1.3512
90-Day Forward . . .	.7420	.7424	1.3477	1.3470
180-Day Forward . . .	.7453	.7457	1.3418	1.3410
Chile (Peso)	.002491	.002419	413.35	413.45
China (Renminbi)	.1200	.1200	8.3315	8.3307
Colombia (Peso)	.0009847	.0009847	1015.50	1015.50
Czech. Rep. (Koruna) . .			. . . . .	. . . . .
Commercial rate . . .	.03679	.03655	27.180	27.360
Denmark (Krone)	.1708	.1706	5.8545	5.8625
Ecuador (Sucre)			. . . .	. . . .
Floating rate	.0003051	.0003047	3278.00	3282.00
Finland (Markka)	.2192	.2187	4.5619	4.5723
France (Franc)	.1936	.1933	5.1655	5.1730
30-Day Forward . . .	.1939	.1937	5.1566	5.1638
90-Day Forward . . .	.1946	.1943	5.1390	5.1467
180-Day Forward . . .	.1956	.1952	5.1131	5.1217
Germany (Mark)	.6537	.6531	1.5297	1.5311
30-Day Forward . . .	.6550	.6545	1.5267	1.5279
90-Day Forward . . .	.6577	.6570	1.5205	1.5220
180-Day Forward . . .	.6617	.6609	1.5113	1.5130
Greece (Drachma)	.004167	.004154	239.98	240.71
Hong Kong (Dollar) . . .	.1293	.1293	7.7320	7.7323
Hungary (Forint)	.006310	.006296	158.47	158.84
India (Rupee)	.02801	.02807	35.705	35.630
Indonesia (Rupiah) . . .	.0004309	.0004306	2320.75	2322.25
Ireland (Punt)	1.6026	1.6018	.6240	.6243
Israel (Shekel)	.3135	.3135	3.1903	3.1903
Italy (Lira)	.0006585	.0006588	1518.50	1518.00
Japan (Yen)	.008953	.008993	111.69	111.20
30-Day Forward . . .	.008992	.009034	111.21	110.69
90-Day Forward . . .	.009071	.009110	110.25	109.78
180-Day Forward . . .	.009183	.009225	108.90	108.40
Jordan (Dinar)	1.4065	1.4065	.7110	.7110
Kuwait (Dinar)	3.3344	3.3434	.2999	.2991
Lebanon (Pound)	.0006420	.0006420	1557.75	1557.75
Malaysia (Ringgit)	.3996	.3998	2.5027	2.5010
Malta (Lira)	2.7739	2.7701	.3605	.3610
Mexico (Peso)			. . . . .	. . . . .
Floating rate	.1326	.1329	7.5440	7.5260
Netherland (Guilder) . .	.5826	.5822	1.7163	1.7177
New Zealand (Dollar) .	.6916	.6912	1.4459	1.4468
Norway (Krone)	.1539	.1537	6.4970	6.5065
Pakistan (Rupee)	.02744	.02735	36.440	36.560
Peru (new Sol)	.3988	.3979	2.5074	2.5134
Philippines (Peso)	.03807	.03807	26.267	26.269
Poland (Zloty)	.3563	.3554	2.8070	2.8135
Portugal (Escudo)	.006461	.006470	154.78	154.56
Russia (Ruble) (a)	.0001846	.0001846	5417.00	5418.00
Saudia Arabia (Riyal) . .	.2666	.2666	3.7505	3.7505
Singapore (Dollar)	.7087	.7084	1.4111	1.4116
Slovak Rep. (Koruna) . .	.03263	.03263	30.650	30.650
South Africa (Rand) . . .	.2205	.2205	4.5360	4.5355
South Korea (Won) . . .	.001206	.001208	828.85	827.65
Spain (Peseta)	.007772	.007764	128.67	128.80
Sweden (Krona)	.1520	.1512	6.5808	6.6133
Switzerland (Franc) . .	.7974	.7971	1.2540	1.2545
30-Day Forward . . .	.8002	.8000	1.2497	1.2500
90-Day Forward . . .	.8054	.8051	1.2416	1.2421
180-Day Forward . . .	.8134	.8131	1.2294	1.2298
Taiwan (Dollar)	.03637	.03638	27.495	27.485
Thailand (Baht)	.03932	.03929	25.434	25.453
Turkey (Lira)	.00001079	.00001079	92650.00	92646.00
United Arab (Dirham) . .	.2723	.2723	3.6720	3.6720
Uruguay (New Peso) .			. . . . .	. . . . .
Financial	.1190	.1198	8.4000	8.3500
Venezuela (Bolivar) b .	.002151	.002148	465.00	465.62
Brady Rate	.002148	.002148	465.50	465.50
SDR	1.4409	1.4385	.6940	.6952
ECU	1.2531	1.2494	. . . .	. . . .

Special Drawing Rights (SDR) are based on exchange rates for the U.S., German, British, French, and Japanese currencies.
Source: International Monetary Fund.
European Currency Unit (ECU) is based on a basket of community currencies.
a-fixing, Moscow Interbank Currency Exchange.
b-Changed to market rate effective Apr. 22.

Source: Wall Street Journal, October 9, 1996, p. C15.

Such reasoning leads to the following conclusion: ***When a country's currency appreciates (rises in value relative to other currencies), the country's goods abroad become more expensive and foreign goods in that country become cheaper (holding domestic prices constant in the two countries). Conversely, when a country's currency depreciates, its goods abroad become cheaper and foreign goods in that country become more expensive.***

Appreciation of a currency can make it harder for domestic manufacturers to sell their goods abroad and can increase competition at home from foreign goods because they cost less. From 1980 to early 1985, the appreciating dollar hurt U.S. industries. For instance, the U.S. steel industry was hurt not just because sales abroad of the more expensive American steel declined but also because sales of relatively cheap foreign steel in the United States increased. Although appreciation of the U.S. dollar hurt some domestic businesses, American consumers benefited because foreign goods were less expensive. Japanese videocassette recorders and cameras and the cost of vacationing in Europe fell in price as a result of the strong dollar.

How Is Foreign Exchange Traded?

You cannot go to a centralized location to watch exchange rates being determined; currencies are not traded on exchanges such as the New York Stock Exchange. Instead, the foreign exchange market is organized as an over-the-counter market in which several hundred dealers (mostly banks) stand ready to buy and sell deposits denominated in foreign currencies. Because these dealers are in constant telephone and computer contact, the market is very competitive; in effect, it functions no differently from a centralized market.

An important point to note is that while banks, companies, and governments talk about buying and selling currencies in foreign exchange markets, they do not take a fistful of dollar bills and sell them for British pound notes. Rather, most trades involve the buying and selling of bank deposits denominated in different currencies. So when we say that a bank is buying dollars in the foreign exchange market, what we actually mean is that the bank is buying *deposits denominated in dollars*.

Trades in the foreign exchange market consist of transactions in excess of $1 million. The market that determines the exchange rates in the "Following the Financial News" box is not where one would buy foreign currency for a trip abroad. Instead, we buy foreign currency in the retail market from dealers such as American Express or from banks. Because retail prices are higher than wholesale, when we buy foreign exchange, we obtain fewer units of foreign currency per dollar than exchange rates in the box indicate.

EXCHANGE RATES IN THE LONG RUN

Like the price of any good or asset in a free market, exchange rates are determined by the interaction of supply and demand. To simplify our analysis of exchange rates in a free market, we divide it into two parts. First, we examine how exchange rates are determined in the long run; then we use our knowledge of the long-run determinants of the exchange rate to help us understand how they are determined in the short run.

Law of One Price

The starting point for understanding how exchange rates are determined is a simple idea called the **law of one price:** If two countries produce an identical good, the price of the good should be the same throughout the world no matter which country produces it. Suppose that American steel costs $100 per ton and identical Japanese steel costs 10,000 yen per ton. The law of one price suggests that the exchange rate between the yen and the dollar must be 100 yen per dollar ($0.01 per yen) in order for one ton of American steel to sell for 10,000 yen in Japan (the price of Japanese steel) and one ton of Japanese steel to sell for $100 in the United States (the price of U.S. steel). If the exchange rate were 200 yen to the dollar, Japanese steel would sell for $50 per ton in the United States or half the price of American steel, and American steel would sell for 20,000 yen per ton in Japan, twice the price of Japanese steel. Because American steel would be more expensive than Japanese steel in both countries and is identical to Japanese steel, the demand for American steel would go to zero. Given a fixed dollar price for American steel, the resulting excess supply of American steel will be eliminated only if the exchange rate falls to 100 yen per dollar, making the price of American steel and Japanese steel the same in both countries.

Theory of Purchasing Power Parity

One of the most prominent theories of how exchange rates are determined is the **theory of purchasing power parity (PPP).** It states that exchange rates between any two currencies will adjust to reflect changes in the price levels of the two countries. The theory of PPP is simply an application of the law of one price to national price levels rather than to individual prices. Suppose that the yen price of Japanese steel rises 10 percent (to 11,000 yen) relative to the dollar price of American steel (unchanged at $100). For the law of one price to hold, the exchange rate must rise to 110 yen to the dollar, a 10 percent appreciation of the dollar. Applying the law of one price to the price levels in the two countries produces the theory of purchasing power parity, which maintains that if the Japanese price level rises 10 percent relative to the U.S. price level, the dollar will appreciate by 10 percent.

As our U.S./Japanese example demonstrates, the theory of PPP suggests that if one country's price level rises relative to another's, its currency should depreciate (the other country's currency should appreciate). As you can see in Figure 2, this prediction is borne out in the long run. From 1973 to the end of 1996, the British price level rose 80 percent relative to the U.S. price level, and as the theory of PPP predicts, the dollar appreciated against sterling, though by 35 percent, an amount smaller than the 80 percent increase predicted by PPP.

Yet, as the same figure indicates, PPP theory often has little predictive power in the short run. From early 1985 to the end of 1987, for example, the British price level rose relative to that of the United States. Instead of appreciating, as PPP the-

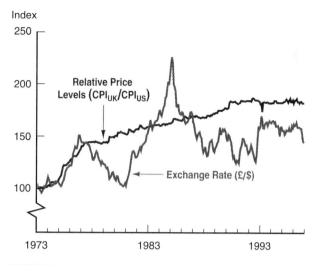

FIGURE 2 Purchasing Power Parity, United States/United Kingdom, 1973–1996 (Index: March 1973 = 100.)

Source: International Financial Statistics.

ory predicts, the U.S. dollar actually depreciated by 40 percent. So even though PPP theory provides some guidance to the long-run movement of exchange rates, it is not perfect and in the short run is a particularly poor predictor. What explains PPP theory's failure to predict well?

Why the Theory of Purchasing Power Parity Cannot Fully Explain Exchange Rates

The PPP conclusion that exchange rates are determined solely by changes in relative price levels rests on the assumption that all goods are identical in both countries. When this assumption is true, the law of one price states that the relative prices of all these goods (that is, the relative price level between the two countries) will determine the exchange rate. The assumption that goods are identical may not be too unreasonable for American and Japanese steel, but is it a reasonable assumption for American and Japanese cars? Is a Toyota the equivalent of a Chevrolet?

Because Toyotas and Chevys are obviously not identical, their prices do not have to be equal. Toyotas can be more expensive relative to Chevys and both Americans and Japanese will still purchase Toyotas. Because the law of one price does not hold for all goods, a rise in the price of Toyotas relative to Chevys will not necessarily mean that the yen must depreciate by the amount of the relative price increase of Toyotas over Chevys.

PPP theory furthermore does not take into account that many goods and services (whose prices are included in a measure of a country's price level) are not traded across borders. Housing, land, and services such as restaurant meals, haircuts, and golf lessons are not traded goods. So even though the prices of these items might rise and lead to a higher price level relative to another country's, there would be little direct effect on the exchange rate.

Factors That Affect Exchange Rates in the Long Run

Our analysis indicates that relative price levels and additional factors affect the exchange rate. In the long run, there are four major ones: relative price levels, tariffs and quotas, preferences for domestic versus foreign goods, and productivity. We examine how each of these factors affects the exchange rate while holding the others constant.

The basic reasoning proceeds along the following lines: Anything that increases the demand for domestic goods relative to foreign goods tends to appreciate the domestic currency because domestic goods will continue to sell well even when the value of the domestic currency is higher. Similarly, anything that increases the demand for foreign goods relative to domestic goods tends to depreciate the domestic currency because domestic goods will continue to sell well only if the value of the domestic currency is lower.

RELATIVE PRICE LEVELS In line with PPP theory, when prices of American goods rise (holding prices of foreign goods constant), the demand for American goods falls and the dollar tends to depreciate so that American goods can still sell well. By contrast, if prices of Japanese goods rise so that the relative prices of American goods fall, the demand for American goods increases, and the dollar tends to appreciate because American goods will continue to sell well even with a higher value of the domestic currency. ***In the long run, a rise in a country's price level (relative to the foreign price level) causes its currency to depreciate, and a fall in the country's relative price level causes its currency to appreciate.***

TARIFFS AND QUOTAS Barriers to free trade such as **tariffs** (taxes on imported goods) and **quotas** (restrictions on the quantity of foreign goods that can be imported) can affect the exchange rate. Suppose that the United States imposes a tariff or a quota on Japanese steel. These trade barriers increase the demand for American steel, and the dollar tends to appreciate because American steel will still sell well even with a higher value of the dollar. ***Tariffs and quotas cause a country's currency to appreciate in the long run.***

PREFERENCES FOR DOMESTIC VERSUS FOREIGN GOODS If the Japanese develop an appetite for American goods—say, for Florida oranges and American movies—the increased demand for American goods (exports) tends to appreciate the dollar because the American goods will continue to sell well even at a higher value for the dollar. Likewise, if Americans decide that they prefer Japanese cars to American cars, the increased demand for Japanese goods (imports) tends to depreciate the dollar. ***Increased demand for a country's exports causes its currency to appreciate in the long run; conversely, increased demand for imports causes the domestic currency to depreciate.***

PRODUCTIVITY If one country becomes more productive than other countries, businesses in that country can lower the prices of domestic goods relative to foreign goods and still earn a profit. As a result, the demand for domestic goods rises, and the domestic currency tends to appreciate because domestic goods will continue to sell well at a higher value for the currency. If, however, its productivity lags behind that of other countries, its goods become relatively more expensive,

—————— S U M M A R Y ——————

TABLE 1   Factors That Affect Exchange Rates in the Long Run

Factor	Change in Factor	Response of the Exchange Rate, E^*
Domestic price level†	↑	↓
Tariffs and quotas†	↑	↑
Import demand	↑	↓
Export demand	↑	↑
Productivity†	↑	↑

*Units of foreign currency per dollar: ↑ indicates currency appreciation; ↓, depreciation.

†Relative to other countries.

Note: Only increase (↑) in the factors are shown; the effects of decreases in the variables on the exchange rate are the opposite of those indicated in the "Response" column.

and the currency tends to depreciate. ***In the long run, as a country becomes more productive relative to other countries, its currency appreciates.***[1]

Study Guide   The trick to figuring out what long-run effect a factor has on the exchange rate is to remember the following: **If a factor increases the demand for domestic goods relative to foreign goods, the domestic currency will appreciate, and if a factor decreases the relative demand for domestic goods, the domestic currency will depreciate.** See how this works by explaining what happens to the exchange rate when any of the factors in Table 1 declines rather than increases.

Our long-run theory of exchange rate behavior is summarized in Table 1. We use the convention that the exchange rate E is quoted so that an appreciation of the currency corresponds to a rise in the exchange rate. In the case of the United States, this means that we are quoting the exchange rate as units of foreign currency per dollar (say, yen per dollar).[2]

---

[1]A country might be so small that a change in productivity or the preferences for domestic or foreign goods would have no effect on prices of these goods relative to foreign goods. In this case, changes in productivity or changes in preferences for domestic or foreign goods affect the country's income but will not necessarily affect the value of the currency. In our analysis, we are assuming that these factors can affect relative prices and consequently the exchange rate.

[2]In professional writing, many economists quote exchange rates as units of domestic currency per foreign currency so that an appreciation of the domestic currency is portrayed as a fall in the exchange rate. The opposite convention is used in the text here because it is more intuitive to think of an appreciation of the domestic currency as a rise in the exchange rate.

EXCHANGE RATES IN THE SHORT RUN

We have developed a theory of the long-run behavior of exchange rates. However, if we are to understand why exchange rates exhibit such large changes (sometimes several percent) from day to day, we must develop a theory of how current exchange rates (spot exchange rates) are determined in the short run.

The key to understanding the short-run behavior of exchange rates is to recognize that an exchange rate is the price of domestic bank deposits (those denominated in the domestic currency) in terms of foreign bank deposits (those denominated in the foreign currency). Because the exchange rate is the price of one asset in terms of another, the natural way to investigate the short-run determination of exchange rates is through an asset market approach that relies heavily on the theory of portfolio choice developed in Chapter 5. As you will see, however, the long-run determinants of the exchange rate we have just outlined also play an important role in the short-run asset market approach.[3]

Earlier approaches to exchange rate determination emphasized the role of import and export demand. The more modern asset market approach used here does not emphasize the flows of purchases of exports and imports over short periods because these transactions are quite small relative to the amount of domestic and foreign bank deposits at any given time. For example, foreign exchange transactions in the United States each year are well over 25 times greater than the amount of U.S. exports and imports. Thus over short periods such as a year, decisions to hold domestic or foreign assets play a much greater role in exchange rate determination than the demand for exports and imports does.

Comparing Expected Returns on Domestic and Foreign Deposits

In this analysis, we treat the United States as the home country, so domestic bank deposits are denominated in dollars. For simplicity, we use francs to stand for any foreign country's currency, so foreign bank deposits are denominated in francs. The theory of portfolio choice suggests that the most important factor affecting the demand for domestic (dollar) deposits and foreign (franc) deposits is the expected return on these assets relative to each other. When Americans or foreigners expect the return on dollar deposits to be high relative to the return on foreign deposits, there is a higher demand for dollar deposits and a correspondingly lower demand for franc deposits. To understand how the demands for dollar and foreign deposits change, we need to compare the expected returns on dollar deposits and foreign deposits.

To illustrate further, suppose that dollar deposits have an interest rate (expected return payable in dollars) of i^D, and foreign bank deposits have an interest rate (expected return payable in the foreign currency, francs) of i^F. To compare the expected returns on dollar deposits and foreign deposits, investors must convert the returns into the currency unit they use.

[3]For a further description of the modern asset market approach to exchange rate determination that we use here, see Paul Krugman and Maurice Obstfeld, *International Economics,* 4th ed. (Reading, Mass.: Addison Wesley Longman, 1997).

First let us examine how François the Foreigner compares the returns on dollar deposits and foreign deposits denominated in his currency, the franc. When he considers the expected return on dollar deposits in terms of francs, he recognizes that it does not equal i^D; instead, the expected return must be adjusted for any expected appreciation or depreciation of the dollar. If the dollar were expected to appreciate by 7 percent, for example, the expected return on dollar deposits in terms of francs would be 7 percent higher because the dollar has become worth 7 percent more in terms of francs. Thus if the interest rate on dollar deposits is 10 percent, with an expected appreciation of the dollar of 7 percent, the expected return on dollar deposits in terms of francs is 17 percent: the 10 percent interest rate plus the 7 percent expected appreciation of the dollar. Conversely, if the dollar were expected to depreciate by 7 percent over the year, the expected return on dollar deposits in terms of francs would be only 3 percent: the 10 percent interest rate minus the 7 percent expected depreciation of the dollar.

Writing the currency exchange rate (the spot exchange rate) as E_t and the expected exchange rate for the next period as E^e_{t+1}, we can write the expected rate of appreciation of the dollar as $(E^e_{t+1} - E_t)/E_t$. Our reasoning indicates that the expected return on dollar deposits RET^D in terms of foreign currency can be written as the sum of the interest rate on dollar deposits plus the expected appreciation of the dollar[4]:

$$RET^D \text{ in terms of francs} = i^D + \frac{E^e_{t+1} - E_t}{E_t}$$

However, François's expected return on foreign deposits RET^F in terms of francs is just i^F. Thus in terms of francs, the relative expected return on dollar deposits (that is, the difference between the expected return on dollar deposits and franc deposits) is calculated by subtracting i^F from the expression just given to yield

$$\text{Relative } RET^D = i^D - i^F + \frac{E^e_{t+1} - E_t}{E_t} \qquad (1)$$

As the relative expected return on dollar deposits increases, foreigners will want to hold more dollar deposits and fewer foreign deposits.

---

[4]This expression is actually an approximation of the expected return in terms of francs, which can be more precisely calculated by thinking how a foreigner invests in the dollar deposit. Suppose that François decides to put one franc into dollar deposits. First he buys $1/E_t$ of U.S. dollar deposits (recall that E_t, the exchange rate between dollar and franc deposits, is quoted in francs per dollar), and at the end of the period he is paid $(1 + i^D)(1/E_t)$ in dollars. To convert this amount into the number of francs he expects to receive at the end of the period, he multiplies this quantity by E^e_{t+1}. François's expected return on his initial investment of one franc can thus be written as $(1 + i^D)(E^e_{t+1}/E_t)$ minus his initial investment of one franc:

$$(1 + i^D)\left(\frac{E^e_{t+1}}{E_t}\right) - 1$$

which can be rewritten as

$$i^D\left(\frac{E^e_{t+1}}{E_t}\right) + \frac{E^e_{t+1} - E_t}{E_t}$$

which is approximately equal to the expression in the text because E^e_{t+1}/E_t is typically close to 1.

Next let us look at the decision to hold dollar deposits versus franc deposits from Al the American's point of view. Following the same reasoning we used to evaluate the decision for François, we know that the expected return on foreign deposits RET^F in terms of dollars is the interest rate on foreign deposits i^F plus the expected appreciation of the foreign currency, equal to minus the expected appreciation of the dollar, $-(E_{t+1}^e - E_t)/E_t$, that is,

$$RET^F \text{ in terms of dollars} = i^F - \frac{E_{t+1}^e - E_t}{E_t}$$

If the interest rate on franc deposits is 5 percent, for example, and the dollar is expected to appreciate by 4 percent, then the expected return on franc deposits in terms of dollars is 1 percent. Al earns the 5 percent interest rate, but he expects to lose 4 percent because he expects the franc to be worth 4 percent less in terms of dollars as a result of the dollar's appreciation.

Al's expected return on the dollar deposits RET^D in terms of dollars is just i^D. Hence in terms of dollars, the relative expected return on dollar deposits is calculated by subtracting the expression just given from i^D to obtain

$$\text{Relative } RET^D = i^D - \left(i^F - \frac{E_{t+1}^e - E_t}{E_t} \right) = i^D - i^F + \frac{E_{t+1}^e - E_t}{E_t}$$

This equation is the same as the one describing François's relative expected return on dollar deposits (calculated in terms of francs). The key point here is that the relative expected return on dollar deposits is the same whether it is calculated by François in terms of francs or by Al in terms of dollars. Thus as the relative expected return on dollar deposits increases, both foreigners and domestic residents respond in exactly the same way—both will want to hold more dollar deposits and fewer foreign deposits.

Interest Parity Condition

We currently live in a world in which there is **capital mobility:** Foreigners can easily purchase American assets such as dollar deposits, and Americans can easily purchase foreign assets such as franc deposits. Because foreign bank deposits and American bank deposits have similar risk and liquidity and because there are few impediments to capital mobility, it is reasonable to assume that the deposits are perfect substitutes (that is, equally desirable). When capital is mobile and when bank deposits are perfect substitutes, if the expected return on dollar deposits is above that on foreign deposits, both foreigners and Americans will want to hold only dollar deposits and will be unwilling to hold foreign deposits. Conversely, if the expected return on foreign deposits is higher than on dollar deposits, both foreigners and Americans will not want to hold any dollar deposits and will want to hold only foreign deposits. For existing supplies of both dollar deposits and foreign deposits to be held, it must therefore be true that there is no difference in their expected returns; that is, the relative expected return in Equation 1 must equal zero. This condition can be rewritten as

$$i^D = i^F - \frac{E_{t+1}^e - E_t}{E_t} \tag{2}$$

This equation is called the **interest parity condition,** and it states that the domestic interest rate equals the foreign interest rate minus the expected appreciation of the domestic currency. Equivalently, this condition can be stated in a more intuitive way: The domestic interest rate equals the foreign interest rate plus the expected appreciation of the foreign currency. If the domestic interest rate is above the foreign interest rate, this means that there is a positive expected appreciation of the foreign currency, which compensates for the lower foreign interest rate. A domestic interest rate of 15 percent versus a foreign interest rate of 10 percent means that the expected appreciation of the foreign currency must be 5 percent (or, equivalently, that the expected depreciation of the dollar must be 5 percent).

There are several ways to look at the interest parity condition. First, we should recognize that interest parity means simply that the expected returns are the same on both dollar deposits and foreign deposits. To see this, note that the left side of the interest parity condition (Equation 2) is the expected return on dollar deposits, while the right side is the expected return on foreign deposits, both calculated in terms of a single currency, the U.S. dollar. Given our assumption that domestic and foreign bank deposits are perfect substitutes (equally desirable), the interest parity condition is an equilibrium condition for the foreign exchange market. Only when the exchange rate is such that expected returns on domestic and foreign deposits are equal—that is, when interest parity holds—will the outstanding domestic and foreign deposits be willingly held.

Equilibrium in the Foreign Exchange Market

To see how the interest parity equilibrium condition works in determining the exchange rate, our first step is to examine how the expected returns on franc and dollar deposits change as the current exchange rate changes.

EXPECTED RETURN ON FRANC DEPOSITS   As we demonstrated earlier, the expected return in terms of dollars on foreign deposits RET^F is the foreign interest rate minus the expected appreciation of the domestic currency: $i^F - (E^e_{t+1} - E_t)/E_t$. Suppose that the foreign interest rate i^F is 10 percent and that the expected exchange rate next period E^e_{t+1} is 10 francs per dollar. When the current exchange rate E_t is 9.5 francs per dollar, the expected appreciation of the dollar is $(10.0 - 9.5)/9.5 = 0.052 = 5.2\%$, so the expected return on franc deposits RET^F in terms of dollars is 4.8 percent (equal to the 10 percent foreign interest rate minus the 5.2 percent dollar appreciation). This expected return when $E_t = 9.5$ francs per dollar is plotted as point A in Figure 3. At a higher current exchange rate of $E_t = 10$ francs per dollar, the expected appreciation of the dollar is zero because E^e_{t+1} also equals 10 francs per dollar. Hence RET^F, the expected dollar return on franc deposits, is now just $i^F = 10$ percent. This expected return on franc deposits when $E_t = 10$ francs per dollar is plotted as point B. At an even higher exchange rate of $E_t = 10.5$ francs per dollar, the expected change in the value of the dollar is now -4.8% [$=(10.0 - 10.5)/10.5 = -0.048$], so the expected dollar return on foreign deposits RET^F has now risen to 14.8% [$= 10\% - (-4.8\%)$]. This combination of exchange rate and expected return on franc deposits is plotted as point C.

The curve connecting these points is the schedule for the expected return on franc deposits in Figure 3, labeled RET^F, and as you can see, it slopes upward; that is, as the exchange rate E_t rises, the expected return on franc deposits rises.

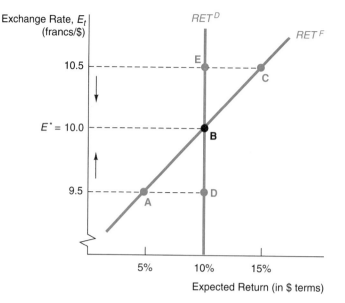

FIGURE 3   Equilibrium in the Foreign Exchange Market
Equilibrium in the foreign exchange market occurs at the intersection of the schedules for the expected return on franc deposits **RET^F** and the expected return on dollar deposits **RET^D** at point B. The equilibrium exchange rate is **E*** = 10 francs per dollar.

The intuition for this upward slope is that because the expected next-period exchange rate is held constant as the current exchange rate rises, there is less expected appreciation of the dollar. Hence a higher current exchange rate means a greater expected appreciation of the foreign currency in the future, which increases the expected return on foreign deposits in terms of dollars.

EXPECTED RETURN ON DOLLAR DEPOSITS The expected return on dollar deposits in terms of dollars RET^D is always the interest rate on dollar deposits i^D no matter what the exchange rate is. Suppose that the interest rate on dollar deposits is 10 percent. The expected return on dollar deposits, whether at an exchange rate of 9.5, 10.0, or 10.5 francs per dollar, is always 10 percent (points D, B, and E). The line connecting these points is the schedule for the expected return on dollar deposits, labeled RET^D in Figure 3.

EQUILIBRIUM The intersection of the schedules for the expected return on dollar deposits RET^D and the expected return on franc deposits RET^F is where equilibrium occurs in the foreign exchange market; in other words,

$$RET^D = RET^F$$

At the equilibrium point B where the exchange rate E^* is 10 francs per dollar, the interest parity condition is satisfied because the expected returns on dollar deposits and on franc deposits are equal.

To see that the exchange rate actually heads toward the equilibrium exchange rate E^*, let's see what happens if the exchange rate is 10.5 francs per dollar, a value above the equilibrium exchange rate. As we can see in Figure 3, the expected return on franc deposits at point C is greater than the expected return on dollar deposits at point E. Since dollar and franc deposits are perfect substitutes, people will not want to hold any dollar deposits, and holders of dollar deposits will try to sell them for franc deposits in the foreign exchange market (which is referred to as "selling dollars" and "buying francs"). However, because the expected return on these dollar deposits is below that on franc deposits, no one holding francs will be willing to exchange them for dollar deposits. The resulting excess supply of dollar deposits means that the price of the dollar deposits relative to franc deposits must fall; that is, the exchange rate (amount of francs per dollar) falls as is illustrated by the downward arrow drawn in the figure at the exchange rate of 10.5 francs per dollar. The decline in the exchange rate will continue until point B is reached at the equilibrium exchange rate of 10 francs per dollar, where the expected return on dollar and franc deposits is now equalized.

Now let us look at what happens when the exchange rate is 9.5 francs per dollar, a value below the equilibrium level. Here the expected return on dollar deposits is greater than that on franc deposits. No one will want to hold franc deposits, and everyone will try to sell them to buy dollar deposits ("sell francs" and "buy dollars"), thus driving up the exchange rate as illustrated by the upward arrow. As the exchange rate rises, there is a smaller expected appreciation of the dollar and so a higher expected appreciation of the franc, thereby increasing the expected return on franc deposits. Finally, when the exchange rate has risen to $E^* = 10$ francs per dollar, the expected return on franc deposits has risen enough so that it again equals the expected return on dollar deposits.

EXPLAINING CHANGES IN EXCHANGE RATES

To explain how an exchange rate changes over time, we have to understand the factors that shift the expected-return schedules for domestic (dollar) deposits and foreign (franc) deposits.

Shifts in the Expected-Return Schedule for Foreign Deposits

As we have seen, the expected return on foreign (franc) deposits depends on the foreign interest rate i^F minus the expected appreciation of the dollar $(E^e_{t+1} - E_t)/E_t$. Because a change in the current exchange rate E_t results in a movement along the expected-return schedule for franc deposits, factors that shift this schedule must work through the foreign interest rate i^F and the expected future exchange rate E^e_{t+1}. We examine the effect of changes in these factors on the expected-return schedule for franc deposits RET^F, holding everything else constant.

··

Study Guide   To grasp how the expected-return schedule for franc deposits shifts, just think of yourself as an investor who is considering putting funds into foreign deposits. When a variable changes (i^F for example), decide whether at a given level of the current exchange rate, holding all other variables constant, you would earn a higher or lower expected return on franc deposits.

CHANGES IN THE FOREIGN INTEREST RATE If the interest rate on foreign deposits i^F increases, holding everything else constant, the expected return on these deposits must also increase. Hence at a given exchange rate, the increase in i^F leads to a rightward shift in the expected-return schedule for franc deposits from RET^F_1 to RET^F_2 in Figure 4. As you can see in the figure, the outcome is a depreciation of the dollar from E_1 to E_2. An alternative way to see this is to recognize that the increase in the expected return on franc deposits at the original equilibrium exchange rate resulting from the rise in i^F means that people will want to buy francs and sell dollars, so the value of the dollar must fall. Our analysis thus generates the following conclusion: ***An increase in the foreign interest rate i^F shifts the RET^F schedule to the right and causes the domestic currency to depreciate ($E\downarrow$).***

Conversely, if i^F falls, the expected return on franc deposits falls, the RET^F schedule shifts to the left, and the exchange rate rises. This yields the following conclusion: ***A decrease in i^F shifts the RET^F schedule to the left and causes the domestic currency to appreciate ($E\uparrow$).***

CHANGES IN THE EXPECTED FUTURE EXCHANGE RATE Any factor that causes the expected future exchange rate E^e_{t+1} to fall decreases the expected appreciation of the dollar and hence raises the expected appreciation of the franc. The result is a higher expected return on franc deposits, which shifts the schedule for the expected return on franc deposits to the right and leads to a decline in the exchange rate as in Figure 4. Conversely, a rise in E^e_{t+1} raises the expected appreciation of the dollar, lowers the expected return on foreign deposits, shifts the RET^F schedule to the left, and raises the exchange rate. To summarize, ***a rise in the expected future exchange rate shifts the RET^F schedule to the left and causes an appreciation of the domestic currency; a fall in the expected future exchange rate shifts the RET^F schedule to the right and causes a depreciation of the domestic currency.***

SUMMARY Our analysis of the long-run determinants of the exchange rate indicates the factors that influence the expected future exchange rate: the relative price level, relative tariffs and quotas, import demand, export demand, and relative productivity (refer to Table 1). The theory of purchasing power parity suggests that if a higher American price level relative to the foreign price level is expected to persist, the dollar will depreciate in the long run. A higher expected relative American price level should thus have a tendency to raise the expected return on franc deposits, shift the RET^F schedule to the right, and lower the current exchange rate.

Similarly, the other long-run determinants of the exchange rate we discussed earlier can also influence the expected return on franc deposits and the current

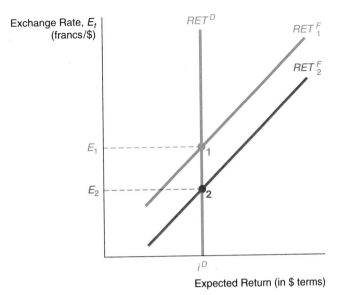

FIGURE 4   Shifts in the Schedule for the Expected Return on Foreign Deposits RET^F
An increase in the expected return on foreign deposits, which occurs when either the foreign interest rate rises or the expected future exchange rate falls, shifts the schedule for the expected return on foreign deposits from RET^F_1 to RET^F_2, and the exchange rate falls from E_1 to E_2.

exchange rate. Briefly, the following changes will increase the expected return on franc deposits, shift the RET^F schedule to the right, and cause a depreciation of the domestic currency, the dollar: (1) expectations of a rise in the American price level relative to the foreign price level, (2) expectations of lower American tariffs and quotas relative to foreign tariffs and quotas, (3) expectations of higher American import demand, (4) expectations of lower foreign demand for American exports, and (5) expectations of lower American productivity relative to foreign productivity.

Shifts in the Expected-Return Schedule for Domestic Deposits

Since the expected return on domestic (dollar) deposits is just the interest rate on these deposits i^D, this interest rate is the only factor that shifts the schedule for the expected return on dollar deposits.

CHANGES IN THE DOMESTIC INTEREST RATE A rise in i^D raises the expected return on dollar deposits, shifts the RET^D schedule to the right, and leads to a rise in the exchange rate, as is shown in Figure 5. Another way of seeing this is to recognize that a rise in i^D, which raises the expected return on dollar deposits, creates an excess demand for dollar deposits at the original equilibrium exchange rate, and the resulting purchases of dollar deposits cause an appreciation of the dollar. *A rise in the domestic interest rate i^D shifts the RET^D schedule to the right and causes an appreciation of the domestic currency; a fall in i^D shifts the RET^D schedule to the left and causes a depreciation of the domestic currency.*

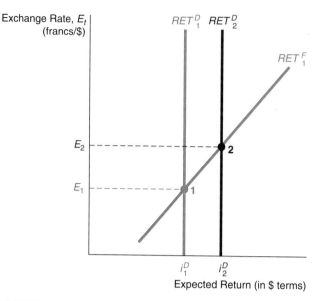

FIGURE 5 Shifts in the Schedule for the Expected Return on Domestic Deposits RET^D
An increase in the expected return on dollar deposits i^D shifts the expected return on domestic (dollar) deposits from RET^D_1 to RET^D_2 and the exchange rate from E_1 to E_2.

Study Guide   As a study aid, the factors that shift the RET^F and RET^D schedules and lead to changes in the current exchange rate E_t are listed in Table 2. The table shows what happens to the exchange rate when there is an increase in each of these variables, holding everything else constant. To give yourself practice, see if you can work out what happens to the RET^F and RET^D schedules and to the exchange rate if each of these factors falls rather than rises. Check your answers by seeing if you get the opposite change in the exchange rate to those indicated in Table 2.

Changes in the Equilibrium Exchange Rate: Two Examples

Our analysis has revealed the factors that affect the value of the equilibrium exchange rate. Now we use this analysis to take a close look at the response of the exchange rate to changes in interest rates and money growth.

Changes in Interest Rates

Changes in domestic interest rates i^D are often cited as a major factor affecting exchange rates. For example, we see headlines in the financial press like this one: "Dollar Recovers As Interest Rates Edge Upward." But is the view presented in this headline always correct?

——— S U M M A R Y ———

TABLE 2 Factors That Shift the RET^F and RET^D Schedules and Affect the Exchange Rate

Factor	Change in Factor	Response of Exchange Rate, E_t	
Domestic interest rate, i^D	↑	↑	
Foreign interest rate, i^F	↑	↓	
Expected domestic price level*	↑	↓	
Expected tariffs and quotas*	↑	↑	
Expected import demand	↑	↓	
Expected export demand	↑	↑	
Expected productivity*	↑	↑	

*Relative to other countries.

Note: Only increases (↑) in the factors are shown; the effects of decreases in the variables on the exchange rate are the opposite of those indicated in the "Response" column.

Not necessarily, because to analyze the effects of interest rate changes, we must carefully distinguish the sources of the changes. The Fisher equation (Chapter 4) states that a (nominal) interest rate equals the *real* interest rate plus expected inflation: $i = i_r + \pi^e$. The Fisher equation indicates that an interest rate i can change for two reasons: Either the real interest rate i_r changes or the expected inflation rate π^e changes. The effect on the exchange rate is quite different, depending on which of these two factors is the source of the change in the nominal interest rate.

Suppose that the domestic real interest rate increases so that the nominal interest rate i^D rises while expected inflation remains unchanged. In this case, it is reasonable to assume that the expected appreciation of the dollar will be unchanged because expected inflation is unchanged, and so the expected return on foreign deposits will remain unchanged for any given exchange rate. The result is that the RET^F schedule stays put and the RET^D schedule shifts to the right, and we end up with the situation depicted in Figure 5, which analyzes an increase in i^D, holding everything else constant. Our model of the foreign exchange market produces the following result: ***When domestic real interest rates rise, the domestic currency appreciates.***

When the nominal interest rate rises because of an increase in expected inflation, we get a different result from the one shown in Figure 5. The rise in expected domestic inflation leads to a decline in the expected appreciation of the dollar (a higher appreciation of the franc), which is typically thought to be larger than the increase in the domestic interest rate i^D.[5] As a result, at any given exchange rate, the expected return on foreign deposits rises more than the expected return on dollar deposits. Thus, as we see in Figure 6, the RET^F schedule shifts to the right more than the RET^D schedule, and the exchange rate falls. Our analysis leads to this conclusion: ***When domestic interest rates rise due to an expected increase in inflation, the domestic currency depreciates.***

Because this conclusion is completely different from the one reached when the rise in the domestic interest rate is associated with a higher real interest rate, we must always distinguish between *real* and *nominal* measures when analyzing the effects of interest rates on exchange rates.

Changes in the Money Supply

Suppose that the Federal Reserve decides to increase the level of the money supply in order to reduce unemployment, which it believes to be excessive. The higher money supply will lead to a higher American price level in the long run (as we will see in Chapter 24) and hence to a lower expected future exchange

[5]This conclusion is standard in asset market models of exchange rate determination; see Rudiger Dornbusch, "Expectations and Exchange Rate Dynamics," *Journal of Political Economy* 84 (1976): 1061–1076. It is also consistent with empirical evidence that suggests that nominal interest rates do not rise one-for-one with increases in expected inflation. See Frederic S. Mishkin, "The Real Interest Rate: An Empirical Investigation," *Carnegie-Rochester Conference Series on Public Policy* 15 (1981): 151–200; and Lawrence Summers, "The Nonadjustment of Nominal Interest Rates: A Study of the Fisher Effect," in *Macroeconomics, Prices and Quantities*, ed. James Tobin (Washington, D.C.: Brookings Institution, 1983), pp. 201–240.

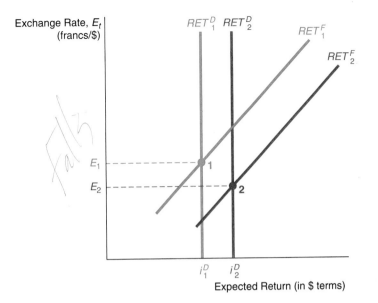

FIGURE 6 Effect of a Rise in the Domestic Nominal Interest Rate as a Result of an Increase in Expected Inflation

Because a rise in domestic expected inflation leads to a decline in expected dollar appreciation that is larger than the resulting increase in the domestic interest rate, the expected return on foreign deposits rises by more than the expected return on domestic (dollar) deposits. **RET^F** shifts to the right more than **RET^D**, and the equilibrium exchange rate falls from **E_1** to **E_2**.

rate. The resulting decline in the expected appreciation of the dollar increases the expected return on foreign deposits at any given current exchange rate and so shifts the RET^F schedule rightward from RET^F_1 to RET^F_2 in Figure 7. In addition, the higher money supply will lead to a higher real money supply M/P because the price level does not immediately increase in the short run. As suggested in Chapter 6, the resulting rise in the real money supply causes the domestic interest rate to fall from i^D_1 to i^D_2 which lowers the expected return on domestic (dollar) deposits, shifting the RET^D schedule in from RET^D_1 to RET^D_2. As we can see in Figure 7, the result is a decline in the exchange rate from E_1 to E_2. The conclusion is this: ***A higher domestic money supply causes the domestic currency to depreciate.***

Exchange Rate Overshooting

Our analysis of the effect of a money supply increase on the exchange rate is not yet over—we still need to look at what happens to the exchange rate in the long run. A basic proposition in monetary theory, called **monetary neutrality,** states that in the long run, a onetime percentage rise in the money supply is matched by the same onetime percentage rise in the price level, leaving unchanged the real money supply and all other economic variables such as interest rates. An intuitive way to understand this proposition is to think of what would happen if our government announced overnight that an old dollar would now be worth 100 new dollars. The money supply in new dollars would be 100 times its old value

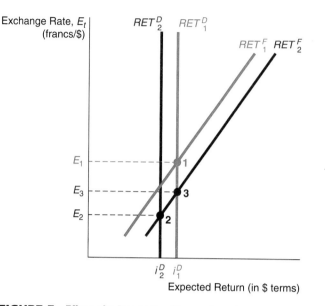

Exchange Rate, E_t
(francs/$)

RET^D_2 RET^D_1

RET^F_1 RET^F_2

E_1 ---------- 1

E_3 ---------- 3

E_2 ---------- 2

i^D_2 i^D_1

Expected Return (in $ terms)

FIGURE 7   Effect of a Rise in the Money Supply

A rise in the money supply leads to a higher domestic price level in the long run, which in turn leads to a lower expected future exchange rate. The resulting decline in the expected appreciation of the dollar raises the expected return on foreign deposits, shifting the RET^F schedule rightward from RET^F_1 to RET^F_2. In the short run, the domestic interest rate i^D falls, shifting RET^D from RET^D_1 to RET^D_2. The short-run outcome is that the exchange rate falls from E_1 to E_2. In the long run, however, the interest rate returns to i^D_1 and RET^D returns to RET^D_1. The exchange rate thus rises from E_2 to E_3 in the long run.

and the price level would also be 100 times higher, but nothing in the economy would really have changed; interest rates and the real money supply would remain the same. Monetary neutrality tells us that in the long run, the rise in the money supply would not lead to a change in the domestic interest rate and so it would return to i^D_1 in the long run, and the schedule for the expected return on domestic deposits would return to RET^D_1. As we can see in Figure 7, this means that the exchange rate would rise from E_2 to E_3 in the long run.

The phenomenon we have described here in which the exchange rate falls by more in the short run than it does in the long run when the money supply increases is called **exchange rate overshooting.** It is important because, as we will see in the following application, it can help explain why exchange rates exhibit so much volatility.

Another way of thinking about why exchange rate overshooting occurs is to recognize that when the domestic interest rate falls in the short run, equilibrium in the foreign exchange market means that the expected return on foreign deposits must be lower. With the foreign interest rate given, this lower expected return on foreign deposits means that there must be an expected appreciation of the dollar (depreciation of the franc) in order for the expected return on foreign deposits to decline when the domestic interest rate falls. This can occur only if the current exchange rate falls below its long-run value.

Why Are Exchange Rates So Volatile?

The high volatility of foreign exchange rates surprises many people. Thirty or so years ago, economists generally believed that allowing exchange rates to be determined in the free market would not lead to large fluctuations in their values. Recent experience has proved them wrong. If we return to Figure 1, we see that exchange rates over the 1980–1996 period have been very volatile.

The asset market approach to exchange rate determination that we have outlined in this chapter gives a straightforward explanation of volatile exchange rates. Because expected appreciation of the domestic currency affects the expected return on foreign deposits, expectations about the price level, inflation, tariffs and quotas, productivity, import demand, export demand, and the money supply play important roles in determining the exchange rate. When expectations about any of these variables change, our model indicates that there will be an immediate effect on the expected return on foreign deposits and therefore on the exchange rate. Since expectations on all these variables change with just about every bit of news that appears, it is not surprising that the exchange rate is volatile. In addition, we have seen that our exchange rate analysis produces exchange rate overshooting when the money supply increases. Exchange rate overshooting is an additional reason for the high volatility of exchange rates.

Because earlier models of exchange rate behavior focused on goods markets rather than asset markets, they did not emphasize changing expectations as a source of exchange rate movements, and so these earlier models could not predict substantial fluctuations in exchange rates. The failure of earlier models to explain volatility is one reason why they are no longer so popular. The more modern approach developed here emphasizes that the foreign exchange market is like any other asset market in which expectations of the future matter. The foreign exchange market, like other asset markets such as the stock market, displays substantial price volatility, and foreign exchange rates are notoriously hard to forecast (see Box 1). Ⓐ

The Dollar and Interest Rates, 1973–1996

In the chapter preview we mentioned that the dollar was weak in the late 1970s, rose substantially from 1980 to 1985, and declined thereafter. We can use our analysis of the foreign exchange market to understand exchange rate movements and help explain the dollar's rise and fall in the 1980s.

Some important information for tracing the dollar's changing value is presented in Figure 8, which plots measures of real and nominal interest rates and the value of the dollar in terms of a basket of foreign currencies (called an **effective exchange rate index**). We can see that the value of the dollar and the

---

B O X 1

Forecasting Exchange Rates

Businesses and financial institutions care a great deal about what foreign exchange rates will be in the future because these rates affect the value of assets on their balance sheet that are denominated in foreign currencies. In addition, financial institutions often engage in trading foreign exchange, both for their own account and for their customers. Businesses and financial institutions therefore need accurate predictions of exchange rates.

Financial institutions and businesses obtain foreign exchange forecasts either by hiring their own staff economists to generate them or by purchasing forecasts from other financial institutions or economic forecasting firms. In predicting exchange rate movements, forecasters look at the factors mentioned in this chapter. For example, if they expect domestic real interest rates to rise, they will predict, in line with our analysis, that the domestic currency will appreciate; conversely, if they expect domestic inflation to increase, they will predict that the domestic currency will depreciate. Exchange rate forecasters are no more or less accurate than other economic forecasters, and they often make large errors. Reports of foreign exchange rate forecasts and how well forecasters are doing appear from time to time in the *Wall Street Journal* and in the trade magazine *Euromoney*.

---

measure of real interest rates rise and fall together. In the late 1970s, real interest rates were at low levels, and so was the value of the dollar. Beginning in 1980, however, real interest rates in the United States began to climb sharply, and at the same time so did the dollar. After 1984, the real interest rate declined substantially, as did the dollar.

Our model of exchange rate determination helps explain the rise and fall in the dollar in the 1980s. As Figure 5 indicates, a rise in the U.S. real interest rate raises the expected return on dollar deposits while leaving the expected return on foreign deposits unchanged. The resulting increased demand for dollar deposits then leads to purchases of dollar deposits (and sales of foreign deposits), which raise the exchange rate. This is exactly what occurred in the 1980–1984 period. The subsequent fall in U.S. real interest rates then lowered the expected return on dollar deposits relative to foreign deposits, and the resulting sales of dollar deposits (and purchases of foreign deposits) lowered the exchange rate.

The plot of *nominal* interest rates in Figure 8 also demonstrates that the correspondence between nominal interest rates and exchange rate movements is not nearly as close as that between *real* interest rates and exchange rate movements. This is also exactly what our analysis predicts. The rise in nominal interest rates in the late 1970s was not reflected in a corresponding rise in the value of the dollar; indeed, the dollar actually fell in the late 1970s. Figure 8 explains why the rise in nominal rates in the late 1970s did not produce a rise in the dollar. As a comparison of the real and nominal interest rates in the late 1970s indicates, the rise in nominal interest rates reflected an increase in expected inflation and not an increase in real interest rates. As our analysis in Figure 6 demonstrates, the rise in nominal interest rates stemming from a rise in expected inflation should lead to a decline in the dollar, and that is exactly what transpired.

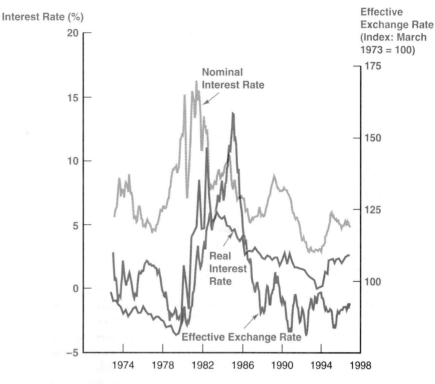

FIGURE 8 Value of the Dollar and Interest Rates, 1973–1996

Sources: International Financial Statistics; Real interest rate from Figure 3 in Chapter 4.

If there is a moral to the story, it is that a failure to distinguish between real and nominal interest rates can lead to poor predictions of exchange rate movements: The weakness of the dollar in the late 1970s and the strength of the dollar in the early 1980s can be explained by movements in *real* interest rates but not by movements in *nominal* interest rates. Ⓐ

Reading the WALL STREET JOURNAL
The "Foreign Exchange" Column

Now that we have an understanding of how exchange rates are determined, we can use our analysis to understand discussions about developments in the foreign exchange market reported in the financial press.

Every day, the *Wall Street Journal* reports on developments in the foreign exchange market on the previous business day in its "Foreign Exchange" column, an example of which is presented in the "Following the Financial News" box.

The column focuses on strong U.S. data and the prospect of higher U.S. and lower German interest rates as the source of the rise in the dollar relative to the

Following the Financial News

The "Foreign Exchange" Column

The "Foreign Exchange" column appears daily in the *Wall Street Journal*; an example is presented here. It is found in the third section, "Money and Investing."

FOREIGN EXCHANGE

Dollar Continues Its Advance on Mark On Strong U.S. Data, Slips Against Yen

BY BETTY W. LIU
AP-Dow Jones News Service

NEW YORK–The dollar continued its climb against the mark yesterday, boosted by the robust U.S. economic outlook and a report indicating Germany could cut interest rates again.

However, the U.S. currency ended off slightly against the yen, though still above the psychologically important 110 yen level as traders took profits from Wednesday's two-month high.

"All the news continues to support the dollar with [U.S.] interest rates moving up, Bundesbank officials commenting that interest rates could move lower . . . and the Iraqi situation," said Roger Chapin, foreign-exchange manager at Bank One Columbus in Columbus, Ohio.

Early in the New York afternoon, Baghdad's official news agency confirmed that Iraq fired missiles at U.S. warplanes over the "no-fly zone" in southern Iraq.

Subdued U.S. producer prices for August showed inflation remains moderate, though the economy is expanding. Bonds and stocks rallied on the numbers, which in turn helped the dollar, traders said.

"We've got the best of all possible worlds here," said Kevin Raphael, foreign-exchange manager at Rabobank Nederland in New York. "We've got high levels of employment and few signs of inflation."

Late in New York, the dollar was quoted at 1.5126 marks, up from 1.5108 marks late Wednesday in New York. The U.S. currency also was quoted at 110.10 yen, down from 110.31 yen. Sterling was trading at $1.5557, up from $1.5551. About noon Friday in Tokyo, the dollar was trading at 1.5127 marks and at 110.16 yen; sterling was quoted at $1.5554.

Klaus Dieter Kuebacher, member of the Bundesbank's policymaking council, said in an interview yesterday that Germany's repurchase, or repo, rate "has leeway to fall some 20 basis points," from its current 3%.

A basis point is one-hundredth of a percentage point. The repo rate is the rate at which the Bundesbank does most of its lending to banks.

U.S. producer prices in August rose a seasonally adjusted 0.3% after remaining unchanged in July.

The Dow Jones Industrial Average ended just shy of its closing high—5778 points, set May 22—at 5771.94, up 17.02 points. The 30-year benchmark Treasury was at 95 30/32, up about $^1/_2$ point to yield 7.07%.

Market players interviewed were convinced the evidence of the economy's strength was overwhelming. Even if today's consumer price data is subdued, they say, it won't keep the Federal Reserve from raising interest rates by its next policy meeting in late September. This, in turn, will keep pushing the dollar up.

The discount and Federal-funds target rates are at 5% and 5.25%, respectively. The discount rate, at which the Fed lends to banks, is considered their fund source of last resort. Banks lend each other excess reserves overnight at the Fed-funds rate.

And a call for a stronger dollar by French central bank Governor Jean-Claude Trichet was an added element of support for the U.S. currency.

Regarding recent comments by Bundesbank officials about interest rates and the dollar, Wayne Grigull, managing director of foreign exchange at Merrill Lynch & Co. in New York, said: "It's vital for an economic union that the countries of Europe start to experience economic growth and that unemployment rates decline. They're not going to decline unless monetary conditions ease" and the mark weakens.

Source: Wall Street Journal, Friday, September 13, 1996, p. C17.

mark. Our analysis of the foreign exchange market explains why these developments lead to an appreciation of the dollar against the mark.

The strong U.S. economy is seen as making it likely that U.S. interest rates will rise in the near future (a view that is consistent with the analysis in Chapter 6). The higher U.S. interest rates will shift the RET^D schedule to the right as in Figure

5 and will thereby cause the exchange rate to rise in the future. The comment from the Bundesbank official implying that German interest rates are likely to fall in the future decreases the expected return on mark deposits, thus shifting the RET^F curve to the left, providing an additional reason why the value of the dollar should rise against the mark in the future. The resulting expectation of a future rise in the dollar against the mark, produces a rise in the dollar today because the expected appreciation of the dollar implies a depreciation of the mark, which decreases the expected return on the mark deposits and shifts the RET^F schedule to the left.

The comment about being in the best of all possible worlds provides an additional reason for the strong dollar because it suggests that although the economy is strong, there are few signs of inflation. The prospect of low inflation in the United States implies that it is more likely that the U.S. price level will be lower relative to the German price level in the future. The lower relative U.S. price level provides an additional reason for an expected appreciation of the dollar, which drives down the expected return on mark deposits because it implies an expected depreciation of the mark, thereby shifting the RET^F schedule to the left. As explained earlier, this leads to a rise in the value of the dollar today.   Ⓐ

S U M M A R Y

1. Foreign exchange rates (the price of one country's currency in terms of another's) are important because they affect the price of domestically produced goods sold abroad and the cost of foreign goods bought domestically.

2. The theory of purchasing power parity suggests that long-run changes in the exchange rate between two countries are determined by changes in the relative price levels of the two countries. Other factors that affect exchange rates in the long run are tariffs and quotas, import demand, export demand, and productivity.

3. Exchange rates are determined in the short run by the interest parity condition, which states that the expected return on domestic deposits is equal to the expected return on foreign deposits.

4. Any factor that changes the expected returns on domestic or foreign deposits will lead to changes in the exchange rate. Such factors include changes in the interest rates on domestic and foreign deposits as well as changes in any of the factors that affect the long-run exchange rate and hence the expected future exchange rate. Changes in the money supply lead to exchange rate overshooting, causing the exchange rate to change by more in the short run than in the long run.

5. The asset market approach to exchange rate determination can explain both the volatility of exchange rates and the rise of the dollar in the 1980–1984 period and its subsequent fall.

K E Y   T E R M S

appreciation, p. 167

capital mobility, p. 176

depreciation, p. 167

effective exchange rate index,

   p. 187

exchange rate, p. 165

exchange rate overshooting,

   p. 186

foreign exchange market, p. 165

forward exchange rate, p. 167

forward transaction, p. 167

interest parity condition, p. 176

law of one price, p. 170

monetary neutrality, p. 185

quotas, p. 172

spot exchange rate, p. 167

spot transaction, p. 167

tariffs, p. 172

theory of purchasing power

   parity (PPP), p. 170

QUESTIONS AND PROBLEMS

1. When the French franc appreciates, are you more likely to drink California or French wine?

*2. "A country is always worse off when its currency is weak (falls in value)." Is this statement true, false, or uncertain? Explain your answer.

3. In a newspaper, check the exchange rates for the foreign currencies listed in the "Following the Financial News" box on page 168. Which of these currencies have appreciated and which have depreciated since October 8, 1996?

*4. If the French price level rises by 5 percent relative to the price level in the United States, what does the theory of purchasing power parity predict will happen to the value of the French franc in terms of dollars?

5. If the demand for a country's exports falls at the same time that tariffs on imports are raised, will the country's currency tend to appreciate or depreciate in the long run?

*6. In the mid- to late 1970s, the yen appreciated relative to the dollar even though Japan's inflation rate was higher than America's. How can this be explained by an improvement in the productivity of Japanese industry relative to American industry?

USING ECONOMIC ANALYSIS TO PREDICT THE FUTURE

Answer the remaining questions by drawing the appropriate exchange market diagrams.

7. The president of the United States announces that he will reduce inflation with a new anti-inflation program. If the public believes him, predict what will happen to the U.S. exchange rate.

*8. If the British central bank prints money to reduce unemployment, what will happen to the value of the pound in the short run and the long run?

9. If the French government unexpectedly announces that it will be imposing higher tariffs and quotas on foreign goods one year from now, what will happen to the value of the franc today?

*10. If nominal interest rates in America rise but real interest rates fall, predict what will happen to the U.S. exchange rate.

11. If American auto companies make a breakthrough in automobile technology and are able to produce a car that gets 60 miles to the gallon, what will happen to the U.S. exchange rate?

*12. If Americans go on a spending spree and buy twice as much French perfume, Japanese TVs, English sweaters, Swiss watches, and Italian wine, what will happen to the value of the U.S. dollar?

13. If expected inflation drops in Europe so that interest rates fall there, predict what will happen to the U.S. exchange rate.

*14. If the German central bank decides to contract the money supply in order to fight inflation, what will happen to the value of the U.S. dollar?

15. If there is a strike in France, making it harder to buy French goods, what will happen to the value of the franc?

PART III

FINANCIAL INSTITUTIONS

Chapter 9

AN ECONOMIC ANALYSIS OF FINANCIAL STRUCTURE

PREVIEW   A healthy and vibrant economy requires a financial system that moves funds from people who save to people who have productive investment opportunities. But how does the financial system make sure that your hard-earned savings get channeled to Paula the Productive Investor rather than to Benny the Bum?

This chapter answers that question by providing an economic analysis of how our financial structure is designed to promote economic efficiency. The analysis focuses on a few simple but powerful economic concepts that enable us to explain features of our financial system such as why financial contracts are written as they are and why financial intermediaries are more important than securities markets for getting funds to borrowers. The analysis also demonstrates the important link between the financial system and the performance of the aggregate economy, which is the subject of Part VI of the book. The economic analysis of financial structure explains how the performance of the financial sector affects economic growth and why financial crises occur and have such severe consequences for aggregate economic activity.

BASIC PUZZLES ABOUT FINANCIAL STRUCTURE THROUGHOUT THE WORLD

The financial system is complex in structure and function throughout the world. There are many different types of institutions: banks, insurance companies, mutual funds, stock and bond markets, and so on—all of which are regulated by government. The financial system channels billions of dollars per year from savers to people with productive investment opportunities. If we take a close look at financial structure all over the world, we find eight basic puzzles that we need to solve in order to understand how the financial system works.

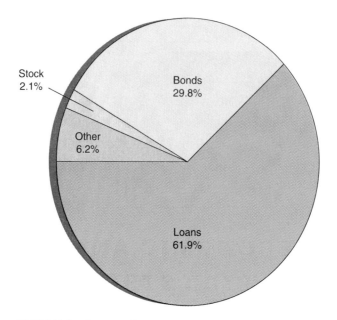

FIGURE 1 Sources of External Funds for Nonfinancial Businesses in the United States

The categories of external funds are as follows: *Loans* is made up primarily of bank loans, but it also includes loans made by other financial intermediaries. *Bonds* includes marketable debt securities such as corporate bonds and commercial paper. *Stock* consists of stock market shares. *Other* includes other loans such as government loans, loans by foreigners, and trade debt (loans made by businesses to other businesses when they purchase goods).

Source: Colin Mayer, "Financial Systems, Corporate Finance, and Economic Development," in *Asymmetric Information, Corporate Finance, and Investment,* ed. R. Glenn Hubbard (Chicago: University of Chicago Press, 1990), p. 312.

The pie chart in Figure 1 indicates how American businesses financed their activities using external funds (those obtained from outside the business itself) in the period 1970–1985. The *loans* category is made up primarily of bank loans, but it also includes loans made by other financial intermediaries; the *bonds* category includes marketable debt securities such as corporate bonds and commercial paper; *stock* consists of stock market shares; and *other* includes other loans such as government loans, loans by foreigners, and trade debt (loans made by businesses to other businesses when they purchase goods). Figure 2 uses the same classifications as Figure 1 and compares the U.S. data to those of five other industrialized countries.

Now let us explore the eight financial puzzles.

*1. **Stocks are not the most important source of external financing for businesses.*** Because so much attention in the media is focused on the stock market, many people have the impression that stocks are the most important sources of financing for American corporations. However, as we can see from the pie chart in Figure 1, the stock market accounted for only a small fraction of the

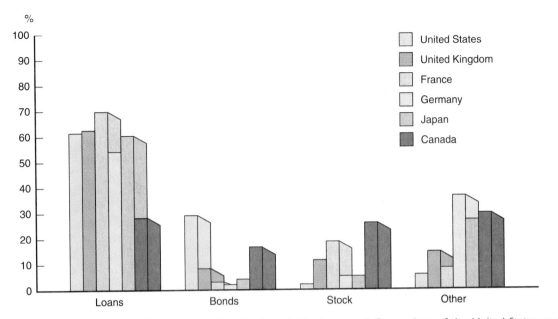

FIGURE 2   Sources of External Funds for Nonfinancial Businesses: A Comparison of the United States and Five Other Industrialized Countries

The categories of external funds are the same as in Figure 1.

Source: Colin Mayer, "Financial Systems, Corporate Finance, and Economic Development," in *Asymmetric Information, Corporate Finance, and Investment,* ed. R. Glenn Hubbard (Chicago: University of Chicago Press, 1990), p. 312.

external financing of American businesses in the 1970–1985 period, 2.1 percent.[1] (In fact, in the mid- to late 1980s, American corporations generally stopped issuing shares to finance their activities; instead they purchased large numbers of shares, meaning that the stock market was actually a *negative* source of corporate finance in those years.) Similarly small figures apply in the other countries presented in Figure 2 as well. Why is the stock market less important than other sources of financing in the United States and other countries?

   *2. **Issuing marketable debt and equity securities is not the primary way in which businesses finance their operations.*** Figure 1 shows that bonds are a far more important source of financing than stocks in the United States (29.8 versus 2.1 percent). However, stocks and bonds combined (31.9

---

[1]The 2.1 percent figure for the percentage of external financing provided by stocks is based on the flows of external funds to corporations. However, this flow figure is somewhat misleading because when a share of stock is issued, it raises funds permanently, whereas when a bond is issued, it raises funds only temporarily until they are paid back at maturity. To see this, suppose that a firm raises $1000 by selling a share of stock and another $1000 by selling a $1000 one-year bond. In the case of the stock issue, the firm can hold on to the $1000 it raised this way, but to hold on to the $1000 it raised through debt, it has to issue a new $1000 bond every year. If we look at the flow of funds to corporations over a 15-year period, as in Figure 1, the firm will have raised $1000 with a stock issue only once in the 15-year period, while it will have raised $1000 with debt 15 times, once in each of the 15 years. Thus it will look like debt is 15 times more important than stocks in raising funds, even though our example indicates that they are actually equally important for the firm.

percent), which make up the total share of marketable securities, still supply less than one-third of the external funds corporations need to finance their activities. The fact that issuing marketable securities is not the most important source of financing is true elsewhere in the world as well. Indeed, as we see in Figure 2, most countries, with the exception of Canada, have a much smaller share of external financing supplied by marketable securities than the United States. Why don't businesses use marketable securities more extensively to finance their activities?

*3. **Indirect finance, which involves the activities of financial intermediaries, is many times more important than direct finance, in which businesses raise funds directly from lenders in financial markets.*** Direct finance involves the sale to households of marketable securities such as stocks and bonds. The 31.9 percent share of stocks and bonds as a source of external financing for American businesses actually greatly overstates the importance of direct finance in our financial system. Since 1970, less than 5 percent of newly issued corporate bonds and commercial paper and around 50 percent of stocks have been sold directly to American households. The rest of these securities have been bought primarily by financial intermediaries such as insurance companies, pension funds, and mutual funds. These figures indicate that direct finance is used in less than 5 percent of the external funding of American business. Because in most countries marketable securities are an even less important source of finance than in the United States, direct finance is also far less important than indirect finance in the rest of the world. Why are financial intermediaries and indirect finance so important in financial markets?

*4. **Banks are the most important source of external funds used to finance businesses.*** As we can see in Figures 1 and 2, the primary sources of external funds for businesses throughout the world are loans (61.9 percent in the United States). Most of these loans are bank loans, so the data suggest that banks have the most important role in financing business activities. An extraordinary fact that surprises most people is that in an average year in the United States, 25 times more funds are raised with bank loans than with stocks. Banks are even more important in countries such as France than they are in the United States, and in developing countries banks play an even more important role in the financial system than they do in the industrialized countries. What makes banks so important to the workings of the financial system?

*5. **The financial system is among the most heavily regulated sectors of the economy.*** You learned in Chapter 2 that the financial system is heavily regulated, not only in the United States but in all other developed countries as well. Governments regulate financial markets primarily to promote the provision of information and to ensure the soundness of the financial system. Why are financial markets so extensively regulated throughout the world?

*6. **Only large, well-established corporations have access to securities markets to finance their activities.*** Individuals and smaller businesses that are not well established almost never raise funds by issuing marketable securities. Instead, they obtain their financing from banks. Why do only large, well-known corporations have the ability to raise funds in securities markets?

*7. **Collateral is a prevalent feature of debt contracts for both households and businesses.*** **Collateral** is property that is pledged to the lender to guarantee payment in the event that the borrower should be unable to make debt payments. Collateralized debt (which is also known as **secured debt** to contrast it with **unsecured debt,** such as credit card debt, which is not collateralized) is the predominant form of household debt and is widely used in business borrowing as well. The majority of household debt in the United States consists of collateralized loans: Your automobile is collateral for your auto loan, and your house is collateral for your mortgage. Commercial and farm mortgages, for which property is pledged as collateral, make up one-quarter of borrowing by nonfinancial businesses; corporate bonds and other bank loans also often involve pledges of collateral. Why is collateral such an important feature of debt contracts?

   8. *Debt contracts are typically extremely complicated legal documents that place substantial restrictions on the behavior of the borrower.* Many students think about a debt contract as a simple IOU that can be written on a single piece of paper. The reality of debt contracts is far different, however. In all countries, bond or loan contracts are typically long legal documents with provisions (called **restrictive covenants**) that restrict and specify certain activities that the borrower can engage in. Restrictive covenants are not just a feature of debt contracts for businesses; for example, personal automobile loan and home mortgage contracts have restrictive covenants that require the borrower to maintain sufficient insurance on the automobile or house purchased with the loan. Why are debt contracts so complex and restrictive?

   As you might recall from Chapter 2, an important feature of financial markets is that they have substantial transaction and information costs. An economic analysis of how these costs affect financial markets provides us with solutions to the eight puzzles, which in turn provide us with a much deeper understanding of how our financial system works. In the next section we examine the impact of transaction costs on the structure of our financial system. Then we turn to how information costs affect financial structure.

TRANSACTION COSTS

Transaction costs are a major problem in financial markets. An example will make this clear.

How Transaction Costs Influence Financial Structure

Say you have $5000 you would like to invest, and you think about investing in the stock market. Because you have only $5000, you can buy only a small number of shares. The stockbroker tells you that your purchase is so small that the brokerage commission for buying the stock you picked will be a large percentage of the purchase price of the shares. If instead you decide to buy a bond, the problem is even worse because the smallest denomination for some bonds you might want to buy is as much as $10,000 and you do not have that much to invest. Indeed, the broker may not even be interested in your business at all because the small size of your account doesn't make spending time on it worthwhile. You are disappointed and realize that you will not be able to use financial markets to earn a return on your hard-earned savings. You can take some consolation, however, in the fact that you are not alone in being stymied by high transaction costs. This is a fact of life for most of us: Most American households never own any securities.

You also face another problem because of transaction costs. Because you have only a small amount of funds available, you can make only a restricted number of investments. That is, you have to put all your eggs in one basket, and your inability to diversify will subject you to a lot of risk.

How Financial Intermediaries Reduce Transaction Costs

This example of the problems posed by transaction costs and the example outlined in Chapter 2 when legal costs kept you from making a loan to Carl the Carpenter illustrate that small savers like you are frozen out of financial markets and are unable to benefit from them. Fortunately, financial intermediaries, an important part of the financial structure, have evolved to reduce transaction costs and allow small savers and borrowers to benefit from the existence of financial markets.

ECONOMIES OF SCALE One solution to the problem of high transaction costs is to bundle the funds of many investors together so that they can take advantage of *economies of scale,* the reduction in transaction costs per dollar of investment as the size (scale) of transactions increases. By bundling investors' funds together, transaction costs for each individual investor are far smaller. Economies of scale exist because the total cost of carrying out a transaction in financial markets increases only a little as the size of the transaction grows. For example, the cost of arranging a purchase of 10,000 shares of stock is not much greater than the cost of arranging a purchase of 50 shares of stock.

The presence of economies of scale in financial markets helps explain why financial intermediaries developed and are such an important part of our financial structure. The clearest example of a financial intermediary that arose because of economies of scale is a mutual fund. A *mutual fund* is a financial intermediary that sells shares to individuals and then invests the proceeds in bonds or stocks. Because it buys large blocks of stocks or bonds, a mutual fund can take advantage of lower transaction costs. These cost savings are then passed on to individual investors after the mutual fund has taken its cut in the form of management fees for administering their accounts. An additional benefit for individual investors is that a mutual fund is large enough to purchase a widely diversified portfolio of securities. The increased diversification for individual investors reduces their risk, thus making them better off.

Economies of scale are also important in lowering the costs of things such as computer technology that financial institutions need to accomplish their tasks. Once a large mutual fund has invested a lot of money in setting up a telecommunications system, for example, it can be used for a huge number of transactions at a low cost per transaction.

EXPERTISE Financial intermediaries also arise because they are better able to develop expertise to lower transaction costs. Mutual funds, banks, and other financial intermediaries develop expertise in computer technology so that they can cheaply provide convenient services such as toll-free numbers that allow you to check on how well your investments are doing or the ability to write checks on your account.

An important outcome of a financial intermediary's low transaction costs is that they allow a financial intermediary to provide its customers with *liquidity services,* services that make it easier for customers to conduct transactions. Money market mutual funds, for example, allow shareholders to write checks that enable them to pay their bills easily while at the same time paying them high interest rates.

ASYMMETRIC INFORMATION: ADVERSE SELECTION AND MORAL HAZARD

The presence of transaction costs in financial markets explains in part why financial intermediaries and indirect finance play such an important role in financial markets (puzzle 3). To understand financial structure more fully, however, we turn to the role of information in financial markets.[2]

Asymmetric information—one party's having insufficient knowledge about the other party involved in a transaction to make accurate decisions—is an important aspect of financial markets. For example, managers of a corporation know whether they are honest or have better information about how well their business is doing than the stockholders do. The presence of asymmetric information leads to adverse selection and moral hazard problems, which were introduced in Chapter 2.

Adverse selection is an asymmetric information problem that occurs *before* the transaction occurs: Potential bad credit risks are the ones who most actively seek out loans. Thus the parties who are the most likely to produce an undesirable outcome are most likely to want to engage in the transaction. For example, big risk takers or outright crooks might be the most eager to take out a loan because they know that they are unlikely to pay it back. Because adverse selection increases the chances that a loan might be made to a bad credit risk, lenders may decide not to make any loans even though there are good credit risks in the marketplace.

Moral hazard arises *after* the transaction occurs: The lender runs the risk that the borrower will engage in activities that are undesirable from the lender's point of view because they make it less likely that the loan will be paid back. For example, once borrowers have obtained a loan, they may take on big risks (which have possible high returns but also run a greater risk of default) because they are playing with someone else's money. Because moral hazard lowers the probability that the loan will be repaid, lenders may decide that they would rather not make a loan.

THE LEMONS PROBLEM: HOW ADVERSE SELECTION INFLUENCES FINANCIAL STRUCTURE

A particular characterization of the adverse selection problem and how it interferes with the efficient functioning of a market was outlined in a famous article by George Akerlof. It is referred to as the "lemons problem" because it resembles

[2]An excellent survey of the literature on information and financial structure that expands on the topics discussed in the rest of this chapter is contained in Mark Gertler, "Financial Structure and Aggregate Economic Activity: An Overview," *Journal of Money, Credit and Banking* 20 (1988): 559–588.

the problem created by lemons in the used-car market.[3] Potential buyers of used cars are frequently unable to assess the quality of the car; that is, they can't tell whether a particular used car is a good car that will run well or a lemon that will continually give them grief. The price that a buyer pays must therefore reflect the *average* quality of the cars in the market, somewhere between the low value of a lemon and the high value of a good car.

The owner of a used car, by contrast, is more likely to know whether the car is a peach or a lemon. If the car is a lemon, the owner is more than happy to sell it at the price the buyer is willing to pay, which, being somewhere between the value of a lemon and a good car, is greater than the lemon's value. However, if the car is a peach, the owner knows that the car is undervalued by the price the buyer is willing to pay, and so the owner may not want to sell it. As a result of this adverse selection, very few good used cars will come to the market. Because the average quality of a used car available in the market will be low and because very few people want to buy a lemon, there will be few sales. The used-car market will then function poorly, if at all.

Lemons in the Stock and Bond Markets

A similar lemons problem arises in securities markets, that is, the debt (bond) and equity (stock) markets. Suppose that our friend Irving the Investor, a potential buyer of securities such as common stock, can't distinguish between good firms with high expected profits and low risk and bad firms with low expected profits and high risk. In this situation, Irving will be willing to pay only a price that reflects the *average* quality of firms issuing securities—a price that lies between the value of securities from bad firms and the value of those from good firms. If the owners or managers of a good firm have better information than Irving and *know* that they are a good firm, they know that their securities are undervalued and will not want to sell them to Irving at the price he is willing to pay. The only firms willing to sell Irving securities will be bad firms (because the price is higher than the securities are worth). Our friend Irving is not stupid; he does not want to hold securities in bad firms, and hence he will decide not to purchase securities in the market. In an outcome similar to that in the used-car market, this securities market will not work very well because few firms will sell securities in it to raise capital.

The analysis is similar if Irving considers purchasing a corporate debt instrument in the bond market rather than an equity share. Irving will buy a bond only if its interest rate is high enough to compensate him for the average default risk of the good and bad firms trying to sell the debt. The knowledgeable owners of a good firm realize that they will be paying a higher interest rate than they should, and so they are unlikely to want to borrow in this market. Only the bad firms will

---

[3]George Akerlof, "The Market for 'Lemons': Quality, Uncertainty and the Market Mechanism," *Quarterly Journal of Economics* 84 (1970): 488–500. Two important papers that have applied the lemons problem analysis to financial markets are Stewart Myers and N. S. Majluf, "Corporate Financing and Investment Decisions When Firms Have Information That Investors Do Not Have," *Journal of Financial Economics* 13 (1984): 187–221, and Bruce Greenwald, Joseph E. Stiglitz, and Andrew Weiss, "Information Imperfections in the Capital Market and Macroeconomic Fluctuations," *American Economic Review* 74 (1984): 194–199.

be willing to borrow, and because investors like Irving are not eager to buy bonds issued by bad firms, they will probably not buy any bonds at all. Few bonds are likely to sell in this market, and so it will not be a good source of financing.

The analysis we have just conducted explains puzzle 2—why marketable securities are not the primary source of financing for businesses in any country in the world. It also partly explains puzzle 1—why stocks are not the most important source of financing for American businesses. The presence of the lemons problem keeps securities markets such as the stock and bond markets from being effective in channeling funds from savers to borrowers.

Tools to Help Solve Adverse Selection Problems

In the absence of asymmetric information, the lemons problem goes away. If buyers know as much about the quality of used cars as sellers so that all involved can tell a good car from a bad one, buyers will be willing to pay full value for good used cars. Because the owners of good used cars can now get a fair price, they will be willing to sell them in the market. The market will have many transactions and will do its intended job of channeling good cars to people who want them.

Similarly, if purchasers of securities can distinguish good firms from bad, they will pay the full value of securities issued by good firms, and good firms will sell their securities in the market. The securities market will then be able to move funds to the good firms that have the most productive investment opportunities.

PRIVATE PRODUCTION AND SALE OF INFORMATION The solution to the adverse selection problem in financial markets is to eliminate asymmetric information by furnishing people supplying funds with full details about the individuals or firms seeking to finance their investment activities. One way to get this material to saver-lenders is to have private companies collect and produce information that distinguishes good from bad firms and then sell it to purchasers of securities. In the United States, companies such as Standard and Poor's, Moody's, and Value Line gather information on firms' balance sheet positions and investment activities, publish these data, and sell them to subscribers (individuals, libraries, and financial intermediaries involved in purchasing securities).

The system of private production and sale of information does not completely solve the adverse selection problem in securities markets, however, because of the so-called **free-rider problem.** The free-rider problem occurs when people who do not pay for information take advantage of the information that other people have paid for. The free-rider problem suggests that the private sale of information will be only a partial solution to the lemons problem. To see why, suppose that you have just purchased information that tells you which firms are good and which are bad. You believe that this purchase is worthwhile because you can make up the cost of acquiring this information, and then some, by purchasing the securities of good firms that are undervalued. However, when our savvy (free-riding) investor Irving sees you buying certain securities, he buys right along with you, even though he has not paid for any information. If many other investors act as Irving does, the increased demand for the undervalued good securities will cause their low price to be bid up immediately to reflect the securities' true value.

As a result of all these free riders, you can no longer buy the securities for less than their true value. Now because you will not gain any extra profits from purchasing the information, you realize that you never should have paid for this information in the first place. If other investors come to the same realization, private firms and individuals may not be able to sell enough of this information to make it worth their while to gather and produce it. The weakened ability of private firms to profit from selling information will mean that less information is produced in the marketplace, and so adverse selection (the lemons problem) will still interfere with the efficient functioning of securities markets.

GOVERNMENT REGULATION The free-rider problem prevents the private market from producing enough information to eliminate all the asymmetric information that leads to adverse selection. Could financial markets benefit from government intervention? The government could, for instance, produce information to help investors distinguish good from bad firms and provide it to the public free of charge. This solution, however, would involve the government in releasing negative information about firms, a practice that might be politically difficult. A second possibility (and one followed by the United States and most governments throughout the world) is for the government to regulate securities markets in a way that encourages firms to reveal honest information about themselves so that investors can determine how good or bad the firms are. In the United States, the Securities and Exchange Commission (SEC) is the government agency that requires firms selling their securities in public markets to adhere to standard accounting principles and to disclose information about their sales, assets, and earnings. Similar regulations are found in other countries.

The asymmetric information problem of adverse selection in financial markets helps explain why financial markets are among the most heavily regulated sectors in the economy (puzzle 5). Government regulation to increase information for investors is needed to reduce the adverse selection problem, which interferes with the efficient functioning of securities (stock and bond) markets.

Although government regulation lessens the adverse selection problem, it does not eliminate it. Even when firms provide information to the public about their sales, assets, or earnings, they still have more information than investors: There is a lot more to knowing the quality of a firm than statistics can provide. Furthermore, bad firms have an incentive to make themselves look like good firms because this would enable them to fetch a higher price for their securities. Bad firms will slant the information they are required to transmit to the public, thus making it harder for investors to sort out the good firms from the bad.

FINANCIAL INTERMEDIATION So far we have seen that private production of information and government regulation to encourage provision of information lessen but do not eliminate the adverse selection problem in financial markets. How, then, can the financial structure help promote the flow of funds to people with productive investment opportunities when there is asymmetric information? A clue is provided by the structure of the used-car market.

An important feature of the used-car market is that most used cars are not sold directly by one individual to another. An individual considering buying a used car might pay for privately produced information by subscribing to a magazine like *Consumer Reports* to find out if a particular make of car has a good repair record. Nevertheless, reading *Consumer Reports* does not solve the adverse selection problem because even if a particular make of car has a good reputation, the specific car someone is trying to sell could be a lemon. The prospective buyer might also bring the used car to a mechanic for a once-over. But what if the prospective buyer doesn't know a mechanic who can be trusted or if the mechanic would charge a high fee to evaluate the car?

Because these roadblocks make it hard for individuals to acquire enough information about used cars, most used cars are not sold directly by one individual to another. Instead, they are sold by an intermediary, a used-car dealer who purchases used cars from individuals and resells them to other individuals. Used-car dealers produce information in the market by becoming experts in determining whether a car is a peach or a lemon. Once they know that a car is good, they can sell it with some form of a guarantee: either a guarantee that is explicit, such as a warranty, or an implicit guarantee in which they stand by their reputation for honesty. People are more likely to purchase a used car because of a dealer's guarantee, and the dealer is able to make a profit on the production of information about automobile quality by being able to sell the used car at a higher price than the dealer paid for it. If dealers purchase and then resell cars on which they have produced information, they avoid the problem of other people free-riding on the information they produced.

Just as used-car dealers help solve adverse selection problems in the automobile market, financial intermediaries play a similar role in financial markets. A financial intermediary such as a bank becomes an expert in the production of information about firms so that it can sort out good credit risks from bad ones. Then it can acquire funds from depositors and lend them to the good firms. Because the bank is able to lend mostly to good firms, it is able to earn a higher return on its loans than the interest it has to pay to its depositors. As a result, the bank earns a profit, which allows it to engage in this information production activity.

An important element in the ability of the bank to profit from the information it produces is that it avoids the free-rider problem by primarily making private loans rather than by purchasing securities that are traded in the open market. Because a private loan is not traded, other investors cannot watch what the bank is doing and bid up the loan's price to the point that the bank receives no compensation for the information it has produced. The bank's role as an intermediary that holds mostly nontraded loans is the key to its success in reducing asymmetric information in financial markets.

Our analysis of adverse selection indicates that financial intermediaries in general, and banks in particular because they hold a large fraction of nontraded loans, should play a greater role in moving funds to corporations than securities markets do. Our analysis thus explains puzzles 3 and 4: why indirect finance is so much more important than direct finance and why banks are the most important source of external funds for financing businesses.

Another important fact that is explained by the analysis here is the greater importance of banks in the financial systems of developing countries. As we have seen, when the quality of information about firms is better, asymmetric information problems will be less severe, and it will be easier for firms to issue securities. Information about private firms is harder to collect in developing countries than in industrialized countries; therefore, the smaller role played by securities markets leaves a greater role for financial intermediaries such as banks. A corollary of this analysis is that as information about firms becomes easier to acquire, the role of banks should decline. A major development in the past 20 years in the United States has been huge improvements in information technology. Thus the analysis here suggests that the lending role of financial institutions such as banks in the United States should have declined, and this is exactly what has occurred (see Chapter 11).

Our analysis of adverse selection also explains which firms are more likely to obtain funds from banks and financial intermediaries, an indirect route, rather than directly from the securities markets. The better known a corporation is, the more information about its activities is available in the marketplace. Thus it is easier for investors to evaluate the quality of the corporation and determine whether it is a good firm or a bad one. Because investors have fewer worries about adverse selection with well-known corporations, they will be willing to invest directly in their securities. Hence we have an explanation for puzzle 6: The larger and more mature a corporation is, the more information investors have about it, and the more likely it is that the corporation can raise funds in securities markets.

COLLATERAL AND NET WORTH Adverse selection interferes with the functioning of financial markets only if a lender suffers a loss when a borrower is unable to make loan payments and thereby defaults. Collateral, property promised to the lender if the borrower defaults, reduces the consequences of adverse selection because it reduces the lender's losses in the event of a default. If a borrower defaults on a loan, the lender can sell the collateral and use the proceeds to make up for the losses on the loan. For example, if you fail to make your mortgage payments, the lender can take title to your house, auction it off, and use the receipts to pay off the loan. Lenders are thus more willing to make loans secured by collateral, and borrowers are willing to supply collateral because the reduced risk for the lender makes it more likely they will get the loan in the first place and perhaps at a better loan rate. The presence of adverse selection in credit markets thus provides an explanation for why collateral is an important feature of debt contracts (puzzle 7).

Net worth (also called **equity capital**), the difference between a firm's assets (what it owns or is owed) and its liabilities (what it owes), can perform a similar role to collateral. If a firm has a high net worth, then even if it engages in investments that cause it to have negative profits and so defaults on its debt payments, the lender can take title to the firm's net worth, sell it off, and use the proceeds to recoup some of the losses from the loan. In addition, the more net worth a firm has in the first place, the less likely it is to default because the firm has a cushion of assets that it can use to pay off its loans. Hence when firms seeking credit have high net worth, the consequences of adverse selection are less important and lenders are more willing to make loans. This analysis lies behind the often-heard lament, "Only the people who don't need money can borrow it!"

SUMMARY So far we have used the concept of adverse selection to explain seven of the eight puzzles about financial structure introduced earlier: The first four emphasize the importance of financial intermediaries and the relative unimportance of securities markets for the financing of corporations; the fifth, that financial markets are among the most heavily regulated sectors of the economy; the sixth, that only large, well-established corporations have access to securities markets; and the seventh, that collateral is an important feature of debt contracts. In the next section we will see that the other asymmetric information concept of moral hazard provides additional reasons for the importance of financial intermediaries and the relative unimportance of securities markets for the financing of corporations, the prevalence of government regulation, and the importance of collateral in debt contracts. In addition, the concept of moral hazard can be used to explain our final puzzle (puzzle 8) of why debt contracts are complicated legal documents that place substantial restrictions on the behavior of the borrower.

HOW MORAL HAZARD AFFECTS THE CHOICE BETWEEN DEBT AND EQUITY CONTRACTS

Moral hazard is the asymmetric information problem that occurs after the financial transaction takes place, when the seller of a security may have incentives to hide information and engage in activities that are undesirable for the purchaser of the security. Moral hazard has important consequences for whether a firm finds it easier to raise funds with debt rather than with equity contracts.

Moral Hazard in Equity Contracts: The Principal-Agent Problem

Equity contracts, such as common stock, are claims to a share in the profits and assets of a business. Equity contracts are subject to a particular type of moral hazard called the **principal-agent problem.** When managers own only a small fraction of the firm they work for, the stockholders who own most of the firm's equity (called the *principals*) are not the same people as the managers of the firm, who are the *agents* of the owners. This separation of ownership and control involves moral hazard in that the managers in control (the agents) may act in their own interest rather than in the interest of the stockholder-owners (the principals) because the managers have less incentive to maximize profits than the stockholder-owners do.

To understand the principal-agent problem more fully, suppose that your friend Steve asks you to become a silent partner in his ice-cream store. The store requires an investment of $10,000 to set up, but Steve has only $1000. So you purchase an equity stake (stock shares) for $9000, which entitles you to 90 percent of the ownership of the firm, while Steve owns only 10 percent. If Steve works hard to make tasty ice cream, keeps the store clean, smiles at all the customers, and hustles to wait on tables quickly, after all expenses (including Steve's salary), the store will have $50,000 in profits per year, of which Steve receives 10 percent ($5000) and you receive 90 percent ($45,000).

But if Steve doesn't provide quick and friendly service to his customers, uses the $50,000 in income to buy artwork for his office, and even sneaks off to the beach while he should be at the store, the store will not earn any profit. Steve can only earn the additional $5000 (his 10 percent share of the profits) over his salary if he works hard and forgoes unproductive investments (such as art for his office). Steve might decide that the extra $5000 just isn't enough to make him want to expend the effort to be a good manager; he might decide that it would be worth his while only if he earned an extra $10,000. If Steve feels this way, he does not have enough incentive to be a good manager and will end up with a beautiful office, a good tan, and a store that doesn't show any profits. Because the store won't show any profits, Steve's decision not to act in your interest will cost you $45,000 (your 90 percent of the profits if he had chosen to be a good manager instead).

The moral hazard arising from the principal-agent problem might be even worse if Steve were not totally honest. Because his ice-cream store is a cash business; Steve has the incentive to pocket $50,000 in cash and tell you that the profits were zero. He now gets a return of $50,000, but you get nothing. The moral hazard incentive to underreport profits is illustrated by the experience with accounting practices in the movie industry described in Box 1.

Further indications that the principal-agent problem created by equity contracts can be severe are provided by examples of managers who build luxurious offices for themselves or drive high-priced corporate automobiles. Besides pursuing personal benefits, managers might also pursue corporate strategies (such as the acquisition of other firms) that enhance their personal power but do not increase the corporation's profitability

The principal-agent problem would not arise if the owners of a firm had complete information about what the managers were up to and could prevent wasteful expenditures or fraud. The principal-agent problem, which is an example of moral hazard, arises only because a manager, like Steve, has more information about his activities than the stockholder does—that is, there is asymmetric information. The principal-agent problem would also not arise if Steve alone owned the store and there were no separation of ownership and control. If this were the case, Steve's hard work and avoidance of unproductive investments would yield him a profit (and extra income) of $50,000, an amount that would make it worth his while to be a good manager.

Tools to Help Solve the Principal-Agent Problem

PRODUCTION OF INFORMATION: MONITORING   You have seen that the principal-agent problem arises because managers have more information about their activities and actual profits than stockholders do. One way for stockholders to reduce this moral hazard problem is for them to engage in a particular type of information production, the monitoring of the firm's activities: auditing the firm frequently and checking on what the management is doing. The problem is that the monitoring process can be expensive in terms of time and money, as reflected in the name economists give it, **costly state verification.** Costly state verification makes the equity contract less desirable, and it explains, in part, why equity is not a more important element in our financial structure.

As with adverse selection, the free-rider problem decreases the amount of information production that would reduce the moral hazard (principal-agent) problem. In this example, the free-rider problem decreases monitoring. If you

BOX 1

"Hollywood Accounting"

Has *Forrest Gump* Been a Money Loser?
Accounting practices in the movie industry are notorious, giving the phrase "Hollywood accounting" a dubious reputation. A standard practice at movie studios is to keep two sets of books, a practice that might not be tolerated in other businesses but is in the movie business, where standards of morality are not always the highest. One set is maintained according to the generally accepted accounting principles in other industries; that set is used to report profits to management and to shareholders. The second set of books, referred to as "contractual accounting," is used when a studio commits to paying out percentages of a movie's "net profits" among actors, directors, writers, and other parties as part of contractual arrangements. Given that the movie studios have a moral hazard incentive to minimize these "net profits,"

not surprisingly they are rarely positive. For example, Forrest Gump, which has taken in over $600 million at the box office, is yet to show any profits according to Paramount, the filmmaker. The same has also been the case for other blockbusters such as the first Batman movie, J.K.F., and Coming to America. Can we really believe that Forrest Gump, one of the most successful movies of all time, is a money loser, or is this just an example of the principal-agent problem at work?

The dubious accounting practices of the movie industry have been coming under attack as a result of numerous lawsuits. In addition, the squeaky-clean Walt Disney Company is trying to change industry practices by going on record that it will not use contractual accounting and a second set of books when it compensates movie actors, directors, and writers.

know that other stockholders are paying to monitor the activities of the company you hold shares in, you can take a free ride on their activities. Then you can use the money you save by not engaging in monitoring to vacation on a Caribbean island. If you can do this, though, so can other stockholders. Perhaps all the stockholders will go to the islands, and no one will spend any resources on monitoring the firm. The moral hazard problem for shares of common stock will then be severe, making it hard for firms to issue them to raise capital.

GOVERNMENT REGULATION TO INCREASE INFORMATION   As with adverse selection, the government has an incentive to try to reduce the moral hazard problem created by asymmetric information. Governments everywhere have laws to force firms to adhere to standard accounting principles that make profit verification easier. They also pass laws to impose stiff criminal penalties on people who commit the fraud of hiding and stealing profits. However, these measures can only be partly effective. Catching this kind of fraud is not easy; fraudulent managers have the incentive to make it very hard for government agencies to find or prove fraud.

FINANCIAL INTERMEDIATION   Financial intermediaries have the ability to avoid the free-rider problem in the face of moral hazard. One financial intermediary that helps reduce the moral hazard arising from the principal-agent problem is the **venture capital firm.** Venture capital firms pool the resources of their partners and use the funds to help budding entrepreneurs start new businesses. In exchange for the use of the venture capital, the firm receives an equity share in the new business. Because verification of earnings and profits is so important in eliminating moral hazard, venture capital firms usually insist on having several of their own people participate as members of the managing body of the firm, the board of directors, so that they can keep a close watch on the firm's activities. When a venture capital firm supplies start-up funds, the equity in the firm is not marketable to anyone *but* the venture capital firm. Thus other investors are unable to take a free ride on the venture capital firm's verification activities. As a result of this arrangement, the venture capital firm is able to garner the full benefits of its verification activities and is given the appropriate incentives to reduce the moral hazard problem.

DEBT CONTRACTS Moral hazard arises with an equity contract, which is a claim on profits in all situations, whether the firm is making or losing money. If a contract could be structured so that moral hazard would exist only in certain situations, there would be a reduced need to monitor managers, and the contract would be more attractive than the equity contract. The debt contract has exactly these attributes because it is a contractual agreement by the borrower to pay the lender *fixed* dollar amounts at periodic intervals. When the firm has high profits, the lender receives the contractual payments and does not need to know the exact profits of the firm. If the managers are hiding profits or are pursuing activities that are personally beneficial but don't increase profitability, the lender doesn't care as long as these activities do not interfere with the ability of the firm to make its debt payments on time. Only when the firm cannot meet its debt payments, thereby being in a state of default, is there a need for the lender to verify the state of the firm's profits. Only in this situation do lenders involved in debt contracts need to act more like equity holders; now they need to know how much income the firm has in order to get their fair share.

The advantage of a less frequent need to monitor the firm, and thus a lower cost of state verification, helps explain why debt contracts are used more frequently than equity contracts to raise capital. The concept of moral hazard thus helps explain puzzle 1, why stocks are not the most important source of financing for businesses.[4]

HOW MORAL HAZARD INFLUENCES FINANCIAL STRUCTURE IN DEBT MARKETS

Even with the advantages just described, debt contracts are still subject to moral hazard. Because a debt contract requires the borrowers to pay out a fixed amount and lets them keep any profits above this amount, the borrowers have an incentive to take on investment projects that are riskier than the lenders would like.

---

[4]Another factor that encourages the use of debt contracts rather than equity contracts in the United States is our tax code. Debt interest payments are a deductible expense for American firms, whereas dividend payments to equity shareholders are not.

For example, suppose that because you are concerned about the problem of verifying the profits of Steve's ice-cream store, you decide not to become an equity partner. Instead, you lend Steve the $9000 he needs to set up his business and have a debt contract that pays you an interest rate of 10 percent. As far as you are concerned, this is a surefire investment because there is a strong and steady demand for ice cream in your neighborhood. However, once you give Steve the funds, he might use them for purposes other than you intended. Instead of opening up the ice-cream store, Steve might use your $9000 loan to invest in chemical research equipment because he thinks he has a 1-in-10 chance of inventing a diet ice cream that tastes every bit as good as the premium brands but has no fat or calories.

Obviously, this is a very risky investment, but if Steve is successful, he will become a multimillionaire. He has a strong incentive to undertake the riskier investment with your money because the gains to him would be so large if he succeeded. You would clearly be very unhappy if Steve used your loan for the riskier investment because if he were unsuccessful, which is highly likely, you would lose most, if not all, of the money you gave him. And if he were successful, you wouldn't share in his success—you would still get only a 10 percent return on the loan because the principal and interest payments are fixed. Because of the potential moral hazard (Steve might use your money to finance a very risky venture), you would probably not make the loan to Steve, even though an ice-cream store in the neighborhood is a good investment that would provide benefits for everyone.

Tools to Help Solve Moral Hazard in Debt Contracts

NET WORTH When borrowers have more at stake because their *net worth* (the difference between their assets and their liabilities) is high, the risk of moral hazard—the temptation to act in a manner that lenders find objectionable—will be greatly reduced because the borrowers themselves have a lot to lose. Let's return to Steve and his ice-cream business. Suppose that the cost of setting up either the ice-cream store or the research equipment is $100,000 instead of $10,000. So Steve needs to put $91,000 of his own money into the business (instead of $1000) in addition to the $9000 supplied by your loan. Now if Steve is unsuccessful in inventing the no-calorie nonfat ice cream, he has a lot to lose, the $91,000 of net worth ($100,000 in assets minus the $9000 loan from you). He will think twice about undertaking the riskier investment and is more likely to invest in the ice-cream store, which is more of a sure thing. Hence when Steve has more of his own money (net worth) in the business, you are more likely to make him the loan.

One way of describing the solution that high net worth provides to the moral hazard problem is to say that it makes the debt contract **incentive-compatible;** that is, it aligns the incentives of the borrower with those of the lender. The greater the borrower's net worth, the greater the borrower's incentive to behave in the way that the lender expects and desires, the smaller the moral hazard problem in the debt contract is, and the easier it is for the firm to borrow. Conversely, when the borrower's net worth is lower, the moral hazard problem is greater, and it is harder for the firm to borrow.

MONITORING AND ENFORCEMENT OF RESTRICTIVE COVENANTS As the example of Steve and his ice-cream store shows, if you could make sure that Steve doesn't invest in anything riskier than the ice-cream store, it would be worth your while to make him the loan. You can ensure that Steve uses your money for the purpose *you* want it to be used for by writing provisions (restrictive covenants) into the debt contract that restrict his firm's activities. By monitoring Steve's activities to see whether he is complying with the restrictive covenants and enforcing the covenants if he is not, you can make sure that he will not take on risks at your expense. Restrictive covenants are directed at reducing moral hazard either by ruling out undesirable behavior or by encouraging desirable behavior. There are four types of restrictive covenants that achieve this objective:

1. Covenants can be designed to lower moral hazard by keeping the borrower from engaging in the undesirable behavior of undertaking risky investment projects. Some such covenants mandate that a loan can be used only to finance specific activities, such as the purchase of particular equipment or inventories. Others restrict the borrowing firm from engaging in certain risky business activities, such as purchasing other businesses.

2. Restrictive covenants can encourage the borrower to engage in desirable activities that make it more likely that the loan will be paid off. One restrictive covenant of this type requires the breadwinner in a household to carry life insurance that pays off the mortgage upon that person's death. Restrictive covenants of this type for businesses focus on encouraging the borrowing firm to keep its net worth high because higher borrower net worth reduces moral hazard and makes it less likely that the lender will suffer losses. These restrictive covenants typically specify that the firm must maintain minimum holdings of certain assets relative to the firm's size.

3. Because collateral is an important protection for the lender, restrictive covenants can encourage the borrower to keep the collateral in good condition and make sure that it stays in the possession of the borrower. This is the type of covenant ordinary people encounter most often. Automobile loan contracts, for example, require the car owner to maintain a minimum amount of collision and theft insurance and prevent the sale of the car unless the loan is paid off. Similarly, the recipient of a home mortgage must have adequate insurance on the home and must pay off the mortgage when the property is sold.

4. Restrictive covenants also require a borrowing firm to provide information about its activities periodically in the form of quarterly accounting and income reports, thereby making it easier for the lender to monitor the firm and reduce moral hazard. This type of covenant may also stipulate that the lender has the right to audit and inspect the firm's books at any time.

We now see why debt contracts are often complicated legal documents with numerous restrictions on the borrower's behavior (puzzle 8): Debt contracts require complicated restrictive covenants to lower moral hazard.

FINANCIAL INTERMEDIATION Although restrictive covenants help reduce the moral hazard problem, they do not eliminate it completely. It is almost impossible to write covenants that rule out *every* risky activity. Furthermore, borrowers may be clever enough to find loopholes in restrictive covenants that make them ineffective.

Another problem with restrictive covenants is that they must be monitored and enforced. A restrictive covenant is meaningless if the borrower can violate it knowing that the lender won't check up or is unwilling to pay for legal recourse. Because monitoring and enforcement of restrictive covenants are costly, the free-rider problem arises in the debt securities (bond) market just as it does in the stock market. If you know that other bondholders are monitoring and enforcing the restrictive covenants, you can free-ride on their monitoring and enforcement. But other bondholders can do the same thing, so the likely outcome is that not enough resources are devoted to monitoring and enforcing the restrictive covenants. Moral hazard therefore continues to be a severe problem for marketable debt.

As we have seen before, financial intermediaries, particularly banks, have the ability to avoid the free-rider problem as long as they primarily make private loans. Private loans are not traded, so no one else can free-ride on the intermediary's monitoring and enforcement of the restrictive covenants. The intermediary making private loans thus receives the benefits of monitoring and enforcement and will work to shrink the moral hazard problem inherent in debt contracts. The concept of moral hazard has provided us with additional reasons why financial intermediaries play a more important role in channeling funds from savers to borrowers than marketable securities do, as described in puzzles 1 through 4.

Summary

The presence of asymmetric information in financial markets leads to adverse selection and moral hazard problems that interfere with the efficient functioning of those markets. Tools to help solve these problems involve the private production and sale of information, government regulation to increase information in financial markets, the importance of collateral and net worth to debt contracts, and the use of monitoring and restrictive covenants. A key finding from our analysis is that the existence of the free-rider problem for traded securities such as stocks and bonds indicates that financial intermediaries, particularly banks, should play a greater role than securities markets in financing the activities of businesses. Economic analysis of the consequences of adverse selection and moral hazard has helped explain the basic features of our financial system and has provided solutions to the eight puzzles about our financial structure outlined at the beginning of this chapter.

Financial Development and Economic Growth

Recent research has found that an important reason why many developing countries experience very low rates of growth is that their financial systems are underdeveloped (a situation referred to as *financial repression*).[5] The economic

---

[5]See Nouriel Roubini and Xavier Sala-i-Martin, "A Growth Model of Inflation, Tax Evasion and Financial Repression," *Journal of Monetary Economics* 35 (1995): 275–301, for a survey of this literature and a list of further references.

analysis of financial structure helps explain how an underdeveloped financial system leads to a low state of economic development and economic growth.

The financial systems in developing countries face several difficulties that keep them from operating efficiently. As we have seen, two important tools used to help solve adverse selection and moral hazard problems in credit markets are collateral and restrictive covenants. In many developing countries, the legal system functions poorly, making it hard to make effective use of these two tools. In these countries, bankruptcy procedures are often extremely slow and cumbersome. For example, in many countries, **creditors** (holders of debt) must first sue the defaulting debtor for payment, which can take several years, and then once a favorable judgment has been obtained, the creditor has to sue again to obtain title to the collateral. The process can take in excess of five years, and by the time the lender acquires the collateral, it well may have been neglected and thus have little value. In addition, governments often block lenders from foreclosing on borrowers in politically powerful sectors such as agriculture. Where the market is unable to use collateral effectively, the adverse selection problem will be worse because the lender will need even more information about the quality of the borrower in order to screen out a good loan from a bad one. The result is that it will be harder for lenders to channel funds to borrowers with the most productive investment opportunities, thereby leading to less productive investment and hence a slower-growing economy. Similarly, a poorly developed legal system may make it extremely difficult for borrowers to enforce restrictive covenants. Thus they may have a much more limited ability to reduce moral hazard on the part of borrowers and so will be less willing to lend. Again the outcome will be less productive investment and a lower growth rate for the economy.

Governments in developing countries have also often decided to use their financial systems to direct credit to themselves or to favored sectors of the economy by setting interest rates at artificially low levels for certain types of loans, by creating so-called development finance institutions to make specific types of loans, or by directing existing institutions to lend to certain entities. As we have seen, private institutions have an incentive to solve adverse selection and moral hazard problems and lend to borrowers with the most productive investment opportunities. Governments have less incentive to do so because they are not driven by the profit motive and so their directed credit programs may not channel funds to sectors that will produce high growth for the economy. The outcome is again likely to result in less efficient investment and slower growth.

In addition, banks in many developing countries have been nationalized by their governments. Again because of the absence of the profit motive, these nationalized banks have little incentive to allocate their capital to the most productive uses. Indeed, the primary loan customer of these nationalized banks is often the government, which does not always use the funds wisely.

We have seen that government regulation can increase the amount of information in financial markets to make them work more efficiently. Many developing countries have an underdeveloped regulatory apparatus that retards the provision of adequate information to the marketplace. For example, developing countries often have weak accounting standards, making it very hard to ascertain the quality of a borrower's balance sheet. As a result, asymmetric information problems are more severe, and the financial system is severely hampered in channeling funds to the most productive uses.

The institutional environment of a poor legal system, weak accounting standards, inadequate government regulation, and government intervention through directed credit programs and nationalization of banks all help explain why many countries stay poor while others grow richer.

FINANCIAL CRISES AND AGGREGATE ECONOMIC ACTIVITY

Our economic analysis of the effects of adverse selection and moral hazard can help us understand **financial crises,** major disruptions in financial markets that are characterized by sharp declines in asset prices and the failures of many financial and nonfinancial firms. Financial crises have been common in most countries throughout modern history. The United States experienced major financial crises in 1819, 1837, 1857, 1873, 1884, 1893, 1907, and 1930–1933 but has had none since then.[6] Studying financial crises is worthwhile because they have led to severe economic downturns in the past and have the potential for doing so in the future.

Financial crises occur when there is a disruption in the financial system that causes such a sharp increase in adverse selection and moral hazard problems in financial markets that the markets are unable to channel funds efficiently from savers to people with productive investment opportunities. As a result of this inability of financial markets to function efficiently, economic activity contracts sharply.

Factors Causing Financial Crises

To understand why banking and financial crises occur and more specifically how they lead to contractions in economic activity, we need to examine the factors that cause them. Four categories of factors can trigger financial crises: increases in interest rates, increases in uncertainty, asset market effects on balance sheets, and bank panics.

INCREASES IN INTEREST RATES As we saw earlier, individuals and firms with the riskiest investment projects are exactly those who are willing to pay the highest interest rates. If market interest rates are driven up sufficiently because of increased demand for credit or because of a decline in the money supply, good credit risks are less likely to want to borrow while bad credit risks are still willing to borrow. Because of the resulting increase in adverse selection, lenders will no longer want to make loans. The substantial decline in lending will lead to a substantial decline in investment and aggregate economic activity.

---

[6]Although we in the United States have not experienced any financial crises since the Great Depression, we have had several close calls—the October 1987 stock market crash, for example. An important reason why we have escaped financial crises is the timely action of the Federal Reserve to prevent them during episodes like that of October 1987. We look at the issue of the Fed's role in preventing financial crises in Chapter 18.

INCREASES IN UNCERTAINTY A dramatic increase in uncertainty in financial markets, due perhaps to the failure of a prominent financial or nonfinancial institution, a recession, or a stock market crash, makes it harder for lenders to screen good from bad credit risks. The resulting inability of lenders to solve the adverse selection problem makes them less willing to lend, which leads to a decline in lending, investment, and aggregate activity.

ASSET MARKET EFFECTS ON BALANCE SHEETS The state of firms' balance sheets has important implications for the severity of asymmetric information problems in the financial system. A sharp decline in the stock market is one factor that can cause a serious deterioration in firms' balance sheets that can increase adverse selection and moral hazard problems in financial markets and provoke a financial crisis. A decline in the stock market means that the net worth of corporations has fallen because share prices are the valuation of a corporation's net worth. The decline in net worth as a result of a stock market decline makes lenders less willing to lend because, as we have seen, the net worth of a firm plays a role similar to that of collateral. When the value of collateral declines, it provides less protection to lenders, meaning that losses on loans are likely to be more severe. Because lenders are now less protected against the consequences of adverse selection, they decrease their lending, which in turn causes investment and aggregate output to decline. In addition, the decline in corporate net worth as a result of a stock market decline increases moral hazard by providing incentives for borrowing firms to make risky investments, as they now have less to lose if their investments go sour. The resulting increase in moral hazard makes lending less attractive—another reason why a stock market decline and hence a decline in net worth leads to decreased lending and economic activity.

In economies in which inflation has been moderate, which characterizes most industrialized countries, many debt contracts are typically of fairly long maturity with fixed interest rates. In this institutional environment, unanticipated declines in the aggregate price level also decrease the net worth of firms. Because debt payments are contractually fixed in nominal terms, an unanticipated decline in the price level raises the value of firms' liabilities in *real* terms (increases the burden of the debt) but does not raise the real value of firms' assets. The result is that net worth in *real* terms (the difference between assets and liabilities in *real* terms) declines. A sharp drop in the price level therefore causes a substantial decline in real net worth and an increase in adverse selection and moral hazard problems facing lenders. An unanticipated decline in the aggregate price level thus leads to a drop in lending and economic activity.

Because of uncertainty about the future value of the domestic currency in developing countries (and in some industrialized countries), many nonfinancial firms, banks, and governments in these countries find it easier to issue debt denominated in foreign currencies. This can lead to a financial crisis in a similar fashion to an unanticipated decline in inflation. With debt contracts denominated in foreign currency, when there is an unanticipated depreciation or devaluation of the domestic currency, the debt burden of domestic firms increases. Since assets are typically denominated in domestic currency, there is a resulting deterioration in firms' balance sheets and a decline in net worth, which then increases adverse selection and moral hazard problems along the lines just described. The increase in asymmetric information problems leads to a decline in investment and economic activity.

Although we have seen that increases in interest rates have a direct effect on increasing adverse selection problems, increases in interest rates also play a role in promoting a financial crisis through their effect on both firms' and households' balance sheets. A rise in interest rates and therefore in households' and firms' interest payments decreases firms' **cash flow,** the difference between cash receipts and cash expenditures. The decline in cash flow causes a deterioration in the balance sheet because it decreases the liquidity of the household or firm and thus makes it harder for lenders to know whether the firm or household will be able to pay its bills. As a result, adverse selection and moral hazard problems become more severe for potential lenders to these firms and households, leading to a decline in lending and economic activity. There is thus an additional reason why sharp increases in interest rates can be an important factor leading to financial crises.

BANK PANICS   Banks perform an important financial intermediation role by engaging in information-producing activities that facilitate productive investment for the economy. Consequently, a financial crisis in which many banks go out of business (called a **bank panic**) reduces the amount of financial intermediation undertaken by banks and so leads to a decline in investment and aggregate economic activity. Indeed, even if the banks do not fail but instead just suffer a substantial contraction in their net worth because of bad loans, the banks will have fewer resources to lend and so bank lending will decline, thereby leading to a contraction in economic activity. A decrease in bank lending during a financial crisis also decreases the supply of funds to borrowers, which in turn leads to higher interest rates. Since a rise in interest rates also increases adverse selection in credit markets, bank panics further intensify the decrease in economic activity through this channel as well.

Financial Crises in the United States

As mentioned, the United States has a long history of banking and financial crises, such crises having occurred every 20 years or so in the nineteenth and early twentieth centuries—in 1819, 1837, 1857, 1873, 1884, 1893, 1907 and 1930-1933. Our analysis of the factors that lead to a financial crisis can explain why these crises took place and why they were so damaging to the U.S. economy.

Study Guide   To understand fully what took place in a U.S. financial crisis, make sure that you can state the reasons why each of the factors—increases in interest rates, increases in uncertainty, asset market effects on balance sheets, and bank panics—increases adverse selection and moral hazard problems, which in turn lead to a decline in economic activity. To help you understand these crises, you might want to refer to Figure 3, a diagram that traces the sequence of events in a U.S. financial crisis.

As shown in Figure 3, most financial crises in the United States have begun with a sharp rise in interest rates (frequently stemming from increases in interest rates abroad), a steep stock market decline, and an increase in uncertainty resulting

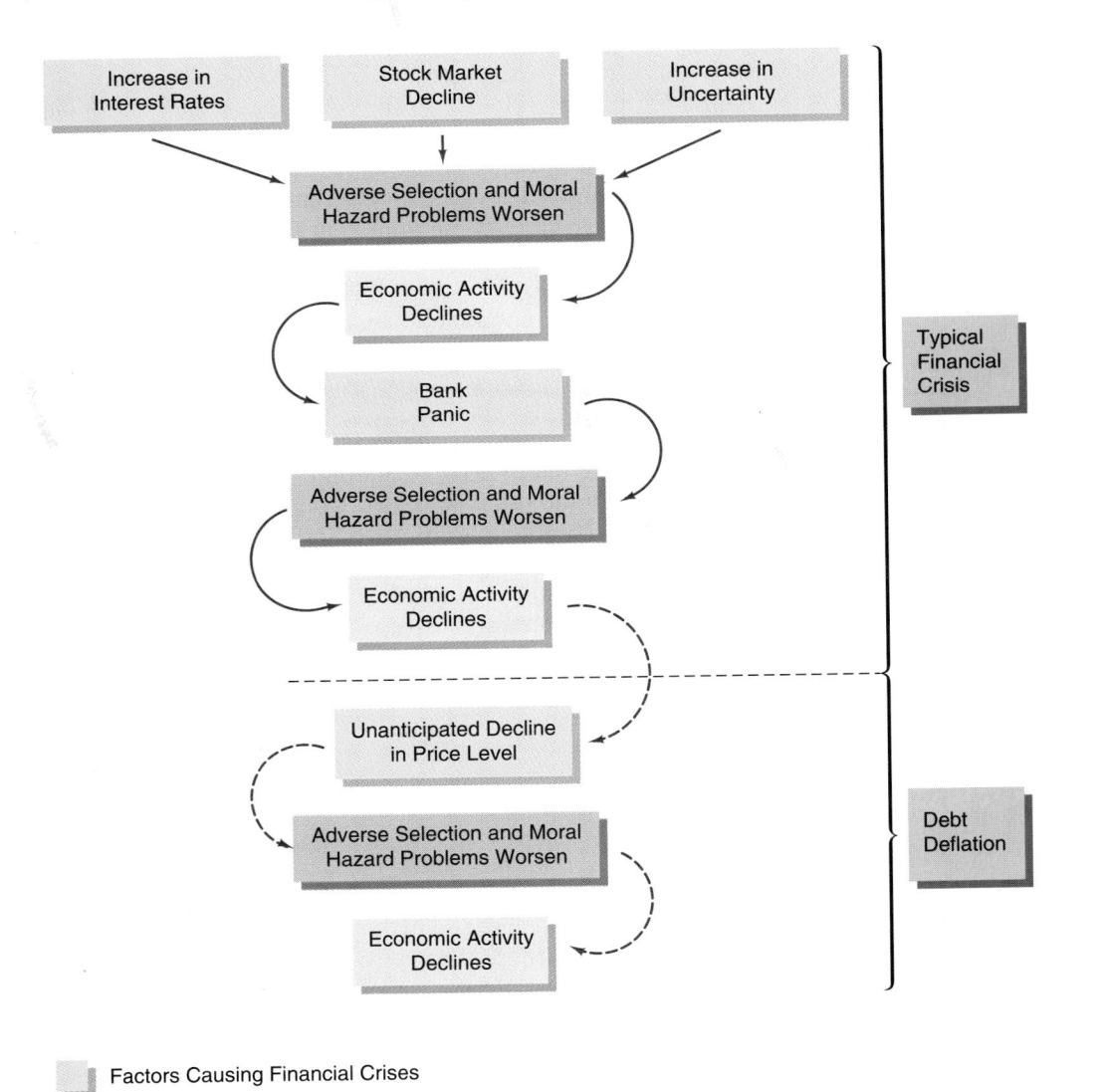

Factors Causing Financial Crises

Consequences of Changes in Factors

FIGURE 3   Sequence of Events in U.S. Financial Crises
The solid arrows trace the sequence of events in a typical financial crisis; the dotted arrows show the additional set of events that occur if the crisis develops into a debt deflation.

from a failure of major financial or nonfinancial firms (the Ohio Life Insurance & Trust Company in 1857, the Northern Pacific Railroad and Jay Cooke & Company in 1873, Grant & Ward in 1884, the National Cordage Company in 1893, the Knickerbocker Trust Company in 1907, and the Bank of the United States in 1930). During these crises, the increase in uncertainty, the rise in interest rates, and the stock market decline increased the severity of adverse selection problems in credit markets; the stock market decline also increased moral hazard problems. The rise in adverse selection and moral hazard problems then made it less attractive for lenders to lend and led to a decline in investment and aggregate economic activity.

Because of the worsening business conditions and uncertainty about their bank's health (perhaps banks would go broke), depositors began to withdraw their funds from banks, which led to bank panics. The resulting decline in the number of banks raised interest rates even further and decreased the amount of financial intermediation by banks. Worsening of the problems created by adverse selection and moral hazard led to further economic contraction.

Finally, there was a sorting out of firms that were **insolvent** (firms that had a negative net worth and hence were bankrupt) from healthy firms by bankruptcy proceedings. The same process occurred for banks, often with the help of public and private authorities. Once this sorting out was complete, uncertainty in financial markets declined, the stock market underwent a recovery, and interest rates fell. The overall result was that adverse selection and moral hazard problems diminished and the financial crisis subsided. With the financial markets able to operate well again, the stage was set for the recovery of the economy.

If, however, the economic downturn led to a sharp decline in prices, the recovery process was short-circuited. In this situation, shown in Figure 3, a process called **debt deflation** occurred, in which a substantial decline in the price level set in, leading to a further deterioration in firms' net worth because of the increased burden of indebtedness. When debt deflation set in, the adverse selection and moral hazard problems continued to increase so that lending, investment spending, and aggregate economic activity remained depressed for a long time. The most significant financial crisis that included debt deflation was the Great Depression, the worst economic contraction in U.S. history (see Box 2). (A)

Financial Crises in Developing Countries: The Case of Mexico, 1994-1995

In recent years, many developing countries have experienced financial crises, the most dramatic of which was the Mexican crisis of 1994-1995. An important puzzle is how a developing country can shift dramatically from a path of reasonable growth before a financial crisis, as was the case in Mexico in 1994, to a sharp decline in economic activity after a crisis occurs that is very damaging to both the economy and the social fabric of the country. We can again apply our asymmetric information analysis of financial crises to explain this puzzle and to understand the Mexican financial crisis of 1994–1995.

BOX 2

Case Study of a Financial Crisis

The Great Depression. Federal Reserve officials viewed the stock market boom of 1928 and 1929, during which stock prices doubled, as excessive speculation. To curb it, they pursued a tight monetary policy to raise interest rates. The Fed got more than it bargained for when the stock market crashed in October 1929.

Although the 1929 crash had a great impact on the minds of a whole generation, most people forget that by the middle of 1930, more than half of the stock market decline had been reversed. What might have been a normal recession turned into something far different, however, with adverse shocks to the agricultural sector, a continuing decline in the stock market after the middle of 1930, and a sequence of bank collapses from October 1930 until March 1933 in which over one-third of the banks in the United States went out of business (events described in more detail in Chapter 19).

The continuing decline in stock prices after mid-1930 (by mid-1932 stocks had declined to 10 percent of their value at the 1929 peak) and the increase in uncertainty from the unsettled business conditions created by the economic contraction made adverse selection and moral hazard problems worse in the credit markets.

The loss of one-third of the banks reduced the amount of financial intermediation. This intensified adverse selection and moral hazard problems, thereby decreasing the ability of financial markets to channel funds to firms with productive investment opportunities. As our analysis predicts, the amount of outstanding commercial loans fell by half from 1929 to 1933, and investment spending collapsed, declining by 90 percent from its 1929 level.

The short-circuiting of the process that kept the economy from recovering quickly, which it does in most recessions, occurred because of a fall in the price level by 25 percent in the 1930–1933 period. This huge decline in prices triggered a debt deflation in which net worth fell because of the increased burden of indebtedness borne by firms. The decline in net worth and the resulting increase in adverse selection and moral hazard problems in the credit markets led to a prolonged economic contraction in which unemployment rose to 25 percent of the labor force. The financial crisis in the Great Depression was the worst ever experienced in the United States, and it explains why this economic contraction was also the most severe one ever experienced by the nation.*

*See Ben Bernanke, "Nonmonetary Effects of the Financial Crisis in the Propagation of the Great Depression," *American Economic Review* 73 (1983): 257–276, for a discussion of the role of asymmetric information problems in the Great Depression period.

Because of the different institutional features of Mexico's debt markets, the sequence of events in the 1994–1995 Mexican banking and financial crisis, which began in December 1994, is different from that which occurred in the United States in the nineteenth and twentieth centuries. Figure 4 provides a diagrammatic exposition of the sequence of events that occurred in the Mexican case.

An important factor leading up to the Mexican financial crisis was the deterioration in banks' balance sheets because of increasing loan losses. When the Mexican banks were privatized in the early 1990s and financial markets were deregulated, a lending boom ensued in which bank credit to the private nonfinancial business sector as a fraction of GDP accelerated dramatically, going from

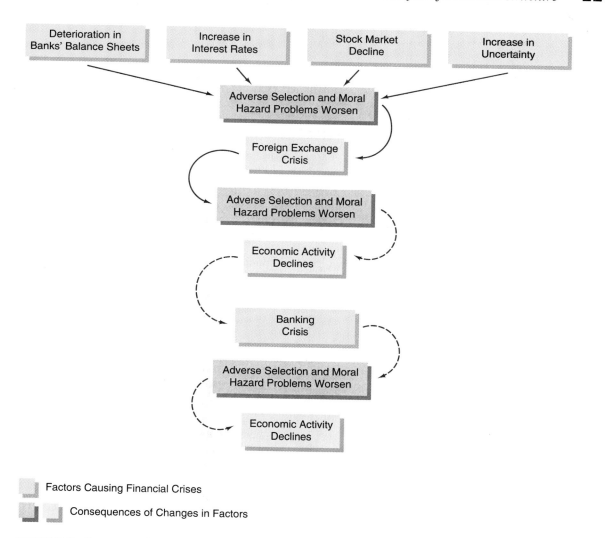

Factors Causing Financial Crises

Consequences of Changes in Factors

FIGURE 4 Sequence of Events in the Mexican Financial Crisis of 1994–1995
The arrows trace the sequence of events during the Mexican financial crisis.

10 percent of GDP in 1988 to over 40 percent of GDP in 1994. Because of weak supervision by bank regulators and a lack of expertise in screening and monitoring borrowers at the commercial banks, losses on their loans began to mount, thereby causing an erosion of banks' net worth (capital). As we have seen, this decline in bank capital would mean that the banks would have fewer resources to lend, and this lack of lending would eventually lead to a contraction in economic activity.

Consistent with the U.S. experience in the nineteenth and early twentieth centuries, another precipitating factor to the Mexican financial crisis was a rise in interest rates abroad. Beginning in February 1994, the Federal Reserve began to raise the federal funds rate to head off inflationary pressures. Although the policy was quite successful in keeping inflation in check in the United States, it put upward pressure on Mexican interest rates, increasing asymmetric information problems in the Mexican financial system. Furthermore, the Mexican central bank, the Banco de Mexico, raised interest rates to protect the value of the peso in the foreign exchange market when the peso came under attack beginning in early 1994. The rise in interest rates directly added to increased adverse selection in Mexican financial markets because, as discussed earlier, it made it more likely that the parties willing to take on the most risk would seek loans.

Even more important, increased interest payments caused reductions in households' and firms' cash flow, which led to a deterioration in their balance sheets. A feature of Mexican debt markets is that debt contracts have very short durations, typically less than one month. Thus the rise in Mexican short-term interest rates, which occurred partly as a result of rising short-term rates in the United States, meant that the effect on cash flow and hence on balance sheets would be substantial. As our asymmetric information analysis suggests, this deterioration in households' and firms' balance sheets increased adverse selection and moral hazard problems in Mexican financial markets, making lenders less willing to lend.

Also consistent with the U.S. experience in the nineteenth and early twentieth centuries, increases in uncertainty in Mexican financial markets and a stock market decline precipitated the full-blown financial crisis. The Mexican economy was hit by political shocks in 1994, specifically the assassination of Luis Donaldo Colosio, the ruling party's presidential candidate, and an uprising in the southern state of Chiapas. These events increased general uncertainty in Mexican financial markets. In addition, by the middle of December 1994, stock prices on the Bolsa (stock exchange) fell nearly 20 percent from their September 1994 peak. As we have seen, an increase in uncertainty and the decrease in net worth as a result of the stock market decline increase asymmetric information problems because it becomes harder to screen out good from bad borrowers and the decline in net worth decreases the value of firms' collateral and increases their incentives to make risky investments because there is less equity to lose if the investments are unsuccessful. The increase in uncertainty and the stock market decline, along with increases in interest rates and the deterioration in banks' balance sheets, were the initial conditions that worsened adverse selection and moral hazard problems (shown in the top of the diagram in Figure 4) and made the Mexican economy ripe for a serious financial crisis when a full-blown speculative attack developed in the foreign exchange market

With the Colosio assassination, the Chiapas uprising, and other political developments, the Mexican peso began to come under attack. Even though the Mexican central bank raised interest rates sharply, it was unable to stem the attack and was forced to devalue the peso on December 20, 1994. (We will return to this in Chapter 20.)

The institutional structure of debt markets in Mexico now interacted with the peso devaluation to propel the economy into a full-fledged financial crisis. When the peso had lost half its value by March 1995, actual and expected inflation rose dramatically, and interest rates on debt denominated in pesos went to sky-high levels, exceeding 100 percent a year. The Mexican stock market crashed, falling another 30 percent in peso terms and over 60 percent in dollar terms. Given the resulting huge increase in interest payments because of the short duration of the

Mexican debt, households' and firms' cash flow dropped dramatically, leading to a deterioration in their balance sheets. In addition, because many firms had debts denominated in dollars, the depreciation of the peso resulted in an immediate sharp increase in their indebtedness in pesos, even though the value of their assets remained unchanged. The depreciation of the peso starting in December 1994 led to an especially sharp negative shock to the net worth of private firms, causing a dramatic increase in adverse selection and moral hazard problems. These asymmetric information problems were severe for domestic lenders and foreign lenders as well because they had difficulty obtaining information about what was going on in the Mexican economy. Foreign lenders were thus eager to pull their funds out of Mexico, and this is exactly what they did. Foreign portfolio investment inflows to Mexico, which had been on the order of $20 billion (a year) in 1993 and early 1994, reversed course, and the outflows exceeded $10 billion a year by the fourth quarter of 1994. Consistent with the theory of financial crises outlined in this chapter, the sharp decline in lending helped lead to a collapse of economic activity, with real GDP growth falling from around 4.0 to 4.5 percent annually in the last half of 1994 to very negative growth rates in the vicinity of -10 percent in 1995. Only in 1996 with financial assistance from the U.S. and the IMF, did the Mexican economy finally start to recover, having suffered serious damage.

As shown in Figure 4, further deterioration to the economy occurred because the collapse in economic activity and the deterioration in the cash flow and balance sheets of both firms and households led to a worsening banking crisis. The problems of firms and households meant that many were no longer able to pay off their debts, resulting in substantial loan losses for the banks. Even more problematic for the Mexican banks was that they had many short-term liabilities denominated in foreign currency, and the sharp increase in the value of these liabilities after the devaluation led to a further deterioration in the banks' balance sheets. Under these circumstances, the banking system would have collapsed in the absence of a government safety net, but the Mexican government came forth with funds to protect depositors, thereby avoiding a bank panic. However, given the banks' loss of capital and the need for the government to intervene to prop up the banks, the banks' ability and willingness to lend were sharply curtailed. As we have seen, a banking crisis of this type hinders the ability of banks to lend and also makes adverse selection and moral hazard problems worse in financial markets because banks are no longer as capable of playing their traditional financial intermediation role. The banking crisis, along with the other factors that increased adverse selection and moral hazard problems in Mexican credit markets, explains the collapse of lending and hence in economic activity in the aftermath of the financial crisis.

SUMMARY

1. There are eight basic puzzles about our financial structure. The first four emphasize the importance of financial intermediaries and the relative unimportance of securities markets for the financing of corporations; the fifth recognizes that financial markets are among the most heavily regulated sectors of the economy; the sixth states that only large, well-established corporations have access to securities markets; the seventh indicates that collateral is an important feature of debt contracts; and the eighth

presents debt contracts as complicated legal documents that place substantial restrictions on the behavior of the borrower.

2. Transaction costs freeze many small savers and borrowers out of direct involvement with financial markets. Financial intermediaries can take advantage of economies of scale and are better able to develop expertise to lower transaction costs, thus enabling their savers and borrowers to benefit from the existence of financial markets.

3. Asymmetric information results in two problems: adverse selection, which occurs before the transaction, and moral hazard, which occurs after the transaction. Adverse selection refers to the fact that bad credit risks are the ones most likely to seek loans, and moral hazard refers to the risk of the borrower's engaging in activities that are undesirable from the lender's point of view.

4. Adverse selection interferes with the efficient functioning of financial markets. Tools to help reduce the adverse selection problem include private production and sale of information, government regulation to increase information, financial intermediation, and collateral and net worth. The free-rider problem occurs when people who do not pay for information take advantage of information that other people have paid for. This problem explains why financial intermediaries, particularly banks, play a more important role in financing the activities of businesses than securities markets do.

5. Moral hazard in equity contracts is known as the principal-agent problem because managers (the agents) have less incentive to maximize profits than stockholders (the principals). The principal-agent problem explains why debt contracts are so much more prevalent in financial markets than equity contracts. Tools to help reduce the principal-agent problem include monitoring, government regulation to increase information, and financial intermediation.

6. Tools to reduce the moral hazard problem in debt contracts include net worth, monitoring and enforcement of restrictive covenants, and financial intermediaries.

7. Financial crises are major disruptions in financial markets. They are caused by increases in adverse selection and moral hazard problems that prevent financial markets from channeling funds to people with productive investment opportunities, leading to a sharp contraction in economic activity. The four types of factors that lead to financial crises are increases in interest rates, increases in uncertainty, asset market effects on balance sheets, and bank panics.

KEY TERMS

bank panic, p. 217

cash flow, p. 217

collateral, p. 198

costly state verification, p. 208

creditor, p. 214

debt deflation, p. 219

financial crisis, p. 215

free-rider problem, p. 203

incentive-compatible, p. 211

insolvent, p. 219

net worth (equity capital), p. 206

principal-agent problem, p. 207

restrictive covenants, p. 199

secured debt, p. 199

unsecured debt, p. 199

venture capital firm, p. 210

QUESTIONS AND PROBLEMS

1. How can economies of scale help explain the existence of financial intermediaries?

*2. Describe two ways in which financial intermediaries help lower transaction costs in the economy.

3. Would moral hazard and adverse selection still arise in financial markets if information were not asymmetric? Explain.

*4. How do standard accounting principles required by the government help financial markets work more efficiently?

5. Do you think the lemons problem would be more severe for stocks traded on the New York Stock Exchange or those traded over-the-counter? Explain.

*6. Which firms are most likely to use bank financing rather than to issue bonds or stocks to finance their activities? Why?

7. How can the existence of asymmetric information provide a rationale for government regulation of financial markets?

*8. Would you be more willing to lend to a friend if she put all of her life savings into her business than you would if she had not done so? Why?

9. Rich individuals often worry that people will seek to marry them only for their money. Is this a problem of adverse selection?

*10. The more collateral there is backing a loan, the less the lender has to worry about adverse selection. Is this statement true, false, or uncertain? Explain your answer.

11. How does the free-rider problem aggravate adverse selection and moral hazard problems in financial markets?

*12. Explain how the separation of ownership and control in American corporations might lead to poor management.

13. Is a financial crisis more likely to occur when the economy is experiencing deflation or inflation? Explain.

*14. How can a stock market crash provoke a financial crisis?

15. How can a sharp rise in interest rates provoke a financial crisis?

Chapter 10

THE BANKING FIRM AND THE MANAGEMENT OF FINANCIAL INSTITUTIONS

PREVIEW Because banks (depository institutions) play such a major role in channeling funds to borrowers with productive investment opportunities, they are important in ensuring that the financial system and the economy run smoothly and efficiently. In the United States, banks supply over $5 trillion of credit annually: They provide loans to businesses, help us finance our college educations or the purchase of a new car or home, and provide us with services such as checking and savings accounts.

In this chapter we examine how banks, the most important of all the financial intermediaries, operate to earn the highest profits possible: how and why they make loans, how they acquire funds and manage their assets and liabilities (debts), and how they earn income. Although we focus on commercial banks because they are the most important financial intermediary, many of the same principles are equally applicable to other types of banking institutions, such as thrifts, and to other nonbank financial institutions as well.

THE BANK BALANCE SHEET

To understand how a bank operates, first we need to examine its **balance sheet,** a list of the bank's assets and liabilities. As the name implies, this list balances; that is, it has the characteristic that

$$\text{Total assets} = \text{total liabilities} + \text{capital}$$

Furthermore, a bank's balance sheet lists *sources* of bank funds (liabilities) and *uses* to which they are put (assets). Banks obtain funds by borrowing and by issuing other liabilities such as deposits. They then use these funds to acquire assets such as securities and loans. Banks make profits by charging an interest rate on their holdings of securities and loans that is higher than the expenses on their liabilities. The balance sheet of all commercial banks at the end of 1996 appears in Table 1.

Liabilities

A bank acquires funds by issuing (selling) liabilities, which are consequently also referred to as *sources of funds*. The funds obtained from issuing liabilities are used to purchase income-earning assets.

CHECKABLE DEPOSITS Checkable deposits are bank accounts that allow the owner of the account to write checks to third parties. Checkable deposits include all accounts on which checks can be drawn: non-interest-bearing checking accounts (demand deposits), interest-bearing NOW (negotiable order of withdrawal) accounts, and money market deposit accounts (MMDAs). Introduced with the Depository Institutions Act in 1982, MMDAs have similar features to money

---

TABLE 1 **Balance Sheet of All Commercial Banks**
(items as a percentage of the total, end of 1996)

Assets (Uses of Funds)*		Liabilities (Sources of Funds)	
Reserves	1	Checkable deposits	17
Cash items in process of collection +		Nontransaction deposits	
deposits at other banks	4	Small-denomination time deposits	
Securities		(< $100,000) + savings deposits	37
U.S. government and agency	15	Large-denomination time deposits	12
State and local government and		Borrowings	26
other securities	6	Bank capital	8
Loans			
Commercial and industrial	18		
Real estate	25		
Consumer	12		
Interbank	5		
Other	8		
Other assets (for example,	6		
physical capital)			
Total	100	Total	100

*In order of decreasing liquidity.
*Source: Federal Reserve *Bulletin*.

market mutual funds and are included in the checkable deposits category. However, MMDAs differ from checkable deposits in that they are not subject to reserve requirements (discussed later in the chapter) like checkable deposits and are not included in the M1 definition of money. Table 1 shows that the category of checkable deposits is an important source of bank funds, making up 17 percent of bank liabilities. Once checkable deposits were the most important source of bank funds (over 60 percent of bank liabilities in 1960), but with the appearance of new, more attractive financial instruments such as money market mutual funds, the share of checkable deposits in total bank liabilities has shrunk over time.

Checkable deposits and money market deposit accounts are payable on demand; that is, if a depositor shows up at the bank and requests payment by making a withdrawal, the bank must pay the depositor immediately. Similarly, if a person who receives a check written on an account from a bank, presents that check at the bank, it must pay the funds out immediately (or credit them to that person's account).

A checkable deposit is an asset for the depositor because it is part of his or her wealth. Conversely, because the depositor can withdraw funds from an account that the bank is obligated to pay, checkable deposits are a liability for the bank. They are usually the lowest-cost source of bank funds because depositors are willing to forgo some interest in order to have access to a liquid asset that can be used to make purchases. The bank's costs of maintaining checkable deposits include interest payments and the costs incurred in servicing these accounts— processing and storing canceled checks, preparing and sending out monthly statements, providing efficient tellers (human or otherwise), maintaining an impressive building and conveniently located branches, and advertising and marketing to entice customers to deposit their funds with a given bank. In recent years, interest paid on deposits (checkable and time) has accounted for around 45 percent of total bank operating expenses, while the costs involved in servicing accounts (employee salaries, building rent, and so on) have been approximately 50 percent of operating expenses.

NONTRANSACTION DEPOSITS Nontransaction deposits are the primary source of bank funds (49 percent of bank liabilities in Table 1). Owners cannot write checks on nontransaction deposits, but the interest rates are usually higher than those on checkable deposits. There are two basic types of nontransaction deposits: savings accounts and time deposits (also called certificates of deposit, or CDs).

Savings accounts were once the most common type of nontransaction deposit. In these accounts, to which funds can be added or from which funds can be withdrawn at any time, transactions and interest payments are recorded in a monthly statement or in a small book (the passbook) held by the owner of the account.

Time deposits have a fixed maturity length, ranging from several months to over five years, and have substantial penalties for early withdrawal (the forfeiture of several months' interest). Small-denomination time deposits (deposits of less than $100,000) are less liquid for the depositor than passbook savings, earn higher interest rates, and are a more costly source of funds for the banks.

Large-denomination time deposits (CDs) are available in denominations of $100,000 or over and are typically bought by corporations or other banks. Large-denomination CDs are negotiable; like bonds, they can be resold in a secondary market before they mature. For this reason, negotiable CDs are held by corporations, money market mutual funds, and other financial institutions as alternative assets to Treasury bills and other short-term bonds. Since 1961, when they first appeared, negotiable CDs have become an important source of bank funds (12 percent).

BORROWINGS Banks obtain funds by borrowing from the Federal Reserve System, other banks, and corporations. Borrowings from the Fed are called **discount loans** (also known as *advances*). Banks also borrow reserves overnight in the federal (fed) funds market from other U.S. banks and financial institutions. Banks borrow funds overnight in order to have enough deposits at the Federal Reserve to meet the amount required by the Fed. Other sources of borrowed funds are loans made to banks by their parent companies (bank holding companies), loan arrangements with corporations (such as repurchase agreements), and borrowings of Eurodollars (deposits denominated in U.S. dollars residing in foreign banks or foreign branches of U.S. banks). Borrowings have become a more important source of bank funds over time: In 1960, they made up only 2 percent of bank liabilities; currently, they exceed 25 percent of bank liabilities.

BANK CAPITAL The final category on the liabilities side of the balance sheet is bank capital, the bank's net worth, which equals the difference between total assets and liabilities (8 percent of total bank assets in Table 1). The funds are raised by selling new equity (stock) or from retained earnings. Bank capital is a cushion against a drop in the value of its assets, which could force the bank into insolvency (when the value of bank assets falls below its liabilities, meaning that the bank is bankrupt). One important component of bank capital is *loan loss reserves*, which are described in Box 1.

Assets

A bank uses the funds that it has acquired by issuing liabilities to purchase income-earning assets. Bank assets are thus naturally referred to as *uses of funds,* and the interest payments earned on them are what enable banks to make profits.

RESERVES All banks hold some of the funds they acquire as deposits in an account at the Fed. **Reserves** are these deposits plus currency that is physically held by banks (called **vault cash** because it is stored in bank vaults overnight). Although reserves currently do not pay any interest, banks hold them for two reasons. First, some reserves, called **required reserves,** are held because by law, the Fed requires that for every dollar of checkable deposits at a bank, a certain fraction (10 cents, for example) must be kept as reserves. This fraction (10 percent in the example) is called the **required reserve ratio.** Banks hold additional reserves, called **excess reserves,** because they are the most liquid of all bank assets and can be used by a bank to meet its obligations when funds are withdrawn, either directly by a depositor or indirectly when a check is written on an account.

BOX 1

Understanding Loan Loss Reserves

Perhaps you have seen headlines in the press about a bank's large increase in loan loss (bad debt) reserves. Often there is confusion about loan loss reserves, perhaps because they have a similar-sounding name to the "reserves" item on a bank's balance sheet. Actually, loan loss reserves have nothing to do with the reserves shown on the assets side of the balance sheet; rather, they are a component of the liabilities item known as bank capital.

To see how loan loss reserves work, suppose that a bank suspects that some of its loans, say, $1 million worth, might prove to be bad debts that will have to be written off (valued at zero) in the future. The bank can set aside $1 million of its earnings and put it into its loan loss reserves account. Because the $1 million is now retained earnings, it adds to the difference between the bank's assets and liabilities and so increases bank capital. The fact that adding to loan loss reserves increases bank capital explains why loan loss reserves are counted as a component of capital. As a result of adding to loan loss reserves, the bank reduces its reported earnings by $1 million, even though it has not yet actually lost the $1 million—in effect, taking its lumps even before the bad debt is written off.

If the bank eventually determines that the $1 million loan will never be paid back and formally writes it off, it reduces the value of its assets by $1 million. The resulting $1 million decline in bank capital is reflected as a decrease in the loan loss reserves account by $1 million. At this time, however, reported earnings are unaffected by the loan write-off because they were reduced earlier when the bank set aside $1 million of earnings as loan loss reserves.

Banks add to loan loss reserves before a bad loan has to be written off because it is better for them to allow for the loss when they have plenty of earnings rather than to wait and find that they must take the loss when they have little in earnings to write the loan off against. In addition, adding to loan loss reserves, which reduces reported earnings, can reduce the amount of taxes a bank has to pay and is also a way of informing the bank's stockholders, depositors, and regulators of potential future losses on loans.

CASH ITEMS IN PROCESS OF COLLECTION Suppose that a check written on an account at another bank is deposited in your bank and the funds for this check have not yet been received (collected) from the other bank. The check is classified as a cash item in process of collection, and it is an asset for your bank because it is a claim on another bank for funds that will be paid within a few days.

DEPOSITS AT OTHER BANKS Many small banks hold deposits in larger banks in exchange for a variety of services, including check collection, foreign exchange transactions, and help with securities purchases. This is an aspect of a system called *correspondent banking*.

Collectively, reserves, cash items in process of collection, and deposits at other banks are often referred to as *cash items*. In Table 1 they constitute only 5 percent of total assets, and their importance has been shrinking over time: In 1960, for example, they accounted for 20 percent of total assets.

SECURITIES A bank's holdings of securities are an important income-earning asset: Securities (made up entirely of debt instruments for commercial banks because banks are not allowed to hold stock) account for 21 percent of bank assets in Table 1, and they provide commercial banks with about 15 percent of their revenue. These securities can be classified into three categories: U.S. government and agency securities, state and local government securities, and other securities. The United States government and agency securities are the most liquid because they can be easily traded and converted into cash with low transaction costs. Because of their high liquidity, short-term U.S. government securities are called **secondary reserves.**

State and local government securities are desirable for banks to hold primarily because state and local governments are more likely to do business with banks that hold their securities. In addition, state and local government securities purchased before August 1986 have substantial tax advantages for banks because their interest payments are deductible from income taxes, and 80 percent of the interest costs associated with the funding of their purchase is deductible. State and local government and other securities are less marketable (hence less liquid) and are also riskier than U.S. government securities, primarily because of default risk: There is some possibility that the issuer of the securities may not be able to make its interest payments or pay back the face value of the securities when they mature.

LOANS   Banks make their profits primarily by issuing loans. In Table 1, some 68 percent of bank assets are in the form of loans, and in recent years they have generally produced more than half of bank revenues. A loan is a liability for the individual or corporation receiving it but an asset for a bank because it provides income to the bank. Loans are typically less liquid than other assets because they cannot be turned into cash until the loan matures. If the bank makes a one-year loan, for example, it cannot get its funds back until the loan comes due in one year. Loans also have a higher probability of default than other assets. Because of the lack of liquidity and higher default risk, the bank earns its highest return on loans.

As you can see in Table 1, the largest categories of loans for commercial banks are commercial and industrial loans made to businesses and real estate loans. Commercial banks also make consumer loans and lend to each other. The bulk of these interbank loans are overnight loans lent in the federal funds market. The major difference in the balance sheets of the various depository institutions is primarily in the type of loan in which they specialize. Savings and loans and mutual savings banks, for example, specialize in residential mortgages, while credit unions tend to make consumer loans.

OTHER ASSETS   The physical capital (bank buildings, computers, and other equipment) owned by the banks is included in this category.

BASIC OPERATION OF A BANK

Before proceeding to a more detailed study of how a bank manages its assets and liabilities in order to make the highest profit, you should understand the basic operation of a bank.

In general terms, banks make profits by selling liabilities with one set of characteristics (a particular combination of liquidity, risk, and return) and using the proceeds to buy assets with a different set of characteristics. This process is often referred to as *asset transformation.* Instead of making a mortgage loan directly to a neighbor, a person can hold a savings deposit that enables a bank to use the funds provided by the deposit to make the loan to the neighbor. The bank has, in effect, transformed the savings deposit (an asset held by the depositor) into a mortgage loan (an asset held by the bank). Another way this process of asset transformation is described is to say that the bank "borrows short and lends long" because it makes long-term loans and funds them by issuing short-dated deposits.

The process of transforming assets and providing a set of services (check clearing, record keeping, credit analysis, and so forth) is like any other production process in a firm. If the bank produces desirable services at low cost and earns substantial income on its assets, it earns profits; if not, the bank suffers losses.

To make our analysis of the operation of a bank more concrete, we use a tool called a **T-account.** A T-account is a simplified balance sheet, with lines in the form of a T, that lists only the changes that occur in balance sheet items starting from some initial balance sheet position. Let's say that Jane Brown has heard that the First National Bank provides excellent service, so she opens a checking account with a $100 bill. She now has a $100 checkable deposit at the bank, which shows up as a $100 liability on the bank's balance sheet. The bank now puts her $100 bill into its vault so that the bank's assets rise by the $100 increase in vault cash. The T-account for the bank looks like this:

FIRST NATIONAL BANK

Assets		Liabilities	
Vault cash	+$100	Checkable deposits	+$100

Since vault cash is also part of the bank's reserves, we can rewrite the T-account as follows:

Assets		Liabilities	
Reserves	+$100	Checkable deposits	+$100

Note that Jane Brown's opening of a checking account leads to *an increase in the bank's reserves equal to the increase in checkable deposits.*

If Jane had opened her account with a $100 check written on an account at another bank, say, the Second National Bank, we would get the same result. The initial effect on the T-account of the First National Bank is as follows:

Assets		Liabilities	
Cash items in process of collection	+$100	Checkable deposits	+$100

Checkable deposits increase by $100 as before, but now the First National Bank is owed $100 by the Second National Bank. This asset for the First National Bank is entered in the T-account as $100 of cash items in process of collection because the First National Bank will now try to collect the funds that it is owed. It could go directly to the Second National Bank and ask for payment of the funds, but if the two banks are in separate states, that would be a time-consuming and costly process. Instead, the First National Bank deposits the check in its account at the Fed, and the Fed collects the funds from the Second National Bank. The result is that the Fed transfers $100 of reserves from the Second National Bank to the First National Bank, and the final balance sheet positions of the two banks are as follows:

FIRST NATIONAL BANK				**SECOND NATIONAL BANK**			
Assets		Liabilities		Assets		Liabilities	
Reserves	+$100	Checkable deposits	+$100	Reserves	−$100	Checkable deposits	−$100

The process initiated by Jane Brown can be summarized as follows: When a check written on an account at one bank is deposited in another, the bank receiving the deposit gains reserves equal to the amount of the check, while the bank on which the check is written sees its reserves fall by the same amount. Therefore, **when a bank receives additional deposits, it gains an equal amount of reserves; when it loses deposits, it loses an equal amount of reserves.**

Study Guide   T-accounts are used to study various topics throughout this text. Whenever you see a T-account, try to analyze what would happen if the opposite action were taken; for example, what would happen if Jane Brown decided to close her $100 account at the First National Bank by writing a $100 check and depositing it in a new checking account at the Second National Bank?

Now that you understand how banks gain and lose reserves, we can examine how a bank rearranges its balance sheet to make a profit when it experiences a change in its deposits. Let's return to the situation when the First National Bank has just received the extra $100 of checkable deposits. As you know, the bank is obliged to keep a certain fraction of its checkable deposits as required reserves.

If the fraction (the required reserve ratio) is 10 percent, the First National Bank's required reserves have increased by $10, and we can rewrite its T-account as follows:

FIRST NATIONAL BANK

Assets		Liabilities	
Required reserves	+$10	Checkable deposits	+$100
Excess reserves	+$90		

Let's see how well the bank is doing as a result of the additional checkable deposits. Because reserves pay no interest, it has no income from the additional $100 of assets. But servicing the extra $100 of checkable deposits is costly because the bank must keep records, pay tellers, return canceled checks, pay for check clearing, and so forth. The bank is making a loss! The situation is even worse if the bank makes interest payments on the deposits, as with NOW accounts. If it is to make a profit, the bank must put to productive use all or part of the $90 of excess reserves it has available.

Let us assume that the bank chooses not to hold any excess reserves but to make loans instead. The T-account then looks like this:

Assets		Liabilities	
Required reserves	+$10	Checkable deposits	+$100
Loans	+$90		

The bank is now making a profit because it holds short-term liabilities such as checkable deposits and uses the proceeds to buy longer-term assets such as loans with higher interest rates. As mentioned earlier, this process of asset transformation is frequently described by saying that banks are in the business of "borrowing short and lending long." For example, if the loans have an interest rate of 10 percent per year, the bank earns $9 in income from its loans over the year. If the $100 of checkable deposits is in a NOW account with a 5 percent interest rate and it costs another $3 per year to service the account, the cost per year of these deposits is $8. The bank's profit on the new deposits is then $1 per year (a 1 percent return on assets).

GENERAL PRINCIPLES OF BANK MANAGEMENT

Now that you have some idea of how a bank operates, let's look at how a bank manages its assets and liabilities in order to earn the highest possible profit. The bank manager has four primary concerns. The first is to make sure that the bank has enough ready cash to pay its depositors when there are **deposit outflows,** that is, when deposits are lost because depositors make withdrawals and demand payment. To keep enough cash on hand, the bank must engage in **liquidity management,** the acquisition of sufficiently liquid assets to meet the bank's obligations to depositors. Second, the bank manager must pursue an acceptably low level of risk by acquiring assets that have a low rate of default and by diversifying asset holdings **(asset management).** The third concern is to acquire funds at low cost **(liability management).** Finally, the manager must decide the amount of capital the bank should maintain and then acquire the needed capital **(capital adequacy management).**

To understand bank and other financial institution management fully, we must go beyond the general principles of bank asset and liability management described next and look in more detail at how a financial institution manages its assets. The two sections following this one provide an in-depth discussion of how a financial institution manages **credit risk,** the risk arising because borrowers may default, and how it manages **interest-rate risk,** the riskiness of earnings and returns on bank assets that results from interest-rate changes.

Liquidity Management and the Role of Reserves

Let us see how a typical bank, the First National Bank, can deal with deposit outflows that occur when its depositors withdraw cash from checking or savings accounts or write checks that are deposited in other banks. In the example that follows, we assume that the bank has ample excess reserves and that all deposits have the same required reserve ratio of 10 percent (the bank is required to keep 10 percent of its time and checkable deposits as reserves). Suppose that the First National Bank's initial balance sheet is as follows:

Assets		Liabilities	
Reserves	$20 million	Deposits	$100 million
Loans	$80 million	Bank capital	$ 10 million
Securities	$10 million		

The bank's required reserves are 10 percent of $100 million, or $10 million. Since it holds $20 million of reserves, the First National Bank has excess reserves of $10 million. If a deposit outflow of $10 million occurs, the bank's balance sheet becomes

Assets		Liabilities	
Reserves	$10 million	Deposits	$90 million
Loans	$80 million	Bank capital	$10 million
Securities	$10 million		

The bank loses $10 million of deposits *and* $10 million of reserves, but since its required reserves are now 10 percent of only $90 million ($9 million), its reserves still exceed this amount by $1 million. In short, *if a bank has ample reserves, a deposit outflow does not necessitate changes in other parts of its balance sheet.*

The situation is quite different when a bank holds insufficient excess reserves. Let's assume that instead of initially holding $10 million in excess reserves, the First National Bank makes loans of $10 million, so that it holds no excess reserves. Its initial balance sheet would be

Assets		Liabilities	
Reserves	$10 million	Deposits	$100 million
Loans	$90 million	Bank capital	$ 10 million
Securities	$10 million		

When it suffers the $10 million deposit outflow, its balance sheet becomes

Assets		Liabilities	
Reserves	$ 0	Deposits	$90 million
Loans	$90 million	Bank capital	$10 million
Securities	$10 million		

After $10 million has been withdrawn from deposits and hence reserves, the bank has a problem: It has a reserve requirement of 10 percent of $90 million, or $9 million, but it has no reserves! To eliminate this shortfall, the bank has four basic options. One is to acquire reserves to meet a deposit outflow by borrowing them from other banks in the federal funds market or by borrowing from corporations.[1] If the First National Bank acquires the $9 million shortfall in reserves by borrowing it from other banks or corporations, its balance sheet becomes

Assets		Liabilities	
Reserves	$ 9 million	Deposits	$90 million
Loans	$90 million	Borrowings from	
Securities	$10 million	other banks or	
		corporations	$ 9 million
		Bank capital	$10 million

---

[1]One way that the First National Bank can borrow from other banks and corporations is by selling negotiable certificates of deposit. This method for obtaining funds is discussed in the section on liability management.

The cost of this activity is the interest rate on these loans, such as the federal funds rate.

A second alternative is for the bank to sell some of its securities to help cover the deposit outflow. For example, it might sell $9 million of its securities and deposit the proceeds with the Fed, resulting in the following balance sheet:

Assets		Liabilities	
Reserves	$ 9 million	Deposits	$90 million
Loans	$90 million	Bank capital	$10 million
Securities	$ 1 million		

The bank incurs some brokerage and other transaction costs when it sells these securities. The U.S. government securities that are classified as secondary reserves are very liquid, so the transaction costs of selling them are quite modest. However, the other securities the bank holds are less liquid, and the transaction cost can be appreciably higher.

A third way that the bank can meet a deposit outflow is to acquire reserves by borrowing from the Fed. In our example, the First National Bank could leave its security and loan holdings the same and borrow $9 million in discount loans from the Fed. Its balance sheet would be

Assets		Liabilities	
Reserves	$ 9 million	Deposits	$90 million
Loans	$90 million	Discount loans	
Securities	$10 million	from the Fed	$ 9 million
		Bank capital	$10 million

There are two costs associated with discount loans. First is the interest rate that must be paid to the Fed (called the **discount rate**). The second is a nonexplicit cost resulting from the Fed's discouragement of too much borrowing from it. If a bank takes out too many discount loans, the Fed may refuse to let it borrow further. In popular parlance, the Fed can "close down the discount window" for that bank.

Finally, a bank can acquire the $9 million of reserves to meet the deposit outflow by reducing its loans by this amount and depositing the $9 million it then receives with the Fed, thereby increasing its reserves by $9 million. This transaction changes the balance sheet as follows:

Assets		Liabilities	
Reserves	$ 9 million	Deposits	$90 million
Loans	$81 million	Bank capital	$10 million
Securities	$10 million		

The First National Bank is once again in good shape because its $9 million of reserves satisfies the reserve requirement.

However, this process of reducing its loans is the bank's costliest way of acquiring reserves when there is a deposit outflow. If the First National Bank has numerous short-term loans renewed at fairly short intervals, it can reduce its total amount of loans outstanding fairly quickly by *calling in* loans—that is, by not renewing some loans when they come due. Unfortunately for the bank, this is likely to antagonize the customers whose loans are not being renewed because they have not done anything to deserve such treatment. Indeed, they are likely to take their business elsewhere in the future, a very costly consequence for the bank.

A second method for reducing its loans is for the bank to sell them off to other banks. Again, this is very costly because other banks do not personally know the customers who have taken out the loans and so may not be willing to buy the loans at their full value.

The foregoing discussion explains why banks hold excess reserves even though loans or securities earn a higher return. When a deposit outflow occurs, holding excess reserves allows the bank to escape the costs of (1) borrowing from other banks or corporations, (2) selling securities, (3) borrowing from the Fed, or (4) calling in or selling off loans. ***Excess reserves are insurance against the costs associated with deposit outflows. The higher the costs associated with deposit outflows, the more excess reserves banks will want to hold.***

Just as you and I would be willing to pay an insurance company to insure us against a casualty loss such as the theft of a car, a bank is willing to pay the cost of holding excess reserves (the opportunity cost, which is the earnings forgone by not holding income-earning assets such as loans or securities) in order to insure against losses due to deposit outflows. Because excess reserves, like insurance, have a cost, banks also take other steps to protect themselves; for example, they might shift their holdings of assets to more liquid securities (secondary reserves).

Study Guide   Bank management is easier to grasp if you put yourself in the banker's shoes and imagine what you would do in the situations described. To understand a bank's possible responses to deposit outflows, imagine how you as a banker might respond to two successive deposit outflows of $10 million.

Asset Management

Now that you understand why a bank has a need for liquidity, we can examine the basic strategy a bank pursues in managing its assets. To maximize its profits, a bank must simultaneously seek the highest returns possible on loans and securities, reduce risk, and make adequate provisions for liquidity by holding liquid assets. Banks try to accomplish these three goals in four basic ways.

First, banks try to find borrowers who will pay high interest rates and are unlikely to default on their loans. They seek out loan business by advertising their borrowing rates and by approaching corporations directly to solicit loans. It is up to the bank's loan officer to decide if potential borrowers are good credit risks who will make interest and principal payments on time. Typically, banks are conservative in their loan policies; the default rate is usually less than 1 percent. It is important, however, that banks not be so conservative that they miss out on attractive lending opportunities that earn high interest rates.

Second, banks try to purchase securities with high returns and low risk. Third, in managing their assets, banks must attempt to lower risk by diversifying. They accomplish this by purchasing many different types of assets (short- and long-term, U.S. Treasury, and municipal bonds) and approving many types of loans to a number of customers. Banks that have not sufficiently sought the benefits of diversification often come to regret it later. For example, banks that had overspecialized in making loans to energy companies, real estate developers, or farmers suffered huge losses in the 1980s with the slump in energy, property, and farm prices. Indeed, many of these banks went broke because they had "put too many eggs in one basket."

Finally, the bank must manage the liquidity of its assets so that it can satisfy its reserve requirements without bearing huge costs. This means that it will hold liquid securities even if they earn a somewhat lower return than other assets. The bank must decide, for example, how much excess reserves must be held to avoid costs from a deposit outflow. In addition, it will want to hold U.S. government securities as secondary reserves so that even if a deposit outflow forces some costs on the bank, these will not be terribly high. Again, it is not wise for a bank to be too conservative. If it avoids all costs associated with deposit outflows by holding only excess reserves, losses are suffered because reserves earn no interest, while the bank's liabilities are costly to maintain. The bank must balance its desire for liquidity against the increased earnings that can be obtained from less liquid assets such as loans.

Liability Management

Before the 1960s, liability management was a staid affair: For the most part, banks took their liabilities as fixed and spent their time trying to achieve an optimal mix of assets. There were two main reasons for the emphasis on asset management. First, over 60 percent of the sources of bank funds were obtained through checkable (demand) deposits that by law could not pay any interest. Thus banks could not actively compete with one another for these deposits, and so their amount was effectively a given for an individual bank. Second, because the markets for making overnight loans between banks were not well developed, banks rarely borrowed from other banks to meet their reserve needs.

Starting in the 1960s, however, large banks (called **money center banks**) in key financial centers, such as New York, Chicago and San Francisco, began to explore ways in which the liabilities on their balance sheets could provide them with reserves and liquidity. This led to an expansion of overnight loan markets, such as the federal funds market, and the development of new financial instruments such as negotiable CDs (first developed in 1961), which enabled money center banks to acquire funds quickly.[2]

This new flexibility in liability management meant that banks could take a different approach to bank management. They no longer needed to depend on

---

[2]Because small banks are not as well known as money center banks and so might be a higher credit risk, they find it harder to raise funds in the negotiable CD market. Hence they do not engage nearly as actively in liability management.

checkable deposits as the primary source of bank funds and as a result no longer treated their sources of funds (liabilities) as given. Instead, they aggressively set target goals for their asset growth and tried to acquire funds (by issuing liabilities) as they were needed.

For example, today, when a money center bank finds an attractive loan opportunity, it can acquire funds by selling a negotiable CD. Or if it has a reserve shortfall, funds can be borrowed from another bank in the federal funds market without incurring high transaction costs. The federal funds market can also be used to finance loans.

The emphasis on liability management explains some of the important changes over the past three decades in the composition of banks' balance sheets. While negotiable CDs and bank borrowings have greatly increased in importance as a source of bank funds in recent years (rising from 2 percent of bank liabilities in 1960 to 38 percent by the end of 1996), checkable deposits have decreased in importance (from 61 percent of bank liabilities in 1960 to 17 percent in 1996). Newfound flexibility in liability management and the search for higher profits have also stimulated banks to increase the proportion of their assets held in loans, which earn higher income (from 46 percent of bank assets in 1960 to 68 percent in 1996).

Capital Adequacy Management

Banks have to make decisions about the amount of capital they need to hold for three reasons. First, bank capital helps prevents *bank failure,* a situation in which the bank cannot satisfy its obligations to pay its depositors and other creditors and so goes out of business. Second, the amount of capital affects returns for the owners (equity holders) of the bank. And third, a minimum amount of bank capital (bank capital requirements) is required by regulatory authorities.

HOW BANK CAPITAL HELPS PREVENT BANK FAILURE Let's consider two banks with identical balance sheets, except that the High Capital Bank has a ratio of capital to assets of 10 percent while the Low Capital Bank has a ratio of 4 percent.

HIGH CAPITAL BANK				LOW CAPITAL BANK			
Assets		Liabilities		Assets		Liabilities	
Reserves	$10 million	Deposits	$90 million	Reserves	$10 million	Deposits	$96 million
Loans	$90 million	Bank capital	$10 million	Loans	$90 million	Bank capital	$ 4 million

Suppose that both banks got caught up in the euphoria of the real estate market in the 1980s, only to find that $5 million of their real estate loans became worthless in the 1990s. When these bad loans are written off (valued at zero), the total value of assets declines by $5 million, and so bank capital, which equals total assets minus liabilities, also declines by $5 million. The balance sheets of the two banks now look like this:

HIGH CAPITAL BANK				LOW CAPITAL BANK			
Assets		Liabilities		Assets		Liabilities	
Reserves	$10 million	Deposits	$90 million	Reserves	$10 million	Deposits	$96 million
Loans	$85 million	Bank capital	$ 5 million	Loans	$85 million	Bank capital	−$ 1 million

The High Capital Bank takes the $5 million loss in stride because its initial cushion of $10 million in capital means that it still has a positive net worth (bank capital) of $5 million after the loss. The Low Capital Bank, however, is in big trouble. Now the value of its assets has fallen below its liabilities, and its net worth is now −$1 million. Because the bank has a negative net worth, it is insolvent (bankrupt): It does not have sufficient assets to pay off all holders of its liabilities (creditors). When a bank becomes insolvent, government regulators close the bank, its assets are sold off, and its managers are fired. Since the owners of the Low Capital Bank will find their investment wiped out, they would clearly have preferred the bank to have had a larger cushion of bank capital to absorb the losses, as was the case for the High Capital Bank. We therefore see an important rationale for a bank to maintain a high level of capital: ***A bank maintains bank capital to lessen the chance that it will become insolvent.***

HOW THE AMOUNT OF BANK CAPITAL AFFECTS RETURNS TO EQUITY HOLDERS
Because owners of a bank must know whether their bank is being managed well, they need good measures of bank profitability. A basic measure of bank profitability is the **return on assets (ROA),** the net profit after taxes per dollar of assets:

$$ROA = \frac{\text{net profit after taxes}}{\text{assets}}$$

The return on assets provides information on how efficiently a bank is being run because it indicates how much profits are generated on average by each dollar of assets.

However, what the bank's owners (equity holders) care about most is how much the bank is earning on their equity investment. This information is provided by the other basic measure of bank profitability, the **return on equity (ROE),** the net profit after taxes per dollar of equity capital:

$$ROE = \frac{\text{net profit after taxes}}{\text{equity capital}}$$

There is a direct relationship between the return on assets (which measures how efficiently the bank is run) and the return on equity (which measures how well the owners are doing on their investment). This relationship is determined by the so-called **equity multiplier *(EM)*,** which is the amount of assets per dollar of equity capital:

$$EM = \frac{\text{assets}}{\text{equity capital}}$$

To see this, we note that

$$\frac{\text{Net profit after taxes}}{\text{Equity capital}} = \frac{\text{net profit after taxes}}{\text{assets}} \times \frac{\text{assets}}{\text{equity capital}}$$

which, using our definitions, yields

$$ROE = ROA \times EM \tag{1}$$

The formula in Equation 1 tells us what happens to the return on equity when a bank holds a smaller amount of capital (equity) for a given amount of assets. As we have seen, the High Capital Bank initially has $100 million of assets and $10 million of equity, which gives it an equity multiplier of 10 (= $100 million/$10 million). The Low Capital Bank, by contrast, has only $4 million of equity, so its equity multiplier is higher, equaling 25 (= $100 million/$4 million). Suppose that these banks have been equally well run so that they both have the same returns on assets of 1 percent. The return on equity for the High Capital Bank equals 1 percent × 10 = 10 percent, while the return on equity for the Low Capital Bank equals 1 percent × 25 = 25 percent. The equity holders in the Low Capital Bank are clearly a lot happier than the equity holders in the High Capital Bank because they are earning more than twice as high a return. We now see why owners of a bank may not want it to hold a lot of capital. *Given the return on assets, the lower the bank capital, the higher the return for the owners of the bank.*

TRADE-OFF BETWEEN SAFETY AND RETURNS TO EQUITY HOLDERS We now see that bank capital has benefits and costs. Bank capital benefits the owners of a bank in that it makes their investment safer by reducing the likelihood of bankruptcy. But bank capital is costly because the higher it is, the lower will be the return on equity for a given return on assets. In determining the amount of bank capital, managers must decide how much of the increased safety that comes with higher capital (the benefit) they are willing to trade off against the lower return on equity that comes with higher capital (the cost).

In more uncertain times, when the possibility of large losses on loans increases, bank managers might want to hold more capital to protect the equity holders. Conversely, if they have confidence that loan losses won't occur, they might want to reduce the amount of bank capital, have a high equity multiplier, and thereby increase the return on equity.

BANK CAPITAL REQUIREMENTS Banks also hold capital because they are required to do so by regulatory authorities. Because of the high costs of holding capital for the reasons just described, bank managers often want to hold less bank capital than is required by the regulatory authorities. In this case, the amount of bank capital is determined by the bank capital requirements. We discuss the details of bank capital requirements and why they are such an important part of bank regulation in Chapter 12.

Strategies for Managing Bank Capital

Suppose that as the manager of the First National Bank, you have to make decisions about the appropriate amount of bank capital. Looking at the balance sheet of the bank, which like the High Capital Bank has a ratio of bank capital to assets of 10 percent ($10 million of capital and $100 million of assets), you are concerned that the large amount of bank capital is causing the return on equity to be too low. You conclude that the bank has a capital surplus and should increase the equity multiplier to increase the return on equity. What should you do?

To lower the amount of capital relative to assets and raise the equity multiplier, you can do any of three things: (1) You can reduce the amount of bank capital by buying back some of the bank's stock. (2) You can reduce the bank's capital by paying out higher dividends to its stockholders, thereby reducing the bank's retained earnings. (3) You can keep bank capital constant but increase the bank's assets by acquiring new funds, say, by issuing CDs, and then seeking out loan business or purchasing more securities with these new funds. Because you think that it would enhance your position with the stockholders, you decide to pursue the second alternative and raise the dividend on the First National Bank stock.

Now suppose that the First National Bank is in a similar situation to the Low Capital Bank and has a ratio of bank capital to assets of 4 percent. You now worry that the bank is short on capital relative to assets because it does not have a sufficient cushion to prevent bank failure. To raise the amount of capital relative to assets, you now have the following three choices: (1) You can raise capital for the bank by having it issue equity (common stock). (2) You can raise capital by reducing the bank's dividends to shareholders, thereby increasing retained earnings that it can put into its capital account. (3) You can keep capital at the same level but reduce the bank's assets by making fewer loans or by selling off securities and then using the proceeds to reduce its liabilities. Suppose that raising bank capital is not easy to do at the current time because capital markets are tight or because shareholders will protest if their dividends are cut. Then you might have to choose the third alternative and decide to shrink the size of the bank.

In recent years, many banks have experienced capital shortfalls and have had to restrict asset growth, as you might have had to do if the First National Bank were short of capital. The important consequences of this for the credit markets are discussed in the application that follows.

Did the Capital Crunch Cause a Credit Crunch in the Early 1990s?

During the 1990–1991 recession and the year following, there occurred a slow-down in the growth of credit that was unprecedented in the post–World War II era. Many economists and politicians have claimed that there was a "credit crunch" during this period in which credit was hard to get, and as a result the performance of the economy in 1990–1992 was very weak. Was the slowdown in credit growth a manifestation of a credit crunch, and if so, what caused it?

Our analysis of how a bank manages bank capital suggests that a credit crunch was likely to have occurred in 1990–1992 and that it was caused at least in part by the so-called capital crunch in which shortfalls of bank capital led to slower credit growth.

The period of the late 1980s saw a boom and then a major bust in the real estate market that led to huge losses for banks on their real estate loans. As our example of how bank capital helps prevent bank failures demonstrates, the loan losses caused a substantial fall in the amount of bank capital. At the same time, regulators were raising capital requirements (a subject discussed in Chapter 12). The resulting capital shortfalls meant that banks had either to raise new capital or to restrict their asset growth by cutting back on lending. Because of the weak economy at the time, raising new capital was extremely difficult for banks, so they chose the latter course. Banks did restrict their lending, and borrowers found it harder to obtain loans, leading to complaints from banks' customers. Only with the stronger recovery of the economy in 1993, helped by a low-interest-rate policy at the Federal Reserve, did these complaints subside. Ⓐ

MANAGING CREDIT RISK

As seen in the earlier discussion of general principles of asset management, banks and also other financial institutions must make successful loans that are paid back in full (and so subject the institution to little credit risk) in order to earn high profits. The economic concepts of adverse selection and moral hazard (introduced in Chapter 2) provide a framework for understanding the principles that financial institutions have to follow to reduce credit risk and make successful loans.[3]

Adverse selection in loan markets occurs because bad credit risks (those most likely to default on their loans) are the ones who usually line up for loans; in other words, those who are most likely to produce an *adverse* outcome are the most likely to be *selected*. Borrowers with very risky investment projects have much to gain if their projects are successful, and so they are the most eager to obtain loans. Clearly, however, they are the least desirable borrowers because of the greater possibility that they will be unable to pay back their loans.

Moral hazard exists in loan markets because borrowers may have incentives to engage in activities that are undesirable from the lender's point of view. In such situations, it is more likely that the lender will be subjected to the *hazard* of default. Once borrowers have obtained a loan, they are more likely to invest in high-risk investment projects—projects that pay high returns to the borrowers if successful. The high risk, however, makes it less likely that they will be able to pay the loan back.

To be profitable, financial institutions must overcome the adverse selection and moral hazard problems that make loan defaults more likely. The attempts of

---

[3]Other financial intermediaries, such as insurance companies, pension funds, and finance companies, also make private loans, and the credit risk management principles we outline here apply to them as well.

financial institutions to solve these problems help explain a number of principles for managing credit risk: screening and monitoring, establishment of long-term customer relationships, loan commitments, collateral, compensating balance requirements, and credit rationing.

Screening and Monitoring

Asymmetric information is present in loan markets because lenders have less information about the investment opportunities and activities of borrowers than borrowers do. This situation leads to two information-producing activities by banks and other financial institutions, screening and monitoring. Indeed, Walter Wriston, a former head of Citicorp, the largest bank corporation in the United States, was often quoted as stating that the business of banking is the production of information.

SCREENING   Adverse selection in loan markets requires that lenders screen out the bad credit risks from the good ones so that loans are profitable to them. To accomplish effective screening, lenders must collect reliable information from prospective borrowers. Effective screening and information collection together form an important principle of credit risk management.

When you apply for a consumer loan (such as a car loan or a mortgage to purchase a house), the first thing you are asked to do is fill out forms that elicit a great deal of information about your personal finances. You are asked about your salary, bank accounts, other assets (such as cars, insurance policies, and furnishings), and outstanding loans; your record of loan, credit card, and charge account repayments; the number of years you've worked and who your employers have been. You also are asked personal questions such as your age, marital status, and number of children. The lender uses this information to evaluate how good a credit risk you are by calculating your "credit score," a statistical measure derived from your answers that predicts whether you are likely to have trouble making your loan payments. Deciding on how good a risk you are cannot be entirely scientific, so the lender must also use judgment. The loan officer, whose job is to decide whether you should be given the loan, might call your employer or talk to some of the personal references you supplied. The officer might even make a judgment based on your demeanor or your appearance. (This is why most people dress neatly and conservatively when they go to a bank to apply for a loan.)

The process of screening and collecting information is similar when a financial institution makes a business loan. It collects information about the company's profits and losses (income) and about its assets and liabilities. The lender also has to evaluate the likely future success of the business. So in addition to obtaining information on such items as sales figures, a loan officer might ask questions about the company's future plans, how the loan will be used, and the competition in the industry. The officer may even visit the company to obtain a firsthand look at its operations. The bottom line is that, whether for personal or business loans, bankers and other financial institutions need to be nosy.

SPECIALIZATION IN LENDING   One puzzling feature of bank lending is that a bank often specializes in lending to local firms or to firms in particular industries, such as energy. In one sense, this behavior seems surprising because it means that the bank is not diversifying its portfolio of loans and thus is exposing itself to more risk. But from another perspective such specialization makes perfect sense. The adverse selection problem requires that the bank screen out bad credit risks. It is easier for the bank to collect information about local firms and determine their creditworthiness than to collect comparable information on firms that are far away. Similarly, by concentrating its lending on firms in specific industries, the bank becomes more knowledgeable about these industries and is therefore better able to predict which firms will be able to make timely payments on their debt.

MONITORING AND ENFORCEMENT OF RESTRICTIVE COVENANTS Once a loan has been made, the borrower has an incentive to engage in risky activities that make it less likely that the loan will be paid off. To reduce this moral hazard, financial institutions must adhere to the principle for managing credit risk that a lender should write provisions (restrictive covenants) into loan contracts that restrict borrowers from engaging in risky activities. By monitoring borrowers' activities to see whether they are complying with the restrictive covenants and by enforcing the covenants if they are not, lenders can make sure that borrowers are not taking on risks at their expense. The need for banks and other financial institutions to engage in screening and monitoring explains why they spend so much money on auditing and information-collecting activities.

Long-Term Customer Relationships

An additional way for banks and other financial institutions to obtain information about their borrowers is through long-term customer relationships, another important principle of credit risk management.

If a prospective borrower has had a checking or savings account or other loans with a bank over a long period of time, a loan officer can look at past activity on the accounts and learn quite a bit about the borrower. The balances in the checking and savings accounts tell the banker how liquid the potential borrower is and at what time of year the borrower has a strong need for cash. A review of the checks the borrower has written reveals the borrower's suppliers. If the borrower has borrowed previously from the bank, the bank has a record of the loan payments. Thus long-term customer relationships reduce the costs of information collection and make it easier to screen out bad credit risks.

The need for monitoring by lenders adds to the importance of long-term customer relationships. If the borrower has borrowed from the bank before, the bank has already established procedures for monitoring that customer. Therefore, the costs of monitoring long-term customers are lower than those for new customers.

Long-term relationships benefit the customers as well as the bank. A firm with a previous relationship will find it easier to obtain a loan at a low interest rate because the bank has an easier time determining if the prospective borrower is a good credit risk and incurs fewer costs in monitoring the borrower.

A long-term customer relationship has another advantage for the bank. No bank can think of every contingency when it writes a restrictive covenant into a loan contract; there will always be risky borrower activities that are not ruled out. However, what if a borrower wants to preserve a long-term relationship with a bank because it will be easier to get future loans at low interest rates? The borrower then has the incentive to avoid risky activities that would upset the bank, even if restrictions on these risky activities are not specified in the loan contract. Indeed, if a bank doesn't like what a borrower is doing even when the borrower isn't violating any restrictive covenants, it has some power to discourage the borrower from such activity: The bank can threaten not to let the borrower have new loans in the future. Long-term customer relationships therefore enable banks to deal with even unanticipated moral hazard contingencies.

The advantages of establishing long-term customer relationships suggest that closer ties between corporations and banks might be beneficial to both. One way to create these ties is for banks to hold equity stakes in companies they lend to and for banks to have members on the boards of directors of these companies. Currently, such financial arrangements do not exist in the United States. They were outlawed by legislation passed in the 1930s for reasons described in Chapter 12. They are, however, an important feature of the Japanese and German financial systems. Box 2 discusses how financial ties work in these countries to help banks cope with asymmetric information.

Loan Commitments

Banks also create long-term relationships and gather information by issuing **loan commitments** to commercial customers. A loan commitment is a bank's commitment (for a specified future period of time) to provide a firm with loans up to a given amount at an interest rate that is tied to some market interest rate. The majority of commercial and industrial loans are made under the loan commitment arrangement. The advantage for the firm is that it has a source of credit when it needs it. The advantage for the bank is that the loan commitment promotes a long-term relationship, which in turn facilitates information collection. In addition, provisions in the loan commitment agreement require that the firm continually supply the bank with information about the firm's income, asset and liability position, business activities, and so on. A loan commitment arrangement is a powerful method for reducing the bank's costs for screening and information collection.

Collateral and Compensating Balances

Collateral requirements for loans are important credit risk management tools. Collateral, which is property promised to the lender as compensation if the borrower defaults, lessens the consequences of adverse selection because it reduces the lender's losses in the case of a loan default. If a borrower defaults on a loan, the lender can sell the collateral and use the proceeds to make up for its losses on the loan. One particular form of collateral required when a bank makes commercial loans is called **compensating balances:** A firm receiving a loan must keep a required minimum amount of funds in a checking account at the bank. For example, a business getting a $10 million loan may be required to keep compensating balances of at least $1 million in its checking account at the bank. This $1 million in compensating balances can then be taken by the bank to make up some of the losses on the loan if the borrower defaults.

Japanese and German Banking Arrangements

A Better Way to Deal with Asymmetric Information? An important feature of the Japanese economic system is the *keiretsu,* or industrial group. Each *keiretsu* is made up of a core group of banks and other financial intermediaries that are linked to a group of industrial firms, many of which trade with each other. Linkages between firms and banks are cemented by each group member's holding equity shares in the other members. Because of their equity holdings, banks have memberships on their *keiretsu* firms' supervisory boards (boards of directors), and former bank executives are often placed in top managerial positions at these firms. Not surprisingly, banks favor firms of their *keiretsu* when making loans and hold a large fraction of these firms' debt.

Although nothing as formal or extensive as the *keiretsu* exists in Germany, German banks also have very close ties with industry through the so-called *Hausbank* system. Bank customers keep equity shares "on deposit" at the bank and give the bank proxies to vote these shares for them. With these voting rights and their own holdings of shares, German banks control the votes of a large share of equity in German corporations and have representation on boards of directors of the majority of the largest German corporations.

The Japanese and German banking arrangements give banks tremendous advantages in collecting information and monitoring activities. Long-term customer relationships are strengthened because banks have ownership rights in firms to which they lend. For the reasons discussed in the text, these stronger long-term relationships make it easier for banks to collect information and monitor firms, thus enabling banks to reduce adverse selection and moral hazard problems. In addition, because the banks have a role in the management of firms, they have timely access to information and the ability to influence management to act in the banks' interest by not investing in projects deemed too risky.

You can see that Japanese and German banking arrangements give their banks an advantage that American banks do not have, which may enable the financial systems in these countries to channel funds more easily to firms with the most productive investment opportunities. However, these advantages do not mean that banks in these countries do not make mistakes and get into serious trouble, as has occurred recently in Japan (see Chapter 12). This raises the interesting issue of whether similar banking arrangements should be allowed in the United States.

Besides serving as collateral, compensating balances help increase the likelihood that a loan will be paid off. They do this by helping the bank monitor the borrower and consequently reduce moral hazard. Specifically, by requiring the borrower to use a checking account at the bank, the bank can observe the firm's check payment practices, which may yield a great deal of information about the borrower's financial condition. For example, a sustained drop in the borrower's checking account balance may signal that the borrower is having financial trouble, or account activity may suggest that the borrower is engaging in risky activities; perhaps a change in suppliers means that the borrower is pursuing new lines of business. Any significant change in the borrower's payment procedures is a signal to the bank that it should make inquiries. Compensating balances therefore make it easier for banks to monitor borrowers more effectively and are another important credit risk management tool.

Credit Rationing

Another way in which financial institutions deal with adverse selection and moral hazard is through **credit rationing:** Lenders refuse to make loans even though borrowers are willing to pay the stated interest rate or even a higher rate. Credit rationing takes two forms. The first occurs when a lender refuses to make a loan *of any amount* to a borrower, even if the borrower is willing to pay a higher interest rate. The second occurs when a lender is willing to make a loan but restricts the size of the loan to less than the borrower would like.

At first you might be puzzled by the first type of credit rationing. After all, even if the potential borrower is a credit risk, why doesn't the lender just extend the loan but at a higher interest rate? The answer is that adverse selection prevents this solution. Individuals and firms with the riskiest investment projects are exactly those that are willing to pay the highest interest rates. If a borrower took on a high-risk investment and succeeded, the borrower would become extremely rich. But a lender wouldn't want to make such a loan precisely because the investment risk is high; the likely outcome is that the borrower will *not* succeed and the lender will not be paid back. Charging a higher interest rate just makes adverse selection worse for the lender; that is, it increases the likelihood that the lender is lending to a bad credit risk. The lender would therefore rather not make any loans at a higher interest rate; instead, it would engage in the first type of credit rationing and would turn down loans.

Financial institutions engage in the second type of credit rationing to guard against moral hazard: They grant loans to borrowers, but not loans as large as the borrowers want. Such credit rationing is necessary because the larger the loan, the greater the benefits from moral hazard. If a bank gives you a $1000 loan, for example, you are likely to take actions that enable you to pay it back because you don't want to hurt your credit rating for the future. However, if the bank lends you $10 million, you are more likely to fly off to Rio to celebrate. The larger your loan, the greater your incentives to engage in activities that make it less likely that you will repay the loan. Since more borrowers repay their loans if the loan amounts are small, financial institutions ration credit by providing borrowers with smaller loans than they seek.

MANAGING INTEREST-RATE RISK

With the increased volatility of interest rates that occurred in the 1980s, banks and other financial institutions became more concerned about their exposure to interest-rate risk, the riskiness of earnings and returns that is associated with changes in interest rates. To see what interest-rate risk is all about, let's again take a look at the First National Bank, which has the following balance sheet:

FIRST NATIONAL BANK

Assets		Liabilities	
Rate-sensitive assets	$20 million	Rate-sensitive liabilities	$50 million
Variable-rate loans		Variable-rate CDs	
Short-term securities		Money market deposit	
Federal funds		accounts	
Fixed-rate assets	$80 million	Fixed-rate liabilities	$50 million
Reserves		Checkable deposits	
Long-term loans		Savings deposits	
Long-term securities		Long-term CDs	
		Equity capital	

A total of $20 million of its assets are rate-sensitive, with interest rates that change frequently (at least once a year), and $80 million of its assets are fixed-rate, with interest rates that remain unchanged for a long period (over a year). On the liabilities side, the First National Bank has $50 million of rate-sensitive liabilities and $50 million of fixed-rate liabilities. Suppose that interest rates rise by 5 percentage points, say, on average from 10 percent to 15 percent. The income on the assets rises by $1 million (= 5 percent × $20 million of rate-sensitive assets), while the payments on the liabilities rise by $2.5 million (= 5 percent × $50 million of rate-sensitive liabilities). The First National Bank's profits now decline by $1.5 million (= $1 million − $2.5 million). Conversely, if interest rates fall by 5 percentage points, similar reasoning tells us that the First National Bank's profits rise by $1.5 million. This example illustrates the following point: *If a bank has more rate-sensitive liabilities than assets, a rise in interest rates will reduce bank profits and a decline in interest rates will raise bank profits.*

Gap and Duration Analysis

The sensitivity of bank profits to changes in interest rates can be measured more directly using **gap analysis,** in which the amount of rate-sensitive liabilities is subtracted from the amount of rate-sensitive assets. In our example, this calculation (called the "gap") is −$30 million (= $20 million − $50 million). By multiplying the gap times the change in the interest rate, we can immediately obtain the effect on bank profits. For example, when interest rates rise by 5 percentage points, the change in profits is 5 percent × −$30 million, which equals −$1.5 million, as we saw.

The analysis we just conducted is known as *basic gap analysis,* and it can be refined in two ways. Clearly, not all assets and liabilities in the fixed-rate category have the same maturity. One refinement, the *maturity bucket approach,* is to measure the gap for several maturity subintervals, called *maturity buckets,* so that effects of interest-rate changes over a multiyear period can be calculated. The second refinement, called *standardized gap analysis,* accounts for the differing degrees of rate sensitivity for different rate-sensitive assets and liabilities.

An alternative method for measuring interest-rate risk, called **duration analysis,** examines the sensitivity of the market value of the bank's total assets and liabilities to changes in interest rates. Duration analysis is based on Macaulay's concept of *duration,* which measures the average lifetime of a security's stream of payments.[4] Duration is a useful concept because it provides a good approximation of the sensitivity of a security's market value to a change in its interest rate:

Percent change in market value of security ≈
− percentage-point change in interest rate × duration in years

where ≈ denotes "approximately equals."

Duration analysis involves using the average (weighted) duration of a financial institution's assets and of its liabilities to see how its net worth responds to a change in interest rates. Going back to our example of the First National Bank, suppose that the average duration of its assets is three years (that is, the average lifetime of the stream of payments is three years), while the average duration of its liabilities is two years. In addition, the First National Bank has $100 million of assets and $90 million of liabilities, so its bank capital is 10 percent of assets. With a 5-percentage-point increase in interest rates, the market value of the bank's assets falls by 15 percent (= −5 percent × 3 years), a decline of $15 million on the $100 million of assets. However, the market value of the liabilities falls by 10 percent (= −5 percent × 2 years), a decline of $9 million on the $90 million of liabilities. The net result is that the net worth (the market value of the assets minus the liabilities) has declined by $6 million, or 6 percent of the total original asset value. Similarly, a 5-percentage-point decline in interest rates increases the net worth of the First National Bank by 6 percent of the total asset value.

As our example makes clear, both duration analysis and gap analysis indicate that the First National Bank will suffer if interest rates rise but will gain if they fall. Duration analysis and gap analysis are thus useful tools for telling a manager of a financial institution its degree of exposure to interest-rate risk.

Strategies for Managing Interest-Rate Risk

Suppose that as the manager of the First National Bank, you have done a duration and gap analysis for the bank as discussed in the text. Now you need to decide what alternative strategies you should pursue to manage the interest-rate risk.

---

[4]Algebraically, Macaulay's duration, D, is defined as

$$D = \sum_{\tau=1}^{N} \tau \frac{CP_\tau}{(1 + i)^\tau} \bigg/ \sum_{\tau=1}^{N} \frac{CP_\tau}{(1 + i)^\tau}$$

where

τ = time until cash payment is made
CP_τ = cash payment (interest plus principal) at time τ
i = interest rate
N = time to maturity of the security

If you firmly believe that interest rates will fall in the future, you may be willing to take no action because you know that the bank has more rate-sensitive liabilities than rate-sensitive assets and so will benefit from the expected interest-rate decline. However, you also realize that the First National Bank is subject to substantial interest-rate risk because there is always a possibility that interest rates will rise rather than fall. What should you do to eliminate this interest-rate risk? One thing you could do is to shorten the duration of the bank's assets to increase their rate sensitivity. Alternatively, you could lengthen the duration of the liabilities. By this adjustment of the bank's assets and liabilities, the bank will be less affected by interest-rate swings.

One problem with eliminating the First National Bank's interest-rate risk by altering the balance sheet is that doing so might be very costly in the short run. The bank may be locked in to assets and liabilities of particular durations because of where its expertise lies. Fortunately, recently developed financial instruments known as financial derivatives—financial forwards and futures, options and swaps—can help the bank reduce its interest-rate risk exposure but do not require that the bank rearrange its balance sheet. We discuss these instruments and how banks and other financial institutions can use them to manage interest-rate risk in Chapter 14.

OFF-BALANCE-SHEET ACTIVITIES

Although asset and liability management has traditionally been the major concern of banks, in the more competitive environment of recent years banks have been aggressively seeking out profits by engaging in off-balance-sheet activities. **Off-balance-sheet activities** involve trading financial instruments and generating income from fees and loan sales, activities that affect bank profits but do not appear on bank balance sheets. Indeed, off-balance-sheet activities have been growing in importance for banks: The income from these activities as a percentage of assets has nearly doubled since 1979.

Loan Sales

One type of off-balance-sheet activity that has grown in importance in recent years involves income generated by loan sales. A **loan sale,** also called a *secondary loan participation,* involves a contract that sells all or part of the cash stream from a specific loan and thereby removes the loan from the bank's balance sheet. Banks earn profits by selling loans for an amount slightly greater than the amount of the original loan. Because the high interest rate on these loans makes them attractive, institutions are willing to buy them even though the higher price means that they earn a slightly lower interest rate than the original interest rate on the loan, usually on the order of 0.15 percentage point.

Generation of Fee Income

Another type of off-balance-sheet activity involves the generation of income from fees that banks receive for providing specialized services to their customers, such as making foreign exchange trades on a customer's behalf, servicing a mortgage-backed security by collecting interest and principal payments and then paying them out, guaranteeing debt securities such as banker's acceptances (the bank promises to make interest and principal payments if the party issuing the security cannot), and providing backup lines of credit. There are several types of backup lines of credit. We have already mentioned the most important, the loan commitment, under which for a fee the bank agrees to provide a loan at the customer's request, up to a given dollar amount, over a specified period of time. Credit lines are also now available to bank depositors with "overdraft privileges"— these bank customers can write checks in excess of their deposit balances and, in effect, write themselves a loan. Other lines of credit for which banks get fees include standby letters of credit to back up issues of commercial paper and other securities and credit lines (called *note issuance facilities,* NIFs, and *revolving underwriting facilities,* RUFs) for underwriting Euronotes, which are medium-term Eurobonds.

Off-balance-sheet activities involving guarantees of securities and backup credit lines increase the risk a bank faces. Even though a guaranteed security does not appear on a bank balance sheet, it still exposes the bank to default risk: If the issuer of the security defaults, the bank is left holding the bag and must pay off the security's owner. Backup credit lines also expose the bank to risk because the bank may be forced to provide loans when it does not have sufficient liquidity or when the borrower is a very poor credit risk.

Trading Activities and Risk Management Techniques

We have already mentioned that banks' attempts to manage interest-rate risk led them to trading in financial futures, options for debt instruments, and interest-rate swaps. Banks engaged in international banking also conduct transactions in the foreign exchange market. All transactions in these markets are off-balance-sheet activities because they do not have a direct effect on the bank's balance sheet. Although bank trading in these markets is often directed toward reducing risk or facilitating other bank business, banks also try to outguess the markets and engage in speculation. This speculation can be a very risky business and indeed has led to bank insolvencies, the most dramatic being the failure of Barings, a British bank, in 1995.

Trading activities, although often highly profitable, are dangerous because they make it easy for financial institutions and their employees to make huge bets quickly. A particular problem for management of trading activities is that the principal-agent problem, discussed in Chapter 9, is especially severe. Given the ability to place large bets, a trader (the agent), whether she trades in bond markets, in foreign exchange markets or in financial derivatives, has an incentive to take on excessive risks: If her trading strategy leads to large profits, she is likely to receive a high salary and bonuses, but if she takes large losses, the financial institution (the principal) will have to cover them. As the Barings Bank failure in 1995 so forcefully demonstrated, a trader subject to the principal-agent problem can take an institution that is quite healthy and drive it into insolvency very fast (see Box 3).

To reduce the principal-agent problem, managers of financial institutions must set up internal controls to prevent debacles like the one at Barings. Such controls include the complete separation of the people in charge of trading

Barings, Daiwa, and Sumitomo

Rogue Traders and the Principal-Agent Problem. The demise of Barings, a venerable British bank over a century old, is a sad morality tale of how the principal-agent problem operating through a rogue trader can take a financial institution that has a healthy balance sheet one month and turn it into an insolvent tragedy the next.

In July 1992, Nick Leeson, Barings's new head clerk at its Singapore branch, began to speculate on the Nikkei, the Japanese version of the Dow Jones index. By late 1992, Leeson had suffered losses of $3 million, which he hid from his superiors by stashing the losses in a secret account. He even fooled his superiors into thinking he was generating large profits, thanks to a failure of internal controls at his firm, which allowed him to execute trades on the Singapore exchange *and* oversee the book-keeping of those trades. (As anyone who runs a cash business, such as a bar, knows, there is always a lower likelihood of fraud if more than one person handles the cash. Similarly for trading operations, you never mix management of the back room with management of the front room; this principle was grossly violated by Barings management.) Things didn't get better for Leeson, who by late 1994 had losses exceeding $250 million. In January and February 1995, he bet the bank. On January 17, 1995, the day of the Kobe earthquake, he lost $75 million, and by the end of the week had lost more than $150 million. When the stock market declined on February 23, leaving him with a further loss of $250 million, he called it quits and fled Singapore. Three days later, he turned himself in at the Frankfurt airport. By the end of his wild ride, Leeson's losses, $1.3 billion in all, ate up Baring's capital and caused the bank to fail.

Our asymmetric information analysis of the principal-agent problem explains Leeson's behavior and the danger of Barings's management lapse. By letting Leeson control both his own trades and the back room, it increased asymmetric information because it reduced the principal's (Barings's) knowledge about Leeson's trading activities. This lapse increased the moral hazard incentive for him to take risks at the bank's expense, as he was now less likely to be caught. Furthermore, once he had experienced large losses, he had even greater incentives to take on even higher risk because if his bets worked out, he could reverse his losses and keep in good standing with the company, whereas if his bets soured, he had little to lose since he was out of a job anyway. Indeed, the bigger his losses, the more he had to gain by bigger bets, which explains the escalation of the amount of his trades as his losses mounted. If Barings's managers had understood the principal-agent problem, they would have been more vigilant in learning what Leeson was up to, and the bank might still be here today.

Unfortunately, Nick Leeson is no longer a rarity in the rogue traders' billionaire club, those who have lost more than $1 billion. Over 11 years, Toshihide Iguchi, an officer in the New York branch of Daiwa Bank, also had control of both the bond trading operation and the back room, and he racked up $1.1 billion in losses over the period. In July 1995, Iguchi disclosed his losses to his superiors, but the management of the bank did not disclose them to its regulators. The result was that Daiwa was slapped with a $340 million fine and the bank was thrown out of the country by U.S. bank regulators. Yasuo Hamanaka is the latest member of the billionaire club. In July 1996, he topped Leeson's and Iguchi's record, losing $2.6 billion for his employer, the Sumitomo Corporation, one of Japan's top trading companies. The moral of these stories is that management of firms engaged in trading activities must reduce the principal-agent problem by closely monitoring their traders' activities.

activities and those in charge of the bookkeeping for trades. In addition, managers must set limits on the total amount of traders' transactions and on the institution's risk exposure. Managers must also scrutinize risk assessment procedures using the latest computer technology. One such method involves the so-called value-at-risk approach. In this approach, the institution develops a statistical model with which it can calculate the maximum loss that its portfolio is likely to sustain over a given time interval, dubbed the value at risk, or VAR. For example, a bank might estimate that the maximum loss that it would be likely to sustain over one day with a probability of 1 in 100 is $1 million; the $1 million figure is the bank's calculated value at risk. Another approach is called "stress testing." In this approach, a manager asks models what would happen if a doomsday scenario occurs; that is, she looks at the losses the institution would sustain if an unusual combination of bad events occurred. With the value-at-risk approach and stress testing, a financial institution can assess its risk exposure and take steps to reduce it.

Because of the increased risk that banks are facing from their off-balance-sheet activities, U.S. bank regulators have become concerned about increased risk from banks' off-balance-sheet activities and, as we will see in Chapter 12, are encouraging banks to pay increased attention to risk management. In addition, the Bank for International Settlements is developing additional bank capital requirements based on value-at-risk calculations for a bank's trading activities.

FINANCIAL INNOVATION

Like other industries, the financial industry is in business to earn profits by selling its products. If a soap company perceives that there is a need in the marketplace for a laundry detergent with fabric softener, it develops a product to fit the need. Similarly, to maximize their profits, financial institutions develop new products to satisfy their own needs as well as those of their customers; in other words, innovation—which can be extremely beneficial to the economy—is driven by the desire to get (or stay) rich. This view of the innovation process leads to the following simple analysis: ***A change in the financial environment will stimulate a search by financial institutions for innovations that are likely to be profitable.***

Starting in the 1960s, individuals and financial institutions operating in financial markets were confronted with drastic changes in the economic environment: Inflation and interest rates climbed sharply and became harder to predict, a situation that changed demand conditions in financial markets. Computer technology advanced rapidly, which changed supply conditions. In addition, financial regulations became more burdensome. Financial institutions found that many of the old ways of doing business were no longer profitable; the financial services and products they had been offering to the public were not selling. Many financial intermediaries found that they were no longer able to acquire funds with their traditional financial instruments, and without these funds they would soon be out of business. To survive in the new economic environment, financial institutions had to research and develop new products and services that would meet customer needs and prove profitable, a process referred to as **financial engineering.** In their case, necessity was the mother of innovation.

Our discussion of why financial innovation occurs suggests that there are three basic types of financial innovations: responses to changes in demand conditions, responses to changes in supply conditions, and avoidance of regulations. Now that we have a framework for understanding why financial institutions such as banks produce innovations, let's look at examples of how financial institutions in their search for profits have produced financial innovations of the three basic types.

Responses to Changes in Demand Conditions

The most significant change in the economic environment that altered the demand for financial products in recent years has been the dramatic increase in the volatility of interest rates. In the 1950s, the interest rate on three-month Treasury bills fluctuated between 1.0 percent and 3.5 percent; in the 1970s, it fluctuated between 4.0 percent and 11.5 percent. This volatility became even more pronounced in the 1980s, during which the three-month T-bill rate ranged from 5 percent to over 15 percent. We have seen in Chapter 4 (Table 2) that a rise in the interest rate from 10 percent to 20 percent would result in a capital loss of nearly 50 percent on a 30-year bond and a negative return of almost 40 percent. Large fluctuations in interest rates lead to substantial capital gains or losses and greater uncertainty about returns on investments. Recall that the risk that is related to the uncertainty about interest-rate movements and returns is called *interest-rate risk*, and high volatility of interest rates, such as we saw in the 1970s and 1980s, leads to a higher level of interest-rate risk.

We would expect the increase in interest-rate risk to increase the demand for financial products and services that could reduce that risk. This change in the economic environment would thus stimulate a search for profitable innovations by financial institutions that meet this new demand and would spur the creation of new financial instruments that help lower interest-rate risk. One financial innovation in the banking industry that appeared in the 1970s confirms this prediction: the development of adjustable-rate mortgages.

ADJUSTABLE-RATE MORTGAGES   Like other investors, financial institutions find that lending is more attractive if interest-rate risk is lower. They would not want to make a mortgage loan at a 10 percent interest rate and two months later find that they could obtain 12 percent in interest on the same mortgage. To reduce interest-rate risk, in 1975 savings and loans in California began to issue adjustable-rate mortgages, that is, mortgage loans on which the interest rate changes when a market interest rate (usually the Treasury bill rate) changes. Initially, an adjustable-rate mortgage might have a 5 percent interest rate. In six months, this interest rate might increase or decrease by the amount of the increase or decrease in, say, the six-month Treasury bill rate, and the mortgage payment would change. Because adjustable-rate mortgages allow mortgage-issuing institutions to earn higher interest rates on mortgages when rates rise, profits are kept higher during these periods.

This attractive feature of adjustable-rate mortgages has encouraged mortgage-issuing institutions to issue adjustable-rate mortgages with lower initial interest rates than on conventional fixed-rate mortgages, making them popular with many households. However, because the mortgage payment on a variable-rate mortgage can increase, many households continue to prefer fixed-rate mortgages. Hence both types of mortgages are widespread.

Responses to Changes in Supply Conditions

The most important source of the changes in supply conditions that stimulate financial innovation has been the improvement in computer and telecommunications technology. These changes have made it profitable for financial institutions to create new financial products and services to the public. When computer technology that substantially lowered the cost of processing financial transactions became available, financial institutions conceived new financial products and instruments dependent on this technology that might appeal to the public, including the bank credit card and electronic banking facilities.

BANK CREDIT AND DEBIT CARDS   Credit cards have been around since well before World War II. Many individual stores (Sears, Macy's, Goldwater's) institutionalized charge accounts by providing customers with credit cards that allowed them to make purchases at these stores without cash. Nationwide credit cards were not established until after World War II, when Diners Club developed one to be used in restaurants all over the country (and abroad). Similar credit card programs were started by American Express and Carte Blanche, but because of the high cost of operating these programs, cards were issued only to selected persons and businesses who could afford expensive purchases.

A firm issuing credit cards earns income from loans it makes to credit card holders and from payments made by stores on credit card purchases (a percentage of the purchase price, say, 5 percent). A credit card program's costs arise from loan defaults, stolen cards, and the expense involved in processing credit card transactions.

Bankers saw the success of Diners Club, American Express, and Carte Blanche and wanted to share in the profitable credit card business. Several commercial banks attempted to expand the credit card business to a wider market in the 1950s, but the cost per transaction when running these programs was so high that their early attempts failed.

In the late 1960s, improved computer technology, which lowered the transaction costs for providing credit card services, made it more likely that bank credit card programs would be profitable. The banks tried to enter this business again, and this time their efforts led to the creation of two successful bank credit card programs: BankAmericard (originally started by the Bank of America but now an independent organization called Visa) and MasterCharge (now MasterCard, run by the Interbank Card Association). These programs have become phenomenally successful; more than 200 million of their cards are in use. Indeed, bank credit cards have been so profitable that nonfinancial institutions such as Sears (which launched the Discover card), General Motors, and AT&T have also entered the credit card business. Consumers have benefited because credit cards are more widely accepted than checks when paying for purchases (particularly abroad), and they allow consumers to take out loans more easily.

The success of bank credit cards has led these institutions to come up with a new financial innovation, *debit cards*. Debit cards often look just like credit cards and can be used to make purchases in an identical fashion. However, in contrast to credit cards, which extend the purchaser a loan that does not have to be paid off immediately, a debit card purchase is immediately deducted from the card holder's bank account. Debit cards depend even more on low costs of processing transactions, since their profits are generated entirely from the fees paid by merchants on debit card purchases at their stores. Debit cards have been growing increasingly popular in recent years.

ELECTRONIC BANKING FACILITIES The wonders of modern computer technology have also enabled banks to lower the cost of bank transactions by having the customer interact with an electronic banking facility rather than with a human being. One important form of electronic banking facility is the automated teller machine (ATM), which has the advantage that it does not have to be paid overtime and never sleeps, thus being available for use 24 hours a day. Not only does this result in cheaper transactions for the bank, but it also provides more convenience for the customer. Furthermore, because of its low cost, ATMs can be put at locations other than a bank or its branches, further increasing customer convenience. The low cost of ATMs has meant that they have sprung up everywhere and now number over 100,000 in the United States alone. Furthermore, it is now as easy to get foreign currency from an ATM when you are traveling in Europe as it is to get cash from your local bank. In addition, transactions with ATMs are so much cheaper for the bank than ones conducted with human tellers that some banks charge customers less if they use the ATM than if they use a human teller.

With the drop in the cost of telecommunications, banks have developed another financial innovation, home banking. It is now cost-effective for banks to set up an electronic banking facility in which the bank's customer is linked up with the bank's computer to carry out transactions either by using a telephone or a personal computer. Now a bank's customers can conduct many of their bank transactions without ever leaving the comfort of home. The advantage for the customer is the convenience of home banking, while banks find that the cost of transactions is substantially less than having the customer come to the bank. Also as we saw in Chapter 3, we are entering a new world in which computer banking is evolving to electronic payment methods that eliminate paper transactions and their associated costs.

With the decline in the price of personal computers and their increasing presence in the home, we have seen a further innovation in the home banking area, the appearance of a new type of banking institution, the **virtual bank,** a bank that has no physical location but rather exists only in cyberspace. In 1995, Security First Network Bank became the first virtual bank, planning to offer an array of banking services on the Internet—accepting checking account and savings deposits, selling certificates of deposits, issuing ATM cards, providing bill paying facilities, and so on. In 1996, Bank of America and Wells Fargo, two of the largest banks in the United States, entered the virtual banking market, providing home banking services via the Internet. The virtual bank thus takes home banking one step further, enabling a customer to have a full set of banking services at home, 24 hours a day.

Avoidance of Existing Regulations

The process of financial innovation we have discussed so far is much like innovation in other areas of the economy: It occurs in response to changes in demand and supply conditions. However, because the financial industry is more heavily regulated than other industries, government regulation is a much greater spur to innovation in this industry. Government regulation leads to financial innovation by creating incentives for firms to skirt regulations that restrict their ability to earn profits. Edward Kane describes this process of avoiding regulations as "loophole mining."[5] The economic analysis of innovation suggests that when the economic environment changes such that regulatory constraints are so burdensome that large profits can be made by avoiding them, loophole mining and innovation are more likely to occur.

Because banking is one of the most heavily regulated industries in America, loophole mining is especially likely to occur. The rise in inflation and interest rates from the late 1960s to 1980 made the regulatory constraints imposed on this industry even more burdensome. Under these circumstances, we would expect the pace of financial innovation in banking to be rapid, and, indeed, it has been.

Two sets of regulations have seriously restricted the ability of banks to make profits: reserve requirements that force banks to keep a certain fraction of their deposits as reserves (deposits in the Federal Reserve System) and restrictions on the interest rates that can be paid on deposits. For the following reasons, these regulations have been among the major forces behind financial innovation in recent years.

RESERVE REQUIREMENTS   The key to understanding why reserve requirements affect financial innovation is to recognize that they act, in effect, as a tax on deposits. Because the Fed does not pay interest on reserves, the opportunity cost of holding them is the interest that a bank could otherwise earn by lending the reserves out. For each dollar of deposits, reserve requirements therefore impose a cost on the bank equal to the interest rate that could be earned if the reserves could be lent out i times the fraction of deposits required as reserves r_D. The cost of $i \times r_D$ imposed on the bank is just like a tax on bank deposits of $i \times r_D$.

It is a great tradition to avoid taxes if possible, and banks also play this game. Just as taxpayers look for loopholes to lower their tax bills, banks seek to increase their profits by mining loopholes and by producing new financial innovations that allow them to escape the tax on deposits imposed by reserve requirements.

RESTRICTIONS ON INTEREST PAID ON DEPOSITS   Until 1980, legislation prohibited banks in most states from paying interest on checking account deposits, and through Regulation Q, the Fed set maximum limits on the interest rate that could be paid on time deposits. The desire to avoid these **deposit rate ceilings** also led to financial innovations.

If market interest rates rose above the maximum rates that banks paid on time deposits under Regulation Q, depositors withdrew funds from banks to put them into higher-yielding securities. This loss of deposits from the banking system restricted the amount of funds that banks could lend (called **disintermediation**)

---

[5]"Banking Takes a Beating," *Time,* December 3, 1984, p. 49.

and thus limited bank profits. Banks had an incentive to get around deposit rate ceilings because by so doing, they could acquire more funds to make loans and earn higher profits.

We can now look at how the desire to avoid restrictions on interest payments and the tax effect of reserve requirements led to several important financial innovations.

EURODOLLARS AND BANK COMMERCIAL PAPER In the late 1960s, inflation was accelerating, and (as we would expect from our analysis of the Fisher effect in Chapter 6) interest rates began to rise. The tax on deposits from reserve requirements $i \times r_D$ also began to rise, and the incentives to avoid this tax increased. In addition, higher interest rates meant that market interest rates exceeded the maximum rate payable on time deposits under Regulation Q, and as market interest rates climbed to then record highs in 1969, investors reduced their time deposits to invest in higher-yielding securities. By the late 1960s, commercial banks had a strong incentive to search for new funds that would not be subject to reserve requirements and so escape the tax of $i \times r_D$ and not be subject to the interest rate ceiling set by Regulation Q.

As the economic analysis of innovation predicts, the banks began to mine loopholes and discovered two sources of funds that avoided both reserve requirements and deposit rate ceilings: Eurodollars and bank commercial paper. Because Eurodollars (deposits abroad denominated in dollars) were borrowed from banks outside the United States, they were not subject to reserve requirements or to Regulation Q. Similarly, commercial paper issued by a bank's parent holding company was not treated as deposits and so was also exempt from these regulations. Not surprisingly, the markets for Eurodollars and bank commercial paper began to expand rapidly in the late 1960s.

NOW ACCOUNTS, ATS ACCOUNTS, AND OVERNIGHT REPOS The rise in interest rates in the late 1960s, which made the avoidance of restrictions on deposit rates profitable, stimulated the development of new types of checking accounts. Because of Regulation Q ceilings, savings and loans and mutual savings banks were hit especially hard by the rise in interest rates in the late 1960s. They lost large amounts of funds to financial instruments that paid higher interest rates, and they needed to find new sources of funds to continue to make profitable loans.

In 1970, as a result of diligent loophole mining, a mutual savings bank in Massachusetts struck gold by discovering a loophole in the prohibition of interest payments on checking accounts. In effect, by calling a check a "negotiable order of withdrawal" (NOW), accounts on which these NOWs could be written were not legally checking accounts. Hence NOW accounts were not subject to regulations on checking accounts and could pay interest. In May 1972, after two years of litigation, mutual savings banks in Massachusetts were allowed to issue NOW accounts that paid interest. Subsequently, in September 1972, the courts approved NOW accounts in New Hampshire.

NOW accounts were immediately successful in Massachusetts and New Hampshire, and they enabled savings and loans and mutual savings banks in those states to earn higher profits because they were able to attract more funds that could be loaned out. Since commercial banks did not want competition from other financial intermediaries for checking account deposits (at the time only commercial banks were legally allowed to issue checking accounts), they mounted a campaign to prevent the spread of these accounts to other states. The result was congressional legislation enacted in January 1974 that limited NOW accounts to New England. Legislation in 1980 finally authorized NOW accounts nationwide for savings and loans, mutual savings banks, and commercial banks, and similar accounts **(share draft accounts)** were authorized for credit unions.

Another innovation that enables banks to pay interest on checking accounts is the ATS (automatic transfer from savings) account. Balances above a certain amount in a checking account are automatically transferred into a savings account that pays interest. When a check is written on the ATS account, the necessary funds to cover the check are automatically transferred from the savings account into the checking account. Thus balances earning interest in a savings account are effectively part of the depositor's checking account because they are available for writing checks. Legally, however, it is the savings account and not the checking account that pays interest to the depositor.

Commercial banks provide a variant of the ATS account to their corporate depositors, which involves the use of a so-called *sweep account* to engage in overnight repurchase agreements (repos). In this type of arrangement, any balances above a certain amount in a corporation's checking account at the end of a business day are "swept out" of the account and invested in overnight repos that pay the corporation interest. (As you may recall from Chapter 2, the repo is an agreement whereby a corporation purchases Treasury bills that the bank agrees to repurchase the next day at a slightly higher price.) Again, although the checking account does not legally pay interest, in effect the corporation is receiving interest on balances that are available for writing checks.

The financial innovations of ATS accounts and overnight repo arrangements were stimulated not only by deposit rate ceilings but also by new technology. Without low-cost computers to process inexpensively the additional transactions required by these accounts, neither of these innovations would be profitable and therefore would not have been developed. Technological factors often combine with other incentives, such as the desire to get around restrictions on deposit rates, to produce financial innovation.

CONCLUSION   Our discussion of financial innovation and the challenges that are facing managers of banks indicate that banking is no longer the staid profession it once was, prompting one banker to state, "Despite all the dark suits worn by its leaders, banking is a very dynamic industry."[6]

SUMMARY

1. The balance sheet of commercial banks can be thought of as a list of the sources and uses of bank funds. The bank's liabilities are its sources of funds, which include checkable deposits, time deposits, discount loans from the Fed, borrowings from other banks and corporations, and bank capital. The bank's assets are its uses of funds, which include reserves, cash items in process of collection, deposits at other banks, securities, loans, and other assets (mostly physical capital).

---

[6]Ibid.

2. Banks make profits through the process of asset transformation: They borrow short (accept deposits) and lend long (make loans). When a bank takes in additional deposits, it gains an equal amount of reserves; when it pays out deposits, it loses an equal amount of reserves.

3. Although more liquid assets tend to earn lower returns, banks still desire to hold them. Specifically, banks hold excess and secondary reserves because they provide insurance against the costs of a deposit outflow. Banks manage their assets to maximize profits by seeking the highest returns possible on loans and securities while at the same time trying to lower risk and making adequate provisions for liquidity. Although liability management was once a staid affair, large (money center) banks now actively seek out sources of funds by issuing liabilities such as negotiable CDs or by actively borrowing from other banks and corporations. Banks manage the amount of capital they hold to prevent bank failure and to meet bank capital requirements set by the regulatory authorities. However, they do not want to hold too much capital because by so doing they will lower the returns to equity holders.

4. The concepts of adverse selection and moral hazard explain many credit risk management principles involving loan activities: screening and monitoring, establishment of long-term customer relationships and loan commitments, collateral and compensating balances, and credit rationing.

5. With the increased volatility of interest rates that occurred in the 1980s, financial institutions became more concerned about their exposure to interest-rate risk. Gap and duration analyses tell a financial insti-

tution if it has more rate-sensitive liabilities than assets (in which case a rise in interest rates will reduce profits and a fall in interest rates will raise profits). Financial institutions manage their interest-rate risk by modifying their balance sheets but can also use strategies (outlined in Chapter 14) involving financial derivatives.

6. Off-balance-sheet activities consist of trading financial instruments and generating income from fees and loan sales, all of which affect bank profits but are not visible on bank balance sheets. Because these off-balance-sheet activities expose banks to increased risk, bank management must pay particular attention to risk assessment procedures and internal controls to restrict employees from taking on too much risk.

7. A change in the economic environment will stimulate financial institutions to search for financial innovations that are likely to be profitable. Changes in demand conditions, especially the rise in interest-rate risk, have stimulated a search for profits that has resulted in financial innovations such as adjustable-rate mortgages, while changes in supply conditions because of advances in computer technology have led to financial innovations such as bank credit cards and electronic banking facilities. Regulation leads to financial innovation by encouraging loophole mining. Starting in the late 1960s, for example, higher interest rates (resulting from higher inflation) combined with deposit rate ceilings and the "tax" on deposits to limit bank profits. The desire to avoid these regulations encouraged financial innovations, including NOW accounts, ATS accounts, and overnight repos.

KEY TERMS

asset management, p. 235

balance sheet, p. 226

capital adequacy management, p. 235

compensating balance, p. 247

credit rationing, p. 249

credit risk, p. 235

deposit outflows, p. 235

deposit rate ceiling, p. 259

discount loans, p. 229

discount rate, p. 237

disintermediation, p. 259

duration analysis, p. 251

equity multiplier *(EM),* p. 242

excess reserves, p. 229

financial engineering, p. 255

gap analysis, p. 250

interest-rate risk, p. 235

liability management, p. 235

liquidity management, p. 235

loan commitment, p. 247

loan sale, p. 252

money center banks, p. 239

off-balance-sheet activities, p. 252

required reserve ratio, p. 229

required reserves, p. 229

reserves, p. 229

return on assets *(ROA),* p. 241

return on equity *(ROE),* p. 241

secondary reserves, p. 231

share draft account, p. 261

T-account, p. 232

vault cash, p. 229

virtual bank, p. 258

QUESTIONS AND PROBLEMS

1. Why might a bank be willing to borrow funds from other banks at a higher rate than it can borrow from the Fed?

*2. Rank the following bank assets from most to least liquid:
   a. Commercial loans
   b. Securities
   c. Reserves
   d. Physical capital

3. Using the T-accounts of the First National Bank and the Second National Bank, describe what happens when Jane Brown writes a $50 check on her account at the First National Bank to pay her friend Joe Green, who in turn deposits the check in his account at the Second National Bank.

*4. What happens to reserves at the First National Bank if one person withdraws $1000 of cash and another person deposits $500 of cash? Use T-accounts to explain your answer.

5. The bank you own has the following balance sheet:

Assets		Liabilities	
Reserves	$ 75 million	Deposits	$500 million
Loans	$525 million	Bank capital	$100 million

If the bank suffers a deposit outflow of $50 million with a required reserve ratio on deposits of 10 percent, what actions must you take to keep your bank from failing?

*6. If a deposit outflow of $50 million occurs, which balance sheet would a bank rather have initially, the balance sheet in Problem 5 or the following balance sheet? Why?

Assets		Liabilities	
Reserves	$100 million	Deposits	$500 million
Loans	$500 million	Bank capital	$100 million

7. Why has the development of overnight loan markets made it more likely that banks will hold fewer excess reserves?

*8. If the bank you own has no excess reserves and a sound customer comes in asking for a loan, should you automatically turn the customer down, explaining that you don't have any excess reserves to loan out? Why or why not? What options are available for you to provide the funds your customer needs?

9. If a bank finds that its *ROE* is too low because it has too much bank capital, what can it do to raise its *ROE*?

*10. If a bank is falling short of meeting its capital requirements by $1 million, what three things can it do to rectify the situation?

11. Why is being nosy a desirable trait for a banker?

*12. A bank almost always insists that the firms it lends to keep compensating balances at the bank. Why?

13. "Because diversification is a desirable strategy for avoiding risk, it never makes sense for a bank to specialize in making specific types of loans." Is this statement true, false, or uncertain? Explain your answer.

*14. Suppose that you are the manager of a bank whose $100 billion of assets have an average duration of four years and whose $90 billion of liabilities have an average duration of six years. Conduct a duration analysis for the bank, and show what will happen to the net worth of the bank if interest rates rise by 2 percentage points. What actions could you take to reduce the bank's interest-rate risk?

15. Suppose that you are the manager of a bank that has $15 million of fixed-rate assets, $30 million of rate-sensitive assets, $25 million of fixed-rate liabilities, and $20 million of rate-sensitive liabilities. Conduct a gap analysis for the bank, and show what will happen to bank profits if interest rates rise by 5 percentage points. What actions could you take to reduce the bank's interest-rate risk?

Chapter **11**

BANKING INDUSTRY: STRUCTURE AND COMPETITION

PREVIEW   The operations of individual banks (how they acquire, use, and manage funds to make a profit) are roughly similar throughout the world. In all countries, banks are financial intermediaries in the business of earning profits. When you consider the structure and operation of the banking industry as a whole, however, the United States is in a class by itself. In most countries, four or five large banks typically dominate the banking industry, but in the United States there are on the order of 10,000 commercial banks, 1500 savings and loan associations, 500 mutual savings banks, and 13,000 credit unions.

Is more better? Does this diversity mean that the American banking system is more competitive and therefore more economically efficient and sound than banking systems in other countries? What in the American economic and political system explains this large number of banking institutions? In this chapter we try to answer these questions by examining the historical trends in the banking industry and its overall structure.

We start by examining the commercial banking industry in detail and then go on to look at the thrift industry, which includes savings and loan associations, mutual savings banks, and credit unions. We spend more time on commercial banks because they are by far the largest depository institutions, accounting for over two-thirds of the deposits in the banking system. In addition to looking at our domestic banking system, we also examine the forces behind the growth in international banking to see how it has affected us in the United States. Finally, we examine how financial innovation has increased the competitive environment for the banking industry and is causing fundamental changes in it.

HISTORICAL DEVELOPMENT OF THE BANKING SYSTEM

The modern commercial banking industry began when the Bank of North America was chartered in Philadelphia in 1782. With the success of this bank, other banks opened for business, and the American banking industry was off and running. (As a study aid, Figure 1 provides a time line of the most important dates in the history of American banking before World War II.)

A major controversy involving the industry in its early years was whether the federal government or the states should charter banks. The Federalists, particularly Alexander Hamilton, advocated greater centralized control of banking and federal chartering of banks. Their efforts led to the creation in 1791 of the Bank of the United States, which had elements of both a private and a **central bank,** a government institution that has responsibility for the amount of money and credit supplied in the economy as a whole. Agricultural and other interests, however, were quite suspicious of centralized power and hence advocated chartering by the states. Furthermore, their distrust of moneyed interests in the big cities led to political pressures to eliminate the Bank of the United States, and in 1811 their efforts met with success when its charter was not renewed. Because of abuses by state banks and the clear need for a central bank to help the federal government raise funds during the War of 1812, Congress was stimulated to create the Second Bank of the United States in 1816. The tensions between advocates and opponents of centralized banking power were a recurrent theme during the operation of this second attempt at central banking in the United States, and with the election of Andrew Jackson, a strong advocate of states' rights, the fate of the Second Bank was sealed. After the election in 1832, Jackson vetoed the rechartering of

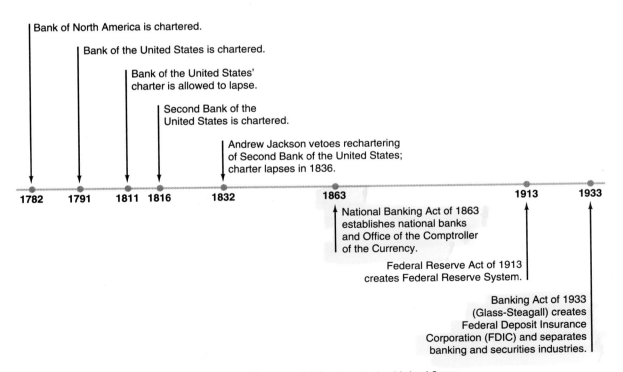

FIGURE 1 Time Line of the Early History of Commercial Banking in the United States

the Second Bank of the United States as a national bank, and its charter lapsed in 1836.

Until 1863, all commercial banks in the United States were chartered by the banking commission of the state in which each operated. No national currency existed, and banks obtained funds primarily by issuing *banknotes* (currency circulated by the banks that could be redeemed for gold). Because banking regulations were extremely lax in many states, banks regularly failed due to fraud or lack of sufficient bank capital; their banknotes became worthless.

To eliminate the abuses of the state-chartered banks (called **state banks**), the National Banking Act of 1863 (and subsequent amendments to it) created a new banking system of federally chartered banks (called **national banks**), supervised by the Office of the Comptroller of the Currency, a department of the U.S. Treasury. This legislation was originally intended to dry up sources of funds to state banks by imposing a prohibitive tax on their banknotes while leaving the banknotes of the federally chartered banks untaxed. The state banks cleverly escaped extinction by acquiring funds by accepting deposits. As a result, today the United States has a **dual banking system** in which banks supervised by the federal government and banks supervised by the states operate side by side.

Central banking did not reappear in this country until the Federal Reserve System (the Fed) was created in 1913 to promote an even safer banking system. All national banks were required to become members of the Federal Reserve System and became subject to a new set of regulations issued by the Fed. State banks could choose (but were not required) to become members of the system, and most did not because of the high costs of membership stemming from the Fed's regulations.

During the Great Depression years 1930–1933, some 9000 bank failures wiped out the savings of many depositors at commercial banks. To prevent future depositor losses from such failures, banking legislation in 1933 established the Federal Deposit Insurance Corporation (FDIC), which provided federal insurance on bank deposits. Member banks of the Federal Reserve System were required to purchase FDIC insurance for their depositors, and non–Federal Reserve commercial banks could choose to buy this insurance (almost all of them did). The purchase of FDIC insurance made banks subject to another set of regulations imposed by the FDIC.

Because investment banking activities of the commercial banks were blamed for many bank failures, provisions in the banking legislation in 1933 (also known as the Glass-Steagall Act) prohibited commercial banks from underwriting or dealing in corporate securities (commercial banks were allowed to sell new issues of government securities, however) and limited banks to the purchase of debt securities approved by the bank regulatory agencies. Likewise it prohibited investment banks from engaging in commercial banking activities. In effect, the Glass-Steagall Act separated the activities of commercial banks from those of the securities industry.

Under the conditions of the Glass-Steagall Act, commercial banks had to sell off their investment banking operations. The First National Bank of Boston, for example, spun off its investment banking operations into the First Boston

Corporation, now one of the most important investment banking firms in America. Investment banking firms typically discontinued their deposit business, although J. P. Morgan discontinued its investment banking business and reorganized as a commercial bank; however, some senior officers of J. P. Morgan went on to organize Morgan Stanley, another one of the largest investment banking firms today.

Multiple Regulatory Agencies

Commercial bank regulation in the United States has developed into a crazy-quilt system of multiple regulatory agencies with overlapping jurisdictions. The Office of the Comptroller of the Currency has the primary supervisory responsibility for the 3000 national banks that own more than half of the assets in the commercial banking system. The Federal Reserve and the state banking authorities have joint primary responsibility for the 1000 state banks that are members of the Federal Reserve System. The Fed also has sole regulatory responsibility over companies that own one or more banks (called **bank holding companies**) and secondary responsibility for the national banks. The FDIC and the state banking authorities jointly supervise the 6000 state banks that have FDIC insurance but are not members of the Federal Reserve System. The state banking authorities have sole jurisdiction over the fewer than 500 state banks without FDIC insurance. (Such banks hold less than 0.2 percent of the deposits in the commercial banking system.)

If you find the U.S. bank regulatory system confusing, imagine how confusing it is for the banks, which have to deal with multiple regulatory agencies. Several proposals have been raised by the U.S. Treasury to rectify this situation by centralizing the regulation of all depository institutions under one independent agency. However, none of these has been successful in Congress, and whether there will be regulatory consolidation in the future is highly uncertain.

STRUCTURE OF THE U.S. COMMERCIAL BANKING INDUSTRY

There are around 10,000 commercial banks in the United States, far more than in any other country in the world. As Table 1 indicates, we have an extraordinary number of small banks. Eighteen percent of the banks have less than $25 million in assets. Far more typical is the size distribution in Canada or the United Kingdom, where five or fewer banks dominate the industry. In contrast, the ten largest commercial banks in the United States (listed in Table 2) together hold just 37 percent of the assets in their industry.

Most industries in the United States have far fewer firms than the commercial banking industry; typically, large firms tend to dominate these industries to a greater extent than in the commercial banking industry. (Consider the computer software industry, which is dominated by Microsoft, or the automobile industry, which is dominated by General Motors, Ford, Chrysler, Toyota, and Honda.) Does the large number of banks in the commercial banking industry and the absence of a few dominant firms suggest that commercial banking is more competitive than other industries?

TABLE 1		Size Distribution of Insured Commercial Banks, End of 1995	
Assets	Number of Banks	Share of Banks (%)	Share of Assets Held (%)
Less than $25 million	1,756	17.7	0.7
$25–$50 million	2,369	23.8	2.0
$50–$100 million	2,534	25.5	4.2
$100–$500 million	2,593	26.1	11.9
$500 million–$1 billion	268	2.7	4.3
$1–$10 billion	346	3.5	24.4
More than $10 billion	75	0.8	52.5
Total	9,941	100.0	100.0

Source: Federal Deposit Insurance Corporation, *1995 Statistics on Banking.*

Restrictions on Branching

The presence of so many commercial banks in the United States actually reflects past regulations that restricted the ability of these financial institutions to open **branches** (additional offices for the conduct of banking operations). Each state had its own regulations on the type and number of branches that a bank could open. Regulations on both coasts, for example, tended to allow banks to open branches throughout a state; in the middle part of the country, regulations on

TABLE 2	Ten Largest U.S. Banks, 1996	
Bank	Assets ($ billions)	Share of All Commercial Bank Assets (%)
1. Citicorp, New York	256.9	6.0
2. BankAmerica Corp., San Francisco	232.4	5.4
3. NationsBank, Charlotte, N.C.	187.3	4.3
4. J. P. Morgan & Co., New York	184.9	4.3
5. Chemical Banking Corp., New York	182.9	4.2
6. First Chicago NBD Corp., Chicago	122.0	2.8
7. Chase Manhattan Corp., New York	121.7	2.8
8. Bankers Trust Corp., New York	104.0	2.4
9. First Union Corp., Charlotte, N.C.	96.7	2.2
10. Banc One Corp., Columbus, Ohio	90.2	2.1
Total	1579.0	36.6

Source: The Banker, June 1996.

branching were more restrictive. The McFadden Act of 1927, which was designed to put national banks and state banks on an equal footing (and the Douglas Amendment of 1970, which closed a loophole in the McFadden Act) effectively prohibited banks from branching across state lines and forced all national banks to conform to the branching regulations in the state of their location.

The result of the McFadden Act and the state branching regulations was that many small banks stayed in existence because a large bank capable of driving them out of business was often restricted from opening a branch nearby. Indeed, it was often easier for a U.S. bank to open a branch in a foreign country than to open one in another state!

Advocates of restrictive state branching regulations argue that these regulations foster competition by keeping so many banks in business. But the existence of large numbers of banks in the United States must be seen as an indication of a *lack* of competition, *not* the presence of vigorous competition. Inefficient banks have been able to remain in business because their customers could not find a conveniently located branch of another bank in which to conduct their business.

The McFadden Act and state branching regulations constituted strong anti-competitive forces in the commercial banking industry. If competition is beneficial to society, why have regulations restricted branching arisen in America? The simplest explanation is that the American public has historically been hostile to large banks. States with the most restrictive branching regulations were typically ones in which populist antibank sentiment was strongest in the nineteenth century. (These states usually had large farming populations whose relations with banks periodically became tempestuous when banks would foreclose on farmers who couldn't pay their debts.) The legacy of nineteenth-century politics was a banking system with restrictive branching regulations and hence an inordinate number of small banks. However, as we will see later in this chapter, branching restrictions are being eliminated, and we are heading toward nationwide banking.

Response to Branching Restrictions

An important feature of the U.S. banking industry is that competition can be repressed by regulation but not completely quashed. As we saw in Chapter 10, the existence of restrictive regulation will stimulate banking institutions to go "loophole mining," coming up with financial innovations that get around these regulations in the banks' search for profits. Regulations restricting branching have stimulated similar economic forces and have promoted the development of three financial innovations: bank holding companies, nonbank banks, and automated teller machines.

BANK HOLDING COMPANIES A holding company is a corporation that owns several different companies. This form of corporate ownership has important advantages for banks in that (1) it has allowed them to circumvent restrictive branching regulations, because the holding company can own a controlling interest in several banks even if branching is not permitted; (2) a bank holding company can engage in other activities related to banking, such as the provision of investment advice, data processing and transmission services, leasing, credit card services, and servicing of loans in other states; and (3) the holding company can issue commercial paper, allowing the bank to tap into nondeposit sources of funds.

At the current time, bank holding companies are restricted to owning businesses that are "closely related to banking." Permissible activities, which are specified by the Federal Reserve's Regulation Y, include the activities mentioned here as well as others, ranging from providing courier services to real estate appraisal. In the past, the Fed and congressional legislation have prohibited bank holding companies from engaging in activities such as brokering real estate, underwriting securities, operating travel agencies, and offering general management consulting. However, in their continuing search for profits, bank holding companies have been seeking ways to get around these regulations and have been entering previously prohibited areas.

Bank holding companies also have the advantage that many states would allow bank holding companies headquartered in other states to purchase banks in their state. In addition, starting in 1982, banks were permitted to purchase out-of-state banks that were failing. For example, bank holding companies headquartered in New York, Ohio, North Carolina, Michigan, and California gained entry into the Texas market by purchasing failing institutions in that state. The result was that the McFadden Act's restrictions on branching no longer prevented these companies from providing banking services in other states.

The growth of the bank holding companies has been dramatic over the past three decades. Today bank holding companies (including Citicorp, BankAmerica, Chase Manhattan, NationsBank, and Wells Fargo) own almost all large banks, and over 90 percent of all commercial bank deposits are held in banks owned by holding companies.

NONBANK BANKS   Another way banks could avoid branching restrictions was through a loophole in the Bank Holding Act of 1956, which defined a bank as a financial institution that accepts deposits *and* makes loans. Once bank holding companies recognized this loophole, they realized that if they opened limited-service banks that either took deposits but did not make commercial loans or did not take deposits but made commercial loans, these so-called **nonbank banks** would not be subject to branching regulations. Thus the bank holding companies discovered a way of branching across state lines. However, the Competitive Equality Bank Act passed in 1987 placed a moratorium on new nonbank banks, thus closing this loophole.

AUTOMATED TELLER MACHINES   Another financial innovation that avoided the restrictions on branching is the electronic banking facility known as the automated teller machine (ATM). Banks realized that if they did not own or rent the ATM, but instead let it be owned by someone else and paid for each transaction with a fee, the ATM would probably not be considered a branch of the bank and thus would not be subject to branching regulations. This is exactly what the regulatory agencies and courts in most states concluded. Because they enable banks to widen their markets, a number of these shared facilities (such as Cirrus and NYCE) have been established nationwide. Furthermore, even when an ATM is owned by a bank, states typically have special provisions that allow wider establishment of ATMs than is permissible for traditional "brick and mortar" branches.

As we saw in Chapter 10, avoiding regulation was not the only reason for the development of the ATM. The advent of cheaper computer and telecommunications technology enabled banks to provide ATMs at low cost, making them a profitable innovation. This further illustrates that technological factors often combine with incentives such as the desire to avoid restrictive regulations like branching restrictions to produce financial innovation.

NATIONWIDE BANKING AND BANK CONSOLIDATION

As we can see in Figure 2, after a remarkable period of stability from 1934 to the mid-1980s, the number of commercial banks has begun to fall dramatically. Why is this sudden decline taking place?

The banking industry hit some hard times in the 1980s and early 1990s, with bank failures running at a rate of over 100 per year from 1985 to 1992 (more on this later in the chapter and in Chapter 12). But bank failures are only part of the story. In the years 1985–1992, the number of banks declined by 3000—more than double the number of failures. And in the period 1992–1996, when the banking industry returned to health, the number of commercial banks declined by a little over 1500, less than 15 percent of which were bank failures, and most of

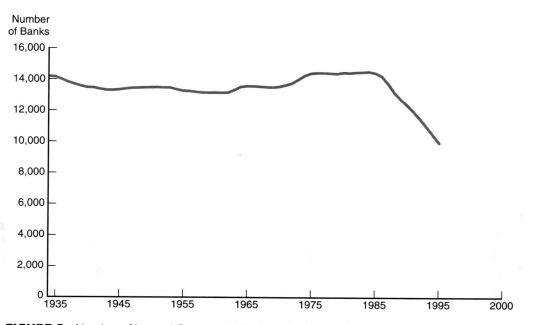

FIGURE 2   Number of Insured Commercial Banks in the United States, 1934–1995

Sources: Federal Deposit Insurance Corporation, *1995 Statistics on Banking; Historical Statistics on Banking.*

these were of small banks. Thus we see that bank failures played an important, though not predominant, role in the decline in the number of banks in the 1985–1992 period and an almost negligible role in the decline in the number of banks since then.

So what explains the rest of the story? The answer is bank consolidation. Banks have been merging to create larger entities or have been buying up other banks. This gives rise to a new question: Why has bank consolidation been taking place in recent years?

As we have seen, loophole mining by banks has reduced the effectiveness of branching restrictions, with the result that many states have recognized that it would be in their best interest if they allowed ownership of banks across state lines. The result has been the formation of regional compacts in which banks in the region are allowed to own banks in other states in the region. In 1975, Maine enacted the first interstate banking legislation that allowed out-of-state bank holding companies to purchase banks in that state. In 1982, Massachusetts enacted a regional compact with other New England states to allow interstate banking, and many other regional compacts were adopted thereafter until by the early 1990s, almost all states allowed some form of interstate banking.

With the barriers to interstate banking breaking down in the early 1980s, banks recognized that they could gain the benefits of diversification because they would now be able to make loans in many states rather than just one. This gave them the advantage that if one state's economy was weak, another in which they operated might be strong, thus decreasing the likelihood that loans in different states would default at the same time. In addition, allowing banks to own banks in other states meant that they could take advantage of economies of scale by increasing their size through out-of-state acquisition of banks or by merging with banks in other states. Mergers and acquisitions explain the first phase of banking consolidation, which has played such an important role in the decline in the number of banks since 1985. Another result of the loosening of restrictions on interstate branching is the development of a new class of bank, the so-called **superregional banks,** bank holding companies that have begun to rival the money center banks in size but whose headquarters are not based in one of the money center cities (New York, Chicago, and San Francisco). Examples of these superregional banks are NationsBank of Charlotte, North Carolina, and Banc One of Columbus, Ohio.

The Riegle-Neal Interstate Banking and Branching Efficiency Act of 1994

Banking consolidation has been given further stimulus by the passage in 1994 of the Riegle-Neal Interstate Banking and Branching Efficiency Act. This legislation expands the regional compacts to the entire nation and overturns the McFadden Act and Douglas Amendment's prohibition of interstate banking. Not only does this act allow bank holding companies to acquire banks in any other state, notwithstanding any state laws to the contrary, but it allows interstate branching by allowing bank holding companies to merge the banks they own into one bank with branches in different states beginning June 1, 1997. States do have the option of allowing interstate branching to occur earlier than this date, and several have done so; they also have the option of opting out of interstate branching, a choice only Texas has made.

The Riegle-Neal Act finally establishes the basis for a true nationwide banking system. Although interstate banking was accomplished previously by out-of-state purchase of banks by bank holding companies, up until 1994 interstate branching was virtually nonexistent because very few states had enacted interstate branching legislation. Allowing banks to conduct interstate banking through branching is especially important because many bankers feel that economies of scale cannot be fully exploited through the bank holding company structure; they can only be fully exploited through branching networks in which all of the bank's operations are fully coordinated.

What Will the Structure of the U.S. Banking Industry Look Like in the Future?

With true nationwide banking becoming a reality, the benefits of bank consolidation for the banking industry have increased substantially, thus driving the next phase of mergers and acquisitions and accelerating the decline in the number of commercial banks. Great changes are occurring in the structure of this industry, and the natural question arises: What will the industry look like in, say, ten years?

One view is that the industry will become more like that in many other countries (see Box 1) and we will end up with only a couple of hundred banks. A more extreme view is that industry will look like that of Canada or the United Kingdom with a few large banks dominating the industry. Research on this question, however, comes up with a different answer. The structure of the U.S. banking industry will still be unique, but not as unique as it once was. Most experts predict that the consolidation surge will settle down as the U.S. banking industry approaches several thousand, rather than several hundred, banks. One simple way of seeing why the number of banks will continue to be substantial is to recognize that California, which has unrestricted branching throughout the state, has close to 400 commercial banks. Blowing up the number of banks by the share of banking assets in California relative to the whole country produces an estimate of the number of banks with unrestricted nationwide branching on the order of 4000. More sophisticated research suggests that the number of banks in the United States will ultimately be somewhat fewer than this, but not much.[1]

Banking consolidation will not only result in a smaller number of banks, but as the recent merger between Chase Manhattan Bank and Chemical Bank and the purchase of Boatsmen's Bank by NationsBank suggest, a shift in assets from smaller banks to larger banks as well. Within ten years, the share of bank assets in banks with less than $100 million in assets is expected to halve, while the amount at the so-called megabanks, those with over $100 billion in assets, is expected to more than double.

---

[1]For example, see Allen N. Berger, Anil K. Kashyap, and Joseph Scalise, "The Transformation of the U.S. Banking Industry: What a Long, Strange Trip It's Been," *Brookings Papers on Economic Activity* 2 (1995): 55-201, and Timothy Hannan and Stephen Rhoades, "Future U.S. Banking Structure, 1990-2010," *Antitrust Bulletin* 37 (1992) 737-798. For a more detailed treatment of the bank consolidation process taking place in the United States, see Frederic S. Mishkin, "Bank Consolidation: A Central Banker's Perspective," National Bureau Working Paper No. 5849, December 1996.

Comparison of Banking Structure in the United States and Abroad

The structure of the commercial banking industry in the United States is radically different from that in other industrialized nations. The United States is the only country that is just now developing a true national banking system in which banks have branches throughout the country. One result is that there are many more banks in the United States than in other industrialized countries. In contrast to the United States, which has on the order of 10,000 commercial banks, every other industrialized country has well under 1000. Japan, for example, has fewer than 100 commercial banks—just 1 percent of the number in the United States, even though its economy and population are half the size of the United States. Another result of the past restrictions on branching in the United States is that our banks tend to be much smaller than those in other countries.

Are Bank Consolidation and Nationwide Banking Good Things?

Advocates of nationwide banking believe that it will produce more efficient banks and a healthier banking system less prone to bank failures. However, critics of bank consolidation fear that it will eliminate small banks, referred to as *community banks*, and that this will result in less lending to small businesses. In addition, they worry that a few banks will come to dominate the industry, making the banking business less competitive.

Most economists are skeptical of these criticisms of bank consolidation. As we have seen, research indicates that even after bank consolidation is completed, the United States will still have plenty of banks. Furthermore, megabanks will not dominate the banking industry. This research suggests that there will be more than ten banks with assets over $100 billion, and their collective share of bank assets will be less than 50 percent. The banking industry will thus remain highly competitive, probably even more so than now considering that banks that have been protected from competition from out-of-state banks will now have to compete with them vigorously to stay in business.

It also does not look as though community banks will disappear. When New York State liberalized branching laws in 1962, there were fears that community banks upstate would be driven from the market by the big New York City banks. Not only did this not happen, but some of the big boys found that the small banks were able to run rings around them in the local markets. Similarly, California, which has had unrestricted statewide branching for a long time, continues to have a thriving collection of community banks.

Economists see some important benefits of bank consolidation and nationwide banking. The elimination of geographic restrictions on banking will increase competition and drive inefficient banks out of business, thus raising the efficiency of the banking sector. The move to larger banking organizations also means that there will be some increase in efficiency because of economies of scale. The increased diversification of banks' loan portfolios may lower the probability of a banking crisis in the future. In the 1980s and early 1990s, bank failures were often concentrated in states with weak economies. For example, after the decline in oil prices in 1986, all the major commercial banks in Texas, which had been very profitable, now found themselves in trouble. At that time, banks in New England were doing fine. However, when the 1990–1991 recession hit New England hard, New England banks started failing. With nationwide banking, a bank could make loans in both New England and Texas and would thus be less likely to fail because when the loans were going sour in one location, they would likely be doing well in the other. Thus nationwide banking is seen as a major step toward creating a healthy banking system that is less prone to banking crises.

The two potential negatives to bank consolidation are that it might lead to a reduction in lending to small businesses because of the reduction in assets at small banks who specialize in small business lending and that the rush of banks to expand into new geographic markets might lead them into increased risk taking, which might lead to bank failures. The jury is still out on these concerns, but most economists see the benefits of bank consolidation and nationwide banking as outweighing the costs.

SEPARATION OF THE BANKING AND SECURITIES INDUSTRIES

Another important feature of the structure of the banking industry in the United States is the separation of the banking and securities industry. The Glass-Steagall Act of 1933 forced a separation between these industries. Glass-Steagall allowed commercial banks to sell new offerings of government securities but prohibited them from underwriting corporate securities or from engaging in brokerage activities. It also prohibited investment banks from engaging in commercial banking activities and thus has protected banks from competition.

Repeal of the Glass-Steagall Act

An issue that has received much attention in Congress is repeal of the Glass-Steagall Act. In 1995 and 1996, Representative Jim Leach, chair of the House Banking Committee, proposed a bill to repeal the Glass-Steagall Act and allow banks to enter the securities business. Leach was unsuccessful in getting the bill passed, but it is clear that Glass-Steagall reform will be on the agenda of future Congresses.

THE CASE FOR ALLOWING BANKS TO ENTER THE SECURITIES BUSINESS   As we have seen, the Glass-Steagall Act of 1933 prohibited banks from engaging in securities market activities such as securities underwriting or the sale of mutual funds. Advocates of allowing banks to participate in securities market activities argue that it is unfair to keep commercial banks from pursuing these activities in competition with investment banking and brokerage firms. Brokerage firms have been able to pursue traditional banking activities with the development of money market mutual funds and cash management accounts. Why shouldn't banks be allowed to compete with brokerage firms in those firms' traditional areas of business, the selling of corporate securities and the management of mutual funds?

Another argument in favor of allowing banks to enter the securities business is increased competition. Bank entry will mean that in the case of a new issue of securities, there will be more bidders to underwrite the issue. As a result, the spread between the price guaranteed to the issuer of the security and the price paid for the security by the general public will fall. This reduction in the spread will mean that both borrowers and lenders in financial markets will be better off: Issuers of securities (borrowers) will receive a higher price for their securities and will thus bear a lower interest cost, while the purchasers of securities (lenders) will be able to buy the securities at a lower price, thereby giving them a higher interest rate. The fact that underwriting spreads for investment-grade bonds have dropped substantially since commercial banks have been allowed to underwrite these securities is powerful evidence in support of this view. Banks' entry into the brokerage business (which has been occurring through bank holding companies) might also increase competition in this industry, which could lead to lower brokerage commissions—another advantage to investors.

THE CASE AGAINST ALLOWING BANKS TO ENTER THE SECURITIES BUSINESS

Opponents of bank entry into the securities business argue that banks have an unfair advantage in competing against brokerage firms. Deposits provide banks with an artificially low cost of funds because they are insured by the FDIC.[2] Brokerage firms have higher costs on the funds they acquire, which are usually obtained through loans from banks.

The securities business, particularly investment banking, may involve more risk than traditional banking activities. An investment bank can suffer substantial losses if it is unable to sell securities it has underwritten for the price that it has agreed to pay the issuer. So allowing commercial banks to engage in investment banking might produce more bank failures and a less stable financial system. This problem would be even more acute because of the existence of federal deposit insurance. Allowing commercial banks to take advantage of additional risky activities increases the potential for moral hazard and adverse selection problems to arise. However, there is no compelling evidence that engaging in investment banking activities increased risk taking by banks before Glass-Steagall was passed.

Another argument against allowing banks to enter the securities business is that commercial banks face a potential conflict of interest if they engage in underwriting of securities. Congressional hearings prior to enactment of the Glass-Steagall Act in 1933 turned up some abuses that were tied to commercial banking's activities in the investment banking area. Banks that were underwriting new issues of securities sold them to trust funds that they managed when they could not sell them to anyone else, and these trust funds often took substantial losses when the securities were sold later. Cases surfaced in which the bank itself

---

[2]Note that the cost of funds will be artificially low only if the FDIC subsidizes the insurance by charging premiums that are too low. The past losses to the FDIC suggest that this was the case until 1991. However, with the development of risk-based deposit insurance premiums, it is no longer clear that the FDIC is subsidizing deposit insurance. So the argument that banks have an unfair advantage because they have an artificially low cost of funds is no longer as persuasive.

would buy securities that it was underwriting when the securities could not be sold elsewhere. The resulting lower quality of the bank's assets could have contributed to a failure later on.

Proponents of allowing banks to enter the securities business counter this argument by saying that the securities markets and commercial banking are very different industries today from what they were before 1933. Bank regulation and the SEC could probably prevent many of the abuses that occurred before the Glass-Steagall Act and the extent of the abuses that occurred before the passage of the act was probably exaggerated. Regulatory authorities now have much greater power than before 1933 to find and punish people who would abuse commercial banking's securities activities, and the erection of "fire walls" to separate various bank operations can help prevent conflicts of interest. Although proponents do not guarantee that no abuses would occur, they suggest that abuses would be infrequent enough that any costs associated with them would be far smaller than the benefits of increased competition in the securities industry.

FUTURE PROSPECTS The debate about whether banks should be involved in securities activities has not been resolved. However, the pursuit of profits and financial innovation has stimulated both banks and other financial institutions to bypass the intent of the Glass-Steagall Act and encroach on each other's traditional territory. In addition, even primarily nonfinancial corporations have entered the banking and securities business. Companies like General Motors, Ford, and General Electric provide installment loans to their customers through their finance company subsidiaries, and retailers like J. C. Penney, Montgomery Ward, and Sears have experimented with selling insurance, securities, money market mutual funds, and real estate in their stores. (However, in 1992, Sears decided that this business was not sufficiently profitable and sold off some of its financial services businesses.)

Because commercial banks' market share in financial services had been falling, in 1987 the Federal Reserve used a loophole in Section 20 of the Glass-Steagall Act to begin to allow bank holding companies to underwrite several previously prohibited classes of securities. The loophole allows affiliates of approved commercial banks to engage in underwriting activities as long as the revenue doesn't exceed a specified amount, currently 25 percent, of the affiliates' total revenue. The remainder of the affiliates' revenue can be obtained by underwriting municipal bonds and selling Treasury securities, activities that were never precluded under Glass-Steagall. After the U.S. Supreme Court validated the Fed's action in July 1988, the Federal Reserve took the historic steps of allowing a commercial bank holding company, J. P. Morgan, to underwrite corporate debt securities (in January 1989) and to underwrite stocks (in September 1990), with the privilege subsequently extended to other bank holding companies. The regulatory agencies have also allowed banks to invest in real estate and to engage in some insurance activities.

The regulatory trend seems to be accepting what has already been occurring in the marketplace. An important factor is that foreign commercial banks are often allowed to engage in the securities business, giving them a competitive edge over

American banks. Regulators may thus be reluctant to restrict commercial banks' securities activities if it puts American banks at a competitive disadvantage relative to foreign banks. The trend away from the separation of banking and the securities industry is therefore likely to continue, and the demise of the Glass-Steagall Act may not be far off.

Separation of the Banking and Securities Industries in Other Countries

Not many other countries have followed the lead of the United States in separating the banking and securities industries. In fact, this separation is the most prominent difference between banking regulation in the United States and in other countries. Around the world, there are three basic frameworks for the banking and securities industries.

The first framework is *universal banking,* which exists in Germany, the Netherlands, and Switzerland. It provides no separation at all between the banking and securities industries. In a universal banking system, commercial banks provide a full range of banking, securities, and insurance services, all within a single legal entity. Banks are allowed to own sizable equity shares in commercial firms, and often they do.

The British-style universal banking system, the second framework, is found in the United Kingdom and countries with close ties to it, such as Canada and Australia. The British-style universal bank engages in securities underwriting, but it differs from the German-style universal bank in three ways: Separate legal subsidiaries are more common, bank equity holdings of commercial firms are less common, and combinations of banking and insurance firms are less common.

The third framework features legal separation of the banking and securities industries, as in the United States and Japan. A major difference between the U.S. and Japanese banking systems is that Japanese banks are allowed to hold substantial equity stakes in commercial firms, whereas American banks cannot. In addition, most American banks use a bank-holding-company structure, but bank holding companies are illegal in Japan. Although the banking and securities industries are legally separated under the Glass-Steagall Act in the United States and Section 65 of the Japanese Securities Act, in both countries commercial banks are increasingly being allowed to engage in securities activities and are thus becoming more like British-style universal banks.

THRIFT INDUSTRY: REGULATION AND STRUCTURE

Not surprisingly, the regulation and structure of the thrift industry (savings and loan associations, mutual savings banks, and credit unions) closely parallels the regulation and structure of the commercial banking industry.

Savings and Loan Associations

Just as there is a dual banking system for commercial banks, savings and loan associations (S&Ls) can be chartered either by the federal government or by the states. Most S&Ls, whether state or federally chartered, are members of the Federal Home Loan Bank System (FHLBS). Established in 1932, the FHLBS was styled after the Federal Reserve System. It has 12 district Federal Home Loan banks, which are supervised by the Office of Thrift Supervision.

Federal deposit insurance (up to $100,000 per account) for S&Ls is provided by the Savings Association Insurance Fund, a subsidiary of the FDIC. The Office of Thrift Supervision regulates federally insured S&Ls by setting minimum capital requirements, requiring periodic reports, and examining the S&Ls. It is also the chartering agency for federally chartered S&Ls, and for these S&Ls it approves mergers and sets the rules for branching.

The branching regulations for S&Ls were more liberal than for commercial banks: In the past, almost all states permitted branching, and since 1980, federally chartered S&Ls were allowed to branch statewide in all states. Since 1981, mergers of financially troubled S&Ls were allowed across state lines, and nationwide branching of S&Ls may soon become common. A result of the less restrictive regulations on S&L branching is that the percentage of S&Ls with under $25 million in assets (3 percent) is less than the percentage of commercial banks with under $25 million in assets (18 percent).

The FHLBS, like the Fed, makes loans to the members of the system (the FHLBS obtains funds for this purpose by issuing bonds). However, in contrast to the Fed's discount loans, which are expected to be repaid quickly, the loans from the FHLBS often need not be repaid for long periods of time. In addition, the rates charged to S&Ls for these loans are often below the rates that the S&Ls must pay when they borrow in the open market. In this way, the FHLBS loan program provides a subsidy to the savings and loan industry (and implicitly to the housing industry, since most of the S&Ls' loans are for residential mortgages).

As we will see in the next chapter, the savings and loans have experienced serious difficulties in recent years. Because savings and loans now engage in many of the same activities as commercial banks, many experts view having a separate charter and regulatory apparatus for S&Ls an anachronism that no longer makes sense. Given the recent troubles of the savings and loan industry, it now looks as though Congress will pass legislation in the near future to merge the S&L and commercial bank charters, thereby eliminating the separate S&L industry.

Mutual Savings Banks

Of the 500 or so mutual savings banks, around half are chartered by the states. Although the mutual savings banks are primarily regulated by the states in which they are located, the majority have their deposits insured by the FDIC up to the limit of $100,000 per account; these banks are also subject to many of the FDIC's regulations for state-chartered banks. As a rule, the mutual savings banks whose deposits are not insured by the FDIC have their deposits insured by state insurance funds.

The branching regulations for mutual savings banks are determined by the states in which they operate. Because these regulations are not too restrictive, there are few mutual savings banks with assets of less than $25 million.

Credit Unions

Credit unions are small cooperative lending institutions organized around a particular group of individuals (union members or employees of a particular firm). They can be chartered either by the states or by the federal government;

over half are federally chartered. The National Credit Union Administration (NCUA) issues federal charters and regulates federally chartered credit unions by setting minimum capital requirements, requiring periodic reports, and examining the credit unions. Federal deposit insurance (up to the $100,000-per-account limit) is provided to both federally chartered and state-chartered credit unions by a subsidiary of the NCUA, the National Credit Union Share Insurance Fund (NCUSIF). Since the majority of credit union lending is for consumer loans with fairly short terms to maturity, they have not suffered the recent financial difficulties of the S&Ls and mutual savings banks.

Because their members share a common bond, credit unions are typically quite small; most hold less than $10 million of assets. In addition, their ties to a particular industry or company make them more likely to fail when large numbers of workers in that industry or company are laid off and have trouble making loan payments. Recent regulatory changes allow individual credit unions to cater to a more diverse group of people, and this has encouraged an expansion in the size of credit unions and may help reduce credit union failures in the future.

Often a credit union's shareholders are dispersed over many states, some even worldwide, so branching across state lines and into other countries is permitted for federally chartered credit unions. The Navy Federal Credit Union, for example, whose shareholders are members of the U.S. Navy and Marine Corps, has branches throughout the world.

INTERNATIONAL BANKING

In 1960, only eight U.S. banks operated branches in foreign countries, and their total assets were less than $4 billion. Currently, over 100 American banks have branches abroad, with assets totaling over $500 billion. The spectacular growth in international banking can be explained by three factors.

First is the rapid growth in international trade and multinational (worldwide) corporations that has occurred since 1960. When American firms operate abroad, they need banking services in foreign countries to help finance international trade. For example, they might need a loan in a foreign currency to operate a factory abroad. And when they sell goods abroad, they need to have a bank exchange the foreign currency they have received for their goods into dollars. Although these firms could use foreign banks to provide them with these international banking services, many of them prefer to do business with the U.S. banks with which they have established long-term relationships and which understand American business customs and practices. As international trade has grown, international banking has grown with it.

Second, when American banks go abroad, they are allowed to pursue activities that are prohibited in the United States under the Glass-Steagall Act. American banks are very active in global investment banking, in which they underwrite foreign securities. They also sell insurance abroad, and they derive substantial profits from these investment banking and insurance activities. The desire to escape burdensome regulations, an important factor that has stimulated financial innovations, has therefore also been a major spur to international banking.

Third, American banks have wanted to tap into the large pool of dollar-denominated deposits in foreign countries known as Eurodollars. To understand the structure of U.S. banking overseas, let us first look at the Eurodollar market, an important source of growth for international banking.

Eurodollar Market

Eurodollars are created when deposits in accounts in the United States are transferred to a bank outside the country and are kept in the form of dollars. For example, if Rolls-Royce PLC deposits a $1 million check, written on an account at an American bank, in its bank in London—specifying that the deposit is payable in dollars—$1 million in Eurodollars is created.[3] Over 90 percent of Eurodollar deposits are time deposits, more than half of them certificates of deposit with maturities of 30 days or more. The total amount of Eurodollars outstanding exceeds $2 trillion, making the Eurodollar market (which was born in an ironic way—see Box 2) one of the most important financial markets in the world economy.

Why would companies like Rolls-Royce want to hold dollar deposits outside the United States? First, the dollar is the most widely used currency in international trade, so Rolls-Royce might want to hold deposits in dollars to conduct its international transactions. Second, Eurodollars are "offshore" deposits—they are held in countries that will not subject them to regulations such as reserve requirements or restrictions (called *capital controls*) on taking the deposits outside the country.[4]

The main center of the Eurodollar market is London, a major international financial center for hundreds of years. Eurodollars are also held outside of Europe in locations that provide offshore status to these deposits—for example, Hong Kong, Singapore, and the Caribbean (Bahamas, Cayman Islands).

The minimum transaction in the Eurodollar market is typically $1 million, and approximately 75 percent of Eurodollar deposits are held by banks. Plainly, you and I are unlikely to come into direct contact with Eurodollars. The Eurodollar market is, however, an important source of funds to U.S. banks, whose borrowing of these deposits is over $100 billion. Rather than using an intermediary and borrowing all the deposits from foreign banks, American banks decided that they could earn higher profits by opening their own branches abroad to attract these deposits. Consequently, the Eurodollar market has been an important stimulus to U.S. banking overseas.

---

[3]Note that the London bank has acquired the deposit at the American bank formerly owned by Rolls-Royce, so the creation of Eurodollars has not caused a reduction in the amount of bank deposits in the United States.

[4]Although most offshore deposits are denominated in dollars, some are also denominated in other currencies. Collectively, these offshore deposits are referred to as Eurocurrencies. A German mark–denominated deposit held in London, for example, is called a Euromark, and a French franc–denominated deposit held in London is called a Eurofranc.

BOX 2

Ironic Birth of the Eurodollar Market

One of capitalism's great ironies is that the Eurodollar market, one of the most important financial markets used by capitalists, was fathered by the Soviet Union. In the early 1950s, during the height of the Cold War, the Soviets had accumulated a substantial amount of dollar balances held by banks in the United States. Because the Russians feared that the U.S. government might freeze these assets in the United States, they wanted to move the deposits to Europe, where they would be safe from expropriation. (This fear was not unjustified —consider the U.S. freeze on Iranian assets in 1979 and Iraqi assets in 1990.) However, they also wanted to keep the deposits in dollars so that they could be used in their international transactions. The solution to the problem was to transfer the deposits to European banks but to keep the deposits denominated in dollars. When the Soviets did this, the Eurodollar was born.

Structure of U.S. Banking Overseas

U.S. banks have most of their foreign branches in Latin America, the Far East, the Caribbean, and London. The largest volume of assets is held by branches in London because it is a major international financial center and the central location for the Eurodollar market. Latin America and the Far East have many branches because of the importance of U.S. trade with these regions. Parts of the Caribbean (especially the Bahamas and the Cayman Islands) have become important as tax havens, with minimal taxation and few restrictive regulations. In actuality, the bank branches in the Bahamas and the Cayman Islands are "shell operations" because they function primarily as bookkeeping centers and do not provide normal banking services.

An alternative corporate structure for U.S. banks that operate overseas is the **Edge Act corporation,** which is a special subsidiary engaged primarily in international banking. This corporate structure, created by the Edge Act of 1919, allows American banks to compete more effectively against foreign banks by exempting Edge Act corporations from certain U.S. banking regulations. For example, Edge Act corporations are exempt from the prohibition on branching across state lines; they can have branches in different states to facilitate the financing of trade with different parts of the world—an office on the West Coast to handle the financing of trade with Japan, an office in Miami to handle the financing of trade with Latin America, and so forth.

U.S. banks (through their holding companies) can also own a controlling interest in foreign banks and in foreign companies that provide financial services, such as finance companies. The international activities of member banks of the Federal Reserve System, bank holding companies, and Edge Act corporations (which account for almost all international banking conducted by U.S. banks) are governed by the Federal Reserve's Regulation K. As in the case of bank holding companies, these international activities must be "closely related to banking."

In late 1981, the Federal Reserve approved the creation of **international banking facilities (IBFs)** within the United States that can accept time deposits from foreigners but are not subject to either reserve requirements or restrictions on interest payments. IBFs are also allowed to make loans to foreigners, but they are not allowed to make loans to domestic residents. States have encouraged the establishment of IBFs by exempting them from state and local taxes. In essence, IBFs are treated like foreign branches of U.S. banks and are not subject to domestic regulations and taxes. The purpose of establishing IBFs is to encourage American and foreign banks to do more banking business in the United States rather than abroad. From this point of view, IBFs have been a success: Their assets climbed to nearly $200 billion in the first two years and currently exceed that amount.

Foreign Banks in the United States

The growth in international trade has not only encouraged U.S. banks to open offices overseas but also encouraged foreign banks to establish offices in the United States. Foreign banks have been extremely successful in the United States. Over the past 20 years, foreign banks have more than doubled their market share in the United States. Currently, they hold more than 20 percent of total U.S. bank assets and do almost as much commercial lending as U.S.-owned banks, with nearly a 50 percent market share of the market lending to U.S. corporations.

Foreign banks engage in banking activities in the United States by operating an agency office of the foreign bank, a subsidiary U.S. bank, or a branch of the foreign bank. An agency office can lend and transfer funds in the United States, but it cannot accept deposits from domestic residents. Agency offices have the advantage of not being subject to regulations that apply to full-service banking offices (such as requirements for FDIC insurance and restrictions on branching). A subsidiary U.S. bank is just like any other U.S. bank (it may even have an American-sounding name) and is subject to the same regulations, but it is owned by the foreign bank. A branch of a foreign bank bears the foreign bank's name and is usually a full-service office. Foreign banks may also form Edge Act corporations and IBFs.

Before 1978, foreign banks were not subject to many regulations that applied to domestic banks: They could open branches across state lines and were not expected to meet reserve requirements, for example. The passage of the International Banking Act of 1978, however, put foreign and domestic banks on a more equal footing. Now foreign banks may open new full-service branches only in the state they designate as their home state or in states that allow the entry of out-of-state banks. Limited-service branches and agency offices in any other state are permitted, however, and foreign banks are allowed to retain any full-service branches opened before ratification of the International Banking Act of 1978.

The internationalization of banking, both by U.S. banks going abroad and by foreign banks entering the United States, has meant that financial markets throughout the world have become more integrated. As a result, there is a growing trend toward international coordination of bank regulation, one example of which is the 1988 Basel agreement to standardize minimum capital requirements in industrialized countries, discussed in Chapter 12. Another development has been the increased importance of foreign banks in international banking. As is

TABLE 3 Ten Largest Banks in the World, 1997	
Bank	**Assets (U.S. $ billions)**
1. Deutche Bank, Germany	503.4
2. Sanwa Bank, Japan	501.0
3. Sumitomo Bank, Japan	499.9
4. Dai-Ichi Kangyo Bank, Japan	498.6
5. Fuji Bank, Japan	487.3
6. Industrial Bank of Japan, Japan	361.4
7. Credit Suisse, Switzerland	358.7
8. HSBC Holdings, United Kingdom	351.6
9. ABN-Amro, Netherlands	340.6
10. Credit Lyonnais, France	339.4

Source: The Banker, February 1997.

shown in Table 3, in 1997, all of the ten largest banks in the world were foreign. The implications of this financial market integration for the operation of our economy is examined further in Chapter 20 when we discuss the international financial system in more detail.

FINANCIAL INNOVATION AND THE DECLINE OF TRADITIONAL BANKING

The traditional financial intermediation role of banking has been to make long-term loans and fund them by issuing short-dated deposits, a process of asset transformation commonly referred to as "borrowing short and lending long." Earlier in the chapter, we saw that changes in regulations restricting bank branching have been increasing the competitive environment in the banking industry in the United States. Another source of increasing competition for this industry is coming from financial innovations. Here we examine how the same economic forces we examined in Chapter 10 have generated financial innovations that present the banking industry with competitive challenges that are causing traditional banking business to decline. The decline in traditional banking has important implications for the future of the banking industry and creates new challenges for regulators.

Behind the Decline: Four Financial Innovations

Four financial innovations have played an important role in the decline of traditional banking: money market mutual funds, junk bonds, the rise of the commercial paper market, and securitization.

MONEY MARKET MUTUAL FUNDS As we saw in Chapter 10, the desire to avoid regulations such as deposit rate ceilings and the restrictions on interest paid on deposits resulted in innovations developed by banks such as NOW and ATS accounts. These same forces produced a new financial institution, the money market mutual fund, that now competes with banks for deposits.

Money market mutual funds issue shares that are redeemable at a fixed price (usually $1) by writing checks. For example, if you buy 5000 shares for $5000, the money market fund uses these funds to invest in short-term money market securities (Treasury bills, certificates of deposit, commercial paper) that provide you with interest payments. In addition, you are able to write checks up to the $5000 held as shares in the money market fund. Although money market fund shares effectively function as checking account deposits that earn interest, they are not legally deposits and so are not subject to reserve requirements or prohibitions on interest payments. For this reason, they can pay higher interest rates than deposits at banks.

The first money market mutual fund was created by two Wall Street mavericks, Bruce Bent and Henry Brown, in 1971. However, the low market interest rates from 1971 to 1977 (which were just slightly above Regulation Q ceilings of 5.25 to 5.5 percent) kept them from being particularly advantageous relative to bank deposits. In early 1978, the situation changed rapidly as market interest rates began to climb over 10 percent, well above the 5.5 percent maximum interest rates payable on savings accounts and time deposits under Regulation Q. In 1977, money market mutual funds had assets under $4 billion; in 1978, their assets climbed to close to $10 billion; in 1979, to over $40 billion; and in 1982, to $230 billion. Currently, their assets are around $900 billion. To say the least, money market mutual funds have been a successful financial innovation, which is exactly what we would have predicted to occur in the late 1970s and early 1980s when interest rates soared beyond Regulation Q ceilings.

JUNK BONDS   Before the advent of computers and advanced telecommunications, it was difficult to acquire information about the financial situation of firms that might want to sell securities. Because of the difficulty in screening out bad from good credit risks, the only firms that were able to sell bonds were very well established corporations that had high credit ratings.[5] Before the 1980s, then, only corporations that could issue bonds with ratings of Baa or above could raise funds by selling newly issued bonds. Some firms that had fallen on bad times, so-called *fallen angels,* had previously issued long-term corporate bonds that now had ratings that had fallen below Baa, bonds that were pejoratively dubbed "junk bonds."

With the improvement in information technology in the 1970s, it became easier for investors to screen out bad from good credit risks, thus making it more likely that they would buy long-term debt securities from less well-known corporations with lower credit ratings. With this change in supply conditions, we would expect that some smart individual would pioneer the concept of selling new public issues of junk bonds, not for fallen angels but for companies that had

---

[5]The discussion of adverse selection problems in Chapter 9 provides a more detailed analysis of why only well-established firms with high credit ratings were able to sell securities.

not yet achieved investment-grade status. This is exactly what Michael Milken of Drexel Burnham, an investment banking firm, started to do in 1977. Junk bonds became an important factor in the corporate bond market, with the amount outstanding exceeding $200 billion by the late 1980s. Although there was a sharp slowdown in activity in the junk bond market after Milken was indicted for securities law violations in 1989, it has heated up again in the 1990s.

COMMERCIAL PAPER MARKET Recall that *commercial paper* is a short-term debt security issued by large banks and corporations. As we saw in Chapter 2, the commercial paper market has undergone tremendous growth since 1970, when there was $33 billion outstanding, to over $750 billion outstanding at the end of 1996. Indeed, commercial paper has been one of the fastest-growing money market instruments.

Improvements in information technology also help provide an explanation for the rapid rise of the commercial paper market. We have seen that the improvement in information technology made it easier for investors to screen out bad from good credit risks, thus making it easier for corporations to issue debt securities. Not only did this make it easier for corporations to issue long-term debt securities as in the junk bond market, but it also meant that they could raise funds by issuing short-term debt securities like commercial paper more easily. Many corporations that used to do their short-term borrowing from banks now frequently raise short-term funds in the commercial paper market instead.

The development of money market mutual funds has been another factor in the rapid growth in the commercial paper market. Because money market mutual funds need to hold liquid, high-quality, short-term assets such as commercial paper, the growth of assets in these funds to around $900 billion has created a ready market in commercial paper. The growth of pension and other large funds that invest in commercial paper has also stimulated the growth of this market.

SECURITIZATION An important example of a financial innovation arising from improvements in both transaction and information technology is securitization, one of the most important financial innovations in the past two decades. **Securitization** is the process of transforming otherwise illiquid financial assets (such as residential mortgages), which have typically been the bread and butter of banking institutions, into marketable capital market securities. As we have seen, improvements in the ability to acquire information have made it easier to sell marketable capital market securities. In addition, with low transaction costs because of improvements in computer technology, financial institutions find that they can cheaply bundle together a portfolio of loans (such as mortgages) with varying small denominations (often less than $100,000), collect the interest and principal payments on the mortgages in the bundle, and then "pass them through" (pay them out) to third parties. By dividing the portfolio of loans into standardized amounts, the financial institution can then sell the claims to these interest and principal payments to third parties as securities. The standardized amounts of these securitized loans make them liquid securities, and the fact that they are made up of a bundle of loans helps diversify risk, making them desirable. The financial institution selling the securitized loans makes a profit by servicing the loans (collecting the interest and principal payments and paying them out) and charging a fee to the third party for this service.

Securitization first started in 1970 when the GNMA (now known as Ginnie Mae) began a program in which it guaranteed interest and principal payments on bundles of standardized mortgages, thereby encouraging the creation of a new financial instrument, the mortgage-backed security. The guarantee of the interest and principal payments made it easy for private financial institutions such as savings and loans and commercial banks to sell a bundle of GNMA-guaranteed mortgages as a security and to pass through these payments to the owner of the security.

In the usual Ginnie Mae pass-through security, the buyer has direct ownership of a pro rata share of the portfolio of mortgage loans. Other types of mortgage-backed securities do not provide ownership of the mortgage portfolio to the buyer but are instead debt obligations of the mortgage-lending institution for which the mortgage loans are the collateral. Mortgage-backed securities continue to be the most common form of securitization. Securitization of mortgages has expanded enormously; two-thirds of all residential mortgages are now securitized, and over $1 trillion of securitized mortgages are currently outstanding.

Securitization has not stopped with mortgages, however: Securitization of automobile loans, credit card receivables, automobile loans, and commercial and computer leases began in the mid-1980s. Securitized credit card receivables have been particularly successful: By 1989, the amount outstanding of these so-called plastic bonds had surpassed $30 billion and is currently over $100 billion.

Computer technology has also enabled financial institutions to tailor securitization to produce securities that have payment streams considered especially desirable by the market. Collateralized mortgage obligations (CMOs), which are bonds that pass through the payments from a portfolio of mortgages, are a good example of such tailoring; they first appeared in 1983. Computerization enables a CMO to be split into several classes known as *tranches*. The first tranches receive interest payments according to the coupon rate on the CMO, with class 1 first receiving all principal payments and prepayments from the collateralized pool of mortgages. After the class 1 bonds have been paid off, the principal payments and prepayments are used to retire the remaining classes sequentially. The last class, called *accrual* or *Z bonds,* receives interest and principal payments only after the other classes have been paid off. The basic CMO described here has the advantage of containing bonds of both short maturity (class 1) and long maturity (the later classes or the accrual bond), thus increasing its potential market. Indeed, the financial innovation process has led to even more complicated CMOs that fit additional niches in the marketplace.

Although securitization could not take place without modern computer technology (think of the cost of collecting payments and paying them out by hand), technology is not the only factor encouraging it; the government has played an important role too. Securitization first started with GNMA guarantees of mortgage payments and even today involves mostly assets directly or indirectly guaranteed by the government. Tax rules have also stimulated new securitized instruments. A change in IRS regulations made possible real estate mortgage investment conduits (REMICs), which are essentially CMOs with a more favorable tax treatment.

Decline of Traditional Banking

In the United States, the importance of commercial banks as a source of funds to nonfinancial borrowers has shrunk dramatically. As we can see in Figure 3, in 1974, commercial banks provided 35 percent of these funds; by 1996, their market share was down to near 20 percent. The decline in market share for thrift institutions has been even more precipitous: from over 20 percent in the late 1970s to below 10 percent today. Another way of viewing the declining role of banking in traditional financial intermediation is to look at the size of banks' balance sheet assets relative to those of other financial intermediaries (see Table 1 in Chapter 13, page 334). Commercial banks' share of total financial intermediary assets has fallen from around 40 percent in the 1960–1980 period to below 30 percent by the end of 1996. Similarly, the share of total financial intermediary assets held by thrift institutions has declined even more from the 20 percent level of the 1960–1980 period to below 10 percent by 1995.

Clearly, the traditional financial intermediation role of banking, whereby banks make loans that are funded with deposits, is no longer as important in our financial system. However, the decline in the market share of banks in total lending and total financial intermediary assets does not necessarily indicate that the banking industry is in decline. If we look at bank profitability relative to GDP, there is no evidence of a declining trend. As we can see in Figure 4, after a dismal performance in the late 1980s and early 1990s, bank profits have rebounded sharply, with strong profits posted every year since 1992. It seems as though the worst is over for the American banking industry and that predictions of its demise may have been over exaggerated.[6]

However, overall bank profitability is not a good indicator of the profitability of traditional banking because it includes an increasing amount of income from nontraditional off-balance-sheet activities discussed in Chapter 10. As you can see in Figure 5, noninterest income derived from off-balance-sheet activities, as a share of total bank income, increased from around 19 percent in the 1960–1980 period to 35 percent of total bank income by 1995. Given that the overall profitability of banks has not risen, the increase in income from off-balance-sheet activities implies that the profitability of traditional banking business has declined. This decline in profitability then explains why banks have been reducing their traditional business.

Reasons for the Decline

To understand why traditional banking business has declined in both size and profitability, we need to look at how the financial innovations described earlier have caused banks to suffer declines in their cost advantages in acquiring funds, that is, on the liabilities side of their balance sheet, while at the same time they have lost income advantages on the assets side of their balance sheet. The

---

[6]For a further discussion of whether the banking industry is in decline, see John H. Boyd and Mark Gertler, "Are Banks Dead? Or Are the Reports Greatly Exaggerated?" in *The Declining(?) Role of Banking* (Chicago: Federal Reserve Bank of Chicago, 1994), pp. 85–117; Gary Gorton and Richard Rosen, "Corporate Control, Portfolio Choice, and the Decline in Banking," *Journal of Finance* (1995); and Franklin Edwards and Frederic S. Mishkin, "The Decline of Traditional Banking: Implications for Financial Stability and Regulatory Policy," Federal Reserve Bank of New York *Economic Policy Review*, July 1995, pp. 27–45.

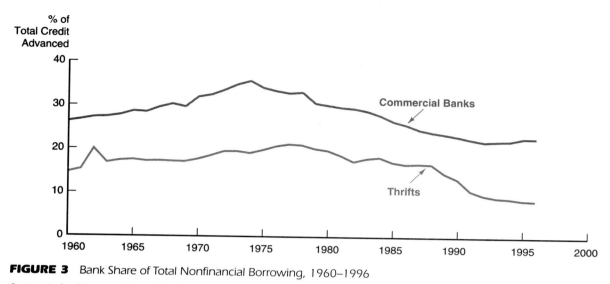

FIGURE 3   Bank Share of Total Nonfinancial Borrowing, 1960–1996

Source: Federal Reserve Flow of Funds Accounts.

FIGURE 4   Commercial Bank Profitability, 1970–1995

Sources: Federal Deposit Insurance Corporation, *Historical Statistics on Banking; Economic Report of the President*.

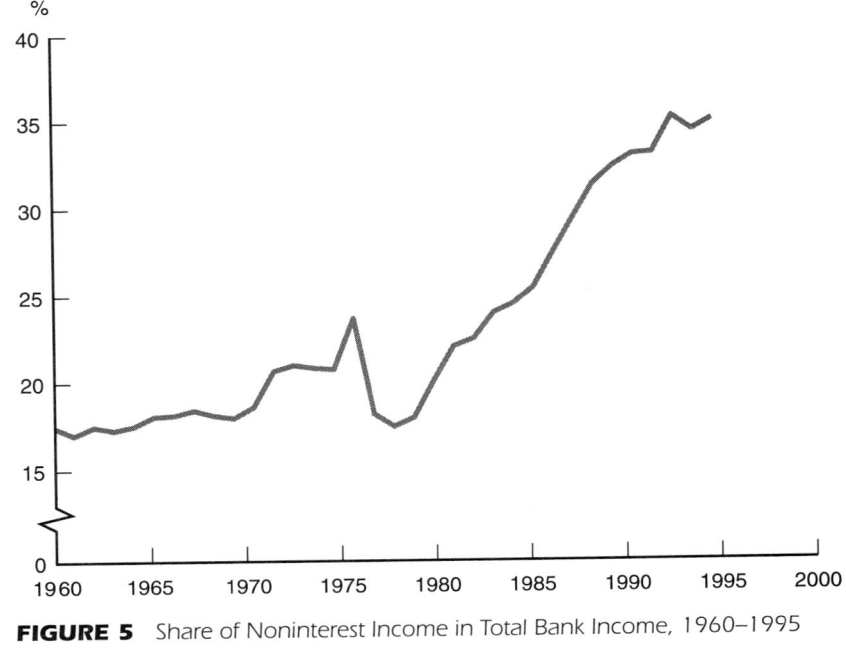

FIGURE 5 Share of Noninterest Income in Total Bank Income, 1960–1995

Sources: Federal Deposit Insurance Corporation, *Historical Statistics on Banking; Quarterly Banking Profile.*

simultaneous decline of cost and income advantages has resulted in reduced profitability of traditional banking and an effort by banks to leave this business and engage in new and more profitable activities.

DECLINE IN COST ADVANTAGES IN ACQUIRING FUNDS (LIABILITIES) Until 1980, banks were subject to deposit rate ceilings that restricted them from paying any interest on checkable deposits and (under Regulation Q) limited them to paying a maximum interest rate of a little over 5 percent on time deposits. Until the 1960s, these restrictions worked to the banks' advantage because their major source of funds (over 60 percent) was checkable deposits, and the zero interest cost on these deposits meant that the banks had a very low cost of funds. Unfortunately, this cost advantage for banks did not last. The rise in inflation from the late 1960s on led to higher interest rates, which made investors more sensitive to yield differentials on different assets. The result was the so-called disintermediation process in which people began to take their money out of banks, with their low interest rates on both checkable and time deposits, and began to seek out higher-yielding investments. Also, as we have seen, at the same time, attempts to get around deposit rate ceilings and reserve requirements led to the financial innovation of money market mutual funds, which put the banks at an even further disadvantage because depositors could now obtain checking account–like services while earning high interest on their money market mutual fund accounts. One manifestation of these changes in the financial system was that the low-cost source of funds, checkable deposits, declined dramatically in importance for banks, falling from over 60 percent of bank liabilities to below 20 percent today.

The growing difficulty for banks in raising funds led to their supporting legislation in the 1980s that eliminated Regulation Q ceilings on time deposit interest rates and allowed checkable deposits like NOW accounts that paid interest. Although these changes in regulation helped make banks more competitive in their quest for funds, it also meant that their cost of acquiring funds had risen substantially, thereby reducing their earlier cost advantage over other financial institutions.

Our discussion of international banking earlier in the chapter documented the encroachment of foreign (particularly Japanese) banks in U.S. financial markets. The loss of cost advantages of American banks helps explain this trend. With the high savings by the Japanese public, Japanese banks were able to tap a large savings pool and thus had access to a cheaper source of funds than American banks. This cost advantage for Japanese banks meant that they could more aggressively seek out loan business in the United States, which is exactly what they did. As a result, they grew at the expense of American banks. Before 1980, two U.S. banks, Citicorp and BankAmerica, were at the top of the heap, whereas in the 1990s, neither even ranks in the top ten of the world's largest banks.

DECLINE IN INCOME ADVANTAGES ON USES OF FUNDS (ASSETS) The loss of cost advantages on the liabilities side of the balance sheet for American banks is one reason that they have become less competitive, but they have also been hit by a decline in income advantages on the assets side from the financial innovations we discussed earlier, junk bonds, securitization, and the rise of the commercial paper market.

We have seen that improvements in information technology have made it easier for firms to issue securities directly to the public. This has meant that instead of going to banks to finance short-term credit needs, many of the banks' best business customers now find it cheaper to go to the commercial paper market for funds instead. The loss of this competitive advantage for banks is evident in the fact that before 1970, nonfinancial commercial paper equaled less than 5 percent of commercial and industrial bank loans, whereas the figure has risen to over 20 percent today. In addition, this growth in the commercial paper market has allowed finance companies, which depend primarily on commercial paper to acquire funds, to expand their operations at the expense of banks. Finance companies, which lend to many of the same businesses that borrow from banks, have increased their market share relative to banks: Before 1980, finance company loans to business equaled around 30 percent of commercial and industrial bank loans; currently, they are over 60 percent.

The rise of the junk bond market has also eaten into banks' loan business, as the following headline from the *Wall Street Journal* indicated: "Wall Street Is Using Junk Bonds to Take Another Slice of Banks' Lending Pie."[7] Improvements in information technology have made it easier for corporations to sell their bonds to the public directly, thereby bypassing banks. Although *Fortune* 500 companies started taking this route in the 1970s, now lower-quality corporate borrowers are using banks less often because they have access to the junk bond market.

---

[7]May 18, 1993, p. C1.

We have also seen that improvements in computer technology have led to securitization, whereby illiquid financial assets such as bank loans or mortgages are transformed into marketable securities. Computers enable other financial institutions to originate loans because they can now accurately evaluate credit risk with statistical methods, while computers have lowered transaction costs, making it possible to bundle these loans and sell them as securities. As a result, banks no longer have an advantage in making loans when default risk can be easily evaluated with computers. Without their former advantages, banks have lost loan business to other financial institutions even though the banks themselves are involved in the process of securitization. Securitization has been a particular problem for mortgage-issuing institutions such as S&Ls because most residential mortgages are now securitized.

Banks' Responses

In any industry, a decline in profitability usually results in exit from the industry (often due to widespread bankruptcies) and a shrinkage of market share. This occurred in the banking industry in the United States during the 1980s via consolidations and bank failures. As we see in Figure 6, in the 1960–1980 period, bank failures in the United States averaged fewer than ten per year, but during the 1980s, bank failures soared, exceeding 200 a year by the end of the decade.

In an attempt to survive and maintain adequate profit levels, many U.S. banks face two alternatives. First, they can attempt to maintain their traditional lending activity by expanding into new and riskier areas of lending. For example, U.S. banks have increased their risk taking by placing a greater percentage of their total funds in commercial real estate loans, traditionally a riskier type of loan. In addition, they have increased lending for corporate takeovers and leveraged buyouts, which are highly leveraged transaction loans. The decline in the profitability of banks' traditional business may thus have helped lead to the crisis in banking that we discuss in Chapter 12.

The second way banks have sought to maintain former profit levels is to pursue new off-balance-sheet activities that are more profitable. As we saw in Figure 5, U.S. commercial banks did this during the early 1980s, nearly doubling the share of their income coming from off-balance-sheet, noninterest-income activities.[8] This strategy, however, has generated concerns about what are proper activities for banks and about whether nontraditional activities might be riskier and result in banks taking excessive risks.

The decline of banks' traditional business has thus meant that the banking industry has been driven to seek out new lines of business. This could be beneficial because by so doing, banks can keep vibrant and healthy. Indeed, bank profitability has been high in recent years, and nontraditional, off-balance-sheet activities have been playing an important role in the resurgence of bank profits. However, there is a danger that the new directions in banking could lead to increased risk taking, and thus the decline in traditional banking requires regulators to be more vigilant. It also poses new challenges for bank regulators, who,

---

[8]Note that some off-balance-sheet activities, such as loan commitments and letters of credit, which produce fee income, can be classified as being in the category of traditional banking business. The data in Figure 5 overstate somewhat the importance of nontraditional banking business.

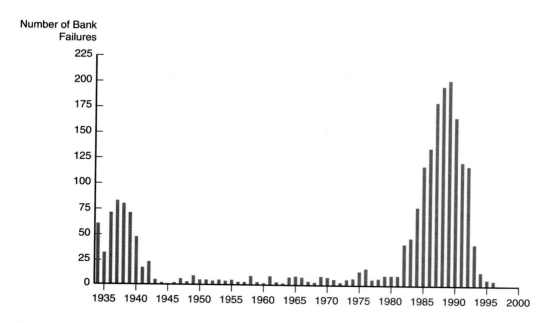

Number of Bank Failures

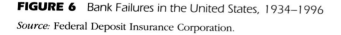

FIGURE 6   Bank Failures in the United States, 1934–1996

Source: Federal Deposit Insurance Corporation.

as we will see in Chapter 12, must now be far more concerned about banks' off-balance-sheet activities.

Decline of Traditional Banking in Other Industrialized Countries

Similar forces to those in the United States have been leading to the decline of traditional banking in other industrialized countries. The loss of banks' monopoly power over depositors has occurred outside the United States as well. Financial innovation and deregulation are occurring worldwide and have created attractive alternatives for both depositors and borrowers. In Japan, for example, deregulation has opened a wide array of new financial instruments to the public, causing a disintermediation process similar to that in the United States. In European countries, innovations have steadily eroded the barriers that have traditionally protected banks from competition.

In other countries, banks have also faced increased competition from the expansion of securities markets. Both financial deregulation and fundamental economic forces in other countries have improved the availability of information in securities markets, making it easier and less costly for firms to finance their activities by issuing securities rather than going to banks. Further, even in countries where securities markets have not grown, banks have still lost loan business because their best corporate customers have had increasing access to foreign and offshore capital markets, such as the Eurobond market. In smaller economies, like

Australia, which still do not have well-developed corporate bond or commercial paper markets, banks have lost loan business to international securities markets. In addition, the same forces that drove the securitization process in the United States are at work in other countries and will undercut the profitability of traditional banking in these countries as well. Thus although the decline of traditional banking has occurred earlier in the United States than in other countries, the same forces are resulting in competitive problems for banks in these countries as well.

The increase in the competitive environment for foreign banks has meant that some of them have found themselves in financial difficulties. Return on assets and return on equity have fallen in Japan and many European countries, and banks in these countries have sometimes been finding themselves in financial difficulties. France's largest bank, Crédit Lyonnais, required a $10 billion bailout in 1995, and the following year, the Italian government injected over $1 billion to help keep the Banco di Napoli afloat. Even in countries like Switzerland and Germany, banks have been running into trouble. For example, in January 1993, BfG Bank, a German bank, needed a capital infusion from its parent company, Crédit Lyonnais, because it suffered huge losses in 1992. In the following chapter, we will discuss the extensive problems in the Japanese banking industry. The United States is not unique in seeing its banks face a more difficult competitive environment.

S U M M A R Y

1. The history of banking in the United States has left us with a dual banking system, with commercial banks chartered by the states and the federal government. Multiple agencies regulate commercial banks: the Office of the Comptroller, the Federal Reserve, the FDIC, and the state banking authorities.

2. Restrictive state branching regulations and the McFadden Act, which prohibits branching across state lines, have led to a large number of small commercial banks. The large number of commercial banks in the United States reflects the past *lack* of competition, not the presence of vigorous competition. Bank holding companies, nonbank banks, and ATMs were important responses to branching restrictions that have weakened the restrictions' anticompetitive effect.

3. Since the mid-1980s, bank consolidation has been occurring at a rapid pace. The first phase of bank consolidation was the result of bank failures and the reduced effectiveness of branching restrictions. The second phase has been stimulated by the Riegle-Neal Interstate Banking and Branching Efficiency Act of 1994, which establishes the basis for a nationwide banking system. Once banking consolidation has settled down, we are likely to be left with a banking system with several thousand banks. Most economists believe that the benefits of bank consolidation and nationwide banking will outweigh the costs.

4. The Glass-Steagall Act separated commercial banking from the securities industry. Competitive forces have been bypassing the intent of the act, causing a breakdown in the separation of the banking and the securities industries, and the Glass-Steagall Act's days may be numbered.

5. The regulation and structure of the thrift industry (savings and loan associations, mutual savings banks, and credit unions) parallel closely the regulation and structure of the commercial banking industry. Savings and loans are primarily regulated by the Office of Thrift Supervision, and deposit insurance is administered by the FDIC. Mutual savings banks are regulated by the states, and federal deposit insurance is provided by the FDIC. Credit unions are regulated by the National Credit Union Administration, and deposit insurance is provided by the National Credit Union Share Insurance Fund.

6. With the rapid growth of world trade since 1960, international banking has grown dramatically. United States banks engage in international banking activities by opening branches abroad, owning controlling interests in foreign banks, forming Edge Act corporations, and operating international banking facilities (IBFs) located in the United States. Foreign banks operate in the United States by owning a subsidiary American bank or by operating branches or agency offices in the United States.

7. Financial innovation has caused banks to suffer declines in cost advantages in acquiring funds and in income advantages on their assets. The resulting squeeze has hurt profitability in banks' traditional lines of business and has led to a decline in traditional banking.

KEY TERMS

bank holding companies, p. 267

branches, p. 268

central bank, p. 265

dual banking system, p. 266

Edge Act corporation, p. 282

international banking facilities

    (IBFs), p. 282

national banks, p. 266

nonbank banks, p. 270

securitization, p. 286

state banks, p. 266

superregional banks, p. 272

QUESTIONS AND PROBLEMS

1. Why was the United States one of the last of the major industrialized countries to have a central bank?

*2. Which regulatory agency has the primary responsibility for supervising the following categories of commercial banks?
   a. National banks
   b. Bank holding companies
   c. Non–Federal Reserve state banks
   d. Federal Reserve member state banks

3. "The commercial banking industry in Canada is less competitive than the commercial banking industry in the United States because in Canada only a few large banks dominate the industry, while in the United States there are around 10,000 commercial banks." Is this statement true, false, or uncertain? Explain your answer.

*4. Why has new technology made it harder to enforce limitations on bank branching?

5. Why has there been such a dramatic increase in bank holding companies?

*6. Why is there a higher percentage of banks with under $25 million of assets among commercial banks than among savings and loans and mutual savings banks?

7. Unlike commercial banks, savings and loans, and mutual savings banks, credit unions do not have restrictions on locating branches in other states. Why, then, are credit unions typically smaller than the other depository institutions?

*8. What incentives have regulatory agencies created to encourage international banking? Why have they done this?

9. How could the approval of international banking facilities (IBFs) by the Fed in 1981 have reduced employment in the banking industry in Europe?

*10. If the bank at which you keep your checking account is owned by Saudi Arabians, should you worry that your deposits are less safe than if the bank were owned by Americans?

11. If reserve requirements were eliminated in the future, as some economists advocate, what effects would this have on the size of money market mutual funds?

*12. Why have banks been losing cost advantages in acquiring funds in recent years?

13. "If inflation had not risen in the 1960s and 1970s, the banking industry might be healthier today." Is this statement true, false, or uncertain? Explain your answer.

*14. Why have banks been losing income advantages on their assets in recent years?

15. "The invention of the computer is the major factor behind the decline of the banking industry." Is this statement true, false, or uncertain? Explain your answer.

Chapter 12

ECONOMIC ANALYSIS OF BANKING REGULATION

PREVIEW   As we have seen in the previous chapters, the financial system is among the most heavily regulated sectors of the economy, and banks are among the most heavily regulated of financial institutions. In this chapter we develop an economic analysis of why regulation of banking takes the form it does.

Unfortunately, the regulatory process may not always work very well, as evidenced by recent crises in the banking systems, not only in the United States but in many countries throughout the world. Here we also use our economic analysis of banking regulation to explain the worldwide crises in banking and how the regulatory system can be reformed to prevent future disasters.

ASYMMETRIC INFORMATION AND BANK REGULATION

In earlier chapters we have seen how asymmetric information, the fact that different parties in a financial contract do not have the same information, leads to adverse selection and moral hazard problems that have an important impact on our financial system. The concepts of asymmetric information, adverse selection, and moral hazard are especially useful in understanding why government has chosen the form of banking regulation we see in the United States and in other countries. There are seven basic categories of banking regulation: the government safety net, restrictions on bank asset holdings and capital requirements, chartering and bank examination, disclosure requirements, consumer protection, restrictions on competition, and separation of the banking and securities industries.

Government Safety Net: Deposit Insurance and the FDIC

As we saw in Chapter 9, banks are particularly well suited to solving adverse selection and moral hazard problems because they make private loans that help avoid the free-rider problem. However, this solution to the free-rider problem creates another asymmetric information problem because depositors lack information about the quality of these private loans. This asymmetric information problem leads to two reasons why the banking system might not function well.

First, before the FDIC started operations in 1934, a **bank failure** (in which a bank is unable to meet its obligations to pay its depositors and other creditors and so must go out of business) meant that depositors would have to wait to get their deposit funds until the bank was liquidated (until its assets had been turned into cash); at that time, they would be paid only a fraction of the value of their deposits. Unable to learn if bank managers were taking on too much risk or were outright crooks, depositors would be reluctant to put money in the bank, thus making banking institutions less viable. Second is that depositors' lack of information about the quality of bank assets can lead to bank panics, which, as we saw in Chapter 9, can have serious harmful consequences for the economy. To see this, consider the following situation. There is no deposit insurance, and an adverse shock hits the economy. As a result of the shock, 5 percent of the banks have such large losses on loans that they become insolvent (have a negative net worth and so are bankrupt). Because of asymmetric information, depositors are unable to tell whether their bank is a good bank or one of the 5 percent that are insolvent. Depositors at bad *and* good banks recognize that they may not get back 100 cents on the dollar for their deposits and will want to withdraw them. Indeed, because banks operate on a "sequential service constraint" (a first-come, first-served basis), depositors have a very strong incentive to show up at the bank first because if they are last in line, the bank may run out of funds and they will get nothing. Uncertainty about the health of the banking system in general can lead to runs on banks both good and bad, and the failure of one bank can hasten the failure of others (referred to as the *contagion effect*). If nothing is done to restore the public's confidence, a bank panic can ensue.

Indeed, bank panics were a fact of American life in the nineteenth and early twentieth centuries, with major ones occurring every 20 years or so in 1819, 1837, 1857, 1873, 1884, 1893, 1907, and 1930–1933. Bank failures were a serious problem even during the boom years of the 1920s, when the number of bank failures averaged around 600 per year.

A government safety net for depositors can short-circuit runs on banks and bank panics, and by providing protection for the depositor, it can overcome reluctance to put funds in the banking system. One form of the safety net is deposit insurance, a guarantee such as that provided by the Federal Deposit Insurance Corporation (FDIC) in the United States in which depositors are paid off in full on the first $100,000 they have deposited in the bank no matter what happens to the bank. With fully insured deposits, depositors don't need to run to the bank to make withdrawals—even if they are worried about the bank's health—because their deposits will be worth 100 cents on the dollar no matter what. From 1930 to 1933, the years immediately preceding the creation of the FDIC, the number of bank failures averaged over 2000 per year. After the establishment of the FDIC in 1934, bank failures averaged fewer than 15 per year until 1981.

The FDIC uses two primary methods to handle a failed bank. In the first, called the *payoff method,* the FDIC allows the bank to fail and pays off deposits up to the $100,000 insurance limit (with funds acquired from the insurance premiums paid by the banks who have bought FDIC insurance). After the bank has been liquidated, the FDIC lines up with other creditors of the bank and is paid its share of the proceeds from the liquidated assets. Typically, when the payoff method is used, account holders with deposits in excess of the $100,000 limit get back more than 90 cents on the dollar, although the process can take several years to complete.

In the second method, called the *purchase and assumption method,* the FDIC reorganizes the bank, typically by finding a willing merger partner who assumes (takes over) all of the failed bank's deposits so that no depositor loses a penny. The FDIC may help the merger partner by providing it with subsidized loans or by buying some of the failed bank's weaker loans. The net effect of the purchase and assumption method is that the FDIC has guaranteed *all* deposits, not just those under the $100,000 limit. The purchase and assumption method was the FDIC's most common procedure for dealing with a failed bank before new banking legislation in 1991.

Deposit insurance is not the only way in which governments provide a safety net for depositors. In other countries, governments have often stood ready to provide support to domestic banks when they face runs even in the absence of explicit deposit insurance. This support is sometimes provided by lending from the central bank to troubled institutions and is often referred to as the "lender of last resort" role of the central bank. In other cases, funds are provided directly by the government to troubled institutions, or these institutions are taken over by the government and the government then guarantees that depositors will receive their money in full.

MORAL HAZARD AND THE GOVERNMENT SAFETY NET   Although a government safety net has been successful at protecting depositors and preventing bank panics, it is a mixed blessing. The most serious drawback of the government safety net stems from moral hazard, the incentives of one party to a transaction to engage in activities detrimental to the other party. Moral hazard is an important concern in insurance arrangements in general because the existence of insurance provides increased incentives for taking risks that might result in an insurance payoff. For example, some drivers with automobile collision insurance that has a low deductible might be more likely to drive recklessly because if they get into an accident, the insurance company pays most of the costs for damage and repairs.

Moral hazard is a prominent concern in government arrangements to provide a safety net. Because with a safety net depositors know that they will not suffer losses if a bank fails, they do not impose the discipline of the marketplace on banks by withdrawing deposits when they suspect that the bank is taking on too much risk. Consequently, banks with a government safety net have an incentive to take on greater risks than they otherwise would.

ADVERSE SELECTION AND THE GOVERNMENT SAFETY NET   A further problem with a government safety net like deposit insurance arises because of adverse selection, the fact that the people who are most likely to produce the adverse outcome insured against (bank failure) are those who most want to take advantage of the insurance. For example, bad drivers are more likely than good drivers to take out automobile collision insurance with a low deductible. Because depositors protected by a government safety net have little reason to impose discipline on the bank, risk-loving entrepreneurs might find the banking industry a particularly attractive one to enter—they know that they will be able to engage in highly risky activities. Even worse, because protected depositors have so little reason to monitor the bank's activities, without government intervention outright crooks might also find banking an attractive industry for their activities because it is easy for them to get away with fraud and embezzlement.

"TOO BIG TO FAIL" The moral hazard created by a government safety net and the desire to prevent bank failures have presented bank regulators with a particular quandary. Because the failure of a very large bank makes it more likely that a major financial disruption will occur, bank regulators are naturally reluctant to allow a big bank to fail and cause losses to its depositors. Indeed, consider Continental Illinois, one of the ten largest banks in the United States when it became insolvent in May 1984. Not only did the FDIC guarantee depositors up to the $100,000 insurance limit, but it also guaranteed accounts exceeding $100,000 and even prevented losses for Continental Illinois bondholders. Shortly thereafter, the Comptroller of the Currency (the regulator of national banks) testified to Congress that the FDIC's policy was to regard the 11 largest banks as "too big to fail"—in other words, the FDIC would bail them out so that no depositor or creditor would suffer a loss. The FDIC would do this by using the purchase and assumption method, giving the insolvent bank a large infusion of capital and then finding a willing merger partner to take over the bank and its deposits. As Box 1 indicates, the too-big-to-fail policy has been extended to big banks that are not even among the 11 largest. (Note that "too big to fail" is somewhat misleading because when a bank is closed or merged into another bank, the managers are usually fired and the stockholders in the bank lose their investment.)

One problem with the too-big-to-fail policy is that it increases the moral hazard incentives for big banks. If the FDIC were willing to close a bank using the alternative payoff method, paying depositors only up to the $100,000 limit, large depositors with more than $100,000 would suffer losses if the bank failed. Thus they would have an incentive to monitor the bank by examining the bank's activities closely and pulling their money out if the bank was taking on too much risk. To prevent such a loss of deposits, the bank would be more likely to engage in less risky activities. However, once large depositors know that a bank is too big to fail, they have no incentive to monitor the bank and pull out their deposits when it takes on too much risk: No matter what the bank does, large depositors will not suffer any losses. The result of the too-big-to-fail policy is that big banks might take on even greater risks, thereby making bank failures more likely.[1]

---

[1] Recent evidence reveals, as our analysis predicts, that large banks have taken on riskier loans than smaller banks and that this has led to higher loan losses for big banks; see John Boyd and Mark Gertler, "U.S. Commercial Banking: Trends, Cycles and Policy," *NBER Macroeconomics Annual, 1993,* pp. 319–368.

BOX 1

A Tale of Two Bank Collapses

Bank of New England and Freedom National Bank. The FDIC's procedures for handling two bank collapses, those of the Bank of New England and Freedom National Bank, illustrate how the too-big-to-fail policy works.

The Bank of New England, based in Boston, was the thirty-third-largest bank holding company in the United States, with over $20 billion of assets. In the 1980s, it was the region's most aggressive real estate lender; over 30 percent of its loan portfolio was in commercial real estate. With the collapse of real estate prices in New England beginning in the late 1980s (commercial real estate values dropped by more than 25 percent), many of the bank's loans went sour. On Friday, January 4, 1991, the bank announced a projected $450 million fourth-quarter loss that exceeded the bank's capital of $255 million. Expecting the failure of the bank, in the next 48 hours depositors lined up at the bank and withdrew over $1 billion in funds, much of it from automated teller machines.

The chairman of the FDIC, William Seidman, expressed his concern over the ramifications of the potential failure: "Given the condition of the financial system in New England, it would be unwise to send a signal that large depositors weren't going to be protected."* The FDIC invoked its too-big-to-fail policy. Sunday night, January 6, the FDIC moved in to stop the run on the bank and agreed to guarantee all Bank of New England deposits, including those in excess of the $100,000 insurance limit. To keep the bank in operation until a buyer could be found and the purchase and assumption method could be used to make sure that no depositors would suffer any loss, the FDIC created what is called a *bridge bank*. In this arrangement, the FDIC creates a new corporation to run the bank and

immediately injects capital ($750 million in the case of the Bank of New England). The FDIC and the buyer of the bank then put additional capital into the bank over time, and eventually the acquirer buys out the FDIC's share. The net result of these transactions was that the FDIC spent $2.3 billion bailing out the Bank of New England, the third-costliest bailout in the FDIC's history. However, when all was said and done and spent, none of the depositors lost a penny.

The very different FDIC treatment of a small insolvent bank in Harlem several months earlier raised serious questions of fairness. The Freedom National Bank was founded in 1964 by baseball great Jackie Robinson and other minority investors. Despite its small size (under $100 million of deposits), it was one of the most prominent black-owned banks.

As a result of many speculative loans that went bad, the bank became insolvent in November 1990. Due to the bank's small size, the FDIC was not concerned that the failure of the bank would have a serious impact on the rest of the banking system, so it closed the bank on November 9 using the payoff method. The bank was liquidated, and large depositors were paid only 50 cents on the dollar for deposits in excess of $100,000. Not only fat cats suffered losses when this bank failed: Charitable organizations like the United Negro College Fund, the National Urban League, and several churches were among the large depositors. Seidman described the unfairness of the treatment of the Freedom National Bank to Congress: "My first testimony when I came to this job was that it's unfair to treat big banks in a way that covers all depositors but not small banks. I promised to do my best to change that. Five years later, I can report that my best wasn't good enough."†

*Quoted in John Meehan, "A Shock to the System: How Far Will Banking's Crisis of Confidence Spread?" *Business Week,* January 21, 1991, p. 26.

†Quoted in Kenneth H. Bacon, "Failures of a Big Bank and a Little Bank Bring Fairness of Deposit-Security Policy into Question," *Wall Street Journal,* December 5, 1990, p. A18.

Another serious problem with the too-big-to-fail policy is that it is basically unfair. Small banks are put at a competitive disadvantage because they will be allowed to fail, creating potential losses for their large depositors, while big banks' large depositors are immune from losses. The unfairness of the too-big-to-fail doctrine came to a head with the different FDIC treatment of two insolvent banks in late 1990 and early 1991 described in Box 1.

Restrictions on Asset Holdings and Bank Capital Requirements

As we have seen, the moral hazard associated with a government safety net encourages too much risk taking on the part of banks. Bank regulations that restrict asset holdings and bank capital requirements are directed at minimizing this moral hazard, which can cost the taxpayers dearly.

Even in the absence of a government safety net, banks still have the incentive to take on too much risk. Risky assets may provide the bank with higher earnings when they pay off; but if they do not pay off and the bank fails, depositors are left holding the bag. If depositors were able to monitor the bank easily by acquiring information on its risk-taking activities, they would immediately withdraw their deposits if the bank was taking on too much risk. To prevent such a loss of deposits, the bank would be more likely to reduce its risk-taking activities. Unfortunately, acquiring information on a bank's activities to learn how much risk the bank is taking can be a difficult task. Hence most depositors are incapable of imposing discipline that might prevent banks from engaging in risky activities. A strong rationale for government regulation to reduce risk taking on the part of banks therefore existed even before the establishment of federal deposit insurance.

Bank regulations that restrict banks from holding risky assets such as common stock are a direct means of making banks avoid too much risk. Bank regulations also promote diversification, which reduces risk by limiting the amount of loans in particular categories or to individual borrowers. Requirements that banks have sufficient bank capital are another way to change the bank's incentives to take on less risk. When a bank is forced to hold a large amount of equity capital, the bank has more to lose if it fails and is thus more likely to pursue less risky activities.

Bank capital requirements take three forms. The first type is based on the so-called **leverage ratio,** the amount of capital divided by the bank's total assets. To be classified as well capitalized, a bank's leverage ratio must exceed 5 percent; a lower leverage ratio, especially one below 3 percent, triggers increased regulatory restrictions on the bank. Through most of the 1980s, minimum bank capital in the United States was set solely by specifying a minimum leverage ratio.

In the wake of the Continental Illinois and savings and loans bailouts, regulators in the United States and the rest of the world have become increasingly worried about banks' holdings of risky assets and about the increase in banks' **off-balance-sheet activities,** activities that involve trading financial instruments and generating income from fees, which do not appear on bank balance sheets but nevertheless expose banks to risk. Under an agreement among banking officials from industrialized nations (who met under the auspices of the Bank for International Settlements in Basel, Switzerland), the Federal Reserve, the FDIC, and the Office of the Comptroller of the Currency have implemented an additional second type of bank-based capital requirement, which was fully phased in by December 1992. Under this risk-based capital requirement, which was fully phased in by December 1992. Under this risk-based capital requirement, which the banks must meet along with the leverage ratio capital requirement, minimum capital standards are linked to off-balance-sheet activities such as interest-rate swaps and trading positions in futures and options. Box 2 outlines the structure of these capital requirements in more detail.

In addition, in 1996, the Federal Reserve announced a third type of capital requirement to take effect by January 1998 to cover risk in trading activities at the largest banks. The Fed will require these banks to use their own internal models to calculate how much they could lose over a ten-day period and then set aside additional capital equal to three times that amount. Banks can meet this new capital requirement with more standard forms of capital or by issuing a new form of capital, called Tier 3, which consists of short-term securities that holders can't cash in at maturity if the bank is undercapitalized.

Bank Supervision: Chartering and Examination

Overseeing who operates banks and how they are operated, referred to as **bank supervision** or more generally as **prudential supervision,** is an important method for reducing adverse selection and moral hazard in the banking business. Because banks can be used by crooks or overambitious entrepreneurs to engage in highly speculative activities, such undesirable people would be eager to run a bank. (Charles Keating Jr., discussed later in this chapter, was one such person.) Chartering banks is one method for preventing this adverse selection problem; through chartering, proposals for new banks are screened to prevent undesirable people from controlling them.

Regular on-site bank examinations, which allow regulators to monitor whether the bank is complying with capital requirements and restrictions on asset holdings, also function to limit moral hazard. Bank examiners give banks a so-called *CAMEL rating* (the acronym is based on the five areas assessed: capital adequacy, asset quality, management, earnings, and liquidity). With this information about a bank's activities, regulators can enforce regulations by taking such formal actions as *cease and desist orders* to alter the bank's behavior or even close a bank if its CAMEL rating is sufficiently low. Actions taken to reduce moral hazard by restricting banks from taking on too much risk help reduce the adverse selection problem further because with less opportunity for risk taking, risk-loving entrepreneurs will be less likely to be attracted to the banking industry.[2]

A commercial bank obtains a charter either from the Comptroller of the Currency (in the case of a national bank) or from a state banking authority (in the

---

[2]Note that the methods regulators use to cope with adverse selection and moral hazard have their counterparts in private financial markets (see Chapter 9). Chartering is similar to the screening of potential borrowers, regulations restricting risky asset holdings are similar to restrictive covenants that prevent borrowing firms from engaging in risky investment activities, bank capital requirements act like restrictive covenants that require minimum amounts of net worth for borrowing firms, and regular bank examinations are similar to the monitoring of borrowers by lending institutions.

BOX 2

The Basel Accord on Risk-Based Capital Requirements

The increased integration of financial markets across countries and the need to make the playing field level for banks from different countries led to the June 1988 Basel accord to standardize bank capital requirements internationally. The stated purposes of the agreement were (1) to promote world financial stability by coordinating supervisory definitions of capital, risk assessments, and standards for capital adequacy across countries and (2) to link a bank's capital requirements systematically to the riskiness of its activities, including various off-balance-sheet forms of risk exposure.

The Basel capital requirements work as follows. Assets and off-balance-sheet activities are allocated into four categories, each with a different weight to reflect the degree of credit risk. The lowest risk category carries a zero weight and includes items that have no default risk, such as reserves and government securities. The next lowest risk category has a weight of 20 percent and includes assets with a low default risk, such as interbank deposits, fully backed mortgage bonds, and securities issued by government agencies. The third category has a weight of 50 percent and includes municipal bonds and residential mortgages. The last risk category has the maximum weight of 100 percent and includes all remaining securities (such as commercial paper), loans (such as commercial and real

estate construction loans), and fixed assets (bank building, computers, and other property). Off-balance-sheet activities are treated in a similar manner by assigning a credit-equivalent percentage that converts them to on-balance-sheet items, and then the appropriate risk weight applies. For example, a standby letter of credit backing a customer's commercial paper is assigned a 100 percent credit equivalent percentage and then has a risk weight of 100 percent because it exposes the bank to the same risk as a direct loan to this customer.

Once all the bank's assets and off-balance-sheet items have been assigned to a risk category, they are weighted by the corresponding risk factor and are added up to compute the total "risk-adjusted assets." The bank must then meet two capital requirements: It must have "core" or Tier 1 capital (stockholder equity capital) of at least 4 percent of total risk-adjusted assets, and total capital (Tier 1 capital plus Tier 2 capital, which is made up of loan loss reserves and subordinated debt) must come to 8 percent of total risk-adjusted assets. (Subordinated debt is debt that is paid off only after depositors and other creditors have been paid.) For regulators to classify a bank as well capitalized, it must meet an even more stringent total-capital requirement of 10 percent of risk-adjusted assets and Tier 1 capital of 6 percent of risk-adjusted assets.

case of a state bank). To obtain a charter, the people planning to organize the bank must submit an application that shows how they plan to operate the bank. In evaluating the application, the regulatory authority looks at whether the bank is likely to be sound by examining the quality of the bank's intended management, the likely earnings of the bank, and the amount of the bank's initial capital. Before 1980, the chartering agency typically explored the issue of whether the community needed a new bank. Often a new bank charter would not be granted if existing banks in a community would be severely hurt by its presence. Today this anticompetitive stance (justified by the desire to prevent bank failures of existing banks) is no longer as strong in the chartering agencies.

Once a bank has been chartered, it is required to file periodic (usually quarterly) *call reports* that reveal the bank's assets and liabilities, income and dividends, ownership, foreign exchange operations, and other details. The bank is also subject to examination by the bank regulatory agencies to ascertain its financial condition at least once a year. To avoid duplication of effort, the three federal agencies work together and usually accept each other's examinations. This means that, typically, national banks are examined by the Office of the Comptroller of the Currency, the state banks that are members of the Federal Reserve System are examined by the Fed, and nonmember state banks are examined by the FDIC.

Bank examinations are conducted by bank examiners, who sometimes make unannounced visits to the bank (so that nothing can be "swept under the rug" in anticipation of their examination). The examiners study a bank's books to see whether it is complying with the rules and regulations that apply to its holdings of assets. If a bank is holding securities or loans that are too risky, the bank examiner can force the bank to get rid of them. If a bank examiner decides that a loan is unlikely to be repaid, the examiner can force the bank to declare the loan worthless (to write off the loan). If, after examining the bank, the examiner feels that it does not have sufficient capital or has engaged in dishonest practices, the bank can be declared a "problem bank" and will be subject to more frequent examinations.

A New Trend in Bank Supervision: Assessment of Risk Management

Traditionally, on-site bank examinations have focused primarily on assessment of the quality of the bank's balance sheet at a point in time and whether it complies with capital requirements and restrictions on asset holdings. Although the traditional focus is important for reducing excessive risk taking by banks, it is no longer felt to be adequate in today's world in which financial innovation has produced new markets and instruments that make it easy for banks and their employees to make huge bets easily and quickly. In this new financial environment, a bank that is quite healthy at a particular point in time can be driven into insolvency extremely rapidly from trading losses, as forcefully demonstrated by the failure of Barings in 1995 (discussed in Chapter 10). Thus an examination that focuses only on a bank's position at a point in time, may not be effective in indicating whether a bank will in fact be taking on excessive risk in the near future.

This change in the financial environment for banking institutions has resulted in a major shift in thinking about the bank supervisory process throughout the world. Bank examiners are now placing far greater emphasis on evaluating the soundness of a bank's management processes with regard to controlling risk. This shift in thinking was reflected in a new focus on risk management in the Federal Reserve System's 1993 guidelines to examiners on trading and derivatives activities. The focus was expanded and formalized in the Trading Activities Manual issued early in 1994, which provided bank examiners with tools to evaluate risk management systems. In late 1995, the Federal Reserve and the Comptroller of the Currency announced that they would be assessing risk management processes at the banks they supervise. Now bank examiners give a separate risk management rating from 1 to 5 that feeds into the overall management rating as part of the CAMEL system. Four elements of sound risk management are assessed to come up with the risk management rating: (1) The quality of oversight provided by the board of directors and senior management, (2) the adequacy of policies and limits for all activities that present significant risks, (3) the quality of the risk measurement and monitoring systems, and (4) the adequacy of internal controls to prevent fraud or unauthorized activities on the part of employees.

This shift toward focusing on management processes is also reflected in recent guidelines adopted by the U.S. bank regulatory authorities to deal with interest-rate risk. At one point, U.S. regulators were contemplating requiring banks to use a standard model to calculate the amount of capital a bank would need to have to allow for the interest-rate risk it bears. Because coming up with a one-size-fits-all model that would work for all banks has proved difficult, the regulatory agencies have instead decided to adopt guidelines for the management of interest-rate risk, although bank examiners will continue to consider interest-rate risk in deciding on the bank's capital requirements. These guidelines require the bank's board of directors to establish interest-rate risk limits, appoint officials of the bank to manage this risk, and monitor the bank's risk exposure. The guidelines also require that senior management of a bank develop formal risk management policies and procedures, to ensure that the board of director's risk limits are not violated and to implement internal controls to monitor interest-rate risk and compliance with the board's directives.

Disclosure Requirements

The free-rider problem described in Chapter 9 indicates that individual depositors and other bank creditors will not have enough incentive to produce private information about the quality of a bank's assets. To ensure that there is better information for depositors and the marketplace, regulators can require that banks adhere to certain standard accounting principles and disclose a wide range of information that helps the market assess the quality of a bank's portfolio and the amount of the bank's exposure to risk. More public information about the risks incurred by banks and the quality of their portfolio can better enable stockholders, creditors, and depositors to evaluate and monitor banks and so act as a deterrent to excessive risk taking. This view is consistent with a recent position paper issued by the Eurocurrency Standing Committee of the G-10 Central Banks, which recommends that estimates of financial risk generated by firms' own internal risk management systems be adapted for public disclosure purposes.[3] Such information would supplement disclosures based on traditional accounting conventions by providing information about risk exposure and risk management that is not normally included in conventional balance sheet and income statement reports. Disclosure requirements can also be the primary focus of a bank regulatory system, as with a new approach recently implemented in New Zealand (Box 3).

---

[3]See Eurocurrency Standing Committee of Central Banks of Group of Ten Countries (Fisher Group), "Discussion Paper on Public Disclosure of Markets and Credit Risks by Financial Intermediaries," September 1994, and a companion piece to this report, Federal Reserve Bank of New York, "A Discussion Paper on Public Disclosure of Risks Related to Market Activity," September 1994.

New Zealand's Disclosure-Based Experiment in Bank Regulation

Until 1995, New Zealand took a conventional approach to bank regulation that relied on regular examinations by the central bank to ensure that the banks complied with capital requirements and asset restrictions and followed good management practices. At the start of 1996, this system was scrapped for one based on disclosure requirements that uses the market to police the behavior of the banks.

As part of this new system, every bank in New Zealand must supply a comprehensive, quarterly financial statement that provides information on the quality of its assets, its lending activities, and its ratings from private credit-rating agencies, among other things. These financial statements must be audited two times a year, and not only must they be provided to the central bank, which will monitor them, but they must also be made public, with a two-page summary posted in all bank branches. In addition, bank directors are required to validate these statements and state publicly that their bank's risk management systems are adequate and being properly implemented. A most unusual feature of this system is that a bank's directors now face unlimited liability—that is, they can lose all their assets, not just their holdings in the bank—if they are found to have made false or misleading statements. Directors are thus in the dangerous position that they can be sued by creditors for everything they are worth if the bank goes bust.

The rationale for this approach is that the market will now provide the necessary discipline to prevent bankers from taking excessive risks because it will have sufficient information about banks' activities—depositors have the incentive to monitor the banks because there is no deposit insurance in New Zealand. Furthermore, banks will now have the incentive to improve their financial health in order to acquire good credit ratings. The system also has the advantage that it reduces regulatory costs for the banks because it will eliminate examination fees and burdensome rules on management procedures.

Critics of New Zealand's new approach point out that even with the new disclosure requirements, the asymmetric information problem may still not be solved. Banks may be less willing to admit to problems if the information has to be made public. In addition, depositors may not have the sophistication to understand fully the information provided and thus may not impose the necessary discipline on the banks. Furthermore, unlimited liability for directors might discourage top people from taking these positions, thereby weakening the management of the banks.

Although advocates of the New Zealand system think that it may prove to be a model for the rest of the world, skeptics point out that it might work only because of the peculiar features of the New Zealand banking system. Almost all New Zealand banks are foreign-owned, and around 90 percent of deposits are at foreign-owned banks. Thus these skeptics contend that in effect, bank regulation has been outsourced to the regulators of the foreign banks that own the New Zealand banks—central banks such as the Bank of England and the Reserve Bank of Australia that supervise the banks with subsidiaries in New Zealand.

BOX 4

The Community Reinvestment Act

A Political Hot Button. The Community Reinvestment Act (CRA) has become more controversial recently because of the strengthening of its provisions in recent years and increased enforcement by bank regulators. Banks now have new reporting requirements on such items as small business lending and community involvement, and they complain that the increased paperwork is both burdensome and costly. The CRA has also received more attention recently because of increased merger activity in the banking industry, which raises its importance because meeting its provisions affects the merger approval process.

Many congressional Republicans regard the act as a heavy-handed affirmative action program that increases the burden of regulation unnecessarily and have strongly advocated its abolishment or at least the exemption of many banks and savings and loans from its provisions. Advocates of the act, who feel just as strongly, have pointed out that in the past minorities have been discriminated against by banks, and it has increased lending to minorities, which has recently begun to rise at a much faster rate than to whites. Considering that affirmative action has become a hot political button, the Community Reinvestment Act is sure to remain controversial.

Consumer Protection

The existence of asymmetric information also suggests that consumers may not have enough information to protect themselves fully. Consumer protection regulation has taken several forms. First is "truth in lending," mandated under the Consumer Protection Act of 1969, which requires all lenders, not just banks, to provide information to consumers about the cost of borrowing including a standardized interest rate (called the annual percentage rate, or APR) and the total finance charges on the loan. The Fair Credit Billing Act of 1974 requires creditors, especially credit card issuers, to provide information on the method of assessing finance charges and requires that billing complaints be handled quickly. Both of these acts are administered by the Federal Reserve System under Regulation Z.

Congress has also passed legislation to reduce discrimination in credit markets. The Equal Credit Opportunity Act of 1974 and its extension in 1976 forbid discrimination by lenders based on race, gender, marital status, age, or national origin. It is administered by the Federal Reserve under Regulation B. The Community Reinvestment Act (CRA) of 1977 was enacted to prevent "redlining," a lender's refusal to lend in a particular area (marked off by a hypothetical red line on a map). The Community Reinvestment Act requires that banks show that they lend in all areas in which they take deposits, and if banks are found to be in noncompliance with the act, regulators can reject their applications for mergers, branching, or other new activities. The increased enforcement of CRA provisions in recent years has been controversial (see Box 4).

Restrictions on Competition

Increased competition can also increase moral hazard incentives for banks to take on more risk. Declining profitability as a result of increased competition could tip the incentives of bankers toward assuming greater risk in an effort to maintain former profit levels. Thus governments in many countries have instituted regulations to protect banks from competition. These regulations have taken two forms in the United States. First are restrictions on branching, such as those described in Chapter 11, which reduce competition between banks. The second form involves preventing nonbank institutions from competing with banks by engaging in banking business.

Although restricting competition may prop up the health of banks, restrictions on competition can also have serious disadvantages: They can lead to higher charges to consumers and can decrease the efficiency of banking institutions, which do not have to compete as hard. Thus although the existence of asymmetric information provides a rationale for anticompetitive regulations, it does not mean that they will be beneficial. Indeed, in recent years, the impulse of governments in industrialized countries to restrict competition has been waning.

Separation of the Banking and Securities Industries: The Glass-Steagall Act

Before 1933, commercial banks engaged in investment banking activities as well as traditional banking activities. Because investment banking is inherently risky, allowing banks to pursue these activities may have increased their moral hazard opportunities for risk taking. After sensational congressional hearings documenting abuses of commercial banks in their securities activities during the Great Depression collapse—which were as widely followed by the public as the Watergate or Iran-*contra* hearings in recent decades—Congress passed the Glass-Steagall Act in 1933. Glass-Steagall allowed commercial banks to sell new offerings of government securities but prohibited them from underwriting corporate securities or from engaging in brokerage activities. It also prohibited investment banks from engaging in commercial banking activities and has thus protected banks from competition. Additional regulations prohibited banks from selling insurance and engaging in other nonbank activities that were considered risky.

Study Guide Because so many laws regulating banking have been passed in the United States, it is hard to keep track of them all. As a study aid, Table 1 lists the major banking legislation in the twentieth century and its key provisions.

 ## INTERNATIONAL BANKING REGULATION

Because asymmetric information problems in the banking industry are a fact of life throughout the world, bank regulation in other countries is similar to that in the United States. Banks are chartered and supervised by government regulators, just as they are in the United States—for example, by the Ministry of Finance in Japan and by the Bank of England in the United Kingdom. Deposit insurance is also a feature of the regulatory systems in most other developed countries, although its coverage is often smaller than in the United States and is purposely not advertised. We have also seen that bank capital requirements are in the process of being standardized across countries with agreements like the Basel accord.

TABLE 1	Major Banking Legislation in the United States in the Twentieth Century

Federal Reserve Act (1913)
Created the Federal Reserve System

McFadden Act of 1927
Put national and state banks on equal footing regarding branching
Effectively prohibited banks from branching across state lines

Banking Act of 1933 (Glass-Steagall) and 1935
Created the FDIC
Separated commercial banking from the securities industry
Prohibited interest on checkable deposits and restricted such deposits to commercial banks
Put interest-rate ceilings on other deposits

Bank Holding Company Act (1956) and Douglas Amendment (1970)
Clarified the status of bank holding companies (BHCs)
Gave the Federal Reserve regulatory responsibility for BHCs

Depository Institutions Deregulation and Monetary Control Act (DIDMCA) of 1980
Gave thrift institutions wider latitude in activities
Approved NOW and ATS accounts nationwide
Phased out interest rate ceilings on deposits
Imposed uniform reserve requirements on depository institutions
Eliminated usury ceilings on loans
Increased deposit insurance to $100,000 per account

Depository Institutions Act of 1982 (Garn–St Germain)
Gave the FDIC and the FSLIC emergency powers to merge banks and thrifts across state lines
Allowed depository institutions to offer money market deposit accounts (MMDAs)
Granted thrifts wider latitude in commercial and consumer lending

Competitive Equality in Banking Act (CEBA) of 1987
Provided $10.8 billion to the FSLIC
Made provisions for regulatory forbearance in depressed areas

Financial Institutions Reform, Recovery, and Enforcement Act (FIRREA) of 1989
Provided funds to resolve S&L failures
Eliminated the FSLIC and the Federal Home Loan Bank Board
Created the Office of Thrift Supervision to regulate thrifts
Created the Resolution Trust Corporation to resolve insolvent thrifts
Raised deposit insurance premiums
Reimposed restrictions on S&L activities

Federal Deposit Insurance Corporation Improvement Act (FDICIA) of 1991
Recapitalized the FDIC
Limited brokered deposits and the too-big-to-fail policy
Set provisions for prompt corrective action   *(continued)*

TABLE 1	Major Banking Legislation in the United States in the Twentieth Century *(continued)*

Federal Deposit Insurance Corporation Improvement Act (FDICIA) of 1991 (cont.)

Instructed the FDIC to establish risk-based premiums

Increased examinations, capital requirements, and reporting requirements

Included the Foreign Bank Supervision Enhancement Act (FBSEA), which strengthened the Fed's Authority to supervise foreign banks

Riegle-Neal Interstate Banking and Branching Efficiency Act of 1994

Overturned prohibition of interstate banking

Allowed branching across state lines

Problems in Regulating International Banking

Particular problems in bank regulation occur when banks are engaged in international banking and thus can readily shift their business from one country to another. Bank regulators closely examine the domestic operations of banks in their country, but they often do not have the knowledge or ability to keep a close watch on bank operations in other countries, either by domestic banks' foreign affiliates or by foreign banks with domestic branches. In addition, when a bank operates in many countries, it is not always clear which national regulatory authority should have primary responsibility for keeping the bank from engaging in overly risky activities. The difficulties inherent in regulating international banking were highlighted by the BCCI scandal discussed in Box 5. Cooperation among regulators in different countries and standardization of regulatory requirements provide potential solutions to the problems of regulating international banking. The world has been moving in this direction through agreements like the Basel accord on capital requirements in 1988 and the new regulatory oversight procedures announced by the Basel Committee in July 1992 (see Box 2). However, whether agreements of this type will solve the problem of regulating international banking in the future is an open question.

Summary

Asymmetric information analysis explains what types of banking regulations are needed to reduce moral hazard and adverse selection problems in the banking system. However, understanding the theory behind regulation does not mean that regulation and supervision of the banking system are easy in practice. Getting bank regulators and supervisors to do their job properly is difficult for several reasons. First, as we learned in the discussion of financial innovation in Chapter 10, in their search for profits, financial institutions have strong incentives to avoid existing regulations by loophole mining. Thus regulation applies to a moving target: Regulators are continually playing cat and mouse with financial institutions—financial institutions think up clever ways to avoid regulations, which then causes regulators to modify their regulation activities. Regulators continually face new challenges in a dynamically changing financial system, and

BOX 5

The BCCI Scandal

The Bank of Credit and Commerce International (BCCI) was chartered in Luxembourg in 1972 by a Pakistani businessman, Agha Hasan Abedi. The bank grew rapidly to $20 billion in assets and by 1991 was operating in more than 70 countries. Unfortunately, the bank was siphoning off funds to secret accounts in the Cayman Islands, where much of this money was stolen. Indeed, estimates suggest that nearly half of the bank's assets may have "disappeared." Fraud was not the only shady activity BCCI engaged in. BCCI supposedly helped dictators such as Saddam Hussein of Iraq, Manuel Noriega of Panama, and Ferdinand Marcos of the Philippines steal huge sums from their countries, helped the CIA channel funds to the *contra* rebels in Nicaragua, and acted as a banker for the notorious Abu Nidal terrorist group. Not surprisingly, BCCI has been dubbed the "Bank of Crooks and Criminals, Inc."

How did BCCI get away with these fraudulent activities for so long? The answer illustrates the difficulties of regulating banks with operations in many countries. Although BCCI's headquarters were in London, regulatory oversight fell to the chartering country, Luxembourg, whose tiny bank regulator, the Institut Monétaire Luxembourgeois (IML), was not up to the task. As a result, BCCI effectively operated free of government regulatory oversight for 15 years. In 1987, the IML reached an agreement with seven other countries' regulators to oversee BCCI jointly, but even this larger group was unable to keep track of the bank's activities. Only in spring 1990 did these regulators uncover some evidence of fraud, and not until July 1991 did the Price Waterhouse accounting firm document the pervasiveness of the fraud to the Bank of England, which then closed BCCI down.

The losses to depositors and stockholders from the BCCI collapse were immense, and national regulators, particularly the Bank of England, have been severely criticized for their slowness in uncovering the scandal. A year after the BCCI collapse, in July 1992, the Basel Committee announced an agreement to standardize further the regulation of international banks. Now a bank's worldwide operations will be under the scrutiny of a single home-country regulator with enhanced powers to acquire information on the bank's activities. Furthermore, regulators in other countries will have the right to restrict operations of a foreign bank if they feel that it lacks effective oversight. Despite this improvement in the regulation of international banks, fears remain that another BCCI-like scandal could happen again.

unless they can respond rapidly to change, they may not be able to keep financial institutions from taking on excessive risk. This problem can be exacerbated if regulators and supervisors do not have the resources or expertise to keep up with clever people in financial institutions who think up ways to hide what they are doing or to get around the existing regulations.

Bank regulation and supervision are difficult for two other reasons. In the regulation and supervision game, the devil is in the details. Subtle differences in the details may have unintended consequences; unless regulators get the regulation and supervision just right, they may be unable to prevent excessive risk taking.

In addition, regulators and supervisors may be subject to political pressure not to do their jobs properly. For all these reasons, there is no guarantee that bank regulators and supervisors will be successful in promoting a healthy financial system. Indeed, as we will see, bank regulation and supervision have not always worked well, leading to banking crises in the United States and throughout the world.

THE 1980s U.S. BANKING CRISIS: WHY?

Before the 1980s, federal deposit insurance seemed to work exceedingly well. In contrast to the pre-1934 period, when bank failures were common and depositors frequently suffered losses, the period from 1934 to 1980 was one in which bank failures were a rarity, averaging 15 a year for commercial banks and fewer than 5 a year for savings and loans. After 1981, this rosy picture changed dramatically. Failures in both commercial banks and savings and loans climbed to levels more than ten times greater than in earlier years. Why did this happen? How did a deposit insurance system that seemed to be working well for half a century find itself in so much trouble?

Early Stages of the Crisis

The story starts with the burst of financial innovation in the 1960s, 1970s, and early 1980s: NOW accounts, money market mutual funds, junk bonds, securitization and the rise of the commercial paper market (discussed in Chapters 10 and 11). Financial innovation decreased the profitability of certain traditional business for commercial banks. Banks now faced increased competition for their sources of funds from new financial institutions such as money market mutual funds while they were losing commercial lending business to the commercial paper market and securitization.

With the decreasing profitability of their traditional business, by the mid-1980s commercial banks were forced to seek out new and potentially risky business to keep their profits up, by placing a greater percentage of their total loans in real estate and in credit extended to assist corporate takeovers and leveraged buyouts (called *highly leveraged transaction loans*).

The existence of deposit insurance increased moral hazard for banks because insured depositors had little incentive to keep the banks from taking on too much risk. Regardless of how much risk banks were taking, deposit insurance guaranteed that depositors would not suffer any losses.

Adding fuel to the fire, financial innovation produced new financial instruments that widened the scope for risk taking. New markets in financial futures, junk bonds, swaps, and other instruments made it easier for banks to take on extra risk—making the moral hazard problem more severe. New legislation that deregulated the banking industry in the early 1980s, the Depository Institutions Deregulation and Monetary Control Act (DIDMCA) of 1980 and the Depository Institutions (Garn–St Germain) Act of 1982, gave expanded powers to the S&Ls and mutual savings banks to engage in new risky activities. These thrift institutions, which had been restricted almost entirely to making loans for home mortgages, now were allowed to have up to 40 percent of their assets in commercial real estate loans, up to 30 percent in consumer lending, and up to 10 percent in commercial loans and leases. In the wake of this legislation, S&L regulators allowed up to 10 percent of assets to be in junk bonds or in direct investments (common stocks, real estate, service corporations, and operating subsidiaries).

In addition, DIDMCA increased the mandated amount of federal deposit insurance from $40,000 per account to $100,000 and phased out Regulation Q deposit-rate ceilings. Banks and S&Ls that wanted to pursue rapid growth and take on risky projects could now attract the necessary funds by issuing larger-denomination insured certificates of deposit with interest rates much higher than those being offered by their competitors. Without deposit insurance, high interest rates would not have induced depositors to provide the high-rolling banks with funds because of the realistic expectation that they might not get the funds back. But with deposit insurance, the government was guaranteeing that the deposits were safe, so depositors were more than happy to make deposits in banks with the highest interest rates.

A financial innovation that made it even easier for high-rolling banks to raise funds is known as **brokered deposits,** which enable depositors to circumvent the $100,000 limit on deposit insurance. Brokered deposits work as follows: A large depositor with $10 million goes to a broker, who breaks the $10 million into 100 packages of $100,000 each and then buys $100,000 CDs at 100 different banks. Because the amount of each CD is within the $100,000 limit for deposits at each bank, the large depositor has in effect obtained deposit insurance on all $10 million. The federal deposit insurance agencies passed a regulation to ban brokered deposits in 1984, but a federal court overturned the ban.

Financial innovation and deregulation in the permissive atmosphere of the Reagan years led to expanded powers for the S&L industry that led to several problems. First, many S&L managers did not have the required expertise to manage risk appropriately in these new lines of business. Second, the new expanded powers meant that there was a rapid growth in new lending, particularly to the real estate sector. Even if the required expertise was available initially, rapid credit growth may outstrip the available information resources of the banking institution, resulting in excessive risk taking. Third, these new powers of the S&Ls and the lending boom meant that their activities were expanding in scope and were becoming more complicated, requiring an expansion of regulatory resources to monitor these activities appropriately. Unfortunately, regulators of the S&Ls at the Federal Savings and Loan Insurance Corporation (FSLIC) had neither the expertise nor the resources that would have enabled them to monitor these new activities sufficiently. Given the lack of expertise in both the S&L industry and the FSLIC, the weakening of the regulatory apparatus, and the moral hazard incentives provided by deposit insurance, it is no surprise that S&Ls took on excessive risks, which led to huge losses on bad loans.

In addition, the incentives of moral hazard were increased dramatically by an historical accident: the combination of sharp increases in interest rates from late 1979 until 1981 and a severe recession in 1981–1982, both of which were engineered by the Federal Reserve to bring down inflation. The sharp rises in interest rates produced rapidly rising costs of funds for the savings and loans that were not matched by higher earnings on the S&Ls' principal asset, long-term residential mortgages (whose rates had been fixed at a time when interest rates were far lower). The 1981–1982 recession and a collapse in the prices of energy and farm products hit the economies of certain parts of the country such as Texas very hard. As a result, there were defaults on many S&Ls' loans. Losses for savings and loan institutions mounted to $10 billion in 1981–1982, and by some estimates over half of the S&Ls in the United States had a negative net worth and were thus insolvent by the end of 1982.

Later Stages of the Crisis: Regulatory Forbearance

At this point, a logical step might have been for the S&L regulators—the Federal Home Loan Bank Board and its deposit insurance subsidiary, the Federal Savings and Loan Insurance Fund (FSLIC), both now abolished—to close the insolvent S&Ls. Instead, these regulators adopted a stance of **regulatory forbearance:** They refrained from exercising their regulatory right to put the insolvent S&Ls out of business. To sidestep their responsibility to close ailing S&Ls, they adopted irregular regulatory accounting principles that in effect substantially lowered capital requirements. For example, they allowed S&Ls to include in their capital calculations a high value for intangible capital, called *goodwill*.

There were three main reasons why the Federal Home Loan Bank Board and FSLIC opted for regulatory forbearance. First, the FSLIC did not have sufficient funds in its insurance fund to close the insolvent S&Ls and pay off their deposits. Second, the Federal Home Loan Bank Board was established to encourage the growth of the savings and loan industry, so the regulators were probably too close to the people they were supposed to be regulating. Third, because bureaucrats do not like to admit that their own agency is in trouble, the Federal Home Loan Bank Board and the FSLIC preferred to sweep their problems under the rug in the hope that they would go away.

Regulatory forbearance increases moral hazard dramatically because an operating but insolvent S&L (nicknamed a "zombie S&L" by Edward Kane of Ohio State University because it is the "living dead") has almost nothing to lose by taking on great risk and "betting the bank": If it gets lucky and its risky investments pay off, it gets out of insolvency. Unfortunately, if, as is likely, the risky investments don't pay off, the zombie S&L's losses will mount, and the deposit insurance agency will be left holding the bag.

This strategy is similar to the "long bomb" strategy in football. When a football team is almost hopelessly behind and time is running out, it often resorts to a high-risk play: the throwing of a long pass to try to score a touchdown. Of course, the long bomb is unlikely to be successful, but there is always a small chance that it will work. If it doesn't, the team has lost nothing, since it would have lost the game anyway.

Given the sequence of events we have discussed here, it should be no surprise that savings and loans began to take huge risks: They built shopping centers in the desert, bought manufacturing plants to convert manure to methane, and purchased billions of dollars of high-risk, high-yield junk bonds. The S&L industry was no longer the staid industry that once operated on the so-called *3-6-3 rule:* You took in money at 3 percent, lent it at 6 percent, and played golf at 3 P.M. Although many savings and loans were making money, losses at other S&Ls were colossal.

Another outcome of regulatory forbearance was that with little to lose, zombie S&Ls attracted deposits away from healthy S&Ls by offering higher interest rates. Because there were so many zombie S&Ls in Texas pursuing this strategy, above-market interest rates on deposits at Texas S&Ls were said to have a "Texas premium." Potentially healthy S&Ls now found that to compete for deposits, they had to pay higher interest rates, which made their operations less profitable and frequently pushed them into the zombie category. Similarly, zombie S&Ls in pursuit of asset growth made loans at below-market interest rates, thereby lowering loan interest rates for healthy S&Ls, and again made them less profitable. The zombie S&Ls had actually taken on attributes of vampires—their willingness to pay above-market rates for deposits and take below-market interest rates on loans was sucking the lifeblood (profits) out of healthy S&Ls.

Competitive Equality in Banking Act of 1987

Toward the end of 1986, the growing losses in the savings and loan industry were bankrupting the insurance fund of the FSLIC. The Reagan administration sought $15 billion in funds for the FSLIC, a completely inadequate sum considering that many times this amount was needed to close down insolvent S&Ls. The legislation passed by Congress, the Competitive Equality in Banking Act (CEBA) of 1987, did not even meet the administration's requests. It allowed the FSLIC to borrow only $10.8 billion through a subsidiary corporation called Financing Corporation (FICO) and, what was worse, included provisions that directed the Federal Home Loan Bank Board to continue to pursue regulatory forbearance (allow insolvent institutions to keep operating), particularly in economically depressed areas such as Texas.

The failure of Congress to deal with the savings and loan crisis was not going to make the problem go away, and consistent with our analysis, the situation deteriorated rapidly. Losses in the savings and loan industry surpassed $10 billion in 1988 and approached $20 billion in 1989. The crisis was reaching epidemic proportions. The collapse of the real estate market in the late 1980s led to additional huge loan losses that greatly exacerbated the problem.

POLITICAL ECONOMY OF THE SAVINGS AND LOAN CRISIS

Although we now have a grasp of the regulatory and economic forces that created the S&L crisis, we still need to understand the political forces that produced the regulatory structure and activities that led to it. The key to understanding the political economy of the S&L crisis is to recognize that the relationship between voter-taxpayers and the regulators and politicians creates a particular type of moral hazard problem, discussed in Chapter 9: the *principal-agent problem,* which occurs when representatives (agents) such as managers have incentives that differ from those of their employer (the principal) and so act in their own interest rather than in the interest of the employer.

Principal-Agent Problem for Regulators and Politicians

Regulators and politicians are ultimately agents for voter-taxpayers (principals) because in the final analysis, taxpayers bear the cost of any losses by the deposit insurance agency. The principal-agent problem occurs because the agent (a politician or regulator) does not have the same incentives to minimize costs to the economy as the principal (the taxpayer).

To act in the taxpayer's interest and lower costs to the deposit insurance agency, regulators have several tasks, as we have seen. They must set tight restrictions on holding assets that are too risky, must impose high capital requirements, and must not adopt a stance of regulatory forbearance, which allows insolvent institutions to continue to operate. However, because of the principal-agent problem, regulators have incentives to do the opposite. Indeed, as our sad saga of the S&L debacle indicates, they have at times loosened capital requirements and restrictions on risky asset holdings and pursued regulatory forbearance. One important incentive for regulators that explains this phenomenon is their desire to escape blame for poor performance by their agency. By loosening capital requirements and pursuing regulatory forbearance, regulators can hide the problem of an insolvent bank and hope that the situation will improve. Edward Kane characterizes such behavior on the part of regulators as "bureaucratic gambling."

Another important incentive for regulators is that they want to protect their careers by acceding to pressures from the people who most influence their careers. These people are not the taxpayers but the politicians who try to keep regulators from imposing tough regulations on institutions that are major campaign contributors. Members of Congress have often lobbied regulators to ease up on a particular S&L that contributed large sums to their campaigns (as we will see in the following application). Regulatory agencies that have little independence from the political process are more vulnerable to these pressures.

In addition, both Congress and the presidential administration promoted banking legislation in 1980 and 1982 that made it easier for savings and loans to engage in risk-taking activities. After the legislation passed, the need for monitoring the S&L industry increased because of the expansion of permissible activities. The S&L regulatory agencies needed more resources to carry out their monitoring activities properly, but Congress (successfully lobbied by the S&L industry) was unwilling to allocate the necessary funds. As a result, the S&L regulatory agencies became so short-staffed that they actually had to cut back on their on-site examinations just when these were needed most. In the period from January 1984 to July 1986, for example, several hundred S&Ls were not examined once. Even worse, spurred on by the intense lobbying efforts of the S&L industry, Congress passed the Competitive Equality in Banking Act of 1987, which, as we have seen, provided inadequate funding to close down the insolvent S&Ls and also hampered the S&L regulators from doing their job properly by including provisions encouraging regulatory forbearance.

As these examples indicate, the structure of our political system has created a serious principal-agent problem; politicians have strong incentives to act in their own interests rather than in the interests of taxpayers. Because of the high cost of running campaigns, American politicians must raise substantial contributions. This situation may provide lobbyists and other campaign contributors with the opportunity to influence politicians to act against the public interest, as we see in the following application.

Principal-Agent Problem in Action: Charles Keating and the Lincoln Savings and Loan Scandal

We see that the principal-agent problem for regulators and politicians creates incentives that may cause excessive risk taking on the part of banking institutions, which then cause substantial losses to the taxpayer. The scandal associated with Charles H. Keating, Jr. and the Lincoln Savings and Loan Association provides a graphic example of the principal-agent problem at work. As Edwin Gray, a former chairman of the Federal Home Loan Bank Board, stated, "This is a story of incredible corruption. I can't call it anything else."[4]

Charles Keating was allowed to acquire Lincoln Savings and Loan of Irvine, California, in early 1984, even though he had been accused of fraud by the SEC less than five years earlier. For Keating, whose construction firm, American Continental, planned to build huge real estate developments in Arizona, the S&L was a gold mine: In the lax regulatory atmosphere at the time, controlling the S&L gave his firm easy access to funds without being scrutinized by outside bankers. Within days of acquiring control, Keating got rid of Lincoln's conservative lending officers and internal auditors, even though he had promised regulators he would keep them. Lincoln then plunged into high-risk investments such as currency futures, junk bonds, common stock, hotels, and vast tracts of desert land in Arizona.

Because of a shortage of savings and loan examiners at the time, Lincoln was able to escape a serious examination until 1986, whereupon examiners from the Federal Home Loan Bank of San Francisco discovered that Lincoln had exceeded the 10 percent limit on equity investments by $600 million. Because of these activities and some evidence that Lincoln was deliberately trying to mislead the examiners, the examiners recommended federal seizure of the bank and all its assets. Keating was not about to take this lying down; he engaged hordes of lawyers—eventually 77 law firms—and accused the bank examiners of bias. He also sued unsuccessfully to overturn the 10 percent equity limit. Keating is said to have bragged that he spent $50 million fighting regulators.

Lawyers were not Keating's only tactic for keeping regulators off his back. After receiving $1.3 million of contributions to their campaigns from Keating, five senators—Dennis De Concini and John McCain of Arizona, Alan Cranston of California, John Glenn of Ohio, and Donald Riegle of Michigan (subsequently nicknamed the "Keating Five")—met with Edwin Gray, the chairman of the Federal Home Loan Board, and later with four top regulators from San Francisco in April 1987. They complained that the regulators were being too tough on Lincoln and urged the regulators to quit dragging out the investigation. After Gray was replaced by M. Danny Wall, Wall took the unprecedented step of removing the San Francisco examiners from the case in September 1987 and transferred the investigation to the bank board's headquarters in Washington. No examiners

---

[4]Quoted in Tom Morganthau, Rich Thomas, and Eleanor Clift, "The S&L Scandal's Biggest Blowout," *Newsweek,* November 6, 1989, p. 35.

called on Lincoln for the next ten months, and as one of the San Francisco examiners described it, Lincoln dropped into a "regulatory black hole."

Lincoln Savings and Loan finally failed in April 1989, with estimated costs to taxpayers of $2.6 billion, making it possibly the most costly S&L failure in history. Keating was convicted for abuses (such as having Lincoln pay him and his family $34 million) but after serving four and a half years in jail, his conviction was overturned in 1996. Wall was forced to resign as head of the Office of Thrift Supervision because of his involvement in the Keating scandal. As a result of their activities on behalf of Keating, the Keating Five senators were made the object of a congressional ethics investigation, but given Congress's propensity to protect its own, they were subjected only to minor sanctions. Ⓐ

SAVINGS AND LOAN BAILOUT: FINANCIAL INSTITUTIONS REFORM, RECOVERY, AND ENFORCEMENT ACT OF 1989

Immediately after taking office, the Bush administration proposed new legislation to provide adequate funding to close down the insolvent S&Ls. The resulting legislation, the Financial Institutions Reform, Recovery, and Enforcement Act (FIRREA), was signed into law on August 9, 1989. It was the most significant legislation to affect the thrift industry since the 1930s. FIRREA's major provisions were as follows: The regulatory apparatus was significantly restructured, eliminating the Federal Home Loan Bank Board and the FSLIC, both of which had failed in their regulatory tasks. The regulatory role of the Federal Home Loan Bank Board was relegated to the Office of Thrift Supervision (OTS), a bureau within the U.S. Treasury Department, and its responsibilities are similar to those that the Office of the Comptroller of the Currency has over the national banks. The regulatory responsibilities of the FSLIC were given to the FDIC, and the FDIC became the sole administrator of the federal deposit insurance system with two separate insurance funds: the Bank Insurance Fund (BIF) and the Savings Association Insurance Fund (SAIF). Another new agency, the Resolution Trust Corporation (RTC), was established to manage and resolve insolvent thrifts placed in conservatorship or receivership. It was made responsible for selling more than $450 billion of real estate owned by failed institutions. After seizing the assets of about 750 insolvent S&Ls, over 25 percent of the industry, the RTC sold over 95 percent of them, with a recovery rate of over 85 percent. After this success, the RTC went out of business on December 31, 1995.

Initially, the total cost of the bailout was estimated to be $159 billion over the ten-year period through 1999, but more recent estimates indicated that the cost would be far higher. Indeed, the General Accounting Office placed a cost for the bailout at more than $500 billion over 40 years. However, as pointed out in Box 1 in Chapter 4, this estimate was misleading because, for example, the value of a payment 30 years from now is worth much less in today's dollars. The present value of the bailout cost actually ended up being on the order of $150 billion. The funding for the bailout came partly from capital in the Federal Home Loan Banks (owned by the S&L industry) but mostly from the sale of government debt by both the Treasury and the Resolution Funding Corporation (RefCorp).

To replenish the reserves of the Savings Association Insurance Fund, insurance premiums for S&Ls were increased from 20.8 cents per $100 of deposits to 23 cents and can rise as high as 32.5 cents. Premiums for banks immediately rose from 8.3 cents to 15 cents per $100 of deposits and were raised further to 23 cents in 1991.

FIRREA also imposed new restrictions on thrift activities that in essence reregulated the S&L industry to the asset choices it had before 1982. S&Ls can no longer purchase junk bonds and had to sell their holdings by 1994. Commercial real estate loans are restricted to four times capital rather than the previous limit of 40 percent of assets, and so this new restriction is a reduction for all institutions whose capital is less than 10 percent of assets. S&Ls must also hold at least 70 percent—up from 60 percent—of their assets in investments that are primarily housing-related. Troubled thrifts are not allowed to accept brokered deposits. Among the most important provisions of FIRREA was the increase in the core-capital leverage requirement from 3 percent to 8 percent and the eventual adherence to the same risk-based capital standards imposed on commercial banks.[5]

FIRREA also enhanced the enforcement powers of thrift regulators by making it easier for them to remove managers, issue cease and desist orders, and impose civil money penalties. The Justice Department was also given $75 million per year for three years to uncover and prosecute fraud in the banking industry, and maximum fines rose substantially.

FIRREA was a serious attempt to deal with some of the problems created by the S&L crisis in that it provided substantial funds to close insolvent thrifts. However, the losses that continued to mount for the FDIC in 1990 and 1991 would have depleted its Bank Insurance Fund by 1992, requiring that this fund be recapitalized. In addition, FIRREA did not focus on the underlying adverse selection and moral hazard problems created by deposit insurance. FIRREA did, however, mandate that the U.S. Treasury produce a comprehensive study and plan for reform of the federal deposit insurance system. After this study appeared in 1991, Congress passed the Federal Deposit Insurance Corporation Improvement Act (FDICIA), which engendered major reforms in the bank regulatory system.

FEDERAL DEPOSIT INSURANCE CORPORATION IMPROVEMENT ACT OF 1991

FDICIA's provisions were designed to serve two purposes: to recapitalize the Bank Insurance Fund of the FDIC and to reform the deposit insurance and regulatory system so that taxpayer losses would be minimized.

FDICIA recapitalized the Bank Insurance Fund by increasing the FDIC's ability to borrow from the Treasury to $30 billion (up from $5 billion). FDICIA also allowed the FDIC to borrow $45 billion for working capital—money that would

---

[5]This change in accounting rules for calculating bank capital has resulted in an interesting legal development that may substantially increase the cost of the S&L bailout. In July 1996, the Supreme Court ruled that the government acted improperly when it altered the accounting rules and is thus liable for resulting costs to the S&Ls. The potential cost to the taxpayer of this ruling has been estimated to be as high as $10 billion.

be repaid as the FDIC sold the assets of failed banks. FDICIA also mandated that the FDIC assess higher deposit insurance premiums until it could pay back its loans and achieve a level of reserves in its insurance funds that would equal 1.25 percent of insured deposits within 15 years, a goal that was reached for the Bank Insurance Fund (BIF) more than ten years earlier in 1995 because of the return to health of the commercial banking industry. However, despite a return to profitability of most S&Ls, the Savings Association Insurance Fund was still far from the mandated goal, leading to legislation in 1996 to return this fund to health (see Box 6).

The bill reduced the scope of deposit insurance in several ways. First, the FDIC is allowed to insure brokered deposits or accounts only if they are established under pension plans at well-capitalized banks. Second, and more important, the too-big-to-fail doctrine has been substantially limited: The FDIC must now close failed banks using the least-costly method, thus making it far more likely that uninsured depositors will suffer losses. An exception to this provision, whereby a bank would be declared too big to fail so that all depositors, both insured and uninsured, would be fully protected, would be allowed only if not doing so would "have serious adverse effects on economic conditions or financial stability." Furthermore, to invoke the too-big-to-fail policy, a two-thirds majority of both the Board of Governors of the Federal Reserve System and the directors of the FDIC, as well as the approval of the secretary of the Treasury, would be required. Furthermore, FDICIA requires that the Fed share in the FDIC's losses if long-term Fed lending to a bank that fails increases the FDIC's losses.

Probably the most important feature of FDICIA is its prompt corrective action provisions, which require the FDIC to intervene earlier and more vigorously when a bank gets into trouble. Banks are now classified into five groups based on bank capital. Group 1, classified as "well capitalized," are banks that significantly exceed minimum capital requirements and are allowed privileges such as insurance on brokered deposits and the ability to do some securities underwriting. Banks in group 2, classified as "adequately capitalized," meet minimum capital requirements and are not subject to corrective actions but are not allowed the privileges of the well-capitalized banks. Banks in group 3, "undercapitalized," fail to meet capital requirements. Banks in groups 4 and 5 are "significantly undercapitalized" and "critically undercapitalized," respectively, and are not allowed to pay interest on their deposits at rates that are higher than average. In addition, for group 3 banks, the FDIC is required to take prompt corrective actions such as requiring them to submit a capital restoration plan, restrict their asset growth, and seek regulatory approval to open new branches or develop new lines of business. Banks that are so undercapitalized as to have equity capital less than 2 percent of assets fall into group 5, and the FDIC must take steps to close them down.

FDICIA also instructed the FDIC to come up with risk-based insurance premiums. The system the FDIC has put in place uses the bank capital classifications just outlined and other supervisory criteria to assess these premiums. For example, after a reduction in insurance premiums in September 1995 when the Bank Insurance Fund reached its mandated level, well-capitalized banks with the best

BOX 6

The SAIF Fix and the Future of the S&L Industry

Although the FDIC's Bank Insurance Fund (BIF) has returned to health and has reached its mandated level of 1.25 percent of insured deposits, this was not yet true for the FDIC's Savings Association Insurance Fund (SAIF) in 1996. The primary reason for the poor state of SAIF is the drain from the nearly $8 billion of outstanding Financing Corporation (FICO) bonds that were used to finance S&L bailouts under the Competitive Equality Banking Act of 1987. Insurance premiums from the S&Ls, which would otherwise be used to beef up SAIF, must first be used to pay off the interest on the FICO bonds instead. The result is that the funds in SAIF were well below the mandated level so that insurance premiums for even the best-capitalized S&Ls remained at 23 cents per $100 of deposits, a level more than five times the premium of 4 cents for well-capitalized commercial banks. The higher premiums for S&Ls put them at a serious competitive disadvantage, and this caused a substantial shrinkage of S&Ls' deposits relative to commercial banks. Indeed, the shrinkage of S&L deposits was so severe that there was fear that there would not be enough insurance premiums collected to cover the FICO bond payments, with the result that these bonds could default.

The growing SAIF-FICO problem was resolved by legislation passed in late 1996 that tapped not only savings institutions but also commercial banks for the needed funds to make the FICO bond payments and to beef up SAIF. The law levied a onetime assessment of nearly $5 billion (an estimated 68 cents per $100 of deposits) on savings institutions to restore the funds in SAIF to the statutory 1.25 percent of insured deposits. Then through 1999, the savings institutions would pay 6.5 cents per $100 of deposits, compared to 1.3 cents for commercial banks, to make the payments on the FICO bonds. If the two industries remain separate, each would pay equal rates of 2.4 cents per $100 of deposits beginning in the year 2000. However, the law expects the merging of savings and loan charters into commercial bank charters and the merger of BIF-SAIF into one fund before the year 2000. Thus the final cleanup of the S&L mess may be the demise of the S&L industry.

supervisory rating (over 90 percent of the banks) only had to pay an insurance premium of 4 cents per $100, while the most undercapitalized banks with a low supervisory rating had to pay 31 cents per $100. (The current premium ranges from zero cents to 27 cents with over 90 percent of banks with over 95 percent of total deposits paying zero.) However, because the Savings Association Insurance Fund had not yet reached its mandated level, S&Ls continued to pay higher premiums.

Other provisions of FDICIA require regulators to perform annual on-site examinations, restrict real estate lending, and mandate stricter and more burdensome reporting requirements. The act also requires that the existing risk-based capital standards, which focus solely on credit risk, be modified to take account of interest-rate risk as well. FDICIA also provides securities firms with access to Federal Reserve discount lending during a financial crisis.

FDICIA also includes the Foreign Bank Supervision Enhancement Act (FBSEA), which in the wake of the BCCI scandal gives supervisory responsibility for foreign banks to the Federal Reserve and gives the Fed increased powers to acquire information on the foreign banks' activities. In addition, the Fed now has the right to prevent the operation of a foreign bank in the United States if it feels that the home country's supervision is not adequate or if the foreign bank is engaging in unsound banking practices.

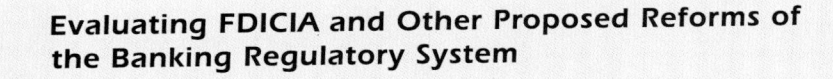

Evaluating FDICIA and Other Proposed Reforms of the Banking Regulatory System

FDICIA is a major step in reforming the banking regulatory system. How well will it work to solve the adverse selection and moral hazard problems of the bank regulatory system? Let's use the analysis in the chapter to evaluate the most important provisions of this legislation to answer this question.

Study Guide   Before looking at the evaluation for each set of provisions and proposals in this application, try to reason out how well they will solve the current problems with banking regulation. This exercise will help you develop a deeper understanding of the material in this chapter.

Limits on the Scope of Deposit Insurance

FDICIA's reduction of the scope of deposit insurance by limiting insurance on brokered deposits and restricting the use of the too-big-to-fail policy might have increased the incentives for uninsured depositors to monitor banks and to withdraw funds if the bank is taking on too much risk. Because banks might now fear the loss of deposits when they engage in risky activities, they might have less incentive to take on too much risk. Limitations on the use of the too-big-to-fail policy starting in 1992 have resulted in increased losses to uninsured depositors at failed banks as planned.

Although the cited elements of FDICIA strengthen the incentive of depositors to monitor banks, some critics of FDICIA would take these limitations on the scope of deposit insurance even further. Some suggest that deposit insurance should be eliminated entirely or should be reduced in amount from the current $100,000 limit to, say, $50,000 or $20,000. Another proposed reform would institute a system of **coinsurance** in which only a percentage of a deposit, say, 90 percent, would be covered by insurance. In this system, the insured depositor would suffer a percentage of the losses along with the deposit insurance agency. Because depositors facing a lower limit on deposit insurance or coinsurance would suffer losses if the bank goes broke, they will have an incentive to monitor the bank's activities. Other critics believe that FDICIA still contains too much scope for the too-big-to-fail policy. Because under FDICIA the Fed, the Treasury, and the FDIC can still agree to implement too-big-to-fail and thus bail out uninsured as well as insured depositors, big banks will not be subjected to enough discipline by uninsured depositors. These critics advocate eliminating the too-big-to-fail policy entirely, thereby decreasing the incentives of big banks to take on too much risk.

However, other experts do not believe that depositors are capable of monitoring banks and imposing discipline on them. The basic problem with reducing the scope of deposit insurance even further as proposed is that banks would be subject to runs, sudden withdrawals by nervous depositors. Such runs could by themselves lead to bank failures. In addition to protecting individual depositors, the purpose of deposit insurance is to prevent a large number of bank failures, which would lead to an unstable banking system and an unstable economy as occurred periodically before the establishment of federal deposit insurance in 1934. From this perspective, federal deposit insurance has been a resounding success. Bank panics, in which there are simultaneous failures of many banks and consequent disruption of the financial system, have not occurred since federal deposit insurance was established.

On the one hand, evidence that the largest banks benefiting from the de facto too-big-to-fail policy before 1991 were also the ones that took on the most risk suggests that limiting its application, as FDICIA does, may substantially reduce risk taking. On the other hand, eliminating the too-big-to-fail policy altogether would also cause some of the same problems that would occur if deposit insurance were eliminated or reduced: The probability of bank panics would increase. If a big bank were allowed to fail, the repercussions in the financial system might be immense. Other banks with a correspondent relationship with the failed bank (those that have deposits at the bank in exchange for a variety of services) would suffer large losses and might fail in turn, leading to a full-scale panic. In addition, the problem of liquidating the big bank's loan portfolio might create a major disruption in the financial market.

Prompt Corrective Action

The prompt corrective action provisions of FDICIA should also substantially reduce incentives for bank risk taking and reduce taxpayer losses. FDICIA uses a carrot-and-stick approach to get banks to hold more capital. If they are well capitalized, they receive valuable privileges; if their capital ratio falls, they are subject to more and more onerous regulation. Increased bank capital reduces moral hazard incentives for the bank because the bank now has more to lose if it fails and so is less likely to take on too much risk.

In addition, encouraging banks to hold more capital reduces potential losses for the FDIC because increased bank capital is a cushion that makes bank failure less likely. Furthermore, forcing the FDIC to close banks once their net worth is less than 2 percent (group 5) rather than waiting until net worth has fallen to zero makes it more likely that when a bank is closed, it will still have a positive net worth, thus limiting FDIC losses.

Prompt corrective action, which requires regulators to intervene early when bank capital begins to fall, is a serious attempt to reduce the principal-agent problem for politicians and regulators. With prompt corrective action provisions, regulators no longer have the option of regulatory forbearance, which, as we have seen, can greatly increase moral hazard incentives for banks.

Some critics of FDICIA feel that there are too many loopholes in the bill that still allow regulators too much discretion, thus leaving open the possibility of regulatory forbearance. However, an often overlooked part of the bill increases the accountability of regulators. FDICIA requires a mandatory review of any bank failure that imposes costs on the FDIC. The resulting report must be made available to any member of Congress and to the general public upon request, and the General Accounting Office must do an annual review of these reports. Opening up the actions of the regulators to public scrutiny will make regulatory forbearance less attractive to them, thereby reducing the principal-agent problem. It will also reduce the incentives of politicians to lean on regulators to relax their regulatory supervision of banks.

Risk-Based Insurance Premiums

Under FDICIA, banks deemed to be taking on greater risk, in the form of lower capital or riskier assets, will be subjected to higher insurance premiums. Risk-based insurance premiums will consequently reduce the moral hazard incentives for banks to take on higher risk because if they do so, they will have to pay higher premiums. In addition, the fact that risk-based premiums drop as the bank's capital increases encourages the bank to hold more capital, which has the benefits already mentioned.

One problem with risk-based premiums is that the scheme for determining the amount of risk the bank is taking may not be very accurate. For example, it might be hard for regulators to determine when a bank's loans are risky. Some critics have also pointed out that the classification of banks by such measures as the Basel risk-based capital standard solely reflects credit risk and does not take sufficient account of interest-rate risk. The regulatory authorities, however, are encouraged by FDICIA to modify existing risk-based standards to include interest-rate risk and, as we have seen earlier in this chapter, have proposed guidelines to encourage banks to manage interest-rate risk.

Other FDICIA Provisions

FDICIA's requirements that regulators perform bank examinations at least once a year are necessary for monitoring banks' compliance with bank capital requirements and asset restrictions. As the S&L debacle illustrates, frequent supervisory examinations of banks are necessary to keep them from taking on too much risk or committing fraud. Similarly, beefing up the ability of the Federal Reserve to monitor foreign banks might help dissuade international banks from engaging in these undesirable activities.

The stricter and more burdensome reporting requirements for banks have the advantage of providing more information to regulators to help them monitor bank activities. However, these reporting requirements have been criticized by banks, which claim that the requirements make it harder to lend to small businesses.

Other Proposed Changes in Banking Regulations

REGULATORY CONSOLIDATION The current bank regulatory system in the United States has banking institutions supervised by four federal agencies: the FDIC, the Office of the Comptroller of the Currency, the Office of Thrift Supervision, and the Federal Reserve. Critics of this system of multiple regulatory agencies with overlapping jurisdictions believe that it creates a system that is too complex and too costly because it is rife with duplication. The Clinton administration proposed a consolidation in which the duties of the four regulatory agencies would be given to a new Federal Banking Commission governed by a five-member board with one member from the Treasury, one from the Federal Reserve, and three independent members appointed by the president and confirmed by the Senate. The Federal Reserve strongly opposed this proposal because it believed that it needed to have hands-on supervision of the largest banks through their bank holding companies (as is the case currently) in order to have the information that would enable the Fed to respond sufficiently quickly in a crisis. The Fed also pointed out that a monolithic regulator might be less effective than two or more regulators in providing checks and balances for regulatory supervision. The Clinton administration's proposal was not passed by Congress, but the issue of regulatory consolidation is sure to come up again.

MARKET-VALUE ACCOUNTING FOR CAPITAL REQUIREMENTS We have seen that the requirement that a bank have substantial equity capital makes the bank less likely to fail. The requirement is also advantageous because a bank with high equity capital has more to lose if it takes on risky investments and so will have less incentive to hold risky assets. Unfortunately, capital requirements, including new risk-based measures, are calculated on an historical-cost (book value) basis in which the value of an asset is set at its initial purchase price. The problem with historical-cost accounting is that changes in the value of assets and liabilities because of changes in interest rates or default risk are not reflected in the calculation of the firm's equity capital. Yet changes in the market value of assets and liabilities and hence changes in the market value of equity capital are what indicate if a firm is truly insolvent. Furthermore, it is the market value of capital that determines the incentives for a bank to hold risky assets.

Market-value accounting when calculating capital requirements is another reform that receives substantial support. All assets and liabilities could be updated to market value periodically, say, every three months, to determine if a bank's capital is sufficient to meet the minimum requirements. This market-value accounting information would let the deposit insurance agency know quickly when a bank was falling below its capital requirement. The bank could then be closed down before its net worth fell below zero, thus preventing a loss to the deposit insurance agency. The market-value-based capital requirement would also ensure that banks would not be operating with negative capital, thereby preventing the bet-the-bank strategy of taking on excessive risk.

Objections to market-value-based capital requirements center on the difficulty of making accurate and straightforward market-value estimates of capital. Historical-cost accounting has an important advantage in that accounting rules are easier to define and standardize when the value of an asset is simply set at its purchase price. Market-value accounting, by contrast, requires estimates and approximations that are harder to standardize. For example, it might be hard to assess the market value of your friend Joe's car loan, whereas it would be quite easy to value a government bond. In addition, conducting market-value accounting would prove costly to banks because estimation of market values requires the collection of more information about the characteristics of assets and liabilities.

Nevertheless, proponents of market-value accounting for capital requirements point out that although market-value accounting involves some estimates and approximations, it would still provide regulators with more accurate assessment of bank equity capital than historical-cost accounting does.

Overall Evaluation

FDICIA appears to be an important step in the right direction because it increases the incentives for banks to hold capital and decreases their incentives to take on excessive risk. However, more could be done to improve the incentives for banks to limit their risk taking. Yet eliminating deposit insurance and the too-big-to-fail policy altogether may be going too far because these proposals might make the banking system too prone to a banking panic. Ⓐ

BANKING CRISES THROUGHOUT THE WORLD

Because misery likes company, it might make you feel better to know that the United States has by no means been alone in suffering a banking crisis. Indeed, as Table 2 and Figure 1 illustrate, banking crises have struck a large number of countries throughout the world, and many of them have been substantially worse than ours. We will examine what took place in several of these other countries and see that the same forces that produced a banking crisis in the United States have been at work elsewhere too.

Scandinavia

As in the United States, an important factor in the banking crises in Norway, Sweden, and Finland was the financial liberalization that occurred in the 1980s.

TABLE 2	The Cost of Rescuing Banks in Several Countries	
Date	**Country**	**Cost as a % of GDP**
1980–1982	Argentina	55
1981–1983	Chile	41
1994–1995	Venezuela	18
1995	Mexico	12–15
1994–1995	Brazil	5–10
1991–1993	Finland	8
1981–1984	Uruguay	7
1991	Sweden	6
1982–1987	Colombia	5
1987–1989	Norway	4
1984–1991	United States	3

Source: Gerard Caprio Jr. and Daniela Klingbiel, "Bank Insolvency: Bad Luck, Bad Policy, or Bad Banking?" paper prepared for the World Bank's *Annual Bank Conference on Development Economics,* Washington, D.C., April 25–26, 1996.

FIGURE 1 Banking Crises Throughout the World Since 1970

Source: Gerard Caprio Jr. and Daniela Klingbiel, "Bank Insolvency: Bad Luck, Bad Policy, or Bad Banking?" paper prepared for the World Bank's *Annual Bank Conference on Development Economics,* Washington, D.C., April 25–26, 1996.

Before the 1980s, banks in these Scandinavian countries were highly regulated and subject to restrictions on the interest rates they could pay to depositors and on the interest rates they could earn on loans. In this noncompetitive environment, and with artificially low rates on both deposits and loans, these banks lent only to the best credit risks, and both banks and their regulators had little need to develop expertise in screening and monitoring borrowers. With the deregulated environment, a lending boom ensued, particularly in the real estate sector. Given the lack of expertise in both the banking industry and its regulatory authorities in keeping risk taking in check, banks engaged in risky lending. When real estate prices collapsed in the late 1980s, massive loan losses resulted. The outcome of this process was similar to what happened in the savings and loan industry in the United States. The government was forced to bail out almost the entire banking industry in these countries in the late 1980s and early 1990s on a scale that was even larger relative to GDP than in the United States (see Table 2).

Latin America The Latin American banking crises show a similar pattern to those in the United States and in Scandinavia. Before the 1980s, banks in many Latin American countries were owned by the government and were subject to interest-rate restrictions as in Scandinavia. Their lending was restricted to the government and other low-risk borrowers. With the deregulation trend that was occurring worldwide, many of these countries liberalized their credit markets and privatized their banks. We then see the same pattern we saw in the United States and Scandinavia, a lending boom in the face of inadequate expertise on the part of both bankers and regulators. The result was again massive loan losses and the inevitable government bailout. What is particularly striking about the Latin American experience is that the cost of the bailout relative to GDP dwarfs that in the United States. For example, in the recent banking crises in Mexico and Venezuela, the cost to the taxpayer of the government bailouts exceeded 10 percent of GDP.

Eastern Europe Before the end of the Cold War, in the communist countries of Eastern Europe and the Soviet Union, banks were owned by the state. When the downfall of communism occurred, banks in these countries had little expertise in screening and monitoring loans. Furthermore, bank regulatory and supervisory apparatus that could rein in the banks and keep them from taking on excessive risk barely existed. Given the lack of expertise on the part of regulators and banks, not surprisingly, substantial loan losses ensued, resulting in the failure or government bailout of many banks. For example, in the second half of 1993, eight banks in Hungary with 25 percent of the financial system's assets were insolvent, and in Bulgaria, an estimated 75 percent of all loans in the banking system were estimated to be substandard in 1995. On August 24, 1995, a bank panic requiring government intervention occurred in Russia when the interbank loan market seized up and stopped functioning because of concern about the solvency of many new banks.

Japan Japan was a latecomer to the banking crisis game. Before 1990, the vaunted Japanese economy looked unstoppable. Unfortunately, it has recently experienced many of the same pathologies that we have seen in other countries. Before the 1980s, Japan's financial markets were among the most heavily regulated in the world, with very strict restrictions on the issuing of securities and interest rates. Financial deregulation and innovation produced a more competitive environment that set off a lending boom, with banks lending aggressively in the real estate sector. As in the other countries we have examined here, financial disclosure and monitoring by regulators did not keep pace with the new financial environment. The result was that banks could and did take on excessive risks, and when property values collapsed in the early 1990s, the banks were left holding massive amounts of bad loans. For example, Japanese banks decided to get into the mortgage lending market by setting up the so-called *jusen,* home mortgage lending companies that raised funds by borrowing from banks and then loaned these funds out to households. Seven of these *jusen* are now insolvent, leaving banks with $60 billion or so of bad loans.

The result is that the Japanese have experienced their first bank failures since World War II. In July 1995, Tokyo-based Cosmo Credit Corporation, Japan's fifth-largest credit union, failed and on August 30, the Osaka authorities announced the imminent closing of Kizu Credit Cooperative, Japan's second-largest credit union. (Kizu's story is remarkably similar to that of many U.S. savings and loans. Kizu, like many American S&Ls, began offering high rates on large time deposits and grew at a blistering pace, with deposits rising from $2.2 billion in 1988 to $12 billion by 1995 and real estate loans growing by a similar amount. When the property market collapsed, so did Kizu.) On the same day, the Ministry of Finance announced that it was liquidating Hyogo Bank, a midsize Kobe bank that was the first commercial bank to fail. Other banks have followed the same path. The Ministry of Finance has estimated total loan losses for the banking sector to be on the order of $350 billion, although many private analysts think the number may be far higher.

The Japanese seem to be going through the same cycle of forbearance as occurred in the United States. It has proved very difficult to arrange bailout packages to close down insolvent banking institutions, and so, not surprisingly, regulators have been reluctant to close them down. Bank regulators have promised that none of Japan's 21 largest banks will be allowed to fail, an admission of a too-big-to-fail policy similar to that found in the United States.

"Déjà Vu All Over Again"

What we see in banking crises in these different countries is that history has kept on repeating itself. The parallels between the banking crisis episodes in all these countries are remarkably similar, leaving us with a feeling of déjà vu. Although financial liberalization is generally a good thing because it promotes competition and can make a financial system more efficient, as we have seen in the countries examined here, it can lead to an increase in moral hazard, risk taking on the part of banks if there is lax regulation and supervision; the result can then be banking crises. However, these episodes do differ in that deposit insurance has not played an important role in many of the countries experiencing banking crises. For example, the size of the Japanese equivalent of the FDIC, the Deposit Insurance Corporation, was so tiny relative to the FDIC that it did not play a prominent role in the banking system and exhausted its resources almost immediately with the first bank failures. This means that deposit insurance is not to blame for some of these banking crises. However, what is common to all the countries discussed here is the existence of a government safety net, in which the government stands ready to bail out banks whether deposit insurance is an important feature of the regulatory environment or not. It is the existence of a government safety net, and not deposit insurance per se, that increases moral hazard incentives for excessive risk taking on the part of banks.

SUMMARY

1. The concepts of asymmetric information, adverse selection, and moral hazard help explain the seven types of banking regulation that we see in the United States and other countries: the government safety net, restrictions on bank asset holdings and capital requirements, bank supervision, disclosure

requirements, consumer protection, restrictions on competition, and the separation of the banking and securities industries.

2. Because asymmetric information problems in the banking industry are a fact of life throughout the world, bank regulation in other countries is similar to that in the United States. It is particularly problematic to regulate banks engaged in international banking because they can readily shift their business from one country to another.

3. Because of financial innovation, deregulation, and a set of historical accidents, adverse selection and moral hazard problems increased in the 1980s and resulted in huge losses for the U.S. savings and loan industry and for taxpayers.

4. Regulators and politicians are subject to the principal-agent problem, meaning that they may not have sufficient incentives to minimize the costs of deposit insurance to taxpayers. As a result, regulators and politicians relaxed capital standards, removed restrictions on holdings of risky assets, and relied on regulatory forbearance, thereby increasing the costs of the S&L bailout.

5. The Financial Institutions Reform, Recovery, and Enforcement Act (FIRREA) of 1989 provided funds for the S&L bailout; created the Resolution Trust Corporation to manage the resolution of insolvent thrifts; eliminated the Federal Home Loan Bank Board and gave its regulatory role to the Office of Thrift Supervision; eliminated the FSLIC, whose insurance role and regulatory responsibilities were taken over by the FDIC; imposed restrictions on thrift activities similar to those in effect before 1982; increased the capital requirements to those adhered to by commercial banks; and increased the enforcement powers of thrift regulators.

6. The Federal Deposit Insurance Corporation Improvement Act (FDICIA) of 1991 recapitalized the Bank Insurance Fund of the FDIC and included reforms for the deposit insurance and regulatory system so that taxpayer losses would be minimized. This legislation limited brokered deposits and the use of the too-big-to-fail policy, mandated prompt corrective action to deal with troubled banks, and instituted risk-based deposit insurance premiums. These provisions have helped reduce the incentives of banks to take on excessive risk and so should help reduce taxpayer exposure in the future.

7. Proposals for reforming the banking regulatory system include elimination of deposit insurance, lower limits on the amount of deposit insurance, outright elimination of the too-big-to-fail policy, coinsurance, risk-based insurance premiums, regulatory consolidation, and market-value accounting for capital requirements.

8. The parallels between the banking crisis episodes that have occurred in countries throughout the world are striking, indicating that similar forces are at work.

KEY TERMS

bank failure, p. 297

bank supervision (prudential supervision), p. 302

brokered deposits, p. 313

coinsurance, p. 322

leverage ratio, p. 301

off-balance-sheet activities, p. 301

regulatory forbearance, p. 314

QUESTIONS AND PROBLEMS

1. Give one example each of moral hazard and adverse selection in private insurance arrangements.

*2. If casualty insurance companies provided fire insurance without any restrictions, what kind of adverse selection and moral hazard problems might result?

3. What bank regulation is designed to reduce adverse selection problems for deposit insurance? Will it always work?

*4. What bank regulations are designed to reduce moral hazard problems created by deposit insurance? Will they completely eliminate the moral hazard problem?

5. What are the costs and benefits of a too-big-to-fail policy?

*6. Why did the S&L crisis not occur until the 1980s?

7. Why is regulatory forbearance a dangerous strategy for a deposit insurance agency?

Chapter 13

NONBANK FINANCIAL INSTITUTIONS

PREVIEW   Although banks (depository institutions) may be the financial institutions we deal with most often, they are not the only financial institutions we come in contact with. Suppose that you purchase insurance from an insurance company, take out an installment loan on your new car from a finance company, or buy a share of common stock with the help of a broker. In each of these transactions, you are dealing with a nonbank financial institution. In our economy, nonbank financial institutions also play an important role in channeling funds from lender-savers to borrower-spenders. Furthermore, the process of financial innovation has increased the importance of nonbank financial institutions. Through innovation, nonbank financial institutions now compete more directly with banks by providing banklike services to their customers. This chapter examines in more detail how the major nonbank financial institutions operate, how they are regulated, and recent trends in the nonbank financial industry.

INSURANCE COMPANIES

Every day we face the possibility of the occurrence of certain catastrophic events that could lead to large financial losses. A spouse's earnings might disappear due to death or illness; a car accident might result in costly repair bills or payments to an injured party. Because financial losses from crises could be large relative to our financial resources, we protect ourselves against them by purchasing insurance coverage that will pay a sum of money if catastrophic events occur. Life insurance companies sell policies that provide income if a person dies, is incapacitated by illness, or retires. Property and casualty companies specialize in policies that pay for losses incurred as a result of accidents, fire, or theft.

Life Insurance Companies

The first life insurance company in the United States (Presbyterian Ministers' Fund in Philadelphia) was established in 1759 and is still in existence. There are currently about 2000 life insurance companies, which are organized in two forms: as stock companies or as mutuals. Stock companies are owned by stockholders; mutuals are technically owned by the policyholders. Although over 90 percent of life insurance companies are organized as stock companies, the largest ones (including Prudential Insurance Company and Metropolitan Life) are organized as mutuals; indeed, over half the assets in the industry are owned by mutual companies.

Life insurance companies have never experienced widespread failures like commercial banks and other depository institutions, so the federal government has not seen the need to regulate the industry. Instead, regulation is left to the states in which a company operates. State regulation is directed at sales practices, the provision of adequate liquid assets to cover losses, and restrictions on the amount of risky assets (such as common stock) that the companies can hold. The regulatory authority is typically a state insurance commissioner.

Because death rates for the population as a whole are predictable with a high degree of certainty, life insurance companies can accurately predict what their payouts to policyholders will be in the future. Consequently, they hold long-term assets that are not particularly liquid—corporate bonds and commercial mortgages as well as some corporate stock.

There are two principal forms of life insurance policies: permanent life insurance (such as whole, universal, and variable life) and temporary insurance (such as term). Permanent life insurance policies have a constant premium throughout the life of the policy. In the early years of the policy, the size of this premium exceeds the amount needed to insure against death because the probability of death is low. Thus the policy builds up a cash value in its early years, but in later years the cash value declines because the constant premium falls below the amount needed to insure against death, the probability of which is now higher. The policyholder can borrow against the cash value of the permanent life policy or can claim it by canceling the policy.

Term insurance, by contrast, has a premium that is matched every year to the amount needed to insure against death during the period of the term (such as one year or five years). As a result, term policies have premiums that rise over time as the probability of death rises (or level premiums with a decline in the amount of death benefits). Term policies have no cash value and thus, in contrast to permanent life policies, provide insurance only, with no savings aspect.

Weak investment returns on permanent life insurance in the 1960s and 1970s led to slow growth of demand for life insurance products. The result was a shrinkage in the size of the life insurance industry relative to other financial intermediaries, with their share of total financial intermediary assets falling from 19.6 percent at the end of 1960 to 11.5 percent at the end of 1980. (See Table 1, which shows the relative shares of financial intermediary assets for each of the financial intermediaries discussed in this chapter.)

Beginning in the mid-1970s, life insurance companies began to restructure their business to become managers of assets for pension funds. An important

TABLE 1   **Relative Shares of Total Financial Intermediary Assets, 1960–1996 (percent)**

	1960	1970	1980	1990	1996
Insurance Companies					
Life insurance	19.6	15.3	11.5	12.5	12.4
Property and casualty	4.4	3.8	4.5	4.9	4.5
Pension Funds					
Private	6.4	8.4	12.5	14.9	16.8
Public (state and local government)	3.3	4.6	4.9	6.7	9.6
Finance Companies	4.7	4.9	5.1	5.6	5.0
Mutual Funds					
Stock and bond	2.9	3.6	1.7	5.9	13.0
Money market	0.0	0.0	1.9	4.6	5.0
Depository Institutions (Banks)					
Commercial banks	38.6	38.5	36.7	30.4	26.1
S&L and mutual savings banks	19.0	19.4	19.6	12.5	5.8
Credit unions	1.1	1.4	1.6	2.0	1.8
Total	100.0	100.0	100.0	100.0	100.0

Source: Federal Reserve Flow of Funds Accounts.

factor behind this restructuring was 1974 legislation that encouraged pension funds to turn over fund management to life insurance companies. Now more than half of the assets managed by life insurance companies are for pension funds and not for life insurance. Insurance companies have also begun to sell investment vehicles for retirement such as **annuities,** arrangements whereby the customer pays an annual premium in exchange for a future stream of annual payments beginning at a set age, say, 65, and continuing until death. The result of this new business has been that the market share of life insurance companies as a percentage of total financial intermediary assets has increased since 1980.

Property and Casualty Insurance Companies

There are over 3000 property and casualty insurance companies in the United States, the two largest of which are State Farm and Allstate. Property and casualty companies are organized as both stock and mutual companies and are regulated by the states in which they operate.

Although property and casualty insurance companies have seen a slight increase in their share of total financial intermediary assets since 1960 (see Table 1), in recent years they have not fared well, and insurance rates have skyrocketed. With the high interest rates in the 1970s, insurance companies had high investment income that enabled them to keep insurance rates low. Since then, however, investment income has fallen with the decline in interest rates, while the growth in lawsuits involving property and casualty insurance and the explosion in amounts awarded in such cases have produced substantial losses for companies.

To return to profitability, insurance companies have raised their rates dramatically—sometimes doubling or even tripling premiums—and have refused to provide coverage for some people. They have also campaigned actively for limits on insurance payouts, particularly for medical malpractice. In the search for profits, insurance companies are also branching out into uncharted territory by insuring the payment of interest on municipal and corporate bonds and on mortgage-backed securities. One worry is that the insurance companies may be taking on excessive risk in order to boost their profits. One result of the concern about the health of the property and casualty insurance industry is that insurance regulators have proposed new rules that would impose risk-based capital requirements on these companies based on the riskiness of their assets and operations.

The investment policies of these companies are affected by two basic facts. First, because they are subject to federal income taxes, the largest share of their assets is held in tax-exempt municipal bonds. Second, because property losses are more uncertain than the death rate in a population, these insurers are less able to predict how much they will have to pay policyholders than life insurance companies are. Natural disasters such as the Los Angeles earthquake in 1994 or the two major hurricanes in 1992, Andrew and Iniki, that devastated parts of Florida and Hawaii, respectively, exposed the property and casualty insurance companies to billions of dollars of losses. Therefore, property and casualty insurance companies hold more liquid assets than life insurance companies; municipal bonds and U.S. government securities amount to over half their assets, and most of the remainder is held in corporate bonds and corporate stock.

Property and casualty insurance companies will insure against losses from almost any type of event, including fire, theft, negligence, malpractice, earthquakes, and automobile accidents. If a possible loss being insured is too large for any one firm, several firms may join together to write a policy in order to share the risk. The most famous risk-sharing operation is Lloyd's of London, an association in which different insurance companies can underwrite a fraction of an insurance policy. Lloyd's of London has claimed that it will insure against any contingency—for a price. Unfortunately, the problems in the insurance industry have not been restricted to the United States, and even the venerable Lloyd's of London has recently found itself in trouble (see Box 1).

The Competitive Threat from the Banking Industry

Until recently, banks have been restricted in their ability to sell life insurance products. This has been changing rapidly, however. Over two-thirds of the states allow banks to sell life insurance in one form or another. In recent years, the bank regulatory authorities, particularly the Office of the Comptroller of the Currency (OCC), have also encouraged banks to enter the insurance field because getting into insurance would help diversify banks' business, thereby improving their economic health and making bank failures less likely. For example, in 1990, the OCC ruled that selling annuities was a form of investment that was incidental to the

The Woes of Lloyd's of London

In June 1993, Lloyd's of London announced the biggest loss in its history, $4.33 billion for the year 1990 (Lloyd's waits three years to allow all claims to be processed before reporting profits or losses). The chairman of Lloyd's stated that the 1990 deficit "represents in every way the low point of Lloyd's history in the last 305 years."* Things continued to get worse for Lloyd's, with losses continuing until 1992, for a cumulative amount of more than $12 billion over the five-year period 1988–1992.

Lloyd's began in 1688 in a London coffeehouse owned by Edward Lloyd, which was a meeting place for merchants, shipowners, and sea captains. Lloyd's became a marketplace in which members, known as "names," trade pieces of insurance policies in order to spread the risk, a process called *reinsurance*. An unusual feature of Lloyd's is that names are directly exposed to losses because they accept unlimited personal liability for any claims they have to pay. Many of those participating in

Lloyd's have come to regret it in recent years, having lost their entire personal fortunes. Indeed, the average loss per name was over $150,000 in 1990. The losses at Lloyd's have also resulted in a slew of lawsuits, with members suing each other right and left over who should be responsible for paying claims.

To survive, the basic structure of Lloyd's has had to change. Lloyd's has opened itself up to corporate capital with only limited liability, has taken measures to lower central spending by the organization, and has altered the way it is governed. In 1996, Lloyd's was able to announce record profits for the year 1993. However, to settle its lawsuits, Lloyd's offered a $4.8 billion rescue package to its 34,000 names, including the creation of a new corporation called Equitas that took over Lloyd's liabilities incurred before 1993. A victim of the worldwide woes of the property and casualty insurance industry, Lloyd's of London, after three centuries, will never be the same.

*"Lloyd's of London Posts Big Loss, Raising Fears on Market's Viability," *Wall Street Journal*, June 23, 1993, p. A10.

banking business and so was a permissible banking activity. As a result, the banks' share of the annuities market has surpassed 20 percent. Currently, more than 40 percent of banks sell insurance products, and the number is expected to grow in the future.

Insurance companies and their agents have reacted to this competitive threat with both lawsuits and lobbying actions to block banks from entering the insurance business. Their efforts have been set back by several Supreme Court rulings that favored the banks. Particularly important was a ruling in favor of Barnett Bank in March 1996, which held that state laws to prevent banks from selling insurance can be superseded by federal rulings from banking regulators that allow banks to sell insurance. The decision gave banks a green light to further their insurance activities, and barring restrictive legislation from Congress, banks will continue to take insurance business away from the insurance companies in the future.

BOX 2

Are Independent Insurance Agents Going the Way of the Milkman?

Twenty years ago, most insurance was sold by independent insurance agents, small independent businessmen who acted as agents for insurance companies but were not employees of the insurance companies. Today, independent insurance agents are facing two competitive challenges that threaten their livelihood. First, new competitors such as banks have been entering the insurance field, taking away some of the independent agents' business. Second, new technology and ways of selling insurance are enabling insurance companies to bypass the independent agents. Insurance companies and banks have used mass-marketing techniques such as toll-free phone numbers and targeted mailings to sell insurance policies. Selling insurance has even

begun to enter cyberspace, with customers able to purchase insurance over the Internet. Just as technology and new merchandising techniques have all but eliminated the door-to-door milkman, independent insurance agents may be on their way out.

American International Group (AIG), a publicly traded company that is the largest seller of commercial insurance, recently jettisoned most of its agents. The result of these competitive forces is that independent insurance agents now sell less than one-third of personal insurance policies. Not surprisingly, independent insurance agents are not taking this lying down and have become very active lobbyists to keep competitors such as banks out of their business.

Competition from banks and other financial institutions is rapidly changing the way insurance is sold and is threatening the livelihood of independent insurance agents (see Box 2).

Insurance Management

Insurance companies, like banks, are in the financial intermediation business of transforming one type of asset into another for the public. Insurance companies use the premiums paid on policies to invest in assets such as bonds, stocks, mortgages, and other loans; the earnings from these assets are then used to pay out claims on the policies. In effect, insurance companies transform assets such as bonds, stocks, and loans into insurance policies that provide a set of services (for example, claim adjustments, savings plans, friendly insurance agents). If the insurance company's production process of asset transformation efficiently provides its customers with adequate insurance services at low cost and if it can earn high returns on its investments, it will make profits; if not, it will suffer losses.

In Chapter 10 the economic concepts of adverse selection and moral hazard allowed us to understand principles of bank management related to managing credit risk; many of these same principles also apply to the lending activities of insurance companies. Here again we apply the adverse selection and moral hazard concepts to explain many management practices specific to the insurance industry.

In the case of an insurance policy, moral hazard arises when the existence of insurance encourages the insured party to take risks that increase the likelihood of an insurance payoff. For example, a person covered by burglary insurance might not take as many precautions to prevent a burglary because the insurance company will reimburse most of the losses if a theft occurs. Adverse selection holds that the people most likely to receive large insurance payoffs are the ones who will want to purchase insurance the most. For example, a person suffering from a terminal disease would want to take out the biggest life and medical insurance policies possible, thereby exposing the insurance company to potentially large losses. Both adverse selection and moral hazard can result in large losses to insurance companies because they lead to higher payouts on insurance claims. Lowering adverse selection and moral hazard to reduce these payouts is therefore an extremely important goal for insurance companies, and this goal explains the insurance practices we will discuss here.

Screening

To reduce adverse selection, insurance companies try to screen out good insurance risks from poor ones. Effective information collection procedures are therefore an important principle of insurance management.

When you apply for auto insurance, the first thing your insurance agent does is ask you questions about your driving record (number of speeding tickets and accidents), the type of car you are insuring, and certain personal matters (age, marital status). If you are applying for life insurance, you go through a similar grilling, but you are asked even more personal questions about such things as your health, smoking habits, and drug and alcohol use. The life insurance company even orders a medical evaluation (usually done by an independent company) that involves taking blood and urine samples. Just as a bank calculates a credit score to evaluate a potential borrower, the insurance company uses the information you provide to allocate you to a risk class—a statistical estimate of how likely you are to have an insurance claim. Based on this information, the insurance company can decide whether to accept you for the insurance or to turn you down because you pose too high a risk and thus would be an unprofitable customer for the insurance company.

Risk-Based Premiums

Charging insurance premiums on the basis of how much risk a policyholder poses for the insurance company is a time-honored principle of insurance management. Adverse selection explains why this principle is so important to insurance company profitability.

To understand why an insurance company finds it necessary to have risk-based premiums, let's examine an example of risk-based insurance premiums that at first glance seems unfair. Harry and Sally, both college students with no accidents or speeding tickets, apply for auto insurance. Normally, Harry will be charged a much higher premium than Sally. Insurance companies do this because young males have a much higher accident rate than young females. Suppose, though, that one insurance company did not base its premiums on a risk classification but rather just charged a premium based on the average combined risk for males and females. Then Sally would be charged too much and Harry too little. Sally could go to another insurance company and get a lower rate, while Harry would sign up for the insurance. Because Harry's premium isn't high enough to cover the accidents he is likely to have, on average the company would lose money on Harry. Only with a premium based on a risk classification, so that Harry is charged more, can the insurance company make a profit.[1]

Restrictive Provisions

Restrictive provisions in policies are another insurance management tool for reducing moral hazard. Such provisions discourage policyholders from engaging in risky activities that make an insurance claim more likely. One type of restrictive provision keeps the policyholder from benefiting from behavior that makes a claim more likely. For example, life insurance companies have provisions in their policies that eliminate death benefits if the insured person commits suicide within the first two years that the policy is in effect. Restrictive provisions may also require certain behavior on the part of the insured that makes a claim less likely. A company renting motor scooters may be required to provide helmets for renters in order to be covered for any liability associated with the rental. The role of restrictive provisions is not unlike that of restrictive covenants on debt contracts described in Chapter 9: Both serve to reduce moral hazard by ruling out undesirable behavior.

Prevention of Fraud

Insurance companies also face moral hazard because an insured person has an incentive to lie to the company and seek a claim even if the claim is not valid. For example, a person who has not complied with the restrictive provisions of an insurance contract may still submit a claim. Even worse, a person may file claims for events that did not actually occur. Thus an important management principle for insurance companies is conducting investigations to prevent fraud so that only policyholders with valid claims receive compensation.

Cancellation of Insurance

Being prepared to cancel policies is another insurance management tool. Insurance companies can discourage moral hazard by threatening to cancel a policy when the insured person engages in activities that make a claim more likely. If your auto insurance company makes it clear that if a driver gets too many speeding tickets, coverage will be canceled, you will be less likely to speed.

Deductibles

The **deductible** is the fixed amount by which the insured's loss is reduced when a claim is paid off. A $250 deductible on an auto policy, for example, means that

---

[1]Note that the example here is in fact the lemons problem described in Chapter 9.

if you suffer a loss of $1000 because of an accident, the insurance company will pay you only $750. Deductibles are an additional management tool that helps insurance companies reduce moral hazard. With a deductible, you experience a loss along with the insurance company when you make a claim. Because you also stand to lose when you have an accident, you have an incentive to drive more carefully. A deductible thus makes a policyholder act more in line with what is profitable for the insurance company; moral hazard has been reduced. And because moral hazard has been reduced, the insurance company can lower the premium by more than enough to compensate the policyholder for the existence of the deductible.

Coinsurance

When a policyholder shares a percentage of the losses along with the insurance company, their arrangement is called *coinsurance*. For example, some medical insurance plans provide coverage for 80 percent of medical bills, and the insured person pays 20 percent after a certain deductible has been met. Coinsurance works to reduce moral hazard in exactly the same way that a deductible does. A policyholder who suffers a loss along with the insurance company has less incentive to take actions, such as going to the doctor unnecessarily, that involve higher claims. Coinsurance is thus another useful management tool for insurance companies.

Limits on the Amount of Insurance

Another important principle of insurance management is that there should be limits on the amount of insurance provided, even though a customer is willing to pay for more coverage. The higher the insurance coverage, the more the insured person can gain from risky activities that make an insurance payoff more likely and hence the greater the moral hazard. For example, if Zelda's car were insured for more than its true value, she might not take proper precautions to prevent its theft, such as making sure that the key is always removed or putting in an alarm system. If it were stolen, she comes out ahead because the excessive insurance payment would allow her to buy an even better car. By contrast, when the insurance payments are lower than the value of her car, she will suffer a loss if it is stolen and will thus take the proper precautions to prevent this from happening. Insurance companies must always make sure that their coverage is not so high that moral hazard leads to large losses.

Summary

Effective insurance management requires several practices: information collection and screening of potential policyholders, risk-based premiums, restrictive provisions, prevention of fraud, cancellation of insurance, deductibles, coinsurance, and limits on the amount of insurance. All of these practices reduce moral hazard and adverse selection by making it harder for policyholders to benefit from engaging in activities that increase the amount and likelihood of claims. With smaller benefits available, the poor insurance risks (those who are more likely to engage in the activities in the first place) see less benefit from the insurance and are thus less likely to seek it out.

PENSION FUNDS

In performing the financial intermediation function of asset transformation, pension funds provide the public with another kind of protection: income payments on retirement. Employers, unions, or private individuals can set up pension plans, which acquire funds through contributions paid in by the plan's participants. As we can see in Table 1, pension plans both public and private have grown in importance, with their share of total financial intermediary assets rising from 10 percent at the end of 1960 to 26 percent at the end of 1996. Federal tax policy has been a major factor behind the rapid growth of pension funds because employer contributions to employee pension plans are tax-deductible. Furthermore, tax policy has also encouraged employee contributions to pension funds by making them tax-deductible as well and enabling self-employed individuals to open up their own tax-sheltered pension plans, Keogh plans, and individual retirement accounts (IRAs).

Because the benefits paid out of the pension fund each year are highly predictable, pension funds invest in long-term securities, with the bulk of their asset holdings in bonds, stocks, and long-term mortgages. The key management issues for pension funds revolve around asset management: Pension fund managers try to hold assets with high expected returns and lower risk through diversification. They also use techniques we discussed in Chapter 10 to manage credit and interest-rate risk. The investment strategies of pension plans have changed radically over time. In the aftermath of World War II, most pension fund assets were held in government bonds, with less than 1 percent held in stock. However, the strong performance of stocks in the 1950s and 1960s afforded pension plans higher returns, causing them to shift their portfolios into stocks, currently on the order of 40 percent of their assets. As a result, pension plans now have a much stronger presence in the stock market: In the early 1950s, they held on the order of 1 percent of corporate stock outstanding, while currently they hold on the order of 25 percent. Pension funds are now the dominant players in the stock market.

Although the purpose of all pension plans is the same, they can differ in a number of attributes. First is the method by which payments are made: If the benefits are determined by the contributions into the plan and their earnings, the pension is a **defined-contribution plan;** if future income payments (benefits) are set in advance, the pension is a **defined-benefit plan.** In the case of a defined-benefit plan, a further attribute is related to how the plan is funded. A defined-benefit plan is **fully funded** if the contributions into the plan and their earnings over the years are sufficient to pay out the defined benefits when they come due. If the contributions and earnings are not sufficient, the plan is **underfunded.** For example, if Jane Brown contributes $100 per year into her pension plan and the interest rate is 10 percent, after ten years the contributions and their earnings would be worth $1753.[2] If the defined benefit on her pension plan pays her $1753

---

[2]The $100 contributed in year 1 would become worth $100 \times (1 + 0.10)^{10} = $259.37 at the end of ten years; the $100 contributed in year 2 would become worth $100 \times (1 + 0.10)^9 = $235.79; and so on until the $100 contributed in year 10 would become worth $100 \times (1 + 0.10) = $110. Adding these together, we get the total value of these contributions and their earnings at the end of ten years:

$$\$259.37 + \$235.79 + \$214.36 + \$194.87 + \$177.16$$
$$+ \$161.05 + \$146.41 + \$133.10 + \$121.00 + \$110.00 = \$1753.11$$

or less after ten years, the plan is fully funded because her contributions and earnings will fully pay for this payment. But if the defined benefit is $2000, the plan is underfunded because her contributions and earnings do not cover this amount.

A second characteristic of pension plans is their *vesting,* the length of time that a person must be enrolled in the pension plan (by being a member of a union or an employee of a company) before being entitled to receive benefits. Typically, firms require that an employee work five years for the company before being vested and qualifying to receive pension benefits; if the employee leaves the firm before the five years are up, either by quitting or being fired, all rights to benefits are lost.

Private Pension Plans

Private pension plans are administered by a bank, a life insurance company, or a pension fund manager. In employer-sponsored pension plans, contributions are usually shared between employer and employee. Many companies' pension plans are underfunded because they plan to meet their pension obligations out of current earnings when the benefits come due. As long as companies have sufficient earnings, underfunding creates no problems, but if not, they may not be able to meet their pension obligations. Because of potential problems caused by corporate underfunding, mismanagement, fraudulent practices, and other abuses of private pension funds (Teamsters pension funds are notorious), Congress enacted the Employee Retirement Income Security Act (ERISA) in 1974. This act established minimum standards for the reporting and disclosure of information, set rules for vesting and the degree of underfunding, placed restrictions on investment practices, and assigned the responsibility of regulatory oversight to the Department of Labor.

ERISA also created the Pension Benefit Guarantee Corporation (called "Penny Benny"), which performs a role similar to that of the FDIC. It insures pension benefits up to a limit (currently over $30,000 per year per person) if a company with an underfunded pension plan goes bankrupt or is unable to meet its pension obligations for other reasons. Penny Benny charges pension plans premiums to pay for this insurance, and it can also borrow funds up to $100 million from the U.S. Treasury. Unfortunately, the problem of pension plan underfunding has been growing worse in recent years. In 1993, the secretary of labor indicated that underfunding had reached levels in excess of $45 billion, with one company's pension plan alone, that of General Motors, underfunded to the tune of $11.8 billion. As a result, Penny Benny, which insures the pensions of one of every three workers, may have to foot the bill if companies with large underfunded pensions go broke.

Public Pension Plans

The most important public pension plan is Social Security (Old Age and Survivors' Insurance Fund), which covers virtually all individuals employed in the private sector. Funds are obtained from workers through Federal Insurance Contribution Act (FICA) deductions from their paychecks and from employers through payroll taxes. Social Security benefits include retirement income, Medicare payments, and aid to the disabled.

Will Social Security Be Privatized?

In recent years, public confidence in the Social Security system has reached a new low. Some surveys suggest that young people have more confidence in the existence of flying saucers than they do in the government's promise to pay them their Social Security benefits. Without some overhaul of the system, Social Security will not be able to meet its future obligations, prompting the Clinton administration to appoint a bipartisan advisory panel on Social Security headed by Edward Gramlich of the University of Michigan. In 1996, the panel proposed three possible options to reform the Social Security system, all involving some privatization. Currently, the assets of the Social Security system, which reside in a trust fund, are all invested in U.S. Treasury securities. However,

to generate higher returns for the trust fund so that the system can meet its obligations, all three proposals suggest investing part of the Social Security trust fund in corporate securities. In one plan, 40 percent of the Social Security trust funds would be invested in common stock, and the rest would be split between corporate and government bonds. The other two plans would allow individuals to take part of their Social Security taxes and invest them in individual retirement accounts.

It is not clear whether steps toward privatization of Social Security will be taken. However, Chile recently privatized its social security system, and the experiment has been deemed highly successful. Will the United States go where Chile has gone?

When Social Security was established in 1935, the federal government intended to operate it like a private pension fund. However, unlike a private pension plan, paid-out benefits are not tied closely to a participant's past contributions, so typically they are paid out from current contributions. This "pay as you go" system at one point led to a massive underfunding, estimated at over $1 trillion.

The problems of the Social Security system could become worse in the future because today's aging American population will lead to a higher number of retired people relative to the working population. Congress has been grappling with the problems of the Social Security system for years, but the prospect of a huge bulge in new retirees when the baby boomers start to retire in 2008 has resulted in calls for radical surgery on Social Security (see Box 3).

State and local governments and the federal government, like private employers, have also set up pension plans for their employees. These plans are almost identical in operation to private pension plans and hold similar assets. Underfunding of the plans is also prevalent, and some investors in municipal bonds worry that it may lead to future difficulties in the ability of state and local governments to meet their debt obligations.

FINANCE COMPANIES

Finance companies acquire funds by issuing commercial paper or stocks and bonds or borrowing from banks, and they use the proceeds to make loans (often for small amounts) that are particularly well suited to consumer and business needs. The financial intermediation process of finance companies can be described by saying that they borrow in large amounts but often lend in small amounts—a process quite different from that of banking institutions, which collect deposits in small amounts and then often make large loans.

A key feature of finance companies is that although they lend to many of the same customers that borrow from banks, they are virtually unregulated compared to commercial banks and thrift institutions. States regulate the maximum amount they can loan to individual consumers and the terms of the debt contract, but there are no restrictions on branching, the assets they hold, or how they raise their funds. The lack of restrictions enables finance companies to tailor their loans to customer needs better than banking institutions can.

As we can see in Table 1, while banking institutions have shrunk dramatically relative to other financial intermediaries, finance companies have held their own in the 1980s and 1990s. Finance companies have benefited from the rapid growth of the commercial paper market because it has given them access to a low-cost source of funds. This access has in turn given them competitive advantages over banks. (Chapter 11 explains in more detail why the commercial paper market has grown so rapidly and how this has benefited finance companies.) Although finance companies often have loans with higher default rates, they have been profitable because they are able to charge higher interest rates on these loans.

There are three types of finance companies: sales, consumer, and business.

1. Sales finance companies are owned by a particular retailing or manufacturing company and make loans to consumers to purchase items from that company. Sears, Roebuck Acceptance Corporation, for example, finances consumer purchases of all goods and services at Sears stores, and General Motors Acceptance Corporation finances purchases of GM cars. Sales finance companies compete directly with banks for consumer loans and are used by consumers because loans can frequently be obtained faster and more conveniently at the location where an item is purchased.

2. Consumer finance companies make loans to consumers to buy particular items such as furniture or home appliances, to make home improvements, or to help refinance small debts. Consumer finance companies are separate corporations (like Household Finance Corporation) or are owned by banks (Citicorp owns Person-to-Person Finance Company, which operates offices nationwide). Typically, these companies make loans to consumers who cannot obtain credit from other sources and charge higher interest rates.

3. Business finance companies provide specialized forms of credit to businesses by making loans and purchasing accounts receivable (bills owed to the firm) at a discount; this provision of credit is called *factoring*. For example, a dressmaking firm might have outstanding bills (accounts receivable) of $100,000 owed by the retail stores that have bought its dresses. If this firm needs cash to buy 100 new sewing machines, it can sell its accounts receivable for, say, $90,000 to a finance company, which is now entitled to collect the $100,000 owed to the firm. Besides factoring, business finance companies also specialize in leasing equipment (such as railroad cars, jet planes, and computers), which they purchase and then lease to businesses for a set number of years.

MUTUAL FUNDS

Mutual funds are financial intermediaries that pool the resources of many small investors by selling them shares and using the proceeds to buy securities. Through the asset transformation process of issuing shares in small denominations and buying large blocks of securities, mutual funds can take advantage of volume discounts on brokerage commissions and purchase diversified holdings (portfolios) of securities. Mutual funds allow the small investor to obtain the benefits of lower transaction costs in purchasing securities and to take advantage of the reduction of risk by diversifying the portfolio of securities held.

Mutual funds have seen a large increase in their market share since 1980 (see Table 1), due primarily to the booming stock market. Another source of growth has been mutual funds that specialize in debt instruments, which first appeared in the 1970s. Before 1970, mutual funds invested almost solely in common stocks. Funds that purchase common stocks may specialize even further and invest solely in foreign securities or in specialized industries, such as energy or high technology. Funds that purchase debt instruments may specialize further in corporate, U.S. government, or tax-exempt municipal bonds or in long-term or short-term securities.[3]

Mutual funds are structured in two ways. The more common structure is an **open-end fund,** from which shares can be redeemed at any time at a price that is tied to the asset value of the fund. Mutual funds also can be structured as a **closed-end fund,** in which a fixed number of nonredeemable shares are sold at an initial offering and are then traded in the over-the-counter market like a common stock. The market price of these shares fluctuates with the value of the assets held by the fund. In contrast to the open-end fund, however, the price of the shares may be above or below the value of the assets held by the fund, depending on factors such as the liquidity of the shares or the quality of the management. The greater popularity of the open-end funds is explained by the greater liquidity of their redeemable shares relative to the nonredeemable shares of closed-end funds.

Originally, shares of most open-end mutual funds were sold by salespeople (usually brokers) who were paid a commission. Since this commission is paid at the time of purchase and is immediately subtracted from the redemption value of the shares, these funds are called **load funds.** Most mutual funds are currently **no-load funds;** they are sold directly to the public with no sales commissions. In both types of funds, the managers earn their living from management fees paid by the shareholders. These fees amount to approximately 0.5 percent of the asset value of the fund per year.

Mutual funds are regulated by the Securities and Exchange Commission, which was given the ability to exercise almost complete control over investment companies in the Investment Company Act of 1940. Regulations require periodic disclosure of information on these funds to the public and restrictions on the methods of soliciting business.

---

[3]Tax-exempt bond funds did not appear until after 1976, when a change in the tax law allowed mutual funds to pass through to shareholders the tax exemption on the interest income from municipal bonds.

Money Market Mutual Funds

An important addition to the family of mutual funds resulting from the financial innovation process described in earlier chapters is the money market mutual fund. Recall that this type of mutual fund invests in short-term debt (money market) instruments of very high quality, such as Treasury bills, commercial paper, and bank certificates of deposit. There is some fluctuation in the market value of these securities, but because their maturity is typically less than six months, the change in the market value is small enough that these funds allow their shares to be redeemed at a fixed value. (Changes in the market value of the securities are figured into the interest paid out by the fund.) Because these shares can be redeemed at a fixed value, the funds allow shareholders to redeem shares by writing checks above some minimum amount (usually $500) on the fund's account at a commercial bank. In this way, shares in money market mutual funds effectively function as checkable deposits that earn market interest rates on short-term debt securities.

In 1977, the assets in money market mutual funds were less than $4 billion; by 1980, they had climbed to over $50 billion and now stand at $900 billion, with a share of financial intermediary assets that has grown to 5 percent (see Table 1). Currently, money market mutual funds account for around one-quarter of the asset value of all mutual funds.

GOVERNMENT FINANCIAL INTERMEDIATION

The government has become involved in financial intermediation in two basic ways: first, by setting up federal credit agencies that directly engage in financial intermediation and, second, by supplying government guarantees for private loans.

Federal Credit Agencies

To promote residential housing, the government has created three government agencies that provide funds to the mortgage market by selling bonds and using the proceeds to buy mortgages: the Government National Mortgage Association (GNMA, or "Ginnie Mae"), Fannie Mae, and Freddie Mac. Except for Ginnie Mae, which is a federal agency and is thus an entity of the U.S. government, the other agencies are federally sponsored agencies that function as private corporations with close ties to the government. As a result, the debt of sponsored agencies is not explicitly backed by the U.S. government, as is the case for Treasury bonds. As a practical matter, however, it is unlikely that the federal government would allow a default on the debt of these sponsored agencies.

Agriculture is another area in which financial intermediation by government agencies plays an important role. The Farm Credit System (composed of Banks for Cooperatives, Farm Credit banks, and various farm credit associations) issues securities and then uses the proceeds to make loans to farmers.

Students also benefit from government financial intermediation. The Student Loan Marketing Association (called "Sallie Mae") provides funds for higher education primarily by purchasing student loans granted by private financial institutions under the Guaranteed Student Loan Program.

In recent years, government financial intermediaries have been experiencing financial difficulties. The Farm Credit System is one example. The rising tide of farm bankruptcies meant losses in the billions of dollars for the Farm Credit System, and as a result it required a bailout from the federal government in 1987. The agency was authorized to borrow up to $4 billion to be repaid over a 15-year period and to date has received over $1 billion in assistance. Sallie Mae has also experienced losses on some of its loan portfolio. There is growing concern in Washington about the health of the federal credit agencies. To head off government bailouts like that for the Farm Credit System, the Federal Credit Reform Act of 1990 set new rules that require such agencies to increase their capital to provide a greater cushion to offset any potential losses.

Government Loan Guarantees: Another Crisis Waiting to Happen?

Another important government role in promoting financial intermediation has been the provision of government loan guarantees. A government loan guarantee acts just like insurance: It insures the lender, say, a bank, from any loss if the borrower defaults. In the housing market, government loan guarantees are provided by the Federal Housing Administration (FHA), the Veterans Administration (VA), and the Department of Housing and Urban Development (HUD). The Education Department guarantees student loans, and the Farmer's Home Administration guarantees loans to farmers.

Government loan guarantees have been growing at a rapid rate, increasing more than tenfold in the past 20 years, and now exceed $1 trillion. They have been particularly attractive to Congress because they subsidize activities that our politicians believe in, like going to college and owning a home, and yet do not involve any direct expenditure on the part of the government. An important economic principle that you hear all the time is "You don't get something for nothing," and this is just as true for the government. The problem with government loan guarantees is the same as that with government deposit insurance: Both are insurance schemes that create moral hazard problems that result in losses to the government. Because banks and other institutions making the loans don't suffer any losses if the loans default, they have little incentive to be careful to whom they make their loans.

The resulting lax lending practices can cause substantial losses for the government agencies that provide the loan guarantees. Notorious is the nearly one-in-three default rate on government-guaranteed loans for students in trade schools. The costs of loan guarantees have recently been hitting the government hard. In 1990, the General Accounting Office startled Congress by predicting that losses on government loan guarantees could end up exceeding $100 billion. The Federal Credit Reform Act of 1990 has required that agencies issuing these guarantees make provisions for anticipated losses in their credit programs, which in 1995 were between $180 billion and $300 billion. An additional problem is that the government bureaucracy to screen and monitor these loans has been shrinking, potentially making the adverse selection and moral hazard problems worse for these loans (see Box 4). Unless the government does a good job of coping with the adverse selection and moral hazard problems inherent in their loan guarantees, taxpayers may be hit with another costly bailout of the same magnitude as that required for the savings and loan industry.

BOX 4

The Downside of Government Downsizing

Owing to increasing public concern about "big government," government downsizing has become an increasingly popular political agenda. But is government downsizing always a good thing?

Beginning with the Reagan administration, there have been cuts in the number of auditors, inspectors, and regulators that oversee federal loan guarantees. This process has continued with the Clinton administration's plan to "reinvent government," one result being a cut in the staff of the General Accounting Office (GAO), the auditing agency of the federal government, by around 30 percent in the 1992–1996 period. Although less government is often desirable, it has a hidden downside. Recent audits by the GAO have found that there are currently too few financial systems

and managers in place to provide adequate screening and monitoring of the loans that the federal government has been guaranteeing—and yet the rapid expansion in loan guarantees will require even more monitoring in the future. We have already seen in the savings and loan bailout of 1989 what can happen when the resources to control adverse selection and moral hazard problems arising from a government insurance guarantee are inadequate: Recall that one reason for high costs in the S&L bailout was the inadequate resources provided to the FSLIC to examine the insured S&L institutions. Thus the push to downsize government may have the unintended consequence of costing taxpayers money by leading to large losses on loans that have received government loan guarantees.

SECURITIES MARKET INSTITUTIONS

The smooth functioning of securities markets, in which bonds and stocks are traded, involves several financial institutions, including securities brokers and dealers, investment banks, and organized exchanges. None of these institutions were included in our list of financial intermediaries because they do not perform the intermediation function of acquiring funds by issuing liabilities and then using the funds to acquire financial assets. Nonetheless, they are important in the process of channeling funds from savers to spenders.

First, however, we must recall the distinction between primary and secondary securities markets discussed in Chapter 2. In a primary market, new issues of a security are sold to buyers by the corporation or government agency borrowing the funds. A secondary market then trades the securities that have been sold in the primary market (and so are secondhand). *Investment banks* assist in the initial sale of securities in the primary market; *securities brokers* and *dealers* assist in the trading of securities in the secondary markets, some of which are organized into exchanges.

Investment Banks

When a corporation wishes to borrow (raise) funds, it normally hires the services of an investment bank to help sell its securities. (Despite its name, an investment bank is not a bank in the ordinary sense; that is, it is not a financial intermediary that takes in deposits and then lends them out.) Some of the well-known U.S.

BOX 5

America Is Number One—at Least in Investment Banking

In contrast to the American commercial banking industry, which as we have seen in Chapter 11 has come under increasing competitive pressure from foreigners, the American investment banks have been fending off the foreign challenge and have emerged on top in the global finance field. Seven of the top ten investment banks in the world are American, and two of the others are partly American-owned. Furthermore, the top four global underwriters in the 1992–1995 period were American firms, with Goldman, Sachs & Co. at the top of the heap in 1995. Not only have the American firms been dominant in the U.S. market, but they have been just as successful in underwriting securities abroad. The competitive environment of U.S. financial markets has prepared them to excel in arranging huge loans abroad, underwriting foreign securities, and negotiating multinational mergers. American investment banking firms are recognized for making use of the latest technology and being the most innovative; that image alone explains much of their ascent to the number one position in global finance.

investment banking firms are Morgan Stanley, Merrill Lynch, Salomon Brothers, First Boston Corporation, and Goldman, Sachs, which have been very successful not only in the United States but outside it as well (see Box 5).

Investment bankers assist in the sale of securities as follows. First, they advise the corporation on whether it should issue bonds or stock. If they suggest that the corporation issue bonds, investment bankers give advice on what the maturity and interest payments on the bonds should be. When the corporation decides which kind of financial instrument it will issue, it offers them to **underwriters**—investment banks that guarantee the corporation a price on the securities and then sell them to the public. If the issue is small, only one investment bank underwrites it (usually the original investment banking firm hired to provide advice on the issue). If the issue is large, several investment banking firms form a syndicate to underwrite the issue jointly, thus limiting the risk that any one investment bank must take. The underwriters sell the securities to the general public by contacting potential buyers, such as banks and insurance companies, directly and by placing advertisements in newspapers like the *Wall Street Journal* (see the "Following the Financial News" box).

The activities of investment banks and the operation of primary markets are heavily regulated by the Securities and Exchange Commission (SEC), which was created by the Securities and Exchange Acts of 1933 and 1934 to ensure that adequate information reaches prospective investors. Issuers of new securities to the general public (for amounts greater than $1.5 million in a year with a maturity longer than 270 days) must file a registration statement with the SEC and must provide to potential investors a prospectus containing all relevant information on the securities. The issuer must then wait 20 days after the registration statement is filed with the SEC before it can sell any of the securities. If the SEC does not object during the 20-day waiting period, the securities can be sold.

Following the Financial News

New Securities Issues

Information about new securities being issued is presented in distinctive advertisements published in the *Wall Street Journal* and other newspapers. These advertisements, called "tombstones" because of their appearance, are typically found in the "Money and Investing" section of the *Wall Street Journal*.

The tombstone indicates the number of shares of stock being issued (3.2 million shares for Safeskin Corporation) and the investment banks involved in selling them. Three of the most important investment banks (listed in the middle of the advertisement) are involved in underwriting these securities as well as many others.

Source: Wall Street Journal, February 4, 1997, p. C22.

This announcement constitutes neither an offer to sell nor a solicitation of an offer to buy these securities. The offering is made only by the Prospectus, copies of which may be obtained in any State from such of the undersigned and others as may lawfully offer these securities in such State.

February 4, 1997

3,200,000 Shares

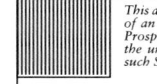

SAFESKIN®

Common Stock

Price $23.25 per Share

Smith Barney Inc.

Donaldson, Lufkin & Jenrette
Securities Corporation

Merrill Lynch & Co.

Bear, Stearns & Co. Inc.	Alex. Brown & Sons Incorporated	Dean Witter Reynolds Inc.
A.G. Edwards & Sons, Inc.	Goldman, Sachs & Co.	Montgomery Securities
Salomon Brothers Inc	Wasserstein Perella Securities, Inc.	The Seidler Companies Incorporated
Branch, Cabell & Co.	Chatsworth Securities, LLC	Cleary Gull Reiland & McDevitt Inc.
D. A. Davidson & Co.	Dominick & Dominick Incorporated	Madison Securities, Inc.
Morgan Keegan & Company, Inc.		Olde Discount Corporation
The Robinson-Humphrey Company, Inc.		Scott & Stringfellow, Inc.
Southeast Research Partners, Inc.	Tucker Anthony Incorporated	Van Kasper & Company

---

Securities Brokers and Dealers

Securities brokers and dealers conduct trading in secondary markets. Brokers are pure middlemen who act as agents for investors in the purchase or sale of securities. Their function is to match buyers with sellers, a function for which they are paid brokerage commissions. In contrast to brokers, dealers link buyers and sellers by standing ready to buy and sell securities at given prices. Therefore, dealers hold inventories of securities and make their living by selling these securities for a slightly higher price than they paid for them—that is, on the "spread" between the asked price and the bid price. This can be a high-risk business because dealers hold securities that can rise or fall in price; in recent years, several firms specializing in bonds have collapsed. Brokers, by contrast, are not as exposed to risk because they do not own the securities involved in their business dealings.

Brokerage firms engage in all three securities market activities, acting as brokers, dealers, and investment bankers. The largest in the United States is Merrill Lynch; other well-known ones are PaineWebber, Dean Witter Reynolds, and Smith Barney. The SEC not only regulates the investment banking operation of the firms but also restricts brokers and dealers from misrepresenting securities and from trading on *insider information,* nonpublic information known only to the management of a corporation.

The forces of competition led to an important development: Brokerage firms started to engage in activities traditionally conducted by commercial banks. In 1977, Merrill Lynch developed the cash management account (CMA), which provides a package of financial services that includes credit cards, immediate loans, check-writing privileges, automatic investment of proceeds from the sale of securities into a money market mutual fund, and unified record keeping. CMAs were adopted by other brokerage firms and spread rapidly. The result is that the distinction between banking activities and the activities of nonbank financial institutions has become blurred. Walter Wriston, former head of Citicorp (the largest bank holding company in the country), has been quoted as saying, "The bank of the future already exists, and it's called Merrill Lynch."[4]

Organized Exchanges

As discussed in Chapter 2, secondary markets can be organized either as over-the-counter markets, in which trades are conducted using dealers, or as organized exchanges, in which trades are conducted in one central location. The New York Stock Exchange (NYSE), trading thousands of securities, is the largest organized exchange in the world, and the American Stock Exchange (AMEX) is a distant second. A number of smaller regional exchanges, which trade only a small number of securities (under 100), exist in places such as Boston and Los Angeles.

Organized stock exchanges actually function as a hybrid of an auction market (in which buyers and sellers trade with each other in a central location) and a dealer market (in which dealers make the market by buying and selling securities at given prices). Securities are traded on the floor of the exchange with the help of a special kind of dealer-broker called a **specialist.** A specialist matches buy and sell orders submitted at the same price and so performs a brokerage function. However, if buy and sell orders do not match up, the specialist buys stocks or sells from a personal inventory of securities, in this manner performing a dealer function. By assuming both functions, the specialist maintains orderly trading of the securities for which he or she is responsible.

Organized exchanges in which securities are traded are also regulated by the SEC. Not only does the SEC have the authority to impose regulations that govern the behavior of brokers and dealers involved with exchanges, but it also has the authority to alter the rules set by exchanges. In 1975, for example, the SEC disallowed rules that set minimum brokerage commission rates. The result was a sharp drop in brokerage commission rates, especially for institutional investors (mutual funds and pension funds), which purchase large blocks of stock. The Securities

---

[4]"Banking Takes a Beating," *Time,* December 3, 1984, p. 50.

Amendments Act of 1975 confirmed the SEC's action by outlawing the setting of minimum brokerage commissions.

Furthermore, the Securities Amendments Act directed the SEC to facilitate a national market system that consolidates trading of all securities listed on the national and regional exchanges as well as those traded in the over-the-counter market using the National Association of Securities Dealers' automated quotation system (NASDAQ). Computers and advanced telecommunications, which reduce the costs of linking these markets, have encouraged the expansion of a national market system. We thus see that legislation and modern computer technology are leading the way to a more competitive securities industry.

The growing internationalization of capital markets has encouraged another trend in securities trading. Increasingly, foreign companies are being listed on U.S. stock exchanges, and the markets are moving toward trading stocks internationally, 24 hours a day.

S U M M A R Y

1. Insurance companies, which are regulated by the states, acquire funds by selling policies that pay out benefits if catastrophic events occur. Property and casualty insurance companies hold more liquid assets than life insurance companies because of greater uncertainty regarding the benefits they will have to pay out. All insurance companies face moral hazard and adverse selection problems that explain the use of insurance management tools, such as information collection and screening of potential policyholders, risk-based premiums, restrictive provisions, prevention of fraud, cancellation of insurance, deductibles, coinsurance, and limits on the amount of insurance.

2. Pension plans provide income payments to people when they retire after contributing to the plans for many years. Pension funds have experienced very rapid growth as a result of encouragement by federal tax policy and now play an important role in the stock market. Many pension plans are underfunded, which means that in future years they will have to pay out higher benefits than the value of their contributions and earnings. The problem of underfunding is especially acute for public pension plans such as Social Security. To prevent abuses, Congress enacted the Employee Retirement Income Security Act (ERISA), which established minimum standards for reporting, vesting, and degree of underfunding of private pension plans. This act also created the Pension Benefit Guarantee Corporation, which insures pension benefits.

3. Finance companies raise funds by issuing commercial paper and stocks and bonds and use the proceeds to make loans that are particularly suited to consumer and business needs. Virtually unregulated in comparison to commercial banks and thrift institutions, finance companies have been able to tailor their loans to customer needs very quickly and have grown rapidly.

4. Mutual funds sell shares and use the proceeds to buy securities. Open-end funds issue shares that can be redeemed at any time at a price tied to the asset value of the firm. Closed-end funds issue nonredeemable shares, which are traded like common stock. They are less popular than open-end funds because their shares are not as liquid. Money market mutual funds hold only short-term, high-quality securities, allowing shares to be redeemed at a fixed value using checks. Shares in these funds effectively function as checkable deposits that earn market interest rates. All mutual funds are regulated by the Securities and Exchange Commission (SEC).

5. Investment banks are firms that assist in the initial sale of securities in primary markets, whereas securities brokers and dealers assist in the trading of securities in the secondary markets, some of which are organized into exchanges. The SEC regulates the financial institutions in the securities markets and ensures that adequate information reaches prospective investors.

KEY TERMS

annuities, p. 334

brokerage firms, p. 351

closed-end fund, p. 345

deductible, p. 339

defined-benefit plan, p. 341

defined-contribution plan, p. 341

fully funded, p. 341

load funds, p. 345

no-load funds, p. 345

open-end fund, p. 345

specialist, p. 351

underfunded, p. 341

underwriters, p. 349

QUESTIONS AND PROBLEMS

*1. If death rates were to become less predictable than they are, how would life insurance companies change the types of assets they hold?

2. Why do property and casualty insurance companies have large holdings of municipal bonds while life insurance companies do not?

*3. Why are all defined contribution pension plans fully funded?

4. How can favorable tax treatment of pension plans encourage saving?

*5. "In contrast to private pension plans, government pension plans are rarely underfunded." Is this statement true, false, or uncertain? Explain your answer.

6. What explains the widespread use of deductibles in insurance policies?

*7. Why might insurance companies restrict the amount of insurance a policyholder can buy?

8. Why are restrictive provisions a necessary part of insurance policies?

*9. If you needed to take out a loan, why might you first go to your local bank rather than to a finance company?

10. Explain why shares in closed-end mutual funds typically sell for less than the market value of the stocks they hold.

*11. Why might you buy a no-load mutual fund instead of a load fund?

12. Why can a money market mutual fund allow its shareholders to redeem shares at a fixed price while other mutual funds cannot?

*13. Why might government loan guarantees be a high-cost way for the government to subsidize certain activities?

14. If you like to take risks, would you rather be a dealer, a broker, or a specialist? Why?

*15. Is investment banking a good career for someone who is afraid of taking risks? Why or why not?

Chapter 14

FINANCIAL DERIVATIVES

P R E V I E W Starting in the 1970s and increasingly in the 1980s and 1990s, the world became a riskier place for the financial institutions described in this part of the book. Swings in interest rates widened, and the bond and stock markets went through some episodes of increased volatility. As a result of these developments, managers of financial institutions have become more concerned with reducing the risk their institutions face. Given the greater demand for risk reduction, the process of financial innovation described in Chapter 10 came to the rescue by producing new financial instruments that help financial institution managers manage risk better. These instruments, called **financial derivatives,** have payoffs that are linked to previously issued securities and are extremely useful risk reduction tools.

In this chapter we look at the most important financial derivatives that managers of financial institutions use to reduce risk: forward contracts, financial futures, options, and swaps. We examine not only how markets for each of these financial derivatives work but also how they can be used by financial institutions to manage risk. We also study financial derivatives because they have become an important source of profits for financial institutions, particularly larger banks, who, as we saw in Chapter 11, have found their traditional business declining.

FORWARD MARKETS

Forward contracts are agreements by two parties to engage in a financial transaction at a future (forward) point in time. Here we focus on forward contracts that are linked to debt instruments, called **interest-rate forward contracts;** later in the chapter we discuss forward contracts for foreign currencies.

Interest-Rate Forward Contracts Interest-rate forward contracts involve the future sale of a debt instrument and have several dimensions: (1) specification of the actual debt instrument that will be delivered at a future date, (2) amount of the debt instrument to be delivered,

(3) price (interest rate) on the debt instrument when it is delivered, and (4) date on which delivery will take place. An example of an interest-rate forward contract might be an agreement for the First National Bank to sell to the Rock Solid Insurance Company, one year from today, $5 million face value of the 8s of 2015 Treasury bonds (coupon bonds with an 8 percent coupon rate that mature in 2015) at a price that yields the same interest rate on these bonds as today's, say, 8 percent. Because Rock Solid will buy the securities at a future date, it is said to have taken a **long position,** while the First National Bank, which will sell the securities, is said to have taken a **short position.**

Hedging with Interest-Rate Forward Contracts

Why would the First National Bank want to enter into this forward contract with Rock Solid Insurance Company in the first place?

The reason is that the First National Bank is able to **hedge** (protect itself) against interest-rate risk in case it wants to sell the bonds before they mature. For its part, the First National Bank, which is currently holding the $5 million of the 8s of 2015, may worry that if interest rates rise in the future, the price of these bonds will fall and expose it to a capital loss if they are sold. When it enters into the forward contract, it locks in the future price and so also eliminates the price risk it faces from interest-rate changes. We thus see that interest-rate forward contracts can allow financial institution managers to reduce (hedge against) interest-rate risk.

Why would the Rock Solid Insurance Company want to enter into the futures contract with the First National Bank? Rock Solid expects to receive premiums of $5 million in one year's time that it will want to invest in the 8s of 2015 but worries that interest rates on these bonds will decline between now and next year. By using the forward contract, it is able to lock in the 8 percent interest rate on the Treasury bonds (which will be sold to it by the First National Bank). (A)

Pros and Cons of Forward Contracts

The advantage of forward contracts is that they can be as flexible as the parties involved want them to be. This means that an institution like the First National Bank may be able to hedge completely the interest-rate risk for the exact security it is holding in its portfolio, just as it has in our example.

However, forward contracts suffer from two problems that severely limit their usefulness. The first is that it may be very hard for an institution like the First National Bank to find another party (called a *counterparty*) to make the contract with. There are brokers to facilitate the matching up of parties like the First National Bank with the Rock Solid Insurance Company, but there may be few institutions that want to engage in a forward contract specifically for the 8s of 2015. This means that it may prove impossible to find a counterparty when a financial institution like the First National Bank wants to make a specific type of forward contract. Furthermore, even if the First National Bank finds a counterparty, it may have to sell for a price lower than it thinks it should for the bonds it wants to sell because there may not be anyone else to make the deal with. A serious problem for the market in interest-rate forward contracts, then, is that it may be difficult to make the financial transaction or that it will have to be made at a disadvantageous price; in the parlance of financial economists, this market suffers from a *lack of liquidity*. (Note that this use of the term *liquidity* when it is applied to a market is somewhat broader than its use when it is applied to an asset. For an asset, liquidity refers to the ease with which the asset can be turned into cash, whereas for a market, liquidity refers to the ease of carrying out financial transactions.)

The second problem with forward contracts is that they are subject to default risk. Suppose that in one year's time, interest rates rise so that the price of the 8s of 2015 falls. The Rock Solid Insurance Company might then decide that it would like to default on the forward contract with the First National Bank because it can now buy the bonds at a price lower than the agreed price in the forward contract. Or perhaps Rock Solid may not have been rock solid and will have gone bust during the year and so is no longer available to complete the terms of the forward contract. Because there is no outside organization guaranteeing the contract, the only recourse is for the First National Bank to go to the courts to sue Rock Solid, but this process will be costly. Furthermore, if Rock Solid is already bankrupt, the First National Bank will suffer a loss; the bank can no longer sell the 8s of 2015 at the price it had agreed with Rock Solid but instead will have to sell at a price well below that because the price of these bonds has fallen.

The presence of default risk in forward contracts means that parties to these contracts must check each other out to be sure that the counterparty is both financially sound and likely to be honest and live up to its contractual obligations. Because this is a costly process and because all the adverse selection and moral hazard problems discussed in earlier chapters apply, default risk is a major barrier to the use of interest-rate forward contracts. When the default risk problem is combined with a lack of liquidity, we see that these contracts may be of limited usefulness to financial institutions. Although there is a market for interest-rate forward contracts, particularly in Treasury and mortgage-backed securities, it is not nearly as large as the financial futures market, to which we turn next.

FINANCIAL FUTURES MARKETS

Given the default risk and liquidity problems in the interest-rate forward market, another solution to hedging interest-rate risk was needed. This solution was provided by the development of financial futures contracts by the Chicago Board of Trade starting in 1975.

Financial Futures Contracts

A **financial futures contract** is similar to an interest-rate forward contract in that it specifies that a debt instrument must be delivered by one party to another on a stated future date. However, it differs from an interest-rate forward contract in sev-

Following the Financial News

Financial Futures

The prices for financial futures contracts are published daily. In the *Wall Street Journal,* these prices are found in the "Commodities" section under the "Interest Rate" heading of the "Future Prices" columns. An excerpt is reproduced here.

Interest Rate

TREASURY BONDS (CBT)-$100,000; PTS. 32NDS OF 100%.

	Open	High	Low	Settle	Change	Lifetime High	Lifetime Low	Open Interest
Mar	110-07	110-24	110-04	110-18	+ 10	120-00	99-26	493,083
June	109-24	110-07	109-21	110-02	+ 10	118-21	99-16	32,303
Sept	109-11	109-20	109-11	109-20	+ 10	117-21	100-18	5,821
Dec	108-26	109-06	108-26	109-06	+ 10	118-08	100-08	4,439

Est vol 475,000; vol Wed 560,366; open int 535,705, + 10,484.

Information for each contract is presented in columns, as follows. (The Chicago Board of Trade's contract for delivery of long-term Treasury bonds in March 1997 is used as an example.)

Open: Opening price; each point corresponds to $1000 of face value—110 7/32 is $110,219 for the March contract

High: Highest traded price that day—110 24/32 is $110,750 for the March contract

Low: Lowest traded price that day—110 4/32 is $110,125 for the March contract

Settle: Settlement price, the closing price that day—110 18/32 is $110,523 for the March contract

Chg: Change in the settlement price from the previous trading day— + 10/32 is +$313 for the March contract

Lifetime High: Highest price ever—120 is $120,000 for the March contract

Lifetime Low: Lowest price ever—99 26/32 is $99,813 for the March contract

Open Interest: Number of contracts outstanding—493,083 for the March contract, with a face value of $49 billion (493,083 × $100,000)

Source: Wall Street Journal, January 31, 1997, p. C14.

eral ways that overcome some of the liquidity and default problems of forward markets.

To understand what financial futures contracts are all about, let's look at one of the most widely traded futures contracts, that for Treasury bonds, which are traded on the Chicago Board of Trade. (An illustration of how prices on these contracts are quoted can be found in the "Following the Financial News" box.) The contract value is for $100,000 face value of bonds. Prices are quoted in points, with each point equal to $1000, and the smallest change in price is one thirty-second of a point ($31.25). This contract specifies that the bonds to be delivered must have at least 15 years to maturity at the delivery date (and must also not be callable, that is, redeemable by the Treasury at its option, in less than 15 years). If the Treasury bonds delivered to settle the futures contract have a coupon rate different from the 8 percent specified in the futures contract, the amount of bonds to be delivered is adjusted to reflect the difference in value between the delivered bonds and the 8 percent coupon bond. In line with the terminology used for forward contracts, parties who have bought a futures contract and thereby agreed to buy (take delivery of) the bonds are said to have taken a *long position,* and parties who have sold a futures contract and thereby agreed to sell (deliver) the bonds have taken a *short position.*

To make our understanding of this contract more concrete, let's consider what happens when you buy or sell one of these Treasury bond futures contracts. Let's say that on February 1, you sell one $100,000 June contract at a price of 115 (that is, $115,000). By selling this contract, you agree to deliver $100,000 face value of the long-term Treasury bonds to the contract's counterparty at the end of June for $115,000. By buying the contract at a price of 115, the buyer has agreed to pay $115,000 for the $100,000 face value of bonds when you deliver them at the end of June. If interest rates on long-term bonds rise so that when the contract matures at the end of June the price of these bonds has fallen to 110 ($110,000 per $100,000 of face value), the buyer of the contract will have lost $5000 because he or she paid $115,000 for the bonds but can sell them only for the market price of $110,000. But you, the seller of the contract, will have gained $5000 because you can now sell the bonds to the buyer for $115,000 but have to pay only $110,000 for them in the market.

It is even easier to describe what happens to the parties who have purchased futures contracts and those who have sold futures contracts if we recognize the following fact: ***At the expiration date of a futures contract, the price of the contract is the same as the price of the underlying asset to be delivered.*** To see why this is the case, consider what happens on the expiration date of the June contract at the end of June when the price of the underlying $100,000-face-value Treasury bond is 110 ($110,000). If the futures contract is selling below 110, say, at 109, a trader can buy the contract for $109,000, take delivery of the bond, and immediately sell it for $110,000, thereby earning a quick profit of $1000. Because earning this profit involves no risk, it is a great deal that everyone would like to get in on. That means that everyone will try to buy the contract, and as a result, its price will rise. Only when the price rises to 110 will the profit opportunity cease to exist and the buying pressure disappear. Conversely, if the price of the futures contract is above 110, say, at 111, everyone will want to sell the contract. Now the sellers get $111,000 from selling the futures contract but have to pay only $110,000 for the Treasury bonds that they must deliver to the buyer of the contract, and the $1000 difference is their profit. Because this profit involves no risk, traders will continue to sell the futures contract until its price falls back down to 110, at which price there are no longer any profits to be made. The elimination of riskless profit opportunities in the futures market is referred to as **arbitrage,** and it guarantees that the price of a futures contract at expiration equals the price of the underlying asset to be delivered.[1]

Armed with the fact that a futures contract at expiration equals the price of the underlying asset makes it even easier to see who profits and loses from such a contract when interest rates change. When interest rates have risen so that the

---

[1]In actuality, futures contracts sometimes set conditions for delivery of the underlying assets that cause the price of the contract at expiration to differ slightly from the price of the underlying assets. Because the difference in price is extremely small, we ignore it in this chapter.

price of the Treasury bond is 110 on the expiration day at the end of June, the June Treasury bond futures contract will also have a price of 110. Thus if you bought the contract for 115 in February, you have a loss of 5 points, or $5000 (5 percent of $100,000). But if you sold the futures contract at 115 in February, the decline in price to 110 means that you have a profit of 5 points, or $5000.

Hedging with Financial Futures

First National Bank can also use financial futures contracts to hedge the interest-rate risk on its holdings of $5 million of the 8s of 2015. To see how it can do this, suppose that the 8s of 2015 are the long-term bonds that would be delivered in the T-bond futures contract expiring one year in the future and that the interest rate on these bonds is expected to remain at 8 percent over the next year so that both the 8s of 2015 and the futures contract are selling at par. It should be easy for you to see that First National can hedge its interest-rate risk by selling $5 million of the T-bond futures contract, that is, 50 contracts ($5 million divided by $100,000 per contract). Then if the interest rate on this bond rises from 8 percent to, say, 10 percent next year when the contract expires, both the futures contract and the bond price will fall by exactly the same percentage so that the capital loss on the bonds is exactly matched by the capital gain on First National's sale of the futures contracts.[2]

The hedge just described is called a **micro hedge** because the financial institution is hedging the interest-rate risk for a specific asset it is holding. A second type of hedge that financial institutions engage in is called a **macro hedge,** in which the hedge is for the institution's entire portfolio. For example, if a bank has more rate-sensitive liabilities than assets, we have seen in Chapter 10 that a rise in interest rates will cause the value of the bank to decline. By selling interest-rate future contracts that will yield a profit when interest rates rise, the bank can offset the losses on its overall portfolio from an interest-rate rise and thereby hedge its interest-rate risk.

Organization of Trading in Financial Futures Markets

Financial futures contracts are traded in the United States on organized exchanges such as the Chicago Board of Trade, the Chicago Mercantile Exchange, the New York Futures Exchange, the MidAmerica Commodity Exchange, and the Kansas City Board of Trade. These exchanges are highly competitive with one another, and each organization tries to design contracts and set rules that will increase the amount of futures trading on its exchange.

The futures exchanges and all trades in financial futures in the United States are regulated by the Commodity Futures Trading Commission (CFTC), which was

---

[2]In the real world, designing a hedge is somewhat more complicated than the example here because the bond that is most likely to be delivered might not be an 8 of 2015. See Frederic S. Mishkin, *Financial Markets and Institutions.* 2d ed. (Reading, Mass.: Addison Wesley Longman, 1998) for a discussion of how to construct the hedge in a more realistic case.

created in 1974 to take over the regulatory responsibilities for futures markets from the Department of Agriculture. The CFTC oversees futures trading and the futures exchanges to ensure that prices in the market are not being manipulated, and it also registers and audits the brokers, traders, and exchanges to prevent fraud and to ensure the financial soundness of the exchanges. In addition, the CFTC approves proposed futures contracts to make sure that they serve the public interest. The most widely traded financial futures contracts listed in the *Wall Street Journal* and the exchanges where they are traded (along with the number of contracts outstanding, called **open interest,** on March 5, 1997) are listed in Table 1.[3]

Given the globalization of other financial markets in recent years, it is not surprising that increased competition from abroad has been occurring in financial futures markets as well.

The Globalization of Financial Futures Markets

Because American futures exchanges were the first to develop financial futures, they dominated the trading of financial futures in the early 1980s. For example, in 1985, all of the top ten futures contracts were traded on exchanges in the United States. With the rapid growth of financial futures markets and the resulting high profits made by the American exchanges, foreign exchanges saw a profit opportunity and began to enter this business. By the 1990s, Eurodollar contracts traded on the London International Financial Futures Exchange, Japanese government bond contracts and Euroyen contracts traded on the Tokyo Stock Exchange, French government bond contracts traded on the Marché à Terme International de France, and Nikkei 225 contracts traded on the Osaka Securities Exchange all became among the most widely traded futures contracts in the world. Even developing countries are getting into the act. In 1996, seven developing countries (also referred to as *emerging-market countries*) established futures exchanges, and this number is expected to double within a few years.

Foreign competition has also spurred knockoffs of the most popular financial futures contracts initially developed in the United States. These contracts traded on foreign exchanges are virtually identical to those traded in the United States and have the advantage that they can be traded when the American exchanges are closed. The movement to 24-hour-a-day trading in financial futures has been further stimulated by the development of the Globex electronic trading system, which allows traders throughout the world to trade futures even when the exchanges are not officially open. Financial futures trading is thus well on the way to being completely internationalized, and competition between U.S. and foreign exchanges will continue to be intense in the future.

Explaining the Success of Futures Markets

The tremendous success of the financial futures market in Treasury bonds is evident from the fact that the total open interest of Treasury bond contracts was over 530,000 on March 5, 1997, for a total value of over $53 billion (531,833 × $100,000). There are several differences between financial futures and forward

---

[3]For a more detailed treatment of financial futures and option markets, see Franklin R. Edwards and Cindy W. Ma, *Futures and Options* (New York: McGraw-Hill, 1992).

TABLE 1   Widely Traded Financial Futures Contracts

Type of Contract	Contract Size	Exchange*	Open Interest March 5, 1997
Interest-Rate Contracts			
Treasury bonds	$100,000	CBT	531,833
Treasury bonds	$50,000	MCE	11,213
Treasury notes	$100,000	CBT	312,442
Five-year Treasury notes	$100,000	CBT	217,587
Two-year Treasury notes	$200,000	CBT	26,512
Thirty-day Fed funds	$5 million	CBT	20,172
Treasury bills	$1 million	CME	9,970
One-month LIBOR	$3 million	CME	34,044
Municipal Bond Index	$1000	CBT	17,934
Eurodollar	$1 million	CME	2,388,907
Euroyen	100 million	CME	27,439
Euroyen	100 million	SIMEX	369,666
Sterling	£500,000	LIFFE	523,575
Long Gilt	£50,000	LIFFE	260,656
Euromark	DM 1 million	LIFFE	1,250,658
Euroswiss franc	SF 1 million	LIFFE	111,320
German government bonds	DM 250,000	LIFFE	290,276
Ten-year French govt. bonds	500,000 francs	MATIF	154,440
Italian government bonds	Lit 200 billion	LIFFE	127,539
Canadian banker's acceptance	C$1,000,000	ME	110,419
Ten-year Canadian government bonds	C$100,000	ME	29,965
Stock Index Contracts			
Standard & Poor's 500 Index	$500 × index	CME	204,656
Standard & Poor's MIDCAP 400	$500 × index	CME	11,415
Nasdaq 100	$100 × index	CME	7,548
Nikkei 225 Stock Average	$5 × index	CME	19,263
Financial Times–Stock Exchange 100-Share Index Composite Index	£25 per index point	LIFFE	71,816
Currency Contracts			
Yen	12,500,000 yen	CME	78,819
Deutschemark	125,000 marks	CME	112,867
Canadian dollar	100,000 Canadian $	CME	62,862

(continued)

| TABLE 1 | **Widely Traded Financial Futures Contracts (*continued*)** |

Currency Contracts (*continued*)

British pound	62,500 pounds	CME	38,791
Swiss Franc	125,000 francs	CME	52,904
Mexican peso	500,000 new pesos	CME	40,166

*Exchange abbreviations: CBT, Chicago Board of Trade; CME, Chicago Mercantile Exchange; LIFFE, London International Financial Futures Exchange; MATIF, Marché à Terme International de France; MCE, MidAmerica Commodity Exchange; ME, Montreal Exchange; NYFE, New York Futures Exchange; SIMEX, Singapore International Monetary Exchange.

Source: Wall Street Journal, March 5, 1997, p. C14.

contracts and in the organization of their markets that help explain why financial futures markets like those for Treasury bonds have been so successful.

Several features of futures contracts were designed to overcome the liquidity problem inherent in forward contracts. The first feature is that, in contrast to forward contracts, the quantities delivered and the delivery dates of futures contracts are standardized, making it more likely that different parties can be matched up in the futures market, thereby increasing the liquidity of the market. In the case of the Treasury bond contract, the quantity delivered is $100,000 face value of bonds, and the delivery dates are set to be the last business day of March, June, September, and December. The second feature is that after the futures contract has been bought or sold, it can be traded (bought or sold) again at any time until the delivery date. In contrast, once a forward contract is agreed on, it typically cannot be traded. The third feature is that in a futures contract, not just one specific type of Treasury bond is deliverable on the delivery date, as in a forward contract. Instead, any Treasury bond that matures in more than 15 years and is not callable for 15 years is eligible for delivery. Allowing continuous trading also increases the liquidity of the futures market, as does the ability to deliver a range of Treasury bonds rather than one specific bond.

Another reason why futures contracts specify that more than one bond is eligible for delivery is to limit the possibility that someone might corner the market and "squeeze" traders who have sold contracts. To corner the market, someone buys up all the deliverable securities so that investors with a short position cannot obtain from anyone else the securities that they contractually must deliver on the delivery date. As a result, the person who has cornered the market can set exorbitant prices for the securities that investors with a short position must buy to fulfill their obligations under the futures contract. The person who has cornered the market makes a fortune, but investors with a short position take a terrific loss. Clearly, the possibility that corners might occur in the market will discourage people from taking a short position and might therefore decrease the size of the market. By allowing many different securities to be delivered, the futures contract makes it harder for anyone to corner the market because a much larger amount of securities would have to be purchased to establish the corner. Corners are more

BOX 1

The Hunt Brothers and the Silver Crash

In early 1979, two Texas billionaires, W. Herbert Hunt and his brother, Nelson Bunker Hunt, decided that they were going to get into the silver market in a big way. Herbert stated his reasoning for purchasing silver as follows: "I became convinced that the economy of the United States was in a weakening condition. This reinforced my belief that investment in precious metals was wise . . . because of rampant inflation." Although the Hunts' stated reason for purchasing silver was that it was a good investment, others felt that their real motive was to establish a corner in the silver market. Along with other associates, several of them from the Saudi royal family, the Hunts purchased close to 300 million ounces of silver in the form of either actual bullion or silver futures contracts. The result was that the price of silver rose from $6 an ounce to over $50 an ounce by January 1980.

Once the regulators and the futures exchanges got wind of what the Hunts were up to, they decided to take action to eliminate the possibility of a corner by limiting to 2000 the number of contracts that any single trader could hold. This limit, which was equivalent to 10 million ounces, was only a small fraction of what the Hunts were holding, and so they were forced to sell. The silver market collapsed soon afterward, with the price of silver declining back to below $10 an ounce. The losses to the Hunts were estimated to be in excess of $1 billion, and they soon found themselves in financial difficulty. They had to go into debt to the tune of $1.1 billion, mortgaging not only the family's holdings in the Placid Oil Company but also 75,000 head of cattle, a stable of Thoroughbred horses, paintings, jewelry, and even such mundane items as irrigation pumps and lawn mowers. Eventually both Hunt brothers were forced into declaring personal bankruptcy, earning them the dubious distinction of declaring the largest personal bankruptcies ever in the United States.

Nelson and Herbert Hunt paid a heavy price for their excursion into the silver market, but at least Nelson retained his sense of humor. When asked right after the collapse of the silver market how he felt about his losses, he said, "A billion dollars isn't what it used to be."

Source: G. Christian Hill, "Dynasty's Decline: The Current Question About the Hunts of Dallas: How Poor Are They?" *Wall Street Journal,* November 14, 1984, p. C28.

than a theoretical possibility, as Box 1 indicates, and are a concern to both regulators and the organized exchanges that design futures contracts.

Trading in the futures market has been organized differently from trading in forward markets to overcome the default risk problems arising in forward contracts. In both types, for every contract, there must be a buyer who is taking a long position and a seller who is taking a short position. However, the buyer and seller of a futures contract make their contract not with each other but with the clearinghouse associated with the futures exchange. This setup means that the buyer of the futures contract does not need to worry about the financial health or trustworthiness of the seller, or vice versa, as in the forward market. As long as the clearinghouse is financially solid, buyers and sellers of futures contracts do not have to worry about default risk.

To make sure that the clearinghouse is financially sound and does not run into financial difficulties that might jeopardize its contracts, buyers or sellers of futures contracts must put an initial deposit, called a **margin requirement,** of perhaps $2000 per Treasury bond contract into a margin account kept at their brokerage firm. Futures contracts are then **marked to market** every day. What this means is that at the end of every trading day, the change in the value of the futures contract is added to or subtracted from the margin account. Suppose that after buying the Treasury bond contract at a price of 115 on Wednesday morning, its closing price at the end of the day, the *settlement price,* falls to 114. You now have a loss of 1 point, or $1000, on the contract, and the seller who sold you the contract has a gain of 1 point, or $1000. The $1000 gain is added to the seller's margin account, making a total of $3000 in that account, and the $1000 loss is subtracted from your account, so you now only have $1000 in your account. If the amount in this margin account falls below the maintenance margin requirement (which can be the same as the initial requirement but is usually a little less), the trader is required to add money to the account. For example, if the maintenance margin requirement is also $2000, you would have to add $1000 to your account to bring it up to $2000. Margin requirements and marking to market make it far less likely that a trader will default on a contract, thus protecting the futures exchange from losses.

A final advantage that futures markets have over forward markets is that most futures contracts do not result in delivery of the underlying asset on the expiration date, whereas forward contracts do. A trader who sold a futures contract is allowed to avoid delivery on the expiration date by making an offsetting purchase of a futures contract. Because the simultaneous holding of the long and short positions means that the trader would in effect be delivering the bonds to itself, under the exchange rules the trader is allowed to cancel both contracts. Allowing traders to cancel their contracts in this way lowers the cost of conducting trades in the futures market relative to the forward market in that a futures trader can avoid the costs of physical delivery, which is not so easy with forward contracts.

Some Problems with Financial Futures Markets

Although financial futures markets can help financial institutions reduce interest-rate risk, managers of these institutions can run into two basic problems when they try to hedge with financial futures.

BASIS RISK The first problem is associated with **basis risk,** the risk associated with the possibility that the prices of the hedged asset and the asset underlying the futures contract do not move together over time. The interest rates on the long-term bonds deliverable in the Treasury bond futures contract may not move completely in tandem with the interest rates on the security that a financial institution might want to hedge. Basis risk is often not large because interest rates on most bonds do move fairly closely together, but sometimes it can be. For example, suppose that the First National Bank was attempting to hedge its holdings of long-term municipal bonds by taking a short position in the Treasury bond futures contract and that sometime before the delivery date, a major default occurred in this market. (Such a default occurred in 1983 when the Washington State Public Power Supply System defaulted on $2.25 billion of its municipal bonds.) Such a default might cause a sharp upward movement in interest rates on municipal bonds because perceptions of higher default risk would shrink demand for them, while demand for default-free Treasury bonds would increase, possibly lowering their interest rates. The result could then be that interest rates on municipal bonds and on the Treasury bond futures contract would move in opposite directions. The rise in municipal bonds would produce a loss on the municipal bonds the bank is holding, but the fall in interest rates on the Treasury bonds would result in an additional loss on the bank's short position in the futures contract. In this case, the futures hedge could make the situation even worse for the bank. The example here is quite extreme, but it does show that the dangers of basis risk are real.

ACCOUNTING PROBLEMS A second problem with futures hedges arises from the system of accounting that financial institutions use. Under generally accepted accounting principles, when a macro hedge is made that hedges not a specific financial asset but a financial institution's entire portfolio, profits or losses the institution makes on the hedge cannot be offset by the unrealized gains or losses on the institution's portfolio (so-called paper gains or losses that are not realized because sales of the items in the portfolio have not yet occurred). To see what this could mean, suppose that a bank manager's hedge works out perfectly, so when interest rates rise and this results in a decrease in the value of the bank by, say, $1 million, the hedge with futures contracts shows an exactly offsetting profit of $1 million. Although the bank has been completely immunized against the change in interest rates, the bank is required to show an increase in profits of the $1 million it makes on the hedge but is not allowed to offset this profit with the losses it suffered on the rest of its portfolio. This example illustrates that hedging with financial futures might result in apparent (but not real) fluctuations in income that could be misinterpreted by the markets or have adverse tax consequences.

STOCK INDEX FUTURES

As we saw in Chapter 13, institutional investors, including pension and mutual funds, have become a more important force in the stock market. In addition, many small investors recognized that mutual funds have a hard time beating the market, and index funds (mutual funds that focus on producing returns similar to those on broad market indexes) became increasingly popular. The increased importance of institutional investors along with the increased focus on tracking market indexes led to an increased demand for a more liquid market in a basket of stocks that track the market.

Given this need in the marketplace, a natural extension to the already successful markets in financial futures occurred in 1982. The financial innovation was futures trading in stock price indexes at the Chicago Board of Trade (CBT), the Chicago Mercantile Exchange (CME), the Kansas City Board of Trade (KCBT), and the New York Futures Exchange (NYFE), a subsidiary of the New York Stock Exchange. The futures trading in stock price indexes is now quite controversial (see Box 2) because critics assert that it has led to substantial increases in market volatility, especially in such episodes as 1987's Black Monday crash.

BOX 2

Program Trading and Portfolio Insurance

Were They to Blame for the Stock Market Crash of 1987? In the aftermath of the Black Monday crash on October 19, 1987, in which the stock market declined by over 20 percent in one day, trading strategies involving stock price index futures markets have been accused (especially by the Brady Commission, which was appointed by President Reagan to study the stock market) of being culprits in the market collapse. One such strategy, called program trading, involves computer-directed trading between the stock index futures and the stocks whose prices are reflected in the stock price index. Program trades are a form of arbitrage conducted to keep stock index futures and stock prices in line with each other. For example, when the price of the stock index futures contract is far below the prices of the underlying stocks in the index, program traders buy index futures, thereby increasing their price, and sell the stocks, thereby lowering their price. Critics of program trading assert that the sharp fall in stock index futures prices on Black Monday led to massive selling in the stock market to keep stock prices in line with the stock index futures prices.

Some experts also blame portfolio insurance for amplifying the crash because they feel that when the stock market started to fall, uncertainty in the market increased, and the resulting increased desire to hedge stocks led to massive selling of stock index futures. The resulting large price declines in stock index futures contracts then led to massive selling of stocks by program traders to keep prices in line.

Because they view program trading and portfolio insurance as causes of the October 1987 market collapse, critics of stock index futures have advocated restrictions on their trading. In response, certain brokerage firms, as well as organized exchanges, have placed limits on program trading. For example, the New York Stock Exchange has curbed computerized program trading when the Dow Jones Industrial Average moves by more than 50 points in one day. However, some prominent finance scholars (among them Nobel laureate Merton Miller of the University of Chicago) do not accept the hypothesis that program trading and portfolio insurance provoked the stock market crash. They believe that the prices of stock index futures primarily reflect the same economic forces that move stock prices—changes in the market's underlying assessment of the value of stocks.

Stock Index Futures Contracts

To understand stock index futures contracts, let's look at the Standard & Poor's 500 Index futures contract, the most widely traded stock index futures contract in the United States. (The S&P 500 Index measures the value of 500 of the most widely traded stocks.) Stock index futures contracts differ from most other financial futures contracts in that they are settled with a cash delivery rather than with the delivery of a security. Cash settlement gives these contracts the advantage of a high degree of liquidity and also rules out the possibility of anyone's cornering the market. In the case of the S&P 500 Index contract, at the final settlement date, the cash delivery due is $500 times the index, so if the index is at 800 on the final settlement date, $400,000 would be the amount due. The price quotes for this contract are also quoted in terms of index points, so a change of 1 point represents a change of $500 in the contract's value.

To understand what all this means, let's look at what happens when you buy or sell this futures contract. Suppose that on February 1, you sell one June contract at a price of 800 (that is, $400,000). By selling the contract, you agree to a delivery amount due of $500 times the S&P 500 Index on the expiration date at the end of June. By buying the contract at a price of 800, the buyer has agreed to pay $400,000 for the delivery amount due of $500 times the S&P 500 Index at the expiration date at the end of June. If the stock market falls so that the S&P 500 Index declines to 700 on the expiration date, the buyer of the contract will have lost $50,000 because he or she has agreed to pay $400,000 for the contract but has a delivery amount due of only $350,000 (700 × $500). But you, the seller of the contract, will have a profit of $50,000 because you agreed to receive a $400,000 purchase price for the contract but have a delivery amount due of only $350,000. Because the amount payable and due are netted out, only $50,000 will change hands; you, the seller of the contract, receive $50,000 from the buyer.

OPTIONS

Another vehicle for hedging interest-rate and stock market risk involves the use of options on financial instruments. **Options** are contracts that give the purchaser the option, or *right,* to buy or sell the underlying financial instrument at a specified price, called the **exercise price** or **strike price,** within a specific period of time (the *term to expiration*). The seller (sometimes called the *writer*) of the option is *obligated* to buy or sell the financial instrument to the purchaser if the owner of the option exercises the right to sell or buy. These option contract features are important enough to be emphasized: The *owner* or buyer of an option does not have to exercise the option; he or she can let the option expire without using it. Hence the *owner* of an option is *not obligated* to take any action but rather has the *right* to exercise the contract if he or she so chooses. The *seller* of an option, by contrast, has no choice in the matter; he or she *must* buy or sell the financial instrument if the owner exercises the option.

Because the right to buy or sell a financial instrument at a specified price has value, the owner of an option is willing to pay an amount for it called a **premium.** There are two types of option contracts: **American options** can be exercised *at any time up to* the expiration date of the contract, and **European options** can be exercised only *on* the expiration date.

Option contracts are written on a number of financial instruments (an example of which is shown in the "Following the Financial News" box). Options on individual stocks are called **stock options,** and such options have existed for a long time. Option contracts on financial futures called **financial futures options** or, more commonly, **futures options,** were developed in 1982 and have become the most widely traded option contracts.

You might wonder why option contracts are more likely to be written on financial futures than on underlying debt instruments such as bonds or certificates of deposit. As you saw earlier in the chapter, at the expiration date, the price of the futures contract and of the deliverable debt instrument will be the same because of arbitrage. So it would seem that investors should be indifferent about

Following the Financial News
Futures Options

The prices for financial futures options are published daily. In the *Wall Street Journal*, they are found in the section "Futures Options Prices" under the "Interest Rate" heading. An excerpt from this listing is reproduced here.

Interest Rate
T-Bonds (CBT)
$100,000; points and 64ths of 100%

Strike Price	Calls-Settle			Puts-Settle		
	Mar	Jun	Sep	Mar	Jun	Sep
109	2-09	....	....	0.37	....	....
110	1-31	2-28	3-03	0-59	2-23	3-26
111	0-62	....	....	1-26	....	....
112	0-37	1-36	2-14	2-01	3-30	4-35
113	0-20	....	....	2-48	....	....
114	0-10	0-60	1-34	3-38	4-52	....

Est. vol. 125,000;
Wd vol. 108,679 calls; 67,341 puts
Op. Int. Wed 426,350 calls; 266,623 puts

Information for each contract is reported in columns, as follows. (The Chicago Board of

Source: Wall Street Journal, January 21, 1997, p. C14.

Trade's option on its Treasury bonds futures contract is used as an example.)

Strike Price: Strike (exercise) price of each contract, which runs from 109 to 114

Calls-Settle: Premium (price) at settlement for call options on the Treasury bond futures expiring in the month listed, with each full point representing $1000 and 64ths of a point listed to the right of the hyphen; at a strike price of 110, the March call option's premium is 1 31/64, or $1,484 per contract

Puts-Settle: Premium (price) at settlement for put options on the Treasury bond futures expiring in the month listed, with each full point representing $1000 and 64ths of a point listed to the right of the hyphen; at a strike price of 110, the March put option's premium is 59/64, or $922 per contract

having the option written on the debt instrument or on the futures contract. However, financial futures contracts have been so well designed that their markets are often more liquid than the markets in the underlying debt instruments. So investors would rather have the option contract written on the more liquid instrument, in this case the futures contract. That explains why the most popular futures options are written on many of the same futures contracts listed in Table 1.

The regulation of option markets is split between the Securities and Exchange Commission (SEC), which regulates stock options, and the Commodity Futures Trading Commission (CFTC), which regulates futures options. Regulation focuses on ensuring that writers of options have enough capital to make good on their contractual obligations and on overseeing traders and exchanges to prevent fraud and ensure that the market is not being manipulated.

Option Contracts

A **call option** is a contract that gives the owner the right to *buy* a financial instrument at the exercise price within a specific period of time. A **put option** is a contract that gives the owner the right to *sell* a financial instrument at the exercise price within a specific period of time.

. . . .

Study Guide   Remembering which is a call option and which is a put option is not always easy. To keep them straight, just remember that having a call option to buy a financial instrument is the same as having the option to **call** in the instrument for delivery at a specified price. Having a put option to sell a financial instrument is the same as having the option to **put** up an instrument for the other party to buy.

. . . .

Profits and Losses on Option and Futures Contracts

To understand option contracts more fully, let's first examine the option on the same June Treasury bond futures contract that we looked at earlier in the chapter. Recall that if you buy this futures contract at a price of 115 (that is, $115,000), you have agreed to pay $115,000 for $100,000 face value of long-term Treasury bonds when they are delivered to you at the end of June. If you sold this futures contract at a price of 115, you agreed, in exchange for $115,000, to deliver $100,000 face value of the long-term Treasury bonds at the end of June. An option contract on the Treasury bond futures contract has several key features: (1) It has the same expiration date as the underlying futures contract, (2) it is an American option and so can be exercised at any time before the expiration date, and (3) the premium (price) of the option is quoted in points that are the same as in the futures contract, so each point corresponds to $1000. If, for a premium of $2000, you buy one call option contract on the June Treasury bond contract with an exercise price of 115, you have purchased the right to buy (call in) the June Treasury bond futures contract for a price of 115 ($115,000 per contract) at any time through the expiration date of this contract at the end of June. Similarly, when for $2000 you buy a put option on the June Treasury bond contract with an exercise price of 115, you have the right to sell (put up) the June Treasury bond futures contract for a price of 115 ($115,000 per contract) at any time until the end of June.

Futures option contracts are somewhat complicated, so to explore how they work and how they can be used to hedge risk, let's first examine how profits and losses on the call option on the June Treasury bond futures contract occur. In February, our old friend Irving the Investor buys, for a $2000 premium, a call option on the $100,000 June Treasury bond futures contract with a strike price of 115. (We assume that if Irving exercises the option, it is on the expiration date at the end of June and not before.) On the expiration date at the end of June, suppose that the underlying Treasury bond for the futures contract has a price of 110. Recall that on the expiration date, arbitrage forces the price of the futures contract to be the same as the price of the underlying bond, so it too has a price of 110 on the expiration date at the end of June. If Irving exercises the call option and buys the futures contract at an exercise price of 115, he will lose money by buying at 115 and selling at the lower market price of 110. Because Irving is smart, he will not exercise the option, but he will be out the $2000 premium he paid. In such a situation, in which the price of the underlying financial instrument is below the exercise price, a call option is said to be "out of the money." At the price of 110 (less than the exercise price), Irving thus suffers a loss on the option contract of the $2000 premium he paid. This loss is plotted as point A in panel (a) of Figure 1.

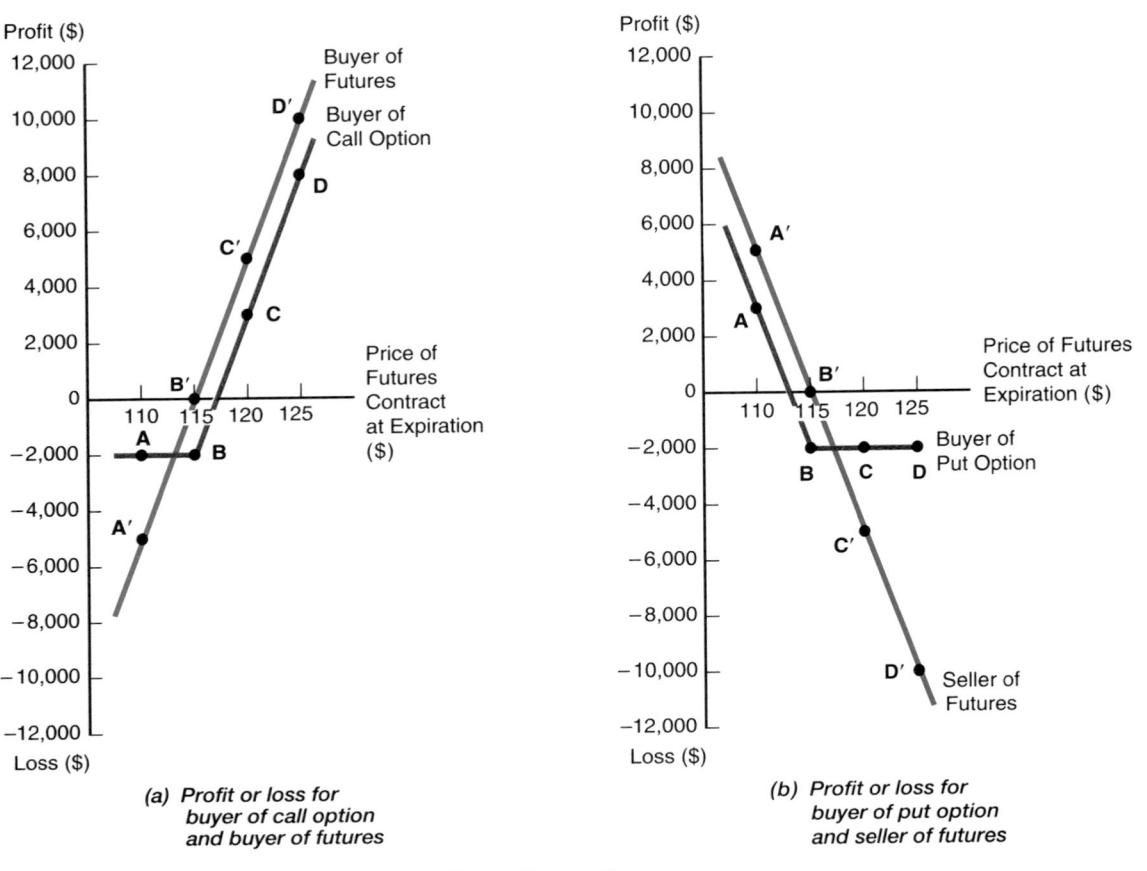

FIGURE 1 Profits and Losses on Options Versus Futures Contracts

The futures contract is the $100,000 June Treasury bond contract, and the option contracts are written on this futures contract with an exercise price of 115. Panel (a) shows the profits and losses for the buyer of the call option and the buyer of the futures contract, and panel (b) shows the profits and losses for the buyer of the put option and the seller of the futures contract.

On the expiration date, if the price of the futures contract is 115, the call option is "at the money," and Irving is indifferent whether he exercises his option to buy the futures contract or not, since exercising the option at 115 when the market price is also at 115 produces no gain or loss. Because he has paid the $2000 premium, at the price of 115 his contract again has a net loss of $2000, plotted as point B.

If the futures contract instead has a price of 120 on the expiration day, the option is "in the money," and Irving benefits from exercising the option: He would buy the futures contract at the exercise price of 115 and then sell it for 120, thereby earning a 5-point gain ($5000 profit) on the $100,000 Treasury bond contract. Because Irving paid a $2000 premium for the option contract, however, his net profit is $3000 ($5000 − $2000). The $3000 profit at a price of 120 is plotted as point C. Similarly, if the price of the futures contract rose to 125, the option contract would yield a net profit of $8000 ($10,000 from exercising the option minus the $2000 premium), plotted as point D. Plotting these points, we get the kinked profit curve for the call option that we see in panel (a).

Suppose that instead of purchasing the futures *option* contract in February, Irving decides instead to buy the $100,000 June Treasury bond *futures* contract at the price of 115. If the price of the bond on the expiration day at the end of June declines to 110, meaning that the price of the futures contract also falls to 110, Irving suffers a loss of 5 points, or $5000. The loss of $5000 on the futures contract at a price of 110 is plotted as point A′ in panel (a). At a price of 115 on the expiration date, Irving would have a zero profit on the futures contract, plotted as point B′. At a price of 120, Irving would have a profit on the contract of 5 points, or $5000 (point C′), and at a price of 125, the profit would be 10 percentage points, or $10,000 (point D′). Plotting these points, we get the linear (straight-line) profit curve for the futures contract that appears in panel (a).

Now we can see the major difference between a futures contract and an option contract. As the profit curve for the futures contract in panel (a) indicates, the futures contract has a linear profit function: Profits grow by an equal dollar amount for every point increase in the price of the underlying financial instrument. By contrast, the kinked profit curve for the option contract is nonlinear, meaning that profits do not always grow by the same amount for a given change in the price of the underlying financial instrument. The reason for this nonlinearity is that the call option protects Irving from having losses that are greater than the amount of the $2000 premium. In contrast, Irving's loss on the futures contract is $5000 if the price on the expiration day falls to 110, and if the price falls even further, Irving's loss will be even greater. This insurance-like feature of option contracts explains why their purchase price is referred to as a premium. Once the underlying financial instrument's price rises above the exercise price, however, Irving's profits grow linearly. Irving has given up something by buying an option rather than a futures contract. As we see in panel (a), when the price of the underlying financial instrument rises above the exercise price, Irving's profits are always less than that on the futures contract by exactly the $2000 premium he paid.

Panel (b) plots the results of the same profit calculations if Irving buys not a call but a put option (an option to sell) with an exercise price of 115 for a premium of $2000 and if he sells the futures contract rather than buying one. In this case, if on the expiration date the Treasury bond futures have a price above the 115 exercise price, the put option is "out of the money." Irving would not want to exercise the put option and then have to sell the futures contract he owns as a result of exercising the put option at a price below the market price and lose money. He would not exercise his option, and he would be out only the $2000 premium he paid. Once the price of the futures contract falls below the 115 exercise price, Irving benefits from exercising the put option because he can sell the futures contract at a price of 115 but can buy it at a price below this. In such a situation, in which the price of the underlying instrument is below the exercise price, the put option is "in the money," and profits rise linearly as the price of the futures contract falls. The profit function for the put option illustrated in panel (b) of Figure 1 is kinked, indicating that Irving is protected from losses greater than the amount of the premium he paid. The profit curve for the sale of the futures contract is just the negative of the profit for the futures contract in panel (a) and is therefore linear.

Panel (b) of Figure 1 confirms the conclusion from panel (a) that profits on option contracts are nonlinear but profits on futures contracts are linear.

Study Guide   To make sure you understand how profits and losses on option and futures contracts are generated, calculate the net profits on the put option and the short position in the futures contract at prices on the expiration day of 110, 115, 120, and 125. Then verify that your calculations correspond to the points plotted in panel (b) of Figure 1.

Two other differences between futures and option contracts must be mentioned. The first is that the initial investment on the contracts differs. As we saw earlier in the chapter, when a futures contract is purchased, the investor must put up a fixed amount, the margin requirement, in a margin account. But when an option contract is purchased, the initial investment is the premium that must be paid for the contract. The second important difference between the contracts is that the futures contract requires money to change hands daily when the contract is marked to market, whereas the option contract requires money to change hands only when it is exercised.

Hedging with Futures Options

Earlier in the chapter, we saw how the First National Bank could hedge the interest-rate risk on its $5 million holdings of 8s of 2015 by selling $5 million of T-bond futures. A rise in interest rates and the resulting fall in bond prices and bond futures contracts would lead to profits on the bank's sale of the futures contracts that would exactly offset the losses on the 8s of 2015 the bank is holding.

As panel (b) of Figure 1 suggests, an alternative way for the manager to protect against a rise in interest rates and hence a decline in bond prices is to buy $5 million of put options written on the same Treasury bond futures. As long as the exercise price is not too far from the current price as in panel (b), the rise in interest rates and decline in bond prices will lead to profits on the futures and the futures put options, profits that will offset any losses on the $5 million of Treasury bonds.

The one problem with using options rather than futures is that the First National Bank will have to pay premiums on the options contracts, thereby lowering the bank's profits in order to hedge the interest-rate risk. Why might the bank manager be willing to use options rather than futures to conduct the hedge? The answer is that the option contract, unlike the futures contract, allows the First National Bank to gain if interest rates decline and bond prices rise. With the hedge using futures contracts, the First National Bank does not gain from increases in bond prices because the profits on the bonds it is holding are offset by the losses from the futures contracts it has sold. However, as panel (b) of Figure 1 indicates, the situation when the hedge is conducted with put options is quite different: Once bond prices rise above the exercise price, the bank does not suffer additional losses on the option contracts. At the same time, the value of the Treasury bonds the bank is holding will increase, thereby leading to a profit for the bank.

Thus using options rather than futures to conduct the micro hedge allows the bank to protect itself from rises in interest rates but still allows the bank to benefit from interest-rate declines (although the profit is reduced by the amount of the premium).

Similar reasoning indicates that the bank manager might prefer to use options to conduct the macro hedge to immunize the entire bank portfolio from interest-rate risk. Again, the strategy of using options rather than futures has the disadvantage that the First National Bank has to pay the premiums on these contracts up front. By contrast, using options allows the bank to keep the gains from a decline in interest rates (which will raise the value of the bank's assets relative to its liabilities) because these gains will not be offset by large losses on the option contracts.

In the case of a macro hedge, there is another reason why the bank might prefer option contracts to futures contracts. Recall that profits and losses on futures contracts can cause accounting problems for banks because such profits and losses are not allowed to be offset by unrealized changes in the value of the rest of the bank's portfolio. Consider the case when interest rates fall. If First National sells futures contracts to conduct the macro hedge, then when interest rates fall and the prices of the Treasury bond futures contracts rise, it will have large losses on these contracts. Of course, these losses are offset by unrealized profits in the rest of the bank's portfolio, but the bank is not allowed to offset these losses in its accounting statements. So even though the macro hedge is serving its intended purpose of immunizing the bank's portfolio from interest-rate risk, the bank would experience large accounting losses when interest rates fall. Indeed, bank managers have lost their jobs when perfectly sound hedges with interest-rate futures have led to large accounting losses. Not surprisingly, bank managers might shrink from using financial futures to conduct macro hedges for this reason.

Futures options, however, can come to the rescue of the managers of banks and other financial institutions. Suppose that First National conducted the macro hedge by buying put options instead of selling Treasury bond futures. Now if interest rates fall and bond prices rise well above the exercise price, the bank will not have large losses on the option contracts because it will just decide not to exercise its options. The bank will not suffer the accounting problems produced by hedging with financial futures. Because of the accounting advantages of using futures options to conduct macro hedges, option contracts have become important interest-rate-risk-hedging tools for financial institution managers. Ⓐ

Factors Affecting the Prices of Option Premiums

If we again look closely at the *Wall Street Journal* entry for Treasury bond futures options in the "Following the Financial News" box, we learn several interesting facts about how the premiums on option contracts are priced. The first thing you might have noticed is that when the strike (exercise) price is higher, the premium for the call option is lower and the premium for the put option is higher. For example, when the strike price rises from 109 to 114, the premium for the March call option falls from 2 9/64 to 10/64, and the premium for the March put option rises from 37/64 to 3 38/64.

Our understanding of the profit function for option contracts illustrated in Figure 1 helps explain this fact. As we saw in panel (a), a higher price for the underlying financial instrument (in this case a Treasury bond futures contract) relative to the option's exercise price results in higher profits on the call (buy) option. Thus the lower the strike price, the higher the profits on the call option contract and the greater the premium that investors like Irving are willing to pay. Similarly, we saw in panel (b) that a higher price for the underlying financial instrument relative to the exercise price lowers profits on the put (sell) option, so that a higher strike price increases profits and thus causes the premium to increase.

The second thing you might have noticed in the *Wall Street Journal* entry is that as the period of time over which the option can be exercised (the term to expiration) gets longer, the premiums for both call and put options rise. For example, at a strike price of 110, the premium on the call option increases from 1 31/64 in March to 2 28/64 in June and to 3 3/64 in September. Similarly, the premium on the put option increases from 59/64 in March to 2 23/64 in June and to 3 26/64 in September. The fact that premiums increase with the term to expiration is also explained by the nonlinear profit function for option contracts. As the term to expiration lengthens, there is a greater chance that the price of the underlying financial instrument will be very high or very low by the expiration date. If the price becomes very high and goes well above the exercise price, the call (buy) option will yield a high profit, but if the price becomes very low and goes well below the exercise price, the losses will be small because the owner of the call option will simply decide not to exercise the option. The possibility of greater variability of the underlying financial instrument as the term to expiration lengthens raises profits on average for the call option.

Similar reasoning tells us that the put (sell) option will become more valuable as the term to expiration increases because the possibility of greater price variability of the underlying financial instrument increases as the term to expiration increases. The greater chance of a low price increases the chance that profits on the put option will be very high. But the greater chance of a high price does not produce substantial losses for the put option because the owner will again just decide not to exercise the option.

Another way of thinking about this reasoning is to recognize that option contracts have an element of "heads, I win; tails, I don't lose too badly." The greater variability of where the prices might be by the expiration date increases the value of both kinds of options. Since a longer term to the expiration date leads to greater variability of where the prices might be by the expiration date, a longer term to expiration raises the value of the option contract.

The reasoning that we have just developed also explains another important fact about option premiums. When the volatility of the price of the underlying instrument is great, the premiums for both call and put options will be higher. Higher volatility of prices means that for a given expiration date, there will again be greater variability of where the prices might be by the expiration date. The "heads, I win; tails, I don't lose too badly" property of options then means that the greater variability of possible prices by the expiration date increases average profits for the option and thus increases the premium that investors are willing to pay.

Summary

Our analysis of how profits on options are affected by price movements for the underlying financial instrument leads to the following conclusions about the factors that determine the premium on an option contract:

1. The higher the strike price, everything else being equal, the lower the premium on call (buy) options and the higher the premium on put (sell) options.
2. The greater the term to expiration, everything else being equal, the higher the premiums for both call and put options.
3. The greater the volatility of prices of the underlying financial instrument, everything else being equal, the higher the premiums for both call and put options.

The results we have derived here appear in more formal models, such as the Black-Scholes model, which analyze how the premiums on options are priced. You might study such models in finance courses.

INTEREST-RATE SWAPS

In addition to forwards, futures, and options, financial institutions use one other important financial derivative to manage risk. **Swaps** are financial contracts that obligate one party to exchange (swap) a set of payments it owns for another set of payments owned by another party. There are two basic kinds of swaps: **Currency swaps** involve the exchange of a set of payments in one currency for a set of payments in another currency. **Interest-rate swaps** involve the exchange of one set of interest payments for another set of interest payments, all denominated in the same currency. We first focus on interest-rate swaps; later in the chapter we discuss currency swaps.

Interest-Rate Swap Contracts

Interest-rate swaps are an important tool for managing interest-rate risk, and they first appeared in the United States in 1982 when, as we have seen, there was an increase in the demand for financial instruments that could be used to reduce interest-rate risk. The most common type of interest-rate swap (called the *plain vanilla swap*) specifies (1) the interest rate on the payments that are being exchanged; (2) the type of interest payments (variable or fixed-rate); (3) the amount of **notional principal,** which is the amount on which the interest is being paid; and (4) the time period over which the exchanges continue to be made. There are many other more complicated versions of swaps, including forward swaps and swap options (called *swaptions*), but here we will look only at the plain vanilla swap. Figure 2 illustrates an interest-rate swap between the Midwest Savings Bank and the Friendly Finance Company. Midwest Savings agrees to pay Friendly Finance a fixed rate of 7 percent on $1 million of notional principal for the next ten years, and Friendly Finance agrees to pay Midwest Savings the one-year Treasury bill rate plus 1 percent on $1 million of notional principal for the same period. Thus as shown in Figure 2, every year, the Midwest Savings Bank would be paying the Friendly Finance Company 7 percent on $1 million, while Friendly Finance would be paying Midwest Savings the one-year T-bill rate plus 1 percent on $1 million.

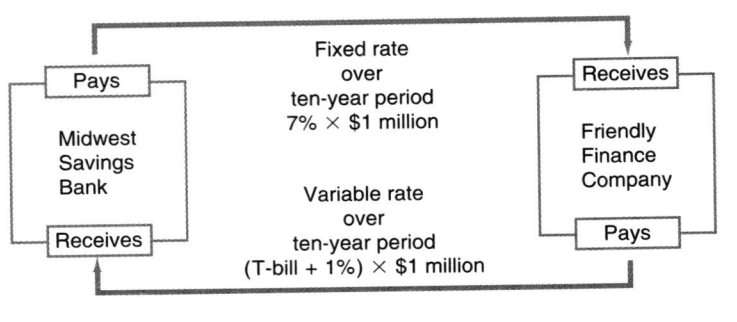

FIGURE 2 Interest-Rate Swap Payments

In this swap arrangement with a notional principal of $1 million and a term of ten years, the Midwest Savings Bank pays a fixed rate of 7 percent × $1 million to the Friendly Finance Company, which in turn agrees to pay the one-year Treasury bill rate plus 1 percent × $1 million to the Midwest Savings Bank.

Hedging with Interest-Rate Swaps

You might wonder why these two parties find it advantageous to enter into this swap agreement. The answer is that it may help both of them hedge interest-rate risk.

Suppose that the Midwest Savings Bank, which tends to borrow short-term and then lend long-term in the mortgage market, has $1 million less of rate-sensitive assets than it has rate-sensitive liabilities. As we learned in Chapter 10, this situation means that as interest rates rise, the rise in the cost of funds (liabilities) is greater than the rise in interest payments it receives on its assets, many of which are fixed-rate. The result of rising interest rates is thus a shrinking of Midwest Savings' net interest margin and a decline in its profitability. As we saw in Chapter 10, to avoid this interest-rate risk, Midwest Savings would like to convert $1 million of its fixed-rate assets into $1 million of rate-sensitive assets, in effect making rate-sensitive assets equal rate-sensitive liabilities, thereby eliminating the gap. This is exactly what happens when it engages in the interest-rate swap. By taking $1 million of its fixed-rate income and exchanging it for $1 million of rate-sensitive Treasury bill income, it has converted income on $1 million of fixed-rate assets into income on $1 million of rate-sensitive assets. Now when interest rates increase, the rise in rate-sensitive income on its assets exactly matches the rise in the rate-sensitive cost of funds on its liabilities, leaving the net interest margin and bank profitability unchanged.

The Friendly Finance Company, which issues long-term bonds to raise funds and uses them to make short-term loans, finds that it is in exactly the opposite situation to Midwest Savings: It has $1 million more of rate-sensitive assets than rate-sensitive liabilities. It is therefore concerned that a fall in interest rates, which will result in a larger drop in income from its assets than the decline in the cost of funds on its liabilities, will cause a decline in profits. By doing the interest-rate swap, it eliminates this interest-rate risk because it has converted $1 million of rate-sensitive income into $1 million of fixed-rate income. Now the Friendly Finance Company finds that when interest rates fall, the decline in rate-sensitive income is smaller and so is matched by the decline in the rate-sensitive cost of funds on its liabilities, leaving its profitability unchanged. Ⓐ

Advantages of Interest-Rate Swaps

To eliminate interest-rate risk, both the Midwest Savings Bank and the Friendly Finance Company could have rearranged their balance sheets by converting fixed-rate assets into rate-sensitive assets, and vice versa, instead of engaging in an interest-rate swap. However, this strategy would have been costly for both financial institutions for several reasons. The first is that financial institutions incur substantial transaction costs when they rearrange their balance sheets. Second, different financial institutions have informational advantages in making loans to certain customers who may prefer certain maturities. Thus, adjusting the balance sheet to eliminate interest-rate risk may result in a loss of these informational advantages, which the financial institution is unwilling to give up. Interest-rate swaps solve these problems for financial institutions because in effect they allow the institutions to convert fixed-rate assets into rate-sensitive assets without affecting the balance sheet. Large transaction costs are avoided, and the financial institutions can continue to make loans where they have an informational advantage.

We have seen that financial institutions can also hedge interest-rate risk with other financial derivatives such as futures contracts and futures options. Interest-rate swaps have one big advantage over hedging with these other derivatives: They can be written for very long horizons, sometimes as long as 20 years, whereas financial futures and futures options typically have much shorter horizons, not much more than a year. If a financial institution needs to hedge interest-rate risk for a long horizon, financial futures and option markets may not do it much good. Instead it can turn to the swap market.

Disadvantages of Interest-Rate Swaps

Although interest-rate swaps have important advantages that make them very popular with financial institutions, they also have disadvantages that limit their usefulness. Swap markets, like forward markets, can suffer from a lack of liquidity. Let's return to looking at the swap between the Midwest Savings Bank and the Friendly Finance Company. As with a forward contract, it might be difficult for the Midwest Savings Bank to link up with the Friendly Finance Company to arrange the swap. In addition, even if the Midwest Savings Bank could find a counterparty like the Friendly Finance Company, it might not be able to negotiate a good deal because it couldn't find any other institution to negotiate with.

Swap contracts also are subject to the same default risk that we encountered for forward contracts. If interest rates rise, the Friendly Finance Company would love to get out of the swap contract because the fixed-rate interest payments it receives are less than it could get in the open market. It might then default on the contract, exposing Midwest Savings to a loss. Alternatively, the Friendly Finance

Company could go bust, meaning that the terms of the swap contract would not be fulfilled.

Financial Intermediaries in Interest-Rate Swaps

As we have just seen, financial institutions do have to be aware of the possibility of losses from a default on swaps. As with a forward contract, each party to a swap must have a lot of information about the other party to make sure that the contract is likely to be fulfilled. The need for information about counterparties and the liquidity problems in swap markets could limit the usefulness of these markets. However, as we saw in Chapter 9, when informational and liquidity problems crop up in a market, financial intermediaries come to the rescue. That is exactly what happens in swap markets. Intermediaries such as investment banks and especially large commercial banks have the ability to acquire information cheaply about the creditworthiness and reliability of parties to swap contracts and are also able to match up parties to a swap. Hence large commercial banks and investment banks have set up swap markets in which they act as intermediaries.

Figure 3 shows how a swap contract works in a more realistic setting in which a commercial bank such as Citibank acts as the intermediary between Midwest Savings and Friendly Finance. Now both Midwest Savings and Friendly Finance make their swap contracts directly with Citibank rather than with each other. Midwest Savings agrees to exchange with Citibank a 7.05 percent fixed-rate interest payment for the one-year Treasury bill rate payment plus 0.95 percent. As we see in the figure, Citibank makes the counterpart swap agreement with the Friendly Finance Company, in which it exchanges a 6.95 percent fixed-rate payment for the one-year Treasury bill rate payment plus 1.05 percent. As in Figure 2, the notional amount of principal is $1 million, and the term of the swap agreement is ten years. Citibank makes a profit because it receives 7.05 percent from Midwest Savings but passes on only 6.95 percent to Friendly Finance, earning a spread of 0.1 percent. Citibank earns an additional spread of 0.1 percent by receiving the one-year bill rate plus 1.05 percent from Friendly Finance while paying out only the one-year bill rate plus 0.95 percent to Midwest Savings. The result is that Citibank makes a total of 0.2 percent × $1 million = $2000 from acting as an intermediary in this interest-rate swap.

Comparing Figures 2 and 3, we see that both Midwest Savings and Friendly Finance give up a little bit by entering into the swap agreement with Citibank—they each receive an interest payment that is 0.05 percent less and pay an interest payment that is 0.05 percent more—but this arrangement has two major advantages for them. First, Citibank has been able to match up both parties, which probably would not have been possible without Citbank's help. Second, both parties know Citibank well and are confident that there will be no default risk on the swap contract. Because the Midwest Savings Bank and the Friendly Finance Company do not know each other well, their concerns about default risk might have prevented them from entering directly into the swap with each other. These two advantages of dealing with Citibank rather than with each other are why Midwest Savings and Friendly Finance are more likely to use Citibank as an intermediary when they conduct swaps and be willing to pay for the right to do so.

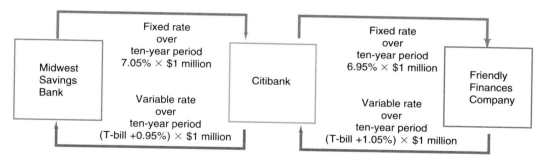

FIGURE 3 Interest-Rate Swap Payments with an Intermediary

In the swap arrangement with an intermediary (Citibank), the Midwest Savings Bank agrees to pay a fixed rate of 7.05 percent × $1 million to Citibank, which in turn pays the one-year Treasury bill rate plus 0.95 percent × $1 million to the Midwest Savings Bank. At the same time, Citibank agrees to pay a fixed rate of 6.95 percent × $1 million to the Friendly Finance Company, which in turn pays the one-year Treasury bill rate plus 1.05 percent × $1 million. The result is that Citibank earns a spread of 0.1 percent on the Treasury bill payments and 0.1 percent on the fixed-rate payments, for a total of 0.2 percent × $1 million = $2000.

Clearly, interest-rate swaps do pose some risk to commercial banks acting as intermediaries such as Citibank in our example. As we have seen in Chapter 12, concerns about the risks posed to banks by interest-rate swaps have led to regulations that force banks to hold more capital when they engage in the intermediation process in the swap market.

Hedging Foreign Exchange Risk

As we discussed in Chapter 8, foreign exchange rates have been highly volatile in recent years. The large fluctuations in exchange rates subject financial institutions and other businesses to significant foreign exchange risk because they generate substantial gains and losses. Luckily for financial institution managers, the financial derivatives discussed in this chapter—forward and financial futures contracts—can be used to hedge foreign exchange risk.

To understand how financial institution managers manage foreign exchange risk, let's suppose that in January, the First National Bank's customer, Frivolous Luxuries, Inc., is due a payment of 20 million deutsche marks (DM) in two months for $10 million worth of goods it has just sold in Germany. Frivolous Luxuries is concerned that if the value of the deutsche mark falls substantially from its current value of 50 cents, the company might suffer a large loss because the DM 20 million payment will no longer be worth $10 million. So Sam, the CEO of Frivolous Luxuries, calls up his friend Mona, the manager of the First National Bank, and asks her to hedge this foreign exchange risk for his company. Let's see how the bank manager does this using forward and financial futures contracts.

Hedging Foreign Exchange Risk with Forward Contracts

Forward markets in foreign exchange have been highly developed by commercial banks and investment banking operations that engage in extensive foreign exchange trading and so are widely used to hedge foreign exchange risk. Mona knows that she can use this market to hedge the foreign exchange risk for Frivolous Luxuries. Such a hedge is quite straightforward for her to execute. She just enters a forward contract that obligates her to sell DM 20 million two months from now in exchange for dollars at the current forward rate of $0.50 per mark.[4]

In two months, when her customer receives the DM 20 million, the forward contract ensures that it is exchanged for dollars at an exchange rate of $0.50 per mark, thus yielding $10 million. No matter what happens to future exchange rates, Frivolous Luxuries will be guaranteed $10 million for the goods it sold in Germany. Mona calls up her friend Sam to let him know that his company is now protected from any foreign exchange movements, and he thanks her for her help.

Hedging Foreign Exchange Risk with Futures Contracts

As an alternative, Mona could have used the currency futures market to hedge the foreign exchange risk. In this case, she would see that the Chicago Mercantile Exchange has a March deutsche mark contract with a contract amount of DM 125,000 and a price of $0.50 per mark. To do the hedge, Mona must sell DM 20 million of the March futures, and since the contract size is DM 125,000, she sells 20 million ÷ 125,000 = 160 contracts. Given the $0.50-per-mark price, the sale of the contracts yields 160 × DM 125,000 × $0.50 = $10 million. The futures hedge thus again enables her to lock in the exchange rate for Frivolous Luxuries so that it gets its payment of $10 million.

One advantage of using the futures market is that the contract size of DM 125,000, worth $62,500, is quite a bit smaller than the minimum size of a forward contract, which is usually $1 million or more. However, in this case, the bank manager is making a large enough transaction that she can use either the forward or the futures market. Her choice depends on whether the transaction costs are lower in one market than in the other. If the First National Bank is active in the forward market, that market would probably have the lower transaction costs, but if First National rarely deals in foreign exchange forward contracts, the bank manager may do better by sticking with the futures market.

---

[4]The forward exchange rate will probably differ slightly from the current spot rate of 50 cents per mark because the interest rates in Germany and the United States may not be equal. In that case, as we saw in Equation 2 in Chapter 8, the future expected exchange rate will not equal the current spot rate and neither will the forward rate. However, since interest differentials have typically been less than 6 percent at an annual rate (1 percent bimonthly), the expected appreciation or depreciation of the mark over a two-month period has always been less than 1 percent. Thus the forward rate is always close to the current spot rate, and so our assumption in the example that the forward rate and the spot rate are the same is a reasonable one.

Hedging Foreign Exchange Risk with Currency Options

Our analysis shows that the bank manager could hedge the foreign exchange risk by selling 160 March deutsche mark futures contracts with a contract amount of DM 125,000 and a price of $0.50 per mark. To do the hedge with options, the bank manager just needs to buy the same amount of 160 put options written on the same March deutsche mark futures contract, with an exercise price of $0.50 per mark. Then if the deutsche mark falls in value, she will exercise the contract and sell the DM 20 million at the $0.50 exercise price, again guaranteeing Frivolous Luxuries its $10 million. To do this, however, the bank manager has to pay a premium for the options, say, 1 cent per mark, for a cost of $1250 per contract and a total cost of $200,000 (= 160 × $1250).

The advantage of hedging with options is that if the deutsche mark rises in value, say, to $0.60, the bank manager will not exercise the option, but the DM 20 million payment will rise in value to $12 million, giving Frivolous Luxuries a net profit of $1.8 million ($2 million minus the $200,000 premium). Thus Frivolous Luxuries is protected from any losses due to a depreciation of the deutsche mark but will gain from any appreciation of the mark. If Sam, the CEO of Frivolous Luxuries, thinks that there is a good possibility that the deutsche mark might appreciate in the next two months to $0.60 but still wants to protect his company from any loss arising from a depreciation of the mark, he will prefer to have the bank manager hedge the foreign exchange risk with options. The $200,000 premium is a small cost to pay for the hedge when he believes that Frivolous Luxuries has a good possibility of making $1.8 million from the appreciation.

Hedging Foreign Exchange Risk with Currency Swaps

Suppose that Frivolous Luxuries expects to sell DM 20 million of goods not just this year but every year for the next seven years. Since futures markets do not offer contracts that far in the future, the bank manager can't use them to hedge Frivolous Luxuries' foreign exchange risk. She might be able to use a set of forward contracts to hedge the risk, but another, possibly cheaper, alternative is to use a currency swap. A currency swap involves an exchange of a periodic set of payments in one currency for a periodic set of payments in another currency.

To see how a currency swap works in a simple example, suppose that the exchange rate is expected to stay at $0.50 per deutsche mark in the future.[5] To hedge the DM 20 million payment that Frivolous Luxuries receives over the next seven years, the bank manager needs to arrange a seven-year swap in which Frivolous Luxuries exchanges DM 20 million each year for $10 million. By making this swap arrangement, Mona has protected Frivolous Luxuries' DM 20 million cash flow from any foreign exchange risk for the next seven years. Ⓐ

---

[5]If the interest rates in the two countries differ, then as we saw from the interest parity condition in Chapter 8, there is an expected change in the exchange rate. Now for interest parity to hold, the party receiving the currency from the country with the higher interest rate must continually increase the payments in the other currency to reflect the expected exchange rate change and the interest-rate differential. In other words, if German interest rates are higher by 2 percentage points than U.S. interest rates, meaning that there is an expected appreciation of the dollar of 2 percent per year, the party receiving the German marks would have to pay 2 percent more in dollars at the end of the first year, 4 percent more at the end of the second year, and so on.

Are Financial Derivatives a Worldwide Time Bomb?

With the bankruptcies of Orange County in 1994 (see Box 3) and the Barings Bank in 1995 (discussed in Chapter 10)—both of which involved trades in financial derivatives—politicians, the media, and regulators have become very concerned about the dangers of derivatives. This concern is international and has spawned a slew of reports issued by such organizations as the Bank for International Settlements (BIS), the Bank of England, the Group of Thirty, the Office of the Comptroller of the Currency (OCC), the Commodity Futures Trading Commission (CFTC), and the Government Accounting Office (GAO). Particularly scary are the notional amounts of derivatives contracts—tens of trillions of dollars worldwide—and the fact that banks, which are subject to bank panics, are major players in the derivatives markets. As a result of these fears, some politicians have called for restrictions on banks' involvement in the derivatives markets. Are financial derivatives a time bomb that could bring down the world financial system?

There are three major concerns about financial derivatives. First is that financial derivatives allow financial institutions to increase their leverage; that is, they can in effect control a proportion of the underlying asset that is many times greater than the amount of money they have had to put up. Increasing their leverage enables them to take huge bets on currency and interest-rate movements, which if they are wrong can bring down the bank, as was the case for Barings in 1995. This concern is valid. As we saw earlier in the chapter, the amount of money placed in margin accounts is only a small fraction of the price of the futures contract, meaning that small movements in the price of a contract can produce losses that are many times the size of the initial amount put in the margin account. Thus although financial derivatives can be used to hedge risk, they can also be used by financial institutions to take on excessive risk.

The second concern is that financial derivatives are too sophisticated for managers of financial institutions because they are so complicated. Although it is true that some financial derivatives can be so complex that some financial managers are not sophisticated enough to use them—a possibility in the Orange County case—this seems unlikely to apply to the big international financial institutions that are the major players in the derivatives markets. Indeed, in the Barings case, the bank was brought down not by trades in complex derivatives but rather by trades in one of the simplest of derivatives, stock index futures. (Recall from Chapter 10 that Barings's problem was more a lack of internal controls at the bank than a problem with derivatives per se.)

A third concern is that banks have holdings of huge notional amounts of financial derivatives, particularly swaps, that greatly exceed the amount of bank capital, and so these derivatives expose the banks to serious risk of failure. Banks are indeed major players in the financial derivatives markets, particularly the swaps market, where our earlier analysis has shown that they are the natural market-makers because they can act as intermediaries between two coun-

BOX 3

The Orange County Bankruptcy

Orange County, California, one of the richest counties in the United States, was forced to declare bankruptcy on December 6, 1994, in the largest municipal bankruptcy filing ever. Orange County's downfall were the investment activities of its treasurer, Robert Citron, who was in charge of the $7.8 billion investment fund, which had not only $4.7 billion of funds from Orange County agencies but also $3.1 billion from 180 other municipalities and local government agencies. For years, the Orange County fund looked like a good investment, with the annual returns averaging 10 percent over the 15-year period to 1994. Unfortunately, these high returns were obtained with a highly leveraged strategy in which the fund purchased quantities of medium- to long-term bonds that were a multiple of the fund's assets and financed these purchases by borrowing with repurchase agreements. Everything was fine until interest rates began to rise in late 1993 and early 1994 and bond prices declined, leaving the fund with large losses.

We have already seen in our discussion of the Barings collapse how the principal-agent problem becomes especially severe once a trader or a manager of a fund starts to experience sizable losses. Once in the hole, the manager of the fund knows that his or her future depends on reversing these losses promptly. In this situation, the fund manager has a strong moral hazard incentive to take excessive risks. This is exactly what Citron did in late 1993 and early 1994 when he began buying large amounts of "inverse floaters," highly risky derivative securities that have high payoffs if long-term bond rates decline.

Unfortunately for Citron, interest rates continued to rise, and the fund slipped deeper in the hole. When Peter Swan, the president of the Irvine Ranch Water District, became suspicious about the financial situation of the fund in November 1994 and asked to redeem $400 million, the jig was up for Citron because the fund did not have the cash to meet this redemption. Finally, on December 5, Citron was forced to resign, and the following day, Orange County declared bankruptcy. When bankruptcy was declared, the fund had estimated losses of $1.5 billion, and was found to have $20 billion of securities, $8.5 billion of which were derivatives, a risky portfolio indeed.

Although the role of derivatives in the Orange County debacle has often been emphasized, the problem here was really one of leverage and the principal-agent problem at work. Indeed, an important reason that Citron was able to get away with such a risky strategy, particularly after the fund sustained large losses, was that disclosure requirements were not as strong as they could be for municipal investment funds in the state of California. In contrast to other states, which require monthly or even daily disclosure of the market value of their municipal investment funds, California required this disclosure only once a year. If California had stricter disclosure requirements, investors in Citron's fund would have found out more quickly the risks he was taking, making it more likely that they would have pulled out their funds. This might have prevented Citron from taking on the risks that he did, and the Orange County bankruptcy would have been avoided.

terparties who would not make the swap without their involvement. However, looking at the notional amount of swaps at banks gives a very misleading picture of their risk exposure. First is that because banks act as intermediaries in the swap markets, as in the swap in Figure 3, they are typically exposed only to credit risk—a default by one of their counterparties. Furthermore, swaps, unlike loans, do not involve payments of the notional amount but rather the much smaller interest payments based on the notional amounts. For example, in the swaps that Citibank arranges in Figure 3, the payments on each of the swaps are only the interest rate times the $1 million notional amount. In the case of a 7 percent interest rate, the payment is only $70,000 for the $1 million swap. Estimates of the credit exposure from swap contracts indicate that they are on the order of 1 percent of the notional value of the contracts and that credit exposure at banks from derivatives is generally less than a quarter of their total credit exposure from loans. Banks' credit exposure from their derivatives activities are thus not out of line with other credit exposures they face. Furthermore, an analysis by the GAO indicates that actual credit losses incurred by banks in their derivatives contracts have been very small, on the order of 0.2 percent of their gross credit exposure.

The conclusion is that financial derivatives do have dangers for financial institutions, but some of these dangers have been overplayed. The biggest danger occurs in trading activities of financial institutions, and as we have seen in Chapter 12, regulators have been paying increased attention to this danger and have issued new disclosure requirements and regulatory guidelines for how derivatives trading should be done. The credit risk exposure posed by derivatives, by contrast, seems to be manageable with standard methods of dealing with credit risk, both by managers of financial institutions and their regulators.

SUMMARY

1. Interest-rate forward contracts, which are agreements to sell a debt instrument at a future (forward) point in time, can be used to hedge interest-rate risk. The advantage of forward contracts is that they are flexible, but the disadvantages are that they are subject to default risk and their market is illiquid.

2. A financial futures contract is similar to an interest-rate forward contract in that it specifies that a debt instrument must be delivered by one party to another on a stated future date. However, it has advantages over a forward contract in that it is not subject to default risk and is more liquid. Forward and futures contracts can be used by financial institutions to hedge (protect) against interest-rate risk.

3. Stock index futures are financial futures whose underlying financial instrument is a stock market index like the Standard & Poor's 500 Index.

4. An option contract gives the purchaser the right to buy (call option) or sell (put option) a security at the exercise (strike) price within a specific period of time. The profit function for options is nonlinear—profits do not always grow by the same amount for a given change in the price of the underlying financial instrument. The nonlinear profit function for options explains why their value (as reflected by the premium paid for them) is negatively related to the exercise price for call options, positively related to the exercise price for put options, positively related to the term to expiration for both call and put options, and positively related to the volatility of the prices of the underlying financial instrument for both call and put options. Financial institutions use futures options to hedge interest-rate risk in a similar fashion to the way they use financial futures and forward contracts. Futures options may be preferred for macro hedges because they suffer from fewer accounting problems than financial futures.

5. Interest-rate swaps involve the exchange of one set of interest payments for another set of interest payments and have default risk and liquidity problems similar to those of forward contracts. As a result, interest-rate swaps often involve intermediaries such as large commercial banks and investment banks that make a market in swaps. Financial institutions find that interest-rate swaps are useful ways to hedge interest-rate risk. Interest-rate swaps have one big advantage over financial futures and options: They can be written for very long horizons.

6. Forwards, futures, options, and swaps are useful for hedging not only interest-rate risk but also foreign exchange risk.

7. There are three concerns about the dangers of derivatives: They allow financial institutions more easily to increase their leverage and take big bets (by effectively enabling them to hold a larger amount of the underlying assets than the amount of money put down), are too complex for managers of financial institutions to understand, and expose financial institutions to large credit risks because of the huge notional amounts of derivative contracts greatly exceed the capital of these institutions. The second two dangers seem to be overplayed, but the danger from increased leverage using derivatives is real.

KEY TERMS

American option, p. 367

arbitrage, p. 358

basis risk, p. 364

call option, p. 368

currency swap, p. 375

European option, p. 367

exercise price (strike price), p. 367

financial derivatives, p. 354

financial futures contract, p. 356

financial futures option (futures option), p. 367

forward contract, p. 354

hedge, p. 355

interest-rate forward contract, p. 354

interest-rate swap, p. 375

long position, p. 355

macro hedge, p. 359

margin requirement, p. 364

marked to market, p. 364

micro hedge, p. 359

notional principal, p. 375

open interest, p. 360

option, p. 367

premium, p. 367

put option, p. 368

short position, p. 355

stock option, p. 367

swap, p. 375

QUESTIONS AND PROBLEMS

1. If the pension fund you manage expects to have an inflow of $120 million six months from now, what forward contract would you seek to enter into to lock in current interest rates?

*2. If the portfolio you manage is holding $25 million of 8s of 2015 Treasury bonds with a price of 110, what forward contract would you enter into to hedge the interest-rate risk on these bonds over the coming year?

3. If at the expiration date, the deliverable Treasury bond is selling for 101 but the Treasury bond futures contract is selling for 102, what will happen to the futures price? Explain your answer.

*4. If you buy a $100,000 June Treasury bond contract for 108 and the price of the deliverable Treasury bond at the expiration date is 102, what is your profit or loss on the contract?

5. Suppose that the pension you are managing is expecting an inflow of funds of $100 million next year and you want to make sure that you will earn the current interest rate of 8 percent when you invest the incoming funds in long-term bonds.

How would you use the futures market to do this?

*6. How would you use the options market to accomplish the same thing as in Problem 5? What are the advantages and disadvantages of using an options contract rather than a futures contract?

7. If you buy a put option on a $100,000 Treasury bond futures contract with an exercise price of 95 and the price of the Treasury bond is 120 at expiration, is the contract in the money, out of the money, or at the money? What is your profit or loss on the contract if the premium was $4000?

*8. Suppose that you buy a call option on a $100,000 Treasury bond futures contract with an exercise price of 110 for a premium of $1500. If on expiration the futures contract has a price of 111, what is your profit or loss on the contract?

9. Explain why greater volatility or a longer term to maturity leads to a higher premium on both call and put options.

*10. Why does a lower strike price imply that a call option will have a higher premium and a put option a lower premium?

11. If the finance company you manage has an income gap of +$5 million, describe an interest-rate swap that would eliminate the company's income gap.

*12. If the savings and loan you manage has an income gap of −$42 million, describe an interest-rate swap that would eliminate the S&L's income risk from changes in interest rates.

13. If your company has a payment of 200 million deutsche marks due one year from now, how would you hedge the foreign exchange risk in this payment with DM 125,000 futures contracts?

*14. Suppose that interest rates in the United States and Great Britain are equal, the exchange rate is $1.50 per pound sterling, and your company is due a payment of £200,000 every year for the next five years. What currency swap would you make to hedge the foreign exchange risk on these payments?

15. If your company has to make a DM 125 million payment to a German company three months from now, how would you hedge the foreign exchange risk in this payment with option contracts on DM 125,000 futures contracts?

PART IV

CENTRAL BANKING
and the
CONDUCT
of
MONETARY
POLICY

Chapter 15

STRUCTURE OF CENTRAL BANKS AND THE FEDERAL RESERVE SYSTEM

PREVIEW   The most important players in financial markets throughout the world are central banks, the government authorities in charge of monetary policy. Central banks' actions affect interest rates, the amount of credit, and the money supply, all of which have direct impacts not only on financial markets but also on aggregate output and inflation. To understand the role that central banks play in financial markets and the overall economy, we need to understand how these organizations work. Who controls central banks and determines their actions? What motivates their behavior? Who holds the reins of power?

In this chapter we look at the institutional structure of major central banks and particularly focus on the Federal Reserve System, the most important central bank in the world. We start by focusing on the formal institutional structure of the Fed and then examine the more relevant informal structure that determines where the true power within the Federal Reserve System lies. By understanding who makes the decisions, we will have a better idea of how they are made. We then look at several other major central banks and see how they are organized. With this information, we will be more able to comprehend the actual conduct of monetary policy described in the following chapters.

ORIGINS OF THE FEDERAL RESERVE SYSTEM

Of all the central banks in the world, the Federal Reserve System probably has the most unusual structure. To understand why this structure arose, we must go back before 1913, when the Federal Reserve System was created.

Before the twentieth century, a major characteristic of American politics was the fear of centralized power, as seen in the checks and balances of the Constitution and the preservation of states' rights. This fear of centralized power was one source of the American resistance to the establishment of a central bank (see Chapter 11). Another source was the traditional American distrust of moneyed interests, the most prominent symbol of which was a central bank. The open hostility of the American public to the existence of a central bank resulted in the demise of the first two experiments in central banking, whose function was to police the banking system: The First Bank of the United States was disbanded in 1811, and the national charter of the Second Bank of the United States expired in 1836 after its renewal was vetoed in 1832 by President Andrew Jackson.

The termination of the Second Bank's national charter in 1836 created a severe problem for American financial markets because there was no lender of last resort who could provide reserves to the banking system to avert a bank panic. Hence in the nineteenth and early twentieth centuries, nationwide bank panics became a regular event, occurring every twenty years or so, culminating in the panic of 1907. The 1907 panic resulted in such widespread bank failures and such substantial losses to depositors that the public was finally convinced that a central bank was needed to prevent future panics.

The hostility of the American public to banks and centralized authority created great opposition to the establishment of a single central bank like the Bank of England. Fear was rampant that the moneyed interests on Wall Street (including the largest corporations and banks) would be able to manipulate such an institution to gain control over the economy and that federal operation of the central bank might result in too much government intervention in the affairs of private banks. Serious disagreements existed over whether the central bank should be a private bank or a government institution. Because of the heated debates on these issues, a compromise was struck. In the great American tradition, Congress wrote an elaborate system of checks and balances into the Federal Reserve Act of 1913, which created the Federal Reserve System with its 12 regional Federal Reserve banks (see Box 1).

FORMAL STRUCTURE OF THE FEDERAL RESERVE SYSTEM

The formal structure of the Federal Reserve System was intended by writers of the Federal Reserve Act to diffuse power along regional lines, between the private sector and the government, and among bankers, businesspeople, and the public. This initial diffusion of power has resulted in the evolution of the Federal Reserve System to include the following entities: the **Federal Reserve banks,** the **Board of Governors of the Federal Reserve System,** the **Federal Open Market Committee (FOMC),** the Federal Advisory Council, and around 4000 member commercial banks. Figure 1 outlines the relationships of these entities to one another and to the three policy tools of the Fed (open market operations, the discount rate, and reserve requirements) discussed in Chapters 16 to 18.

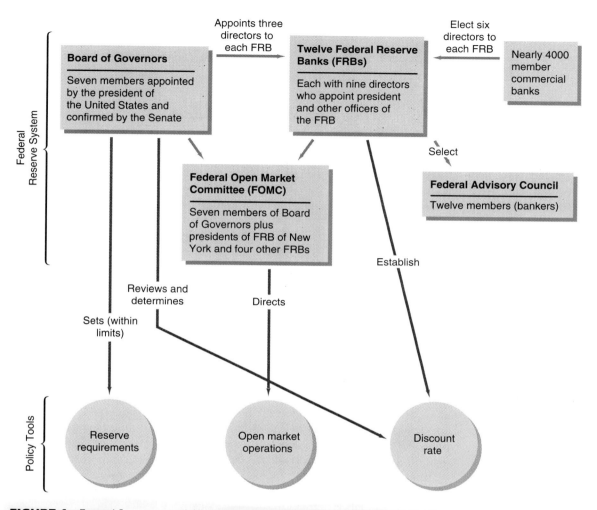

FIGURE 1   Formal Structure and Allocation of Policy Tools in the Federal Reserve

Federal Reserve Banks

Each of the 12 Federal Reserve districts has one main Federal Reserve bank, which may have branches in other cities in the district. The locations of these districts, the Federal Reserve banks, and their branches are shown in Figure 2. The three largest Federal Reserve banks in terms of assets are those of New York, Chicago, and San Francisco—combined they hold over 50 percent of the assets (discount loans, securities, and other holdings) of the Federal Reserve System. The New York bank, with around one-quarter of the assets, is the most important of the Federal Reserve banks (see Box 2).

Each of the Federal Reserve banks is a quasi-public (part private, part government) institution owned by the private commercial banks in the district who are members of the Federal Reserve System. These member banks have purchased stock in their district Federal Reserve bank (a requirement of membership), and the dividends paid by that stock are limited by law to 6 percent

The Political Genius of the Founders of the Federal Reserve System

The history of the United States has been one of public hostility to banks and especially to a central bank. How were the politicians who founded the Federal Reserve able to design a system that has become one of the most prestigious institutions in the United States?

The answer is that the founders recognized that if power was too concentrated in either Washington or New York, cities that Americans love to hate, an American central bank might not have enough public support to operate effectively. They thus decided to set up a decentralized system with 12 Federal Reserve banks spread throughout the country to make sure that all regions of the country were represented in monetary policy deliberations. In addition, they made the Federal Reserve banks quasi-private institutions overseen by directors from the private sector living in that district who represent views from that region and are in close contact with the president of the Federal Reserve bank. The unusual structure of the Federal Reserve System has promoted a concern in the Fed with regional issues as is evident in Federal Reserve bank publications. Without this unusual structure, the Federal Reserve System might have been far less popular with the public, making the institution far less effective.

annually. The member banks elect six directors for each district bank; three more are appointed by the Board of Governors. Together, these nine directors appoint the president of the bank (subject to the approval of the Board of Governors).

The directors of a district bank are classified into three categories, A, B, and C: The three A directors (elected by the member banks) are professional bankers, and the three B directors (also elected by the member banks) are prominent leaders from industry, labor, agriculture, or the consumer sector. The three C directors, who are appointed by the Board of Governors to represent the public interest, are not allowed to be officers, employees, or stockholders of banks. This design for choosing directors was intended by the framers of the Federal Reserve Act to ensure that the directors of each Federal Reserve bank would reflect all constituencies of the American public.

The 12 Federal Reserve banks perform the following functions:

- Clear checks
- Issue new currency
- Withdraw damaged currency from circulation
- Evaluate proposed mergers and applications for banks to expand their activities
- Administer and make discount loans to banks in their districts
- Act as liaisons between the business community and the Federal Reserve System
- Examine bank holding companies and state-chartered member banks
- Collect data on local business conditions

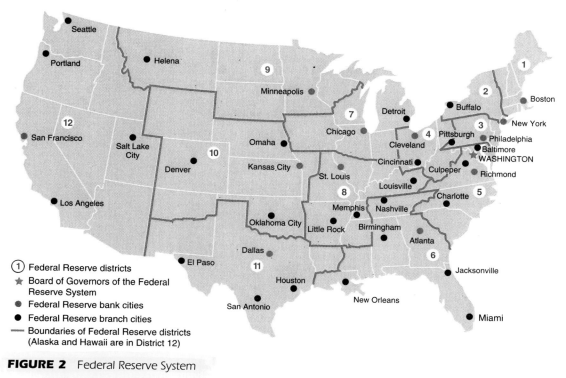

FIGURE 2   Federal Reserve System

Source: Federal Reserve *Bulletin.*

- Use their staffs of professional economists to research topics related to the conduct of monetary policy

The 12 Federal Reserve banks are involved in monetary policy in several ways:

1. Their directors "establish" the discount rate (although the discount rate in each district is reviewed and determined by the Board of Governors).
2. They decide which banks, member and nonmember alike, can obtain discount loans from the Federal Reserve bank.
3. Their directors select one commercial banker from each bank's district to serve on the Federal Advisory Council, which consults with the Board of Governors and provides information that helps in the conduct of monetary policy.
4. Five of the 12 bank presidents each have a vote in the Federal Open Market Committee, which directs **open market operations** (the purchase and sale of government securities that affect both interest rates and the amount of reserves in the banking system). As explained in Box 2, the president of the New York Fed always has a vote in the FOMC, making it the most important of the banks; the other four votes allocated to the district banks rotate annually among the remaining 11 presidents.

Special Role of the Federal Reserve Bank of New York

The Federal Reserve Bank of New York plays a special role in the Federal Reserve System for several reasons. First, its district contains many of the largest commercial banks in the United States, the safety and soundness of which are paramount to the health of the U.S. financial system. The Federal Reserve Bank of New York conducts examinations of bank holding companies and state-chartered banks in its district, making it the supervisor of some of the most important financial institutions in our financial system. Not surprisingly, given this responsibility, the Bank Supervision group is one of the largest units of the New York Fed and is by far the largest bank supervision group in the Federal Reserve System.

The second reason for the New York Fed's special role is its active involvement in the bond and foreign exchange markets. The New York Fed houses the open market desk, which conducts open market operations—the purchase and sale of bonds—that determine the amount of reserves in the banking system. Because of this involvement in the Treasury securities market, as well as its walking-distance location near the New York and American Stock Exchanges, the officials at the Federal Reserve Bank of New York are in constant contact with the major domestic financial markets in the United States. In addition, the Federal Reserve Bank of New York also houses the foreign exchange desk, which conducts foreign exchange interventions on behalf of the Federal Reserve System and the U.S. Treasury. Its involvement

in these financial markets means that the New York Fed is an important source of information on what is happening in domestic and foreign financial markets, particularly during crisis periods, as well as a liaison between officials in the Federal Reserve System and private participants in the markets.

The third reason for the Federal Reserve Bank of New York's prominence is that it is the only Federal Reserve bank to be a member of the Bank for International Settlements (BIS). Thus the president of the New York Fed, along with the chairman of the Board of Governors, represent the Federal Reserve System in its regular monthly meetings with other major central bankers at the BIS. This close contact with foreign central bankers and interaction with foreign exchange markets means that the New York Fed has a special role in international relations, both with other central bankers and with private market participants. Adding to its prominence in international circles is that the New York Fed is the repository for over $100 billion of the world's gold, an amount greater than the gold at Fort Knox.

Finally, the president of the Federal Reserve Bank of New York, currently William McDonough, is the only permanent member of the FOMC among the Federal Reserve bank presidents, serving as the vice chairman of the committee. Thus he, the chairman, and the vice chairman of the Board of Governors are the three most important officials in the Federal Reserve System.

Member Banks   All *national banks* (commercial banks chartered by the Office of the Comptroller of the Currency) are required to be members of the Federal Reserve System. Commercial banks chartered by the states are not required to be members, but they can choose to join. Currently, around one-third of the commercial banks in the United States are members of the Federal Reserve System, having declined from a peak figure of 49 percent in 1947.

Before 1980, only member banks were required to keep reserves as deposits at the Federal Reserve banks. Nonmember banks were subject to reserve requirements determined by their states, which typically allowed them to hold much of their reserves in interest-bearing securities. Because no interest is paid on reserves deposited at the Federal Reserve banks, it was costly to be a member of the system, and as interest rates rose, the relative cost of membership rose, and more and more banks left the system.

This decline in Fed membership was a major concern of the Board of Governors (one reason was that it lessened the Fed's control over the money supply, making it more difficult for the Fed to conduct monetary policy). The chairman of the Board of Governors repeatedly called for new legislation that required all commercial banks to be members of the Federal Reserve System. One result of the Fed's pressure on Congress was a provision in the Depository Institutions Deregulation and Monetary Control Act of 1980: All depository institutions became subject (by 1987) to the same requirements to keep deposits at the Fed, so member and nonmember banks would be on an equal footing in terms of reserve requirements. In addition, all depository institutions were given access to the Federal Reserve facilities, such as the discount window (discussed in Chapter 18) and Fed check clearing, on an equal basis. These provisions ended the decline in Fed membership and reduced the distinction between member and nonmember banks.

Board of Governors of the Federal Reserve System

At the head of the Federal Reserve System is the seven-member Board of Governors, headquartered in Washington, D.C. Each governor is appointed by the president of the United States and confirmed by the Senate. To limit the president's control over the Fed and insulate the Fed from other political pressures, the governors serve one nonrenewable 14-year term, with one governor's term expiring every other January.[1] The governors (many are professional economists) are required to come from different Federal Reserve districts to prevent the interests of one region of the country from being overrepresented. The chairman of the Board of Governors is chosen from among the seven governors and serves a four-year term. It is expected that once a new chairman is chosen, the old chairman resigns from the Board of Governors, even if there are many years left to his or her term as a governor.

The Board of Governors is actively involved in decisions concerning the conduct of monetary policy. All seven governors are members of the FOMC and vote on the conduct of open market operations. Because there are only 12 voting members on this committee (seven governors and five presidents of the district banks), the board has the majority of the votes. The board also sets reserve requirements (within limits imposed by legislation) and effectively controls the

---

[1]Although technically the governor's term is nonrenewable, a governor can resign just before the term expires and then be reappointed by the president. This explains how one governor, William McChesney Martin Jr., served for 28 years. Since Martin, the chairman from 1951 to 1970, retired from the board in 1970, the practice of extending a governor's term beyond 14 years has become a rarity.

discount rate by the "review and determination" process, whereby it approves or disapproves the discount rate "established" by the Federal Reserve banks. The chairman of the board advises the president of the United States on economic policy, testifies in Congress, and speaks for the Federal Reserve System to the media. The chairman and other governors may also represent the United States in negotiations with foreign governments on economic matters. The board has a staff of professional economists (larger than those of individual Federal Reserve banks), which provides economic analysis that the board uses in making its decisions. (Box 3 discusses the role of the research staff.)

Through legislation, the Board of Governors has often been given duties not directly related to the conduct of monetary policy. In the past, for example, the board set the maximum interest rates payable on certain types of time deposits under Regulation Q. (Since Regulation Q was eliminated in 1986, the board no longer has this authority.) Under the Credit Control Act of 1969 (which expired in 1982), the board had the ability to regulate and control credit once the president of the United States approved. The Board of Governors also sets margin requirements, the fraction of the purchase price of the securities that has to be paid for with cash rather than borrowed funds. It also sets the salary of the president and all officers of each Federal Reserve bank and reviews each bank's budget. Finally, the board has substantial bank regulatory functions: It approves bank mergers and applications for new activities, specifies the permissible activities of bank holding companies, and supervises the activities of foreign banks in the United States.

Federal Open Market Committee (FOMC)

The FOMC usually meets eight times a year (about every six weeks) and makes decisions regarding the conduct of open market operations, which influence the monetary base. The committee consists of the seven members of the Board of Governors, the president of the Federal Reserve Bank of New York, and presidents of four other Federal Reserve banks. The chairman of the Board of Governors also presides as the chairman of the FOMC. Even though only presidents of five of the Federal Reserve banks are voting members of the FOMC, the other seven presidents of the district banks attend FOMC meetings and participate in discussions. Hence they have some input into the committee's decisions.

Because open market operations are the most important policy tool that the Fed has for controlling the money supply, the FOMC is necessarily the focal point for policymaking in the Federal Reserve System. Although reserve requirements and the discount rate are not actually set by the FOMC, decisions in regard to these policy tools are effectively made there. The FOMC does not actually carry out securities purchases or sales. Rather it issues directives to the trading desk at the Federal Reserve Bank of New York, where the manager for domestic open market operations supervises a roomful of people who execute the purchases and sales of the government or agency securities. The manager communicates daily with the FOMC members and their staffs concerning the activities of the trading desk.

BOX 3 INSIDE THE FED

Role of the Research Staff

The Federal Reserve System is the largest employer of economists not just in the United States but in the world. The system's research staff has around 1000 people, about half of whom are economists. Of these 500 economists, 250 are at the Board of Governors, 100 are at the Federal Reserve Bank of New York, and the remainder are at the other Federal Reserve banks. What do all these economists do?

The most important task of the Fed's economists is to follow the incoming data from government agencies and private sector organizations on the economy and provide guidance to the policymakers on where the economy may be heading and what the impact of monetary policy actions on the economy might be. Before each FOMC meeting, the research staff at each Federal Reserve bank briefs its president and the senior management of the bank on its forecast for the U.S. economy and the issues that are likely to be discussed at the meeting. The research staff also provides briefing materials or a formal briefing on the economic outlook for the bank's region, something that each president discusses at the FOMC meeting. Meanwhile, at the Board of Governors, economists maintain a large econometric model (a model whose equations are estimated with statistical procedures) that helps them produce their forecasts of the national economy, and they too brief the governors on the national economic outlook.

The research staffers at the banks and the board also provide support for the bank supervisory staff, tracking developments in the banking sector and other financial markets and institutions and providing bank examiners with technical advice that they might need in the course of their examinations. Because the Board of Governors has to decide on whether to approve bank mergers, the research staff at both the board and the bank in whose district the merger is to take place prepare information on what effect the proposed merger might have on the competitive environment. To assure compliance with the Community Reinvestment Act, economists also analyze a bank's performance in its lending activities in different communities.

Because of the increased influence of developments in foreign countries on the U.S. economy, the research staff, particularly at the New York Fed and the board, produce reports on the major foreign economies. They also conduct research on developments in the foreign exchange market because of its growing importance in the monetary policy process and to support the activities of the foreign exchange desk. Economists also help support the operation of the open market desk by projecting reserve growth and the growth of the monetary aggregates.

Staff economists also engage in basic research on the effects of monetary policy on output and inflation, developments in the labor markets, international trade, international capital markets, banking and other financial institutions, financial markets, and the regional economy, among other topics. This research is published widely in academic journals and in Reserve bank publications. (Federal Reserve bank reviews are a good source of supplemental material for money and banking students.)

Another important activity of the research staff primarily at the Reserve banks is in the public education area. Staff economists are called on frequently to make presentations to the board of directors at their banks or to make speeches to the public in their district.

The FOMC Meeting

The FOMC meeting takes place in the boardroom on the second floor of the main building of the Board of Governors in Washington. The seven governors and the 12 Reserve Bank presidents, along with the secretary of the FOMC, the board's director of the Research and Statistics Division and his deputy, and the directors of the Monetary Affairs and International Finance Divisions, sit around a massive conference table. Although only five of the Reserve Bank presidents have voting rights on the FOMC at any given time, all actively participate in the deliberations. Seated around the sides of the room are the directors of research at each of the Reserve banks and other senior board and Reserve Bank officials, who, by tradition, do not speak at the meeting.

Except for the meetings before the February and July testimony by the chairman of the Board of Governors before Congress, the meeting starts on Tuesday at 9:00 A.M. sharp with a quick approval of the minutes of the previous meeting of the FOMC. The first substantive agenda item is the report by the manager of system open market operations on foreign currency and domestic open market operations and other issues related to these topics. After the governors and Reserve Bank presidents finish asking questions and discussing these reports, a vote is taken to ratify them.

The next stage in the meeting is a presentation of the board staff's national economic forecast, which is referred to as the "green book" forecast (see Box 4), by the director of the Research and Statistics Division at the board. After the governors and Reserve Bank presidents have queried the division director about the forecast, the so-called *go-round* occurs: Each bank president presents an overview of economic conditions in his or her district and the bank's assessment of the national outlook, and each governor, except for the chairman, gives a view of the national outlook. By tradition, remarks avoid the topic of monetary policy at this time.

After a coffee break, everyone returns to the boardroom and the agenda turns to current monetary policy and the domestic policy directive. The board's director of the Monetary Affairs Division then leads off the discussion by outlining the different scenarios for monetary policy actions outlined in the blue book (see Box 4) and may describe an issue relating to how monetary policy should be conducted. After a question-and-answer period, the chairman (currently Alan Greenspan) sets the stage for the following discussion by presenting his views on the state of the economy and then typically makes a recommendation for what monetary policy action should be taken. Then each of the FOMC members as well as the nonvoting bank presidents express his or her views on monetary policy, and the chairman summarizes the discussion and proposes specific wording for the directive to the open market desk (see Box 5). The secretary of the FOMC formally reads the proposed directive, and the members of the FOMC vote.[2]

Then there is an informal buffet lunch, and while eating, the participants hear a presentation on the latest developments in Congress on banking legislation and other legislation relevant to the Federal Reserve. Around 2:15 P.M. the meeting breaks up and the public announcement is made about the outcome of the meeting: whether the federal funds rate and discount rate have been raised, lowered,

---

[2]The decisions expressed in the directive may not be unanimous, and the dissenting views are made public. However, except in rare cases, the chairman's vote is always on the winning side.

Green, Blue, and Beige

What Do These Colors Mean at the Fed?
Three research documents play an important role in the monetary policy process and at Federal Open Market Committee meetings. The national forecast for the next two years, generated by the Federal Reserve Board of Governors' Research and Statistics Division, is placed between green covers and is thus known as the "green book." It is provided to all who attend the FOMC meeting. The "blue book," in blue covers, is also provided to all participants at the FOMC meeting. It contains the projections for the monetary aggregates prepared by the Monetary Affairs Division at the Board of Governors and contains typically three alternative scenarios for the stance of monetary policy (labeled A, B, and C). The "beige book," with beige covers, is produced by the Reserve banks and details evidence gleaned either from surveys or from talks with key businesses and financial institutions on the state of the economy in each of the Federal Reserve districts. This is the only one of the three books that is distributed publicly, and it often receives a lot of attention in the press.

or left unchanged.[3] The postmeeting announcement is an innovation initiated in 1994. Before then, no such announcement was made, and the markets had to guess what policy action was taken. The decision to announce this information was a step in the direction of greater openness by the Fed.

INFORMAL STRUCTURE OF THE FEDERAL RESERVE SYSTEM

The Federal Reserve Act and other legislation give us some idea of the formal structure of the Federal Reserve System and who makes decisions at the Fed. What is written in black and white, however, does not necessarily reflect the reality of the power and decision-making structure.

As envisioned in 1913, the Federal Reserve System was to be a highly decentralized system designed to function as 12 separate, cooperating central banks. In the original plan, the Fed was not responsible for the health of the economy through its control of the money supply and its ability to affect interest rates. Over time, it has acquired the responsibility for promoting a stable economy, and this

---

[3]The meetings before the February and July chairman's testimony before Congress, required by the Humphrey-Hawkins legislation, have a somewhat different format. Rather than start Tuesday morning at 9:00 A.M. like the other meetings, they start at 2:30 on Tuesday and go over to Wednesday, with the usual announcement around 2:15 P.M. These longer meetings have the additional agenda item of a discussion and vote on the ranges for the monetary aggregates, which are transmitted to Congress, a requirement of the Humphrey-Hawkins Act. Because, as we will see in Chapter 19, monetary aggregates have been deemphasized in the conduct of monetary policy, this agenda item is not as important as it once was.

BOX 5 INSIDE THE FED

Decoding the FOMC Directive

The FOMC directive to the open market desk is released to the public after the following FOMC meeting. Thus it appears in the Federal Reserve *Bulletin* six weeks or so after the policy action was taken. The final operational paragraph provides much information about the stance of monetary policy, but it has nuances that require a magic decoder ring to unscramble its meaning. The first sentence of the operational paragraph reads as follows (italics indicate where the alternative words fit in).

> In the implementation of policy for the immediate future, the Committee seeks to *(increase, decrease, maintain) (slightly, somewhat, significantly)* the existing degree of pressure on reserve positions.

"Increase" implies that the federal funds rate is to be raised, "decrease" means the rate is to be lowered, and "maintain" means the rate is to remain unchanged. The next word indicates the extent of the change: "slightly" means one-quarter of a percentage point, "somewhat" means one-half of a percentage point, and "significantly" means three-fourths of a percentage point. Thus if "decrease somewhat" is used, the federal funds rate is to be lowered by 0.5 percent.

A directive can also be described in FOMC jargon as "symmetric" or "asymmetric." A *symmetric directive* means the committee has no bias as to what should happen to the monetary policy stance between meetings. In this case, the chairman has the discretion to change the federal funds rate by a quarter of a percentage point without consulting the committee but is unlikely to do so without consultation. An *asymmetric directive* means that the FOMC has a bias toward how monetary policy should be changed. If the directive is asymmetric, the chairman has the authority to direct the open market desk to change the federal funds rate in the direction specified by up to half a percentage point without consultation with the committee.

Whether a directive is symmetric or asymmetric can be discerned from the second sentence in the operational paragraph. If the second sentence reads "somewhat greater or somewhat lesser reserve restraint would be acceptable in the intermeeting period," the directive is symmetric, and there is no bias to the monetary policy stance. If it says "somewhat greater reserve restraint would or slightly lesser reserve restraint might be acceptable in the intermeeting period," it is asymmetric in the direction of raising interest rates, and if it is worded "slightly greater reserve restraint might or somewhat lesser reserve restraint would be acceptable in the intermeeting period," it is asymmetric with a bias toward lowering rates.

Now let's use our magic decoder ring to interpret the final operational paragraph of the directive from the FOMC meeting held on August 20, 1996. (The underlined phrases are the ones that change from directive to directive and tell us the stance of policy.)

> In the implementation of policy for the immediate future, the Committee seeks to <u>maintain</u> the existing degree of pressure on reserve positions. In the context of the Committee's long-run objectives for price stability and sustainable economic growth, and giving careful consideration to economic, financial, and monetary developments, <u>somewhat greater reserve restraint would or slightly lesser reserve restraint might</u> be acceptable in the intermeeting period. The contemplated reserve conditions are expected to be consistent with moderate growth in M2 and M3 over the coming months.

The first sentence indicates the stance on monetary policy was unchanged, leaving the federal funds rate as it was. However, the second sentence indicates the directive was asymmetric, with a bias toward raising the federal funds rate in the intermeeting period.

responsibility has caused the Federal Reserve System to evolve slowly into a more unified central bank.

The framers of the Federal Reserve Act of 1913 intended the Fed to have only one basic tool of monetary policy, the control of discount loans to member banks. The use of open market operations as a tool for monetary control was not yet well understood, and reserve requirements were fixed by the Federal Reserve Act. The discount tool was to be controlled by the joint decision of the Federal Reserve banks and the Federal Reserve Board (which later became the Board of Governors), so that both would share equally in the determination of monetary policy. However, the board's ability to "review and determine" the discount rate effectively allowed it to dominate the district banks in setting this policy.

Banking legislation during the Great Depression years centralized power within the newly created Board of Governors by giving it effective control over the remaining two tools of monetary policy, open market operations and changes in reserve requirements. The Banking Act of 1933 granted the FOMC authority to determine open market operations, and the Banking Act of 1935 gave the board the majority of votes in the FOMC. The Banking Act of 1935 also gave the board authority to change reserve requirements.

Since the 1930s, then, the Board of Governors has acquired the reins of control over the tools for conducting monetary policy. In recent years, the power of the board has become even greater. Although the directors of a Federal Reserve bank choose its president with the approval of the board, the board sometimes suggests a choice (often a professional economist) for president of a Federal Reserve bank to the directors of the bank, who then often follow the board's suggestions. Since the board sets the salary of the bank's president and reviews the budget of each Federal Reserve bank, it has further influence over the district banks' activities.

If the Board of Governors has so much power, what power do the Federal Advisory Council and the "owners" of the Federal Reserve banks—the member banks—actually have within the Federal Reserve System? The answer is almost none. Although member banks own stock in the Federal Reserve banks, they have none of the usual benefits of ownership. First, they have no claim on the earnings of the Fed and get paid only a 6 percent annual dividend, regardless of how much the Fed earns. Second, they have no say over how their property is used by the Federal Reserve System, in contrast to stockholders of private corporations. Third, there is usually only a single candidate for each of the six A and B directorships "elected" by the member banks, and this candidate is frequently suggested by the president of the Federal Reserve bank (who, in turn, is approved by the Board of Governors). The net result is that member banks are essentially frozen out of the political process at the Fed and have little effective power. Fourth, as its name implies, the Federal Advisory Council has only an advisory capacity and has no authority over Federal Reserve policymaking. Although the member bank "owners" do not have the usual power associated with being a stockholder, they do play an important but subtle role in the Federal Reserve System (see Box 6).

A fair characterization of the Federal Reserve System as it has evolved is that it functions as a central bank, headquartered in Washington, D.C., with branches

Role of Member Banks in the Federal Reserve System

Although the member bank stockholders in each Federal Reserve bank have little direct power in the Federal Reserve System, they do play an important role. Their six representatives on the board of directors of each bank have a major oversight function. Along with the three public interest directors, they oversee the audit process for the Federal Reserve bank, making sure it is being run properly, and also share their management expertise with the senior management of the bank. Because they vote on recommendations by each bank to raise, lower, or maintain the discount rate at its current level, they engage in discussions about monetary policy and transmit their private sector views to the president and senior management of the bank. They also get to understand the inner workings of the Federal Reserve banks and the system so that they can help explain the position of the Federal Reserve to their contacts in the private and political sectors. Advisory councils like the Federal Advisory Council and others that are often set up by the district banks—for example, the Small Business and Agriculture Advisory Council and the Thrift Advisory Council at the New York Fed—are a conduit for the private sector to express views on both the economy and the state of the banking system.

So even though the owners of the Reserve banks do not have the usual voting rights, they are important to the Federal Reserve System because they make sure it does not get out of touch with the needs and opinions of the private sector.

in 12 cities. Because all aspects of the Federal Reserve System are essentially controlled by the Board of Governors, who controls the board? Although the chairman of the Board of Governors does not have legal authority to exercise control over this body, he effectively does so through his ability to act as spokesperson for the Fed and negotiate with Congress and the president of the United States. He also exercises control by setting the agenda of board and FOMC meetings. For example, the fact that the agenda at the FOMC has the chairman speak first about monetary policy enables him to have greater influence over what the policy action will be. The chairman also influences the board through the force of stature and personality. Chairmen of the Board of Governors (including Marriner S. Eccles, William McChesney Martin Jr., Arthur Burns, Paul A. Volcker, and Alan Greenspan) have typically had strong personalities and have wielded great power.

The chairman also exercises power by supervising the board's staff of professional economists and advisers. Because the staff gathers information for the board and conducts the analyses that the board uses in its decisions, it also has some influence over monetary policy. In addition, in the past, several appointments to the board itself have come from within the ranks of its professional staff, making the chairman's influence even farther-reaching and longer-lasting than a four-year term.

The informal power structure of the Fed, in which power is centralized in the chairman of the Board of Governors, is summarized in Figure 3.

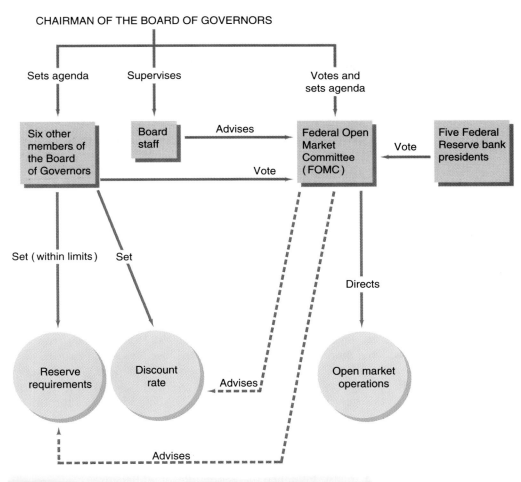

CHAIRMAN OF THE BOARD OF GOVERNORS

Sets agenda

Supervises

Votes and
sets agenda

Six other
members of
the Board
of Governors

Board
staff

Advises

Federal Open
Market
Committee
(FOMC)

Vote

Five Federal
Reserve bank
presidents

Vote

Set (within limits)

Set

Directs

Reserve
requirements

Discount
rate

Advises

Open market
operations

Advises

FIGURE 3   Informal Power Structure of the Federal Reserve System

HOW INDEPENDENT IS THE FED?

When we look, in the next four chapters, at how the Federal Reserve conducts monetary policy, we will want to know why it decides to take certain policy actions but not others. To understand its actions, we must understand the incentives that motivate the Fed's behavior. How free is the Fed from presidential and congressional pressures? Do economic, bureaucratic, or political considerations guide it? Is the Fed truly independent of outside pressures?

The Federal Reserve appears to be remarkably free of the political pressures that influence other government agencies. Not only are the members of the Board of Governors appointed for a 14-year term (and so cannot be ousted from office), but also the term is technically not renewable, eliminating some of the incentive for the governors to curry favor with the president and Congress.

Probably even more important to its independence from the whims of Congress is the Fed's independent and substantial source of revenue from its holdings of securities and, to a lesser extent, from its loans to banks. In recent years, for example, the Fed has had net earnings after expenses of around $20 billion per year—not a bad living if you can find it! Because it returns the bulk of these earnings to the Treasury, it does not get rich from its activities, but this income gives the Fed an important advantage over other government agencies: It is not subject to the appropriations process usually controlled by Congress. Indeed, the General Accounting Office, the auditing agency of the federal government, cannot audit the monetary policy or foreign exchange market functions of the Federal Reserve. Because the power to control the purse strings is usually synonymous with the power of overall control, this feature of the Federal Reserve System contributes to its independence more than any other factor.

Yet the Federal Reserve is still subject to the influence of Congress because the legislation that structures it is written by Congress and is subject to change at any time. When legislators are upset with the Fed's conduct of monetary policy, they frequently threaten to take control of the Fed's finances and force it to submit a budget request like other government agencies. A recent example is the call by Senators Dorgan and Reid in 1996 for Congress to have budgetary authority over the nonmonetary activities of the Federal Reserve. This is a powerful club to wave, and it certainly has some effect in keeping the Fed from straying too far from congressional wishes.

Congress has also passed legislation to make the Federal Reserve more accountable for its actions. In 1975, Congress passed House Concurrent Resolution 133, which requires the Fed to announce its objectives for the growth rates of the monetary aggregates. In the Full Employment and Balanced Growth Act of 1978 (the Humphrey-Hawkins Act), the Fed is required to explain how these objectives are consistent with the economic plans of the president of the United States. In recent years, Representative Henry Gonzalez, the former chairman of the House Banking Committee, has pressured the Fed to be less secretive in its deliberations about monetary policy—with some success, as the Fed's move to a post-FOMC announcement testifies.

The president can also influence the Federal Reserve. Because congressional legislation can affect the Fed directly or affect its ability to conduct monetary policy, the president can be a powerful ally through his influence on Congress. Second, although ostensibly a president might be able to appoint only one or two members to the Board of Governors during each presidential term, in actual practice the president appoints members far more often. One reason is that most governors do not serve out a full 14-year term. (Governors' salaries are substantially below what they can earn in the private sector, thus providing an incentive for them to take private sector jobs before their term expires.) In addition, the president is able to appoint a new chairman of the Board of Governors every four years, and a chairman who is not reappointed is expected to resign from the board so that a new member can be appointed.

The power that the president enjoys through his appointments to the Board of Governors is limited, however. Because the term of the chairman is not necessarily concurrent with that of the president, a president may have to deal with a chairman of the Board of Governors appointed by a previous administration. Alan Greenspan, for example, was appointed chairman in 1987 by President Ronald Reagan and was reappointed to another term by another Republican president, George Bush. When Bill Clinton, a Democrat, became president in 1993, Greenspan had several years left to his term. Clinton was put under tremendous pressure to reappoint Greenspan when his term expired and did so in 1996, even though Greenspan is a Republican.[4]

You can see that the Federal Reserve has extraordinary independence for a government agency and is one of the most independent central banks in the world. Nonetheless, the Fed is not free from political pressures. Indeed, to understand the Fed's behavior, we must recognize that public support for the actions of the Federal Reserve plays a very important role.

STRUCTURE AND INDEPENDENCE OF FOREIGN CENTRAL BANKS

In contrast to the Federal Reserve System, which is decentralized into 12 district banks, which are privately owned, central banks in other industrialized countries consist of one centralized unit that is owned by the government. Here we examine the structure and degree of independence of four of the most important foreign central banks: the Bank of England, the Bundesbank in Germany, the Bank of Canada, and the Bank of Japan.

Bank of England

The Bank of England is the oldest central bank, having been founded in 1694. The Bank Act of 1946 gave the government statutory authority over the Bank of England. The governor of the Bank of England, currently Eddie George, is appointed by the government for a four-year term, as are the 16 directors.

Because the government has statutory power over the bank, it is the least independent of the central banks examined in this chapter. Indeed, the Bank of England can only make recommendations as to what monetary policy should be, as the decision to raise or lower interest rates resides not with the governor of the Bank of England but with the chancellor of the Exchequer (the equivalent of the U.S. secretary of the Treasury). Recently, the government has made three major institutional changes that have increased somewhat the independence of the Bank of England. First, in February 1993, the monthly meeting between the chancellor and the governor to set monetary policy was formalized. Second, beginning in November 1993, the bank has been given more discretion to decide the timing of any interest-rate change decided by the chancellor, as long as the change is made before the next meeting. Third, since April 1994, the minutes of the meeting between the chancellor and the governor have been released two weeks after the next monthly meeting, a lag of six weeks. (Previously, the lag was 30 years—quite a change.) These measures have given the Bank of England a more public role in the setting of interest rates. However, several recent examples where the

---

[4]Similarly, William McChesney Martin Jr., the chairman from 1951 to 1970, was appointed by President Truman (Dem.) but was reappointed by Presidents Eisenhower (Rep.), Kennedy (Dem.), and Nixon (Rep.). Also Paul Volcker, the chairman from 1979 to 1987, was appointed by President Carter (Dem.) but was reappointed by President Reagan (Rep.).

government has overruled the governor on interest-rate changes indicate that the Bank of England is still subservient to the government.

Deutsche Bundesbank

The Deutsche Bundesbank, more commonly referred to as the Bundesbank or as Buba by financial market participants, was founded in 1957 but had its predecessor in the Prussian Bank, founded in 1846. Like the Federal Reserve, the Bundesbank has a mix of national and regional appointees on the Direktorium, the monetary policymaking body of the bank. The state governments appoint heads of their state central banks, who are also directors of the Bundesbank. National directors, all of whom serve six-year terms, are appointed by the parliament. The governor of the Bundesbank, currently Hans Tietmayer, is appointed by the directors for an eight-year term.

The Bundesbank, along with the Swiss National Bank, is considered the most independent central bank in the world. Monetary policy is determined by the Bundesbank on its own authority, and there is no obligation for the bank to provide credit to the government. Furthermore, in contrast to the Federal Reserve, whose chairman is required to testify before Congress, the Bundesbank is not required to report to parliament or any other part of the federal government. In addition, the Bundesbank is the only central bank of the five discussed here who has the pursuit of price stability as its sole, formally stated primary mission.

Bank of Canada

Canada was late in establishing a central bank: The Bank of Canada was founded in 1934. Its directors are appointed by the government to three-year terms, and they appoint the governor, currently Gordon Thiesen, who has a seven-year term. The directors oversee a governing council of the four deputy governors and the governor.

The Bank Act was amended in 1967 to give the ultimate responsibility for monetary policy to the government. So on paper, the Bank of Canada is not as independent as the Federal Reserve. In practice, however, the Bank of Canada does essentially control monetary policy. In the event of a disagreement between the bank and the government, the minister of finance can issue a directive that the bank must follow. However, because the directive must be in writing and specific and applicable for a specified period, it is unlikely that such a directive would be issued, and none has been to date.

Bank of Japan

The Bank of Japan (Nippon Ginko) was founded in 1882 during the Meiji Restoration. Monetary policy is determined by the seven-member Policy Board, composed of the governor, currently Yasuo Matsushita, who is appointed by the government to a five-year term, and four members taken from the banking, commercial, or industrial sector appointed by the cabinet to three-year terms. Two nonvoting government representatives also sit on the Policy Board.

The Bank of Japan is not formally independent of the government, with the ultimate power residing with the Ministry of Finance. In addition, Ministry of Finance bureaucrats alternate with officials from the Bank of Japan as governor of the bank. However, by tradition it is understood that the government should not override the Bank of Japan's decisions about monetary policy, and the government has never invoked the provisions allowing it to override the bank. Therefore, the Bank of Japan, although not independent on paper, has a fair degree of independence in practice. Legislation is currently pending that would further increase the Bank of Japan's independence from the Ministry of Finance.

<table>
<tr><td>

The Trend Toward Greater Independence

</td><td>

Our survey of the structure and independence of these major central banks indicates that the Bundesbank (and also the Swiss National Bank) are the most independent, followed closely by the Federal Reserve. The European Central Bank, which will come into being if European monetary union occurs in 1999 as planned, will have a structure like the Federal Reserve System in which central banks for each country would have a role similar to that of the Reserve banks. The European Central Bank would be highly independent, on a par with the Bundesbank; it would be independent from both the European Union (EU) and the national governments and would have complete control over monetary policy. In addition, like the Bundesbank, the European Central Bank's primary mission would be the pursuit of price stability. A trend in recent years is that more and more governments have been granting greater independence to their central banks; recent examples have been France and Spain. Both theory and experience suggest that more independent central banks produce better monetary policy, thus providing an impetus for this trend.

</td></tr>
</table>

EXPLAINING CENTRAL BANK BEHAVIOR

One view of government bureaucratic behavior is that bureaucracies serve the public interest (this is the *public interest view*). Yet some economists have developed a theory of bureaucratic behavior that suggests other factors that influence how bureaucracies operate. The *theory of bureaucratic behavior* suggests that the objective of a bureaucracy is to maximize its own welfare, just as a consumer's behavior is motivated by the maximization of personal welfare and a firm's behavior is motivated by the maximization of profits. The welfare of a bureaucracy is related to its power and prestige. Thus this theory suggests that an important factor affecting a central bank's behavior is its attempt to increase its power and prestige.

What predictions does this view of a central bank like the Fed suggest? One is that the Federal Reserve will fight vigorously to preserve its autonomy, a prediction verified time and time again as the Fed has continually counterattacked congressional attempts to control its budget. In fact, it is extraordinary how effectively the Fed has been able to mobilize a lobby of bankers and businesspeople to preserve its independence when threatened.

Another prediction is that the Federal Reserve will try to avoid conflict with powerful groups that may threaten to curtail its power and reduce its autonomy. The Fed's behavior may take several forms. One possible factor explaining why the Fed is sometimes slow to increase interest rates and so smooths out their fluctuations is that it wishes to avoid a conflict with the president and Congress over increases in interest rates. The desire to avoid conflict with Congress and the president may also explain why in the past the Fed (particularly the chairman of the Board of Governors) devised clever stratagems to avoid blame for its past mistakes (see Box 7).

The desire of the Fed to hold as much power as possible also explains why it vigorously pursued a campaign to gain control over more banks. The campaign culminated in legislation that expanded jurisdiction of the Fed's reserve requirements to *all* banks (not just the member commercial banks) by 1987.

The theory of bureaucratic behavior seems applicable to the Federal Reserve's actions, but we must recognize that this view of the Fed as being solely concerned with its own self-interest is too extreme. Maximizing one's welfare does not rule out altruism. (You might give generously to a charity because it makes you feel good about yourself, but in the process you are helping a worthy cause.) The Fed is surely concerned that it conduct monetary policy in the public interest. However, much uncertainty and disagreement exist over what monetary policy should be.[5] When it is unclear what is in the public interest, other motives may influence the Fed's behavior. In these situations, the theory of bureaucratic behavior may be a useful guide to predicting what motivates the Fed.

SHOULD THE FED BE INDEPENDENT?

As we have seen, the Federal Reserve is probably the most independent government agency in the United States. Every few years, the question arises in Congress as to whether the independence of the Fed should be curtailed. Politicians who strongly oppose a Fed policy often want to bring it under their supervision in order to impose a policy more to their liking. Should the Fed be independent, or would we be better off with a central bank under the control of the president or Congress?

The Case for Independence

The strongest argument for an independent Federal Reserve rests on the view that subjecting the Fed to more political pressures would impart an inflationary bias to monetary policy. In the view of many observers, politicians in a democratic society are shortsighted because they are driven by the need to win their next election. With this as the primary goal, they are unlikely to focus on long-run objectives, such as promoting a stable price level. Instead, they will seek short-run solutions to problems, like high unemployment and high interest rates, even if the short-run solutions have undesirable long-run consequences. For example, we saw in Chapter 6 that high money growth might lead initially to a drop in interest rates but might cause an increase later as inflation heats up. Would a Federal Reserve under the control of Congress or the president be more likely to pursue a policy of excessive money growth when interest rates are high, even though it would eventually lead to inflation and even higher interest rates in the future? The

---

[5]One example of the uncertainty over how best to conduct monetary policy was discussed in Chapter 3: Economists are not sure how to measure money. So even if economists agreed that controlling the quantity of money is the appropriate way to conduct monetary policy (a controversial position, as we will see in later chapters), the Fed cannot be sure which monetary aggregate it should control.

BOX 7 INSIDE THE FED

Games the Fed Plays

As the theory of bureaucratic behavior predicts, the Fed may play games to obscure its actions in order to avoid congressional interference in its activities. In 1975, Congress passed House Concurrent Resolution 133, which instructed the Fed to report quarterly to the banking committees of the House and the Senate its target ranges for the growth in the monetary aggregates over the next 12 months and how successful it had been in achieving its previous targets. One game that the Fed played was to report on several monetary aggregates (such as M1, M2, and M3) rather than on one: When the Fed testified to Congress on its success in achieving its past targets, it would focus on the particular monetary aggregate whose growth rate was closest to the target range.

In addition to this clever tactic, the Fed devised a procedure for setting its target for monetary aggregates (called *base drift*) that made it more likely that it would hit its targets, thereby avoiding conflict with Congress. Every quarter, the Fed would revise the target values for monetary aggregates by applying target growth rates to the amount at which the aggregate had ended up (a new base). When

the Fed overshot its targets, as frequently occurred after 1975, it revised future target values upward, making it less likely that the monetary aggregates would exceed target ranges in the future. Similarly, if the Fed undershot its targets, it revised future target values downward, making it less likely that the monetary aggregates would fall below the target ranges in the future. Subsequent legislation now restricts the Fed to changing the base for its target ranges only once a year, reducing the extent of base drift.

Another indication that the Fed actively wanted to obscure its actions was its desire for secrecy, as reflected in the active defense of its delay in releasing FOMC directives to Congress or to the public. A former Fed official has stated that "a lot of staffers would concede that [secrecy] is designed to shield the Fed from political oversight." However, this official also stated that this was not a bad thing because "most politicians have a shorter time horizon than is optimal for monetary policy."* However, as discussed earlier, the Fed has provided more information about its monetary policy decisions in recent years.

*Quoted in "Monetary Zeal: How Federal Reserve Under Volcker Finally Slowed Down Inflation," *Wall Street Journal,* December 7, 1984, p. 23.

advocates of an independent Federal Reserve say yes. They believe that a politically insulated Fed is more likely to be concerned with long-run objectives and thus be a defender of a sound dollar and a stable price level.

A variation on the preceding argument is that the political process in America leads to the so-called **political business cycle,** in which just before an election, expansionary policies are pursued to lower unemployment and interest rates. After the election, the bad effects of these policies—high inflation and high interest rates—come home to roost, requiring contractionary policies that politicians hope the public will forget before the next election. There is some evidence that such a political business cycle exists in the United States, and a Federal Reserve under the control of Congress or the president might make the cycle even more pronounced.

Putting the Fed under the control of the president (making it more subject to influence by the Treasury) is also considered dangerous because the Fed can be used to facilitate Treasury financing of large budget deficits by its purchases of Treasury bonds.[6] Treasury pressure on the Fed to "help out" might lead to a more inflationary bias in the economy. An independent Fed is better able to resist this pressure from the Treasury.

Another argument for Fed independence is that control of monetary policy is too important to leave to politicians, a group that has repeatedly demonstrated a lack of expertise at making hard decisions on issues of great economic importance, such as reducing the budget deficit or reforming the banking system. Another way to state this argument is in terms of the principal-agent problem discussed in Chapters 9 and 12. Both the Federal Reserve and politicians are agents of the public (the principals), and as we have seen, both politicians and the Fed have incentives to act in their own interest rather than in the interest of the public. The argument supporting Federal Reserve independence is that the principal-agent problem is worse for politicians than for the Fed because politicians have fewer incentives to act in the public interest.

Indeed, some politicians may prefer to have an independent Fed, which can be used as a public "whipping boy" to take some of the heat off their shoulders. It is possible that a politician who in private opposes an inflationary monetary policy will be forced to support such a policy in public for fear of not being reelected. An independent Fed can pursue policies that are politically unpopular yet in the public interest.

The Case Against Independence

Proponents of a Fed under the control of the president or Congress argue that it is undemocratic to have monetary policy (which affects almost everyone in the economy) controlled by an elite group responsible to no one. The current lack of accountability of the Federal Reserve has serious consequences: If the Fed performs badly, there is no provision for replacing members (as there is with politicians). True, the Fed needs to pursue long-run objectives, but elected officials of Congress vote on long-run issues also (foreign policy, for example). If we push the argument further that policy is always performed better by elite groups like the Fed, we end up with such conclusions as the Joint Chiefs of Staff should determine military budgets or the IRS should set tax policies with no oversight from the president or Congress. Would you advocate this degree of independence for the Joint Chiefs or the IRS?

The public holds the president and Congress responsible for the economic well-being of the country, yet they lack control over the government agency that may well be the most important factor in determining the health of the economy.

---

[6]The Federal Reserve Act prohibited the Fed from buying Treasury bonds directly from the Treasury (except to roll over maturing securities); instead the Fed buys Treasury bonds on the open market. One possible reason for this prohibition is consistent with the foregoing argument: The Fed would find it harder to facilitate Treasury financing of large budget deficits.

In addition, to achieve a cohesive program that will promote economic stability, monetary policy must be coordinated with fiscal policy (management of government spending and taxation). Only by placing monetary policy under the control of the politicians who also control fiscal policy can these two policies be prevented from working at cross-purposes.

Another argument against Federal Reserve independence is that an independent Fed has not always used its freedom successfully. The Fed failed miserably in its stated role as lender of last resort during the Great Depression, and its independence certainly didn't prevent it from pursuing an overly expansionary monetary policy in the 1960s and 1970s that contributed to rapid inflation in this period.

Our earlier discussion also suggests that the Federal Reserve is not immune from political pressures.[7] Its independence may encourage it to pursue a course of narrow self-interest rather than the public interest.

There is yet no consensus on whether Federal Reserve independence is a good thing, although public support for independence of the central bank seems to have been growing in both the United States and abroad. As you might expect, people who like the Fed's policies are more likely to support its independence, while those who dislike its policies advocate a less independent Fed.

Central Bank Independence and Macroeconomic Performance in Seventeen Countries

We have seen that advocates of an independent central bank believe that macroeconomic performance will be improved by making the central bank more independent. Recent research seems to support this conjecture: When central banks are ranked from 1 (least independent) to 4 (most independent), inflation performance is found to be the best for countries with the most independent central banks.[8] As you can see in Figure 4, Germany and Switzerland, with the two most independent central banks, were also the countries with the lowest inflation rates in the 1973–1988 period. By contrast, the countries with the highest inflation in those years—Spain, New Zealand, Australia, and Italy—were also the countries with the least independent central banks. (The Spanish and New Zealand central banks have since gained greater independence.) Although a more independent central bank appears to lead to a lower inflation rate, this is not achieved at the expense of poorer real economic performance. Countries with independent central banks are no more likely to have high unemployment or greater output fluctuations than countries with less independent central banks.

---

[7]For evidence on this issue, see Robert E. Weintraub, "Congressional Supervision of Monetary Policy," *Journal of Monetary Economics* 4 (1978): 341–362. Some economists suggest that lessening the independence of the Fed might even reduce the incentive for politically motivated monetary policy; see Milton Friedman, "Monetary Policy: Theory and Practice," *Journal of Money, Credit and Banking* 14 (1982): 98–118.

[8]Alberto Alesina and Lawrence H. Summers, "Central Bank Independence and Macroeconomic Performance: Some Comparative Evidence," *Journal of Money, Credit and Banking* 25 (1993): 151–162. However, Adam Posen, "Central Bank Independence and Disinflationary Credibility: A Missing Link," Federal Reserve Bank of New York Staff Report No. 1, May 1995, has cast some doubt on whether the causality runs from central bank independence to improved inflation performance.

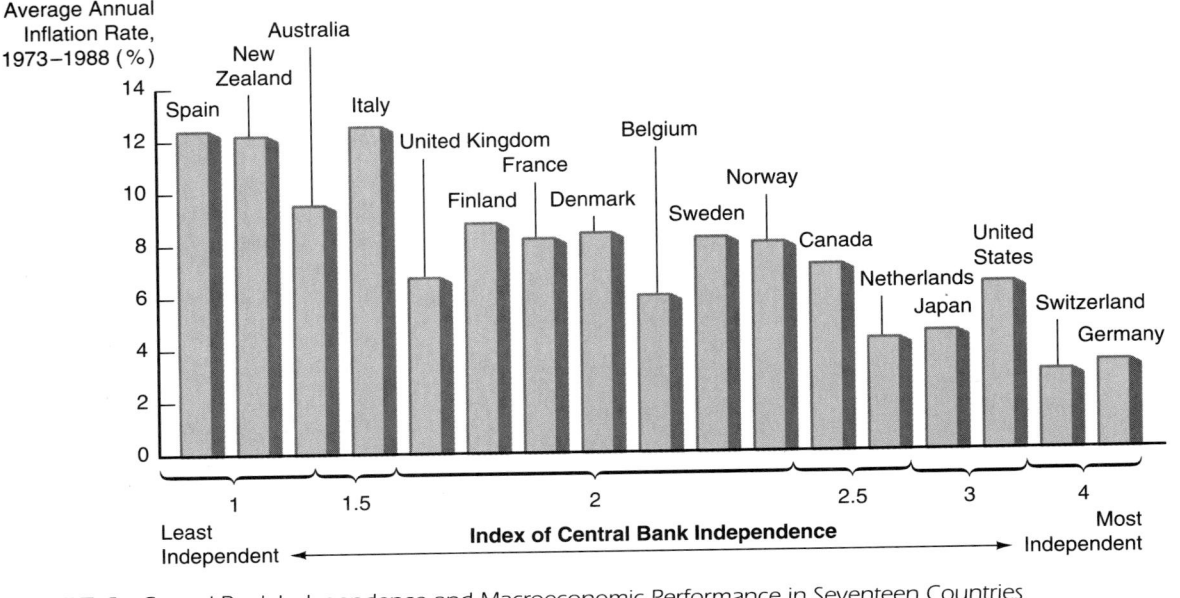

FIGURE 4 Central Bank Independence and Macroeconomic Performance in Seventeen Countries

On the horizontal axis, the 17 central banks are rated from least independent, 1, to most independent, 4. More independent banks have generally produced lower inflation than less independent central banks.

Source: Alberto Alesina and Lawrence H. Summers, "Central Bank Independence and Macroeconomic Performance: Some Comparative Evidence," *Journal of Money, Credit and Banking* 25 (1993): 151–162.

S U M M A R Y

1. The Federal Reserve System was created in 1913 to lessen the frequency of bank panics. Because of public hostility to central banks and the centralization of power, the Federal Reserve System was created with many checks and balances to diffuse power.

2. The formal structure of the Federal Reserve System consists of 12 regional Federal Reserve banks, around 4000 member commercial banks, the Board of Governors of the Federal Reserve System, the Federal Open Market Committee, and the Federal Advisory Council.

3. Although on paper the Federal Reserve System appears to be decentralized, in practice it has come to function as a unified central bank controlled by the Board of Governors, especially the board's chairman.

4. The Federal Reserve is more independent than most agencies of the U.S. government, but it is still subject to political pressures because the legislation that structures the Fed is written by Congress and can be changed at any time. The theory of bureaucratic behavior indicates that one factor driving the Fed's behavior is its attempt to increase its power and prestige. This view explains many of the Fed's actions, although the agency may also try to act in the public interest.

5. The case for an independent Federal Reserve rests on the view that curtailing the Fed's independence and subjecting it to more political pressures would impart an inflationary bias to monetary policy. An independent Fed can afford to take the long view and not respond to short-run problems that will result in expansionary monetary policy and a political business cycle. The case against an independent Fed holds that it is undemocratic to have monetary policy (so important to the public) controlled by an elite that is not accountable to the public. An independent Fed also makes the coordination of monetary and fiscal policy difficult.

KEY TERMS

Board of Governors of the
Federal Reserve System,
p. 390

Federal Open Market
Committee (FOMC), p. 390

Federal Reserve banks, p. 390

open market operations, p. 393

political business cycle, p. 409

QUESTIONS AND PROBLEMS

*1. Why was the Federal Reserve System set up with 12 regional Federal Reserve banks rather than one central bank, as in other countries?

2. What political realities might explain why the Federal Reserve Act of 1913 placed two Federal Reserve banks in Missouri?

*3. "The Federal Reserve System resembles the U.S. Constitution in that it was designed with many checks and balances." Discuss.

4. In what ways can the regional Federal Reserve banks influence the conduct of monetary policy?

*5. Which entities in the Federal Reserve System control the discount rate? Reserve requirements? Open market operations?

6. Do you think that the 14-year nonrenewable terms for governors effectively insulate the Board of Governors from political pressure?

*7. Over time, which entities have gained power in the Federal Reserve System and which have lost power? Why do you think this has happened?

8. The Fed is the most independent of all U.S. government agencies. What is the main difference between it and other government agencies that explains its greater independence?

*9. What is the primary tool that Congress uses to exercise some control over the Fed?

10. In the 1960s and 1970s, the Federal Reserve System lost member banks at a rapid rate. How can the theory of bureaucratic behavior explain the Fed's campaign for legislation to require all commercial banks to become members? Was the Fed successful in this campaign?

*11. "The theory of bureaucratic behavior indicates that the Fed never operates in the public interest." Is this statement true, false, or uncertain? Explain your answer.

12. Why might eliminating the Fed's independence lead to a more pronounced political business cycle?

*13. "The independence of the Fed leaves it completely unaccountable for its actions." Is this statement true, false, or uncertain? Explain your answer.

14. "The independence of the Fed has meant that it takes the long view and not the short view." Is this statement true, false, or uncertain? Explain your answer.

*15. The Fed promotes secrecy by not releasing FOMC directives to Congress or the public immediately. Discuss the pros and cons of this policy.

Chapter 16

MULTIPLE DEPOSIT CREATION AND THE MONEY SUPPLY PROCESS

PREVIEW   As we saw in Chapter 6 and will see in later chapters on monetary theory, movements in the money supply affect interest rates and the overall health of the economy and thus affect us all. Because of its far-reaching effects on economic activity, it is important to understand how the money supply is determined. Who controls it? What causes it to change? How might control of it be improved? In this and subsequent chapters we answer these questions by providing a detailed description of the *money supply process*, the mechanism that determines the level of the money supply.

Because deposits at banks are by far the largest component of the money supply, understanding how these deposits are created is the first step in understanding the money supply process. This chapter provides an overview of how the banking system creates deposits. In addition, it outlines the basic building blocks needed in later chapters for you to understand in greater depth how the money supply is determined.

FOUR PLAYERS IN THE MONEY SUPPLY PROCESS

The "cast of characters" in the money supply story is as follows:

1. The central bank—the government agency that oversees the banking system and is responsible for the conduct of monetary policy; in the United States, the Federal Reserve System
2. Banks (depository institutions)—the financial intermediaries that accept deposits from individuals and institutions and make loans: commercial banks, savings and loan associations, mutual savings banks, and credit unions
3. Depositors—individuals and institutions that hold deposits in banks

4. Borrowers from banks—individuals and institutions that borrow from the depository institutions and institutions that issue bonds that are purchased by the depository institutions

Of the four players, the central bank, the Federal Reserve System, is the most important. Its conduct of monetary policy involves actions that affect its balance sheet (holdings of assets and liabilities), to which we turn now.

THE FED'S BALANCE SHEET AND THE MONETARY BASE

Just as any other bank has a balance sheet that lists its assets and liabilities, so does the Fed. We examine each of the categories of assets and liabilities because changes in them have an important impact on the money supply.

Assets

1. Securities. These are the Fed's holdings of securities, which consist primarily of Treasury securities but in the past have also included banker's acceptances. The total amount of securities is controlled by open market operations (the Fed's purchase and sale of these securities). As shown in Table 1, "Securities" is by far the largest category of assets in the Fed's balance sheet.

2. Discount loans. These are loans the Fed makes to banks, and the amount is affected by the Fed's setting the discount rate, the interest rate the Fed charges banks for these loans.

These first two Fed assets are important because they earn interest. Because the liabilities of the Fed do not pay interest, the Fed makes billions of dollars every year—its assets earn income, and its liabilities cost nothing. Although it returns most of its earnings to the federal government, the Fed does spend some of it on "worthy causes," such as supporting economic research.

3. Gold and SDR certificate accounts. Special drawing rights (SDRs) are issued to governments by the International Monetary Fund (IMF) to settle international debts and have replaced gold in international financial transactions. When the Treasury acquires gold or SDRs, it issues certificates to the Fed that are claims on the gold or SDRs and is in turn credited with deposit balances at the Fed. The gold and SDR accounts are made up of these certificates issued by the Treasury.

4. Coin. This is the smallest item in the balance sheet, and it consists of Treasury currency (mostly coins) held by the Fed.

5. Cash items in process of collection. These arise from the Fed's check-clearing process. When a check is given to the Fed for clearing, the Fed will present it to the bank on which it is written and will collect funds by deducting the amount of the check from the bank's deposits (reserves) with the Fed. Before these funds are collected, the check is a cash item in process of collection and is a Fed asset.

6. Other Federal Reserve assets. These include deposits and bonds denominated in foreign currencies as well as physical goods such as computers, office equipment, and buildings owned by the Federal Reserve.

Liabilities

1. Federal Reserve notes (currency) outstanding. The Fed issues currency (those green-and-gray pieces of paper in your wallet that say "Federal Reserve

TABLE 1	Consolidated Balance Sheet of the Federal Reserve System ($ billions, end of 1996)		
Assets		**Liabilities**	
Securities: U.S. government and agency securities and banker's acceptances	414.7	Federal Reserve notes outstanding *M1*	426.5
		Bank deposits	24.5
Discount loans	0.1	U.S. Treasury deposits	7.7
Gold and SDR certificate accounts	20.7	Foreign and other deposits	1.1
Coin *I.O.U.*	0.6	Deferred-availability cash items	7.5
Cash items in process of collection	12.8	Other Federal Reserve liabilities	
Other Federal Reserve assets	32.2	and capital accounts	13.8
Total	481.1	Total	481.1

Source: Federal Reserve *Bulletin*.

note" at the top). The Federal Reserve notes outstanding are the amount of this currency that is in the hands of the public. (Currency held by depository institutions is also a liability of the Fed but is counted as part of the reserves liability.)

Federal Reserve notes are IOUs from the Fed to the bearer and are also liabilities, but unlike most liabilities, they promise to pay back the bearer solely with Federal Reserve notes; that is, they pay off IOUs with other IOUs. Accordingly, if you bring a $100 bill to the Federal Reserve and demand payment, you will receive two $50s, five $20s, ten $10s, or one hundred $1 bills.

People are more willing to accept IOUs from the Fed than from you or me because Federal Reserve notes are a recognized medium of exchange; that is, they are accepted as a means of payment and so function as *money*. Unfortunately, neither you nor I can convince people that our IOUs are worth anything more than the paper they are written on.[1]

2. Reserves. All banks have an account at the Fed in which they hold deposits. Reserves consist of deposits at the Fed plus currency that is physically held by banks (called *vault cash* because it is stored in bank vaults). **Reserves** are assets for the banks but liabilities for the Fed because the banks can demand

---

[1]The "Federal Reserve notes outstanding" item on the Fed's balance sheet refers only to currency in circulation, the amount in the hands of the public. Currency that has been printed by the U.S. Bureau of Printing and Engraving is not automatically a liability of the Fed. For example, consider the importance of having $1 million of your own IOUs printed up. You give out $100 worth to other people and keep the other $999,900 in your pocket. The $999,900 of IOUs does not make you richer or poorer and does not affect your indebtedness. You care only about the $100 of liabilities from the $100 of circulated IOUs. The same reasoning applies for the Fed in regard to its Federal Reserve notes.

For similar reasons, the currency component of the money supply, no matter how it is defined, includes only currency in circulation. It does not include any additional currency that is not yet in the hands of the public. The fact that currency has been printed but is not circulating means that it is not anyone's asset or liability and thus cannot affect anyone's behavior. Therefore, it makes sense not to include it in the money supply.

payment on them at any time and the Fed is required to satisfy its obligation by paying Federal Reserve notes. As you will see, an increase in reserves leads to an increase in the level of deposits and hence in the money supply.

Total reserves can be divided into two categories: reserves that the Fed requires banks to hold (**required reserves**) and any additional reserves the banks choose to hold (**excess reserves**). For example, the Fed might require that for every dollar of deposits at a depository institution, a certain fraction (say, 10 cents) must be held as reserves. This fraction (10 percent) is called the **required reserve ratio.** Currently, the Fed pays no interest on reserves.

3. U.S. Treasury deposits. The Treasury keeps deposits at the Fed, against which it writes all its checks.

4. Foreign and other deposits. These include the deposits with the Fed owned by foreign governments, foreign central banks, international agencies (such as the World Bank and the United Nations), and U.S. government agencies (such as the FDIC and Federal Home Loan banks).

5. Deferred-availability cash items. Like cash items in process of collection, these also arise from the Fed's check-clearing process. When a check is submitted for clearing, the Fed does not immediately credit the bank that submitted the check. Instead, it promises to credit the bank within a certain prearranged time limit, which never exceeds two days. These promises are the deferred-availability items and are a liability of the Fed.

6. Other Federal Reserve liabilities and capital accounts. This item includes all the remaining Federal Reserve liabilities not included elsewhere on the balance sheet. For example, stock in the Federal Reserve System purchased by member banks is included here.

Monetary Base

The first two liabilities on the balance sheet, Federal Reserve notes (currency) outstanding and reserves, are often referred to as the *monetary liabilities* of the Fed. When we add to these liabilities the U.S. Treasury's monetary liabilities (Treasury currency in circulation, primarily coins), we get a construct called the **monetary base.** The monetary base is an important part of the money supply because increases in it will lead to a multiple increase in the money supply (everything else being constant). This is why the monetary base is also called **high-powered money.** Recognizing that Treasury currency and Federal Reserve currency can be lumped together into the category *currency in circulation,* denoted by C, the monetary base equals the sum of currency in circulation plus reserves, R. The monetary base MB is expressed as[2]

$$MB = \text{(Federal Reserve notes + Treasury currency − coin) + reserves}$$
$$= C + R$$

The items on the right-hand side of this equation indicate how the base is used and are called the **uses of the base.** Unfortunately, this equation does not

---

[2]In the member bank reserves data that the Fed publishes every week, Treasury currency outstanding is defined to include Treasury currency that is held at the Treasury (called "Treasury cash holdings"). What we have defined as "Treasury currency" is actually equal to "Treasury currency outstanding" minus "Treasury cash holdings."

tell us the factors that determine the base (the **sources of the base**), but the Federal Reserve balance sheet in Table 1 comes to the rescue because like all balance sheets, it has the property that the total assets on the left-hand side must equal the total liabilities on the right-hand side. Because the "Federal Reserve notes" and "reserves" items in the uses of the base are Federal Reserve liabilities, the "assets equals liabilities" property of the Fed balance sheet enables us to solve for these items in terms of the Fed balance sheet items that are included in the sources of the base: Specifically, Federal Reserve notes and reserves equal the sum of all the Fed assets minus all the other Fed liabilities:

Federal Reserve notes + reserves = Securities + discount loans + gold and SDRs + coin + cash items in process of collection + other Federal Reserve assets − Treasury deposits − foreign and other deposits − deferred-availability cash items − other Federal Reserve liabilities and capital

The two balance sheet items related to check clearing can be collected into one term called **float,** defined as "Cash items in process of collection" minus "Deferred-availability cash items." Substituting all the right-hand-side items in the equation for "Federal Reserve notes + reserves" in the uses-of-the-base equation, we obtain the following expression describing the sources of the monetary base:

$$MB = \text{Securities + discount loans + gold and SDRs + float + other Federal Reserve assets + Treasury currency − Treasury deposits −}$$
$$\text{foreign and other deposits − other Federal Reserve liabilities and capital (1)}$$

Accounting logic has led us to a useful equation that clearly identifies the nine factors affecting the monetary base listed in Table 2. As Equation 1 and Table 2 depict, increases in the first six factors increase the monetary base, and increases in the last three reduce the monetary base.

CONTROL OF THE MONETARY BASE

The Federal Reserve exercises control over the monetary base via the first two factors listed in Table 2: through its purchases or sales of government securities in the open market, called **open market operations,** and through its extension of discount loans to banks.

Federal Reserve Open Market Operations

As Table 2 suggests, the primary way in which the Fed causes changes in the monetary base is through its open market operations. A purchase of bonds by the Fed is called an **open market purchase,** and a sale of bonds by the Fed is called an **open market sale.**

OPEN MARKET PURCHASE FROM A BANK   Suppose that the Fed purchases $100 of bonds from a bank and pays for them with a $100 check. The bank will either

─── S U M M A R Y ───

TABLE 2   Factors Affecting the Monetary Base

Factor	Value ($ billions, end of 1996)	Change in Factor	Change in Monetary Base
Factors That Increase the Monetary Base			
1. Securities: U.S. government and agency securities and banker's acceptances	414.7	↑	↑
2. Discount loans	0.1	↑	↑
3. Gold and SDR certificate accounts	20.8	↑	↑
4. Float	4.3	↑	↑
5. Other Federal Reserve assets	32.2	↑	↑
6. Treasury currency	25.0	↑	↑
Subtotal 1	497.1		
Factors That Decrease the Monetary Base			
7. Treasury deposits with the Fed	7.7	↑	↓
8. Foreign and other deposits with the Fed	7.9	↑	↓
9. Other Federal Reserve liabilities and capital accounts	13.8	↑	↓
Subtotal 2	29.4		
Monetary Base			
Subtotal 1 − Subtotal 2	467.7		

Source: Federal Reserve *Bulletin.*

deposit the check in its account with the Fed or cash it in for currency, which will be counted as vault cash. To understand what occurs as a result of this transaction, we look at *T-accounts*, which list only the changes that occur in balance sheet items starting from the initial balance sheet position. Either action means that the bank will find itself with $100 more reserves and a reduction in its holdings of securities of $100. The T-account for the banking system, then, is

BANKING SYSTEM

Assets		Liabilities
Securities	−$100	
Reserves	+$100	

The Fed meanwhile finds that its liabilities have increased by the additional $100 of reserves, while its assets have increased by the $100 of additional securities that it now holds. Its T-account is

FEDERAL RESERVE SYSTEM

Assets		Liabilities	
Securities	+$100	Reserves	+$100

The net result of this open market purchase is that reserves have increased by $100, the amount of the open market purchase. Because there has been no change of currency in circulation, the monetary base has also risen by $100.

OPEN MARKET PURCHASE FROM THE NONBANK PUBLIC To understand what happens when there is an open market purchase from the nonbank public, we must look at two cases. First, let's assume that the person or corporation that sells the $100 of bonds to the Fed deposits the Fed's check in the local bank. The nonbank public's T-account after this transaction is

NONBANK PUBLIC

Assets		Liabilities
Securities	−$100	
Checkable deposits	+$100	

When the bank receives the check, it credits the depositor's account with the $100 and then deposits the check in its account with the Fed, thereby adding to its reserves. The banking system's T-account becomes

BANKING SYSTEM

Assets		Liabilities	
Reserves	+$100	Checkable deposits	+$100

The effect on the Fed's balance sheet is that it has gained $100 of securities in its assets column, while it has an increase of $100 of reserves in its liabilities column:

FEDERAL RESERVE SYSTEM

Assets		Liabilities	
Securities	+$100	Reserves	+$100

As you can see in the above T-account, when the Fed's check is deposited in a bank, the net result of the Fed's open market purchase from the nonbank public is identical to the effect of its open market purchase from a bank: Reserves increase by the amount of the open market purchase, and the monetary base increases by the same amount.

If, however, the person or corporation selling the bonds to the Fed cashes the Fed's check either at a local bank or at a Federal Reserve bank for currency, the effect on reserves is different.[3] This seller will receive currency of $100 while reducing holdings of securities by $100. The bond seller's T-account will be

NONBANK PUBLIC

Assets		Liabilities
Securities	−$100	
Currency	+$100	

The Fed now finds that it has exchanged $100 of currency for $100 of securities, so its T-account is

FEDERAL RESERVE SYSTEM

Assets		Liabilities
Securities	+$100	Currency in circulation +$100

The net effect of the open market purchase in this case is that reserves are unchanged, while currency in circulation increases by the $100 of the open market purchase. Thus the monetary base increases by the $100 amount of the open market purchase, while reserves do not. This contrasts with the case in which the seller of the bonds deposits the Fed's check in a bank; in that case, reserves increase by $100, and so does the monetary base.

The analysis reveals that ***the effect of an open market purchase on reserves depends on whether the seller of the bonds keeps the proceeds from the sale in currency or in deposits.*** If the proceeds are kept in currency, the open market purchase has no effect on reserves; if the proceeds are kept as deposits, reserves increase by the amount of the open market purchase.

The effect of an open market purchase on the monetary base, however, is always the same (the monetary base increases by the amount of the purchase) whether the seller of the bonds keeps the proceeds in

---

[3]If the bond seller cashes the check at the local bank, its balance sheet will be unaffected because the $100 of vault cash that it pays out will be exactly matched by the deposit of the $100 check at the Fed. Thus its reserves will remain the same, and there will be no effect on its T-account. That is why a T-account for the banking system does not appear here.

deposits or in currency. The impact of an open market purchase on reserves is much more uncertain than its impact on the monetary base.

OPEN MARKET SALE If the Fed sells $100 of bonds to a bank or the nonbank public, the monetary base will decline by $100. For example, if the Fed sells the bonds to an individual who pays for them with currency, the buyer exchanges $100 of currency for $100 of bonds, and the resulting T-account is

NONBANK PUBLIC

Assets		Liabilities
Securities	+$100	
Currency	−$100	

The Fed, for its part, has reduced its holdings of securities by $100 and has also lowered its monetary liability by accepting the currency as payment for its bonds, thereby reducing the amount of currency in circulation by $100:

FEDERAL RESERVE SYSTEM

Assets		Liabilities	
Securities	−$100	Currency in circulation	−$100

The effect of the open market sale of $100 of bonds is to reduce the monetary base by an equal amount, although reserves remain unchanged. Manipulations of T-accounts in cases in which the buyer of the bonds is a bank or the buyer pays for the bonds with a check written on a checkable deposit account at a local bank lead to the same $100 reduction in the monetary base, although the reduction occurs because the level of reserves has fallen by $100.

Study Guide The best way to learn how open market operations affect the monetary base is to use T-accounts. Using T-accounts, try to verify that an open market sale of $100 of bonds to a bank or to a person who pays with a check written on a bank account leads to a $100 reduction in the monetary base.

The following conclusion can now be drawn from our analysis of open market purchases and sales: ***The effect of open market operations on the monetary base is much more certain than the effect on reserves.*** Therefore, the Fed can control the monetary base with open market operations more effectively than it can control reserves.

BOX 1

Foreign Exchange Rate Intervention and the Monetary Base

It is common to read in the newspaper about a Federal Reserve intervention in the foreign exchange market to buy or sell dollars. Can this also be a factor that affects the monetary base? The answer is yes because a Federal Reserve intervention in the foreign exchange market involves a purchase or sale of assets denominated in a foreign currency, which affects the "Other Federal Reserve assets" category in the Fed's balance sheet.

Suppose that the Fed purchases $100 of deposits denominated in French francs in exchange for $100 of deposits at the Fed (a sale of dollars for francs). A Federal Reserve purchase of any asset, whether it be a U.S. government bond or a deposit denominated in a foreign currency, is still just an open market purchase and so leads to an equal rise in the monetary base. One way to see this is

to look at Table 2 and recognize that $100 of deposits denominated in francs belongs in the "Other Federal Reserve assets" category. Thus a $100 purchase of franc deposits leads to a $100 increase in the "Other Federal Reserve assets" item in Table 2 and hence a $100 increase in the monetary base. Similarly, a sale of foreign currency deposits leads to a decline in "Other Federal Reserve assets" and a decline in the monetary base. Another way to see this is to realize that the T-accounts from a $100 purchase or sale of deposits foreign currency are identical to those in the text for a $100 open market purchase or sale except the word *securities* would be replaced by *foreign-currency-denominated deposits*. Federal Reserve interventions in the foreign exchange market are thus an important influence on the monetary base, a topic that we discuss further in Chapter 20.

Open market operations can also be done in other assets besides government bonds and have the same effects on the monetary base we have described here. One example of this is a foreign exchange intervention by the Fed (see Box 1).

Shifts from Deposits into Currency

Even if the Fed does not conduct open market operations, a shift from deposits to currency will affect the reserves in the banking system. However, such a shift will have no effect on the monetary base, another reason why the Fed has more control over the monetary base than over reserves.

Let's suppose that Jane Brown (who opened a $100 checking account at the First National Bank in Chapter 10) decides that tellers are so abusive in all banks that she closes her account by withdrawing the $100 balance in cash and vows never to deposit it in a bank again. The effect on the T-account of the nonbank public is

NONBANK PUBLIC

Assets		Liabilities
Checkable deposits	−$100	
Currency	+$100	

The banking system loses $100 of deposits and hence $100 of reserves:

BANKING SYSTEM

Assets		Liabilities	
Reserves	−$100	Checkable deposits	−$100

For the Fed, Jane Brown's action means that there is $100 of additional currency circulating in the hands of the public, while reserves in the banking system have fallen by $100. The Fed's T-account is

FEDERAL RESERVE SYSTEM

Assets		Liabilities	
		Currency in circulation	+$100
		Reserves	−$100

The net effect on the monetary liabilities of the Fed is a wash; the monetary base is unaffected by Jane Brown's disgust at the banking system. But reserves are affected. Random fluctuations of reserves can occur as a result of random shifts into currency and out of deposits, and vice versa. The same is not true for the monetary base, making it a more stable variable.

Discount Loans   In this chapter so far we have seen changes in the monetary base solely as a result of open market operations. However, the monetary base is also affected when the Fed makes a discount loan to a bank. When the Fed made a $100 discount loan to the First National Bank, the bank was credited with $100 of reserves from the proceeds of the loan. The effects on the balance sheet of the banking system and the Fed are illustrated by the following T-accounts:

BANKING SYSTEM				**FEDERAL RESERVE SYSTEM**			
Assets		Liabilities		Assets		Liabilities	
Reserves	+$100	Discount loans	+$100	Discount loans	+$100	Reserves	+$100

The monetary liabilities of the Fed have now increased by $100, and the monetary base, too, has increased by this amount. However, if a bank pays off a loan from the Fed, thereby reducing its borrowings from the Fed by $100, the T-accounts of the banking system and the Fed are as follows:

BANKING SYSTEM				**FEDERAL RESERVE SYSTEM**			
Assets		Liabilities		Assets		Liabilities	
Reserves	−$100	Discount loans	−$100	Discount loans	−$100	Reserves	−$100

The net effect on the monetary liabilities of the Fed, and hence on the monetary base, is then a reduction of $100. We see that the monetary base changes one-for-one with the change in the borrowings from the Fed.

Overview of the Fed's Ability to Control the Monetary Base

The factor that most affects the monetary base is the Fed's holdings of securities, which are completely controlled by the Fed through its open market operations. Factors not controlled by the Fed (for example, float and Treasury deposits with the Fed) undergo substantial short-run variations and can be important sources of fluctuations in the monetary base over time periods as short as a week. However, these fluctuations are usually quite predictable and so can be offset through open market operations. ***Although float and Treasury deposits with the Fed undergo substantial short-run fluctuations, which complicate control of the monetary base, they do not prevent the Fed from accurately controlling it.***

MULTIPLE DEPOSIT CREATION: A SIMPLE MODEL

With our understanding of how the Federal Reserve controls the monetary base and how banks operate (Chapter 10), we now have the tools necessary to explain how deposits are created. When the Fed supplies the banking system with $1 of additional reserves, deposits increase by a multiple of this amount—a process called **multiple deposit creation.**

Deposit Creation: The Single Bank

Suppose that the $100 open market purchase described earlier was conducted with the First National Bank. After the Fed has bought the $100 bond from the First National Bank, the bank finds that it has an increase in reserves of $100. To analyze what the bank will do with these additional reserves, assume that the bank does not want to hold excess reserves because it earns no interest on them. We begin the analysis with the following T-account:

FIRST NATIONAL BANK

Assets		Liabilities
Securities	−$100	
Reserves	+$100	

Because the bank has no increase in its checkable deposits, required reserves remain the same, and the bank finds that its additional $100 of reserves means that its excess reserves have increased by $100. Let's say that the bank decides to make a loan equal in amount to the $100 increase in excess reserves. When the bank makes the loan, it sets up a checking account for the borrower and puts the proceeds of the loan into this account. In this way the bank alters its balance sheet by increasing its liabilities with $100 of checkable deposits and at the same time increasing its assets with the $100 loan. The resulting T-account looks like this:

FIRST NATIONAL BANK

Assets		Liabilities	
Securities	−$100	Checkable deposits	+$100
Reserves	+$100		
Loans	+$100		

The bank has created checkable deposits by its act of lending. Because checkable deposits are part of the money supply, the bank's act of lending has in fact created money.

In its current balance sheet position, the First National Bank still has excess reserves and so might want to make additional loans. However, these reserves will not stay at the bank for very long. The borrower took out a loan not to leave $100 idle at the First National Bank but to purchase goods and services from other individuals and corporations. When the borrower makes these purchases by writing checks, they will be deposited at other banks, and the $100 of reserves will leave the First National Bank. *A bank cannot safely make loans for an amount greater than the excess reserves it has before it makes the loan.*

The final T-account of the First National Bank is

FIRST NATIONAL BANK

Assets		Liabilities
Securities	−$100	
Loans	+$100	

The increase in reserves of $100 has been converted into additional loans of $100 at the First National Bank, plus an additional $100 of deposits that have made their way to other banks. (All the checks written on accounts at the First National Bank are deposited in banks rather than converted into cash because we are assuming that the public does not want to hold any additional currency.) Now let's see what happens to these deposits at the other banks.

Deposit Creation: The Banking System

To simplify the analysis, let us assume that the $100 of deposits created by First National Bank's loan is deposited at Bank A and that this bank and all other banks hold no excess reserves. Bank A's T-account becomes

BANK A

Assets		Liabilities	
Reserves	+$100	Checkable deposits	+$100

If the required reserve ratio is 10 percent, this bank will now find itself with a $10 increase in required reserves, leaving it $90 of excess reserves. Because Bank A (like the First National Bank) does not want to hold on to excess reserves, it will make loans for the entire amount. Its loans and checkable deposits will then increase by $90, but when the borrower spends the $90 of checkable deposits, they and the reserves at Bank A will fall back down by this same amount. The net result is that Bank A's T-account will look like this:

BANK A

Assets		Liabilities	
Reserves	+$10	Checkable deposits	+$100
Loans	+$90		

If the money spent by the borrower to whom Bank A lent the $90 is deposited in another bank, such as Bank B, the T-account for Bank B will be

BANK B

Assets		Liabilities	
Reserves	+$90	Checkable deposits	+$90

The checkable deposits in the banking system have increased by another $90, for a total increase of $190 ($100 at Bank A plus $90 at Bank B). In fact, the distinction between Bank A and Bank B is not necessary to obtain the same result on the overall expansion of deposits. If the borrower from Bank A writes checks to someone who deposits them at Bank A, the same change in deposits would occur. The T-accounts for Bank B would just apply to Bank A, and its checkable deposits would increase by the total amount of $190.

Bank B will want to modify its balance sheet further. It must keep 10 percent of $90 ($9) as required reserves and has 90 percent of $90 ($81) in excess reserves and so can make loans of this amount. Bank B will make an $81 loan to a borrower, who spends the proceeds from the loan. Bank B's T-account will be

BANK B

Assets		Liabilities	
Reserves	+$ 9	Checkable deposits	+$90
Loans	+$81		

The $81 spent by the borrower from Bank B will be deposited in another bank (Bank C). Consequently, from the initial $100 increase of reserves in the banking system, the total increase of checkable deposits in the system so far is $271 (= $100 + $90 + $81).

Following the same reasoning, if all banks make loans for the full amount of their excess reserves, further increments in checkable deposits will continue (at Banks C, D, E, and so on), as depicted in Table 3. Therefore, the total increase in deposits from the initial $100 increase in reserves will be $1000: The increase is tenfold, the reciprocal of the 0.10 reserve requirement.

If the banks choose to invest their excess reserves in securities, the result is the same. If Bank A had taken its excess reserves and purchased securities instead of making loans, its T-account would have looked like this:

BANK A

Assets		Liabilities	
Reserves	+$10	Checkable deposits	+$100
Securities	+$90		

When the bank buys $90 of securities, it writes a $90 check to the seller of the securities, who in turn deposits the $90 at a bank such as Bank B. Bank B's checkable deposits rise by $90, and the deposit expansion process is the same as before. ***Whether a bank chooses to use its excess reserves to make loans or to purchase securities, the effect on deposit expansion is the same.***

TABLE 3 **Creation of Deposits (assuming 10 percent reserve requirement and a $100 increase in reserves)**

Bank	Increase in Deposits ($)	Increase in Loans ($)	Increase in Reserves ($)
First National	0.00	100.00	0.00
A	100.00	90.00	10.00
B	90.00	81.00	9.00
C	81.00	72.90	8.10
D	72.90	65.61	7.29
E	65.61	59.05	6.56
F	59.05	53.14	5.91
.	.	.	.
.	.	.	.
.	.	.	.
Total for all banks	1000.00	1000.00	100.00

You can now see the difference in deposit creation for the single bank versus the banking system as a whole. Because a single bank can create deposits equal only to the amount of its excess reserves, it cannot by itself generate multiple deposit expansion. A single bank cannot make loans greater in amount than its excess reserves because the bank will lose these reserves as the deposits created by the loan find their way to other banks. However, the banking system as a whole can generate a multiple expansion of deposits because when a bank loses its excess reserves, these reserves do not leave the banking system even though they are lost to the individual bank. So as each bank makes a loan and creates deposits, the reserves find their way to another bank, which uses them to make additional loans and create additional deposits. As you have seen, this process continues until the initial increase in reserves results in a multiple increase in deposits.

The multiple increase in deposits generated from an increase in the banking system's reserves is called the **simple deposit multiplier.**[4] In our example with a 10 percent required reserve ratio, the simple deposit multiplier is 10. More generally, the simple deposit multiplier equals the reciprocal of the required reserve ratio, expressed as a fraction ($10 = 1/0.10$), so the formula for the multiple expansion of deposits can be written as

$$\Delta D = \frac{1}{r_D} \times \Delta R \qquad (2)$$

[4]This multiplier should not be confused with the Keynesian multiplier, which is derived through a similar step-by-step analysis. That multiplier relates an increase in income to an increase in investment, whereas the simple deposit multiplier relates an increase in deposits to an increase in reserves.

where ΔD = change in total checkable deposits in the banking system

r_D = required reserve ratio (0.10 in the example)

ΔR = change in reserves for the banking system ($100 in the example)[5]

Multiple Deposit Contraction

The multiple deposit creation process should also work in reverse; that is, when the Fed withdraws reserves from the banking system, there should be a multiple contraction of deposits. To prove this, let us trace the effect of a reduction of reserves in the banking system when again we assume that banks do not hold any excess reserves.

Let's start our analysis with a $100 reduction in the reserves of the First National Bank (by the Fed's sale of a $100 bond to the bank). The First National Bank finds that it has lost $100 of reserves, and because it has not been holding any excess reserves, its holdings of reserves are $100 short of the required amount. It can obtain the reserves needed by selling $100 of securities or by demanding repayment of $100 of loans. When it sells the securities, it will receive $100 of checks written on an account with another bank that will be deposited at the Fed, thus raising its reserves by the same amount. Similarly, the repayment of the loan will also be made with checks written on an account with another bank. In both cases, the reserves at the First National Bank will be increased by $100, but the bank on which the checks are drawn (such as Bank A) will lose $100 of checkable deposits and $100 of reserves. Bank A's T-account will be

BANK A

Assets		Liabilities	
Reserves	−$100	Checkable deposits	−$100

Bank A will now find that it cannot meet its reserve requirements—it will be $90 short. Its reserves have fallen by $100, but its required reserves have also fallen by $10 (10 percent of the $100 decline in checkable deposits). To meet this reserve shortfall, Bank A will reduce its holdings of loans or securities by $90, transforming its T-account to

---

[5]A formal derivation of this formula follows. Using the reasoning in the text, the change in checkable deposits is $100 (= $\Delta R \times 1$) plus $90 [= $\Delta R \times (1 - r_D)$] plus $81 [= $\Delta R \times (1 - r_D)^2$ and so on, which can be rewritten as

$$\Delta D = \Delta R \times [1 + (1 - r_D) + (1 - r_D)^2 + (1 - r_D)^3 + \cdots]$$

Using the formula for the sum of an infinite series found in footnote 5 in Chapter 4, this can be rewritten as

$$\Delta D = \Delta R \times \frac{1}{1 - (1 - r_D)} = \frac{1}{r_D} \times \Delta R$$

BANK A

Assets		Liabilities	
Reserves	$-\$10$	Checkable deposits	$-\$100$
Loans and securities	$-\$90$		

If the checks that Bank A receives as a result of reducing its loans or securities were written on accounts at Bank B, Bank B would then find itself with the following T-account:

BANK B

Assets		Liabilities	
Reserves	$-\$90$	Checkable deposits	$-\$90$

Bank B now has a reserve shortfall of $81 ($90 minus 10 percent of $90), and so it reduces its loans and securities by this amount, lowering another bank's checkable deposits by $81. This process keeps on going, with the level of checkable deposits in the banking system changing by

$$-\$100 - \$90 - \$81 - \$72.90 - \$65.61 - \$59.05 - \ldots = -\$1000$$

You can see that the process of multiple deposit contraction is symmetrical to the process of multiple deposit creation.

Deriving the Formula for Multiple Deposit Creation

The formula for the multiple creation of deposits can also be derived directly using algebra. We obtain the same answer for the relationship between a change in deposits and a change in reserves, but more quickly.

Our assumption that banks do not hold on to any excess reserves means that the total amount of required reserves for the banking system RR will equal the total reserves in the banking system R:

$$RR = R$$

The total amount of required reserves equals the required reserve ratio r_D times the total amount of checkable deposits D:

$$RR = r_D \times D$$

Substituting $r_D \times D$ for RR in the first equation,

$$r_D \times D = R$$

and dividing both sides of the preceding equation by r_D gives us

$$D = \frac{1}{r_D} \times R$$

Taking the change in both sides of this equation and using delta to indicate a change,

$$\Delta D = \frac{1}{r_D} \times \Delta R$$

which is the same formula for deposit creation found in Equation 2.

This derivation provides us with another way of looking at the multiple creation of deposits because it forces us to look directly at the banking system as a whole rather than one bank at a time. For the banking system as a whole, deposit creation (or contraction) will stop only when all excess reserves in the banking system are gone; that is, the banking system will be in equilibrium when the total amount of required reserves equals the total amount of reserves, as seen in the equation $RR = R$. When $r_D \times D$ is substituted for RR, the resulting equation $R = r_D \times D$ tells us how high checkable deposits will have to be in order for required reserves to equal total reserves. Accordingly, a given level of reserves in the banking system determines the level of checkable deposits when the banking system is in equilibrium (when $ER = 0$); put another way, the given level of reserves supports a given level of checkable deposits.

In our example, the required reserve ratio is 10 percent. If reserves increase by $100, checkable deposits must rise to $1000 in order for total required reserves also to increase by $100. If the increase in checkable deposits is less than this, say, $900, then the increase in required reserves of $90 remains below the $100 increase in reserves, so there are still excess reserves somewhere in the banking system. The banks with the excess reserves will now make additional loans, creating new deposits, and this process will continue until all reserves in the system are used up. This occurs when checkable deposits have risen to $1000.

We can also see this by looking at the T-account of the banking system as a whole (including the First National Bank) that results from this process:

BANKING SYSTEM

Assets		Liabilities	
Securities	−$ 100	Checkable deposits	+$1000
Reserves	+$ 100		
Loans	+$1000		

The procedure of eliminating excess reserves by loaning them out means that the banking system (First National Bank and Banks A, B, C, D, and so on) continues to make loans up to the $1000 amount until deposits have reached the $1000 level. In this way, $100 of reserves supports $1000 (ten times the quantity) of deposits.

Critique of the Simple Model

Our model of multiple deposit creation seems to indicate that the Federal Reserve is able to exercise complete control over the level of checkable deposits by setting the required reserve ratio and the level of reserves. The actual creation of deposits is much less mechanical than the simple model indicates. If proceeds from Bank A's $90 loan are not deposited but are kept in cash, nothing is deposited in Bank B, and the deposit creation process stops dead in its tracks. The total increase in checkable deposits is only $100—considerably less than the $1000 we calculated. So if some proceeds from loans are used to raise the holdings of currency, checkable deposits will not increase by as much as our streamlined model of multiple deposit creation tells us.

Another situation ignored in our model is one in which banks do not make loans or buy securities in the full amount of their excess reserves. If Bank A decides to hold on to all $90 of its excess reserves, no deposits would be made in Bank B, and this would also stop the deposit creation process. The total increase in deposits would again be only $100 and not the $1000 increase in our example. Hence if banks choose to hold all or some of their excess reserves, the full expansion of deposits predicted by the simple model of multiple deposit creation does not occur.

Our examples rightly indicate that the Fed is not the only player whose behavior influences the level of deposits and therefore the money supply. Banks' decisions regarding the amount of excess reserves they wish to hold and depositors' decisions regarding how much currency to hold can cause the money supply to change. In the next chapter we stress the behavior and interactions of the four players in constructing a more realistic model of the money supply process.

S U M M A R Y

1. There are four players in the money supply process: the central bank, banks (depository institutions), depositors, and borrowers from banks.

2. The monetary base consists of currency in circulation and reserves. Nine factors affect the monetary base: (1) the Fed's holdings of securities, (2) discount loans, (3) gold and SDR accounts, (4) float, (5) other Federal Reserve assets, (6) Treasury currency outstanding, (7) Treasury deposits with the Fed, (8) foreign and other deposits with the Fed, and (9) other Federal Reserve liabilities and capital accounts. Increases in the first six add to the monetary base; increases in the others reduce the monetary base.

3. The Federal Reserve controls the monetary base through open market operations and extension of discount loans to banks and has better control over the monetary base than over reserves. Although float and Treasury deposits with the Fed undergo substantial short-run fluctuations, which complicate control of the monetary base, they do not prevent the Fed from accurately controlling it.

4. A single bank can make loans up to the amount of its excess reserves, thereby creating an equal amount of deposits. The banking system can create a multiple expansion of deposits because as each bank makes a loan and creates deposits, the reserves find their way to another bank, which uses them to make loans and create additional deposits. In the simple model of multiple deposit creation in which banks do not hold on to excess reserves and the public holds no currency, the multiple increase in checkable deposits (simple deposit multiplier) equals the reciprocal of the required reserve ratio.

5. The simple model of multiple deposit creation has serious deficiencies. Decisions by depositors to increase their holdings of currency or of banks to hold excess reserves will result in a smaller expansion of deposits than the simple model predicts. All four players—the Fed, banks, depositors, and borrowers from banks—are important in the determination of the money supply.

KEY TERMS

excess reserves, p. 417

float, p. 418

high-powered money, p. 417

monetary base, p. 417

multiple deposit creation,
   p. 425

open market operations, p. 418

open market purchase, p. 418

open market sale, p. 418

required reserve ratio, p. 417

required reserves, p. 417

reserves, p. 416

simple deposit multiplier,
   p. 429

sources of the base, p. 418

uses of the base, p. 417

QUESTIONS AND PROBLEMS

1. If the Fed sells $2 million of bonds to the First National Bank, what happens to reserves and the monetary base? Use T-accounts to explain your answer.

*2. If the Fed sells $2 million of bonds to Irving the Investor, who pays for the bonds with a briefcase filled with currency, what happens to reserves and the monetary base? Use T-accounts to explain your answer.

*3. If the Fed lends five banks an additional total of $100 million but depositors withdraw $50 million and hold it as currency, what happens to reserves and the monetary base? Use T-accounts to explain your answer.

4. The First National Bank receives an extra $100 of reserves but decides not to loan any of these reserves out. How much deposit creation takes place for the entire banking system?

Unless otherwise noted, the following assumptions are made in all the remaining problems: The required reserve ratio on checkable deposits is 10 percent, banks do not hold on to excess reserves, and the public's holdings of currency do not change.

*5. Using T-accounts, show what happens to checkable deposits in the banking system when the Fed loans an additional $1 million to the First National Bank.

6. Using T-accounts, show what happens to checkable deposits in the banking system when the Fed sells $2 million of bonds to the First National Bank.

*7. Suppose that the Fed buys $1 million of bonds from the First National Bank. If the First National Bank and all other banks use the resulting increase in reserves to purchase securities only and not to make loans, what will happen to checkable deposits?

8. If the Fed buys $1 million of bonds from the First National Bank, but an additional 10 percent of any deposit is held as excess reserves, what is the total increase in checkable deposits? (*Hint:* Use T-accounts to show what happens at each step of the multiple expansion process.)

*9. If a bank depositor withdraws $1000 of currency from an account, what happens to reserves and checkable deposits?

10. If reserves in the banking system increase by $1 billion as a result of discount loans of $1 billion and checkable deposits increase by $9 billion, why isn't the banking system in equilibrium? What will continue to happen in the banking system until equilibrium is reached? Show the T-account for the banking system in equilibrium.

*11. If the Fed reduces reserves by selling $5 million worth of bonds to the banks, what will the T-account of the banking system look like when the banking system is in equilibrium? What will have happened to the level of checkable deposits?

12. If the required reserve ratio on checkable deposits increases to 20 percent, how much multiple deposit creation will take place when reserves are increased by $100?

*13. If a bank decides that it wants to hold $1 million of excess reserves, what effect will this have on checkable deposits in the banking system?

14. If a bank sells $10 million of bonds back to the Fed in order to pay back $10 million on the discount loan it owes, what will be the effect on the level of checkable deposits?

*15. If you decide to hold $100 less cash than usual and therefore deposit $100 in cash in the bank, what effect will this have on checkable deposits in the banking system if the rest of the public keeps its holdings of currency constant?

Chapter 17

DETERMINANTS OF
THE MONEY SUPPLY

P R E V I E W   In Chapter 16 we developed a simple model of multiple deposit creation that showed how the Fed can control the level of checkable deposits by setting the required reserve ratio and the level of reserves. Unfortunately for the Fed, life isn't that simple; control of the money supply is far more complicated. Our critique of this model indicated that decisions by depositors about their holdings of currency and by banks about their holdings of excess reserves also affect the money supply. To deal with these criticisms, in this chapter we develop a money supply model in which depositors and banks assume their important roles. The resulting framework provides an in-depth description of the money supply process to help you understand the complexity of the Fed's role.

To simplify the analysis, we separate the development of our model into several steps. First, because the Fed can exert more precise control over the monetary base (currency in circulation plus total reserves in the banking system) than it can over total reserves alone, our model links changes in the money supply to changes in the monetary base. This link is achieved by deriving a **money multiplier** (a ratio that relates the change in the money supply to a given change in the monetary base). Finally, we examine the determinants of the money multiplier.

Study Guide   One reason for breaking the money supply model into its component parts is to help you answer questions using intuitive step-by-step logic rather than memorizing how changes in the behavior of the Fed, depositors, or banks will affect the money supply.

In deriving a model of the money supply process, we focus here on a simple definition of money (currency plus checkable deposits), which corresponds to M1. Although other broader definitions of money are frequently used in policy-making, particularly M2, we conduct the analysis with an M1 definition because it is less complicated and yet provides a basic understanding of the money supply process. Furthermore, all analyses and results using the M1 definition apply equally well to the M2 definition. A somewhat more complicated money supply model for the M2 definition is developed in the appendix to this chapter.

THE MONEY SUPPLY MODEL AND THE MONEY MULTIPLIER

Because, as we saw in Chapter 16, the Fed can control the monetary base better than it can control reserves, it makes sense to link the money supply M to the monetary base MB through a relationship such as the following:

$$M = m \times MB \qquad (1)$$

The variable m is the money multiplier, which tells us how much the money supply changes for a given change in the monetary base MB. This multiplier tells us what multiple of the monetary base is transformed into the money supply. Because the money multiplier is larger than 1, the alternative name for the monetary base, *high-powered money*, is logical; a $1 change in the monetary base leads to more than a $1 change in the money supply.

The money multiplier reflects the effect on the money supply of other factors besides the monetary base, and the following model will explain the factors that determine the size of the money multiplier. Depositors' decisions about their holdings of currency and checkable deposits are one set of factors affecting the money multiplier. Another involves the reserve requirements imposed by the Fed on the banking system. Banks' decisions about excess reserves also affect the money multiplier.

Deriving the Money Multiplier

In our model of multiple deposit creation in Chapter 16, we ignored the effects on deposit creation of changes in the public's holdings of currency and banks' holdings of excess reserves. Now we incorporate these changes into our model of the money supply process by assuming that the desired level of currency C and excess reserves ER grows proportionally with checkable deposits D; in other words, we assume that the ratios of these items to checkable deposits are constants in equilibrium:

$$\{C/D\} = \text{currency ratio}$$
$$\{ER/D\} = \text{excess reserves ratio}$$

where the braces indicate that we are treating the ratio as a constant in equilibrium.

We will now derive a formula that describes how the currency ratio desired by depositors, the excess reserves ratio desired by banks, and the required reserve ratio set by the Fed affect the multiplier m. We begin the derivation of the model of the money supply with the equation

$$R = RR + ER$$

which states that the total amount of reserves in the banking system R equals the sum of required reserves RR and excess reserves ER. (Note that this equation corresponds to the equilibrium condition $RR = R$ in Chapter 16, where excess reserves were assumed to be zero.)

The total amount of required reserves equals the required reserve ratio r_D times the amount of checkable deposits D:

$$RR = r_D \times D$$

Substituting $r_D \times D$ for RR in the first equation yields an equation that links reserves in the banking system to the amount of checkable deposits and excess reserves they can support:

$$R = (r_D \times D) + ER$$

A key point here is that the Fed sets the required reserve ratio r_D to be less than 1. Thus $1 of reserves can support more than $1 of deposits, and the multiple expansion of deposits can occur.

Let's see how this works in practice. If excess reserves are held at zero ($ER = 0$), the required reserve ratio is set at $r_D = 0.10$, and the level of checkable deposits in the banking system is $800 billion, the amount of reserves needed to support these deposits is $80 billion (= $0.10 \times 800 billion). The $80 billion of reserves can support ten times this amount in checkable deposits, just as in Chapter 16, because multiple deposit creation will occur.

Because the monetary base MB equals currency C plus reserves R, we can generate an equation that links the amount of monetary base to the levels of checkable deposits and currency by adding currency to both sides of the equation:

$$MB = R + C = (r_D \times D) + ER + C$$

Another way of thinking about this equation is to recognize that it reveals the amount of the monetary base that is needed to support the existing amounts of checkable deposits, currency, and excess reserves.

An important feature of this equation is that an additional dollar of MB that arises from an additional dollar of currency does not support any additional deposits. This occurs because such an increase leads to an identical increase in the right-hand side of the equation with no change occurring in D. The currency component of MB does not lead to multiple deposit creation as the reserves component does. Put another way, ***an increase in the monetary base that goes into currency is not multiplied, whereas an increase that goes into supporting deposits is multiplied.***

Another important feature of this equation is that an additional dollar of MB that goes into excess reserves ER does not support any additional deposits or currency. The reason for this is that when a bank decides to hold excess reserves, it does not make additional loans, so these excess reserves do not lead to the creation of deposits. Therefore, if the Fed injects reserves into the banking system and they are held as excess reserves, there will be no effect on deposits or currency and hence no effect on the money supply. In other words, you can think of excess reserves as an idle component of reserves that are not being used to support any deposits (although they are important for bank liquidity management, as we saw in Chapter 10). This means that for a given level of reserves, a higher amount of excess reserves implies that the banking system in effect has fewer reserves to support deposits.

To derive the money multiplier formula in terms of the currency ratio {C/D} and the excess reserves ratio {ER/D}, we rewrite the last equation, specifying C as {C/D} $\times$ D and ER as {ER/D} $\times$ D:

$$MB = (r_D \times D) + (\{ER/D\} \times D) + (\{C/D\}) \times D) = (r_D + \{ER/D\} + \{C/D\}) \times D$$

We next divide both sides of the equation by the term inside the parentheses to get an expression linking checkable deposits D to the monetary base MB:

$$D = \frac{1}{r_D + \{ER/D\} + \{C/D\}} \times MB \qquad (2)$$

Using the definition of the money supply as currency plus checkable deposits ($M = D + C$) and again specifying C as {C/D} $\times$ D,

$$M = D + (\{C/D\} \times D) = (1 + \{C/D\}) \times D$$

Substituting in this equation the expression for D from Equation 2, we have

$$M = \frac{1 + [C/D]}{r_D + \{ER/D\} + \{C/D\}} \times MB \qquad (3)$$

Finally, we have achieved our objective of deriving an expression in the form of our earlier Equation 1. As you can see, the ratio that multiplies MB is the money multiplier that tells how much the money supply changes in response to a given change in the monetary base (high-powered money). The money multiplier m is thus

$$m = \frac{1 + \{C/D\}}{r_D + \{ER/D\} + \{C/D\}} \qquad (4)$$

and it is a function of the currency ratio set by depositors {C/D}, the excess reserves ratio set by banks {ER/D}, and the required reserve ratio set by the Fed r_D.

Although the algebraic derivation we have just completed shows you how the money multiplier is constructed, you need to understand the basic intuition behind it in order to be able to understand and apply the money multiplier concept without having to memorize it.

Intuition Behind the Money Multiplier

To get a feel for what the money multiplier means, let us again construct a numerical example with realistic numbers for the following variables:

r_D = required reserve ratio = 0.10
C = currency in circulation = $400 billion
D = checkable deposits = $800 billion
ER = excess reserves = $0.8 billion
M = money supply (M1) = $C + D$ = $1200 billion

From these numbers we can calculate the values for the currency ratio {C/D} and the excess reserves ratio {ER/D}:

$$\{C/D\} = \frac{\$400 \text{ billion}}{\$800 \text{ billion}} = 0.5$$

$$\{ER/D\} = \frac{\$0.8 \text{ billion}}{\$800 \text{ billion}} = 0.001$$

The resulting value of the money multiplier is

$$m = \frac{1 + 0.5}{0.1 + 0.001 + 0.5} = \frac{1.5}{0.601} = 2.5$$

The money multiplier of 2.5 tells us that given the required reserve ratio of 10 percent on checkable deposits and the behavior of depositors as represented by $\{C/D\} = 0.5$ and banks as represented by $\{ER/D\} = 0.001$, a \$1 increase in the monetary base leads to a \$2.50 increase in the money supply (M1).

An important characteristic of the money multiplier is that it is less than the simple deposit multiplier of 10 found in Chapter 16. The key to understanding this result and our money supply model is to realize that ***although there is multiple expansion of deposits, there is no such expansion for currency.*** Thus if some portion of the increase in high-powered money finds its way into currency, this portion does not undergo multiple deposit expansion. In our analysis in Chapter 16, we did not allow for this possibility, and so the increase in reserves led to the maximum amount of multiple deposit creation. However, in our current model of the money multiplier, the level of currency does increase when the monetary base MB and checkable deposits D increase because $\{C/D\}$ is greater than zero. As previously stated, any increase in MB that goes into an increase in currency is not multiplied, so only part of the increase in MB is available to support checkable deposits that undergo multiple expansion. The overall level of multiple deposit expansion must be lower, meaning that the increase in M, given an increase in MB, is smaller than the simple model in Chapter 16 indicated.[1]

FACTORS THAT DETERMINE THE MONEY MULTIPLIER

To develop our intuition of the money multiplier even further, let us look at how this multiplier changes in response to changes in the variables in our model: $\{C/D\}$, $\{ER/D\}$, and r_D. The "game" we are playing is a familiar one in economics: We ask what happens when one of these variables changes, leaving all other variables the same *(ceteris paribus)*.

Changes in the Required Reserve Ratio r_D

If the required reserve ratio on checkable deposits increases while all the other variables stay the same, the same level of reserves cannot support as large an amount of checkable deposits; more reserves are needed because required reserves for these checkable deposits have risen. The resulting deficiency in

---

[1]Another reason that the money multiplier is smaller is that $\{ER/D\}$ is a constant fraction greater than zero, indicating that an increase in MB and D leads to higher excess reserves. The resulting higher amount of excess reserves means that the amount of reserves used to support checkable deposits will not increase as much as it otherwise would. Hence the increase in checkable deposits and the money supply will be lower, and the money multiplier will be smaller. However, because $\{ER/D\}$ is currently so tiny, around 0.001, the impact of this ratio on the money multiplier is now quite small. But there have been periods when the $\{ER/D\}$ ratio has been much larger and so has had a more important role in lowering the money multiplier.

reserves then means that banks must contract their loans, causing a decline in deposits and hence in the money supply. The reduced money supply relative to the level of *MB*, which has remained unchanged, indicates that the money multiplier has declined as well. Another way to see this is to realize that when r_D is higher, less multiple expansion of checkable deposits occurs. With less multiple deposit expansion, the money multiplier must fall.[2]

We can verify that the foregoing analysis is correct by seeing what happens to the value of the money multiplier in our numerical example when r_D increases from 10 percent to 15 percent (leaving all the other variables unchanged). The money multiplier becomes

$$m = \frac{1 + 0.5}{0.15 + 0.001 + 0.5} = \frac{1.5}{0.651} = 2.3$$

which, as we would expect, is less than 2.5.

The analysis just conducted can also be applied to the case in which the required reserve ratio falls. In this case, there will be more multiple expansion for checkable deposits because the same level of reserves can now support more checkable deposits, and the money multiplier will rise. For example, if r_D falls from 10 percent to 5 percent, plugging this value into our money multiplier formula (leaving all the other variables unchanged) yields a money multiplier of

$$m = \frac{1 + 0.5}{0.05 + 0.001 + 0.5} = \frac{1.5}{0.551} = 2.72$$

which is above the initial value of 2.5.

We can now state the following result: ***The money multiplier and the money supply are negatively related to the required reserve ratio r_D.***

Changes in the Currency Ratio {C/D}

Next, what happens to the money multiplier when depositor behavior causes {*C/D*} to increase with all other variables unchanged? An increase in {*C/D*} means that depositors are converting some of their checkable deposits into currency. As shown before, checkable deposits undergo multiple expansion while currency does not. Hence when checkable deposits are being converted into currency, there is a switch from a component of the money supply that undergoes multiple expansion to one that does not. The overall level of multiple expansion declines, and so must the multiplier.[3]

This reasoning is confirmed by our numerical example, where {*C/D*} rises from 0.50 to 0.75. The money multiplier then falls from 2.5 to

$$m = \frac{1 + 0.75}{0.1 + 0.001 + 0.75} = \frac{1.75}{0.851} = 2.06$$

We have now demonstrated another result: ***The money multiplier and the money supply are negatively related to the currency ratio {C/D}.***

---

[2]This result can be demonstrated from the Equation 4 formula as follows: When r_D rises, the denominator of the money multiplier rises, and therefore the money multiplier must fall.

[3]As long as r_D + {*ER/D*} is less than 1 (as is the case using the realistic numbers we have used), an increase in {*C/D*} raises the denominator of the money multiplier proportionally by more than it raises the numerator. The increase in {*C/D*} causes the multiplier to fall.

Changes in the Excess Reserves Ratio {ER/D}

When banks increase their holdings of excess reserves relative to checkable deposits, the banking system in effect has fewer reserves to support checkable deposits. This means that given the same level of *MB*, banks will contract their loans, causing a decline in the level of checkable deposits and a decline in the money supply, and the money multiplier will fall.[4]

This reasoning is supported in our numerical example when {*ER/D*} rises from 0.001 to 0.005. The money multiplier declines from 2.5 to

$$m = \frac{1 + 0.5}{0.1 + 0.005 + 0.5} = \frac{1.5}{0.605} = 2.48$$

Note that although the excess reserves ratio has risen fivefold, there has been only a small decline in the money multiplier. This decline is small because in recent years the {*ER/D*} ratio has been extremely small, so changes in it have only a small impact on the money multiplier. However, there have been times, particularly during the Great Depression, when this ratio was far higher, and its movements had a substantial effect on the money supply and the money multiplier. Thus our final result is still an important one: ***The money multiplier and the money supply are negatively related to the excess reserves ratio {ER/D}.***

To understand the factors that determine the level of {*ER/D*} in the banking system, we must look at the costs and benefits to banks of holding excess reserves. When the costs of holding excess reserves rise, we would expect the level of excess reserves and hence {*ER/D*} to fall; when the benefits of holding excess reserves rise, we would expect the level of excess reserves and {*ER/D*} to rise. Two primary factors affect these costs and benefits and hence affect the excess reserves ratio: market interest rates and expected deposit outflows.

MARKET INTEREST RATES As you may recall from our analysis of bank management in Chapter 10, the cost to a bank of holding excess reserves is its opportunity cost, the interest that could have been earned on loans or securities if they had been held instead of excess reserves. For the sake of simplicity, we assume that loans and securities earn the same interest rate *i*, which we call the market interest rate. If *i* increases, the opportunity cost of holding excess reserves rises, and the desired ratio of excess reserves to deposits will fall. A decrease in *i*, conversely, will reduce the opportunity cost of excess reserves, and {*ER/D*} will rise. ***The banking system's excess reserves ratio {ER/D} is negatively related to the market interest rate i.***

Another way of understanding the negative effect of market interest rates on {*ER/D*} is to return to the theory of portfolio choice, which states that if the expected returns on alternative assets rise relative to the expected returns on an asset, the demand for that asset will decrease. As the market interest rate increases, the expected return on loans and securities rises relative to the zero return on excess reserves, and the excess reserves ratio falls.

---

[4]This result can be demonstrated from the Equation 4 formula as follows: When {*ER/D*} rises, the denominator of the money multiplier rises, and so the money multiplier must fall.

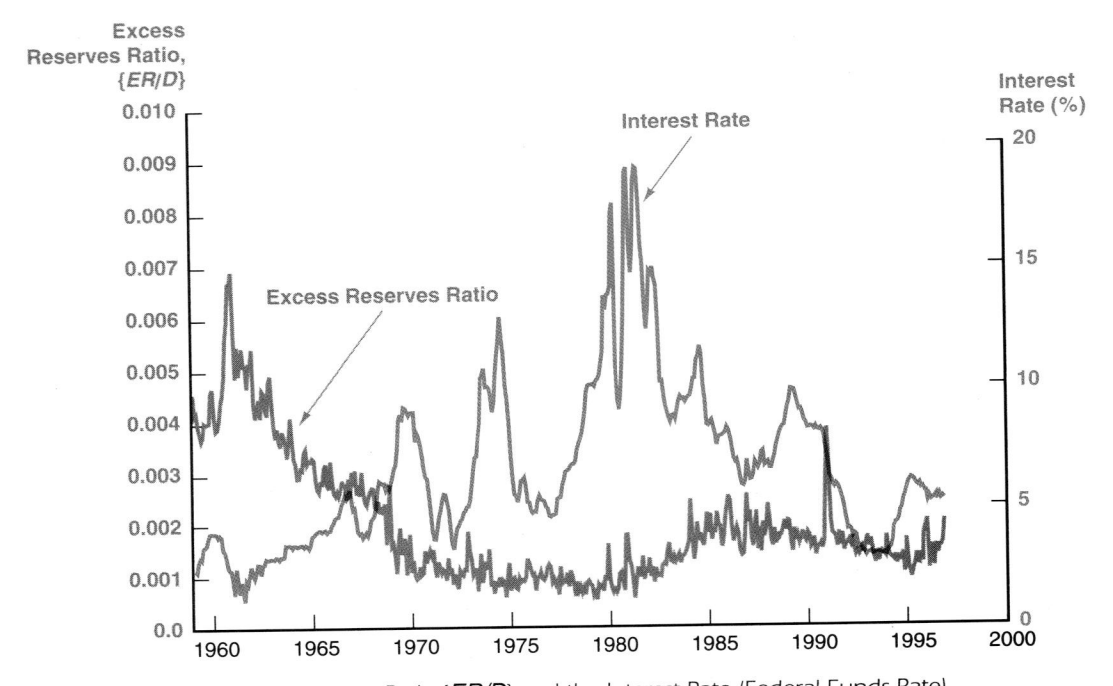

FIGURE 1   The Excess Reserves Ratio {*ER/D*} and the Interest Rate (Federal Funds Rate)

Figure 1 shows us (as the theory of portfolio choice predicts) that there is a negative relationship between the excess reserves ratio and a representative market interest rate, the federal funds rate. The period 1960–1981 saw an upward trend in the federal funds rate and a declining trend in {*ER/D*}, whereas in the period 1980–1996, a decline in the federal funds rate is associated with a rise in {*ER/D*}. The empirical evidence thus supports our analysis that the excess reserves ratio is negatively related to market interest rates.

EXPECTED DEPOSIT OUTFLOWS Our analysis of bank management in Chapter 10 also indicated that the primary benefit to a bank of holding excess reserves is that they provide insurance against losses due to deposit outflows; that is, they enable the bank experiencing deposit outflows to escape the costs of calling in loans, selling securities, borrowing from the Fed or other corporations, or bank failure. If banks fear that deposit outflows are likely to increase (that is, if expected deposit outflows increase), they will want more insurance against this possibility and will increase the excess reserves ratio. Another way to put it is this: If expected deposit outflows rise, the expected benefits, and hence the expected returns for holding excess reserves, increase. As the theory of portfolio choice predicts, excess reserves will then rise. Conversely, a decline in expected deposit outflows will reduce the insurance benefit of excess reserves, and their level should fall. We have the following result: *The excess reserves ratio {ER/D} is positively related to expected deposit outflows.*

ADDITIONAL FACTORS THAT DETERMINE THE MONEY SUPPLY

So far we have been assuming that the Fed has complete control over the monetary base. However, whereas the amount of open market purchases or sales is completely controlled by the Fed's placing orders with dealers in bond markets, the central bank lacks complete control over the monetary base because it cannot unilaterally determine, and therefore perfectly predict, the amount of borrowing by banks from the Fed. The Federal Reserve sets the discount rate (interest rate on discount loans), and then banks make decisions about whether to borrow. The amount of discount loans, though influenced by the Fed's setting of the discount rate, is not completely controlled by the Fed; banks' decisions play a role too.[5]

Therefore, we might want to split the monetary base into two components: one that the Fed can control completely and another that is less tightly controlled. The less tightly controlled component is the amount of the base that is created by discount loans from the Fed. The remainder of the base (called the **nonborrowed monetary base**) is under the Fed's control because it results primarily from open market operations.[6] The nonborrowed monetary base is formally defined as the monetary base minus discount loans from the Fed:

$$MB_n = MB - DL$$

where
MB_n = nonborrowed monetary base
MB = monetary base
DL = discount loans from the Fed

The reason for distinguishing the nonborrowed monetary base MB_n from the monetary base MB is that the nonborrowed monetary base, which is tied to open market operations, is directly under the control of the Fed, whereas the monetary base, which is also influenced by discount loans from the Fed, is not.

To complete the money supply model, we use the fact that $MB = MB_n + DL$ and rewrite the money supply model as

$$M = m \times (MB_n + DL) \tag{5}$$

where the money multiplier m is defined as in Equation 4. Thus in addition to the effects on the money supply of the required reserve ratio, currency ratio, and excess reserves ratio, the expanded model stipulates that the money supply is also affected by changes in MB_n and DL. Because the money multiplier is positive, Equation 5 immediately tells us that the money supply is positively related to both

---

[5]The Fed, like any banker, can also decide whether or not to make such a loan, thus giving it further control over the amount of borrowings from the Fed. The key point, however, is not altered by this fact. Decisions of the banks as well as the Fed are important to the level of discount loans from the Fed.

[6]Actually, there are other items on the Fed's balance sheet (discussed in Chapter 16) that affect the magnitude of the nonborrowed monetary base. Since their effects on the nonborrowed base relative to open market operations are both small and predictable, these other items do not present the Fed with difficulties in controlling the nonborrowed base.

the nonborrowed monetary base and discount loans. However, it is still worth developing the intuition for these results.

Changes in the Nonborrowed Monetary Base MB_n

As shown in Chapter 16, the Fed's open market purchases increase the nonborrowed monetary base, and its open market sales decrease it. Holding all other variables constant, an increase in MB_n arising from an open market purchase increases the amount of the monetary base that is available to support currency and deposits, so the money supply will increase. Similarly, an open market sale that decreases MB_n will shrink the amount of the monetary base available to support currency and deposits, thereby causing the money supply to decrease.

We have the following result: ***The money supply is positively related to the nonborrowed monetary base MB_n.***

Changes in Discount Loans DL from the Fed

With the nonborrowed monetary base MB_n unchanged, more discount loans from the Fed provide additional reserves (and hence higher MB) to the banking system, and these are used to support more currency and deposits. As a result, the increase in DL will lead to a rise in the money supply. If banks reduce the level of their discount loans, with all other variables held constant, the amount of MB available to support currency and deposits will decline, causing the money supply to decline.

The result is this: ***The money supply is positively related to the level of discount loans DL from the Fed.***

Market Interest Rates and the Discount Rate

Our analysis of what determines discount loan borrowing from the Federal Reserve relies on identifying the costs and benefits of borrowing from the Fed. Two primary factors affect these costs and benefits and subsequently the volume of discount loans: market interest rates and the discount rate.

The principal benefit for a bank when it borrows from the Fed is straightforward. With additional borrowed reserves, a bank can acquire loans and securities, which earn the market interest rate i. The primary cost of borrowing for the bank, however, is the discount rate i_d, the interest rate the Fed charges on its loans to banks.[7] The greater the difference between the benefits (earnings) obtained from the use of borrowed funds i and the cost of borrowing i_d, the more a bank will borrow from the Fed. Thus discount loan borrowing is positively related to $i - i_d$. This relationship in turn implies that ***the amount of discount loans DL is positively related to the market interest rate i and negatively related to the discount rate i_d.***

---

[7]Changes in the discount rate i_d can also have an effect on the excess reserves ratio $\{ER/D\}$. The cost to a bank experiencing a deposit outflow rises when i_d rises because it is more costly to borrow from the Fed when an outflow occurs. Thus a rise in i_d increases the benefits of holding excess reserves, and $\{ER/D\}$ rises. This effect of the discount rate on the excess reserves ratio has not been emphasized in the text because it is believed to be small.

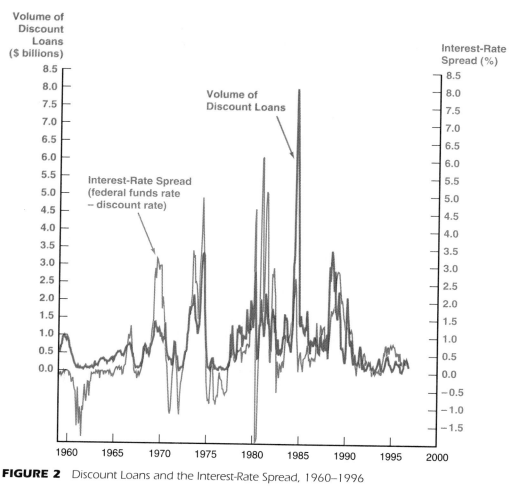

FIGURE 2 Discount Loans and the Interest-Rate Spread, 1960–1996

Sources: Federal Reserve *Bulletin;* Citibase databank.

Again, empirical evidence strongly confirms this analysis. Figure 2 shows a strong positive relationship between the volume of discount loans and the difference between a representative market interest rate (the federal funds rate) and the discount rate.

OVERVIEW OF THE MONEY SUPPLY PROCESS

We now have a model of the money supply process in which all four of the players—the Federal Reserve System, depositors, banks, and borrowers from banks—directly influence the money supply. As a study aid, Table 1 charts the money supply (M1) response to the five variables discussed and gives a brief synopsis of the reasoning behind each result.

——— **S U M M A R Y** ———

TABLE 1 Money Supply (M1) Response

Player	Variable	Change in Variable	Money Supply Response	Reason
Federal Reserve System	r_D	↑	↓	Less multiple deposit expansion
	MB_n	↑	↑	More *MB* to support currency and checkable deposits
	i_d	↑	↓	*DL* ↓ so less *MB* to support *D* and *C*
Depositors	$\{C/D\}$	↑	↓	Less multiple deposit expansion
Depositors and banks	Expected deposit outflows	↑	↓	$\{ER/D\}$ ↑ so fewer reserves to support *D*
Borrowers from banks and the other three players	i	↑	↑	$\{ER/D\}$ ↓ so more reserves to support *D*; *DL* ↑ so more *MB* to support *D* and *C*

Note: Only increases (↑) in the variables are shown. The effects of decreases on the money supply would be the opposite of those indicated in the "Response" column.

··

Study Guide   To improve your understanding of the money supply process, slowly work through the logic behind the results in Table 1 rather than just memorizing the results. Then see if you can construct your own table in which all the variables decrease rather than increase.

··

The variables are grouped by the player or players who either influence the variable or are most influenced by it. The Federal Reserve, for example, influences the money supply by controlling the first three variables—r_D, MB_n, and i_d, also known as the tools of the Fed. (How these tools are used is discussed in subsequent chapters.) Depositors influence the money supply through their decisions about the currency ratio $\{C/D\}$, while banks influence the money supply by their decisions about $\{ER/D\}$, which are affected by their expectations about deposit outflows. Because depositors' behavior also influences bankers' expectations about deposit outflows, this variable also reflects the role of both depositors and bankers in the money supply process. Market interest rates, as represented by i, affect the money supply through the excess reserves ratio, $\{ER/D\}$. As shown in Chapter 6, the demand for loans by borrowers influences market interest rates, as does the supply of money. Therefore, all four players are important in the determination of i.

Explaining Movements in the Money Supply, 1980–1996

To make the theoretical analysis of this chapter more concrete, we need to see whether the model of the money supply process developed here helps us understand recent movements of the money supply. We look at money supply movements from 1980 to 1996, a particularly interesting period because the growth rate of the money supply displayed unusually high variability.

Figure 3 shows the movements of the money supply (M1) from 1980 to 1996, with the percentage next to each bracket representing the annual growth rate for the bracketed period: From January 1980 to October 1984, for example, the money supply grew at a 7.2 percent annual rate. The variability of money growth in the 1980–1996 period is quite apparent, swinging from 7.2 percent to 13.1 percent, down to 3.3 percent, then up to 11.1 percent and finally back down to −1.5 percent. What explains these sharp swings in the growth rate of the money supply?

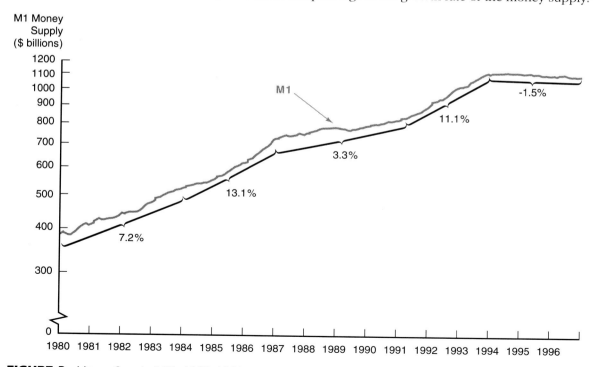

FIGURE 3 Money Supply (M1), 1980–1996

Percentage for each bracket indicates the annual growth rate of the money supply over the bracketed period.

Source: Citibase databank.

Our money supply model, as represented by Equation 5, suggests that the movements in the money supply that we see in Figure 3 are explained by either changes in $MB_n + DL$ (the nonborrowed monetary base plus discount loans) or by changes in m (the money multiplier). Figure 4 plots these variables and shows their growth rates for the same bracketed periods as in Figure 3. Notice that the money multiplier m fluctuates within a fairly narrow band between 2.3 and 3.3.

Over the whole period, the average growth rate of the money supply (6.1 percent) is fairly well explained by the average growth rate of the nonborrowed monetary base MB_n (7.2 percent). In addition, we see that DL is rarely an important source of fluctuations in the money supply since $MB_n + DL$ is closely tied to MB_n except for the unusual period in 1984 when discount loans increased dramatically (the Fed extended $5 billion of loans to the financially troubled Continental Illinois National Bank).

The conclusion drawn from our analysis is this: ***Over long periods, the primary determinant of movements in the money supply is the nonborrowed monetary base MB$_n$, which is controlled by Federal Reserve open market operations.***

For shorter time periods, the link between the growth rates of the nonborrowed monetary base and the money supply is not always close, primarily because the money multiplier m experiences substantial short-run swings that have a major impact on the growth rate of the money supply. The currency ratio $\{C/D\}$, which is also plotted in Figure 4, explains most of these movements in the money multiplier.

From January 1980 until October 1984, $\{C/D\}$ is relatively constant. Not surprisingly, there is almost no trend in the money multiplier m, so the growth rate of the money supply and the nonborrowed monetary base have similar magnitudes. The upward movement in the money multiplier from October 1984 to January 1987 is explained by the downward trend in the currency ratio. The decline in $\{C/D\}$ meant that there was a shift from one component of the money supply with less multiple expansion (currency) to one with more (checkable deposits), so the money multiplier rose. In the period from January 1987 to April 1991, $\{C/D\}$ underwent a substantial rise. As our money supply model predicts, the rise in $\{C/D\}$ led to a fall in the money multiplier because there was a shift from checkable deposits, with more multiple expansion, to currency, which had less. From April 1991 to December 1993, $\{C/D\}$ fell somewhat. The decline in $\{C/D\}$ led to a rise in the money multiplier because there was again a shift from the currency component of the money supply with less multiple expansion to the checkable deposits component with more. Finally, the sharp rise in $\{C/D\}$ from December 1993 to December 1996 should have led to a decline in the money multiplier because the shift into currency produces less multiple deposit expansion. As our money supply model predicts, the money multiplier did indeed fall sharply in this period, and there was a dramatic deceleration of money growth.

Although our examination of the 1980–1996 period indicates that factors such as changes in the $\{C/D\}$ ratio can have a major impact on the money supply over short periods, we must not forget that over the entire period, the growth rate of the money supply is closely linked to the growth rate of the nonborrowed monetary base, MB_n. Indeed, empirical evidence suggests that more than three-fourths of the fluctuation in the money supply can be attributed to Federal Reserve open market operations, which determine MB_n.

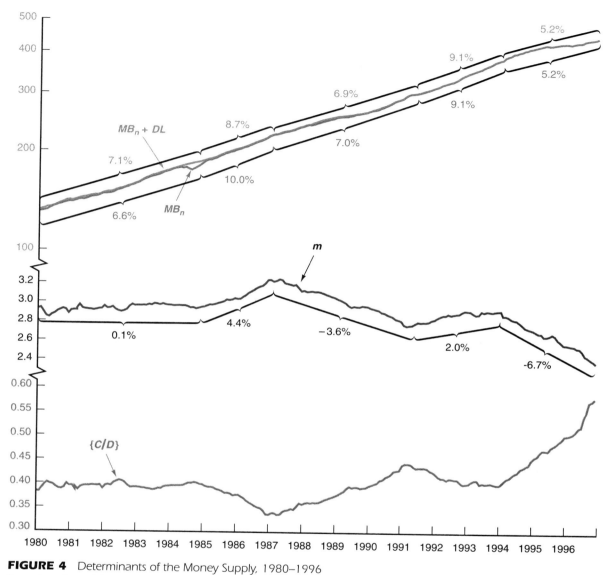

FIGURE 4   Determinants of the Money Supply, 1980–1996

Percentage for each bracket indicates the annual growth rate of the series over the bracketed period.

Source: Citibase databank.

The Great Depression Bank Panics, 1930–1933

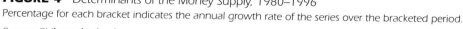

We can also use our money supply model to help us understand major movements in the money supply that have occurred in the past. In this application, we use the model to explain the monetary contraction that occurred during the Great

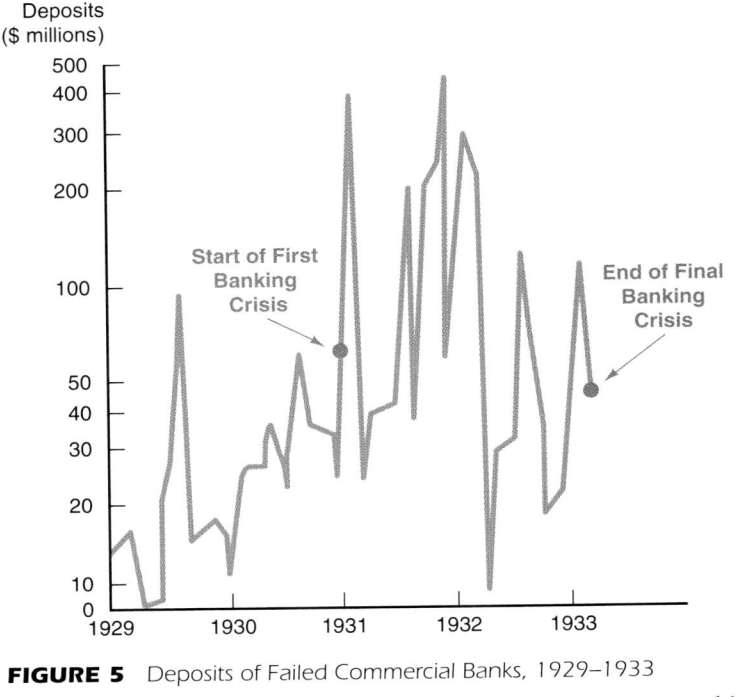

FIGURE 5   Deposits of Failed Commercial Banks, 1929–1933

Source: Milton Friedman and Anna Jacobson Schwartz, *A Monetary History of the United States, 1867–1960* (Princeton, N.J.: Princeton University Press, 1963), p. 309.

Depression, the worst economic downturn in U.S. history. In Chapter 9 we discussed bank panics and saw that they could harm the economy by making asymmetric information problems more severe in credit markets, as they did during the Great Depression. Here we can see that another consequence of bank panics is that they can cause a substantial reduction in the money supply. As we will see in the chapters on monetary theory later in the book, such reductions can also cause severe damage to the economy.

Figure 5 traces the bank crisis during the Great Depression by showing the volume of deposits at failed commercial banks from 1929 to 1933. In their classic book *A Monetary History of the United States, 1867–1960*, Milton Friedman and Anna Schwartz describe the onset of the first banking crisis in late 1930 as follows:

Before October 1930, deposits of suspended [failed] commercial banks had been somewhat higher than during most of 1929 but not out of line with experience during the preceding decade. In November 1930, they were more than double the highest value recorded since the start of monthly data in 1921. A crop of bank failures, particularly in Missouri, Indiana, Illinois, Iowa, Arkansas, and North Carolina, led to widespread attempts to convert checkable and time deposits into currency, and also, to a much lesser extent, into postal savings deposits. A contagion of fear spread among depositors, starting from the agricultural areas, which had experienced the heaviest impact of bank failures in the twenties. But failure of 256 banks with $180 million of deposits in November 1930 was followed by the failure of 532 with over $370 million of deposits in December (all figures seasonally unadjusted), the most dramatic being the failure on December 11 of the Bank of the United States with over $200 million of deposits. That failure was especially important. The Bank of United States was the largest commercial bank, as measured by volume of deposits, ever to have failed up to that time in U.S. history. Moreover, though it was just an ordinary commercial bank, the Bank of the United States's name had led many at home and abroad to regard it somehow as an official bank, hence its failure constituted more of a blow to confidence than would have been administered by the fall of a bank with a less distinctive name.[8]

The first bank panic, from October 1930 to January 1931, is clearly visible in Figure 5 at the end of 1930, when there is a rise in the amount of deposits at failed banks. Because there was no deposit insurance at the time (the FDIC wasn't established until 1934), when a bank failed, depositors would receive only partial repayment of their deposits. Therefore, when banks were failing during a bank panic, depositors knew that they would be likely to suffer substantial losses on deposits and thus the expected return on deposits would be negative. The theory of portfolio choice predicts that with the onset of the first bank crisis, depositors

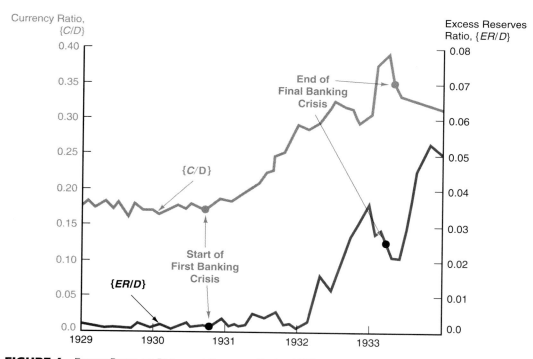

FIGURE 6   Excess Reserves Ratio and Currency Ratio, 1929–1933

Sources: Federal Reserve *Bulletin;* Milton Friedman and Anna Jacobson Schwartz, *A Monetary History of the United States, 1867–1960* (Princeton, N.J.: Princeton University Press, 1963), p. 333.

---

[8]Milton Friedman and Anna Jacobson Schwartz, *A Monetary History of the United States, 1867–1960* (Princeton, N.J.: Princeton University Press, 1963), pp. 308–311.

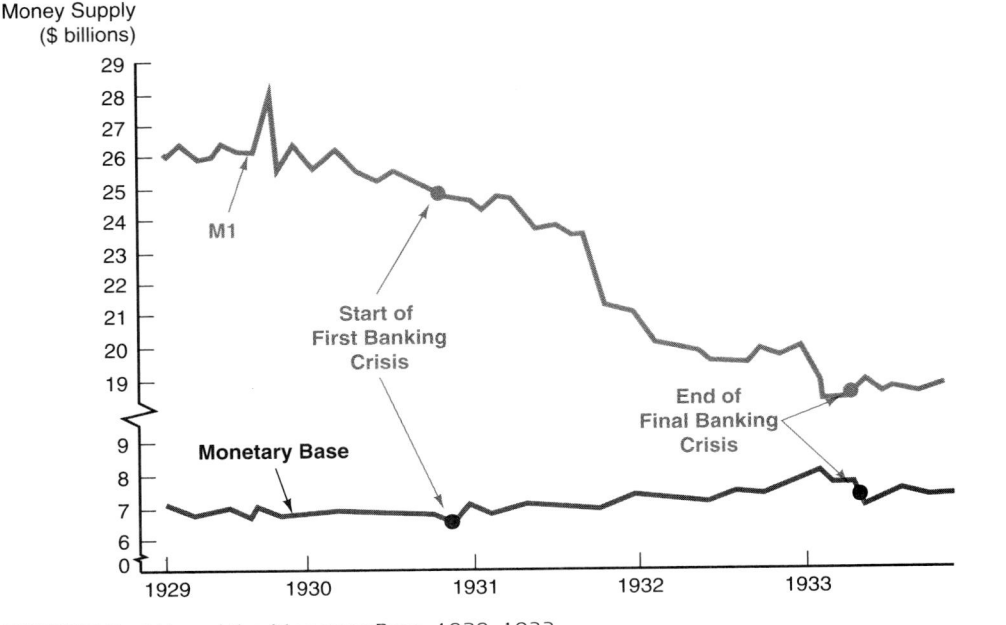

FIGURE 7   M1 and the Monetary Base, 1929–1933

Source: Milton Friedman and Anna Jacobson Schwartz, *A Monetary History of the United States, 1867–1960* (Princeton, N.J.: Princeton University Press, 1963), p. 333.

would shift their holdings from checkable deposits to currency by withdrawing currency from their bank accounts, and {C/D} would rise. Our earlier analysis of the excess reserves ratio suggests that the resulting surge in deposit outflows would cause the banks to protect themselves by substantially increasing their excess reserves ratio {ER/D}. Both of these predictions are borne out by the data in Figure 6. {C/D} began to climb during the first bank panic (October 1930–January 1931). Even more striking is the behavior of {ER/D}, which more than doubled from November 1930 to January 1931.

The money supply model predicts that when {ER/D} and {C/D} increase, the money supply will fall. The rise in {C/D} results in a decline in the overall level of multiple deposit expansion, leading to a smaller money multiplier and a decline in the money supply, while the rise in {ER/D} reduces the amount of reserves available to support deposits and also causes the money supply to fall. Thus our model predicts that the rise in {ER/D} and {C/D} after the onset of the first bank crisis would result in a decline in the money supply—a prediction borne out by the evidence in Figure 7. The money supply declined sharply in December 1930 and January 1931 during the first bank panic.

Banking crises continued to occur from 1931 to 1933, and the pattern predicted by our model persisted: {C/D} continued to rise, and so did {ER/D}. By the end of the crises in March 1933, the money supply (M1) had declined by over 25 percent—by far the largest decline in all of American history—and it coincided with the nation's worst economic contraction (see Chapter 9). Even more remarkable is that this decline occurred despite a 20 percent rise in the level of the monetary base—which illustrates how important the changes in {*C/D*} and {*ER/D*} during bank panics can be in the determination of the money supply. It also illustrates that the Fed's job of conducting monetary policy can be complicated by depositor and bank behavior. Ⓐ

SUMMARY

1. We developed a model to describe how the money supply is determined. First, we linked the monetary base to the money supply using the concept of the money multiplier, which tells us how much the money supply changes when there is a change in the monetary base.

2. The money supply is negatively related to the required reserve ratio r_D, the currency ratio {*C/D*}, and the excess reserves ratio {*ER/D*}. It is positively related to the level of discount loans *DL* from the Fed and the nonborrowed base MB_n, which is determined by Fed open market operations. The money

supply model therefore allows for the behavior of all four players in the money supply process: the Fed through its setting of the required reserve ratio, the discount rate, and open market operations; depositors through their decisions about the currency ratio; the banks through their decisions about the excess reserves ratio and discount loans from the Fed; and borrowers from banks indirectly through their effect on market interest rates, which affect bank decisions regarding the excess reserves ratio and borrowings from the Fed.

KEY TERMS

money multiplier, p. 435

nonborrowed monetary base, p. 443

QUESTIONS AND PROBLEMS

*1. "The money multiplier is necessarily greater than 1." Is this statement true, false, or uncertain? Explain your answer.

2. "If reserve requirements on checkable deposits were set at zero, the amount of multiple deposit expansion would go on indefinitely." Is this statement true, false, or uncertain? Explain.

*3. During the Great Depression years 1930–1933, the currency ratio {*C/D*} rose dramatically. What do you think happened to the money supply? Why?

4. During the Great Depression, the excess reserves ratio {*ER/D*} rose dramatically. What do you think happened to the money supply? Why?

*5. Traveler's checks have no reserve requirements and are included in the M1 measure of the money supply. When people travel during the summer and convert some of their checking account

deposits into traveler's checks, what happens to the money supply? Why?

6. If Jane Brown closes her account at the First National Bank and uses the money instead to open up a money market mutual fund account, what happens to M1 and M2? Why?

*7. Some experts have suggested that reserve requirements on checkable deposits and time deposits should be set equal because this would improve control of M2. Does this argument make sense? (*Hint:* Think about what happens when checkable deposits are converted into time deposits or vice versa.)

8. Why might the procyclical behavior of interest rates (rising during business cycle expansions and falling during recessions) lead to procyclical movements in the money supply?

USING ECONOMIC ANALYSIS TO PREDICT THE FUTURE

*9. The Fed buys $100 million of bonds from the public and also lowers r_D. What will happen to the money supply?

10. The Fed has been discussing the possibility of paying interest on excess reserves. If this occurred, what would happen to the level of {*ER/D*}?

*11. If the Fed sells $1 million of bonds and banks reduce their discount loans by $1 million, predict what will happen to the money supply.

12. Predict what will happen to the money supply if there is a sharp rise in the currency ratio.

*13. What do you predict would happen to the money supply if expected inflation suddenly increased?

14. If the economy starts to boom and loan demand picks up, what do you predict will happen to the money supply?

*15. Milton Friedman once suggested that Federal Reserve discount lending should be abolished. Predict what would happen to the money supply if Friedman's suggestion were put into practice.

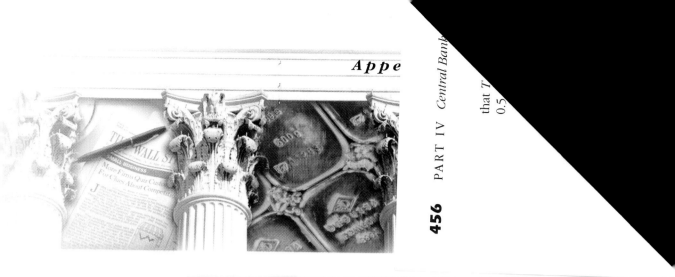

THE M2 MONEY MULTIPLIER

The derivation of a money multiplier for the M2 definition of money requires only slight modifications to the analysis in the chapter. The definition of M2 is

$$M2 = D + C + T + MMF$$

where C = currency in circulation
D = checkable deposits
T = time and savings deposits
MMF = primarily money market mutual fund shares and money market deposit accounts, plus overnight repurchase agreements and overnight Eurodollars

We again assume that all desired quantities of these variables rise proportionally with checkable deposits so that the equilibrium ratios $\{C/D\}$, $\{T/D\}$, and $\{MMF/D\}$ set by depositors are treated as constants. Replacing C by $\{C/D\} \times D$, T by $\{T/D\} \times D$, and MMF by $\{MMF/D\} \times D$ in the definition of M2 just given, we get

$$M2 = D + (\{C/D\} \times D) + (\{T/D\} \times D) + (\{MMF/D\} \times D)$$
$$= (1 + \{C/D\} + \{T/D\} + \{MMF/D\}) \times D$$

Substituting in the expression for D from Equation 2 in the chapter,[1] we have

$$M2 = \frac{1 + \{C/D\} + \{T/D\} + \{MMF/D\}}{r_D + \{ER/D\} + \{C/D\}} \times MB \tag{1}$$

To see what this formula implies about the M2 money multiplier, we continue with the same numerical example in the chapter, with the additional information

---

[1]From the derivation here it is clear that the quantity of checkable deposits D is unaffected by the depositor ratios $\{T/D\}$ and $\{MMF/D\}$ even though time deposits and money market mutual fund shares are included in M2. This is just a consequence of the absence of reserve requirements on time deposits and money market mutual fund shares, so T and MMF do not appear in any of the equations in the derivation of D in the chapter.

= \$2400 billion and *MMF* = \$400 billion so that {T/D} = 3 and {MMF/D} =

The resulting value of the multiplier for M2 is

$$m_2 = \frac{1 + 0.5 + 3 + 0.5}{0.10 + 0.001 + 0.5} = \frac{5.0}{0.601} = 8.32$$

An important feature of the M2 multiplier is that it is substantially above the M1 multiplier of 2.5 that we found in the chapter. The crucial concept in understanding this difference is that a lower required reserve ratio for time deposits or money market mutual fund shares means that they undergo more multiple expansion because fewer reserves are needed to support the same amount of them. Time deposits and *MMFs* have a lower required reserve ratio than checkable deposits—zero—and they will therefore have more multiple expansion than checkable deposits will. Thus the overall multiple expansion for the sum of these deposits will be greater than for checkable deposits alone, and so the M2 money multiplier will be greater than the M1 money multiplier.

FACTORS THAT DETERMINE THE M2 MONEY MULTIPLIER

Changes in r_D, {C/D}, and {ER/D}

The economic reasoning analyzing the effect of changes in the required reserve ratio and the currency ratio on the M2 money multiplier is identical to that used for the M1 multiplier in the chapter. An increase in the required reserve ratio r_D will decrease the amount of multiple deposit expansion, thus lowering the M2 money multiplier. An increase in {C/D} means that deposits have shifted out of checkable deposits into currency, and since currency has no multiple deposit expansion, the overall level of multiple deposit expansion for M2 must also fall, lowering the M2 multiplier. An increase in the excess reserves ratio {ER/D} means that banks use fewer reserves to support deposits, so deposits and the M2 money multiplier fall.

We thus have the same results we found for the M1 multiplier: *The M2 money multiplier and M2 money supply are negatively related to the required reserve ratio r_D, the currency ratio {C/D}, and the excess reserves ratio {ER/D}.*

Response to Changes in {T/D} and {MMF/D}

An increase in either {T/D} or {MMF/D} leads to an increase in the M2 multiplier because the required reserve ratios on time deposits and money market mutual fund shares are zero and hence are lower than the required reserve ratio on checkable deposits.

Both time deposits and money market mutual fund shares undergo more multiple expansion than checkable deposits. Thus a shift out of checkable deposits into time deposits or money market mutual funds, increasing {T/D} or {MMF/D}, implies that the overall level of multiple expansion will increase, raising the M2 money multiplier.

A decline in {T/D} or {MMF/D} will result in less overall multiple expansion, and the M2 money multiplier will decrease, leading to the following conclusion:

——— S U M M A R Y ———

TABLE A1   **Response of the M2 Money Supply to Changes in MB_n, DL, r_D, $\{ER/D\}$, $\{C/D\}$, $\{T/D\}$, and $\{MMF/D\}$**

Variable	Change in Variable	M2 Money Supply Response	Reason
MB_n	↑	↑	More *MB* to support *C* and *D*
DL	↑	↑	More *MB* to support *C* and *D*
r_D	↑	↓	Less multiple deposit expansion
$\{ER/D\}$	↑	↓	Fewer reserves to support *C* and *D*
$\{C/D\}$	↑	↓	Less overall deposit expansion
$\{T/D\}$	↑	↑	More multiple deposit expansion
$\{MMF/D\}$	↑	↑	More multiple deposit expansion

Note: Only increases (↑) in the variables are shown; the effects of decreases in the variables on the money multiplier would be the opposite of those indicated in the "Response" column.

The M2 money multiplier and M2 money supply are positively related to both the time deposit ratio $\{T/D\}$ and the money market fund ratio $\{MMF/D\}$.

The response of the M2 money supply to all the depositor and required reserve ratios is summarized in Table A1.

Chapter 18

TOOLS OF MONETARY POLICY

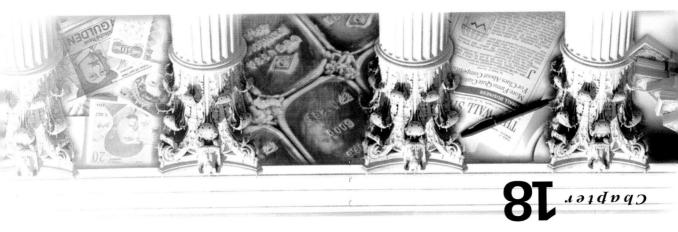

P R E V I E W   In the chapters describing the structure of the Federal Reserve System and the money supply process, we mentioned three policy tools that the Fed can use to manipulate the money supply and interest rates: open market operations, which affect the money supply and interest rates; changes in the discount rate, which affect interest rates and the monetary base by influencing the quantity of discount loans; and changes in reserve requirements, which affect the money multiplier. Because the Fed's use of these policy tools has such an important impact on economic activity, it is important to understand how the Fed wields them in practice and how relatively useful each tool is. In this chapter we also seek an answer to the following question: How can the use of these policy tools be modified to improve control over the money supply?

OPEN MARKET OPERATIONS

Open market operations are the most important monetary policy tool because they are the primary determinants of changes in interest rates and the monetary base, the main source of fluctuations in the money supply. Open market purchases expand the monetary base, thereby raising the money supply and lowering short-term interest rates, and open market sales shrink the monetary base, lowering the money supply and raising short-term interest rates. Now that we understand from Chapter 16 the factors that influence the monetary base, we can examine how the Federal Reserve conducts open market operations with the object of controlling short-term interest rates and the money supply.

There are two types of open market operations: **Dynamic open market operations** are intended to change the level of reserves and the monetary base, and **defensive open market operations** are intended to offset movements in other factors that affect reserves and the monetary base, such as changes in Treasury deposits with the Fed or float. The Fed conducts open market operations in U.S.

Treasury and government agency securities, especially U.S. Treasury bills.[1] The Fed conducts most of its open market operations in Treasury securities because the market for these securities is the most liquid and has the largest trading volume. It has the capacity to absorb the Fed's substantial volume of transactions without experiencing excessive price fluctuations that would disrupt the market.

As we saw in Chapter 15, the decision-making authority for open market operations is the Federal Open Market Committee (FOMC). The actual execution of these operations, however, is conducted by the trading desk at the Federal Reserve Bank of New York. The best way to see how these transactions are executed is to look at a typical day at the trading desk, located in a newly built trading room on the ninth floor of the Federal Reserve Bank of New York.

A Day at the Trading Desk

The head of domestic open market operations, currently Sandy Krieger, supervises the analysts and traders who execute the purchases and sales of securities. To get a grip on what might happen in the federal funds market that day, her workday and her staff's begins with a review of developments in the federal funds market the previous day and with an update on the actual amount of reserves in the banking system the day before. Later in the morning, Sandy's staff issues updated reports that contain detailed forecasts of what will be happening to some of the short-term factors affecting the supply and demand of reserves (discussed in Chapter 16). For example, if float is predicted to decrease because good weather throughout the country is speeding up check delivery, Sandy knows that she will have to conduct a defensive open market operation (in this case a *purchase* of securities) to offset the expected decline in reserves and the monetary base from the decreased float. However, if Treasury deposits with the Fed are predicted to fall, a defensive open market *sale* would be needed to offset the expected increase in reserves. The report also predicts the change in the public's holding of currency. If currency holdings are expected to rise, then, as we have seen in Chapters 16 and 17, reserves fall, and an open market purchase is needed to raise reserves back up again.

This information will help Sandy and her staff decide how large a change in reserves is needed to obtain a desired level of the federal funds rate. If the amount of reserves in the banking system is too large, many banks will have excess reserves to lend that other banks may have little desire to hold, and the federal funds rate will probably fall. If the level of reserves is too low, banks seeking to borrow reserves from the few banks that have excess reserves to lend may push the funds rate higher than the desired level. Also during the morning, the staff will monitor the behavior of the federal funds rate and contact some of the major participants in the funds market, which may provide independent information about whether a change in reserves is needed to achieve the desired level of the federal funds rate. Early in the morning, members of Sandy's staff contact several representatives of the so-called **primary dealers,** government securities dealers (who operate out of private firms or commercial banks) that the open market desk

---

[1]To avoid conflicts of interest, the Fed does not conduct open market operations in privately issued securities. (For example, think of the conflict if the Federal Reserve purchased bonds issued by a company owned by the chairman's brother-in-law.)

trades with. Her staff finds out how the dealers view market conditions to get a feel for what may happen to the prices of the securities they trade in over the course of the day. They also call the Treasury to get updated information on the expected level of Treasury balances at the Fed in order to refine their estimates of the supply of reserves.

Afterward, members of the Monetary Affairs Division at the Board of Governors are contacted, and the New York Fed's forecasts of reserve supply and demand are compared with the Board's. On the basis of these projections and the observed behavior of the federal funds market, the desk will formulate and propose a course of action to be taken that day, which may involve plans to add reserves to or drain reserves from the banking system through open market operations. If an operation is contemplated, the type, size, and maturity will be discussed.

The whole process is currently completed by midmorning, at which time a daily conference call is arranged linking the desk with the Office of the Director of Monetary Affairs at the Board and with one of the four voting Reserve Bank presidents outside of New York. During the call, a member of Sandy's unit will outline the desk's proposed reserve management strategy for the day. After the plan is approved, the desk is instructed to execute immediately any temporary open market operations that were planned for that day. (Outright operations, to be described shortly, may be conducted at other times of the day.)

The desk is linked electronically with its domestic open market trading counterparties by a computer system called TRAPS (Trading Room Automated Processing System), and all open market operations are now performed over this system. A message will be electronically transmitted simultaneously to all the primary dealers over TRAPS indicating the type and maturity of the operation being arranged. The dealers are given several minutes to respond via TRAPS with their propositions. The propositions are then assembled and displayed on a computer screen for evaluation. The desk will select all propositions, beginning with the most attractively priced, up to the point where the desired amount is purchased or sold, and it will then notify each dealer via TRAPS which of its propositions have been chosen. The entire selection process is typically completed in a matter of minutes.

These temporary transactions are of two basic types. In a **repurchase agreement** (often called a **repo**), the Fed purchases securities with an agreement that the seller will repurchase them in a short period of time, anywhere from 1 to 15 days from the original date of purchase. Because the effects on reserves of a repo are reversed on the day the agreement matures, a repo is actually a temporary open market purchase and is an especially desirable way of conducting a defensive open market purchase that will be reversed shortly. When the Fed wants to conduct a temporary open market sale, it engages in a **matched sale-purchase transaction** (sometimes called a **reverse repo**) in which the Fed sells securities and the buyer agrees to sell them back to the Fed in the near future.

At times, the desk may see the need to address a persistent reserve shortage or surplus and wish to arrange an operation that will have a permanent impact on the supply of reserves. Outright transactions, which involve a purchase or sale of securities that is not self-reversing, are also conducted over TRAPS. These operations are traditionally executed at times of day when temporary operations are not being conducted.

Open market operations have several advantages over the other tools of monetary policy.

1. Open market operations occur at the initiative of the Fed, which has complete control over their volume. This control is not found, for example, in discount operations, in which the Fed can encourage or discourage banks to take out discount loans by altering the discount rate but cannot directly control the volume of discount loans.

2. Open market operations are flexible and precise; they can be used to any extent. No matter how small a change in reserves or the monetary base is desired, open market operations can achieve it with a small purchase or sale of securities. Conversely, if the desired change in reserves or the base is very large, the open market operations tool is strong enough to do the job through a very large purchase or sale of securities.

3. Open market operations are easily reversed. If a mistake is made in conducting an open market operation, the Fed can immediately reverse it. If the Fed decides that the federal funds rate is too low because it has made too many open market purchases, it can immediately make a correction by conducting open market sales.

4. Open market operations can be implemented quickly; they involve no administrative delays. When the Fed decides that it wants to change the monetary base or reserves, it just places orders with securities dealers, and the trades are executed immediately.

DISCOUNT POLICY

Discount policy, which primarily involves changes in the discount rate, affects the money supply by affecting the volume of discount loans and the monetary base. A rise in discount loans adds to the monetary base and expands the money supply; a fall in discount loans reduces the monetary base and shrinks the money supply. The Federal Reserve facility at which discount loans are made to banks is called the **discount window.** It is easiest to understand how the Fed affects the volume of discount loans by looking at how the discount window operates.

The Fed can affect the volume of discount loans in two ways: by affecting the *price* of the loans (the discount rate) or by affecting the *quantity* of the loans through its administration of the discount window.[2]

The mechanism through which the Fed's discount rate affects the volume of discount loans is straightforward: A higher discount rate raises the cost of borrowing from the Fed, so banks will take out fewer discount loans; a lower discount rate makes discount loans more attractive to banks, and loan volume will increase.

To examine how the Fed affects the quantity of discount loans through its administration of the discount window, we have to examine more closely how these loans are made.

---

[2]Each Federal Reserve bank administers its own discount window facility. In our discussion here of discount policy, when we discuss the Fed's administration of the discount window, we are actually referring to the district banks' administration of their discount window facilities.

Why Has Adjustment Credit Borrowing Shrunk to Such Low Levels in the 1990s?

In recent years, adjustment credit borrowing has declined to very low levels, averaging below $100 million, making discount lending less important to the monetary policy process. Why has this occurred?

The Federal Reserve has not changed its rules on this kind of lending or discouraged its use, so the answer must lie with choices made by the borrowing banks. The problems in the banking industry in the late 1980s and early 1990s described in Chapter 12 provide a likely explanation for the decline in adjustment credit borrowing. Banks became reluctant to go to the discount window to borrow because

often market participants are able to guess who had done so. In an environment of concern about the health of banks, some banks fear that if they are perceived as seeking increased liquidity from the discount window, market participants will become concerned that the bank is in trouble and may begin pulling funds out of the bank. Consequently, even though perfectly healthy banks may need short-term liquidity, they have been reluctant to come to the discount window. With the return to health of the banking industry in recent years, these fears may diminish, and adjustment credit lending may increase again.

The Fed's discount loans to the banks are of three types: adjustment credit, seasonal credit, and extended credit. *Adjustment credit loans* are the discount loans that play the most important role in monetary policy. They are intended to be used by banks to help them with short-term liquidity problems that may result from a temporary deposit outflow, and the rate charged on them is the basic discount rate established by the Federal Reserve banks and approved by the Board of Governors. Adjustment credit, which can be obtained with a phone call, is expected to be repaid fairly quickly—by the end of the next business day for the larger banks. In the 1990s, adjustment credit has shrunk to very low levels, with the result that discount lending has been playing a less important role in monetary policy (see Box 1).

Seasonal credit is given to meet the needs of a limited number of banks in vacation and agricultural areas that have a seasonal pattern. Since 1992, the interest rate charged on seasonal credit is tied to the monthly average federal funds and certificate of deposit rates, with the basic discount rate as a floor. *Extended credit*, given to banks that have experienced severe liquidity problems because of deposit outflows, is not expected to be repaid quickly. The interest rate on these loans is set at one-half of a percentage point above the interest rate charged on seasonal credit. Banks obtaining extended credit have to submit a proposal outlining the need for extended credit and a plan for restoring the liquidity of the bank. The most important example of extended credit to a bank was the Fed's loans to Continental Illinois in 1984, which exceeded $5 billion.

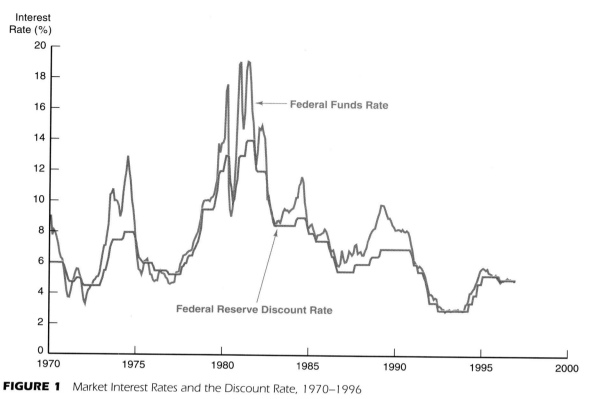

FIGURE 1 Market Interest Rates and the Discount Rate, 1970–1996

Source: Federal Reserve *Bulletin*.

The Fed administers the discount window in several ways to prevent its credit funds from being misused and to limit this borrowing. In recent years, as depicted in Figure 1, the discount rate has frequently been below market interest rates, so there is an incentive for banks to take out low-interest discount loans from the Fed and use the proceeds to make loans or purchase securities with higher interest rates. (Figure 2 in Chapter 17 shows that the volume of discount loans has risen abruptly when the discount rate fell below market interest rates.) Banks are not supposed to make a profit from discount loans, and the Fed tries to prevent that by indicating to individual banks that they should not come to the discount window too often. If a bank comes to the discount window too frequently, the Fed will deny it loans in the future. Its position is that coming to the discount window is a privilege, not a right.

A bank faces three costs when it borrows from the discount window: the interest cost represented by the discount rate, the cost of concerns that might be raised about the health of the bank if the market guesses that the bank has gone to the discount window, and the cost of being more likely to be turned down for a discount loan in the future because of too frequent trips to the discount window. The Fed's setting of rules for use of the discount window is frequently referred to as *moral suasion*.

Discounting to Troubled Banks

Franklin National and Continental Illinois. In May 1974, the public learned that Franklin National Bank, the twentieth-largest bank in the United States, with deposits close to $3 billion, had suffered large losses in foreign exchange trading and had made many bad loans. Large depositors, whose accounts exceeded the $100,000 limit insured by the FDIC, began to withdraw their deposits, and the failure of the bank was imminent. Because the immediate failure of Franklin National would have had repercussions on other vulnerable banks, possibly leading to more bank failures, the Fed announced that discount loans would be made available to Franklin National so that depositors, including the largest, would not suffer any losses. By the time Franklin National was merged into the European-American Bank in October 1974, the Fed had lent Franklin National the sum of $1.75 billion, nearly 5% of the total amount of reserves in the banking system. The quick Fed action was completely successful in preventing any other bank failures, and a possible bank panic was avoided.

A 1984 episode involved Continental Illinois National Bank and the Fed in a similar action. Continental Illinois had made many bad loans (primarily to businesses in the energy industry and to foreign countries), and rumors of financial trouble in early May 1984 caused large depositors to withdraw over $10 billion of deposits from the bank. The FDIC arranged a rescue effort in July 1984, that culminated in a $4.5 billion commitment of funds to save the bank; still, the Fed had to lend Continental Illinois over $5 billion—making its $1.75 billion loan to Franklin National look like small potatoes! The Fed's action prevented further bank failures, and again a potential bank panic was averted.

Lender of Last Resort

In addition to its use as a tool to influence the monetary base and the money supply, discounting is important in preventing financial panics. When the Federal Reserve System was created, its most important role was intended to be as the **lender of last resort;** it was to provide reserves to banks when no one else would in order to prevent bank failures from spinning out of control, thereby preventing bank and financial panics. Discounting is a particularly effective way to provide reserves to the banking system during a banking crisis because reserves are immediately channeled to the banks that need them most.

Using the discount tool to avoid financial panics by performing the role of lender of last resort is an extremely important requirement of successful monetary policymaking. As we demonstrated with our money supply analysis in Chapter 17, the bank panics in the 1930–1933 period were the cause of the sharpest decline in the money supply in U.S. history, which many economists see as the driving force behind the collapse of the economy during the Great Depression. Financial panics can also severely damage the economy because they interfere with the ability of financial intermediaries and markets to move funds to people with productive investment opportunities (see Chapter 9).

Unfortunately, the discount tool has not always been used by the Fed to prevent financial panics, as the massive failures during the Great Depression attest. The Fed learned from its mistakes of that period and has performed admirably in its role of lender of last resort in the post–World War II period. Two examples of the use of the Fed's discount weapon to avoid bank panics are the provisions of huge loans to Franklin National Bank in 1974 and to Continental Illinois ten years later (see Box 2).

At first glance, it might appear as though the presence of the FDIC, which insures depositors from losses due to a bank's failure up to a limit of $100,000 per account, would make the lender-of-last-resort function of the Fed superfluous. (The FDIC is described in detail in Chapter 12.) There are two reasons why this is not the case. First, it is important to recognize that the FDIC's insurance fund amounts to around 1 percent of the amount of these deposits outstanding. If a large number of bank failures occurred, the FDIC would not be able to cover all the depositors' losses. Indeed, the large number of bank failures in the 1980s and early 1990s, described in Chapter 12, led to large losses and a shrinkage in the FDIC's insurance fund, which reduced the FDIC's ability to cover depositors' losses. This fact has not weakened the confidence of small depositors in the banking system because the Fed has been ready to stand behind the banks to provide whatever reserves are needed to prevent bank panics. Second, the nearly $500 billion of large-denomination deposits in the banking system are not guaranteed by the FDIC because they exceed the $100,000 limit. A loss of confidence in the banking system could still lead to runs on banks from the large-denomination depositors, and bank panics could still occur despite the existence of the FDIC. The importance of the Federal Reserve's role as lender of last resort is, if anything, more important today because of the high number of bank failures experienced in the 1980s and early 1990s.

Not only can the Fed be a lender of last resort to banks, but it can also play the same role for the financial system as a whole. The existence of the Fed's discount window can help prevent financial panics that are not triggered by bank failures, as was the case during the Black Monday stock market crash of 1987 (see Box 3).

Although the Fed's role as the lender of last resort has the benefit of preventing bank and financial panics, it does have a cost. If a bank expects that the Fed will provide it with discount loans when it gets into trouble, as occurred with Continental Illinois, it will be willing to take on more risk knowing that the Fed will come to the rescue. The Fed's lender-of-last-resort role has thus created a moral hazard problem similar to the one created by deposit insurance (discussed in Chapter 12): Banks take on more risk, thus exposing the deposit insurance agency, and hence taxpayers, to greater losses. The moral hazard problem is most severe for large banks, which may believe that the Fed and the FDIC view them as "too big to fail"; that is, they will always receive Fed loans when they are in trouble because their failure would be likely to precipitate a bank panic.

Similarly, Federal Reserve actions to prevent financial panic, as occurred after the October 1987 stock market crash, may encourage financial institutions other than banks to take on greater risk. They, too, expect the Fed to ensure that they could get loans if a financial panic seemed imminent. When the Fed considers using the discount weapon to prevent panics, it therefore needs to consider the

Discounting to Prevent a Financial Panic

The Black Monday Stock Market Crash of 1987. Although October 19, 1987, dubbed "Black Monday," will go down in the history books as the largest one-day decline in stock prices to date (the Dow Jones Industrial Average declined by more than 500 points) it was on Tuesday, October 20, 1987, that financial markets almost stopped functioning. Felix Rohatyn, one of the most prominent men on Wall Street, stated flatly: "Tuesday was the most dangerous day we had in 50 years."* Much of the credit for prevention of a market meltdown after Black Monday must be given to the Federal Reserve System and the chairman of the Board of Governors, Alan Greenspan.

The stress of keeping markets functioning during the sharp decline in stock prices on Monday, October 19, meant that many brokerage houses and specialists (dealer-brokers who maintain orderly trading on the stock exchanges) were severely in need of additional funds to finance their activities. However, understandably enough, New York banks, as well as foreign and regional U.S. banks, growing very nervous about the financial health of securities firms, began to cut back credit to the securities industry at the very time when it was most needed. Panic was in the air. One chairman of a large specialist firm commented that on Monday, "from 2 P.M. on, there was

total despair. The entire investment community fled the market. We were left alone on the field." It was time for the Fed, like the cavalry, to come to the rescue.

Upon learning of the plight of the securities industry, Alan Greenspan and E. Gerald Corrigan, then president of the Federal Reserve Bank of New York and the Fed official most closely in touch with Wall Street, became fearful of a spreading collapse of securities firms. To prevent this from occurring, Greenspan announced before the market opened on Tuesday, October 20, the Federal Reserve System's "readiness to serve as a source of liquidity to support the economic and financial system." In addition to this extraordinary announcement, the Fed made it clear that it would provide discount loans to any bank that would make loans to the securities industry, although this did not prove to be necessary. As one New York banker said, the Fed's message was, "We're here. Whatever you need, we'll give you."

The outcome of the Fed's timely action was that a financial panic was averted. The markets kept functioning on Tuesday, and a market rally ensued that day, with the Dow Jones Industrial Average climbing over 100 points.

*"Terrible Tuesday: How the Stock Market Almost Disintegrated a Day After the Crash," *Wall Street Journal,* November 20, 1987, p. 1. This article provides a fascinating and more detailed view of the events described here and is the source of all the quotations cited.

trade-off between the moral hazard cost of its role as lender of last resort and the benefit of preventing financial panics. This trade-off explains why the Fed must be careful not to perform its role as lender of last resort too frequently.

Announcement Effect

Discount policy serves another function for the Federal Reserve: It can be used to signal the Fed's intentions about future monetary policy. Hence if the Fed decides to slow the expansion of the economy by increasing the federal funds rate, it can amplify the announcement that it makes after the FOMC meeting by also raising the discount rate. This signal alone may rein in economic expansion because the public will expect monetary policy to be less expansionary in the future.

The problem with the announcement effect is that it is subject to misinterpretation. We saw in Chapter 17 that if the federal funds rate is rising relative to the discount rate, the volume of discount loans will rise. In such a situation, the Fed may have no intention of amplifying the announcement of a federal funds rate increase, but to keep the amount of discounting from becoming excessive, it may raise the discount rate to keep it more in line with market interest rates. When the discount rate rises, the market may interpret this as a signal that the Fed is moving to a more contractionary policy, even if that is not the case. The announcement effect may be a hindrance rather than a help. Another approach is for the Fed to communicate directly with the public by announcing its intentions about monetary policy outright and then carrying them out. Fed announcements would be believed, and the market would respond accordingly.

Advantages and Disadvantages of Discount Policy

The most important advantage of discount policy is that the Fed can use it to perform its role of lender of last resort. Experiences with Continental Illinois, Franklin National Bank, and the Black Monday crash indicate that this role has become more important in the past couple of decades. Yet two significant disadvantages of discount policy cause many economists to suggest that it should not be used as a tool of monetary control. First is the confusion about the Federal Reserve's intentions that may be created by the announcement of discount rate changes. Second, when the Fed sets the discount rate at a particular level, large fluctuations will occur in the spread between market interest rates and the discount rate $(i - i_d)$ as market interest rates change. As we have noted (see Figure 2 in Chapter 17), these fluctuations in the past led to large unintended fluctuations in the volume of discount loans and hence in the money supply. Discount policy can make it harder to control the money supply.

The use of discount policy to control the money supply seems to have little to recommend it. Not only does it suffer from the two disadvantages described, but it is also less effective than open market operations for two additional reasons: Open market operations are completely at the discretion of the Fed, whereas the volume of discount loans is not—the Fed can change the discount rate, but it can't make banks borrow. In addition, open market operations are more easily reversed than changes in discount policy.

Evaluating Proposed Reforms of Discount Policy

The disadvantages of discount policy as a tool of monetary control have prompted economists to suggest two proposed reforms of discount policy: abolishing discounting entirely and tying the discount rate to a market rate of interest. Here we evaluate whether either of these suggested reforms would be a good idea.

Should Discounting Be Abolished?

Milton Friedman and other economists have proposed that the Fed should terminate its discount facilities in order to establish better monetary control.[3] Friedman has contended that the presence of the FDIC eliminates the possibility of bank panics; therefore, the use of discounting is no longer as necessary. Abolishing discounting would eliminate fluctuations in the monetary base due to changes in the volume of discount loans and so would reduce unintended fluctuations in the money supply.

Critics of Friedman's proposal emphasize that the FDIC is effective at preventing bank panics only because the Fed stands behind it and plays the role of lender of last resort. Furthermore, as we have seen in the case of the Black Monday crash, the existence of the Federal Reserve's discount facilities can help avert a financial panic unrelated to bank failures. Because of the increased number of bank failures in recent years, the need for the Fed's use of the discount facility to preserve the health of the financial system has become more apparent. Hence most economists do not support Friedman's proposal.

Should the Discount Rate Be Tied to a Market Rate of Interest?

An alternative proposal, much less radical than abolishing discounting, is that the discount rate be tied to a market rate of interest, such as the three-month U.S. Treasury bill rate or the federal funds rate. One version of this proposal, called the *penalty discount rate concept,* involves setting the discount rate at a fixed amount above the market interest rate—say, at 3 percentage points above the three-month bill rate—and allowing banks to borrow all the funds they want at that rate.

The advantages of tying the discount rate to a market rate of interest are many. First, the Fed could continue to use discounting to perform its role of lender of last resort. Second, most fluctuations in the spread between market interest rates and the discount rate $(i - i_d)$ would be eliminated, removing a major source of fluctuations in the volume of discount loans. Third, if the penalty discount rate concept were used, the administration of the discount window would be greatly simplified because there no longer would be a need to ration discount loans since they would cost more than any profits that could be earned by using the proceeds to make additional loans. Fourth, because discount rate changes would be automatic, there would be no false signals about the Federal Reserve's intentions, and the announcement effect would disappear.

Tying the discount rate to a market rate of interest is supported by many professional economists. However, other economists have opposed this proposed reform because they think that keeping the discount rate fixed when market interest rates change would reduce fluctuations in market interest rates. Such a policy would cause discount loans and hence reserves to rise when market interest rates rise, possibly countering some of the rise in market interest rates.

---

[3]Milton Friedman, *A Program for Monetary Stability* (New York: Fordham University Press, 1960); Marvin Goodfriend and Robert G. King, "Financial Deregulation, Monetary Policy, and Central Banking," Federal Reserve Bank of Richmond *Review* 74 (1988): 3–22.

Even though the Federal Reserve does not formally tie the discount rate to a market rate of interest, we can see from Figure 1 that the Fed already pursues a discount policy that is not too far removed from this proposal. It does not let the discount rate move too far away from market rates of interest because it does not want to let the volume of discount loans get out of hand.   Ⓐ

RESERVE REQUIREMENTS

As we saw in Chapter 17, changes in reserve requirements affect the money supply by causing the money supply multiplier to change. A rise in reserve requirements reduces the amount of deposits that can be supported by a given level of the monetary base and will lead to a contraction of the money supply. Conversely, a decline in reserve requirements leads to an expansion of the money supply because more multiple deposit creation can take place. The Fed has had the authority to vary reserve requirements since the 1930s, and this is a powerful way of affecting the money supply. Indeed, changes in reserve requirements have such large effects on the money supply that the Fed rarely resorts to using this tool to control it.

The Depository Institutions Deregulation and Monetary Control Act of 1980 provided a simpler scheme for setting reserve requirements. All depository institutions, including commercial banks, savings and loan associations, mutual savings banks, and credit unions, are now subject to the same reserve requirements, as follows: Required reserves on all checkable deposits—including non-interest-bearing checking accounts, NOW accounts, super-NOW accounts, and ATS (automatic transfer savings) accounts—are equal to 3 percent of the bank's first $49.3 million of checkable deposits[4] and 10 percent of the checkable deposits over $49.3 million, and the percentage set initially at 10 percent can be varied between 8 and 14 percent, at the Fed's discretion. In extraordinary circumstances, the percentage can be raised as high as 18 percent.

Advantages and Disadvantages of Reserve Requirement Changes

The main advantage of using reserve requirements to control the money supply is that they affect all banks equally and have a powerful effect on the money supply. The fact that changing reserve requirements is a powerful tool, however, is probably more of a curse than a blessing because small changes in the money supply are hard to engineer by varying reserve requirements. With checkable deposits currently hovering near the $700 billion level, a $\frac{1}{2}$-percentage-point increase in the reserve requirement on these deposits would reduce excess reserves by $35 billion. Because this decline in excess reserves would result in multiple deposit contraction, the decline in the money supply would be even greater. It is true that small changes in the money supply could be obtained by extremely small changes in reserve requirements (say, by 0.001 percentage point), but because it is so expensive to administer changes in reserve requirements, such a strategy is not practical. Using reserve requirements to fine-tune the money supply is like trying to use a jackhammer to cut a diamond.

---

[4]The $49.3 million figure is as of the end of 1996. Each year, the figure is adjusted upward by 80 percent of the percentage increase in checkable deposits in the United States.

Another disadvantage of using reserve requirements to control the money supply is that raising the requirements can cause immediate liquidity problems for banks with low excess reserves. When the Fed has raised these requirements in the past, it has usually softened the blow by conducting open market purchases or by making the discount window more available, thus providing reserves to banks that needed them. Continually fluctuating reserve requirements would also create more uncertainty for banks and make their liquidity management more difficult.

The policy tool of changing reserve requirements does not have much to recommend it, and it is rarely used.

Evaluating Proposed Reforms of Reserve Requirements

Two extreme proposals have been suggested to reform reserve requirements. One is to abolish reserve requirements entirely, and the other is to set required reserves at 100 percent of deposits. Again we examine whether reforms like this make sense.

Should Reserve Requirements Be Abolished?

As we will see in the following application, central banks in many countries have been reducing reserve requirements, and some have eliminated them entirely. If you had studied only the simple deposit multiplier (Chapter 16), you might think that abolishing reserve requirements would result in an infinite money supply. However, as our more sophisticated money supply model (Chapter 17) indicates, this reasoning would be incorrect. Banks would still want to hold reserves to protect themselves against deposit outflows, and there would still be a demand for currency. Both these factors would limit the size of the money supply.

The case for keeping reserve requirements must rest on the proposition that having reserve requirements results in a more stable money multiplier and hence a more controllable money supply. Since the evidence for or against this view is limited, the desirability of this proposed reform remains an open question.

Should Reserve Requirements Be Raised to 100 Percent?

At the same time that Milton Friedman suggested abolishing discounting, he also suggested that required reserves be set equal to 100 percent of deposits.[5] With a 100 percent reserve requirement, the money supply could be strictly controlled by the Fed because it would be equal to the monetary base. The advantage of this proposal is clear, but several major disadvantages surface. Banks would no longer be able to make loans because with a 100 percent reserve requirement, no excess reserves would be available. Loans would have to be made by other financial intermediaries. Not only would this restructuring of the banking system be

---

[5]Friedman, *Program for Monetary Stability*. This proposal was outlined earlier by Henry Simons in *Economic Policy for a Free Society* (Chicago: University of Chicago Press, 1948).

extremely costly, but the financial intermediaries not subject to reserve requirements might develop ways of making their liabilities function more like checkable deposits in order to attract funds.[6] The outcome might be that the Fed would enjoy complete control of the *official* money supply, but the *economically relevant* money supply might be even less under the Fed's control because it would be affected by the activities of nonbank financial intermediaries. In addition, the Fed's control over the financial system could be weakened further because all the loan activity would be in the hands of financial institutions not subject to the Fed's reserve requirements.   Ⓐ

Why Have Reserve Requirements Been Declining Worldwide?

In recent years, central banks in many countries in the world have been reducing or eliminating their reserve requirements. In the United States, the Federal Reserve eliminated reserve requirements on time deposits in December 1990 and lowered reserve requirements on checkable deposits from 12 percent to 10 percent in April 1992. As a result, the majority of U.S. depository institutions—but not the largest ones with the bulk of deposits—find that reserve requirements are not binding: In order to service their depositors, many depository institutions need to keep sufficient vault cash on hand (which counts toward meeting reserve requirements) that they more than meet reserve requirements voluntarily. Canada has gone a step further: Financial market legislation taking effect in June 1992 eliminated all reserve requirements over a two-year period. The central banks of Switzerland, New Zealand, and Australia have also eliminated reserve requirements entirely. What explains the downward trend for reserve requirements in most countries?

You may recall from Chapter 10 that reserve requirements act as a tax on banks. Because central banks typically do not pay interest on reserves, the bank earns nothing on them and loses the interest that could have been earned if the bank held loans instead. The cost imposed on banks from reserve requirements means that banks, in effect, have a higher cost of funds than intermediaries not subject to reserve requirements, making them less competitive. We have already seen in Chapter 11 that additional market forces have been making banks less competitive, weakening the health of banking systems throughout the world. Central banks have thus been reducing reserve requirements to make banks more competitive and stronger.[7] The Federal Reserve was explicit about this rationale for its April 1992 reduction when it announced it on February 18, 1992, stating in its press release that the reduction "will reduce funding costs for depositories and strengthen their balance sheets. Over time, it is expected that most of these cost savings will be passed on to depositors and borrowers."   Ⓐ

---

[6]We would expect this to happen because it would trigger the process of financial innovation discussed in Chapter 10.

[7]Many economists believe that the Fed should pay market interest rates on reserves, another suggestion for dealing with this problem.

SUMMARY

1. The amount of an open market operation conducted on any given day by the trading desk of the Federal Reserve Bank of New York is determined by the amount of the dynamic open market operation intended to change reserves and the monetary base and by the amount of the defensive open market operation used to offset other factors that affect reserves and the monetary base. Open market operations are the primary tool used by the Fed to control the money supply because they occur at the initiative of the Fed, are flexible, are easily reversed, and can be implemented quickly.

2. The volume of discount loans is affected by the discount rate and the discouragement of borrowing by moral suasion. Besides its effect on the monetary base and the money supply, discounting allows the Fed to perform its role as the lender of last resort. However, discount policy does make control of the money supply more difficult because it results in unintended fluctuations in the volume of discount loans and hence in the money supply. Many economists support tying the discount rate to a market interest rate to reduce these unintended fluctuations in the volume of discount loans.

3. Changing reserve requirements is too blunt a tool to use for controlling the money supply, and hence it is rarely used.

KEY TERMS

defensive open market operations, p. 458

discount window, p. 461

dynamic open market operations, p. 458

lender of last resort, p. 464

matched sale-purchase transaction (reverse repo), p. 460

primary dealers, p. 459

repurchase agreement (repo), p. 460

QUESTIONS AND PROBLEMS

*1. If the manager of the open market desk hears that a snowstorm is about to strike New York City, making it difficult to present checks for payment there and so raising the float, what defensive open market operations will the manager undertake?

2. During Christmastime, when the public's holdings of currency increase, what defensive open market operations typically occur? Why?

*3. If the Treasury has just paid for a supercomputer and as a result its deposits with the Fed fall, what defensive open market operations will the manager of the open market desk undertake?

4. If float decreases below its normal level, why might the manager of domestic operations consider it more desirable to use repurchase agreements to affect the monetary base rather than an outright purchase of bonds?

*5. Most open market operations are currently repurchase agreements. What does this tell us about the likely volume of defensive open market operations relative to dynamic open market operations?

6. "The only way that the Fed can affect the level of discount loans is by adjusting the discount rate." Is this statement true, false, or uncertain? Explain your answer.

*7. If the Fed did not administer the discount window to limit borrowing, what do you predict would happen to the money supply if the discount rate were several percentage points below the interest rate on loans?

8. "If the discount rate were always kept above the interest rate on loans, the Fed would rarely have to administer the discount window to limit borrowing." Is this statement true, false, or uncertain? Explain your answer.

*9. "Discounting is no longer needed because the presence of the FDIC eliminates the possibility of bank panics." Discuss.

10. The benefits of using Fed discount operations to prevent bank panics are straightforward. What are the costs?

*11. You often read in the newspaper that the Fed has just lowered the discount rate. Does this signal that the Fed is moving to a more expansionary monetary policy? Why or why not?

12. How can the procyclical movement of interest rates (rising during business cycle expansions and falling during business cycle contractions) lead to a procyclical movement in the money supply as a result of Fed discounting? Why might this movement of the money supply be undesirable?

*13. Which proposal would lead to tighter control of the money supply: abolishing discounting or tying the discount rate to a market rate of interest? Which of the two proposals would you prefer and why?

14. "Considering that raising reserve requirements to 100 percent makes complete control of the money supply possible, Congress should authorize the Fed to raise reserve requirements to this level." Discuss.

*15. Compare the use of open market operations, discounting, and changes in reserve requirements to control the money supply on the following criteria: flexibility, reversibility, effectiveness, and speed of implementation.

Chapter 19

CONDUCT OF MONETARY POLICY: GOALS AND TARGETS

PREVIEW   Now that we understand the tools central banks like the Federal Reserve use to conduct monetary policy, we can proceed to see how monetary policy is actually conducted by central banks. Understanding the conduct of monetary policy is important because it not only affects the money supply and interest rates but also has a major influence on the level of economic activity and hence on our well-being.

To explore this subject, we look at the goals that the Fed and other countries' central banks establish for monetary policy and their strategies for attaining them. After examining the goals and strategies, we can evaluate the Fed's and other central banks' conduct of monetary policy in the past, with the hope that it will give us some clues to where monetary policy may head in the future.

GOALS OF MONETARY POLICY

Six basic goals are continually mentioned by personnel at the Federal Reserve and other central banks when they discuss the objectives of monetary policy: (1) high employment, (2) economic growth, (3) price stability, (4) interest-rate stability, (5) stability of financial markets, and (6) stability in foreign exchange markets.

High Employment

The Employment Act of 1946 and the Full Employment and Balanced Growth Act of 1978 (more commonly called the Humphrey-Hawkins Act) commit the U.S. government to promoting high employment consistent with a stable price level. High employment is a worthy goal for two main reasons: (1) the alternative situation, high unemployment, causes much human misery, with families suffering financial distress, loss of personal self-respect, and increase in crime (though this last conclusion is highly controversial), and (2) when unemployment is high, the economy has not only idle workers but also idle resources (closed factories and unused equipment), resulting in a loss of output (lower GDP).

Although it is clear that high employment is desirable, how high should it be? At what point can we say that the economy is at full employment? At first, it might seem that full employment is the point at which no worker is out of a job, that is, when unemployment is zero. But this definition ignores the fact that some unemployment, called *frictional unemployment*, which involves searches by workers and firms to find suitable matchups, is beneficial to the economy. For example, a worker who decides to look for a better job might be unemployed for a while during the job search. Workers often decide to leave work temporarily to pursue other activities (raising a family, travel, returning to school), and when they decide to reenter the job market, it may take some time for them to find the right job. The benefit of having some unemployment is similar to the benefit of having a nonzero vacancy rate in the market for rental apartments. As many of you who have looked for an apartment have discovered, when the vacancy rate in the rental market is too low, you will have a difficult time finding the right apartment.

Another reason that unemployment is not zero when the economy is at full employment is due to what is called *structural unemployment*, a mismatch between job requirements and the skills or availability of local workers. Clearly, this kind of unemployment is undesirable. Nonetheless, it is something that monetary policy can do little about.

The goal for high employment should therefore not seek an unemployment level of zero but rather a level above zero consistent with full employment at which the demand for labor equals the supply of labor. This level is called the **natural rate of unemployment.**

Although this definition sounds neat and authoritative, it isn't because it leaves a troublesome question unanswered: What unemployment rate is consistent with full employment? On the one hand, in some cases, it is obvious that the unemployment rate is too high: The unemployment rate in excess of 20 percent during the Great Depression, for example, was clearly far too high. In the early 1960s, on the other hand, policymakers thought that a reasonable goal was 4 percent, a level that was probably too low because it led to accelerating inflation. Current estimates of the natural rate of unemployment place it between 5 and 6 percent, but even this estimate is subject to a great deal of uncertainty and disagreement. In addition, it is possible that appropriate government policy, such as the provision of better information about job vacancies or job training programs, might decrease the natural rate of unemployment.

Economic Growth

The goal of steady economic growth is closely related to the high-employment goal because businesses are more likely to invest in capital equipment to increase productivity and economic growth when unemployment is low. Conversely, if unemployment is high and factories are idle, it does not pay for a firm to invest in additional plants and equipment. Although the two goals are closely related, policies can be specifically aimed at promoting economic growth by directly encouraging firms to invest or by encouraging people to save, which provides more funds for firms to invest. In fact, this is the stated purpose of so-called supply-side economics policies, which are intended to spur economic growth by providing tax incentives for businesses to invest in facilities and equipment and for taxpayers to save more. The public, politicians, and the media in the United

States have become much more concerned about economic growth in recent years because of the dramatic slowdown since the early 1970s. In the 1950s and 1960s, real GDP grew in excess of $3\frac{1}{2}$ percent per year on average, whereas since 1973, it has grown at 2 to $2\frac{1}{2}$ percent. This has generated an active debate over what can be done to increase our growth rate and whether monetary policy can play a role in boosting growth.

Price Stability

Over the past two decades, policymakers in the United States have become more aware of the social and economic costs of inflation and more concerned with a stable price level as a goal of economic policy. (The growing commitment to price stability is also evident in Europe—see Box 1.) Price stability is desirable because a rising price level (inflation) creates uncertainty in the economy, and that may hamper economic growth. For example, the information conveyed by the prices of goods and services is harder to interpret when the overall level of prices is changing, which complicates decision making for consumers, businesses, and government. Not only do public opinion surveys indicate that the public is very hostile to inflation, but also a growing body of evidence suggests that inflation leads to lower economic growth.[1] The most extreme example of unstable prices is *hyperinflation*, such as Argentina and Brazil experienced until recently. Many economists attribute the slower growth that these countries have experienced to their problems with hyperinflation.

Inflation also makes it hard to plan for the future. For example, it is more difficult to decide how much funds should be put aside to provide for a child's college education in an inflationary environment. Further, inflation may strain a country's social fabric: Conflict may result because each group in the society may compete with other groups to make sure that its income keeps up with the rising level of prices.

Interest-Rate Stability

Interest-rate stability is desirable because fluctuations in interest rates can create uncertainty in the economy and make it harder to plan for the future. Fluctuations in interest rates that affect consumers' willingness to buy houses, for example, make it more difficult for consumers to decide when to purchase a house and for construction firms to plan how many houses to build. A central bank may also want to reduce upward movements in interest rates for the reasons we discussed in Chapter 15: Upward movements in interest rates generate hostility toward central banks like the Fed and lead to demands that their power be curtailed.

Stability of Financial Markets

As our analysis in Chapter 9 showed, financial crises can interfere with the ability of financial markets to channel funds to people with productive investment opportunities, thereby leading to a sharp contraction in economic activity. The promotion of a more stable financial system in which financial crises are avoided

---

[1]For example, see Stanley Fischer, "The Role of Macroeconomic Factors in Growth," *Journal of Monetary Economics* 32 (1993): 485–512.

BOX 1

The Growing European Commitment to Price Stability

Not surprisingly, given Germany's experience with hyperinflation in the 1920s, its central bank has the strongest commitment to price stability. In contrast to statutes for the German central bank, the statutes of other central banks in Europe set various objectives for policy, including all the goals outlined here in the text. However, European policymakers have been coming around to the view that the primary objective for a central bank should be price stability. The increased importance of this goal is reflected in the December 1991 Treaty of European Union, known as the Maastricht Treaty, which proposed the creation of the European System of Central Banks, which would function very much like the Federal Reserve System. The statute of the European System of Central Banks sets price stability as the primary objective of this system and indicates that the general economic policies of the European Union are to be supported only if they are not in conflict with price stability.

is thus an important goal for a central bank. Indeed, as discussed in Chapter 15, the Federal Reserve System was created in response to the bank panic of 1907 to promote financial stability.

The stability of financial markets is also fostered by interest-rate stability because fluctuations in interest rates create great uncertainty for financial institutions. An increase in interest rates produces large capital losses on long-term bonds and mortgages, losses that can cause the failure of the financial institutions holding them. In recent years, more pronounced interest-rate fluctuations have been a particularly severe problem for savings and loan associations and mutual savings banks, many of which got into serious financial trouble in the 1980s and early 1990s (as we have seen in Chapter 12).

Stability in Foreign Exchange Markets

With the increasing importance of international trade to the U.S. economy, the value of the dollar relative to other currencies has become a major consideration for the Fed. As we saw in Chapter 8, a rise in the value of the dollar makes American industries less competitive with those abroad, and declines in the value of the dollar stimulate inflation in the United States. In addition, preventing large changes in the value of the dollar makes it easier for firms and individuals purchasing or selling goods abroad to plan ahead. Stabilizing extreme movements in the value of the dollar in foreign exchange markets is thus viewed as a worthy goal of monetary policy. In other countries, which are even more dependent on foreign trade, stability in foreign exchange markets takes on even greater importance.

Conflict Among Goals

Although many of the goals mentioned are consistent with each other—high employment with economic growth, interest-rate stability with financial market stability—this is not always the case. The goal of price stability often conflicts with the goals of interest-rate stability and high employment in the short run (but probably not in the long run). For example, when the economy is expanding and unemployment is falling, both inflation and interest rates may start to rise. If the central bank tries to prevent a rise in interest rates, this may cause the economy to overheat and stimulate inflation. But if a central bank raises interest rates to prevent inflation, in the short run unemployment may rise. The conflict among goals may thus present central banks like the Federal Reserve with some hard choices. We return to the issue of how central banks should choose conflicting goals in later chapters when we examine how monetary policy affects the economy.

CENTRAL BANK STRATEGY: USE OF TARGETS

The central bank's problem is that it wishes to achieve certain goals, such as price stability with high employment, but it does not directly influence the goals. It has a set of tools to employ (open market operations, changes in the discount rate, and changes in reserve requirements) that can affect the goals indirectly after a period of time (typically more than a year). If the central bank waits to see what the price level and employment will be one year later, it will be too late to make any corrections to its policy—mistakes will be irreversible.

All central banks consequently pursue a different strategy for conducting monetary policy by aiming at variables that lie between its tools and the achievement of its goals. The strategy is as follows: After deciding on its goals for employment and the price level, the central bank chooses a set of variables to aim for, called **intermediate targets,** such as the monetary aggregates (M1, M2, or M3) or interest rates (short- or long-term), which have a direct effect on employment and the price level. However, even these intermediate targets are not directly affected by the central bank's policy tools. Therefore, it chooses another set of variables to aim for, called **operating targets,** or alternatively called *instruments*, such as reserve aggregates (reserves, nonborrowed reserves, monetary base, or nonborrowed base) or interest rates (federal funds rate or Treasury bill rate), which are more responsive to its policy tools. (Recall that nonborrowed reserves are total reserves minus borrowed reserves, which are the amount of discount loans; the nonborrowed base is the monetary base minus borrowed reserves; and the federal funds rate is the interest rate on funds loaned overnight between banks.)[2]

The central bank pursues this strategy because it is easier to hit a goal by aiming at targets than by aiming at the goal directly. Specifically, by using intermediate and operating targets, it can more quickly judge whether its policies are on the right track, rather than waiting until it sees the final outcome of its policies on employment and the price level.[3] By analogy, NASA employs the strategy of using

---

[2]There is some ambiguity as to whether to call a particular variable an operating target or an intermediate target. The monetary base and the Treasury bill rate are often viewed as possible intermediate targets, even though they may function as operating targets as well. In addition, if the Fed wants to pursue a goal of interest-rate stability, an interest rate can be both a goal and a target.

[3]This reasoning for the use of monetary targets has come under attack because information on employment and the price level can be useful in evaluating policy. See Benjamin M. Friedman, "The Inefficiency of Short-Run Monetary Targets for Monetary Policy," *Brookings Papers on Economic Activity* 2 (1977): 292–346.

Tools of the Central Bank

Open market operations
Discount policy
Reserve requirements

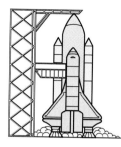

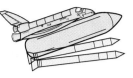

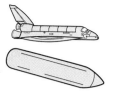

Operating Targets

Reserve aggregates
(reserves, nonborrowed
reserves, monetary base,
nonborrowed base)
Interest rates (short-term
such as federal funds rate)

Intermediate Targets

Monetary aggregates
(M1, M2, M3)
Interest rates (short-
and long-term)

Goals

High employment,
price stability,
financial market
stability and so on.

FIGURE 1 *Central Bank Strategy*

targets when it is trying to send a spaceship to the moon. It will check to see whether the spaceship is positioned correctly as it leaves the atmosphere (we can think of this as NASA's "operating target"). If the spaceship is off course at this stage, NASA engineers will adjust its thrust (a policy tool) to get it back on target. NASA may check the position of the spaceship again when it is halfway to the moon (NASA's "intermediate target") and can make further midcourse corrections if necessary.

The central bank's strategy works in a similar way. Suppose that the central bank's employment and price-level goals are consistent with a nominal GDP growth rate of 5 percent. If the central bank feels that the 5 percent nominal GDP growth rate will be achieved by a 4 percent growth rate for M2 (its intermediate target), which will in turn be achieved by a growth rate of $3\frac{1}{2}$ percent for the monetary base (its operating target), it will carry out open market operations (its tool) to achieve the $3\frac{1}{2}$ percent growth in the monetary base. After implementing this policy, the central bank may find that the monetary base is growing too slowly, say, at a 2 percent rate; then it can correct this too slow growth by increasing the amount of its open market purchases. Somewhat later, the central bank will begin to see how its policy is affecting the growth rate of the money supply. If M2 is growing too fast, say, at a 7 percent rate, the central bank may decide to reduce its open market purchases or make open market sales to reduce the M2 growth rate.

One way of thinking about this strategy (illustrated in Figure 1) is that the central bank is using its operating and intermediate targets to direct monetary policy (the spaceship) toward the achievement of its goals. After the initial setting of the policy tools (the liftoff), an operating target such as the monetary base, which the central bank can control fairly directly, is used to reset the tools so that monetary policy is channeled toward achieving the intermediate target of a certain rate of money supply growth. Midcourse corrections in the policy tools can be made again when the central bank sees what is happening to its intermediate target, thus directing monetary policy so that it will achieve its goals of high employment and price stability (the spaceship reaches the moon).

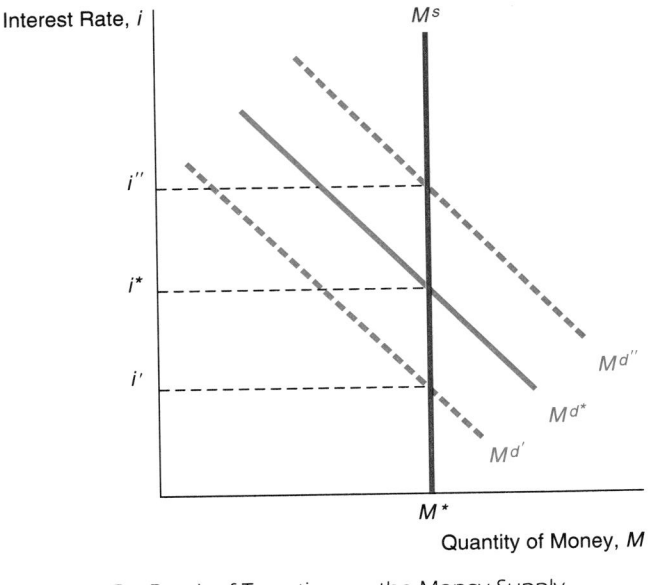

FIGURE 2 Result of Targeting on the Money Supply
Targeting on the money supply at **M*** will lead to fluctuations in the interest rate between *i'* and *i"*
because of fluctuations in the money demand curve between $M^{d'}$ and $M^{d"}$.

CHOOSING THE TARGETS

As we see in Figure 1, there are two different types of target variables: interest
rates and aggregates (monetary aggregates and reserve aggregates). In our example, the central bank chose a 4 percent growth rate for M2 to achieve a 5 percent
rate of growth for nominal GDP. It could have chosen to lower the interest rate
on the three-month Treasury bills to, say, 3 percent to achieve the same goal. Can
the central bank choose to pursue both of these targets at the same time? The
answer is no. The application of the supply and demand analysis of the money
market that we covered in Chapter 6 explains why a central bank must choose
one or the other.

Let's first see why a monetary aggregate target involves losing control of the
interest rate. Figure 2 contains a supply and demand diagram for the money market. Although the central bank expects the demand curve for money to be at
M^{d*}, it fluctuates between $M^{d'}$ and $M^{d"}$ because of unexpected increases or
decreases in output or changes in the price level. The money demand curve might
also shift unexpectedly because the public's preferences about holding bonds versus money may change. If the central bank's monetary aggregate target of a 4 percent growth rate in M2 results in a money supply of M^*, it expects that the interest
rate will be i^*. However, as the figure indicates, the fluctuations in the money
demand curve between $M^{d'}$ and $M^{d"}$ will result in an interest rate fluctuating
between i' and $i"$. Pursuing a monetary aggregate target implies that interest rates
will fluctuate.

The supply and demand diagram in Figure 3 shows the consequences of an
interest-rate target set at i^*. Again, the central bank expects the money demand

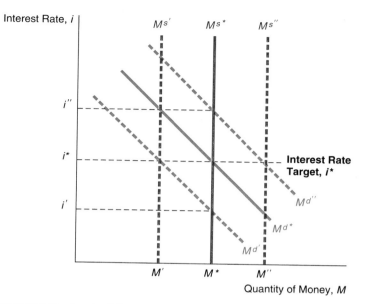

FIGURE 3   Result of Targeting on the Interest Rate
Targeting the interest rate at i^* will lead to fluctuations of the money supply between M' and M'' because of fluctuations in the money demand curve between $M^{d'}$ and $M^{d''}$.

curve to be at M^{d^*}, but it fluctuates between $M^{d'}$ and $M^{d''}$ due to unexpected changes in output, the price level, or the public's preferences toward holding money. If the demand curve falls to $M^{d'}$, the interest rate will begin to fall below i^*, and the price of bonds will rise. With an interest-rate target, the central bank will prevent the interest rate from falling by selling bonds to drive their price back down and the interest rate back up to its former level. The central bank will make open market sales until the money supply declines to $M^{s'}$, at which point the equilibrium interest rate is again i^*. Conversely, if the demand curve rises to $M^{d''}$ and drives up the interest rate, the central bank would keep interest rates from rising by buying bonds to keep their prices from falling. The central bank will make open market purchases until the money supply rises to $M^{s''}$ and the equilibrium interest rate is i^*. The central bank's adherence to the interest-rate target thus leads to a fluctuating money supply as well as fluctuations in reserve aggregates such as the monetary base.

The conclusion from the supply and demand analysis is that interest-rate and monetary aggregate targets are incompatible: A central bank can hit one or the other but not both. Because a choice between them has to be made, we need to examine what criteria should be used to decide on the target variable.

Criteria for Choosing Intermediate Targets

The rationale behind a central bank's strategy of using targets suggests three criteria for choosing an intermediate target: It must be measurable, it must be controllable by the central bank, and it must have a predictable effect on the goal.

MEASURABILITY Quick and accurate measurement of an intermediate-target variable is necessary because the intermediate target will be useful only if it signals when policy is off track more rapidly than the goal. What good does it do for the central bank to plan to hit a 4 percent growth rate for M2 if it has no way of quickly and accurately measuring M2? Data on the monetary aggregates are obtained after a two-week delay, and interest-rate data are available almost immediately. Data on a variable like GDP that serves as a goal, by contrast, are compiled quarterly and are made available with a month's delay. In addition, the GDP data are less accurate than data on the monetary aggregates or interest rates. On these grounds alone, focusing on interest rates and monetary aggregates as intermediate targets rather than on a goal like GDP can provide clearer signals about the status of the central bank's policy.

At first glance, interest rates seem to be more measurable than monetary aggregates and hence more useful as intermediate targets. Not only are the data on interest rates available more quickly than on monetary aggregates, but they are also measured more precisely and are rarely revised, in contrast to the monetary aggregates, which are subject to a fair amount of revision (as we saw in Chapter 3). However, as we learned in Chapter 4, the interest rate that is quickly and accurately measured, the nominal interest rate, is typically a poor measure of the real cost of borrowing, which indicates with more certainty what will happen to GDP. This real cost of borrowing is more accurately measured by the real interest rate—the interest rate adjusted for expected inflation ($i_r = i - \pi^e$). Unfortunately, the real interest rate is extremely hard to measure because we have no direct way to measure expected inflation. Since both interest rate and monetary aggregates have measurability problems, it is not clear whether one should be preferred to the other as an intermediate target.

CONTROLLABILITY A central bank must be able to exercise effective control over a variable if it is to function as a useful target. If the central bank cannot control an intermediate target, knowing that it is off track does little good because the central bank has no way of getting the target back on track. Some economists have suggested that nominal GDP should be used as an intermediate target, but since the central bank has little direct control over nominal GDP, it will not provide much guidance on how the Fed should set its policy tools. A central bank does, however, have a good deal of control over the monetary aggregates and interest rates.

Our discussion of the money supply process and the central bank's policy tools indicates that a central bank does have the ability to exercise a powerful effect on the money supply, although its control is not perfect. We have also seen that open market operations can be used to set interest rates by directly affecting the price of bonds. Because a central bank can set interest rates directly whereas it cannot completely control the money supply, it might appear that interest rates dominate the monetary aggregates on the controllability criterion. However, a central bank cannot set real interest rates because it does not have control over expectations of inflation. So again, a clear-cut case cannot be made that interest rates are preferable to monetary aggregates as an intermediate target or vice versa.

PREDICTABLE EFFECT ON GOALS The most important characteristic a variable must have to be useful as an intermediate target is that it must have a predictable impact on a goal. If a central bank can accurately and quickly measure the price of tea in China and can completely control its price, what good will it do? The central bank cannot use the price of tea in China to affect unemployment or the price level in its country. Because the ability to affect goals is so critical to the usefulness of an intermediate-target variable, the linkage of the money supply and interest rates with the goals—output, employment, and the price level—is a matter of much debate. The evidence on whether these goals have a closer (more predictable) link with the money supply than with interest rates is discussed in Chapter 25.

Criteria for Choosing Operating Targets

The choice of an operating target can be based on the same criteria used to evaluate intermediate targets. Both the federal funds rate and reserve aggregates are measured accurately and are available daily with almost no delay; both are easily controllable using the policy tools that we discussed in Chapter 18. When we look at the third criterion, however, we can think of the intermediate target as the goal for the operating target. An operating target that has a more predictable impact on the most desirable intermediate target is preferred. If the desired intermediate target is an interest rate, the preferred operating target will be an interest-rate variable like the federal funds rate because interest rates are closely tied to each other (as we saw in Chapter 7). However, if the desired intermediate target is a monetary aggregate, our money supply model in Chapters 16 and 17 shows that a reserve aggregate operating target such as the monetary base will be preferred. Because there does not seem to be much reason to choose an interest rate over a reserve aggregate on the basis of measurability or controllability, the choice of which operating target is better rests on the choice of the intermediate target (the goal of the operating target).

FED POLICY PROCEDURES: HISTORICAL PERSPECTIVE

The well-known adage "The road to hell is paved with good intentions" applies as much to the Federal Reserve as it does to human beings. Understanding a central bank's goals and the strategies it can use to pursue them cannot tell us how monetary policy is actually conducted. To understand the practical results of the theoretical underpinnings, we have to look at how central banks have actually conducted policy in the past. First we will look at the Federal Reserve's past policy procedures: its choice of goals, policy tools, operating targets, and intermediate targets. This historical perspective will not only show us how our central bank carries out its duties but will also help us interpret the Fed's activities and see where U.S. monetary policy may be heading in the future. Once we are done studying the Fed, we will then examine central banks' experiences in other countries.

The following discussion of the Fed's policy procedures and their effect on the money supply provides a review of the money supply process and how the Fed's policy tools work. If you have trouble understanding how the particular policies described affect the money supply, it might be helpful to review the material in Chapters 16 and 17.

The Early Years: Discount Policy as the Primary Tool

When the Fed was created, changing the discount rate was the primary tool of monetary policy—the Fed had not yet discovered that open market operations were a more powerful tool for influencing the money supply, and the Federal Reserve Act made no provisions for changes in reserve requirements. The guiding principle for the conduct of monetary policy was that as long as loans were being made for "productive" purposes—that is, to support the production of goods and services—providing reserves to the banking system to make these loans would not be inflationary.[4] This theory, now thoroughly discredited, became known as the **real bills doctrine.** In practice, it meant that the Fed would make loans to member commercial banks when they showed up at the discount window with *eligible paper*, loans to facilitate the production and sale of goods and services. (Note that since the 1920s, the Fed has not conducted discount operations in this way.) The Fed's act of making loans to member banks was initially called *rediscounting* because the original bank loans to businesses were made by discounting (loaning less than) the face value of the loan, and the Fed would be discounting them again. (Over time, when the Fed's emphasis on eligible paper diminished, the Fed's loans to banks became known as *discounts*, and the interest rate on these loans the *discount rate*, which is the terminology we use today.)

By the end of World War I, the Fed's policy of rediscounting eligible paper and keeping interest rates low to help the Treasury finance the war had led to a raging inflation; in 1919 and 1920, the inflation rate averaged 14 percent. The Fed decided that it could no longer follow the passive policy prescribed by the real bills doctrine because it was inconsistent with the goal of price stability, and for the first time the Fed accepted the responsibility of playing an active role in influencing the economy. In January 1920, the Fed raised the discount rate from $4\frac{3}{4}$ percent to 6 percent, the largest jump in its history, and eventually raised it further to 7 percent in June 1920, where it remained for nearly a year. The result of this policy was a sharp decline in the money supply and an especially sharp recession in 1920–1921. Although the blame for this severe recession can clearly be laid at the Fed's doorstep, in one sense the Fed's policy was very successful: After an initial decline in the price level, the inflation rate went to zero, paving the way for the prosperous Roaring Twenties.

Discovery of Open Market Operations

In the early 1920s, a particularly important event occurred: The Fed accidentally discovered open market operations. When the Fed was created, its revenue came exclusively from the interest it received on the discount loans that it made to member banks. After the 1920–1921 recession, the volume of discount loans

---

[4]Another guiding principle was the maintenance of the gold standard, which we will discuss in Chapter 20.

shrank dramatically, and the Fed was pressed for income. It solved this problem by purchasing income-earning securities. In doing so, the Fed noticed that reserves in the banking system grew and there was a multiple expansion of bank loans and deposits. This result is obvious to us now (we studied the multiple deposit creation process in Chapter 16), but to the Fed at that time it was a revelation. A new monetary policy tool was born, and by the end of the 1920s, it was the most important weapon in the Fed's arsenal.

The Great Depression

The stock market boom in 1928 and 1929 created a dilemma for the Fed. It wanted to temper the boom by raising the discount rate, but it was reluctant to do so because that would mean raising interest rates to businesses and individuals who had legitimate needs for credit. Finally, in August 1929, the Fed raised the discount rate, but by then it was too late; the speculative excesses of the market boom had already occurred, and the Fed's action only hastened the stock market crash and pushed the economy into recession.

The weakness of the economy, particularly in the agricultural sector, led to a "contagion of fear" that triggered substantial withdrawals from banks, building to a full-fledged panic in November and December 1930. For the next two years, the Fed sat idly by while one bank panic after another occurred, culminating in the final panic in March 1933, at which point the new president, Franklin Delano Roosevelt, declared a bank holiday. (Why the Fed failed to engage in its lender-of-last-resort role during this period is discussed in Box 2.) The spate of bank panics from 1930 to 1933 were the most severe in U.S. history, and Roosevelt aptly summed up the problem in his statement "The only thing we have to fear is fear itself." By the time the panics were over in March 1933, more than one-third of the commercial banks in the United States had failed.

In Chapter 17, we examined how the bank panics of this period led to a decline in the money supply by over 25 percent. The resulting unprecedented decline in the money supply during this period is thought by many economists, particularly monetarists, to have been the major contributing factor to the severity of the depression, never equaled before or since.

Reserve Requirements as a Policy Tool

The Thomas Amendment to the Agricultural Adjustment Act of 1933 provided the Federal Reserve's Board of Governors with emergency power to alter reserve requirements with the approval of the president of the United States. In the Banking Act of 1935, this emergency power was expanded to allow the Fed to alter reserve requirements without the president's approval.

The first use of reserve requirements as a tool of monetary control proved that the Federal Reserve was capable of adding to the blunders that it had made during the bank panics of the early 1930s. By the end of 1935, banks had increased their holdings of excess reserves to unprecedented levels, a sensible strategy considering their discovery during the 1930–1933 period that the Fed would not always perform its intended role as lender of last resort. Bankers now understood that they would have to protect themselves against a bank run by holding substantial amounts of excess reserves. The Fed viewed these excess reserves as a

BOX 2 INSIDE THE FED

Bank Panics of 1930–1933: Why Did the Fed Let Them Happen?

The Federal Reserve System was totally passive during the bank panics of the Great Depression period and did not perform its intended role of lender of last resort to prevent them. In retrospect, the Fed's behavior seems quite extraordinary, but hindsight is always clearer than foresight.

The primary reason for the Fed's inaction was that Federal Reserve officials did not understand the negative impact bank failures could have on the money supply and economic activity. Friedman and Schwartz report that the Federal Reserve officials "tended to regard bank failures as regrettable consequences of bank management or bad banking practices, or as inevitable reactions to prior speculative excesses, or as a consequence but hardly a cause of the financial and economic collapse in process." In addition, bank failures in the early stages of the bank panics "were concentrated among smaller banks and, since the most influential figures in the system were big-city bankers who deplored the existence of smaller banks, their disappearance may have been viewed with complacency."*

Friedman and Schwartz also point out that political infighting may have played an important role in the passivity of the Fed during this period. The Federal Reserve Bank of New York, which until 1928 was the dominant force in the Federal Reserve System, strongly advocated an active program of open market purchases to provide reserves to the banking system during the bank panics. However, other powerful figures in the Federal Reserve System opposed the New York bank's position, and the bank was outvoted. (Friedman and Schwartz's discussion of the politics of the Federal Reserve System during this period makes for fascinating reading, and you might enjoy their highly readable book.)

*Milton Friedman and Anna Jacobson Schwartz, *A Monetary History of the United States, 1867–1960* (Princeton, N.J.: Princeton University Press, 1963), p. 358.

---

nuisance that made it harder to exercise monetary control. Specifically, the Fed worried that these excess reserves might be loaned out and would produce "an uncontrollable expansion of credit in the future."[5]

To improve monetary control, the Fed raised reserve requirements in three steps: August 1936, January 1937, and May 1937. The result of this action was, as we would expect from our money supply model, a slowdown of money growth toward the end of 1936 and an actual decline in 1937. The recession of 1937–1938, which commenced in May 1937, was a severe one and was especially upsetting to the American public because even at its outset unemployment was intolerably high. So not only does it appear that the Fed was at fault for the severity of the

---

[5]Milton Friedman and Anna Jacobson Schwartz, *A Monetary History of the United States,* 1867–1960 (Princeton, N.J.: Princeton University Press, 1963), p. 524.

Great Depression contraction in 1929–1933, but to add insult to injury, it appears that it was also responsible for aborting the subsequent recovery. The Fed's disastrous experience with varying its reserve requirements made it far more cautious in the use of this policy tool in the future.

War Finance and the Pegging of Interest Rates: 1942–1951

With the entrance of the United States into World War II in late 1941, government spending skyrocketed, and to finance it, the Treasury issued huge amounts of bonds. The Fed agreed to help the Treasury finance the war cheaply by pegging interest rates at the low levels that had prevailed before the war: $\frac{3}{8}$ percent on Treasury bills and $2\frac{1}{2}$ percent on long-term Treasury bonds. Whenever interest rates would rise above these levels and the price of bonds would begin to fall, the Fed would make open market purchases, thereby bidding up bond prices and driving interest rates down again. The result was a rapid growth in the monetary base and the money supply. The Fed had thus in effect relinquished its control of monetary policy to meet the financing needs of the government.

When the war ended, the Fed continued to peg interest rates, and because there was little pressure on them to rise, this policy did not result in an explosive growth in the money supply. When the Korean War broke out in 1950, however, interest rates began to climb, and the Fed found that it was again forced to expand the monetary base at a rapid rate. Because inflation began to heat up (the consumer price index rose 8 percent between 1950 and 1951), the Fed decided that it was time to reassert its control over monetary policy by abandoning the interest-rate peg. An often bitter debate ensued between the Fed and the Treasury, which wanted to keep its interest costs down and so favored a continued pegging of interest rates at low levels. In March 1951, the Fed and the Treasury came to an agreement known as the Accord, in which pegging was abandoned but the Fed promised that it would not allow interest rates to rise precipitously. After Eisenhower's election as president in 1952, the Fed was given complete freedom to pursue its monetary policy objectives.

Targeting Money Market Conditions: The 1950s and 1960s

With its freedom restored, the Federal Reserve, then under the chairmanship of William McChesney Martin Jr., took the view that monetary policy should be grounded in intuitive judgment based on a feel for the money market. The policy procedure that resulted can be described as one in which the Fed targeted on money market conditions, a vague collection of variables that were supposed to describe supply and demand conditions in the money market. Included among these variables were short-term interest rates and **free reserves** FR, equal to excess reserves in the banking system ER minus the volume of discount loans DL:

$$FR = ER - DL$$

The Fed considered free reserves a particularly good indicator of money market conditions because it thought that they represented the amount of slack in the banking system. The Fed viewed banks as having a first priority in using their excess reserves to repay their discount loans, so only the excess reserves not borrowed from the Fed represented the *free* reserves that could be used to make loans and create deposits. The Fed interpreted an increase in free reserves as an easing of money market conditions and used open market sales to withdraw reserves from the banking system. A fall in free reserves meant a tightening of money market conditions, and the Fed made open market purchases.

An important characteristic of this policy procedure is that it led to more rapid growth in the money supply when the economy was expanding and a slowing of money growth when the economy was in recession. The so-called *procyclical monetary policy* (a positive association of money supply growth with the business cycle) is explained by the following step-by-step reasoning. As we learned in Chapter 6, a rise in national income ($Y\uparrow$) leads to a rise in market interest rates ($i\uparrow$), thus raising the opportunity cost of holding excess reserves and causing excess reserves to decline ($ER\downarrow$). The rise in interest rates also increases the incentives to borrow from the discount window because bank loans become more profitable and so the volume of discount loans will rise ($DL\uparrow$). The decline in excess reserves and the rise in the volume of discount loans then imply that free reserves will fall ($FR\downarrow = ER\downarrow - DL\uparrow$). When the Fed reacts to the decline in free reserves by making open market purchases, it raises the monetary base ($MB\uparrow$) and hence the money supply ($M\uparrow$). The reasoning outlined can be summarized as follows:

$$Y\uparrow \Rightarrow i\uparrow \Rightarrow ER\downarrow, DL\uparrow \Rightarrow FR\downarrow \Rightarrow MB\uparrow \Rightarrow M\uparrow$$

A business cycle contraction causes the opposite chain of events so that the fall in income leads to a fall in the money supply ($Y\downarrow \Rightarrow M\downarrow$). Thus the Fed's use of a free reserves target results in a positive association of money supply movements with national income and hence a procyclical monetary policy.

During this period, many economists, especially Karl Brunner and Allan Meltzer, criticized the Fed's use of free reserves as a target variable because of the procyclical monetary policy that it created. When the money supply grows more rapidly during a business cycle expansion, it can add to inflationary pressures; when it grows more slowly during a recession, it is likely to make the economic contraction worse. Indeed, a stated objective of the Fed during this period was that monetary policy should "lean against the wind": In other words, monetary policy should be anticyclical—contractionary when there is a business cycle expansion and expansionary when there is a business cycle contraction.

The Fed's other primary operating target, short-term interest rates, performed no better as a target variable than free reserves and also led to procyclical monetary policy. If the Fed saw interest rates rising as a result of a rise in income, it would purchase bonds to bid their price up and lower interest rates to their target level. The resulting increase in the monetary base caused the money supply to rise and the business cycle expansion to be accompanied by a faster rate of money growth. In summary,

$$Y\uparrow \Rightarrow i\uparrow \Rightarrow MB\uparrow \Rightarrow M\uparrow$$

In a recession, the opposite sequence of events would occur, and the decline in income would be accompanied by a slower rate of growth in the money supply ($Y\downarrow \Rightarrow M\downarrow$).

A further problem with using interest rates as the primary operating target is that they might encourage an inflationary spiral to get out of control. As we saw in Chapter 6, when inflation and hence expected inflation rises, nominal interest rates rise via the Fisher effect. If the Fed attempted to prevent this increase by purchasing bonds, this would also lead to a rise in the monetary base and the money supply:

$$\pi\uparrow \Rightarrow \pi^e\uparrow \Rightarrow i\uparrow \Rightarrow MB\uparrow \Rightarrow M\uparrow$$

Higher inflation could thus lead to an increase in the money supply, which would increase inflationary pressures further.

By the late 1960s, the rising chorus of criticism of procyclical monetary policy and concerns about inflation finally led the Fed to abandon its focus on money market conditions.

Targeting Monetary Aggregates: The 1970s

In 1970, Arthur Burns was appointed chairman of the Board of Governors, and soon thereafter the Fed stated that it was committing itself to the use of monetary aggregates as intermediate targets. Did monetary policy cease to be procyclical? A glance at Figure 4 in Chapter 1 indicates that monetary policy was as procyclical in the 1970s as in the 1950s and 1960s. What went wrong? Why did the conduct of monetary policy not improve? The answers to these questions lie in the Fed's operating procedures during the period, which suggest that its commitment to targeting monetary aggregates was not very strong.

Every six weeks, the Federal Open Market Committee would set target ranges for the growth rate of various monetary aggregates and would determine what federal funds rate (the interest rate on funds loaned overnight between banks) it thought consistent with these aims. The target ranges for the growth in monetary aggregates were fairly broad—a typical range for M1 growth might be 3 percent to 6 percent; for M2, 4 percent to 7 percent—while the range for the federal funds rate was a narrow band, say, from $7\frac{1}{2}$ percent to $8\frac{1}{4}$ percent. The trading desk at the Federal Reserve Bank of New York was then instructed to meet both sets of targets, but as we saw earlier, interest-rate targets and monetary aggregate targets might not be compatible. If the two targets were incompatible—say, the federal funds rate began to climb higher than the top of its target band when M1 was growing too rapidly—the trading desk was instructed to give precedence to the federal funds rate target. In the situation just described, this would mean that although M1 growth was too high, the trading desk would make open market purchases to keep the federal funds rate within its target range.

The Fed was actually using the federal funds rate as its operating target. During the six-week period between FOMC meetings, an unexpected rise in income (which would cause the federal funds rate to hit the top of its target band) would then induce open market purchases and a too rapid growth of the money supply. When the FOMC met again, it would try to bring money supply growth back on track by raising the target range on the federal funds rate. However, if income continued to rise unexpectedly, money growth would overshoot again. This is exactly what occurred from June 1972 to June 1973, when the economy boomed unexpectedly: M1 growth greatly exceeded its target, increasing at approximately an 8 percent rate, while the federal funds rate climbed from $4\frac{1}{2}$ percent to $8\frac{1}{2}$ percent. The economy soon became overheated, and inflationary pressures began to mount.

The opposite chain of events occurred at the end of 1974, when the economic contraction was far more severe than anyone had predicted. The federal funds rate fell dramatically from over 12 percent to 5 percent and persistently bumped against the bottom of its target range. The trading desk conducted open market sales to keep the federal funds rate from falling, and money growth dropped precipitously, actually turning negative by the beginning of 1975. Clearly, this sharp drop in money growth when the United States was experiencing one of the worst economic contractions of the postwar era was a serious mistake.

Using the federal funds rate as an operating target promoted a procyclical monetary policy despite the Fed's lip service to monetary aggregate targets. If the Federal Reserve really intended to pursue monetary aggregate targets, it seems peculiar that it would have chosen an interest rate for an operating target rather than a reserve aggregate. (However, as the discussion of the conduct of Japanese monetary policy later in this chapter makes clear, more effective monetary control can be achieved even when an interest rate is used as an operating target.) The explanation for why the Fed chose an interest rate as an operating target is that it was still very concerned with achieving interest-rate stability and was reluctant to relinquish control over interest-rate movements. The incompatibility of the Fed's policy procedure with its stated intent of targeting on the monetary aggregates had become very clear by October 1979, when the Fed's policy procedures underwent drastic revision.

New Fed Operating Procedures: October 1979– October 1982

In October 1979, two months after Paul Volcker became chairman of the Board of Governors, the Fed finally deemphasized the federal funds rate as an operating target by widening its target range more than fivefold: A typical range might be from 10 percent to 15 percent. The primary operating target became nonborrowed reserves, which the Fed would set after estimating the volume of discount loans the banks would borrow. Figure 4 shows what happened to the federal funds rate and the growth rate of the M1 money supply both before and after October 1979. Not surprisingly, the federal funds rate underwent much greater fluctuations after it was deemphasized as an operating target. What is surprising, however, is that the deemphasis of the federal funds target did not result in improved monetary control: After October 1979, the fluctuations in the rate of money supply growth *increased* rather than decreased as would have been expected. In addition, the Fed missed its M1 growth target ranges in all three years of the 1979–1982 period.[6] What went wrong?

---

[6]The M1 target ranges and actual growth rates for 1980–1982 were as follows:

Year	Target Range (%)	Actual (%)
1980	4.5–7.0	7.5
1981	6.0–8.5	5.1
1982	2.5–5.5	8.8

Source: Board of Governors of the Federal Reserve System, *Monetary Policy Objectives, 1981–1983.*

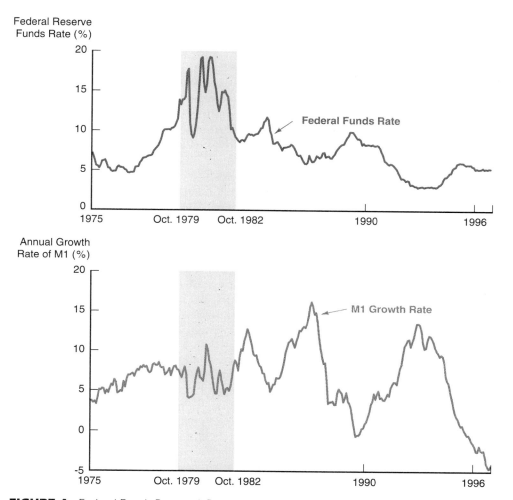

FIGURE 4   *Federal Funds Rate and Growth Rate of the Money Supply: Before and After October 1979*
Sources: Federal Reserve *Bulletin;* Board of Governors of the Federal Reserve System.

There are several possible answers to this question. The first is that the economy was exposed to several shocks during this period that made monetary control more difficult: the acceleration of financial innovation and deregulation, which added new categories of deposits such as NOW accounts to the measures of monetary aggregates; the imposition by the Fed of credit controls from March to July 1980, which restricted the growth of consumer and business loans; and the back-to-back recessions of 1980 and 1981–1982.[7]

[7]Another explanation focuses on the technical difficulties of monetary control when using a nonborrowed reserves operating target under a system of lagged reserve requirements, in which required reserves for a given week are calculated on the basis of the level of deposits two weeks earlier. See David Lindsey, "Nonborrowed Reserve Targeting and Monetary Control," in *Improving Money Stock Control*, ed. Laurence Meyer (Boston: Kluwer-Nijhoff, 1983), pp. 3–41.

A more persuasive explanation for poor monetary control, however, is that controlling the money supply was never really the intent of Volcker's policy shift. Despite Volcker's statements about the need to target monetary aggregates, he was not committed to these targets. Rather, he was far more concerned with using interest-rate movements to wring inflation out of the economy. Volcker's primary reason for changing the Fed's operating procedure was to free his hand to manipulate interest rates in order to fight inflation. It was necessary to abandon interest-rate targets if Volcker were to be able to raise interest rates sharply when a slowdown in the economy was required to dampen inflation. This view of Volcker's strategy suggests that the Fed's announced attachment to monetary aggregate targets may have been a smokescreen to keep the Fed from being blamed for the high interest rates that would result from the new policy.

The interest-rate movements in Figure 4 support this interpretation of Fed strategy. After the October 1979 announcement, short-term interest rates were driven up by nearly 5 percent, until in March 1980 they exceeded 15 percent. With the imposition of credit controls in March 1980 and the rapid decline in real GDP in the second quarter of 1980, the Fed eased up on its policy and allowed interest rates to decline sharply. When recovery began in July 1980, inflation remained persistent, still exceeding 10 percent. Because the inflation fight was not yet won, the Fed tightened the screws again, sending short-term rates above the 15 percent level for a second time. The 1981–1982 recession and its large decline in output and high unemployment began to bring inflation down. With inflationary psychology apparently broken, interest rates were allowed to fall.

The Fed's anti-inflation strategy during the October 1979–October 1982 period was neither intended nor likely to produce smooth growth in the monetary aggregates. Indeed, the large fluctuations in interest rates and the business cycle, along with financial innovation, helped generate volatile money growth.

Deemphasis of Monetary Aggregates: October 1982– Early 1990s

In October 1982, with inflation in check, the Fed returned, in effect, to a policy of smoothing interest rates. It did this by placing less emphasis on monetary aggregate targets and shifting to borrowed reserves (discount loan borrowings) as an operating target. To see how a borrowed reserves target produces interest-rate smoothing, let's consider what happens when the economy expands ($Y\uparrow$) so that interest rates are driven up. The rise in interest rates ($i\uparrow$) increases the incentives for banks to borrow more from the Fed, so borrowed reserves rise ($DL\uparrow$). To prevent the resulting rise in borrowed reserves from exceeding the target level, the Fed must lower interest rates by bidding up the price of bonds through open market purchases. The outcome of targeting on borrowed reserves, then, is that the Fed prevents a rise in interest rates. In doing so, however, the Fed's open market purchases increase the monetary base ($MB\uparrow$) and lead to a rise in the money supply ($M\uparrow$), which produces a positive association of money and national income ($Y\uparrow \Rightarrow M\uparrow$). Schematically,

$$Y\uparrow \Rightarrow i\uparrow \Rightarrow DL\uparrow \Rightarrow MB\uparrow \Rightarrow M\uparrow$$

A recession causes the opposite chain of events: The borrowed reserves target prevents interest rates from falling and results in a drop in the monetary base, leading to a fall in the money supply ($Y\downarrow \Rightarrow M\downarrow$).

The deemphasis of monetary aggregates and the change to a borrowed reserves target are visible in Figure 4, where we see much smaller fluctuations in the federal funds rate after October 1982 but continue to have large fluctuations in money supply growth. Finally, in February 1987, the Fed announced that it would no longer even set M1 targets. The abandonment of M1 targets was defended on two grounds. The first was that the rapid pace of financial innovation and deregulation had made the definition and measurement of money very difficult. The second is that there had been a breakdown in the stable relationship between M1 and economic activity (discussed in Chapter 21). These two arguments suggested that a monetary aggregate such as M1 might no longer be a reliable guide for monetary policy. As a result, the Fed switched its focus to the broader monetary aggregate M2, which it felt had a more stable relationship with economic activity. However, in the early 1990s, this relationship also broke down, and in July 1993, Board of Governors Chairman Alan Greenspan testified in Congress that the Fed would no longer use any monetary targets, including M2, as a guide for conducting monetary policy.

Federal Funds Targeting Again: Early 1990s and Beyond

Having abandoned monetary aggregates as a guide for monetary policy, the Federal Reserve returned to using a federal funds target in the early 1990s. Indeed, from late 1992 until February 1994, a period of a year and a half, the Fed kept the federal funds rate targeted at the constant rate of 3 percent, a low level last seen in the 1960s. The explanation for this unusual period of keeping the federal funds rate pegged so low for such a long period of time was fear on the part of the Federal Reserve that the credit crunch mentioned in Chapter 10 was putting a drag on the economy (the "headwinds" referred to by Greenspan) that was producing a sluggish recovery from the 1990–1991 recession. Starting in February 1994, after the economy had returned to rapid growth, the Fed began to raise the federal funds rate in order to head off any future inflationary pressures, but with a new policy procedure. Instead of keeping the federal funds rate target secret, as it had done previously, the Fed now announced any federal funds target change. As mentioned in Chapter 15, around 2:15 P.M. after every FOMC meeting, the Fed now announces whether the federal funds rate target has been raised, lowered, or kept the same. As a result of this announcement, the outcome of the FOMC meeting is now big news, and the media devote much more attention to FOMC meetings because an announced change in the federal funds rate feeds into changes in other interest rates that affect consumers and businesses.

International Considerations

The increasing importance of international trade to the American economy has brought international considerations to the forefront of Federal Reserve policy-making in recent years. By 1985, the strength of the dollar had contributed to a deterioration in American competitiveness with foreign businesses. In public pronouncements, Chairman Volcker and other Fed officials made it clear that the dollar was at too high a value and needed to come down. Because, as we saw in Chapter 8, expansionary monetary policy is one way to lower the value of the dollar, it is no surprise that the Fed engineered an acceleration in the growth rates

BOX 3

International Policy Coordination

The Plaza Agreement and the Louvre Accord. By 1985, the decrease in the competitiveness of American corporations as a result of the strong dollar was raising strong sentiment in Congress for restricting imports. This protectionist threat to the international trading system stimulated finance ministers and the heads of central banks from the Group of Five (G-5) industrial countries—the United States, the United Kingdom, France, West Germany, and Japan—to reach an agreement at New York's Plaza Hotel in September 1985 to bring down the value of the dollar. From September 1985 until the beginning of 1987, the value of the dollar did indeed undergo a substantial decline, falling by 35 percent on average relative to foreign currencies. At this point, there was growing controversy over the decline in the dollar, and another meeting of policymakers from the G-5 countries plus Canada took place in February 1987 at the Louvre Museum in Paris. There the policymakers agreed that exchange rates should be stabilized around the levels currently prevailing. Although the value of the dollar did continue to fluctuate relative to foreign currencies after the Louvre Accord, its downward trend had been checked as intended.

Because subsequent exchange rate movements were pretty much in line with the Plaza Agreement and the Louvre Accord, these attempts at international policy coordination have been considered successful. However, other aspects of the agreements were not adhered to by all signatories. For example, West German and Japanese policymakers agreed that their countries should pursue more expansionary policies by increasing government spending and cutting taxes, and the United States agreed to try to bring down its budget deficit. At that time, the United States was not particularly successful in lowering its deficit, and the Germans were reluctant to pursue expansionary policies because of their concerns about inflation.

---

of the monetary aggregates in 1985 and 1986 and that the value of the dollar declined. By 1987, policymakers at the Fed agreed that the dollar had fallen sufficiently, and sure enough, monetary growth in the United States slowed. These monetary policy actions by the Fed were encouraged by the process of **international policy coordination** (agreements among countries to enact policies cooperatively) that led to the Plaza Agreement in 1985 and the Louvre Accord in 1987 (see Box 3). International considerations, although not the primary focus of the Federal Reserve, are likely to be a major factor in the conduct of American monetary policy in the future.

MONETARY TARGETING IN OTHER COUNTRIES

To understand more fully how monetary policy is conducted, we must compare our own experiences with those of other countries. Here we examine how central banks in other countries have conducted monetary policy. Not surprisingly, many of their experiences parallel those in the United States.

As we noted in our study of the conduct of U.S. monetary policy, the Federal Reserve has flirted with monetary targeting as its basic monetary policy strategy.

And the Fed was not alone in adopting a monetary targeting framework in the 1970s; so did many other countries' central banks as well. Why did monetary targeting become so popular in the 1970s?[8]

The primary reason was the rise in inflation throughout the industrialized world. Central banks realized that using nominal interest rates as a target variable could lead to rising inflationary pressures. They believed that monetary aggregates could serve as a guidepost, or *nominal anchor*, that could promote a less inflationary monetary policy. Of probably even more importance, central banks believed that monetary targets could help send almost immediate signals to both the public and markets about the stance of monetary policy and the intentions of the policymakers to keep inflation in check. These signals might then help fix inflation expectations and help produce lower wage and price increases and thus less actual inflation.

We examine the experiences of four foreign countries—the United Kingdom, Canada, Germany, and Japan—to evaluate the extent to which monetary targeting has been a successful strategy for monetary policy.

United Kingdom

As in the United States, the British introduced monetary targeting in late 1973 in response to mounting concerns about inflation. The Bank of England targeted M3, a broader monetary target than the Fed used, but did not pursue it seriously: Announced targets were consistently overshot, and the Bank of England frequently revised its targets midstream or abandoned them entirely. The outcome was greater volatility of British monetary aggregates compared to American ones. After inflation accelerated in the late 1970s, Prime Minister Margaret Thatcher in 1980 introduced the Medium-Term Financial Strategy, which proposed a gradual deceleration of M3 growth. Unfortunately, the M3 targets ran into problems similar to those of the M1 targets in the United States: They were not reliable indicators of the tightness of monetary policy. After 1983, arguing that financial innovation was wreaking havoc with the relationship between M3 and national income, the Bank of England began to deemphasize M3 in favor of a narrower monetary aggregate, M0 (the monetary base). The target for M3 was temporarily suspended in October 1985 and was completely dropped in 1987, and monetary targets were abandoned altogether when the nation tied its exchange rate to the deutsche mark and became part of the European Monetary System (EMS) in October 1990.

Canada

The Canadian experience with monetary policy closely parallels that of the United States. This is not surprising given the strong ties between the two economies and the fact that the value of the Canadian dollar has been closely linked to the U.S dollar.

---

[8]The discussion here is based on Ben Bernanke and Frederic S. Mishkin, "Central Bank Behavior and the Strategy of Monetary Policy: Observations from Six Industrialized Countries," in *NBER Macroeconomics Annual, 1992*, ed. Oliver Blanchard and Stanley Fischer (Cambridge, Mass.: MIT Press, 1992), pp. 183–228.

In response to rising inflation in the early 1970s, the Bank of Canada introduced a program of "monetary gradualism" under which M1 growth would be controlled within a gradually falling target range. Monetary gradualism was no more successful in Canada than the initial attempts at monetary targeting in the United States and the United Kingdom. By 1978, only three years after monetary targeting had begun, the Bank of Canada began to distance itself from this strategy out of concern for the exchange rate. Because of the conflict with exchange rate goals, as well as the uncertainty about M1 as a reliable guide to monetary policy, the M1 targets were abandoned in November 1982. From November 1982 to January 1988, the Bank of Canada pursued a monetary policy strategy without an explicit nominal anchor, but in January 1988, John Crow, the governor (head) of the Bank of Canada, announced that the bank would subsequently pursue an objective of price stability.

Germany

Germany's central bank, the Bundesbank, also responded to rising inflation in the early 1970s by adopting monetary targets in 1975. The monetary aggregate chosen was a narrow one known as *central bank money*, the sum of currency in circulation and bank deposits weighted by the 1974 required reserve ratios. The Bundesbank has allowed growth outside of its target ranges for periods of two to three years, and overshoots of its targets have subsequently been reversed. The primary reason for allowing deviations from its targets has been exchange rate considerations, which have been important to international agreements such as the European Monetary System, the Plaza Agreement, and the Louvre Accord. In 1988, the Bundesbank switched targets from central bank money to M3. German monetary policy using monetary targeting has been quite successful in maintaining a low and stable inflation rate.

The reunification of Germany in 1990 created some difficult problems for monetary policy. The Bundesbank was torn between trying to restrain the inflationary pressures created by reunification and keeping its exchange rate in line with those in other European countries. These strains contributed to an exchange rate crisis in Europe in September 1992, which will be discussed further in Chapter 20. The Bundesbank continues to subscribe to monetary targeting, but recent research suggests that its commitment may be weaker than its rhetoric suggests.[9]

Japan

The increase in oil prices in late 1973 was a major shock for Japan, which experienced a huge jump in the inflation rate to greater than 20 percent in 1974—a surge facilitated by money growth in 1973 in excess of 20 percent. The Bank of Japan, like the other central banks discussed here, began to pay more attention to money growth rates. In 1978, the Bank of Japan began to announce "forecasts" at the beginning of each quarter for M2 + CDs. Although the Bank of Japan was not officially committed to monetary targeting, monetary policy appeared to be more money-focused after 1978. For example, after the second oil price shock in

---

[9]See Richard Clarida and Mark Gertler, "How the Bundesbank Conducts Monetary Policy," National Bureau of Economic Research, Working Paper #5581, May 1996.

1979, the Bank of Japan quickly reduced M2 + CDs growth, rather than allowing it to shoot up as occurred after the first oil shock. The Bank of Japan conducted monetary policy with operating procedures that are similar in many ways to those that the Federal Reserve has used in the United States. The Bank of Japan uses the interest rate in the Japanese interbank market (which has a function similar to that of the federal funds market in the United States) as its daily operating target, just as the Fed has done.

The Bank of Japan's monetary policy performance during the 1978–1987 period was much better than the Fed's. Money growth in Japan slowed gradually, beginning in the mid-1970s, and was much less variable than in the United States. The outcome was a more rapid braking of inflation and an average inflation rate that was lower in Japan. In addition, these excellent results on inflation were achieved with lower variability in real output in Japan than in the United States. The success of Japanese monetary policy in the 1978–1987 period using an interest rate as an operating target, in contrast to the lack of success in the 1970–1979 period in the United States when the Fed used a similar operating procedure, suggests that using an interest rate as an operating target is not necessarily a barrier to successful monetary policy. More important might be a commitment to a low inflation rate, something that was true for the Bank of Japan in this period.

In parallel with the United States, financial innovation and deregulation in Japan began to reduce the usefulness of the M2 + CDs monetary aggregate as an indicator of monetary policy. Because of concerns about the appreciation of the yen, the Bank of Japan significantly increased the rate of money growth from 1987 to 1989. Many observers blame speculation in Japanese land and stock prices (the so-called bubble economy) on the increase in money growth, and to reduce this speculation, in 1989 the Bank of Japan switched to a tighter monetary policy aimed at slower money growth. The aftermath has been a substantial decline in land and stock prices and the collapse of the bubble economy.

Lessons from Monetary Targeting Experiences

There are several lessons to be drawn from the experience with monetary targeting in these four countries and the United States. First, successful use of monetary targeting seems to require that the central bank pursue its targeting strategy seriously. Countries like the United States, Canada, and especially the United Kingdom were unable to use monetary targeting to bring inflation under control because the procedures they used to implement the targets did not imply a strong commitment to the strategy and they consistently overshot their monetary targets. Germany and Japan, by contrast, were more successful in using monetary aggregates to keep inflation in check. This did not mean that the Bundesbank and the Bank of Japan always met their targets; more critical to their success was that they subsequently reversed overshoots of the targets. A further lesson from the Japanese experience is that the success of monetary targeting can be achieved with operating procedures that focus on interest rates as the operating target. The final lesson is that the breakdown in the relationship between monetary aggregates and the goal variables, nominal GDP and inflation, in many countries made the monetary targeting strategy untenable. As the former governor of the Bank of Canada, John Crow, is said to have stated, "We didn't abandon monetary aggregates; they abandoned us."

THE NEW INTERNATIONAL TREND IN MONETARY POLICY STRATEGY: INFLATION TARGETING

Although central banks have abandoned monetary targeting, the reasons they adopted it in the first place remain. Central banks still see the need to have a nominal anchor that will promote price stability. Another nominal anchor for monetary policy can be the foreign exchange rate. As we will see in Chapter 20, some countries have achieved low inflation by tying the value of their currency to the currency of a country with a good inflation record. However, the problem with this strategy is that, as shown in Chapter 20, with a fixed exchange rate, a country no longer exercises control over its own monetary policy and so cannot use monetary policy to respond to domestic shocks.

The search for a nominal anchor has led many countries to pursue inflation targeting as their basic monetary strategy. To understand what inflation targeting is all about, we look at the experience in three countries, New Zealand, which was the first to adopt this strategy; Canada; and the United Kingdom.

New Zealand

As part of a general reform of the government's role in the economy, the New Zealand parliament in 1989 passed the Reserve Bank of New Zealand Act, which became effective on February 1, 1990. Besides increasing the independence of the central bank, the Reserve Bank of New Zealand, transforming it from one of the least independent to one of the most independent among the developed countries, the act also committed the Reserve Bank to the sole objective of price stability. The act stipulated that the minister of finance and the governor of the Reserve Bank should negotiate and make public a "policy targets agreement" that sets out the targets against which monetary policy performance will be evaluated. These agreements have specified numerical target ranges for inflation and the dates by which they were to be reached. An unusual feature of the New Zealand legislation is that the governor of the Reserve Bank is held personally accountable for the success of monetary policy. If the goals set forth in the policy targets agreement are not met, the governor is subject to dismissal.

The first policy targets agreement, signed by the minister of finance and the governor of the Reserve Bank on March 2, 1990, directed the Reserve Bank to achieve an annual inflation rate within the 0 to 2 percent range, and subsequent agreements stuck with this range until November 1996 when the range was widened to 0 to 3 percent. As a result of tight monetary policy, the inflation rate was brought down from above 5 percent to below 2 percent by the end of 1992, but at the cost of a deep recession and a sharp rise in unemployment. Through 1996, inflation has typically remained within the 0 to 2 percent range, with the exception of a brief period in 1995, when it exceeded the range by a few tenths of a percentage point. (Under the Reserve Bank Act, the governor, Don Brash, could have been dismissed, but after parliamentary debate, he was retained in his job.) Since 1992, New Zealand's growth rate has been very high, with some years exceeding 5 percent, and unemployment has diminished significantly.

Canada

On February 26, 1991, a joint announcement by the minister of finance and the governor of the Bank of Canada established formal inflation targets. The target ranges were 2 to 4 percent by the end of 1992, 1.5 to 3.5 percent by June 1994, and 1 to 3 percent by December 1996. After the new government took office in late 1993, the target range was set at 1 to 3 percent from December 1995 until December 1998. Canadian inflation has also fallen dramatically since the adoption of inflation targets, from above the 5 percent level in 1991 to a 0 percent rate in 1995, well below the target range of 1 to 3 percent. However, as was the case in New Zealand, this decline was not without cost: Unemployment soared to above the 10 percent level from 1991 until 1994 but has since fallen.

United Kingdom

When the United Kingdom left the European Monetary System after the speculative attack on the pound in September 1992 (more on this in Chapter 20), the British decided to turn to inflation targets to replace the exchange rate as the nominal anchor. As you may recall from Chapter 15, the central bank in the United Kingdom, the Bank of England, does not have statutory authority over monetary policy; it can only make recommendations. Thus it was the chancellor of the Exchequer (the equivalent of the U.S. Treasury secretary) who announced an inflation target for the nation on October 8, 1992. Three weeks later, he "invited" the governor of the Bank of England to begin producing an inflation report on a quarterly basis that would report on the progress being made in achieving the target—an invitation that the governor accepted. The inflation target range was set at 1 to 4 percent until the next election, in spring 1997, with the intent that the inflation rate should settle down to the lower half of the range (below 2.5 percent). Along with this inflation target, the government instituted the three institutional changes mentioned in Chapter 15, which, along with the publication of the inflation report, gave the Bank of England a more independent voice on monetary policy.

Before the adoption of inflation targets, inflation had already been falling in the United Kingdom, from a peak of 9 percent at the beginning of 1991 to 4 percent at the time of adoption. After a small upward movement in early 1993, inflation continued to fall until by the third quarter of 1994, it was at 2.2 percent, within the intended range articulated by the chancellor. Subsequently inflation rose, climbing above the 2.5 percent level by 1996. Meanwhile, growth of the U.K. economy was strong, causing a reduction in the unemployment rate.

Lessons from Inflation Targeting Experiences

Several lessons can be drawn from the inflation targeting experiences in these three countries. First, as the New Zealand and Canadian experience indicates, inflation targets have not been able to produce a decline in inflation without a substantial decline in output and a rise in unemployment. Hopes that inflation targets would lead to disinflation at a lower cost have not been realized. Second, inflation targets have so far worked well in keeping inflation at moderate levels. One important advantage of inflation targets is that they keep the goal of price stability in the public's eye, thus making the central bank more accountable for keeping inflation low, which can also help reduce political pressures on the central bank to pursue inflationary monetary policy.

How successful will inflation targeting be at keeping inflation low in the countries examined here? It is still too early to tell. Nonetheless, many other countries have followed New Zealand, Canada, and the United Kingdom in adopting inflation targets, including Australia, Finland, Israel, Spain, and Sweden. The growing popularity of inflation targeting indicates that it might become the wave of the future for central bank strategy.

S U M M A R Y

1. The six basic goals of monetary policy are high employment, economic growth, price stability, interest-rate stability, stability of financial markets, and stability in foreign exchange markets.

2. By using intermediate and operating targets, a central bank like the Fed can more quickly judge whether its policies are on the right track and make midcourse corrections, rather than waiting to see the final outcome of its policies on such goals as employment and the price level. The Fed's policy tools directly affect its operating targets, which in turn affect the intermediate targets, which in turn affect the goals.

3. Because interest-rate and monetary aggregate targets are incompatible, a central bank must choose between them on the basis of three criteria: measurability, controllability, and the ability to affect goal variables predictably. Unfortunately, these criteria do not establish an overwhelming case for one set of targets over another.

4. The historical record of the Fed's conduct of monetary policy reveals that the Fed has switched its operating targets many times, returning to a federal funds rate target in recent years.

5. In response to the rise in inflation in the early 1970s, central banks around the world also began to target monetary aggregates. Monetary targeting seems to have been most effective when pursued seriously, which does not mean that targets are always met; more critical to success was a reversal of overshoots of the targets. Unfortunately, the breakdown in many countries of the relationship between monetary aggregates and the goal variables, nominal GDP and inflation, made the monetary targeting strategy untenable.

6. After disappointments with monetary targeting, the search for a nominal anchor has led several countries to pursue inflation targeting as their basic monetary strategy. Although inflation targeting so far has been successful in keeping inflation rates low in countries that have adopted it, hopes that inflation targets would lead to disinflation at a lower cost have not been realized.

K E Y   T E R M S

free reserves, p. 487

intermediate targets, p. 478

international policy
   coordination, p. 494

natural rate of unemployment,
   p. 475

operating target, p. 478

real bills doctrine, p. 484

Q U E S T I O N S   A N D   P R O B L E M S

*1. "Unemployment is a bad thing, and the government should make every effort to eliminate it." Do you agree or disagree? Explain your answer.

2. Classify each of the following as either an operating target or an intermediate target, and explain why.

a. The three-month Treasury bill rate

b. The monetary base

c. M2

*3. "If the demand for money did not fluctuate, the Fed could pursue both a money supply target and an interest-rate target at the same time." Is this statement true, false, or uncertain? Explain your answer.

4. If the Fed has an interest-rate target, why will an increase in money demand lead to a rise in the money supply?

*5. What procedures can the Fed use to control the three-month Treasury bill rate? Why does control of this interest rate imply that the Fed will lose control of the money supply?

6. Compare the monetary base to M2 on the grounds of controllability and measurability. Which do you prefer as an intermediate target? Why?

*7. "Interest rates can be measured more accurately and more quickly than the money supply. Hence an interest rate is preferred over the money supply as an intermediate target." Do you agree or disagree? Explain your answer.

8. Explain why the rise in the discount rate in 1920 led to a sharp decline in the money supply.

*9. How did the Fed's failure to perform its role as the lender of last resort contribute to the decline of the money supply in the 1930–1933 period?

10. Excess reserves are frequently called *idle reserves,* suggesting that they are not useful. Does the episode of the rise in reserve requirements in 1936–1937 bear out this view?

*11. "When the economy enters a recession, either a free reserves target or an interest-rate target will lead to a slower rate of growth for the money supply." Explain why this statement is true. What does it say about the use of free reserves or interest rates as targets?

12. "The failure of the Fed to control the money supply in the 1970s and 1980s suggests that the Fed is not able to control the money supply." Do you agree or disagree? Explain your answer.

*13. Which is more likely to produce smaller fluctuations in the federal funds rate, a nonborrowed reserves target or a borrowed reserves target? Why?

14. How can bank behavior and the Fed's behavior cause money supply growth to be procyclical (rising in booms and falling in recessions)?

*15. Why might the Fed say that it wants to control the money supply but in reality not be serious about doing so?

Chapter 20

THE INTERNATIONAL FINANCIAL SYSTEM

PREVIEW   Thanks to the growing interdependence between the U.S. economy and the economies of the rest of the world, a country's monetary policy can no longer be conducted without taking international considerations into account. In this chapter we examine how international financial transactions and the structure of the international financial system affect monetary policy. We also examine the evolution of the international financial system during the past half century and where it may be heading in the future.

INTERVENTION IN THE FOREIGN EXCHANGE MARKET

In Chapter 8 we analyzed the foreign exchange market as if it were a completely free market that responds to all market pressures. However, the foreign exchange market, like many others, is not free of government intervention; central banks regularly engage in international financial transactions called **foreign exchange interventions** in order to influence exchange rates. In our current international financial arrangement, called a **managed float regime** (or a **dirty float**), exchange rates fluctuate from day to day, but central banks attempt to influence their countries' exchange rates by buying and selling currencies. The exchange rate analysis we developed in Chapter 8 is used here to explain the impact that central bank intervention has on the foreign exchange market.

Foreign Exchange Intervention and the Money Supply   The first step in understanding how central bank intervention in the foreign exchange market affects exchange rates is to see the impact on the monetary base from a central bank sale in the foreign exchange market of some of its holdings of assets denominated in a foreign currency (called **international reserves**). Suppose that the Fed decides to sell $1 billion of its foreign assets in exchange for $1 billion of U.S. currency. (This transaction is done at the foreign exchange desk at the Federal Reserve Bank of New York—see Box 1.) The Fed's purchase of dollars has two effects. First, it reduces the Fed's holding of international reserves by $1 billion. Second, because its purchase of currency removes it from the hands of the public, currency in circulation falls by $1 billion. We can see this in the following T-account for the Federal Reserve:

FEDERAL RESERVE SYSTEM

Assets		Liabilities	
Foreign assets (international reserves)	−$1 billion	Currency in circulation	−$1 billion

Because the monetary base is made up of currency in circulation plus reserves, this decline in currency implies that the monetary base has fallen by $1 billion.

If instead of paying for the foreign assets sold by the Fed with currency, the persons buying the foreign assets pay for them by checks written on accounts at domestic banks, then the Fed deducts the $1 billion from the deposit accounts these banks have with the Fed. The result is that deposits with the Fed (reserves) decline by $1 billion, as shown in the following T-account:

FEDERAL RESERVE SYSTEM

Assets		Liabilities	
Foreign assets (international reserves)	−$1 billion	Deposits with the Fed (reserves)	−$1 billion

In this case, the outcome of the Fed sale of foreign assets and the purchase of dollar deposits is a $1 billion decline in reserves and a $1 billion decline in the monetary base because reserves are also a component of the monetary base.

We now see that the outcome for the monetary base is exactly the same when a central bank sells foreign assets to purchase domestic bank deposits or domestic currency. This is why when we say that a central bank has purchased its domestic currency, we do not have to distinguish whether it actually purchased currency or bank deposits denominated in the domestic currency. We have thus reached an important conclusion: ***A central bank's purchase of domestic currency and corresponding sale of foreign assets in the foreign exchange market leads to an equal decline in its international reserves and the monetary base.***

We could have reached the same conclusion by a more direct route. A central bank sale of a foreign asset is no different from an open market sale of a government bond. We learned in our exploration of the money supply process that

BOX 1 INSIDE THE FED

A Day at the Federal Reserve Bank of New York's Foreign Exchange Desk

Although the U.S. Treasury is primarily responsible for foreign exchange policy, decisions to intervene in the foreign exchange market are made jointly by the U.S. Treasury and the Federal Reserve as represented by the FOMC (Federal Open Market Committee). The actual conduct of foreign exchange intervention is the responsibility of the foreign exchange desk at the Federal Reserve Bank of New York, which is right next to the open market desk.

Dino Kos, the head of foreign exchange operations at the New York Fed, supervises the traders and analysts who follow developments in the foreign exchange market. Every morning at 7:30, a trader on Kos's staff who has arrived at the New York Fed in the predawn hours speaks on the telephone with counterparts at the U.S. Treasury and provides an update on overnight activity in overseas financial and foreign exchange markets. Later in the morning, at 9:30, Kos and his staff hold a conference call with senior staff at the Board of Governors of the Federal Reserve in Washington. In the afternoon, at 2:30, they have a second conference call, which is a joint briefing of officials at the board and the Treasury. Although by statute the Treasury has the lead role in setting foreign exchange policy, it strives to reach a consensus among all three parties—the Treasury, the Board of Governors, and the Federal Reserve Bank of New York. If they decide that a foreign exchange intervention is necessary that day—an unusual occurrence, as a year may go by without a U.S. foreign exchange intervention—Kos instructs his traders to carry out the agreed-on purchase or sale of foreign currencies. Because funds for exchange rate intervention are held separately by the Treasury (in its Exchange Stabilization Fund) and the Federal Reserve, Kos and his staff are not trading the funds of the Federal Reserve Bank of New York; rather they act as an agent for the Treasury and the FOMC in conducting these transactions.

As part of their duties, before every FOMC meeting, Kos and his staff help prepare a lengthy document full of data for the FOMC members, other Reserve bank presidents, and Treasury officials that describes developments in the domestic and foreign markets over the previous five or six weeks, a task that keeps them especially busy right before the FOMC meeting.

an open market sale leads to an equal decline in the monetary base; therefore, a sale of foreign assets also leads to an equal decline in the monetary base. By similar reasoning, a central bank purchase of foreign assets paid for by selling domestic currency, like an open market purchase, leads to an equal rise in the monetary base. Thus we reach the following conclusion: ***A central bank's sale of domestic currency to purchase foreign assets in the foreign exchange market results in an equal rise in its international reserves and the monetary base.***

The intervention we have just described, in which a central bank allows the purchase or sale of domestic currency to have an effect on the monetary base, is called an **unsterilized foreign exchange intervention.** But what if the central bank does not want the purchase or sale of domestic currency to affect the monetary base? All it has to do is to counter the effect of the foreign exchange intervention by conducting an offsetting open market operation in the government bond market. For example, in the case of a $1 billion purchase of dollars by the Fed and a corresponding $1 billion sale of foreign assets, which we have seen would decrease the monetary base by $1 billion, the Fed can conduct an open market purchase of $1 billion of government bonds, which would increase the monetary base by $1 billion. The resulting T-account for the foreign exchange intervention and the offsetting open market operation leaves the monetary base unchanged:

FEDERAL RESERVE SYSTEM

Assets		Liabilities	
Foreign assets (inter-national reserves)	−$1 billion	Monetary base (reserves)	0
Government bonds	+$1 billion		

A foreign exchange intervention with an offsetting open market operation that leaves the monetary base unchanged is called a **sterilized foreign exchange intervention.**

Now that we understand that there are two types of foreign exchange interventions, unsterilized and sterilized, let's look at how each affects the exchange rate.

Unsterilized Intervention

Your intuition might lead you to suspect that if a central bank wants to lower the value of the domestic currency, it should sell its currency in the foreign exchange market and purchase foreign assets. Indeed, this intuition is correct for the case of an unsterilized intervention.

Recall that in an unsterilized intervention, if the Federal Reserve decides to sell dollars in order to buy foreign assets in the foreign exchange market, this works just like an open market purchase of bonds to increase the monetary base. Hence the sale of dollars leads to an increase in the money supply, and we find ourselves analyzing exactly the situation already described in Figure 7 of Chapter 8, which is reproduced here as Figure 1. The higher money supply leads to a higher U.S. price level in the long run and so to a lower expected future exchange rate. The resulting decline in the expected appreciation of the dollar increases the expected return on foreign deposits and shifts the RET^F schedule to the right. In addition, the increase in the money supply will lead to a higher real money supply in the short run, which causes the interest rate on dollar deposits to fall. The resulting lower expected return on dollar deposits translates as a leftward shift in the RET^D schedule. The fall in the expected return on dollar deposits and the increase in the expected return on foreign deposits means that foreign assets have a higher expected return than dollar deposits at the old equilibrium exchange rate. Hence people will try to sell their dollar deposits, and the exchange rate will fall. Indeed, as we saw in Chapter 8, the increase in the money supply will lead to exchange rate overshooting, whereby the exchange rate falls by more in the short run than it does in the long run.

Our analysis leads us to the following conclusion about unsterilized interventions in the foreign exchange market: ***An unsterilized intervention in which domestic currency is sold to purchase foreign assets leads to a gain in international reserves, an increase in the money supply, and a depreciation of the domestic currency.***

The reverse result is found for an unsterilized intervention in which domestic currency is purchased by selling foreign assets. The purchase of domestic currency by selling foreign assets (reducing international reserves) works like an open market sale to reduce the monetary base and the money supply. The decrease in the money supply raises the interest rate on dollar deposits and shifts RET^D rightward while causing RET^F to shift leftward because it leads to a lower U.S. price level in the long run and thus to a higher expected appreciation of the dollar and hence a lower expected return on foreign deposits. The increase in the expected return on dollar deposits relative to foreign deposits will mean that people will want to buy more dollar deposits, and the exchange rate will rise. ***An unsterilized intervention in which domestic currency is purchased by selling foreign assets leads to a drop in international reserves, a decrease in the money supply, and an appreciation of the domestic currency.***

Sterilized Intervention

The key point to remember about a sterilized intervention is that the central bank engages in offsetting open market operations so that there is no impact on the monetary base and the money supply. In the context of the model of exchange rate determination we have developed here, it is straightforward to show that a sterilized intervention has *no effect* on the exchange rate. Remember that in our model, foreign and domestic deposits are perfect substitutes, so equilibrium in the foreign exchange market occurs when the expected returns on foreign and domestic deposits are equal. A sterilized intervention leaves the money supply unchanged and so has no way of directly affecting interest rates or the expected future exchange rate.[1] Because the expected returns on dollar and foreign deposits are unaffected, the expected return schedules remain at RET^D_1 and RET^F_1 in Figure 1, and the exchange rate remains unchanged at E_1.

At first it might seem puzzling that a central bank purchase or sale of domestic currency that is sterilized does not lead to a change in the exchange rate. A

---

[1]Note that a sterilized intervention could indicate what central banks want to happen to the future exchange rate and so might provide a signal about the course of future monetary policy. In this way, a sterilized intervention could lead to shifts in the RET^F schedule, but in reality it is the future change in monetary policy, not the sterilized intervention, that is the ultimate source of exchange rate effects. For a discussion of the signaling effect, see Maurice Obstfeld, "The Effectiveness of Foreign Exchange Intervention: Recent Experience, 1985–1988," in *International Policy Coordination and Exchange Rate Fluctuations,* ed. William H. Branson, Jacob A. Frenkel, and Morris Goldstein (Chicago: University of Chicago Press, 1990), pp. 197–237.

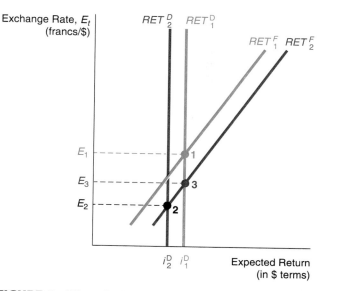

FIGURE 1   Effect of a Sale of Dollars and a Purchase of Foreign Assets

A sale of dollars and the consequent open market purchase of foreign assets increase the monetary base. The resulting rise in the money supply leads to a higher domestic price level in the long run, which leads to a lower expected future exchange rate. The resulting decline in the expected appreciation of the dollar raises the expected return on foreign deposits, shifting the **RET**^{F} schedule rightward from **RET**$^F_1$ to **RET**$^F_2$. In the short run, the domestic interest rate i^D falls, shifting **RET**^{D} from **RET**$^D_1$ to **RET**$^D_2$. The short-run outcome is that the exchange rate falls from **E**$_1$ to **E**$_2$. In the long run, however, the interest rate returns to i^D_1, and **RET**^{D} returns to **RET**$^D_1$. The exchange rate therefore rises from **E**$_2$ to **E**$_3$ in the long run.

central bank purchase of domestic currency cannot raise the exchange rate because with no effect on the domestic money supply or interest rates, any resulting rise in the exchange rate would mean that the expected return on foreign deposits would be greater than the expected return on domestic deposits. Given our assumption that foreign and domestic deposits are perfect substitutes (equally desirable), this would mean that no one would want to hold domestic deposits.[2] So the exchange rate would have to fall back to its previous level, where the expected returns on domestic and foreign deposits were equal.

BALANCE OF PAYMENTS

Because international financial transactions such as foreign exchange interventions have considerable effects on monetary policy, it is worth knowing how these transactions are measured. The **balance of payments** is a bookkeeping

---

[2]If domestic and foreign deposits are not perfect substitutes, a sterilized intervention can affect the exchange rate. However, most studies find little evidence to support the position that sterilized intervention has a significant impact on foreign exchange rates. For a further discussion of the effects of sterilized versus unsterilized intervention, see Paul Krugman and Maurice Obstfeld, *International Economics,* 4th ed. (Reading, Mass.: Addison Wesley Longman, 1997).

system for recording all payments that have a direct bearing on the movement of funds between a nation (private sector and government) and foreign countries.

The balance-of-payments account in the accompanying "Following the Financial News" box uses a standard double-entry bookkeeping system much like one that you or I might use to keep a record of payments and receipts. All transactions involving payments from foreigners to Americans are entered in the "Receipts" column with a plus sign (+) to reflect that they are credits; that is, they result in a flow of funds to Americans. Receipts include foreign purchases of American products such as computers and wheat (exports), purchases from foreign tourists (services), income earned from American investment abroad (investment income), foreign gifts and pensions paid to Americans (unilateral transfers), and foreign payments for American assets (capital inflows).

All payments to foreigners are entered in the "Payments" column with a minus sign (−) to reflect that they are debits because they result in flows of funds to other countries. Payments include American purchases of foreign products such as French wine and Japanese cars (imports), American travel abroad (services), income earned by foreigners from investments in the United States (investment income), foreign aid and gifts and pensions paid to foreigners (unilateral transfers), and American payments for foreign assets (capital outflows).

Current Account

The **current account** shows international transactions that involve currently produced goods and services. The difference between merchandise exports (line 1) and imports (line 2) is called the **trade balance.** When merchandise imports are greater than exports (here by $175 billion), we have a trade balance deficit; if exports are greater than imports, we have a trade balance surplus.

The next three items in the current account are the net payments or receipts that arise from investment income, the purchase and sale of services, and unilateral transfers (gifts, pensions, and foreign aid). In 1995, for example, net investment income was minus $11 billion (in line 3) for the United States because Americans received less investment income from abroad than they paid out. Americans bought less in services from foreigners than foreigners bought from Americans, so net services generated $63 billion in receipts (line 4). Since Americans made more unilateral transfers to foreign countries (especially foreign aid) than foreigners made to the United States, a $30 billion payment is shown in line 5.

The sum of the items in lines 1 through 5 is the current account balance, which in 1995 showed a deficit of $153 billion. The current account balance is an important balance-of-payment concept for several reasons. As we can see from the balance-of-payments account, any surplus or deficit in the current account must be balanced either by capital account transactions (lending or borrowing abroad) or by changes in government reserve asset items:

Current account + capital account = change in government reserve assets

The current account balance tells us whether the United States (private sector and government combined) is increasing or decreasing its claims on foreign wealth. A surplus indicates that America is increasing its claims on foreign wealth,

Following the Financial News

The Balance of Payments

Newspapers periodically report information on the balance of payments. Balance-of-trade figures (merchandise exports minus imports) are reported monthly in the last week of the month. The complete set of items in the balance of payments is published on a quarterly basis, with the previous quarter's figures published between the eighteenth and twentieth day of the last month of the following quarter. An example of the balance-of-payments accounts for the United States appears here.

U.S. Balance of Payments, 1995 ($ billions)			
	Receipts (+)	Payments (−)	Balance
Current Account			
(1) Merchandise exports	+575		
(2) Merchandise imports		−750	
Trade balance			−175
(3) Net investment income		−11	
(4) Net services	+63		
(5) Net unilateral transfers		−30	
Current account balance: (1) + (2) + (3) + (4) + (5)			−153
Capital Account			
(6) Capital outflows		−270	
(7) Capital inflows	+316		
(8) Statistical discrepancy	+7		
Official reserve transactions balance: (1) + (2) + (3) + (4) + (5) + (6) + (7) + (8)			−100
Method of Financing			
(9) Increase in U.S. official reserve assets		−10	
(10) Increase in foreign official assets	+110		
Total financing of surplus: (9) + (10)			+100
Balance of Payments			
Sum: (1) through (10)			0

Source: Survey of Current Business, April 1996.

and a deficit, as in 1995, indicates that the country is reducing its claims on foreign wealth.[3]

Financial analysts follow the current account balance closely because they believe that it can provide information on the future movement of exchange rates. The current account balance provides some indication of what is happening to the demand for imports and exports, which, as we saw in Chapter 8, can affect the exchange rate. In addition, the current account balance provides information about what will be happening to U.S. claims on foreign wealth in the long run. Because a movement of foreign wealth to American residents can affect the demand for dollar assets, changes in U.S. claims on foreign wealth, reflected in the current account balance, can affect the exchange rate over time.[4]

Capital Account

The **capital account** describes the flow of capital between the United States and other countries. Capital outflows are American purchases of foreign assets (a "Payments" item), and capital inflows are foreign purchases of American assets (a "Receipts" item). The capital outflows (line 6) are less than the capital inflows (line 7), resulting in a net flow of $46 billion in funds from foreigners in exchange for claims against American individuals and corporations.

The statistical discrepancy (line 8) represents errors due to unrecorded transactions involving smuggling and other capital flows. The statistical discrepancy, which keeps the balance-of-payments account in balance, is +$7 billion, which suggests that some of the other items in the balance of payments may not be measured very accurately. Many experts believe that the statistical discrepancy is primarily the result of large hidden capital flows, and so the item has been placed in the capital account part of the balance of payments.

Official Reserve Transactions Balance

The sum of lines 1 through 8, called the **official reserve transactions balance,** equals the current account balance plus the items in the capital account. When we refer to a surplus or a deficit in the balance of payments, we actually mean a surplus or deficit in the official reserve transactions balance. Because the balance-of-payments account must balance, the official reserve transactions balance tells us the net amount of international reserves that must move between central banks to finance international transactions. One reason we are particularly interested in the movements of international reserves is that, as we saw earlier in the chapter, these movements have an important impact on the money supply and exchange rates.

---

[3]The current account balance can also be viewed as showing by how much total saving exceeds private sector and government investment in the United States. We can see this by noting that total U.S. saving equals the increase in total wealth held by the U.S. private sector and government. Total investment equals the increase in the U.S. capital stock (wealth physically in the United States). The difference between them is the increase in U.S. claims on foreign wealth.

[4]If American residents have a greater preference for dollar assets than foreigners do, a movement of foreign wealth to American residents when there is a balance-of-payments surplus will increase the demand for dollar assets over time and will cause the dollar to appreciate.

Methods of Financing the Balance of Payments

Because most countries' currencies are not held by other countries as international reserves, these countries must finance an excess of payments over receipts (a deficit in the balance of payments) by providing international reserves to foreign governments and central banks. A balance-of-payments deficit is associated with a loss of international reserves; likewise, a balance-of-payments surplus is associated with a gain.

In contrast to other countries' currencies, the U.S. dollar and dollar-denominated assets are the major component of international reserves held by other countries. Thus a U.S. balance-of-payments deficit can be financed by a decrease in U.S. international reserves, an increase in foreign central banks' holdings of international reserves (dollar assets), or both. Conversely, a U.S. balance-of-payments surplus can be financed by an increase in U.S. international reserves, a decrease in foreign central banks' international reserves, or both.

For the United States in 1995, the official reserve transactions deficit of $100 billion was financed by a $10 billion increase in U.S. international reserves (-10 in the "Payments" column of line 9) and a $110 billion increase of foreign holdings of dollars (in the "Receipts" column of line 10).[5] On net, the United States' indebtedness to foreign governments (central banks) increased by $100 billion (the $110 billion foreign increase in holdings of U.S. dollars minus the $10 billion increase in U.S. holdings of international reserves). This $100 billion increase in net U.S. government indebtedness just matches the $100 billion official reserve transactions deficit, so the sum of lines 1 through 10 is zero, and the account balances.

EVOLUTION OF THE INTERNATIONAL FINANCIAL SYSTEM

Before examining the impact of international financial transactions on monetary policy, we need to understand the past and current structure of the international financial system.

Gold Standard

Before World War I, the world economy operated under the **gold standard,** meaning that the currency of most countries was convertible directly into gold. American dollar bills, for example, could be turned in to the U.S. Treasury and exchanged for approximately $\frac{1}{20}$ ounce of gold. Likewise, the British Treasury would exchange $\frac{1}{4}$ ounce of gold for £1 sterling. Because an American could convert $20 into 1 ounce of gold, which could be used to buy £4, the exchange rate between the pound and the dollar was effectively fixed at $5 to the pound. Tying currencies to gold resulted in an international financial system with fixed exchange rates between currencies. The fixed exchange rates under the gold standard had the

---

[5]At first it may seem strange that when the United States gains $10 billion of international reserves, it is entered in the balance of payments as a payment with a negative sign. Recall, however, that when a central bank loses international reserves, it has sold foreign assets. Thus a decrease in international reserves is just like an inflow of capital in the capital account and appears as a payment with a negative sign.

important advantage of encouraging world trade by eliminating the uncertainty that occurs when exchange rates fluctuate.

To see how the gold standard operated in practice, let us see what occurs if, under the gold standard, the British pound begins to appreciate above the $5 par value. If an American importer of £100 of English tweed tries to pay for the tweed with dollars, it costs more than the $500 it cost before. Nevertheless, the importer has another option involving the purchase of gold that can reduce the cost of the tweed. Instead of using dollars to pay for the tweed, the American importer can exchange the $500 for gold, ship the gold to Britain, and convert it into £100. The shipment of gold to Britain is cheaper as long as the British pound is above the $5 par value (plus a small amount to pay for the cost of shipping the gold).

The appreciation of the pound leads to a British gain of international reserves (gold) and an equal U.S. loss. Because a change in a country's holdings of international reserves (gold) leads to an equal change in its monetary base, the movement of gold from the United States to Britain causes the British monetary base to rise and the American monetary base to fall. The resulting rise in the British money supply raises the British price level, while the fall in the U.S. money supply lowers the U.S. price level. The resulting increase in the British price level relative to the United States then causes the pound to depreciate. This process will continue until the value of the pound falls back down to its $5 par value.

A depreciation of the pound below the $5 par value, on the contrary, stimulates gold shipments from Britain to the United States. These shipments raise the American money supply and lower the British money supply, causing the pound to appreciate back toward the $5 par value. We thus see that under the gold standard, a rise or fall in the exchange rate sets in motion forces that return it to the par value.

As long as countries abided by the rules under the gold standard and kept their currencies backed by and convertible into gold, exchange rates remained fixed. However, adherence to the gold standard meant that a country had no control over its monetary policy because its money supply was determined by gold flows between countries. Furthermore, monetary policy throughout the world was greatly influenced by the production of gold and gold discoveries. When gold production was low in the 1870s and 1880s, the money supply throughout the world grew slowly and did not keep pace with the growth of the world economy. The result was deflation (falling price levels). Gold discoveries in Alaska and South Africa in the 1890s then greatly expanded gold production, which caused money supplies to increase rapidly and price levels to rise (inflation) until World War I.

Bretton Woods System and the IMF

World War I caused massive trade disruptions. Countries could no longer convert their currencies into gold, and the gold standard collapsed. Despite attempts to revive it in the interwar period, the worldwide depression, beginning in 1929, led to its permanent demise. As the Allied victory in World War II was becoming certain in 1944, the Allies met in Bretton Woods, New Hampshire, to develop a new international monetary system to promote world trade and prosperity after the war. In the agreement worked out among the Allies, central banks bought and sold their own currencies to keep their exchange rates fixed at a certain level (called a **fixed exchange rate regime**). The agreement lasted from 1945 to 1971 and was known as the **Bretton Woods system.**

The Bretton Woods agreement created the **International Monetary Fund (IMF),** headquartered in Washington, D.C., which had 30 original member countries in 1945 and currently has over 150. The IMF was given the task of promoting the growth of world trade by setting rules for the maintenance of fixed exchange rates and by making loans to countries that were experiencing balance-of-payments difficulties.[6] As part of its role of monitoring the compliance of member countries with its rules, the IMF also took on the job of collecting and standardizing international economic data.

The Bretton Woods agreement also set up the International Bank for Reconstruction and Development, commonly referred to as the **World Bank,** also headquartered in Washington, D.C., which provides long-term loans to help developing countries build dams, roads, and other physical capital that would contribute to their economic development. The funds for these loans are obtained primarily by issuing World Bank bonds, which are sold in the capital markets of the developed countries.[7]

Because the United States emerged from World War II as the world's largest economic power, with over half of the world's manufacturing capacity and the greater part of the world's gold, the Bretton Woods system of fixed exchange rates was based on the convertibility of U.S. dollars into gold (for foreign governments and central banks only) at $35 per ounce. The fixed exchange rates were to be maintained by intervention in the foreign exchange market by central banks in countries besides the United States who bought and sold dollar assets, which they held as international reserves. The U.S. dollar, which was used by other countries to denominate the assets that they held as international reserves, was called the **reserve currency.** Thus an important feature of the Bretton Woods system was the establishment of the United States as the reserve currency country.

HOW A FIXED EXCHANGE RATE REGIME WORKS   The most important feature of the Bretton Woods system was that it set up a fixed exchange rate regime. Figure 2 shows how a fixed exchange rate regime works in practice using the model of exchange rate determination we learned in Chapter 8. Panel (a) describes a situation in which the domestic currency is initially overvalued: The schedule for the expected return on foreign deposits RET_1^F intersects the schedule for the expected return on domestic deposits RET_1^D at exchange rate E_1, which is lower than the par (fixed) value of the exchange rate E_{par}. To keep the exchange rate at E_{par}, the central bank must intervene in the foreign exchange market to purchase domestic currency by selling foreign assets, and this action, like an open market sale,

---

[6]Rules for the conduct of trade between countries (the setting of tariffs and quotas) were given to the General Agreement on Tariffs and Trade (GATT), headquartered in Geneva. For a discussion of how this agency operates, see John Williamson, *The Open Economy and the World Economy* (New York: Basic Books, 1983).

[7]In 1960, the World Bank established an affiliate, the International Development Association (IDA), which provides particularly attractive loans to third-world countries (with 50-year maturities and zero interest rates, for example). Funds for these loans are obtained by direct contributions of member countries.

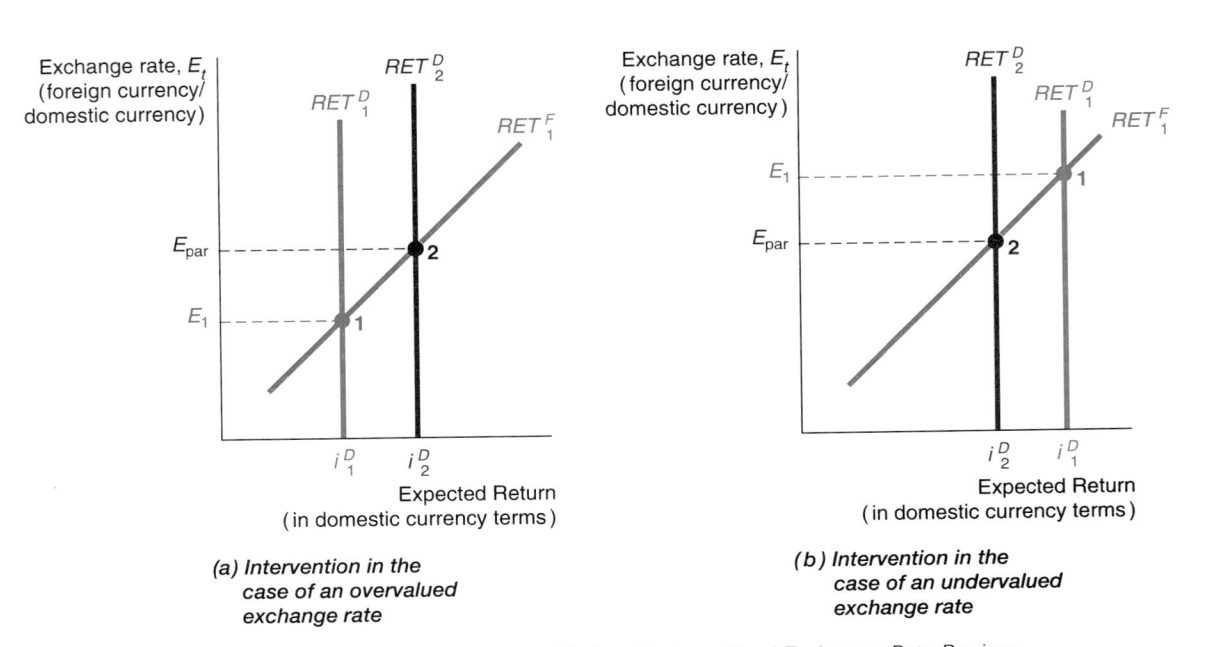

(a) Intervention in the case of an overvalued exchange rate

(b) Intervention in the case of an undervalued exchange rate

FIGURE 2 Intervention in the Foreign Exchange Market Under a Fixed Exchange Rate Regime

In panel (a), the exchange rate at E_{par} is overvalued. To keep the exchange rate at E_{par} (point 2), the central bank must purchase domestic currency to shift the schedule for the expected return on domestic deposits to RET_2^D. In panel (b), the exchange rate at E_{par} is undervalued, so a central bank sale of domestic currency is needed to shift RET^D to RET_2^D to keep the exchange rate at E_{par} (point 2).

means that the monetary base and the money supply decline. Because the exchange rate will continue to be fixed at E_{par}, the expected future exchange rate remains unchanged, and so the schedule for the expected return on foreign deposits remains at RET_1^F. However, the purchase of domestic currency, which leads to a fall in the money supply, also causes the interest rate on domestic deposits i^D to rise. This increase in turn shifts the expected return on domestic deposits RET^D to the right. The central bank will continue purchasing domestic currency and selling foreign assets until the RET^D curve reaches RET_2^D and the equilibrium exchange rate is at E_{par} at point 2 in panel (a).

We have thus come to the conclusion that ***when the domestic currency is overvalued, the central bank must purchase domestic currency to keep the exchange rate fixed, but as a result it loses international reserves.***

Panel (b) in Figure 2 shows how a central bank intervention keeps the exchange rate fixed at E_{par} when the exchange rate is initially undervalued, that is, when RET_1^F and the initial RET_1^D intersect at exchange rate E_1, which is above E_{par}. Here the central bank must sell domestic currency and purchase foreign assets, and this works like an open market purchase to raise the money supply and lower the interest rate on domestic deposits i^D. The central bank keeps selling domestic currency and lowers i^D until RET^D shifts all the way to RET_2^D, where the equilibrium exchange rate is at E_{par}—point 2 in panel (b). Our analysis thus leads us to the following result: ***When the domestic currency is undervalued,***

the central bank must sell domestic currency to keep the exchange rate fixed, but as a result it gains international reserves.

As we have seen, if a country's currency has an overvalued exchange rate, its central bank's attempts to keep the currency from depreciating will result in a loss of international reserves. If the country's central bank eventually runs out of international reserves, it cannot keep its currency from depreciating, and a **devaluation** must occur, meaning that the par exchange rate is reset at a lower level.

If, by contrast, a country's currency has an undervalued exchange rate, its central bank's intervention to keep the currency from appreciating leads to a gain of international reserves. Because, as we will see shortly, the central bank might not want to acquire these international reserves, it might want to reset the par value of its exchange rate at a higher level (a **revaluation**).

Note that if domestic and foreign deposits are perfect substitutes, as is assumed in the model of exchange rate determination used here, a sterilized exchange rate intervention would not be able to keep the exchange rate at E_{par} because, as we have seen in Chapter 8, neither RET^F nor RET^D will shift. For example, if the exchange rate is overvalued, a sterilized purchase of domestic currency will still leave the expected return on domestic deposits below the expected return on foreign deposits at the par exchange rate—so pressure for a depreciation of the domestic currency is not removed. If the central bank keeps on purchasing its domestic currency but continues to sterilize, it will just keep on losing international reserves until it finally runs out of them and is forced to let the value of the currency seek a lower level.

One implication of the foregoing analysis is that a country that ties its exchange rate to a larger country's currency loses control of its monetary policy. If the larger country pursues a more contractionary monetary policy and decreases its money supply, this would lead to lower expected inflation in the larger country, thus causing an appreciation of the larger country's currency and a depreciation of the smaller country's currency. The smaller country, having locked in its exchange rate, will now find its currency overvalued and will therefore have to sell the larger country's currency and buy its own to keep its currency from depreciating. The result of this foreign exchange intervention will then be a decline in the smaller country's international reserves, a contraction of the monetary base, and thus a decline in its money supply. Sterilization of this foreign exchange intervention is not an option because this would just lead to a continuing loss of international reserves until the smaller country was forced to devalue. The smaller country no longer controls its monetary policy because movements in its money supply are completely determined by movements in the larger country's money supply.

Smaller countries are often willing to tie their exchange rate to that of a larger country in order to inherit the more disciplined monetary policy of their bigger neighbor, thus ensuring a lower inflation rate. An extreme example of such a strategy is the currency board, which has been used by Hong Kong and has recently been adopted by countries such as Argentina (see Box 2), Latvia, and Estonia.

BRETTON WOODS SYSTEM OF FIXED EXCHANGE RATES Under the Bretton Woods system, exchange rates were supposed to change only when a country was experiencing a "fundamental disequilibrium," that is, large persistent deficits

BOX 2

Argentina's Currency Board

Argentina has a long history of monetary instability, with inflation rates fluctuating dramatically and sometimes surging to beyond 1,000 percent a year. To end this cycle of inflationary surges, Argentina decided to adopt a currency board in April 1991. A *currency board system* is one in which the domestic currency has 100 percent backing in foreign reserves and in which the note-issuing authority, whether the central bank or the government, establishes a fixed exchange rate against a particular foreign currency and then stands ready to exchange domestic currency for foreign currency at that rate whenever the public requests it.

The Argentine currency board works as follows. Under Argentina's convertibility law, the peso/dollar exchange rate is fixed at one to one, and a member of the public can go to the Argentine central bank and exchange a peso for a dollar, or vice versa, at any time. A currency board is just a variant of a fixed exchange rate regime in which the commitment to the fixed exchange rate is especially strong because the conduct of monetary policy is in effect put on autopilot and is completely taken out of the hands of the central bank and the government. The money supply can expand only when dollars are exchanged for pesos at the central bank, meaning that the increased amount of pesos is matched by an equal increase in foreign exchange reserves. The central bank therefore no longer has the ability to print money and thereby cause inflation.

The early years of Argentina's currency board looked stunningly successful. Inflation, which had been running at an 800 percent annual rate in 1990, fell to less than 5 percent by the end of 1994, and economic growth was rapid, averaging almost 8 percent annually from 1991 to 1994. However, a currency board is not without its problems. In the aftermath of the Mexican peso crisis, concern about the health of the Argentine economy resulted in the public's pulling money out of the banks (deposits fell by 18 percent) and exchanging pesos for dollars, thus causing a contraction of the Argentine money supply. The result was a sharp drop in Argentine economic activity, with real GDP shrinking by more than 5 percent in 1995 and the unemployment rate jumping above 15 percent. Only in 1996 did the economy begin to recover. Because the central bank of Argentina has no control over monetary policy under the currency board system, it was relatively helpless to counteract the contractionary monetary policy stemming from the public's behavior. Furthermore, because the currency board does not allow the central bank to create pesos and lend them to the banks, it has very little capability to act as a lender of last resort. With help from international agencies, such as the IMF, the World Bank, and the Interamerican Development Bank, who lent Argentina over $5 billion to help shore up its banking system, the currency board still survives. However, the Argentine public is not as enamored with the currency board as it once was.

or surpluses in its balance of payments. To maintain fixed exchange rates when countries had balance-of-payments deficits and were losing international reserves, the IMF would loan deficit countries international reserves contributed by other members. As a result of its power to dictate loan terms to borrowing countries, the IMF could encourage deficit countries to pursue contractionary monetary policies that would strengthen their currency or eliminate their balance-of-payment deficits.

If the IMF loans were not sufficient to prevent depreciation of a currency, the country was allowed to devalue its currency by setting a new, lower exchange rate.

A notable weakness of the Bretton Woods system was that although deficit countries losing international reserves could be pressured into devaluing their currency or pursuing contractionary policies, the IMF had no way to force surplus countries to revise their exchange rates upward or pursue more expansionary policies. Particularly troublesome in this regard was the fact that the reserve currency country, the United States, could not devalue its currency under the Bretton Woods system even if the dollar was overvalued. When the United States attempted to reduce domestic unemployment in the 1960s by pursuing an inflationary monetary policy, a fundamental disequilibrium of an overvalued dollar developed. Because surplus countries were not willing to revise their exchange rates upward, adjustment in the Bretton Woods system did not take place, and the system collapsed in 1971. Attempts to patch up the Bretton Woods system with the Smithsonian Agreement in December 1971 proved unsuccessful, and by 1973, America and its trading partners had agreed to allow exchange rates to float.

Managed Float

Although exchange rates are currently allowed to change daily in response to market forces, central banks have not been willing to give up their option of intervening in the foreign exchange market. Preventing large changes in exchange rates makes it easier for firms and individuals purchasing or selling goods abroad to plan into the future. Furthermore, countries with surpluses in their balance of payments frequently do not want to see their currencies appreciate because it makes their goods more expensive abroad and foreign goods cheaper in their country. Because an appreciation might hurt sales for domestic businesses and increase unemployment, surplus countries have often sold their currency in the foreign exchange market and acquired international reserves.

Countries with balance-of-payments deficits do not want to see their currency lose value because it makes foreign goods more expensive for domestic consumers and can stimulate inflation. To keep the value of the domestic currency high, deficit countries have often bought their own currency in the foreign exchange market and given up international reserves.

The current international financial system is a hybrid of a fixed and a flexible exchange rate system. Rates fluctuate in response to market forces but are not determined solely by them. Furthermore, many countries continue to keep the value of their currency fixed against other currencies, as in the European Monetary System (to be described shortly).

The IMF continues to function as a data collector and international lender but does not attempt to encourage fixed exchange rates. The IMF's role of international lender has also become important recently because of the situations like the third-world debt crisis of the 1980s and the more recent Mexican peso crisis (discussed later in the chapter). The IMF has been directly involved in helping developing countries with difficulties in repaying their loans and provided large loans to Mexico and other countries in the aftermath of the Mexican peso crisis.

Another important feature of the current system is the continuing deemphasis of gold in international financial transactions. Not only has the United States suspended convertibility of dollars into gold for foreign central banks, but since 1970 the IMF has been issuing a paper substitute for gold, called **special drawing rights (SDRs).** Like gold in the Bretton Woods system, SDRs function as international reserves. Unlike gold, whose quantity is determined by gold discoveries and the rate of production, SDRs can be created by the IMF whenever it decides that there is a need for additional international reserves to promote world trade and economic growth.

The use of gold in international transactions was further deemphasized by the IMF's elimination of the official gold price in 1975 and by the sale of gold by the U.S. Treasury and the IMF to private interests in order to demonetize it. Currently, the price of gold is determined in a free market. Investors who want to speculate in it are able to purchase and sell at will, as are jewelers and dentists who use gold in their businesses.

European Monetary System (EMS)

In March 1979, eight members of the European Economic Community (Germany, France, Italy, the Netherlands, Belgium, Luxembourg, Denmark, and Ireland) set up the European Monetary System (EMS), in which they agreed to fix their exchange rates vis-à-vis one another and to float jointly against the U.S. dollar. Spain joined the EMS in June 1989, the United Kingdom in October 1990, and Portugal in April 1992. The EMS created a new monetary unit, the *European currency unit* (ECU), whose value is tied to a basket of specified amounts of European currencies. Each member of the EMS is required to contribute 20 percent of its holdings of gold and dollars to the European Monetary Cooperation Fund and in return receives an equivalent amount of ECUs.

The exchange rate mechanism (ERM) of the European Monetary System works as follows. The exchange rate between every pair of currencies of the participating countries is not allowed to fluctuate outside narrow limits around a fixed exchange rate. (The limits were typically ±2.25 percent but were raised to ±15 percent after the September 1992 foreign exchange crisis.) When the exchange rate between two countries' currencies moves outside of these limits, the central banks of both countries are supposed to intervene in the foreign exchange market. If, for example, the French franc depreciates below its lower limit against the German mark, the Bank of France must buy francs and sell marks, thereby giving up international reserves. Similarly, the German central bank must also intervene to buy marks and sell francs and consequently increase its international reserves. The EMS thus requires that intervention be symmetric when a currency falls outside the limits, with the central bank with the weak currency giving up international reserves and the one with the strong currency gaining them. Central bank intervention is also very common even when the exchange rate is within the limits, but in this case, if one central bank intervenes, no others are required to intervene as well.

A serious shortcoming of fixed exchange rate systems such as the Bretton Woods system or the European Monetary System is that they can lead to foreign exchange crises involving a "speculative attack" on a currency—massive sales of a weak currency or purchases of a strong currency to cause a sharp change in the exchange rate. In the following application, we use our model of exchange rate determination to understand how the September 1992 exchange rate crisis that rocked the European Monetary System came about.

September 1992 Foreign Exchange Crisis

In the aftermath of German reunification in October 1990, the German central bank, the Bundesbank, faced rising inflationary pressures, with inflation having accelerated from below 3 percent in 1990 to near 5 percent by 1992. To get monetary growth under control and to dampen inflation, the Bundesbank raised German interest rates to near double-digit levels. Figure 3 shows the consequences of these actions by the Bundesbank in the foreign exchange market for sterling. Note that in the diagram, the pound sterling is the domestic currency and RET^D is the expected return on sterling deposits, while the foreign currency is the German mark (deutsche mark, DM), so RET^F is the expected return on mark deposits.

The increase in German interest rates i^F shifted the RET^F schedule rightward to RET^F_2 in Figure 3, so that the intersection of the RET^D_1 and the RET^F_2 schedules at point 1′ was below the lower exchange rate limit (2.778 marks per pound, denoted E_{par}) under the exchange rate mechanism. To lower the value of the mark relative to the pound and restore the pound/mark exchange rate to within the ERM limits, either the Bank of England had to pursue a contractionary monetary policy, thereby raising British interest rates to i^D_2 and shifting the RET^D_1 schedule to the right to point 2, or the Bundesbank could pursue an expansionary monetary policy, thereby lowering German interest rates, which would shift the RET^F schedule to the left to move back to point 1. (The shifts in RET^D to point 2 or RET^F to point 1 are not shown in the figure.)

The catch was that the Bundesbank, whose primary goal is fighting inflation, was unwilling to pursue an expansionary monetary policy, while the British, who were facing their worst recession in the postwar period, were unwilling to pursue a contractionary monetary policy to prop up the pound. This impasse became clear when in response to great pressure from other members of the EMS, the Bundesbank was willing to lower its lending rates by only a token amount on September 14 after a speculative attack was mounted on the currencies of the Scandinavian countries. So at some point in the near future, the value of the pound would have to decline to point 1′. Speculators now knew that the appreciation of the mark was imminent and hence that the value of foreign (mark) deposits would rise in value relative to the pound. As a result, the expected return on mark deposits increased sharply, shifting the RET^F schedule to RET^F_3 in Figure 3.

The huge potential losses on pound deposits and potential gains on mark deposits caused a massive sell-off of pounds (and purchases of marks) by speculators. The need for the British central bank to intervene to raise the value of the pound now became much greater and required a huge rise in British interest rates all the way to i^D_3. After a major intervention effort on the part of the Bank of England, which included a rise in its lending rate from 10 percent to 15 percent, which still wasn't enough, the British were finally forced to give up on September 16: They pulled out of the ERM indefinitely, allowing the pound to depreciate by 10 percent against the mark.

Speculative attacks on other currencies forced devaluation of the Spanish peseta by 5 percent and the Italian lira by 15 percent. To defend its currency, the

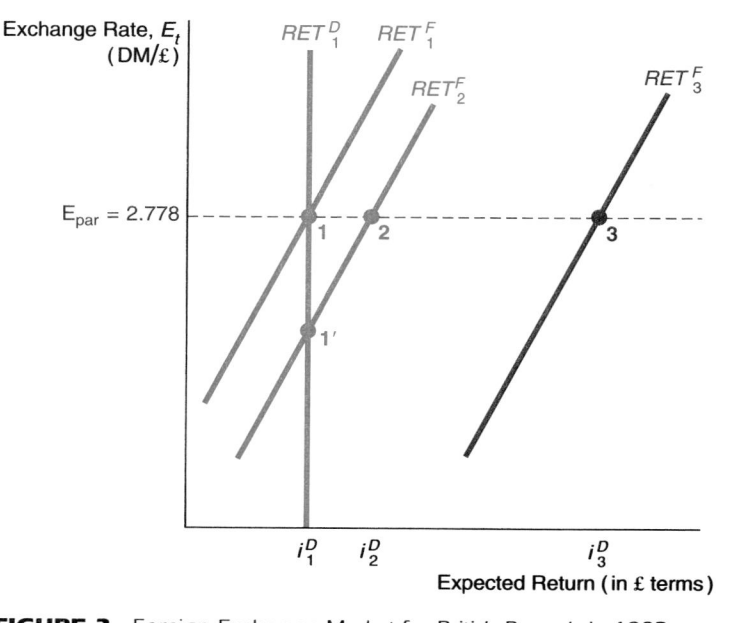

FIGURE 3 Foreign Exchange Market for British Pounds in 1992
The realization by speculators that the United Kingdom would soon devalue the pound increased the expected return on foreign (German mark, DM) deposits and shifted RET_2^F rightward to RET_3^F. The result was the need for a much greater purchase of pounds by the British central bank to raise the interest rate to i_3^D to keep the exchange rate at 2.778 German marks per pound.

Swedish central bank was forced to raise its daily lending rate to the astronomical level of 500 percent! By the time the crisis was over, the British, French, Italian, Spanish, and Swedish central banks had intervened to the tune of $100 billion; the Bundesbank alone had laid out $50 billion for foreign exchange intervention. Because foreign exchange crises lead to large changes in central banks' holdings of international reserves and thus affect the official reserve asset items in the balance of payments, these crises are also referred to as **balance-of-payments crises.**

The attempt to prop up the European Monetary System was not cheap for these central banks. It is estimated that they lost $4 to $6 billion as a result of exchange rate intervention during the crisis. What the central banks lost, the speculators gained. A speculative fund run by George Soros ran up $1 billion of profits during the crisis, and Citibank traders are reported to have made $200 million. When an exchange rate crisis comes, life can certainly be sweet for exchange rate speculators. Ⓐ

Mexican Peso Crisis of December 1994

As part of a reform plan initiated in 1987 to stabilize the Mexican economy, the Mexican government decided to put limits on the movements of the peso against the dollar. When the ruling party's presidential candidate was assassinated in March 1994, investors became concerned that the government might devalue the currency despite promises not to do so. The result was a speculative attack on the peso that not only brought down the peso but also threatened to bring down the currencies of other developing countries, particularly those in Latin America (jauntily referred to as the "Tequila effect"). Figure 3 can be used to understand the sequence of events during the Mexican peso crisis. We just need to recognize that RET^D is now the expected return on peso deposits and, since the foreign currency is the dollar, RET^F is the expected return on dollar deposits, with both denominated in the domestic currency, the peso.

Because of investors' concerns that the peso might be devalued after the March assassination, the expected return on dollar deposits rose, thus moving the RET^F schedule from RET^F_1 to RET^F_2 in Figure 3. The result was that the intersection of RET^D_1 and RET^F_2 was below the lower exchange limit E_{par} of around 30 cents per peso. To keep the peso from falling through this limit, the Mexican authorities needed to buy pesos and sell dollars, to raise interest rates to i^D_2 by shifting the RET^D curve to the right. This is exactly what they did, raising interest rates from around 10 percent to over 20 percent and losing close to half of their $30 billion in international reserves in the process. For the time being, the peso held, but more bad luck was to hit the Mexicans. An uprising in the southern state of Chiapas, the assassination of another high official in the ruling party, and concerns about the large current account deficit and the new untried president, who was inaugurated on December 1, led to further rumors of devaluation. Now the RET^F curve shifted even farther to the right, say, to RET^F_3, and the Mexican authorities intervened further, doubling interest rates again and almost completely exhausting the nation's foreign exchange reserves. Once speculators guessed that the Mexicans were running out of reserves, the game was up. With near certainty that the Mexican government would be forced to devalue, the expected return on dollar deposits increased sharply, shifting RET^F even farther to the right, making a devaluation inevitable. On December 20, Mexico's government had to devalue the peso; it had less than half its former value by early 1995.

The aftermath of this crisis was not only speculative attacks on other developing countries' currencies but also a full-scale financial crisis in Mexico that, as we saw in Chapter 9, severely damaged the nation's economy. The foreign exchange rate crisis that shocked the European Monetary System in September 1992 cost central banks a lot of money, but the public in European countries was not seriously affected. The Mexican public was not so lucky; as described in Chapter 9, the speculative attack that caused the collapse of the peso produced a severe depression that cost all Mexicans dearly. Ⓐ

INTERNATIONAL CONSIDERATIONS AND MONETARY POLICY

Our analysis in this chapter so far has suggested several ways in which monetary policy can be affected by international matters. Awareness of these effects can have significant implications for the way monetary policy is conducted.

Direct Effects of the Foreign Exchange Market on the Money Supply

When central banks intervene in the foreign exchange market, they acquire or sell off international reserves, and their monetary base is affected. When a central bank intervenes in the foreign exchange market, it gives up some control of its money supply. For example, in the early 1970s, the German central bank faced a dilemma. In attempting to keep the German mark from appreciating too much against the U.S. dollar, the Germans acquired huge quantities of international reserves, leading to a rapid rate of money growth that the German central bank considered inflationary.

The Bundesbank could have tried to halt the growth of the money supply by stopping its intervention in the foreign exchange market and reasserting control over its own money supply. Such a strategy has a major drawback when the central bank is under pressure not to allow its currency to appreciate: The lower price of imports and higher price of exports as a result of an appreciation in its currency will hurt domestic producers and increase unemployment.

Because the U.S. dollar has been a reserve currency, the U.S. monetary base and money supply have been less affected by developments in the foreign exchange market. As long as foreign central banks, rather than the Fed, intervene to keep the value of the dollar from changing, American holdings of international reserves are unaffected. The ability to conduct monetary policy is typically easier when a country's currency is a reserve currency.[8]

Balance-of-Payments Considerations

Under the Bretton Woods system, balance-of-payments considerations were more important than they are under the current managed float regime. When a nonreserve currency country is running balance-of-payments deficits, it necessarily gives up international reserves. To keep from running out of these reserves, under the Bretton Woods system it had to implement contractionary monetary policy to strengthen its currency. Exactly that occurred in the United Kingdom before its devaluation of the pound in 1967. When policy became expansionary, the balance of payments deteriorated, and the British were forced to "slam on the brakes" by implementing a contractionary policy. Once the balance of payments improved, policy became more expansionary until the deteriorating balance of payments again forced the British to pursue a contractionary policy. Such on-again, off-again actions became known as a "stop-go" policy, and the domestic instability it created was criticized severely.

Because the United States is a major reserve currency country, it can run large balance-of-payments deficits without losing huge amounts of international reserves. This does not mean, however, that the Federal Reserve is never influenced by developments in the U.S. balance of payments. Current account deficits in the United States suggest that American businesses may be losing some of their ability to compete because the value of the dollar is too high. In addition, large U.S. balance-of-payments deficits lead to balance-of-payments surpluses in other countries, which can in turn lead to large increases in their holdings of international reserves (this was especially true under the Bretton Woods system).

---

[8]However, the central bank of a reserve currency country must worry about a shift away from the use of its currency for international reserves.

money supply." Is this statement true, false, or uncertain? Explain your answer.

*10. Why can balance-of-payments deficits force some countries to implement a contractionary monetary policy?

11. "Balance-of-payments deficits always cause a country to lose international reserves." Is this statement true, false, or uncertain? Explain your answer.

*12. How can persistent U.S. balance-of-payments deficits stimulate world inflation?

13. "Inflation is not possible under the gold standard." Is this statement true, false, or uncertain? Explain your answer.

*14. Why is it that in a pure flexible exchange rate system, the foreign exchange market has no direct effects on the money supply? Does this mean that the foreign exchange market has no effect on monetary policy?

15. "The abandonment of fixed exchange rates after 1973 has meant that countries have pursued more independent monetary policies." Is this statement true, false, or uncertain? Explain your answer.

PART V

MONETARY THEORY

Chapter 21

THE DEMAND FOR MONEY

PREVIEW   In earlier chapters we spent a lot of time and effort learning what the money supply is, how it is determined, and what role the Federal Reserve System plays in it. Now we are ready to explore the role of the money supply in determining the price level and total production of goods and services (aggregate output) in the economy. The study of the effect of money on the economy is called **monetary theory,** and we examine this branch of economics in the chapters of Part V.

When economists mention *supply*, the word *demand* is sure to follow, and the discussion of money is no exception. The supply of money is an essential building block in understanding how monetary policy affects the economy because it suggests the factors that influence the quantity of money in the economy. Not surprisingly, another essential part of monetary theory is the demand for money.

This chapter describes how the theories of the demand for money have evolved. We begin with the classical theories refined at the start of the twentieth century by economists such as Irving Fisher, Alfred Marshall, and A. C. Pigou; then we move on to the Keynesian theories of the demand for money. We end with Milton Friedman's modern quantity theory.

A central question in monetary theory is whether or to what extent the quantity of money demanded is affected by changes in interest rates. Because this issue is crucial to how we view money's effects on aggregate economic activity, we focus on the role of interest rates in the demand for money.[1]

QUANTITY THEORY OF MONEY

Developed by the classical economists in the nineteenth and early twentieth centuries, the quantity theory of money is a theory of how the nominal value of aggregate income is determined. Because it also tells us how much money is held

---

[1]In Chapter 23 we will see that the responsiveness of the quantity of money demanded to changes in interest rates has important implications for the relative effectiveness of monetary policy and fiscal policy in influencing aggregate economic activity.

for a given amount of aggregate income, it is also a theory of the demand for money. The most important feature of this theory is that it suggests that interest rates have no effect on the demand for money.

Velocity of Money and Equation of Exchange

The clearest exposition of the classical quantity theory approach is found in the work of the American economist Irving Fisher, in his influential book *The Purchasing Power of Money*, published in 1911. Fisher wanted to examine the link between the total quantity of money M (the money supply) and the total amount of spending on final goods and services produced in the economy $P \times Y$, where P is the price level and Y is aggregate output (income). (Total spending $P \times Y$ is also thought of as aggregate nominal income for the economy or as nominal GDP.) The concept that provides the link between M and $P \times Y$ is called the **velocity of money** (often reduced simply to *velocity*), the rate of turnover of money, that is, the average number of times per year that a dollar is spent in buying the total amount of goods and services produced in the economy. Velocity V is defined more precisely as total spending $P \times Y$ divided by the quantity of money M:

$$V = \frac{P \times Y}{M} \tag{1}$$

If, for example, nominal GDP ($P \times Y$) in a year is $5 trillion and the quantity of money is $1 trillion, velocity is 5, meaning that the average dollar bill is spent five times in purchasing final goods and services in the economy.

By multiplying both sides of this definition by M, we obtain the **equation of exchange,** which relates nominal income to the quantity of money and velocity:

$$M \times V = P \times Y \tag{2}$$

The equation of exchange thus states that the quantity of money multiplied by the number of times that this money is spent in a given year must be equal to nominal income (the total nominal amount spent on goods and services in that year).[2]

As it stands, Equation 2 is nothing more than an identity—a relationship that is true by definition. It does not tell us, for instance, that when the money supply M changes, nominal income ($P \times Y$) changes in the same direction; a rise in M, for example, could be offset by a fall in V that leaves $M \times V$ (and therefore $P \times Y$) unchanged. To convert the equation of exchange (*an identity*) into a *theory* of how nominal income is determined requires an understanding of the factors that determine velocity.

---

[2]Fisher actually first formulated the equation of exchange in terms of the nominal value of transactions in the economy PT:

$$MV_T = PT$$

where
P = average price per transaction
T = number of transactions conducted in a year
$V_T = PT/M$ = transactions velocity of money

Because the nominal value of transactions T is difficult to measure, the quantity theory has been formulated in terms of aggregate output Y, as follows: T is assumed to be proportional to Y so that $T = vY$, where v is a constant of proportionality. Substituting vY for T in Fisher's equation of exchange yields $MV_T = vPY$, which can be written as Equation 2 in the text in which $V = V_T/v$.

Irving Fisher reasoned that velocity is determined by the institutions in an economy that affect the way individuals conduct transactions. If people use charge accounts and credit cards to conduct their transactions and consequently use money less often when making purchases, less money is required to conduct the transactions generated by nominal income ($M\downarrow$ relative to $P \times Y$), and velocity ($P \times Y$)/M will increase. Conversely, if it is more convenient for purchases to be paid for with cash or checks (both of which are money), more money is used to conduct the transactions generated by the same level of nominal income, and velocity will fall. Fisher took the view that the institutional and technological features of the economy would affect velocity only slowly over time, so velocity would normally be reasonably constant in the short run.

Quantity Theory

Fisher's view that velocity is fairly constant in the short run transforms the equation of exchange into the **quantity theory of money,** which states that nominal income is determined solely by movements in the quantity of money: When the quantity of money M doubles, $M \times V$ doubles and so must $P \times Y$, the value of nominal income. To see how this works, let's assume that velocity is 5, nominal income (GDP) is initially $5 trillion, and the money supply is $1 trillion. If the money supply doubles to $2 trillion, the quantity theory of money tells us that nominal income will double to $10 trillion (= 5 × $2 trillion).

Because the classical economists (including Fisher) thought that wages and prices were completely flexible, they believed that the level of aggregate output Y produced in the economy during normal times would remain at the full-employment level, so Y in the equation of exchange could also be treated as reasonably constant in the short run. The quantity theory of money then implies that if M doubles, P must also double in the short run because V and Y are constant. In our example, if aggregate output is $5 trillion, the velocity of 5 and a money supply of $1 trillion indicate that the price level equals 1 because 1 times $5 trillion equals the nominal income of $5 trillion. When the money supply doubles to $2 trillion, the price level must also double to 2 because 2 times $5 trillion equals the nominal income of $10 trillion.

For the classical economists, the quantity theory of money provided an explanation of movements in the price level: ***Movements in the price level result solely from changes in the quantity of money.***

Quantity Theory of Money Demand

Because the quantity theory of money tells us how much money is held for a given amount of aggregate income, it is in fact a theory of the demand for money. We can see this by dividing both sides of the equation of exchange by V, thus rewriting it as

$$M = \frac{1}{V} \times PY$$

where nominal income $P \times Y$ is written as PY. When the money market is in equilibrium, the quantity of money M that people hold equals the quantity of money demanded M^d, so we can replace M in the equation by M^d. Using k to represent the quantity $1/V$ (a constant because V is a constant), we can rewrite the equation as

$$M^d = k \times PY \qquad (3)$$

Equation 3 tells us that because k is a constant, the level of transactions generated by a fixed level of nominal income PY determines the quantity of money M^d that people demand. Therefore, Fisher's quantity theory of money suggests that the demand for money is purely a function of income, and interest rates have no effect on the demand for money.

Fisher came to this conclusion because he believed that people hold money only to conduct transactions and have no freedom of action in terms of the amount they want to hold. The demand for money is determined (1) by the level of transactions generated by the level of nominal income PY and (2) by the institutions in the economy that affect the way people conduct transactions that determine velocity and hence k.

CAMBRIDGE APPROACH TO MONEY DEMAND

While Fisher was developing his quantity theory approach to the demand for money, a group of classical economists in Cambridge, England, which included Alfred Marshall and A. C. Pigou, were studying the same topic. Although their analysis led them to an equation identical to Fisher's money demand equation ($M^d = k \times PY$), their approach differed significantly. Instead of studying the demand for money by looking solely at the level of transactions and the institutions that affect the way people conduct transactions as the key determinants, the Cambridge economists asked how much money individuals would want to hold, given a set of circumstances. In the Cambridge model, then, individuals are allowed some flexibility in their decision to hold money and are not completely bound by institutional constraints such as whether they can use credit cards to make purchases. Accordingly, the Cambridge approach did not rule out the effects of interest rates on the demand for money.

The classical Cambridge economists recognized that two properties of money motivate people to want to hold it: its utility as a *medium of exchange* and as a store of wealth.

Because it is a medium of exchange, people can use money to carry out transactions. The Cambridge economists agreed with Fisher that the demand for money would be related to (but not determined solely by) the level of transactions and that there would be a transactions component of money demand proportional to nominal income.

That money also functions as a store of wealth led the Cambridge economists to suggest that the level of people's wealth also affects the demand for money. As wealth grows, an individual needs to store it by holding a larger quantity of assets—one of which is money. Because the Cambridge economists believed that wealth in nominal terms is proportional to nominal income, they also believed that the wealth component of money demand is proportional to nominal income.

The Cambridge economists concluded that the demand for money would be proportional to nominal income and expressed the demand for money function as

$$M^d = k \times PY$$

where k is the constant of proportionality. Because this equation looks just like Fisher's (Equation 3), it would seem that the Cambridge group agreed with Fisher that interest rates play no role in the demand for money in the short run. However, that is not the case.

Although the Cambridge economists often treated k as a constant and agreed with Fisher that nominal income is determined by the quantity of money, their approach allowed individuals to choose how much money they wished to hold. It allowed for the possibility that k could fluctuate in the short run because the decisions about using money to store wealth would depend on the yields and expected returns on other assets that also function as stores of wealth. If these characteristics of other assets changed, k might change too. Although this seems a minor distinction between the Fisher and Cambridge approaches, you will see that when John Maynard Keynes (a later Cambridge economist) extended the Cambridge approach, he arrived at a very different view from the quantity theorists on the importance of interest rates to the demand for money.

To summarize, both Irving Fisher and the Cambridge economists developed a classical approach to the demand for money in which the demand for money is proportional to income. However, the two approaches differ in that Fisher's emphasized technological factors and ruled out any possible effect of interest rates on the demand for money in the short run, whereas the Cambridge approach emphasized individual choice and did not rule out the effects of interest rates.

IS VELOCITY A CONSTANT?

The classical economists' conclusion that nominal income is determined by movements in the money supply rested on their belief that velocity PY/M could be treated as reasonably constant.[3] Is it reasonable to assume that velocity is constant? To answer this, let's look at Figure 1, which shows the year-to-year changes in velocity from 1915 to 1996 (nominal income is represented by nominal GDP and the money supply by M1 and M2).

What we see in Figure 1 is that even in the short run, velocity fluctuates too much to be viewed as a constant. Prior to 1950, velocity exhibited large swings up and down. This may reflect the substantial instability of the economy in this period, which included two world wars and the Great Depression. (Velocity actually falls, or at least its rate of growth declines, in years when recessions are taking place.) After 1950, velocity appears to have more moderate fluctuations, yet there are large differences in the growth rate of velocity from year to year. The percentage change in M1 velocity (GDP/M1) from 1981 to 1982, for example, was −2.5 percent, whereas from 1980 to 1981 velocity grew at a rate of 4.2 percent. This difference of 6.7 percent means that nominal GDP was 6.7 percent lower

---

[3]Actually, the classical conclusion still holds if velocity grows at some uniform rate over time that reflects changes in transaction technology. Hence the concept of a constant velocity should more accurately be thought of here as a lack of upward and downward fluctuations in velocity.

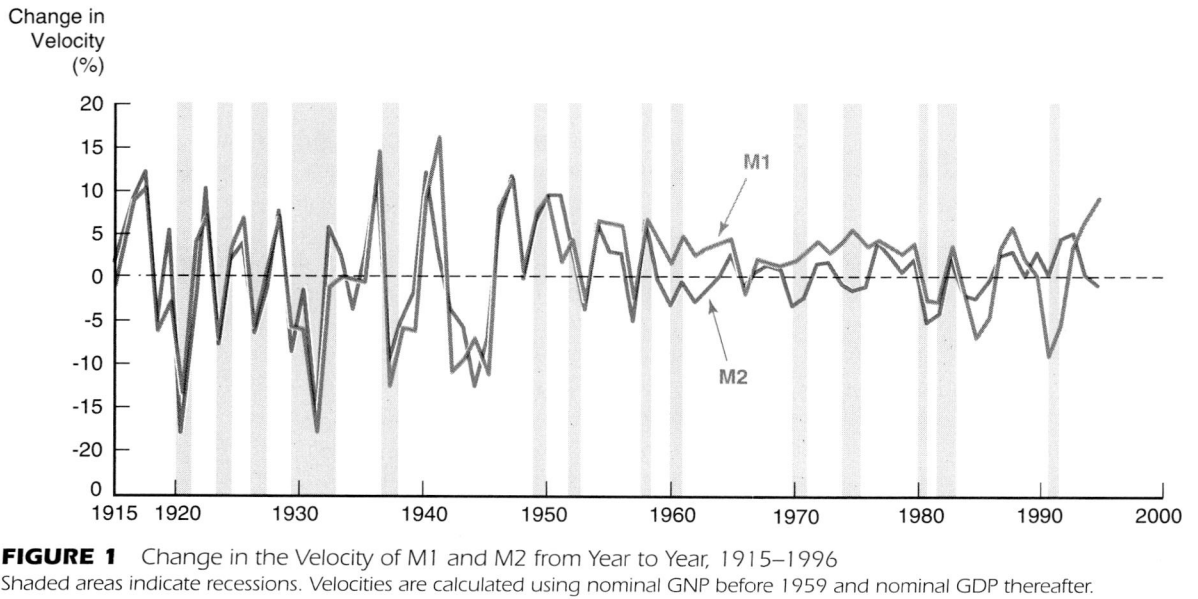

FIGURE 1 Change in the Velocity of M1 and M2 from Year to Year, 1915–1996

Shaded areas indicate recessions. Velocities are calculated using nominal GNP before 1959 and nominal GDP thereafter.

Sources: Economic Report of the President; Banking and Monetary Statistics; Citibase databank.

than it would have been if velocity had kept growing at the same rate as in 1980–1981.[4] The drop is enough to account for the severe recession that took place in 1981–1982. After 1982, M1 velocity appears to have become even more volatile, a fact that has puzzled researchers when they examine the empirical evidence on the demand for money (discussed later in this chapter). M2 velocity remained more stable than M1 velocity after 1982, with the result that the Federal Reserve dropped its M1 targets in 1987 and began to focus more on M2 targets. However, instability of M2 velocity in the early 1990s resulted in the Fed's announcement in July 1993 that it no longer felt that any of the monetary aggregates, including M2, was a reliable guide for monetary policy.

Until the Great Depression, economists did not recognize that velocity declines sharply during severe economic contractions. Why did the classical economists not recognize this fact when it is easy to see in the pre-depression period in Figure 1? Unfortunately, accurate data on GDP and the money supply did not exist before World War II. (Only after the war did the government start to collect these data.) Economists had no way of knowing that their view of velocity as a constant was demonstrably false. The decline in velocity during the Great Depression years was so great, however, that even the crude data available to

---

[4]We reach a similar conclusion if we use M2 velocity. The percentage change in M2 velocity (GDP/M2) from 1981 to 1982 was −5.0 percent, whereas from 1980 to 1981 it was +2.3 percent. This difference of 7.3 percent means that nominal GDP was 7.3 percent lower than it would have been if M2 velocity had kept growing at the same rate as in 1980–1981.

economists at that time suggested that velocity was not constant. This explains why, after the Great Depression, economists began to search for other factors influencing the demand for money that might help explain the large fluctuations in velocity.

Let us now examine the theories of money demand that arose from this search for a better explanation of the behavior of velocity.

KEYNES'S LIQUIDITY PREFERENCE THEORY

In his famous 1936 book *The General Theory of Employment, Interest and Money,* John Maynard Keynes abandoned the classical view that velocity was a constant and developed a theory of money demand that emphasized the importance of interest rates. Keynes, at Cambridge at the time, naturally enough followed the approach developed by his Cambridge predecessors. His theory of the demand for money, which he called the **liquidity preference theory,** also asked the question, Why do individuals hold money? But Keynes was far more precise than his predecessors regarding what influences the individuals' decisions. He postulated that there are three motives behind the demand for money: the transactions motive, the precautionary motive, and the speculative motive.

Transactions Motive

In both the Fisher and Cambridge classical approaches, individuals are assumed to hold money because it is a medium of exchange that can be used to carry out everyday transactions. Following the classical tradition, Keynes emphasized that this component of the demand for money is determined primarily by the level of people's transactions. Because he believed that these transactions were proportional to income, like the classical economists, he took the transactions component of the demand for money to be proportional to income.

Precautionary Motive

Keynes went beyond the classical analysis by recognizing that in addition to holding money to carry out current transactions, people hold money as a cushion against an unexpected need. Suppose that you've been thinking about buying a fancy stereo; you walk by a store that is having a 50 percent-off sale on the one you want. If you are holding money as a precaution for just such an occurrence, you can purchase the stereo right away; if you are not holding precautionary money balances, you cannot take advantage of the sale. Precautionary money balances also come in handy if you are hit with an unexpected bill, say, for car repair or hospitalization.

Keynes believed that the amount of precautionary money balances people want to hold is determined primarily by the level of transactions that they expect to make in the future and that these transactions are proportional to income. Therefore, he postulated, the demand for precautionary money balances is proportional to income.

Speculative Motive

If Keynes had ended his theory with the transactions and precautionary motives, income would be the only important determinant of the demand for money, and he would not have added much to the Cambridge approach. However, Keynes agreed with the classical Cambridge economists that money is a store of wealth and called this reason for holding money the speculative motive. Since he also agreed with the classical Cambridge economists that wealth is tied closely to income, the speculative component of money demand would be related to income. However, Keynes looked more carefully at the factors that influence the decisions regarding how much money to hold as a store of wealth. Unlike the classical Cambridge economists, who were willing to treat the wealth component of money demand as proportional to income, Keynes believed that interest rates, too, have an important role to play.

Keynes divided the assets that can be used to store wealth into two categories: money and bonds. He then asked the following question: Why would individuals decide to hold their wealth in the form of money rather than bonds?

Thinking back to the discussion of the theory of portfolio choice (Chapter 5), you would want to hold money if its expected return was greater than the expected return from holding bonds. Keynes assumed that the expected return on money was zero because in his time, unlike today, most checkable deposits did not earn interest. For bonds, there are two components of the expected return: the interest payment and the *expected* rate of capital gains.

You learned in Chapter 4 that when interest rates rise, the price of a bond falls. If you expect interest rates to rise, you expect the price of the bond to fall and therefore suffer a negative capital gain—that is, a capital loss. If you expect the rise in interest rates to be substantial enough, the capital loss might outweigh the interest payment, and your *expected* return on the bond would be negative. In this case, you would want to store your wealth as money because its expected return is higher; its zero return exceeds the negative return on the bond.

Keynes assumed that individuals believe that interest rates gravitate to some normal value (an assumption less plausible in today's world). If interest rates are below this normal value, individuals expect the interest rate on bonds to rise in the future and so expect to suffer capital losses on them. As a result, individuals will be more likely to hold their wealth as money rather than bonds, and the demand for money will be high.

What would you expect to happen to the demand for money when interest rates are above the normal value? In general, people will expect interest rates to fall, bond prices to rise, and capital gains to be realized. At higher interest rates, they are more likely to expect the return from holding a bond to be positive, thus exceeding the expected return from holding money. They will be more likely to hold bonds than money, and the demand for money will be quite low. From Keynes's reasoning we can conclude that as interest rates rise, the demand for money falls, and therefore ***money demand is negatively related to the level of interest rates.***

Putting the Three Motives Together

In putting the three motives for holding money balances together into a demand for money equation, Keynes was careful to distinguish between nominal quantities and real quantities. Money is valued in terms of what it can buy. If, for example, all prices in the economy double (the price level doubles), the same nominal quantity of money will be able to buy only half as many goods. Keynes thus reasoned that people want to hold a certain amount of **real money balances** (the quantity of money in real terms)—an amount that his three motives indicated would be related to real income Y and to interest rates i.[5] Keynes wrote down the following demand for money equation, known as the *liquidity preference function*, which says that the demand for real money balances M^d/P is a function of (related to) i and Y:

$$\frac{M^d}{P} = f(\underset{-}{i}, \underset{+}{Y}) \tag{4}$$

The minus sign below i in the liquidity preference function means that the demand for real money balances is negatively related to the interest rate i, and the plus sign below Y means that the demand for real money balances and real income Y are positively related. This money demand function is the same one that was used in our analysis of money demand discussed in Chapter 6.

Keynes's conclusion that the demand for money is related not only to income but also to interest rates is a major departure from Fisher's view of money demand, in which interest rates can have no effect on the demand for money, but it is less of a departure from the Cambridge approach, which did not rule out possible effects of interest rates. However, the classical Cambridge economists did not explore the explicit effects of interest rates on the demand for money.

By deriving the liquidity preference function for velocity PY/M, we can see that Keynes's theory of the demand for money implies that velocity is not constant but instead fluctuates with movements in interest rates. The liquidity preference equation can be rewritten as

$$\frac{P}{M^d} = \frac{1}{f(i, Y)}$$

Multiplying both sides of this equation by Y and recognizing that M^d can be replaced by M because they must be equal in money market equilibrium, we solve for velocity:

$$V = \frac{PY}{M} = \frac{Y}{f(i, Y)} \tag{5}$$

We know that the demand for money is negatively related to interest rates; when i goes up, $f(i, Y)$ declines, and therefore velocity rises. In other words, a rise in interest rates encourages people to hold lower real money balances for a given level of income; therefore, the rate of turnover of money (velocity) must be higher. This reasoning implies that because interest rates have substantial fluctuations, the liquidity preference theory of the demand for money indicates that velocity has substantial fluctuations as well.

---

[5]The classical economists' money demand equation can also be written in terms of real money balances by dividing both sides of Equation 3 by the price level P to obtain

$$\frac{M^d}{P} = k \times Y$$

An interesting feature of Equation 5 is that it explains some of the velocity movements in Figure 1, in which we noted that when recessions occur, velocity falls or its rate of growth declines. What fact regarding the cyclical behavior of interest rates that we discussed in Chapter 6 might help us explain this phenomenon? You might recall that interest rates are procyclical, rising in expansions and falling in recessions. The liquidity preference theory indicates that a rise in interest rates will cause velocity to rise also. The procyclical movements of interest rates should induce procyclical movements in velocity, and that is exactly what we see in Figure 1.

Keynes's model of the speculative demand for money provides another reason why velocity might show substantial fluctuations. What would happen to the demand for money if the view of the normal level of interest rates changes? For example, what if people expect the future normal interest rate to be higher than the current normal interest rate? Because interest rates are then expected to be higher in the future, more people will expect the prices of bonds to fall and anticipate capital losses. The expected returns from holding bonds will decline, and money will become more attractive relative to bonds. As a result, the demand for money will increase. This means that $f(i, Y)$ will increase and so velocity will fall. Velocity will change as expectations about future normal levels of interest rates change, and unstable expectations about future movements in normal interest rates can lead to instability of velocity. This is one more reason why Keynes rejected the view that velocity could be treated as a constant.

Study Guide Keynes's explanation of how interest rates affect the demand for money will be easier to understand if you think of yourself as an investor who is trying to decide whether to invest in bonds or to hold money. Ask yourself what you would do if you expected the normal interest rate to be lower in the future than it is currently. Would you rather be holding bonds or money?

To sum up, Keynes's liquidity preference theory is an extension of the classical Cambridge approach but is far more precise about the reasons why people hold money. Specifically, Keynes postulated three motives for holding money: the transactions motive, the precautionary motive, and the speculative motive. Although Keynes took the transactions and precautionary components of the demand for money to be proportional to income, he reasoned that the speculative motive would be negatively related to the level of interest rates.

Keynes's model of the demand for money has the important implication that velocity is not constant but instead is positively related to interest rates, which fluctuate substantially. His theory also rejected the constancy of velocity because changes in people's expectations about the normal level of interest rates would cause shifts in the demand for money that would cause velocity to shift as well. Thus Keynes's liquidity preference theory casts doubt on the classical quantity theory that nominal income is determined primarily by movements in the quantity of money.

FURTHER DEVELOPMENTS IN THE KEYNESIAN APPROACH

After World War II, economists began to take the Keynesian approach to the demand for money even further by developing more precise theories to explain the three Keynesian motives for holding money. Because interest rates were viewed as a crucial element in monetary theory, a key focus of this research was to understand better the role of interest rates in the demand for money.

Transactions Demand

William Baumol and James Tobin independently developed similar demand for money models, which demonstrated that even money balances held for transactions purposes are sensitive to the level of interest rates.[6] In developing their models, they considered a hypothetical individual who receives a payment once a period and spends it over the course of this period. In their model, money, which earns zero interest, is held only because it can be used to carry out transactions.

To refine this analysis, let's say that Grant Smith receives $1000 at the beginning of the month and spends it on transactions that occur at a constant rate during the course of the month. If Grant keeps the $1000 in cash in order to carry out his transactions, his money balances follow the sawtooth pattern displayed in Figure 2. At the beginning of the month he has $1000, and by the end of the

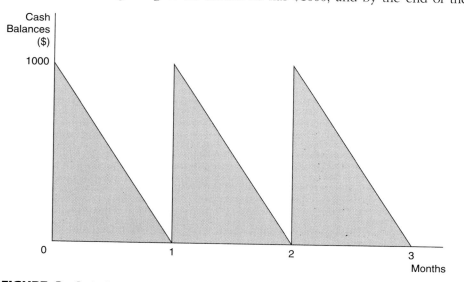

FIGURE 2 *Cash Balances for an Individual Who Keeps the Entire Monthly Payment in Cash*

The $1000 payment at the beginning of each month is held entirely as cash and is spent at a constant rate until it is exhausted by the end of the month. At this point, a new $1000 payment is received, and the whole process begins again.

---

[6]William J. Baumol, "The Transactions Demand for Cash: An Inventory Theoretic Approach," *Quarterly Journal of Economics* 66 (1952): 545–556; James Tobin, "The Interest Elasticity of the Transactions Demand for Cash," *Review of Economics and Statistics* 38 (1956): 241–247.

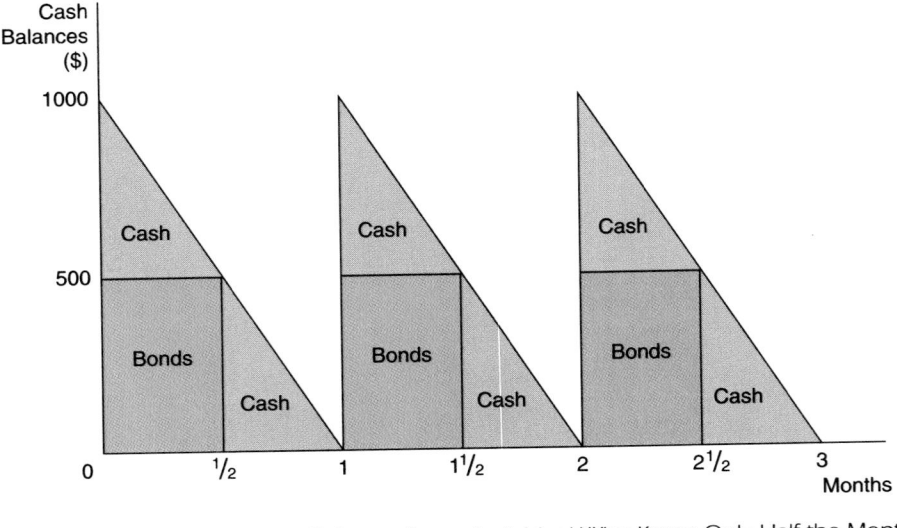

FIGURE 3 Cash and Bond Balances for an Individual Who Keeps Only Half the Monthly Payment in Cash
Half of a monthly $1000 payment is put into bonds, and half is held as cash. At the middle of the month, cash balances reach zero, and bonds must be sold to bring balances up to $500. By the end of the month, cash balances dwindle to zero.

month he has no cash left because he has spent it all. Over the course of the month, his holdings of money will on average be $500 (his holdings at the beginning of the month, $1000, plus his holdings at the end of the month, $0, divided by 2).

At the beginning of the next month, Grant receives another $1000 payment, which he holds as cash, and the same decline in money balances begins again. This process repeats monthly, and his average money balance during the course of the year is $500. Since his yearly nominal income is $12,000 and his holdings of money average $500, the velocity of money ($V = PY/M$) is $12,000/$500 = 24.

Suppose that as a result of taking a money and banking course, Grant realizes that he can improve his situation by not always holding cash. In January, then, he decides to hold part of his $1000 in cash and puts part of it into an income-earning security such as bonds. At the beginning of each month, Grant keeps $500 in cash and uses the other $500 to buy a Treasury bond. As you can see in Figure 3, he starts out each month with $500 of cash and $500 of bonds, and by the middle of the month, his cash balance has run down to zero. Because bonds cannot be used directly to carry out transactions, Grant must sell them and turn them into cash so that he can carry out the rest of the month's transactions. At the middle of the month, then, Grant's bond holdings drop to zero and his cash balance rises back up to $500. By the end of the month, the cash is gone. When he again receives his next $1000 monthly payment, he again divides it into $500 of cash and $500 of bonds, and the process continues. The net result of this process is that the average cash balance held during the month is $500/2 = $250 —just half of what it was before. Velocity has doubled to $12,000/$250 = 48.

What has Grant Smith gained from his new strategy? He has earned interest on $500 of bonds that he held for half the month. If the interest rate is 1 percent per month, he has earned an additional $2.50 (= $\frac{1}{2}$ × $500 × 1 percent) per month.

Sounds like a pretty good deal, doesn't it? In fact, if he had kept $333.33 in cash at the beginning of the month, he would have been able to hold $666.67 in bonds for the first third of the month. Then he could have sold $333.33 of bonds and held on to $333.34 of bonds for the next third of the month. Finally, two-thirds of the way through the month, he would have had to sell the remaining bonds to raise cash. The net result of this is that Grant would have earned $3.33 per month [= ($\frac{1}{3}$ × $666.67 × 1 percent) + ($\frac{1}{3}$ × $333.34 × 1 percent)]. This is an even better deal. His average cash holdings in this case would be $333.33/2 = $166.67. Clearly, the lower his average cash balance, the more interest he will earn.

As you might expect, there is a catch to all this. In buying bonds, Grant incurs transaction costs of two types. First, he must pay a straight brokerage fee for the buying and selling of the bonds. These fees increase when average cash balances are lower because Grant will be buying and selling bonds more often. Second, by holding less cash, he will have to make more trips to the bank to get the cash, once he has sold some of his bonds. Because time is money, this must also be counted as part of the transaction costs.

Grant faces a trade-off. If he holds very little cash, he can earn a lot of interest on bonds, but he will incur greater transaction costs. If the interest rate is high, the benefits of holding bonds will be high relative to the transaction costs, and he will hold more bonds and less cash. Conversely, if interest rates are low, the transaction costs involved in holding a lot of bonds may outweigh the interest payments, and Grant would then be better off holding more cash and fewer bonds.

The conclusion of the Baumol-Tobin analysis may be stated as follows: As interest rates increase, the amount of cash held for transactions purposes will decline, which in turn means that velocity will increase as interest rates increase.[7] Put another way, the ***transactions component of the demand for money is negatively related to the level of interest rates.***

The basic idea in the Baumol-Tobin analysis is that there is an opportunity cost of holding money—the interest that can be earned on other assets. There is also a benefit to holding money—the avoidance of transaction costs. When interest rates increase, people will try to economize on their holdings of money for transactions purposes because the opportunity cost of holding money has increased. By using simple models, Baumol and Tobin revealed something that we might not otherwise have seen: that the transactions demand for money, and

---

[7]Similar reasoning leads to the conclusion that as brokerage fees increase, the demand for transactions money balances increases as well. When these fees rise, the benefits from holding transactions money balances increase because by holding these balances, an individual will not have to sell bonds as often, thereby avoiding these higher brokerage costs. The greater benefits to holding money balances relative to the opportunity cost of interest forgone, then, lead to a higher demand for transactions balances.

not just the speculative demand, will be sensitive to interest rates. The Baumol-Tobin analysis presents a nice demonstration of the value of economic modeling.

Study Guide The idea that as interest rates increase, the opportunity cost of holding money increases so that the demand for money falls can be stated equivalently with the terminology of expected returns used earlier. As interest rates increase, the expected return on the other asset, bonds, increases, causing the relative expected return on money to fall, thereby lowering the demand for money. These two explanations are in fact identical because as we saw in Chapter 6, changes in the opportunity cost of an asset are just a description of what is happening to the relative expected return. The opportunity cost terminology was used by Baumol and Tobin in their work on the transactions demand for money, and that is why we used this terminology in the text. To make sure you understand the equivalence of the two terminologies, try to translate the reasoning in the precautionary demand discussion from opportunity cost terminology to expected returns terminology.

Precautionary Demand

Models that explore the precautionary motive of the demand for money have been developed along lines similar to the Baumol-Tobin framework, so we will not go into great detail about them here. We have already discussed the benefits of holding precautionary money balances, but weighed against these benefits must be the opportunity cost of the interest forgone by holding money. We therefore have a trade-off similar to the one for transactions balances. As interest rates rise, the opportunity cost of holding precautionary balances rises, and so the holdings of these money balances fall. We then have a result similar to the one found for the Baumol-Tobin analysis.[8] ***The precautionary demand for money is negatively related to interest rates.***

Speculative Demand

Keynes's analysis of the speculative demand for money was open to several serious criticisms. It indicated that an individual holds only money as a store of wealth when the expected return on bonds is less than the expected return on money and holds only bonds when the expected return on bonds is greater than the expected return on money. Solely in the rare instance when people have expected returns on bonds and money that are exactly equal would they hold both. Keynes's analysis therefore implies that practically no one holds a diversified portfolio of bonds and money simultaneously as a store of wealth. Since diversification is apparently a sensible strategy for choosing which assets to hold (recall Chapter 5), the fact that it rarely occurs in Keynes's analysis is a serious shortcoming of his theory of the speculative demand for money.

---

[8]These models of the precautionary demand for money also reveal that as uncertainty about the level of future transactions grows, the precautionary demand for money increases. This is so because greater uncertainty means that individuals are more likely to incur transaction costs if they are not holding precautionary balances. The benefit of holding such balances then increases relative to the opportunity cost of forgone interest, and so the demand for them rises.

Tobin developed a model of the speculative demand for money that attempted to avoid this criticism of Keynes's analysis.[9] His basic idea was that not only do people care about the expected return on one asset versus another when they decide what to hold in their portfolio, but they also care about the riskiness of the returns from each asset. Specifically, Tobin assumed that most people are risk-averse—that they would be willing to hold an asset with a lower expected return if it is less risky. An important characteristic of money is that its return is certain; Tobin assumed it to be zero. Bonds, by contrast, can have substantial fluctuations in price, and their returns can be quite risky and sometimes negative. So even if the expected returns on bonds exceed the expected return on money, people might still want to hold money as a store of wealth because it has less risk associated with its return than bonds do.

The Tobin analysis also shows that people can reduce the total amount of risk in a portfolio by diversifying, that is, by holding both bonds and money. The model suggests that individuals will hold bonds and money simultaneously as stores of wealth. Since this is probably a more realistic description of people's behavior than Keynes's, Tobin's rationale for the speculative demand for money seems to rest on more solid ground.

Tobin's attempt to improve on Keynes's rationale for the speculative demand for money was only partly successful, however. It is still not clear that the speculative demand even exists. What if there are assets that have no risk—like money—but earn a higher return? Will there be any speculative demand for money? No, because an individual will always be better off holding such an asset rather than money. The resulting portfolio will enjoy a higher expected return yet has no higher risk. Do such assets exist in the American economy? The answer is yes. U.S. Treasury bills, money market mutual fund shares, and other assets that have no default risk provide certain returns that are greater than those available on money. Therefore, why would anyone want to hold money balances as a store of wealth (ignoring for the moment transactions and precautionary reasons)?

Although Tobin's analysis did not explain why money is held as a store of wealth, it was an important development in our understanding of how people should choose among assets. Indeed, his analysis was an important step in the development of the academic field of finance, which examines asset pricing and portfolio choice (the decision to buy one asset over another).

To sum up, further developments of the Keynesian approach have attempted to give a more precise explanation for the transactions, precautionary, and speculative demand for money. The attempt to improve Keynes's rationale for the speculative demand for money has been only partly successful; it is still not clear that this demand even exists. However, the models of the transactions and precautionary demand for money indicate that these components of money demand are negatively related to interest rates. Hence Keynes's proposition that the demand for money is sensitive to interest rates—suggesting that velocity is not constant and that nominal income might be affected by factors other than the quantity of money—is still supported.

---

[9]James Tobin, "Liquidity Preference as Behavior Towards Risk," *Review of Economic Studies* 25 (1958): 65–86.

FRIEDMAN'S MODERN QUANTITY THEORY OF MONEY

In 1956, Milton Friedman developed a theory of the demand for money in a famous article, "The Quantity Theory of Money: A Restatement."[10] Although Friedman frequently refers to Irving Fisher and the quantity theory, his analysis of the demand for money is actually closer to that of Keynes and the Cambridge economists than it is to Fisher's.

Like his predecessors, Friedman pursued the question of why people choose to hold money. Instead of analyzing the specific motives for holding money, as Keynes did, Friedman simply stated that the demand for money must be influenced by the same factors that influence the demand for any asset. Friedman then applied the theory of portfolio choice to money.

The theory of portfolio choice (Chapter 5) indicates that the demand for money should be a function of the resources available to individuals (their wealth) and the expected returns on other assets relative to the expected return on money. Like Keynes, Friedman recognized that people want to hold a certain amount of real money balances (the quantity of money in real terms). From this reasoning, Friedman expressed his formulation of the demand for money as follows:

$$\frac{M^d}{P} = f(\underset{+}{Y_p},\ \underset{-}{r_b - r_m},\ \underset{-}{r_e - r_m},\ \underset{-}{\pi^e - r_m}) \tag{6}$$

where M^d/P = demand for real money balances

Y_p = Friedman's measure of wealth, known as *permanent income* (technically, the present discounted value of all expected future income, but more easily described as expected average long-run income)

r_m = expected return on money

r_b = expected return on bonds

r_e = expected return on equity (common stocks)

π^e = expected inflation rate

and the signs underneath the equation indicate whether the demand for money is positively $(+)$ related or negatively $(-)$ related to the terms that are immediately above them.[11]

Let us look in more detail at the variables in Friedman's money demand function and what they imply for the demand for money.

Because the demand for an asset is positively related to wealth, money demand is positively related to Friedman's wealth concept, permanent income

---

[10]Milton Friedman, "The Quantity Theory of Money: A Restatement," in *Studies in the Quantity Theory of Money*, ed. Milton Friedman (Chicago: University of Chicago Press, 1956), pp. 3–21.

[11]Friedman also added to his formulation a term h that represented the ratio of human to nonhuman wealth. He reasoned that if people had more permanent income coming from labor income and thus from their human capital, they would be less liquid than if they were receiving income from financial assets. In this case, they might want to hold more money because it is a more liquid asset than the alternatives. The term h plays no essential role in Friedman's theory and has no important implications for monetary theory. That is why we ignore it in the money demand function.

(indicated by the plus sign beneath it). Unlike our usual concept of income, permanent income (which can be thought of as expected average long-run income) has much smaller short-run fluctuations because many movements of income are transitory (short-lived). For example, in a business cycle expansion, income increases rapidly, but because some of this increase is temporary, average long-run income does not change very much. Hence in a boom, permanent income rises much less than income. During a recession, much of the income decline is transitory, and average long-run income (hence permanent income) falls less than income. One implication of Friedman's use of the concept of permanent income as a determinant of the demand for money is that the demand for money will not fluctuate much with business cycle movements.

An individual can hold wealth in several forms besides money; Friedman categorized them into three types of assets: bonds, equity (common stocks), and goods. The incentives for holding these assets rather than money are represented by the expected return on each of these assets relative to the expected return on money, the last three terms in the money demand function. The minus sign beneath each indicates that as each term rises, the demand for money will fall.

The expected return on money r_m, which appears in all three terms, is influenced by two factors:

1. The services provided by banks on deposits included in the money supply, such as provision of receipts in the form of canceled checks or the automatic paying of bills. When these services are increased, the expected return from holding money rises.
2. The interest payments on money balances. NOW accounts and other deposits that are included in the money supply currently pay interest. As these interest payments rise, the expected return on money rises.

The terms $r_b - r_m$ and $r_e - r_m$ represent the expected return on bonds and equity relative to money; as they rise, the relative expected return on money falls, and the demand for money falls. The final term, $\pi^e - r_m$, represents the expected return on goods relative to money. The expected return from holding goods is the expected rate of capital gains that occurs when their prices rise and hence is equal to the expected inflation rate π^e. If the expected inflation rate is 10 percent, for example, then goods' prices are expected to rise at a 10 percent rate, and their expected return is 10 percent. When $\pi^e - r_m$ rises, the expected return on goods relative to money rises, and the demand for money falls.

DISTINGUISHING BETWEEN THE FRIEDMAN AND KEYNESIAN THEORIES

There are several differences between Friedman's theory of the demand for money and the Keynesian theories. One is that by including many assets as alternatives to money, Friedman recognized that more than one interest rate is important to the operation of the aggregate economy. Keynes, for his part, lumped financial assets other than money into one big category—bonds—because he felt that their returns generally move together. If this is so, the expected return on bonds will be a good indicator of the expected return on other financial assets, and there will be no need to include them separately in the money demand function.

Also in contrast to Keynes, Friedman viewed money and goods as substitutes; that is, people choose between them when deciding how much money to hold. That is why Friedman included the expected return on goods relative to money as a term in his money demand function. The assumption that money and goods are substitutes indicates that changes in the quantity of money may have a direct effect on aggregate spending.

In addition, Friedman stressed two issues in discussing his demand for money function that distinguish it from Keynes's liquidity preference theory. First, Friedman did not take the expected return on money to be a constant, as Keynes did. When interest rates rise in the economy, banks make more profits on their loans, and they want to attract more deposits to increase the volume of their now more profitable loans. If there are no restrictions on interest payments on deposits, banks attract deposits by paying higher interest rates on them. Because the industry is competitive, the expected return on money held as bank deposits then rises with the higher interest rates on bonds and loans. The banks compete to get deposits until there are no excess profits, and in doing so they close the gap between interest earned on loans and interest paid on deposits. The net result of this competition in the banking industry is that $r_b - r_m$ stays relatively constant when the interest rate i rises.[12]

What if there are restrictions on the amount of interest that banks can pay on their deposits? Will the expected return on money be a constant? As interest rates rise, will $r_b - r_m$ rise as well? Friedman thought not. He argued that although banks might be restricted from making pecuniary payments on their deposits, they can still compete on the quality dimension. For example, they can provide more services to depositors by providing more tellers, paying bills automatically, or providing more cash machines at more accessible locations. The result of these improvements in money services is that the expected return from holding deposits will rise. So despite the restrictions on pecuniary interest payments, we might still find that a rise in market interest rates will raise the expected return on money sufficiently so that $r_b - r_m$ will remain relatively constant.[13] ***Unlike Keynes's theory, which indicates that interest rates are an important determinant of the demand for money, Friedman's theory suggests that changes in interest rates should have little effect on the demand for money.***

Therefore, Friedman's money demand function is essentially one in which

---

[12]Friedman does suggest that there is some increase in $r_b - r_m$ when i rises because part of the money supply (especially currency) is held in forms that cannot pay interest in a pecuniary or nonpecuniary form. See, for example, Milton Friedman, "Why a Surge of Inflation Is Likely Next Year," *Wall Street Journal*, September 1, 1983, p. 24.

[13]Competing on the quality of services is characteristic of many industries that are restricted from competing on price. For example, in the 1960s and early 1970s, when airfares were set high by the Civil Aeronautics Board, airlines were not allowed to lower their fares to attract customers. Instead, they improved the quality of their service by providing free wine, fancier food, piano bars, movies, and wider seats.

permanent income is the primary determinant of money demand, and his money demand equation can be approximated by

$$\frac{M^d}{P} = f(Y_p) \tag{7}$$

In Friedman's view, the demand for money is insensitive to interest rates—not because he viewed the demand for money as insensitive to changes in the incentives for holding other assets relative to money but rather because changes in interest rates should have little effect on these incentive terms in the money demand function. The incentive terms remain relatively constant because any rise in the expected returns on other assets as a result of the rise in interest rates would be matched by a rise in the expected return on money.

The second issue Friedman stressed is the stability of the demand for money function. In contrast to Keynes, Friedman suggested that random fluctuations in the demand for money are small and that the demand for money can be predicted accurately by the money demand function. When combined with his view that the demand for money is insensitive to changes in interest rates, this means that velocity is highly predictable. We can see this by writing down the velocity that is implied by the money demand equation (7):

$$V = \frac{Y}{f(Y_p)} \tag{8}$$

Because the relationship between Y and Y_p is usually quite predictable, a stable money demand function (one that does not undergo pronounced shifts so that it predicts the demand for money accurately) implies that velocity is predictable as well. If we can predict what velocity will be in the next period, a change in the quantity of money will produce a predictable change in aggregate spending. Even though velocity is no longer assumed to be constant, the money supply continues to be the primary determinant of nominal income as in the quantity theory of money. Therefore, Friedman's theory of money demand is indeed a restatement of the quantity theory because it leads to the same conclusion about the importance of money to aggregate spending.

You might recall that we said that the Keynesian liquidity preference function (in which interest rates are an important determinant of the demand for money) is able to explain the procyclical movements of velocity that we find in the data. Can Friedman's money demand formulation explain this procyclical velocity phenomenon as well?

The key clue to answering this question is the presence of permanent income rather than measured income in the money demand function. What happens to permanent income in a business cycle expansion? Because much of the increase in income will be transitory, permanent income rises much less than income. Friedman's money demand function then indicates that the demand for money rises only a small amount relative to the rise in measured income, and as Equation 8 indicates, velocity rises. Similarly, in a recession, the demand for money falls less than income because the decline in permanent income is small relative to income, and velocity falls. In this way, we have the procyclical movement in velocity.

To summarize, Friedman's theory of the demand for money used a similar approach to that of Keynes and the earlier Cambridge economists but did not go into detail about the motives for holding money. Instead, Friedman made use of the theory of portfolio choice to indicate that the demand for money will be a function of permanent income and the expected returns on alternative assets relative to the expected return on money. There are two major differences between Friedman's theory and Keynes's. Friedman believed that changes in interest rates have little effect on the expected returns on other assets relative to money. Thus, in contrast to Keynes, he viewed the demand for money as insensitive to interest rates. In addition, he differed from Keynes in stressing that the money demand function does not undergo substantial shifts and so is stable. These two differences also indicate that velocity is predictable, yielding a quantity theory conclusion that money is the primary determinant of aggregate spending.

EMPIRICAL EVIDENCE ON THE DEMAND FOR MONEY

As we have seen, the alternative theories of the demand for money can have very different implications for our view of the role of money in the economy. Which of these theories is an accurate description of the real world is an important question, and it is the reason why evidence on the demand for money has been at the center of many debates on the effects of monetary policy on aggregate economic activity. Here we examine the empirical evidence on the two primary issues that distinguish the different theories of money demand and affect their conclusions about whether the quantity of money is the primary determinant of aggregate spending: Is the demand for money sensitive to changes in interest rates, and is the demand for money function stable over time?

Interest Rates and Money Demand

Earlier in the chapter we saw that if interest rates do not affect the demand for money, velocity is more likely to be a constant—or at least predictable—so that the quantity theory view that aggregate spending is determined by the quantity of money is more likely to be true. However, the more sensitive the demand for money is to interest rates, the more unpredictable velocity will be, and the link between the money supply and aggregate spending will be less clear. Indeed, there is an extreme case of ultrasensitivity of the demand for money to interest rates, called the *liquidity trap*, in which monetary policy has no effect on aggregate spending because a change in the money supply has no effect on interest rates. (If the demand for money is ultrasensitive to interest rates, a tiny change in interest rates produces a very large change in the quantity of money demanded. Hence in this case, the demand for money is completely flat in the supply and demand diagrams of Chapter 6. Therefore, a change in the money supply that shifts the money demand curve to the right or left only shifts the curve onto itself, leaving its position and the interest rate unchanged.)

James Tobin conducted one of the earliest studies on the link between interest rates and money demand using U.S. data.[14] Tobin separated out transactions balances from other money balances, which he called "idle balances," assuming

---

[14]James Tobin, "Liquidity Preference and Monetary Policy," *Review of Economics and Statistics* 29 (1947): 124–131.

that transactions balances were proportional to income only, and idle balances were related to interest rates only. He then looked at whether his measure of idle balances was inversely related to interest rates in the period 1922–1941 by plotting the average level of idle balances each year against the average interest rate on commercial paper that year. When he found a clear-cut inverse relationship between interest rates and idle balances, Tobin concluded that the demand for money is sensitive to interest rates.[15]

Additional empirical evidence on the demand for money strongly confirms Tobin's finding.[16] Does this sensitivity ever become so high that we approach the case of the liquidity trap in which monetary policy is ineffective? The answer is almost certainly no. Keynes suggested in *The General Theory* that a liquidity trap might occur when interest rates are extremely low. (However, he did state that he had never yet seen an occurrence of a liquidity trap.)

Typical of the evidence demonstrating that the liquidity trap has never occurred is that of David Laidler, Karl Brunner, and Allan Meltzer, who looked at whether the interest sensitivity of money demand increased in periods when interest rates were very low.[17] Laidler and Meltzer looked at this question by seeing if the interest sensitivity of money demand differed across periods, especially in periods such as the 1930s when interest rates were particularly low.[18] They found that there was no tendency for interest sensitivity to increase as interest rates fell—in fact, interest sensitivity did not change from period to period. Brunner and Meltzer explored this question by recognizing that higher interest sensitivity in the 1930s as a result of a liquidity trap implies that a money demand function estimated for this period should not predict well in more normal periods. What Brunner and Meltzer found was that a money demand function, estimated mostly with data from the 1930s, accurately predicted the demand for money in the 1950s. This result provided little evidence in favor of the existence of a liquidity trap during the Great Depression period.

The evidence on the interest sensitivity of the demand for money found by different researchers is remarkably consistent. Neither extreme case is supported

---

[15]A problem with Tobin's procedure is that idle balances are not really distinguishable from transactions balances. As the Baumol-Tobin model of transactions demand for money makes clear, transactions balances will be related to both income and interest rates, just like idle balances.

[16]See David E. W. Laidler, *The Demand for Money: Theories and Evidence,* 4th ed. (New York: HarperCollins, 1993). Only one major study has found that the demand for money is insensitive to interest rates: Milton Friedman, "The Demand for Money: Some Theoretical and Empirical Results," *Journal of Political Economy* 67 (1959): 327–351. He concluded that the demand for money is not sensitive to interest-rate movements, but as later work by David Laidler (using the same data as Friedman) demonstrated, Friedman used a faulty statistical procedure that biased his results: David Laidler, "The Rate of Interest and the Demand for Money: Some Empirical Evidence," *Journal of Political Economy* 74 (1966): 545–555. When Laidler employed the correct statistical procedure, he found the usual result that the demand for money is sensitive to interest rates. In later work, Friedman has also concluded that the demand for money is sensitive to interest rates.

[17]David E. W. Laidler, "Some Evidence on the Demand for Money," *Journal of Political Economy* 74 (1966): 55–68; Allan H. Meltzer, "The Demand for Money: The Evidence from the Time Series," *Journal of Political Economy* 71 (1963): 219–246; Karl Brunner and Allan H. Meltzer, "Predicting Velocity: Implications for Theory and Policy," *Journal of Finance* 18 (1963): 319–354.

[18]Interest sensitivity is measured by the interest elasticity of money demand, which is defined as the percentage change in the demand for money divided by the percentage change in the interest rate.

by the data: The demand for money is sensitive to interest rates, but there is little evidence that a liquidity trap has ever existed.

Stability of Money Demand

If the money demand function, like Equation 4 or 6, is unstable and undergoes substantial unpredictable shifts, as Keynes thought, then velocity is unpredictable, and the quantity of money may not be tightly linked to aggregate spending, as it is in the modern quantity theory. The stability of the money demand function is also crucial to whether the Federal Reserve should target interest rates or the money supply (see Chapter 23). Thus it is important to look at the question of whether the money demand function is stable or not because it has important implications for how monetary policy should be conducted.

As our discussion of the Brunner and Meltzer article indicates, evidence on the stability of the demand for money function is related to the evidence on the existence of a liquidity trap. Brunner and Meltzer's finding that a money demand function estimated using data mostly from the 1930s predicted the demand for money well in the postwar period not only suggests that a liquidity trap did not exist in the 1930s but also indicates that the money demand function has been stable over long periods of time. The evidence that the interest sensitivity of the demand for money did not change from period to period also suggests that the money demand function is stable, since a changing interest sensitivity would mean that the demand for money function estimated in one period would not be able to predict well in another period.

By the early 1970s, the evidence using quarterly data from the postwar period strongly supported the stability of the money demand function when M1 was used as the definition of the money supply. For example, a well-known study by Stephen Goldfeld published in 1973 found not only that the interest sensitivity of M1 money demand did not undergo changes in the postwar period but also that the M1 money demand function predicted extremely well throughout the postwar period.[19] As a result of this evidence, the M1 money demand function became the conventional money demand function used by economists.

THE CASE OF THE MISSING MONEY The stability of the demand for money, then, was a well-established fact when, starting in 1974, the conventional M1 money demand function began to severely overpredict the demand for money. Stephen Goldfeld labeled this phenomenon of instability in the demand for money function "the case of the missing money."[20] It presented a serious challenge to the usefulness of the money demand function as a tool for understanding how monetary policy affects aggregate economic activity. In addition, it had important implications for how monetary policy should be conducted. As a result, the instability of the M1 money demand function stimulated an intense search for a solution to the mystery of the missing money so that a stable money demand function could be resurrected.

---

[19]Stephen M. Goldfeld, "The Demand for Money Revisited," *Brookings Papers on Economic Activity* 3 (1973): 577–638.

[20]Stephen M. Goldfeld, "The Case of the Missing Money," *Brookings Papers on Economic Activity* 3 (1976): 683–730.

The search for a stable money demand function took two directions. The first direction focused on whether an incorrect definition of money could be the reason why the demand for money function had become so unstable. Inflation, high nominal interest rates, and advances in computer technology, caused the payments mechanism and cash management techniques to undergo rapid changes after 1974. In addition, many new financial instruments emerged and have grown in importance. This has led some researchers to suspect that the rapid pace of financial innovation since 1974 has meant that the conventional definitions of the money supply no longer apply. They searched for a stable money demand function by actually looking directly for the missing money; that is, they looked for financial instruments that have been incorrectly left out of the definition of money used in the money demand function.

Overnight repurchase agreements (RPs) are one example. These are one-day loans with little default risk because they are structured to provide Treasury bills as collateral. (Chapter 2 gives a more detailed discussion of the structure of this type of loan.) Corporations with demand deposit accounts at commercial banks frequently loan out substantial amounts of their account balances overnight with these RPs, lowering the measures of the money supply. However, the amounts loaned out are very close substitutes for money, since the corporation can quickly make a decision to decrease these loans if it needs more money in its demand deposit account to pay its bills. Gillian Garcia and Simon Pak, for example, found that including overnight RPs in measures of the money supply substantially reduced the degree to which money demand functions overpredicted the money supply.[21] More recent evidence using later data has cast some doubt on whether including overnight RPs and other highly liquid assets in measures of the money supply produces money demand functions that are stable.[22]

The second direction of search for a stable money demand function was to look for new variables to include in the money demand function that will make it stable. Michael Hamburger, for example, found that including the average dividend-price ratio on common stocks (average dividends divided by average price) as a measure of their interest rate resulted in a money demand function that is stable.[23] Other researchers, such as Heller and Khan, added the entire term structure of interest rates to their money demand function and found that this produces a stable money demand function.[24]

These attempts to produce a stable money demand function have been criticized on the grounds that these additional variables do not accurately measure

[21]Gillian Garcia and Simon Pak, "Some Clues in the Case of the Missing Money," *American Economic Review* 69 (1979): 330–334.

[22]See the survey in John P. Judd and John L. Scadding, "The Search for a Stable Money Demand Function," *Journal of Economic Literature* 20 (1982): 993–1023.

[23]Michael Hamburger, "Behavior of the Money Stock: Is There a Puzzle?" *Journal of Monetary Economics* 3 (1977): 265–288. The stability of his money demand function also depends on his assumption that the income elasticity of the demand for money is unity. This assumption has been strongly criticized by many critics, including R. W. Hafer and Scott E. Hein, "Evidence on the Temporal Stability of the Demand for Money Relationship in the United States," Federal Reserve Bank of St. Louis *Review* (1979): 3–14, who find that this assumption is strongly rejected by the data.

[24]H. Heller and Moshin S. Khan, "The Demand for Money and the Term Structure of Interest Rates," *Journal of Political Economy* 87 (1979): 109–129.

the opportunity cost of holding money, and so the theoretical justification for including them in the money demand function is weak.[25] Also, later research questions whether these alterations to the money demand function will lead to continuing stability in the future.[26]

VELOCITY SLOWDOWN IN THE 1980S The woes of conventional money demand functions increased in the 1980s. We have seen that they overpredicted money demand in the middle and late 1970s; that is, they underpredicted velocity (PY/M), which rose faster than expected. The tables turned beginning in 1982; as can be seen in Figure 1, economists now faced a surprising slowdown in M1 velocity, which conventional money demand functions also could not predict. Although researchers have tried to explain this velocity slowdown, they have not been entirely successful.[27]

M2 TO THE RESCUE? As we saw in Figure 1, M2 velocity remained far more stable than M1 velocity in the 1980s. The relative stability of M2 velocity suggests that money demand functions in which the money supply is defined as M2 might perform substantially better than those in which the money supply is defined as M1. Researchers at the Federal Reserve found that M2 money demand functions performed well in the 1980s, with M2 velocity moving quite closely with the opportunity cost of holding M2 (market interest rates minus an average of the interest paid on deposits and financial instruments that make up M2).[28] However, in the early 1990s, M2 growth has shown a dramatic slowdown, which some researchers believe cannot be explained by traditional money demand functions.[29] Doubts continue to arise about the stability of money demand.

CONCLUSION The main conclusion from the research on the money demand function seems to be that the most likely cause of its instability is the rapid pace of financial innovation occurring after 1973, which has changed what items can be counted as money. The evidence is still somewhat tentative, however, and a truly stable and satisfactory money demand function has not yet been found. And so the search for a stable money demand function goes on.

---

[25]Frederic S. Mishkin, "Discussion of Asset Substitutability and the Impact of Federal Deficits," in *The Economic Consequences of Government Deficits,* ed. Laurence H. Meyer (Boston: Kluwer-Nijhoff, 1983), pp. 117–120; Frederic S. Mishkin, "Discussion of Recent Velocity Behavior: The Demand for Money and Monetary Policy," in *Monetary Targeting and Velocity* (San Francisco: Federal Reserve Bank of San Francisco, 1983), pp. 129–132.

[26]This research is discussed in Judd and Scadding (note 22).

[27]See, for example, Robert H. Rasche, "M1 Velocity and Money-Demand Functions: Do Stable Relationships Exist?" *Empirical Studies of Velocity, Real Exchange Rates, Unemployment and Productivity, Carnegie-Rochester Conference Series on Public Policy* 17 (Autumn 1987), pp. 9–88.

[28]See David H. Small and Richard D. Porter, "Understanding the Behavior of M2 and V2," *Federal Reserve Bulletin* 75 (1989): 244–254.

[29]See, for example, Bryon Higgins, "Policy Implications of Recent M2 Behavior," Federal Reserve Bank of Kansas City *Economic Review* (Third Quarter 1992): 21–36. For a contrary view, see Robert L. Hetzel, "How Useful Is M2 Today," Federal Reserve Bank of Richmond *Economic Review* (September-October 1992): 12–26.

The recent instability of the money demand function calls into question whether our theories and empirical analyses are adequate.[30] It also has important implications for the way monetary policy should be conducted because it casts doubt on the usefulness of the money demand function as a tool to provide guidance to policymakers. In particular, because the money demand function has become unstable, velocity is now harder to predict, and setting rigid money supply targets in order to control aggregate spending in the economy may not be an effective way to conduct monetary policy.

S U M M A R Y

1. Irving Fisher developed a transactions-based theory of the demand for money in which the demand for real balances is proportional to real income and is insensitive to interest-rate movements. An implication of his theory is that velocity, the rate of turnover of money, is constant. This generates the quantity theory of money, which implies that aggregate spending is determined solely by movements in the quantity of money.

2. The classical Cambridge approach tried to answer the question of how much money individuals want to hold. This approach also viewed the demand for real balances as proportional to real income, but it differs from Fisher's analysis in that it does not rule out interest-rate effects on the demand for money.

3. The classical view that velocity can be effectively treated as a constant is not supported by the data. The nonconstancy of velocity became especially clear to the economics profession after the sharp drop in velocity during the years of the Great Depression.

4. John Maynard Keynes extended the Cambridge approach by suggesting three motives for holding money: the transactions motive, the precautionary motive, and the speculative motive. His resulting liquidity preference theory views the transactions and precautionary components of money demand as proportional to income. However, the speculative component of money demand is viewed as sensitive to interest rates as well as to expectations about the

future movements of interest rates. This theory, then, implies that velocity is unstable and cannot be treated as a constant.

5. Further developments in the Keynesian approach provided a better rationale for the three Keynesian motives for holding money. Interest rates were found to be important to the transactions and precautionary components of money demand as well as to the speculative component.

6. Milton Friedman's theory of money demand used a similar approach to that of Keynes and the classical Cambridge economists. Treating money like any other asset, Friedman used the theory of portfolio choice to derive a demand for money that is a function of the expected returns on other assets relative to the expected return on money and permanent income. In contrast to Keynes, Friedman believed that the demand for money is stable and insensitive to interest-rate movements. His belief that velocity is predictable (though not constant) in turn leads to the quantity theory conclusion that money is the primary determinant of aggregate spending.

7. There are two main conclusions from the research on the demand for money: The demand for money is sensitive to interest rates, but there is little evidence that the liquidity trap has ever existed; and since 1973, money demand has been found to be unstable, with the most likely source of the instability being the rapid pace of financial innovation.

K E Y   T E R M S

equation of exchange, p. 530

liquidity preference theory,
p. 535

monetary theory, p. 529

quantity theory of money,
p. 531

real money balances, p. 537

velocity of money, p. 530

---

[30]Thomas F. Cooley and Stephen F. Le Roy, "Identification and Estimation of Money Demand," *American Economic Review* 71 (1981): 825–844, is especially critical of the empirical research on the demand for money.

QUESTIONS AND PROBLEMS

*1. The money supply M has been growing at 10 percent per year, and nominal GDP *PY* has been growing at 20 percent per year. The data are as follows (in billions of dollars):

	1998	*1999*	*2000*
M	100	110	121
PY	1000	1200	1440

Calculate the velocity in each year. At what rate is velocity growing?

2. Calculate what happens to nominal GDP if velocity remains constant at 5 and the money supply increases from $200 billion to $300 billion.

*3. What happens to nominal GDP if the money supply grows by 20 percent but velocity declines by 30 percent?

4. If credit cards were made illegal by congressional legislation, what would happen to velocity? Explain your answer.

*5. If velocity and aggregate output are reasonably constant (as the classical economists believed), what happens to the price level when the money supply increases from $1 trillion to $4 trillion?

6. If velocity and aggregate output remain constant at 5 and 1000, respectively, what happens to the price level if the money supply declines from $400 billion to $300 billion?

*7. "Considering that both Fisher and the classical Cambridge economists ended with the same equation for the demand for money, $M^d = k \times PY$, their theories are equivalent." Is this statement true, false, or uncertain? Explain your answer.

8. Using data from the *Economic Report of the President,* calculate velocity for the M2 definition of the money supply in the past five years. Does velocity appear to be constant?

*9. In Keynes's analysis of the speculative demand for money, what will happen to money demand if people suddenly decide that the normal level of the interest rate has declined? Why?

10. Why is Keynes's analysis of the speculative demand for money important to his view that velocity will undergo substantial fluctuations and thus cannot be treated as constant?

*11. If interest rates on bonds go to zero, what does the Baumol-Tobin analysis suggest Grant Smith's average holdings of money balances should be?

12. If brokerage fees go to zero, what does the Baumol-Tobin analysis suggest Grant Smith's average holdings of money should be?

*13. "In Tobin's analysis of the speculative demand for money, people will hold both money and bonds, even if bonds are expected to earn a positive return." Is this statement true, false, or uncertain? Explain your answer.

14. Both Keynes's and Friedman's theories of the demand for money suggest that as the relative expected return on money falls, demand for it will fall. Why does Friedman think that money demand is unaffected by changes in interest rates, but Keynes thought that it is affected?

*15. Why does Friedman's view of the demand for money suggest that velocity is predictable, whereas Keynes's view suggests the opposite?

Chapter 22

THE KEYNESIAN FRAMEWORK AND THE *ISLM* MODEL

PREVIEW   In the media, you often see forecasts of GDP and interest rates by economists and government agencies. At times, these forecasts seem to come from a crystal ball, but economists actually make their predictions using a variety of economic models. One model widely used by economic forecasters is the *ISLM* model, which was developed by Sir John Hicks in 1937 and is based on the analysis in John Maynard Keynes's influential book *The General Theory of Employment, Interest and Money,* published in 1936.[1] The *ISLM* model explains how interest rates and total output produced in the economy (aggregate output or, equivalently, aggregate income) are determined, given a fixed price level.

The *ISLM* model is valuable not only because it can be used in economic forecasting but also because it provides a deeper understanding of how government policy can affect aggregate economic activity. In Chapter 24 we use it to evaluate the effects of monetary and fiscal policy on the economy and to learn some lessons about how monetary policy might best be conducted.

In this chapter we begin by developing the simplest framework for determining aggregate output, in which all economic actors (consumers, firms, and others) except the government play a role. Government fiscal policy (spending and taxes) is then added to the framework to see how it can affect the determination of aggregate output. Finally, we achieve a complete picture of the *ISLM* model by adding monetary policy variables: the money supply and the interest rate.

DETERMINATION OF AGGREGATE OUTPUT

Keynes was especially interested in understanding movements of aggregate output because he wanted to explain why the Great Depression had occurred and how government policy could be used to increase employment in a similar

---

[1]John Hicks, "Mr. Keynes and the Classics: A Suggested Interpretation," *Econometrica* (1937): 147–159.

economic situation. Keynes's analysis started with the recognition that the total quantity demanded of an economy's output was the sum of four types of spending: (1) **consumer expenditure** (*C*), the total demand for consumer goods and services (hamburgers, stereos, rock concerts, visits to the doctor, and so on); (2) **planned investment spending** (*I*), the total planned spending by businesses on new physical capital (machines, computers, factories, raw materials, and the like) plus planned spending on new homes; (3) **government spending** (*G*), the spending by all levels of government on goods and services (typewriters, aircraft carriers, government workers, red tape, and so forth); and (4) **net exports** (*NX*), the net foreign spending on domestic goods and services, equal to exports minus imports.[2] The total quantity demanded of an economy's output, called **aggregate demand** (Y^{ad}), can be written as

$$Y^{ad} = C + I + G + NX \tag{1}$$

Using the commonsense concept from supply and demand analysis, Keynes recognized that equilibrium would occur in the economy when total quantity of output supplied (aggregate output produced), *Y*, equals quantity of output demanded Y^{ad}, that is, when

$$Y = Y^{ad} \tag{2}$$

When this equilibrium condition is satisfied, producers are able to sell all of their output and have no reason to change their production. Keynes's analysis explains two things: (1) why aggregate output is at a certain level (which involves understanding what factors affect each component of aggregate demand) and (2) how the sum of these components can add up to an output smaller than the economy is capable of producing, resulting in less than full employment of resources.

Keynes was especially concerned with explaining the low level of output and employment during the Great Depression. Because inflation was not a serious problem during this period, he assumed that output could change without causing a change in prices. ***Keynes's analysis assumes that the price level is fixed;*** that is, dollar amounts for variables such as consumer expenditure, investment, and aggregate output do not have to be adjusted for changes in the price level to tell us how much the real quantities of these variables change. Because the price level is assumed to be fixed, when we talk in this chapter about changes in nominal quantities, we are talking about changes in real quantities as well.

Our discussion of Keynes's analysis begins with a simple framework of aggregate output determination in which the role of government, net exports, and the possible effects of money and interest rates are ignored. Because we are assuming that government spending and net exports are zero (*G* = 0 and *NX* = 0), we need only examine consumer expenditure and investment spending to explain how aggregate output is determined. This simple framework is unrealistic because both government and monetary policy are left out of the picture and because it makes other simplifying assumptions, such as a fixed price level. Still, the model is worth studying because its simplified view helps us understand the

---

[2]Imports are subtracted from exports in arriving at the net exports component of the total quantity demanded of an economy's output because imports are already counted in *C, I,* and *G* but do not add to the demand for the economy's output.

key factors that explain how the economy works. It also clearly illustrates the Keynesian idea that the economy can come to rest at a level of aggregate output below the full employment level. Once you understand this simple framework, we can proceed to more complex and more realistic models.

Consumer Expenditure and the Consumption Function

Ask yourself what determines how much you spend on consumer goods and services. Your likely response is that your income is the most important factor because if your income rises, you will be willing to spend more. Keynes reasoned similarly that consumer expenditure is related to **disposable income,** the total income available for spending, equal to aggregate income (which is equivalent to aggregate output) minus taxes $(Y - T)$. He called this relationship between disposable income Y_D and consumer expenditure C the **consumption function** and expressed it as

$$C = a + (mpc \times Y_D) \tag{3}$$

The term *mpc,* the **marginal propensity to consume,** is the slope of the consumption function line $(\Delta C/\Delta Y_D)$ and reflects the change in consumer expenditure that results from an additional dollar of disposable income. Keynes assumed that *mpc* was a constant between the values of 0 and 1. If, for example, a $1.00 increase of disposable income leads to an increase in consumer expenditure of $0.50, then *mpc* = 0.5.

The term *a* stands for **autonomous consumer expenditure,** the amount of consumer expenditure that is independent of disposable income. It tells us how much consumers will spend when disposable income is 0 (they still must have food, clothing, and shelter). If *a* is $200 billion when disposable income is 0, consumer expenditure will equal $200 billion.[3]

A numerical example of a consumption function using the values of *mpc* = 0.5 and *a* = 200 will clarify the preceding concept. The $200 billion of consumer expenditure at a disposable income of 0 is listed in the first row of Table 1 and is plotted as point E in Figure 1. (Remember that throughout this chapter, dollar amounts for all variables in the figures correspond to real quantities because Keynes assumed that the price level is fixed.) Because *mpc* = 0.5, when disposable income increases by $400 billion, the change in consumer expenditure—ΔC in column 3 of Table 1—is $200 billion (0.5 × $400 billion). Thus when disposable income is $400 billion, consumer expenditure is $400 billion (initial value of $200 billion when income is 0 plus the $200 billion change in consumer expenditure). This combination of consumer expenditure and disposable income is listed in the second row of Table 1 and is plotted as point F in Figure 1. Similarly, at point G, where disposable income has increased by another $400 billion to $800 billion, consumer expenditure will rise by another $200 billion to $600 billion. By the same reasoning, at point H, at which disposable income is $1200 billion, consumer expenditure will be $800 billion. The line connecting these points in Figure 1 graphs the consumption function.

---

[3]Consumer expenditure can exceed income if people have accumulated savings to tide them over bad times. An alternative is to have parents who will give you money for food (or to pay for school) when you have no income. The situation in which consumer expenditure is greater than disposable income is called *dissaving.*

TABLE 1	Consumption Function: Schedule of Consumer Expenditure *C* When *mpc* = 0.5 and *a* = 200 ($ billions)			
Point in Figure 1	Disposable income Y_D (1)	Change in Disposable Income ΔY_D (2)	Change in Consumer Expenditure ΔC (0.5 × ΔY_D) (3)	Consumer Expenditure *C* (4)
E	0	—	—	200 (= *a*)
F	400	400	200	400
G	800	400	200	600
H	1200	400	200	800

Study Guide   The consumption function is an intuitive concept that you can readily understand if you think about how your own spending behavior changes as you receive more disposable income. One way to make yourself more comfortable with this concept is to estimate your marginal propensity to consume (for example, it might be 0.8) and your level of consumer expenditure when your disposable income is 0 (it might be $2000) and then construct a consumption function similar to that in Table 1.

Investment Spending

It is important to understand that there are two types of investment. The first type, **fixed investment,** is the spending by firms on equipment (machines, com-

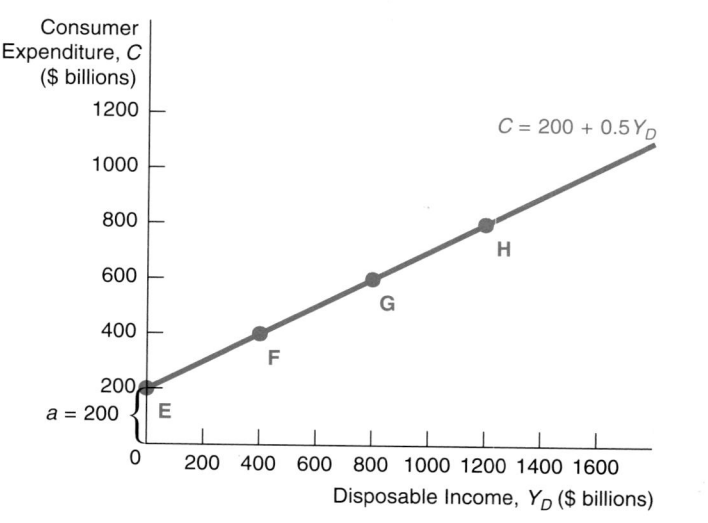

FIGURE 1   Consumption Function
The consumption function plotted here is from Table 1; *mpc* = 0.5 and *a* = 200.

```
B O X   1
```

Meaning of the Word Investment

Economists use the word *investment* somewhat differently from other people. When people say that they are making an investment, they are normally referring to the purchase of common stocks or bonds, purchases that do not necessarily involve newly produced goods and services. But when economists speak of investment spending, they are referring to the purchase of *new* physical assets such as new machines or new houses—purchases that add to aggregate demand.

puters, airplanes) and structures (factories, office buildings, shopping centers) and planned spending on residential housing. The second type, **inventory investment,** is spending by firms on additional holdings of raw materials, parts, and finished goods, calculated as the change in holdings of these items in a given time period, say, a year. (Box 1 explains how economists' use of the word investment differs from everyday use of the term.)

Suppose that Compaq, a company that produces personal computers, has 100,000 computers sitting in its warehouses on December 31, 1997, ready to be shipped to dealers. If each computer has a wholesale price of $1000, Compaq has an inventory worth $100 million. If by December 31, 1998, its inventory of personal computers has risen to $150 million, its inventory investment in 1998 is $50 million, the *change* in the level of its inventory over the course of the year ($150 million minus $100 million). Now suppose that there is a drop in the level of inventories; inventory investment will then be negative.

Compaq may also have additional inventory investment if the level of raw materials and parts that it is holding to produce these computers increases over the course of the year. If on December 31, 1997, it holds $20 million of computer chips used to produce its computers and on December 31, 1998, it holds $30 million, it has an additional $10 million of inventory investment in 1998.

An important feature of inventory investment is that—in contrast to fixed investment, which is always planned—some inventory investment can be unplanned. Suppose that the reason that Compaq finds itself with an additional $50 million of computers on December 31, 1998, is that $50 million less of its computers were sold in 1998 than expected. This $50 million of inventory investment in 1998 was unplanned. In this situation, Compaq is producing more computers than it can sell and will cut production.

Planned investment spending, a component of aggregate demand Y^{ad}, is equal to planned fixed investment plus the amount of inventory investment *planned* by firms. Keynes mentioned two factors that influence planned investment spending: interest rates and businesses' expectations about the future. How these factors affect investment spending is discussed later in this chapter. For now, planned investment spending will be treated as a known value. At this stage, we want to see how aggregate output is determined for a given level of planned investment spending; once we understand this, we can examine how interest rates and business expectations influence aggregate output by affecting planned investment spending.

Equilibrium and the Keynesian Cross Diagram

We have now assembled the building blocks (consumer expenditure and planned investment spending) that will enable us to see how aggregate output is determined when we ignore the government. Although unrealistic, this stripped-down analysis clarifies the basic principles of output determination. In the next section, government enters the picture and makes our model more realistic.

The diagram in Figure 2, known as the *Keynesian cross diagram*, shows how aggregate output is determined. The vertical axis measures aggregate demand, and the horizontal axis measures the level of aggregate output. The 45° line shows all the points at which aggregate output Y equals aggregate demand Y^{ad}; that is, it shows all the points at which the equilibrium condition $Y = Y^{ad}$ is satisfied. Since government spending and net exports are zero ($G = 0$ and $NX = 0$), aggregate demand is

$$Y^{ad} = C + I$$

Because there is no government sector to collect taxes, there are none in our simplified economy; disposable income Y_D then equals aggregate output Y (remember that aggregate income and aggregate output are equivalent; see the appendix to Chapter 1). Thus the consumption function with $a = 200$ and $mpc = 0.5$ plotted in Figure 1 can be written as $C = 200 + 0.5Y$ and is plotted in Figure 2. Given that planned investment spending is $300 billion, aggregate demand can then be expressed as

$$Y^{ad} = C + I = 200 + 0.5Y + 300 = 500 + 0.5Y$$

This equation, plotted in Figure 2, represents the quantity of aggregate demand at any given level of aggregate output and is called the **aggregate demand function.**

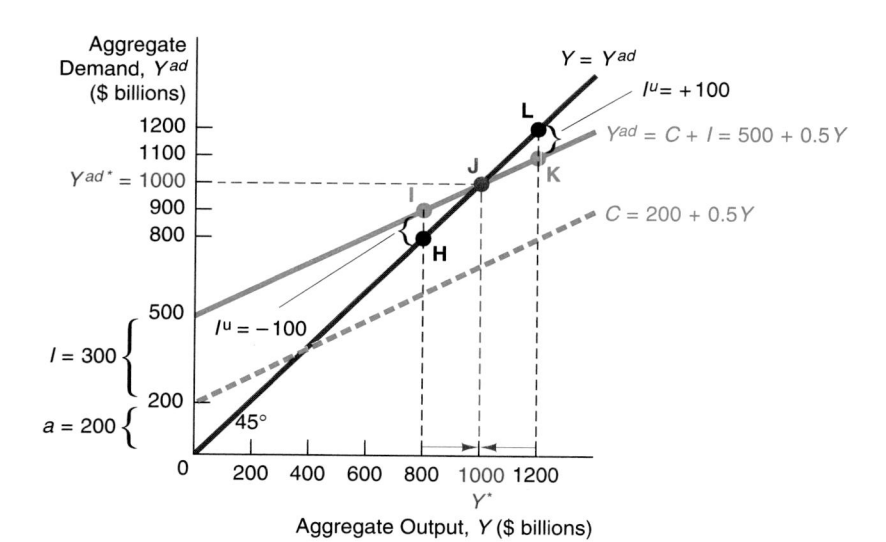

FIGURE 2 Keynesian Cross Diagram
When $I = 300$ and $C = 200 + 0.5Y$, equilibrium output occurs at $Y^* = 1000$, where the aggregate demand function $Y^{ad} = C + I$ intersects with the 45° line $Y = Y^{ad}$.

The aggregate demand function $Y^{ad} = C + I$ is the vertical sum of the consumption function line ($C = 200 + 0.5Y$) and planned investment spending ($I = 300$). The point at which the aggregate demand function crosses the 45° line $Y = Y^{ad}$ indicates the equilibrium level of aggregate demand and aggregate output. In Figure 2, equilibrium occurs at point J, with both aggregate output Y^* and aggregate demand Y^{ad*} at $1000 billion.

As you learned in Chapter 6, the concept of equilibrium is useful only if there is a tendency for the economy to settle there. To see whether the economy heads toward the equilibrium output level of $1000 billion, let's first look at what happens if the amount of output produced in the economy is $1200 billion and is therefore above the equilibrium level. At this level of output, aggregate demand is $1100 billion (point K), $100 billion less than the $1200 billion of output (point L on the 45° line). Since output exceeds aggregate demand by $100 billion, firms are saddled with $100 billion of unsold inventory. To keep from accumulating unsold goods, firms will cut production. As long as it is above the equilibrium level, output will exceed aggregate demand and firms will cut production, sending aggregate output toward the equilibrium level.

Another way to observe a tendency of the economy to head toward equilibrium at point J is from the viewpoint of inventory investment. When firms do not sell all output produced, they add unsold output to their holdings of inventory, and inventory investment increases. At an output level of $1200 billion, for instance, the $100 billion of unsold goods leads to $100 billion of unplanned inventory investment, which firms do not want. Companies will decrease production to reduce inventory to the desired level, and aggregate output will fall (indicated by the arrow near the horizontal axis). This viewpoint means that unplanned inventory investment for the entire economy I^u equals the excess of output over aggregate demand. In our example, at an output level of $1200 billion, $I^u = \$100$ billion. If I^u is positive, firms will cut production and output will fall. Output will stop falling only when it has returned to its equilibrium level at point J, where $I^u = 0$.

What happens if aggregate output is below the equilibrium level of output? Let's say output is $800 billion. At this level of output, aggregate demand at point I is $900 billion, $100 billion higher than output (point H on the 45° line). At this level, firms are selling $100 billion more goods than they are producing, so inventory falls below the desired level. The negative unplanned inventory investment ($I^u = -\$100$ billion) will induce firms to increase their production in order to raise inventory to desired levels. As a result, output rises toward the equilibrium level, shown by the arrow in Figure 2. As long as output is below the equilibrium level, unplanned inventory investment will remain negative, firms will continue to raise production, and output will continue to rise. We again see the tendency for the economy to settle at point J, where aggregate demand Y equals output Y^{ad} and unplanned inventory investment is zero ($I^u = 0$).

Expenditure Multiplier

Now that we understand that equilibrium aggregate output is determined by the position of the aggregate demand function, we can examine how different factors shift the function and consequently change aggregate output. We will find that either a rise in planned investment spending or a rise in autonomous consumer expenditure shifts the aggregate demand function upward and leads to an increase in aggregate output.

OUTPUT RESPONSE TO A CHANGE IN PLANNED INVESTMENT SPENDING Suppose that a new electric motor is invented that makes all factory machines three times more efficient. Because firms are suddenly more optimistic about the profitability of investing in new machines that use this new motor, planned investment spending increases by $100 billion from an initial level of $I_1 = \$300$ billion to $I_2 = \$400$ billion. What effect does this have on output?

The effects of this increase in planned investment spending are analyzed in Figure 3 using a Keynesian cross diagram. Initially, when planned investment spending I_1 is $300 billion, the aggregate demand function is Y_1^{ad}, and equilibrium occurs at point 1, where output is $1000 billion. The $100 billion increase in planned investment spending adds directly to aggregate demand and shifts the aggregate demand function upward to Y_2^{ad}. Aggregate demand now equals output at the intersection of Y_2^{ad} with the 45° line $Y = Y^{ad}$ (point 2). As a result of the $100 billion increase in planned investment spending, equilibrium output rises by $200 billion to $1200 billion ($Y_2$). For every dollar increase in planned investment spending, aggregate output has increased twofold.

The ratio of the change in aggregate output to a change in planned investment spending, $\Delta Y/\Delta I$, is called the **expenditure multiplier.** (This multiplier should not be confused with the money supply multiplier developed in Chapter

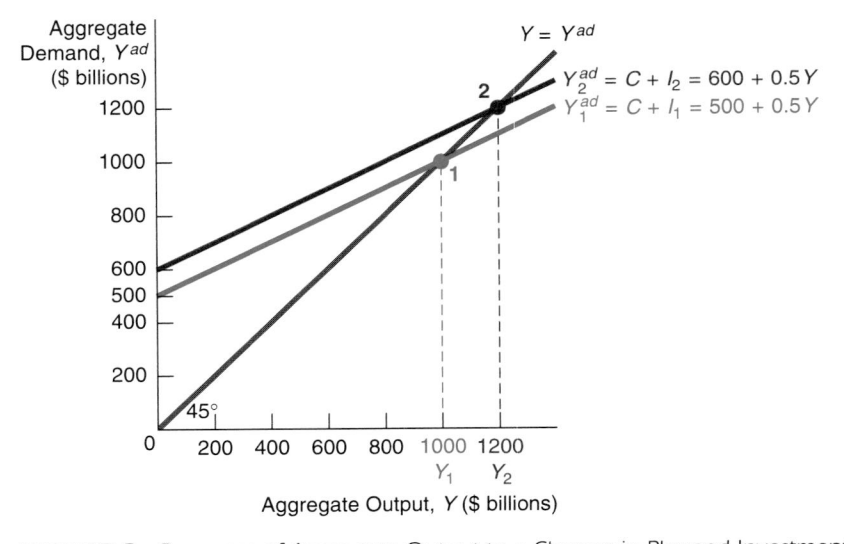

FIGURE 3 Response of Aggregate Output to a Change in Planned Investment
A $100 billion increase in planned investment spending from $I_1 = 300$ to $I_2 = 400$ shifts the aggregate demand function upward from Y_1^{ad} to Y_2^{ad}. The equilibrium moves from point 1 to point 2, and equilibrium output rises from $Y_1 = 1000$ to $Y_2 = 1200$.

16, which measures the ratio of the change in the money supply to a change in the monetary base.) In Figure 3, the expenditure multiplier is 2.

Why does a change in planned investment spending lead to an even larger change in aggregate output so that the expenditure multiplier is greater than 1? The expenditure multiplier is greater than 1 because an increase in planned investment spending, which raises output, also leads to an additional increase in consumer expenditure ($mpc \times \Delta Y$). The increase in consumer expenditure in turn raises aggregate demand and output further, resulting in a multiple change of output from a given change in planned investment spending. This conclusion can be derived algebraically by solving for the unknown value of Y in terms of a, mpc, and I, resulting in the following equation:[4]

$$Y = (a + I) \times \frac{1}{1 - mpc} \tag{4}$$

Because I is multiplied by the term $1/(1 - mpc)$, this equation tells us that a $1 change in I leads to a $1/(1 - mpc)$ change in aggregate output; thus $1/(1 - mpc)$ is the expenditure multiplier. When $mpc = 0.5$, the change in output for a $1 change in I is $2 [= 1/(1 - 0.5)]$; if $mpc = 0.8$, the change in output for a $1 change in I is $5. The larger the marginal propensity to consume, the higher the expenditure multiplier.

RESPONSE TO CHANGES IN AUTONOMOUS SPENDING Because a is also multiplied by the term $1/(1 - mpc)$ in Equation 4, a $1 change in autonomous consumer expenditure a also changes aggregate output by $1/(1 - mpc)$, the amount of the expenditure multiplier. Therefore, we see that the expenditure multiplier applies equally well to changes in autonomous consumer expenditure. In fact, Equation 4 can be rewritten as

$$Y = A \times \frac{1}{1 - mpc} \tag{5}$$

in which A = autonomous spending = $a + I$.

This rewritten equation tells us that any change in autonomous spending, whether from a change in a, in I, or in both, will lead to a multiplied change in Y. If both a and I decrease by $100 billion each and $mpc = 0.5$, the expenditure multiplier is $2 [= 1/(1 - 0.5)]$, and aggregate output Y will fall by $2 \times $200 billion = $400 billion. Conversely, a rise in I by $100 billion that is offset by a $100 billion decline in a will leave autonomous spending A, and hence Y, unchanged. The

---

[4]Substituting the consumption function $C = a + (mpc \times Y)$ into the aggregate demand function $Y^{ad} = C + I$ yields

$$Y^{ad} = a + (mpc \times Y) + I$$

In equilibrium, where aggregate output equals aggregate demand,

$$Y = Y^{ad} = a + (mpc \times Y) + I$$

Subtracting the term $mpc \times Y$ from both sides of this equation in order to collect the terms involving Y on the left side, we have

$$Y - (mpc \times Y) = Y(1 - mpc) = a + I$$

Dividing both sides by $1 - mpc$ to solve for Y leads to Equation 4 in the text.

expenditure multiplier $1/(1 - mpc)$ can therefore be defined more generally as the ratio of the change in aggregate output to a change in autonomous spending $(\Delta Y/\Delta A)$.

Another way to reach this conclusion—that any change in autonomous spending will lead to a multiplied change in aggregate output—is to recognize that the shift in the aggregate demand function in Figure 3 did not have to come from an increase in I; it could also have come from an increase in a, which directly raises consumer expenditure and therefore aggregate demand. Alternatively, it could have come from an increase in both a and I. Changes in the attitudes of consumers and firms about the future, which cause changes in their spending, will result in multiple changes in aggregate output.

Keynes believed that changes in autonomous spending are dominated by unstable fluctuations in planned investment spending, which is influenced by emotional waves of optimism and pessimism—factors he referred to as **"animal spirits."** His view was colored by the collapse in investment spending during the Great Depression, which he saw as the primary reason for the economic contraction. We will examine the consequences of this fall in investment spending in the following application.

The Collapse of Investment Spending and the Great Depression

From 1929 to 1933, the U.S. economy experienced the largest percentage decline in investment spending ever recorded. One explanation for the investment collapse was the ongoing set of financial crises during this period, described in Chapter 9. In 1992 dollars, investment spending fell from $200 billion to $33 billion—a decline of over 80 percent. What does the Keynesian analysis developed so far suggest should have happened to aggregate output in this period?

Figure 4 demonstrates how the $167 billion drop in planned investment spending would shift the aggregate demand function downward from Y_1^{ad} to Y_2^{ad}, moving the economy from point 1 to point 2. Aggregate output would then fall sharply; real GDP actually fell by $303 billion (a multiple of the $167 billion drop in investment spending), from $1019 billion to $716 billion (in 1992 dollars). Because the economy was at full employment in 1929, the fall in output resulted in massive unemployment, with over 25 percent of the labor force unemployed in 1933.

Government's Role

After witnessing the events in the Great Depression, Keynes took the view that an economy would continually suffer major output fluctuations because of the volatility of autonomous spending, particularly planned investment spending. He was especially worried about sharp declines in autonomous spending, which would inevitably lead to large declines in output and an equilibrium with high unemployment. If autonomous spending fell sharply, as it did during the Great Depression, how could an economy be restored to higher levels of output and more reasonable levels of unemployment? Not by an increase in autonomous

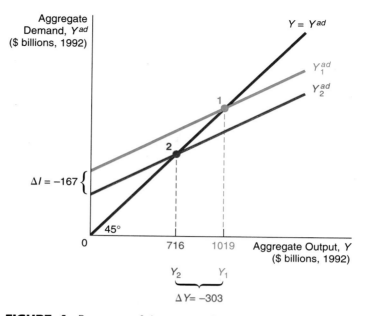

FIGURE 4   Response of Aggregate Output to the Collapse of Investment Spending, 1929–1933

The decline of $167 billion (in 1992 dollars) in planned investment spending from 1929 to 1933 shifted the aggregate demand function down from Y_1^{ad} to Y_2^{ad} and caused the economy to move from point 1 to point 2, where output fell by $303 billion.

Source: Economic Report of the President.

spending, since the business outlook was so grim. Keynes's answer to this question involved looking at the role of government in determining aggregate output.

Keynes realized that government spending and taxation could also affect the position of the aggregate demand function and hence be manipulated to restore the economy to full employment. As shown in the aggregate demand equation $Y^{ad} = C + I + G + NX$, government spending G adds directly to aggregate demand. Taxes, however, do not affect aggregate demand directly, as government spending does. Instead, taxes lower the amount of income that consumers have available for spending and affect aggregate demand by influencing consumer expenditure; that is, when there are taxes, disposable income Y_D does not equal aggregate output; it equals aggregate output Y minus taxes T: $Y_D = Y - T$. The consumption function $C = a + (mpc \times Y_D)$ can be rewritten as follows:

$$C = a + [mpc \times (Y - T)] = a + (mpc \times Y) - (mpc \times T) \qquad (6)$$

This consumption function looks similar to the one used in the absence of taxes, but it has the additional term $-(mpc \times T)$ on the right side. This term indicates that if taxes increase by $100, consumer expenditure declines by mpc times this amount; if $mpc = 0.5$, consumer expenditure declines by $50. This occurs because consumers view $100 of taxes as equivalent to a $100 reduction in income and reduce their expenditure by the marginal propensity to consume times this amount.

To see how the inclusion of government spending and taxes modifies our analysis, first we will observe the effect of a positive level of government spending on aggregate output in the Keynesian cross diagram of Figure 5. Let's say that in the absence of government spending or taxes, the economy is at point 1, where the aggregate demand function $Y_1^{ad} = C + I = 500 + 0.5Y$ crosses the 45° line $Y = Y^{ad}$. Here equilibrium output is at $1000 billion. Suppose, however, that the economy reaches full employment at an aggregate output level of $1800 billion. How can government spending be used to restore the economy to full employment at $1800 billion of aggregate output?

If government spending is set at $400 billion, the aggregate demand function shifts upward to $Y_2^{ad} = C + I + G = 900 + 0.5Y$. The economy moves to point 2, and aggregate output rises by $800 billion to $1800 billion. Figure 5 indicates that aggregate output is positively related to government spending and that a change in government spending leads to a multiplied change in aggregate output, equal to the expenditure multiplier, $1/(1 - mpc) = 1/(1 - 0.5) = 2$. Therefore, declines in planned investment spending that produce high unemployment (as occurred during the Great Depression) can be offset by raising government spending.

What happens if the government decides that it must collect taxes of $400 billion to balance the budget? Before taxes are raised, the economy is in equilibrium

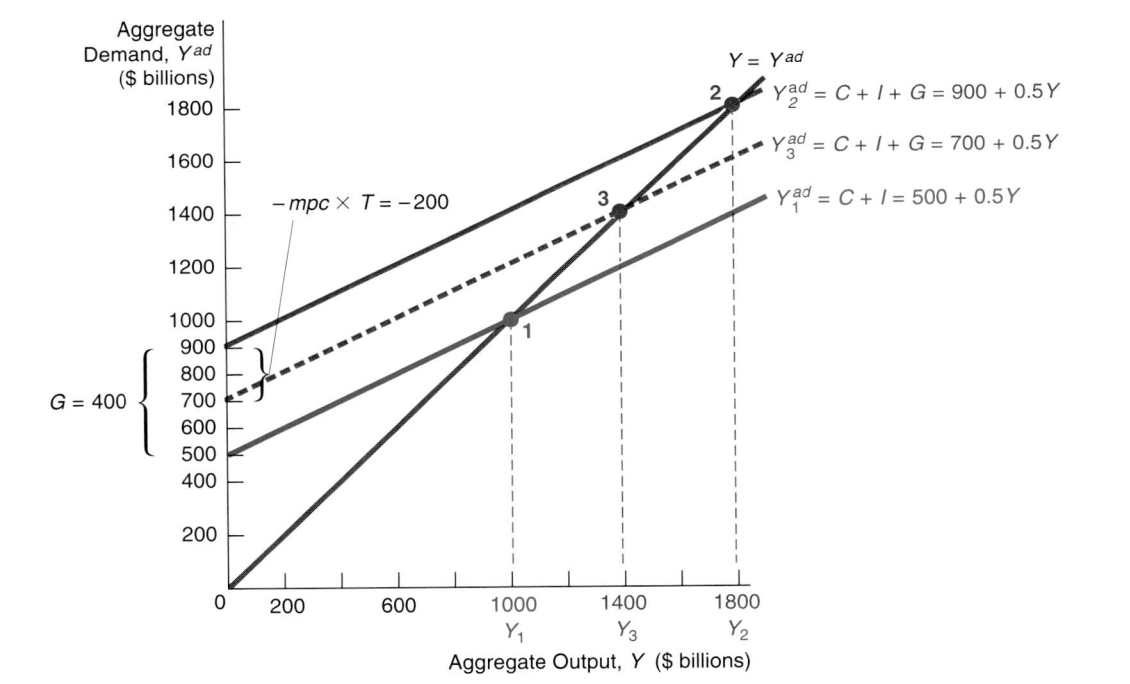

FIGURE 5 Response of Aggregate Output to Government Spending and Taxes

With no government spending or taxes, the aggregate demand function is Y_1^{ad}, and equilibrium output is $Y_1 = 1000$. With government spending of $400 billion, the aggregate demand function shifts upward to Y_2^{ad}, and aggregate output rises by $800 billion to $Y_2 = $1800 billion. Taxes of $400 billion lower consumer expenditure and the aggregate demand function by $200 billion from Y_2^{ad} to Y_3^{ad}, and aggregate output falls by $400 billion to $Y_3 = $1400 billion.

at the same point 2 found in Figure 5. Our discussion of the consumption function (which allows for taxes) indicates that taxes T reduce consumer expenditure by $mpc \times T$ because there is T less income now available for spending. In our example, $mpc = 0.5$, so consumer expenditure and the aggregate demand function shift downward by \$200 billion ($= 0.5 \times 400$); at the new equilibrium, point 3, the level of output has declined by twice this amount (the expenditure multiplier) to \$1400 billion.

Although you can see that aggregate output is negatively related to the level of taxes, it is important to recognize that the change in aggregate output from the \$400 billion increase in taxes ($\Delta Y = -\$400$ billion) is smaller than the change in aggregate output from the \$400 billion increase in government spending ($\Delta Y = \$800$ billion). If both taxes and government spending are raised equally by \$400 billion, as occurs in going from point 1 to point 3 in Figure 5, aggregate output will rise.

The Keynesian framework indicates that the government can play an important role in determining aggregate output by changing the level of government spending or taxes. If the economy enters a deep recession, in which output drops severely and unemployment climbs, the analysis we have just developed provides a prescription for restoring the economy to health. The government might raise aggregate output by increasing government spending, or it could lower taxes and reverse the process described in Figure 5 (that is, a tax cut makes more income available for spending at any level of output, shifting the aggregate demand function upward and causing the equilibrium level of output to rise).

Role of International Trade

International trade also plays a role in determining aggregate output because net exports (exports minus imports) are a component of aggregate demand. To analyze the effect of net exports in the Keynesian cross diagram of Figure 6, suppose that initially net exports are equal to zero ($NX_1 = 0$) so that the economy is at point 1, where the aggregate demand function $Y_1^{ad} = C + I + G + NX_1 = 500 + 0.5Y$ crosses the 45° line $Y = Y_1^{ad}$. Equilibrium output is again at \$1000 billion. Now foreigners suddenly get an urge to buy more American products so that net exports rise to \$100 billion ($NX_2 = 100$). The \$100 billion increase in net exports adds directly to aggregate demand and shifts the aggregate demand function upward to $Y_2^{ad} = C + I + G + NX_2 = 600 + 0.5Y$. The economy moves to point 2, and aggregate output rises by \$200 billion to \$1200 billion (Y_2). Figure 6 indicates that just as we found for planned investment spending and government spending, a rise in net exports leads to a multiplied rise in aggregate output, equal to the expenditure multiplier, $1/(1 - mpc) = 1/(1 - 0.5) = 2$. Therefore, changes in net exports can be another important factor affecting fluctuations in aggregate output.

Summary of the Determinants of Aggregate Output

Our analysis of the Keynesian framework so far has identified five autonomous factors (factors independent of income) that shift the aggregate demand function and hence the level of aggregate output:

1. Changes in autonomous consumer expenditure (a)
2. Changes in planned investment spending (I)

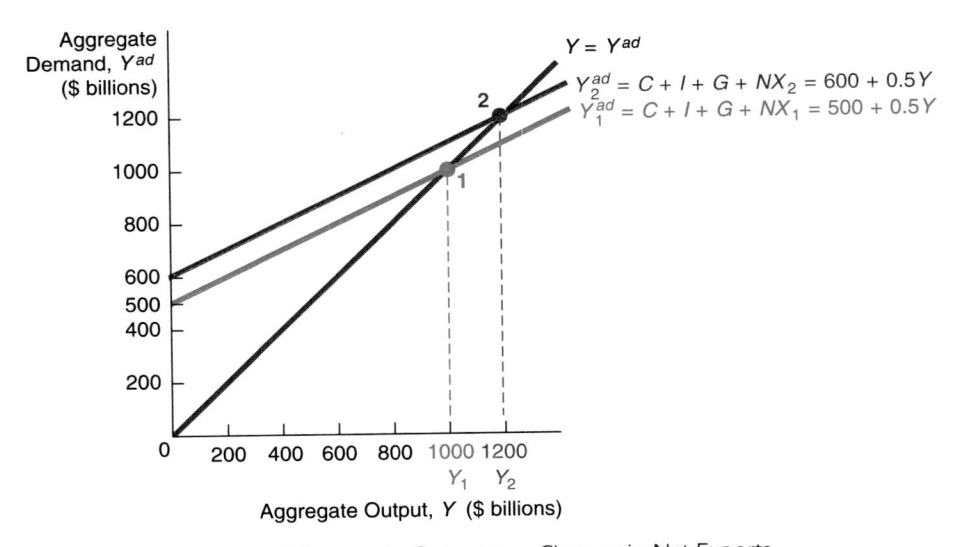

FIGURE 6 Response of Aggregate Output to a Change in Net Exports

A $100 billion increase in net exports from $NX_1 = 0$ to $NX_2 = 100$ shifts the aggregate demand function upward from Y_1^{ad} to Y_2^{ad}. The equilibrium moves from point 1 to point 2, and equilibrium output rises from $Y_1 = \$1000$ billion to $Y_2 = \$1200$ billion.

3. Changes in government spending (G)
4. Changes in taxes (T)
5. Changes in net exports (NX)

The effects of changes in each of these variables on aggregate output are summarized in Table 2 and discussed next in the text.

CHANGES IN AUTONOMOUS CONSUMER SPENDING (**a**) A rise in autonomous consumer expenditure a (say, because consumers become more optimistic about the economy when the stock market booms) directly raises consumer expenditure and shifts the aggregate demand function upward, resulting in an increase in aggregate output. A decrease in a causes consumer expenditure to fall, leading ultimately to a decline in aggregate output. Therefore, ***aggregate output is positively related to autonomous consumer expenditure a.***

CHANGES IN PLANNED INVESTMENT SPENDING (**I**) A rise in planned investment spending adds directly to aggregate demand, thus raising the aggregate demand function and aggregate output. A fall in planned investment spending lowers aggregate demand and causes aggregate output to fall. Therefore, ***aggregate output is positively related to planned investment spending I.***

CHANGES IN GOVERNMENT SPENDING (**G**) A rise in government spending also adds directly to aggregate demand and raises the aggregate demand function, increasing aggregate output. A fall directly reduces aggregate demand, lowers the aggregate demand function, and causes aggregate output to fall. Therefore, ***aggregate output is positively related to government spending G.***

———— S U M M A R Y ————

TABLE 2	**Response of Aggregate Output *Y* to Autonomous Changes in *a, I, G, T,* and *NX***	

Variable	Change in Variable	Response of Aggregate Output, Y	
Autonomous consumer expenditure, *a*	↑	↑	
Investment, *I*	↑	↑	
Government spending, *G*	↑	↑	
Taxes, *T*	↑	↓	
Net exports, *NX*	↑	↑	

Note: Only increases (↑) in the variables are shown; the effects of decreases in the variables on aggregate output would be the opposite of those indicated in the "Response" column.

CHANGES IN TAXES *(T)*   A rise in taxes does not affect aggregate demand directly but does lower the amount of income available for spending, reducing consumer expenditure. The decline in consumer expenditure then leads to a fall in the aggregate demand function, resulting in a decline in aggregate output. A lowering of taxes makes more income available for spending, raises consumer expenditure, and leads to higher aggregate output. Therefore, ***aggregate output is negatively related to the level of taxes T.***

CHANGES IN NET EXPORTS (NX) A rise in net exports adds directly to aggregate demand and raises the aggregate demand function, increasing aggregate output. A fall directly reduces aggregate demand, lowers the aggregate demand function, and causes aggregate output to fall. Therefore, ***aggregate output is positively related to net exports NX.***

SIZE OF THE EFFECTS FROM THE FIVE FACTORS The aggregate demand function in the Keynesian cross diagrams shifts vertically by the full amount of the change in *a, I, G,* or *NX,* resulting in a multiple effect on aggregate output through the effects of the expenditure multiplier, $1/(1 - mpc)$. A change in taxes has a smaller effect on aggregate output because consumer expenditure changes only by *mpc* times the change in taxes ($-mpc \times \Delta T$), which in the case of $mpc = 0.5$ means that aggregate demand shifts vertically by only half of the change in taxes.

If there is a change in one of these autonomous factors that is offset by a change in another (say, *I* rises by $100 billion, but *a, G,* or *NX* falls by $100 billion or *T* rises by $200 billion when $mpc = 0.5$), the aggregate demand function will remain in the same position, and aggregate output will remain unchanged.[5]

Study Guide   To test your understanding of the Keynesian analysis of how aggregate output changes in response to changes in the factors described, see if you can use Keynesian cross diagrams to illustrate what happens to aggregate output when each variable decreases rather than increases. Also, be sure to do the problems at the end of the chapter that ask you to predict what will happen to aggregate output when certain economic variables change.

---

[5]These results can be derived algebraically as follows. Substituting the consumption function allowing for taxes (Equation 6) into the aggregate demand function (Equation 1), we have

$$Y^{ad} = a - (mpc \times T) + (mpc \times Y) + I + G + NX$$

If we assume that taxes *T* are unrelated to income, we can define autonomous spending in the aggregate demand function to be

$$A = a - (mpc \times T) + I + G + NX$$

The expenditure equation can be rewritten as

$$Y^{ad} = A + (mpc \times Y)$$

In equilibrium, aggregate demand equals aggregate output,

$$Y = A + (mpc \times Y)$$

which can be solved for *Y.* The resulting equation,

$$Y = A \times \frac{1}{1 - mpc}$$

is the same equation that links autonomous spending and aggregate output in the text (Equation 5), but it now allows for additional components of autonomous spending in *A.* We see that any increase in autonomous expenditure leads to a multiple increase in output. Thus any component of autonomous spending that enters *A* with a positive sign (*a, I, G,* and *NX*) will have a positive relationship with output, and any component with a negative sign ($-mpc \times T$) will have a negative relationship with output. This algebraic analysis also shows us that any rise in a component of *A* that is offset by a movement in another component of *A,* leaving *A* unchanged, will also leave output unchanged.

THE *ISLM* MODEL

So far our analysis has excluded monetary policy. We now include money and interest rates in the Keynesian framework in order to develop the more intricate *ISLM* model of how aggregate output is determined, in which monetary policy plays an important role. Why another complex model? The *ISLM* model is more versatile and allows us to understand economic phenomena that cannot be analyzed with the simpler Keynesian cross framework used earlier. The *ISLM* model will help you understand how monetary policy affects economic activity and interacts with fiscal policy (changes in government spending and taxes) to produce a certain level of aggregate output; how the level of interest rates is affected by changes in investment spending as well as by changes in monetary and fiscal policy; how best to conduct monetary policy; and how the *ISLM* model generates the aggregate demand curve, an essential building block for the aggregate supply and demand analysis used in Chapter 24 and thereafter.

Like our simplified Keynesian model, the full Keynesian *ISLM* model examines an equilibrium in which aggregate output produced equals aggregate demand, and since it assumes a fixed price level, real and nominal quantities are the same. The first step in constructing the *ISLM* model is to examine the effect of interest rates on planned investment spending and hence on aggregate demand. Next we use a Keynesian cross diagram to see how the interest rate affects the equilibrium level of aggregate output. The resulting relationship between equilibrium aggregate output and the interest rate is known as the **IS curve.**

Just as a demand curve alone cannot tell us the quantity of goods sold in a market, the *IS* curve by itself cannot tell us what the level of aggregate output will be because the interest rate is still unknown. We need another relationship, called the **LM curve,** which describes the combinations of interest rates and aggregate output for which the quantity of money demanded equals the quantity of money supplied. When the *IS* and *LM* curves are combined in the same diagram, the intersection of the two determines the equilibrium level of aggregate output as well as the interest rate. Finally, we will have obtained a more complete analysis of the determination of aggregate output in which monetary policy plays an important role.

Equilibrium in the Goods Market: The IS Curve

In Keynesian analysis, the primary way that interest rates affect the level of aggregate output is through their effects on planned investment spending and net exports. After explaining why interest rates affect planned investment spending and net exports, we will use Keynesian cross diagrams to learn how interest rates affect equilibrium aggregate output.[6]

INTEREST RATES AND PLANNED INVESTMENT SPENDING Businesses make investments in physical capital (machines, factories, and raw materials) as long as

---

[6]More modern Keynesian approaches suggest that consumer expenditure, particularly for consumer durables (cars, furniture, appliances), is influenced by the interest rate. This interest sensitivity of consumer expenditure can be allowed for in the model here by defining planned investment spending more generally to include the interest-sensitive component of consumer expenditure.

they expect to earn more from the physical capital than the interest cost of a loan to finance the investment. When the interest rate is high, few investments in physical capital will earn more than the cost of borrowed funds, so planned investment spending is low. When the interest rate is low, many investments in physical capital will earn more than the interest cost of borrowed funds. Therefore, when interest rates are lower, business firms are more likely to undertake an investment in physical capital, and planned investment spending will be higher.

Even if a company has surplus funds and does not need to borrow to undertake an investment in physical capital, its planned investment spending will be affected by the interest rate. Instead of investing in physical capital, it could purchase a security, such as a bond. If the interest rate on this security is high, the opportunity cost (forgone interest earnings) of an investment is high, and planned investment spending will be low because the firm would probably prefer to purchase the security than to invest in physical capital. As the interest rate and the opportunity cost of investing fall, planned investment spending will increase because investments in physical capital are more likely than the security to earn greater income for the firm.

The relationship between the amount of planned investment spending and any given level of the interest rate is illustrated by the investment schedule in panel (a) of Figure 7. The downward slope of the schedule reflects the negative relationship between planned investment spending and the interest rate. At a low interest rate i_1, the level of planned investment spending I_1 is high; for a high interest rate i_3, planned investment spending I_3 is low.

INTEREST RATES AND NET EXPORTS As discussed in more detail in Chapter 8, when interest rates rise in the United States (with the price level fixed), U.S. dollar bank deposits become more attractive relative to deposits denominated in foreign currencies, thereby causing a rise in the value of dollar deposits relative to other currency deposits, that is, a rise in the exchange rate. The higher value of the dollar resulting from the rise in interest rates makes domestic goods more expensive than foreign goods, thereby causing a fall in net exports. Therefore, as the interest rate rises, the value of the dollar rises, domestic goods become more expensive, and net exports fall. The resulting negative relationship between interest rates and net exports is shown in panel (b) of Figure 7. At a low interest rate i_1, the exchange rate is low and net exports NX_1 are high; at a high interest rate i_3, the exchange rate is high and net exports NX_3 are low.

DERIVING THE *IS* CURVE We can now use what we have learned about the relationship of interest rates to planned investment spending and net exports in panels (a) and (b) to examine the relationship between interest rates and the equilibrium level of aggregate output (holding government spending and autonomous consumer expenditure constant). The three levels of planned investment spending and net exports in panels (a) and (b) are represented in the three aggregate demand functions in the Keynesian cross diagram of panel (c). The lowest interest rate i_1 has the highest level of both planned investment spending i_1 and net exports NX_1 and hence the highest aggregate demand function Y_1^{ad}.

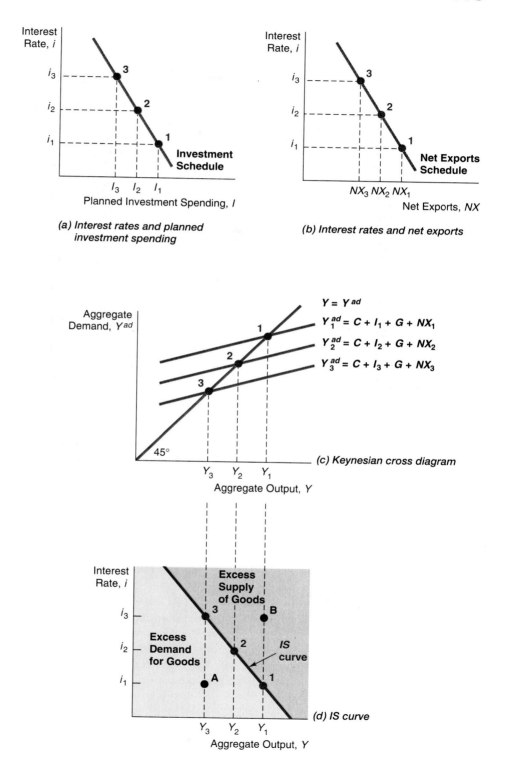

(a) *Interest rates and planned investment spending*

(b) *Interest rates and net exports*

(c) *Keynesian cross diagram*

(d) *IS curve*

FIGURE 7

Deriving the *IS* Curve
The investment schedule in panel (a) shows that as the interest rate rises from i_1 to i_2 to i_3, planned investment spending falls from I_1 to I_2 to I_3, and panel (b) shows that net exports also fall from NX_1 to NX_2 to NX_3 as the interest rate rises. Panel (c) then indicates the levels of equilibrium output Y_1, Y_2, and Y_3 that correspond to those three levels of planned investment and net exports. Finally, panel (d) plots the level of equilibrium output corresponding to each of the three interest rates; the line that connects these points is the *IS* curve.

Point 1 in panel (d) shows the resulting equilibrium level of output Y_1, which corresponds to interest rate i_1. As the interest rate rises to i_2, both planned investment spending and net exports fall, to I_2 and NX_2, so equilibrium output falls to Y_2. Point 2 in panel (d) shows the lower level of output Y_2, which corresponds to interest rate i_2. Finally, the highest interest rate i_3 leads to the lowest level of planned investment spending and net exports and hence the lowest level of equilibrium output, which is plotted as point 3.

The line connecting the three points in panel (d), the *IS* curve, shows the combinations of interest rates and equilibrium aggregate output for which aggregate output produced equals aggregate demand.[7] The negative slope indicates that higher interest rates result in lower planned investment spending and net exports and hence lower equilibrium output.

WHAT THE *IS* CURVE TELLS US   The *IS* curve traces out the points at which the total quantity of goods produced equals the total quantity of goods demanded. It describes points at which the goods market is in equilibrium. For each given level of the interest rate, the *IS* curve tells us what aggregate output must be for the goods market to be in equilibrium. As the interest rate rises, planned investment spending and net exports fall, which in turn lowers aggregate demand; aggregate output must be lower in order for it to equal aggregate demand and satisfy goods market equilibrium.

The *IS* curve is a useful concept because output tends to move toward points on the curve that satisfy goods market equilibrium. If the economy is located in the area to the right of the *IS* curve, it has an excess supply of goods. At point B, for example, aggregate output Y_1 is greater than the equilibrium level of output Y_3 on the *IS* curve. This excess supply of goods results in unplanned inventory accumulation, which causes output to fall toward the *IS* curve. The decline stops only when output is again at its equilibrium level on the *IS* curve.

If the economy is located in the area to the left of the *IS* curve, it has an excess demand for goods. At point A, aggregate output Y_3 is below the equilibrium level of output Y_1 on the *IS* curve. The excess demand for goods results in an unplanned decrease in inventory, which causes output to rise toward the *IS* curve, stopping only when aggregate output is again at its equilibrium level on the *IS* curve.

Significantly, equilibrium in the goods market does not produce a unique equilibrium level of aggregate output. Although we now know where aggregate output will head for a given level of the interest rate, we cannot determine aggregate output because we do not know what the interest rate is. To complete our analysis of aggregate output determination, we need to introduce another market that produces an additional relationship that links aggregate output and interest rates. The market for money fulfills this function with the *LM* curve. When the *LM* curve is combined with the *IS* curve, a unique equilibrium that determines both aggregate output and the interest rate is obtained.

---

[7]The *IS* was so named by Sir John Hicks because in the simplest Keynesian framework with no government sector, equilibrium in the Keynesian cross diagram occurs when investment spending *I* equals saving *S*.

Equilibrium in the Market for Money: The LM Curve

Just as the *IS* curve is derived from the equilibrium condition in the goods market (aggregate output equals aggregate demand), the *LM* curve is derived from the equilibrium condition in the market for money, which requires that the quantity of money demanded equal the quantity of money supplied. The main building block in Keynes's analysis of the market for money is the demand for money he called *liquidity preference*. Let us briefly review his theory of the demand for money (discussed at length in Chapters 6 and 21).

Keynes's liquidity preference theory states that the demand for money in real terms M^d/P depends on income Y (aggregate output) and interest rates i. The demand for money is positively related to income for two reasons. First, a rise in income raises the level of transactions in the economy, which in turn raises the demand for money because it is used to carry out these transactions. Second, a rise in income increases the demand for money because it increases the wealth of individuals who want to hold more assets, one of which is money. The opportunity cost of holding money is the interest sacrificed by not holding other assets (such as bonds) instead. As interest rates rise, the opportunity cost of holding money rises, and the demand for money falls. According to the liquidity preference theory, the demand for money is positively related to aggregate output and negatively related to interest rates.

DERIVING THE *LM* CURVE   In Keynes's analysis, the level of interest rates is determined by equilibrium in the market for money, at which point the quantity of money demanded equals the quantity of money supplied. Figure 8 depicts what happens to equilibrium in the market for money as the level of output changes. Because the *LM* curve is derived holding the money supply at a fixed level, it is fixed at the level of $\overline{M}$, in panel (a).[8] Each level of aggregate output has its own money demand curve because as aggregate output changes, the level of transactions in the economy changes, which in turn changes the demand for money.

When aggregate output is Y_1, the money demand curve is $M^d(Y_1)$: It slopes downward because a lower interest rate means that the opportunity cost of holding money is lower, so the quantity of money demanded is higher. Equilibrium in the market for money occurs at point 1, at which the interest rate is i_1. When aggregate output is at the higher level Y_2, the money demand curve shifts rightward to $M^d(Y_2)$ because the higher level of output means that at any given interest rate, the quantity of money demanded is higher. Equilibrium in the market for money now occurs at point 2, at which the interest rate is at the higher level of i_2. Similarly, a still higher level of aggregate output, Y_3, results in an even higher level of the equilibrium interest rate, i_3.

Panel (b) plots the equilibrium interest rates that correspond to the different output levels, with points 1, 2, and 3 corresponding to the equilibrium points 1, 2, and 3 in panel (a). The line connecting these points is the *LM* curve, which shows the combinations of interest rates and output for which the market for

---

[8]As pointed out in earlier chapters on the money supply process, the money supply is positively related to interest rates, and so the M^s curve in panel (a) should actually have a positive slope. The M^s curve is assumed to be vertical in panel (a) in order to simplify the graph, but allowing for a positive slope leads to identical results.

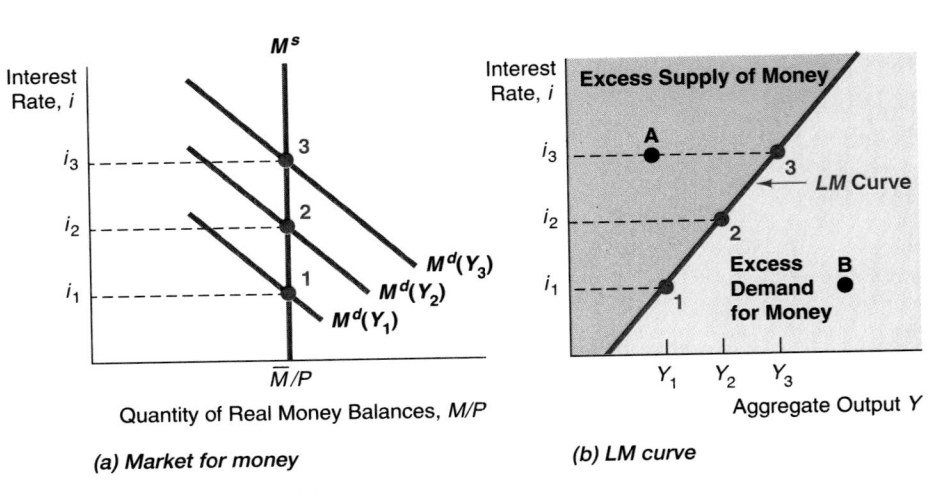

FIGURE 8 Deriving the **LM** Curve

Panel (a) shows the equilibrium levels of the interest rate in the market for money that arise when aggregate output is at Y_1, Y_2, and Y_3. Panel (b) plots the three levels of the equilibrium interest rate i_1, i_2, and i_3 corresponding to these three levels of output; the line that connects these points is the **LM** curve.

money is in equilibrium.[9] The positive slope arises because higher output raises the demand for money and thus raises the equilibrium interest rate.

WHAT THE **LM** CURVE TELLS US The *LM* curve traces out the points that satisfy the equilibrium condition that the quantity of money demanded equals the quantity of money supplied. For each given level of aggregate output, the *LM* curve tells us what the interest rate must be for there to be equilibrium in the market for money. As aggregate output rises, the demand for money increases and the interest rate rises, so that money demanded equals money supplied and the market for money is in equilibrium.

Just as the economy tends to move toward the equilibrium points represented by the *IS* curve, it also moves toward the equilibrium points on the *LM* curve. If the economy is located in the area to the left of the *LM* curve, there is an excess supply of money. At point A, for example, the interest rate is i_3 and aggregate output is Y_1. The interest rate is above the equilibrium level, and people are holding more money than they want to. To eliminate their excess money balances, they will purchase bonds, which causes the price of the bonds to rise and their interest rate to fall. (The inverse relationship between the price of a bond and its interest rate is discussed in Chapter 4.) As long as an excess supply of money exists, the interest rate will fall until it comes to rest on the *LM* curve.

If the economy is located in the area to the right of the *LM* curve, there is an excess demand for money. At point B, for example, the interest rate i_1 is below the equilibrium level, and people want to hold more money than they currently

---

[9]Hicks named this the *LM* curve to indicate that it represents the combinations of interest rates and output for which money demand, which Keynes denoted as *L* to represent liquidity preference, equals money supply *M*.

do. To acquire this money, they will sell bonds and drive down bond prices, and the interest rate will rise. This process will stop only when the interest rate rises to an equilibrium point on the *LM* curve.

ISLM APPROACH TO AGGREGATE OUTPUT AND INTEREST RATES

Now that we have derived the *IS* and *LM* curves, we can put them into the same diagram (Figure 9) to produce a model that enables us to determine both aggregate output and the interest rate. The only point at which the goods market and the market for money are in simultaneous equilibrium is at the intersection of the *IS* and *LM* curves, point E. At this point, aggregate output equals aggregate demand (*IS*) and the quantity of money demanded equals the quantity of money supplied (*LM*). At any other point in the diagram, at least one of these equilibrium conditions is not satisfied, and market forces move the economy toward the general equilibrium, point E.

To learn how this works, let's consider what happens if the economy is at point A, which is on the *IS* curve but not the *LM* curve. Even though at point A the goods market is in equilibrium, so that aggregate output equals aggregate demand, the interest rate is above its equilibrium level, so the demand for money is less than the supply. Because people have more money than they want to hold, they will try to get rid of it by buying bonds. The resulting rise in bond prices causes a fall in interest rates, which in turn causes both planned investment

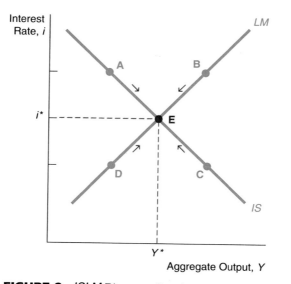

FIGURE 9   *ISLM* Diagram: Simultaneous Determination of Output and the Interest Rate
Only at point E, when the interest rate is i and output is Y*, is there equilibrium simultaneously in both the goods market (as measured by the **IS** curve) and the market for money (as measured by the **LM** curve). At other points, such as A, B, C, or D, one of the two markets is not in equilibrium, and there will be a tendency to head toward the equilibrium, point E.*

spending and net exports to rise, and thus aggregate output rises. The economy then moves down along the *IS* curve, and the process continues until the interest rate falls to i^* and aggregate output rises to Y^*—that is, until the economy is at equilibrium point E.

If the economy is on the *LM* curve but off the *IS* curve at point B, it will also head toward the equilibrium at point E. At point B, even though money demand equals money supply, output is higher than the equilibrium level and exceeds aggregate demand. Firms are unable to sell all their output, and unplanned inventory accumulates, prompting them to cut production and lower output. The decline in output means that the demand for money will fall, lowering interest rates. The economy then moves down along the *LM* curve until it reaches equilibrium point E.

Study Guide   To test your understanding of why the economy heads toward equilibrium point E at the intersection of the **IS** and **LM** curves, see if you can provide the reasoning behind the movement to point E from points such as C and D in the figure.

We have finally developed a model, the *ISLM* model, that tells us how both interest rates and aggregate output are determined when the price level is fixed. Although we have demonstrated that the economy will head toward an aggregate output level of Y^*, there is no reason to assume that at this level of aggregate output the economy is at full employment. If the unemployment rate is too high, government policymakers might want to increase aggregate output to reduce it. The *ISLM* apparatus indicates that they can do this by manipulating monetary and fiscal policy. We will conduct an *ISLM* analysis of how monetary and fiscal policy can affect economic activity in the next chapter.

SUMMARY

1. In the simple Keynesian framework in which the price level is fixed, output is determined by the equilibrium condition in the goods market that aggregate output equals aggregate demand. Aggregate demand equals the sum of consumer expenditure, planned investment spending, government spending, and net exports. Consumer expenditure is described by the consumption function, which indicates that consumer expenditure will rise as disposable income increases. Keynes's analysis shows that aggregate output is positively related to autonomous consumer expenditure, planned investment spending, government spending, and net exports and negatively related to the level of taxes. A change in any of these factors leads, through the expenditure multiplier, to a multiple change in aggregate output.

2. The *ISLM* model determines aggregate output and the interest rate for a fixed price level using the *IS* and *LM* curves. The *IS* curve traces out the combinations of the interest rate and aggregate output for which the goods market is in equilibrium, and the *LM* curve traces out the combinations for which the market for money is in equilibrium. The *IS* curve slopes downward because higher interest rates lower planned investment spending and so lower equilibrium output. The *LM* curve slopes upward because higher aggregate output raises the demand for money and so raises the equilibrium interest rate.

3. The simultaneous determination of output and interest rates occurs at the intersection of the *IS* and *LM* curves, where both the goods market and the market for money are in equilibrium. At any other level of interest rates and output, at least one of the markets will be out of equilibrium, and forces will move the economy toward the general equilibrium point at the intersection of the *IS* and *LM* curves.

KEY TERMS

aggregate demand, p. 556

aggregate demand function,
   p. 560

"animal spirits," p. 564

autonomous consumer
   expenditure, p. 557

consumer expenditure, p. 556

consumption function, p. 557

disposable income, p. 557

expenditure multiplier, p. 562

fixed investment, p. 558

government spending, p. 556

inventory investment, p. 559

IS curve, p. 571

LM curve, p. 571

marginal propensity to
   consume, p. 557

net exports, p. 556

planned investment spending,
   p. 556

QUESTIONS AND PROBLEMS

1. Calculate the value of the consumption function at each level of disposable income in Table 1 if *a* = 100 and *mpc* = 0.9.

*2. Why do companies cut production when they find that their unplanned inventory investment is greater than zero? If they didn't cut production, what effect would this have on their profits? Why?

3. Plot the consumption function $C = 100 + 0.75Y$ on graph paper.
   a. Assuming no government sector, if planned investment spending is 200, what is the equilibrium level of aggregate output? Show this equilibrium level on the graph you have drawn.
   b. If businesses become more pessimistic about the profitability of investment and planned investment spending falls by 100, what happens to the equilibrium level of output?

*4. If the consumption function is $C = 100 + 0.8Y$ and planned investment spending is 200, what is the equilibrium level of output? If planned investment falls by 100, how much does the equilibrium level of output fall?

5. Why are the multipliers in Problems 3 and 4 different? Explain intuitively why one is higher than the other.

*6. If firms suddenly become more optimistic about the profitability of investment and planned investment spending rises by $100 billion, while consumers become more pessimistic and autonomous consumer spending falls by $100 billion, what happens to aggregate output?

7. "A rise in planned investment spending by $100 billion at the same time that autonomous consumer expenditure falls by $50 billion has the same effect on aggregate output as a rise in autonomous consumer expenditure alone by $50

billion." Is this statement true, false, or uncertain? Explain your answer.

*8. If the consumption function is $C = 100 + 0.75Y$, $I = 200$, and government spending is 200, what will be the equilibrium level of output? Demonstrate your answer with a Keynesian cross diagram. What happens to aggregate output if government spending rises by 100?

9. If the marginal propensity to consume is 0.5, how much will government spending have to rise in order to raise output by $1000 billion?

*10. Suppose that government policymakers decide that they will change taxes to raise aggregate output by $400 billion, and *mpc* = 0.5. By how much will taxes have to be changed?

11. What happens to aggregate output if both taxes and government spending are lowered by $300 billion and *mpc* = 0.5? Explain your answer.

*12. Will aggregate output rise or fall if an increase in autonomous consumer expenditure is matched by an equal increase in taxes?

13. If a change in the interest rate has no effect on planned investment spending, trace out what happens to the equilibrium level of aggregate output as interest rates fall. What does this imply about the slope of the *IS* curve?

*14. Using a supply and demand diagram for the market for money, show what happens to the equilibrium level of the interest rate as aggregate output falls. What does this imply about the slope of the *LM* curve?

15. "If the point describing the combination of the interest rate and aggregate output is not on either the *IS* or *LM* curve, the economy will have no tendency to head toward the intersection of the two curves." Is this statement true, false, or uncertain? Explain your answer.

Chapter 23

MONETARY AND FISCAL POLICY IN THE *ISLM* MODEL

P R E V I E W   Since World War II, government policymakers have tried to promote high employment without causing inflation. If the economy experiences a recession such as the one that occurred at the time of Iraq's invasion of Kuwait in 1990, policymakers have two principal sets of tools that they can use to affect aggregate economic activity: *monetary policy,* the control of interest rates or the money supply, and *fiscal policy,* the control of government spending and taxes.

The *ISLM* model can help policymakers predict what will happen to aggregate output and interest rates if they decide to increase the money supply or increase government spending. In this way, *ISLM* analysis enables us to answer some important questions about the usefulness and effectiveness of monetary and fiscal policy on economic activity.

But which is better? When is monetary policy more effective than fiscal policy at controlling the level of aggregate output, and when is it less effective? Will fiscal policy be more effective if it is conducted by changing government spending rather than changing taxes? Should the monetary authorities conduct monetary policy by manipulating the money supply or interest rates?

In this chapter we use the *ISLM* model to help answer these questions and to learn how the model generates the aggregate demand curve featured prominently in the aggregate demand and supply framework (examined in Chapter 24), which is used to understand changes not only in aggregate output but in the price level as well. Our analysis will show why economists focus so much attention on topics such as the stability of the demand for money function and whether the demand for money is strongly influenced by interest rates.

First, however, let's examine the *ISLM* model in more detail to see how the *IS* and *LM* curves developed in Chapter 22 shift and the implications of these shifts. (We continue to assume that the price level is fixed so that real and nominal quantities are the same.)

FACTORS THAT CAUSE THE *IS* CURVE TO SHIFT

You have already learned that the *IS* curve describes equilibrium points in the goods market—the combinations of aggregate output and interest rate for which aggregate output produced equals aggregate demand. The *IS* curve shifts whenever a change in autonomous factors (independent of aggregate output) occurs that is unrelated to the interest rate. (A change in the interest rate that affects equilibrium aggregate output only causes a movement along the *IS* curve.) We have already identified five candidates as autonomous factors that can shift aggregate demand and hence affect the level of equilibrium output. We can now ask how changes in each of these factors affect the *IS* curve.

1. Changes in Autonomous Consumer Expenditure. A rise in autonomous consumer expenditure shifts aggregate demand upward and shifts the *IS* curve to the right (see Figure 1). To see how this shift occurs, suppose that the *IS* curve is initially at IS_1 in panel (a) and a huge oil field is discovered in Wyoming, perhaps containing more oil than in Saudi Arabia. Consumers now become more optimistic about the future health of the economy, and autonomous consumer expenditure rises. What happens to the equilibrium level of aggregate output as a result of this rise in autonomous consumer expenditure when the interest rate is held constant at i_A?

The IS_1 curve tells us that equilibrium aggregate output is at Y_A when the interest rate is at i_A (point A). Panel (b) shows that this point is an equilibrium in the goods market because the aggregate demand function Y_1^{ad} at an interest rate i_A crosses the 45° line $Y = Y^{ad}$ at an aggregate output level of Y_A. When autonomous consumer expenditure rises because of the oil discovery, the aggregate demand function shifts upward to Y_2^{ad} and equilibrium output rises to $Y_{A'}$. This rise in equilibrium output from Y_A to $Y_{A'}$ when the interest rate is i_A is plotted in panel (a) as a movement from point A to point A'. The same analysis can be applied to every point on the initial IS_1 curve; therefore, the rise in autonomous consumer expenditure shifts the *IS* curve to the right from IS_1 to IS_2 in panel (a).

A decline in autonomous consumer expenditure reverses the direction of the analysis. For any given interest rate, the aggregate demand function shifts downward, the equilibrium level of aggregate output falls, and the *IS* curve shifts to the left.

2. Changes in Investment Spending Unrelated to the Interest Rate. In Chapter 22 we learned that changes in the interest rate affect planned investment spending and hence the equilibrium level of output, but this change in investment spending merely causes a movement along the *IS* curve and not a shift. A rise in planned investment spending unrelated to the interest rate (say, because companies become more confident about investment profitability after the Wyoming oil discovery) shifts the aggregate demand function upward, as in panel (b) of Figure 1. For any given interest rate, the equilibrium level of aggregate output rises, and the *IS* curve will shift to the right, as in panel (a).

A decrease in investment spending because companies become more pessimistic about investment profitability shifts the aggregate demand function downward for any given interest rate; the equilibrium level of aggregate output falls, shifting the *IS* curve to the left.

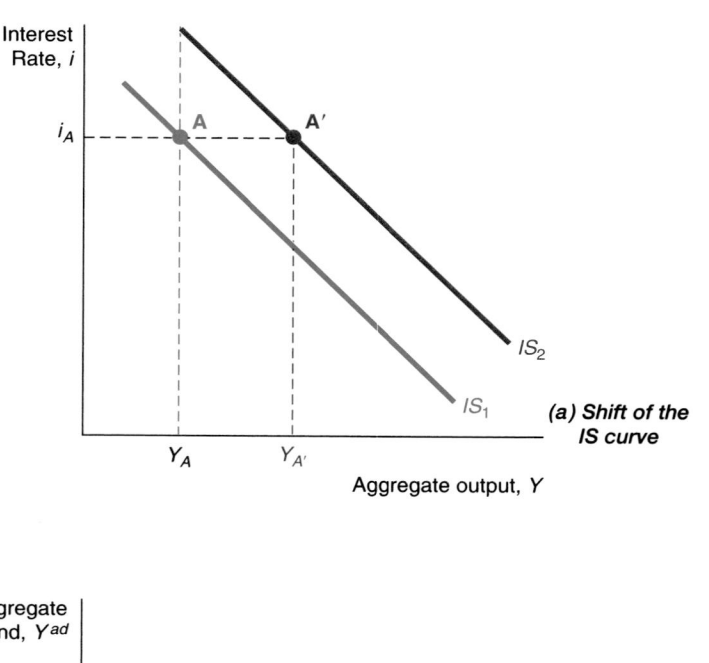

(a) Shift of the IS curve

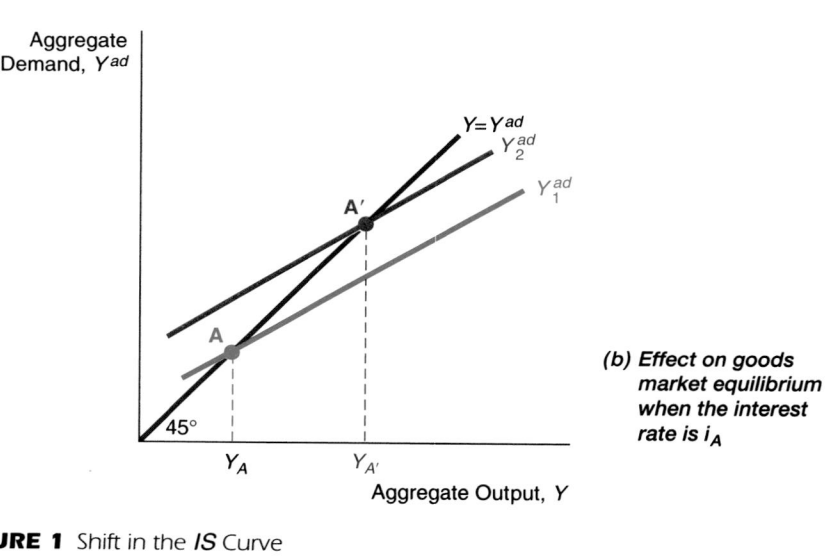

(b) Effect on goods market equilibrium when the interest rate is i_A

FIGURE 1 Shift in the *IS* Curve
The *IS* curve will shift from IS_1 to IS_2 as a result of (1) an increase in autonomous consumer spending, (2) an increase in planned investment spending due to business optimism, (3) an increase in government spending, (4) a decrease in taxes, or (5) an increase in net exports that is unrelated to interest rates. Panel (b) shows how changes in these factors lead to the rightward shift in the *IS* curve using a Keynesian cross diagram. For any given interest rate (here i_A), these changes shift the aggregate demand function upward and raise equilibrium output from Y_A to $Y_{A'}$.

3. Changes in Government Spending. An increase in government spending will also cause the aggregate demand function at any given interest rate to shift upward, as in panel (b). The equilibrium level of aggregate output rises at any given interest rate, and the *IS* curve shifts to the right. Conversely, a decline in government spending shifts the aggregate demand function downward, and the equilibrium level of output falls, shifting the *IS* curve to the left.

4. Changes in Taxes. Unlike changes in other factors that directly affect the aggregate demand function, a decline in taxes shifts the aggregate demand function by raising consumer expenditure and shifting the aggregate demand function upward at any given interest rate. A decline in taxes raises the equilibrium level of aggregate output at any given interest rate and shifts the *IS* curve to the right (as in Figure 1). Recall, however, that a change in taxes has a smaller effect on aggregate demand than an equivalent change in government spending. So for a given change in taxes, the *IS* curve will shift less than for an equal change in government spending.

A rise in taxes lowers the aggregate demand function and reduces the equilibrium level of aggregate output at each interest rate. Therefore, a rise in taxes shifts the *IS* curve to the left.

5. Changes in Net Exports Unrelated to the Interest Rate. As with planned investment spending, changes in net exports arising from a change in interest rates merely cause a movement along the *IS* curve and not a shift. An autonomous rise in net exports unrelated to the interest rate—say, because American-made jeans become more chic than French-made jeans—shifts the aggregate demand function upward and causes the *IS* curve to shift to the right, as in Figure 1. Conversely, an autonomous fall in net exports shifts the aggregate demand function downward, and the equilibrium level of output falls, shifting the *IS* curve to the left.

FACTORS THAT CAUSE THE *LM* CURVE TO SHIFT

The *LM* curve describes the equilibrium points in the market for money—the combinations of aggregate output and interest rate for which the quantity of money demanded equals the quantity of money supplied. Whereas five factors can cause the *IS* curve to shift (changes in autonomous consumer expenditure, planned investment spending unrelated to the interest rate, government spending, taxes, and net exports unrelated to the interest rate), only two factors can cause the *LM* curve to shift: autonomous changes in money demand and changes in the money supply. How do changes in these two factors affect the *LM* curve?

1. Changes in the Money Supply. A rise in the money supply shifts the *LM* curve to the right, as shown in Figure 2. To see how this shift occurs, suppose that the *LM* curve is initially at LM_1 in panel (a) and the Federal Reserve conducts open market purchases that increase the money supply. If we consider point A, which is on the initial LM_1 curve, we can examine what happens to the equilibrium level of the interest rate, holding output constant at Y_A.

Panel (b), which contains a supply and demand diagram for the market for money, depicts the equilibrium interest rate initially as i_A at the intersection of the supply curve for money M_1^s and the demand curve for money M^d. The rise in the quantity of money supplied shifts the supply curve to M_2^s, and, holding output constant at Y_A, the equilibrium interest rate falls to $i_{A'}$. In panel (a), this decline in the equilibrium interest rate from i_A to $i_{A'}$ is shown as a movement from point A to point A'. The same analysis can be applied to every point on the initial LM_1 curve, leading to the conclusion that at any given level of aggregate output, the

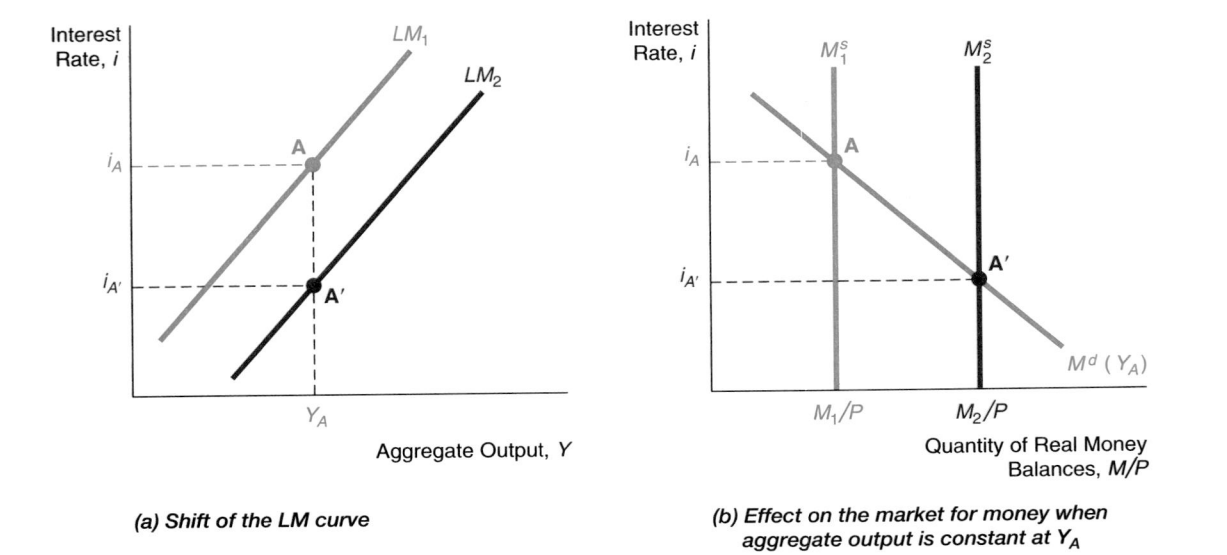

FIGURE 2 Shift in the **LM** Curve from an Increase in the Money Supply
The **LM** curve shifts to the right from **LM**₁ to **LM**₂ when the money supply increases because, as indicated in panel (b), at any given level of aggregate output (say, Y_A), the equilibrium interest rate falls (point A to A').

equilibrium interest rate falls when the money supply increases. Thus LM_2 is below and to the right of LM_1.

Reversing this reasoning, a decline in the money supply shifts the *LM* curve to the left. A decline in the money supply results in a shortage of money at points on the initial *LM* curve. This condition of excess demand for money can be eliminated by a rise in the interest rate, which reduces the quantity of money demanded until it again equals the quantity of money supplied.

2. Autonomous Changes in Money Demand. The theory of portfolio choice outlined in Chapter 5 indicates that there can be an autonomous rise in money demand (not caused by a change in the price level, aggregate output, or the interest rate). For example, an increase in the volatility of bond returns would make bonds riskier relative to money and would increase the quantity of money demanded at any given interest rate, price level, or amount of aggregate output. The resulting autonomous increase in the demand for money shifts the *LM* curve to the left, as shown in Figure 3. Consider point A on the initial LM_1 curve. Suppose that a massive financial panic occurs, sending many companies into bankruptcy. Because bonds have become a riskier asset, people want to shift from holding bonds to holding money; they will hold more money at all interest rates and output levels. The resulting increase in money demand at an output level of Y_A is shown by the shift of the money demand curve from M_1^d to M_2^d in panel (b). The new equilibrium in the market for money now indicates that if aggregate output is constant at Y_A, the equilibrium interest rate will rise to $i_{A'}$, and the point of equilibrium moves from A to A'.

Conversely, an autonomous decline in money demand would lead to a rightward shift in the *LM* curve. The fall in money demand would create an excess

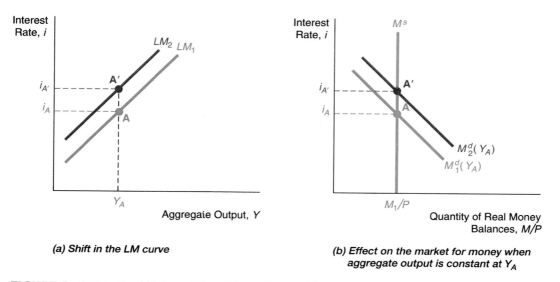

(a) Shift in the LM curve

(b) Effect on the market for money when aggregate output is constant at Y_A

FIGURE 3   Shift in the *LM* Curve When Money Demand Increases
The *LM* curve shifts to the left from *LM*₁ to *LM*₂ when money demand increases because, as indicated in panel (b), at any given level of aggregate output (say, Y_A) , the equilibrium interest rate rises (point A to A').

supply of money, which is eliminated by a rise in the quantity of money demanded from a decline in the interest rate.

CHANGES IN EQUILIBRIUM LEVEL OF THE INTEREST RATE AND AGGREGATE OUTPUT

You can now use your knowledge of factors that cause the *IS* and *LM* curves to shift for the purpose of analyzing how the equilibrium levels of the interest rate and aggregate output change in response to changes in monetary and fiscal policies.

Response to a Change in Monetary Policy

Figure 4 illustrates the response of output and interest rate to an increase in the money supply. Initially, the economy is in equilibrium for both the goods market and the market for money at point 1, the intersection of IS_1 and LM_1. Suppose that at the resulting level of aggregate output Y_1, the economy is suffering from an unemployment rate of 20 percent, and the Federal Reserve decides that it should try to raise output and reduce unemployment by raising the money supply. Will the Fed's change in monetary policy have the intended effect?

The rise in the money supply causes the *LM* curve to shift rightward to LM_2, and the equilibrium point for both the goods market and the market for money moves to point 2 (intersection of IS_1 and LM_2). As a result of an increase in the money supply, the interest rate declines to i_2, as we found in Chapter 6, and aggregate output rises to Y_2; the Fed's policy has been successful in improving the health of the economy.

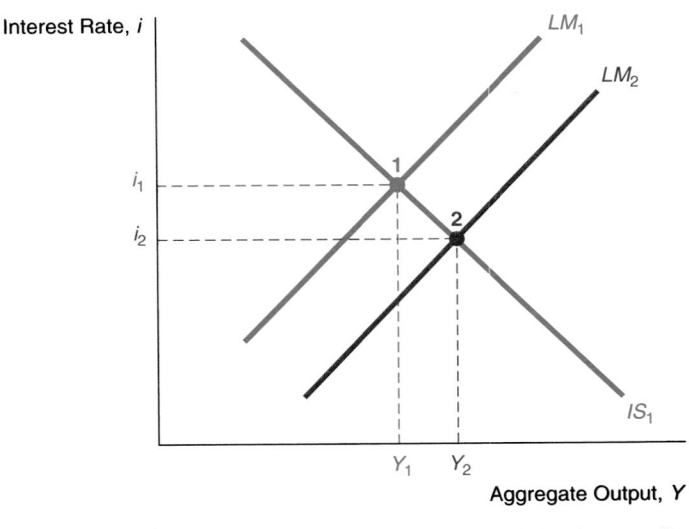

FIGURE 4 Response of Aggregate Output and the Interest Rate to an Increase in the Money Supply
The increase in the money supply shifts the **LM** curve to the right from **LM₁** to **LM₂**; the economy moves to point 2, where output has increased to **Y₂** and the interest rate has declined to i_2

For a clear understanding of why aggregate output rises and the interest rate declines, think about exactly what has happened in moving from point 1 to point 2. When the economy is at point 1, the increase in the money supply (rightward shift of the *LM* curve) creates an excess supply of money, resulting in a decline in the interest rate. The decline causes investment spending and net exports to rise, which in turn raises aggregate demand and causes aggregate output to rise. The excess supply of money is eliminated when the economy reaches point 2 because both the rise in output and the fall in the interest rate have raised the quantity of money demanded until it equals the new higher level of the money supply.

A decline in the money supply reverses the process; it shifts the *LM* curve to the left, causing the interest rate to rise and output to fall. Accordingly, ***aggregate output is positively related to the money supply;*** aggregate output expands when the money supply increases and falls when it decreases.

Response to a Change in Fiscal Policy

Suppose that the Federal Reserve is not willing to increase the money supply when the economy is suffering from a 20 percent unemployment rate at point 1. Can the federal government come to the rescue and manipulate government spending and taxes to raise aggregate output and reduce the massive unemployment?

The *ISLM* model demonstrates that it can. Figure 5 depicts the response of output and the interest rate to an expansionary fiscal policy (increase in government spending or decrease in taxes). An increase in government spending or a

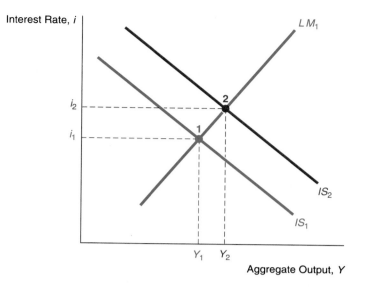

FIGURE 5   Response of Aggregate Output and the Interest Rate to an Expansionary Fiscal Policy

Expansionary fiscal policy (a rise in government spending or a decrease in taxes) shifts the **IS** curve to the right from **IS**$_1$ to **IS**$_2$; the economy moves to point 2, aggregate output increases to **Y**$_2$, and the interest rate rises to i_2.

decrease in taxes causes the *IS* curve to shift to *IS*$_2$, and the equilibrium point for both the goods market and the market for money moves to point 2 (intersection of *IS*$_2$ with *LM*$_1$). The result of the change in fiscal policy is a rise in aggregate output to *Y*$_2$ and a rise in the interest rate to i_2. Note the difference in the effect on the interest rate of an expansionary fiscal policy from an expansionary monetary policy. In the case of an expansionary fiscal policy, the interest rate rises, whereas in the case of an expansionary monetary policy, the interest rate falls.

   Why does an increase in government spending or a decrease in taxes move the economy from point 1 to point 2, causing a rise in both aggregate output and the interest rate? An increase in government spending raises aggregate demand directly; a decrease in taxes makes more income available for spending and raises aggregate demand by raising consumer expenditure. The resulting increase in aggregate demand causes aggregate output to rise. The higher level of aggregate output raises the quantity of money demanded, creating an excess demand for money, which in turn causes the interest rate to rise. At point 2, the excess demand for money created by a rise in aggregate output has been eliminated by a rise in the interest rate, which lowers the quantity of money demanded.

   A contractionary fiscal policy (decrease in government spending or increase in taxes) reverses the process described in Figure 5; it causes aggregate demand to fall, which shifts the *IS* curve to the left and causes both aggregate output and the interest rate to fall. ***Aggregate output and the interest rate are positively related to government spending and negatively related to taxes.***

Study Guide   As a study aid, Table 1 indicates the effect on aggregate output and interest rates of a change in the seven factors that shift the *IS* and *LM* curves. In addition, the table provides schematics describing the reason for the output and interest-rate response. *ISLM* analysis is best learned by practicing applications. To get this practice, you might try to develop the reasoning for your own Table 1 in which all the factors decrease rather than increase or answer Problems 5–7 and 13–15 at the end of this chapter.

The Vietnam War Buildup and the Rise in Interest Rates, 1965–1966

From early 1965 to the end of 1966, America dramatically increased its involvement in the Vietnam War by increasing the number of troops in Vietnam from under 25,000 to over 350,000. The troop buildup resulted in a substantial rise in military spending, which led to a $66 billion (in 1992 dollars) increase in government spending from 1965 to 1966 (from $682 billion to $748 billion). What does our *ISLM* model predict should have happened to aggregate output and interest rates as a result?

Figure 6 shows that the increase in government spending would have shifted the *IS* curve to the right from IS_1 to IS_2, while the *LM* curve remained unchanged because the money supply (M1) remained almost constant in real terms: $711 billion in 1965 and $704 billion (in 1992 dollars) in 1966. The *ISLM* model then predicts that the economy moves from point 1 to point 2, meaning that both GDP

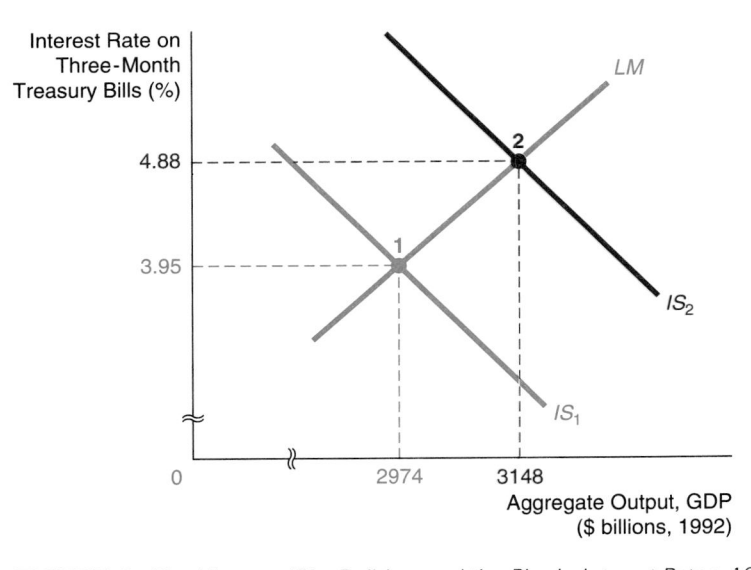

FIGURE 6 The Vietnam War Buildup and the Rise in Interest Rates, 1965–1966
The rise in military spending from 1965 to 1966 led to a rightward shift of the *IS* curve from IS_1 to IS_2, which moved the economy from point 1 to point 2, thereby raising both aggregate output and the interest rate.

— S U M M A R Y —

TABLE 1		**Effects from Factors That Shift the *IS* and *LM* Curves**		
Factor	**Change in Factor**	**Response**	**Reason**	
Consumer expenditure, C	$\uparrow$	$Y\uparrow, i\uparrow$	$C\uparrow \Rightarrow Y^{ad}\uparrow \Rightarrow$ IS shifts right	
Investment, I	$\uparrow$	$Y\uparrow, i\uparrow$	$I\uparrow \Rightarrow Y^{ad}\uparrow \Rightarrow$ IS shifts right	
Government spending, G	$\uparrow$	$Y\uparrow, i\uparrow$	$G\uparrow \Rightarrow Y^{ad}\uparrow \Rightarrow$ IS shifts right	
Taxes, T	$\uparrow$	$Y\downarrow, i\downarrow$	$T\uparrow \Rightarrow C\downarrow \Rightarrow Y^{ad}\downarrow \Rightarrow$ IS shifts left	
Net exports, NX	$\uparrow$	$Y\uparrow, i\uparrow$	$NX\uparrow \Rightarrow Y^{ad}\uparrow \Rightarrow$ IS shifts right	
Money supply, M^s	$\uparrow$	$Y\uparrow, i\downarrow$	$M^s\uparrow \Rightarrow i\downarrow \Rightarrow$ LM shifts right	
Money supply, M^d	$\uparrow$	$Y\downarrow, i\uparrow$	$M^d\uparrow \Rightarrow i\uparrow \Rightarrow$ LM shifts left	

Note: Only increases ($\uparrow$) in the factors are shown. The effect of decreases in the factors would be the opposite of those indicated in the "Response" column.

and interest rates rise, and that is exactly what happened from 1965 to 1966: GDP rose by $174 billion (a multiple of the $66 billion increase in government spending), from $2974 billion to $3148 billion, while the interest rate on three-month Treasury bills rose from 3.95 percent to 4.88 percent.[1]

Economists at the time agreed that taxes needed to be increased to keep the economy from overheating and to reduce interest rates by shifting the *IS* curve back to the left. Unfortunately, President Lyndon Johnson thought it politically infeasible to raise taxes to pay for what was rapidly becoming America's most unpopular war. Taxes were not increased until 1968, and by then the overheated economy had burst into inflation and the then record-high interest rates. (A)

EFFECTIVENESS OF MONETARY VERSUS FISCAL POLICY

Our discussion of the effects of fiscal and monetary policy suggests that a government can easily lift an economy out of a recession by implementing any of a number of policies (changing the money supply, government spending, or taxes). But how can policymakers decide which of these policies to use if faced with too much unemployment? Should they decrease taxes, increase government spending, raise the money supply, or do all three? And if they decide to increase the money supply, by how much? Economists do not pretend to have all the answers, and although the *ISLM* model will not clear the path to aggregate economic bliss, it can help policymakers decide which policies might be most effective under certain circumstances.

Monetary Policy Versus Fiscal Policy: The Case of Complete Crowding Out

The *ISLM* model developed so far in this chapter shows that both monetary and fiscal policy affect the level of aggregate output. To understand when monetary policy is more effective than fiscal policy, we will examine a special case of the *ISLM* model in which money demand is unaffected by the interest rate (money demand is said to be interest-inelastic) so that monetary policy affects output but fiscal policy does not.

Consider the slope of the *LM* curve if the demand for money is unaffected by changes in the interest rate. If point 1 in panel (a) of Figure 7 is such that the quantity of money demanded equals the quantity of money supplied, then it is on the *LM* curve. If the interest rate rises to, say, i_2, the quantity of money demanded is unaffected, and it will continue to equal the *unchanged* quantity of money supplied only if aggregate output remains *unchanged* at Y_1 (point 2). Equilibrium in the market for money will occur at the same level of aggregate output regardless of the interest rate, and the *LM* curve will be vertical, as shown in both panels of Figure 7.

---

[1]An alternative explanation of why interest rates rose from 1965 to 1966 is that expected inflation increased over this period, causing nominal interest rates to rise. (See Chapter 6 for an explanation of why a rise in expected inflation can raise nominal interest rates.) Note that this explanation and the *ISLM* explanation are not inconsistent; both the rise in expected inflation and the rightward shift of the *IS* curve may have contributed to the rise in interest rates in this period.

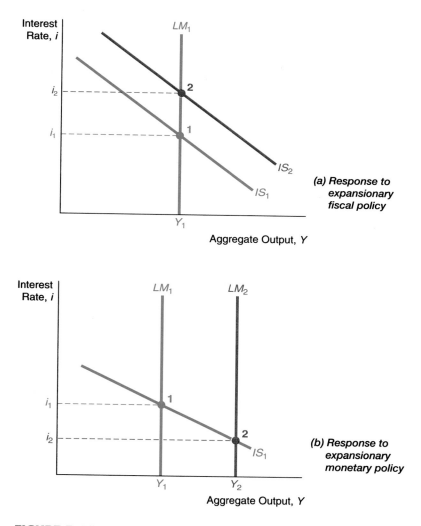

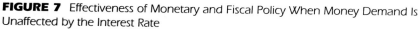

FIGURE 7   Effectiveness of Monetary and Fiscal Policy When Money Demand Is Unaffected by the Interest Rate

When the demand for money is unaffected by the interest rate, the **LM** curve is vertical. In panel (a), an expansionary fiscal policy (increase in government spending or a cut in taxes) shifts the **IS** curve from IS_1 to IS_2 and leaves aggregate output unchanged at Y_1. In panel (b), an increase in the money supply shifts the **LM** curve from LM_1 to LM_2 and raises aggregate output from Y_1 to Y_2. Therefore, monetary policy is effective, but fiscal policy is not.

Suppose that the economy is suffering from a high rate of unemployment, which policymakers try to eliminate with either expansionary fiscal or monetary policy. Panel (a) depicts what happens when an expansionary fiscal policy (increase in government spending or cut in taxes) is implemented, shifting the *IS* curve to the right from IS_1 to IS_2. As you can see in panel (a), the fiscal expansion has no effect on output; aggregate output remains at Y_1 when the economy moves from point 1 to point 2.

In our earlier analysis, expansionary fiscal policy always increased aggregate demand and raised the level of output. Why doesn't that happen in panel (a)? The answer is that because the *LM* curve is vertical, the rightward shift of the *IS* curve raises the interest rate to i_2, which causes investment spending and net exports to fall enough to offset completely the increased spending of the expansionary fiscal policy. Put another way, increased spending that results from expansionary fiscal policy has *crowded out* investment spending and net exports, which decrease because of the rise in the interest rate. This situation in which expansionary fiscal policy does not lead to a rise in output is frequently referred to as a case of **complete crowding out.**[2]

Panel (b) shows what happens when the Federal Reserve tries to eliminate high unemployment through an expansionary monetary policy (increase in the money supply). Here the *LM* curve shifts to the right from LM_1 to LM_2 because at each interest rate, output must rise so that the quantity of money demanded rises to match the increase in the money supply. Aggregate output rises from Y_1 to Y_2 (the economy moves from point 1 to point 2), and expansionary monetary policy does affect aggregate output in this case.

We conclude from the analysis in Figure 7 that if the demand for money is unaffected by changes in the interest rate (money demand is interest-inelastic), monetary policy is effective but fiscal policy is not. An even more general conclusion can be reached: ***The less interest-sensitive money demand is, the more effective monetary policy is relative to fiscal policy.***

Because the interest sensitivity of money demand is important to policymakers' decisions regarding the use of monetary or fiscal policy to influence economic activity, the subject has been studied extensively by economists and has been the focus of many debates. Findings on the interest sensitivity of money demand are discussed in Chapter 21.

Targeting Money Supply Versus Interest Rates

In the 1970s and early 1980s, central banks in many countries pursued a strategy of monetary targeting—that is, they used their policy tools to hit a money supply target (tried to make the money supply equal to a target value). However, as we have seen in Chapter 19, many of these central banks abandoned monetary targeting in the 1980s because of the breakdown of the stable relationship between the money supply and economic activity to pursue interest-rate targeting instead. The *ISLM* model has important implications for which variable a central bank

---

[2]When the demand for money is affected by the interest rate, the usual case in which the *LM* curve slopes upward but is not vertical, some crowding out occurs. The rightward shift of the *IS* curve also raises the interest rate, which causes investment spending and net exports to fall somewhat. However, as Figure 5 indicates, the rise in the interest rate is not sufficient to reduce investment spending and net exports to the point where aggregate output does not increase. Thus expansionary fiscal policy increases aggregate output, and only partial crowding out occurs.

should target and we can apply it to explain why central banks have abandoned monetary targeting for interest-rate targeting.[3]

As we saw in Chapter 19, when the Federal Reserve attempts to hit a money supply target, it cannot at the same time pursue an interest-rate target; it can hit one target or the other but not both. Consequently, it needs to know which of these two targets will produce more accurate control of aggregate output.

In contrast to the textbook world you have been inhabiting, in which the *IS* and *LM* curves are assumed to be fixed, the real world is one of great uncertainty in which *IS* and *LM* curves shift unexpectedly because of unanticipated changes in autonomous spending and money demand. To understand whether the Fed should use a money supply target or an interest-rate target, we need to look at two cases: first, one in which uncertainty about the *IS* curve is far greater than uncertainty about the *LM* curve and another in which uncertainty about the *LM* curve is far greater than uncertainty about the *IS* curve.

The *ISLM* diagram in Figure 8 illustrates the outcome of the two targeting strategies for the case in which the *IS* curve is unstable and uncertain and so it fluctuates around its expected value of IS^* from IS' and IS'', while the *LM* curve is stable and certain so it stays at LM^*. Since the central bank knows that the expected position of the *IS* curve is at IS^* and desires aggregate output of Y^*, it will set its interest-rate target at i^* so that the expected level of output is Y^*. This policy of targeting the interest rate at i^* is labeled "Interest-Rate Target."

How would the central bank keep the interest rate at its target level of i^*? Recall from Chapter 19 that the Fed can hit its interest-rate target by buying and selling bonds when the interest rate differs from i^*. When the *IS* curve shifts out to IS'', the interest rate would rise above i^* with the money supply unchanged. However, to counter this rise in interest rates, the central bank would need to buy bonds just until their price is driven back up so that the interest rate comes back down to i^*. (The result of these open market purchases is that, as we have seen in Chapters 16 and 17, the monetary base and the money supply rise until the *LM* curve shifts to the right to intersect the IS'' curve at i^*—not shown in the diagram for simplicity.) When the interest rate is below i^*, the central bank needs to sell bonds to lower their price and raise the interest rate back up to i^*. (These open market sales reduce the monetary base and the money supply until the *LM* curve shifts to the left to intersect the *IS* curve at IS'—again not shown in the diagram.) The result of pursuing the interest-rate target is that aggregate output fluctuates between Y'_I and Y''_I in Figure 8.

If, instead, the Fed pursues a money supply target, it will set the money supply so that the resulting *LM* curve LM^* intersects the IS^* curve at the desired output level of Y^*. This policy of targeting the money supply is labeled "Money Supply Target." Because it is not changing the money supply and so keeps the *LM* curve at LM^*, aggregate output will fluctuate between Y'_M and Y''_M for the money supply target policy.

---

[3]The classic paper on this topic is William Poole, "The Optimal Choice of Monetary Policy Instruments in a Simple Macro Model," *Quarterly Journal of Economics* 84 (1970): 192–216. A less mathematical version of his analysis, far more accessible to students, is contained in William Poole, "Rules of Thumb for Guiding Monetary Policy," in *Open Market Policies and Operating Procedures: Staff Studies* (Washington, D.C.: Board of Governors of the Federal Reserve System, 1971).

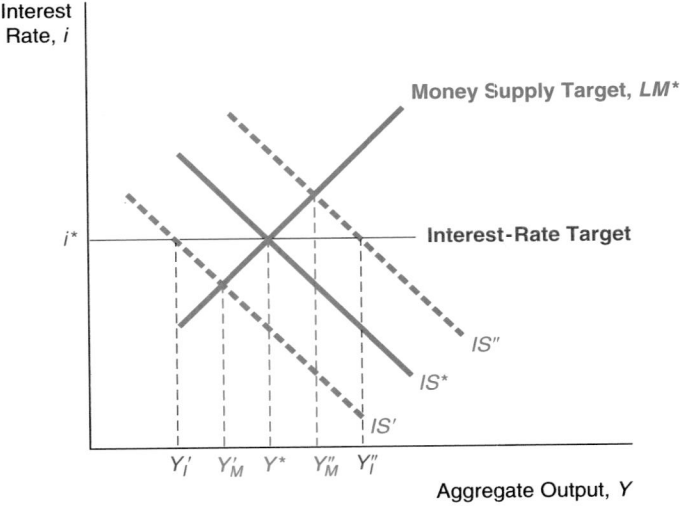

FIGURE 8 Money Supply and Interest-Rate Targets When the *IS* Curve Is Unstable and the *LM* Curve Is Stable

The unstable *IS* curve fluctuates between *IS'* and *IS"*. The money supply target produces smaller fluctuations in output (Y'_M to Y''_M) than the interest rate targets (Y'_I to Y''_I). Therefore, the money supply target is preferred.

As you can see in the figure, the money supply target leads to smaller output fluctuations around the desired level than the interest-rate target. A rightward shift of the *IS* curve to *IS"*, for example, causes the interest rate to rise, given a money supply target, and this rise in the interest rate leads to a lower level of investment spending and net exports and hence to a smaller increase in aggregate output than occurs under an interest-rate target. Because smaller output fluctuations are desirable, the conclusion is that *if the IS curve is more unstable than the LM curve, a money supply target is preferred.*

The outcome of the two targeting strategies for the case of a stable *IS* curve and an unstable *LM* curve is illustrated in Figure 9. Again, the interest-rate and money supply targets are set so that the expected level of aggregate output equals the desired level Y^*. Because the *LM* curve is now unstable, it fluctuates between *LM'* and *LM"* even when the money supply is fixed, causing aggregate output to fluctuate between Y'_M and Y''_M.

The interest-rate target, by contrast, is not affected by uncertainty about the *LM* curve because it is set by the Fed's adjusting the money supply whenever the interest rate tries to depart from i^*. When the interest rate begins to rise above i^* because of an increase in money demand, the central bank again just buys bonds, driving up their price and bringing the interest rate back down to i^*. The result of these open market purchases is a rise in the monetary base and the money supply. Similarly, if the interest rate falls below i^*, the central bank sells bonds to lower their price and raise the interest rate back to i^*, thereby causing a decline in the monetary base and the money supply. The only effect of the fluctuating *LM* curve, then, is that the money supply fluctuates more as a result of the interest-

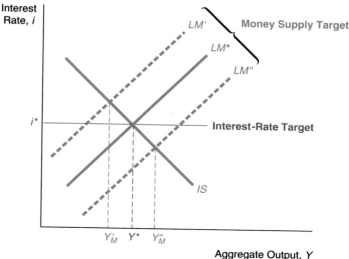

FIGURE 9   Money Supply and Interest-Rate Targets When the **LM** Curve Is Unstable and the **IS** Curve Is Stable

The unstable **LM** curve fluctuates between **LM′** and **LM″**. The money supply target then produces bigger fluctuations in output (Y'_M to Y''_M) than the interest-rate target (which leaves output fixed at Y^*). Therefore, the interest-rate target is preferred.

rate target policy. The outcome of the interest-rate target is that output will be exactly at the desired level with no fluctuations.

Since smaller output fluctuations are desirable, the conclusion from Figure 9 is that ***if the LM curve is more unstable than the IS curve, an interest-rate target is preferred.***

We can now see why many central banks decided to abandon monetary targeting for inflation targeting in the 1980s. With the rapid proliferation of new financial instruments whose presence can affect the demand for money (see Chapter 21), money demand (which is embodied in the *LM* curve) became highly unstable in many countries. Thus central banks in these countries recognized that they were more likely to be in the situation in Figure 9 and decided that they would be better off with an interest-rate target than a money supply target.[4]   Ⓐ

---

[4]It is important to recognize, however, that the crucial factor in deciding which target is preferred is the *relative* instability of the *IS* and *LM* curves. Although the *LM* curve has been unstable recently, the evidence supporting a stable *IS* curve is also weak. Instability in the money demand function does not automatically mean that money supply targets should be abandoned for an interest-rate target. Furthermore, the analysis so far has been conducted assuming that the price level is fixed. More realistically, when the price level can change so that there is uncertainty about expected inflation, the case for an interest-rate target is less strong. As we learned in Chapters 4 and 6, the interest rate that is more relevant to investment decisions is not the nominal interest rate but the real interest rate (the nominal interest rate minus expected inflation). Hence when expected inflation rises, at each given nominal interest rate, the real interest rate falls and investment and net exports rise, shifting the *IS* curve to the right. Similarly, a fall in expected inflation raises the real interest rate at each given nominal interest rate, lowers investment and net exports, and shifts the *IS* curve to the left. Since in the real world, expected inflation undergoes large fluctuations, the *IS* curve in Figure 9 will also have substantial fluctuations, making it less likely that the interest-rate target is better than the money supply target.

ISLM MODEL IN THE LONG RUN

So far in our *ISLM* analysis, we have been assuming that the price level is fixed so that nominal values and real values are the same. This is a reasonable assumption for the short run, but in the long run the price level does change. To see what happens in the *ISLM* model in the long run, we make use of the concept of the **natural rate level of output** (denoted by Y_n), which is the rate of output at which the price level has no tendency to rise or fall. When output is above the natural rate level, the booming economy will cause prices to rise; when output is below the natural rate level, the slack in the economy will cause prices to fall.

Because we now want to examine what happens when the price level changes, we can no longer assume that real and nominal values are the same. The spending variables that affect the *IS* curve (consumer expenditure, investment spending, government spending, and net exports) describe the demand for goods and services and are *in real terms*; they describe the physical quantities of goods that people want to buy. Because these quantities do not change when the price level changes, a change in the price level has no effect on the *IS* curve, which describes the combinations of the interest rate and aggregate output *in real terms* that satisfy goods market equilibrium.

Figure 10 shows what happens in the *ISLM* model when output rises above the natural rate level, which is marked by a vertical line at Y_n. Suppose that initially the *IS* and *LM* curves intersect at point 1, where output $Y = Y_n$. Panel (a) examines what happens to output and interest rates when there is a rise in the money supply. As we saw in Figure 2, the rise in the money supply causes the *LM* curve to shift to LM_2, and the equilibrium moves to point 2 (the intersection of IS_1 and LM_2), where the interest rate falls to i_2 and output rises to Y_2. However, as we can see in panel (a), the level of output at Y_2 is greater than the natural rate level Y_n, and so the price level begins to rise.

In contrast to the *IS* curve, which is unaffected by a rise in the price level, the *LM* curve is affected by the price level rise because the liquidity preference theory states that the demand for money *in real terms* depends on real income and interest rates. This makes sense because money is valued in terms of what it can buy. However, the money supply that you read about in newspapers is not the money supply in real terms; it is a nominal quantity. As the price level rises, the quantity of money *in real terms* falls, and the effect on the *LM* curve is identical to a fall in the nominal money supply with the price level fixed. The lower value of the real money supply creates an excess demand for money, causing the interest rate to rise at any given level of aggregate output, and the *LM* curve shifts back to the left. As long as the level of output exceeds the natural rate level, the price level will continue to rise, shifting the *LM* curve to the left, until finally output is back at the natural rate level Y_n. This occurs when the *LM* curve has returned to LM_1, where real money balances M/P have returned to the original level and the economy has returned to the original equilibrium at point 1. The result of the expansion in the money supply in the long run is that the economy has the same level of output and interest rates.

The fact that the increase in the money supply has left output and interest rates unchanged in the long run is referred to as **long-run monetary neutrality.** The only result of the increase in the money supply is a higher price level, which

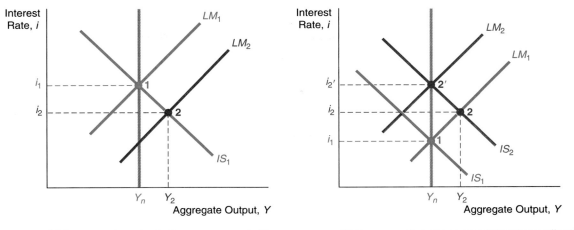

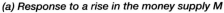
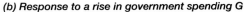

(a) *Response to a rise in the money supply M*   (b) *Response to a rise in government spending G*

FIGURE 10 The ISLM Model in the Long Run

In panel (a), a rise in the money supply causes the *LM* curve to shift rightward to *LM*₂, and the equilibrium moves to point 2, where the interest rate falls to i_2 and output rises to Y_2. Because output at Y_2 is above the natural rate level Y_n, the price level rises, the real money supply falls, and the *LM* curve shifts back to *LM*₁; the economy has returned to the original equilibrium at point 1. In panel (b), an increase in government spending shifts the *IS* curve to the right to *IS*₂, and the economy moves to point 2, at which the interest rate has risen to i_2 and output has risen to Y_2. Because output at Y_2 is above the natural rate level Y_n, the price level begins to rise, real money balances *M/P* begin to fall, and the *LM* curve shifts to the left to *LM*₂. The long-run equilibrium at point 2' has an even higher interest rate at $i_{2'}$, and output has returned to Y_n.

has increased proportionally to the increase in the money supply so that real money balances *M/P* are unchanged.

Panel (b) looks at what happens to output and interest rates when there is expansionary fiscal policy such as an increase in government spending. As we saw earlier, the increase in government spending shifts the *IS* curve to the right to *IS*₂, and in the short run the economy moves to point 2 (the intersection of *IS*₂ and *LM*₁), where the interest rate has risen to i_2 and output has risen to Y_2. Because output at Y_2 is above the natural rate level Y_n, the price level begins to rise, real money balances *M/P* begin to fall, and the *LM* curve shifts to the left. Only when the *LM* curve has shifted to *LM*₂ and the equilibrium is at point 2', where output is again at the natural rate level Y_n, does the price level stop rising and the *LM* curve come to rest. The resulting long-run equilibrium at point 2' has an even higher interest rate at $i_{2'}$ and output has not risen from Y_n. Indeed, what has occurred in the long run is complete crowding out: The rise in the price level, which has shifted the *LM* curve to *LM*₂, has caused the interest rate to rise to $i_{2'}$, causing investment and net exports to fall enough to offset the increased government spending completely. What we have discovered is that even though complete crowding out does not occur in the short run in the *ISLM* model (when the *LM* curve is not vertical), it does occur in the long run.

Our conclusion from examining what happens in the *ISLM* model from an expansionary monetary or fiscal policy is that ***although monetary and fiscal policy can affect output in the short run, neither affects output in the long run.*** Clearly, an important issue in deciding on the effectiveness of monetary and fiscal policy to raise output is how soon the long run occurs. This is a topic that we explore in the next chapter.

ISLM MODEL AND THE AGGREGATE DEMAND CURVE

We now examine further what happens in the *ISLM* model when the price level changes. When we conduct the *ISLM* analysis with a changing price level, we find that as the price level falls, the level of aggregate output rises. Thus we obtain a relationship between the price level and quantity of aggregate output for which the goods market and the market for money are in equilibrium, called the **aggregate demand curve.** This aggregate demand curve is a central element in the aggregate supply and demand analysis of Chapter 24, which allows us to explain changes not only in aggregate output but also in the price level.

Deriving the Aggregate Demand Curve

Now that you understand how a change in the price level affects the *IS* and *LM* curves, we can analyze what happens in the *ISLM* diagram when the price level changes. This exercise is carried out in Figure 11. Panel (a) contains an *ISLM* diagram for a given value of the nominal money supply. Let us first consider a price level of P_1. The *LM* curve at this price level is $LM(P_1)$, and its intersection with the *IS* curve is at point 1, where output is Y_1. The equilibrium output level Y_1 that occurs when the price level is P_1 is also plotted in panel (b) as point 1. If the price level rises to P_2, then *in real terms* the money supply has fallen. The effect on the *LM* curve is identical to a decline in the nominal money supply when the price level is fixed: The *LM* curve will shift leftward to $LM(P_2)$. The new equilibrium level of output has fallen to Y_2 because planned investment and net exports fall when the interest rate rises. Point 2 in panel (b) plots this level of

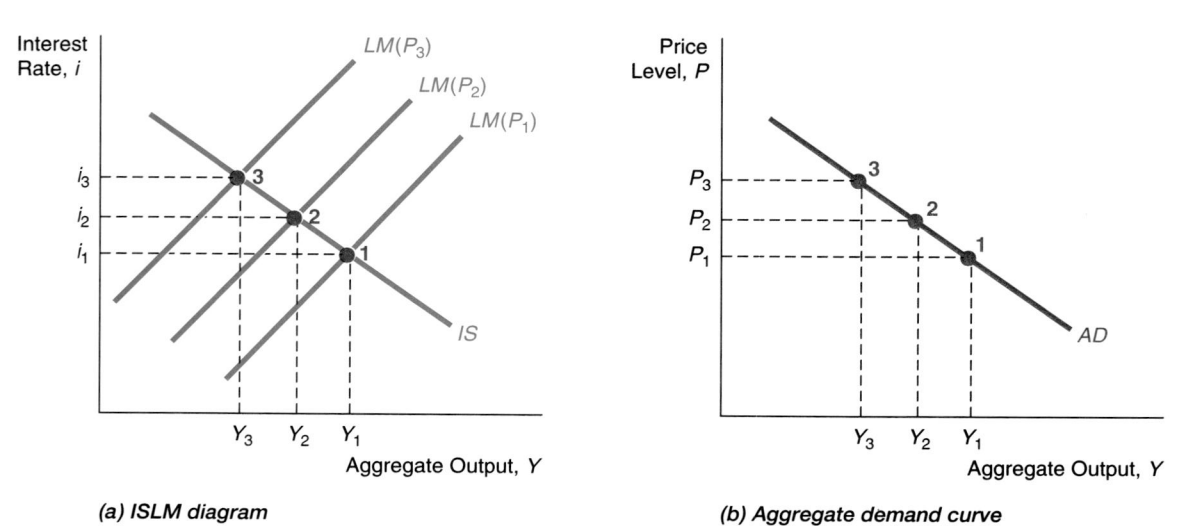

(a) ISLM diagram   **(b) Aggregate demand curve**

FIGURE 11 Deriving the Aggregate Demand Curve
The *ISLM* diagram in panel (a) shows that as the price level rises from P_1 to P_2 to P_3, the *LM* curve shifts to the left, and equilibrium output falls. The combinations of the price level and equilibrium output from panel (a) are then plotted in panel (b), and the line connecting them is the aggregate demand curve *AD*.

output for price level P_2. A further increase in the price level to P_3 causes a further decline in the real money supply, leading to a further decline in planned investment and net exports, and output declines to Y_3. Point 3 in panel (b) plots this level of output for price level P_3.

The line that connects the three points in panel (b) is the aggregate demand curve AD, and it indicates the level of aggregate output consistent with equilibrium in the goods market and the market for money at any given price level. This aggregate demand curve has the usual downward slope because a higher price level reduces the money supply in real terms, raises interest rates, and lowers the equilibrium level of aggregate output.

Factors That Cause the Aggregate Demand Curve to Shift

ISLM analysis demonstrates how the equilibrium level of aggregate output changes for a given price level. A change in any factor that causes the *IS* or *LM* curve to shift (except a change in the price level) causes the aggregate demand curve to shift. To see how this works, let's first look at what happens to the aggregate demand curve when the *IS* curve shifts.

SHIFTS IN THE **IS** CURVE Five factors cause the *IS* curve to shift: changes in autonomous consumer spending, changes in investment spending related to business confidence, changes in government spending, changes in taxes, and autonomous changes in net exports. How changes in these factors lead to a shift in the aggregate demand curve is examined in Figure 12.

Suppose that initially the aggregate demand curve is at AD_1 and there is a rise, for example, in government spending. The *ISLM* diagram in panel (b) shows what

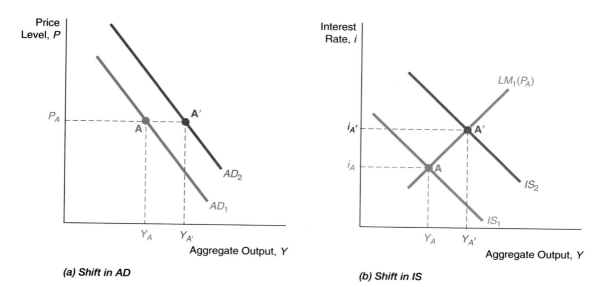

(a) Shift in AD   **(b) Shift in IS**

FIGURE 12 Shift in the Aggregate Demand Curve from a Shift in the **IS** Curve

Expansionary fiscal policy, a rise in net exports, or more optimistic consumers and firms shift the **IS** curve to the right in panel (b), and at a price level of P_A, equilibrium output rises from Y_A to $Y_{A'}$. This change in equilibrium output is shown as a movement from point **A** to point **A'** in panel (a); hence the aggregate demand curve shifts to the right from AD_1 to AD_2.

then happens to equilibrium output, holding the price level constant at P_A. Initially, equilibrium output is at Y_A at the intersection of IS_1 and LM_1. The rise in government spending (holding the price level constant at P_A) shifts the IS curve to the right and raises equilibrium output to $Y_{A'}$. In panel (a), this rise in equilibrium output is shown as a movement from point A to point A', and the aggregate demand curve shifts to the right (to AD_2).

The conclusion from Figure 12 is that ***any factor that shifts the IS curve shifts the aggregate demand curve in the same direction.*** Therefore, "animal spirits" that encourage a rise in autonomous consumer spending or planned investment spending, a rise in government spending, a fall in taxes, or an autonomous rise in net exports—all of which shift the IS curve to the right—will also shift the aggregate demand curve to the right. Conversely, a fall in autonomous consumer spending, a fall in planned investment spending, a fall in government spending, a rise in taxes, or a fall in net exports will cause the aggregate demand curve to shift to the left.

SHIFTS IN THE *LM* CURVE Shifts in the LM curve are caused by either an autonomous change in money demand (not caused by a change in P, Y, or i) or a change in the money supply. Figure 13 shows how either of these changes leads to a shift in the aggregate demand curve. Again, we are initially at the AD_1 aggregate demand curve, and we look at what happens to the level of equilibrium output when the price level is held constant at P_A. A rise in the money supply shifts the LM curve to the right and raises equilibrium output to $Y_{A'}$. This rise in equilibrium output is shown as a movement from point A to point A' in panel (a), and the aggregate demand curve shifts to the right.

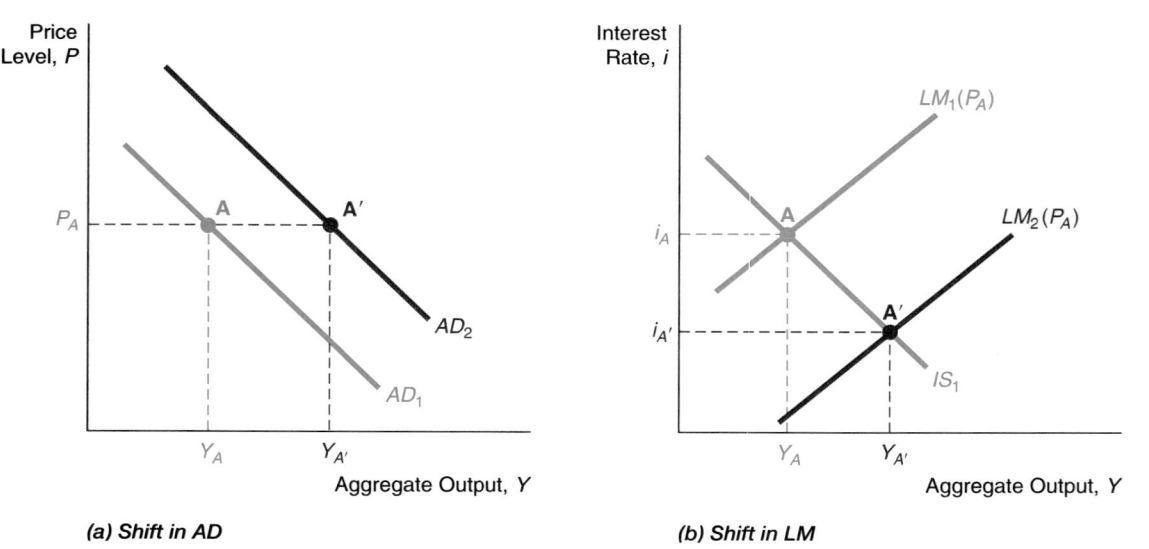

(a) Shift in AD   (b) Shift in LM

FIGURE 13 Shift in the Aggregate Demand Curve from a Shift in the LM Curve

A rise in the money supply or a fall in money demand shifts the **LM** curve to the right in panel (b), and at a price level of P_A, equilibrium output rises from Y_A to $Y_{A'}$. This change in equilibrium output is shown as a movement from point A to point A' in panel (a); hence the aggregate demand curve shifts to the right from AD_1 to AD_2.

Our conclusion from Figure 13 is similar to that of Figure 12: ***Any factor that shifts the LM curve shifts the aggregate demand curve in the same direction.*** Therefore, a decline in money demand as well as an increase in the money supply, both of which shift the *LM* curve to the right, also shift the aggregate demand curve to the right. The aggregate demand curve will shift to the left, however, if the money supply declines or money demand rises.

You have now derived and analyzed the aggregate demand curve—an essential element in the aggregate demand and supply framework that we examine in Chapter 24. The aggregate demand and supply framework is particularly useful because it demonstrates how the price level is determined and enables us to examine factors that affect aggregate output when the price level varies.

S U M M A R Y

1. The *IS* curve is shifted to the right by a rise in autonomous consumer spending, a rise in planned investment spending related to business confidence, a rise in government spending, a fall in taxes, or an autonomous rise in net exports. A movement in the opposite direction of these five factors will shift the *IS* curve to the left.

2. The *LM* curve is shifted to the right by a rise in the money supply or an autonomous fall in money demand; it is shifted to the left by a fall in the money supply or an autonomous rise in money demand.

3. A rise in the money supply raises equilibrium output but lowers the equilibrium interest rate. Expansionary fiscal policy (a rise in government spending or a fall in taxes) raises equilibrium output but, in contrast to expansionary monetary policy, also raises the interest rate.

4. The less interest-sensitive money demand is, the more effective monetary policy is relative to fiscal policy.

5. The *ISLM* model provides the following conclusion about the conduct of monetary policy: When the *IS* curve is more unstable than the *LM* curve, pursuing a money supply target provides smaller output fluctuations than pursuing an interest-rate target and is preferred; when the *LM* curve is more unstable than the *IS* curve, pursuing an interest-rate target leads to smaller output fluctuations and is preferred.

6. The conclusion from examining what happens in the *ISLM* model from an expansionary monetary or fiscal policy is that although monetary and fiscal policy can affect output in the short run, neither affects output in the long run.

7. The aggregate demand curve tells us the level of aggregate output consistent with equilibrium in the goods market and the market for money for any given price level. It slopes downward because a lower price level creates a higher level of the real money supply, lowers the interest rate, and raises equilibrium output. The aggregate demand curve shifts in the same direction as a shift in the *IS* or *LM* curve; hence it shifts to the right when government spending increases, taxes decrease, "animal spirits" encourage consumer and business spending, autonomous net exports increase, the money supply increases, or money demand decreases.

K E Y   T E R M S

aggregate demand curve, p. 598

complete crowding out, p. 592

long-run monetary neutrality, p. 596

natural rate level of output, p. 596

QUESTIONS AND PROBLEMS

1. If taxes and government spending rise by equal amounts, what will happen to the position of the *IS* curve? Explain this with a Keynesian cross diagram.

*2. What happened to the *IS* curve during the Great Depression when investment spending collapsed? Why?

3. What happens to the position of the *LM* curve if the Fed decides that it will decrease the money supply to fight inflation and if, at the same time, the demand for money falls?

*4. "An excess demand for money resulting from a rise in the demand for money can be eliminated only by a rise in the interest rate." Is this statement true, false, or uncertain? Explain your answer.

In Problems 5–15, demonstrate your answers with an *ISLM* diagram.

5. In late 1969, the Federal Reserve reduced the money supply while the government raised taxes. What do you think should have happened to interest rates and aggregate output?

*6. "The high level of interest rates and the rapidly growing economy during Ronald Reagan's third and fourth years as president can be explained by a tight monetary policy combined with an expansionary fiscal policy." Do you agree? Why or why not?

7. Suppose that the Federal Reserve wants to keep interest rates from rising when the government sharply increases military spending. How can the Fed do this?

*8. Evidence indicates that lately the demand for money has become quite unstable. Why is this finding important to Federal Reserve policymakers?

9. "As the price level rises, the equilibrium level of output determined in the *ISLM* model also rises." Is this statement true, false, or uncertain? Explain your answer.

*10. What will happen to the position of the aggregate demand curve if the money supply is reduced when government spending increases?

11. An equal rise in government spending and taxes will have what effect on the position of the aggregate demand curve?

*12. If money demand is unaffected by changes in the interest rate, what effect will a rise in government spending have on the position of the aggregate demand curve?

USING ECONOMIC ANALYSIS TO PREDICT THE FUTURE

13. Predict what will happen to interest rates and output if a stock market crash causes autonomous consumer expenditure to fall.

*14. Predict what will happen to interest rates and aggregate output when there is an autonomous export boom.

15. If a series of defaults in the bond market make bonds riskier and as a result the demand for money rises, predict what will happen to interest rates and aggregate output.

Chapter 24

AGGREGATE DEMAND AND SUPPLY ANALYSIS

PREVIEW   In earlier chapters we focused considerable attention on monetary policy because it touches our everyday lives by affecting the prices of the goods we buy and the quantity of available jobs. In this chapter we develop a basic tool, aggregate demand and supply analysis, that will enable us to study the effects of money on output and prices. **Aggregate demand** is the total quantity of an economy's final goods and services demanded at different price levels. **Aggregate supply** is the total quantity of final goods and services that firms in the economy want to sell at different price levels. As with other supply and demand analyses, the actual quantity of output and the price level are determined by equating aggregate demand and aggregate supply.

Aggregate demand and supply analysis will enable us to explore how aggregate output and the price level are determined. (The "Following the Financial News" box indicates when data on aggregate output and the price level are published.) Not only will the analysis help us interpret recent episodes in the business cycle, but it will also enable us to understand the debates on how economic policy should be conducted.

AGGREGATE DEMAND

The first building block of aggregate supply and demand analysis is the **aggregate demand curve,** which describes the relationship between the quantity of aggregate output demanded and the price level when all other variables are held constant. **Monetarists** (led by Milton Friedman) view the aggregate demand curve as downward-sloping with one primary factor that causes it to shift—changes in the quantity of money. **Keynesians** (followers of Keynes) also view the aggregate demand curve as downward-sloping, but they believe that changes in government spending and taxes or in consumer and business willingness to spend can also cause it to shift.

--- **Following the Financial News** ---

Aggregate Output, Unemployment, and the Price Level

Newspapers periodically report data that provide information on the level of aggregate output, unemployment, and the price level. Here is a list of the relevant data series, their frequency, and when they are published.

Aggregate Output and Unemployment

Real GDP: Quarterly (January–March, April–June, July–September, October–December); published three to four weeks after the end of a quarter.

Industrial production: Monthly. Industrial production is not as comprehensive a measure of aggregate output as real GDP because it measures only manufacturing output; the estimate for the previous month is reported in the middle of the following month.

Unemployment rate: Monthly; previous month's figure is usually published on Friday of the first week of the following month.

Price Level

GDP deflator: Quarterly. This comprehensive measure of the price level (described in the appendix to Chapter 1) is published at the same time as the real GDP data.

Consumer price index (CPI): Monthly. The CPI is a measure of the price level for consumers (also described in the appendix to Chapter 1); the value for the previous month is published in the third or fourth week of the following month.

Producer price index (PPI): Monthly. The PPI is a measure of the average level of wholesale prices charged by producers and is published at the same time as industrial production data.

Monetarist View of Aggregate Demand

The monetarist view of aggregate demand links the quantity of money M with total nominal spending on goods and services $P \times Y$ (P = price level and Y = aggregate real output or, equivalently, aggregate real income). To do this it uses the concept of the **velocity of money:** the average number of times per year that a dollar is spent on final goods and services. More formally, velocity V is calculated by dividing nominal spending $P \times Y$ by the money supply M:

$$V = \frac{P \times Y}{M}$$

Suppose that the total nominal spending in a year was $2 trillion and the money supply was $1 trillion; velocity would then be $2 trillion/$1 trillion = 2. On average, the money supply supports a level of transactions associated with 2 times its value in final goods and services in the course of a year. By multiplying both sides by M, we obtain the **equation of exchange,** which relates the money supply to aggregate spending:

$$M \times V = P \times Y \tag{1}$$

At this point, the equation of exchange is nothing more than an identity; that is, it is true by definition. It does not tell us that when M rises, aggregate spending will rise as well. For example, the rise in M could be offset by a fall in V, with the result that $M \times V$ does not rise. However, Friedman's analysis of the demand for money (discussed in detail in Chapter 21) suggests that velocity varies over time in a predictable manner unrelated to changes in the money supply. With this analysis, the equation of exchange is transformed into a theory of how aggregate spending is determined and is called the **modern quantity theory of money.**

To see how the theory works, let's look at an example. If velocity is predicted to be 2 and the money supply is $1 trillion, the equation of exchange tells us that aggregate spending will be $2 trillion (2 × $1 trillion). If the money supply doubles to $2 trillion, Friedman's analysis suggests that velocity will continue to be 2 and aggregate spending will double to $4 trillion (2 × $2 trillion). Thus Friedman's modern quantity theory of money concludes that *changes in aggregate spending are determined primarily by changes in the money supply.*

DERIVING THE AGGREGATE DEMAND CURVE To learn how the modern quantity theory of money generates the aggregate demand curve, let's look at an example in which we measure aggregate output in trillions of 1992 dollars, with the price level in 1992 having a value of 1.0. As just shown, with a predicted velocity of 2 and a money supply of $1 trillion, aggregate spending will be $2 trillion. If the price level is given at 2.0, the quantity of aggregate output demanded is $1 trillion because aggregate spending $P \times Y$ then continues to equal 2.0 × $1 trillion = $2 trillion, the value of $M \times V$. This combination of a price level of 2.0 and aggregate output of 1 is marked as point A in Figure 1. If the price level is given as 1.0 instead, aggregate output demanded is $2 trillion (point B), so aggregate spending continues to equal $2 trillion (= 1.0 × 2 trillion). Similarly, at an even lower price level of 0.5, the quantity of output demanded rises to $4 trillion, shown by point C. The curve connecting these points, marked AD_1, is the aggregate demand curve, given a money supply of $1 trillion. As you can see, it has the usual downward slope of a demand curve, indicating that as the price level falls (everything else held constant), the quantity of output demanded rises.

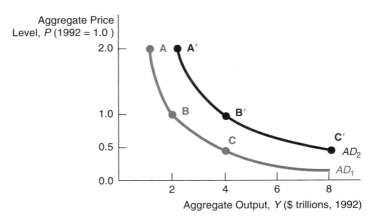

FIGURE 1 Aggregate Demand Curve
An aggregate demand curve is drawn for a **fixed** level of the money supply. A rise in the money supply from $1 trillion to $2 trillion leads to a shift in the aggregate demand curve from **AD**₁ to **AD**₂.

SHIFTS IN THE AGGREGATE DEMAND CURVE In Friedman's modern quantity theory, changes in the money supply are the primary source of the changes in aggregate spending and shifts in the aggregate demand curve. To see how a change in the money supply shifts the aggregate demand curve in Figure 1, let's look at what happens when the money supply increases to $2 trillion. Now aggregate spending rises to $2 \times $2 trillion = $4 trillion, and at a price level of 2.0, the quantity of aggregate output demanded will rise to $2 trillion so that 2.0×2 trillion = $4 trillion. Therefore, at a price level of 2.0, the aggregate demand curve moves from point A to A'. At a price level of 1.0, the quantity of output demanded rises from $2 to $4 trillion (from point B to B'), and at a price level of 0.5, output demanded rises from $4 to $8 trillion (from point C to C'). The result is that the rise in the money supply to $2 trillion shifts the aggregate demand curve outward to AD_2.

Similar reasoning indicates that a decline in the money supply lowers aggregate spending proportionally and reduces the quantity of aggregate output demanded at each price level. Thus a decline in the money supply shifts the aggregate demand curve to the left.

Keynesian View of Aggregate Demand

Rather than determining aggregate demand from the equation of exchange, Keynesians analyze aggregate demand in terms of its four component parts: **consumer expenditure**, the total demand for consumer goods and services; **planned investment spending**,[1] the total planned spending by business firms on new machines, factories, and other inputs to production, plus planned spending on new homes; **government spending**, spending by all levels of government (federal, state, and local) on goods and services (paper clips, computers, computer programming, missiles, government workers, and so on); and **net exports**, the net foreign spending on domestic goods and services, equal to exports minus imports. Using the symbols C for consumer expenditure, I for planned investment spending, G for government spending, and NX for net exports, we can write the following expression for aggregate demand Y^{ad}:

$$Y^{ad} = C + I + G + NX \qquad (2)$$

AGGREGATE DEMAND CURVE Keynesian analysis, like monetarist analysis, suggests that the aggregate demand curve is downward-sloping because a lower price level ($P\downarrow$), holding the nominal quantity of money (M) constant, leads to a larger quantity of money in real terms (in terms of the goods and services that it can buy, $M/P\uparrow$). The larger quantity of money in real terms ($M/P\uparrow$) that results from the lower price level causes interest rates to fall ($i\downarrow$), as suggested in Chapter 6. The resulting lower cost of financing purchases of new physical capital makes investment more profitable and stimulates planned investment spending ($I\uparrow$). Because, as shown in Equation 2, the increase in planned investment spending adds directly to aggregate demand ($Y^{ad}\uparrow$), the lower price level leads to a higher

---

[1]Recall that economists restrict use of the word *investment* to the purchase of new physical capital, such as a new machine or a new house, that adds to expenditure.

level of aggregate demand ($P\downarrow \Rightarrow Y^{ad}\uparrow$). Schematically, we can write the mechanism just described as follows:

$$P\downarrow \Rightarrow M/P\uparrow \Rightarrow i\downarrow \Rightarrow I\uparrow \Rightarrow Y^{ad}\uparrow$$

Another mechanism that generates a downward-sloping aggregate demand curve operates through international trade. Because a lower price level ($P\downarrow$) leads to a larger quantity of money in real terms ($M/P\uparrow$) and lower interest rates ($i\downarrow$), U.S. dollar bank deposits become less attractive relative to deposits denominated in foreign currencies, thereby causing a fall in the value of dollar deposits relative to other currency deposits (a decline in the exchange rate, denoted by $E\downarrow$). The lower value of the dollar, which makes domestic goods cheaper relative to foreign goods, then causes net exports to rise, which in turn increases aggregate demand:

$$P\downarrow \Rightarrow M/P\uparrow \Rightarrow i\downarrow \Rightarrow E\downarrow \Rightarrow NX\uparrow \Rightarrow Y^{ad}\uparrow$$

The mechanisms described also indicate why Keynesian analysis suggests that changes in the money supply shift the aggregate demand curve. For a given price level, a rise in the money supply causes the real money supply to increase ($M/P\uparrow$), which leads to an increase in aggregate demand, as shown. Thus an increase in the money supply shifts the aggregate demand curve to the right (as in Figure 1) because it lowers interest rates and stimulates planned investment spending and net exports. Similarly, a decline in the money supply shifts the aggregate demand curve to the left.[2]

In contrast to monetarists, Keynesians believe that other factors (manipulation of government spending and taxes, changes in net exports, and changes in consumer and business spending) are also important causes of shifts in the aggregate demand curve. For instance, if the government spends more ($G\uparrow$) or net exports increase ($NX\uparrow$), aggregate demand rises, and the aggregate demand curve shifts to the right. A decrease in government taxes ($T\downarrow$) leaves consumers with more income to spend, so consumer expenditure rises ($C\uparrow$). Aggregate demand also rises, and the aggregate demand curve shifts to the right. Finally, if consumer and business optimism increases, consumer expenditure and planned investment spending rise ($C\uparrow$, $I\uparrow$), again shifting the aggregate demand curve to the right. Keynes described these waves of optimism and pessimism as **"animal spirits"** and considered them a major factor affecting the aggregate demand curve and an important source of business cycle fluctuations.

The Crowding-Out Debate

You have seen that both monetarists and Keynesians agree that the aggregate demand curve is downward-sloping and shifts in response to changes in the money supply. However, monetarists see only one important source of movements in the aggregate demand curve—changes in the money supply—while Keynesians suggest that other factors—fiscal policy, net exports, and "animal spirits"—are equally important sources of shifts in the aggregate demand curve.

---

[2]A complete demonstration of the Keynesian analysis of the aggregate demand curve is given in Chapters 22 and 23.

Because aggregate demand can be written as the sum of $C + I + G + NX$, it might appear as though any factor that affects one of its components must cause aggregate demand to change. Then it would seem as though a fiscal policy change such as a rise in government spending (holding the money supply constant) would necessarily shift the aggregate demand curve. Because monetarists view changes in the money supply as the only important source of shifts in the aggregate demand curve, they must have an explanation as to why the foregoing reasoning is invalid.

Monetarists agree that an increase in government spending will raise aggregate demand if the other components of aggregate demand, C, I, and NX, remained unchanged after the government spending rise. They contend, however, that the increase in government spending will *crowd out* private spending (C, I, and NX), which will fall by exactly the amount of the government spending increase. This phenomenon of an exactly offsetting movement of private spending to an expansionary fiscal policy, such as a rise in government spending, is called **complete crowding out.**

How might complete crowding out occur? When government spending increases ($G\uparrow$), the government has to finance this spending by competing with private borrowers for funds in the credit market. Interest rates will rise ($i\uparrow$), increasing the cost of financing purchases of both physical capital and consumer goods and lowering net exports. The result is that private spending will fall ($C\downarrow$, $I\downarrow$, $NX\downarrow$), and so aggregate demand may remain unchanged. This chain of reasoning can be summarized as follows:

$$G\uparrow \Rightarrow i\uparrow \Rightarrow C\downarrow, I\downarrow, NX\downarrow$$

Therefore, $C + I + G + NX = Y^{ad}$ is unchanged.

Keynesians do not deny the validity of the first set of steps. They agree that an increase in government spending raises interest rates, which in turn lowers private spending; indeed, this is a feature of the Keynesian analysis of aggregate demand (See Chapters 22 and 23). However, they contend that in the short run only **partial crowding out** occurs—some decline in private spending that does not completely offset the rise in government spending.

The Keynesian crowding-out picture suggests that when government spending rises, aggregate demand does increase, and the aggregate demand curve shifts to the right. The extent to which crowding out occurs is the issue that separates monetarist and Keynesian views of the aggregate demand curve. We will discuss the evidence on this issue in Chapter 25.

AGGREGATE SUPPLY

The key feature of aggregate supply is that as the price level increases, the quantity of output supplied increases *in the short run*. Figure 2 illustrates the positive relationship between quantity of output supplied and price level. Suppose that initially the quantity of output supplied at a price level of 1.0 is $4 trillion, represented by point A. A rise in the price level to 2.0 leads, in the short run, to an increase in the quantity of output supplied to $6 trillion (point B). The line AS_1 connecting points A and B describes the relationship between the quantity of

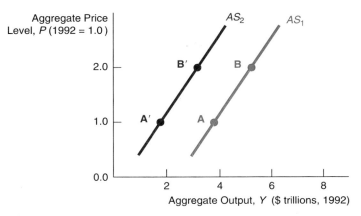

FIGURE 2 Aggregate Supply Curve in the Short Run
A rise in the costs of production shifts the supply curve leftward from **AS**₁ to **AS**₂.

output supplied in the short run and the price level and is called the **aggregate supply curve;** as you can see, it is upward-sloping.

To understand why the aggregate supply curve slopes upward, we have to look at the factors that cause the quantity of output supplied to change. Because the goal of business is to maximize profits, the quantity of output supplied is determined by the profit made on each unit of output. If profit rises, more output will be produced, and the quantity of output supplied will increase; if it falls, less output will be produced, and the quantity of output supplied will fall.

Profit on a unit of output equals the price for the unit minus the costs of producing it. In the short run, costs of many factors that go into producing goods and services are fixed; wages, for example, are often fixed for periods of time by labor contracts (sometimes as long as three years), and raw materials are often bought by firms under long-term contracts that fix the price. Because these costs of production are fixed in the short run, when the overall price level rises, the price for a unit of output will be rising relative to the costs of producing it, and the profit per unit will rise. Because the higher price level results in higher profits in the short run, firms increase production, and the quantity of aggregate output supplied rises, resulting in an upward-sloping aggregate supply curve.

Frequent mention of the *short run* in the preceding paragraph hints that the aggregate supply curve (AS_1 in Figure 2) may not remain fixed as time passes. To see what happens over time, we need to understand what makes the aggregate supply curve shift.[3]

Shifts in the Aggregate Supply Curve

We have seen that the profit on a unit of output determines the quantity of output supplied. If the cost of producing a unit of output rises, profit on a unit of output falls, and the quantity of output supplied falls. To learn what this implies

---

[3]The aggregate supply curve is closely linked to the Phillips curve discussed in macroeconomics. The relationship between those two concepts is described in the appendix to this chapter.

for the position of the aggregate supply curve, let's consider what happens at a price level of 1.0 when the costs of production increase. Now that firms are earning a lower profit per unit of output, they reduce production, and the quantity of aggregate output supplied falls from $4 (point A) to $2 trillion (point A'). Applying the same reasoning at point B indicates that aggregate output supplied falls to point B'. What we see is that *the aggregate supply curve shifts to the left when costs of production increase and to the right when costs of production decrease.*

EQUILIBRIUM IN AGGREGATE SUPPLY AND DEMAND ANALYSIS

The equilibrium level of aggregate output and the price level will occur at the point where the quantity of aggregate output demanded equals the quantity of aggregate output supplied. However, in the context of aggregate supply and demand analysis, there are two types of equilibrium: short-run and long-run.

Equilibrium in the Short Run

Figure 3 illustrates an equilibrium in the short run in which the quantity of aggregate output demanded equals the quantity of output supplied; that is, where the aggregate demand curve AD and the aggregate supply curve AS intersect at point E. The equilibrium level of aggregate output equals Y^*, and the equilibrium price level equals P^*.

As in our earlier supply and demand analyses, equilibrium is a useful concept only if there is a tendency for the economy to head toward it. We can see that the economy heads toward the equilibrium at point E by first looking at what happens when we are at a price level above the equilibrium price level P^*. If the price level is at P', the quantity of aggregate output supplied at point D is greater than the quantity of aggregate output demanded at point A. Because people want to

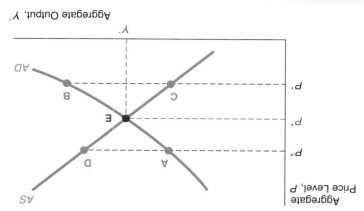

FIGURE 3   Equilibrium in the Short Run

Equilibrium occurs at point E at the intersection of the aggregate demand curve AD and the aggregate supply curve AS.

sell more goods and services than others want to buy (a condition of *excess supply*), the prices of goods and services will fall, and the aggregate price level will drop. This decline in the price level will continue until it has reached its equilibrium level of P^* at point E.

When the price level is below the equilibrium price level, say, at P', the quantity of output demanded is greater than the quantity of output supplied. Now the price level will rise because people want to buy more goods than others want to sell (a condition of *excess demand*). This rise in the price level will continue until it has again reached its equilibrium level of P^* at point E.

Equilibrium in the Long Run

Usually in supply and demand analysis, once we find the equilibrium at which the quantity demanded equals the quantity supplied, there is no need for additional discussion. In *aggregate* supply and demand analysis, however, that is not the case. Even when the quantity of aggregate output demanded equals the quantity supplied, forces operate that can cause the equilibrium to move over time. To understand why, we must remember that if costs of production change, the aggregate supply curve will shift.

The most important component of production costs is wages (approximately 70 percent of production costs), which are determined in the labor market. If the economy is booming, employers will find that they have difficulty hiring qualified workers and may even have a hard time keeping their present employees. In this case, the labor market is tight because the demand for labor exceeds the supply; employers will raise wages to attract needed workers, and this raises the costs of production. The higher costs of production lower the profits per unit of output at each price level, and the aggregate supply curve shifts to the left (see Figure 2).

By contrast, if the economy enters a recession and the labor market is slack because demand for labor is less than supply, workers who cannot find jobs will be willing to work for lower wages. In addition, employed workers may be willing to make wage concessions to keep from losing their jobs (as airline and steel workers did in the 1980s).[4] Therefore, in a slack labor market in which the demand for labor is less than the supply, wages and hence costs of production will fall, profits per unit of output will rise, and the aggregate supply curve will shift to the right.

Our analysis suggests that the aggregate supply curve will shift depending on whether the labor market is tight or slack. How do we decide which it is? One helpful concept is the **natural rate of unemployment,** the rate of unemployment to which the economy gravitates in the long run at which demand for labor equals supply. (A related concept is the **NAIRU,** the **nonaccelerating inflation rate of unemployment,** the rate of unemployment at which there is no tendency for inflation to change.) Many economists believe that the rate is currently around 6 percent. When unemployment is at, say, 4 percent, below the natural rate of unemployment of 6 percent, the labor market is tight; wages will rise, and the

---

[4]Airline and steel workers may have lost jobs because of other market forces besides overall high unemployment in the economy, specifically, airline deregulation and a change in the competitiveness of the American auto industry compared to the rest of the world.

aggregate supply curve will shift leftward. When unemployment is at, say, 8 percent, above the natural rate of unemployment, the labor market is slack; wages will fall, and the aggregate supply curve will shift rightward. Only when unemployment is at the natural rate will no pressure exist from the labor market for wages to rise or fall, so the aggregate supply need not shift.

The level of aggregate output produced at the natural rate of unemployment is called the **natural rate level of output.** Because, as we have seen, the aggregate supply curve will not remain stationary when unemployment and aggregate output differ from their natural rate levels, we need to look at how the short-run equilibrium changes over time in response to two situations: when equilibrium is initially below the natural rate level and when it is initially above the natural rate level.

In panel (a) of Figure 4, the initial equilibrium occurs at point 1, the intersection of the aggregate demand curve AD and the initial aggregate supply curve AS_1. Because the level of equilibrium output Y_1 is greater than the natural rate level Y_n, unemployment is less than the natural rate, and excessive tightness exists in the labor market. This tightness drives wages up, raises production costs, and shifts the aggregate supply curve to AS_2. The equilibrium is now at point 2, and output falls to Y_2. Because aggregate output Y_2 is still above the natural rate level, Y_n, wages continue to be driven up, eventually shifting the aggregate supply curve to AS_3. The equilibrium reached at point 3 is on the vertical line at Y_n and is a long-run equilibrium. Because output is at the natural rate level, there is no further pressure on wages to rise and thus no further tendency for the aggregate supply curve to shift.

The movements in panel (a) indicate that the economy will not remain at a level of output higher than the natural rate level because the aggregate supply curve will shift to the left, raise the price level, and cause the economy to slide upward along the aggregate demand curve until it comes to rest at a point on the vertical line through the natural rate level of output Y_n. Because the vertical line through Y_n is the only place at which the aggregate supply curve comes to rest, this vertical line indicates the quantity of output supplied in the long run for any given price level. We can characterize this as the **long-run aggregate supply curve.**

In panel (b), the initial equilibrium at point 1 is one at which output Y_1 is below the natural rate level. Because unemployment is higher than the natural rate, wages begin to fall, shifting the aggregate supply curve rightward until it comes to rest at AS_3. The economy slides downward along the aggregate demand curve until it reaches the long-run equilibrium point 3, the intersection of the aggregate demand curve AD and the long-run aggregate supply curve at Y_n. Here, as in panel (a), the economy comes to rest when output has again returned to the natural rate level.

A striking feature of both panels of Figure 4 is that regardless of where output is initially, it returns eventually to the natural rate level. This feature is described by saying that the economy has a **self-correcting mechanism.**

An important issue for policymakers is how rapidly this self-correcting mechanism works. Many economists, particularly Keynesians, believe that the self-correcting mechanism takes a long time, so the approach to long-run equilibrium is slow. This view is reflected in Keynes's often quoted remark, "In the long run, we are all dead." These economists view the self-correcting mechanism as slow because wages are inflexible, particularly in the downward direction when unem-

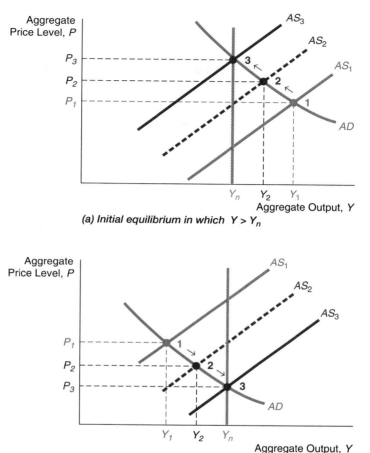

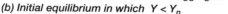

FIGURE 4 Adjustment to Long-Run Equilibrium in Aggregate Supply and Demand Analysis
In both panels, the initial equilibrium is at point 1 at the intersection of **AD** and **AS**$_1$. In panel (a), $Y_1 >$ Y_n, so the aggregate supply curve keeps shifting to the left until it reaches **AS**$_3$, where output has returned to Y_n. In panel (b), $Y_1 < Y_n$, so the aggregate supply curve keeps shifting to the right until output is again returned to Y_n. Hence in both cases, the economy displays a self-correcting mechanism that returns it to the natural rate level of output.

ployment is high. The resulting slow wage and price adjustments mean that the aggregate supply curve does not move quickly to restore the economy to the natural rate of unemployment. Hence when unemployment is high, these economists (called **activists**) are more likely to see the need for active government policy to restore the economy to full employment.

Other economists, particularly monetarists, believe that wages are sufficiently flexible that the wage and price adjustment process is reasonably rapid. As a result of this flexibility, adjustment of the aggregate supply curve to its long-run position and the economy's return to the natural rate levels of output and unemployment will occur quickly. Thus these economists (called **nonactivists**) see much less need for active government policy to restore the economy to the natural rate levels of output and unemployment when unemployment is high. Indeed, monetarists advocate the use of a rule whereby the money supply or the monetary base grows at a constant rate so as to minimize fluctuations in aggregate demand that might lead to output fluctuations. We will return to the debate about whether active government policy to keep the economy near full employment is beneficial in Chapter 26.

Shifts in Aggregate Demand

You are now ready to analyze what happens when the aggregate demand curve shifts. Our discussion of the Keynesian and monetarist views of aggregate demand indicates that six factors can affect the aggregate demand curve: the money supply, government spending, net exports, taxes, consumer optimism, and business optimism—the last two ("animal spirits") affecting willingness to spend. The possible effect on the aggregate demand curve of these six factors is summarized in Table 1.

Figure 5 depicts the effect of a rightward shift in the aggregate demand curve caused by an increase in the money supply ($M\uparrow$), an increase in government spending ($G\uparrow$), an increase in net exports ($NX\uparrow$), a decrease in taxes ($T\downarrow$), or an increase in the willingness of consumers and businesses to spend because they become more optimistic ($C\uparrow$, $I\uparrow$). The figure has been drawn so that initially the economy is in long-run equilibrium at point 1, where the initial aggregate demand curve AD_1 intersects the aggregate supply AS_1 curve at Y_n. When the aggregate demand curve shifts rightward to AD_2, the economy moves to point 1′, and both output and the price level rise. However, the economy will not remain at point 1′ because output at $Y_{1'}$ is above the natural rate level. Wages will rise, eventually shifting the aggregate supply curve leftward to AS_2, where it finally comes to rest. The economy thus slides up the aggregate demand curve from point 1′ to point

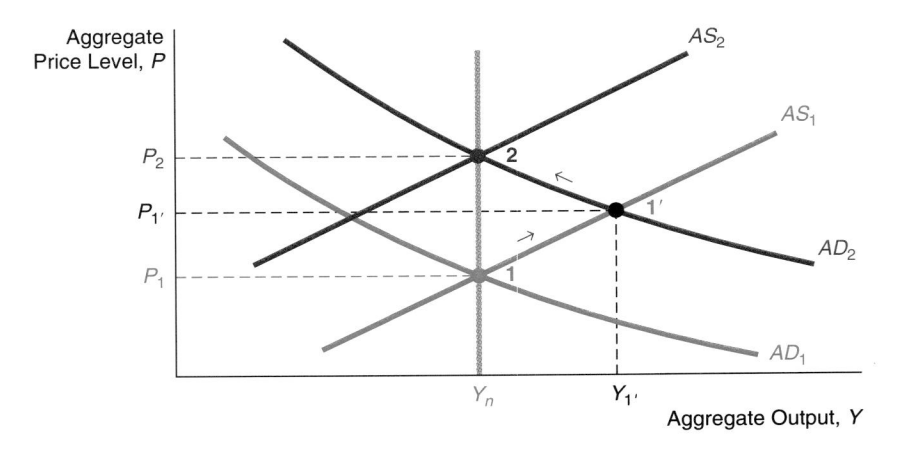

FIGURE 5 Response of Output and the Price Level to a Shift in the Aggregate Demand Curve

A shift in the aggregate demand curve from AD_1 to AD_2 moves the economy from point 1 to point 1′. Because $Y_{1'} > Y_n$, the aggregate supply curve begins to shift leftward, eventually reaching AS_2, where output returns to Y_n and the price level has risen to P_2.

———— S U M M A R Y ————

TABLE 1	Factors That Shift the Aggregate Demand Curve	
Factor	**Change**	**Shift in the Aggregate Demand Curve**
Money supply, M	↑	
Government, G	↑	
Taxes, T	↑	
Net exports, NX	↑	
Consumer optimism, C	↑	
Business optimism, I	↑	

Note: Only increases (↑) in the factors are shown. The effect of decreases in the factors would be the opposite of those indicated in the "Shift" column. Note that monetarists view only the money supply as an important cause of shifts in the aggregate demand curve.

2, which is the point of long-run equilibrium at the intersection of AD_2 and Y_n. ***Although the initial short-run effect of the rightward shift in the aggregate demand curve is a rise in both the price level and output, the ultimate long-run effect is only a rise in the price level.***

Shifts in Aggregate Supply

Not only can shifts in aggregate demand be a source of fluctuations in aggregate output (the business cycle), but so can shifts in aggregate supply. Factors that cause the aggregate supply curve to shift are the ones that affect the costs of production: (1) tightness of the labor market, (2) expectations of inflation, (3) workers' attempts to push up their real wages, and (4) changes in the production costs that are unrelated to wages (such as energy costs). The first three factors shift the aggregate supply curve by affecting wage costs; the fourth affects other costs of production.

TIGHTNESS OF THE LABOR MARKET Our analysis of the approach to long-run equilibrium has shown us that when the labor market is tight ($Y > Y_n$), wages and hence production costs rise, and when the labor market is slack ($Y < Y_n$), wages and production costs fall. The effects on the aggregate supply curve are as follows: ***When aggregate output is above the natural rate level, the aggregate supply curve shifts to the left; when aggregate output is below the natural rate level, the aggregate supply curve shifts to the right.***

EXPECTED PRICE LEVEL Workers and firms care about wages in real terms, that is, in terms of the goods and services that wages can buy. When the price level increases, a worker earning the same nominal wage will be able to buy fewer goods and services. A worker who expects the price level to rise will thus demand a higher nominal wage in order to keep the real wage from falling. For example, if Chuck the Construction Worker expects prices to increase by 5 percent, he will want a wage increase of at least 5 percent (more if he thinks he deserves an increase in real wages). Similarly, if Chuck's employer knows that the houses he is building will rise in value at the same rate as inflation (5 percent), his employer will be willing to pay Chuck 5 percent more. An increase in the expected price level leads to higher wages, which in turn raise the costs of production, lower the profit per unit of output at each price level, and shift the aggregate supply curve to the left (see Figure 2). Therefore, ***a rise in the expected price level causes the aggregate supply curve to shift to the left; the greater the expected increase in price level (that is, the higher the expected inflation), the larger the shift.***

WAGE PUSH Suppose that Chuck and his fellow construction workers decide to strike and succeed in obtaining higher real wages. This wage push will then raise the costs of production, and the aggregate supply curve will shift leftward. ***A successful wage push by workers will cause the aggregate supply curve to shift to the left.***

CHANGES IN PRODUCTION COSTS UNRELATED TO WAGES Changes in technology and in the supply of raw materials (called **supply shocks**) can also shift the aggregate supply curve. A negative supply shock, such as a reduction in the availability of raw materials (like oil), which raises their price, increases production costs and shifts the aggregate supply curve leftward. A positive supply shock, such as unusually good weather that leads to a bountiful harvest and lowers the cost of food, will reduce production costs and shift the aggregate supply curve rightward. Similarly, the development of a new technology that lowers production costs, perhaps by raising worker productivity, can also be considered a positive supply shock that shifts the aggregate supply curve to the right.

The effect on the aggregate supply curve of changes in production costs unrelated to wages can be summarized as follows: ***A negative supply shock that raises production costs shifts the aggregate supply curve to the left; a positive supply shock that lowers production costs shifts the aggregate supply curve to the right.***[5]

· ·

Study Guide   As a study aid, factors that shift the aggregate supply curve are listed in Table 2.

· ·

Now that we know what factors can affect the aggregate supply curve, we can examine what occurs when they cause the aggregate supply curve to shift leftward, as in Figure 6. Suppose that the economy is initially at the natural rate level of output at point 1 when the aggregate supply curve shifts from AS_1 to AS_2 because of a negative supply shock (a sharp rise in energy prices). The economy will move from point 1 to point 2, where the price level rises but aggregate output *falls*. A situation of a rising price level but a falling level of aggregate output, as pictured in Figure 6, has been labeled *stagflation* (a combination of words *stagnation* and *inflation*). At point 2, output is below the natural rate level, so wages fall and shift the aggregate supply curve back to where it was initially at AS_1. The result is that the economy slides down the aggregate demand curve AD_1 (assuming that the aggregate demand curve remains in the same position), and the economy returns to the long-run equilibrium at point 1. ***Although a leftward shift in the aggregate supply curve initially raises the price level and lowers output, the ultimate effect is that output and price level are unchanged (holding the aggregate demand curve constant).***

Shifts in the Long-Run Aggregate Supply Curve: Real Business Cycle Theory and Hysteresis

To this point we have assumed that the natural rate level of output Y_n and hence the long-run aggregate supply curve (the vertical line through Y_n) are given. However, over time, the natural rate level of output increases as a result of economic growth. If the productive capacity of the economy is growing at a steady

---

[5]Developments in the foreign exchange market can also shift the aggregate supply curve by changing domestic production costs. As discussed in more detail in Chapter 8, when the dollar increases in value, it makes foreign goods cheaper in the United States. The decline in prices of foreign goods and hence foreign factors of production lowers U.S. production costs and thus raises the profit per unit of output at each price level in the United States. An increase in the value of the dollar therefore shifts the aggregate supply curve to the right. Conversely, a decline in the value of the dollar, which makes foreign factors of production more expensive, shifts the aggregate supply curve to the left.

—————— S U M M A R Y ——————

TABLE 2	Factors That Shift the Aggregate Supply Curve

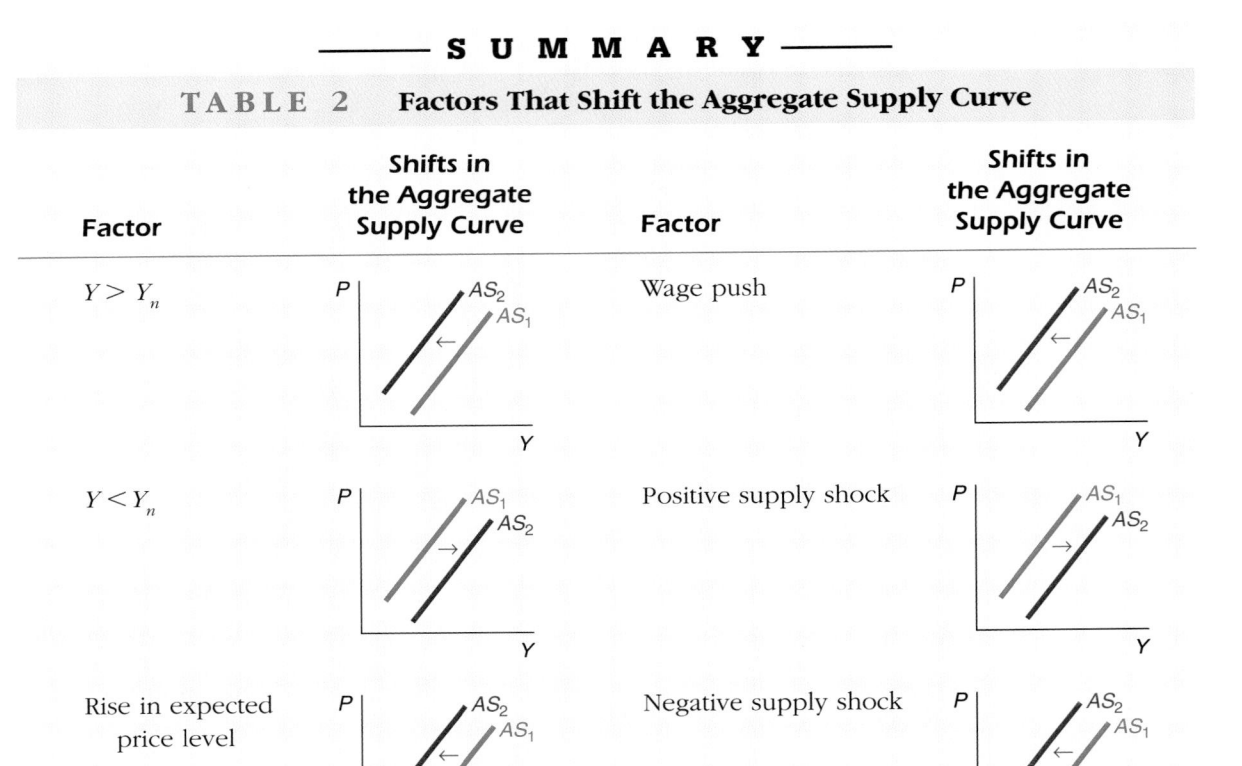

Factor	Shifts in the Aggregate Supply Curve	Factor	Shifts in the Aggregate Supply Curve
$Y > Y_n$		Wage push	
$Y < Y_n$		Positive supply shock	
Rise in expected price level		Negative supply shock	

rate of 3 percent per year, for example, this means that every year, Y_n will grow by 3 percent and the long-run aggregate supply curve at Y_n will shift to the right by 3 percent. To simplify the analysis when Y_n grows at a steady rate, Y_n and the long-run aggregate supply curve are drawn as fixed in the aggregate demand and supply diagrams. Keep in mind, however, that the level of aggregate output pictured in these diagrams is actually best thought of as the level of aggregate output relative to its normal rate of growth (trend).

The usual assumption when conducting aggregate demand and supply analysis is that shifts in either the aggregate demand or aggregate supply curve have no effect on the natural rate level of output (which grows at a steady rate). Movements of aggregate output around the Y_n level in the diagram then describe short-run (business cycle) fluctuations in aggregate output. However, some economists take issue with the assumption that Y_n is unaffected by aggregate demand and supply shocks.

One group, led by Edward Prescott of the University of Minnesota, has developed a theory of aggregate economic fluctuations called **real business cycle theory** in which aggregate supply (real) shocks do affect the natural rate level of

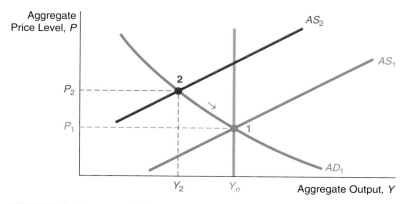

FIGURE 6 Response of Output and the Price Level to a Shift in Aggregate Supply
A shift in the aggregate supply curve from AS_1 to AS_2 moves the economy from point 1 to point 2. Because $Y_2 < Y_n$, the aggregate supply curve begins to shift back to the right, eventually returning to AS_1, where the economy is again at point 1.

output Y_n. This theory views shocks to tastes (workers' willingness to work, for example) and technology (productivity) as the major driving forces behind short-run fluctuations in the business cycle because these shocks lead to substantial short-run fluctuations in Y_n. Shifts in the aggregate demand curve, say, as a result of changes in monetary policy, by contrast, are not viewed as being particularly important to aggregate output fluctuations. Because real business cycle theory views most business cycle fluctuations as resulting from fluctuations in the natural rate level of output, it does not see much need for activist policy to eliminate high unemployment. Real business cycle theory is highly controversial and is currently the subject of intensive research.[6]

Another group of economists disagrees with the assumption that the natural rate level of output Y_n is unaffected by aggregate demand shocks. These economists contend that the natural rate level of unemployment and output are subject to **hysteresis,** a departure from full employment levels as a result of past high unemployment.[7] When unemployment rises because of a reduction of aggregate demand that shifts the *AD* curve inward, the natural rate of unemployment is viewed as rising above the full employment level. This could occur because the unemployed become discouraged and fail to look hard for work or because employers may be reluctant to hire workers who have been unemployed for a long time, thinking that it is a signal that the worker is undesirable. The outcome is that the natural rate of unemployment shifts upward after unemployment has become high, and Y_n falls below the full employment level. In this situation, the self-correcting mechanism will be able to return the economy only to

---

[6]See Charles Plosser, "Understanding Real Business Cycles," *Journal of Economic Perspectives* (1989): 51–77, for a detailed review of the literature on real business cycle theory.

[7]For a further discussion of hysteresis, see Olivier Blanchard and Lawrence Summers, "Hysteresis in the European Unemployment Problem," *NBER Macroeconomics Annual*, 1986, 1, ed. Stanley Fischer (Cambridge, Mass.: M.I.T. Press, 1986) pp. 15–78.

the natural rate levels of output and unemployment, not to the full employment level. Only with expansionary policy to shift the aggregate demand curve to the right and raise aggregate output can the natural rate of unemployment be lowered (Y_n raised) to the full employment level. Proponents of hysteresis are thus more likely to promote activist, expansionary policies to restore the economy to full employment.

Study Guide   *Aggregate supply and demand analysis are best learned by practicing applications. In this section, we have traced out what happens to aggregate output when there is an increase in the money supply or a negative supply shock. Make sure that you can also draw the appropriate shifts in the aggregate demand and supply curves and analyze what happens when other variables such as taxes or the expected price level change.*

Conclusions

Aggregate demand and supply analysis yields the following conclusions (under the usual assumption that the natural rate level of output is unaffected by aggregate demand and supply shocks):

1. A shift in the aggregate demand curve—which can be caused by changes in monetary policy (the money supply), fiscal policy (government spending or taxes), international trade (net exports), or "animal spirits" (business and consumer optimism)—affects output only in the short run and has no effect in the long run. Furthermore, the initial change in the price level is less than is achieved in the long run, when the aggregate supply curve has fully adjusted.

2. A shift in the aggregate supply curve—which can be caused by changes in expected inflation, workers' attempts to push up real wages, or a supply shock—affects output and prices only in the short run and has no effect in the long run (holding the aggregate demand curve constant).

3. The economy has a self-correcting mechanism, which will return it to the natural rate levels of unemployment and aggregate output over time.

Explaining Past Business Cycle Episodes

Aggregate supply and demand analysis is an extremely useful tool for analyzing aggregate economic activity; we will apply it to several business cycle episodes. In addition, since a good economic model must be able to predict the future as well as explain the past, we will look at how aggregate supply and demand analysis can be used to predict the response of aggregate output and the price level to events that might happen in the future. To simplify our analysis, we always assume, in this application and the next, that aggregate output is initially at the natural rate level.

TABLE 3	Unemployment and Inflation During the Vietnam War Buildup, 1964–1970	
Year	**Unemployment Rate (%)**	**Inflation (Year to Year) (%)**
1964	5.0	1.3
1965	4.4	1.6
1966	3.7	2.9
1967	3.7	3.1
1968	3.5	4.2
1969	3.4	5.5
1970	4.8	5.7

Source: *Economic Report of the President.*

Vietnam War Buildup, 1964–1970

America's involvement in Vietnam began to escalate in the early 1960s, and after 1964, the United States was fighting a full-scale war. Beginning in 1965, the resulting increases in military expenditure raised government spending, while at the same time the Federal Reserve increased the rate of money growth in an attempt to keep interest rates from rising. What does aggregate supply and demand-analysis suggest should have happened to aggregate output and the price level as a result of the Vietnam War buildup?

The rise in government spending and the higher rate of money growth would shift the aggregate demand curve to the right (shown in Figure 5). As a result, aggregate output would rise, unemployment would fall, and the price level would rise. Table 3 demonstrates that this is exactly what happened: The unemployment rate fell steadily from 1964 to 1969, remaining well below what economists now think was the natural rate of unemployment during that period (around 5 percent), and inflation began to rise. As Figure 5 predicts, unemployment would eventually begin to return to the natural rate level because of the economy's self-correcting mechanism. This is exactly what we saw occurring in 1970, when the inflation rate rose even higher and unemployment increased.

Negative Supply Shocks, 1973–1975 and 1978–1980

In 1973, the U.S. economy was hit by a series of negative supply shocks. As a result of the oil embargo stemming from the Arab-Israeli war of 1973, the Organization of Petroleum Exporting Countries (OPEC) was able to engineer a quadrupling of oil prices by restricting oil production. In addition, a series of crop failures throughout the world led to a sharp increase in food prices. Another factor was the termination of wage and price controls in 1973 and 1974, which led to a push by workers to obtain wage increases that had been prevented by the controls. The triple thrust of these events caused the aggregate supply curve to shift sharply leftward, and as the aggregate demand and supply diagram in Figure 6 predicts, both the price level and unemployment began to rise dramatically (see Table 4).

The 1978–1980 period was almost an exact replay of the 1973–1975 period. By 1978, the economy had just about fully recovered from the 1973–1974 supply

TABLE 4 **Unemployment and Inflation During the Supply Shock Periods, 1973–1975 and 1978–1980**

Year	Unemployment Rate (%)	Inflation (Year to Year) (%)	Year	Unemployment Rate (%)	Inflation (Year to Year) (%)
1973	4.8	6.2	1978	6.0	7.6
1974	5.5	11.0	1979	5.8	11.3
1975	8.3	9.1	1980	7.0	13.5

Source: Economic Report of the President.

shocks when poor harvests and a doubling of oil prices (as a result of the over-throw of the shah of Iran) again led to another sharp leftward shift of the aggregate supply curve. The pattern predicted by Figure 6 played itself out again—inflation and unemployment both shot upward (see Table 4).

APPLICATION

Predicting Future Economic Activity

Now let's see what will happen to aggregate output and the price level if certain events that have a reasonable probability of occurring in the near future actually do occur.

Elimination of Japanese Trade Barriers

The U.S. and Japanese governments have been engaged in talks about eliminating barriers to exports of U.S. goods to Japan. If the talks are successful in tearing down these barriers, what might we predict would happen to output and the price level in the United States?

Our aggregate supply and demand analysis of the elimination of Japanese trade barriers would be that pictured in Figure 5. The elimination of Japanese trade barriers would cause U.S. net exports to rise, leading to a rightward shift of the aggregate demand curve, which would initially raise aggregate output and the price level (increasing inflation) in the United States. In the long run, however, aggregate output would return to its natural rate level, and the price level would stop rising, so the increase in inflation would be only temporary.

Reduction in the Size of the U.S. Military

The Congress and the Clinton administration have been significantly downsizing the U.S. military, a move that includes the closing of many military bases. What effect will cuts in military spending have on the economy?

The reduction in military spending would probably lead to less government spending and a leftward shift of the aggregate demand curve. The outcome would be opposite that pictured in Figure 5: The price level would fall, lowering the inflation rate, and aggregate output would also fall at first; in the long run, however, aggregate output would return to the natural rate level.

....

Study Guide   Many examples of future events with implications for shifts in the aggregate demand and supply curves come to mind. Try to think of some yourself, and then use aggregate supply and demand analysis to predict what will happen to the economy. Such exercises will help you master aggregate supply and demand analysis (and may even be fun).

....

S U M M A R Y

1. The aggregate demand curve indicates the quantity of aggregate output demanded at each price level, and it is downward-sloping. Monetarists view changes in the money supply as the primary source of shifts in the aggregate demand curve. Keynesians believe that not only are changes in the money supply important to shifts in the aggregate demand curve, but so are changes in fiscal policy (government spending and taxes), net exports, and the willingness of consumers and businesses to spend ("animal spirits").

2. In the short run, the aggregate supply curve slopes upward because a rise in the price level raises the profit earned on each unit of production, and the quantity of output supplied rises. Four factors can cause the aggregate supply curve to shift: tightness of the labor market as represented by unemploy-

ment relative to the natural rate, expectations of inflation, workers' attempts to push up their real wages, and supply shocks unrelated to wages that affect production costs.

3. Equilibrium in the short run occurs at the point where the aggregate demand curve intersects the aggregate supply curve. Although this is where the economy heads temporarily, it has a self-correcting mechanism, which leads it to settle permanently at the long-run equilibrium where aggregate output is at its natural rate level. Shifts in either the aggregate demand or the aggregate supply curve can produce changes in aggregate output and the price level.

4. Aggregate supply and demand analysis can be used either to explain past business cycle episodes or to predict the response of aggregate output and the price level to future events.

K E Y   T E R M S

activist, p. 613

aggregate demand, p. 603

aggregate demand curve, p. 603

aggregate supply, p. 603

aggregate supply curve, p. 609

"animal spirits", p. 607

complete crowding out, p. 608

consumer expenditure, p.606

equation of exchange, p. 604

government spending, p. 606

hysteresis, p. 619

Keynesian, p. 603

long-run aggregate supply curve, p. 612

modern quantity theory of money, p. 605

monetarist, p. 603

natural rate level of output, p. 612

natural rate of unemployment, p. 611

net exports, p. 606

nonaccelerating inflation rate of unemployment (NAIRU), p. 611

nonactivist, p. 613

partial crowding out, p. 608

planned investment spending, p. 606

real business cycle theory, p. 618

self-correcting mechanism, p. 612

supply shock, p. 616

velocity, p. 604

velocity of money, p. 604

QUESTIONS AND PROBLEMS

1. Given that a monetarist predicts velocity to be 5, graph the aggregate demand curve that results if the money supply is $400 billion. If the money supply falls to $50 billion, what happens to the position of the aggregate demand curve?

*2. Milton Friedman states, "Money is all that matters to nominal income." How is this statement built into the aggregate demand curve in the monetarist framework?

3. Suppose that government spending is raised at the same time that the money supply is lowered. What will happen to the position of the Keynesian aggregate demand curve? The monetarist aggregate demand curve?

*4. Why does the Keynesian aggregate demand curve shift when "animal spirits" change, but the monetarist aggregate demand curve does not?

5. If the dollar increases in value relative to foreign currencies so that foreign goods become cheaper in the United States, what will happen to the position of the aggregate supply curve? The aggregate demand curve?

*6. "Profit-maximizing behavior on the part of firms explains why the aggregate supply curve is upward-sloping." Is this statement true, false, or uncertain? Explain your answer.

7. If huge budget deficits cause the public to think that there will be higher inflation in the future, what is likely to happen to the aggregate supply curve when budget deficits rise?

*8. If a pill were invented that made workers twice as productive but their wages did not change, what would happen to the position of the aggregate supply curve?

9. When aggregate output is below the natural rate level, what will happen to the price level over time if the aggregate demand curve remains unchanged? Why?

*10. Show how aggregate supply and demand analysis can explain why both aggregate output and the price level fell sharply when investment spending collapsed during the Great Depression.

11. "An important difference between monetarists and Keynesians rests on how long they think the long run actually is." Is this statement true, false, or uncertain? Explain your answer.

USING ECONOMIC ANALYSIS TO PREDICT THE FUTURE

*12. Predict what will happen to aggregate output and the price level if the Federal Reserve increases the money supply at the same time that Congress implements an income tax cut.

13. Suppose that the public believes that a newly announced anti-inflation program will work and so lowers its expectations of future inflation. What will happen to aggregate output and the price level in the short run?

*14. Proposals have come before Congress that advocate the implementation of a national sales tax. Predict the effect of such a tax on both the aggregate supply and demand curves and on aggregate output and the price level.

15. With the decline in the value of the dollar since 1985, some experts predict a dramatic improvement in the ability of American firms to compete abroad. Predict what would happen to output and the price level in the United States as a result.

AGGREGATE SUPPLY AND THE PHILLIPS CURVE: HISTORICAL PERSPECTIVE

In this appendix we examine how economists' view of aggregate supply has evolved over time and how the concept called the **Phillips curve,** which described the relationship between unemployment and inflation, fits into the analysis of aggregate supply.

The classical economists, who predated Keynes, believed that wages and prices were extremely flexible, so the economy would always adjust quickly to the natural rate level of output Y_n. This view is equivalent to assuming that the aggregate supply curve is vertical at an output level of Y_n even in the short run.

With the advent of the Great Depression in 1929 and the subsequent long period of high unemployment, the classical view of an economy that adjusts quickly to the natural rate level of output became less tenable. The teachings of John Maynard Keynes emerged as the dominant way of thinking about the determination of aggregate output, and the view that aggregate supply is vertical was abandoned. Instead, Keynesians in the 1930s, 1940s, and 1950s assumed that for all practical purposes, the price level could be treated as fixed. They viewed aggregate supply as a horizontal curve along which aggregate output could increase without an increase in the price level.

In 1958, A. W. Phillips published a famous paper that outlined a relationship between unemployment and inflation.[1] This relationship was popularized by Paul Samuelson and Robert Solow of the Massachusetts Institute of Technology in the early 1960s, and naturally enough, it became know as the *Phillips curve,* after its discoverer. The Phillips curve indicates that the rate of change of wages $\Delta w/w$,

---

[1]A. W. Phillips, "The Relationship Between Unemployment and the Rate of Change of Money Wages in the United Kingdom, 1861–1957," *Economica* 25 (1958): 283–299.

called *wage inflation,* is negatively related to the difference between the actual unemployment rate U and the natural rate of unemployment U_n:

$$\frac{\Delta w}{w} = -h\,(U - U_n)$$

where h is a constant that indicates how much wage inflation changes for a given change in $U - U_n$. If h were 2, for example, a 1 percent increase in the unemployment rate relative to the natural rate would result in a 2 percent decline in wage inflation.

The Phillips curve provides a view of aggregate supply because it indicates that a rise in aggregate output that lowers the unemployment rate will raise wage inflation and thus lead to a higher level of wages and the price level. In other words, the Phillips curve implies that the aggregate supply curve will be upward-sloping. In addition, it indicates that when $U > U_n$ (the labor market is slack), $\Delta w/w$ is negative and wages decline over time. Hence the Phillips curve supports the view of aggregate supply in Chapter 24 that when the labor market is slack, production costs will fall and the aggregate supply curve will shift to the right.[2]

Figure A1 shows what the Phillips curve relationship looks like for the United States. As we can see from panel (a), the relationship works well until 1969 and seems to indicate an apparent trade-off between unemployment and wage inflation: If the public wants to have a lower unemployment rate, it can "buy" this by accepting a higher rate of wage inflation.

In 1967, however, Milton Friedman pointed out a severe flaw in the Phillips curve analysis: It left out an important factor that affects wage changes, workers' expectations of inflation.[3] Friedman noted that firm and workers are concerned with real wages not nominal wages; they are concerned with the wage adjusted for any expected increase in the price level—that is, they look at the rate of change of wages minus expected inflation. When unemployment is high relative to the natural rate, real (not nominal) wages should fall ($\Delta w/w - \pi^e < 0$); when unemployment is low relative to the natural rate, real wages should rise ($\Delta w/w - \pi^e > 0$). The Phillips curve relationship thus needs to be modified by replacing $\Delta w/w$ by $\Delta w/w - \pi^e$. This results in an *expectations-augmented Phillips curve,* expressed as

$$\frac{\Delta w}{w} - \pi^e = -h\,(U - U_n) \qquad \text{or} \qquad \frac{\Delta w}{w} = -h\,(U - U_n) + \pi^e$$

---

[2]Because workers normally become more productive over time as a result of new technology and increases in physical capital, their real wages grow over time, even when the economy is at the natural rate of unemployment. To reflect this, the Phillips curve should include a term that reflects the growth in real wages due to higher worker productivity. We have left this term out of the equation in the text because higher productivity that results in high real wages will not cause the aggregate supply curve to shift. If, for example, workers become 3 percent more productive every year and their real wages grow at 3 percent per year, the effective cost of workers to the firm (called *unit labor costs*) remains unchanged, and the aggregate supply curve does not shift. Thus the $\Delta w/w$ term in the Phillips curve is more accurately thought of as the change in the unit labor costs.

[3]This criticism of the Phillips curve was outlined in Milton Friedman's famous presidential address to the American Economic Association: Milton Friedman, "The Role of Monetary Policy," *American Economic Review* 58 (1968): 1–17.

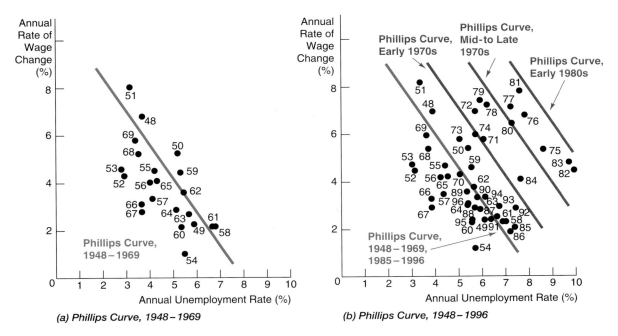

FIGURE A1 Phillips Curve in the United States

Although the Phillips curve relationship worked fairly well from 1948 to 1969, after this period it appeared to shift upward, as is clear from panel (b). Looking at the whole period after World War II, there is no apparent trade-off between unemployment and inflation.

Source: Economic Report of the President.

The expectations-augmented Phillips curve implies that as expected inflation rises, nominal wages will be increased to prevent real wages from falling, and the Phillips curve will shift upward. The resulting rise in production costs will then shift the aggregate supply curve leftward. The conclusion from Friedman's modification of the Phillips curve is therefore that the higher inflation is expected to be, the larger the leftward shift in the aggregate supply curve; this conclusion is built into the analysis of the aggregate supply curve in the chapter.

Friedman's modification of the Phillips curve analysis was remarkably clairvoyant: As inflation increased in the late 1960s, the Phillips curve did indeed begin to shift upward, as we can see from panel (b). An important feature of panel (b) is that a trade-off between unemployment and wage inflation is no longer apparent; there is no clear-cut relationship between unemployment and wage inflation—a high rate of wage inflation does not mean that unemployment is low, nor does a low rate of wage inflation mean that unemployment is high. This is exactly what the expectations-augmented Phillips curve predicts: A rate of unemployment permanently below the natural rate of unemployment cannot be "bought" by accepting a higher rate of inflation because no long-run trade-off between unemployment and wage inflation exists.[4]

A further refinement of the concept of aggregate supply came from research by Milton Friedman, Edmund Phelps, and Robert Lucas, who explored the implications of the expectations-augmented Phillips curve for the behavior of unemployment. Solving the expectations-augmented Phillips curve for U leads to the following expression:

$$U = U_n - \frac{\Delta w/w - \pi^e}{b}$$

Because wage inflation and price inflation are closely tied to each other, π can be substituted for $\Delta w/w$ in this expression to obtain

$$U = U_n - \frac{\pi - \pi^e}{b}$$

This expression, often referred to as the *Lucas supply function,* indicates that deviations of unemployment and aggregate output from the natural rate levels respond to unanticipated inflation (actual inflation minus expected inflation, $\pi - \pi^e$). When inflation is greater than anticipated, unemployment will be below the natural rate (and aggregate output above the natural rate). When inflation is below its anticipated value, unemployment will rise above the natural rate level. The conclusion from this view of aggregate supply is that only unanticipated policy can cause deviations from the natural rate of unemployment and output. The implications of this view are explored in detail in Chapter 28.

---

[4]This predicition can be derived from the expectations-augmented Phillips curve as follows. When wage inflation is held at a constant level, inflation and expected inflation will eventually equal wage inflation. Thus in the long run, $\pi^e = \Delta w/w$. Substituting the long-run value of π^e into the expectations-augmented Phillips curve gives

$$\frac{\Delta w}{w} = -b(U - U_n) + \frac{\Delta w}{w}$$

Subtracting $\Delta w/w$ from both sides of the equation gives $0 = -b(U - U_n)$, which implies that $U = U_n$. This tells us that in the long run, for any level of wage inflation, unemployment will settle to its natural rate level; hence the long-run Phillips curve is vertical, and there is no long-run trade-off between unemployment and wage inflation.

Chapter 25

TRANSMISSION MECHANISMS OF MONETARY POLICY: THE EVIDENCE

PREVIEW Since 1980, the U.S. economy has been on a roller coaster, with output, unemployment, and inflation undergoing drastic fluctuations. At the start of the 1980s, inflation was running at double-digit levels, and the recession of 1980 was followed by one of the shortest economic expansions on record. After a year, the economy plunged into the 1981–1982 recession, the most severe economic contraction in the postwar era—the unemployment rate climbed to over 10 percent, and only then did the inflation rate begin to come down to below the 5 percent level. The 1981–1982 recession was then followed by a long economic expansion that reduced the unemployment rate to below 6 percent in the 1987–1990 period. With Iraq's invasion of Kuwait and a rise in oil prices in the second half of 1990, the economy again plunged into recession. Subsequent growth in the economy was sluggish at first but eventually sped up, lowering the unemployment rate to below 5 percent by early 1997. In light of large fluctuations in aggregate output (reflected in the unemployment rate) and inflation, and the economic instability that accompanies them, policymakers face the following dilemma: What policy or policies, if any, should be implemented to reduce output and inflation fluctuations in the future?

To answer this question, monetary policymakers must have an accurate assessment of the timing and effect of their policies on the economy. To make this assessment, they need to understand the mechanisms through which monetary policy affects the economy. In this chapter we examine empirical evidence on the effect of money on economic activity. We first look at a framework for evaluating empirical evidence and then use this framework to understand why there are still deep disagreements on the importance of money to the economy. We then go on to examine the transmission mechanisms of monetary policy and the empirical evidence on them so as better to understand the role that monetary policy plays in the economy. We will see that these monetary transmission mechanisms emphasize the link between the financial system (which we studied in the first three parts of this book) and monetary theory, the subject of this part of the book.

FRAMEWORK FOR EVALUATING EMPIRICAL EVIDENCE

To develop a framework for understanding how to evaluate empirical evidence, we need to recognize that there are two basic types of empirical evidence in economics and other scientific disciplines: **Structural model evidence** examines whether one variable affects another by using data to build a model that explains the channels through which this variable affects the other; **reduced-form evidence** examines whether one variable has an effect on another simply by looking directly at the relationship between the two variables.

Suppose that you were interested in whether drinking coffee leads to heart disease. Structural model evidence would involve developing a model that analyzed data on how coffee is metabolized by the human body, how it affects the operation of the heart, and how its effects on the heart lead to heart attacks. Reduced-form evidence would involve looking directly at whether coffee drinkers tend to experience heart attacks more frequently than non–coffee drinkers.

How you look at the evidence—whether you focus on structural model evidence or reduced-form evidence—can lead to different conclusions. This is particularly true for the debate between monetarists and Keynesians. Monetarists tend to focus on reduced-form evidence and feel that changes in the money supply are more important to economic activity than Keynesians do; Keynesians, for their part, focus on structural model evidence. To understand the differences in their views about the importance of monetary policy, we need to look at the nature of the two types of evidence and the advantages and disadvantages of each.

Structural Model Evidence

The Keynesian analysis discussed in Chapter 24 is specific about the channels through which the money supply affects economic activity (called the **transmission mechanisms of monetary policy**). Keynesians typically examine the effect of money on economic activity by building a **structural model,** a description of how the economy operates using a collection of equations that describe the behavior of firms and consumers in many sectors of the economy. These equations then show the channels through which monetary and fiscal policy affect aggregate output and spending. A Keynesian structural model might have behavioral equations that describe the workings of monetary policy with the following schematic diagram:

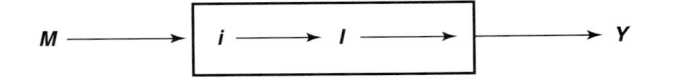

The model describes the transmission mechanism of monetary policy as follows: The money supply M affects interest rates i, which in turn affect investment spending I, which in turn affects aggregate output or aggregate spending Y. The Keynesians examine the relationship between M and Y by looking at empirical evidence (structural model evidence) on the specific channels of monetary influence, such as the link between interest rates and investment spending.

Reduced-Form Evidence

Monetarists do not describe specific ways in which the money supply affects aggregate spending. Instead, they examine the effect of money on economic activity by looking at whether movements in Y are tightly linked to (have a high correlation with) movements in M. Using reduced-form evidence, monetarists analyze the effect of M on Y as if the economy were a black box whose workings cannot be seen. The monetarist way of looking at the evidence can be represented by the following schematic diagram, in which the economy is drawn as a black box with a question mark:

Now that we have seen how monetarists and Keynesians look at the empirical evidence on the link between money and economic activity, we can consider the advantages and disadvantages of their approaches.

Advantages and Disadvantages of Structural Model Evidence

The structural model approach, used primarily by Keynesians, has the advantage of giving us an understanding of how the economy works. If the structure is correct—if it contains all the transmission mechanisms and channels through which monetary and fiscal policy can affect economic activity, the structural model approach has three major advantages over the reduced-form approach.

1. Because we can evaluate each transmission mechanism separately to see whether it is plausible, we will obtain more pieces of evidence on whether money has an important effect on economic activity. If we find important effects of money on economic activity, for example, we will have more confidence that changes in money actually cause the changes in economic activity; that is, we will have more confidence on the direction of causation between M and Y.

2. Knowing how changes in money affect economic activity may help us predict the effect of M on Y more accurately. Expansions in the money supply might be found to be less effective when interest rates are low. Then, when interest rates are higher, we would be able to predict that an expansion in the money supply would have a larger impact on Y than would otherwise be the case.

3. By knowing how the economy operates, we may be able to predict how institutional changes in the economy might affect the link between M and Y. For instance, before 1980, when Regulation Q was still in effect, restrictions on interest payments on savings deposits meant that the average consumer would not earn more on savings when interest rates rose. Since the termination of Regulation Q, the average consumer now earns more on savings when interest rates rise. If we understand how earnings on savings affect consumer spending, we might be able to say that a change in the money supply, which affects interest rates, will have a different effect today than it would have had before 1980. Because of the rapid pace of financial innovation, the advantage of being able to predict how institutional changes affect the link between M and Y may be even more important now than in the past.

These three advantages of the structural model approach suggest that this approach is better than the reduced-form approach *if we know the correct structure of the model.* Put another way, structural model evidence is only as good as the structural model it is based on; it is best only if all the transmission mechanisms are fully understood. This is a big *if*, as failing to include one or two relevant transmission mechanisms for monetary policy in the structural model might result in a serious underestimate of the impact of M on Y.

Monetarists worry that many Keynesian structural models may ignore the transmission mechanisms for monetary policy that are most important. For example, if the most important monetary transmission mechanisms involve consumer spending rather than investment spending, the Keynesian structural model (such as the $M\uparrow \Rightarrow i\downarrow \Rightarrow I\uparrow \Rightarrow Y\uparrow$ one we used earlier), which focuses on investment spending for its monetary transmission mechanism, may underestimate the importance of money to economic activity. In other words, monetarists reject the interpretation of evidence from many Keynesian structural models because they believe that the channels of monetary influence are too narrowly defined. In a sense, they accuse Keynesians of wearing blinders that prevent them from recognizing the full importance of monetary policy.

Advantages and Disadvantages of Reduced-Form Evidence

The main advantage of reduced-form evidence over structural model evidence is that no restrictions are imposed on the way monetary policy affects the economy. If we are not sure that we know what all the monetary transmission mechanisms are, we may be more likely to spot the full effect of M on Y by looking at whether movements in Y correlate highly with movements in M. Monetarists favor reduced-form evidence because they believe that the particular channels through which changes in the money supply affect Y are diverse and continually changing. They contend that it may be too difficult to identify all the transmission mechanisms of monetary policy.

The most notable objection to reduced-form evidence is that it may misleadingly suggest that changes in M cause changes in Y when that is not the case. A basic principle applicable to all scientific disciplines, including economics, states that **correlation does not necessarily imply causation.** The fact that the movement of one variable is linked to another doesn't necessarily mean that one variable *causes* the other.

Suppose that you notice that wherever criminal activity abounds, more police patrol the street. Should you conclude that police patrols cause criminal activity and recommend that pulling police off the street would lower the crime rate? The

Perils of Reverse Causation

A Russian Folk Tale. A Russian folk tale illustrates the problems that can arise from reverse causation. As the story goes, there once was a severe epidemic in the Russian countryside and many doctors were sent to the towns where the epidemic was at its worst. The peasants in the towns noticed that wherever doctors went, many people were dying. So to reduce the death rate, they killed all the doctors.

Were the peasants better off? Clearly not.

answer is clearly no, because police patrols do not cause criminal activity; criminal activity causes police patrols. This situation is called **reverse causation** and can lead to misleading conclusions when interpreting correlations (see Box 1).

The reverse causation problem may be present when examining the link between money and aggregate output or spending. Our discussion of the conduct of monetary policy in Chapter 19 suggested that when the Federal Reserve has an interest-rate or a free reserves target, higher output may lead to a higher money supply. If most of the correlation between M and Y occurs because of the Fed's interest-rate target, controlling the money supply will not help control aggregate output because it is actually Y that is causing M rather than the other way around.

Another facet of the correlation-causation question is that an outside factor, yet unknown, could be the driving force behind two variables that move together. Coffee drinking might be associated with heart disease not because coffee drinking causes heart attacks but because coffee drinkers tend to be people who are under a lot of stress and the stress causes heart attacks. Getting people to stop drinking coffee, then, would not lower the incidence of heart disease. Similarly, if there is an unknown outside factor that causes M and Y to move together, controlling M will not improve control of Y. (The perils of ignoring an outside driving factor are illustrated in Box 2.)

Conclusions

No clear-cut case can be made that reduced-form evidence is preferable to structural model evidence or vice versa. The structural model approach, used primarily by Keynesians, offers an understanding of how the economy works. If the structure is correct, it predicts the effect of monetary policy more accurately, allows predictions of the effect of monetary policy when institutions change, and provides more confidence in the direction of causation between M and Y. If the structure of the model is not correctly specified because it leaves out important transmission mechanisms of monetary policy, it could be very misleading.

The reduced-form approach, used primarily by monetarists, does not restrict the way monetary policy affects the economy and may be more likely to spot the full effect of M on Y. However, reduced-form evidence cannot rule out reverse causation, whereby changes in output cause changes in money, or the possibility that an outside factor drives changes in both output and money. A high correlation of money and output might then be misleading because controlling the money supply would not help control the level of output.

BOX 2

Perils of Ignoring an Outside Driving Factor

How to Lose a Presidential Election. Ever since Muncie, Indiana, was dubbed "Middletown" by two sociology studies over half a century ago, it has produced a vote for president that closely mirrors the national vote; that is, in every election, there has been a very high correlation between Muncie's vote and the national vote. Noticing this, a political adviser to a presidential candidate recommends that the candidate's election will be assured if *all* the candidate's campaign funds are spent in Muncie. Should the presidential candidate promote or fire this adviser? Why?

It is very unlikely that the vote in a small town like Muncie drives the vote in a national election. Rather it is more likely that national preferences are a third driving factor that determines the vote in Muncie and also determines the vote in the national election. Changing the vote in Muncie will thus only break the relationship between that town's vote and national preferences and will have almost no impact on the election. Spending all the campaign money on this town will therefore be a waste of money.

The presidential candidate should definitely fire the adviser.

Armed with the framework to evaluate empirical evidence we have outlined here, we can now use it to evaluate the empirical debate between monetarists and Keynesians on the importance of money to the economy.

EARLY KEYNESIAN EVIDENCE ON THE IMPORTANCE OF MONEY

Although Keynes proposed his theory for analyzing aggregate economic activity in 1936, his views reached their peak of popularity among economists in the 1950s and early 1960s, when the majority of economists had accepted his framework. Although Keynesians currently believe that money has important effects on economic activity, the early Keynesians of the 1950s and early 1960s characteristically held the view that *monetary policy does not matter at all* to movements in aggregate output and hence to the business cycle.

Their belief in the ineffectiveness of monetary policy stemmed from three pieces of structural model evidence:

1. During the Great Depression, interest rates on U.S. Treasury securities fell to extremely low levels; the three-month Treasury bill rate, for example, declined to below 1 percent. Early Keynesians viewed monetary policy as affecting aggregate demand solely through its effect on nominal interest rates, which in turn affect investment spending; they believed that low interest rates during the depression indicated that monetary policy was easy because it encouraged investment spending and so could not have played a contractionary role during this period. Seeing that monetary policy was not capable of explaining why the worst economic contraction in U.S. history had taken place, they concluded that changes in the money supply have no effect on aggregate output—in other words, money doesn't matter.

2. Early empirical studies found no linkage between movements in nominal interest rates and investment spending. Because early Keynesians saw this link as the channel through which changes in the money supply affect aggregate demand, finding that the link was weak also led them to the conclusion that changes in the money supply have no effect on aggregate output.

3. Surveys of businesspeople revealed that their decisions on how much to invest in new physical capital were not influenced by market interest rates. This evidence further confirmed that the link between interest rates and investment spending was weak, strengthening the conclusion that money doesn't matter. The result of this interpretation of the evidence was that most economists paid only scant attention to monetary policy until the mid-1960s.

Study Guide   Before reading about the objections that were raised against early Keynesian interpretations of the evidence, use the ideas on the disadvantages of structural model evidence to see if you can come up with some objections yourself. This will help you learn to apply the principles of evaluating evidence discussed earlier.

Objections to Early Keynesian Evidence

While Keynesian economics was reaching its ascendancy in the 1950s and 1960s, a small group of economists at the University of Chicago, led by Milton Friedman, adopted what was then the unfashionable view that money *does* matter to aggregate demand. Friedman and his disciples, who later became known as *monetarists,* objected to the early Keynesian interpretation of the evidence on the grounds that the structural model used by the early Keynesians was severely flawed. Because structural model evidence is only as good as the model it is based on, the monetarist critique of this evidence needs to be taken seriously.

In 1963, Friedman and Anna Schwartz published their classic monetary history of the United States, which showed that contrary to the early Keynesian beliefs, monetary policy during the Great Depression was not easy; indeed, it had never been more contractionary.[1] Friedman and Schwartz documented the massive bank failures of this period and the resulting decline in the money supply—the largest ever experienced in the United States (see Chapter 17). Hence monetary policy could explain the worst economic contraction in U.S. history, and the Great Depression could not be singled out as a period that demonstrates the ineffectiveness of monetary policy.

A Keynesian could still counter Friedman and Schwartz's argument that money was contractionary during the Great Depression by citing the low level of interest rates. But were these interest rates really so low? Referring to Figure 1 in Chapter 7, you will note that although interest rates on U.S. Treasury securities and high-grade corporate bonds were low during the Great Depression, interest rates on lower-grade bonds, such as Baa corporate bonds, rose to unprecedented high levels during the sharpest part of the contraction phase (1930–1933). By the

---

[1]Milton Friedman and Anna Jacobson Schwartz, *A Monetary History of the United States, 1867–1960* (Princeton, N.J.: Princeton University Press, 1963).

standard of these lower-grade bonds, then, interest rates were high and monetary policy was tight.

There is a moral to this story. Although much aggregate economic analysis proceeds as though there is only *one* interest rate, we must always be aware that there are *many* interest rates, which may tell different stories. During normal times, most interest rates move in tandem, so lumping them all together and looking at one representative interest rate may not be too misleading. But that is not always so. Unusual periods (like the Great Depression), when interest rates on different securities begin to diverge, do occur. This is exactly the kind of situation in which a structural model (like the early Keynesians') that looks at only the interest rates on a low-risk security such as a U.S. Treasury bill or bond can be very misleading.

There is a second, potentially more important reason why the early Keynesian structural model's focus on nominal interest rates provides a misleading picture of the tightness of monetary policy during the Great Depression. In a period of deflation, when there is a declining price level, low *nominal* interest rates do not necessarily indicate that the cost of borrowing is low and that monetary policy is easy—in fact, the cost of borrowing could be quite high. If, for example, the public expects the price level to decline at a 10 percent rate, then even though nominal interest rates are at zero, the real cost of borrowing would be as high as 10 percent. [Recall from Chapter 4 that the real rate equals the nominal rate, 0, minus the expected rate of inflation, −10 percent, so the real rate equals 0 − (−10 percent) = 10 percent.]

You can see in Figure 1 that this is exactly what happened during the Great Depression: Real interest rates on U.S. Treasury bills were far higher during the 1931–1933 contraction phase of the depression than was the case throughout the next 40 years.[2] As a result, movements of *real* interest rates indicate that contrary to the early Keynesians' beliefs, monetary policy was extremely tight during the Great Depression. Because an important role for monetary policy during this depressed period could no longer be ruled out, most economists were forced to rethink their position regarding whether money matters.

Monetarists also objected to the early Keynesian structural model's view that a weak link between nominal interest rates and investment spending indicates that investment spending is unaffected by monetary policy. A weak link between *nominal* interest rates and investment spending does not rule out a strong link between *real* interest rates and investment spending. As depicted in Figure 1, nominal interest rates are often a very misleading indicator of real interest rates— not only during the Great Depression but in later periods as well. Because real interest rates more accurately reflect the true cost of borrowing, they should be more relevant to investment decisions than nominal interest rates. Accordingly, the two pieces of early Keynesian evidence indicating that nominal interest rates

---

[2]In the 1980s, real interest rates rose to exceedingly high levels, approaching those of the Great Depression period. Recent research has tried to explain this phenomenon, some of which points to monetary policy as the source of high real rates in the 1980s. For example, see Oliver J. Blanchard and Lawrence H. Summers, "Perspectives on High World Interest Rates," *Brookings Papers on Economic Activity* 2 (1984): 273–324; and John Huizinga and Frederic S. Mishkin, "Monetary Policy Regime Shifts and the Unusual Behavior of Real Interest Rates," *Carnegie-Rochester Conference Series on Public Policy* 24 (1986): 231–274.

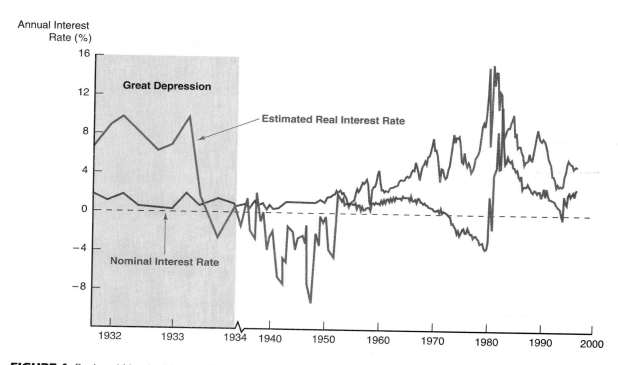

FIGURE 1 Real and Nominal Interest Rates on Three-Month Treasury Bills, 1931–1996
Source: Citibase databank.

have little effect on investment spending do not rule out a strong effect of changes in the money supply on investment spending and hence on aggregate demand.

Monetarists also assert that interest-rate effects on investment spending might be only one of many channels through which monetary policy affects aggregate demand. Monetary policy could then have a major impact on aggregate demand even if interest-rate effects on investment spending are small, as was suggested by the early Keynesians.

Study Guide As you read the monetarist evidence presented in the next section, again try to think of objections to the evidence. This time use the ideas on the disadvantages of reduced-form evidence.

EARLY MONETARIST EVIDENCE ON THE IMPORTANCE OF MONEY

In the early 1960s, Milton Friedman and his followers published a series of studies based on reduced-form evidence that promoted the case for a strong effect of money on economic activity. In general, reduced-form evidence can be broken down into three categories: *timing evidence,* which looks at whether the movements in one variable typically occur before another; *statistical evidence,* which performs formal statistical tests on the correlation of the movements of one variable with another; and *historical evidence,* which examines specific past episodes to see whether movements in one variable appear to cause another. Let's look at the monetarist evidence on the importance of money that falls into each of these three categories.

Timing Evidence

Monetarist timing evidence reveals how the rate of money supply growth moves relative to the business cycle. The evidence on this relationship was first presented by Friedman and Schwartz in a famous paper published in 1963.[3] Friedman and Schwartz found that in every business cycle they studied over nearly a century, the money growth rate always turned down before output did. On average, the peak in the rate of money growth occurred 16 months before the peak in the level of output. However, this lead time could vary, ranging from a few months to more than two years. The conclusion that these authors reached on the basis of this evidence is that money growth causes business cycle fluctuations, but its effect on the business cycle operates with "long and variable lags."

Timing evidence is based on the philosophical principle first stated in Latin as *post hoc, ergo propter hoc,* which means that if one event occurs after another, the second event must have been caused by the first. This principle is valid only if we know that the first event is an *exogenous* event, an event occurring as a result of an independent action that could not possibly be caused by the event following it or by some outside factor that might affect both events. If the first event is exogenous, when the second event follows the first, we can be more confident that the first event is causing the second.

An example of an exogenous event is a controlled experiment. A chemist mixes two chemicals; suddenly his lab blows up and he with it. We can be absolutely sure that the cause of his demise was the act of mixing the two chemicals together. The principle of *post hoc, ergo propter hoc* is extremely useful in scientific experimentation.

Unfortunately, economics does not enjoy the precision of hard sciences like physics or chemistry. Often we cannot be sure that an economic event, such as a decline in the rate of money growth, is an exogenous event—it could have been caused, itself, by an outside factor or by the event it is supposedly causing. When another event (such as a decline in output) typically follows the first event (a decline in money growth), we cannot conclude with certainty that one caused the other. Timing evidence is clearly of a reduced-form nature because it looks directly at the relationship of the movements of two variables. Money growth could lead output, or both could be driven by an outside factor.

Because timing evidence is of a reduced-form nature, there is also the possibility of reverse causation, in which output growth causes money growth. How

---

[3]Milton Friedman and Anna Jacobson Schwartz, "Money and Business Cycles," *Review of Economics and Statistics* 45, Suppl. (1963): 32–64.

can this reverse causation occur while money growth still leads output? There are several ways in which this can happen, but we will deal with just one example.[4]

Suppose that you are in a hypothetical economy with a very regular business cycle movement, plotted in panel (a) of Figure 2, that is four years long (four years from peak to peak). Let's assume that in our hypothetical economy, there is reverse causation from output to the money supply, so movements in the money supply and output are perfectly correlated; that is, the money supply M and output Y move upward and downward at the same time. The result is that the peaks and troughs of the M and Y series in panels (a) and (b) occur at exactly the same time; therefore, no lead or lag relationship exists between them.

Now let's construct the rate of money supply growth from the money supply series in panel (b). This is done in panel (c). What is the rate of growth of the money supply at its peaks in years 1 and 5? At these points, it is not growing at all; the rate of growth is zero. Similarly, at the trough in year 3, the growth rate is zero. When the money supply is declining from its peak in year 1 to its trough in year 3, it has a negative growth rate, and its decline is fastest sometime between years 1 and 3 (year 2). Translating to panel (c), the rate of money growth is below zero from years 1 to 3, with its most negative value reached at year 2. By similar reasoning, you can see that the growth rate of money is positive in years 0 to 1 and 3 to 5, with the highest values reached in years 0 and 4. When we connect all these points together, we get the money growth series in panel (c), in which the peaks are at years 0 and 4, with a trough in year 2.

Now let's look at the relationship of the money growth series of panel (c) with the level of output in panel (a). As you can see, the money growth series consistently has its peaks and troughs exactly one year before the peaks and troughs of the output series. We conclude that in our hypothetical economy, the rate of money growth always decreases one year before output does. This evidence does not, however, imply that money growth *drives* output. In fact, by assumption, we know that this economy is one in which causation actually runs from output to the level of money supply, and there is no lead or lag relationship between the two. Only by our judicious choice of using the *growth rate* of the money supply rather than its *level* have we found a leading relationship.

This example shows how easy it is to misinterpret timing relationships. Furthermore, by searching for what we hope to find, we might focus on a variable, such as a growth rate, rather than a level, which suggests a misleading relationship. Timing evidence can be a dangerous tool for deciding on causation.

Stated even more forcefully, "one person's lead is another person's lag." For example, you could just as easily interpret the relationship of money growth and output in Figure 2 to say that the money growth rate lags output by three years—after all, the peaks in the money growth series occur three years after the peaks in the output series. In short, you could say that output leads money growth.

---

[4]A famous article by James Tobin, "Money and Income: *Post Hoc, Ergo Propter Hoc,*" *Quarterly Journal of Economics* 84 (1970): 301–317, describes an economic system in which changes in aggregate output cause changes in the growth rate of money but changes in the growth rate of money have no effect on output. Tobin shows that such a system with reverse causation could yield timing evidence similar to that found by Friedman and Schwartz.

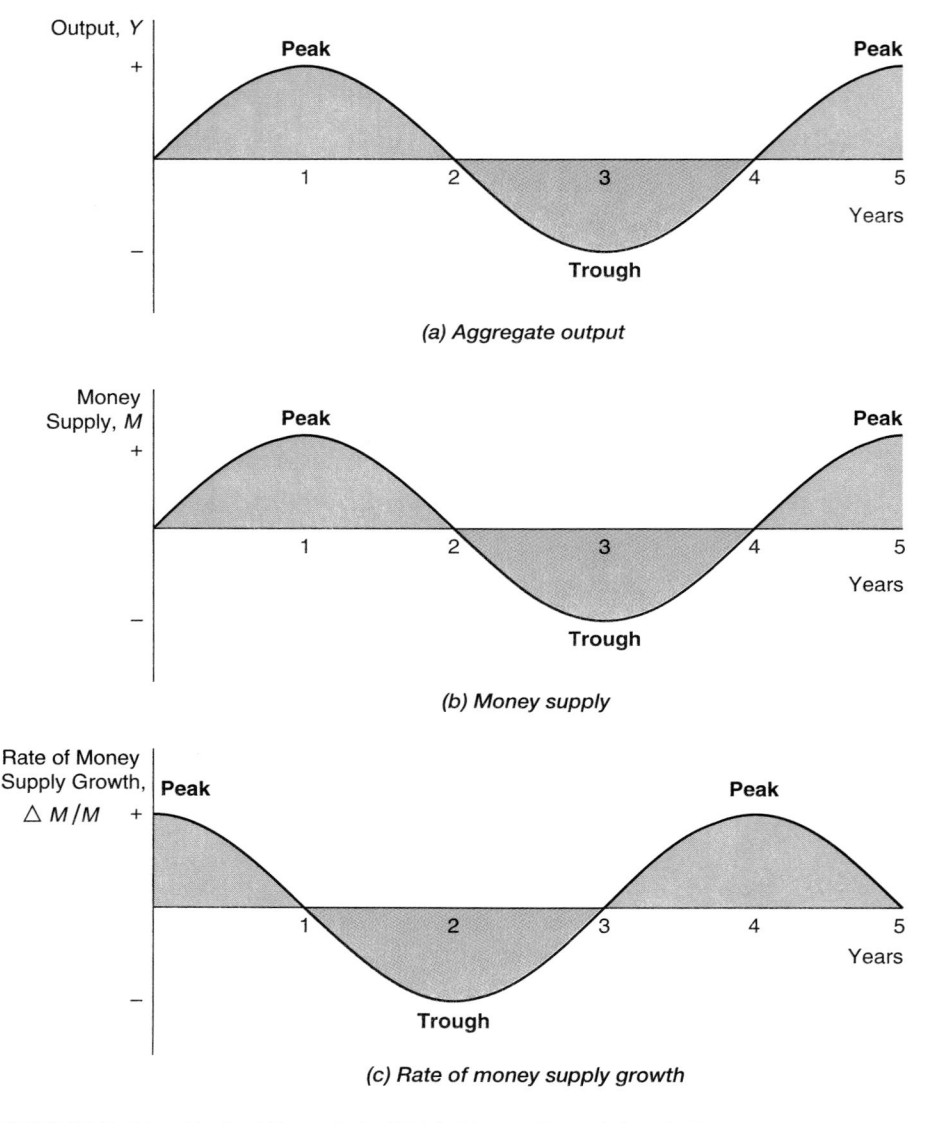

FIGURE 2 Hypothetical Example in Which Money Growth Leads Output
Although neither **M** nor **Y** leads the other (that is, their peaks and troughs coincide), Δ**M/M** has its peaks and troughs one year ahead of **M** and **Y**, thus leading both series. (Note that **M** and **Y** in the panels are drawn as movements around a positive average value; a plus sign indicates a value above the average, and a minus sign indicates a value below the average, not a negative value.)

We have seen that timing evidence is extremely hard to interpret. Unless we can be sure that changes in the leading variable are exogenous events, we cannot be sure that the leading variable is actually causing the following variable. And it is all too easy to find what we seek when looking for timing evidence. Perhaps the best way of describing this danger is to say that "timing evidence may be in the eyes of the beholder."

**Statistical
Evidence**

Monetarist statistical evidence examines the correlations between money and aggregate output or aggregate spending by performing formal statistical tests. Again in 1963 (obviously a vintage year for the monetarists), Milton Friedman and David Meiselman published a paper that proposed the following test of a monetarist model against a Keynesian model.[5] In the Keynesian framework, investment and government spending are sources of fluctuations in aggregate demand, so Friedman and Meiselman constructed a "Keynesian" autonomous expenditure variable *A* equal to investment spending plus government spending. They characterized the Keynesian model as saying that *A* should be highly correlated with aggregate spending *Y*, while the money supply *M* should not. In the monetarist model, the money supply is the source of fluctuations in aggregate spending, and *M* should be highly correlated with *Y*, while *A* should not.

A logical way to find out which model is better would be to see which is more highly correlated with *Y*: *M* or *A*. When Friedman and Meiselman conducted this test for many different periods of U.S. data, they discovered that *the monetarist model wins!*[6] They concluded that monetarist analysis gives a better description than Keynesian analysis of how aggregate spending is determined.

Several objections were raised against the Friedman-Meiselman evidence.

1. The standard criticisms of this reduced-form evidence are the ones we have already discussed: Reverse causation could occur, or an outside factor might drive both series.

2. The test may not be fair because the Keynesian model is characterized too simplistically. Keynesian structural models commonly include hundreds of equations. The one-equation Keynesian model that Friedman-Meiselman tested may not adequately capture the effects of autonomous expenditure. Furthermore, Keynesian models usually include the effects of other variables. By ignoring them, the effect of monetary policy might be overestimated and the effect of autonomous expenditure underestimated.

3. The Friedman-Meiselman measure of autonomous expenditure *A* might be constructed poorly, preventing the Keynesian model from performing well. For example, orders for military hardware affect aggregate demand before they appear as spending in the autonomous expenditure variable that Friedman and Meiselman used. A more careful construction of the autonomous expenditure variable should take account of the placing of orders for military hardware. When the autonomous expenditure variable was constructed more carefully by critics of the Friedman-Meiselman study, they found that the results were reversed: The Keynesian model won.[7] A more recent postmortem on the appropriateness of

[5]Milton Friedman and David Meiselman, "The Relative Stability of Monetary Velocity and the Investment Multiplier," in *Stabilization Policies,* ed. Commission on Money and Credit (Upper Saddle River, N.J.: Prentice Hall, 1963), pp. 165–268.

[6]Friedman and Meiselman did not actually run their tests using the *Y* variable because they felt that this gave an unfair advantage to the Keynesian model in that *A* is included in *Y*. Instead, they subtracted *A* from *Y* and tested for the correlation of *Y* − *A* with *M* or *A*.

[7]See, for example, Albert Ando and Franco Modigliani, "The Relative Stability of Monetary Velocity and the Investment Multiplier," *American Economic Review* 55 (1965): 693–728.

various ways of determining autonomous expenditure does not give a clear-cut victory to either the Keynesian or the monetarist model.[8]

Historical Evidence

The monetarist historical evidence, found in Friedman and Schwartz's *Monetary History,* has been very influential in gaining support for the monetarist position. We have already seen that the book was extremely important as a criticism of early Keynesian thinking, showing as it did that the Great Depression was not a period of easy monetary policy and that the depression could be attributed to the sharp decline in the money supply from 1930 to 1933 resulting from bank panics. In addition, the book documents in great detail that the growth rate of money leads business cycles because it declines before every recession. This timing evidence is, of course, subject to all the criticisms raised earlier.

The historical evidence contains one feature, however, that makes it different from other monetarist evidence we have discussed so far. Several episodes occur in which changes in the money supply appear to be exogenous events. These episodes are almost like controlled experiments, so the *post hoc, ergo propter hoc* principle is far more likely to be valid: If the decline in the growth rate of the money supply is soon followed by a decline in output in these episodes, much stronger evidence is presented that money growth is the driving force behind the business cycle.

One of the best examples of such an episode is the increase in reserve requirements in 1936–1937 (discussed in Chapter 19), which led to a sharp decline in the money supply and in its rate of growth. The increase in reserve requirements was implemented because the Federal Reserve wanted to improve its control of monetary policy; it was not implemented in response to economic conditions. We can thus rule out reverse causation from output to the money supply. Also, it is hard to think of an outside factor that could have driven the Fed to increase reserve requirements and that could also have directly affected output. Therefore, the decline in the money supply in this episode can probably be classified as an exogenous event with the characteristics of a controlled experiment. Soon after this experiment, the very severe recession of 1937–1938 occurred. We can conclude with confidence that in this episode, the change in the money supply due to the Fed's increase in reserve requirements was indeed the source of the business cycle contraction that followed.

A Monetary History also documents other historical episodes, such as the bank panic of 1907 and other years in which the decline in money growth again appears to have been an exogenous event. The fact that recessions have frequently followed apparently exogenous declines in money growth is very strong evidence that changes in the growth rate of the money supply do have an impact on aggregate output. Recent work by Christina and David Romer, both of the University of California, Berkeley, applies the historical approach to more recent data using more sophisticated statistical techniques and also finds that monetary policy shifts have had an important impact on the aggregate economy.[9]

---

[8]See William Poole and Edith Kornblith, "The Friedman-Meiselman CMC Paper: New Evidence on an Old Controversy," *American Economic Review* 63 (1973): 908–917.

[9]Christina Romer and David Romer, "Does Monetary Policy Matter? A New Test in the Spirit of Friedman and Schwartz," *NBER Macroeconomics Annual, 1989,* 4, ed. Stanley Fischer (Cambridge Mass.: M.I.T. Press, 1989) 121–170.

OVERVIEW OF THE MONETARIST EVIDENCE

Where does this discussion of the monetarist evidence leave us? We have seen that because of reverse causation and outside-factor possibilities, there are some serious doubts about the conclusions that can be drawn from timing and statistical evidence alone. However, some of the historical evidence in which exogenous declines in money growth are followed by business cycle contractions does provide stronger support for the monetarist position. When historical evidence is combined with timing and statistical evidence, the conclusion that money does matter seems warranted.

As you can imagine, the economics profession was quite shaken by the appearance of the monetarist evidence, as up to that time most economists believed that money does not matter at all. Monetarists had demonstrated that this early Keynesian position was probably wrong, and it won them a lot of converts. Recognizing the fallacy of the position that money does not matter does not necessarily mean that we must accept the position that money is *all* that matters. Many Keynesian economists shifted their views toward the monetarist position, but not all the way. Instead, they adopted an intermediate position compatible with the Keynesian aggregate supply and demand analysis described in Chapter 24: They allowed that money, fiscal policy, net exports, and "animal spirits" all contributed to fluctuations in aggregate demand. The result has been a convergence of the Keynesian and monetarist views on the importance of money to economic activity. However, proponents of a new theory of aggregate fluctuations called *real business cycle theory* do not accept the monetarist reduced-form evidence that money is important to business cycle fluctuations because they believe there is reverse causation from the business cycle to money (see Box 3).

TRANSMISSION MECHANISMS OF MONETARY POLICY

Economic research went in two directions after the successful monetarist attack against the early Keynesian position. One direction was to use more sophisticated monetarist reduced-form models to test for the importance of money to economic activity.[10] The second direction was to pursue a structural model approach and to develop a better understanding of channels (other than interest-rate effects on investment) through which monetary policy affects aggregate demand. In this section we examine some of these channels, or *transmission mechanisms*, beginning with interest-rate channels because they are the key monetary transmission mechanism in the Keynesian *ISLM* and *AD/AS* models you have seen in Chapters 22, 23, and 24.

---

[10]The most prominent example of more sophisticated reduced-form research is the so-called St. Louis model, which was developed at the Federal Reserve Bank of St. Louis in the late 1960s and early 1970s. It provided support for the monetarist position but is subject to the same criticisms of reduced-form evidence outlined in the text. The St. Louis model was first outlined in Leonall Andersen and Jerry Jordan, "Monetary and Fiscal Actions: A Test of Their Relative Importance in Economic Stabilization," Federal Reserve Bank of St. Louis *Review,* 50 (November 1968): 11–23.

Real Business Cycle Theory and the Debate on Money and Economic Activity

New entrants to the debate on money and economic activity are advocates of *real business cycle theory,* which states that real shocks to tastes and technology (rather than monetary shocks) are the driving forces behind business cycles. Proponents of this theory do not accept the monetarist view that money matters to business cycles because they believe that the correlation of output with money reflects reverse causation; that is, the business cycle drives money, rather than the other way around. An important piece of evidence they offer to support the reverse causation argument is that almost none of the correlation between money and output comes from the monetary base, which is controlled by the monetary authorities.* Instead, the money-output correlation stems from other sources of money supply movements that, as we saw in Chapters 16 and 17, are affected by the actions of banks, depositors, and borrowers from banks and are more likely to be influenced by the business cycle.

Although real business cycle theory reserves no role for money in the business cycle, it does view money as an important determinant of inflation. So monetary policy still plays a crucial role in the economy.

*Robert King and Charles Plosser, "Money, Credit and Prices in a Real Business Cycle," *American Economic Review* 74 (1984): 363–380; Charles Plosser, "Understanding Real Business Cycles," *Journal of Economic Perspectives* 3 (Summer 1989): 51–78.

Traditional Interest-Rate Channels

The traditional Keynesian view of the monetary transmission mechanism can be characterized by the following schematic showing the effect of a monetary expansion:

$$M\uparrow \Rightarrow i_r\downarrow \Rightarrow I\uparrow \Rightarrow Y\uparrow \tag{1}$$

where $M\uparrow$ indicates an expansionary monetary policy leading to a fall in real interest rates ($i_r\downarrow$), which in turn lowers the cost of capital, causing a rise in investment spending ($I\uparrow$), thereby leading to an increase in aggregate demand and a rise in output ($Y\uparrow$).

Although Keynes originally emphasized this channel as operating through businesses' decisions about investment spending, the search for new monetary transmission mechanisms recognized that consumers' decisions about housing and **consumer durable expenditure** (spending by consumers on durable items such as automobiles and refrigerators) also are investment decisions. Thus the interest-rate channel of monetary transmission outlined in Equation 1 applies equally to consumer spending in which I represents residential housing and consumer durable expenditure.

An important feature of the interest-rate transmission mechanism is its emphasis on the *real* rather than the nominal interest rate as the rate that affects consumer and business decisions. In addition, it is often the real *long*-term interest rate and not the short-term interest rate that is viewed as having the major impact on spending. How is it that changes in the short-term nominal interest rate induced by a central bank result in a corresponding change in the real interest rate on both short- and long-term bonds? The key is the phenomenon known as *sticky prices*, the fact that the aggregate price level adjusts slowly over time, meaning that expansionary monetary policy, which lowers the short-term nominal interest rate, also lowers the short-term *real* interest rate. The expectations hypothesis of the term structure described in Chapter 7, which states that the long-term interest rate is an average of expected future short-term interest rates, suggests that the lower real short-term interest rate leads to a fall in the real long-term interest rate. These lower real interest rates then lead to rises in business fixed investment, residential housing investment, inventory investment, consumer durable expenditure, and residential housing, all of which produce the rise in aggregate output.

The fact that it is the real interest rate that affects spending rather than the nominal rate provides an important mechanism for how monetary policy can stimulate the economy, even if nominal interest rates hit a floor of zero during a deflationary episode. With nominal interest rates at a floor of zero, an expansion in the money supply ($M\uparrow$) can raise the expected price level ($P^e\uparrow$) and hence expected inflation ($\pi^e\uparrow$), thereby lowering the real interest rate ($i_r = i - \pi^e\downarrow$) even when the nominal interest rate is fixed at zero and stimulating spending through the interest-rate channel:

$$M\uparrow \Rightarrow P^e\uparrow \Rightarrow \pi^e\uparrow \Rightarrow i_r\downarrow \Rightarrow I\uparrow \Rightarrow Y\uparrow \qquad (2)$$

This mechanism thus indicates that monetary policy can still be effective even when nominal interest rates have already been driven down to zero by the monetary authorities. Indeed, this mechanism is a key element in monetarist discussions of why the U.S. economy was not stuck in a liquidity trap (in which increases in the money supply might be unable to lower interest rates, discussed in Chapter 21) during the Great Depression and why expansionary monetary policy could have prevented the sharp decline in output during that period.

Some economists such as John Taylor of Stanford University take the position that there is strong empirical evidence for substantial interest-rate effects on consumer and investment spending through the cost of capital, making the interest-rate monetary transmission mechanism a strong one. His position is highly controversial, and many researchers, including Ben Bernanke of Princeton University and Mark Gertler of New York University, believe that the empirical evidence does not support strong interest-rate effects operating through the cost of capital.[11] Indeed, these researchers see the empirical failure of traditional interest-rate monetary transmission mechanisms as having provided the stimulus for the search for other transmission mechanisms of monetary policy.

These other transmission mechanisms fall into two basic categories: those operating through asset prices other than interest rates and those operating through asymmetric information effects on credit markets (the so-called **credit view**). (All these mechanisms are summarized in the schematic diagram in Figure 3.)

---

[11]See John Taylor, "The Monetary Transmission Mechanism: An Empirical Framework," *Journal of Economic Perspectives* 9 (Fall 1995): 11–26, and Ben Bernanke and Mark Gertler, "Inside the Black Box: The Credit Channel of Monetary Policy Transmission," *Journal of Economic Perspectives* 9 (Fall 1995): 27–48.

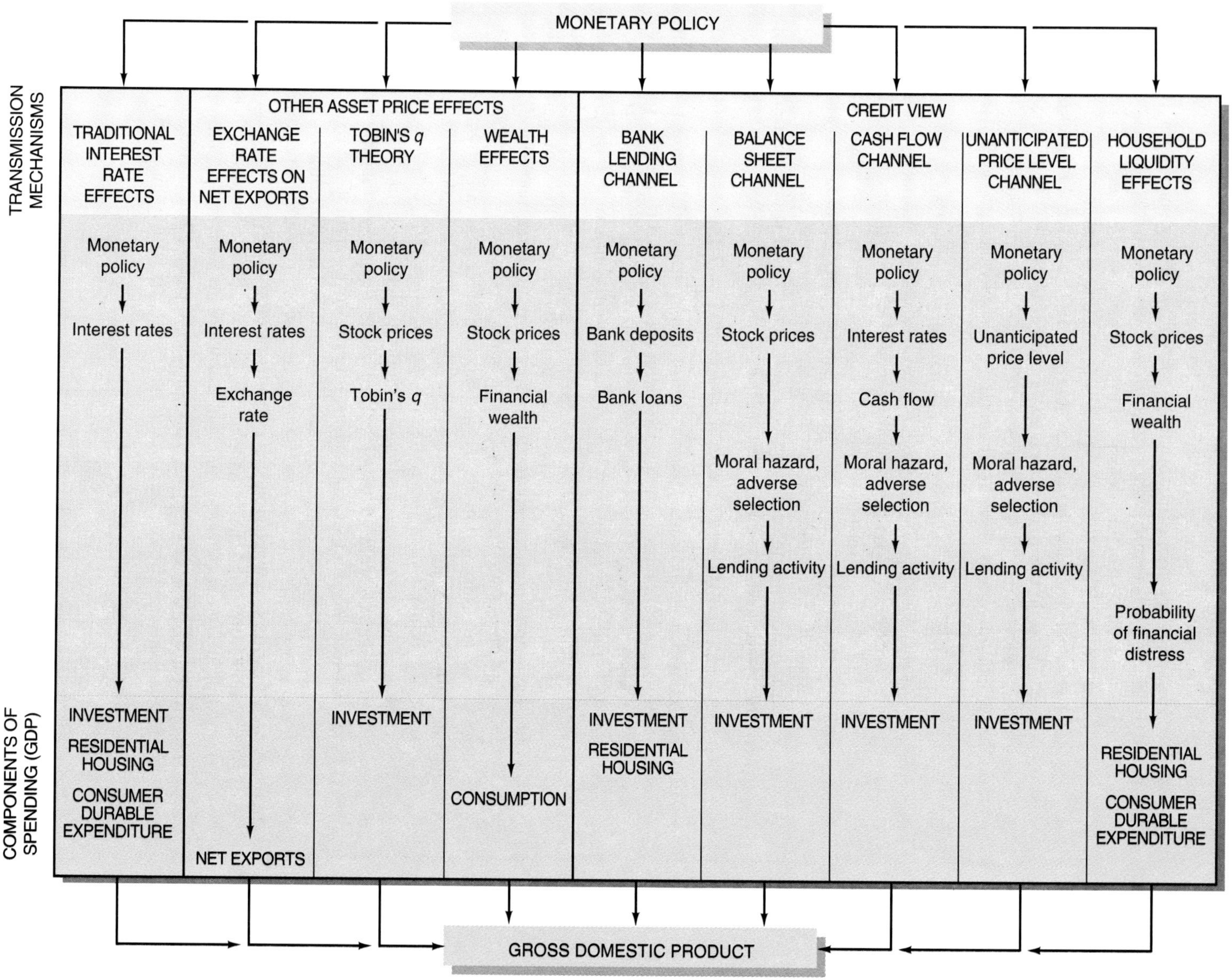

FIGURE 3 The Link Between Monetary Policy and GDP: Monetary Transmission Mechanisms

Other Asset Price Channels

As we have seen earlier in the chapter, a key monetarist objection to the Keynesian analysis of monetary policy effects on the economy is that it focuses on only one asset price, the interest rate, rather than on many asset prices. Monetarists envision a transmission mechanism in which other relative asset prices and real wealth transmit monetary effects onto the economy. In addition to bond prices, two other asset prices receive substantial attention as channels for monetary policy effects: foreign exchange and equities (stocks).

EXCHANGE RATE EFFECTS ON NET EXPORTS With the growing internationalization of economies throughout the world and the advent of flexible exchange rates, more attention has been paid to how monetary policy affects exchange rates, which in turn affect net exports and aggregate output.

This channel also involves interest-rate effects because, as we have seen in Chapter 8, when domestic real interest rates fall, domestic dollar deposits become less attractive relative to deposits denominated in foreign currencies. As a result, the value of dollar deposits relative to other currency deposits falls, and the dollar depreciates (denoted by $E\downarrow$). The lower value of the domestic currency makes domestic goods cheaper than foreign goods, thereby causing a rise in net exports ($NX\uparrow$) and hence in aggregate output ($Y\uparrow$). The schematic for the monetary transmission mechanism that operates through the exchange rate is

$$M\uparrow \Rightarrow i_r\downarrow \Rightarrow E\downarrow \Rightarrow NX\uparrow \Rightarrow Y\uparrow \tag{3}$$

Recent research has found that this exchange rate channel plays an important role in how monetary policy affects the domestic economy.[12]

TOBIN'S *q* THEORY James Tobin developed a theory, referred to as *Tobin's q Theory*, that explains how monetary policy can affect the economy through its effects on the valuation of equities (stock). Tobin defines q as the market value of firms divided by the replacement cost of capital. If q is high, the market price of firms is high relative to the replacement cost of capital, and new plant and equipment capital is cheap relative to the market value of firms. Companies can then issue stock and get a high price for it relative to the cost of the facilities and equipment they are buying. Investment spending will rise because firms can buy a lot of new investment goods with only a small issue of stock.

Conversely, when q is low, firms will not purchase *new* investment goods because the market value of firms is low relative to the cost of capital. If companies want to acquire capital when q is low, they can buy another firm cheaply and acquire old capital instead. Investment spending, the purchase of new investment goods, will then be very low. Tobin's q theory gives a good explanation for the extremely low rate of investment spending during the Great Depression. In that period, stock prices collapsed, and by 1933, stocks were worth only one-tenth of their value in late 1929; q fell to unprecedented low levels.

---

[12]For example, see Ralph Bryant, Peter Hooper, and Catherine Mann, *Evaluating Policy Regimes: New Empirical Research in Empirical Macroeconomics* (Washington, D.C.: Brookings Institution, 1993), and John B. Taylor, *Macroeconomic Policy in a World Economy: From Econometric Design to Practical Operation* (New York: Norton, 1993).

The crux of this discussion is that a link exists between Tobin's q and investment spending. But how might monetary policy affect stock prices? Quite simply, when money supply increases, the public finds that it has more money than it wants and so gets rid of it through spending. One place the public spends is in the stock market, increasing the demand for stocks and consequently raising their prices.[13] Combining this with the fact that higher stock (equity) prices (P_e) will lead to a higher q and thus higher investment spending I leads to the following transmission mechanism of monetary policy:[14]

$$M\uparrow \Rightarrow P_e\uparrow \Rightarrow q\uparrow \Rightarrow I\uparrow \Rightarrow Y\uparrow \qquad (4)$$

(Note that P_e represents the price of equity, whereas P^e, in an earlier schematic, represents the expected price level.)

WEALTH EFFECTS In their search for new monetary transmission mechanisms, researchers also looked at how consumers' balance sheets might affect their spending decisions. Franco Modigliani was the first to take this tack, using his famous life cycle hypothesis of consumption. **Consumption** is spending by consumers on nondurable goods and services.[15] It differs from *consumer expenditure* in that it does not include spending on consumer durables. The basic premise of Modigliani's theory is that consumers smooth out their consumption over time. Therefore, what determines consumption spending is the lifetime resources of consumers, not just today's income.

An important component of consumers' lifetime resources is their financial wealth, a major component of which is common stocks. When stock prices rise, the value of financial wealth increases, thereby increasing the lifetime resources of consumers, and consumption should rise. Considering that, as we have seen, expansionary monetary policy can lead to a rise in stock prices, we now have another monetary transmission mechanism:

$$M\uparrow \Rightarrow P_e\uparrow \Rightarrow \text{wealth } \uparrow \Rightarrow \text{consumption } \uparrow \Rightarrow Y\uparrow \qquad (5)$$

Modigliani's research found this relationship to be an extremely powerful mechanism that adds substantially to the potency of monetary policy.[16]

The wealth and Tobin's q channels allow for a general definition of equity, so the Tobin q framework can also be applied to the housing market, where housing is equity. An increase in house prices, which raises their prices relative to replace-

---

[13]See James Tobin, "A General Equilibrium Approach to Monetary Theory," *Journal of Money, Credit, and Banking* 1 (1969): 15–29. A somewhat more Keynesian story with the same outcome is that the increase in the money supply lowers interest rates on bonds so that the yields on alternatives to stocks fall. This makes stocks more attractive relative to bonds, so demand for them increases, raises their price, and thereby lowers their yield.

[14]An alternative way of looking at the link between stock prices and investment spending is that higher stock prices lower the yield on stocks and reduce the cost of financing investment spending through issuing equity. This way of looking at the link between stock prices and investment spending is formally equivalent to Tobin's q approach; see Barry Bosworth, "The Stock Market and the Economy," *Brookings Papers on Economic Activity* 2 (1975): 257–290.

[15]Consumption also includes another small component, the services that a consumer receives from the ownership of housing and consumer durables.

[16]See Franco Modigliani, "Monetary Policy and Consumption," in *Consumer Spending and Money Policy: The Linkages* (Boston: Federal Reserve Bank, 1971), pp. 9–84.

ment cost, leads to a rise in Tobin's q for housing, thereby stimulating its production. Similarly, housing and land prices are extremely important components of wealth, and so rises in these prices increase wealth, thereby raising consumption. Monetary expansion, which raises land and housing prices through the Tobin's q and wealth mechanisms described here, thus leads to a rise in aggregate demand.

Credit View

Dissatisfaction with the conventional stories that interest-rate effects explain the impact of monetary policy on expenditures on durable assets has led to a new explanation based on the problem of asymmetric information in financial markets (see Chapter 9). This explanation, referred to as the *credit view*, proposes that two types of monetary transmission channels arise as a result of information problems in credit markets: those that operate through effects on bank lending and those that operate through effects on firms' and households' balance sheets.[17]

BANK LENDING CHANNEL The bank lending channel is based on the analysis in Chapter 9, which demonstrated that banks play a special role in the financial system because they are especially well suited to solve asymmetric information problems in credit markets. Because of banks' special role, certain borrowers will not have access to the credit markets unless they borrow from banks. As long as there is no perfect substitutability of retail bank deposits with other sources of funds, the bank lending channel of monetary transmission operates as follows. Expansionary monetary policy, which increases bank reserves and bank deposits, increases the quantity of bank loans available. Because many borrowers are dependent on bank loans to finance their activities, this increase in loans will cause investment (and possibly consumer) spending to rise. Schematically, the monetary policy effect is

$$M\uparrow \Rightarrow \text{bank deposits} \uparrow \Rightarrow \text{bank loans} \uparrow \Rightarrow I\uparrow \Rightarrow Y\uparrow \tag{6}$$

An important implication of the credit view is that monetary policy will have a greater effect on expenditure by smaller firms, which are more dependent on bank loans, than it will on large firms, which can access the credit markets directly through stock and bond markets (and not only through banks).

Though this result has been confirmed by researchers, doubts about the bank lending channel have been raised in the literature, and there are reasons to suspect that the bank lending channel in the United States may not be as powerful as it once was.[18] The first reason this channel is not as powerful is that the current U.S. regulatory framework no longer imposes restrictions on banks that

---

[17]Recent surveys of the credit view can be found in Ben Bernanke, "Credit in the Macroeconomy," *Federal Reserve Bank of New York Quarterly Review*, Spring 1993, pp. 50–70; Ben Bernanke and Mark Gertler, "Inside the Black Box: The Credit Channel of Monetary Policy Transmission," *Journal of Economic Perspectives* 9 (Fall 1995): 27–48; Stephen G. Cecchetti, "Distinguishing Theories of the Monetary Transmission Mechanism," Federal Reserve Bank of St. Louis *Review* 77 (May-June 1995): 83–97; and R. Glenn Hubbard, "Is There a 'Credit Channel' for Monetary Policy?" Federal Reserve Bank of St. Louis *Review* 77 (May-June 1995): 63–74.

[18]For example, see Valerie Ramey, "How Important Is the Credit Channel in the Transmission of Monetary Policy?" *Carnegie-Rochester Conference Series on Public Policy* 39 (1993): 1–45, and Allan H. Meltzer, "Monetary, Credit (and Other) Transmission Processes: A Monetarist Perspective," *Journal of Economic Perspectives* 9 (Fall 1995): 49–72.

hinder their ability to raise funds (see Chapter 10). Prior to the mid-1980s, certificates of deposit (CDs) were subjected to reserve requirements and Regulation Q deposit rate ceilings, which made it hard for banks to replace deposits that flowed out of the banking system during a monetary contraction. With these regulatory restrictions abolished, banks can more easily respond to a decline in bank reserves and a loss of retail deposits by issuing CDs at market interest rates that are not required to be backed up by required reserves. Second, the worldwide decline of the traditional bank lending business (see Chapter 11) has rendered the bank lending channel less potent. Nonetheless, many economists believe that the bank lending channel played an important role in the slow recovery in the U.S. from the 1990–91 recession, as the application on page 653 indicates.

BALANCE SHEET CHANNEL Even though the bank lending channel may be declining in importance, it is by no means clear that this is the case for the other credit channel, the balance sheet channel. Like the bank lending channel, the balance sheet channel also arises from the presence of asymmetric information problems in credit markets. In Chapter 9, we saw that the lower the net worth of business firms, the more severe the adverse selection and moral hazard problems in lending to these firms. Lower net worth means that lenders in effect have less collateral for their loans, and so potential losses from adverse selection are higher. A decline in net worth, which raises the adverse selection problem, thus leads to decreased lending to finance investment spending. The lower net worth of businesses also increases the moral hazard problem because it means that owners have a lower equity stake in their firms, giving them more incentive to engage in risky investment projects. Since taking on riskier investment projects makes it more likely that lenders will not be paid back, a decrease in businesses' net worth leads to a decrease in lending and hence in investment spending.

Monetary policy can affect firms' balance sheets in several ways. Expansionary monetary policy ($M\uparrow$), which causes a rise in equity prices ($P_e\uparrow$) along lines described earlier, raises the net worth of firms and so leads to higher investment spending ($I\uparrow$) and aggregate demand ($Y\uparrow$) because of the decrease in adverse selection and moral hazard problems. This leads to the following schematic for one balance sheet channel of monetary transmission:

$$M\uparrow \Rightarrow P_e\uparrow \Rightarrow \text{adverse selection} \downarrow, \text{moral hazard} \downarrow \Rightarrow \text{lending} \uparrow \Rightarrow I\uparrow \Rightarrow Y\uparrow \quad (7)$$

CASH FLOW CHANNEL Another balance sheet channel operates through its effects on *cash flow,* the difference between cash receipts and cash expenditures. Expansionary monetary policy, which lowers nominal interest rates, also causes an improvement in firms' balance sheets because it raises cash flow. The rise in cash flow causes an improvement in the balance sheet because it increases the liquidity of the firm (or household) and thus makes it easier for lenders to know whether the firm (or household) will be able to pay its bills. The result is that adverse selection and moral hazard problems become less severe, leading to an increase in lending and economic activity. The following schematic describes this additional balance sheet channel:

$$M\uparrow \Rightarrow i\downarrow \Rightarrow \text{cash flow} \uparrow \Rightarrow \text{adverse selection} \downarrow,$$
$$\text{moral hazard} \downarrow \Rightarrow \text{lending} \uparrow \Rightarrow I\uparrow \Rightarrow Y\uparrow \quad (8)$$

An important feature of this transmission mechanism is that it is *nominal* interest rates that affect firms' cash flow. Thus this interest-rate mechanism differs from the traditional interest-rate mechanism discussed earlier in which it is the real rather than the nominal interest rate that affects investment. Furthermore, the short-term interest rate plays a special role in this transmission mechanism because it is interest payments on short-term rather than long-term debt that typically have the greatest impact on households' and firms' cash flow.

A related mechanism involving adverse selection through which expansionary monetary policy that lowers interest rates can stimulate aggregate output involves the credit-rationing phenomenon. As we discussed in Chapter 9, credit rationing occurs in cases where borrowers are denied loans even when they are willing to pay a higher interest rate. This is because individuals and firms with the riskiest investment projects are exactly the ones who are willing to pay the highest interest rates, for if the high-risk investment succeeds, they will be the primary beneficiaries. Thus higher interest rates increase the adverse selection problem, and lower interest rates reduce it. When expansionary monetary policy lowers interest rates, less risk-prone borrowers make up a higher fraction of those demanding loans, and so lenders are more willing to lend, raising both investment and output, along the lines of parts of the schematic in Equation 8.

UNANTICIPATED PRICE LEVEL CHANNEL A third balance sheet channel operates through monetary policy effects on the general price level. Because debt payments are contractually fixed in nominal terms, an unanticipated rise in the price level lowers the value of firms' liabilities in real terms (decreases the burden of the debt) but should not lower the real value of the firms' assets. Monetary expansion that leads to an unanticipated rise in the price level ($P\uparrow$) therefore raises real net worth, which lowers adverse selection and moral hazard problems, thereby leading to a rise in investment spending and aggregate output as in the following schematic:

$$M\uparrow \Rightarrow \text{unanticipated } P\uparrow \Rightarrow \text{adverse selection } \downarrow,$$
$$\text{moral hazard } \downarrow \Rightarrow \text{lending } \uparrow \Rightarrow I\uparrow \Rightarrow Y\uparrow \tag{9}$$

The view that unanticipated movements in the price level have important effects on aggregate demand has a long tradition in economics: It is the key feature in the debt-deflation view of the Great Depression we outlined in Chapter 9.

HOUSEHOLD LIQUIDITY EFFECTS Although most of the literature on the credit channel focuses on spending by businesses, the credit view should apply equally as well to consumer spending, particularly on consumer durables and housing. Declines in bank lending induced by a monetary contraction should cause a decline in durables and housing purchases by consumers who do not have access to other sources of credit. Similarly, increases in interest rates cause a deterioration in household balance sheets because consumers' cash flow is adversely affected.

Another way of looking at how the balance sheet channel may operate through consumers is to consider liquidity effects on consumer durable and housing expenditures—found to have been important factors during the Great Depression (see Box 4). In the liquidity effects view, balance sheet effects work through their impact on consumers' desire to spend rather than on lenders' desire

BOX 4

Consumers' Balance Sheets and the Great Depression

The years between 1929 and 1933 witnessed the worst deterioration in consumers' balance sheets ever seen in the United States. The stock market crash in 1929, which caused a slump that lasted until 1933, reduced the value of consumers' wealth by $635 billion (in 1992 dollars), and as expected, consumption dropped sharply (by over $95 billion). Because of the decline in the price level in that period, the level of real debt consumers owed also increased sharply (by over 20 percent). Consequently, the value of financial assets relative to the amount of debt declined sharply, increasing the likelihood of financial distress. Not surprisingly, spending on consumer durables and housing fell precipitously: From 1929 to 1933, consumer durable expenditure declined by over 50 percent, while expenditure on housing declined by 80 percent.*

*For further discussion of the effect of consumers' balance sheets on spending during the Great Depression, see Frederic S. Mishkin, "The Household Balance Sheet and the Great Depression," *Journal of Economic History* 38 (1978): 918–937.

to lend. Because of asymmetric information about their quality, consumer durables and housing are very illiquid assets. If, as a result of a bad income shock, consumers needed to sell their consumer durables or housing to raise money, they would expect a big loss because they could not get the full value of these assets in a distress sale. (This is just a manifestation of the lemons problem described in Chapter 9.) In contrast, if consumers held financial assets (such as money in the bank, stocks, or bonds), they could easily sell them quickly for their full market value and raise the cash. Hence if consumers expect a higher likelihood of finding themselves in financial distress, they would rather be holding fewer illiquid consumer durable or housing assets and more liquid financial assets.

A consumer's balance sheet should be an important influence on his or her estimate of the likelihood of suffering financial distress. Specifically, when consumers have a large amount of financial assets relative to their debts, their estimate of the probability of financial distress is low, and they will be more willing to purchase consumer durables or housing. When stock prices rise, the value of financial assets rises as well; consumer durable expenditure will also rise because consumers have a more secure financial position and a lower estimate of the likelihood of suffering financial distress. This leads to another transmission mechanism for monetary policy, operating through the link between money and equity prices:[19]

$$M\uparrow \Rightarrow P_e\uparrow \Rightarrow \text{financial assets} \uparrow \Rightarrow \text{likelihood of financial distress} \downarrow$$
$$\Rightarrow \text{consumer durable and housing expenditure} \uparrow \Rightarrow Y\uparrow \qquad (10)$$

The illiquidity of consumer durable and housing assets provides another reason why a monetary expansion, which lowers interest rates and thereby raises cash flow to consumers, leads to a rise in spending on consumer durables and housing. A rise in consumer cash flow decreases the likelihood of financial dis-

---

[19]See Frederic S. Mishkin, "What Depressed the Consumer? The Household Balance Sheet and the 1973–1975 Recession," *Brookings Papers on Economic Activity* 1 (1977): 123–164.

tress, which increases the desire of consumers to hold durable goods or housing, thus increasing spending on them and hence aggregate output. The only difference between this view of cash flow effects and that outlined in Equation 8 is that it is not the willingness of lenders to lend to consumers that causes expenditure to rise but the willingness of consumers to spend.

Why Are Credit Channels Likely to Be Important?

There are three reasons to believe that credit channels are important monetary transmission mechanisms. First, a large body of evidence on the behavior of individual firms supports the view that credit market imperfections of the type crucial to the operation of credit channels do affect firms' employment and spending decisions.[20] Second, there is evidence that small firms (which are more likely to be credit-constrained) are hurt more by tight monetary policy than large firms, which are unlikely to be credit-constrained.[21] Third, and maybe most compelling, the asymmetric information view of credit market imperfections at the core of the credit channel analysis is a theoretical construct that has proved useful in explaining many other important phenomena, such as why many of our financial institutions exist, why our financial system has the structure that it has, and why financial crises are so damaging to the economy (all topics discussed in Chapter 9). The best support for a theory is when it is found to be useful in a wide range of applications. By this standard, the asymmetric information theory supporting the existence of credit channels as an important monetary transmission mechanism has much to recommend it.

Credit Crunch and Slow Recovery from the 1990–1991 Recession

The Iraqi invasion of Kuwait in the summer of 1990 caused a collapse in consumer confidence and threatened to drive oil prices permanently higher. The resulting decline in consumer expenditure caused the aggregate demand curve to shift to the left, and, consistent with our aggregate demand and supply analysis, unemployment rose and inflation fell (see Table 1). What is surprising about the resulting recession in 1990–1991 is not that it occurred but that recovery from it was so sluggish.

After a typical recession, aggregate output grows quite rapidly, with growth rates ordinarily exceeding 4 percent. A rapid recovery might have been expected to be even more likely after the Western victory in the 1991 Gulf War, which quickly returned oil prices to their previous level. However, recovery from the 1990–1991 recession did not follow the typical pattern. From the middle of 1991, when the recession was officially declared over, until the end of 1992, real gross domestic product grew at an anemic rate, less than 2 percent. This caused the unemployment rate to keep rising in 1992, as Table 1 indicates. Only in 1993 did

---

[20]For a survey of this evidence, see Hubbard, "Is There a 'Credit Channel'?" (note 17).

[21]See Mark Gertler and Simon Gilchrist, "Monetary Policy, Business Cycles, and the Behavior of Small Manufacturing Firms," *Quarterly Journal of Economics,* 109 (May 1994): 309–340.

TABLE 1	Unemployment and Inflation During the 1990–1992 Credit Crunch	
Year	Unemployment Rate (%)	Inflation (Year to Year) (%)
1990	5.4	5.4
1991	6.6	4.2
1992	7.3	3.0

Source: Economic Report of the President.

the economy begin to pick up steam. Why was recovery from the recession so sluggish?

The explanation seems to be related to the bank lending view, which suggests that a reduction in bank lending could cause a decline in business and consumer spending that would reduce aggregate demand. The period from 1990 to 1992 saw an unprecedented slowdown in the growth of bank lending. According to our discussion of the bank lending channel, the reduction might have come about because of tight monetary policy, but in this particular episode, the credit slowdown stemmed from other sources. As we discussed in Chapter 10, banks found themselves with capital shortfalls for two reasons: Huge losses on their loans, particularly in real estate, eroded their capital, and increases in capital requirements in the aftermath of the banking crisis described in Chapter 12 required them to obtain more capital. The resulting capital shortfalls restrained asset growth for banks and hence restricted bank lending. In addition, the deterioration in companies' balance sheets as a result of the huge run-up of debt in the 1980s exacerbated adverse selection and moral hazard problems for lenders such as banks, which made them less likely to make loans. The resulting credit crunch is viewed by most analysts as an important factor in causing the 1990–1991 recession and accounts for the anemic recovery.

LESSONS FOR MONETARY POLICY

What useful implications for central banks' conduct of monetary policy can we draw from the analysis in this chapter? There are four basic lessons to be drawn.

1. It is dangerous always to associate the easing or tightening of monetary policy with a fall or a rise in short-term nominal interest rates.

Because most central banks use short-term nominal interest rates, typically the interbank rate, as the key operating instrument for monetary policy, there is a danger that central banks and the public will focus too much on short-term nominal interest rates as an indicator of the stance of monetary policy. Indeed, it is quite common to see statements that always associate monetary tightenings with a rise in the interbank rate and monetary easings with a decline in the rate. This view is highly problematic because, as we have seen in our discussion of the Great Depression period, movements in nominal interest rates do not always correspond to movements in real interest rates, and yet, it is typically the real and not the nominal interest rate that is an element in the channel of monetary policy transmission. For example, we have seen that during the contraction phase of the Great Depression in the United States, short-term interest rates fell to near zero and yet real interest rates were extremely high. Short-term interest rates that are near zero therefore do not indicate that monetary policy is easy if the economy is undergoing deflation, as was true during the contraction phase of the Great Depression. Indeed, as Milton Friedman and Anna Schwartz have emphasized, the period of near-zero short-term interest rates during the contraction phase of the Great Depression was one of highly contractionary monetary policy rather than the reverse.

*2. **Other asset prices besides those on short-term debt instruments contain important information about the stance of monetary policy because they are important elements in various monetary policy transmission mechanisms.*** As we have seen in this chapter, economists have come a long way in understanding that other asset prices besides interest rates have major effects on aggregate demand. The view in Figure 3 that other asset prices, such as stock prices, foreign exchange rates, and housing and land prices, play an important role in monetary transmission mechanisms is held by both monetarists and Keynesians. An important feature of the credit channels is their emphasis on the ways in which monetary policy affects the economy through other asset prices besides interest rates. Furthermore, the discussion of such additional channels as those operating through the exchange rate, Tobin's q, and wealth effects provides additional reasons why other asset prices play such an important role in the monetary transmission mechanisms. Although there are strong disagreements among economists about which channels of monetary transmission are the most important—not surprising, given that economists, particularly those in academia, always like to disagree—they do agree that other asset prices play an important role in the way monetary policy affects the economy.

The view that other asset prices besides short-term interest rates matter has important implications for monetary policy. When we try to assess the stance of policy, it is critical that we look at other asset prices besides short-term interest rates. For example, if short-term interest rates are low or even zero and yet stock prices are low, land prices are low, and the value of the domestic currency is high, monetary policy is clearly tight, *not* easy.

*3. **Monetary policy can be highly effective in reviving a weak economy even if short-term interest rates are already near zero.*** We have recently entered a world where inflation is not always the norm. Japan, for example, recently experienced a period of deflation, when the price level was actually falling. One common view is that when a central bank has driven down short-term nominal interest rates to near zero, there is nothing more that monetary policy can do to stimulate the economy. The transmission mechanisms of monetary policy described here indicate that this view is false. As our discussion of the factors that affect the monetary base in Chapter 16 indicated, expansionary monetary policy to increase liquidity in the economy can be conducted with open market purchases, which do not have to be solely in short-term government securities. For example, purchase of foreign currencies, like purchases of government bonds, lead to an increase in the monetary base and in the money supply. This increased liquidity helps revive the economy by raising general price-level expectations and by reflating other asset prices, which then stimulate aggregate demand through the channels outlined here. Therefore, monetary policy can be a potent force for reviving economies that are undergoing deflation and have short-term interest rates near zero. Indeed, because of the lags inherent in fiscal policy and the political constraints on its use, expansionary monetary policy is the key policy action that is required to revive an economy experiencing deflation.

    4. *Avoiding unanticipated fluctuations in the price level is an important objective of monetary policy, thus providing a rationale for price stability as the primary long-run goal for monetary policy.* As we saw in Chapter 19, central banks in recent years have been putting greater emphasis on price stability as the primary long-run goal for monetary policy. Several rationales have been proposed for this goal, including the undesirable effects of uncertainty about the future price level on business decisions and hence on productivity, distortions associated with the interaction of nominal contracts and the tax system with inflation, and increased social conflict stemming from inflation. The discussion here of monetary transmission mechanisms provides an additional reason why price stability is so important. As we have seen, unanticipated movements in the price level can cause unanticipated fluctuations in output, an undesirable outcome. Particularly important in this regard is that, as we saw in Chapter 9, price deflations can be an important factor leading to a prolonged financial crisis, as occurred during the Great Depression. An understanding of the monetary transmission mechanisms thus makes it clear that the goal of price stability is desirable because it reduces uncertainty about the future price level. Thus the price stability goal implies that a negative inflation rate is at least as undesirable as too high an inflation rate. Indeed, because of the threat of financial crises, central banks must work very hard to prevent price deflations.

SUMMARY

1. There are two basic types of empirical evidence: reduced-form evidence and structural model evidence. Both have advantages and disadvantages. The main advantage of structural model evidence is that it provides us with an understanding of how the economy works and gives us more confidence in the direction of causation between money and output. However, if the structure is not correctly specified because it ignores important monetary transmission mechanisms, it could seriously underestimate the effectiveness of monetary policy. Reduced-form evidence has the advantage of not restricting the way monetary policy affects economic activity and so may be more likely to capture the full effects of monetary policy. However, reduced-form evidence cannot rule out the possibility of reverse causation or an outside driving factor, which could lead to misleading conclusions about the importance of money.

2. The early Keynesians believed that money does not matter because they found weak links between interest rates and investment and because low interest rates on Treasury securities convinced them that monetary policy was easy during the worst economic contraction in U.S. history, the Great Depression. Monetarists objected to this interpretation of the evidence on the grounds that (a) the focus on nominal rather than real interest rates may have obscured any link between interest rates and investment, (b) interest-rate effects on investment might be only one of many channels through which monetary policy affects aggregate demand, and (c) by the standards of real interest rates and interest rates on lower-grade bonds, monetary policy was extremely contractionary during the Great Depression.

3. Early monetarist evidence falls into three categories: timing, statistical, and historical. Because of reverse

causation and outside-factor possibilities, some serious doubts exist regarding conclusions that can be drawn from timing and statistical evidence alone. However, some of the historical evidence in which exogenous declines in money growth are followed by recessions provides stronger support for the monetarist position that money matters. As a result of empirical research, Keynesian and monetarist opinion has converged to the view that money does matter to aggregate economic activity and the price level. However, Keynesians do not agree with the monetarist position that money is *all* that matters.

4. The transmission mechanisms of monetary policy include traditional interest-rate channels which operate through the cost of capital and affect investment; other asset price channels such as exchange rate effects, Tobin's q theory, and wealth effects; and the credit view channels—the bank lending channel, the balance sheet channel, the cash flow channel, and household liquidity effects.

5. Four lessons for monetary policy can be drawn from this chapter: (a) It is dangerous always to associate monetary policy easing or tightening with a fall or a rise in short-term nominal interest rates; (b) other asset prices besides those on short-term debt instruments contain important information about the stance of monetary policy because they are important elements in the monetary policy transmission mechanisms; (c) monetary policy can be highly effective in reviving a weak economy even if short-term interest rates are already near zero; and (d) avoiding unanticipated fluctuations in the price level is an important objective of monetary policy, thus providing a rationale for price stability as the primary long-run goal for monetary policy.

KEY TERMS

consumer durable expenditure, p. 644

consumption, p. 648

credit view, p. 645

reduced-form evidence, p. 630

reverse causation, p. 633

structural model, p. 630

structural model evidence, p. 630

transmission mechanisms of monetary policy, p. 630

QUESTIONS AND PROBLEMS

1. Suppose that a researcher is trying to determine whether jogging is good for a person's health. She examines this question in two ways. In method A, she looks to see whether joggers live longer than nonjoggers. In method B, she looks to see whether jogging reduces cholesterol in the bloodstream and lowers blood pressure; then she asks whether lower cholesterol and blood pressure prolong life. Which of these two methods will produce reduced-form evidence and which will produce structural model evidence?

2. If research indicates that joggers do not have lower cholesterol and blood pressure than nonjoggers, is it still possible that jogging is good for your health? Give a concrete example.

3. If research indicates that joggers live longer than nonjoggers, is it possible that jogging is not good for your health? Give a concrete example.

*4. Suppose that you plan to buy a car and want to know whether a General Motors car is more reliable than a Ford. One way to find out is to ask owners of both cars how often their cars go into the shop for repairs. Another way is to visit the factory producing the cars and see which one is built better. Which procedure will provide reduced-form evidence and which structural model evidence?

*5. If the GM car you plan to buy has a better repair record than a Ford, does this mean that the GM car is necessarily more reliable? (GM car owners might, for example, change their oil more frequently than Ford owners.)

*6. Suppose that when you visit the Ford and GM car factories to examine how the cars are built, you only have time to see how well the engine is put together. If Ford engines are better built than GM engines, does that mean that the Ford will be more reliable than the GM car?

7. How might bank behavior (described in Chapter 17) lead to causation running from output to the money supply? What does this say about evidence that finds a strong correlation between money and output?

*8. What operating procedures of the Fed (described in Chapter 19) might explain how movements in output might cause movements in the money supply?

9. "In every business cycle in the past 100 years, the rate at which the money supply is growing always decreases before output does. Therefore, the money supply causes business cycle movements." Do you agree? What objections can you raise against this argument?

*10. How did the research strategies of Keynesian and monetarist economists differ after they were exposed to the earliest monetarist evidence?

11. In the 1973–1975 recession, the value of common stocks in real terms fell by nearly 50 percent. How might this decline in the stock market have affected aggregate demand and thus contributed to the severity of this recession? Be specific about the mechanisms through which the stock market decline affected the economy.

*12. "The cost of financing investment is related only to interest rates; therefore, the only way that monetary policy can affect investment spending is through its effects on interest rates." Is this statement true, false, or uncertain? Explain your answer.

13. Predict what will happen to stock prices if the money supply rises. Explain why you are making this prediction.

*14. Franco Modigliani found that the most important transmission mechanisms of monetary policy involve consumer expenditure. Describe how at least two of these mechanisms work.

15. "The monetarists have demonstrated that the early Keynesians were wrong in saying that money doesn't matter at all to economic activity. Therefore, we should accept the monetarist position that money is all that matters." Do you agree? Why or why not?

Chapter 26

MONEY AND INFLATION

PREVIEW Since the early 1960s, when the inflation rate hovered between 1 and 2 percent, the economy has suffered from higher and more variable rates of inflation. By the late 1960s, the inflation rate had climbed beyond 5 percent, and by 1974, it reached the double-digit level. After moderating somewhat during the 1975–1978 period, it shot above 10 percent in 1979 and 1980, slowed to around 5 percent from 1982 to 1990, and declined further to around 3 percent in the 1992–1996 period. Inflation, the condition of a continually rising price level, has become a major concern of politicians and the public, and how to control it frequently dominates the discussion of economic policy.

How do we prevent the inflationary fire from igniting and end the roller-coaster ride in the inflation rate of the past 30 years? Milton Friedman provides an answer in his famous proposition that "inflation is always and everywhere a monetary phenomenon." He postulates that the source of all inflation episodes is a high growth rate of the money supply: Simply by reducing the growth rate of the money supply to low levels, inflation can be prevented.

In this chapter we use aggregate demand and supply analysis from Chapter 24 to reveal the role of monetary policy in creating inflation. You will find that as long as inflation is defined as the condition of a continually and rapidly rising price level, monetarists and Keynesians both agree with Friedman's proposition that inflation is a monetary phenomenon.

But what *causes* inflation? How does inflationary monetary policy come about? You will see that inflationary monetary policy is an offshoot of other government policies: the attempt to hit high employment targets or the running of large budget deficits. Examining how these policies lead to inflation will point us toward ways of preventing it at minimum cost in terms of unemployment and output loss.

MONEY AND INFLATION: EVIDENCE

The evidence for Friedman's statement is straightforward. ***Whenever a country's inflation rate is extremely high for a sustained period of time, its rate of money supply growth is also extremely high.***

Consider the inflation experienced in Latin America from 1986 to 1996. A popular belief is that something structural in the Latin American economies (say, militant labor unions or unstable political systems) causes high inflation. In reality, the experience of inflation in Latin America is varied; some Latin American countries, such as Honduras, had average annual inflation rates below 10 percent during this period, while others, such as Argentina, Brazil, and Nicaragua, suffered from inflation rates exceeding 100 percent.

The graph in Box 1, which plots the inflation rates for Latin American countries against the growth rates of their money supply, reveals that the countries with very high inflation also have the highest rates of money growth. Evidence for the Latin American countries, as well as countries elsewhere in the world (see Figure 6 in Chapter 1), seems to support the proposition that extremely high inflation is the result of a high rate of money growth. Keep in mind, however, that you are looking at reduced-form evidence, which focuses solely on the correlation of two variables: money growth and the inflation rate. As with all reduced-form evidence, reverse causation (inflation causing money supply growth) or an outside factor that drives both money growth and inflation could be involved.

How might you rule out these possibilities? First, you might look for historical episodes in which an increase in money growth appears to be an exogenous event; a high inflation rate for a sustained period following the increase in money growth would provide strong evidence that high money growth is the driving force behind the inflation. Luckily for our analysis, such clear-cut episodes—hyperinflations (extremely rapid inflations with inflation rates exceeding 50 percent per month)—have occurred, the most notorious being the German hyperinflation of 1921–1923.

German Hyperinflation, 1921–1923

In 1921, the need to make reparations and reconstruct the economy after World War I caused the German government's expenditures greatly to exceed revenues. The government could have obtained revenues to cover these increased expenditures by raising taxes, but that solution was, as always, politically unpopular and would have taken much time to implement. The government could also have financed the expenditure by borrowing from the public, but the amount needed was far in excess of its capacity to borrow. There was only one route left: the printing press. The government could pay for its expenditures simply by printing more currency (increasing the money supply) and using it to make payments to the individuals and companies that were providing it with goods and services. As shown in Figure 1, this is exactly what the German government did; in late 1921, the money supply began to increase rapidly, and so did the price level.

In 1923, the budgetary situation of the German government deteriorated even further. Early that year, the French invaded the Ruhr because Germany had failed to make its scheduled reparations payments. A general strike in the region then ensued to protest the French action, and the German government actively supported this "passive resistance" by making payments to striking workers. As a result, government expenditures climbed dramatically, and the government printed currency at an even faster rate to finance this spending. As displayed in

Inflation and Money Growth Rates in Latin America, 1986–1996

This graph plots for a group of Latin American countries the average inflation rate over the period 1986–1996 against the average money growth rate over the same period. It demonstrates that high inflation in these countries is generally associated with a high rate of money growth. (Countries such as Brazil and Nicaragua do not appear in the graph because their data were unavailable for the 1986–1996 period.)

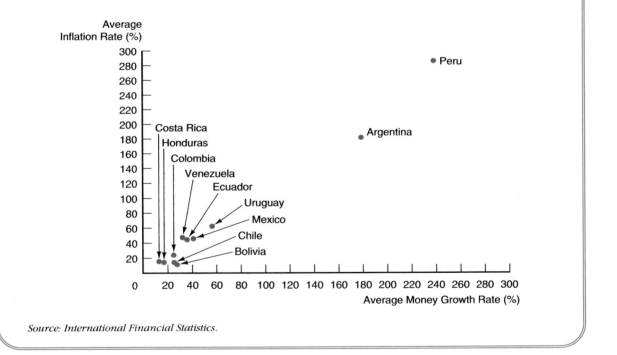

Source: International Financial Statistics.

Figure 1, the result of the explosion in the money supply was that the price level blasted off, leading to an inflation rate for 1923 that exceeded 1 million percent!

The invasion of the Ruhr and the printing of currency to pay striking workers fit the characteristics of an exogenous event. Reverse causation (that the rise in the price level caused the French to invade the Ruhr) is highly implausible, and it is hard to imagine a third factor that could have been a driving force behind both inflation and the explosion in the money supply. Therefore, the German hyperinflation qualifies as a "controlled experiment" that supports Friedman's proposition that inflation is a monetary phenomenon.

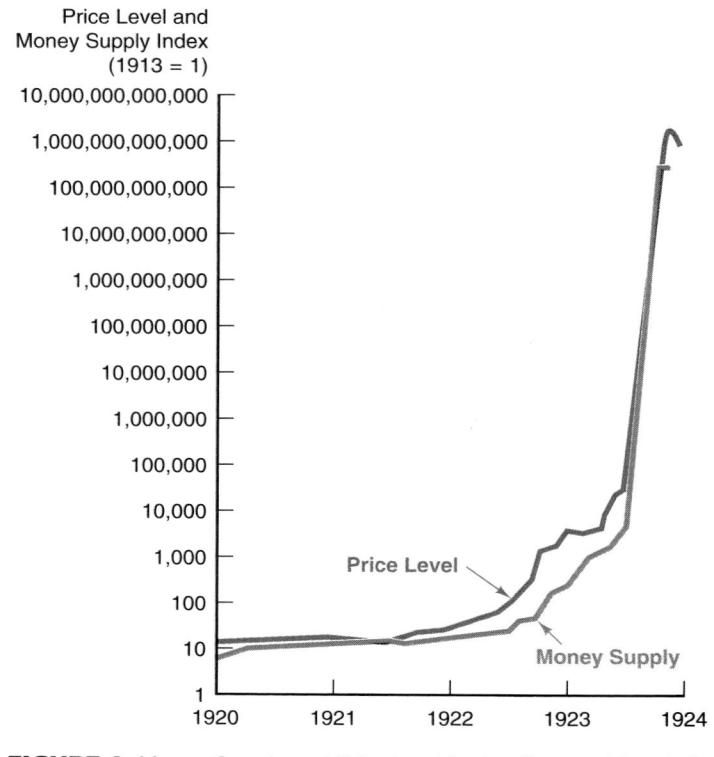

FIGURE 1 Money Supply and Price Level in the German Hyperinflation

Source: Frank D. Graham, *Exchange, Prices and Production in Hyperinflation: Germany, 1920–25* (Princeton, N.J.: Princeton University Press, 1930), pp. 105–106.

Recent Episodes of Rapid Inflation

Although recent rapid inflations have not been as dramatic as the German hyperinflation, many countries in the 1980s and 1990s experienced rapid inflations in which the high rates of money growth can also be classified as exogenous events. For example, of all Latin American countries in the decade from 1986 to 1996, Argentina, Brazil, and Nicaragua had both the highest rates of money growth and the highest average inflation rates. However, in the last couple of years, inflation in these countries has been brought down considerably.

The explanation for the high rates of money growth in these countries is similar to the explanation for Germany during its hyperinflation: The unwillingness of Argentina, Brazil, and Nicaragua to finance government expenditures by raising taxes led to large budget deficits (sometimes over 15 percent of GDP), which were financed by money creation.

That the inflation rate is high in all cases in which the high rate of money growth can be classified as an exogenous event (including episodes in Argentina, Brazil, Nicaragua, and Germany) is strong evidence that high money growth causes high inflation.

MEANING OF *INFLATION*

You may have noticed that all the empirical evidence on the relationship of money growth and inflation discussed so far looks only at cases in which the price level is continually rising at a rapid rate. It is this definition of inflation that Friedman and other economists use when they make statements such as "inflation is always and everywhere a monetary phenomenon." This is not what your friendly newscaster means when reporting the monthly inflation rate on the nightly news. The newscaster is only telling you how much, in percentage terms, the price level has changed from the previous month. For example, when you hear that the monthly inflation rate is 1 percent (12 percent annual rate), this merely indicates that the price level has risen by 1 percent in that month. This could be a one-shot change, in which the high inflation rate is merely temporary, not sustained. Only if the inflation rate remains high for a substantial period of time (greater than 1 percent per month for several years) will economists say that inflation has been high.

Accordingly, Milton Friedman's proposition actually says that upward movements in the price level are a monetary phenomenon *only* if this is a sustained process. When *inflation* is defined as a continuing and rapid rise in the price level, most economists, whether monetarist or Keynesian, will agree with Friedman's proposition that money alone is to blame.

VIEWS OF INFLATION

Now that we understand what Friedman's proposition means, we can use the aggregate supply and demand analysis learned in Chapter 24 to show that large and persistent upward movements in the price level (high inflation) can occur only if there is a continually increasing money supply.

Monetarist View

First, let's look at the outcome of a continually increasing money supply using monetarist analysis (see Figure 2). Initially, the economy is at point 1, with output at the natural rate level and the price level at P_1 (the intersection of the aggregate demand curve AD_1 and the aggregate supply curve AS_1). If the money supply increases steadily over the course of the year, the aggregate demand curve shifts rightward to AD_2. At first, for a very brief time, the economy may move to point $1'$ and output may increase above the natural rate level to Y', but the resulting decline in unemployment below the natural rate level will cause wages to rise, and the aggregate supply curve will quickly begin to shift leftward. It will stop shifting only when it reaches AS_2, at which time the economy has returned to the natural rate level of output on the long-run aggregate supply curve.[1] At the new equilibrium, point 2, the price level has increased from P_1 to P_2.

---

[1]In monetarist analysis, the aggregate supply curve may immediately shift in toward AS_2 because workers and firms may expect the increase in the money supply, so expected inflation will be higher. In this case, the movement to point 2 will be very rapid, and output need not rise above the natural rate level. (Further support for this scenario, from the theory of rational expectations, is discussed in Chapter 27.)

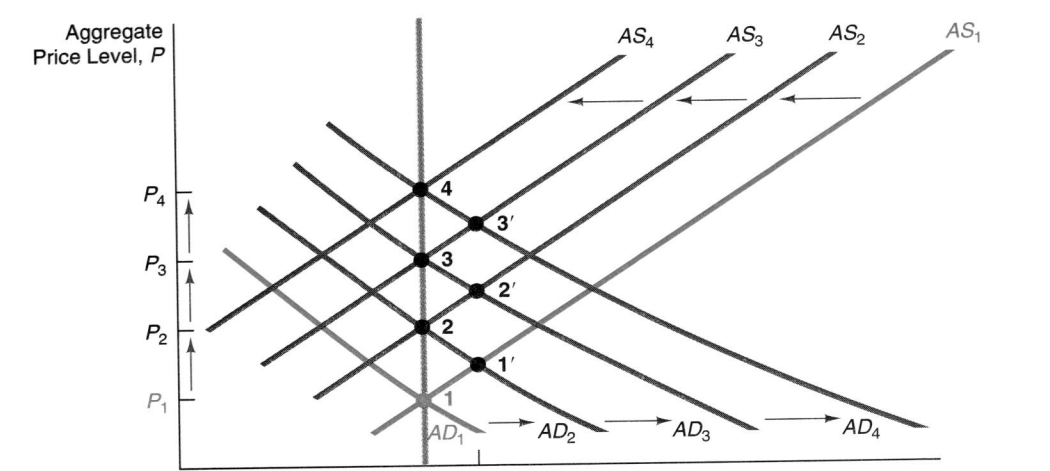

FIGURE 2 Response to a Continually Rising Money Supply
A continually rising money supply shifts the aggregate demand curve to the right from AD_1 to AD_2 to AD_3 to AD_4, while the supply curve shifts to the left from AS_1 to AS_2 to AS_3 to AS_4. The result is that the price level rises continually from P_1 to P_2 to P_3 to P_4.

If the money supply increases the next year, the aggregate demand curve will shift to the right again to AD_3, and the aggregate supply curve will shift from AS_2 to AS_3; the economy will then move to point 2′ and then 3, where the price level has risen to P_3. If the money supply continues to grow in subsequent years, the economy will continue to move to higher and higher price levels. As long as the money supply grows, this process will continue, and inflation will occur.

Do monetarists believe that a continually rising price level can be due to any source other than money supply growth? The answer is no. In monetarist analysis, the money supply is viewed as the sole source of shifts in the aggregate demand curve, so there is nothing else that can move the economy from point 1 to 2 to 3 and beyond. ***Monetarist analysis indicates that rapid inflation must be driven by high money supply growth.***

Keynesian View

Keynesian analysis indicates that the continually increasing money supply will have the same effect on the aggregate demand and supply curves that we see in Figure 2: The aggregate demand curve will keep on shifting to the right, and the aggregate supply curve will keep shifting to the left.[2] The conclusion is the same

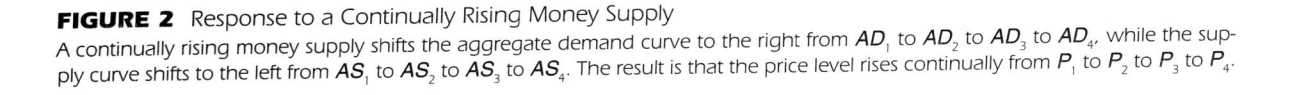

[2]The only difference in the two analyses is that Keynesians believe that the aggregate supply curve would shift leftward more slowly than monetarists do. Thus Keynesian analysis suggests that output might tend to stay above the natural rate longer than monetarist analysis does.

one that the monetarists reach: A rapidly growing money supply will cause the price level to rise continually at a high rate, thus generating inflation.

Could a factor other than money generate high inflation in the Keynesian analysis? The answer is no. This result probably surprises you, for in Chapter 24 you learned that Keynesian analysis allows other factors besides changes in the money supply (such as fiscal policy and supply shocks) to affect the aggregate demand and supply curves. To see why Keynesians also view high inflation as a monetary phenomenon, let's examine whether their analysis allows other factors to generate high inflation in the absence of a high rate of money growth.

CAN FISCAL POLICY BY ITSELF PRODUCE INFLATION? To examine this question, let's look at Figure 3, which demonstrates the effect of a one-shot permanent increase in government expenditure (say, from $500 billion to $600 billion) on aggregate output and the price level. Initially, we are at point 1, where output is at the natural rate level and the price level is P_1. The increase in government expenditure shifts the aggregate demand curve to AD_2, and we move to point 1′, where output is above the natural rate level at $Y_{1′}$. The aggregate supply curve will begin to shift leftward, eventually reaching AS_2, where it intersects the aggregate demand curve AD_2 at point 2, at which output is again at the natural rate level and the price level has risen to P_2.

The net result of a one-shot permanent increase in government expenditure is a one-shot permanent increase in the price level. What happens to the inflation

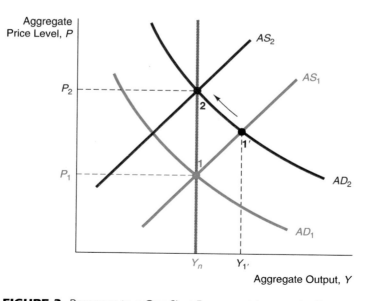

FIGURE 3 Response to a One-Shot Permanent Increase in Government Expenditure
A one-shot permanent increase in government expenditure shifts the aggregate demand curve rightward from AD_1 to AD_2, moving the economy from point 1 to point 1′. Because output now exceeds the natural rate level Y_n, the aggregate supply curve eventually shifts leftward to AS_2, and the price level rises from P_1 to P_2, a one-shot permanent increase but not a continuing increase.

rate? When we move from point 1 to 1′ to 2, the price level rises, and we have a positive inflation rate. But when we finally get to point 2, the inflation rate returns to zero. We see that the one-shot increase in government expenditure leads to only a *temporary* increase in the inflation rate, not to an inflation in which the price level is continually rising.

If, however, government spending increased continually, we *could* get a continuing rise in the price level. It appears, then, that Keynesian analysis could reject Friedman's proposition that inflation is always the result of money growth. The problem with this argument is that a continually increasing level of government expenditure is not a feasible policy. There is a limit on the total amount of possible government expenditure; the government cannot spend more than 100 percent of GDP. In fact, well before this limit is reached, the political process would stop the increases in government spending. As revealed in the continual debates in Congress over balanced budgets and government spending, both the public and politicians have a particular target level of government spending they deem appropriate; although small deviations from this level might be tolerated, large deviations would not. Indeed, public and political perceptions impose tight limits on the degree to which government expenditures can increase.

What about the other side of fiscal policy, taxes? Could continual tax cuts generate an inflation? Again the answer is no. The analysis in Figure 3 also describes the price and output response to a one-shot decrease in taxes. There will be a one-shot increase in the price level, but the increase in the inflation rate will be only temporary. We can increase the price level by cutting taxes even more, but this process would have to stop—once taxes reach zero, they can't be reduced further. We must conclude, then, that **Keynesian analysis indicates that high inflation cannot be driven by fiscal policy alone.**[3]

CAN SUPPLY-SIDE PHENOMENA BY THEMSELVES PRODUCE INFLATION? Because supply shocks and workers' attempts to increase their wages can shift the aggregate supply curve leftward, you might suspect that these supply-side phenomena by themselves could stimulate inflation. Again, we can show that this suspicion is incorrect.

Suppose that there is a negative supply shock—for example, an oil embargo—that raises oil prices (or workers could have successfully pushed up their wages). As displayed in Figure 4, the negative supply shock shifts the aggregate supply curve from AS_1 to AS_2. If the money supply remains unchanged, leaving the aggregate demand curve at AD_1, we move to point 1′, where output $Y_{1'}$ is below the natural rate level and the price level $P_{1'}$ is higher. The aggregate supply curve will now shift back to AS_1 because unemployment is above the natural rate, and the economy slides down AD_1 from point 1′ to point 1. The net result of the supply shock is that we return to full employment at the initial price level,

---

[3]The argument here demonstrates that "animal spirits" also cannot be the source of inflation. Although consumer and business optimism, which stimulates their spending, can produce a one-shot shift in the aggregate demand curve and a temporary inflation, it cannot produce continuing shifts in the aggregate demand curve and inflation in which the price level rises continually. The reasoning is the same as before: Consumers and businesses cannot continue to raise their spending without limit because their spending cannot exceed 100 percent of GDP.

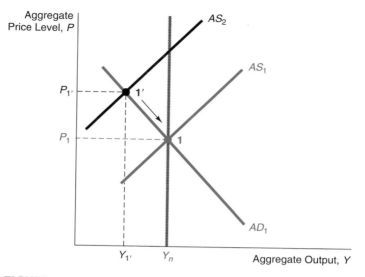

FIGURE 4   Response to a Supply Shock

A negative supply shock (or a wage push) shifts the aggregate supply curve leftward to **AS**$_2$ and results in high unemployment at point 1′. As a result, the aggregate supply curve shifts back to the right to **AS**$_1$, and the economy returns to point 1, where the price level has returned to **P**$_1$.

and there is no continuing inflation. Additional negative supply shocks that again shift the aggregate supply curve leftward will lead to the same outcome: The price level will rise temporarily, but inflation will not result. The conclusion that we have reached is the following: ***Supply-side phenomena cannot be the source of high inflation.***[4]

Summary

Our aggregate demand and supply analysis shows that Keynesian and monetarist views of the inflation process are not very different. Both believe that high inflation can occur only with a high rate of money growth. Recognizing that by inflation we mean a continuing increase in the price level at a rapid rate, most economists agree with Milton Friedman that "inflation is always and everywhere a monetary phenomenon."

ORIGINS OF INFLATIONARY MONETARY POLICY

Although we now know *what* must occur to generate a rapid inflation—a high rate of money growth—we still can't understand *why* high inflation occurs until we have learned how and why inflationary monetary policies come about. If everyone agrees that inflation is not a good thing for an economy, why do we see so much of it? Why do governments pursue inflationary monetary policies? Since there is nothing intrinsically desirable about inflation and since we know that a

---

[4]Supply-side phenomena that alter the natural rate level of output (and shift the long-run aggregate supply curve at Y_n) can produce a permanent one-shot change in the price level. However, this resulting one-shot change results in only a temporary inflation, not a continuing rise in the price level.

high rate of money growth doesn't happen of its own accord, it must follow that in trying to achieve other goals, governments end up with a high money growth rate and high inflation. In this section we will examine the government policies that are the most common sources of inflation.

High Employment Targets and Inflation

The first goal most governments pursue that often results in inflation is high employment. The U.S. government is committed by law (the Employment Act of 1946 and the Humphrey-Hawkins Act of 1978) to promoting high employment. Though it is true that both laws require a commitment to a high level of employment consistent with a stable price level, in practice our government has often pursued a high employment target with little concern about the inflationary consequences of its policies. This was true especially in the mid-1960s and 1970s when the government began to take a more active role in attempting to stabilize unemployment.

Two types of inflation can result from an activist stabilization policy to promote high employment: **cost-push inflation,** which occurs because of negative supply shocks or a push by workers to get higher wages, and **demand-pull inflation,** which results when policymakers pursue policies that shift the aggregate demand curve to the right. We will now use aggregate demand and supply analysis to examine how a high employment target can lead to both types of inflation.

COST-PUSH INFLATION In Figure 5, the economy is initially at point 1, the intersection of the aggregate demand curve AD_1 and the aggregate supply curve AS_1. Suppose that workers decide to seek higher wages either because they want to increase their real wages (wages in terms of the goods and services they can buy) or because they expect inflation to be high and wish to keep up with inflation. The effect of such an increase (similar to a negative supply shock) is to shift the aggregate supply curve leftward to AS_2.[5] If government fiscal and monetary policy remains unchanged, the economy would move to point $1'$ at the intersection of the new aggregate supply curve AS_2 and the aggregate demand curve AD_1. Output would decline to below its natural rate level Y_n, and the price level would rise to $P_{1'}$.

What would activist policymakers with a high employment target do if this situation developed? Because of the drop in output and resulting increase in unemployment, they would implement policies to raise the aggregate demand curve to AD_2 so that we would return to the natural rate level of output at point 2 and price level P_2. The workers who have increased their wages have not fared too badly. The government has stepped in to make sure that there is no excessive unemployment, and they have achieved their goal of higher wages. Because the government has, in effect, given in to the demands of workers for higher wages, an activist policy with a high employment target is often referred to as an **accommodating policy.**

The workers, having eaten their cake and had it too, might be encouraged to seek even higher wages. In addition, other workers might now realize that their

---

[5]The cost-push inflation we describe here might also occur as a result of either firms' attempts to obtain higher prices or negative supply shocks.

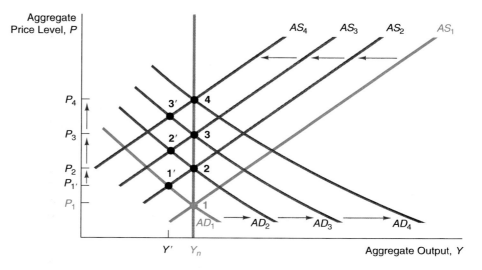

FIGURE 5 Cost-Push Inflation with an Activist Policy to Promote High Employment
In a cost-push inflation, the leftward shifts of the aggregate supply curve from **AS**$_1$ to **AS**$_2$ to **AS**$_3$ and so on cause a government with a high employment target to shift the aggregate demand curve to the right continually to keep unemployment and output at their natural rate levels. The result is a continuing rise in the price level from **P**$_1$ to **P**$_2$ to **P**$_3$ and so on.

wages have fallen relative to their fellow workers', and because they don't want to be left behind, these workers will seek to increase their wages. The result is that the aggregate supply curve shifts leftward again to AS_3. Unemployment develops again when we move to point 2', and the activist policies will once more be used to shift the aggregate demand curve rightward to AD_3 and return the economy to full employment at a price level of P_3. If this process continues, the result will be a continuing increase in the price level—a cost-push inflation.

What role does monetary policy play in a cost-push inflation? A cost-push inflation can occur only if the aggregate demand curve is shifted continually to the right. In Keynesian analysis, the first shift of the aggregate demand curve to AD_2 could be achieved by a one-shot increase in government expenditure or a one-shot decrease in taxes. But what about the next required rightward shift of the aggregate demand curve to AD_3, and the next, and the next? The limits on the maximum level of government expenditure and the minimum level of taxes would prevent the use of this expansionary fiscal policy for very long. Hence it cannot be used continually to shift the aggregate demand curve to the right. But the aggregate demand curve *can* be shifted continually rightward by continually increasing the money supply, that is, by going to a higher rate of money growth. Therefore, ***a cost-push inflation is a monetary phenomenon because it cannot occur without the monetary authorities pursuing an accommodating policy of a higher rate of money growth.***

DEMAND-PULL INFLATION The goal of high employment can lead to inflationary monetary policy in another way. Even at full employment, unemployment is always present because of frictions in the labor market, which make it difficult to match workers with employers. An unemployed auto worker in Detroit may not know about a job opening in the electronics industry in California or, even if he or she did, may not want to move or be retrained. So the unemployment rate when there is full employment (the natural rate of unemployment) will be greater than zero. If policymakers set a target for unemployment that is too low because it is less than the natural rate of unemployment, this can set the stage for a higher rate of money growth and a resulting inflation. Again we can show how this can happen using an aggregate supply and demand diagram (see Figure 6).

If policymakers have an unemployment target (say, 4 percent) that is below the natural rate (estimated to be between 5 and 6 percent currently), they will try to achieve an output target greater than the natural rate of output. This target level of output is marked Y_T in Figure 6. Suppose that we are initially at point 1; the economy is at the natural rate of output but below the target level of output Y_T. To hit the unemployment target of 4 percent, policymakers enact policies to increase aggregate demand, and the effects of these policies shift the aggregate demand curve until it reaches AD_2 and the economy moves to point 1'. Output is at Y_T, and the 4 percent unemployment rate goal has been reached.

If the targeted unemployment rate was at the natural rate level between 5 and 6 percent, there would be no problem. However, because at Y_T, the 4 percent unemployment rate is below the natural rate level, wages will rise and the aggregate supply curve will shift in to AS_2, moving the economy from point 1' to point 2. The economy is back at the natural rate of unemployment but at a higher price

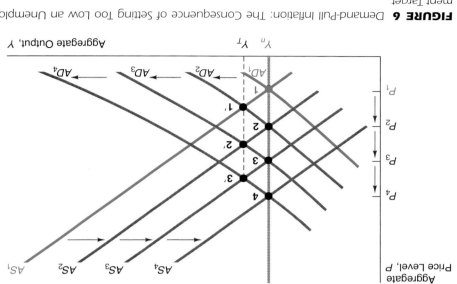

FIGURE 6 Demand-Pull Inflation: The Consequence of Setting Too Low an Unemployment Target

Too low an unemployment target (too high an output target of Y_T) causes the government to shift the aggregate demand curve rightward from AD_1 to AD_2, to AD_3, and so on, while the aggregate supply curve shifts leftward from AS_1 to AS_2, to AS_3, and so on. The result is a continuing rise in the price level known as a demand-pull inflation.

level of P_2. We could stop there, but because unemployment is again higher than the target level, policymakers would again shift the aggregate demand curve rightward to AD_3 to hit the output target at point 2′, and the whole process would continue to drive the economy to point 3 and beyond. The overall result is a steadily rising price level—an inflation.

How can policymakers continually shift the aggregate demand curve rightward? We have already seen that they cannot do it through fiscal policy because of the limits on raising government expenditures and reducing taxes. Instead they will have to resort to expansionary monetary policy: a continuing increase in the money supply and hence a high money growth rate.

Pursuing too high an output target or, equivalently, too low an unemployment rate is the source of inflationary monetary policy in this situation, but it seems senseless for policymakers to do this. They have not gained the benefit of a permanently higher level of output but have generated the burden of an inflation. If, however, they do not realize that the target rate of unemployment is below the natural rate, the process that we see in Figure 6 will be well under way before they realize their mistake.

Because the inflation described results from policymakers' pursuing policies that shift the aggregate demand curve to the right, it is called a *demand-pull inflation*. In contrast, a *cost-push inflation* occurs when workers push their wages up. Is it easy to distinguish between them in practice? The answer is no. We have seen that both types of inflation will be associated with higher money growth, so we cannot distinguish them on this basis. Yet as Figures 5 and 6 demonstrate, demand-pull inflation will be associated with periods when unemployment is below the natural rate level, whereas cost-push inflation is associated with periods when unemployment is above the natural rate level. To decide which type of inflation has occurred, we can look at whether unemployment has been above or below its natural rate level. This would be easy if economists and policymakers actually knew how to measure the natural rate of unemployment; unfortunately, this very difficult research question is still not fully resolved by the economics profession. In addition, the distinction between cost-push and demand-pull inflation is blurred because a cost-push inflation can be initiated by a demand-pull inflation: When a demand-pull inflation produces higher inflation rates, expected inflation will eventually rise and cause workers to demand higher wages so that their real wages do not fall. In this way, demand-pull inflation can eventually trigger cost-push inflation.

Budget Deficits and Inflation

Our discussion of the evidence on money and inflation suggested that budget deficits are another possible source of inflationary monetary policy. To see if this could be the case, we need to look at how a government finances its budget deficits.

GOVERNMENT BUDGET CONSTRAINT Because the government has to pay its bills just as we do, it has a budget constraint. There are two ways we can pay for our spending: raise revenue (by working) or borrow. The government also enjoys these two options: raise revenue by levying taxes or go into debt by issuing government bonds. Unlike us, however, it has a third option: The government can create money and use it to pay for the goods and services it buys.

Methods of financing government spending are described by an expression called the **government budget constraint,** which states the following: The government budget deficit *DEF,* which equals the excess of government spending *G* over tax revenue *T,* must equal the sum of the change in the monetary base ΔMB and the change in government bonds held by the public ΔB. Algebraically, this expression can be written as

$$DEF = G - T = \Delta MB + \Delta B \qquad (1)$$

To see what the government budget constraint means in practice, let's look at the case in which the only government purchase is a $100 million supercomputer. If the government convinces the electorate that such a computer is worth paying for, it will probably be able to raise the $100 million in taxes to pay for it, and the budget deficit will equal zero. The government budget constraint then tells us that no issue of money or bonds is needed to pay for the computer because the budget is balanced. If taxpayers think that supercomputers are too expensive and refuse to pay taxes for them, the budget constraint indicates that the government must pay for it by selling $100 million of new bonds to the public or by printing $100 million of currency to pay for the computer. In either case, the budget constraint is satisfied; the $100 million deficit is balanced by the change in the stock of government bonds held by the public (ΔB = $100 million) or by the change in the monetary base (ΔMB = $100 million).

The government budget constraint thus reveals two important facts: *If the government deficit is financed by an increase in bond holdings by the public, there is no effect on the monetary base and hence on the money supply. But, if the deficit is not financed by increased bond holdings by the public, the monetary base and the money supply increase.*

There are several ways to understand why a deficit leads to an increase in the monetary base when the public's bond holdings do not increase. The simplest case is when the government's treasury has the legal right to issue currency to finance its deficit. Financing the deficit is then very straightforward: The government just pays for the spending that is in excess of its tax revenues with new currency. Because this increase in currency adds directly to the monetary base, the monetary base rises and the money supply with it through the process of multiple deposit creation described in Chapters 16 and 17.

In the United States, however, and in many other countries, the government does not have the right to issue currency to pay for its bills. In this case, the government must finance its deficit by first issuing bonds to the public to acquire the extra funds to pay its bills. Yet if these bonds do not end up in the hands of the public, the only alternative is that they are purchased by the central bank. For the government bonds not to end up in the hands of the public, the central bank must conduct an open market purchase, which, as we saw in Chapters 16 and 17, leads to an increase in the monetary base and in the money supply. This method of financing government spending is called **monetizing the debt** because, as the two-step process described indicates, government debt issued to finance government spending has been removed from the hands of the public and has been replaced by high-powered money. This method of financing, or the more direct method when a government just issues the currency directly, is also, somewhat inaccurately, referred to as **printing money** because high-powered money (the monetary base) is created in the process. The use of the word *printing* is misleading because what is essential to this method of financing government spending is not the actual printing of money but rather the issuing of monetary liabilities to the public after the money has been printed.

We thus see that a budget deficit can lead to an increase in the money supply if it is financed by the creation of high-powered money. However, earlier in this chapter you have seen that inflation can develop only when the stock of money grows continually. Can a budget deficit financed by printing money do this? The answer is yes, if the budget deficit persists for a substantial period of time. In the first period, if the deficit is financed by money creation, the money supply will rise, shifting the aggregate demand curve to the right and leading to a rise in the price level (see Figure 2). If the budget deficit is still present in the next period, it has to be financed all over again. The money supply will rise again, and the aggregate demand curve will again shift to the right, causing the price level to rise further. As long as the deficit persists and the government resorts to printing money to pay for it, this process will continue. ***Financing a persistent deficit by money creation will lead to a sustained inflation.***

A critical element in this process is that the deficit is persistent. If temporary, it would not produce an inflation because the situation would then be similar to that shown in Figure 3, in which there is a one-shot increase in government expenditure. In the period when the deficit occurs, there will be an increase in money to finance it, and the resulting rightward shift of the aggregate demand curve will raise the price level. If the deficit disappears next period, there is no longer a need to print money. The aggregate demand curve will not shift further, and the price level will not continue to rise. Hence the one-shot increase in the money supply from the temporary deficit generates only a one-shot increase in the price level, and no inflation develops.

To summarize, ***a deficit can be the source of a sustained inflation only if it is persistent rather than temporary and if the government finances it by creating money rather than by issuing bonds to the public.***

If inflation is the result, why do governments frequently finance persistent deficits by creating money? The answer is the key to understanding how budget deficits may lead to inflation.

BUDGET DEFICITS AND MONEY CREATION IN OTHER COUNTRIES   Although the United States has well-developed money and capital markets in which huge quantities of its government bonds, both short- and long-term, can be sold, this is not the situation in many developing countries. If developing countries run budget deficits, they cannot finance them by issuing bonds and must resort to their only other alternative, printing money. As a result, when they run large deficits relative to GDP, the money supply grows at substantial rates, and inflation results.

Earlier we cited Latin American countries with high inflation rates and high money growth as evidence that inflation is a monetary phenomenon. The Latin

American countries with high money growth are precisely the ones that have persistent and extremely large budget deficits relative to GDP. The only way to finance the deficits is to print more money, so the ultimate source of their high inflation rates is their large budget deficits.

In all episodes of hyperinflation, huge government budget deficits are also the ultimate source of inflationary monetary policies. The budget deficits during hyperinflations are so large that even if a capital market exists to issue government bonds, it does not have sufficient capacity to handle the quantity of bonds that the government wishes to sell. In this situation, the government must also resort to the printing press to finance the deficits.

BUDGET DEFICITS AND MONEY CREATION IN THE UNITED STATES So far we have seen why budget deficits in some countries must lead to money creation and inflation. Either the deficit is huge, or the country does not have sufficient access to capital markets in which it can sell all government bonds. But neither of these scenarios seems to describe the situation in the United States. True, the United States' deficits have increased in the recent past, but even so, the magnitude of these deficits relative to GDP is small compared to the deficits of countries that have experienced hyperinflations: The U.S. deficit as a percent of GDP reached a peak of 6 percent in 1983, whereas Argentina's budget deficit has often exceeded 15 percent of GDP. Furthermore, since the United States has the best-developed government bond market of any country in the world, it can issue large quantities of bonds to finance its deficit.

Whether the budget deficit influences the monetary base and the money supply or not depends critically on how the Federal Reserve chooses to conduct monetary policy. If the Fed pursues a policy goal of preventing high interest rates (a likely possibility, as we have seen in Chapter 19), many economists contend that a budget deficit will lead to the printing of money. Their reasoning, using the supply and demand analysis of the bond market in Chapter 6, is as follows: When the Treasury issues bonds to the public, the supply of bonds rises (from B_1^s to B_2^s in Figure 7), causing interest rates to rise from i_1 to i_2 and bond prices to fall. If the Fed considers the rise in interest rates undesirable, it will buy bonds to prop up bond prices and reduce interest rates. The net result is that the government budget deficit has led to Federal Reserve open market purchases, which raise the monetary base (create high-powered money) and raise the money supply. If the budget deficit persists so that the quantity of bonds supplied keeps on growing, the upward pressure on interest rates will continue, the Fed will purchase bonds again and again, and the money supply will continually rise, resulting in an inflation.

Economists such as Robert Barro of Harvard University, however, do not agree that budget deficits influence the monetary base in the manner just described. Their analysis (which Barro named **Ricardian equivalence** after the nineteenth-century British economist David Ricardo) contends that when the government runs deficits and issues bonds, the public recognizes that it will be subject to higher taxes in the future to pay off these bonds. The public then saves more in anticipation of these future taxes, with the net result that the public demand for bonds increases to match the increased supply. The demand curve

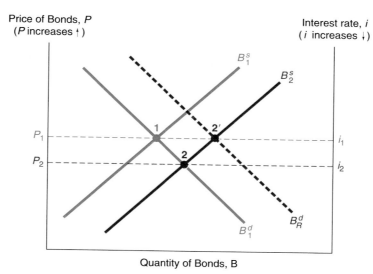

Price of Bonds, P
(P increases ↑)

Interest rate, i
(i increases ↓)

Quantity of Bonds, B

FIGURE 7 Interest Rates and the Government Budget Deficit
When the Treasury issues bonds to finance the budget deficit, the supply curve for bonds shifts rightward from B_1^s to B_2^s. Many economists take the position that the equilibrium moves to point 2 because the bond demand curve remains unchanged, with the result that the bond price falls from P_1 to P_2 and the interest rate rises from i_1 to i_2. Adherents of Ricardian equivalence, however, suggest that the demand curve for bonds also increases to B_R^d, moving the equilibrium to point 2′, where the interest rate is unchanged at i_1. (Note that P and i increase in opposite directions. P on the left vertical axis increases as we go up the axis, whereas i on the right vertical axis increases as we go down the axis.)

for bonds shifts rightward to B_R^d in Figure 7, leaving the interest rate unchanged at i_1. There is now no need for the Fed to purchase bonds to keep the interest rate from rising.

To sum up, although high inflation is "always and everywhere a monetary phenomenon" in the sense that it cannot occur without a high rate of money growth, there are reasons why this inflationary monetary policy might come about. The two underlying reasons are the adherence of policymakers to a high employment target and the presence of persistent government budget deficits.

Explaining the Rise in U.S. Inflation, 1960–1980

Now that we have examined the underlying sources of inflation, let's apply this knowledge to understanding the causes of the rise in U.S. inflation from 1960 to 1980.

Figure 8 documents the rise in inflation in those years. At the beginning of the period, the inflation rate is close to 1 percent at an annual rate; by the late 1970s, it is averaging around 8 percent. How does the analysis of this chapter explain this rise in inflation?

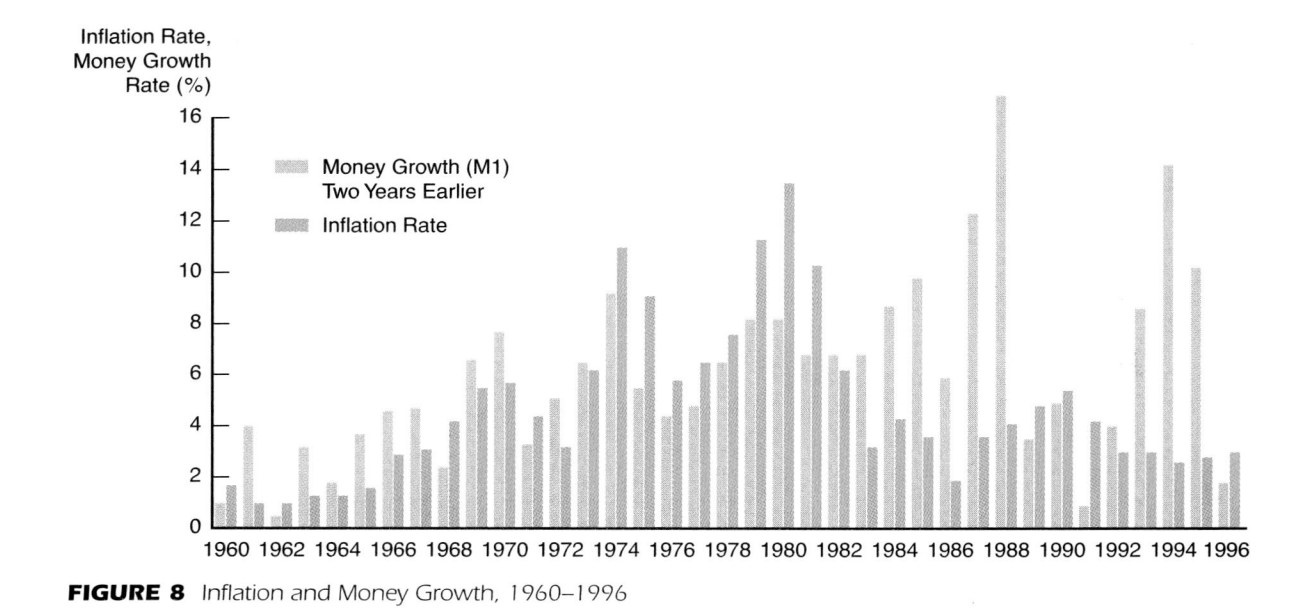

FIGURE 8 Inflation and Money Growth, 1960–1996

Source: Economic Report of the President.

The conclusion that inflation is a monetary phenomenon is given a fair amount of support by the period from 1960 through 1980. As Figure 8 shows, in this period there is a close correspondence between movements in the inflation rate and the monetary growth rate from two years earlier. (The money growth rates are from two years earlier because research indicates that a change in money growth takes that long to affect the inflation rate.) The rise in inflation from 1960 to 1980 can be attributed to the rise in the money growth rate over this period. But you have probably noticed that in 1974–1975 and 1979–1980, the inflation rate is well above the money growth rate from two years earlier. You may recall from Chapter 24 that temporary upward bursts of the inflation rate in those years can be attributed to supply shocks from oil and food price increases that occurred in 1973–1975 and 1978–1980.

However, the linkage between money growth and inflation after 1980 is not at all evident in Figure 8. This is the result of substantial gyrations in velocity in the 1980s (documented in Chapter 21). Indeed, the early 1980s was a period of rapid disinflation (a substantial fall in the inflation rate), yet the money growth rates in Figure 8 do not display a visible downward trend until after the disinflation was over. (The disinflationary process in the 1980s will be discussed in another application later in this chapter.) Although some economists see the 1980s as evidence against the money-inflation link, others view the 1980s as an unusual period characterized by large fluctuations in interest rates and by rapid financial innovation that made the correct measurement of money far more difficult (see Chapter 3). In their view, the 1980s was an aberration, and the close correspondence of money and inflation is sure to reassert itself. However, this has not yet occurred in the 1990s.

What is the underlying cause of the increased rate of money growth that we see occurring from 1960 to 1980? We have identified two possible sources of infla-

Debt (% of GDP)

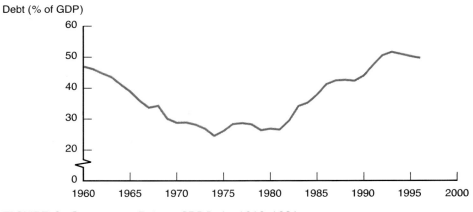

FIGURE 9 Government Debt-to-GDP Ratio, 1960–1996

Source: Economic Report of the President.

tionary monetary policy: government adherence to a high employment target and budget deficits. Let's see if budget deficits can explain the move to an inflationary monetary policy by plotting the ratio of government debt to GDP in Figure 9. This ratio provides a reasonable measure of whether government budget deficits put upward pressure on interest rates. Only if this ratio is rising might there be a tendency for budget deficits to raise interest rates because the public is then being asked to hold more government bonds relative to their capacity to buy them. Surprisingly, over the course of the 20-year period from 1960 to 1980, this ratio was falling, not rising. Thus U.S. budget deficits in this period did not raise interest rates and so could not have encouraged the Fed to expand the money supply by buying bonds. Therefore, Figure 9 tells us that we can rule out budget deficits as a source of the rise in inflation in this period.

Because politicians were frequently bemoaning the budget deficits in this period, why did deficits not lead to an increase in the debt-GDP ratio? The reason is that in this period, U.S. budget deficits were sufficiently small that the increase in the stock of government debt was still slower than the growth in nominal GDP, and the ratio of debt to GDP declined. You can see that interpreting budget deficit numbers is a tricky business.[6]

We have ruled out budget deficits as the instigator; what else could be the underlying cause of the higher rate of money growth and more rapid inflation in the 1960s and 1970s? Figure 10, which compares the actual unemployment rate to the natural rate of unemployment, shows that the economy was experiencing

---

[6]Another way of understanding the decline in the debt-GDP ratio is to recognize that a rise in the price level reduces the value of the outstanding government debt in real terms, that is, in terms of the goods and services it can buy. So even though budget deficits did lead to a somewhat higher nominal amount of debt in this period, the continually rising price level (inflation) produced a lower real value of the government debt. The decline in the real amount of debt at the same time that real GDP was rising in this period then resulted in the decline in the debt-GDP ratio. For a fascinating discussion of how tricky it is to interpret deficit numbers, see Robert Eisner and Paul J. Pieper, "A New View of the Federal Debt and Budget Deficits," *American Economic Review* 74 (1984): 11–29.

unemployment below the natural rate in all but one year between 1965 and 1973. This suggests that in 1965–1973, the American economy was experiencing the demand-pull inflation described in Figure 6.

Policymakers apparently pursued policies that continually shifted the aggregate demand curve to the right in trying to achieve an output target that was too high, thus causing the continual rise in the price level outlined in Figure 6. This occurred because policymakers, economists, and politicians had become committed in the mid-1960s to a target unemployment rate of 4 percent, the level of unemployment they thought was consistent with price stability. In hindsight, most economists today agree that the natural rate of unemployment was substantially higher in this period, on the order of 5 to 6 percent, as shown in Figure 10. The result of the inappropriate 4 percent unemployment target was the beginning of the most sustained inflationary episode in American history.

After 1975, the unemployment rate was regularly above the natural rate of unemployment, yet inflation continued. It appears that we have the phenomenon of a cost-push inflation described in Figure 5 (the impetus for which was the earlier demand-pull inflation). The persistence of inflation can be explained by the public's knowledge that government policy continued to be concerned with achieving high employment. With a higher rate of expected inflation arising initially from the demand-pull inflation, the aggregate supply curve in Figure 5 continued to shift leftward, causing a rise in unemployment that policymakers would

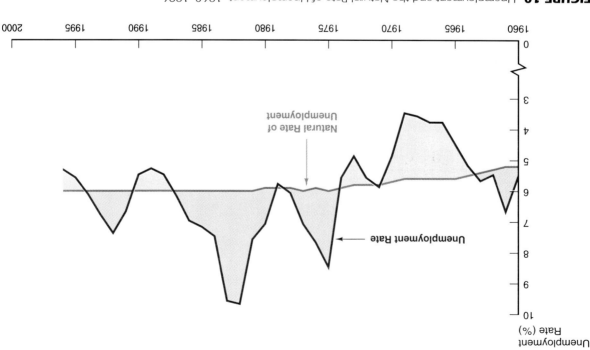

FIGURE 10 Unemployment and the Natural Rate of Unemployment, 1960–1996

Sources: Economic Report of the President; Robert Gordon, Macroeconomics, 6th ed. (New York: HarperCollins, 1996).

try to eliminate by shifting the aggregate demand curve to the right. The result was a continuation of the inflation that had started in the 1960s.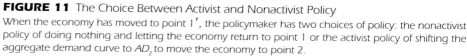

ACTIVIST/NONACTIVIST POLICY DEBATE

All economists have similar policy goals—they want to promote high employment and price stability—and yet they often have very different views on how policy should be conducted. Activists regard the self-correcting mechanism through wage and price adjustment (see Chapter 24) as very slow and hence see the need for the government to pursue active, accommodating, discretionary policy to eliminate high unemployment whenever it develops. Nonactivists, by contrast, believe that the performance of the economy would be improved if the government avoided active policy to eliminate unemployment. We will explore the activist/nonactivist policy debate by first looking at what the policy responses might be when the economy experiences high unemployment.

Responses to High Unemployment

Suppose that policymakers confront an economy that has moved to point 1' in Figure 11. At this point, aggregate output $Y_{1'}$ is lower than the natural rate level, and the economy is suffering from high unemployment. Policymakers have two viable choices: If they are nonactivists and do nothing, the aggregate supply curve will eventually shift rightward over time, driving the economy from point 1' to point 1, where full employment is restored. The accommodating, activist alternative is to try to eliminate the high unemployment by attempting to shift the aggregate demand curve rightward to AD_2 by pursuing expansionary policy (an increase

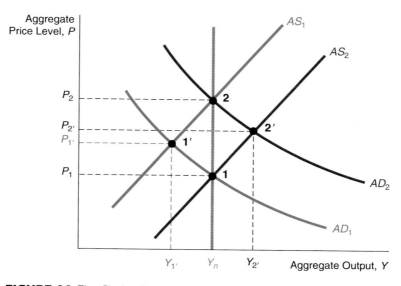

FIGURE 11 The Choice Between Activist and Nonactivist Policy

When the economy has moved to point 1', the policymaker has two choices of policy: the nonactivist policy of doing nothing and letting the economy return to point 1 or the activist policy of shifting the aggregate demand curve to AD_2 to move the economy to point 2.

in the money supply, increase in government spending, or lowering of taxes). If policymakers could shift the aggregate demand curve to AD_2 instantaneously, the economy would immediately move to point 2, where there is full employment. However, several types of lags prevent this immediate movement from occurring.

1. The *data lag* is the time it takes for policymakers to obtain the data that tell them what is happening in the economy. Accurate data on GDP, for example, are not available until several months after a given quarter is over.

2. The *recognition lag* is the time it takes for policymakers to be sure of what the data are signaling about the future course of the economy. For example, to minimize errors, the National Bureau of Economic Research (the organization that officially dates business cycles) will not declare the economy to be in recession until at least six months after it has determined that one has begun.

3. The *legislative lag* represents the time it takes to pass legislation to implement a particular policy. The legislative lag does not exist for most monetary policy actions such as open market operations. It can, however, be quite important for the implementation of fiscal policy, when it can sometimes take six months to a year to get legislation passed to change taxes or government spending.

4. The *implementation lag* is the time it takes for policymakers to change policy instruments once they have decided on the new policy. Again, this lag is unimportant for the conduct of open market operations because the Fed's trading desk can purchase or sell bonds almost immediately upon being told to do so by the Federal Open Market Committee. Actually implementing fiscal policy may take time, however; for example, getting government agencies to change their spending habits takes time, as does changing tax tables.

5. The *effectiveness lag* is the time it takes for the policy actually to have an impact on the economy. An important element of the monetarist viewpoint is that the effectiveness lag for changes in the money supply is long and variable (from several months to several years). Keynesians usually view fiscal policy as having a shorter effectiveness lag than monetary policy (fiscal policy takes approximately a year until its full effect is felt), but there is substantial uncertainty about how long this lag is.

Activist and Nonactivist Positions

Now that we understand the considerations that affect decisions by policymakers on whether to pursue an activist or nonactivist policy, we can examine when each of these policies would be preferable.

CASE FOR AN ACTIVIST POLICY Activists, such as the Keynesians, view the wage and price adjustment process as extremely slow. They consider a nonactivist policy costly because the slow movement of the economy back to full employment results in a large loss of output. However, even though the five lags described result in delay of a year or two before the aggregate demand curve shift to AD_2, the aggregate supply curve moves very little during this time. The appropriate path for policymakers to pursue is thus an activist policy of moving the economy to point 2 in Figure 11.

CASE FOR A NONACTIVIST POLICY Nonactivists, such as the monetarists, view the wage and price adjustment process as more rapid than activists and consider nonactivist policy less costly because output is soon back at the natural rate level. They suggest that an activist, accommodating policy of shifting the aggregate demand curve to AD_2 is costly because it produces more volatility in both the price level and output. The reason for this volatility is that the time it takes to shift the aggregate demand curve to AD_2 is substantial, whereas the wage and price adjustment process is more rapid. Hence before the aggregate demand curve shifts to the right, the aggregate supply curve will have shifted rightward to AS_2, and the economy will have moved from point 1′ to point 1, where it has returned to the natural rate level of output Y_n. After adjustment to the AS_2 curve is complete, the shift of the aggregate demand curve to AD_2 finally takes effect, leading the economy to point 2′ at the intersection of AD_2 and AS_2. Aggregate output at $Y_{2'}$ is now greater than the natural rate level ($Y_{2'} > Y_n$), so the aggregate supply curve will now shift leftward back to AS_1, moving the economy to point 2, where output is again at the natural rate level.

Although the activist policy eventually moves the economy to point 2 as policymakers intended, it leads to a sequence of equilibrium points—1′, 1, 2′, and 2—at which both output and the price level have been highly variable: Output overshoots its target level of Y_n, and the price level falls from $P_{1'}$ to P_1 and then rises to $P_{2'}$ and eventually to P_2. Because this variability is undesirable, policymakers would be better off pursuing the nonactivist policy, which moved the economy to point 1 and left it there.

Expectations and the Activist/Nonactivist Debate

Our analysis of inflation in the 1970s demonstrated that expectations about policy can be an important element in the inflation process. Allowing for expectations about policy to affect how wages are set (the wage-setting process) provides an additional reason for pursuing a nonactivist policy.

DO EXPECTATIONS FAVOR A NONACTIVIST APPROACH? Does the possibility that expectations about policy matter to the wage-setting process strengthen the case for a nonactivist policy? The case for an activist policy states that with slow wage and price adjustment, the activist policy returns the economy to full employment at point 2 far more quickly than it takes to get to full employment at point 1 under nonactivist policy. However, the activist argument does not allow for the possibility (1) that expectations about policy matter to the wage-setting process and (2) that the economy might initially have moved from point 1 to point 1′ because an attempt by workers to raise their wages or a negative supply shock shifted the aggregate supply curve from AS_2 to AS_1. We must therefore ask the following question about activist policy: Will the aggregate supply curve continue to shift to the left after the economy has reached point 2, leading to cost-push inflation?

The answer to this question is yes *if* expectations of policy matter. Our discussion of cost-push inflation in Figure 5 suggested that if workers know that policy will be accommodating in the future, they will continue to push their wages up, and the aggregate supply curve will keep on shifting leftward. As a result, policymakers are forced to accommodate the cost push by continuing to shift the aggregate demand curve to the right to eliminate the unemployment that develops. The accommodating, activist policy with its high employment target has the hidden cost or disadvantage that it may well lead to inflation.[7]

The main advantage of a nonaccommodating, nonactivist policy, in which policymakers do not try to shift the aggregate demand curve in response to the cost push, is that it will prevent inflation. As depicted in Figure 4, the result of an upward push on wages in the face of a nonaccommodating, nonactivist policy will be a period of unemployment above the natural rate level, which will eventually shift the aggregate supply curve and the price level back to their initial positions. The main criticism of this nonactivist policy is that the economy will suffer protracted periods of unemployment when the aggregate supply curve shifts leftward. Workers, however, would probably not push for higher wages to begin with if they knew that policy would be nonaccommodating, because their wage gains will lead to a protracted period of unemployment. A nonaccommodating, nonactivist policy may have not only the advantage of preventing inflation but also the hidden benefit of discouraging leftward shifts in the aggregate supply curve that lead to excessive unemployment.

In conclusion, *if workers' options about whether policy is accommodating or nonaccommodating matter to the wage-setting process, the case for a nonactivist policy is much stronger.*

DO EXPECTATIONS ABOUT POLICY MATTER TO THE WAGE-SETTING PROCESS?

The answer to this question is crucial to deciding whether activist or nonactivist policy is preferred and so has become a major topic of current research for economists, but the evidence is not yet conclusive. We can ask, however, whether expectations about policy do affect people's behavior in other contexts. This information will help us know if expectations regarding whether or not policy is accommodating are important to the wage-setting process.

As any good negotiator knows, convincing your opponent that you will be nonaccommodating is crucial to getting a good deal. If you are bargaining with a car dealer over price, for example, you must convince him that you can just as easily walk away from the deal and buy a car from a dealer on the other side of town. This principle also applies to conducting foreign policy—it is to your advantage to convince your opponent that you will go to war (be nonaccommodating) if your demands are not met. Similarly, if your opponent thinks that you will be accommodating, he will almost certainly take advantage of you (for an example, see Box 2). Finally, anyone who has dealt with a 2-year-old child knows that the more you give in (pursue an accommodating policy), the more demanding the child becomes. In conclusion, people's expectations about policy do affect

---

[7]The issue that is being described here is the dynamic inconsistency of policy described by Finn Kydland and Edward Prescott, "Rules Rather than Discretion: The Inconsistency of Optimal Plans," *Journal of Political Economy* 85 (1977): 473–491. A much less technical discussion of this subject can be found in Edward Prescott, "Should Control Theory Be Used for Economic Stabilization?" *Carnegie-Rochester Conference Series on Public Policy* 7 (1977): 13–38.

> ## BOX 2
>
> ### *Perils of Accommodating Policy*
>
> **The Terrorism Dilemma.** A major dilemma confronting our foreign policy in recent years is whether to cave in to the demands of terrorists when they are holding American hostages. Because our hearts go out to the hostages and their families, we might be tempted to pursue an accommodating policy of giving in to the terrorists to bring the hostages safely back home. However, pursuing this accommodating policy is likely to encourage terrorists to take hostages in the future.
>
> The terrorism dilemma illustrates the principle that opponents are more likely to take advantage of you in the future if you accommodate them now. Recognition of this principle, which demonstrates the perils of accommodating policy, explains why governments in countries such as the United States and Israel have been reluctant to give in to terrorist demands even though it has sometimes resulted in the death of hostages.

their behavior. Consequently, it is quite plausible that expectations about policy also affect the wage-setting process.[8]

Rules Versus Discretion: Conclusions

The following conclusions can be generated from our analysis: Activists believe in the use of discretionary policy to eliminate excessive unemployment whenever it develops because they view the wage and price adjustment process as sluggish and unresponsive to expectations about policy. Nonactivists, by contrast, believe that a discretionary policy that reacts to excessive unemployment is counterproductive because wage and price adjustment is rapid and because expectations about policy can matter to the wage-setting process. Nonactivists thus advocate the use of a policy rule to keep the aggregate demand curve from fluctuating away from the trend rate of growth of the natural rate level of output. Monetarists, who adhere to the nonactivist position and who also see money as the sole source of fluctuations in the aggregate demand curve, therefore advocate a policy rule whereby the Federal Reserve keeps the money supply growing at a constant rate. This monetarist rule is referred to as a **constant-money-growth-rate rule.**

As our analysis indicates, an important element for the success of a nonaccommodating policy rule is that it be *credible:* The public must believe that policymakers will be tough and not accede to a cost push by shifting the aggregate demand curve to the right to eliminate unemployment. In other words, government policymakers need credibility as inflation fighters in the eyes of the public. Otherwise, workers will be more likely to push for higher wages, which will shift the aggregate supply curve leftward after the economy reaches full employment

---

[8]A recent development in monetary theory, new classical macroeconomics, strongly suggests that expectations about policy are crucial to the wage-setting process and the movements of the aggregate supply curve. We will explore why new classical macroeconomics comes to this conclusion in Chapters 27 and 28 , when we discuss the implications of the rational expectations hypothesis, which states that expectations are formed using all available information, including expectations about policy.

at a point such as point 2 in Figure 11 and lead to unemployment or inflation (or both). Alternatively, a credible, nonaccommodating policy rule has the benefit that it makes a cost push less likely and thus helps prevent inflation and potential increases in unemployment. The following application suggests that recent historical experience is consistent with the importance of credibility to successful policymaking.

Importance of Credibility to Volcker's Victory over Inflation

In the period from 1965 through the 1970s, policymakers had little credibility as inflation fighters—a well-deserved reputation, as they pursued an accommodating policy to achieve high employment. As we have seen, the outcome was not a happy one. Inflation soared to double-digit levels, while the unemployment rate remained high. To wring inflation out of the system, the Federal Reserve under Chairman Paul Volcker put the economy through two back-to-back recessions in 1980 and 1981–1982 (see Chapter 19). (The data on inflation, money growth, and unemployment in this period are shown in Figures 8 and 10.) Only after the 1981–1982 recession—the most severe in the postwar period, with unemployment above the 10 percent level—did Volcker establish credibility for the Fed's anti-inflation policy. By the end of 1982, inflation was running at a rate of less than 5 percent.

One indication of Volcker's credibility came in 1983 when the money growth rate accelerated dramatically and yet inflation did not rise. Workers and firms were convinced that if inflation reared its head, Volcker would pursue a nonaccommodating policy of quashing it. They did not raise wages and prices, which would have shifted the aggregate supply curve leftward and would have led to both inflation and unemployment. The success of Volcker's anti-inflation policy continued throughout the rest of his term as chairman, which ended in 1987; unemployment fell steadily, while the inflation rate remained below 5 percent. Volcker's triumph over inflation was achieved because he obtained credibility the hard way; he earned it.

SUMMARY

1. Milton Friedman's famous proposition that "inflation is always and everywhere a monetary phenomenon" is supported by the following evidence: Every country that has experienced a sustained, high inflation has also experienced a high rate of money growth.

2. Aggregate demand and supply analysis shows that Keynesian and monetarist views of the inflation process are not very different. Both believe that high inflation can occur only if there is a high rate of money growth. As long as we recognize that by inflation we mean a rapid and continuing increase in the price level, almost all economists agree with Friedman's proposition.

3. Although high inflation is "always and everywhere a monetary phenomenon" in the sense that it cannot occur without a high rate of money growth, there are reasons why inflationary monetary policy comes about. The two underlying reasons are the adher-

ence of policymakers to a high employment target and the presence of persistent government budget deficits.

4. Activists believe in the use of discretionary policy to eliminate excessive unemployment whenever it occurs because they view wage and price adjust-

ment as sluggish and unresponsive to expectations about policy. Nonactivists take the opposite view and believe that discretionary policy is counterproductive. In addition, they regard the credibility of a nonaccommodating (nonactivist) anti-inflation policy as crucial to its success.

KEY TERMS

accommodating policy, p. 668

constant-money-growth-rate
  rule, p. 683

cost-push inflation, p. 668

demand-pull inflation, p. 668

government budget constraint,
  p. 672

monetizing the debt, p. 672

printing money, p. 673

Ricardian equivalence, p. 674

QUESTIONS AND PROBLEMS

1. "There are frequently years when the inflation rate is high and yet money growth is quite low. Therefore, the statement that inflation is a monetary phenomenon cannot be correct." Comment.

*2. Why do economists focus on historical episodes of hyperinflation to decide whether inflation is a monetary phenomenon?

3. "Since increases in government spending raise the aggregate demand curve in Keynesian analysis, fiscal policy by itself can be the source of inflation." Is this statement true, false, or uncertain? Explain your answer.

*4. "A cost-push inflation occurs as a result of workers' attempts to push up their wages. Therefore, inflation does not have to be a monetary phenomenon." Is this statement true, false, or uncertain? Explain your answer.

5. "Because government policymakers do not consider inflation desirable, their policies cannot be the source of inflation." Is this statement true, false, or uncertain? Explain your answer.

*6. "A budget deficit that is only temporary cannot be the source of inflation." Is this statement true, false, or uncertain? Explain your answer.

7. How can the Fed's desire to prevent high interest rates lead to inflation?

*8. "If the data and recognition lags could be reduced, activist policy would more likely be beneficial to the economy." Is this statement true, false, or uncertain? Explain your answer.

9. "The more sluggish wage and price adjustment is, the more variable output and the price level are

when an activist policy is pursued." Is this statement true, false, or uncertain? Explain your answer.

*10. "If the public believes that the monetary authorities will pursue an accommodating policy, a cost-push inflation is more likely to develop." Is this statement true, false, or uncertain? Explain your answer.

11. Why are activist policies to eliminate unemployment more likely to lead to inflation than nonactivist policies?

*12. "The less important expectations about policy are to movements of the aggregate supply curve, the stronger the case is for activist policy to eliminate unemployment." Is this statement true, false, or uncertain? Explain your answer.

13. If the economy's self-correcting mechanism works slowly, should the government necessarily pursue an activist policy to eliminate unemployment?

*14. "To prevent inflation, the Fed should follow Teddy Roosevelt's advice: 'Speak softly and carry a big stick.'" What would the Fed's "big stick" be? What is the statement trying to say?

15. In a speech early in the Iraq-Kuwait crisis, President George Bush stated that although his heart went out to the hostages held by Saddam Hussein, he would not let this hostage taking deter the United States from insisting on the withdrawal of Iraq from Kuwait. Do you think that Bush's position made sense? Explain why or why not.

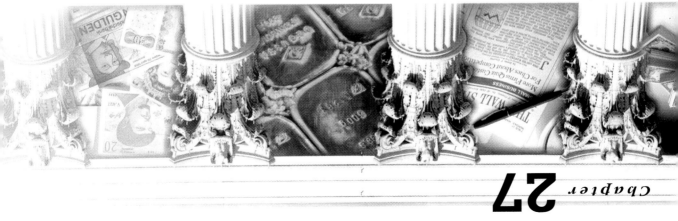

Chapter 27

THEORY OF RATIONAL EXPECTATIONS AND EFFICIENT CAPITAL MARKETS

PREVIEW   Throughout our discussion of the many facets of money, banking, and financial markets, you may have noticed that the subject of expectations keeps cropping up again and again. If consumers expect that they will be richer in the future, for example, they spend more today, and aggregate output will increase; if banks expect deposit outflows to occur, they increase their holdings of excess reserves, which causes the money supply to fall; and if participants in the capital markets expect interest rates to rise and anticipate capital losses on long-term bonds, they will decrease their demand for long-term bonds, and the bond prices will fall. Expectations influence the behavior of all participants in the economy and have a major impact on economic activity.

The *theory of rational expectations* attempts to explain how economic agents form their expectations. It is at the center of many recent debates about how monetary policy and fiscal policy should be conducted (discussed in Chapter 28). In addition, when this theory is applied to financial markets, where it is called the *theory of efficient capital markets* (or, more simply, *efficient markets theory*), it has important implications about what factors determine securities prices and how these prices move over time.

In this chapter we examine the basic reasoning behind the theory of rational expectations and apply it to financial markets. In addition to helping us understand the factors that influence the formation of business and consumer expectations, rational expectations theory explains some puzzling features of the operation and behavior of financial markets. You will see, for example, that it explains why changes in stock prices are unpredictable and why listening to a stockbroker's hot tips may not be a good idea.

Theoretically, rational expectations theory should be a powerful tool for analyzing behavior. But to establish that it is *in reality* a useful tool, we must compare the theory with the data. Does the empirical evidence support the theory? Although the evidence is somewhat mixed and is very controversial, it indicates that for many purposes, this theory is a good starting point for analyzing expectations.

ROLE OF EXPECTATIONS IN ECONOMIC ACTIVITY

It is difficult to think of any sector of the economy in which expectations exert no influence on the effects of policy and the way markets behave. To point up the critical role of expectations in influencing economic activity, it might be useful to list the various avenues in which they have come into play in our study of money, banking, and financial markets.

Study Guide Before you read on, try to list examples from this book in which expectations influence economic behavior and then compare your list to the examples that follow. This is an excellent way for you to review how the material we have studied so far fits together.

1. *Asset demand and the determination of interest rates.* Because expectations of returns are an important factor in determining the quantity of an asset people demand, expectations are central to the behavior of asset prices in a financial market (Chapters 5 and 6). For example, we have seen that expectations of inflation have a major impact on bond prices and interest rates through the Fisher effect. The speed with which expectations of inflation respond to a higher rate of money growth is an important factor determining whether interest rates rise or fall when money growth increases.

2. *Risk and term structure of interest rates.* Expectations are also central in the determination of the risk and term structure of interest rates (Chapter 7). Expectations about the likelihood of bankruptcy are probably the most important factors in determining the risk structure of interest rates. Expectations of future short-term interest rates play a central role in determining long-term interest rates.

3. *Foreign exchange rates.* Recall that the exchange rate is the price of one asset (deposits denominated in the domestic currency) in terms of another (deposits denominated in the foreign currency). Thus the expected returns on foreign deposits relative to domestic deposits are a central element in the determination of foreign exchange rates (Chapter 8). Because expected appreciation or depreciation of the domestic currency affects the expected return on foreign deposits relative to domestic deposits, expectations about the price level, inflation, tariffs and quotas, import and export demand, and the money supply play an important role in determining the exchange rate. In addition, expectations that a central bank is about to devalue or revalue its domestic currency are a key feature of a speculative attack on a currency (Chapter 20).

4. *Asymmetric information and financial structure.* Expectations are what make the asymmetric information problems of adverse selection and moral hazard we encountered in Part III important in determining financial structure. Financial

intermediaries engage in information collection because they have expectations that adverse selection will occur, that is, that the least desirable credit risks will be the most likely to seek loans. Similarly, expectations that borrowers will increase moral hazard by taking on too much risk are what drives financial institutions to take steps to limit moral hazard through monitoring and enforcement of restrictive covenants. The greater the expectations of the effects of adverse selection and moral hazard, the greater the efforts of financial institutions to engage in activities to reduce these asymmetric information problems and hence the greater the impact of asymmetric information on our financial structure.

5. Financial innovation. Because financial institutions are concerned with the future profitability of the new financial instruments they issue, expectations about interest-rate movements and the nature of the regulatory environment in the future affect financial innovation (Chapters 10 and 11). Furthermore, in deciding on which regulations to impose on financial markets, regulators must guess how financial institutions will behave in response to new regulations. The result can be a complicated game between regulators and regulated in which each tries to outguess the other.

6. Bank asset and liability management. Banks' decisions about which assets to hold are influenced by their expectations about the returns, risk, and liquidity of various assets (Chapter 10). Their decisions about which liabilities to assume are influenced by their expectations about the future cost of taking on various liabilities. In addition, because banks must manage liquidity to remain solvent, expectations about deposit outflows will affect their decisions about whether to hold more or fewer liquid assets.

7. The money supply process. As you will recall from Chapters 16 and 17, depositor behavior and bank behavior are important in the money supply process. Depositors' decisions to hold currency versus demand or time deposits are affected primarily by expectations of the relative returns on these assets. Banks' decisions about excess reserves and borrowing from the Fed are influenced by their expectations of the returns they can earn on loans. In addition, the amount of excess reserves is affected by bankers' expectations concerning depositor outflows.

The role of expectations in bank panics and the resulting declines in the money supply are especially important (Chapter 17). Depositors' expectations that a bank or banks are in trouble cause them to withdraw deposits, which in turn causes banks to fail, which causes more banks to fail. Bankers' expectations of deposit outflows make the situation even worse because their scramble for liquidity and the resulting increase in excess reserves can lead to more bank failures. The net result of this process is that the currency–checkable deposits ratio and excess reserves rise, causing a sharp drop in the money supply.

8. Federal Reserve. The Fed's expectations of inflation and the state of the economy affect the targets it sets for monetary policy. Its expectations of short-term interest rates can be a factor in the procedures it uses to control the money supply (Chapter 19).

9. Demand for money. Because money is just another asset, its expected return relative to other assets is an important factor in determining its demand (Chapter 21). Expectations about the level of lifetime resources (usually represented by permanent income) are frequently thought to be another major determinant of the demand for money.

10. Aggregate demand. Expectations play a prominent role in determining aggregate demand. Our discussion of the *ISLM* model (Chapters 22 and 23) and the transmission mechanisms of monetary policy (Chapter 25) reveals that consumer expenditure is related to consumers' expectations of the future resources available to them and of the likelihood of financial distress. Investment spending depends on firms' expectations of future profits from investment projects as well as expectations about the cost of financing the project. It is no wonder that Keynes emphasized "animal spirits" (expectations) as a major factor driving aggregate demand and the business cycle.

11. Aggregate supply and inflation. Analysis of the aggregate supply curve (Chapter 24) indicated that workers' expectations about inflation and the likely response of government policy to unemployment affect the position of the aggregate supply curve. Expectations about inflation and government policy influence workers' willingness to push wages higher, and so these expectations play a central role in cost-push inflation, whereby the aggregate supply curve shifts farther and farther to the left (Chapter 26). The public's expectations of government policy, which are affected by the credibility of government policymakers, have implications for the desirability of pursuing activist or nonactivist policies.

In conclusion, expectations are important in every sector of the economy through their effects on policy and market behavior. Next we outline the theory of rational expectations, currently the most widely used theory to describe the formation of business and consumer expectations.

THEORY OF RATIONAL EXPECTATIONS

In the 1950s and 1960s, economists regularly viewed expectations as formed from past experience only. Expectations of inflation, for example, were typically viewed as being an average of past inflation rates. This view of expectation formation, called **adaptive expectations,** suggests that changes in expectations will occur slowly over time as past data change.[1] So if inflation had formerly been steady at a 5 percent rate, expectations of future inflation would be 5 percent too. If inflation rose to a steady rate of 10 percent, expectations of future inflation would rise toward 10 percent, but slowly: In the first year, expected inflation might rise only to 6 percent; in the second year, to 7 percent; and so on.

Adaptive expectations have been faulted on the grounds that people use more information than just past data on a single variable to form their expectations

---

[1]More specifically, adaptive expectations, say, of inflation, are written as a weighted average of past inflation rates:

$$\pi_t^e = (1 - \lambda)\sum_{j=0}^{\infty}\lambda^j \pi_{t-j}$$

where

π_t^e = adaptive expectation of inflation at time t
π_{t-j} = inflation at time $t - j$
λ = a constant between the values of 0 and 1

of that variable. Their expectations of inflation will almost surely be affected by their predictions of future monetary policy as well as by current and past monetary policy. In addition, people often change their expectations quickly in the light of new information. To meet these objections to adaptive expectations, John Muth developed an alternative theory of expectations, called **rational expectations**, which can be stated as follows: *Expectations will be identical to optimal forecasts (the best guess of the future) using all available information.[2]*

What exactly does this mean? To explain it more clearly, let's use the theory of rational expectations to examine how expectations are formed in a situation that most of us encounter at some point in our lifetime: our drive to work. Suppose that when Joe Commuter travels when it is not rush hour, it takes him an average of 30 minutes for his trip. Sometimes it takes him 35 minutes, other times 25 minutes, but the average non-rush-hour driving time is 30 minutes. If, however, Joe leaves for work during the rush hour, it takes him, on average, an additional 10 minutes to get to work. Given that he leaves for work during the rush hour, the best guess of the driving time—the **optimal forecast**—is 40 minutes.

If the only information available to Joe before he leaves for work that would have a potential effect on his driving time is that he is leaving during the rush hour, what does rational expectations theory allow you to predict about Joe's expectations of his driving time? Since the best guess of his driving time using all available information is 40 minutes, Joe's expectation should also be the same. Clearly, an expectation of 35 minutes would not be rational because it is not equal to the optimal forecast, the best guess of the driving time.

Suppose that the next day, given the same conditions and the same expectations, it takes Joe 45 minutes to drive because he hits an abnormally large number of red lights, and the day after that he hits all the lights right and it takes him only 35 minutes. Do these variations mean that Joe's 40-minute expectation is irrational? No, an expectation of 40 minutes' driving time is still a rational expectation. In both cases, the forecast is off by 5 minutes, so the expectation has not been perfectly accurate. However, the forecast does not have to be perfectly accurate to be rational—it need only be the *best possible* given the available information; that is, it has to be correct *on average*, and the 40-minute expectation meets this requirement. Since there is bound to be some randomness in Joe's driving time regardless of driving conditions, an optimal forecast will never be completely accurate.

The example makes the following important point about rational expectations: *Even though a rational expectation equals the optimal forecast using all available information, a prediction based on it may not always be perfectly accurate.*

What if an item of information relevant to predicting driving time is unavailable or ignored? Suppose that on Joe's usual route to work there is an accident that causes a two-hour traffic jam. If Joe has no way of ascertaining this information, his rush-hour expectation of 40 minutes' driving time is still rational because the accident information is not available to him for incorporation into his optimal

---

[2]John Muth, "Rational Expectations and the Theory of Price Movements," *Econometrica* 29 (1961): 315–335.

forecast. However, if there was a radio or TV traffic report about the accident that Joe did not bother to listen to or heard but ignored, his 40-minute expectation is no longer rational. In light of the availability of this information, Joe's optimal forecast should have been two hours and 40 minutes.

Accordingly, there are two reasons why an expectation may fail to be rational:

1. People might be aware of all available information but find it takes too much effort to make their expectation the best guess possible.
2. People might be unaware of some available relevant information, so their best guess of the future will not be accurate.

Nonetheless, it is important to recognize that if an additional factor is important but information about it is not available, an expectation that does not take account of it can still be rational.

Formal Statement of the Theory

We can state the theory of rational expectations somewhat more formally. If X stands for the variable that is being forecast (in our example, Joe Commuter's driving time), X^e for the expectation of this variable (Joe's expectation of his driving time), and X^{of} for the optimal forecast of X using all available information (the best guess possible of his driving time), the theory of rational expectations then simply says

$$X^e = X^{of} \tag{1}$$

That is, the expectation of X equals the optimal forecast using all available information.

Rationale Behind the Theory

Why do people try to make their expectations match their best possible guess of the future using all available information? The simplest explanation is that it is costly for people not to do so. Joe Commuter has a strong incentive to make his expectation of the time it takes him to drive to work as accurate as possible. If he underpredicts his driving time, he will often be late to work and risk being fired. If he overpredicts, he will, on average, get to work too early and will have given up sleep or leisure time unnecessarily. Accurate expectations are desirable, and there are strong incentives for people to try to make them equal to optimal forecasts by using all available information.

The same principle applies to businesses. Suppose that an appliance manufacturer, say, General Electric, knows that interest-rate movements are important to the sales of appliances. If GE makes poor forecasts of interest rates, it will earn less profit because it might either produce too many appliances or too few. There are strong incentives for GE to acquire all available information to help it forecast interest rates and use the information to make the best possible guess of future interest-rate movements.

The incentives for equating expectations with optimal forecasts are especially strong in financial markets. In these markets, people with better forecasts of the future get rich. The application of the theory of rational expectations to financial markets (where it is called **efficient markets theory**) is thus particularly useful.

Implications of the Theory

Rational expectations theory leads to two commonsense implications for the forming of expectations that are important in the analysis of the aggregate economy.

    1. If there is a change in the way a variable moves, the way in which expectations of this variable are formed will change as well. This tenet of rational expectations theory can be most easily understood through a concrete example. Suppose that Keynes was correct in believing that interest rates move in such a way that they tend to return to a "normal" level in the future (Chapter 21). If today's interest rate is high relative to the normal level, an optimal forecast of the interest rate in the future is that it will decline to the normal level. Rational expectations theory would imply that when today's interest rate is high, the expectation is that it will fall in the future.

    Suppose now that the way in which the interest rate moves changes so that when the interest rate is high, it stays high. In this case, when today's interest rate is high, the optimal forecast of the future interest rate, and hence the rational expectation, is that it will stay high. Expectations of the future interest rate will no longer indicate that the interest rate will fall. The change in the way the interest-rate variable moves has therefore led to a change in the way that expectations of future interest rates are formed. The rational expectations analysis here is generalizable to expectations of any variable. Hence when there is a change in the way any variable moves, the way in which expectations of this variable are formed will change too.

    2. The forecast errors of expectations will on average be zero and cannot be predicted ahead of time. The forecast error of an expectation is $X - X^e$, the difference between the realization of a variable X and the expectation of the variable; that is, if Joe Commuter's driving time on a particular day is 45 minutes and his expectation of the driving time is 40 minutes, the forecast error is 5 minutes.

    Suppose that in violation of the rational expectations tenet, Joe's forecast error is not, on average, equal to zero; instead, it equals 5 minutes. The forecast error is now predictable ahead of time because Joe will soon notice that he is, on average, 5 minutes late for work and can improve his forecast by increasing it by 5 minutes. Rational expectations theory implies that this is exactly what Joe will do because he will want his forecast to be the best guess possible. When Joe has revised his forecast upward by 5 minutes, on average, the forecast error will equal zero so that it cannot be predicted ahead of time. Rational expectations theory implies that forecast errors of expectations cannot be predicted.

EFFICIENT MARKETS THEORY: RATIONAL EXPECTATIONS IN FINANCIAL MARKETS

While the theory of rational expectations was being developed by monetary economists, financial economists were developing a parallel theory of expectation formation in financial markets. It led them to the same conclusion as the rational expectations theorists: Expectations in financial markets are equal to optimal forecasts using all available information.[3] Although financial economists gave their theory another name, calling it the *theory of efficient capital markets* or *efficient markets theory,* in fact their theory is just an application of rational expectations to the pricing of securities.

Efficient markets theory is based on the assumption that prices of securities in financial markets fully reflect all available information. You may recall from Chapter 4 that the rate of return from holding a security equals the sum of the capital gain on the security (the change in the price) plus any cash payments, divided by the initial purchase price of the security:

$$RET = \frac{P_{t+1} - P_t + C}{P_t} \tag{2}$$

where RET = rate of return on the security held from time t to $t + 1$ (say, the end of 1997 to the end of 1998)

P_{t+1} = price of the security at time $t + 1$, the end of the holding period

P_t = price of the security at time t, the beginning of the holding period

C = cash payment (coupon or dividend payments) made in the period t to $t + 1$

Let's look at the expectation of this return at time t, the beginning of the holding period. Because the current price P_t and the cash payment C are known at the beginning, the only variable in the definition of the return that is uncertain is the price next period P_{t+1}.[4] Denoting the expectation of the security's price at the end of the holding period as P_{t+1}^e, the expected return RET^e is

$$RET^e = \frac{P_{t+1}^e - P_t + C}{P_t}$$

Efficient markets theory also views expectations of future prices as equal to optimal forecasts using all currently available information. In other words, the market's expectations of future securities prices are rational, so that

$$P_{t+1}^e = P_{t+1}^{of}$$

which in turn implies that the expected return on the security will equal the optimal forecast of the return:

$$RET^e = RET^{of} \tag{3}$$

Unfortunately, we cannot observe either RET^e or P_{t+1}^e, so the rational expectations equations by themselves do not tell us much about how the financial market behaves. However, if we can devise some way to measure the value of RET^e, these equations will have important implications for how prices of securities change in financial markets.

---

[3]The development of efficient markets theory was not wholly independent of the development of rational expectations theory in that financial economists were aware of Muth's work.

[4]There are cases where C might not be known at the beginning of the period, but that does not make a substantial difference to the analysis. We would in that case assume that not only price expectations but also the expectations of C are optimal forecasts using all available information.

The supply and demand analysis of the bond market developed in Chapter 6 shows us that the expected return on a security (the interest rate in the case of the bond examined) will have a tendency to head toward the equilibrium return that equates the quantity demanded to the quantity supplied. Supply and demand analysis enables us to determine the expected return on a security with the following equilibrium condition: The expected return on a security RET^e equals the equilibrium return RET^*, which equates the quantity of the security demanded to the quantity supplied; that is,

$$RET^e = RET^* \tag{4}$$

The academic field of finance explores the factors (risk and liquidity, for example) that influence the equilibrium returns on securities. For our purposes, it is sufficient to know that we can determine the equilibrium return and thus determine the expected return with the equilibrium condition.

We can derive an equation to describe pricing behavior in an efficient market by using the equilibrium condition to replace RET^e with RET^* in the rational expectations equation (Equation 3). In this way we obtain

$$RET^{of} = RET^* \tag{5}$$

This equation tells us that ***current prices in a financial market will be set so that the optimal forecast of a security's return using all available information equals the security's equilibrium return.*** Financial economists state it more simply: A security's price fully reflects all available information in an efficient market.

Rationale Behind the Theory

Let's see what the efficient markets condition means in practice and why it is a sensible characterization of pricing behavior. Suppose that the equilibrium return on a security, say, Exxon common stock, is 10 percent at an annual rate, and its current price P_t is lower than the optimal forecast of tomorrow's price P^{of}_{t+1} so that the optimal forecast of the return at an annual rate is 50 percent, which is greater than the equilibrium return of 10 percent. We are now able to predict that, on average, Exxon's return would be abnormally high. This situation is called an **unexploited profit opportunity** because, on average, people would be earning more than they should, given the characteristics of that security. Knowing that, on average, you can earn such an abnormally high rate of return on Exxon because $RET^{of} > RET^*$, you would buy more, which would in turn drive up its current price P_t relative to the expected future price P^{of}_{t+1}, thereby lowering RET^{of}. When the current price had risen sufficiently so that RET^{of} equals RET^* and the efficient markets condition (Equation 5) is satisfied, the buying of Exxon will stop, and the unexploited profit opportunity will have disappeared.

Similarly, a security for which the optimal forecast of the return is -5 percent while the equilibrium return is 10 percent ($RET^{of} < RET^*$) would be a poor investment because, on average, it earns less than the equilibrium return. In such a case, you would sell the security and drive down its current price relative to the expected future price until RET^{of} rose to the level of RET^* and the efficient markets condition is again satisfied. What we have shown can be summarized as follows:

$$RET^{of} > RET^* \rightarrow P_t\uparrow \rightarrow RET^{of}\downarrow$$
$$RET^{of} < RET^* \rightarrow P_t\downarrow \rightarrow RET^{of}\uparrow$$
$$\text{until}$$
$$RET^{of} = RET^*$$

Another way to state the efficient markets condition is this: ***In an efficient market, all unexploited profit opportunities will be eliminated.***

An extremely important factor in this reasoning is that ***not everyone in a financial market must be well informed about a security or have rational expectations for its price to be driven to the point at which the efficient markets condition holds.*** Financial markets are structured so that many participants can play. As long as a few keep their eyes open for unexploited profit opportunities, they will eliminate the profit opportunities that appear because in so doing, they make a profit. The theory of efficient markets makes sense because it does not require everyone in a market to be cognizant of what is happening to every security.

Stronger Version of Efficient Markets Theory

Many financial economists take efficient markets theory one step further in their analysis of financial markets. Not only do they define efficient markets as those in which expectations are rational, that is, equal to optimal forecasts using all available information, but they also add the condition that an efficient market is one in which prices reflect the true fundamental (intrinsic) value of the securities. Thus in an efficient market, all prices are always correct and reflect **market fundamentals** (items that have a direct impact on future income streams of the securities). This stronger view of market efficiency has several important implications in the academic field of finance. First, it implies that in an efficient capital market, one investment is as good as any other because the securities' prices are correct. Second, it implies that a security's price reflects all available information about the intrinsic value of the security. Third, it implies that security prices can be used by managers of both financial and nonfinancial firms to assess their cost of capital (cost of financing their investments) accurately and hence that security prices can be used to help them make the correct decisions about whether a specific investment is worth making or not. The stronger version of market efficiency is a basic tenet of much analysis in the finance field.

EVIDENCE ON EFFICIENT MARKETS THEORY

Early evidence on efficient markets theory was quite favorable to it, but in recent years, deeper analysis of the evidence suggests that the theory may not always be entirely correct. Let's first look at the earlier evidence in favor of the theory and then examine some of the more recent evidence that casts some doubt on it.

Evidence in Favor of Market Efficiency

Evidence in favor of market efficiency has examined the performance of investment analysts and mutual funds, whether stock prices reflect publicly available information, the random-walk behavior of stock prices, and the success of so-called technical analysis.

PERFORMANCE OF INVESTMENT ANALYSTS AND MUTUAL FUNDS We have seen that one implication of efficient markets theory is that when purchasing a security, you cannot expect to earn an abnormally high return, a return greater than the equilibrium return. This implies that it is impossible to beat the market. Many studies shed light on whether investment advisers and mutual funds (some of which charge steep sales commissions to people who purchase them) beat the market. One common test that has been performed is to take buy and sell recommendations from a group of advisers or mutual funds and compare the performance of the resulting selection of stocks with the market as a whole. Sometimes the advisers' choices have even been compared to a group of stocks chosen by putting a copy of the financial page of the newspaper on a dartboard and throwing darts. The *Wall Street Journal,* for example, has a regular feature called "Investment Dartboard" that compares how well stocks picked by investment advisers do relative to stocks picked by throwing darts. Do the advisers win? To their embarrassment, the dartboard beats them as often as they beat the dartboard. Furthermore, even when the comparison includes only advisers who have been successful in the past in predicting the stock market, the advisers still don't regularly beat the dartboard.

In studies of mutual fund performance, mutual funds are separated into groups according to whether they had the highest or lowest profits in a chosen period. When their performance is compared to a subsequent period, the mutual funds that did well in the first period do not beat the market in the second.[5]

The conclusion from the study of investment advisers and mutual fund performance is this: ***Having performed well in the past does not indicate that an investment adviser or a mutual fund will perform well in the future.*** This is not pleasing news to investment advisers, but it is exactly what the theory of efficient markets predicts. It says that some advisers will be lucky and some will be unlucky. Being lucky does not mean that a forecaster actually has the ability to beat the market. (An exception that proves the rule is discussed in Box 1.)

DO STOCK PRICES REFLECT PUBLICLY AVAILABLE INFORMATION? Efficient markets theory predicts that stock prices will reflect all publicly available information. Thus if information is already publicly available, a positive announcement about a company will not, on average, raise the price of its stock because this information is already reflected in the stock price. Early empirical evidence also confirmed this conjecture from efficient markets theory: Favorable earnings announcements or announcements of stock splits (a division of a share of stock

---

[5]An early study that found that mutual funds do not outperform the market is Michael C. Jensen, "The Performance of Mutual Funds in the Period 1945–64," *Journal of Finance* 23 (1968): 389–416. More recent studies on mutual fund performance are Mark Grimblatt and Sheridan Titman, "Mutual Fund Performance: An Analysis of Quarterly Portfolio Holdings," *Journal of Business* 62 (1989): 393–416, and R. A. Ippolito, "Efficiency with Costly Information: A Study of Mutual Fund Performance, 1965–84," *Quarterly Journal of Economics* 104 (1989): 1–23.

BOX 1

An Exception That Proves the Rule

Ivan Boesky. Efficient markets theory indicates that investment advisers should not have the ability to beat the market. Yet that is exactly what Ivan Boesky was able to do until 1986, when he was charged by the Securities and Exchange Commission with making unfair profits (rumored to be in the hundreds of millions of dollars) by trading on inside information. In an out-of-court settlement, Boesky was banned from the securities business, fined $100 million, and sentenced to three years in jail. (After serving his sentence, Boesky was released from jail in 1990.) If the stock market is efficient, can the SEC legitimately claim that Boesky was able to beat the market? The answer is yes.

Ivan Boesky was the most successful of the so-called *arbs* (short for *arbitrageurs*) who made hundreds of millions in profits for himself and his clients by investing in the stocks of firms that were about to be taken

over by other firms at an above-market price. Boesky's continuing success was assured by an arrangement whereby he paid cash (sometimes in a suitcase) to Dennis Levine, an investment banker who had inside information about when a takeover was to take place because his firm was arranging the financing of the deal. When Levine found out that a firm was planning a takeover, he would inform Boesky, who would then buy the stock of the company being taken over and sell it after the stock had risen.

Boesky's ability to make millions year after year in the 1980s is an exception that proves the rule that financial analysts cannot continually outperform the market; yet it supports the efficient markets claim that only information *unavailable to the market* enables an investor to do so. Boesky profited from knowing about takeovers before the rest of the market; this information was known to him but unavailable to the market.

into multiple shares, which is usually followed by higher earnings) do not, on average, cause stock prices to rise.[6]

RANDOM-WALK BEHAVIOR OF STOCK PRICES The term **random walk** describes the movements of a variable whose future changes cannot be predicted (are random) because, given today's value, the variable is just as likely to fall as to rise. An important implication of efficient markets theory is that stock prices should approximately follow a random walk; that is, ***future changes in stock prices should, for all practical purposes, be unpredictable.*** The random-walk implication of efficient markets theory is the one most commonly mentioned in the press because it is the most readily comprehensible to the public. In fact, when people mention the "random-walk theory of stock prices," they are in reality referring to efficient markets theory.

The case for random-walk stock prices can be demonstrated. Suppose that people could predict that the price of Happy Feet Corporation (HFC) stock would rise 1 percent in the coming week. The predicted rate of capital gains and rate

---

[6]Ray Ball and Philip Brown, "An Empirical Evaluation of Accounting Income Numbers," *Journal of Accounting Research* 6, (1968):159–178, and Eugene F. Fama, Lawrence Fisher, Michael C. Jensen, and Richard Roll, "The Adjustment of Stock Prices to New Information," *International Economic Review*, 10 (1969): 1–21.

of return on HFC stock would then be over 50 percent at an annual rate. Since this is very likely to be far higher than the equilibrium rate of return on HFC stock ($RET^{of} > RET^*$), the theory of efficient markets indicates that people would immediately buy this stock and bid up its current price. The action would stop only when the predictable change in the price dropped to near zero so that $RET^{of} = RET^*$.

Similarly, if people could predict that the price of HFC stock would fall by 1 percent, the predicted rate of return would be negative ($RET^{of} < RET^*$), and people would immediately sell. The current price would fall until the predictable change in the price rose back to near zero, where the efficient markets condition again holds. Efficient markets theory suggests that the predictable change in stock prices will be near zero, leading to the conclusion that stock prices will generally follow a random walk.[7]

Financial economists have used two types of tests to explore the hypothesis that stock prices follow a random walk. In the first, they examine stock market records to see if changes in stock prices are systematically related to past changes and hence could have been predicted on that basis. The second type of test examines the data to see if publicly available information other than past stock prices could have been used to predict changes. These tests are somewhat more stringent because additional information (money supply growth, government spending, interest rates, corporate profits) might be used to help forecast stock returns. Early results from both types of tests generally confirmed the efficient markets view that stock prices are not predictable and follow a random walk.[8]

TECHNICAL ANALYSIS A popular technique used to predict stock prices, called *technical analysis*, is to study past stock price data and search for patterns such as trends and regular cycles. Rules for when to buy and sell stocks are then established on the basis of the patterns that emerge. The theory of efficient markets suggests that technical analysis is a waste of time. The simplest way to understand why is to use the random-walk result derived from efficient markets theory that holds that past stock price data cannot help predict changes. Therefore, technical analysis, which relies on such data to produce its forecasts, cannot successfully predict changes in stock prices.

---

[7]Note that the random-walk behavior of stock prices is only an *approximation* derived from efficient markets theory. It would hold exactly only for a stock for which an unchanged price leads to its having the equilibrium return. Then, when the predictable change in the stock price is exactly zero, $RET^{of} = RET^*$.

[8]The first type of test, using only stock market data, is referred to as a test of *weak-form efficiency* because the information that can be used to predict stock prices is restricted solely to past price data. The second type of test is referred to as a test of *semistrong-form efficiency* because the information set is expanded to include all publicly available information, not just past stock prices. A third type of test is called a test of *strong-form efficiency* because the information set includes insider information, known only to the owners of the corporation, as when they plan to declare a high dividend. Strong-form tests do sometimes indicate that insider information can be used to predict changes in stock prices. This finding does not contradict efficient markets theory because the information is not available to the market and hence cannot be reflected in market prices. In fact, there are strict laws against using insider information to trade in financial markets. For an early survey on the three forms of tests, see Eugene F. Fama, "Efficient Capital Markets: A Review of Theory and Empirical Work," *Journal of Finance* 25 (1970): 383–416.

Two types of tests bear directly on the value of technical analysis. The first performs the empirical analysis described earlier to evaluate the performance of any financial analyst, technical or otherwise. The results are exactly what efficient markets theory predicts: Technical analysts fare no better than other financial analysts; on average, they do not outperform the market, and successful past forecasting does not imply that their forecasts will outperform the market in the future. The second type of test (first performed by Sidney Alexander) takes the rules developed in technical analysis for when to buy and sell stocks and applies them to new data.[9] The performance of these rules is then evaluated by the profits that would have been made using them. These tests also discredit technical analysis: It does not outperform the overall market.

Should Foreign Exchange Rates Follow a Random Walk?

Efficient markets theory can be used to show that foreign exchange rates, like stock prices, should generally follow a random walk. To see why this is the case, consider what would happen if people could predict that a currency would appreciate by 1 percent in the coming week. By buying this currency, they could earn a greater than 50 percent return at an annual rate, which is likely to be far above the equilibrium return for holding a currency. As a result, people would immediately buy the currency and bid up its current price, thereby reducing the expected return. The process would stop only when the predictable change in the exchange rate dropped to near zero so that the optimal forecast of the return no longer differed from the equilibrium return. Likewise, if people could predict that the currency would depreciate by 1 percent in the coming week, they would sell it until the predictable change in the exchange rate was again near zero. Efficient markets theory therefore implies that future changes in exchange rates should, for all practical purposes, be unpredictable; in other words, exchange rates should follow random walks. This is exactly what empirical evidence finds.[10] Ⓐ

Evidence Against Market Efficiency

All the early evidence supporting efficient markets theory appeared to be overwhelming, causing Eugene Fama, a prominent financial economist, to state in his famous 1970 survey of the empirical evidence on efficient markets theory, "The evidence in support of the efficient markets model is extensive, and (somewhat uniquely in economics) contradictory evidence is sparse."[11] However, in recent

---

[9]Sidney Alexander, "Price Movements in Speculative Markets: Trends or Random Walks?" *Industrial Management Review,* May 1961, pp. 7–26, and Sidney Alexander, "Price Movements in Speculative Markets: Trends or Random Walks? No. 2," in *The Random Character of Stock Prices,* ed. Paul Cootner (Cambridge, Mass.: MIT Press, 1964), pp. 338–372.

[10]See Richard A. Meese and Kenneth Rogoff, "Empirical Exchange Rate Models of the Seventies: Do They Fit out of Sample?" *Journal of International Economics* 14 (1983): 3–24.

[11]Eugene F. Fama, "Efficient Capital Markets: A Review of Theory and Empirical Work," *Journal of Finance* 25 (1970): 383–416.

years, the theory has begun to show a few cracks, referred to as *anomalies*, and empirical evidence indicates that efficient markets theory may not always be generally applicable.

SMALL-FIRM EFFECT One of the earliest reported anomalies in which the stock market did not appear to be efficient is called the *small-firm effect*. Many empirical studies have shown that small firms have earned abnormally high returns over long periods of time, even when the greater risk for these firms has been taken into account.[12] The small-firm effect seems to have diminished in recent years but is still a challenge to the theory of efficient markets. Various theories have been developed to explain the small-firm effect, suggesting that it may be due to rebalancing of portfolios by institutional investors, tax issues, low liquidity of small-firm stocks, large information costs in evaluating small firms, or an inappropriate measurement of risk for small-firm stocks.

JANUARY EFFECT Over long periods of time, stock prices have tended to experience an abnormal price rise from December to January that is predictable and hence inconsistent with random-walk behavior. This so-called **January effect** seems to have diminished in recent years for shares of large companies but still occurs for shares of small companies.[13] Some financial economists argue that the January effect is due to tax issues. Investors have an incentive to sell stocks before the end of the year in December because they can then take capital losses on their tax return and reduce their tax liability. Then when the new year starts in January, they can repurchase the stocks, driving up their prices and producing abnormally high returns. Although this explanation seems sensible, it does not explain why institutional investors such as private pension funds, which are not subject to income taxes, do not take advantage of the abnormal returns in January and buy stocks in December, thus bidding up their price and eliminating the abnormal returns.[14]

MARKET OVERREACTION Recent research suggests that stock prices may overreact to news announcements and that the pricing errors are corrected only slowly.[15] When corporations announce a major change in earnings, say, a large decline, the stock price may overshoot, and after an initial large decline, it may

---

[12]For example, see Marc R. Reinganum, "The Anomalous Stock Market Behavior of Small Firms in January: Empirical Tests of Tax Loss Selling Effects," *Journal of Financial Economics* 12 (1983): 89–104; Jay R. Ritter, "The Buying and Selling Behavior of Individual Investors at the Turn of the Year," *Journal of Finance* 43, (1988): 701–717; and Richard Roll, "Vas Ist Das? The Turn-of-the-Year Effect: Anomaly or Risk Mismeasurement?" *Journal of Portfolio Management* 9 (1988): 18–28.

[13]For example, see Donald B. Keim, "The CAPM and Equity Return Regularities," *Financial Analysts Journal* 42 (May-June 1986): 19–34.

[14]Another anomaly that makes the stock market seem less than efficient is the fact that the *Value Line Survey*, one of the most prominent investment advice newsletters, has produced stock recommendations that have yielded abnormally high returns on average. See Fischer Black, "Yes, Virginia, There Is Hope: Tests of the Value Line Ranking System," *Financial Analysts Journal* 29 (September-October 1973): 10–14, and Gur Huberman and Shmuel Kandel, "Market Efficiency and Value Line's Record," *Journal of Business* 63 (1990): 187–216. Whether the excellent performance of the *Value Line Survey* will continue in the future is, of course, a question mark.

[15]Werner De Bondt and Richard Thaler, "Further Evidence on Investor Overreaction and Stock Market Seasonality," *Journal of Finance* 62 (1987): 557–580.

rise back to more normal levels over a period of several weeks. This violates efficient markets theory because an investor could earn abnormally high returns, on average, by buying a stock immediately after a poor earnings announcement and then selling it after a couple of weeks when it has risen back to normal levels.

EXCESSIVE VOLATILITY   A closely related phenomenon to market overreaction is that the stock market appears to display excessive volatility; that is, fluctuations in stock prices may be much greater than is warranted by fluctuations in their fundamental value. In an important paper, Robert Shiller of Yale University found that fluctuations in the S&P 500 stock index could not be justified by the subsequent fluctuations in the dividends of the stocks making up this index. There has been much subsequent technical work criticizing these results, but Shiller's work, along with research that finds that there are smaller fluctuations in stock prices when stock markets are closed, has produced a consensus that stock market prices appear to be driven by factors other than fundamentals.[16]

MEAN REVERSION   Some researchers have also found that stock returns display **mean reversion:** Stocks with low returns today tend to have high returns in the future, and vice versa. Hence stocks that have done poorly in the past are more likely to do well in the future because mean reversion indicates that there will be a predictable positive change in the future price, suggesting that stock prices are not a random walk. Other researchers have found that mean reversion is not nearly as strong in data after World War II and so have raised doubts about whether it is currently an important phenomenon. The evidence on mean reversion remains controversial.[17]

Overview of the Evidence on Efficient Markets Theory

As you can see, the debate on efficient markets theory is far from over. The evidence seems to suggest that efficient markets theory may be a reasonable starting point for evaluating behavior in financial markets. However, there do seem to be important violations of market efficiency that suggest that efficient markets theory may not be the whole story and so may not be generalizable to all behavior in financial markets.

---

[16]Robert Shiller, "Do Stock Prices Move Too Much to Be Justified by Subsequent Changes in Dividends?" *American Economic Review* 71 (1981): 421–436, and Kenneth R. French and Richard Roll, "Stock Return Variances: The Arrival of Information and the Reaction of Traders," *Journal of Financial Economics* 17 (1986): 5–26.

[17]Evidence for mean reversion has been reported by James M. Poterba and Lawrence H. Summers, "Mean Reversion in Stock Prices: Evidence and Implications," *Journal of Financial Economics* 22 (1988): 27–59; Eugene F. Fama and Kenneth R. French, "Permanent and Temporary Components of Stock Prices," *Journal of Political Economy* 96 (1988): 246–273; and Andrew W. Lo and A. Craig MacKinlay, "Stock Market Prices Do Not Follow Random Walks: Evidence from a Simple Specification Test," *Review of Financial Studies* 1 (1988): 41–66. However, Myung Jig Kim, Charles R. Nelson, and Richard Startz, in "Mean Reversion in Stock Prices? A Reappraisal of the Evidence," *Review of Economic Studies* 58 (1991): 515–528, question whether some of these findings are valid. For an excellent summary of this evidence, see Charles Engel and Charles S. Morris, "Challenges to Stock Market Efficiency: Evidence from Mean Reversion Studies," *Federal Reserve Bank of Kansas City Economic Review*, September-October 1991, pp. 21–35. See also N. Jegadeesh and Sheridan Titman, "Returns to Buying Winners and Selling Losers: Implications for Stock Market Efficiency," *Journal of Finance* 48 (1993): 65–92, which shows that mean reversion also occurs for individual stocks.

Practical Guide to Investing in the Stock Market

Efficient markets theory has numerous applications to the real world. It is especially valuable because it can be applied directly to an issue that concerns many of us: how to get rich (or at least not get poor) in the stock market. (The "Following the Financial News" box shows how stock prices are reported daily.) A practical guide to investing in the stock market, which we develop here, provides a better understanding of the use and implications of efficient markets theory.

How Valuable Are Published Reports by Investment Advisers?

Suppose that you have just read in the "Heard on the Street" column of the *Wall Street Journal* that investment advisers are predicting a boom in oil stocks because an oil shortage is developing. Should you proceed to withdraw all your hard-earned savings from the bank and invest it in oil stocks?

Efficient markets theory tells us that when purchasing a security, we cannot expect to earn an abnormally high return, a return greater than the equilibrium return. Information in newspapers and in the published reports of investment advisers is readily available to many market participants and is already reflected in market prices. So acting on this information will not yield abnormally high returns, on average. As we have seen, the empirical evidence for the most part confirms that recommendations from investment advisers cannot help us outperform the general market. Indeed, as Box 2 suggests, human investment advisers in San Francisco do not on average even outperform an orangutan!

Probably no other conclusion is met with more skepticism by students than this one when they first hear it. We all know or have heard of somebody who has been successful in the stock market for a period of many years. We wonder, how could someone be so consistently successful if he or she did not really know how to predict when returns would be abnormally high? The following story, reported in the press, illustrates why such anecdotal evidence is not reliable.

A get-rich-quick artist invented a clever scam. Every week, he wrote two letters. In letter A, he would pick team A to win a particular football game, and in letter B, he would pick the opponent, team B. A mailing list would then be separated into two groups, and he would send letter A to the people in one group and letter B to the people in the other. The following week he would do the same thing but would send these letters only to the group who had received the first letter with the correct prediction. After doing this for ten games, he had a small cluster of people who had received letters predicting the correct winning team for every game. He then mailed a final letter to them, declaring that since he was obviously an expert predictor of the outcome of football games (he had picked winners ten weeks in a row) and since his predictions were profitable for the recipients who bet on the games, he would continue to send his predictions only if he were paid a substantial amount of money. When one of his clients figured out what he was up to, the con man was prosecuted and thrown in jail!

Following the Financial News

Stock Prices

Stock prices are published daily, and in the *Wall Street Journal* they are reported in the sections "NYSE—Composite Transactions," "Amex—Composite Transactions," and "Over-the-Counter Markets." The New York Stock Exchange (NYSE) and American Stock Exchange (Amex) stocks' prices are quoted in the following format:

52 Weeks		Stock	Sym	Div	Yld %	PE	Vol 100s	Hi	Lo	Close	Net Chg
Hi	**Lo**										
31	24	IntAlum	IAL	1.00	3.7	17	52	$27\frac{1}{8}$	27	$27\frac{1}{8}$	$-\frac{1}{8}$
$170\frac{1}{8}$	$89\frac{1}{8}$	IBM	IBM	1.40	.9	15	45740	$158\frac{1}{4}$	$155\frac{3}{4}$	$157\frac{1}{4}$	$+\frac{7}{8}$
$27\frac{1}{2}$	$25\frac{1}{2}$	IBM dep pf		1.88	7.1	...	372	$26\frac{5}{8}$	$26\frac{3}{8}$	$26\frac{5}{8}$	$+\frac{1}{4}$
$19\frac{1}{8}$	$12\frac{7}{8}$	IntFamEntn B	FAM		...	42	328	18	$17\frac{5}{8}$	18	$+\frac{1}{8}$
$4\frac{1}{4}$	$3\frac{3}{8}$	IntFinBear wt			...	...	83	$3\frac{1}{2}$	$3\frac{1}{4}$	$3\frac{1}{2}$	...

Source: Wall Street Journal, January 30, 1997, p. C5.

The following information is included in each column. International Business Machines (IBM) common stock is used as an example.

52 Weeks Hi: Highest price of a share in the past 52 weeks: $170\frac{1}{8}$ for IBM stock

52 Weeks Lo: Lowest price of a share in the past 52 weeks: $89\frac{1}{8}$ for IBM stock

Stock: Company name: IBM for International Business Machines

Sym: Symbol that identifies company: IBM

Div: Annual dividends: $1.40 for IBM

Yld %: Yield for stock expressed as annual dividends divided by today's closing price: 0.9% (= 1.40 ÷ $157\frac{1}{4}$) for IBM stock

PE: Price-earnings ratio; the stock price divided by the annual earnings per share: 15.

Vol 100s: Number of shares (in hundreds) traded that day: 4,574,000 shares for IBM

Hi: Highest price of a share that day: $158\frac{1}{4}$

Lo: Lowest price of a share that day: $155\frac{3}{4}$

Close: Closing price (last price) that day: $157\frac{1}{4}$

Net Chg: Change in the closing price from the previous day: $+\frac{7}{8}$

Prices quoted for shares traded over-the-counter (through dealers rather than on an organized exchange) are sometimes quoted with the same information, but in many cases only the bid price (the price the dealer is willing to pay for the stock) and the asked price (the price the dealer is willing to sell the stock for) are quoted.

What is the lesson of the story? Even if no forecaster is an accurate predictor of the market, there will always be a group of consistent winners. A person who has done well regularly in the past cannot guarantee that he or she will do well in the future. Note that there will also be a group of persistent losers, but you rarely hear about them because no one brags about a poor forecasting record.

BOX 2

Should You Hire an Ape as Your Investment Adviser?

The *San Francisco Chronicle* has come up with an amusing way of evaluating how successful investment advisers are at picking stocks. They ask eight analysts to pick five stocks at the beginning of the year and then compare the performance of their stock picks to those chosen by Jolyn, an orangutan living at Marine World/Africa USA in Vallejo, California. Consistent with the results found in the "Investment Dartboard" feature of the *Wall Street Journal,* Jolyn beats the investment advisers as often as they beat her. Given this result, you might be just as well off hiring an orangutan as your investment adviser as you would hiring a human being!

Should You Be Skeptical of Hot Tips?

Suppose that your broker phones you with a hot tip to buy stock in the Happy Feet Corporation (HFC) because it has just developed a product that is completely effective in curing athlete's foot. The stock price is sure to go up. Should you follow this advice and buy HFC stock?

Efficient markets theory indicates that you should be skeptical of such news. If the stock market is efficient, it has already priced HFC stock so that its expected return will equal the equilibrium return. The hot tip is not particularly valuable and will not enable you to earn an abnormally high return.

You might wonder, though, if the hot tip is based on new information and would give you an edge on the rest of the market. If other market participants have gotten this information before you, the answer is no. As soon as the information hits the street, the unexploited profit opportunity it creates will be quickly eliminated. The stock's price will already reflect the information, and you should expect to realize only the equilibrium return. But if you are one of the first to know the new information (as Ivan Boesky was—see Box 1), it can do you some good. Only then can you be one of the lucky ones who, on average, will earn an abnormally high return by helping eliminate the profit opportunity by buying HFC stock.

Do Stock Prices Always Rise When There Is Good News?

If you follow the stock market, you might have noticed a puzzling phenomenon: When good news about a stock, such as a particularly favorable earnings report, is announced, the price of the stock frequently does not rise. Efficient markets theory and the random-walk behavior of stock prices explain this phenomenon.

Because changes in stock prices are unpredictable, when information is announced that has already been expected by the market, the stock price will remain unchanged. The announcement does not contain any new information that should lead to a change in stock prices. If this were not the case and the announcement led to a change in stock prices, it would mean that the change was predictable. Because that is ruled out in an efficient market, **stock prices will respond to announcements only when the information being announced is**

new and unexpected. If the news is expected, there will be no stock price response. This is exactly what the evidence we described earlier, which shows that stock prices reflect publicly available information, suggests will occur.

Sometimes a stock price declines when good news is announced. Although this seems somewhat peculiar, it is completely consistent with the workings of an efficient market. Suppose that although the announced news is good, it is not as good as expected. HFC's earnings may have risen 15 percent, but if the market expected earnings to rise by 20 percent, the new information is actually unfavorable, and the stock price declines.

Efficient Markets Prescription for the Investor

What does the theory of efficient markets recommend for investing in the stock market? It tells us that hot tips, investment advisers' published recommendations, and technical analysis—all of which make use of publicly available information—cannot help an investor outperform the market. Indeed, it indicates that anyone without better information than other market participants cannot expect to beat the market. So what is an investor to do?

Efficient markets theory leads to the conclusion that such an investor (and almost all of us fit into this category) should not try to outguess the market by constantly buying and selling securities. This process does nothing but boost the income of brokers, who earn commissions on each trade.[18] Instead, the investor should pursue a "buy and hold" strategy—purchase stocks and hold them for long periods of time. This will lead to the same returns, on average, but the investor's net profits will be higher because fewer brokerage commissions will have to be paid.[19]

It is frequently a sensible strategy for a small investor, whose costs of managing a portfolio may be high relative to its size, to buy into a mutual fund rather than individual stocks. Because efficient markets theory indicates that no mutual fund can consistently outperform the market, an investor should not buy into one that has high management fees or that pays sales commissions to brokers but rather should purchase a no-load (commission-free) mutual fund that has low management fees.

As we have seen, the evidence indicates that it will not be easy to beat the prescription suggested here, although some of the anomalies to efficient markets theory suggest that an extremely clever investor (which rules out most of us) may be able to outperform a buy-and-hold strategy.

EVIDENCE ON RATIONAL EXPECTATIONS IN OTHER MARKETS

Evidence in other financial markets also supports efficient markets theory and hence the rationality of expectations. For example, there is little evidence that

---

[18]The investor may also have to pay Uncle Sam capital gains taxes on any profits that are realized when a security is sold—an additional reason why continual buying and selling does not make sense.

[19]As we saw in Chapter 5, the investor can also minimize risk by holding a diversified portfolio. The investor will be better off by pursuing a buy-and-hold strategy with a diversified portfolio or with a mutual fund that has a diversified portfolio.

financial analysts are able to outperform the bond market.[20] The returns on bonds appear to conform to the efficient markets condition of Equation 5.

Rationality of expectations is, however, much harder to test in markets other than financial markets because price data that reflect expectations are not as readily available. The most common tests of rational expectations in these markets make use of survey data on the forecasts of market participants. For example, one well-known study by James Pesando used a survey of inflation expectations collected from prominent economists and inflation forecasters.[21] In that survey, these people were asked what they predicted the inflation rate would be over the next six months and over the next year. Because rational expectations theory implies that forecast errors should on average be zero and cannot be predicted, tests of the theory involve asking whether the forecast errors in a survey could be predicted ahead of time using publicly available information. The evidence from Pesando's and subsequent studies is mixed. Sometimes the forecast errors cannot be predicted, and at other times they can. The evidence is not as supportive of rational expectations theory as the evidence from financial markets.

Does the fact that forecast errors from surveys are often predictable suggest that we should reject rational expectations theory in these other markets? The answer is not necessarily. One problem with this evidence is that the expectations data are obtained from surveys rather than from actual economic decisions of market participants. That is a serious criticism of this evidence. Survey responses are not always reliable because there is little incentive for participants to tell the truth. For example, when people are asked in surveys how much television they watch, responses greatly underestimate the actual time spent. Neither are people very truthful about the shows they watch. Often they say they watch ballet on public television. We know they are actually watching Vanna White turn letters on *Wheel of Fortune* instead, because it, not ballet, gets high Nielsen ratings. How many people will admit to being regular watchers of *Wheel of Fortune?*

A second problem with survey evidence is that a market's behavior may not be equally influenced by the expectations of all the survey participants, making survey evidence a poor guide to market behavior. For example, we have already seen that prices in financial markets often *behave* as if expectations are rational even though many of the market participants do not have rational expectations.[22] Proof is not yet conclusive on the validity of rational expectations theory in markets other than financial markets. One important conclusion, however, that is supported by the survey evidence is that *if there is a change in the way a variable moves, there will be a change in the way expectations of this variable are formed as well.*

---

[20]See the discussion in Frederic S. Mishkin, "Efficient Markets Theory: Implications for Monetary Policy," *Brookings Papers on Economic Activity* 3 (1978): 707–768, of the results in Michael J. Prell, "How Well Do the Experts Forecast Interest Rates?" *Federal Reserve Bank of Kansas City Monthly Review,* September-October 1973, pp. 3–15.

[21]James Pesando, "A Note on the Rationality of the Livingston Price Expectations," *Journal of Political Economy* 83 (1975): 845–858.

[22]There is some fairly strong evidence for this proposition. For example, Frederic S. Mishkin, "Are Market Forecasts Rational?" *American Economic Review* 71 (1981): 295–306, finds that although survey forecasts of short-term interest rates are not rational, the bond market *behaves* as if the expectations of these interest rates are rational.

What Does the Stock Market Crash of 1987 Tell Us About Rational Expectations and Efficient Markets?

Many economists have suggested that the October 19, 1987, stock market crash should make us question the validity of efficient markets and rational expectations. They do not believe that a rational marketplace could have produced such a massive swing in share prices. To what degree should the stock market crash make us doubt the validity of rational expectations and efficient markets theory?

Nothing in rational expectations theory rules out large one-day changes in stock prices. A large change in stock prices can result from new information that produces a dramatic change in optimal forecasts of the future valuation of firms. Some economists have pointed out that there are many possible explanations for why rational expectations of the future value of firms dropped dramatically on October 19, 1987: moves in Congress to restrict corporate takeovers, the disappointing performance of the trade deficit, congressional failure to reduce the budget deficit substantially, increased fears of inflation, the decline of the dollar, and increased fears of financial distress in the banking industry. Other economists doubt whether these explanations are enough to explain the stock market drop because none of these market fundamentals seems important enough.

One lesson from the Black Monday stock market crash appears to be that factors other than market fundamentals may have had an effect on stock prices. The crash of 1987 has therefore convinced many economists that the stronger version of efficient markets theory, which states that asset prices reflect the true fundamental (intrinsic) value of securities, is incorrect. They attribute a large role in determination of stock prices to market psychology and to the institutional structure of the marketplace. However, nothing in this view contradicts the basic reasoning behind rational expectations or efficient markets theory—that market participants eliminate unexploited profit opportunities. Even though stock market prices may not always solely reflect market fundamentals, this does not mean that rational expectations do not hold. As long as the stock market crash was unpredictable, the basic lessons of the theory of rational expectations hold.

Some economists have come up with theories of what they call *rational bubbles* to explain events such as the stock market crash. A **bubble** is a situation in which the price of an asset differs from its fundamental market value. In a rational bubble, investors can have rational expectations that a bubble is occurring because the asset price is above its fundamental value but continue to hold the asset anyway. They might do this because they believe that someone else will buy the asset for a higher price in the future. In a rational bubble, asset prices can therefore deviate from their fundamental value for a long time because the bursting of the bubble cannot be predicted and so there are no unexploited profit opportunities.

However, other economists believe that the stock market crash of 1987 suggests that there may be unexploited profit opportunities and that the theory of rational expectations and efficient markets theory may be fundamentally flawed. The controversy over whether capital markets are efficient or expectations are rational continues.

SUMMARY

1. Expectations are important to almost all economic behavior.
2. The theory of rational expectations states that expectations will not differ from optimal forecasts (the best guesses of the future) using all available information. Rational expectations theory makes sense because it is costly for people not to have the best forecast of the future. The theory has two important implications: (a) If there is a change in the way a variable moves, there will be a change in the way expectations of this variable are formed, too, and (b) the forecast errors of expectations are unpredictable.
3. Efficient markets theory is the application of rational expectations to the pricing of securities in financial markets. Current security prices will fully reflect all available information because in an efficient market, all unexploited profit opportunities are eliminated. The elimination of unexploited profit opportunities necessary for a financial market to be efficient does not require that all market participants be well informed and have rational expectations.
4. The evidence on efficient markets theory is quite mixed. Early evidence on the performance of investment analysts and mutual funds, whether stock prices reflect publicly available information, the random-walk behavior of stock prices, and the success of so-called technical analysis was quite favorable to efficient markets theory. However, in recent years, evidence on the small-firm effect, the January effect, the *Value Line Survey*, market overreaction, excessive volatility, and mean reversion suggests that the theory may not always be entirely correct. The evidence seems to suggest that efficient markets theory may be a reasonable starting point for evaluating behavior in financial markets but may not be generalizable to all behavior in financial markets.
5. Efficient markets theory indicates that hot tips, investment advisers' published recommendations, and technical analysis cannot help an investor outperform the market. The prescription for investors is to pursue a buy-and-hold strategy—purchase stocks and hold them for long periods of time. Empirical evidence generally supports these implications of efficient markets theory in the stock market.
6. Although the evidence supporting rational expectations in financial markets is strong, the evidence in other markets is more mixed. However, even for these other markets, there is support for the rational expectations conclusion that a change in the way a variable moves will change the way that expectations of the variable are formed.
7. The stock market crash of 1987 has convinced many economists that the stronger version of efficient markets theory, which states that asset prices reflect the true fundamental (intrinsic) value of securities, is not correct. It is less clear that the stock market crash shows that rational expectations theory is wrong. Even if the stock market was driven by factors other than fundamentals, the crash does not clearly demonstrate that expectations were not rational as long as the crash could not have been predicted.

KEY TERMS

adaptive expectations, p. 689

bubble, p. 707

efficient markets theory, p. 691

January effect, p. 700

market fundamentals, p. 695

mean reversion, p. 701

optimal forecast, p. 690

random walk, p. 697

rational expectations, p. 690

unexploited profit opportunity, p. 694

QUESTIONS AND PROBLEMS

*1. "Forecasters' predictions of inflation are notoriously inaccurate, so their expectations of inflation cannot be rational." Is this statement true, false, or uncertain? Explain your answer.

2. "Whenever it is snowing when Joe Commuter gets up in the morning, he misjudges how long it will take him to drive to work. Otherwise, his expectations of the driving time are perfectly accurate. Considering that it snows only once every ten years where Joe lives, Joe's expectations are almost always perfectly accurate." Are Joe's expectations rational? Why or why not?

*3. If a forecaster spends hours every day studying data to forecast interest rates but his expectations are not as accurate as predicting that tomorrow's interest rates will be identical to today's interest rate, are his expectations rational?

4. "If stock prices did not follow a random walk, there would be unexploited profit opportunities in the market." Is this statement true, false, or uncertain? Explain your answer.

*5. In Chapter 25 you studied why stock prices might rise when the money supply rises. Does this mean that when you see that the money supply has risen sharply in the past week, you should go out and buy stocks? Why or why not?

6. If the public expects a corporation to lose $5 a share this quarter and it actually loses $4, which is still the largest loss in the history of the company, what does efficient markets theory say will happen to the price of the stock when the $4 loss is announced?

*7. If I read in the *Wall Street Journal* that the "smart money" on Wall Street expects stock prices to fall, should I follow that lead and sell all my stocks?

8. If my broker has been right in her five previous buy and sell recommendations, should I continue listening to her advice?

*9. Can a person with rational expectations expect the price of IBM to rise by 10 percent in the next month?

10. "If most participants in the stock market do not follow what is happening to the monetary aggregates, prices of common stocks will not fully reflect information about them." Is this statement true, false, or uncertain? Explain your answer.

*11. "An efficient market is one in which no one ever profits from having better information than the rest." Is this statement true, false, or uncertain? Explain your answer.

12. If higher money growth is associated with higher future inflation and if announced money growth turns out to be extremely high but is still less than the market expected, what do you think would happen to long-term bond prices?

*13. "Foreign exchange rates, like stock prices, should follow a random walk." Is this statement true, false, or uncertain? Explain your answer.

14. Can we expect the value of the dollar to rise by 2 percent next week if our expectations are rational?

*15. "Human fear is the source of stock market crashes, so these crashes indicate that expectations in the stock market cannot be rational." Is this statement true, false, or uncertain? Explain your answer.

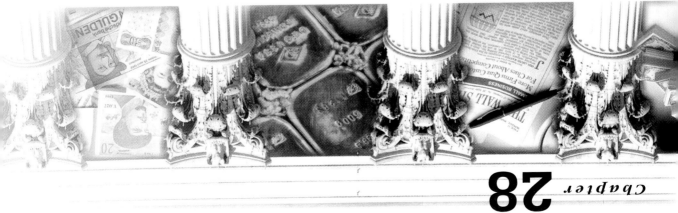

Chapter 28

RATIONAL EXPECTATIONS: IMPLICATIONS FOR POLICY

P R E V I E W

After World War II, economists, armed with Keynesian models (such as the *ISLM* model), that described how government policies could be used to manipulate employment and output, felt that activist policies could reduce the severity of business cycle fluctuations without creating inflation. In the 1960s and 1970s, these economists got their chance to put their policies into practice (see Chapter 26), but the results were not what they had anticipated. The economic record for that period is not a happy one: Inflation accelerated, the rate often climbing above 10 percent, while unemployment figures deteriorated from those of the 1950s.[1]

In the 1970s and 1980s, economists, including Robert Lucas of the University of Chicago and Thomas Sargent of Stanford University and the University of Chicago, used rational expectations theory to examine why activist policies appear to have performed so poorly. Their analysis cast doubt on whether macro-economic models can be used to evaluate the potential effects of policy or whether policy can be effective if the public *expects* that it will be implemented. Because the analysis of Lucas and Sargent has such strong implications for the way policy should be conducted, it has been labeled the *rational expectations revolution.*[2]

This chapter examines the analysis behind the rational expectations revolution. We start first with the Lucas critique, which indicates that because expectations are important in economic behavior, it may be quite difficult to predict what the outcome of an activist policy will be. We then discuss the effect of rational expectations on the aggregate demand and supply analysis developed in Chapter 24 by exploring three models that incorporate expectations in different ways.

---

[1] Some of the deterioration can be attributed to supply shocks in 1973–1975 and 1978–1980.

[2] Other economists who have been active in promoting the rational expectations revolution are Robert Barro of Harvard University, Bennett McCallum of Carnegie-Mellon University, Edward Prescott of the University of Minnesota, and Neil Wallace of the University of Miami.

A comparison of all three models indicates that the existence of rational expectations makes activist policies less likely to be successful and raises the issue of credibility as an important element affecting policy outcomes. With rational expectations, an essential ingredient to a successful anti-inflation policy is the credibility of the policy in the eyes of the public. The rational expectations revolution is now at the center of many of the current debates in monetary theory that have major implications for how monetary and fiscal policy should be conducted.

THE LUCAS CRITIQUE OF POLICY EVALUATION

In his famous paper "Econometric Policy Evaluation: A Critique," Robert Lucas presented an argument that had devastating implications for the usefulness of conventional **econometric models** (models whose equations are estimated with statistical procedures) for evaluating policy.[3] Economists developed these models for two purposes: to forecast economic activity and to evaluate the effects of different policies. Although Lucas's critique had nothing to say about the usefulness of these models as forecasting tools, he argued that they could not be relied on to evaluate the potential impact of particular policies on the economy.

Econometric Policy Evaluation

To understand Lucas's argument, we must first understand econometric policy evaluation: how econometric models are used to evaluate policy. For example, we can examine how the Federal Reserve uses its econometric model in making decisions about the future course of monetary policy. The model contains equations that describe the relationships among hundreds of variables. These relationships are assumed to remain constant and are estimated using past data. Let's say that the Fed wants to know the effect on unemployment and inflation of an increase in the rate of money growth from 5 percent to 10 percent. It feeds the new, higher rate of money growth into a computer that contains the model, and the model then provides an answer about how much unemployment will fall as a result of the higher money growth and how much the inflation rate will rise. Other possible policies, such as a decline in money growth to 1 percent, might also be fed into the model. After a series of these policies have been tried out, the policymakers at the Fed can see which policies produce the most desirable outcome for unemployment and inflation.

Lucas's challenge to this procedure for evaluating policies is based on a simple principle of rational expectations theory: *The way in which expectations are formed (the relationship of expectations to past information) changes when the behavior of forecasted variables changes.* So when policy changes, the relationship between expectations and past information will change, and because expectations affect economic behavior, the relationships in the econometric model will change. The econometric model, which has been estimated with past data, is then no longer the correct model for evaluating the response to this policy change and may consequently prove highly misleading.

[3]Robert Lucas, Jr., "Econometric Policy Evaluation: A Critique," *Carnegie-Rochester Conference Series on Public Policy* 1 (1976): 19–46.

Example: The Term Structure of Interest Rates

The best way to understand Lucas's argument is to look at a concrete example involving only one equation typically found in econometric models: the term structure equation. The equation relates the long-term interest rate to current and past values of the short-term interest rate. It is one of the most important equations in Keynesian econometric models because the long-term interest rate, not the short-term rate, is the one believed to have an impact on aggregate demand.

In Chapter 7 we learned that the long-term interest rate is related to an average of expected future short-term interest rates. Suppose that in the past, when the short-term rate rose, it quickly fell back down again; that is, any increase was temporary. Because rational expectations theory suggests that any rise in the short-term interest rate is expected to be only temporary, a rise should have only a minimal effect on the average of expected future short-term rates. It will cause the long-term interest rate to rise by a negligible amount. The term structure relationship estimated using past data will then show only a weak effect on the long-term interest rate of changes in the short-term rate.

Suppose that the Fed wants to evaluate what will happen to the economy if it pursues a policy that is likely to raise the short-term interest rate from a current level of 5 percent to a permanently higher level of 8 percent. The term structure equation that has been estimated using past data will indicate that there will be just a small change in the long-term interest rate. However, if the public recognizes that the short-term rate is rising to a permanently higher level, rational expectations theory indicates that people will no longer expect a rise in the short-term rate to be temporary. Instead, when they see the interest rate rise to 8 percent, they will expect the average of future short-term interest rates to rise substantially, and so the long-term interest rate will rise greatly, not minimally as the estimated term structure equation suggests. You can see that evaluating the likely outcome of the change in Fed policy with an econometric model can be highly misleading.

The term structure example also demonstrates another aspect of the Lucas critique. The effects of a particular policy depend critically on the public's expectations about the policy. If the public expects the rise in the short-term interest rate to be merely temporary, the response of long-term interest rates, as we have seen, will be negligible. If, however, the public expects the rise to be more permanent, the response of long-term rates will be far greater. ***The Lucas critique points out not only that conventional econometric models cannot be used for policy evaluation but also that the public's expectations about a policy will influence the response to that policy.***

The term structure equation discussed here is only one of many equations in econometric models to which the Lucas critique applies. In fact, Lucas uses the examples of consumption and investment equations in his paper. One attractive feature of the term structure example is that it deals with expectations in a financial market, a sector of the economy for which the theory and empirical evidence supporting rational expectations are very strong. The Lucas critique should also apply, however, to sectors of the economy for which rational expectations theory is more controversial because the basic principle of the Lucas critique is not that expectations are always rational but rather that the formation of expectations changes when the behavior of a forecasted variable changes. This less stringent principle is supported by the evidence in sectors of the economy other than financial markets.

NEW CLASSICAL MACROECONOMIC MODEL

We now turn to the implications of rational expectations for the aggregate demand and supply analysis we studied in Chapter 24. The first model we examine that views expectations as rational is the *new classical macroeconomic model* developed by Robert Lucas and Thomas Sargent, among others. In the new classical model, all wages and prices are completely flexible with respect to expected changes in the price level; that is, a rise in the expected price level results in an immediate and equal rise in wages and prices because workers try to keep their *real* wages from falling when they expect the price level to rise.

This view of how wages and prices are set indicates that a rise in the expected price level causes an immediate leftward shift in the aggregate supply curve, which leaves real wages unchanged and aggregate output at the natural rate (full-employment) level if expectations are realized. This model then suggests that anticipated policy has no effect on aggregate output and unemployment; only unanticipated policy has an effect.

Effects of Unanticipated and Anticipated Policy

First, let us look at the short-run response to an unanticipated (unexpected) policy such as an unexpected increase in the money supply.

In Figure 1, the aggregate supply curve AS_1 is drawn for an expected price level P_1. The initial aggregate demand curve AD_1 intersects AS_1 at point 1, where the realized price level is at the expected price level P_1 and aggregate output is at

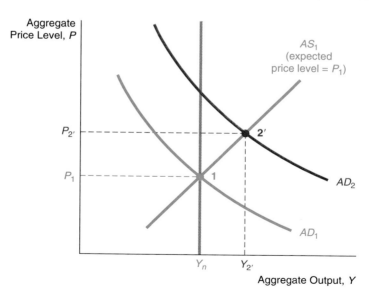

FIGURE 1 Short-Run Response to Unanticipated Expansionary Policy in the New Classical Model

Initially, the economy is at point 1 at the intersection of AD_1 and AS_1 (expected price level = P_1). An expansionary policy shifts the aggregate demand curve to AD_2, but because this is unexpected, the aggregate supply curve remains fixed at AS_1. Equilibrium now occurs at point 2'—aggregate output has increased above the natural rate level to $Y_{2'}$, and the price level has increased to $P_{2'}$.

the natural rate level Y_n. Because point 1 is also on the long-run aggregate supply curve at Y_n, there is no tendency for the aggregate supply to shift. The economy remains in long-run equilibrium.

Suppose that the Fed suddenly decides that the unemployment rate is too high and so makes a large bond purchase that is unexpected by the public. The money supply increases, and the aggregate demand curve shifts rightward to AD_2. Because this shift is unexpected, the expected price level remains at P_1 and the aggregate supply curve remains at AS_1. Equilibrium is now at point 2', the intersection of AD_2 and AS_1. Aggregate output increases above the natural rate level to $Y_{2'}$ and the realized price level increases to $P_{2'}$.

If, by contrast, the public expects that the Fed will make these open market purchases in order to lower unemployment because they have seen it done in the past, the expansionary policy will be anticipated. The outcome of such anticipated expansionary policy is illustrated in Figure 2. Because expectations are rational, workers and firms recognize that an expansionary policy will shift the aggregate demand curve to the right and will expect the aggregate price level to rise to P_2. Workers will demand higher wages so that their real earnings will remain the same when the price level rises. The aggregate supply curve then shifts leftward to AS_2 and intersects AD_2 at point 2, an equilibrium point where aggregate output is at the natural rate level Y_n and the price level has risen to P_2.

The new classical macroeconomic model demonstrates that aggregate output does not increase as a result of anticipated expansionary policy and that the economy immediately moves to a point of long-run equilibrium (point 2) where aggre-

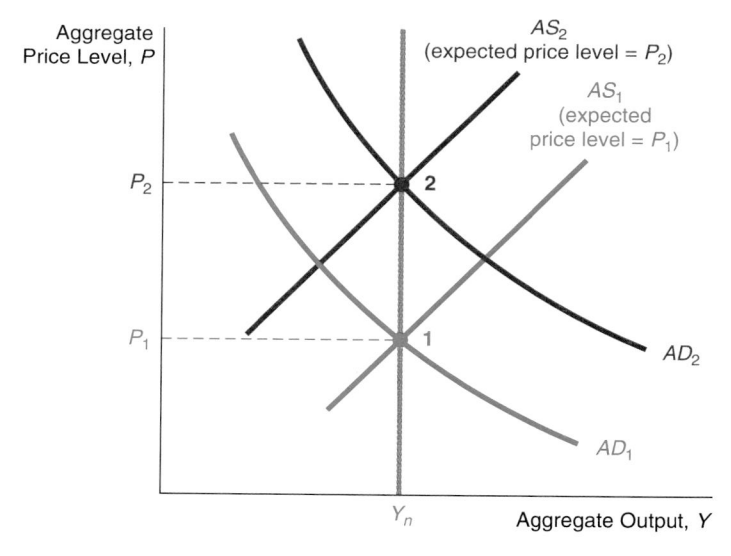

FIGURE 2 *Short-Run Response to Anticipated Expansionary Policy in the New Classical Model*

The expansionary policy shifts the aggregate demand curve rightward to ***AD₂****, but because this policy is expected, the aggregate supply curve shifts leftward to* ***AS₂****. The economy moves to point 2, where aggregate output is still at the natural rate level but the price level has increased to* ***P₂****.*

BOX 1

Proof of the Policy Ineffectiveness Proposition

The proof that in the new classical macro-economic model aggregate output *necessarily* remains at the natural rate level when there is anticipated expansionary policy is as follows. In the new classical model, the expected price level for the aggregate supply curve occurs at its intersection with the long-run aggregate supply curve (see Figure 2). The optimal forecast of the price level is given by the intersection of the aggregate supply curve with the anticipated aggregate demand curve AD_2. If the aggregate supply curve is to the right of AS_2 in Figure 2, it will intersect AD_2 at a price level lower than the expected level (at the intersection of this aggregate supply curve and the Y_n line). The optimal forecast of the price level will then not equal the expected price level, thereby violating the rationality of expectations. A similar argument can be made to show that when the aggregate supply curve is to the left of AS_2, the assumption of rational expectations is violated. Only when the aggregate supply curve is at AS_2 (corresponding to an expected price level of P_2) are expectations rational because the optimal forecast equals the expected price level. As we see in Figure 2, the AS_2 curve implies that aggregate output remains at the natural rate level as a result of the anticipated expansionary policy.

gate output is at the natural rate level. Although Figure 2 suggests why this occurs, we have not yet proved why an anticipated expansionary policy shifts the aggregate supply curve to exactly AS_2 (corresponding to an expected price level of P_2) and hence why aggregate output *necessarily* remains at the natural rate level. The proof is somewhat difficult and is dealt with in Box 1.

The new classical model has the word *classical* associated with it because when policy is anticipated, the new classical model has a property that is associated with the classical economists of the nineteenth and early twentieth centuries: Aggregate output remains at the natural rate level. Yet the new classical model allows aggregate output to fluctuate away from the natural rate level as a result of *unanticipated* movements in the aggregate demand curve. The conclusion from the new classical model is a striking one: ***Anticipated policy has no effect on the business cycle; only unanticipated policy matters.***[4]

This conclusion has been called the **policy ineffectiveness proposition** because it implies that one anticipated policy is just like any other; it has no effect on output fluctuations. You should recognize that this proposition does not rule out output effects from policy changes. If the policy is a surprise (unanticipated), it will have an effect on output.[5]

---

[4]Note that the new classical view in which anticipated policy has no effect on the business cycle does not imply that anticipated policy has no effect on the overall health of the economy. For example, the new classical analysis does not rule out possible effects of anticipated policy on the natural rate of output Y_n, which can benefit the public.

[5]Thomas Sargent and Neil Wallace, "'Rational' Expectations, the Optimal Monetary Instrument, and the Optimal Money Supply Rule," *Journal of Political Economy* 83 (1975): 241–254, first demonstrated the full implications of the policy ineffectiveness proposition.

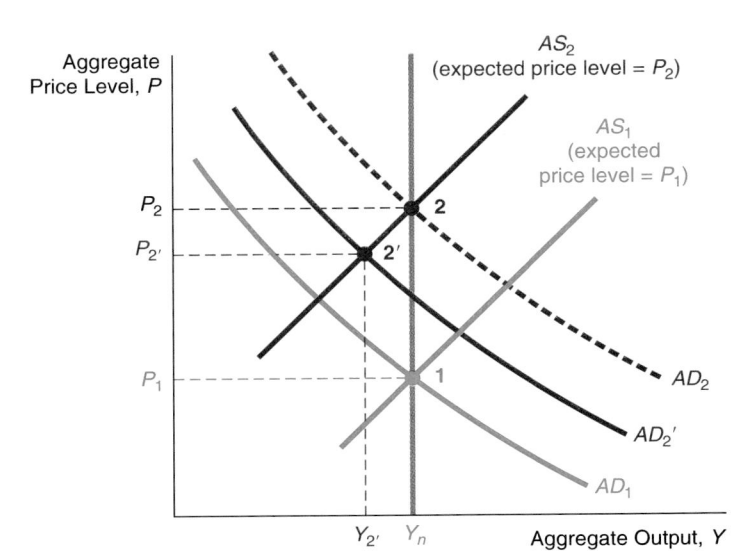

FIGURE 3 Short-Run Response to an Expansionary Policy That Is Less Expansionary than Expected in the New Classical Model
Because the public expects the aggregate demand curve to shift to **AD**$_2$, the aggregate supply curve shifts to **AS**$_2$ (expected price level = **P**$_2$). When the actual expansionary policy falls short of the public's expectation (the aggregate demand curve merely shifts to **AD**$_{2'}$), the economy ends up at point 2', at the intersection of **AD**$_{2'}$ and **AS**$_2$. Despite the expansionary policy, aggregate output falls to **Y**$_{2'}$.

Can an Expansionary Policy Lead to a Decline in Aggregate Output?

Another important feature of the new classical model is that an expansionary policy, such as an increase in the rate of money growth, can lead to a *decline* in aggregate output if the public expects an even more expansionary policy than the one actually implemented. There will be a surprise in the policy, but it will be negative and drive output down. Policymakers cannot be sure if their policies will work in the intended direction.

To see how an expansionary policy can lead to a decline in aggregate output, let us turn to the aggregate supply and demand diagram in Figure 3. Initially we are at point 1, the intersection of AD_1 and AS_1; output is Y_n, and the price level is P_1. Now suppose that the public expects the Fed to increase the money supply in order to shift the aggregate demand curve to AD_2. As we saw in Figure 2, the aggregate supply curve shifts leftward to AS_2 because the price level is expected to rise to P_2. Suppose that the expansionary policy engineered by the Fed actually falls short of what was expected so that the aggregate demand curve shifts only to $AD_{2'}$. The economy will move to point 2', the intersection of the aggregate supply curve AS_2 and the aggregate demand curve $AD_{2'}$. The result of the mistaken expectation is that output falls to $Y_{2'}$, while the price level rises to $P_{2'}$ rather than P_2. An expansionary policy that is less expansionary than anticipated leads to an output movement directly opposite to that intended.

Study Guide Mastering the new classical macroeconomic model, as well as the new Keynesian model in the next section, requires practice. Make sure that you can draw the aggregate demand

and supply curves that explain what happens in each model when there is a contractionary policy that is (1) unanticipated, (2) anticipated, and (3) less contractionary than anticipated.

Implications for Policymakers

The new classical model, with its policy ineffectiveness proposition, has two important lessons for policymakers: It illuminates the distinction between the effects of anticipated versus unanticipated policy actions, and it demonstrates that policymakers cannot know the outcome of their decisions without knowing the public's expectations regarding them.

At first you might think that policymakers can still use policy to stabilize the economy. Once they figure out the public's expectations, they can know what effect their policies will have. There are two catches to such a conclusion. First, it may be nearly impossible to find out what the public's expectations are, given that the public consists of more than 260 million U.S. citizens. Second, even if it were possible, policymakers would run into further difficulties in that because the public has rational expectations, it will try to guess what policymakers plan to do. Public expectations do not remain fixed while policymakers are plotting a surprise—the public will revise its expectations, and policies will have no predictable effect on output.[6]

Where does this lead us? Should the Fed and other policymaking agencies pack up, lock the doors, and go home? In a sense, the answer is yes. The new classical model implies that discretionary stabilization policy cannot be effective and might have undesirable effects on the economy. Policymakers' attempts to use discretionary policy may create a fluctuating policy stance that leads to unpredictable policy surprises, which in turn cause undesirable fluctuations around the natural rate level of aggregate output. To eliminate these undesirable fluctuations, the Fed and other policymaking agencies should abandon discretionary policy and generate as few policy surprises as possible.

As we have seen in Figure 2, even though anticipated policy has no effect on aggregate output in the new classical model, it *does* have an effect on the price level. The new classical macroeconomists care about anticipated policy and suggest that policy rules be designed so that the price level will remain stable. One natural suggestion for achieving this goal, as well as for reducing uncertainty about policy, is for the monetary authorities to follow a constant money growth rule, keeping the rate of money growth consistent with price stability. Some adherents of the new classical macroeconomics in the end support this monetarist policy prescription (see Chapter 26).

NEW KEYNESIAN MODEL

In the new classical model, all wages and prices are completely flexible with respect to expected changes in the price level; that is, a rise in the expected price level results in an immediate and equal rise in wages and prices. Many econo-

---

[6]This result follows from one of the implications of rational expectations: The forecast error of expectations about policy (the deviation of actual policy from expectations of policy) must be unpredictable. Because output is affected only by unpredictable (unanticipated) policy changes in the new classical model, policy effects on output must be unpredictable as well.

mists who accept rational expectations as a working hypothesis do not accept the characterization of wage and price flexibility in the new classical model. These critics of the new classical model, called *new Keynesians,* object to complete wage and price flexibility and identify factors in the economy that prevent some wages and prices from rising fully with a rise in the expected price level.

Long-term labor contracts are one source of rigidity that prevents wages and prices from responding fully to changes in the expected price level (called *wage-price stickiness*). For example, workers might find themselves at the end of the first year of a three-year wage contract that specifies the wage rate for the coming two years. Even if new information appeared that would make them raise their expectations of the inflation rate and the future price level, they could not do anything about it because they are locked into a wage agreement. Even with a high expectation about the price level, the wage rate will not adjust. In two years, when the contract is renegotiated, both workers and firms may build the expected inflation rate into their agreement, but they cannot do so immediately.

Another source of rigidity is that firms may be reluctant to change wages frequently even when there are no explicit wage contracts because it may affect the work effort of the labor force. For example, a firm may not want to lower workers' wages when unemployment is high because this might result in poorer worker performance. Price stickiness may also occur because firms engage in fixed-price contracts with their suppliers or because it is costly for firms to change prices frequently. All of these rigidities (which diminish wage and price flexibility), even if they are not present in all wage and price arrangements, suggest that an increase in the expected price level might not translate into an immediate and complete adjustment of wages and prices.

Although the new Keynesians do not agree with the complete wage and price flexibility of the new classical macroeconomics, they nevertheless recognize the importance of expectations to the determination of aggregate supply and are willing to accept rational expectations theory as a reasonable characterization of how expectations are formed. The model they have developed, the *new Keynesian model,* assumes that expectations are rational but does not assume complete wage and price flexibility; instead, it assumes that wages and prices are sticky. Its basic conclusion is that unanticipated policy has a larger effect on aggregate output than anticipated policy (as in the new classical model). However, in contrast to the new classical model, the policy ineffectiveness proposition does not hold: Anticipated policy *does* affect aggregate output and the business cycle.

Effects of Unanticipated and Anticipated Policy

In panel (a) of Figure 4, we look at the short-run response to an unanticipated expansionary policy for the new Keynesian model. The analysis is identical to that of the new classical model. We again start at point 1, where the aggregate demand curve AD_1 intersects the aggregate supply curve AS_1 at the natural rate level of output and price level P_1. When the Fed pursues its expansionary policy of purchasing bonds and raising the money supply, the aggregate demand curve shifts

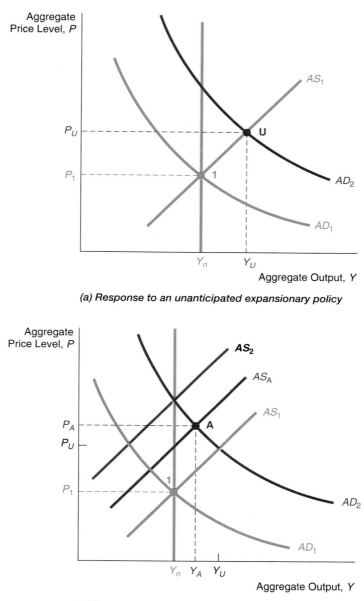

(a) Response to an unanticipated expansionary policy

(b) Response to an anticipated expansionary policy

FIGURE 4 Short-Run Response to Expansionary Policy in the New Keynesian Model
The expansionary policy that shifts aggregate demand to AD_2 has a bigger effect on output when it is unanticipated than when it is anticipated. When the expansionary policy is unanticipated in panel (a), the short-run aggregate supply curve does not shift, and the economy moves to point U so that aggregate output increases to Y_U and the price level rises to P_U. When the policy is anticipated in panel (b), the short-run aggregate supply curve shifts to AS_A (but not all the way to AS_2 because rigidities prevent complete wage and price adjustment), and the economy moves to point A so that aggregate output rises to Y_A (which is less than Y_U) and the price level rises to P_A (which is higher than P_U).

rightward to AD_2. Because the expansionary policy is unanticipated, the expected price level remains unchanged, leaving the aggregate supply curve unchanged. Thus the economy moves to point U, where aggregate output has increased to Y_U and the price level has risen to P_U.

In panel (b), we see what happens when the Fed's expansionary policy that shifts the aggregate demand curve from AD_1 to AD_2 is anticipated. Because the expansionary policy is anticipated and expectations are rational, the expected price level increases, causing wages to increase and the aggregate supply curve to shift to the left. Because of rigidities that do not allow *complete* wage and price adjustment, the aggregate supply curve does not shift all the way to AS_2 as it does in the new classical model. Instead, it moves to AS_A, and the economy settles at point A, the intersection of AD_2 and AS_A. Aggregate output has risen above the natural rate level to Y_A, while the price level has increased to P_A. **Unlike the new classical model, anticipated policy does have an effect on aggregate output in the new Keynesian model.**

We can see in Figure 4 that Y_U is greater than Y_A, meaning that the output response is greater to unanticipated policy than to anticipated policy. It is greater because the aggregate supply curve does not shift when policy is unanticipated, causing a lower price level and hence a higher level of output. We see that **like the new classical model, the new Keynesian model distinguishes between the effects of anticipated versus unanticipated policy, with unanticipated policy having a greater effect.**

Implications for Policymakers

Because the new Keynesian model indicates that anticipated policy has an effect on aggregate output, it does not rule out beneficial effects from activist stabilization policy, in contrast to the new classical model. It does warn the policymaker that designing such a policy will not be an easy task because the effects of anticipated and unanticipated policy can be quite different. As in the new classical model, to predict the outcome of their actions, policymakers must be aware of the public's expectations about those actions. Policymakers face similar difficulties in devising successful policies in both the new classical and new Keynesian models.

COMPARISON OF THE TWO NEW MODELS WITH THE TRADITIONAL MODEL

To obtain a clearer picture of the impact of the rational expectations revolution on our analysis of the aggregate economy, we can compare the two rational expectations models (the new classical macroeconomic model and the new Keynesian model) to a model we call, for lack of a better name, the *traditional model*. In the traditional model, expectations are *not* rational. That model uses adaptive expectations (mentioned in Chapter 27), expectations based solely on past experience. The traditional model views expected inflation as an average of past inflation rates. This average is not affected by the public's predictions of future policy; hence predictions of future policy do not affect the aggregate supply curve.

First we will examine the short-run output and price responses in the three models. Then we will examine the implications of these models for both stabilization and anti-inflation policies.

Study Guide   As a study aid, the comparison of the three models is summarized in Table 1. You may want to refer to the table as we proceed with the comparison.

Short-Run Output and Price Responses

Figure 5 compares the response of aggregate output and the price level to an expansionary policy in the three models. Initially, the economy is at point 1, the intersection of the aggregate demand curve AD_1 and the aggregate supply curve AS_1. When the expansionary policy occurs, the aggregate demand curve shifts to AD_2. If the expansionary policy is *unanticipated,* all three models show the same short-run output response. The traditional model views the aggregate supply curve as given in the short run, while the other two view it as remaining at AS_1 because there is no change in the expected price level when the policy is a surprise. Hence when policy is *unanticipated,* all three models indicate a movement to point 1′, where the AD_2 and AS_1 curves intersect and where aggregate output and the price level have risen to $Y_{1'}$ and $P_{1'}$ respectively.

The response to the *anticipated* expansionary policy is, however, quite different in the three models. In the traditional model in panel (a), the aggregate supply curve remains at AS_1 even when the expansionary policy is anticipated because adaptive expectations imply that anticipated policy has no effect on expectations and hence on aggregate supply. It indicates that the economy moves to point 1′, which is where it moved when the policy was unanticipated. The traditional model does not distinguish between the effects of anticipated and unanticipated policy: Both have the same effect on output and prices.

In the new classical model in panel (b), the aggregate supply curve shifts leftward to AS_2 when policy is anticipated because when expectations of the higher price level are realized, aggregate output will be at the natural rate level. Thus it indicates that the economy moves to point 2; aggregate output does not rise, but prices do, to P_2. This outcome is quite different from the move to point 1′ when policy is unanticipated. The new classical model distinguishes between the short-run effects of anticipated and unanticipated policies: Anticipated policy has no effect on output, but unanticipated policy does. However, anticipated policy has a bigger impact than unanticipated policy on price level movements.

The new Keynesian model in panel (c) is an intermediate position between the traditional and new classical models. It recognizes that anticipated policy affects the aggregate supply curve, but due to rigidities such as long-term contracts, wage and price adjustment is not as complete as in the new classical model. Hence the aggregate supply curve shifts only to AS_2 in response to anticipated policy, and the economy moves to point 2′, where output at $Y_{2'}$ is lower than the $Y_{1'}$ level reached when the expansionary policy is unanticipated. But the price level at $P_{2'}$ is higher than the level $P_{1'}$ that resulted from the unanticipated policy. Like the new classical model, the new Keynesian model distinguishes between

───── **S U M M A R Y** ─────

TABLE 1	The Three Models

Model	Response to Unanticipated Expansionary Policy	Response to Anticipated Expansionary Policy	Can Activist Policy Be Beneficial?	Response to Unanticipated Anti-inflation Policy	Response to Anticipated Anti-inflation Policy	Is Credibility Important to Successful Anti-inflation Policy?
Traditional model	$Y\uparrow, P\uparrow$	$Y\uparrow, P\uparrow$ by same amount as when policy is unanticipated	Yes	$Y\downarrow, \pi\downarrow$	$Y\downarrow, \pi\downarrow$ by same amount as when policy is unanticipated	No
New classical macroeconomic model	$Y\uparrow, P\uparrow$	Y unchanged, $P\uparrow$ by more than when policy is unanticipated	No	$Y\downarrow, \pi\downarrow$	Y unchanged, $\pi\downarrow$ by more than when policy is unanticipated	Yes
New Keynesian model	$Y\uparrow, P\uparrow$	$Y\uparrow$ by less than when policy is unanticipated, $P\uparrow$ by more than when policy is unanticipated	Yes, but designing a beneficial policy is difficult	$Y\downarrow, \pi\downarrow$	$Y\downarrow$ by less than when policy is unanticipated, $\pi\downarrow$ by more than when policy is unanticipated	Yes

Note: π represents the inflation rate.

the effects of anticipated and unanticipated policies: Anticipated policy has a smaller effect on output than unanticipated policy but a larger effect on the price level. However, in contrast to the new classical model, anticipated policy does affect output fluctuations.

Stabilization Policy

The three models have different views of the effectiveness of *stabilization policy,* policy intended to reduce output fluctuations. Because the effects of anticipated and unanticipated policy are identical in the traditional model, policymakers do not have to concern themselves with the public's expectations. This makes it easier for them to predict the outcome of their policy, an essential matter if their actions are to have the intended effect. In the traditional model, it is possible for an activist policy to stabilize output fluctuations.

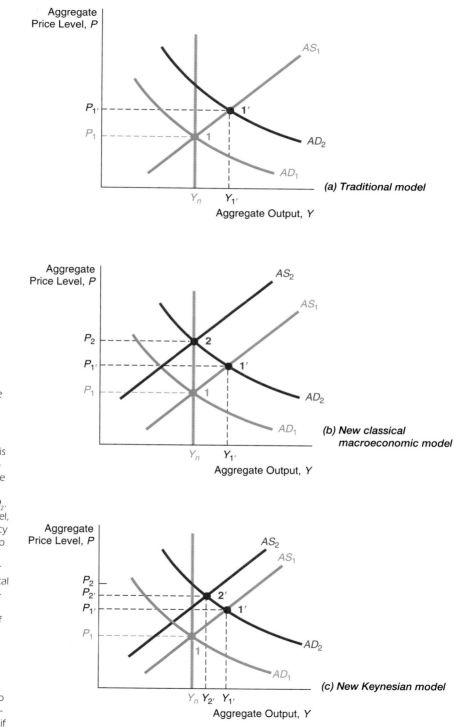

(a) Traditional model

(b) New classical macroeconomic model

(c) New Keynesian model

FIGURE 5

Comparison of the Short-Run Response to Expansionary Policy in the Three Models

Initially, the economy is at point 1. The expansionary policy shifts the aggregate demand curve from AD_1 to AD_2. In the traditional model, the expansionary policy moves the economy to point 1' whether the policy is anticipated or not. In the new classical model, the expansionary policy moves the economy to point 1' if it is unanticipated and to point 2 if it is anticipated. In the new Keynesian model, the expansionary policy moves the economy to point 1' if it is unanticipated and to point 2' if it is anticipated.

The new classical model takes the extreme position that activist stabilization policy serves to aggravate output fluctuations. In this model, only unanticipated policy affects output; anticipated policy does not matter. Policymakers can affect output only by surprising the public. Because the public is assumed to have rational expectations, it will always try to guess what policymakers plan to do.

In the new classical model, the conduct of policy can be viewed as a game in which the public and the policymakers are always trying to outfox each other by guessing the other's intentions and expectations. The sole possible outcome of this process is that an activist stabilization policy will have no predictable effect on output and cannot be relied on to stabilize economic activity. Instead it may create a lot of uncertainty about policy that will increase random output fluctuations around the natural rate level of output. Such an undesirable effect is exactly the opposite of what the activist stabilization policy is trying to achieve. The outcome in the new classical view is that policy should follow a nonactivist rule in order to promote as much certainty about policy actions as possible.

The new Keynesian model again takes an intermediate position between the traditional and the new classical models. Contrary to the new classical model, it indicates that anticipated policy *does* matter to output fluctuations. Policymakers can count on some output response from their anticipated policies and can use them to stabilize the economy.

In contrast to the traditional model, however, the new Keynesian model recognizes that the effects of anticipated and unanticipated policy will not be the same. Policymakers will encounter more uncertainty about the outcome of their actions because they cannot be sure to what extent the policy is anticipated or not. Hence an activist policy is less likely to operate always in the intended direction and is less likely to achieve its goals. The new Keynesian model raises the possibility that an activist policy could be beneficial, but uncertainty about the outcome of policies in this model may make the design of such a beneficial policy extremely difficult.

Anti-inflation Policies

So far we have focused on the implications of these three models for policies whose intent is to eliminate fluctuations in output. By the end of the 1970s, the high inflation rate (which exceeded 10 percent) helped shift the primary concern of policymakers to the reduction of inflation. What do these models have to say about anti-inflation policies designed to eliminate upward movements in the price level? The aggregate demand and supply diagrams in Figure 6 will help us answer the question.

Suppose that the economy has settled into a sustained 10 percent inflation rate caused by a high rate of money growth that shifts the aggregate demand curve so that it moves up by 10 percent every year. If this inflation rate has been built into wage and price contracts, the aggregate supply curve shifts so as to rise at the same rate. We see this in Figure 6 as a shift in the aggregate demand curve from AD_1 in year 1 to AD_2 in year 2, while the aggregate supply curve moves from AS_1 to AS_2. (Note that the figure is not drawn to scale.) In year 1, the economy is at point 1 (intersection of AD_1 and AS_1); in the second year, the economy moves to point 2 (intersection of AD_2 and AS_2), and the price level has risen 10 percent from P_1 to P_2.

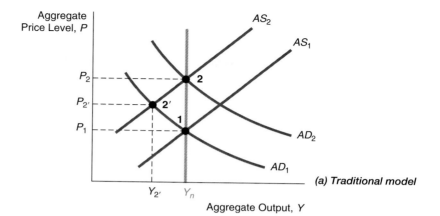

(a) Traditional model

FIGURE 6

Anti-inflation Policy in the Three Models

With an ongoing inflation in which the economy is moving from point 1 to point 2, the aggregate demand curve is shifting from AD_1 to AD_2 and the short-run aggregate supply curve from AS_1 to AS_2. The anti-inflation policy, when implemented, prevents the aggregate demand curve from rising, holding it at AD_1. (a) In the traditional model, the economy moves to point 2′ whether the anti-inflation policy is anticipated or not. (b) In the new classical model, the economy moves to point 2′ if the policy is unanticipated and to point 1 if it is anticipated. (c) In the new Keynesian model, the economy moves to point 2′ if the policy is unanticipated and to point 2″ if it is anticipated.

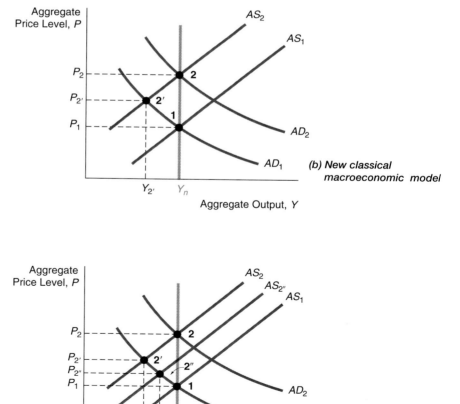

(b) New classical macroeconomic model

(c) New Keynesian model

Now suppose that a new Federal Reserve chairman is appointed who decides that inflation must be stopped. He convinces the Board of Governors to stop the high rate of money growth so that the aggregate demand curve will not rise from AD_1. The policy of halting money growth immediately could be costly if it led to a fall in output. Let's use our three models to explore the degree to which aggregate output will fall as a result of an anti-inflation policy.

First, look at the outcome of this policy in the traditional model's view of the world in panel (a). The movement of the aggregate supply curve to AS_2 is already set in place and is unaffected by the new policy of keeping the aggregate demand curve at AD_1 (whether the effort is anticipated or not). The economy moves to point 2' (the intersection of the AD_1 and AS_2 curves), and the inflation rate slows down because the price level increases only to $P_{2'}$ rather than P_2. The reduction in inflation has not been without cost: Output has declined to $Y_{2'}$, which is well below the natural rate level.

The late Arthur Okun of the Brookings Institution estimated that in the traditional model, the cost in terms of lost output for each 1 percent reduction in the inflation rate is 9 percent of a year's real GDP. The high cost of reducing inflation in the traditional model is one reason why some economists are reluctant to advocate an anti-inflation policy of the sort tried here. They question whether the cost of high unemployment is worth the benefits of a reduced inflation rate.

If you adhere to the new classical philosophy, you would not be as pessimistic about the high cost of reducing the inflation rate. If the public *expects* the monetary authorities to stop the inflationary process by ending the high rate of money growth, it will occur without any output loss. In panel (b), the aggregate demand curve will remain at AD_1, but because this is expected, wages and prices can be adjusted so that they will not rise, and the aggregate supply curve will remain at AS_1 instead of moving to AS_2. The economy will stay put at point 1 (the intersection of AD_1 and AS_1), and aggregate output will remain at the natural rate level while inflation is stopped because the price level is unchanged.

An important element in the story is that the anti-inflation policy be anticipated by the public. If the policy is *not* expected, the aggregate demand curve remains at AD_1, but the aggregate supply curve continues its shift to AS_2. The outcome of the unanticipated anti-inflation policy is a movement of the economy to point 2'. Although the inflation rate slows in this case, it is not entirely eliminated as it was when the anti-inflation policy was anticipated. Even worse, aggregate output falls below the natural rate level to $Y_{2'}$. An anti-inflation policy that is unanticipated, then, is far less desirable than one that is.

The new Keynesian model in panel (c) also leads to the conclusion that an unanticipated anti-inflation policy is less desirable than an anticipated one. If the policy of keeping the aggregate demand curve at AD_1 is *not* expected, the aggregate supply curve will continue its shift to AS_2, and the economy moves to point 2', at the intersection of AD_1 and AS_2. The inflation rate slows, but output declines to $Y_{2'}$, well below the natural rate level.

If, by contrast, the anti-inflation policy is *expected,* the aggregate supply curve will not move all the way to AS_1. Instead it will shift only to $AS_{2''}$ because some wages and prices (but not all) can be adjusted, so wages and the price level will not rise at their previous rates. Instead of moving to point 2' (as occurred when the anti-inflation policy was not expected), the economy moves to point 2'', the intersection of the AD_1 and $AS_{2''}$ curves. The outcome is more desirable than when the policy is unanticipated—the inflation rate is lower (the price level rises only to $P_{2''}$ and not $P_{2'}$), and the output loss is smaller as well ($Y_{2''}$ is higher than $Y_{2'}$).

Credibility in Fighting Inflation

Both the new classical and new Keynesian models indicate that for an anti-inflation policy to be successful in reducing inflation at the lowest output cost, the public must believe (expect) that it will be implemented. In the new classical view of the world, the best anti-inflation policy (when it is credible) is to go "cold turkey." The rise in the aggregate demand curve from AD_1 should be stopped immediately. Inflation would be eliminated at once with no loss of output *if the policy is credible.* In a new Keynesian world, the cold-turkey policy, *even if credible,* is not as desirable because it will produce some output loss.

John Taylor, a proponent of the new Keynesian model, has demonstrated that a more gradual approach to reducing inflation may be able to eliminate inflation without producing a substantial output loss.[7] An important catch here is that this gradual policy must somehow be made credible, which may be harder to achieve than a cold-turkey anti-inflation policy, which demonstrates immediately that the policymakers are serious about fighting inflation. Taylor's contention that inflation can be reduced with little output loss may be overly optimistic.

Incorporating rational expectations into aggregate supply and demand analysis indicates that a successful anti-inflation policy must be credible. Evidence that credibility plays an important role in successful anti-inflation policies is provided by the dramatic end of the Bolivian hyperinflation in 1985 (see Box 2). Establishing credibility is easier said than done. You might think that an announcement by policymakers at the Federal Reserve that they plan to pursue an anti-inflation policy might do the trick. The public would expect this policy and would act accordingly. However, it implies that the public will believe the policymakers' announcement. Unfortunately, that is not how the real world works.

Our historical review of Federal Reserve policymaking in Chapter 19 suggests that the Fed has not always done what it set out to do. In fact, during the 1970s, the chairman of the Federal Reserve Board, Arthur Burns, repeatedly announced that the Fed would pursue a vigorous anti-inflation policy. The actual policy pursued, however, had quite a different outcome: The rate of growth of the money supply increased rapidly during the period, and inflation soared. Such episodes have reduced the credibility of the Federal Reserve in the eyes of the public and, as predicted by the new classical and new Keynesian models, have had serious consequences. The reduction of inflation that occurred from 1981 to 1984 was bought at a very high cost; the 1981–1982 recession that helped bring the inflation rate down was the most severe recession in the post–World War II period. Unless some method of restoring credibility to anti-inflation policy is achieved, eliminating inflation will be a costly affair because such policy will be unanticipated.

---

[7]John Taylor, "The Role of Expectations in the Choice of Monetary Policy," in *Monetary Policy Issues in the 1980s* (Kansas City: Federal Reserve Bank, 1982), pp. 47–76.

BOX 2

Ending the Bolivian Hyperinflation

Case Study of a Successful Anti-inflation Program.   The most remarkable anti-inflation program in recent times was implemented in Bolivia. In the first half of 1985, Bolivia's inflation rate was running at 20,000 percent and rising. Indeed, the inflation rate was so high that the price of a movie ticket often rose while people waited in line to buy it. In August 1985, Bolivia's new president announced his anti-inflation program, the New Economic Policy. To rein in money growth and establish credibility, the new government took drastic actions to slash the budget deficit by shutting down many state-owned enterprises, eliminating subsidies, freezing public sector salaries, and collecting a new wealth tax. The finance ministry was put on a new footing; the budget was balanced on a day-by-day basis. Without exceptions, the finance minister would not authorize spending in excess of the amount of tax revenue that had been collected the day before.

Arthur Okun's rule of thumb that a reduction of 1 percent in the inflation rate requires a 9 percent loss of a year's aggregate output indicates that ending the Bolivian hyperinflation would have required halving Bolivian aggregate output for 400 years! Instead, the Bolivian inflation was stopped in its tracks within one month, and the output loss was minor (less than 5 percent of GDP).

Certain hyperinflations before World War II were also ended with small losses of output using policies similar to Bolivia's,* and a more recent anti-inflation program in Israel that also involved substantial reductions in budget deficits sharply reduced inflation without any clear loss of output. There is no doubt that credible anti-inflation policies can be highly successful in eliminating inflation.

*For an excellent discussion of the end of four hyperinflations in the 1920s, see Thomas Sargent, "The Ends of Four Big Inflations," in *Inflation: Causes and Consequences,* ed. Robert E. Hall (Chicago: University of Chicago Press, 1982), pp. 41–98.

The U.S. government can play an important role in establishing the credibility of anti-inflation policy. We have seen that large budget deficits may help stimulate inflationary monetary policy, and when the government and the Fed announce that they will pursue a restrictive anti-inflation policy, it is less likely that they will be believed *unless* the federal government demonstrates fiscal responsibility. Another way to say this is to use the old cliché "actions speak louder than words." When the government takes actions that will help the Fed adhere to anti-inflation policy, the policy will be more credible. Unfortunately, this lesson has sometimes been ignored by politicians in the United States and in other countries.

Credibility and the Reagan Budget Deficits

The Reagan administration was strongly criticized for creating huge budget deficits by cutting taxes in the early 1980s. In the Keynesian framework, we usually think of tax cuts as stimulating aggregate demand and increasing aggregate output. Could the expectation of large budget deficits have helped create a more severe recession in 1981–1982 after the Federal Reserve implemented an anti-inflation monetary policy?

Some economists answer yes, using diagrams like panels (b) and (c) of Figure 6. They claim that the prospect of large budget deficits made it harder for the public to believe that an anti-inflationary policy would actually be pursued when the Fed announced its intention to do so. Consequently, the aggregate supply curve would continue to rise from AS_1 to AS_2 as in panels (b) and (c). When the Fed actually kept the aggregate demand curve from rising to AD_2 by slowing the rate of money growth in 1980–1981 and allowing interest rates to rise, the economy moved to a point like 2′ in panels (b) and (c), and much unemployment resulted. As our analysis in panels (b) and (c) of Figure 6 predicts, the inflation rate did slow substantially, falling below 5 percent by the end of 1982, but this was very costly: Unemployment reached a peak of 10.7 percent.

If the Reagan administration had actively tried to reduce deficits instead of raising them by cutting taxes, what might have been the outcome of the anti-inflation policy? Instead of moving to point 2′, the economy might have moved to point 2″ in panel (c)—or even to point 1 in panel (b), if the new classical macroeconomists are right. We would have had an even more rapid reduction in inflation and a smaller loss of output. No wonder some economists were so hostile to Reagan's budget policies!

Reagan is not the only head of state who ran large budget deficits while espousing an anti-inflation policy. Britain's Margaret Thatcher preceded Reagan in this activity, and economists such as Thomas Sargent assert that the reward for her policy was a climb of unemployment in Britain to unprecedented levels.[8]

Although many economists agree that the Fed's anti-inflation program lacked credibility, especially in its initial phases, not all of them agree that the Reagan budget deficits were the cause of that lack of credibility. The conclusion that the Reagan budget deficits helped create a more severe recession in 1981–1982 is controversial.

IMPACT OF THE RATIONAL EXPECTATIONS REVOLUTION

The theory of rational expectations has caused a revolution in the way most economists now think about the conduct of monetary and fiscal policies and their effects on economic activity. One result of this revolution is that economists are now far more aware of the importance of expectations to economic decision making and to the outcome of particular policy actions. Although the rationality of expectations in all markets is still controversial, most economists now accept the following principle suggested by rational expectations: Expectation formation will change when the behavior of forecasted variables changes. As a result, the Luca

---

[8]Thomas Sargent, "Stopping Moderate Inflations: The Methods of Poincaré and Thatcher," in *Infla Debt, and Indexation,* ed. Rudiger Dornbusch and M. H. Simonsen (Cambridge, Mass.: MIT 1983), pp. 54–96, discusses the problems that Thatcher's policies caused and contrasts them wit' successful anti-inflation policies pursued by the Poincaré government in France during the 1'

critique of policy evaluation using conventional econometric models is now taken seriously by most economists. The Lucas critique also demonstrates that the effect of a particular policy depends critically on the public's expectations about that policy. This observation has made economists much less certain that policies will have their intended effect. An important result of the rational expectations revolution is that economists are no longer as confident in the success of activist stabilization policies as they once were.

Has the rational expectations revolution convinced economists that there is no role for activist stabilization policy? Those who adhere to the new classical macroeconomics think so. Because anticipated policy does not affect aggregate output, activist policy can lead only to unpredictable output fluctuations. Pursuing a nonactivist policy in which there is no uncertainty about policy actions is then the best that we can do. Such a position is not accepted by many economists because the empirical evidence on the policy ineffectiveness proposition is mixed. Some studies find that only unanticipated policy matters to output fluctuations, while other studies find a significant impact of anticipated policy on output movements.[9] In addition, some economists question whether the degree of wage and price flexibility required in the new classical model actually exists.

The result is that many economists take an intermediate position that recognizes the distinction between the effects of anticipated versus unanticipated policy but believe that anticipated policy can affect output. They are still open to the possibility that activist stabilization policy can be beneficial, but they recognize the difficulties of designing it.

The rational expectations revolution has also highlighted the importance of credibility to the success of anti-inflation policies. Economists now recognize that if an anti-inflation policy is not believed by the public, it may be less effective in reducing the inflation rate when it is actually implemented and may lead to a larger loss of output than is necessary. Achieving credibility (not an easy task in that policymakers often say one thing but do another) should then be an important goal for policymakers. To achieve credibility, policymakers must be consistent in their course of action.

The rational expectations revolution has caused major rethinking about the way economic policy should be conducted and has forced economists to recognize that we may have to accept a more limited role for what policy can do for us. Rather than attempting to fine-tune the economy so that all output fluctuations are eliminated, we may have to settle for policies that create less uncertainty and thereby promote a more stable economic environment.

---

[9]Studies with findings that only unanticipated policy matters include Thomas Sargent, "A Classical Macroeconometric Model for the United States," *Journal of Political Economy* 84 (1976): 207–237; Robert J. Barro, "Unanticipated Money Growth and Unemployment in the United States," *American Economic Review* 67 (1977): 101–115; and Robert J. Barro and Mark Rush, "Unanticipated Money and Economic Activity," in *Rational Expectations and Economic Policy,* ed. Stanley Fischer (Chicago: University of Chicago Press, 1980), pp. 23–48. Studies that find a significant impact of anticipated policy are Frederic S. Mishkin, "Does Anticipated Monetary Policy Matter? An Econometric Investigation," *Journal of Political Economy* 90 (1982): 22–51, and Robert J. Gordon, "Price Inertia and Policy Effectiveness in the United States, 1890–1980," *Journal of Political Economy* 90 (1982): 1087–1117.

S U M M A R Y

1. The simple principle (derived from rational expectations theory) that expectation formation changes when the behavior of forecasted variables changes led to the famous Lucas critique of econometric policy evaluation. Lucas argued that when policy changes, expectation formation changes; hence the relationships in an econometric model will change. An econometric model that has been estimated on the basis of past data will no longer be the correct model for evaluating the effects of this policy change and may prove to be highly misleading. The Lucas critique also points out that the effects of a particular policy depend critically on the public's expectations about the policy.

2. The new classical macroeconomic model assumes that expectations are rational and that wages and prices are completely flexible with respect to the expected price level. It leads to the policy ineffectiveness proposition that anticipated policy has no effect on output; only unanticipated policy matters.

3. The new Keynesian model also assumes that expectations are rational but views wages and prices as sticky. Like the new classical model, the new Keynesian model distinguishes between the effects from anticipated and unanticipated policy: Anticipated policy has a smaller effect on aggregate output than unanticipated policy. However, anticipated policy does matter to output fluctuations.

4. The new classical model indicates that activist policy can only be counterproductive, while the new Keynesian model suggests that activist policy might be beneficial. However, since both indicate that there is uncertainty about the outcome of a particular policy, the design of a beneficial activist policy may be very difficult. A traditional model in which expectations about policy have no effect on the aggregate supply curve does not distinguish between the effects of anticipated or unanticipated policy. This model favors activist policy because the outcome of a particular policy is less uncertain.

5. If expectations about policy affect the aggregate supply curve, as they do in the new classical and new Keynesian models, an anti-inflation policy will be more successful (will produce a faster reduction in inflation with smaller output loss) if it is credible.

6. The rational expectations revolution has forced economists to be less optimistic about the effective use of activist stabilization policy and has made them more aware of the importance of credibility to successful policymaking.

K E Y   T E R M S

econometric model, p. 711

policy ineffectiveness
proposition, p. 715

Q U E S T I O N S   A N D   P R O B L E M S

1. If the public expects the Fed to pursue a policy that is likely to raise short-term interest rates permanently to 12 percent but the Fed does not go through with this policy change, what will happen to long-term interest rates? Explain your answer.

*2. If consumer expenditure is related to consumers' expectations of their average income in the future, will an income tax cut have a larger effect on consumer expenditure if the public expects the tax cut to last for one year or for ten years?

Use an aggregate supply and demand diagram to illustrate your answer in all the following questions.

3. Having studied the new classical model, the new chairman of the Federal Reserve Board has thought up a surefire plan for reducing inflation

and lowering unemployment. He announces that the Fed will lower the rate of money growth from 10 percent to 5 percent and then persuades the FOMC to keep the rate of money growth at 10 percent. If the new classical view of the world is correct, can his plan achieve the goals of lowering inflation and unemployment? How? Do you think his plan will work? If the traditional model's view of the world is correct, will the Fed chairman's surefire plan work?

*4. "The costs of fighting inflation in the new classical and new Keynesian models are lower than in the traditional model." Is this statement true, false, or uncertain? Explain your answer.

5. The new classical model is sometimes characterized as an offshoot of the monetarist model

because the two models have similar views of aggregate supply. What are the differences and similarities between the monetarist and new classical views of aggregate supply?

*6. "The new classical model does not eliminate policymakers' ability to reduce unemployment because they can always pursue policies that are more expansionary than the public expects." Is this statement true, false, or uncertain? Explain your answer.

7. What principle of rational expectations theory is used to prove the proposition that stabilization policy can have no predictable effect on aggregate output in the new classical model?

*8. "The Lucas critique by itself casts doubt on the ability of activist stabilization policy to be beneficial." Is this statement true, false, or uncertain? Explain your answer.

9. "The more credible the policymakers who pursue an anti-inflation policy, the more successful that policy will be." Is this statement true, false, or uncertain? Explain your answer.

*10. Many economists are worried that a high level of budget deficits may lead to inflationary monetary policies in the future. Could these budget deficits have an effect on the current rate of inflation?

USING ECONOMIC ANALYSIS TO PREDICT THE FUTURE

11. Suppose that a treaty is signed limiting armies throughout the world. The result of the treaty is that the public expects military and hence government spending to be reduced. If the new classical view of the economy is correct and government spending does affect the aggregate demand curve, predict what will happen to aggregate output and the price level when government spending is reduced in line with the public's expectations.

12. How would your prediction differ in Problem 11 if the new Keynesian model provides a more realistic description of the economy? What if the traditional model provides the most realistic description of the economy?

*13. The chairman of the Federal Reserve Board announces that over the next year, the rate of money growth will be reduced from its current rate of 10 percent to a rate of 2 percent. If the

chairman is believed by the public but the Fed actually reduces the rate of money growth to 5 percent, predict what will happen to the inflation rate and aggregate output if the new classical view of the economy is correct.

*14. How would your prediction differ in Problem 13 if the new Keynesian model provides a more accurate description of the economy? What if the traditional model provides the most realistic description of the economy?

15. If, in a surprise victory, a new administration is elected to office that the public believes will pursue inflationary policy, predict what might happen to the level of output and inflation even before the new administration comes into power. Would your prediction differ depending on which of the three models—traditional, new classical, and new Keynesian—you believed in?

A MATHEMATICAL TREATMENT OF THE BAUMOL-TOBIN AND TOBIN MEAN-VARIANCE MODELS

BAUMOL-TOBIN MODEL OF TRANSACTIONS DEMAND FOR MONEY

The basic idea behind the Baumol-Tobin model was laid out in the chapter. Here we explore the mathematics that underlie the model. The assumptions of the model are as follows:

1. An individual receives income of T_0 at the beginning of every period.
2. An individual spends this income at a constant rate, so at the end of the period, all income T_0 has been spent.
3. There are only two assets—cash and bonds. Cash earns a nominal return of zero, and bonds earn an interest rate i.
4. Every time an individual buys or sells bonds to raise cash, a fixed brokerage fee of b is incurred.

Let us denote the amount of cash that the individual raises for each purchase or sale of bonds as C, and $n =$ the number of times the individual conducts a transaction in bonds. As we saw in Figure 3 in the chapter, where $T_0 = 1000$, $C = 500$, and $n = 2$,

$$n = \frac{T_0}{C}$$

Because the brokerage cost of each bond transaction is b, the total brokerage costs for a period are

$$nb = \frac{bT_0}{C}$$

Not only are there brokerage costs, but there is also an opportunity cost to holding cash rather than bonds. This opportunity cost is the bond interest rate i times average cash balances held during the period, which, from the discussion in the chapter, we know is equal to $C/2$. The opportunity cost is then

$$\frac{iC}{2}$$

Combining these two costs, we have the total costs for an individual equal to

$$\text{Costs} = \frac{bT_0}{C} + \frac{iC}{2}$$

The individual wants to minimize costs by choosing the appropriate level of C. This is accomplished by taking the derivative of costs with respect to C and setting it to zero.[1] That is,

$$\frac{d\,\text{Costs}}{dC} = \frac{-bT_0}{C^2} + \frac{i}{2} = 0$$

Solving for C yields the optimal level of C:

$$C = \sqrt{\frac{2bT_0}{i}}$$

Because money demand M^d is the average desired holding of cash balances $C/2$,

$$M^d = \frac{1}{2}\sqrt{\frac{2bT_0}{i}} = \sqrt{\frac{bT_0}{2i}} \tag{1}$$

This is the famous *square root rule*.[2] It has these implications for the demand for money:

---

[1] To minimize costs, the second derivative must be greater than zero. We find that it is, because

$$\frac{d^2\,\text{Costs}}{dC^2} = \frac{-2}{C^3}(-bT_0) = \frac{2bT_0}{C^3} > 0$$

[2] An alternative way to get Equation 1 is to have the individual maximize profits, which equal the interest on bonds minus the brokerage costs. The average holding of bonds over a period is just

$$\frac{T_0}{2} - \frac{C}{2}$$

Thus profits are

$$\text{Profits} = -\frac{i}{2}(T_0 - C) - \frac{bT_0}{C}$$

Then

$$\frac{d\,\text{Profits}}{dC} = \frac{-i}{2} + \frac{bT_0}{C^2} = 0$$

This equation yields the same square root rule as Equation 1.

1. The transactions demand for money is negatively related to the interest rate i.
2. The transactions demand for money is positively related to income, but there are economies of scale in money holdings—that is, the demand for money rises less than proportionally with income. For example, if T_0 quadruples in Equation 1, the demand for money only doubles.
3. A lowering of the brokerage costs due to technological improvements would decrease the demand for money.
4. There is no money illusion in the demand for money. If the price level doubles, both T_0 and b will double. Equation 1 then indicates that M will double as well. Thus the demand for real money balances remains unchanged, which makes sense because neither the interest rate nor real income has changed.

TOBIN MEAN-VARIANCE MODEL

Tobin's mean-variance analysis of money demand is just an application of the basic ideas in the theory of portfolio choice outlined in Chapter 5. Tobin assumes that the utility that people derive from their assets is positively related to the expected return on their portfolio of assets and is negatively related to the riskiness of this portfolio as represented by the variance (or standard deviation) of its returns. This framework implies that an individual has indifference curves that can be drawn as in Figure 1. Notice that these indifference curves slope upward because an individual is willing to accept more risk if offered a higher expected return. In addition, as we go to higher indifference curves, utility is higher because for the same level of risk, the expected return is higher.

Tobin looks at the choice of holding money, which earns a certain zero return, or bonds, whose return

$$R_B = i + g$$

where i = interest rate on the bond and g = capital gain. Tobin also assumes that the expected capital gain is zero[3] and its variance is σ_g^2. That is,

$$E(g) = 0 \qquad \text{and so} \qquad E(R_B) = i + 0 = i$$

$$Var(g) = E[g - E(g)]^2 = E(g^2) = \sigma_g^2$$

where E = expectation of the variable inside the parentheses and Var = variance of the variable inside the parentheses.

If A is the fraction of the portfolio put into bonds ($0 \leq A \leq 1$) and $1 - A$ is the fraction of the portfolio held as money, the return R on the portfolio can be written as

$$R = AR_B + (1 - A)(0) = AR_B = A(i + g)$$

---

[3]This assumption is not critical to the results. If $E(g) \neq 0$, it can be added to the interest term i, and the analysis proceeds as indicated.

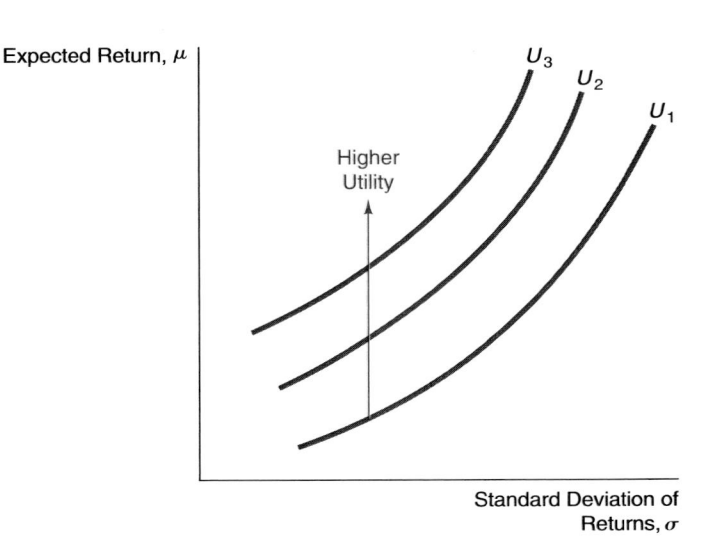

FIGURE 1 Indifference Curves in a Mean-Variance Model

The indifference curves are upward-sloping, and higher indifference curves indicate that utility is higher. In other words, $U_3 > U_2 > U_1$.

Then the mean and variance of the return on the portfolio, denoted respectively as μ and σ^2, can be calculated as follows:

$$\mu = E(R) = E(AR_B) = AE(R_B) = Ai$$

$$\sigma^2 = E(R - \mu)^2 = E[A(i + g) - Ai]^2 = E(Ag)^2 = A^2 E(g^2) = A^2 \sigma_g^2$$

Taking the square root of both sides of the equation directly above and solving for A yields

$$A = \frac{1}{\sigma_g}\sigma \qquad (2)$$

Substituting for A in the equation $\mu = Ai$ using the preceding equation gives us

$$\mu = \frac{i}{\sigma_g}\sigma \qquad (3)$$

Equation 3 is known as the *opportunity locus* because it tells us the combinations of μ and σ that are feasible for the individual. This equation is written in a form in which the μ variable corresponds to the y axis and the σ variable to the x axis. The opportunity locus is a straight line going through the origin with a slope of i/σ_g. It is drawn in the top half of Figure 2 along with the indifference curves from Figure 1.

The highest indifference curve is reached at point B, the tangency of the indifference curve and the opportunity locus. This point determines the optimal level of risk σ^* in the figure. As Equation 2 indicates, the optimal level of A, A^* is

$$A^* = \frac{\sigma^*}{\sigma_g}$$

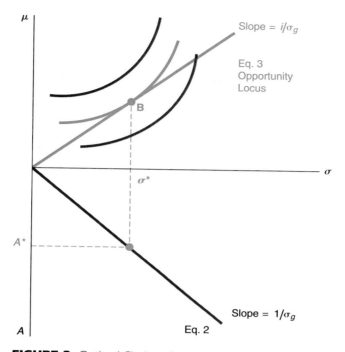

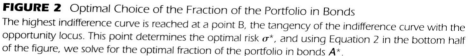

FIGURE 2 Optimal Choice of the Fraction of the Portfolio in Bonds
The highest indifference curve is reached at a point B, the tangency of the indifference curve with the opportunity locus. This point determines the optimal risk σ^*, and using Equation 2 in the bottom half of the figure, we solve for the optimal fraction of the portfolio in bonds **A***.

This equation is solved in the bottom half of Figure 2. Equation 2 for A is a straight line through the origin with a slope of $1/\sigma_g$. Given σ^*, the value of A read off this line is the optimal value A^*. Notice that the bottom part of the figure is drawn so that as we move down, A is increasing.

Now let's ask ourselves what happens when the interest rate increases from i_1 to i_2. This situation is shown in Figure 3. Because σ_g is unchanged, the Equation 2 line in the bottom half of the figure does not change. However, the slope of the opportunity locus does increase as i increases. Thus the opportunity locus rotates up and we move to point C at the tangency of the new opportunity locus and the indifference curve. As you can see, the optimal level of risk increases from σ_1^* to σ_2^*, and the optimal fraction of the portfolio in bonds rises from A_1^* to A_2^*. The result is that as the interest rate on bonds rises, the demand for money falls; that is, $1 - A$, the fraction of the portfolio held as money, declines.[4]

---

[4]The indifference curves have been drawn so that the usual result is obtained that as i goes up, A^* goes up as well. However, there is a subtle issue of income versus substitution effects. If, as people get wealthier, they are willing to bear less risk, and if this income effect is larger than the substitution effect, then it is possible to get the opposite result that as i increases, A^* declines. This set of conditions is unlikely, which is why the figure is drawn so that the usual result is obtained. For a discussion of income versus substitution effects, see David Laidler, *The Demand for Money: Theories and Evidence,* 4th ed. (New York: HarperCollins, 1993).

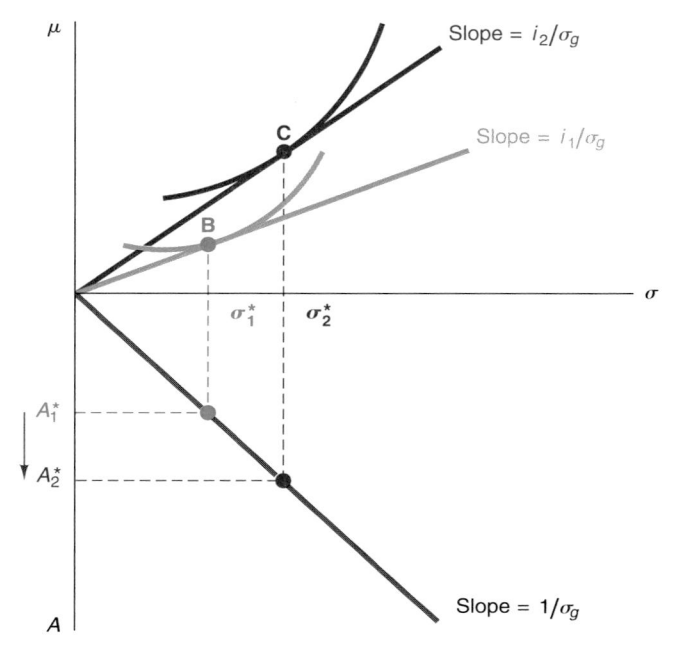

FIGURE 3 Optimal Choice of the Fraction of the Portfolio in Bonds as the Interest Rate Rises

The interest rate on bonds rises from i_1 to i_2, rotating the opportunity locus upward. The highest indifference curve is now at point **C** where it is tangent to the new opportunity locus. The optimal level of risk rises from σ_1^* to σ_2^*, and then Equation 2, in the bottom half of the figure, shows that the optimal fraction of the portfolio in bonds rises from A_1^* to A_2^*.

Tobin's model then yields the same result as Keynes's analysis of the speculative demand for money: It is negatively related to the level of interest rates. This model, however, makes two important points that Keynes's model does not:

1. Individuals diversify their portfolios and hold money *and* bonds at the same time.
2. Even if the expected return on bonds is greater than the expected return on money, individuals will still hold money as a store of wealth because its return is more certain.

ALGEBRA OF THE *ISLM* MODEL

The use of algebra to analyze the *ISLM* model allows us to extend the multiplier analysis in Chapter 22 and to obtain many of the results of Chapters 22 and 23 very quickly.

BASIC CLOSED-ECONOMY *ISLM* MODEL

The goods market can be described by the following equations:

Consumption function:	$C = \overline{C} + mpc\,(Y - T)$	(1)
Investment function:	$I = \overline{I} - di$	(2)
Taxes:	$T = \overline{T}$	(3)
Government spending:	$G = \overline{G}$	(4)
Goods market equilibrium condition:	$Y = Y^{ad} = C + I + G$	(5)

The money market is described by these equations:

Money demand function:	$M^d = \overline{M}^d + eY - fi$	(6)
Money supply:	$M^s = \overline{M}$	(7)
Money market equilibrium condition:	$M^d = M^s$	(8)

The uppercase terms are the variables of the model; $\overline{G}$, $\overline{T}$, and $\overline{M}$, are the values of the policy variables that are set exogenously (outside the model); and $\overline{C}$, $\overline{I}$, and $\overline{M}^d$ are autonomous components of consumer expenditure, investment spending, and money demand that are also determined exogenously (outside the model). Except for the interest rate i, the lowercase terms are the parameters, the givens of the model, and all are assumed to be positive. The definitions of these variables and parameters are as follows:

$$C = \text{consumer spending}$$
$$I = \text{investment spending}$$
$$G = \overline{G} = \text{government spending}$$
$$Y = \text{output}$$
$$T = \overline{T} = \text{taxes}$$

$$M^d = \text{money demand}$$
$$M^s = \overline{M} = \text{money supply}$$
$$i = \text{interest rate}$$
$$\overline{C} = \text{autonomous consumer spending}$$
$$d = \text{interest sensitivity of investment spending}$$
$$\overline{I} = \text{autonomous investment spending related to business confidence}$$
$$\overline{M}^d = \text{autonomous money demand}$$
$$e = \text{income sensitivity of money demand}$$
$$f = \text{interest sensitivity of money demand}$$
$$mpc = \text{marginal propensity to consume}$$

**IS and LM
Curves**

Substituting for *C*, *I*, and *G* in the goods market equilibrium condition and then solving for *Y*, we obtain the *IS* curve:

$$Y = \frac{1}{1 - mpc} (\overline{C} + \overline{I} - mpc\,\overline{T} + \overline{G} - di) \tag{9}$$

Solving for *i* from Equations 6, 7, and 8, we obtain the *LM* curve:

$$i = \frac{\overline{M}^d - \overline{M} + eY}{f} \tag{10}$$

**Solution of
the Model**

The solution to the model occurs at the intersection of the *IS* and *LM* curves, which involves solving for *Y* and *i* simultaneously, using Equations 9 and 10, as follows:

$$Y = \frac{1}{1 - mpc + de/f} \left(\overline{C} + \overline{I} - mpc\,\overline{T} + \overline{G} - \frac{d\overline{M}^d}{f} + \frac{d\overline{M}}{f} \right) \tag{11}$$

$$i = \frac{1}{f(1 - mpc) + d} \left[e(\overline{C} + \overline{I} - mpc\,\overline{T} + \overline{G}) + \overline{M}^d(1 - mpc) - \overline{M}(1 - mpc) \right] \tag{12}$$

Implications

The conclusions reached with these algebraic solutions are the same as those reached in Chapters 22 and 23; for example:

1. Because all the coefficients are positive, Equation 11 indicates that a rise in $\overline{C}, \overline{I}, \overline{G},$ and $\overline{M}$ leads to a rise in *Y* and that a rise in $\overline{T}$ or $\overline{M}^d$ leads to a fall in *Y*.
2. Equation 12 indicates that a rise in $\overline{C}, \overline{I}, \overline{G},$ and $\overline{M}^d$ leads to a rise in *i* and that a rise in $\overline{M}$ or $\overline{T}$ leads to a fall in *i*.
3. As *f*, the interest sensitivity of money demand, increases, the multiplier term

$$\frac{1}{1 - mpc + de/f}$$

increases, and so fiscal policy ($\overline{G}$, $\overline{T}$) has more effect on output; conversely, the term multiplying $\overline{M}$,

$$\frac{d}{f}\left(\frac{1}{1 - mpc + de/f}\right) = \frac{d}{f(1 - mpc) + de}$$

declines, so monetary policy has less effect on output.

4. By similar reasoning, as d, the interest sensitivity of investment spending, increases, monetary policy has more effect on output and fiscal policy has less effect on output.

OPEN-ECONOMY *ISLM* MODEL

To make the basic *ISLM* model into an open-economy model, we need to include net exports in the goods market equilibrium condition so that Equation 5 becomes Equation 5′:

$$Y = Y^{ad} = C + I + G + NX \qquad (5')$$

As the discussion in Chapter 23 suggests, the net exports and exchange rate relations can be written

$$NX = \overline{NX} - bE \qquad (13)$$
$$E = \overline{E} + ji \qquad (14)$$

where

NX = net exports
$\overline{NX}$ = autonomous net exports
b = exchange rate sensitivity of net exports
E = exchange rate (value of domestic currency)
$\overline{E}$ = autonomous exchange rate
j = interest sensitivity of exchange rate

Substituting for net exports in the goods market equilibrium condition (Equation 5′) using the net exports and exchange rate relations and then solving for Y as in the basic model, we obtain the open-economy *IS* curve:

$$Y = \frac{1}{1 - mpc}\left[\overline{C} + \overline{I} - mpc\,\overline{T} + \overline{G} + \overline{NX} - b\overline{E} - (d + bj)i\right] \qquad (15)$$

The *LM* curve is the same as in the basic model, and so the solutions for Y and i are as follows:

$$Y = \frac{1}{1 - mpc + (d + bj)e/f}$$
$$\times (\overline{C} + \overline{I} - mpc\,\overline{T} + \overline{G} - \frac{d + bj}{f}\overline{M}^d + \frac{d + bj}{f}\overline{M} + \overline{NX} - b\overline{E}) \qquad (16)$$

$$i = \frac{1}{f(1 - mpc) + (d + bj)e}$$
$$\times \left[e(\overline{C} + \overline{I} - mpc\,\overline{T} + \overline{G} + \overline{NX} - b\overline{E}) + \overline{M}^d(1 - mpc) - \overline{M}(1 - mpc)\right] \qquad (17)$$

Implications

1. As the *IS* curve in Equation 15 indicates, including net exports in aggregate demand provides an additional reason for the negative relationship between Y and i (the downward slope of the *IS* curve). This additional reason for the negative relationship of Y and i is represented by hj in the term $-(d + hj)i$.

2. Equations 16 and 17 indicate that all the results we found for the basic model still hold.

3. Equation 16 indicates that a rise in $\overline{NX}$ leads to a rise in Y and that an autonomous rise in the value of the domestic currency $\overline{E}$ leads to a decline in Y.

4. Equation 17 indicates that a rise in $\overline{NX}$ leads to a rise in i and that a rise in $\overline{E}$ leads to a decline in i.

GLOSSARY

accommodating policy   An activist policy in pursuit of a high employment target. **668**

activist   An economist who views the self-correcting mechanism through wage and price adjustment to be very slow and hence sees the need for the government to pursue active, discretionary policy to eliminate high unemployment whenever it develops. **613**

adaptive expectations   Expectations of a variable based on an average of past values of the variable. **689**

adverse selection   The problem created by asymmetric information *before* a transaction occurs: The people who are the most undesirable from the other party's point of view are the ones who are most likely to want to engage in the financial transaction. **35**

aggregate demand   The total quantity of output demanded in the economy at different price levels. **556, 603**

aggregate demand curve   A relationship between the price level and the quantity of aggregate output demanded when the goods and money markets are in equilibrium. **598, 603**

aggregate demand function   The relationship between aggregate output and aggregate demand that shows the quantity of aggregate output demanded for each level of aggregate output. **560**

aggregate income   The total income of factors of production (land, labor, capital) in the economy. **17**

aggregate output   The total production of final goods and services in the economy. **9**

aggregate price level   The average price of goods and services in an economy. **10**

aggregate supply   The quantity of aggregate output supplied by the economy at different price levels. **603**

aggregate supply curve   The relationship between the quantity of output supplied in the short run and the price level. **609**

American option   An option that can be exercised at any time up to the expiration date of the contract. **697**

"animal spirits"   Waves of optimism and pessimism that affect consumers' and businesses' willingness to spend. **564, 607**

annuities   Financial contracts under which a customer pays an annual premium in exchange for a future stream of annual payments beginning at a set age, say, 65, and ending when the person dies. **334**

appreciation   Increase in a currency's value. **167**

arbitrage   Elimination of a riskless profit opportunity in a market. **358**

asset   A financial claim or piece of property that is a store of value. **4, 94**

asset management   The acquisition of assets that have a low rate of default and diversification of asset holdings to increase profits. **235**

asset market approach   An approach to determine asset prices using stocks of assets rather than flows. **109**

asymmetric information   The unequal knowledge that each party to a transaction has about the other party. **35**

autonomous consumer expenditure   The amount of consumer expenditure that is independent of disposable income. **557**

balance of payments   A bookkeeping system for recording all payments that have a direct bearing on the movement of funds between a country and foreign countries. **507**

balance-of-payments crisis   A foreign exchange crisis stemming from problems in a country's balance of payments. **520**

balance sheet   A list of the assets and liabilities of a bank (or firm) that balances: Total assets equal total liabilities plus capital. **226**

bank failure   A situation in which a bank cannot satisfy its obligations to pay its depositors and other creditors and so goes out of business. **297**

bank holding companies   Companies that own one or more banks. **267**

bank panic   The simultaneous failure of many banks, as during a financial crisis. **217**

banks   Financial institutions that accept money deposits and make loans (such as commercial banks, savings and loan associations, and credit unions). **8**

bank supervision   Overseeing who operates banks and how they are operated. **302**

basis point   One one-hundredth of a percentage point. **84**

basis risk The risk associated with the possibility that the prices of a hedged asset and the asset underlying the futures contract do not move closely together over time. **364**

beta A measure of the sensitivity of an asset's return to changes in the value of the market portfolio, which is also a measure of the asset's marginal contribution to the risk of the market portfolio. **100**

Board of Governors of the Federal Reserve System A board with seven governors (including the chairman) that plays an essential role in decision making within the Federal Reserve System. **390**

bond A debt security that promises to make payments periodically for a specified period of time. **4**

branches Additional offices of banks that conduct banking operations. **268**

Bretton Woods system The international monetary system in use from 1945 to 1971 in which exchange rates were fixed and the U.S. dollar was freely convertible into gold (by foreign governments and central banks only). **513**

brokerage firms Firms that participate in securities markets as brokers, dealers, and investment bankers. **351**

brokered deposits Deposits that enable depositors to circumvent the $100,000 limit on federal deposit insurance by breaking up a large deposit into smaller packages of less than $100,000 at each bank so that the total amount deposited is fully insured. **313**

brokers Agents for investors who match buyers with sellers. **24**

bubble A situation in which the price of an asset differs from its fundamental market value. **707**

budget deficit The excess of government expenditure over tax revenues. **13**

business cycles The upward and downward movement of aggregate output produced in the economy. **9**

call option An option contract that provides the right to buy a security at a specified price. **368**

capital account An account that describes the flow of capital between the United States and other countries. **510**

capital adequacy management A bank's decision about the amount of capital it should maintain and then acquisition of the needed capital. **235**

capital market A financial market in which longer-term debt (maturity of greater than one year) and equity instruments are traded. **25**

capital mobility A situation in which foreigners can easily purchase a country's assets and the country's residents can easily purchase foreign assets. **176**

cash flow The difference between cash receipts and cash expenditures. **217**

central bank The government agency that oversees the banking system and is responsible for the amount of money and credit supplied in the economy; in the United States, the Federal Reserve System. **13, 265**

closed-end fund A mutual fund in which a fixed number of nonredeemable shares are sold at an initial offering, then traded in the over-the-counter market like common stock. **345**

coinsurance A situation in which only a portion of losses are covered by insurance, so that the insured suffers a percentage of the losses along with the insurance agency. **322**

collateral Property that is pledged to the lender to guarantee payment in the event that the borrower should be unable to make debt payments. **208**

commodity money Money made up of precious metals or another valuable commodity. **52**

compensating balance A required minimum amount of funds that a firm receiving a loan must keep in a checking account at the lending bank. **247**

complete crowding out The situation in which expansionary fiscal policy, such as an increase in government spending, does not lead to a rise in output because there is an exactly offsetting movement in private spending. **592, 608**

consol A perpetual bond with no maturity date and no repayment of principal that periodically makes fixed coupon payments. **77**

constant-money-growth-rate rule A policy rule advocated by monetarists whereby the Federal Reserve keeps the money supply growing at a constant rate. **683**

consumer durable expenditure Spending by consumers on durable items such as automobiles and household appliances. **644**

consumer expenditure The total demand for (spending on) consumer goods and services. **556, 606**

consumption Spending by consumers on nondurable goods and services (including services related to the ownership of homes and consumer durables). **648**

consumption function The relationship between disposable income and consumer expenditure. **557**

costly state verification Monitoring a firm's activities, an expensive process in both time and money. **208**

cost-push inflation Inflation that occurs because of the push by workers to obtain higher wages. **668**

coupon bond A credit market instrument that pays the owner a fixed interest payment every year until the maturity date, when a specified final amount is repaid. **70**

coupon rate The dollar amount of the yearly coupon payment expressed as a percentage of the face value of a coupon bond. **70**

creditor A holder of debt. **214**

credit rationing A lender's refusing to make loans even though borrowers are willing to pay the stated interest rate or even a higher rate or restricting the size of loans made to less than the full amount sought. **249**

credit risk The risk arising from the possibility that the borrower will default. **235**

credit view Monetary transmission mechanisms operating through asymmetric information effects on credit markets. **645**

currency Paper money (such as dollar bills) and coins. **26**

currency swap The exchange of a set of payments in one currency for a set of payments in another currency. **375**

current account An account that shows international transactions involving currently produced goods and services. **508**

current yield An approximation of the yield to maturity that equals the yearly coupon payment divided by the price of a coupon bond. **79**

dealers People who link buyers with sellers by buying and selling securities at stated prices. **24**

debt deflation A situation in which a substantial decline in the price level sets in, leading to a further deterioration in firms' net worth because of the increased burden of indebtedness. **226**

deductible The fixed amount by which the insured's loss is reduced when a claim is paid off. **339**

default A situation in which the party issuing a debt instrument is unable to make interest payments or pay off the amount owed when the instrument matures. **26**

default-free bonds Bonds with no default risk, such as U.S. government bonds. **144**

default risk The chance that the issuer of a debt instrument will be unable to make interest pay-

ments or pay off the face value when the instrument matures. **144**

defensive open market operations Open market operations intended to offset movements in other factors that affect the monetary base (such as changes in Treasury deposits with the Fed or changes in float). **458**

defined-benefit plan A pension plan in which benefits are set in advance. **341**

defined-contribution plan A pension plan in which benefits are determined by the contributions into the plan and their earnings. **341**

demand curve A curve depicting the relationship between quantity demanded and price when all other economic variables are held constant. **104**

demand-pull inflation Inflation that results when policymakers pursue policies that shift the aggregate demand curve. **668**

deposit outflows Losses of deposits when depositors make withdrawals or demand payment. **235**

deposit rate ceiling Restriction on the maximum interest rate payable on deposits. **259**

depreciation Decrease in a currency's value. **167**

devaluation Resetting of the fixed value of a currency at a lower level. **515**

dirty float See *managed float regime.* **502**

discount bond A credit market instrument that is bought at a price below its face value and whose face value is repaid at the maturity date; it does not make any interest payments. Also called a *zero-coupon bond.* **70**

discount loans A bank's borrowings from the Federal Reserve System; also known as *advances.* **229**

discount rate The interest rate that the Federal Reserve charges banks on discount loans. **237**

discount window The Federal Reserve facility at which discount loans are made to banks. **461**

discount yield See *yield on a discount basis.* **80**

disintermediation A reduction in the flow of funds into the banking system that causes the amount of financial intermediation to decline. **259**

disposable income Total income available for spending, equal to aggregate income minus taxes. **557**

diversification The holding of a variety of risky assets. **98**

dividends Periodic payments made by equities to shareholders. **23**

dual banking system The system in the United States in which banks supervised by the federal government and banks supervised by the states operate side by side. **266**

duration analysis A measurement of the sensitivity of the market value of a bank's assets and liabilities to changes in interest rates. **251**

dynamic open market operations Open market operations that are intended to change the level of reserves and the monetary base. **458**

econometric model A model whose equations are estimated using statistical procedures. **711**

economies of scale The reduction in transaction costs per dollar of transaction as the size (scale) of transactions increases. **35**

Edge Act corporation A special subsidiary of a U.S. bank that is engaged primarily in international banking. **282**

effective exchange rate index An index reflecting the value of a basket of representative foreign currencies. **187**

efficient markets theory The application of the theory of rational expectations to financial markets. **691**

electronic money (e-money) Money that is stored electronically. **55**

equation of exchange The equation $MV = PY$, which relates nominal income to the quantity of money. **530, 604**

equities Claims to share in the net income and assets of a corporation (such as common stock). **23**

equity capital See *net worth*. **206**

equity multiplier *(EM)* The amount of assets per dollar of equity capital. **241**

Eurobonds Bonds denominated in a currency other than that of the country in which they are sold. **32**

Eurodollars U.S. dollars that are deposited in foreign banks outside of the United States or in foreign branches of U.S. banks. **29**

European option An option that can be exercised only at the expiration date of the contract. **367**

excess demand A situation in which quantity demanded is greater than quantity supplied. **107**

excess reserves Reserves in excess of required reserves. **229, 417**

excess supply A situation in which quantity supplied is greater than quantity demanded. **107**

exchange rate The price of one currency in terms of another. **165**

exchange rate overshooting A phenomenon whereby the exchange rate changes by more in the short run than it does in the long run when the money supply changes. **186**

exchanges Secondary markets in which buyers and sellers of securities (or their agents or brokers) meet in one central location to conduct trades. **24**

exercise price The price at which the purchaser of an option has the right to buy or sell the underlying financial instrument. Also known as the *strike price*. **367**

expectations hypothesis The proposition that the interest rate on a long-term bond will equal the average of the short-term interest rates that people expect to occur over the life of the long-term bond. **152**

expected return The return on an asset expected over the next period. **95**

expenditure multiplier The ratio of a change in aggregate output to a change in investment spending (or autonomous spending). **562**

face value A specified final amount paid to the owner of a coupon bond at the maturity date. Also called *par value*. **70**

federal funds rate The interest rate on overnight loans of deposits at the Federal Reserve. **28**

Federal Open Market Committee (FOMC) The committee that makes decisions regarding the conduct of open market operations; composed of the seven members of the Board of Governors of the Federal Reserve System, the president of the Federal Reserve Bank of New York, and the presidents of four other Federal Reserve banks on a rotating basis. **390**

Federal Reserve banks The 12 district banks in the Federal Reserve System. **390**

Federal Reserve System (the Fed) The central banking authority responsible for monetary policy in the United States. **13**

fiat money Paper currency decreed by a government as legal tender but not convertible into coins or precious metal. **53**

financial crisis A major disruption in financial markets that is characterized by sharp declines in asset prices and the failures of many financial and nonfinancial firms. **223**

financial derivatives Instruments that have payoffs that are linked to previously issued securities, used as risk reduction tools. **354**

financial engineering The process of researching and developing new financial products and services that would meet customer needs and prove profitable. **255**

financial futures contract   A futures contract in which the standardized commodity is a particular type of financial instrument. **356**

financial futures option   An option in which the underlying instrument is a futures contract. Also called a futures option. **367**

financial intermediaries   Institutions (such as banks, insurance companies, mutual funds, pension funds, and finance companies) that borrow funds from people who have saved and then make loans to others. **7**

financial intermediation   The process of indirect finance whereby financial intermediaries link lender-savers and borrower-spenders. **34**

financial markets   Markets in which funds are transferred from people who have a surplus of available funds to people who have a shortage of available funds. **3**

financial panic   The widespread collapse of financial markets and intermediaries in an economy. **42**

Fisher effect   The outcome that when expected inflation occurs, interest rates will rise; named after economist Irving Fisher. **117**

fixed exchange rate regime   A regime in which central banks buy and sell their own currencies to keep their exchange rates fixed at a certain level. **513**

fixed investment   Spending by firms on equipment (computers, airplanes) and structures (factories, office buildings) and planned spending on residential housing. **558**

fixed-payment loan   A credit market instrument that provides a borrower with an amount of money that is repaid by making a fixed payment periodically (usually monthly) for a set number of years. **70**

float   Cash items in process of collection at the Fed minus deferred-availability cash items. **418**

foreign bonds   Bonds sold in a foreign country and denominated in that country's currency. **32**

foreign exchange intervention   An international financial transaction in which a central bank buys or sells currency to influence foreign exchange rates. **502**

foreign exchange market   The market in which exchange rates are determined. **6**

foreign exchange rate   See *exchange rate.* **6**

forward contract   An agreement by two parties to engage in a financial transaction at a future (forward) point in time. **354**

forward exchange rate   The exchange rate for a forward transaction. **167**

forward transaction   A transaction that involves the exchange of bank deposits denominated in different currencies at some specified future date. **167**

free reserves   Excess reserves in the banking system minus the volume of discount loans. **487**

free-rider problem   The problem that occurs when people who do not pay for information take advantage of the information that other people have paid for. **203**

fully funded   Describing a pension plan in which the contributions to the plan and their earnings over the years are sufficient to pay out the defined benefits when they come due. **341**

futures option   See *financial futures option.* **367**

gap analysis   A measurement of the sensitivity of bank profits to changes in interest rates, calculated by subtracting the amount of rate-sensitive liabilities from the amount of rate-sensitive assets. **250**

gold standard   A regime under which a currency is directly convertible into gold. **511**

government budget constraint   The requirement that the government budget deficit equal the sum of the change in the monetary base and the change in government bonds held by the public. **672**

government spending   Spending by all levels of government on goods and services. **556, 606**

gross domestic product (GDP)   The value of all final goods and services produced in the economy during the course of a year. **17**

hedge   To protect oneself against risk. **355**

high-powered money   The monetary base. **417**

hyperinflation   An extreme inflation in which the inflation rate exceeds 50 percent per month. **52**

hysteresis   A departure from full employment levels as a result of past high unemployment. **619**

incentive-compatible   Aligning the incentives of both parties to a contract. **211**

income   The flow of earnings. **49**

indexed bond   A bond whose interest and principal payments are adjusted for changes in the price level, and whose interest rate thus provides a direct measure of a real interest rate. **92**

inflation   The condition of a continually rising price level. **10**

inflation rate   The rate of change of the price level, usually measured as a percentage change per year. **11**

insolvent   In a situation in which the value of a

firm's or bank's assets have fallen below its liabilities; bankrupt. 266

interest parity condition   The observation that the domestic interest rate equals the foreign interest rate plus the expected appreciation in the foreign currency. 176

interest rate   The cost of borrowing or the price paid for the rental of funds (usually expressed as a percentage per year.) 4

interest-rate forward contract   A forward contract that is linked to a debt instrument. 354

interest-rate risk   The possible reduction in returns that is associated with changes in interest rates. 87, 235

interest-rate swap   A financial contract that allows one party to exchange (swap) a set of interest payments for another set of interest payments owned by another party. 375

intermediate target   Any of a number of variables, such as monetary aggregates or interest rates, that have a direct effect on employment and the price level and that the Fed seeks to influence. 478

intermediate-term   With reference to a debt instrument, having a maturity of between one and ten years. 23

international banking facilities (IBFs)   Banking establishments in the United States that can accept time deposits from foreigners but are not subject to either reserve requirements or restrictions on interest payments. 282

International Monetary Fund (IMF)   The international organization created by the Bretton Woods agreement whose objective is to promote the growth of world trade by making loans to countries experiencing balance-of-payments difficulties. 513

international policy coordination   Agreements among countries to enact policies cooperatively. 494

international reserves   Central bank holdings of assets denominated in foreign currencies. 502

inventory investment   Spending by firms on additional holdings of raw materials, parts, and finished goods. 559

inverted yield curve   A yield curve that is downward-sloping. 152

investment banks   Firms that assist in the initial sale of securities in the primary market. 24

IS curve   The relationship that describes the combinations of aggregate output and interest rates for which the total quantity of goods produced equals the total quantity demanded (goods market equilibrium). 571

January effect   An abnormal rise in stock prices from December to January. 700

junk bonds   Bonds with ratings below Baa (or BBB) that have a high default risk. 146

Keynesian   A follower of John Maynard Keynes who believes that movements in the price level and aggregate output are driven by changes not only in the money supply but also in government spending and fiscal policy and who does not regard the economy as inherently stable. 603

L   A measure of highly liquid assets that adds to M3 short-term Treasury securities, commercial paper, long-term Eurodollars, savings bonds, and banker's acceptances. 59

law of one price   The principle that if two countries produce an identical good, the price of this good should be the same throughout the world no matter which country produces it. 170

lender of last resort   Provider of reserves to financial institutions when no one else would provide them in order to prevent a financial crisis. 463

leverage ratio   A bank's capital divided by its assets. 301

liabilities   IOUs or debts. 21

liability management   The acquisition of funds at low cost to increase profits. 235

liquid   Easily converted into cash. 24

liquidity   The relative ease and speed with which an asset can be converted into cash. 51, 95

liquidity management   The decisions made by a bank to maintain sufficient liquid assets to meet the bank's obligations to depositors. 235

liquidity preference framework   A model developed by John Maynard Keynes that predicts the equilibrium interest rate on the basis of the supply of and demand for money. 122

liquidity preference theory   John Maynard Keynes's theory of the demand for money. 535

liquidity premium theory   The theory that the interest rate on a long-term bond will equal an average of short-term interest rates expected to occur over the life of the long-term bond plus a positive term (liquidity) premium. 158

LM curve   The relationship that describes the combinations of interest rates and aggregate output for which the quantity of money demanded equals the quantity of money supplied (money market equilibrium). 521

load funds   Open-end mutual funds sold by salespeople who receive a commission that is paid at the time of purchase and is immediately subtracted from the redemption value of the shares. **345**

loanable funds   The quantity of loans. **108**

loanable funds framework   Determining the equilibrium interest rate by analyzing the supply of and demand for bonds (loanable funds). **108**

loan commitment   A bank's commitment (for a specified future period of time) to provide a firm with loans up to a given amount at an interest rate that is tied to some market interest rate. **247**

loan sale   The sale under a contract (also called a *secondary loan participation*) of all or part of the cash stream from a specific loan, thereby removing the loan from the bank's balance sheet. **252**

long position   A contractual obligation to take delivery of an underlying financial instrument. **355**

long-run aggregate supply curve   The quantity of output supplied in the long run at any given price level. **612**

long-run monetary neutrality   See *monetary neutrality*. **596**

long-term   With reference to a debt instrument, having a maturity of ten years or more. **23**

luxury   An asset for which the wealth elasticity of demand is greater than 1. **96**

M1   A measure of money that includes currency, traveler's checks, and checkable deposits. **58**

M2   A measure of money that adds to M1 money market deposit accounts, money market mutual fund shares, small-denomination time deposits, savings deposits, overnight repurchase agreements, and overnight Eurodollars. **58**

M3   A measure of money that adds to M2 large-denomination time deposits, long-term repurchase agreements, and institutional money market fund shares. **59**

macro hedge   A hedge of interest-rate risk for a financial institution's entire portfolio. **359**

managed float regime   The current international financial environment in which exchange rates fluctuate from day to day but central banks attempt to influence their countries' exchange rates by buying and selling currencies. Also known as a *dirty float*. **502**

marginal propensity to consume   The slope of the consumption function line that measures the change in consumer expenditure resulting from an additional dollar of disposable income. **557**

margin requirement   A sum of money that must be kept in an account (the margin account) at a brokerage firm. **364**

marked to market   Repriced and settled in the margin account at the end of every trading day to reflect any change in the value of the futures contract. **364**

market equilibrium   A situation occurring when the quantity that people are willing to buy (demand) equals the quantity that people are willing to sell (supply). **107**

market fundamentals   Items that have a direct impact on future income streams of a security. **695**

matched sale-purchase transaction   An arrangement whereby the Fed sells securities and the buyer agrees to sell them back to the Fed in the near future; sometimes called a *reverse repo*. **460**

maturity   Time to the expiration date (maturity date) of a debt instrument. **23**

mean reversion   The phenomenon that stocks with low returns today tend to have high returns in the future, and vice versa. **701**

medium of exchange   Anything that is used to pay for goods and services. **49**

micro hedge   A hedge for a specific asset. **359**

modern quantity theory of money   The theory that changes in aggregate spending are determined primarily by changes in the money supply. 605

monetarist   A follower of Milton Friedman who sees changes in the money supply as the primary source of movements in the price level and aggregate output and who views the economy as inherently stable. **603**

monetary aggregates   The various measures of the money supply used by the Federal Reserve System (M1, M2, M3, and L). **58**

monetary base   The sum of the Fed's monetary liabilities (currency in circulation and reserves) and the U.S. Treasury's monetary liabilities (Treasury currency in circulation, primarily coins). **417**

monetary neutrality   A proposition that in the long run, a percentage rise in the money supply is matched by the same percentage rise in the price level, leaving unchanged the real money supply and all other economic variables such as interest rates. **185**

monetary policy   The management of the money supply and interest rates. **12**

monetary theory   The theory that relates changes in the quantity of money to changes in economic activity. **10**

monetizing the debt   A method of financing government spending whereby the government debt issued to finance government spending is removed from the hands of the public and is replaced by high-powered money instead. Also called *printing money*. **672**

money Anything that is generally accepted in payment for goods or services or in the repayment of debts. **9**

money center banks Large banks in key financial centers (New York, Chicago, San Francisco). **239**

money market A financial market in which only short-term debt instruments (maturity of less than one year) are traded. **25**

money multiplier A ratio that relates the change in the money supply to a given change in the monetary base. **435**

money supply The quantity of money. **9**

moral hazard The risk that one party to a transaction will engage in behavior that is undesirable from the other party's point of view. **36**

multiple deposit creation The process whereby, when the Fed supplies the banking system with $1 of additional reserves, deposits increase by a multiple of this amount. **425**

NAIRU (nonaccelerating inflation rate of unemployment) The rate of unemployment when demand for labor equals supply, consequently eliminating the tendency for the inflation rate to change. **611**

national banks Federally chartered banks. **266**

natural rate level of output The level of aggregate output produced at the natural rate of unemployment at which there is no tendency for wages or prices to change. **596, 612**

natural rate of unemployment The rate of unemployment consistent with full employment at which the demand for labor equals the supply of labor. **475, 611**

necessity An asset for which as wealth grows, the percentage increase in demand is less than the percentage increase in wealth—in other words, an asset with wealth elasticity less than one. **95**

net exports Net foreign spending on domestic goods and services, equal to exports minus imports. **556, 606**

net worth The difference between a firm's assets (what it owns or is owed) and its liabilities (what it owes). Also called *equity capital*. **206**

no-load funds Mutual funds sold directly to the public on which no sales commissions are charged. **345**

nominal interest rate An interest rate that does not take inflation into account. **89**

nonaccelerating inflation rate of unemployment See *NAIRU*. **611**

nonactivist An economist who believes that the performance of the economy would be improved if the government avoided active policy to eliminate unemployment. **613**

nonbank banks Limited-service banks that either do not make commercial loans or do not take in deposits. **270**

nonborrowed monetary base The monetary base minus discount loans. **443**

nonsystematic risk The component of an asset's risk that is unique to the asset and so can be eliminated by diversification. **100**

notional principal The amount on which interest is being paid in a swap arrangement. **375**

off-balance-sheet activities Bank activities that involve trading financial instruments and the generation of income from fees and loan sales, all of which affect bank profits but are not visible on bank balance sheets. **252, 301**

official reserve transactions balance The current account balance plus items in the capital account. **510**

open-end fund A mutual fund in which shares can be redeemed at any time at a price that is tied to the asset value of the fund. **345**

open interest The number of contracts outstanding. **360**

open market operations The Fed's buying or selling of bonds in the open market. **393, 418**

open market purchase A purchase of bonds by the Fed. **418**

open market sale A sale of bonds by the Fed. **123**

operating target Any of a set of variables, such as reserve aggregates or interest rates, that the Fed seeks to influence and that are responsive to its policy tools. **478**

opportunity cost The amount of interest (expected return) sacrificed by not holding an alternative asset. **123**

optimal forecast The best guess of the future using all available information. **690**

option A contract that gives the purchaser the option (right) to buy or sell the underlying financial instrument at a specified price, called the *exercise price* or *strike price*, within a specific period of time (the term to expiration). **367**

over-the-counter (OTC) market A secondary market in which dealers at different locations who have an inventory of securities stand ready to buy and sell securities "over the counter" to anyone who comes to them and is willing to accept their prices. **24**

partial crowding out The situation in which an increase in government spending leads to a decline in private spending that does not completely offset the rise in government spending. **608**

par value See *face value*. **70**

payments system The method of conducting transactions in the economy. **52**

Phillips curve A relationship between unemployment and inflation discovered by A. W. Phillips. **625**

planned investment spending Total planned spending by businesses on new physical capital (machines, computers, apartment buildings) plus planned spending on new homes. **556, 606**

policy ineffectiveness proposition The conclusion from the new classical model that anticipated policy has no effect on output fluctuations. **715**

political business cycle A business cycle caused by expansionary policies before an election. **409**

preferred habitat theory The theory that the interest rate on a long-term bond will equal the average of the short-term interest rates expected to occur over the life of the long-term bond plus a term premium that responds to supply and demand conditions for that bond. **158**

premium The amount paid for an option contract. **367**

present discounted value See *present value*. **72**

present value Today's value of a payment to be received in the future when the interest rate is *i*. Also called *present discounted value*. **71**

primary dealers Government securities dealers, operating out of private firms or commercial banks, with whom the Fed's open market desk trades. **459**

primary market A financial market in which new issues of a security are sold to initial buyers. **23**

principal-agent problem A moral hazard problem that occurs when the managers in control (the agents) act in their own interest rather than in the interest of the owners (the principals) due to different sets of incentives. **207**

printing money See *monetizing the debt*. **673**

prudential supervision See bank supervision. **302**

put option An option contract that provides the right to sell a security at a specified price. **368**

quantity theory of money The theory that nominal income is determined solely by movements in the quantity of money. **531**

quotas Restrictions on the quantity of foreign goods that can be imported. **172**

random walk The movements of a variable whose future changes cannot be predicted (are random) because the variable is just as likely to fall as to rise from today's value. **697**

rate of capital gain The change in a security's price relative to the initial purchase price. **85**

rate of return See *return*. **85**

rational expectations Expectations that reflect optimal forecasts (the best guess of the future) using all available information. **690**

real bills doctrine A guiding principle (now discredited) for the conduct of monetary policy that states that as long as loans are made to support the production of goods and services, providing reserves to the banking system to make these loans will not be inflationary. **484**

real business cycle theory A theory that views real shocks to tastes and technology as the major driving force behind short-run business cycle fluctuations. **618**

real interest rate The interest rate adjusted for expected changes in the price level (inflation) so that it more accurately reflects the true cost of borrowing. **89**

real money balances The quantity of money in real terms. **553**

real terms Terms reflecting actual goods and services one can buy. **90**

recession A period when aggregate output is declining. **10**

reduced-form evidence Evidence that examines whether one variable has an effect on another by simply looking directly at the relationship between the two variables. **630**

Regulation Q The regulation under which the Federal Reserve System has the power to set maximum interest rates that banks can pay on savings and time deposits. **44**

regulatory forbearance Regulators' refraining from exercising their right to put an insolvent bank out of business. **314**

repurchase agreement (repo) An arrangement whereby the Fed, or another party, purchases securities with the understanding that the seller will repurchase them in a short period of time, usually less than a week. **460**

required reserve ratio The fraction of deposits that the Fed requires be kept as reserves. **229, 417**

required reserves Reserves that are held to meet the Fed's requirement that for every dollar of deposits at a bank, a certain fraction must be kept as reserves. **229, 417**

reserve currency A currency, such as the U.S. dollar, that is used by other countries to denominate the assets they hold as international reserves. **530**

reserve requirements Regulation making it obligatory for depository institutions to keep a certain fraction of their deposits in accounts with the Fed. **45**

reserves Banks' holding of deposits in accounts with the Fed plus currency that is physically held by banks (vault cash). **229, 416**

restrictive covenants Provisions that restrict and specify certain activities that a borrower can engage in. **199**

return The payments to the owner of a security plus the change in the security's value, expressed as a fraction of its purchase price. More precisely called the *rate of return*. **85**

return on assets (ROA) Net profit after taxes per dollar of assets. **266**

return on equity (ROE) Net profit after taxes per dollar of equity capital. **241**

revaluation Resetting of the fixed value of a currency at a higher level. **515**

reverse causation A situation in which one variable is said to cause another variable when in reality the reverse is true. **633**

reverse repo See *matched sale-purchase transaction*. **460**

Ricardian equivalence Named after the Nineteenth-century British economist David Ricardo, it contends that when the government runs deficits and issues bonds, the public recognizes that it will be subject to higher taxes in the future in order to pay off these bonds. **674**

risk The degree of uncertainty associated with the return on an asset. **95**

risk premium The spread between the interest rate on bonds with default risk and the interest rate on default-free bonds. **144**

risk structure of interest rates The relationship among the various interest rates on bonds with the same term to maturity. **143**

secondary market A financial market in which securities that have previously been issued (and are thus secondhand) can be resold. **23**

secondary reserves Short-term U.S. government and agency securities held by banks. **231**

secured debt Debt guaranteed by collateral. **198**

securitization The process of transforming illiquid financial assets into marketable capital market instruments. **286**

security A claim on the borrower's future income that is sold by the borrower to the lender. Also called a *financial instrument*. **4**

segmented markets theory A theory of term structure that sees markets for different-maturity bonds as completely separated and segmented such that the interest rate for bonds of a given maturity is determined solely by supply of and demand for bonds of that maturity. **157**

self-correcting mechanism A characteristic of the economy that causes output to return eventually to the natural rate level regardless of where it is initially. **612**

share draft account An account at a credit union that is similar to a NOW account. **261**

short position A contractual obligation to deliver an underlying financial instrument. **355**

short-term With reference to a debt instrument, having a maturity of one year or less. **23**

simple deposit multiplier The multiple increase in deposits generated from an increase in the banking system's reserves in a simple model in which the behavior of depositor and bank plays no role. **429**

simple loan A credit market instrument providing the borrower with an amount of funds that must be repaid to the lender at the maturity date along with an additional payment (interest). **70**

sources of the base The factors that determine the monetary base. **418**

special drawing rights (SDRs) An IMF-issued paper substitute for gold that functions as international reserves. **518**

specialist A dealer-broker operating in an exchange who maintains orderly trading of the securities for which he or she is responsible. **351**

spot exchange rate The exchange rate for a spot transaction. **167**

spot transaction The predominant type of exchange rate transaction, involving the immediate exchange of bank deposits denominated in different currencies. **167**

state banks State-chartered banks. **266**

sterilized foreign exchange intervention A foreign exchange intervention with an offsetting open market operation that leaves the monetary base unchanged. **505**

stock A security that is a claim on the earnings and assets of a corporation. **4**

stock option An option on an individual stock. **367**

store of value A repository of purchasing power over time. **51**

strike price See *exercise price*. **367**

structural model A description of how the economy operates, using a collection of equations that describe the behavior of firms and consumers in many sectors of the economy. **630**

structural model evidence Evidence that examines whether one variable affects another by using data to build a model illustrating the channels through which this variable affects the other. **630**

superregional banks Bank holding companies similar in size to money center banks, but whose headquarters are not based in one of the money center cities (New York, Chicago, San Francisco). **272**

supply curve A curve depicting the relationship between quantity supplied and price when all other economic variables are held constant. **106**

supply shock Any change in technology or the supply of raw materials that can shift the aggregate supply curve. **616**

swap A financial contract that obligates one party to exchange (swap) a set of payments it owns for a set of payments owned by another party. **375**

systematic risk The component of an asset's risk that cannot be eliminated by diversification. **100**

T-account A simplified balance sheet with lines in the form of a T that lists only the changes that occur in balance sheet items starting from some initial balance sheet position. **232**

tariffs Taxes on imported goods. **172**

term structure of interest rates The relationship among interest rates on bonds with different terms to maturity. **143**

theory of portfolio choice The theory that the quantity demanded of an asset is (1) usually positively related to wealth, (2) positively related to its expected return relative to alternative assets, (3) negatively related to the risk of its return relative to alternative assets, and (4) positively related to its liquidity relative to alternative assets. **97**

theory of purchasing power parity (PPP) The theory that exchange rates between any two currencies will adjust to reflect changes in the price levels of the two countries. **170**

thrift institutions (thrifts) Savings and loan associations, mutual savings banks, and credit unions. **37**

trade balance The difference between merchandise exports and imports. **508**

transaction costs The time and money spent trying to exchange financial assets, goods, or services. **34**

transmission mechanisms of monetary policy The channels through which the money supply affects economic activity. **630**

underfunded Describing a pension plan in which the contributions and their earnings are not sufficient to pay out the defined benefits when they come due. **341**

underwriters Investment banks that guarantee prices on securities to corporations and then sell the securities to the public. **349**

underwriting Guaranteeing prices on securities to corporations and then selling the securities to the public. **24**

unemployment rate The percentage of the labor force not working. **9**

unexploited profit opportunity A situation in which an investor can earn a higher than normal return. **694**

unit of account Anything used to measure value in an economy. **50**

unsecured debt Debt not guaranteed by collateral. **199**

unsterilized foreign exchange intervention A foreign exchange intervention in which a central bank allows the purchase or sale of domestic currency to affect the monetary base. **505**

uses of the base The items accounting for use of the monetary base (Federal Reserve notes, reserves, and Treasury currency outstanding not held by the Fed). **417**

vault cash Currency that is physically held by banks and stored in vaults overnight. **229**

velocity See *velocity of money*. **604**

velocity of money The rate of turnover of money; the average number of times per year that a dollar is spent in buying the total amount of final goods and services produced in the economy. **530**

venture capital firm A financial intermediary that pools the resources of its partners and uses the funds to help entrepreneurs start up new businesses. **210**

virtual bank A bank that has no building but rather exists only in cyberspace. **258**

wealth All resources owned by an individual, including all assets. **49, 95**

wealth elasticity of demand The measure of how much, with everything else unchanged, demand for an asset changes in percentage terms in response to a percentage change in wealth. **95**

World Bank The International Bank for Reconstruction and Redevelopment, an international organization that provides long-term loans to assist developing countries in building dams, roads, and other physical capital that would contribute to their economic development. **513**

yield curve   A plot of the interest rates for particular types of bonds with different terms to maturity. **157**

yield on a discount basis   The measure of interest rates by which dealers in bill markets quote the interest rate on U.S. Treasury bills; formally defined in Equation 8 of Chapter 4. Also known as the *discount yield*. **80**

yield to maturity   The interest rate that equates the present value of payments received from a credit market instrument with its value today. **72**

zero-coupon bond   See *discount bond*. **70**

ANSWERS TO SELECTED QUESTIONS AND PROBLEMS

CHAPTER 1

2. The data in Figures 1, 2, 3, and 4 suggest that real output, the inflation rate, and interest rates would all fall.

4. You might be more likely to buy a house or a car because the cost of financing them would fall, or you might be less likely to save because you earn less on your savings.

6. No. It is true that people who borrow to purchase a house or a car are worse off because it costs them more to finance their purchase; however, savers benefit because they can earn higher interest rates on their savings.

8. They channel funds from people who do not have a productive use for them to people who do, thereby resulting in higher economic efficiency.

10. The lower price for a firm's shares means that it can raise a smaller amount of funds, and so investment in facilities and equipment will fall.

12. It makes foreign goods more expensive, so British consumers will buy fewer foreign goods and more domestic goods.

14. In the mid- to late 1970s and in the late 1980s and early 1990s, the value of the dollar was low, making travel abroad relatively more expensive; thus it was a good time to vacation in the United States and see the Grand Canyon. With the rise of the dollar's value in the early 1980s, travel abroad became relatively cheaper, making it a good time to visit the Tower of London.

CHAPTER 2

1. The share of IBM stock is an asset for its owner because it entitles the owner to a share of the earnings and assets of IBM. The share is a liability for IBM because it is a claim on its earnings and assets by the owner of the share.

3. Yes, because the absence of financial markets means that funds cannot be channeled to people who have the most productive use for them. Entrepreneurs then cannot acquire funds to set up businesses that would help the economy grow rapidly.

5. This statement is false. Prices in secondary markets determine the prices that firms issuing securities receive in primary markets. In addition, secondary markets make securities more liquid and thus easier to sell in the primary markets. Therefore, secondary markets are, if anything, more important than primary markets.

7. Because you know your family member better than a stranger, you know more about the borrower's honesty, propensity for risk taking, and other traits. There is less asymmetric information than with a stranger and less likelihood of an adverse selection problem, with the result that you are more likely to lend to the family member.

9. Loan sharks can threaten their borrowers with bodily harm if borrowers take actions that might jeopardize their paying off the loan. Hence borrowers from a loan shark are less likely to increase moral hazard.

11. Yes, because even if you know that a borrower is taking actions that might jeopardize paying off the loan, you must still stop the borrower from doing so. Because that may be costly, you may not spend the time and effort to reduce moral hazard, and so the problem of moral hazard still exists.

13. Because the costs of making the loan to your neighbor are high (legal fees, fees for a credit check, and so on), you will probably not be able to earn 5 percent on the loan after your expenses even though it has a 10 percent interest rate. You are better off depositing your savings with a financial intermediary and earning 5 percent interest. In addition, you are likely to bear less risk by depositing your savings at the bank rather than lending them to your neighbor.

15. Increased discussion of foreign financial markets in the U.S. press and the growth in markets for international financial instruments such as Eurodollars and Eurobonds.

CHAPTER 3

2. Since the orchard owner likes only bananas but the banana grower doesn't like apples, the banana grower will not want apples in exchange for his bananas, and they will not trade. Similarly, the chocolatier will not be willing to trade with the banana grower because she does not like bananas. The orchard owner will not trade with the chocolatier because he doesn't like chocolate. Hence in

a barter economy, trade among these three people may well not take place because in no case is there a double coincidence of wants. However, if money is introduced into the economy, the orchard owner can sell his apples to the chocolatier and then use the money to buy bananas from the banana grower. Similarly, the banana grower can use the money she receives from the orchard owner to buy chocolate from the chocolatier, and the chocolatier can use the money to buy apples from the orchard owner. The result is that the necessity of a double coincidence of wants is eliminated, and everyone is better off because all three producers are now able to eat what they like best.

4. Because a check was so much easier to transport than gold, people would frequently rather be paid by check even if there were a possibility that the check might bounce. In other words, the lower transactions costs involved in handling checks made people more willing to accept them.

6. Because money was losing value at a slower rate (the inflation rate was lower) in the 1950s than in the 1970s, it was then a better store of value, and you would have been willing to hold more of it.

9. Money loses its value at an extremely rapid rate in hyperinflation, so you want to hold it for as short a time as possible. Thus money is like a hot potato that is quickly passed from one person to another.

11. Not necessarily. Although the total amount of debt has predicted inflation and the business cycle better than M1, M2, or M3, it may not be a better predictor in the future. Without some theoretical reason for believing that the total amount of debt will continue to predict well in the future, we may not want to define money as the total amount of debt.

13. M1 contains the most liquid assets. M3 is the largest measure.

15. Revisions are not a serious problem for long-run movements of the money supply because revisions for short-run (one-month) movements tend to cancel out. Revisions for long-run movements, such as one-year growth rates, are thus typically quite small.

CHAPTER 4

1. Less. It would be worth $1/(1 + 0.20) = \$0.83$ when the interest rate is 20 percent, rather than $1/(1 + 0.10) = \$0.91$ when the interest rate is 10 percent.

3. $\$1100/(1 + 0.10) + \$1210/(1 + 0.10)^2 + \$1331/(1 + 0.10)^3 = \$3000$.

5. $\$2000 = \$100/(1 + i) + \$100/(1 + i)^2 + \cdots + \$100/(1 + i)^{20} + \$1000/(1 + i)^{20}$.

7. 14.9 percent, derived as follows: The present value of the $2 million payment five years from now is $\$2/(1 + i)^5$ million which equals the $1 million loan. Thus $1 = 2/(1 + i)^5$. Solving for i, $(1 + i)^5 = 2$, so that $i = \sqrt[5]{2} - 1 = 0.149 = 14.9$ percent.

9. If the one-year bond did not have a coupon payment, its yield to maturity would be $(\$1000 - \$800)/\$800 = \$200/\$800 = 0.25 = 25$ percent. Since it does have a coupon payment, its yield to maturity must be greater than 25 percent. However, because the current yield is a good approximation of the yield to maturity for a 20-year bond, we know that the yield to maturity on this bond is approximately 15 percent. Therefore, the one-year bond has a higher yield to maturity.

11. You would rather own the Treasury bill because it has a higher yield to maturity. As the example in the text indicates, the discount yield's understatement of the yield to maturity for a one-year bond is substantial, exceeding one percentage point. Thus the yield to maturity on the one-year bill would be greater than 9 percent, the yield to maturity on the one-year Treasury bond.

13. No. If interest rates rise sharply in the future, long-term bonds may suffer such a sharp fall in price that their return might be quite low, possibly even negative.

15. The economists are right. They reason that nominal interest rates were below expected rates of inflation in the late 1970s, making real interest rates negative. The expected inflation rate, however, fell much faster than nominal interest rates in the mid-1980s, so nominal interest rates were above the expected inflation rate and real rates became positive.

CHAPTER 5

2. (a) More, because your wealth has increased; (b) more, because it has become more liquid; (c) less, because its expected return has fallen relative to Polaroid stock; (d) more, because it has become less risky relative to stocks; (e) less, because its expected return has fallen.

4. (a) More, because they have become more liquid; (b) more, because their expected return has risen relative to stocks; (c) less, because they have become less liquid relative to stocks; (d) less, because their expected return has fallen; (e) more, because they have become more liquid.

6. Yes. The higher expected return on stocks, holding everything else constant, would mean a lower rel-

ative expected return on bonds. Thus the demand for bonds would decrease.

8. Purchasing shares in the pharmaceutical company is more likely to reduce my overall risk because the correlation of returns on my investment in a football team with the returns on the pharmaceutical company should be low. By contrast, the correlation of returns on an investment in a football team and an investment in a basketball team are probably pretty high, so in this case there would be little risk reduction if I invested in both.

10. True. When an asset's beta is higher, its systematic risk is higher. Since this systematic risk cannot be diversified away, the asset is less desirable, everything else being equal, and the demand for the asset will be lower. (Note that we assume that investors are risk-averse and hence do not like risk.)

12. It wouldn't matter from a risk point of view because both stocks have a beta of 0.5 and have the same amount of systematic risk.

14. Risk premium $= R^e - R_f = \beta(R_m^e - R_f) = 3(8\% - 5\%) = 9\%$.

CHAPTER 6

1. When the Fed sells bonds to the public, it increases the supply of bonds, thus shifting the supply curve B^s to the right. The result is that the intersection of the supply and demand curves B^s and B^d occurs at a higher equilibrium interest rate, and the interest rate rises. With the liquidity preference framework, the decrease in the money supply shifts the money supply curve M^s to the left, and the equilibrium interest rate rises. The answer from the loanable funds framework is consistent with the answer from the liquidity preference framework.

3. When the price level rises, the quantity of money in real terms falls (holding the nominal supply of money constant); to restore their holdings of money in real terms to their former level, people will want to hold a greater nominal quantity of money. Thus the money demand curve M^d shifts to the right, and the interest rate rises.

6. Interest rates would rise. A sudden increase in people's expectations of future real estate prices raises the expected return on real estate relative to bonds, so the demand for bonds falls. The demand curve B^d shifts to the left, and the equilibrium interest rate rises.

8. In the loanable funds framework, the increased riskiness of bonds lowers the demand for bonds. The demand curve B^d shifts to the left, and the

equilibrium interest rate rises. The same answer is found in the liquidity preference framework. The increased riskiness of bonds relative to money increases the demand for money. The money demand curve M^d shifts to the right, and the equilibrium interest rate rises.

10. Yes, interest rates will rise. The lower commission on stocks makes them more liquid relative to bonds, and the demand for bonds will fall. The demand curve B^d will therefore shift to the left, and the equilibrium interest rate will rise.

12. The interest rate on the AT&T bonds will rise. Because people now expect interest rates to rise, the expected return on long-term bonds such as AT&T's will fall, and the demand for these bonds will decline. The demand curve B^d will therefore shift to the left, and the equilibrium interest rate will rise.

14. Interest rates will rise. When bond prices become volatile and bonds become riskier, the demand for bonds will fall. The demand curve will shift to the left, and the equilibrium interest will rise.

CHAPTER 7

2. U.S. Treasury bills have lower default risk and more liquidity than negotiable CDs. Consequently, the demand for Treasury bills is higher, and they have a lower interest rate.

4. True. When bonds of different maturities are close substitutes, a rise in interest rates for one bond causes the interest rates for others to rise because the expected returns on bonds of different maturities cannot get too far out of line.

6. (a) The yield to maturity would be 5 percent for a one-year bond, 6 percent for a two-year bond, 6.33 percent for a three-year bond, 6.5 percent for a four-year bond, and 6.6 percent for a five-year bond. (b) The yield to maturity would be 5 percent for a one-year bond, 4.5 percent for a two-year bond, 4.33 percent for a three-year bond, 4.25 percent for a four-year bond, and 4.2 percent for a five-year bond. The upward-sloping yield curve in (a) would be even steeper if people preferred short-term bonds over long-term bonds because long-term bonds would then have a positive risk premium. The downward-sloping yield curve in (b) would be less steep and might even have a slight positive upward slope if the long-term bonds have a positive risk premium.

8. The flat yield curve at shorter maturities suggests that short-term interest rates are expected to fall moderately in the near future, while the steep

upward slope of the yield curve at longer maturities indicates that interest rates further into the future are expected to rise. Because interest rates and expected inflation move together, the yield curve suggests that the market expects inflation to fall moderately in the near future but to rise later on.

10. The reduction in income tax rates would make the tax-exempt privilege for municipal bonds less valuable, and they would be less desirable than taxable Treasury bonds. The resulting decline in the demand for municipal bonds and increase in demand for Treasury bonds would raise interest rates on municipal bonds while causing interest rates on Treasury bonds to fall.

12. Lower brokerage commissions for corporate bonds would make them more liquid and thus increase their demand, which would lower their risk premium.

14. You would raise your predictions of future interest rates because the higher long-term rates imply that the average of the expected future short-term rates is higher.

CHAPTER 8

2. False. Although a weak currency has the negative effect of making it more expensive to buy foreign goods or to travel abroad, it may help domestic industry. Domestic goods become cheaper relative to foreign goods, and the demand for domestically produced goods increases. The resulting higher sales of domestic products may lead to higher employment, a beneficial effect on the economy.

4. It predicts that the value of the French franc will fall 5 percent in terms of dollars.

6. Even though the Japanese price level rose relative to the American, the yen appreciated because the increase in Japanese productivity relative to American productivity made it possible for the Japanese to continue to sell their goods at a profit at a high value of the yen.

8. The pound depreciates but overshoots, declining by more in the short run than in the long run. Consider Britain the domestic country. The rise in the money supply leads to a higher domestic price level in the long run, which leads to a lower expected future exchange rate. The resulting expected depreciation of the pound raises the expected return on foreign deposits, shifting RET^F to the right. The rise in the money supply lowers the interest rate on pound deposits in the short run, which shifts RET^D to the left. The short-run outcome is a lower equilibrium exchange rate.

However, in the long run, the domestic interest rate returns to its previous value, and RET^D shifts back to its original position. The exchange rate rises to some extent, although it still remains below its initial position.

10. The dollar will depreciate. A rise in nominal interest rates but a decline in real interest rates implies a rise in expected inflation that produces an expected depreciation of the dollar that is larger than the increase in the domestic interest rate. As a result, the expected return on foreign deposits rises by more than the expected return on domestic deposits. RET^F shifts rightward more than RET^D, so the equilibrium exchange rate falls.

12. The dollar will depreciate. An increased demand for imports would lower the expected future exchange rate and result in an expected appreciation of the foreign currency. The higher resulting expected return on foreign deposits shifts the RET^F schedule to the right, and the equilibrium exchange rate falls.

14. The contraction of the German money supply will increase German interest rates and raise the future value of the mark, both of which will shift RET^F (with Germany as the foreign country) to the right. The result is a decline in the value of the dollar.

CHAPTER 9

2. Financial intermediaries develop expertise in such areas as computer technology so that they can inexpensively provide liquidity services such as checking accounts that lower transactions costs for depositors. Financial intermediaries can also take advantage of economies of scale and engage in large transactions that have a lower cost per dollar per transaction.

4. Standard accounting principles make profit verification easier, thereby reducing adverse selection and moral hazard problems in financial markets and hence making them operate better. Standard accounting principles make it easier for investors to screen out good firms from bad firms, thereby reducing the adverse selection problem in financial markets. In addition, they make it harder for managers to understate profits, thereby reducing the principal-agent (moral hazard) problem.

6. Smaller firms that are not well known are the most likely to use bank financing. Since it is harder for investors to acquire information about these firms, it will be hard for the firms to sell securities in the financial markets. Banks that specialize in collecting information about smaller firms will then be the

only outlet these firms have for financing their activities.

8. Yes. The person who is putting her life savings into her business has more to lose if she takes on too much risk or engages in personally beneficial activities that don't lead to higher profits. So she will act more in the interest of the lender, making it more likely that the loan will be paid off.

10. True. If the borrower turns out to be a bad credit risk and goes broke, the lender loses less because the collateral can be sold to make up any losses on the loan. Thus adverse selection is not as severe a problem.

12. The separation of ownership and control creates a principal-agent problem. The managers (the agents) do not have as strong an incentive to maximize profits as the owners (the principals). Thus the managers might not work hard, might engage in wasteful spending on personal perks, or might pursue business strategies that enhance their personal power but do not increase profits.

14. A stock market crash reduces the net worth of firms and so increases the moral hazard problem. With less of an equity stake, owners have a greater incentive to take on risky projects and spend corporate funds on items that benefit them personally. A stock market crash, which increases the moral hazard problem, thus makes it less likely that lenders will be paid back. So lending and investment will decline, creating a financial crisis in which financial markets do not work well and the economy suffers.

CHAPTER 10

2. The rank from most to least liquid is (c), (b), (a), (d).

4. Reserves drop by $500. The T-account for the First National Bank is as follows:

First National Bank

Assets		Liabilities	
Reserves	−$500	Checkable deposits	−$500

6. The bank would rather have the balance sheet shown in this problem because after it loses $50 million due to deposit outflow, the bank would still have excess reserves of $5 million: $50 million in reserves minus required reserves of $45 million (10 percent of the $450 million of deposits). Thus the bank would not have to alter its balance sheet fur-

ther and would not incur any costs as a result of the deposit outflow. By contrast, with the balance sheet in Problem 5, the bank would have a shortfall of reserves of $20 million ($25 million in reserves minus the required reserves of $45 million). In this case, the bank will incur costs when it raises the necessary reserves through the methods described in the text.

8. No. When you turn a customer down, you may lose that customer's business forever, which is extremely costly. Instead, you might go out and borrow from other banks, corporations, or the Fed to obtain funds so that you can make the customer loans. Alternatively, you might sell negotiable CDs or some of your securities to acquire the necessary funds.

10. It can raise $1 million of capital by issuing new stock. It can cut its dividend payments by $1 million, thereby increasing its retained earnings by $1 million. It can decrease the amount of its assets so that the amount of its capital relative to its assets increases, thereby meeting the capital requirements.

12. Compensating balances can act as collateral. They also help establish long-term customer relationships, which make it easier for the bank to collect information about prospective borrowers, thus reducing the adverse selection problem. Compensating balances help the bank monitor the activities of a borrowing firm so that it can prevent the firm from taking on too much risk, thereby not acting in the interest of the bank.

14. The assets fall in value by $8 million (= $100 million × −2 percent × 4 years) while the liabilities fall in value by $10.8 million (= $90 million × −2 percent × 6 years). Since the liabilities fall in value by $2.8 million more than the assets do, the net worth of the bank rises by $2.8 million. The interest-rate risk can be reduced by shortening the maturity of the liabilities to a duration of four years or lengthening the maturity of the assets to a duration of six years. Alternatively, you could engage in an interest-rate swap, in which you swap the interest earned on your assets with the interest on another bank's assets that have a duration of six years.

CHAPTER 11

2. (a) Office of the Comptroller of the Currency; (b) the Federal Reserve; (c) state banking authorities and the FDIC; (d) the Federal Reserve.

4. New technologies such as electronic banking facilities are frequently shared by several banks, so

these facilities are not classified as branches. Thus they can be used by banks to escape limitations to offering services in other states and, in effect, to escape limitations from restrictions on branching.

6. Because restrictions on branching are stricter for commercial banks than for savings and loans. Thus small commercial banks have greater protection from competition and are more likely to survive than small savings and loans.

8. International banking has been encouraged by giving special tax treatment and relaxed branching regulations to Edge Act corporations and to international banking facilities (IBFs); this was done to make American banks more competitive with foreign banks. The hope is that it will create more banking jobs in the United States.

10. No, because the Saudi-owned bank is subject to the same regulations as the American-owned bank.

12. The rise of inflation and the resulting higher interest rates on alternatives to checkable deposits meant that banks had a big shrinkage in this low-cost way of raising funds. The innovation of money market mutual funds also meant that the banks lost checking account business. The abolishment of Regulation Q and the appearance of NOW accounts did help decrease disintermediation but raised the cost of funds for American banks, which now had to pay higher interest rates on checkable and other deposits. Foreign banks were also able to tap a large pool of domestic savings, thereby lowering their cost of funds relative to American banks.

14. The growth of the commercial paper market and the development of the junk bond market meant that corporations were now able to issue securities rather than borrow from banks, thus eroding the competitive advantage of banks on the lending side. Securitization has enabled other financial institutions to originate loans, again taking away some of the banks' loan business.

CHAPTER 12

2. There would be adverse selection because people who might want to burn their property for some personal gain would actively try to obtain substantial fire insurance policies. Moral hazard could also be a problem because a person with a fire insurance policy has less incentive to take measures to prevent a fire.

4. Regulations that restrict banks from holding risky assets directly decrease the moral hazard of risk taking by the bank. Requirements that force banks to have a large amount of capital also decrease the banks' incentives for risk taking because banks now have more to lose if they fail. Such regulations will not completely eliminate the moral hazard problem because bankers have incentives to hide their holdings of risky assets from the regulators and to overstate the amount of their capital.

6. The S&L crisis did not occur until the 1980s because interest rates stayed low before then, so S&Ls were not subjected to losses from high interest rates. Also, the opportunities for risk taking were not available until the 1980s, when legislation and financial innovation made it easier for S&Ls to take on more risk, thereby greatly increasing the adverse selection and moral hazard problems.

8. FIRREA provided funds for the S&L bailout, created the Resolution Trust Corporation to manage the resolution of insolvent thrifts, eliminated the Federal Home Loan Bank Board and gave its regulatory role to the Office of Thrift Supervision, eliminated the FSLIC and turned its insurance role and regulatory responsibilities over to the FDIC, imposed restrictions on thrift activities similar to those in effect before 1982, increased the capital requirements to those adhered to by commercial banks, and increased the enforcement powers of thrift regulators.

10. If political candidates receive campaign funds from the government and are restricted in the amount they spend, they will have less need to satisfy lobbyists to win elections. As a result, they may have greater incentives to act in the interest of taxpayers (the principals), and so the political process might improve.

12. Eliminating or limiting the amount of deposit insurance would help reduce the moral hazard of excessive risk taking on the part of banks. It would, however, make bank failures and panics more likely, so it might not be a very good idea.

14. The economy would benefit from reduced moral hazard; that is, banks would not want to take on too much risk because doing so would increase their deposit insurance premiums. The problem is, however, that it is difficult to monitor the degree of risk in bank assets because often only the bank making the loans knows how risky they are.

CHAPTER 13

1. Because there would be more uncertainty about how much they would have to pay out in any given year, life insurance companies would tend to hold shorter-term assets that are more liquid.

3. Because benefits paid out are set to equal contributions to the plan and their earnings.

5. False. Government pension plans are often underfunded. Many pension plans for both federal and state employees are not fully funded.

7. Because the bigger the policy, the greater the moral hazard—the incentive for the policyholder to engage in activities that make the insurance payoff more likely. Because payoffs are costly, the insurance company will want to reduce moral hazard by limiting the amount of insurance.

9. Because interest rates on loans are typically lower at banks than at finance companies.

11. Because you do not have to pay a commission on a no-load fund, it is cheaper than a load fund, which does require a commission.

13. Government loan guarantees may be very costly because like any insurance, they increase moral hazard. Because the banks and other institutions making the guaranteed loans do not suffer any losses if the loans default, these institutions have little incentive not to make bad loans. The resulting losses to the government can be substantial, as was true in past years.

15. No. Investment banking is a risky business because if the investment bank cannot sell a security it is underwriting for the price it promised to pay the issuing firm, the investment bank can suffer substantial losses.

CHAPTER 14

2. You would enter into a contract that specifies that you will sell the $25 million of 8s of 2015 at a price of 110 one year from now

4. You have a loss of 6 points, or $6000, per contract.

6. You would buy $100 million worth (1000 contracts) of the put long-term bond option with a delivery date of one year in the future and with a strike price that corresponds to a yield of 8 percent. This means that you would have the option to buy the long bond with the 8 percent interest rate, thereby making sure that you can earn the 8 percent. The disadvantage of the options contract is that you have to pay a premium that you would not have to pay with a futures contract. The advantage of the options contract is that if the interest rate rises and the bond price falls during the next year, you do not have to exercise the option and so will be able to earn a higher rate than 8 percent when the funds come in next year, whereas with the futures contract, you have to take delivery of the bond and will only earn 8 percent.

8. You have a profit of 1 point ($1000) when you exercise the contract, but you have paid a premium of $1500 for the call option, so your net profit is −$500, a loss of $500.

10. Because for any given price at expiration, a lower strike price means a higher profit for a call option and a lower profit for a put option. A lower strike price makes a call option more desirable and raises its premium and makes a put option less desirable and lowers its premium.

12. It would swap interest on $42 million of fixed-rate assets for the interest on $42 million of variable-rate assets, thereby eliminating its income gap.

14. You would swap £200,000 every year for payments of $300,000 every year for five years.

CHAPTER 15

1. Because of traditional American hostility to a central bank and centralized authority, the system of 12 regional banks was set up to diffuse power along regional lines.

3. Like the U.S. Constitution, the Federal Reserve System, originally established by the Federal Reserve Act, has many checks and balances and is a peculiarly American institution. The ability of the 12 regional banks to affect discount policy was viewed as a check on the centralized power of the Board of Governors, just as states' rights are a check on the centralized power of the federal government. The provision that there be three types of directors (A, B, and C) representing different groups (professional bankers, businesspeople, and the public) was again intended to prevent any group from dominating the Fed. The Fed's independence of the federal government and the setting up of the Federal Reserve banks as incorporated institutions were further intended to restrict government power over the banking industry.

5. The Board of Governors sets reserve requirements and the discount rate; the FOMC directs open market operations. In practice, however, the FOMC helps make decisions about reserve requirements and the discount rate.

7. The Board of Governors has clearly gained power at the expense of the regional Federal Reserve banks. This trend toward ever more centralized power is a general one in American government, but in the case of the Fed, it was a natural outgrowth of the Fed's having been given the responsibility for promoting a stable economy. This responsibility has required greater central direction

of monetary policy, the role taken over the years by the Board of Governors and by the FOMC, which the board controls.

9. The threat that Congress will acquire greater control over the Fed's finances and budget.

11. False. Maximizing one's welfare does not rule out altruism. Operating in the public interest is clearly one objective of the Fed. The theory of bureaucratic behavior only points out that other objectives, such as maximizing power, also influence Fed decision making.

13. False. The Fed is still subject to political pressure because Congress can pass legislation limiting the Fed's power. If the Fed is performing badly, Congress can therefore make the Fed accountable by passing legislation that the Fed does not like.

15. The argument for not releasing the FOMC directives immediately is that it keeps Congress off the Fed's back, thus enabling the Fed to pursue an independent monetary policy that is less subject to inflation and political business cycles. The argument for releasing the directive immediately is that it would make the Fed more accountable.

CHAPTER 16

2. Reserves are unchanged, but the monetary base falls by $2 million as indicated by the following T-accounts:

Irving the Investor

Assets	Liabilities
Securities +$2 million	
Currency −$2 million	

Federal Reserve System

Assets	Liabilities
Securities −$2 million	Currency −$2 million

3. Reserves increase by $50 million, but the monetary base increases by $100 million, as the T-accounts for the five banks and the Fed indicate:

Five Banks

Assets	Liabilities
Reserves +$50 million	Discount loans +$100 million
	Deposits −$50 million

Federal Reserve System

Assets	Liabilities
Discount loans +$100 million	Reserves +$50 million
	Currency +$50 million

5. The T-accounts are identical to those in the sections "Deposit Creation: The Single Bank" and "Deposit Creation: The Banking System" except that all the entries are multiplied by 10,000 (that is, $100 becomes $1 million). The net result is that checkable deposits rise by $10 million.

7. The $1 million Fed purchase of bonds increases reserves in the banking system by $1 million, and the total increase in checkable deposits is $10 million. The fact that banks buy securities rather than make loans with their excess reserves makes no difference in the multiple deposit creation process.

9. Reserves in the banking system fall by $1000, and a multiple contraction occurs, reducing checkable deposits by $10,000.

11. The level of checkable deposits falls by $50 million. The T-account of the banking system in equilibrium is as follows:

Banking System

Assets	Liabilities
Reserves −$5 million	Checkable deposits−$50 million
Securities +$5 million	
Loans −$50 million	

13. The $1 million holdings of excess reserves means that the bank has to reduce its holdings of loans or securities, thus starting the multiple contraction process. Because the required reserve ratio is 10 percent, checkable deposits must decline by $10 million.

15. The deposit of $100 in the bank increases its reserves by $100. This starts the process of multiple deposit expansion, leading to an increase in checkable deposits of $1000.

CHAPTER 17

1. Uncertain. As the formula in Equation 4 indicates, if r_D + {ER/D} is greater than 1, the money multiplier is greater than 1. In practice, however, {ER/D} is so small that r_D + {ER/D} is less than 1 and the money multiplier is greater than 1.

3. The money supply fell sharply because when {C/D} rose, there was a shift from one component of the money supply (checkable deposits) with more multiple expansion to another (currency) with less. Overall multiple deposit expansion fell, leading to a decline in the money supply.

5. There is a shift from one component of the money supply (checkable deposits) with less multiple expansion to another (traveler's checks) with more. Multiple expansion therefore increases, and the money supply increases.

7. Yes, because with no reserve requirements on time deposits, a shift from checkable deposits (with less multiple expansion) to time deposits (with more multiple expansion) increases the total amount of deposits and raises M2. However, if reserve requirements were equal for both types of deposits, they would both undergo the same amount of multiple expansion, and a shift from one to the other would have no effect on M2. Thus control of M2 would be better because random shifts from time deposits to checkable deposits or vice versa would not affect M2.

9. Both the Fed's purchase of $100 million of bonds (which raises the monetary base) and the lowering of r_D (which increases the amount of multiple expansion and raises the money multiplier) lead to a rise in the money supply.

11. The Fed's sale of $1 million of bonds shrinks the monetary base by $1 million, and the reduction of discount loans also lowers the monetary base by another $1 million. The resulting $2 million decline in the monetary base leads to a decline in the money supply.

13. A rise in expected inflation would increase interest rates (through the Fisher effect), which would in turn cause {ER/D} to fall and the volume of discount loans to rise. The fall in {ER/D} increases the amount of reserves available to support checkable deposits so that deposits and the money multiplier will rise. The rise in discount loans causes the monetary base to rise. The resulting increase in the money multiplier and the monetary base leads to an increase in the money supply.

15. The money supply would fall because if the discount window were eliminated, banks would need to hold more excess reserves, making fewer reserves available to support deposits. Moreover, abolishing discounting would reduce the volume of discount loans, which would also cause the monetary base and the money supply to fall.

CHAPTER 18

1. The snowstorm would cause float to increase, which would increase the monetary base. To counteract this effect, the manager will undertake a defensive open market sale.

3. As we saw in Chapter 16, when the Treasury's deposits at the Fed fall, the monetary base increases. To counteract this increase, the manager would undertake an open market sale.

5. It suggests that defensive open market operations are far more common than dynamic operations because repurchase agreements are used primarily to conduct defensive operations to counteract temporary changes in the monetary base.

7. The monetary base and the money supply would increase indefinitely. Banks could borrow at the lower discount rate and then lend the proceeds at a higher interest rate. Hence banks would make a profit on every dollar borrowed from the Fed, so they would continue to borrow indefinitely—which would in turn increase the monetary base indefinitely.

9. This statement is incorrect. The FDIC would not be effective in eliminating bank panics without Fed discounting to troubled banks in order to keep bank failures from spreading.

11. Usually not, since most declines in the Fed discount rate occur because market interest rates have fallen and the Fed does not want to let the discount rate get too far out of line with market rates. Hence a reduction in the discount rate frequently says nothing about the future direction of Fed policy.

13. Abolishing discounting would provide tighter control over the money supply because no fluctuation in the volume of discount loans would be possible. By contrast, the proposal to tie the discount rate to market interest rates may be more desirable because it has the advantage that the Fed could still perform its role as lender of last resort.

15. Open market operations are more flexible, reversible, and faster to implement than the other two tools. Discount policy is more flexible, reversible, and faster to implement than changing reserve requirements, but it is less effective than either of the other two tools.

CHAPTER 19

1. Disagree. Some unemployment is beneficial to the economy because the availability of vacant jobs makes it more likely that a worker will find the right job and that the employer will find the right worker for the job.

3. True. In such a world, hitting a monetary target would mean that the Fed would also hit its interest target, or vice versa. Thus the Fed could pursue both a monetary target and an interest-rate target at the same time.

5. The Fed can control the interest rate on three-month Treasury bills by buying and selling them in the open market. When the bill rate rises above the target level, the Fed would buy bills, which would bid up their price and lower the interest rate to its target level. Similarly, when the bill rate falls below the target level, the Fed would sell bills to raise the interest rate to the target level. The resulting open market operations would of course affect the money supply and cause it to change. The Fed would be giving up control of the money supply to pursue its interest-rate target.

7. Disagree. Although *nominal* interest rates are measured more accurately and more quickly than the money supply, the interest-rate variable that is of more concern to policymakers is the *real* interest rate. Because the measurement of real interest rates requires estimates of expected inflation, it is not true that real interest rates are necessarily measured more accurately and more quickly than the money supply. Interest-rate targets are therefore not necessarily better than money supply targets.

9. Because the Fed did not lend to troubled banks during this period, massive bank failures occurred, leading to a decline in the money supply when depositors increased their holdings of currency relative to deposits and banks increased their excess reserves to protect themselves against runs. As the money supply model presented in Chapters 16–17 indicates, these decisions by banks and depositors led to a sharp contraction of the money supply.

11. When the economy enters a recession, interest rates usually fall. If the Fed is targeting interest rates, it tries to prevent a decline in interest rates by selling bonds, thereby lowering their prices and raising interest rates to the target level. The open market sale would then lead to a decline in the monetary base and in the money supply. The decline in interest rates would also cause excess reserves to rise and the volume of discount loans to fall, thereby raising free reserves. With a free reserves target, the Fed would find monetary policy easy and would pursue contractionary policy. Therefore, neither interest-rate nor free reserves targets are very satisfactory because both can lead to a slower rate of money supply growth during a

recession, just when the Fed would not want to slow money supply growth.

13. A borrowed reserves target will produce smaller fluctuations in the federal funds rate. In contrast to when there is a nonborrowed reserves target, when the federal funds rate rises with a borrowed reserves target, the Fed prevents the tendency of discount borrowings to rise by buying bonds to lower interest rates. The result is smaller fluctuations in the federal funds rate with a borrowed reserves target.

15. The Fed may prefer to control interest rates rather than the money supply because it wishes to avoid the conflict with Congress that occurs when interest rates rise. The Fed might also believe that interest rates are actually a better guide to future economic activity.

CHAPTER 20

2. The purchase of dollars involves a sale of foreign assets, which means that international reserves fall and the monetary base falls. The resulting fall in the money supply causes interest rates to rise and RET^D to shift to the right while it lowers the future price level, thereby raising the future expected exchange rate, causing RET^F to shift to the left. The result is a rise in the exchange rate. However, in the long run, the RET^D curve returns to its original position, and so there is overshooting.

4. Because other countries often intervene in the foreign exchange market when the United States has a deficit so that U.S. holdings of international reserves do not change. By contrast, when the Netherlands has a deficit, it must intervene in the foreign exchange market and buy guilders, which results in a reduction of international reserves for the Netherlands.

6. Two francs per dollar.

8. A large balance-of-payments surplus may require a country to finance the surplus by selling its currency in the foreign exchange market, thereby gaining international reserves. The result is that the central bank will have supplied more of its currency to the public, and the monetary base will rise. The resulting rise in the money supply can cause the price level to rise, leading to a higher inflation rate.

10. In order to finance the deficit, the central bank might intervene in the foreign exchange market and buy domestic currency, thereby implementing a contractionary monetary policy. The result is that

they sell off international reserves and their monetary base falls, leading to a decline in the money supply.

12. When other countries buy U.S. dollars to keep their exchange rates from changing vis-à-vis the dollar because of the U.S. deficits, they gain international reserves and their monetary base increases. The outcome is that the money supply in these countries grows faster and leads to higher inflation throughout the world.

14. There are no direct effects on the money supply because there is no central bank intervention in a pure flexible exchange rate regime; therefore, changes in international reserves that affect the monetary base do not occur. However, monetary policy can be affected by the foreign exchange market because monetary authorities may want to manipulate exchange rates by changing the money supply and interest rates.

CHAPTER 21

1. Velocity is approximately 10 in 1995, 11 in 1996, and 12 in 1997. The rate of velocity growth is approximately 10 percent per year.

3. Nominal GDP declines by approximately 10 percent.

5. The price level quadruples.

7. False. The two approaches differ in that Fisher's rules out any possible effect of interest rates on the demand for money, whereas the Cambridge approach does not.

9. The demand for money will decrease. People would be more likely to expect interest rates to fall and therefore more likely to expect bond prices to rise. The increase in the expected return on bonds relative to money will then mean that people would demand less money.

11. Money balances should average one-half of Grant's monthly income because he would hold no bonds, since holding them would entail additional brokerage costs but would not provide him with any interest income.

13. True. Because bonds are riskier than money, risk-averse people would be likely to want to hold both.

15. In Keynes's view, velocity is unpredictable because interest rates, which have large fluctuations, affect the demand for money and hence velocity. In addition, Keynes's analysis suggests that if people's expectations of the normal level of interest rates change, the demand for money changes. Keynes thought that these expectations moved unpredictably, meaning that money demand and velocity are also unpredictable. Friedman sees the demand for money as stable, and because he also believes that changes in interest rates have only small effects on the demand for money, his position is that the demand for money, and hence velocity, is predictable.

CHAPTER 22

2. Companies cut production when their unplanned inventory investment is greater than zero because they are then producing more than they can sell. If they continue at current production, profits will suffer because they are building up unwanted inventory, which is costly to store and finance.

4. The equilibrium level of output is 1500. When planned investment spending falls by 100, the equilibrium level of output falls by 500 to 1000.

6. Nothing. The $100 billion increase in planned investment spending is exactly offset by the $100 billion decline in autonomous consumer expenditure, and autonomous spending and aggregate output remain unchanged.

8. Equilibrium output of 2000 occurs at the intersection of the 45° line $Y = Y^{ad}$ and the aggregate demand function $Y^{ad} = C + I + G = 500 + 0.75Y$. If government spending rises by 100, equilibrium output will rise by 400 to 2400.

10. Taxes should be reduced by $400 billion because the increase in output for a T decrease in taxes is T; that is, it equals the change in autonomous spending $mpc \times T$ times the multiplier $1/(1 - mpc) = (mpc \times T)[1/(1 - mpc)] = 0.5T[1/(1 - 0.5)] = 0.5T/0.5 = T$.

12. Rise. The fall in autonomous spending from an increase in taxes is always less than the change in taxes because the marginal propensity to consume is less than 1. By contrast, autonomous spending rises one-for-one with a change in autonomous consumer expenditure. So if taxes and autonomous consumer expenditure rise by the same amount, autonomous spending must rise, and aggregate output also rises.

14. When aggregate output falls, the demand for money falls, shifting the money demand curve to the left, which causes the equilibrium interest rate to fall. Because the equilibrium interest rate falls when aggregate output falls, there is a positive

association between aggregate output and the equilibrium interest rate, and the LM curve slopes up.

CHAPTER 23

2. When investment spending collapsed, the aggregate demand function in the Keynesian cross diagram fell, leading to a lower level of equilibrium output for any given interest rate. The fall in equilibrium output for any given interest rate implies that the IS curve shifted to the left.

4. False. It can also be eliminated by a fall in aggregate output, which lowers the demand for money and brings it back into equality with the supply of money.

6. The ISLM model gives exactly this result. The tax cuts shifted the IS curve to the right, while tight money shifted the LM curve to the left. The interest rate at the intersection of the new IS and LM curves is necessarily higher than at the initial equilibrium, and aggregate output can be higher.

8. Because it suggests that an interest-rate target is better than a money supply target. The reason is that unstable money demand increases the volatility of the LM curve relative to the IS curve, and as demonstrated in the text, this makes it more likely that an interest-rate target is preferred to a money supply target.

10. The effect on the aggregate demand curve is uncertain. A rise in government spending would shift the IS curve to the right, raising equilibrium output for a given price level. But the reduction in the money supply would shift the LM curve to the left, lowering equilibrium output for a given price level. Depending on which of these two effects on equilibrium output is stronger, the aggregate demand curve could shift either to the right or to the left.

12. No effect. The LM curve would be vertical in this case, meaning that a rise in government spending and a rightward shift in the IS curve would not lead to higher aggregate output but rather only to a rise in the interest rate. For any given price level, therefore, equilibrium output would remain the same, and the aggregate demand curve would not shift.

14. The increase in net exports shifts the IS curve to the right, and the equilibrium level of interest rates and aggregate output will rise.

CHAPTER 24

2. Because the position of the aggregate demand curve is fixed if nominal income $(P \times Y)$ is fixed, Friedman's statement implies that the position of the aggregate demand curve is completely determined by the quantity of money. This is built into the monetarist aggregate demand curve because it shifts only when the money supply changes.

4. The Keynesian aggregate demand curve shifts because a change in "animal spirits" causes consumer expenditure or planned investment spending to change, which then causes the quantity of aggregate output demanded to change at any given price level. In the monetarist view, by contrast, a change in "animal spirits" has little effect on velocity, and aggregate spending $(P \times Y)$ remains unchanged; hence the aggregate demand curve does not shift.

6. True. Given fixed production costs, firms can earn higher profits by producing more when prices are higher. Profit-maximizing behavior on the part of firms thus leads them to increase production when prices are higher.

8. The aggregate supply curve would shift to the right because production costs would fall.

10. The collapse in investment spending during the Great Depression reduced the quantity of output demanded at any given price level and shifted the aggregate demand curve to the left. In an aggregate demand and supply diagram, the equilibrium price level and aggregate output would then fall, which explains the decline in aggregate output and the price level that occurred during the Great Depression.

12. Both the increase in the money supply and the income tax cut will increase the quantity of output demanded at any given price level and so will shift the aggregate demand curve to the right. The intersection of the aggregate demand and aggregate supply curve will be at a higher level of both output and price level in the short run. However, in the long run, the aggregate supply curve will shift leftward, leaving output at the natural rate level, but the price level will be even higher.

14. Because the national sales tax would raise production costs, and the aggregate supply curve would shift to the left. The intersection of the aggregate supply curve with the aggregate demand curve would then be at a higher level of prices and a lower level of aggregate output; put, aggregate output would fall, and the price level would rise.

CHAPTER 25

4. Seeing which car is built better produces structural model evidence because it explains why one car is better than the other (that is, how the car is built).

Asking owners how often their cars undergo repairs produces reduced-form evidence because it looks only at the correlation of reliability with the manufacturer of the car.

5. Not necessarily. If GM car owners change their oil more frequently than Ford owners, GM cars would have better repair records even though they are not more reliable cars. In this case, it is a third factor, the frequency of oil changes, that leads to the better repair record for GM cars.

6. Not necessarily. Although the Ford engine might be built better than the GM engine, the rest of the GM car might be better made than the Ford. The result could be that the GM car is more reliable than the Ford.

8. If the Fed has interest-rate targets, a rise in output that raises interest rates might cause the Fed to buy bonds and bid up their price in order to drive interest rates back down to their target level (see Chapter 6). The result of these open market purchases would be that the increase in output would cause an increase in the monetary base and hence an increase in the money supply. In addition, a rise in output and interest rates would cause free reserves to fall (because excess reserves would fall and the volume of discount loans would rise). If the Fed has a free reserves target, the increase in aggregate output will then cause the Fed to increase the money supply because it believes that money is tight.

10. Monetarists went on to refine their reduced-form models with more sophisticated statistical procedures, one outcome of which was the St. Louis model. Keynesians began to look for transmission mechanisms of monetary policy that they may have ignored.

12. False. Monetary policy can affect stock prices, which affect Tobin's *q*, thereby affecting investment spending. In addition, monetary policy can affect loan availability, which may also influence investment spending.

14. There are three mechanisms involving consumer expenditure. First, a rise in the money supply lowers interest rates and reduces the cost of financing purchases of consumer durables, and consumer durable expenditure rises. Second, a rise in the money supply causes stock prices and wealth to rise, leading to greater lifetime resources for consumers and causing them to increase their consumption. Third, a rise in the money supply that causes stock prices and the value of financial assets to rise also lowers people's probability of financial distress, and so they spend more on consumer durables.

CHAPTER 26

2. Because hyperinflations appear to be examples in which the increase in money supply growth is an exogenous event, the fact that hyperinflation occurs when money growth is high is powerful evidence that a high rate of money growth causes inflation.

4. False. Although workers' attempts to push up their wages can lead to inflation if the government has a high employment target, inflation is still a monetary phenomenon because it cannot occur without accommodating monetary policy.

6. True. If financed with money creation, a temporary budget deficit can lead to a onetime rightward shift in the aggregate demand curve and hence to a one-time increase in the price level. However, once the budget deficit disappears, there is no longer any reason for the aggregate demand curve to shift. Thus a temporary deficit cannot lead to a continuing rightward shift of the aggregate demand curve and therefore cannot produce inflation, a continuing increase in the price level.

8. True. The monetarist objection to activist policy would no longer be as serious. The aggregate demand curve could be quickly moved to AD_2 in Figure 10, and the economy would move quickly to point 2 because the aggregate supply curve would not have as much time to shift. The scenario of a highly variable price level and output would not occur, making an activist policy more desirable.

10. True, if expectations about policy affect the wage-setting process. In this case, workers and firms are more likely to push up wages and prices because they know that if they do so and unemployment develops as a result, the government will pursue expansionary policies to eliminate the unemployment. Therefore, the cost of pushing up wages and prices is lower, and workers and firms will be more likely to do it.

12. True. If expectations about policy have no effect on the aggregate supply curve, a cost-push inflation is less likely to develop when policymakers pursue an activist accommodating policy. Furthermore, if expectations about policy do not matter, pursuing a nonaccommodating, nonactivist policy does not have the hidden benefit of making it less likely that workers will push up their wages and create unemployment. The case for an activist policy is therefore stronger.

CHAPTER 27

1. False. Expectations can be highly inaccurate and still be rational because optimal forecasts are not necessarily accurate: A forecast is optimal if it is the best possible even if the forecast errors are large.

3. No, because he could improve the accuracy of his forecasts by predicting that tomorrow's interest rates will be identical to today's. His forecasts are therefore not optimal, and he does not have rational expectations.

5. No, you shouldn't buy stocks because the rise in the money supply is publicly available information that will be already incorporated into stock prices. So you cannot expect to earn more than the equilibrium return on stocks by acting on the money supply information.

7. No, because this is publicly available information and is already reflected in stock prices. The optimal forecast of stock returns will equal the equilibrium return, so there is no benefit from selling your stocks.

9. No, if the person has no better information than the rest of the market. An expected price rise of 10 percent over the next month implies an annual return of more than 100 percent, which certainly exceeds its equilibrium return. This would mean that there is an unexploited profit opportunity in the market, which would have been eliminated in an efficient market. The only time that the person's expectations could be rational is if the person had information unavailable to the market that allowed the person to beat the market.

11. False. The people with better information are exactly those who make the market more efficient by eliminating unexploited profit opportunities. These people can profit from their better information.

13. True in principle. Foreign exchange rates are a random walk over a short interval such as a week because changes in the exchange rate are unpredictable. If a change were predictable, large unexploited profit opportunities would exist in the foreign exchange market. If the foreign exchange market is efficient, these unexploited profit opportunities cannot exist, and so the foreign exchange rate will approximately follow a random walk.

15. False. Although human fear may be the source of stock market crashes, that does not imply that there are unexploited profit opportunities in the market. Nothing in rational expectations theory rules out large changes in stock prices as a result of fears on the part of the investing public.

CHAPTER 28

2. A tax cut that is expected to last for ten years will have a larger effect on consumer expenditure than the one that is expected to last only one year. The reason is that the longer the tax cut is expected to last, the greater its effect on expected average income and consumer expenditure.

4. True, if the anti-inflation policy is credible. As shown in Figure 6, if anti-inflation policy is believed (and hence expected), there is no output loss than in the new classical model [the economy stays at point 1 in panel (b)], and there is a smaller output loss than would otherwise be the case in the new Keynesian model [the economy goes to point 2" rather than point 2' in panel (c)].

6. Uncertain. It is true that policymakers can reduce unemployment by pursuing a more expansionary policy than the public expects. However, the rational expectations assumption indicates that the public will attempt to anticipate policymakers' actions. Policymakers cannot be sure whether expansionary policy will be more or less expansionary than the public expects and hence use policy to make a predictable impact on unemployment.

8. True, because the Lucas critique indicates that the effect of policy on the aggregate demand curve depends on the public's expectations about that policy. The outcome of a particular policy is therefore less certain than in Lucas's view than if expectations about it do not matter, and it is harder to design a beneficial activist stabilization policy.

10. Yes, if budget deficits are expected to lead to an inflationary monetary policy and expectations about monetary policy affect the aggregate supply curve. In this case, a large budget deficit would cause the aggregate supply curve to shift more to the left because expected inflation would be higher. The result is that the increase in the price level (the inflation rate) would be higher.

13. The aggregate supply curve would shift to the left less than the aggregate demand curve shifts to the

14. The Fed's big stick is the ability to let unemployment develop as a result of a wage push by not trying to eliminate unemployment with expansionary monetary policy. The statement proposes that the Fed should pursue a nonaccommodating policy because this will prevent cost-push inflation and make it less likely that unemployment develops because of workers' attempts to push up their wages.

right; hence at their intersection, aggregate output would rise and the price level would be higher than it would have been if money growth had been reduced to a rate of 2 percent.

14. Using the traditional model, the aggregate supply curve would continue to shift leftward at the same rate, and the smaller rightward shift of the aggregate demand curve because money supply growth has been reduced would mean a smaller increase in the price level and a reduction of aggregate output.

In the new Keynesian model, the effect of this anti-inflation policy on aggregate output is uncertain. The aggregate supply curve would not shift leftward by as much as in the traditional model because the anti-inflation policy is expected, but it would shift to the left by more than in the new classical model. Hence inflation falls, but aggregate output may rise or fall, depending on whether the aggregate supply curve shifts to the left more or less than the aggregate demand curve shifts to the right.

CREDITS

INDEX

Note: Page numbers followed by *n* indicate footnotes.

GUIDE TO COMMONLY USED SYMBOLS

SYMBOL	PAGE WHERE INTRODUCED	TERM
β	101	beta
Δ	430	change in a variable
π^e	89	expected inflation
a	557	autonomous consumer expenditure
AD	598	aggregate demand curve
AS	609	aggregate supply curve
B^d	105	demand for bonds
B^s	106	supply of bonds
C	75	yearly coupon payment
C	417	currency
C	556	consumer expenditure
$\{C/D\}$	436	currency ratio
D	145	demand curve
D	430	checkable deposits
DL	443	discount loans
E	174	exchange (spot) rate
$(E^e_{t+1} - E_t)E_t$	175	expected appreciation of domestic currency
EM	241	equity multiplier
ER	436	excess reserves
$\{ER/D\}$	436	excess reserves ratio
G	556	government spending
i	71	interest rate (yield to maturity)
i_d	444	discount rate
i^D	174	interest rate on domestic assets
i^F	174	interest rate on foreign assets
i_r	89	real interest rate
I	556	investment spending
IS	571	IS curve
LM	571	LM curve
m	436	money multiplier

The Story of

Figure Skating

Michael Boo

WILLIAM MORROW AND COMPANY

New York

Permission for photographs is gratefully acknowledged: pages 2, 19, 43, 46—The World Figure Skating Museum; page 13—The Metropolitan Museum of Art, Rogers Fund, 1911 (11.92); pages 28, 54, 60, 63—*American Skating World*; pages 31, 33—20th Century Fox Film Corporation; pages 35, 89—*Ice Capades/American Skating World*; page 39—courtesy of Candid Productions Incorporated; pages 57, 58, 79—Margaret S. Williamson; pages 62, 110, 133—Lois Elfman/*American Skating World*; page 65—Rhonda Wiles/*American Skating World*; pages 67, 92, 105, 116, 118, 119, 124, 125, 126, 147, 153—George S. Rossano/*American Skating World*; pages 69, 72, 90, 210—David Leonardi/*American Skating World*; page 70—Mentor Management; page 73—Dawn Norman/*American Skating World*; page 77—All Sport Photographic Ltd/*American Skating World*; page 81—Diane Delozier/*American Skating World*; pages 82, 111—Nancy L. Kast/*American Skating World*; page 84—Carole Swan/*American Skating World*; page 91—Sherri Fillingham/*American Skating World*; page 95—Michael Sterling Public Relations/*American Skating World*; pages 98, 100, 107—Don Shelley/*American Skating World*; page 108—Ed Lewi/*American Skating World*; page 113—Jonathan Becker/*American Skating World*; pages 114, 167—Kolette Myers/*American Skating World*; pages 127, 128, 139, 141, 144, 149, 155, 160—Charles C. White/*American Skating World*; page 135—Shirley McLaughlin/*American Skating World*; pages 137, 158—Karen Chande/*American Skating World*; pages 142, 148, 166—Charles E. Covell/*American Skating World*; pages 146, 150, 152, 161, 187—Barb McCutcheon/*American Skating World*; page 172—Deborah J. Nelson/Satin Stitches; page 174—John M. Egbert/*American Skating World*; page 176—SP-Teri; pages 181, 183—Frank J. Zamboni & Co, Inc.; page 185—Ice Castle; page 191—Marco Entertainment

Published by Morrow Junior Books
a division of William Morrow and Company, Inc.
1350 Avenue of the Americas, New York, NY 10019
www.williammorrow.com

Printed in the United States of America.

1 2 3 4 5 6 7 8 9 10

Library of Congress Cataloging-in-Publication Data
Boo, Michael.
The story of figure skating / Michael Boo.
p. cm.
Includes bibliographical references and index.
Summary: Surveys the history of figure skating and examines some of its notable performers.
ISBN 0-688-15820-X
1. Skating—History—Juvenile literature.   2. Skaters—Juvenile literature.
[1. Ice skating.   2. Ice skaters.]   I. Title.
GV850.4.B66 1998   796.91'2'09—dc21   98-13569   CIP AC

To the memory of Harris Collins,
ASSOCIATE PRODUCER/DIRECTOR,
Tour of World Figure Skating Champions (now Champions on Ice)

Special thanks to Jana Bobek, mother of Nicole Bobek; Rosemary Brosnan, Executive Editor, Morrow Junior Books; Michele Coppola, former Associate Editor, Morrow Junior Books; Deborah J. Nelson, President, Satin Stitches; Michael Rosenberg, President, Marco Entertainment; George Spiteri, President, SP-Teri; Thomas Memorial Library (Chesterton, Indiana) research desk librarians; Donald Yontz, President, Entertainment Production Services; and Richard F. Zamboni, President, Frank J. Zamboni, Inc., & Co.

A very special thanks to Kermit Jackson, Owner and Executive Editor, American Skating World.

Also special thanks to my friends at Champions on Ice: Roger Bathurst, Wardrobe Supervisor; Tom Collins, Executive Producer; Elaine DeMore, USFSA Representative; Pat Gale, Media Coordinator; Paul Hendrickson, Production Manager; Eric Lang, Physical Therapist; Lou McClary, Security; and Sandy Reed, Coordinator.

A very special thanks to the dozens of skaters who have allowed me over the years to interview them for American Skating World.

CONTENTS

THIS IS A GREAT TIME IN HISTORY TO BE A FIGURE skating fan. Never before has so much skating been offered on television, giving one a chance to see a multitude of competitions, exhibitions, and theatrical productions. An increasing number of tours are traveling the world, allowing more and more fans to see their favorite skaters in person.

The dramatic increase in tours and professional competitions and exhibitions has encouraged countless well-known skaters to put off retirement, keeping them on the ice and in front of their fans well beyond the age when in previous decades they would have hung up their skates.

Skating clubs are growing, and more children and adults are discovering the joys of lacing up their boots and gliding across the ice, providing more coaches with a chance to make a living from their passion.

It wasn't so long ago that just a handful of skating programs appeared on television, with many broadcast during the holidays. A significant amount of time was dedicated to skating during the broadcast of the Winter Olympics, but the four years in between seemed like a long wait. The National and World Championships were shown without much fanfare each year, but as soon as they were over, fans had little else to look forward to.

Television viewers knew the big names from the past mainly from their memories, as former amateur champions and other professionals had little chance to stay in the spotlight. Many signed on with the glitzy and glamorous skating tours of the day. But these big-name skaters were just the icing on the cake rather than the "main event," often taking a backseat in the advertising to the costumed cartoon and fairy-tale characters. The idea of having professional competitions was a radical one. How could pros stay in shape to compete head-to-head? This seems a strange question today, now that pros are in many instances better athletes than they were as amateurs.

Today the most popular touring shows let the skating speak for itself. While some shows still feature cute animal costumes and cartoon characters, one sees the biggest reactions from the crowd at those shows where the skaters do what they do best, which is to skate with all their heart. Big names from Winter Olympics a decade earlier are still thrilling audiences with their leaps, jumps, and artistry, sometimes skating side by side with names that have just become known to the public.

This book traces the evolutions and revolutions that have occurred in figure skating over the past several decades, and even in previous centuries. It attempts to bring to life the developments, events, and personal sacrifices that have helped shape skating into one of the most popular spectator sports today.

*part***One**

The Birth of Figure Skating

The First Skates

NORTHERN EUROPEANS, QUITE POSSIBLY THE VIKINGS, are credited with creating the first skates some time around the ninth century by fastening lengths of wood or bones to their everyday boots. In the Scandinavian countries, sharpened antlers also were used for blades. Archaeologists have even unearthed blades that were made from walrus teeth.

Skaters today would have an extremely difficult time skating on these ancient blades. Today's metal blades have a hollow groove running their entire length. As shallow as it is, the groove creates two very sharp edges (referred to as the inside edge and the outside edge) that grip the ice.

The earliest blades had no edges to grip the ice and help the skaters push forward, so the skaters had to carry poles. Skaters used the poles not only for balance and to keep from sliding side to side, but also, more importantly, to move forward. The poles propelled the skaters in much the same manner as those used by today's cross-country skiers.

The Dutch are credited with figuring out how to skate without poles when iron blades became available. The first all-metal skate blades showed up in Russia near the end of the 1600s. These early iron blades of the Industrial Revolution allowed skaters to use the sharpened edges to dig into the ice for propulsion.

Skates as known today did not exist centuries ago. Now, when someone mentions the word *skates*, we think of the combination of boot and blade. Back then, the word *skates* meant just the blades, which were fastened to everyday boots with straps. These straps sometimes held the blades on rather flimsily and were prone to breaking from the side-to-side stress.

Later, blades were attached to heavy and structurally weak wooden foot plates, which were then strapped on to boots. These wooden devices were an improvement over blades simply attached to the boots, but they did not absorb much stress before breaking. Leather straps would be a necessary evil until near the end of the eighteenth century, when blades began to be more solidly fastened to boots with clamps.

It wasn't until 1850 that the first modern all-steel skate was created. Philadelphia mechanic E. V. Bushnell's clip-on invention screwed a steel blade of superior hardness directly to a skate boot, eliminating the need for straps or clamps.

With Bushnell's invention, skaters could jump and spin without concern that their blades would separate from the boot. This helped make the mid-1800s a period of substantial recreational skating growth.

Gliding through Europe

In 1380, a girl named Lidwina was born in Holland (the Netherlands). Like most of her friends, she learned to skate almost as soon as she learned to walk. In 1396, she fell while skating on the ice of a frozen canal (legend has it that she was pushed over) and sustained serious internal injuries. Lidwina was bedridden the rest of her life, but before she died in 1433, she was credited with performing a variety of miracles from her bedside and is thought by many to be responsible for miracles even after her death.

Her remains were interred near her hometown of Schiedam, and in 1616 she was beatified by the Roman Catholic church, a step on the way to the sainthood that was bestowed upon her in 1890 by Pope Leo XIII. Scheidam was completely untouched by the Nazi bombing blitz that destroyed so much of Holland during World War II. Locals attribute this to the divine intervention of their hometown patron saint and enthusiastically celebrate Saint Lidwina Feast Day every April 14.

If skating were to have a patron saint, it's no surprise that she would come from the Netherlands, a country practically synonymous with the popularization of skating. The winters of northern Europe are long and cold, creating ample opportunities for skating across the ice of natural bodies of water for much of the year. That's why so many paintings of Dutch ice skating scenes are found in art museums throughout Europe, many by Dutch masters of the fourteenth through the seventeenth centuries.

Skating at Slooten, near Amsterdam, by seventeenth-century Dutch painter Jan Beerstraaten

The Dutch not only loved recreational skating, but they also used skating as an essential mode of transportation. Many villages throughout the Netherlands are connected by rivers and canals that freeze solid during the winter. During that season, long before there was such a thing as a snowplow, it often became impossible to travel the roads between countless villages. Skating became not just the preferred method of getting from one place to another—in some cases it was the only method possible.

The sport of speed skating was born when the many youngsters skating down canals and rivers began to challenge one another to races. The sport, with its extra-long blades for pushing ahead quickly, attracted throngs of cheering onlookers. Casual contests led to actual competitions, and the sport soon spread throughout the region and the nearby countries of Scandinavia. It's no wonder that of the first sixty-five Men's World Speed Skating titles, presented each year since 1893, fifty-five were won by athletes from the Netherlands and the Scandinavian countries of Norway, Sweden, and Finland.

It would take some time for skating to become popular in North America, but by the mid-1700s, the sport had crossed the North Sea. It became enough of a rage in Scotland that the world's first skating club was founded in Edinburgh in 1744.

It was not unheard of for skaters to fall through the ice of the rivers, canals, ponds, and lakes that had become natural skating venues. Mishaps like these were such a problem that when the first skating club was founded in North America in 1849, its members were required to carry ropes to rescue people who fell into frigid waters while skating. The Philadelphia Skating Club and Humane Society was so named because, in addition to skating, its members showed concern for their fellow humans by risking their lives to rescue those in danger.

Skating was enjoying the status of the "in" thing on both sides of the Atlantic.

By that time, skating was so popular in the British Isles that the cover of the very first mass-produced printed Christmas card, manufactured in London, featured a skating scene.

The Quest for Year-round Ice

Many skating enthusiasts dreamed that one day people would skate indoors, mercifully separated from icy winds and cold weather. The first recorded attempts to make artificial ice were in 1812, but it would be decades before anyone got it right. Artificial ice was produced in 1842, but it didn't prove to be solid enough for skating.

Florida inventor Dr. John Gorrie created a machine in 1850 that could make ice by using compressed air, which absorbed the heat in the water. At the time, this was not seen as a practical solution, though much later Gorrie's device laid the groundwork for more successful ice-making machines, including refrigerator ice makers.

The first covered indoor ice rink was the Skating Club House, constructed in Quebec City, Canada, in 1854. However, the ice was made naturally and kept frozen by keeping the windows open. This wasn't the significant progress that many skaters had been hoping for, but at least they could skate indoors.

In the 1860s, a system was created whereby water was flooded over metal tubes, then frozen by the tubes. A big advance came in 1865 or 1876 (history books disagree), when W. A. Parker came up with the idea of mixing brine (water saturated with salt) with carbonic acid (carbon dioxide dissolved in water), creating an artificial ice surface that was more solid and better able to withstand the rigors of skate blades than artificially frozen water alone.

British professor John Gamgee successfully created artificial ice indoors in the mid-1870s. He opened an indoor rink in Chelsea, England, that utilized a process of cooling ice by pumping glycerin and water through copper pipes and keeping the ice refrigerated with ether. The rink was microscopic by today's standards, a scant twenty-four by sixteen feet, about the size of a large residential living room. But it opened the way for larger indoor rinks.

In 1879, Gamgee's method was employed at the Glaciarium in Manchester, England. At twenty-four by forty feet, this was, at the time, the world's largest indoor ice rink.

That same year, the Wizard of Menlo Park, Thomas Alva Edison, shocked the world by inventing the incandescent lightbulb. Within the next decade, ice rinks had installed the new-fangled contraptions so that patrons could skate after dark.

Warm weather, strong winds, darkness—all the elements that had kept people off the ice at one time or another had now been conquered. Ice rinks could be enjoyed even during the summer, and warm-weather locales could now build ice rinks. Nature proved to be no match for the desires and conquests of humanity.

Why It's Called Figure Skating

While many skaters were perfectly happy just to skate around on a pond for enjoyment or to race down a canal for glory, others were starting to create the new sport and art form of figure skating. It wasn't at all like today's figure skating. The early practitioners of the discipline spent countless hours learning how to trace basic forms on the ice, mostly variations of circles and figure eights. These basic figures became known as "school figures," which is how the term *figure skating* originated.

This simple discipline evolved into something far more complex, with skaters sometimes taking hours to produce ornate and intricate figures. The most unusual of these designs became the individual calling cards of those who were best in the world, with "Can you top this?" challenges issued to others. When we look at some of these ornamental figures, it's amazing that anyone could have had enough steadiness of foot and patience to trace these complex pictures onto the ice.

An ornamental figure

In 1772, Robert Jones wrote and published *A Treatise on Skating*, the first comprehensive English-language textbook on figure skating. More than a century later, in 1882, the first international skate meet was held in Vienna, Austria. All the skaters had to demonstrate proficiency in many standardized school figures—there were more than forty variations on the figure eight alone. In addition, the contestants were allowed to perform a figure of their own choosing and to present a free skate routine.

In 1883, Henry Boswell, an iron worker and skater in Oxford, England, created the first skate especially made for figure skating, with a blade that resembles the one we know today. Toe picks (the notches ground into the front of every figure skate) helped the skaters stop on a dime and control their tracings and other movements.

Despite this improvement, the sport seemed to many to be more drudgery than fun. Observers noted that the faces of the figure skaters showed no joy as they immersed themselves in deep concentration to trace the intricate figures.

A century later, as school figures were being considered for elimination at the World and Olympic Championships, many were still saying that despite the self-discipline achieved through learning and perfecting school figures, tracing figures was a huge waste of skaters' time and effort, not to mention that it was something spectators could hardly care less about.

Jackson Haines: Skating's First Superstar

Jackson Haines, the father of contemporary figure skating, was born in New York City in 1840, just prior to the time of the first experiments with artificial ice. (Some books claim that he was born in Chicago.) He excelled at the tracing of figures, bringing grace and beauty to the increasingly mundane art form.

Haines was not at all thrilled by proper skating decorum, which held that skaters had to maintain a stiff, rigid posture, with arms neatly folded. He felt there had to be more to skating than tracing school figures, and he had an intense desire to liberate skating from the restrictions that had been placed upon it.

He believed that figure skating would not truly become an art form until the rules allowed for more individual self-expression. The ballet training he received in Europe and his work as a ballet instructor in Philadelphia prior to the Civil War were strong influences on Haines and allowed him to apply elements of dance to his skating.

There was no official United States Figure Skating Association National Championship until 1914, but in 1863 and 1864 Haines won the predecessor event, the Championships of America. Despite his accomplishments, he was disregarded at best and scorned at worst by fellow American skaters for being too much of a showman. He was not like the rest of them, being fond of fancy costumes and exuding a sense of grace that other skaters thought was less than appropriate.

Too radical for the established skating scene in the United States, Haines packed his bags and sailed to Europe, where he was regarded less with suspicion and more with a sense of wonder. He settled in Vienna and got to know the Strauss family of composers. The famous Johann Strauss wrote waltzes in his honor, and Haines stunned the world by doing something that is taken for granted today: He skated to music. Thomas Edison didn't invent the phonograph until 1877, so Haines employed musicians to sit by the side of the ice and perform. In the process, he taught the Viennese how to waltz on ice.

Sculpture of Jackson Haines, the father of modern figure skating, at the World Figure Skating Museum

Haines created quite a sensation in Vienna and throughout Europe. He made artistry an important element in skating and actively pursued what is now thought of as free skating. Among the moves he's credited with developing are the spiral and the spread eagle, the latter employed more than a century later to such great and memorable effect by Brian Boitano in his stunning free skate (long program) performance at the 1988 Winter Olympics.

The ever-inventive Haines also did the first sit spin, a staple in all advanced skaters' repertoires. In this move, the skater drops almost to the ice while spinning in place on one bent knee, with the other leg extended straight out or bent to the front.

Wanting to spin more freely, Haines developed a blade that was shorter than the conventional skate blade and that allowed him to do tighter turns. (The blades did not have the toe picks that Boswell would add a few years later in 1883.) He also was the first to attach a permanent blade to a boot.

He was so popular that streets were named after him in some of Europe's major cities. He was so influential that he single-handedly gave birth to the International Style of figure skating, the style we recognize and accept today as legitimate figure skating.

It seemed that there was nothing Haines couldn't do. But in 1875, in only his midthirties, he died of pneumonia in Finland while traveling by sled to a skating exhibition. An outcast in his day in his native country, he was buried in Finland under a tombstone that reads, JACKSON HAINES, IN REMEMBRANCE OF AMERICA'S SKATING KING.

The Haines Aftermath

The effect of Haines's life and work cannot be discounted. The International Style truly lived up to its name by spreading to country after country. In 1879, the first-known international skating competition was held in Stockholm, Sweden. Only men were allowed to compete, as competition was deemed "improper" for "proper" women. (Women were eventually allowed into international competitions, but for the sake of modesty they had to wear long dresses that practically touched the ice.)

That same year saw the creation of the world's first organized skating governing body, the National Skating Association of Great Britain. Although speed skaters were the only original members, the organization was eventually opened to the vast number of figure skaters caught up in the craze kindled by Haines's success.

The year 1879 was an active one for the evolution of figure skating, for in addition to the two events just mentioned, the year also saw the first skating carnival take place on manufactured ice. Carnivals were nothing new, with masked skaters in ornate costumes skating about as spectators watched from rinkside seats. But this carnival took place on a large, mechanically frozen surface in New York City's Madison Square Garden, and, as such, it attracted quite a bit of media attention.

Ironically, word of Haines's success began to filter back to the United States, and American skaters started to adopt his more musical and expressive style as their own. Numerous new skating clubs were formed in the country that had at one time seemed to discard him.

As a result, Louis Rubenstein, a Canadian International Style disciple and twelve-time Canadian National Champion, saw a need for the clubs to unite in common purpose. He helped found not only the Amateur Figure Skating Association of Canada in 1878 (which later became the Canadian Figure Skating Association) but also the International Skating Union of America and the National Amateur Skating Association of the United States—organizations comprising many new and previously existing skating clubs.

In 1884, Norwegian all-around skater Axel Paulsen visited North America. (He was an "all-around" skater because he excelled as both a speed skater and a figure skater.) He managed to win indoor track races and long-distance events of ten and twenty-five miles by skating with his arms positioned behind his back over long distances and being more aerodynamic than anyone else.

Paulsen also presented figure skating demonstrations in the International Style and amazed all with his signature jump, for which he leaped into the air forward, rotated one-and-a-half revolutions in the air, and then landed backward on the opposite foot. The jump, known as the axel, is today a staple in every competitive skater's arsenal of tricks, with more advanced skaters pulling off double axels and triple axels, the latter the most difficult of all triple jumps. Despite being a single jump, Paulsen's axel was the most challenging jump yet seen in its day.

In addition to fostering goodwill and camaraderie among figure skaters, organizations such as the United States Figure Skating Association became clearinghouses for the standardization of competitions and proficiency tests. These encourage the use of proper techniques and help skaters move up the competitive ladder.

The International Skating Union (ISU) was formed in 1892, lending its approval to the first World Figure Skating Championships in St. Petersburg, Russia, in 1896, which were won by Gilbert Fuchs, a German. (Ladies' and Pairs events had yet to break onto the internationally judged skating scene, and it would be a long time before Ice Dancing became recognized.)

By the end of the nineteenth century, children all around the world were reading a book by Mary Mapes Dodge that was written in 1885. The main character of the book is a young boy skater growing up in Holland, a country that Dodge described in stunning and picturesque detail despite never having been there. More than a century later, *Hans Brinker and the Silver Skates* remains the most popular book ever written about skating.

Skating Becomes a Spectator Sport

Welcome, Ladies

THE TURN OF THE TWENTIETH CENTURY WAS A TIME of great hope and expectations. Edison's lightbulb, no longer an oddity in homes and workplaces, was changing the way that people lived. Early automobiles were rolling out of factories, changing the way people traveled. Inventors Wilbur and Orville Wright made the first airplane flight in Kitty Hawk, North Carolina, in 1903, giving people a glimpse of commercial transportation in the future. For the most part, the world was at peace.

It was a time of great growth for recreation and for competitive figure skating.

In 1901, Sweden's Ulrich Salchow, creator of the jump that bears his last name and eventual President of the International Skating Union (ISU), won the first of his ten ISU World Figure Skating Championships between that year and 1911, his string of victories interrupted only in 1906. In 1902, he was almost defeated by Great Britain's Madge Syers, the only time men and women ever competed head-to-head at the World Championships.

As one might imagine, a woman's earning the silver medal in singles skating at the most prestigious skating event in the world caused quite a stir. The truth is, no one had seen this as a potential problem, because no one among the rule makers thought that a woman might be that good in a "man's sport," and Syers was the first woman ever to apply to compete in the World Championships.

After Syers's near upset of Salchow—and some sports observers thought she should have won—the rules were changed, and women had to wait until 1906 to compete for the World Championship in their own division. Naturally, the gold medalist of the first two

Ladies' World Championships was none other than Madge Syers.

It's not inconceivable that Syers might have toppled Salchow in 1902 had she spent more of her time as a singles skater. Amazingly, she was also one of the top Pairs in the world, a fact that would have to wait until 1908 to be proven.

The Ladies contestants, once they were formally allowed to compete, had to wear long dresses that came down to the top of their skates to preserve their modesty. "Real" ladies didn't expose their ankles in public. (To this day, women are officially known as Ladies in the language of the ISU.)

It's not known what the women skaters thought of skating's Victorian mind-set. A half century earlier, a German woman was stoned to death for skating, despite the fact that women had been skating in neighboring Holland for centuries.

Whatever the reason, perhaps some of the women skaters who entered the first World and Olympic Championships considered long dresses a small price to pay for being on the ice.

The Era of Summer "Winter" Olympics

The first modern-day Olympics were held in Athens, Greece, in 1896. The ISU had attempted to get figure skating into the schedule but was turned down by the International Olympic Committee (IOC). However, the IOC relented, and in 1908 figure skating was allowed in the Olympics, the only winter sport to be included in the summer games in London, England.

There was a practical reason why skating was the only winter sport to be allowed in the Olympics. There was no separate Winter Olympics until 1924 in Chamonix, France. Artificial ice surfaces for summer skating were not unusual by 1908, but artificial snow for ski jumps and cross-country ski trails was not yet common. And besides, the English had perfected artificial ice and were able to offer a venue that thumbed its nose at the heat of summer.

As expected, Ulrich Salchow won the 1908 Olympic Men's gold

medal, leading the Swedish men to a gold, silver, and bronze medal sweep of the Olympics. Men from Sweden and Austria won every one of the first six Olympic titles in figure skating (1908, 1920, 1924, 1928, 1932, and 1936). Ladies from Great Britain, Sweden, Austria, and Norway and Pairs from Germany, Finland, Austria, and France did the same.

More dramatically, men from Germany, Austria, and Sweden won every one of the first thirty-six World titles (through 1936, with a few years missing during World War I). Up through the same year, Ladies' skaters from Great Britain, Hungary, Austria, and Norway won every one of the first twenty-four World titles. Over that same time frame, Pairs champions came only from Germany, Great Britain, Finland, Austria, France, and Hungary.

What's the point? At least part of every one of those European countries has long winters. Throughout the world, there were still relatively few indoor rinks. Therefore, skaters from the more frigid countries had an advantage. It's also important to note that skaters didn't train with coaches in other countries to the extent that they do now. The best-trained skaters in those days came from cold climates with ample natural ice, just as the best-trained surfers today come from warm climates with ample waves.

But back to the 1908 Olympics: The unsinkable Madge Syers was still in good enough form after nearly upsetting Salchow at Worlds six years earlier to follow her 1906 and 1907 World titles with the first Olympic gold medal presented to a Ladies' Champion.

The Pairs skaters of the 1800s and early 1900s did not do lifts and throws, as they do today. Remember that the women had to wear long dresses, and landing on the dress after an aerial maneuver would have been disastrous. Instead, the Pairs glided around the ice in close contact with each other. If you were to see such a routine today, you would be forgiven for mistaking it for early Ice Dancing.

Anna Hubler and Heinrich Burger of Germany won the 1908 Olympic Pairs title, along with the first-ever World Pairs title the same year and another World Championship two years later. However, the real story in Pairs may have been, once again, Madge Syers. With her husband, Edgar, she captured the Olympic bronze medal in Pairs. She was truly a versatile athlete.

There was no figure skating at the Stockholm, Sweden, Summer Games in 1912, as no satisfactory artificial rink existed in the city, so there was a twelve-year gap between Olympic figure skating titles. (No Olympics were held in 1916 during World War I.)

There would be one more Olympics in which figure skating was a medal event during the Summer Games. The Belgian Summer Games of 1920 in Antwerp saw Sweden's Gillis Grafstrom win the first of his three Olympic gold medals; he won the others in 1924 and 1928. Salchow placed just out of the medals in fourth place, skating on an injured leg, nine years after the last of his ten World Championships and at the "advanced" age of forty-two.

Grafstrom astounded audiences by performing the first "flying" sit spin, a sit spin approached directly from a jump. But over the extensive period of his three Olympics victories, and despite adding many new jumps and spins to his skating repertoire, he won only three World titles—in 1922, 1924, and 1929. We'll never know if Grafstrom could have won additional World gold medals, as there were no ISU World Championships from 1915 through 1921, while the world was at war. Instead of skating against one another, athletes were shooting at one another.

Charlotte: Skating's First Ice Queen

On May 7, 1915, the German military sank the *Lusitania*, an English luxury liner, resulting in a great loss of civilian life. This act of aggression prompted the United States to declare war on Germany. Despite that, one of the most beloved entertainers in America was a German girl who was brought to America the same year the *Lusitania* went down.

Charlotte Oelschlagel was spotted in a Berlin nightclub by Charles

Dillingham, who was in Europe looking for talent to play at his New York City theater, the massive six-thousand-seat Hippodrome. As the Hippodrome was the largest theater in the world, Dillingham wasn't looking for just *any* act—he needed to find real star quality, and he found it in seventeen-year-old Charlotte. The entertainer (who never used her last name professionally) was packing the crowds in for *Charlotte's Ice Revue,* a glitzy ice show with a supporting cast of sixty-five skaters that had been playing the German capital for the previous two years.

Charlotte was the talk of Berlin and very soon, she and her entire cast were the talk of Broadway. Dillingham took a chance that America's first large-scale ice show would be a success, signing the entire entourage to a six-week deal and changing the name of the show to *Flirting in St. Moritz.* His gamble was richly rewarded, as Charlotte's supreme artistry and the show's remarkable staying power filled the massive Hippodrome every day (sometimes twice daily) for three years.

It is said that Charlotte inspired hotels and resorts throughout the eastern United States to build indoor ice rinks for ice shows of their own and that she was the first woman to perform an axel jump. Little girls begged for Charlotte dolls. Popular songs were written about the star. She was a one-person cottage industry—skating's first queen of the ice. Though she never had a World or Olympic skating medal to her name, she created a move with her future husband that all World and Olympic Pairs must now perform if they have any hopes of success—the death spiral. This is the dramatic spin in which the female rotates on one skate around her male partner with the back of her head almost touching the ice. (Some historians state that the first death spiral was performed many years later by Canadian Pairs team Suzanne Morrow and Wallace Diestelmeyer, World bronze medalists in 1948, while others simply state that the pair was the first to do a death spiral in international competition.)

Charlotte also created the "Charlotte Stop," in which she would

glide on one leg, pivoting forward from the waist, and suddenly stop as if she had magical brakes. It's a move that many skaters have exploited since.

Charlotte became skating's first movie star, appearing in the 1916 silent film *The Frozen Warning*. The film, the first skating motion picture to be made, was split into six parts, intended to be viewed in installments, like so many of the "continuing adventure" serials that were popular in the movie houses of the day.

In the film, an up-to-no-good secret agent from a sinister foreign government steals a powerful new weapon from Charlotte's on-screen inventor boyfriend. She learns about the event and attempts to turn the tables on the secret agent during a skating performance. Now this is where things get really good: During her performance, she traces the word *spies* on the ice with her skates and then leaps into the air, pointing toward the villain. The spy is caught, the weapon is recovered, and Charlotte is honored for her courageous heroism. You have to love it.

Sonja Henie: One in a Million

For the most part, the 1920s were years of prosperity throughout the industrialized world. World War I was over, and the Great Depression wouldn't strike until October 1929.

Out of an earlier organization, the United States Figure Skating Association (USFSA) was founded in 1921, with only seven skating clubs as charter members. (Today, there are more than 450 member clubs throughout the United States.) The USFSA immediately joined the ISU and two years later published the first edition of *Skating*, the body's official magazine, which is still published today.

The first true Winter Olympics (in Chamonix, France, in 1924) are remembered less for who won (Grafstrom, among others, with his second Olympic Men's gold) than for those who didn't. The French Pairs team of Andrée Joly and Pierre Brunet took the bronze medal but came back in 1928 and 1932 to win two Olympic Pairs

Charlotte, the German youngster who became skating's first ice queen, demonstrating a dramatic stag leap

gold medals with their trailblazing use of dramatic, gravity-defying lifts. They also had a curious habit of winning the World Championship in alternate years: 1926, 1928, 1930, and 1932.

Pairs skaters had just started to develop movements where they would skate apart from each other, but they were still doing similar movements. The lifts Joly and Brunet were fond of meant that each of the Pairs skaters would undertake a unique and individual role in the partnership. This was radical for its day.

Even though Joly and Brunet didn't win the big one in 1924, at least they got a medal. An eleven-year-old girl who entered the Ladies' competition placed dead last (in thirteenth place) at her first Olympics—although she would someday change the world of figure skating forever.

Sonja Henie was an expert at tracing figures and an advocate of combining ballet with figure skating. She was Norwegian National Champion at the tender age of ten, but she was a bit ahead of her time for international tastes at the 1924 Winter Olympics, wearing white dresses instead of the traditional black. Worse yet, in the eyes of the judges, she wore short dresses so she would have the freedom necessary to jump.

Just three years later, in Oslo, Norway, fourteen-year-old Henie would win the first of her ten consecutive World titles. And four years after her less-than-illustrious Olympic debut, she won the first of her three Olympic singles titles in St. Moritz, Switzerland, also winning Olympic gold in 1932 (in Lake Placid, New York—the first Olympics to be held in North America) and 1936. (The only other skater who has as many World and Olympic titles is Pairs Champion Irina Rodnina, who won her ten World and three Olympic titles with two different partners from 1969 through 1980.)

Three-time Olympic gold medalist Sonja Henie

In between her second and third Olympic gold medals, Henie performed in a 1934 show at the Berlin Ice Palace and was photographed shaking hands with Nazi leader Adolf Hitler. The photo would come back to haunt her years later.

Henie was simply so powerful and athletic, graceful, and artistic that the judges had little choice but to recognize that the world of Ladies' skating was changing right in front of their eyes. She introduced elements of dance into her free skate programs and had more of an impact on the public than even Charlotte did.

Meanwhile, Henie's path crossed that of Chicago sports promoter Arthur M. Wirtz, although neither realized just how important each was to become to the other. Wirtz was famous for his financial interests in a number of sports arenas and teams, and in 1935 he produced a two-night ice show at his cavernous Chicago Stadium. He didn't spend much money to produce it, but he made a financial killing from its commercial success.

Less than two weeks after her 1936 Olympic victory, Henie retired from amateur competition and signed a contract with Wirtz, creating a partnership that lasted fifteen years. During that time, Henie and her *Hollywood Ice Revue* became the biggest single attraction ever to hit arenas in North America, breaking box office records everywhere she went.

In 1937, the first of Henie's eleven movies was released. *One in a Million* broke box office records of its own. When she felt uncomfortable playing a romantic scene in a later movie with Tyrone Power, she suggested that maybe she would feel more at ease if she put on her skates.

In 1940, she teamed up with Wirtz to co-produce *It Happens on Ice* at the Center Theatre in New York City's Rockefeller Center. For ten years, the Center was the only venue in America that featured nothing but ice shows. Although she was just co-producer and not the star of the show, *It Happens on Ice* set attendance records for a Broadway production.

Henie became a U.S. citizen in 1941 and was one of the wealthiest entertainers of her day. The *One in a Million* woman became the first female athlete to become a millionaire. During World War II, she was approached by her fellow Norwegians to contribute finan-

The Famous *Hawaiian* Dance

All of the several special numbers Sonja Henie has created for performance before the American public have been acclaimed, but most popular of all is her famous interpretation of the Hula.

Here the coordination of hands and feet is at its perfect best. Miss Henie devoted much time to the study of hand movements with the greatest Hawaiian dancers, whose genius at telling a story with their hands and fingers is without equal anywhere.

As a result, Miss Henie's Hawaiian Dance is completely authentic, and has the added charm of her rhythmic expertness on skates.

The Hawaiian Dance is being included in the 1947 "Hollywood Ice Revue" because audiences which have seen it before simply wouldn't listen to having it omitted. Besides, it is one of Miss Henie's favorite numbers.

The glamorous Hawaiian dance dress was just one of the many extravagant costumes Sonja Henie wore during the 1947 *Hollywood Ice Revue.*

cially to the Norwegian resistance movement that was fighting the Nazis. She turned them down by stating that she was an American now, and many never forgave her. In addition, they remembered the story about the photo of her with Hitler.

When Nazi troops advanced through Norway, she received a phone call that the troops were closing in on her residence. She instructed that the photo be put on prominent display in the house. When the troops entered the house and saw the photo of Henie with Hitler, they instantly refused to loot her home.

In 1968, she tried to make amends for not helping out her native country during World War II by donating her vast collection of modern art to a public museum she established with her husband near Oslo.

In 1951, Henie parted ways with Wirtz and formed the *Sonja Henie Ice Revue*. While not as successful as the earlier efforts with Wirtz, this tour changed the face of skating by introducing the Zamboni Ice Resurfacer to the world. Before Henie's tour, only one other Zamboni existed—at the ice rink built and managed by inventor Frank Zamboni. Zamboni custom-built a second machine at Henie's request, and everywhere the tour went, rink managers decided they had to have a Zamboni for themselves.

Three years later, she skated in Oslo with *Holiday on Ice*. Over thirty-three days, more people came out to see her skate than resided in Norway's capital city.

Early Ice Extravaganzas

In a repeat of what happened during World War I, there were no World Championships or Winter Olympics during the tumultuous years of World War II. The war eliminated Worlds from 1940 through 1946 and the 1940 and 1944 Olympics.

In 1936, America's first outdoor artificial ice rink opened in the plaza of New York City's Rockefeller Center. It still remains open each winter, and thousands of people gather every week to glide around on the public ice.

Also in 1936 (which was the same year Henie's *Hollywood Ice Revue* took to the road), Shipstads and Johnson *Ice Follies* was founded as the world's first large-scale traveling ice show, breaking attendance records throughout the United States and Canada. Although it was "large-scale," the effects of the Depression meant that the promoters could hire only a couple of dozen skaters at first. This show provided retired amateurs with an opportunity to keep skating past their competitive years, more often than not as members of the chorus line.

Ice Capades brought the flamboyant style and unabashed glitz of a Las Vegas floor show to hundreds of cities throughout the world.

In 1940, *Ice Capades* debuted, bringing movies, books, operas, and other cultural diversions to the ice, and it is largely credited with giving wide exposure to Ice Dancing, which wasn't to become a World Championship sport until 1952 and an Olympic sport until 1976. *Ice Capades* performed a completely new show each year. The operation eventually expanded to three separate touring companies for a period of several years, but through the 1980s and '90s it experienced numerous financial problems and had a number of owners (including Olympic gold medalist Dorothy Hamill).

Holiday on Ice was formed in 1944 and became known for bringing ice spectacles to locales that would otherwise never have had a chance to host one, such as Mexico, Cuba, Central and South America, and the Caribbean islands of the West Indies. The operation traveled with its own refrigeration equipment and could make its own 100- by 60-foot portable ice rink wherever it went.

Eventually, before the production ceased operations, *Holiday on Ice* skaters performed on every continent except Antarctica. In 1959, they became the first ice show to play behind the Iron Curtain, at a time when relationships between the United States and the then–Soviet Union were rather strained. About one million Muscovites saw the production over a two-month run.

Holiday on Ice became *Walt Disney's World on Ice* in 1981 and since then has directed its marketing appeal to children, often focusing on bringing Disney films to life.

Each of the three big ice companies was famous for producing lavish, sometimes garish and "over the top," always spectacular and fabulously costumed production numbers. They brought the flamboyance of a circus troupe to life on the ice. The big-budget productions overwhelmed the senses with visually explosive color, costumes, and pageantry. The operative word seemed to be MORE! The souls of these shows live on today in the grandiose, skimpy-on-costumes-but-big-on-feather-headdresses showgirl productions seen in Las Vegas.

The Early TV Days

The World War II Vacuum

THE HISTORY OF TWENTIETH-CENTURY FIGURE skating in the United States is generally thought of as being either pre-1961 or post-1961, for reasons that will later be discussed. And as for the pre-1961 days, they can be thought of as being pre–Sonja Henie and post–Sonja Henie, so much did she influence the sport and the way it was marketed.

Henie's popularity inspired many skaters to take to the ice. However, the effect of her retirement in 1936 from amateur competition was soon muted by the brewing storm clouds of World War II. Had Henie stayed eligible for amateur competition, she would not have been able to defend her title at the 1940 Winter Olympics. There were none.

In 1936, Nazi Germany staged the Winter Olympics in Garmisch. If the world had known then what it would find out a few years later when the crimes of the Holocaust came to light, there might not have been the 1936 Winter Olympics either. It's ironic that the country that staged the last Winter Olympics prior to World War II would be most responsible for the cancellation of the Winter Olympics in 1940. Germany gave the world no choice, after they invaded Poland in 1939.

Nor were there Winter Olympics in 1944. Also affected by the war were the World Championships, which were canceled for seven years, from 1940 through 1946. There's no telling whose might have been a household name yet today had there been no war.

Many skaters were certainly in their prime during those years, but without a world stage to shine on, those who were not still in their prime when the war was over faded into obscurity. Some probably wanted to compete in top form after the war, but by then time just wasn't on their side.

The Postwar Years and Dick Button

One skater who might have made a greater impact had there been no World War II was Canada's Barbara Ann Scott, Canadian Ladies' Champion in 1944, 1945, 1946, and 1948. In 1947 and 1948, Scott won the ISU's World Ladies' Championship, and she was victorious as well at the 1948 Winter Olympics in St. Moritz, Switzerland. Her 1947 World victory made her the first North American to win an ISU World Championship.

The year of Scott's second World Championship saw other Canadian skaters garner attention as well. Pairs team Suzanne Morrow and Wallace Diestelmeyer is credited with doing the first death spiral at a World Championship, during a performance that earned them the bronze medal.

The Soviets, who would virtually own the World and Olympics Pairs titles from 1964 on and the Ice Dancing titles from 1970 on (Ice Dancing wasn't an Olympic event until 1976), were unknown on the world stage after World War II. In fact, the only Russian/Soviet Pairs medal earned at the World Championships prior to 1962 was a single bronze, won by the Russian team of A. L. Fischer and L. P. Popowa at the 1908 World Championships, the first at which a Pairs competition was held.

In 1946, the world got its first glimpses of a man known by skating fans today as a popular and beloved television skating commentator and a producer of professional skating competitions. That year, Richard "Dick" Button started compiling an impressive string of U.S. Men's gold medal victories, winning the first Men's National Championship to be decided since 1943. This propelled him to prominence as the top male skater in the country as soon as the war was over. He stayed in that position for seven straight years, from 1946 through 1952. He also won five straight World Championships

Dick Button defies gravity during a stunning Russian split.

(1948 through 1952) and won the Men's gold medal at both the 1948 and 1952 Winter Olympics.

His 1948 Olympic victory at the age of eighteen makes him the youngest man ever to win an Olympics singles championship. In addition, it gave the United States its first-ever Olympic skating gold medal in any of the skating disciplines and its first-ever Olympic Men's medal of any color.

Button's 1946 National Championship came just four years after he took his first skating lesson. He was driven to succeed at introducing increasingly more difficult jumps into competitions. At the 1952 Winter Olympics, he became the first skater successfully to perform any triple jump, in this case a triple loop. He was never satisfied with playing it safe, and as he introduced new jumps, other skaters found it harder and harder to keep up with his lead.

Even today, it's amazing to read the list of Dick Button firsts. (Remember that only people who succeed at accomplishing a jump in competition go into the record books. Practices don't count. Lots of almost-firsts have happened in practices.)

In 1945, Button performed the first double salchow, soon adding the double loop and double lutz to his repertoire of jumps. At the 1948 Winter Olympics, he nailed the first two-and-a-half-rotation jump in history, the double axel.

Consider that Axel Paulsen first performed the single axel in 1882, and that wasn't even in a formal competition. It would take sixty-six years before someone was able to stretch an axel out to a double. It would take someone else another thirty years to pull off a triple axel—Canada's Vern Taylor at the 1978 World Championships.

But for all of Button's accomplishments, it was his performance of the first triple loop in 1952 that is most talked about. Today, even junior-level skaters attempt triple loops, the easiest of all triple jumps. But in 1952, Dick Button had no one who could tell him, based on his or her own experience, how it could be done.

American Singles Dominate

The same year of Button's landmark triple, Ice Dancing became a part of the World Championships. Jean Westwood and Lawrence Demmy of Great Britain won the first title and repeated the victory each of the next three years. Three different British Ice Dancing teams would win the next five Worlds (1956 through 1960), and Diane Towler and Bernard Ford would win four more in a row for Great Britain from 1966 through 1969.

In 1950, Karol and Peter Kennedy became the first Americans to win the Pairs World Championship. Ten different Pairs teams won the World Championships from 1947 through 1964. Only one Pairs team seemed to have a lock on the World Championships leading up to Winter Olympics during that same period. Canada's Barbara Wagner and Robert Paul won four Worlds in a row (1957 through 1960) and took gold at the 1960 Winter Olympics.

During the post-Button years, the Men's and Ladies' scene on the world stage was firmly in America's control.

Two brothers would take over the mantle from Button once he retired from amateur competition. Together, with Button, they gave the United States a streak of twelve consecutive Men's World Championships and four consecutive Olympic Men's gold medals. Hayes Alan Jenkins won the 1953, 1954, 1955, and 1956 Worlds and the 1956 Winter Olympics. David Jenkins picked up from his older sibling, winning the 1957, 1958, and 1959 World Championships and the 1960 Winter Olympics. Between the two of them, they also won eight consecutive USFSA Championships, four each, from 1953 through 1960. Skating was a way of life in the Jenkins family. Their sister was an accomplished skater, and their mother served as a USFSA judge.

Tenley Albright won the USFSA Ladies' Championship in 1952, the year she took the silver medal at the Winter Olympics. She recaptured her USFSA crown each of the next four years. In 1953, she became the first American woman to win the World Championship, and repeated as World Champion in 1955, capping off her competitive career with a gold medal performance at the 1956 Winter Olympics in Cortina, Italy.

The year of her Olympic victory was an interesting one in the annals of U.S. Ladies' Champions, for although Albright defeated silver medalist Carol Heiss for the fourth year in a row at the USFSA Championship and would go on to win the Olympics over second-place Heiss, her World team comrade would turn the tables one month after the Olympics by forcing Albright to settle for the silver medal at the 1956 World Championships.

Albright certainly had a bright amateur career, and there is little doubt that she would have had a successful professional career as well, if she had so chosen. However, Albright had other plans. She had wanted to be a doctor for several years and saw skating as a means of accomplishing her higher goal. She had seen her share of doctors as a youth, having been stricken with childhood polio. Many victims of this now virtually unheard-of disease never walked again. Albright fought it and skated to build up her strength step-by-step, eventually becoming a World and Olympic Champion. And after attaining her goal of being the best skater in the world, she completed college, went on to medical school, and became a highly respected surgeon.

Albright never relinquished her amateur status. Remarkably, she remains the only Olympic singles gold medalist, man or woman, since 1928, who did not turn pro.

World and Olympic Champion Carol Heiss

Carol Heiss first appeared on the world stage in 1953, as silver medalist behind Albright at the USFSA Championship and as fourth-place finisher in that year's World Championship. She was only thirteen years old. In the early 1920s, Sonja Henie had been the first Ladies' skater to do a single axel jump. Heiss became the first to do

a double axel. As for placing behind Albright at Nationals, finishing second to her teammate would be something she would have to get used to.

During the last four years (1953 through 1956) of Albright's five-year USFSA winning streak, Heiss had to settle for the silver medal at Nationals and wait her turn for the gold. Patience paid off, and Heiss won four consecutive USFSA and World Championship gold medals in the years immediately afterward, in addition to her upset victory over newly crowned Olympic Champion Albright in 1956 when Heiss was sixteen years old. Today, a sixteen-year-old Ladies' World Champion would not be unusual. When Heiss won her first Worlds in 1956, only Sonja Henie had been younger when she won her first Worlds.

The payoff came in 1960, when Heiss won the Winter Olympics Ladies' gold medal in Squaw Valley, California. But the big news was yet to come, presented at the World Championships just after the Olympics. After winning another Worlds title, she announced her engagement to U.S. World and Olympic Men's Champion Hayes Alan Jenkins. Jenkins became perhaps the man most surrounded by skating family: his mother, sister, brother, and now his wife.

Perhaps partially because of the successes enjoyed by U.S. skaters on the world level, ice arenas started popping up around the country. In 1943, there were only about one hundred rinks in the entire nation. About that same number were added in 1958 alone. That year, Mary Mapes Dodge's 1885 classic novel, *Hans Brinker and the Silver Skates*, was made into a feature-length production by NBC-TV, supposedly the first time that a dramatic television production employed figure skaters.

Interest in skating was at a record high in the United States. Rinks were being built; skating features were being made for television; American touring companies were heading behind the Iron Curtain. American skaters were the dominant force in singles skating. The 1960 Winter Olympics made it two Winter Games in a row that

American singles skaters would take the gold medals, and the third that Men would do so—Button in 1952, Hayes Alan Jenkins and Albright in 1956, and David Jenkins and Heiss in 1960.

It was the best of times for American figure skating. But suddenly, it was the worst of times.

Long Live the Dream: Team USA—1961

In 1961, the world came crashing down around American figure skating.

The big names had turned pro after the 1960 Olympics and World Championships. That allowed a new generation of American skaters to move up the ranks and take the mantle of being best in the country.

The 1961 USFSA Nationals were held in late January in Colorado Springs, Colorado. There were many new faces on the medals stand, names that everyone expected would soon be world famous.

Winning the USFSA Men's Championship was Bradley Lord, who had never before stood on the U.S. Championship medals podium. Winning the Ladies' title was Laurence Owen, whose highest placement at Nationals had been a bronze medal in 1960. Maribel Owen (sister to Laurence) and Dudley Richards won Pairs gold after finishing second the year before. The 1961 USFSA National Ice Dance Championship was won by Dianne Sherbloom and Larry Pierce.

Less than a month after the National Championships, on Tuesday, February 14, the entire U.S. World Team of eighteen skaters—plus sixteen coaches, USFSA officials, family members, and friends—regrouped at New York's Idlewild Airport (now known as Kennedy International).

It was a joyous day, not just because all looked forward to the upcoming World Championships in Prague, Czechoslovakia, but also because it was Valentine's Day.

All boarded the plane and headed off across the Atlantic Ocean in an attempt to bring home more World gold medals. After the reign

of Button, the Jenkins brothers, Albright, and Heiss, the nation's skating fans had come to expect nothing less.

The Boeing 707, carrying seventy-four people, came in for a refueling stop in Brussels, Belgium, the morning of February 15. Close to landing, the plane's landing gear was raised by the pilot, without explanation to the control tower. As the plane pulled out of its landing pattern and started to climb, it began to shake violently and make unusual loud noises. Flight 548 then fell to earth. All aboard were killed. The hopes of a nation were shattered, and skating fans around the world went into mourning.

There can be no argument that February 15, 1961, was the worst day in the history of figure skating.

Stunned by the tragedy, the ISU canceled the World Championships. It would have been unthinkable to continue.

Since 1961, the USFSA's Memorial Fund has served as a living memorial to those who were lost that tragic day. The fund is financed through voluntary contributions from fans, skate clubs, and other organizations, not-for-profit foundations, and corporations. Each year, hundreds of skaters receive financial assistance from the Memorial Fund so that they may continue their training and education.

But even though the memory lives on, a part of the soul and heart of every skating fan perished along with the 1961 U.S. World Team. February 15, 1961, is the day the dream died.

The United States figure skating team and its coaches posing in front of the plane that was to crash—with no survivors—on the way to the 1961 World Championships

part **Two**

The Age of Artistry

American Skating Rebounds

AFTER THE 1961 PLANE CRASH, MANY OBSERVERS predicted that it would be more than a decade before the American competitive skating scene would be back to something that resembled normal. The loss of three of the country's top coaches meant there was a serious lack of coaching talent to train the top skaters of America's cloudy skating future. Italy's Carlo Fassi and other coaches from Europe suddenly found themselves in demand on the North American side of the Atlantic Ocean.

The 1962 U.S. National Championships were held in Boston, Massachusetts. Competing for top honors were a large number of essentially unknown skaters. Monty Hoyt won the Men's Championship, placed third in 1963 and 1964, and then disappeared from the news. Barbara Roles—U.S. bronze medalist in 1959 and silver medalist in 1960 and 1960 World bronze medalist—won the Ladies' Championship, her life having been spared because she wasn't on the podium at the 1961 Nationals. She went on to have a long career in shows and in coaching. Dorotheyann Nelson and Pieter Kollen won Pairs, and Yvonne Littlefield and Peter Betts won Ice Dancing honors.

The 1962 World Championships were held in Prague, Czechoslovakia, the city that was to have hosted the canceled event in 1961. It had to be eerie for the American team to travel to that location and skate in the very arena that was to have been witness to the skating efforts of so many deceased American skaters. As expected, no Americans won medals, the skaters having been forced to carry the mantle of their country years earlier than originally expected. It would be 1965 before an American singles skater, Pairs, or Ice Dancing team would again ascend to the World Championships podium.

A highlight of the 1962 Worlds was Canada's Don Jackson pulling off the first triple lutz jump ever performed in competition, to win the Men's title.

Tragedy struck the world of figure skating once again on Halloween in 1963. A butane tank exploded at the Indianapolis (Indiana) Fairgrounds Coliseum, collapsing part of the building and killing seventy-five and injuring hundreds of skating fans who had come out to see a performance of *Holiday on Ice*.

The years 1963 and 1964 saw no U.S. skaters on the World Championships podium. The drought of American skaters, though expected, was a bit hard for some to accept. There had been at least one American singles on the podium every year from 1947 through 1960, including twenty-six Men's and seventeen Ladies' medals, and six World medals each for U.S. Pairs and Ice Dancing teams.

Though the U.S. Pairs team of Vivian and Ronald Joseph was awarded the bronze medal at the 1964 Winter Olympics, the pair did not have the honor of standing on the medals podium in Innsbruck, Austria. The team of Marika Kilius and Hans Baumler from the Federal Republic of Germany (West Germany) had signed a contract to appear in an ice show before they competed in the Olympics. When this was proven, they had to forfeit their silver medal, moving the bronze medal team up to silver and the fourth-place team of Joseph and Joseph up to bronze. Today, things have totally changed. One might be forgiven for wondering if skaters could be disqualified for *not* having a pro contract in hand before the Olympics.

At the 1965 Worlds, Canada's Petra Burka became the first woman to perform a triple jump (a salchow) in Ladies' World Championship competition.

Slowly, the World Championship medals tide started to turn. Ice Dancers Lorna Dyer and John Carrell captured the World bronze in 1965 and 1966 and took silver in 1967. That year, they were stopped from winning the gold by Great Britain's four-time (1966–1969) World Champions team of Diane Towler and Bernard Ford, the same team that had stopped U.S. team Kristin Fortune and Dennis Sveum in 1966. Ice Dancers Judy Schwomeyer and James Sladky took the bronze in 1969 and the silver in 1970, stopped only by the Soviet Union's Liudmila Pakhomova and Aleksandr Gorshkov, who won the first of their six World golds.

Pairs wouldn't see a U.S. team on the Worlds podium until 1966, when Cynthia and Ronald Kauffman won their first of three straight World bronze medals. Scott Allen captured the Men's silver medal at Worlds in 1965, and Gary Visconti took the bronze in 1966 and 1967. Tim Wood captured silver in 1968 and won the title in 1969 and 1970. But it was in the Ladies' competition that the United States would find the first post-crash, media-savvy, business-whiz, big-smile, everybody-loves-'em banner carrier.

American Sweethearts: Fleming and Lynn

Peggy Fleming was twelve years old when her coach was killed in the 1961 plane crash. She then went to Colorado Springs to study with the Italian coach Carlo Fassi. In 1964, Fleming won the first of five consecutive U.S. Championships. She was sixth at the 1964 Winter Olympics in Innsbruck, Austria, and popped onto the Worlds medal podium with a bronze in 1965. In 1966, 1967, and 1968, she won the World Championship and struck pay dirt by winning the 1968 Winter Olympics in Grenoble, France—the first Winter Olympics to be broadcast worldwide.

Around the world, millions marveled at Fleming's ability to float gently across the ice, seemingly without effort. At nineteen, she was, for the time, the third youngest Ladies' Olympic Champion ever (behind Sonja Henie and Barbara Ann Scott). It was in no small part due to her winning these first globally telecast Winter Olympics (which were also the first Winter Olympics to be broadcast live and in color) that she quickly turned pro and headlined *Ice Follies*.

She was recognized as perhaps the most charming ambassador skating has ever had, which might explain why Snoopy from the "Peanuts" comic strip once had a crush on her. Today she's still in public demand and remains at the forefront of skating, starring in traveling ice shows and serving as a sought-after television commentator for skating competitions.

In 1969, television audiences fell in love with a petite blonde pixie who had captured the U.S. Championship bronze medal the year before. For five years—from 1969 until 1973—Janet Lynn would be America's hope for the next worldwide ice queen. No other U.S. singles skater or team was nearly as dominant during this time. Three-time U.S. Champion Tim Wood won the silver medal at the 1968 Winter Olympics, and took the World titles in 1969 and 1970, but still was overshadowed by Lynn's radiance. Three-time U.S. Pairs Champions JoJo Starbuck and Kenneth Shelley won the World bronze medal in 1971 and 1972, achieving some fame during that time, but they experienced nothing like the adulation afforded Lynn.

Why was Lynn so popular? She won only two medals at the World Championships—a bronze in 1972 and a silver in 1973. She took the bronze medal at the 1972 Winter Olympics in Sapporo, Japan, yet was more popular than Beatrix Schuba, who won the gold.

Lynn was so poetic on the ice because she knew how to combine grace with athleticism. If Lynn had been competing under the rules that are in effect today, she would have won a number of World titles and the 1972 Olympics. She won many of the free programs, but she was not as good in figures. (Eight years later, Switzerland's Denise Biellmann encountered the same fate, placing fourth at the Lake Placid Winter Olympics after winning the nonfigures portions of the competition, because she was a dismal twelfth after the compulsory figures.)

At the 1972 Olympics, Beatrix "Trixi" Schuba, World silver medalist in 1969 and 1970 and World gold medalist in 1971 and

Her grace and gentleness on the ice made Peggy Fleming a skating idol for decades.

1972, was far ahead of Lynn and everyone else at the end of the compulsory figures. She was so far ahead, in fact, that she could afford to free skate as she usually did. And how she usually skated was generally considered to be rather lackluster and lifeless. It didn't matter that she placed ninth in the 1972 Worlds free skate (and it's generally considered that she wouldn't have medaled at all had it not been for her expertise at tracing figures). In 1972, the tracing of the figures (three times around each figure) accounted for a stunning 50 percent of a skater's total score. If someone racked up a big lead, it was hard for others to catch up.

This left Lynn in the lurch. Even though she was the best freestyle skater on the planet, adored by all, she could never overcome the tyranny of the figures. This helped add to the public's sympathy for her. And entering the free skate after being fourth in figures in Sapporo, she was so far above everyone else in grace, athleticism, and poise that she won the event even though she fell. And when she fell, she got up, smiling as if she had just landed the biggest jump ever, and continued. This endeared her even more to the public. Falling and still winning. Winning and still coming in third. The public loved Lynn and hated the system that allowed mediocre freestyle skating to win.

Janet Lynn did not retire after the Olympics. She stayed "eligible" for one more year, partially because compulsory school figures were being devalued to 30 percent of the overall score. A "short" freestyle skate program of required elements was added in 1973. At the 1973 Worlds, Lynn placed second behind Canada's Karen Magnussen, who had moved up from silver at Worlds the year before and bronze the year before that. Lynn had tripped up during the required jumps of the short program. The short program should have been her salvation, but instead, she placed a miserable twelfth leading into the long program. And then, with her typical come-from-behind, can-do spirit, she won the long program, the one that the worldwide television audience would actually see.

The poetic
Janet Lynn

Lynn would not get the crown many thought was due her, but others realized, gold medal or not, that she was ripe for public adoration. Chicago sports promoter Arthur M. Wirtz, who thirty-seven years earlier had signed up Sonja Henie, knew just how valuable Lynn was, no matter where she placed. He signed her to a $1.45 million deal with *Ice Follies*, making her the highest paid female athlete up to that time. Unfortunately, Lynn developed a severe case of asthma and had to retire from exhibitions before her contract expired.

Consummate Artists: Cranston and Curry

The always innovative Toller Cranston changed the face of skating.

Perhaps the most artistically influential skater of the day was Toller Cranston, Canadian Men's Champion for six years in a row, from 1971 to 1976. His only World medal was a bronze in 1974, and in 1976, he received the bronze medal at the Winter Olympics in Innsbruck. Like Janet Lynn, Cranston could have won the World Championships in 1974 and 1975 if not for his poor showing in figures, even though figures had been devalued.

Cranston's style was often more appreciated than understood. His choreography utilized movements, especially in spins, that were sculptural in character. He would transform his spinning body into unique contortions that had never been seen before. His captivating choreography and attention to musical detail made him far more influential than his medal count would suggest, sending skating off in an entirely new direction. He is, without a doubt, the most important skater never to win a World or Olympic gold medal.

Great Britain's John Curry won his first World medal, a bronze, in 1975. Then, in 1976, he won the gold medal at the Olympics and the World Championships. Because much of the television audience prior to the 1990s mostly paid attention to skating only during Olympic years, his 1976 Olympic gold was well timed. So was his decision to train under Carlo Fassi (Peggy Fleming's and Dorothy Hamill's coach) and Gustav Lussi (Dick Button's coach) when it appeared he wasn't moving up as he should in the World Championship rankings.

Curry had long felt that if he could win the Olympics, he would have the ability to take skating off in a new direction when he turned pro. His style was one of pure elegance, heavily influenced by the classical world of ballet. Every detail of his body position was important, down to his fingertips. He wanted to bring ballet to the ice and introduce fans to a new way of looking at figure skating, trusting in their ability to understand and appreciate subtlety and nuance. It would be a hard enough sell even if he did have an Olympic gold medal. Without it, his dream would die before it even got off the ground. But he pursued his ideal, turning down lucrative offers to skate in the more popular ice shows.

As a result of his victory in Innsbruck, Curry was able to pull together a troupe of skaters known as *The John Curry Theatre of Skating*. They brought ballet on ice to audiences in London in 1978 and 1979. Late in 1979, the ensemble came to the United States as *Ice Dancing*. Critics heaped rave reviews on the production, but it had to fold, as it continually lost money. Curry found that the American public might not be ready for what he had to offer.

The John Curry Skating Company was born in 1983, based on the concept of the earlier productions, but with better funding. The ensemble toured the world and performed to live orchestral music,

as Curry felt that the shows would not be as effective with taped music. (In that regard, he repeated what Jackson Haines had done about 120 years earlier.) From Japan to London to the United Arab Emirates and a series of opera houses and cultural centers in the United States, Curry showed audiences that skating could be a thing of pure beauty at a time when other ice shows were putting cartoon characters on the ice.

Curry commissioned some of the leading choreographers of the day to create new and daring works for the ice. Normally, one thinks of a figure skating choreographer as someone who works with a number of figure skaters, helping them develop their own unique and personal style on the ice. Curry went a step further in his desire to turn skating into an art form. He commissioned works for the ice from choreographers in the world of dance, people who had never before worked with figure skaters. These "outside" choreographers found it a challenge to work in the medium of skating. Their standard dance techniques did not allow for gliding across the surface of a stage. But in getting these creative forces to bring their talents to the ice, Curry forged new ideas that henceforward influenced all facets of skating.

Hamill and the Late 1970s

The last of Janet Lynn's five U.S. Championship gold medals was earned in 1973. In second place was Dorothy Hamill, who, like Fleming and Curry, was coached by the legendary Carlo Fassi. Hamill went on to win the next three U.S. titles and the 1976 Winter Olympics and World Championship.

Hamill had a different type of personality from Lynn's. Whereas Lynn was self-assured and confident, Hamill was always nervous before competitions, to the point that her coach couldn't help wondering if she would hold it all together until she got through her program. But television audiences saw her as being the innocent "girl next door," and they loved her for it.

John Curry brought the lyrical classicism of ballet to singles skating.

Olympic gold medalist Dorothy Hamill

In Munich (then in West Germany) in 1974, she was to skate her long program immediately after a West German favorite performed. Just as she was coming onto the ice, the audience started booing the scores of the previous skater. Hamill took the boos personally, broke down on the ice, and had to go to the side of the rink to be comforted by her coach. The audience, realizing what had happened, gave her a tremendous ovation upon her return, possibly giving her the strength to pull off her first World Championship medal, a silver.

She had two trademarks. One was the Hamill Camel, in which she would spin with her torso bent parallel to the ice and then drop into a sit spin. The other trademark was her compact, bowl-like Hamill Wedge hairstyle, which became a fad with schoolgirls throughout the United States.

After leaving amateur competition, Hamill skated for *Ice Capades*. In 1991, she bought the company in an attempt to save it from dissolving. During her tenure at the helm, the company became more balletlike, telling a continuous story instead of performing several unconnected routines. "Cinderella" and "Hansel and Gretel" captivated audiences, but they weren't the glitzy, gaudy showgirl spectacles that people had come to associate with the company. A few years later, she sold it.

Along the way, Hamill has become a television producer and still makes special appearances with a variety of skating shows.

Toward the end of the 1970s, Charles Tickner became the dominant force in American Men's skating, winning the U.S. title in 1977, 1978, 1979, and 1980. Tickner placed on the medal stand at Worlds only twice, winning the gold in 1978 and the bronze in 1980, the same year he took bronze at the Lake Placid (New York) Winter Olympics behind Great Britain's Robin Cousins.

Despite Tickner's winning the 1978 World Championship in Ottawa, Canada, the big news in the Men's competition was a Canadian skater who didn't even make it to the podium. Vern Taylor executed the first successful triple axel—the three-and-a-half-revolution triple jump that's the most difficult of all—in competition at the Worlds. With all the triples now out of

Charles Tickner was the dominant force in American Men's skating in the late 1970s.

the way, skaters could start dreaming about someday pulling off the "impossible" quad jump.

The same year of Taylor's accomplishment, Switzerland's Denise Biellmann became the first woman to pull off a triple lutz in competition.

Linda Fratianne won the U.S. Ladies' gold the same four years as Tickner took the U.S. Men's, and won the World gold medal twice, in 1977 and 1979, plus the silver in 1978 and the bronze in 1980. She took the silver medal behind Anett Pötzsch of the German Democratic Republic (GDR, or East Germany).

Despite winning Ladies' gold at the 1980 Winter Olympics, Pötzsch couldn't capitalize on the glamour of being the Olympic ice queen because of the restrictions of her country's communist political system. The leaders of the GDR (known almost exclusively as East Germany by North Americans and Western Europeans) believed that commercialism was an evil of American capitalism. Making money off one's talent was not in keeping with the spirit of socialism.

For the most part, star athletes from the communist countries weren't allowed to travel freely after their amateur days were over, for fear they would defect to the West. The authorities wanted to prevent defections such as that of the Soviet Pairs team of Ludmila and Oleg Protopopov (known in their amateur days as Belousova and Protopopov). They had won four World golds (1965–1968) and two Olympic golds (1964 and 1968) with their beautiful grace. After their 1980 defection to Switzerland, they became big hits on the ice show tour circuit and in professional contests. More unfortunate in the eyes of the communist authorities, they became vocal and eloquent spokespersons against the communist system. Therefore, star athletes from Soviet bloc nations who traveled to the West knew that their movements were being monitored. They also feared that a defection could have negative implications for family members back home.

Anett Pötzsch, despite having a personality Western audiences

loved and an appreciation for American music—her 1980 Olympic closing ceremony exhibition performance was set to Louis Armstrong's music—would have few of the opportunities that were available to American Ladies' Olympic Champions such as Peggy Fleming and Dorothy Hamill.

Soviets Dominate Pairs and Ice Dancing

Ice Dancing wasn't recognized as an official event at the World Championships until 1952 and didn't become an Olympic event until 1976.

From 1952 through 1960, and from 1966 through 1969, every World Ice Dancing Championship was won by British teams.

Then, in 1970, Liudmila Pakhomova and Aleksandr Gorshkov, who have the most World Championship titles, with six, started a remarkable string of Soviet and, later, Russian victories. Soviet/Russian teams won every Ice Dancing World title through 1979 and twelve of the next eighteen titles up through 1997. Soviet/Russian teams also won five of the first six Ice Dancing titles given at the Winter Olympics, the one exception being Jayne Torvill and Christopher Dean's incredible year in 1984.

In Pairs skating, the Soviet/Russian skaters were also stunningly successful. Belousova and Protopopov's four World and two Olympic titles were followed by the dynasty of Irina Rodnina, who favored athleticism and more difficult side-by-side jumps. She won the first of her ten World Championships in 1969 with partner Alexsei Ulanov, winning three more Worlds in a row with him, as well as the 1972 Olympic crown. However, he fell in love with another Soviet skater, so she began to audition other male skaters with whom she could form a new partnership. With Alexandr Zaitsev, her future husband, she won the Worlds six years in a row, from 1973 through 1978, taking time off in 1979 to have a child. They also won the 1976 Olympics and, after she recovered from having her baby, came back and won the 1980 Olympics as well.

After Rodnina and Zaitsev retired, Soviet/Russian Pairs skaters won eleven of the next fourteen World Championships.

What is it about the Soviets that made them so dominant in Ice Dancing and Pairs? Some have argued that the system they lived under fostered a better competitive environment, that the Soviet skaters were given everything they needed for success—coaches, choreographers, ice time, a place to live, food—while the American skaters were forced to seek public and private sponsorships in order to stay in training. Also, numerous Ice Dancing and Pairs teams behind the former Iron Curtain were married. Many felt that their married status gave them quite an important advantage over most Western skating couples.

In Pairs and Ice Dancing, the man is responsible for showing off the woman. She is the main attraction, he the supporting cast. In

Pairs, he lifts and she rises above his shoulders. He throws and she sails through the air. Both Pairs and Ice Dancing couples have to convince the judges that they are two people united as one, a couple as opposed to two individuals. They have to demonstrate their caring for each other and show great emotion for each other on the ice. It's natural to suspect that married couples would have an easier time convincing judges of their bond. According to this line of thought, the Soviets must have had an advantage. This did nothing to explain, though, why so many unmarried Soviet skating couples were so successful at climbing to the top.

Maia Usova and Alexander Zhulin were among the many Soviet couples who got married partly for economic reasons.

In 1995, several years after the Soviet domination of Pairs and Ice Dancing commenced, Soviet/ Russian Ice Dancer Alexander Zhulin (partner with Maia Usova) talked about this perception. They were third at the 1990 and 1991 Worlds, second in 1992, and first in 1993, as well as recipients of the bronze medal at the 1992 Winter Olympics and silver medal at the 1994 Olympics. Like so many other Soviets, they were married. And then they got divorced, as did so many ex-Soviet skating teams after the Soviet Union dissolved.

Zhulin states: "It's true that many, many Russian skating couples were married and now many, many Russian couples are divorced. The reason, actually, is very simple. I think fifty percent of the couples married because we Russians had nothing—no money, no anything. When they put their money together, they could buy a car, maybe afford a house, or get an apartment.

"Before we married, we got only one hundred rubles a month to skate. That's about twenty dollars of U.S. money. If we were married, we could get an apartment from our [skating] federation. As a married couple, we could get a letter from the federation that would be sent to the government. The letter would go to the government, who would then consider giving us a car so we could get to our training sessions easier and hopefully an apartment so we could have a normal life. Apartments are scarce, so they would rather give one out to a married couple than two to two singles.

"We took a train every day to practice that took one and a half hours each way. We couldn't get a place to stay any closer. And we ate like two dogs. I saw a movie over here in the U.S. about a prison, and all I could concentrate on was the prisoners were eating all this wonderful food.

"We couldn't understand how it was possible for people to live as they did in the United States and West Germany. Going to any city was like going to Disneyland."

So, as it turns out, things weren't all that rosy behind the Iron Curtain. What, then, explains the Soviet/Russian success in Pairs and Ice Dancing for so very long? We see it was difficult to live and train under their system. And yet, incredible Pairs and Ice Dancing couples kept capturing medal after medal.

Perhaps their skaters won so many medals because—and this may be a novel thought to some—they trained harder and ended up being better than everyone else.

Big Changes

Three Cheers for Artistry

IN A PERFECT WORLD, athleticism and artistry in figure skating would be mutually compatible. Over the years, however, skaters, judges, and the International Skating Union have been trying to come to grips with balancing the two ideals.

One year after placing fourth at the Winter Olympics despite winning the short and long programs at the event (because of a poor performance in figures), Switzerland's Denise Biellmann won the 1981 Worlds gold medal and then promptly turned pro. She never had a problem delivering both athleticism and artistry.

Her flexibility was legendary, and everyone waited through each of her routines for her crowning achievement, the "Biellmann Spin." With one leg extended above and behind her head, she looked like a revolving Christmas tree ornament. Such

Denise Biellmann demonstrates the spin that is her trademark.

grace was pure artistry, and such flexibility was the envy of any athlete. Her departure from the ranks of amateur Ladies' skaters left a vacuum. The door was open for less-rounded skaters to specialize as either artists or technicians.

It seems that whenever skaters and their coaches figure out how to pull off bigger and more challenging jumps, artistry has taken a temporary backseat. When one skater perfects a new jump for the first time, everyone else has to learn it so as not to be left behind. When Dick Button did the first triple jump, it wasn't long before every Men's skater was expected to do a triple. It wasn't long after Denise Biellmann became the first Ladies' competitor to execute a triple lutz in 1978 that all Ladies' hopefuls were polishing up their own triple lutzes. The same goes for Pairs lifts and throws and side-by-side jumps. Whoever does something for the first time is not going to be alone for long.

Near the end of the 1970s, more Ladies' entrants were experimenting with increased athleticism, often at the expense of artistry. One skater who refused to sell out her artistry was Lisa-Marie Allen, U.S. silver medalist during the last three years of Linda Fratianne's reign as U.S. Ladies' Champion (1978–1980),

Lisa-Marie Allen stressed beauty of movement over athleticism.

and bronze medalist behind Elaine Zayak in 1981. (She had stayed an amateur one year past the Olympics so she could go out as National Champion, then sprained her ankle and had to skate the long program with it wrapped.)

To many, Allen was the supreme musical stylist on the ice for her time. Like John Curry's, her every movement was smooth and understated. She did not call attention to herself through flashy and meaningless movements—instead she allowed her choreography to "breathe." She put in no movement unless it emphasized the mood of the moment in the music. Allen didn't jump just for the sake of jumping. At 5-9, she was able to exploit height without the biggest jumps.

She was inspired by the artistry of Peggy Fleming, whom she saw skate in *Ice Follies* as a birthday treat. The image of Fleming's grace never left her mind. During Allen's amateur career, increased demands of athleticism started to creep into Ladies' routines. Allen was disturbed by the trend of skaters' spending much of their programs doing little more than setting up big jumps instead of concentrating on creating beautiful lines with their stroking and lovely images with their entire bodies.

Increasingly, there seemed to be little demand for a skater who could melt one's socks off with style but who wouldn't jump unnecessarily if it would cheapen her program. Audiences were enamored of the jump-jump-jumping of tiny Elaine Zayak and seemed to be caring less for Fleming-like beauty and grace. As soon as she finished the 1981 season, with Zayak setting the course for the future of Ladies' skating in America, Allen packed her bags and joined *Ice Capades*.

At this writing, Allen is making quite a name for herself on the professional circuit and is in demand in pro competitions and ice shows, where style and grace are still rewarded. She is also active as co-founder and artistic director of City of Angels Ice Theatre, dedicated to developing the theatrical art form component of skating.

Elaine Zayak
ushered in an
athletic revolution
in Ladies' skating.

Three Cheers for Athleticism

While Allen was the perfect representative of skating as an art, Elaine Zayak was the anointed representative of the new ideal, the self-propelled jumping machine. U.S. gold medalist in 1981, bronze medalist in 1982 and 1984, and silver medalist in 1983 (the last three years behind Rosalynn Sumners), she burst onto the World Championships scene by taking the silver medal in 1981 and the bronze in 1984 and, most important, by her shocking win in 1982.

The press, always looking for a story even when one wasn't there, tried to make Zayak and Sumners out to be bitter rivals. Things got so silly in 1982 that the two skaters issued a joint "friendship statement" to try to put the inaccurate rumors of their alleged disdain for each other to rest.

Sumners was quite an adept technician who seemed at times to be unsure of herself. She was one of the first to admit using a sports psychologist to help her focus on her routine. In that regard, she was something of a pioneer. Sports psychologists are not at all uncommon today, as skaters strive to get every advantage they can over their competitors.

Despite winning the U.S. title in 1982, 1983, and 1984, and the World title in 1983, Sumners was haunted by persistent doubts of her ability to execute certain jumps flawlessly. At the 1984 Winter Olympics, she was on her way to winning the gold medal over Katarina Witt in the long program when she singled a double axel, doubled a triple toe loop combination, and then completely eliminated a triple toe loop and double axel. The

Rosalynn Sumners
could jump
flawlessly when
not plagued with
self-doubt.

result was that she lost the gold by the scantiest of margins——.1 from one judge.

But while Sumners had problems psychologically dealing with jumps she could normally do in her sleep, Zayak loved to jump and did so with effortlessness and abandon, as no rules were in place to stop her from jumping from one end of the rink to the other. The audiences loved it and the judges found they had no choice but to reward her for performing difficult jumps, even if she did them at the expense of artistry.

Feeling pushed by Zayak, other skaters started to pack more triples into their program, whether they fit or not. Falling during one's competition performance became more of a common occurrence. This was at no time any clearer than at the 1982 Worlds in Copenhagen, Denmark. Ladies' entrants were wiping up the ice in rehearsals, attempting jumps they could not yet control. All knew that Zayak's show was packed with triples.

She didn't appear to be much of a threat after taking tenth place in the short program, having a rather miserable time trying to keep things together. This dropped her to seventh overall, factoring in her placement in compulsory figures. In the long program, though, the unthinkable happened. One by one, each of the Ladies' entrants went out on the ice and, trying to keep up with the push toward athleticism, proceeded to fall, and fall, and fall during the "jump fest." Zayak, recovered from her short program, went onto the rink and gave the skating world a lesson in jumping, delivering seven perfect triples and becoming the only top skater to stay on her blades. She was the new World Champion.

The call became louder and louder from those concerned that artistry would disappear under an avalanche of jumps. Already, artistic creativity was suffering as skaters fell into the trap of "1-2-3-jump, 1-2-3-jump." In response, the International Skating Union passed a rule that sought to restore balance to the competition programs.

Under this rule, programs could not contain duplicate triples, although one triple could be done again if it was part of a combination jump. Skaters were also required to do a minimum number of spins and step sequences. The ISU action became informally known as the Zayak Rule.

Arguably, skaters develop technique before artistry, which is why young "jumping machine" skaters tend to be less artistic than older, more mature, and more developed skaters.

Some people with the ISU thought the Zayak Rule would be the last word needed to preserve artistry for all eternity. They did not realize that the ever-decreasing age of Ladies' competitors would send the average age of various nations' world teams spiraling downward.

Just What Is Ice Dancing?

While the big question in Ladies' singles skating during the early 1980s was "Is figure skating a sport or an art?" the big question in Ice Dancing during the same period appeared to be "What is Ice Dancing? Is it ballroom dancing on ice, or can it be something more?"

There are many restrictions in Ice Dancing. For starters, there are no big lifts over the man's head or dramatic throws, as with Pairs. There are no individual elements wherein one partner is apart from the other for several seconds, doing something individualistic, as is allowed in Pairs competition. The couples, for the most part, are always together, skating as a single entity instead of as two people with distinct roles. Footwork—how the feet interact with each other and move—is of far more importance than with Pairs.

Ice Dancing wasn't even an Olympic sport until 1976 and has been recognized at Worlds only since 1952, while there has been a Pairs event since 1908 at both the Olympics and Worlds. It was as if the authorities at the top levels of figure skating at first didn't want Ice Dancing in the world-level competitions at all and, once it was in, they didn't know how to handle it.

For quite some time, the changing of the guard in Ice Dancing had been moving at a glacial pace. Ice Dancing judging was accused of being much too predictable. It seemed that one could see who was going to win in future years by who was next in line. Case in point: At the 1984 Winter Olympics, Great Britain's Jayne Torvill and Christopher Dean won the gold (and then turned pro), followed by two teams from the Soviet Union, Natalia Bestemianova and Andrei Bukin (silver) and Marina Klimova and Sergei Ponomarenko (bronze). At the 1988 Winter Olympics, Bestemianova and Bukin won the gold (and then turned pro), and Klimova and Ponomarenko took the silver. Care to guess who won at the 1992 Winter Olympics?

At Worlds during that same period, things weren't much different. Bestemianova and Bukin waited in third one year and second for three years while Torvill and Dean won in 1981, 1982, 1983, and 1984. Then Bestemianova and Bukin moved up to first in 1985, 1986, 1987, and 1988, each year followed by Klimova and Ponomarenko in second. To no one's surprise, it was Klimova and Ponomarenko's turn on the top podium in 1989, 1990, and 1992, interrupted only by France's brother-and-sister team of Isabelle and Paul Duchesnay in 1991, as the Soviets temporarily took second.

The rankings of Ice Dancing couples were utterly predictable. And because there are no throws or high lifts in the sport, there was little mystery about whether or not a team would get through its program in one piece, unless the team members were to do something dramatic like skate into the wall and not come back to the ice. If a couple were to fall, they might as well pack up and go home. Otherwise, positions seldom changed from one phase of a competition to the next.

To many television viewers, one dance couple looked about the same as any other. The music seemed stuck in the ballrooms of Johann Strauss's nineteenth-century Vienna. There was little variety in styles from one couple to another, and watching the skaters go through the motions of traditional Ice Dancing was about as exciting as watching paint dry.

That all changed with the ascension of Jayne Torvill and Christopher Dean.

And Just Who Do Torvill and Dean Think They Are?

When Torvill and Dean won their first of four straight World titles in 1981, it's doubtful that many had any idea of the extent to which they would shake things up. They hadn't shattered any Ice Dancing stereotypes earlier. It had been too important for them to get established first. Unknown to the world at large, Dean had quite a vivid imagination and was remarkably creative—a surprise to some, because most of the ideas in their earlier days are said to have come from Torvill. In 1982, the team created a free dance program to *Mack and Mabel*, a musical. If they hadn't had the previous year's gold to back them up, the judges might not have accepted the program as well as they did. Instead of straight-ahead ballroom dancing on ice, Torvill and Dean created a unified theme, and each became one of the two lead characters.

Today, that doesn't sound like such a big deal. In 1982, it was on the verge of heresy. But the judges couldn't argue with Torvill and Dean's impeccable technique and stunning choreography. The team, more than any other, redefined choreography as something more than just movement on the ice to music. Torvill and Dean *became* the music. Instead of simply interpreting the music, they

Jayne Torvill and Christopher Dean are the greatest Ice Dancers of all time.

brought new meaning to it by pouring their personalities into it. They didn't keep their distance from the music—they chopped it, diced it, pureed it, and shaped it into a presence of their own creation. They put the stamp of their unique personalities upon the music. This was radical for Ice Dancers of the time.

In 1983, Torvill and Dean presented the musical *Barnum*, bringing a spontaneous circus flair to the ice. The program didn't seem cut and dried; it seemed to evolve anew every time it was skated. And indeed, Torvill and Dean became well known for changing programs up to the last possible moment. Near the end of the program, Dean spun Torvill around the ice like a toy top. The audience at Worlds went bonkers. There was nothing in the rule book to stop them, and indeed they relished staying ahead of the restrictive Ice Dancing rules—not breaking them, but stretching them to the limits.

They were awarded perfect 6.0s in Presentation from all nine judges. They were unquestionably the favorites heading into the 1984 Winter Olympics, but no one at the time could have guessed just what a dramatic impact they would have on the sport one year later.

The year 1983 also produced one of the strangest things ever to happen in Ice Dancing; however, because it happened behind the scenes, few people were aware of it at the time. At Worlds, the designated Original Set Pattern Dance was to be skated to a rock and roll tempo. (For this part of the competition, all dance teams must create a repetitive dance, performed to the same style of music. The style is announced months in advance, giving each team the chance to choose its own musical selection within the framework of the style.)

Canada's Tracy Wilson and Robert McCall decided to perform their Original Set Pattern Dance to the music of Paul Anka. Earlier in the season, international judges told them that their musical selection wasn't rock and roll. A deposition from famed rock and roll singer and songwriter Anka convinced the judges otherwise, and

Wilson and McCall were able to keep the music, without penalty.

Another 1983 judging call was just plain weird. Five-time U.S. Champions (1981–1985) Judy Blumberg and Michael Seibert were told at Worlds by an Italian judge that their Fred Astaire/Ginger Rogers music was "not dance music." *Not dance music?* Tell that to the millions of people in dance halls who have danced the night away to the same music. This judge dumped them because of her opinion, but they still managed to finish with the bronze, as they would do again in 1984 and 1985.

Judy Blumberg and Michael Seibert were one of America's strongest Ice Dancing teams.

For the 1984 Winter Olympics in Sarajevo, Yugoslavia, Blumberg and Seibert put together a dramatic portrait on ice based on the dynamic Mussorgsky tone poem *Scheherazade*. It was not a typical dance program, but it was within the boundaries that were being expanded by Torvill and Dean. The dance team was on its way to winning a silver medal at the Olympics when the same judge who dumped them in 1983 did so again, stating that she didn't like the music, which had already been approved by an international panel. This action knocked Blumberg and Seibert all the way to fourth place. At Worlds a month later, the team did not skate nearly as well as at the Olympics, even by their own admission. Yet they took the bronze. In some ways, this made the Olympic situation hurt even more, as it proved to them that they had been worthy of winning an Olympic medal.

Bolero *and Beyond*

But 1984 will forever be remembered for Torvill and Dean's landmark *Bolero* free dance program, set to the music of Maurice Ravel's famous orchestral work. Perhaps the most heralded program ever presented on the ice, it took the theme concept a step further, since it used a single piece of music instead of snippets from multiple selections. A single repetitive musical statement began softly and continually built to the dynamic conclusion. There were no tempo changes—which was unheard of—and the musical and choreographic flow was continuous.

With *Bolero*, Torvill and Dean didn't just give Ice Dancing a nudge—they pushed it over the cliff.

For several seconds at the beginning, they didn't even skate. Dean, kneeling on the ice, twisted Torvill into several contortions as if he were playing with a stick of licorice. Then, when they stood up to skate, time itself seemed to disappear. Their movements were fluid and seamless. Everything blended from one moment to the next. It was hypnotic to watch, and one was afraid to breathe, lest one ruin the aura of the moment. It was, in short, magic.

At the end, Dean twisted Torvill back and forth in the air, off to his front and side, being careful not to lift her too high, which would violate the rules. It was the closest thing to a Pairs "trick" that Ice Dancing had ever seen, and yet it was perfectly legal. As in 1983, they received nine perfect 6.0s in Presentation, and they added three perfect 6.0s in their technical marks.

Torvill and Dean went on to have a successful professional career and they toured the world with several shows of their own design, continuing to expand the art form and taking Ice Dancing more toward a concept of Ice Theater. Ten years after they changed the face of Ice Dancing, they reinstated as amateurs in order to compete in the 1994 Winter Olympics.

Natalia Bestemianova and Andrei Bukin exploited their flair for the dramatic.

By 1985, the ISU had started to restrain innovation in Ice Dancing, and the sport became more restrictive and headed back to its ballroom roots. Although theatrical presentations were popular with audiences, the ISU officials were concerned that Ice Dancing was selling out and losing its heritage.

Bestemianova and Bukin (popularly known as B&B) won all the World Championships from 1985 through 1988, as well

The sensual and expressive Marina Klimova and her husband, Sergei Ponomarenko

as the 1988 Winter Olympics. They had a wonderfully dramatic flair. Some criticized them for being too flamboyant, with movements that were extremely exaggerated and theatrical. Klimova and Ponomarenko took over the helm in 1989, 1990, and 1992, also winning the 1992 Winter Olympics. The married couple (especially Klimova) brought a searing passion into the rink, just about melting the ice with their obvious love for each other. Though far more ballroom-oriented than Torvill and Dean, they managed to sell their style to the public through their passion.

During the post–Torvill and Dean years, the British team's influence was kept alive by the Ice Dancing brother-and-sister team of Isabelle and Paul Duchesnay, who left Canada to skate for France. Dean choreographed their programs, and the Duchesnays became famous for many unusual body positions. (Dean ended up marrying Isabelle, but the marriage didn't work out. Later, he married 1990 Ladies' Champion, Jill Trenary.)

What Dean came up with in 1988 shocked just about everyone. The *Savage Rites* jungle program the Duchesnays took to the 1988 Winter Olympics found them attired in jungle garb, shocking a number of judges, who were used to pretty dresses and nondescript male attire.

The audience at the European Championships was thrilled to the point of throwing seat cushions in the air, but some judges were aghast at this "impure" intrusion upon their sacred ground. They placed the Duchesnays eighth at the Winter Olympics, proving that they didn't know how to judge the routine by giving them scores that varied by .8 in Presentation. In amateur figure skating events, where judges have only six points to work with, that's a chasm as wide as the Grand Canyon.

Paul remembers why the team made such a dramatic departure from the norm. "Change in Ice Dancing is a slow process. Normally you wait for the ones in front of you to retire and then you will move up ahead. However, our amateur career didn't last that long.

To go from twelfth [in 1986] to first [in 1991 with Missing II, a show inspired by political oppression in South America], we had to create a little bit of a ruckus."

Many expected the team to win the 1992 Winter Olympics, but an operation on Isabelle's foot just a few months before and problems with the French skating federation made things difficult for them. They ended up settling for second behind Klimova and Ponomarenko with a somewhat more traditional (for them) *West Side Story* program that was not their first choice.

Paul talks further of the mind-set among the day's rule makers. "We came up with our first musical choices, and the federation said, 'No, that won't do. It's too much.' The International Skating Union said, 'You have to change music because if you use this you will not win.'

"We asked the referee who was going to judge the music in Albertville [scene of the Olympics], and he said, 'If you choose this music, you will not be in contention. I will personally [Paul then made a slashing movement with his finger across his throat].' Things were difficult because we were forced to use conventional music."

After the 1992 Winter Olympics, Isabelle commented on the Ice Dancing restrictions by stating that the ISU should throw away the rule book. She added, "I think they should throw it away because it's hindering Ice Dancing. There are too many rules regarding music, costuming, and choreography. You don't have the freedom to pick what you want. The innovation is erased before we even start, and we don't have as much variety to pick from as we could. The girl has to wear a skirt; the music can only be ballroom-type with a rhythm."

It's as if the Torvill and Dean revolution never happened.

Good-bye to Figures

The death of compulsory figures was a long and painful one—long for the number of years it took, painful for skaters such as Janet

Judges often didn't know how to respond to the daring costumes and innovative choreography of Isabelle and Paul Duchesnay.

Lynn and Denise Biellmann, who swept the free skate portions of major competitions yet were prevented from winning some titles by their level of expertise in tracing mundane figures.

Up until 1968, compulsory figures were worth 60 percent of a single skater's total score. In 1968, they were reduced to 50 percent. The reduction was the first gasp in the death of figures, but they still accounted for half the score. This explained why someone like Beatrix Schuba could win three major titles despite not even placing in the top six in any of the free skate segments of the competitions.

Figures also gave judges a chance to hold back skaters they didn't like, regardless of how well they performed in that first segment of the competition. It's been said that sometimes certain judges "propped up" their favorite skaters (or skaters from their home country) with high marks in the compulsories and "dumped on" their less favorite skaters (or skaters from other countries) with low marks.

Having to know dozens of variations on a figure eight—some of which had to be steadily traced on one foot, and then retraced twice perfectly over the first tracing—was a bore for singles skaters who really just wanted to go out and show the world how good they were and how much fun they were having.

There were many ways skaters could mess up a required figure: They could push off too lightly, causing them not to make it all the way around the tracing. This was considered "death" to a skater's chance of getting a good score. And the etching itself wasn't all that was scored by the judges. Also important was posture. Control and patience were two of the key elements required to get it just right.

Even at the World Championships, few fans would show up to watch the figures portion of the competition, unless they just wanted to get a glimpse of the top skaters. It was like watching a yacht race: One knew the skater was out there, but one couldn't really tell exactly what was happening.

After a skater traced each figure, the judges would closely observe the etching, getting on their knees if necessary, looking for every little bobble and mistake. Still, voices cried out for figures to be saved. They said that the countless hours spent tracing figures helped skaters learn control and techniques that would help them in free skating.

In 1973, the first short program was introduced. This program required singles skaters to execute specific jumps and use certain techniques, to music of their own choosing. With that, figures were reduced to 30 percent of the total score. In the 1980s, opponents of figures started to raise their voices, proclaiming that it was time to eliminate figures altogether. For 1989 and 1990, the ISU reduced figures to just 20 percent of the total score. Skaters still had to do them, but if they weren't all that good in the discipline, their chances wouldn't be killed entirely.

The last compulsory figures were executed at the 1990 Worlds in Halifax, Nova Scotia. With the elimination of the figures, the short program took on increased importance for singles skaters, counting for one-third of the overall score. If they miss any of the required elements, their chances for overall success can be doomed. With compulsory figures but a distant memory, the discipline seems to have gone the way of the dinosaur.

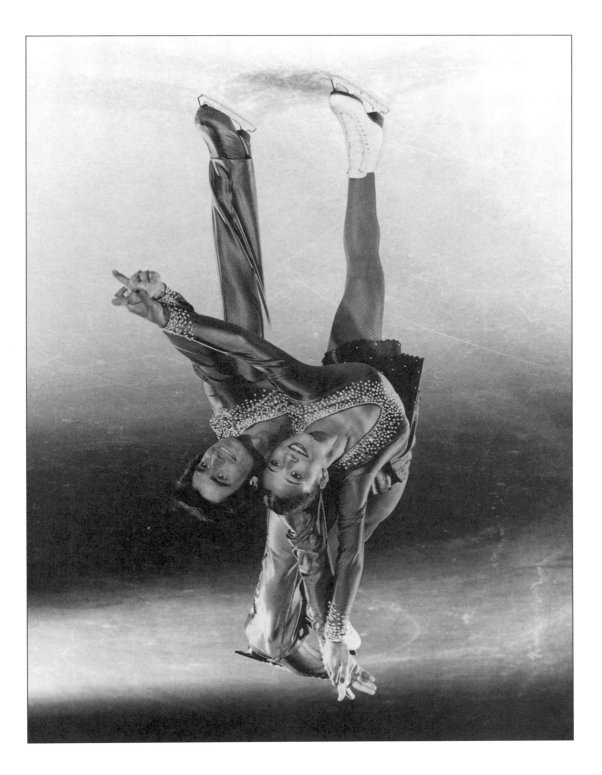

Big Personalities

Olympic Heartbreaks

FEW MOMENTS IN THE HISTORY OF U.S. FIGURE SKATING were as sad as the 1980 Winter Olympics nonperformance of Tai Babilonia and Randy Gardner, U.S. Pairs Champions from 1976 through 1980. Babilonia and Gardner were considered the country's best hope at Olympic gold in Pairs.

At both the 1976 Winter Olympics and Worlds, the year of their first U.S. Championship, the team placed a respectable fifth. They moved up to the bronze medal position in the next two years and won Worlds in 1979, the year ten-time World Champion Irina Rodnina took off to have a baby with her second partner and husband, Alexandr Zaitsev. Babilonia and Gardner's 1979 victory set them up, in the eyes of many, as the team with the most momentum going into the 1980 Olympics, especially because Rodnina and Zaitsev would be coming off a season of noncompetition.

There was something fresh-faced about Babilonia and Gardner, something very all-American. Most of the country's best wishes rested on the shoulders of the one couple who stood the best chance of breaking the Soviet domination of Pairs. Until Babilonia and Gardner's 1979 victory, Soviet Pairs had won every Worlds since 1965 and every Winter Olympics since 1964.

The Pairs 1980 Winter Olympics long program was about to begin. Because the two weeks of festivities were being held in Lake Placid, New York, there was more interest than usual from the American television audience. With cameras focused on the final warm-up session, the unthinkable happened in front of the eyes of the world. Gardner kept falling on the ice, grimacing in pain. Word of a prior muscle pull circulated, and the public watched in shock

Tai Babilonia and Randy Gardner will forever be remembered for their heartbreaking last-minute withdrawal from the Olympics.

as Gardner made it back to his coach and a confused Babilonia.

There was no way he could go through the program and risk serious injury to himself and his partner. At the eleventh hour, the pair had to withdraw from competition. Gardner left the ice in shock. Babilonia left in tears. Throughout the country, people watching on television also had tears in their eyes. The cruelest fate seemed to be to allow such a gifted couple, who had worked their entire lives for this moment, to get so close, yet stay so far away.

For years, skating commentators would refer to the pair as the Heartbreak Kids. They were always warmly received by fans in exhibitions and at pro competitions. But in the back of perhaps every fan's mind was one simple thought: What if?

Canadian skating fans had their own version of the Heartbreak Kids at the 1984 Olympics. Unlike Babilonia and Gardner in Lake Placid, Barbara Underhill and Paul Martini did get a chance to perform in Sarajevo, but what was to be their moment in the sun turned into disaster. Despite having just barely placed in medal position at the previous Worlds, they were perceived by many as having the best shot at winning the 1984 Winter Olympics.

Not long before the Olympics, Underhill changed her boots. This turned out to haunt the team, and they fell—literally—to seventh in Sarajevo. First, Underhill fell during a sit spin in the short program and took Martini down with her. At that moment, their Olympic dream was over. But sadly, things got worse. During the long program, Underhill fell again, and both partners took turns singling side-by-side double salchows.

Underhill went back to her old boots right after the Olympics, and the team went on to win Worlds a few weeks later with a stunning performance in Ottawa, Canada. The audience was cheering so loudly during the last minute that the music was almost drowned out.

Interestingly, the American team of Caitlin and Peter Carruthers's second place at the 1984 Winter Olympics was seen as a victory for them. Not given much of a chance even to medal, they sat in good

New boots proved to be the undoing of Olympic hopes for Barbara Underhill and Paul Martini.

Sister and brother Caitlin and Peter Carruthers became national heroes for their dynamic 1984 Olympic performance.

position after the short program and put on the performance of their lives in the long program. Many felt that they should have beaten Soviets Elena Valova and Oleg Vasiliev, so dynamic was their performance. Carruthers and Carruthers returned home to a heroes' welcome and were the focus of many subsequent ice show performances—not because they placed second in the Olympics, but because they did better than expected.

Ekaterina Gordeeva and Sergei Grinkov captured two Olympic gold medals.

Gordeeva and Grinkov

Soviet skaters Ekaterina Gordeeva and Sergei Grinkov were paired together when he was fifteen and she an incredibly young ten years old. Critics lambasted the pairing, saying that Grinkov was so much taller than Gordeeva that he could throw her around the ice like a rag doll. The criticism of the pair's height and age difference intensified when they won the World Championship in 1986 with many dramatic lifts and throws, but somewhat less successful artistry. But by 1987 and their second World Championship, their classical style started to shine through, leaving critics with little verbal ammunition. They went on to win the 1989 and 1990 Worlds as well and the 1988 Winter Olympics over defending Champions Valova and Vasiliev.

Still, success didn't spare them occasionally weird speculation on their age difference. In 1988, someone in the press asked Gordeeva if she would consider dumping Grinkov for a younger partner. Rather than break up over their physical differences, they fell in love and got married. But, unlike so many other Soviet skating couples, they stayed married, their love growing deeper every year. Their love was the genuine article, and even previous critics, now enamored of their beauty and grace on the ice, would have to admit that their relationship was a model for skating and nonskating couples alike.

After turning pro, the couple joined the *Stars on Ice* tour, continuing to polish and perfect their style even more. They moved to America, like so many other former Soviets, and became the proud parents of a baby girl, Daria, who was "adopted" by all the members of the tour.

When the ISU announced that the 1994 Winter Olympics would be open to professionals, Gordeeva and Grinkov reinstated and took another swing at amateur competition, their classical purity providing a contrast to the heartfelt drama and emotional soul-baring of defending Olympic Pairs Champions Natalia Mishkutenok and Artur Dmitriev. Both pairs were skating not for the now defunct Soviet Union but for their native Russia. Television skating commentator Dick Button mentioned that of all the professional skaters who were reinstating for the Olympics (among them Katarina Witt, Brian Boitano, Viktor Petrenko, Torvill and Dean, and Mishkutenok and Dmitriev), the reinstatement of G&G was the most viable.

Gordeeva and Grinkov won their second Olympic Championship and made big plans for the future. But in November 1995, tragedy struck when Grinkov collapsed and died during practice in Lake Placid for the upcoming *Stars on Ice* tour. Always appearing to be the picture of health, he had undetected severe congenital heart disease. A massive heart attack, with no warning, claimed the life of one of the most gentle people the world of skating has seen.

The skating world was stunned by the tragedy, but it was especially hard on the close-knit company of *Stars on Ice*. However, in true "the show must go on" fashion, the 1995–1996 tour opened less than two weeks later, minus the pair that best exemplified perfection.

After months of mourning, friends of Ekaterina (Katia), including the *Stars on Ice* cast, performed a televised memorial tribute to Sergei. At the beginning of the program, a lone spotlight grazed across the ice, following the invisible pair that was now but a memory. Sergei's skater friends took turns presenting their skating tributes, many of which were not at all sad, in keeping with the spirit of celebrating his life. Twice during the presentation, Katia took to the ice as a new singles skater, sharing her pain and her hope with the teary audience. It was one of the most courageous acts ever witnessed on ice. She knew Sergei would not want her to give up her love and passion for skating.

Hamilton: The "Little Giant"

It's impossible to find anyone who doesn't love Scott Hamilton. Perhaps the most popular skating personality today, he has long been considered the number one spokesperson for figure skating. Respected universally by his fellow skaters and the public, he is one voice that is always trusted as a TV skating commentator.

His exhibition programs—and, later, his professional programs—have long been noted for bringing humor into the rink. Few skaters have had the courage to recognize humor as a legitimate vehicle for serious skating. As film actors and actresses have long said, comedy is much more difficult to perform than "serious" acting, and this perhaps explains why Hamilton's unique sense of what will make people laugh is so special.

Hamilton took up skating partly as a way of overcoming the effects of a childhood illness, Shwachman's disease. The malady causes a failure to metabolize food, sometimes leading to starvation, and often results in lack of growth.

Stars on Ice founder Scott Hamilton has retained a sense of humor in life and on the ice.

Recognized as a fighter with a lot of heart, he was selected by his 1980 Olympic teammates to carry the American flag in the 1980 Winter Olympics Opening Ceremony in Lake Placid, when he was still a relatively unknown skater.

One year later, Hamilton would win the first of his four straight World Championships. In 1982, he became the first American skater since Tim Wood (1969 and 1970) to win back-to-back Worlds. He went on to win the 1983 and 1984 Worlds, as well as the 1984

Winter Olympics, over strong challenges by Canadian Brian Orser.

Hamilton did not win the compulsory figures portion of the 1981, 1982, and 1983 Worlds. Therefore, it came as a surprise to many when he not only placed first in figures at the 1984 Winter Olympics in Sarajevo but also did so with a massive lead. Orser placed seventh in figures, making his gold medal hunt extremely difficult.

Orser won both the short and long programs, and Hamilton presented a substantially less than stellar long program performance, singling a triple flip and doubling a triple salchow. Unknown to many at the time, this was largely the result of an annoying inner ear infection. (The inner ear controls one's sense of balance, something that is crucial to everyone but especially to skaters.)

The media being what they are, Hamilton was bombarded with questions as to whether he was embarrassed to win the gold medal with a sub-par performance. Realizing he was the first American man to win Olympic gold since David Jenkins in 1960, he responded, "I came here for the gold and I did it. It may not have been pretty, but I did it."

Enjoying a solid professional career, he has continued to skate dynamic programs full of zing and zest. Looking for another challenge, he went on to found *Stars on Ice*, a traveling ice show with a cast of famous skaters who often unite as an ensemble to tell a story with costumes, props, and creative lighting.

Then, in early 1997, he was diagnosed with cancer. The news hit during the 1997 Worlds, with the skating world still reeling from the sudden death earlier in the week of famed coach Carlo Fassi. Hamilton fought it hard, went through extensive therapy, and made his way back onto the ice. Later in the year, a televised tribute was held in his honor, featuring performances by many of his closest skating friends. Scott took to the ice at the end and amazed everyone by pulling off two of his famous back flips, demonstrating his courage and heart.

At the end of his performance, he grabbed the microphone and breathlessly proclaimed, "I win. I win." The battle he had won was far more significant than all four World golds and his Olympic gold medal combined.

Boitano: *The Artist Revealed*

When Brian Boitano first hit the world stage in 1983, it's doubtful that many people realized his impending greatness. Scott Hamilton said, about that time, that Boitano was the greatest jumper he had ever seen, so there was reason to keep an eye on him.

Twelve years prior to his first trip to Worlds, Boitano started group lessons with a local San Francisco–area coach, Linda Leaver, who was practically unknown outside of her rink. She recognized his potential so strongly that when her husband had a chance to be transferred to a better job, she persuaded him to turn it down so she could mold Boitano into the champion she was convinced he could become. Her husband agreed to give her a certain amount of time to see if her intuition was correct.

More than a quarter century later, Leaver remains the only coach Boitano has ever had. He stuck with her as he was ascending through the ranks, despite repeated suggestions from others that he should go work with a coach with more "experience." Boitano showed the same faith in Leaver that Leaver had showed in him and that Leaver's husband showed in her.

Along the way, Boitano would win the U.S. Championship from 1985 through 1988, the World Championship in 1986 and 1988, and the 1988 Winter Olympics, plus almost too many professional championships to count.

However, there seemed to be a problem. Boitano was, as Hamilton suggested, the best jumper in the world. His technique was impeccable. He usually did well in figures, and he was fearless in his desire to try jumps most other skaters would shy away from. But observers commented that he wasn't nearly as artistic as he should be.

It was the compulsory figures, which he loved, that would undo him during his first real shot at going to Worlds. In 1982, with Hamilton still riding high, Boitano missed a chance to make the World Team at the U.S. Nationals, a moment he says was his lowest point in skating. Because of a sixth-place finish in figures, he finished fourth place overall after nailing every triple in the book, including the triple axel. His short program was clean; he was the only one to execute a triple flip–triple toe loop combination at a time when double-triples just weren't being done. Also, his long program was a study in how to toss off triples as if they were child's play. But one mistake on one figure doomed his chances to move on, and he asked in frustration, "What do I need to do to make these people want to send me?"

What the skating world didn't know was how devastating that experience was to him at the time. He admits to having had thoughts of hanging up his skates.

In 1983 and 1984, he made the U.S. World Team, finishing seventh in 1983 and sixth in 1984 at Worlds, with a strong fifth-place finish at the 1984 Winter Olympics. He was the U.S. Men's Champion four years in a row, from 1985 through 1988. He moved up to third at Worlds in 1985, and stunned everyone at the 1986 Worlds by laying down a long program that was on the verge of perfection. His victory inspired him to try to be the first to successfully land a quad jump in world competition.

The 1987 Worlds received a lot of publicity in the United States, as they were held in Cincinnati, Ohio. The publicity largely centered on Boitano's attempt to nail the infamous quad toe loop—which was like the fabled Western jackelope, rumored to exist but never actually seen live.

Brian Orser had finished second at Worlds for three years in a row, also finishing second to Hamilton at the 1984 Winter Olympics. Cruelly nicknamed Mr. Second Place by somewhat insensitive skating commentators, he had much to prove in Boitano's

Brian Boitano's backward-leaning spread eagle is one of the most dramatic moves in figure skating.

home country. Orser lit the arena on fire in his short program, not just nailing jumps but also demonstrating his artistic superiority over Boitano—something not lost on coach Leaver.

Boitano had announced he was going to go for the quad in the long program, no matter what. A headline in one of the Cincinnati newspapers screamed out, QUAD LOOMS TONIGHT. Indeed, he had nailed the jump in the open practice session, and all knew he was capable of pulling it off. (To the untrained eye, the quad toe loop appears something like the three-and-a-half-revolution triple axel, but more of a blur. Many skating fans don't really care which edges set up the jumps and which ones land them. But they can recognize a big, big jump when they see it.)

In the long program, Boitano went for the quad as thousands of fans held their breath, and he fell out of it. Mr. Second Place had his first—and only—World Championship, getting the opportunity to retire the undesired nickname. Boitano had to settle for the silver medal. Later Boitano said, "If I had played it conservatively, I think I could have won that competition. But then I wouldn't have made any changes in my mind, in my brain, and then come back stronger the next year."

The changes he made were largely in his artistic approach. After the 1987 Worlds loss, when some analysts commented that he seemed mostly to be just going through the motions, with little care for how the motions were connected together, Leaver called in Canadian Sandra Bezic. Bezic was gaining a reputation as a choreographer sensitive to unleashing artistic senses within skaters, but her work with Boitano would establish her as a miracle worker. She released the artist within him, and less than a year later, Boitano was *the* artistic skater of the 1988 Winter Olympics.

The Olympics were being held in Orser's home country, which partially accounted for his decision to stay eligible after his loss to Hamilton at the big show in 1984. Both he and Boitano ended up doing military-themed presentations for the 1988 long program,

Brian Orser was a silver medalist at two consecutive Olympics.

allowing an even closer comparison of styles between the two—and encouraging the media to declare the Olympic matchup the Battle of the Brians.

When Boitano hit the U.S. Nationals, fans gasped. He wasn't just artistic, he was remarkably artistic, full of soulful energy and emotional delivery. Leaver's decision to "share" him with Bezic turned out to be just what he needed.

For his short program, Bezic choreographed a routine to the waltz music of *Les Patineurs* (*The Skaters*). After a difficult jump, Boitano was to reach down and wipe the ice shavings off his blade, and then casually toss the shavings over his shoulder as if saying, "No big deal." One could not help but make the comparison to tossing salt over one's shoulder for good luck.

Boitano performed no quad that year, but he did a new jump, the Tano triple lutz. He extended his arm above his head during the jump, as opposed to the standard practice of pulling one's arms into the body to help with the rotation. The extended arm seriously throws one's balance off center, making the jump difficult to control. But he did it spectacularly, as if to show that standard laws of physics did not apply to him. It has become a trademark of his.

By the time Boitano hit his lengthy spread eagle in the Olympic long program, with legs wide open and a backward-leaning position that seemed impossible to maintain for a second—not to mention for a complete circle around the rink—there was no doubt that he had transformed himself into a total artist. He won the Olympics with what was instantly described as a "performance of a lifetime," edging a near-solid performance by Orser (who had turned a triple Axel into a double). Orser must have felt as if he had been hit by a ton of bricks.

Oh, about the figure that doomed Boitano at the 1982 U.S. Nationals? It was also required at the 1988 Winter Olympics. He nailed it, perfectly, in one continuous line.

Boitano went on to win the 1988 Worlds over Orser and has since enjoyed one of the most remarkable professional careers ever. He's put together a number of touring events and has been involved in several televised skating shows, realizing that "more people in one night see a TV show than are going to see the entire tour live."

And he still is coached by Leaver whenever possible.

But, despite his victories, he refused to take his awards and go quietly into the night. Boitano became the leading spokesperson for the idea of allowing professional skaters to compete in the Olympics. When the ISU formally agreed to open up the 1994 Winter Olympics to professionals, the ruling became known informally as the Boitano Rule. He, naturally, was the first professional skater to decide to reactivate his eligibility. (We'll take a closer look at the 1994 Olympics in the next chapter.)

Today, people still talk about his remarkable 1988 Olympic performance as if it had taken place yesterday. Boitano reflects on the moment: "The interesting thing is, that was just a practice performance for me, a practice performance that I laid out in front of everybody. That's what was so fulfilling."

America's New Sweetheart Is Not from America

A case can be made that from 1984 through 1988, Katarina Witt was the most popular Ladies' skater among American fans. She had an appeal that was universal, she wasn't afraid to flaunt her femininity, and she was a shameless flirt on the ice. It's said that she received so many letters from male admirers that she had no place to store them except in her bathtub.

And, despite being so popular among Americans, she wasn't even an American skater. In fact, she was a citizen of the German Democratic Republic, more commonly known as East Germany. In many ways, her communist government placed far more restrictions on athletes than the Soviet Union did. But Witt enjoyed freedoms other citizens didn't enjoy, because the authorities realized her public relations value and allowed her unprecedented travel freedom.

She was second to Elaine Zayak at the 1982 Worlds, and at the 1983 Worlds, Witt placed second in the short program and won the long, but she slipped to fourth place overall because she finished eighth in figures. Witt went on to win the 1984 Winter Olympics in Sarajevo over Rosalynn Sumners and the 1984 Worlds over Elaine Zayak, establishing herself as a powerhouse and becoming one of the few figure skating "stories" to emerge from behind the drama of Torvill and Dean's *Bolero* Ice Dancing revolution. But while other top skaters were able to cash in on their Olympic successes, she was unable to do so. Her country's political system would not allow her to accept an offer to be a cover girl for an American cosmetics company.

She went on to win the 1985 Worlds and then slipped to second behind the athleticism of America's Debi Thomas in 1986. But she bounced back in 1987 and once again won the Winter Olympics, in Calgary in 1988, and that year's Worlds as well.

She knew how to work an audience unlike any other skater. At the 1987 Worlds in Cincinnati, she stuck around the auditorium where the compulsory figures competition was being held, going up into the stands to sign autographs. This action earned her a scolding, via the local newspapers, from the camp of Debi Thomas and her coach, Alex McGowan. They said she was trying to win American fans by being so accessible, to which many of those American fans probably responded with "And your point is . . . ?"

She didn't quiet these detractors by her next move, which some feel she planned. Every skater is allowed a block of time to be on the ice during a practice session hours before a free skate event. The music of each skater is played over the arena sound system. Although each skater is given a chance for a full run-through, few actually take the opportunity to do so. They might just skate around a bit to get a feel for the rink and try a few jumps, preferring to save their energy for the actual contest.

At the end of the practice session for the final group of Ladies' skaters, no one was left on the ice but Witt. There was still one more

Katarina Witt became one of the most popular skaters among American audiences.

skater's music selection to be played. The practice session audience started to call out for Witt to do something, and she responded by making up a routine on the spot to the other skater's music. Her movements seemed to fit perfectly. The audience ate it up, and Witt won many new fans.

The Thomas camp, which through the media was trying to get American fans to support Thomas, was not doing cartwheels.

Both skaters performed solid technical programs, but Witt had the edge in artistic marks. Thomas finished a strong second and helped set up a year-long anticipation of the 1988 Winter Olympics.

Ironically, there was a possibility that Witt might not have been allowed to perform at the 1987 Worlds. Each medalist from the four disciplines—Men's, Ladies', Pairs, and Ice Dancing—the year before was given a full-page color photo spread in the program book. Her photo caption identified her as being from East Germany. Officials of the German Democratic Republic demanded that the program book be altered or they would pull her from the competition. Thousands of stickers were printed up, and workers spent several hours frantically sticking them over the offending caption in every souvenir program book.

In 1988, both Witt and Thomas skated to music from the opera *Carmen* at the Calgary Winter Olympics. Witt proclaimed that while Thomas *skated* to music from *Carmen*, she (Witt) "*became* Carmen," the lead character from the opera.

She created controversy with a short program outfit that some felt was far too revealing of her thighs. She added feathers in "strategic" locations after the European Championships but still gave reason for people to talk about her. (And while they talked about her, good or bad, they weren't talking about anyone else. She was, after all, a master at media manipulation.) Thomas added fuel to the media fire by stating, a day before the Olympic long program, "Her costumes belong in an X-rated movie." A twenty-minute press conference with gaga media in Calgary focused on all the distractions, rather than on her skating. Witt was probably pleased with the attention.

She won her second Olympic gold medal despite a lengthy section in the middle of her program where she flirted more than she skated. But she didn't turn out to be the main talk of the Ladies' competition.

Canadian Elizabeth Manley, who had never stood on a Worlds medals podium, caught fire and electrified the largely Canadian audience in the short program, where she was a surprise third, and in the long program, which she won with an especially impressive performance. She took the Olympic silver medal, a fact that seemed hard for her to believe, as she bit the medal on the podium just to be sure it was real.

American hopeful Caryn Kadavy, bronze medalist from the 1987 Worlds, had to withdraw from the Olympics because of the flu, after valiantly competing in the short program. Fellow teammate Jill Trenary moved up to fourth place overall, also feeling flulike symptoms.

And Thomas? She finished third, behind Witt and the surprising Manley. After two-footing the landing of a triple combination jump shortly into

Elizabeth Manley gave one of the most enthusiastic Olympic performances ever seen.

Now a doctor, Debi Thomas made a run for Olympic gold while a full-time pre-med student.

her long program, she admitted, "I just didn't want to be out there anymore." Concentration shattered, she two-footed another triple landing and put her hand down on yet another.

At Worlds a few weeks later, the 1-2-3 results were identical, except now Thomas was married. Even her coach didn't know she had gotten married until someone from the media told him. Considering that Thomas should have kept her concentration focused entirely on skating during that crucial period, getting married just before Worlds was probably not what any coach would recommend. But then, maybe she figured after the Olympics that she couldn't really shatter her dream any further.

As a pro, Witt continued her unique way of toying with the audience and making viewers melt in the palm of her hand. While she was in Chicago with Brian Boitano's *Skating II* tour, a man with a camera yelled out to her as she passed by him in the front row. "Let me take your picture, Katarina," he begged. Normally, skaters would consider such a request as nothing more than an unwanted distraction that could break their focus. Witt, however, immediately altered her program, with the music still playing, and spent about half a minute posing for the surprised shutterbug.

The easing of East German travel restrictions in November 1989 should have been nothing but good news for Witt, who could now do exactly what she wanted, when she wanted. She had been allowed substantially more freedom than the average East German, but, frankly, she was not an "average" East German. She was considered by some of her fellow Germans to be far too friendly with the totalitarian regime that oppressed them, denying them the same travel freedoms that she enjoyed. When she went back home to the former East Germany to appear at a youth rally, she was, to her surprise, emphatically booed and called nasty names.

It seemed such an unexpected and unfortunate happening for someone so beloved outside of her own country. For a moment, at least, perhaps Witt was able to relate to the post–World War II home country reception received by the only other woman to win back-to-back Olympic figure skating titles, Sonja Henie.

Other 1980s Ladies

Debi Thomas enjoyed a substantial professional career after the 1988 Winter Olympics, while holding down a full load of university pre-med classes. She retired from competitions to devote all her time to medical studies. In 1997, she became Dr. Thomas and began her residency program with the goal of eventually practicing orthopedic surgery.

Jill Trenary won the 1987, 1989, and 1990 U.S. Nationals, placing second in 1988 to Thomas. She continually moved up in the world rankings, eventually placing first in 1990 and winning the compulsory figures event the last time it would be held at Worlds. Her fourth-place finish at the 1988 Winter Olympics set her up as a possible medalist in 1992, but she sprained an ankle at the 1991 U.S. Nationals and pulled out of the competition, turning pro as the defending World Champion. This meant she gave up her shot at the

Jill Trenary was equally adept at free skating and performing the once-compulsory figures.

1992 Winter Olympics, the last Olympics not to allow professionals to reinstate.

Because figures played a part in her victory, she is considered by some to be the last "total" Ladies' Champion. Now married to Christopher Dean, she has a much more relaxed feeling about being on the ice, stating, "I realize now that if I don't hit a triple, the program can still be very, very good. It's a matter of focusing more on the entire package, including the costuming and expressions. What happens between *A* and *Z* is more important than what happened at, let's say, *D*." Recognizing the difference between amateur competition and professional exhibitions, she adds, "Of course, I wouldn't have achieved becoming World Champion in 1990 if I had this attitude then."

In 1988, Japanese spark plug Midori Ito became the first Ladies' competitor to pull off a triple axel in competition. She won the 1989 Worlds and then placed second to Trenary at the 1990 Worlds. Her 1989 performance was notable for a dazzling display of jumping that, because of her small stature, seemed to propel her into the air like a missile. And she continually wore a genuine smile that lit up the Paris arena.

At the 1991 Worlds, she jumped right through the hole in the rink wall where a TV camera was sitting. Despite this, she was considered a favorite to win the 1992 Winter Olympics in Albertville, France, but she finished second to Kristi Yamaguchi, amidst an avalanche of Japanese media coverage that put a phenomenal amount of pressure on her. Plus, her concentration was totally shattered by French skater Surya Bonaly, who did a back flip—an illegal move in amateur competition—right in front of her while she was getting ready to set up her own jump during the long program warm-up session.

Midori Ito remains the most famous figure skater to come out of Japan.

Ito is regarded as perhaps the most gracious skater ever to have been on the ice. After her encounter with the wall in 1991, she skated over to the gaping hole to apologize to the cameraman and to pick up pieces of wall that had fallen on the ice. And after her "disappointing" Olympic finish in 1992, she went on Japanese television to apologize to all her countryfolk, whom she felt she had let down.

Elaine Zayak, discussed in an earlier chapter, disappeared for some time, then reinstated her eligibility for the 1994 U.S. Championships. She finished an admirable fourth, having made clear all along that even if she qualified for the Olympics, she would not go. She entered the competition only for personal satisfaction and would not consider "depriving" an amateur skater of being selected for the World and Olympic Team.

Tiffany Chin won the bronze medal at the 1983 and 1986 U.S. Nationals, the silver in 1984, and the gold in 1985. She showed great promise by taking fourth place at the 1984 Winter Olympics, with many feeling that she should have taken the bronze of Soviet Kira Ivanova, a lackluster free skater but more solid in the figures than Chin. She went on to take World bronze in 1985 and 1986, then seemed to burn out. She skates today as a solo and ensemble performer in touring professional ice shows.

Denise Biellmann, 1981 World Champion, has had a phenomenal professional career. Continuing to stretch the athletic and artistic envelopes (as well as her leg during her trademark Biellmann Spin), she's won numerous contests over skaters many years her junior. Her programs occasionally are a bit experimental for some tastes, but she continues to push forward, taking the risk that the audience might not understand her as well as the judges.

Other 1980s Men

David Santee started off the decade with much potential for the future, placing fourth at the 1980 Winter Olympics and Worlds. In 1981, only Scott Hamilton stood between him and the gold medal at Worlds, his one and only time on the Worlds medals podium.

Santee came from a skating family; his brother James also made some impressions at Nationals, although he never appeared on the

Working with
John Curry's ice
ballet company
revealed David
Santee's hidden
artistry.

podium. David Santee was perhaps best known for his semiportrayal of Rocky Balboa from the Sylvester Stallone hit film *Rocky*. After a while, though, it seemed as if he were stalled artistically, and he left amateur competition. Many were surprised when he signed on to skate with John Curry's ice ballet company, but the change did him a world of good and allowed him to discover his artistic inner soul.

Czechoslovakian skater Jozef Sabovcik was a surprise bronze medalist at the 1984 Winter Olympics, as he had no medals from prior Worlds. Because he was sixth at the 1983 Worlds, he felt no pressure at the Olympics. He remembers, "My teammates and I were always worried about our hockey players, and the skiers all had tremendous problems with the snow. I was watching all the other events, and suddenly it was time for me to go and perform and I didn't have any time to dread it. The incredible thing was I ended up with a medal I didn't expect."

He had severe difficulties with his legs and was told by many people to skip the Olympics because his knees might "blow out." However, he had missed a chance to go to the 1980 Winter Olympics in Lake Placid because the Czech skating federation didn't have the money to send any athletes, so he wasn't about to miss out on Sarajevo. He

Jozef Sabovcik has earned the nickname Jumpin' Joe for his huge, dazzling jumps.

says he was taking off his skates after his Olympic long program when someone ran in and yelled that he had come in third. He didn't even realize that meant he had to go out to the podium until it was suggested he should go out to the rink to pick up his medal.

His knees did prevent him from contending in future years. In 1986, he was in second place going into the long program at Worlds, but then his knee acted up. Every landing left him visibly in pain, and by the end of the program, he could barely stand.

A while later, he left Czechoslovakia for Canada, where he became associated with Toller Cranston, saying Cranston doesn't care as much about where the jumps go as he wants him to understand "what is that music trying to portray and what is it trying to tell me?"

At the 1986 European Championships, Sabovcik was the first to stand up on a quad jump, but a mistake on the landing meant that Kurt Browning would get the credit for successfully landing the first quad in international competition. Lately, Sabovcik has enjoyed a competitive rebirth because of all the professional competitions now being held. He is always a threat and has won a number of events, still knocking off big jumps, including quads. This has earned him the respect of fellow skaters and the nickname Jumpin' Joe.

Christopher Bowman was a skater who promised to be one of the biggest names ever. Naturally talented and blessed with a Hollywood flair for the dramatic, he captivated audiences and loved playing to the fans, the judges, and the cameras. He was as much a free spirit as his coach, Frank Carroll, was not. Carroll often tried to get Bowman to focus on disciplining himself, but with all that natural talent and success, Bowman didn't see much reason not to have as much fun as he could along the way, playing up his party image whenever he could.

He first came to the public eye as a baby in television commercials, so the showmanship was practically bred into him. He was called Bowman the Showman by admirers and detractors alike, and he did nothing to discourage the nickname.

Christopher
Bowman was
known as
Bowman the
Showman.

He twice took the silver medal and twice took the bronze at the U.S. Nationals, and he won the gold in 1989. His placements at Worlds from 1987 through 1991 were seventh, fifth, second, third, and fourth. He was seventh in the 1988 Winter Olympics and fourth in 1992, edged for a medal by Czechoslovakian Petr Barna.

He had many run-ins with coach Carroll, but none more publicly than after his 1990 Worlds long program. Carroll had tried to teach Bowman personal responsibility (Bowman referred to himself as Hans Brinker from Hell) and was infuriated when Bowman, after a shaky start, totally rechoreographed his long program as he skated it. Carroll recognized nothing of what the two had worked on for months. When he pointed this out to Bowman after he got off the ice, Bowman insulted Carroll by responding, "All head and no heart." They then went to the "kiss and cry" area to await the scores. Bowman was ecstatic with the high marks that earned him a Worlds bronze medal, but it was clear to everyone watching on TV that Carroll was anything but amused. It was the beginning of the end of their relationship.

Later, Bowman went to study under Toller Cranston, a totally different personality and one who emphasized a balletic approach to choreography. Cranston, when asked how he was going to package Bowman, announced he was going to "dip him in black." And so he attired Bowman in a dignified, solid black costume, turning Bowman into a younger version of himself. Bowman looked very, very uncomfortable with his new, less showy image.

Bowman then made some personal decisions that would haunt him for some time, but he eventually recovered from his lapses to become a respected TV commentator of skating competitions. But there are still some fans, remembering his potential, who wonder what would have happened had his ability to focus on the end result been equal to his natural gifts.

Alexandr Fadeev of the Soviet Union tried for a quad toe loop at the 1986 Worlds but didn't get credit for being the first because it

Alexandr Fadeev was one of the best Men's skaters to come out of the former Soviet Union.

wasn't executed perfectly. In fact, he failed spectacularly, but in doing so he threw down the gauntlet, and other skaters would know that if it could be attempted, it could be achieved. He won the bronze medal at Worlds in 1984, 1986, and 1987 and won Worlds in 1985 with a dizzying performance that left him sweating and looking totally exhausted at the end.

In 1986, he felt pressured to try the quad. What happened next was enough to make him want to crawl under the ice and hide. He fell out of two triples, touched his hand to the ice on another, and over-rotated yet another. The quad was a total disaster. He received dismal marks of 5.4 to 5.6, which should have knocked him off the medals stand altogether. However, the Soviet judge saw fit to award him two marks of 5.8 and 5.9, as if nothing bad had happened. The audience in Switzerland booed loudly, and this obvious act of nationalism went down as one of the most blatant and scandalous ever.

While Fadeev and Sabovcik tried mightily to be the first to get credit for landing a quad jump in international competition, Canadian Champion Kurt Browning is in the record books as the man who did achieve where others failed. He accomplished this feat at the 1988 Worlds, in which—because of the figures—he finished sixth overall (behind Champion Brian Boitano) despite taking third place in the long program.

However, Browning did win the next three Worlds and placed second to Viktor Petrenko in 1992, returning to win the 1993 Worlds over up-and-coming teammate Elvis Stojko. Despite going on to take the silver medal at the 1992 Worlds a few weeks later, he had a devastating time at the 1992 Winter Olympics in Albertville, placing sixth. All his fans felt that he truly deserved better, considering his remarkable achievements up to that time, but in figure skating, despite occasional judging irregularities, you typically get only what you deserve at the moment.

Kurt Browning performed the first quad in international competition.

part **Three**

Skating Turned Upside Down

Pre-Lillehammer

IT SEEMS THAT EVERYTHING THAT HAPPENED IN SKATING in the early 1990s was largely overshadowed by the events of 1994. And yet, some very fine skating took place in the years leading up to the reinstatement of professionals and the bizarre Harding/Kerrigan affair.

Lost in the madness of the 1994 Winter Olympics was the fact that just two years earlier, there was another Winter Olympics, in Albertville, France, the last to be held in the same year as the Summer Olympics.

A few personalities of the early 1990s were discussed in previous chapters, crossing over from the 1980s. Some of those, plus others who didn't become big names until the early 1990s, were Soviets who found that by 1992, the country they used to represent no longer existed.

Viktor Petrenko, World and Olympic bronze medalist in 1988, World silver medalist in 1990 and 1991, and World and Olympic gold medalist in 1992, skated most of his amateur career as a Soviet but was proud to declare himself a Ukrainian in 1992, when the USSR broke up just before the Winter Olympics. However, Ukraine wasn't recognized as an ISU member until 1993, so, in 1992, he and other former Soviets skated under the banner of a country that didn't really exist, the Commonwealth of Independent States.

Petrenko turned pro after his Olympic victory, but he didn't really enjoy it. For one thing, there was a limited number of professional competitions then, and he missed the thrill of competing. He jumped at the chance to reinstate as an amateur for the 1994 Winter Olympics. He won many events as a second-time amateur,

Olympic gold
medalist Viktor
Petrenko

but a mistake in the Olympic short program put him in ninth going into the free skate, killing his chances of earning a medal. With a strong long program, he moved up to fourth.

As a successful professional who reinstated as an amateur singles skater, Petrenko wasn't alone in not living up to past potential during the 1994 Olympics. The Winter Games were not kind to Brian Boitano or Katarina Witt either.

Many thought that American Paul Wylie's silver medal performance in the 1992 Winter Olympics was worthy of the gold. From 1988 through 1992, he alternated between second and third place at the USFSA Nationals, never managing to win. In the three years he was sent to Worlds, he placed ninth, tenth, and eleventh. In 1992, he was chosen for the U.S. Olympic Team, but not to go to the Worlds. Perhaps that's why judges had a little difficulty dealing with his being so "on" in Albertville.

Wylie relishes his expressive dynamism, enjoying skating to programs that tell a story. He was always popular with the audiences as an amateur but just couldn't pull it together to achieve his potential until Albertville. His coach blamed that on his habit of thinking too

Paul Wylie astounded everyone by almost winning Olympic gold at Albertville, France.

much about everything he did. One of the brightest people ever to strap on a pair of skates, he found it difficult to skate with abandon.

After his stellar Olympic performance, he turned pro and had a spectacular pro career, finishing it up in 1998, still in his prime, in order to return to Harvard and pursue a degree in law.

Kristi Yamaguchi was the big story in early 1990s Ladies' skating, placing second at the USFSA Nationals in 1989, 1990, and 1991, winning Worlds in 1991, and winning Nationals, Worlds, and the Winter Olympics in 1992, over Midori Ito and a rising Nancy Kerrigan.

As a five-year-old, Yamaguchi used to skate around her rink while clutching a Dorothy Hamill doll, having taken up the sport because the 1976 Olympic Champion was her idol.

For a while, she excelled in both singles and Pairs skating. In 1989 and 1990, she won the USFSA Pairs Championship with partner Rudy Galindo. Both years they placed fifth at Worlds. However, she suspected that her chances of medaling in Pairs at Worlds or the Olympics were fairly remote, as the Soviet Pairs skaters were so strong. After the 1990 USFSA Pairs victory, she broke up with Galindo and concentrated solely on singles skating. It must have worked, because she went straight to the top the next two years. Galindo became a singles skater as well, struggling competitively and financially until his stunning USFSA Championship performance in 1996.

Yamaguchi has enjoyed an outstanding professional career since turning pro in 1992, excelling in programs that are of a carefree nature.

Natalia Mishkutenok and Artur Dmitriev were products of supercoach Tamara Moskvina. They

Enjoying success in singles and Pairs, Kristi Yamaguchi decided to concentrate solely on singles and went straight to the highest step of the Olympic podium.

placed third at the 1990 Worlds and then won Worlds in 1991 and 1992, also winning the 1992 Winter Olympics. Perhaps no Pairs team since Belousova and Protopopov in the mid-1960s has been more poetic. They were famous for unique spins that flaunted her flexibility—especially their trademark spin wherein she hugged close to his legs while upside down.

After 1992, the team experienced difficulties in keeping their partnership together. They all but disappeared in 1993 and came back for the 1994 Winter Olympics, holding their relationship together by a thread. They performed spectacularly, and some thought they could have beaten Gordeeva and Grinkov. However, they weren't quite as polished as their Russian teammates, though they were dripping with emotion.

After the 1994 Winter Olympics, Dmitriev paired up with Oksana

No Pairs skater had more flexibility than Natalia Mishkutenok, shown with partner Artur Dmitriev.

With Oksana Kazakova, Artur Dmitriev won his second Olympic gold medal.

Kazakova, moving up through the ranks to win the 1998 Winter Olympics. Dmitriev is outspoken about the restrictions of Pairs skating, stating, "We must do three lifts, two throws, three jumps, two spins, two death spirals, and steps. I think we must add more difficulty. If you talk about elements and compare today [1997] to the 1984 Olympic Games, it's the same difficulty level. The same throws, the same jumps, the same twists."

Blurring the Line between Amateurs and Professionals

It had always been accepted that once skaters had a chance to turn professional, they would cheerfully leave the world of amateur skating and enter their postcompetitive days, where they could make money. Before skating became the popular sensation it is today, turning pro often meant signing on with a big tour such as *Ice Capades, Ice Follies,* and *Holiday on Ice.* Only a few skaters became marquee names that attracted paying audience members. Many more became members of the chorus—the ensemble that skated to big, glitzy musical numbers and wore extravagant costumes.

It was easy to know who was an amateur and who was a pro. Amateurs competed—pros didn't. Amateurs didn't make money—pros did. (Under the old ISU rules, amateurs couldn't even make money performing in exhibitions, although trust funds to help defer training expenses were common.)

Dick Button started to change the equation when he held the first big, nationally televised professional competition in 1980, now known as the NutraSweet World Professional Figure Skating Championship. The event gave pros a chance to rediscover the joys of competition, with fewer restrictions than were found in ISU-sanctioned events. (For example, pros could skate to music with words. Amateurs could do so only in exhibitions.) Button's professional competitions required two separate full-length programs, one emphasizing technical proficiency and the other artistry.

After his win at the 1988 Winter Olympics, Brian Boitano entered and won an incredible string of professional competitions, continuing to improve his technique and artistry to the point where no other male skater could catch him. If he for some reason hadn't turned pro, he could have won the 1992 Winter Olympics. And this possibility disturbed him greatly. He became quite vocal that the Olympics should be open to the best athletes in the world, regardless of their amateur or professional status. Boitano pointed out that in many other Olympic sports, professionals were allowed to compete. Certainly the top skiers made a lot of money from endorsements and commercials, as did top summer sports athletes such as track and basketball stars. If Michael Jordan was allowed to play on America's Dream Team, why should Brian Boitano be barred from competing in the most prestigious athletic event in the world?

In 1991, the International Skating Union issued guidelines to allow amateur skaters to receive pay from competitions, exhibitions, and endorsements, yet still remain eligible to compete in ISU events. The catch was that the events had to be sanctioned by the ISU and the funds had to go through the skaters' national governing bodies. However, the ISU still did not allow for professionals to reinstate as amateurs. But allowing amateurs to make money was the first step in cracking the door open for professionals to come back some year into the ISU fold.

After years of considering the possibility and rejecting it, the ISU finally decided that pros could reinstate for the 1994 Winter Olympics, in essence allowing them to reenter the ranks of amateur skating. There was quite a bit of controversy over this decision, with many pointing out that the top pros could end up taking away spots from deserving amateurs who had patiently waited for their chance to go to the Olympics. The ruling allowing professionals to come back to the Olympics became commonly known as the Boitano Rule. Not everyone used the term with endearment.

Many thought that Boitano would be somewhat lonely on the ice, surmising that pros would not want to take the time to train hard to get back into the kind of physical and mental condition necessary for intense amateur competition. But when it came time for pro skaters to announce their intentions to reinstate, Boitano was joined by a number of former Olympic gold medalists, including Viktor Petrenko, Katarina Witt, the Ice Dancing team of Jayne Torvill and Christopher Dean, the Pairs team of Ekaterina Gordeeva and Sergei Grinkov, and the Pairs team of Natalia Mishkutenok and Artur Dmitriev. Elaine Zayak also reinstated, for the USFSA Championships only. Unlike the others, she had no desire to reenter the world stage.

When the dust settled after the 1994 Winter Olympics in Lillehammer, Norway, the professionals who had reinstated went home with mixed results. Gordeeva and Grinkov won their second Olympic gold medal for Pairs, followed by a reenergized Mishkutenok and Dmitriev. Petrenko, Boitano, and four-time World Champion Kurt Browning (still an amateur) experienced calamities that destroyed their medal hopes—falls that almost never plagued them any other time. Browning had hoped to get the Olympic medal that eluded him in 1992.

Like the reinstated Men, Witt also finished out of medal placement, but was never really considered a front-runner to begin with. Hers was more of a personal victory. Her parents had not been allowed to travel out of East Germany to see her win her previous two Olympic gold medals, having to contend with severe travel restrictions placed upon them by a government always fearful of the possibility of embarrassing defections. In Lillehammer, with Germany reunified and the people now free, Witt's parents were finally able to see her skate live in the Winter Olympics.

Torvill and Dean finished third in Ice Dancing, despite overwhelming public sentiment that they were still the best. Ten years after winning the Olympic gold, with *Bolero* still fresh in skating fans' minds, they returned to the amateur scene with a more traditional *Face the Music* program. They realized that in some ways the world of Ice Dancing had moved backward since 1984. They won the European Championship but were told by judges that they weren't "dancing" enough for the rules of 1994. Taking the advice to heart, they changed more than half their program for the Olympics a few weeks later and were beaten by two teams they had defeated at the Europeans.

Harding's Fall from Grace

The reinstatement of professionals was *supposed* to be the big story at the 1994 Winter Olympics, the first Winter Games to be held in a year apart from the Summer Olympics. And then a strange little incident in Detroit, Michigan, changed all that.

Tonya Harding was talented enough to have it all. She was the first American woman to pull off a successful three-and-a-half-revolution triple axel in competition and only the second woman (after Midori Ito) in the world to do one. She was an up-and-coming skater when she won the bronze medal at the 1989 USFSA Championships, but she had a rough year in 1990. She then came back and stunned the skating world by winning Nationals in 1991, defeating eventual 1992 Winter Olympic Champion Kristi Yamaguchi and the person with whom she would become forever connected in the public's eye, Nancy Kerrigan. In 1991, Yamaguchi defeated her at Worlds, but Harding stood on the Worlds medals stand with bronze medalist Kerrigan, for a 1-2-3 American Ladies' medals sweep and what would be her only trip to the podium.

The American public was quite fond of Harding. She was poor. She had had a rough childhood. She trained in a public rink in the wide-open atrium of an indoor shopping center outside Portland, Oregon. She drove a pickup truck. She had real faults and didn't attempt to hide them. Despite suffering from asthma, she smoked cigarettes. She was a fighter—literally. A well-publicized traffic confrontation found her going after another motorist with a baseball bat. Harding was anything but a prim and proper skating icon. She was real, and gritty, and didn't fit in the mold of a traditional skating princess. She was the common person, the underdog, the skater whom parents didn't want their sons to bring home, but the skater with whom the sons were probably most intrigued.

In 1992, Harding took the bronze at Nationals and almost got a medal at the Albertville, France, Winter Olympics. Her trademark triple axel betrayed her in the short program, and she ended up in fourth after the long program. A sixth-place finish at Worlds a few weeks later was the beginning of the slide downward that kept her off the USFSA medals stand in 1993. But her husband, Jeff Gillooly, would eventually formulate a plan to assure that no one would stand in her way in 1994.

Thursday, January 6, 1994, became a day that will live in infamy.

Gillooly had a couple of friends with whom he shared his plan: to take Nancy Kerrigan out of the USFSA Nationals competition in Detroit. One of these friends somehow sneaked backstage after Kerrigan completed a practice session prior to the beginning of the Ladies' competition. In the hallway Kerrigan was passing through, he whacked her hard on her right knee with a collapsible police baton, crippling Kerrigan instantly. He then ran down the hallway, crashed through a window, and disappeared into a waiting escape car.

A handheld video camera was soon on the scene, catching Kerrigan's anguished cries of "Why me?" while she lay on the floor of the hallway in pain. With a chance to win the upcoming Winter Olympics seemingly dashed in an instant of brutal ferocity, she thought everything she had worked for had been taken from her by an act she could not comprehend.

It turned out that Kerrigan's knee wasn't broken, but it was severely bruised and would keep her from defending her 1993

Tonya Harding
was known by
many as skating's
"bad girl."

Nationals title. Harding issued a lukewarm "best wishes" to Kerrigan and went on to win the 1994 USFSA Ladies' title as if she knew nothing about the incident. Kerrigan watched the long program in person, as suspicions started to mount that Harding was somehow involved in the madness.

Because of heavy news coverage of the attack, television viewership of Nationals was high. A USFSA committee soon voted to send Kerrigan to the Olympics, if she recovered in time to compete. Harding was to be sent, too, because it was not yet clear if she'd had any involvement. Michelle Kwan was to be sent as an alternate in case Kerrigan couldn't skate. Because Kerrigan was the only U.S. skater to place in the top ten at the previous year's Worlds, the country was allowed only two Ladies' skaters for the 1994 Olympics and Worlds.

The Winter Olympics Ladies' competition was just seven weeks later in Lillehammer. During that time, Kerrigan went through an astounding training regimen to get back on the ice. As she remembers, "I never worked so hard in my life." It took every ounce of strength she had to try to pull herself back into shape.

Meanwhile, investigators started to close the noose around Harding. Too many things didn't add up. New details appeared nightly on the national networks about what had probably happened. In a short time, the public became convinced that Harding had had something to do with the attack. The USFSA became convinced as well.

Realizing this, Harding took legal action to prevent the USFSA from keeping her out of the Olympics until her role in the attack, if any, was determined beyond a shadow of a doubt. She filed a $25 million lawsuit against the USFSA to prevent it from taking her off the Olympic team. She continued to train as if nothing was wrong, but the TV cameras that flooded the sides of her training rink were enough to let anyone know that the media smelled a hot story and weren't going to miss any of it.

By the time of the Olympics, Harding had been found guilty in the court of public opinion. She stayed away from Norway until the last possible moment, and when she appeared in Lillehammer, the cameras followed her every move. They also focused on Nancy Kerrigan, whose training/rehabilitation regimen had paid off. She was determined to show the world that memories of the attack would not keep her down.

The Ladies' short program from Lillehammer garnered huge television ratings. But it was the long program where the twisted story set new standards for bizarreness. Harding botched a jump early in her program and then suddenly stopped skating. She went over to the judges, crying, showing them that her boot lace had broken. The television commentator said it was a ploy he had seen her use before when she wasn't skating well at the start of a program. No one in her entourage had a spare lace immediately available. She would have to start the program over, but it did not help her. Harding, who had tried to keep the world from caving in on her since the Detroit attack, would finish eighth.

Kerrigan skated brilliantly and was first after the short program. She presented a very fine long program but lost the gold medal by the scantiest of margins. She was placed first by the four judges from the Western countries and was placed second by

Heroically fighting back from a vicious attack on her knee, Nancy Kerrigan won Olympic silver.

four judges from the Eastern countries. Jan Hoffman, the German judge and former Men's World Champion, tied Kerrigan and Oksana Baiul. But he gave Kerrigan a 5.8 in Artistic Impression and Baiul a 5.9. That .1 was the entire tie-breaking margin of victory for Baiul, even though she had two-footed a landing on one of her jumps.

In all the media publicity over the Harding/Kerrigan matchup, defending World Champion Oksana Baiul had almost been lost in the shuffle. She trained in Lillehammer in relative seclusion and took the ice feeling little of the pressure felt by Harding and Kerrigan. And when it was over, with Harding in eighth, there really was no Harding/Kerrigan matchup, after all.

Ukrainian Baiul had come out of nowhere the year before to win the 1993 Worlds at the age of fifteen. In 1992, she wasn't even one of the top ten skaters in the transitional former Soviet Union. Orphaned at an early age, she was supported by 1992 Olympic gold medalist Viktor Petrenko out of the fees he earned as a professional. She moved in with his coach and mother-in-law, Galina Zmievskaya, who became a surrogate mother to her and would work on-ice wonders with her in a short time.

Her expressive artistry was beyond compare, and so was her resolve. The day after a serious collision with another skater in an Olympics practice session, she skated in pain with stitches in her leg. And, after missing a triple in the Olympics long program, she threw another one in toward the end. That, and skating on her cut leg, showed she was as gutsy a performer as Kerrigan, who, at twenty-four, was eight years her senior.

It almost seemed an anticlimax to the Olympics that Kerrigan didn't win. With a silver medal, Kerrigan went on to do many product endorsements and was identified by American Sports Data in 1996 as the number one most-recognized female athlete in America. Plus, Disney signed her to a variety of projects.

And Harding? Well, she became the closest thing the skating world has to a nonperson. Her husband, who soon became her ex-

Oksana Baiul came out of total obscurity to win the World Championship and the 1994 Winter Olympics.

husband, and his two friends were found guilty of planning the attack on Kerrigan and spent time in prison for their crimes. When it was confirmed that Harding had indeed known about the attack and had lied about it to authorities, she was sentenced to perform hundreds of hours of community service and received massive monetary fines.

In June 1994, a USFSA Hearing Panel stripped Harding of her ill-won Ladies' title as punishment for her involvement in the attack. Three months later, the USFSA Executive Committee voted to leave the title vacant, the only time this has ever happened. Officially, there is no USFSA Ladies' Champion for 1994. She was also banned for life from ever competing as an amateur.

She could, however, perform as a professional. But it is virtually certain that this will never happen. While she would sell a lot of tickets, many professional skaters are said to have "Tonya clauses" in their contracts with ice shows and competitions. If she's in, they're out.

It was an unfortunate end to what was one of the most promising careers in all of skating.

Post-Lillehammer Ladies

Japan's Yuka Sato was born to parents who both were Japanese Champions and had represented Japan at the Winter Olympics. A few weeks after Lillehammer, she turned the tables on France's Surya Bonaly at the 1994 Worlds, held in Japan. The competitive field was smaller than at Lillehammer, as is often the case in an Olympic year, with the three Olympic medalists out of the picture. Baiul and Kerrigan had already turned pro, and Lu Chen, Olympic bronze medalist from China, went home to take care of a nagging foot problem.

Bonaly captured the silver medal at three Worlds in a row—1993, 1994, and 1995. She fully expected to win the 1994 event, and at the medal ceremony in Japan, she shocked the skating world by removing her medal from around her neck after it had been presented, holding it in her hand while the Japanese national anthem was played. Considering that the World Championships were in Japan, this created an even bigger stir. Realizing her mistake, she publicly apologized to the Japanese people for her action.

The Japanese people remembered that Bonaly was the skater who threw off Midori Ito's concentration at the 1992 Winter Olympics by doing a back flip in front of her while Ito was setting up a jump in warm-up for the long program. There was little reason for Bonaly, an accomplished gymnast, to try such a jump. Back flips are illegal in amateur competition because the move allegedly cannot be landed on one foot, which is a requirement of all jumps. But in 1994, in the Lillehammer exhibition, where rules are less restrictive, Bonaly not only nailed a back flip but astounded everyone by landing it on one foot. No one else, including all the men who perform it regularly in professional competition, has the incredible strength to do likewise.

Bonaly has a strong opinion about the rule forbidding back flips in amateur competition, stating, "It's stupid. I've done it on one foot, and I can do it in combination with a triple jump—a triple salchow on the same foot right away after the back flip." Although other women have done back flips, she is the only person to do one in a split position, with the legs split. Most men who can do a back flip are afraid to try that one.

She is the only Ladies' skater who can pull off a quad jump, and she actually attempted one in the 1992 Winter Olympics. More impressively, she can do two quads—a salchow and a toe loop—and has pulled them off in exhibitions. But her dedication to jumping comes at a price, as she has long been criticized for not devoting enough time to working on artistry.

Surya Bonaly is the first Ladies' skater to successfully perform a quad.

Bonaly finds the rules for singles skaters to be too restrictive. Her mother, Suzanne, points out, "Skating is the only sport where the rules state, 'You must not do more than this.' It's like being in jail. The rules are like a ceiling. She can do so much, but the rules are holding her back. I think everyone in the public loses, as they don't get a chance to see what can be done."

Lu Chen returned to competition after her foot healed to win the 1995 Worlds over Bonaly and the United States' Nicole Bobek. As big as China is, Chen says there may be fewer than ten rinks in the entire country, so she had no skating tradition to draw on. In 1996, she delivered a breathtaking long program at Worlds, earning some perfect scores of 6.0. Many would have given her another gold medal on the spot, but the United States' Michelle Kwan came out on the ice and earned even more perfect scores. Kwan raised the stakes in the long program by throwing in an extra triple toe at the end of her program, a move that could have knocked her off the medals stand had she failed. Her perfection was enough to beat Chen's perfection. It was a competition where a tie that couldn't have been broken would have been an appropriate solution.

Kwan had had a lot of pressure on her at the 1994 Worlds. With Kerrigan and Harding out of the picture, the thirteen-year-old Olympic alternate was on her own, attempting to salvage two positions for the United States for the 1995 Worlds. To do so, she would have to place among the top ten Ladies' skaters. Additional pressure was thrust upon her when Nicole Bobek fell apart miserably in the qualification round, placing thirteenth in her group. Kwan showed what a fighter she was by finishing in eighth place, and, as a result, she salvaged her own second-place position on the World Team for the next year.

Kwan doesn't worry as much as most other skaters about missing jumps. According to her choreographer, Lori Nichol, "She doesn't get really upset if she misses something. It's just a fact, it's just something that happens, and she'll fix it next time. So nothing ever really gets her down or really gets her too up. She was excited after [1996] Worlds. She kept pinching herself, [asking,] 'Is this real?' And within fifteen minutes, she was talking about the sunglasses she wanted to go buy. So in that fifteen minutes, we were back to reality."

Tara Lipinski made many sacrifices in her quest for the gold. She moved to Detroit to train with her coach, while her father stayed behind in Texas to work and raise money for her training expenses. It's not uncommon for a world-level skater to spend more than $50,000 per year for training, equipment, travel, and other incidentals. The Lipinski family had to take out a second mortgage on their house to pay for her expenses. But the result was worth it—a World Championship and a Winter Olympics crown.

Lipinski won her first USFSA Nationals medal, a bronze, in 1996. One year later she was National and World Champion at the age of fourteen, the youngest World Champion ever, just a few months younger than Sonja Henie had been when she won her first Worlds in 1927. Interestingly, she would not have even qualified to go to Worlds in 1997 under the ISU's new age limit policy, instituted to assure that participants at Worlds would be at least fifteen years old. Lipinski was "grand-

With fluid movement and seamless choreography, Michelle Kwan is the epitome of sophisticated elegance.

fathered" in because she had competed at Worlds the year before.

The reason for such a ruling was to protect the young skaters. The ISU didn't want younger skaters to feel obligated to try some of the maneuvers they would need in order to compete on the world level. The risk of injury to extremely young skaters attempting world-class-level jumps was deemed too great.

While male skaters have to mature to be able to perfect the more explosive jumps, female skaters find it easier to toss off the jumps while they are younger. Males don't have the necessary muscle masses until they're a bit older. Females find that once they have gone through puberty, their center of gravity has changed, and in many cases, they have to learn to jump all over again. There have been many cases in which a Ladies' skater achieved success at a very early age, ran into roadblocks during puberty, and then slowly came back to competitive form afterward.

The discrepancy between age and success for Ladies and Men at Worlds is clear when one looks at the record books. The youngest Ladies' World Champion was Lipinski, at age fourteen. The youngest Men's World Champion was Donald McPherson of Canada, who was eighteen when he won in 1963.

Jill Trenary is concerned about the trend to younger Ladies' skaters, but for reasons of personal—rather than physical—development. She says, "It's hard for me to see some girls being out of school at fifteen or sixteen. They're doing nothing but skating, but I think being in school is important to being a total person. Some of these girls are missing out on having a real life. Hopefully they'll have a strong upbringing that can help them through it all.

"I'm concerned about seeing many young girls achieving fame and glory so soon while they're so young. I hate to say it, but the money that comes with such an early success is not necessarily a good thing. I just hope they stay close to their families and skate because they love skating and not because they're hooked on the TV coverage or money. I hope they do it for themselves."

At fifteen, Tara Lipinski was the youngest Olympic gold medalist in history.

After winning the 1995 USFSA Championship and capturing the bronze medal at Worlds that year, Nicole Bobek had a really rough 1996 and wasn't sent to Worlds after she pulled out of Nationals with an injury. There was precedent to send her, as the USFSA had done so in the past with other skaters who were temporarily injured. Her Worlds medal the year before was in her favor, but in the end, a committee decided to send third-place Lipinski instead.

Some felt that the USFSA was punishing Bobek for not training hard enough heading into Nationals. She participated with teammate Todd Eldredge as a featured skater in *Nutcracker on Ice*, just a month prior to Nationals. The press was merciless about the appearance that both skaters were taking Nationals for granted.

Bobek has long been misunderstood by the mainstream press. She's a free spirit who at times seems to enjoy poking fun at established conventions. The media have interpreted this as meaning that she doesn't care about competing, which is far from the truth. She cares, but she wants to enjoy herself along the way. She has received very little attention for her ongoing work with Touch the Heart and Raise the Spirit, where she goes into elementary schools and talks to students about what it took to achieve success.

The media enjoyed picking on the fact that she has had more than her share of coaches. She would have stuck with the great Carlo Fassi had he not moved back to Italy. Things just weren't right with some of her other coaches, and she longed

Nicole Bobek's training regimen and numerous coaching changes were sometimes frowned upon by the USFSA.

for Fassi. They were able to get together once again for the 1997 season, and through working with him she was able to reclaim a spot on the World Team, behind Lipinski and Kwan. Then, at Worlds in Lausanne, Switzerland, the unthinkable happened. Fassi died of a sudden heart attack. Bobek came unglued in the short program and got her emotional strength together for the long program. At the end, she went to her knees and gave a silent prayer in his memory. It was one of the most touching moments ever witnessed on the ice.

Post-Lillehammer Men

Many thought the dissolution of the Soviet Union in 1992 would negatively affect the development of top skaters there. This was not the case at the 1994 Winter Olympics, as all the gold medalists came from either Russia (Urmanov, Gordeeva and Grinkov, and Grishuk and Platov) or Ukraine (Baiul).

Alexei Urmanov was quite a surprise at the Olympics. He was first seen on the medals stand as bronze medalist at the 1993 Worlds, his last appearance on the Worlds podium. As the favored reinstated professionals fell by the wayside, he performed solidly, if not exactly with much spirit. But there was little to be found wrong with his performance, and his ended up being the best out of a lot of performances that were less than sterling.

Canada's Elvis Stojko attacked the Worlds scene with his unique training in the martial arts. He took the bronze in 1992, and the silver in 1993, and he won it all in 1994, 1995, and 1997, capturing Olympic silver in 1994. He had a rough time in the short program at the 1996 Worlds in Edmonton, Canada, dashing his hopes to win a medal in his home country with an uncharacteristic fall caused by over-rotating a triple axel. But he came back with one of the most startling long programs ever skated.

With the audience going berserk, he grabbed an *Edmonton Sun* newspaper that had come out after the short program and held it up to the cameras. The big headline, plastered across the front page over

Elvis Stojko's black belt training in martial arts inspires his skating.

a picture of the earlier fall, read ELVIS IS DEAD. Stojko comments, "It's so weird how one jump can make all the difference in the way people look at things. The most important thing in [the] sport is not if you fall, but how fast you get up and continue."

Stojko has the most consistent quad in the business, so pulling off triples is normally easy for him. But the fall that cost him a Worlds medal, and probably the gold as well, left him reflecting on the qualities that make him the great performer he is. He says, "Everything happens for a reason. If you go for it all the way and you don't quite make it, you're hungrier the next time, because you're going to do it next time."

Todd Eldredge has demonstrated his ability to fight back. After winning the 1990 and 1991 USFSA Men's Championship, he didn't even make it to the Nationals medals stand for the next three years. In 1995, he blasted back to win the gold and then lost to Rudy Galindo in 1996 when Galindo delivered the performance of several lifetimes in his hometown of San Jose, California. But Eldredge once again fought back and won the gold

Todd Eldredge has often fought back from adversity to achieve great success.

in 1997. He also won the Worlds bronze in 1991, the silver (behind Stojko) in 1995 and 1997, and the gold in 1996, coming back to best Galindo on the world stage.

He admits to being "burned out" in 1993, partially as a result of the back injury that plagued him the year before. He might have regained a spot on the World and Olympic Team in 1994 had he not come down with the flu at the U.S. Nationals, placing fourth.

One reason he was able to come back after assorted disappointments is the outlook he has on skating. It's important to him, but he knows it isn't everything. His advice to skaters who feel down is simple: "If they know in their heart that they love skating, then they should stick with it and try everything they can to make it work. If the time comes when they don't love it anymore, then they should set different goals for themselves. There are other things out there to do than skating." Although he considered hanging up his boots when things were going poorly for him, he knew in his heart that he had to continue.

Russia's Ilia Kulik won the Olympic Men's gold medal in 1998.

Russian Ilia Kulik is one of the great jumpers to come out of the post-Lillehammer days. A World silver medalist in 1996, he trains in the United States, like so many skaters from the former Soviet Union. Many skaters from Europe and Asia, and some of the best Russian coaches, now make their home in America. Professionals spend most of their time in America because that's where most of their work is. Many top amateurs do so because it's getting harder to find good coaches and good ice back in their home countries.

One skater who always knows how to play the audience is France's Philippe Candeloro, World silver medalist in 1994, World bronze medalist in 1995, and Olympic bronze medalist in 1994 and 1998. Candeloro works hard to get into his characterizations. In his Olympic debut, he became the Godfather, in 1997 Napoleon, and in 1998 a

Musketeer—not just skating to the music, but skating as the title characters, complete with mannerisms and attitude.

After Kristi Yamaguchi decided to focus solely on singles skating, Rudy Galindo experienced enough unfortunate circumstances to push less dedicated skaters over the edge. It was bad enough for him to lose the chance to repeat as National Champion in Pairs, which he had won with Yamaguchi in 1989 and 1990. But then, while attempting to make it as a singles skater, he lost his father, a brother, and two coaches.

Living in a mobile home out of economic necessity, he was determined to make his skating pay off. Coached for free by his sister Laura, he built up his singles technique. In 1996, at the age of twenty-six, he finally hit pay dirt. He gave a magical performance in his hometown of San Jose, one that left the audience in tears. Many considered it a fluke, but at the 1996 Worlds, he pulled off a bronze medal, then quickly turned pro. Perhaps more than any other skater, Galindo proved the power of patience and perseverance.

Post-Lillehammer Pairs and Ice Dancers

One of the most painful falls ever seen in the Winter Olympics was that of Germany's Mandy Wötzel and Ingo Steuer in Lillehammer, reminding all just how dangerous Pairs skating can be. The 1993 World silver medalists were poised to try for an Olympic medal when Wötzel's skate

One of the most popular skaters ever, France's Philippe Candeloro

Mandy Wötzel and Ingo Steuer have had their share of misfortunes on the ice.

blade got caught in an indentation in the ice, causing her to fall hard on her chin. Steuer almost fell on top of her, and ended up having to carry her off the ice in the middle of their long program.

Steuer has a few battle scars of his own, having suffered a cut lip from Wötzel's skate and a concussion from a lift mishap. But when they stay injury-free, they can be magnificent, as proven by the Worlds silver medal finish in 1996 and their gold medal finish in 1997.

Canadians Isabelle Brasseur and Lloyd Eisler were the most vocal in their opposition to the idea of pros reinstating as amateurs for the 1994 Winter Olympics. The team thrills audiences with their acrobatics, which helped them win Olympic bronze in 1992, behind the former Soviet teams of Mishkutenok and Dmitriev and Elena Bechke and Denis Petrov. They were perfectly situated to make a run for the Olympic gold in 1994. Though they ended up being the top amateur team, they were defeated in their goal by the two returning professional Russian teams of Gordeeva and Grinkov and Mishkutenok and Dmitriev.

Brasseur explains the team's feeling about professionals who reinstated: "We didn't understand why they would come back when they've already been there. We wouldn't go back because there are younger people who have trained for years, and for us to declare our eligibility for the Olympics in the last year means they wouldn't get to go. It may be their only chance to go to the Olympics."

Brasseur also has an opinion about the state of amateur Pairs skating: "I really believe a pair should be an overall look. They should have interaction between each other. They should have great lifts, a great death spiral, a great side-by-side spin, and an overall good package. I think more and more they're putting emphasis on the jumps, and they're lacking the Pairs package.

"A good Pairs package is Meno and Sand. You look at them and everything is good. Everything is smooth. Things are flowing. They were the only ones that didn't have a triple jump [in 1996], but they were the only ones that had a program that started from the

first seconds and flowed all the way through to the last seconds."

Jenni Meno and Todd Sand each won USFSA Nationals medals with different partners prior to 1993. After getting together just months earlier, they took the silver medal at Nationals in 1993 and won the next three titles, placing second in 1997 behind Kyoko Ina and Jason Dungjen. In 1995 and 1996, they captured the bronze at Worlds. More important, they got married in 1995, although they claim that their artistry stems more from the blending of their styles than the fact that they're married.

Meno says: "We're so close and we spend so much time together that when we're out there [on the ice], we almost know what the other person is thinking. I think that helps us as a pair. It's nice to be out there competing with someone who loves you and someone whom you love."

Realizing how fortunate they are, Meno and Sand gave their grant money from the USFSA Athletes Support to the Junior Pairs Champions at the USFSA National Championships in order that the up-and-coming team could continue with their training.

The media loved Calla Urbanski and Rocky Marval, two Americans who had to work for a living to support their skating, Urbanski as a waitress and Marval as a truck driver. They took the U.S. silver medal in Pairs in 1991 and won the next two titles. But friction caused them to split up temporarily just before the 1994 Winter Olympics season.

Jenni Meno and Todd Sand found success and love with each other.

Calla Urbanski and Rocky Marval, nicknamed "the waitress and the truck driver."

Back together now, they enjoy their pro career, because the pressure is lifted off them and there are so many more opportunities to perform. And they're still referred to in the media as "the waitress and the truck driver." They say they did not create the image—CBS did. The network had a story to sell the public during the 1992 Winter Olympics, where they finished tenth. Urbanski was thirty-one at the time—the oldest skater on the ice by several years. She's proud to proclaim, "I paved the way, saying that 'You don't have to be eighteen to do it.'"

Marval is now married to Isabelle Brasseur.

The Russian/Ukrainian Ice Dancing team of Oksana Grishuk and Evgeny Platov hit the world scene with a bronze medal at the 1992 Worlds; in 1993, they moved up to silver. They then won the next four World titles and the 1994 and 1998 Winter Olympics. Their style is often one of frenetic activity and unabashed enthusiasm.

In the old days, they would bring in gas for their training rink's Zamboni; such were the difficulties they had to contend with as the former Soviet system reinvented itself. Perhaps that's one reason they enjoy living in America so much, along with so many other skaters from Russia. But they have one complaint about American television's treatment of Ice Dancing.

According to Oksana, who now goes by the single name of Pasha, "People enjoy watching Ice Dancing when we're on TV. But some competitions on TV cut out the dance parts. It makes us upset because we did our best job and got our best results. Most [people] don't have a chance to go and see performers in person, so they watch it on TV, and Ice Dancing gets cut off."

This is a phenomenon that indeed is true. Ice Dancing has traditionally been regarded as something less interesting for the public to watch. Americans, especially, like to be excited by figure skating. Perhaps Ice Dancing makes one think too much, as one has to concentrate on the beauty and flow in order to appreciate the sport. Watching singles skaters and Pairs is to witness sheer drama; they

Pasha (formerly
Oksana Grishuk)
and Evgeny Platov
are the only
couple to have
won two Olympic
gold medals in
Ice Dancing.

pull off the aerial fireworks or they fall. For whatever reasons, Ice Dancing typically gets little coverage on American television.

To watch Ice Dancers is to experience romance. There rarely is any drama. In contrast to the microwaved fast food of singles skating and Pairs, Ice Dancing is a meal that takes time to heat up. But if one is patient, it can be the main course that is the most satisfying.

Nagano

Nagano Welcomes a Changed World

THE 1998 WINTER OLYMPICS IN NAGANO, JAPAN, were full of surprises: Tara Lipinski upset Michelle Kwan, and Lu Chen recovered remarkably from near oblivion. But the Winter Games also had their share of melancholy: Nicole Bobek plummeted, Todd Eldredge did not win a medal, and Elvis Stojko suffered a painful injury.

The spotlight focused upon renewed nationalism, which raised its head under the name "bloc judging."

Many geographic and political boundaries seemed to disappear, as several skaters from the former Soviet Union moved to the United States to enjoy substantially better training facilities. These included the Nagano Men's and Ice Dancing gold medalists—Ilia Kulik and Grishuk and Platov—coached by the versatile Tatiana Tarasova. Galina Zmievskaya (Petrenko's and Baiul's coach) also moved her home base. In addition to the incentive of better facilities in the United States, coaches from the former Soviet Union can make as much in two hours in the United States as they made in a month back home.

Four years before Nagano, the Boitano Rule had encouraged many professional skaters to reinstate and take another shot at Olympic glory. In 1998, not a single pro chose to take that step. Perhaps pros thought it would be too much work, or maybe they were concerned their standing in the public eye would be tarnished if they performed poorly. They may have recalled the subpar performances of so many of the reinstated pros in Lillehammer.

Ladies: America's 1-2 Punch

Despite pulling out of competitions and missing several crucial

weeks of practice because of a fractured bone in her foot, Michelle Kwan was stunning at the 1998 USFSA Nationals, earning fifteen Presentation 6.0s between her short and long programs. Up until then, no woman had received even a single 6.0 in a USFSA Nationals short program.

Naturally, Kwan became the favorite for Ladies' Olympic gold. A top skating journalist wrote that if Kwan were to fall in Nagano, her depth of artistry would still be enough to carry her through to the top of the medals podium.

Defending USFSA Nationals Champion Tara Lipinski hadn't fallen in a short program since 1996, but she did just that at the 1998 Nationals. She fought back from fourth place to capture the silver medal. Nicole Bobek finished with the bronze, seeming to have recovered from the 1997 loss of her coach at Worlds. Immediately, there was talk of an American 1-2-3 sweep of the Ladies' medals in Nagano.

The approaches of the American Ladies' Olympic Team members to the Winter Games were quite different. Kwan and Bobek took a safe approach, staying home to practice and arriving after the Olympics were well under way. Lipinski decided to experience the Olympics to the fullest—marching in the opening ceremonies, living in the Olympic village, and attending hockey games.

After the short program, Kwan and Lipinski sat 1-2, followed by Russia's Maria Butyrskaya, a self-proclaimed "romantic woman on the ice," in contrast to what she said was Lipinski's "childish skating." The two top Americans looked strong as they headed into the long program free skate.

The Ladies' free skate in Nagano is said to have been the greatest Ladies' event ever. Kwan skated superbly, but without the spark that ignited her soul at Nationals. She scored nine straight 5.9s in Presentation, but few counted on Lipinski's 5.8s and 5.9s in Presentation, earned by skating with boundless joy and charm. With

Michelle Kwan was the favorite leading into the 1998 Winter Olympics.

superior Technical Merit marks, Lipinski became the youngest Olympic Ladies' Champion in skating history, taking that honor away from Sonja Henie.

China's Lu Chen took bronze over Butyrskaya with an ethereal long program performance that was so delicate it seemed as if she was skating on a cloud. Her remarkable recovery came on the heels of a disastrous 1997, which saw her fail to qualify for the short program at Worlds.

Further down the ranking than one would expect, in tenth place, was potential medalist Surya Bonaly. Despite her placement, she created some of the loudest talk to come out of Nagano. She was still steaming over her short program Technical Merit scores of 4.9 to 5.7, an astounding range of judging inconsistency. She showed her contempt for the system by throwing in an illegal back flip near the end of her long program, then ended her show with her back to the judges.

And what about Bobek? She finished seventeenth in both the short and long programs, falling on several jumps, earning scores as low as 4.4. Every skater has bad days. But few have bad days that happen so publicly and at such an inopportune time. But at least she had a chance to compete. Germany's Tanja Szewczenko had been an Olympic medal favorite, as a result of winning some major international competitions. After courageously battling back from a serious foot injury and a life-threatening illness that had almost killed her, she caught the flu in Nagano and had to withdraw from the Olympics.

Tara Lipinski surprised many people, but not herself, in winning the 1998 Winter Olympics.

Lu Chen won a second Olympic bronze in 1998.

Men: Towering Triumphs and Devastating Defeats

Unlike the predicted Ladies' results, there was no clear leader heading into the Men's competition in Nagano. The only certainty was that there would be a new Men's Champion, as Alexei Urmanov had been forced out of competition earlier in the season with a groin injury.

Russian Ilia Kulik had pulled out of the European Championships with a pinched back nerve. But he was in no pain as he won the Olympic short program, then knocked off a quadruple toe loop as the first skater in the long program's final group. This set a standard that no other skater was able to match, making Kulik the first Men's skater to take the gold medal in his first Olympic appearance since Dick Button did so fifty years earlier.

Canada's Elvis Stojko, more than any other skater, can take credit for the technical revolution in Men's skating. He pulled off the first quadruple jump combined with any other jump, the first quad toe loop–double toe loop, and the first successful landing of a quad-triple combination. But he had long heard from the judges that he should be more artistic, more flowing, "softer" on the ice. He refused to pay attention to any of that, earning his three World Championships with his incredible technique, overshadowing the judges' reservations about his bombastic, martial arts–inspired style.

During the long program, many observers sensed that he was having trouble. He didn't even try his quad, even though Kulik had already landed one. He appeared slower than normal and lacked his typical spunk. At the end of his program, he grimaced in extreme pain and could barely make it off the ice, hardly seeming to notice his scores.

Only a handful of people knew that Stojko had injured a groin muscle a month before the Olympics. He didn't want any sympathy from the judges, choosing heroically to let his skating stand on its own merits. His coach, Doug Leigh, said that if there were a medal for courage, Stojko should get it.

Nagano was the fourth Olympics in a row that saw a Canadian enter competition as the reigning World Champion, each coached by Leigh. In every case, the Olympic gold medal proved out of reach, and Canada has yet to win its first Olympic Men's gold medal.

When the World Championships were in Japan in 1994, the Japanese audience fell head over heels in love with Philippe Candeloro and his antics. His popularity was still riding high when he returned for the Olympics, even though he finished no higher than ninth at the previous two Worlds. But the surprise bronze medalist from Lillehammer four years earlier proved he knows when to peak for maximum effect, capturing the bronze with a magnificently choreographed routine as a dashing Musketeer sword fighter. For sheer spectacle, it was one of the most splendid programs ever witnessed.

And with Candeloro's remarkable performance, former World Champion Todd Eldredge found himself in an uncomfortably familiar situation. Like Kurt Browning before him, he built up to an Olympic medal and didn't get one, even though he became the first skater since Dick Button to win five Men's USFSA titles. He added his fourth-place 1998 finish to his list of personally challenging Olympic experiences, having finished in tenth place in 1992 because of a back injury, and missing out on 1994 opportunities when he caught the flu prior to Nationals.

Entering the long program, he appeared tense, proceeding to water down a triple axel into a single, fumbling his triple-triple combination, and turning the second part of two combination jumps into double axels. He attempted to throw in a triple axel—and fell on it—at the end of his program, a gutsy move that had worked when he won the World Championship in 1996. Like Browning, he quite possibly left the Olympics with a giant "what if" hanging over him.

Because of his injury, Stojko didn't attempt a quad. Candeloro doesn't have one in his arsenal of jumps, and Eldredge (who attempted one and fell at Nationals) chose not to risk it in Nagano.

With Kulik performing one, the 1998 Winter Games became the first Olympics in which the quad determined the final results. Some think that the jump will be so common in the future that it will become a required element in Men's short programs.

Pairs: The Russians Still Have What It Takes

In Pairs competition in Nagano, Tamara Moskvina's teams, still coached in Russia, won gold and silver. This gave Russian skaters their tenth straight Olympic Pairs gold medal since 1964.

Oksana Kazakova and Artur Dmitriev came alive in the long program with a burning passion that was poetry on ice. Dmitriev became the first male Pairs skater to win Olympic gold twice with two different partners, first with Natalia Mishkutenok in 1992, and then with Kazakova.

Silver medalists Elena Bereznaia and Anton Sikharulidze had topped Kazakova and Dmitriev at the Champions Series finals and the European Championships. Since 1968, the winning Pair at every Europeans held in an Olympic year had gone on to win Olympic gold. But a fall by Sikharulidze in the short program dimmed their chances of winning, and both fell, with just seconds to go in the long program, as she was coming down from a star lift.

It might be said the real victory was in Bereznaia's even being on the ice. She had recovered from ongoing abuse from a previous partner and a serious injury that saw his blade slice open her skull during a side-by-side camel spin, the maneuver in which a leg of each skater is extended outward at head level while each rotates close to the other in unison. Soon after her recovery, she and Sikharulidze started to skate together, rapidly becoming a major international force.

Bronze medalists Mandy Wötzel and Ingo Steuer certainly had their share of accidents. Like Bereznaia, Wötzel also spent a few months in the hospital after being hit in the head with a previous partner's skate during a side-by-side camel spin. Then she experienced the horrible fall in the 1994 Olympics. Steuer endured a half dozen knee operations in addition to a cut lip and a concussion from lift mishaps. But it was an accident just two months prior to Nagano that almost kept them from going for a medal. Steuer's right arm was hit by the mirror of a car while he stood on the sidewalk in Germany, tearing shoulder ligaments and giving him lasting headaches and dizziness—two symptoms especially dangerous to someone responsible for safely lifting another skater over his head.

American Champions Kyoko Ina and Jason Dungjen made a valiant try for a medal, missing by just one spot. Their short program scores had them in first place from one judge and seventh from another, causing their coach to ask if the judges were all watching the same program. Others had wondered the same when Sikharulidze's fall in the short program didn't result in a mandatory deduction, and when Kazakova and Dmitriev won first place on the sheets of eight of the nine judges in the long program, but received fourth place on the sheet of the German judge. This led to concern that the German judge had tried to prop up the chances of his country's Wötzel and Steuer.

Jenni Meno and Todd Sand were forced to pull out of the 1998 USFSA Nationals when Meno bruised an ankle bone just hours before the long program. The USFSA sent them to the Olympics, though, after considering their past performance results. Meno spent a few weeks off the ice for rehabilitation before Nagano, but falls reduced them to finishing in eighth place overall.

Dance: "Bloc Judging" Exposed

Twenty-two years after Ice Dancing was first allowed in the Winter Olympics, some people still wondered whether it should be an Olympic sport. The people asking these questions were not comforted by claims in Nagano that Ice Dancing results are sometimes fixed.

To many, Pasha (Oksana Grishuk) and Evgeny Platov seemed the predetermined Olympic Ice Dancing winners. They came into

Russia's Anjelika Krylova and Oleg Ovsiannikov are perfect examples of classical Russian Ice Dancing emotion and drama.

Nagano with a twenty-one-event winning streak stretching all the way back to the 1994 Winter Olympics, and they weren't penalized for falls in three different competitions leading up to the Olympics. (Falls in Ice Dancing are practically unheard of.) And although Pasha almost fell during the first compulsory dance of the Olympics, the team was placed first by seven of the nine judges.

However, in the free dance, the team delivered one of the most remarkable and captivating programs seen since Torvill and Dean's *Bolero*. *Memorial Requiem* exuded a quality that made viewers afraid to breathe, lest they miss something. And when it was all over, Pasha and Platov became the first Ice Dancers to repeat as Olympic gold medalists.

Russians Anjelika Krylova and Oleg Ovsiannikov took the silver medal, and the French team of Marina Anissina (a former Russian skater) and Gwendal Peizerat took the bronze with a thoroughly captivating role-playing program to *Romeo and Juliet*.

The cries of bloc judging were loudest from the camp of Canada's fourth-place Shae-Lynn Bourne and Victor Kraatz, bronze medalists at the 1996 and 1997 World Championships. Despite skating clean compulsory dances, they were already out of the gold medal hunt by the end of the first compulsory dance, in which they finished fifth. This led their coach, Natalia Dubova, to issue the charge of bloc judging among some of the judges.

Bloc judging is where a number of judges from different countries get together and agree to help one anothers' skaters by voting in a predetermined manner. A pair would practically have

Shae-Lynn Bourne and Victor Kraatz are shown "etching a deep line."

to break their legs on the ice to change the results. Dubova's charges were largely based on the fact that the same five judges placed certain teams in the exact same high positions for the compulsories, while all the other judges rated the same teams lower, and the five judges placed other teams in low positions when all the other judges had the same teams in higher positions.

Bloc judging or not, the results in Nagano were very predictable. The only change in position among the top twenty-four couples caused by the free dance results was an exchange of positions between teams in twentieth and twenty-first place. Once couples got set up in the compulsories, they tended to stay put. This led the president of the ISU to say he would ask the federation's congress to increase the value of the free dance, which would decrease the value of the compulsory phase and supposedly hinder bloc judging. Only in Ice Dancing is the final phase not worth more than what comes before it.

Other news in Ice Dancing was that, for the first time ever, vocals were allowed for the original dance, the second phase of the competition. It was shocking for some to hear Elvis Presley and other singers scream out during the required jive rhythm, seeming to blur the lines of distinction between competition and exhibition programs.

Once again, Ice Dancing appeared to be pulled in opposite directions. The leading practitioners of pure Ice Dancing (as defined by the rule book) were Bourne and Kraatz, whose *Riverdance* brought a massive amount of footwork to the rink. The most obvious proponents of Ice Dancing as Ice Theater were Pasha and Platov, leading the discipline into new, uncharted territory.

The old question from the 1980s remained: Is it ballroom dancing on ice—or can it, and should it, be something more?

part *Four*

Fashions

AS SOON AS A SKATER GLIDES ONTO THE ICE FOR A performance, her choice of costuming creates expectations in the minds of judges and fans. Realizing this, the top Ladies' skaters in the world sometimes spend thousands of dollars on custom-made costumes, to give themselves that added push over their competition. For her 1994 Winter Olympics program, Nancy Kerrigan commissioned an original outfit from Vera Wang, one of the best-known designers of wedding gowns for wealthy people. Such taste does not come cheap.

Men's costumes are quite a bit simpler and less expensive. Sometimes sequins will be splashed on for effect, but typically the costumes are not too extravagant. Whatever the gender, the outfit must fit perfectly, allowing for freedom of movement, and must enhance the skater rather than be the main attraction. Costumes won't make a skater, but a bad costume, or one that is too gaudy, could distract the judges enough that it could break the skater. The goal of a custom costume designer, then, is to get a distinctive look while not going overboard.

Deborah Nelson, president of Satin Stitches, has made costumes for countless skaters for more than a quarter century. As a costume designer and creator, she is always searching for new, durable fabrics that will move with the skater's body.

Nelson finds it necessary to stay current with the latest design trends off the ice, drawing inspiration from designs for high fashion, activewear, ballroom dance, pageant gowns, and Broadway and film costuming. Of today's costumes, she says: "Instead of the heavily beaded dresses of past years, emphasis is on pure styling with

distinguished accents. Judicious use of rhinestones and beaded and sequined appliqués gives the hint of glitz that a costume needs to add sparkle to a performance."

Careful attention is given to costumes for Men's skaters so that the look is masculine. Shirts are designed as full body suits so that they always appear to be perfectly tucked in.

The total look of the costume goes beyond the blouse and skirt or pants and shirt. Sometimes it even goes as far as incorporating matching boot covers. Not all skaters can afford to buy a special set of boots in a color matching the costume, so boot covers are a good way to get around that.

On the other end of the wardrobe spectrum are the touring ice shows. Competitive skaters for the most part have to take care of their own costumes. (One popular story is told of Brian Boitano's dying his tights in a hotel sink and hanging them out the window to dry.) But big touring companies often travel with a person whose job it is to keep all the costumes in top shape between performances and to fix problems when they occur during performances.

Wardrobe master Roger Bathurst has spent a number of seasons with *Champions on Ice*. He always has safety pins available for last-second emergency repairs, and while he worked with *Holiday on Ice*, he even sewed performers into their costumes when a zipper broke at the last moment.

Bathurst has taken care of beaded costumes that cost several thousand dollars. The skaters are performing in exhibition, so, unlike the trend toward simplicity that Deborah Nelson sees in competitive skating, Bathurst sees the skaters go to the opposite extreme, toward glamour and glitz. The top Ladies' skaters use a lot of chiffon and Lycra. The Men's skaters lean toward gabardine, a material that always looks nice and pressed and keeps its crease. But while the Ladies' skaters of the *Champions on Ice* tour attempt to create a major ice show look with a lot of sequins and beads, the Men's skaters are increasingly skating in T-shirt–type tops and slacks, with some of the shirts bought right off the rack.

Blades

Blades don't get much press in the skating journals and are not often spoken of as separate items apart from skating boots. When people speak of "skates," they are usually talking about the combination of the blade and the boot.

No one today thinks much about E. V. Bushnell's 1850 creation of a skate boot that, for the first time, contained a screw-on steel blade. But because of his invention, the thin pieces of metal making up the blade allow skaters to glide across the surface of the ice at great

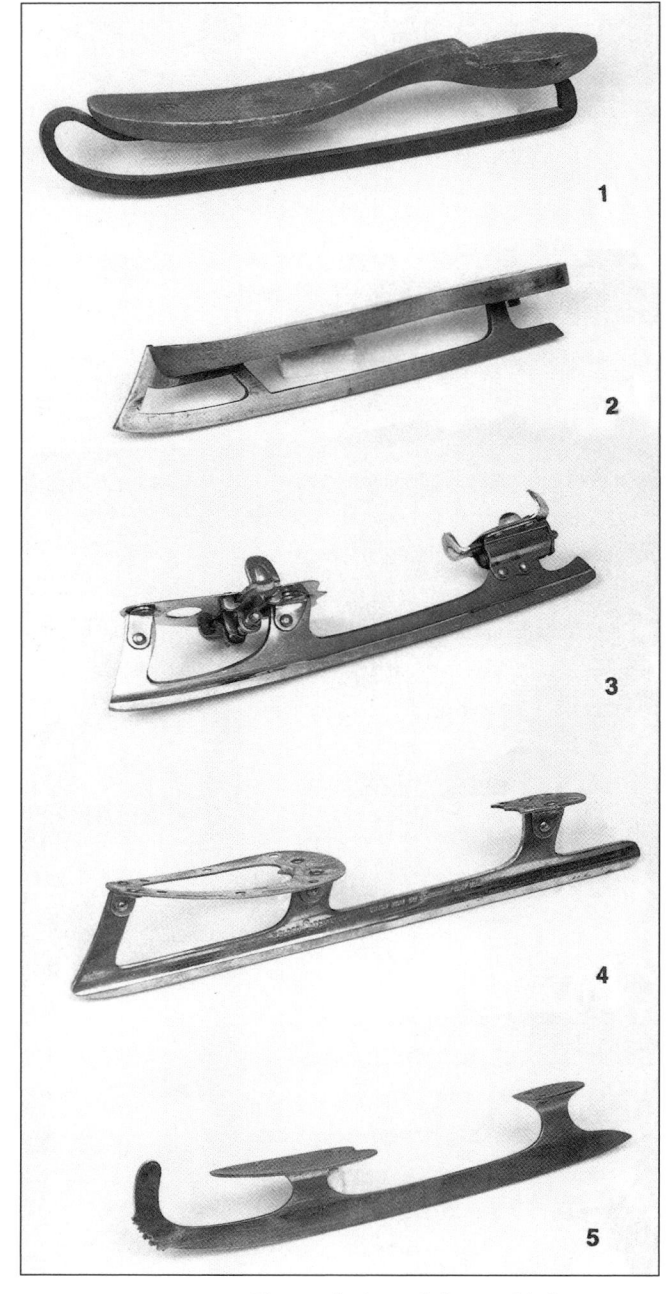

The evolution of skating blades is seen
in this series of photos.

speed. With screw-on blades, they can jump and rotate without fear of the blades separating upon landing. It seems remarkable that everything skaters do, they do on a piece of metal just over one-eighth of an inch wide.

Because sharpening blades requires a grinding wheel and an expert and steady hand, few skaters sharpen their own. If the blades aren't sharpened properly, skaters will have a difficult time attaining the speeds necessary for jumping. There can be no nicks or burrs in the metal; these would slow one down or even trip one up.

A careful sharpening will leave a smooth but sharp inside edge and outside edge on the bottom of each blade, with an equally smooth hollow and rounded concave groove between the two edges. (The inside edge is the edge closest to the other skate. The outside edge is farthest from the other skate.) These edges prevent skaters from sliding to the side and allow them to grip the ice in order to push off for propulsion. The gripping of the ice also allows them to glide, jump, and steer themselves in straight lines or curves. Skaters typically favor one or the other edge unless traveling in a straight line.

And as the area between the edges is concave and not flat, so are the blades not flat from front to back. There is a slight, almost imperceptible curve to the blade, allowing for a smaller part of the blade to come into contact with the ice at any one time. This makes it easier for the skater to maneuver and skate in curved forms.

Figure skate blades are noticeably different from hockey and speed skate blades in that they have teeth, notches in the metal in the front part of the blade, which assist in the takeoffs of jumps and spins. Most skaters who have achieved any level of proficiency will find themselves skating on one of two blade brands: John Wilson or Mitchell & King (better known as MK). Both brands are made in the same factory in England, the two companies having merged in 1997.

Serious skaters skate on blades that have a tempered steel chromium finish, as opposed to the cheaper nickel plating found on some less expensive blades. Incidentally, Ice Dancing blades are shorter than Pairs and singles blades. This allows the couple to do fancy footwork close to each other's blades without the blades' coming in contact.

Boots

While the choice in brands for top blades is quite limited, there is a larger variety of brands and styles of boots available for all levels of skaters. The most important thing a skater needs to remember when choosing a boot is fit, fit, and fit. Without a proper fit, the boot just won't work well and the skater might experience all sorts of problems, from blisters and calluses to ankle injuries.

A serious, growing skater generally wants to have a half size of room to grow into, with a little space left at the end of the big toe. Some parents think it's okay to save money by having their developing skater wear an extra pair of socks to fill in a pair of skates that is way too large. This is a bad idea. Boots that are too wide will

An SP-Teri boot

crease and break down. In the other direction, boots that are too narrow—used after a skater should have moved to a larger size—will cause cramps.

Department store boots often come in just one width and are usually available only in full sizes. A good-quality boot line will be available in several widths and half sizes, such as the line of boots by SP-Teri.

Besides the additional widths and sizes, other factors separate a typical department store skating boot from one of quality. A skater should look for good, firm leather in the ankle area. Soles and heels should be made of leather instead of rubber. Better boots have ankle padding and will have foam padding (instead of less expensive felt padding) on the tongue.

Some mass-merchandised boots combine the soles and heels into one unit, which is not recommended. Also, the blades are sometimes riveted on, so one cannot adjust them. A better boot will allow for the blades to be screwed on, making them adjustable in the future.

To be properly fitted to boots, a skater will go to a local skate shop (which is often located at a training rink). The shop personnel will then put the skater's feet on a measuring device that will determine the foot size for a single specific manufacturer. (Each manufacturer has its own measuring scale.) The skater is measured for length, and then the ball of the foot is measured to determine width. Only then will appropriate boots be tried on. The boot is fitted to the foot; then the blade is fitted to the boot. Skaters with hand-me-down blades should avoid the temptation to go with a boot just because the blade fits.

A boot that is too big will feel comfortable when new. But when the skater skates on it, many problems may occur. The skater may experience blisters and heel slippage. She won't properly feel her toe picks or the edges of the blades. And, she will often re-lace the boot in a futile attempt to get a tighter fit.

One should never discount the importance of a skater's boots' feeling just right. In 1984, at the Sarajevo, Yugoslavia, Winter Olympics, Barbara Underhill and Paul Martini were considered favorites to win the gold medal in Pairs. Underhill felt very uncomfortable in her new boots, which contributed to a fall in the short program—destroying their chances for a medal—and caused her to single a side-by-side double jump in the long program. The team finished in seventh place.

After the Olympics, Underhill, at the suggestion of fellow Canadian skater Brian Orser, took her new blades off her new boots and put them on a pair of old, comfortable boots. With everything feeling right and proper, the team stunned the skating community by winning the World Championship a few weeks later. Underhill attributed the difference in performance to being comfortable in her boots, a vivid lesson for all skaters.

How Ice Is Made

Many venues where touring ice companies perform are arenas that host hockey games, and as such, the buildings already contain ice-making equipment. But sometimes a tour will visit a venue where ice-making equipment is not available. How does the ice get made? The company brings in its own.

No, touring companies don't travel with ice, but they do travel with the equipment necessary to make it. This is where someone like Donald Yontz of Entertainment Production Services comes in. Yontz has been around skating since 1968 and once was a principal skater in *Ice Capades*. He has been at the forefront of ice making for traveling ice shows and has developed some specialized equipment for his state-of-the-art ice-making process.

At the heart of Yontz's system is a five-and-a-half-inch-deep frame not unlike that of a water bed. A plastic liner holds in the water. An inch of high-density foam insulation is laid on the floor over the liner, over which the refrigeration coils are set. Then the rink is flooded and water fills up the area inside the plastic liner. Rinks can be adjusted to fit just about any size stage.

The coils under the ice are an adaptation of solar collector panels like the type one finds throughout Yontz's home state of Florida. They are set in mats known in the ice industry as Yontz Mats. Each mat consists of five three-eighths-inch tubes that are in essence rubber pipes, connected to as many other Yontz Mats as needed. Refrigeration fluid moves through these pipes, bringing in cold to freeze the ice and keep it frozen, and more important, removing heat in the process. Only sixty-five gallons per minute of brine solution—the refrigeration fluid—move through the floor, which isn't a lot, considering that the amount is spread across the entire floor. Quite a bit of heat is moved away from the ice with a very small amount of fluid.

The brine solution is pumped into a machine that sits on a truck outside the venue, a machine very similar to the ones used for stationary ice rinks. A big engine with cooling fans absorbs the heat from the warmed brine; then Glycol, acting like an antifreeze, cools the brine by extracting the heat before the compressor pump sends the brine back through the Yontz Mats for another pass.

Once the ice is set, the crew turns off the cooling machine and lets the ice melt. When it is refrozen, it forms a much more solid surface than before and is considered "cured." This process also helps eliminate air pockets formed during the initial freezing, which could be a problem if a skater were to land on one and crash through the ice.

It takes twenty-four hours to put in a rink completely, from carrying everything needed into the venue to laying it down, setting it up, filling it up, and letting it cure. Only about three of those hours are spent laying down the floor.

One big problem in keeping the ice at the right temperature is the heat produced by the lights used on the stage. When the lights are too hot, the compressor has to work overtime, which risks making the ice too hard. The harder the ice is, the sharper a skater's blades need to be, and the ice tends to shatter when skaters come down from jumps. Keeping ice at the right temperature is a delicate and vitally important process.

Because traveling with a Zamboni is not viable for small rinks, the ice is resurfaced by filling the bad ruts with slush, scraping off the snow, and spreading water over the surface and letting it harden. This has to be accomplished in a short time during intermissions, and the ice may not be totally frozen when skaters first get back on the surface.

Once the performance is over, workers walk onto the ice with twenty-pound poles that have sledgehammers attached to the bottom. They pound the ice and break it up, dumping the pieces outside. To thaw the ice on the stage by heating the coils (and then siphoning off the water) would take a prohibitive amount of time.

Because skating tours will often need portable ice rinks in tour stops just a day apart, Yontz has multiple crews and sets of equipment. He has even produced ice surfaces for outdoor venues in warm locations, such as Las Vegas, Nevada, and at Sea World in San Diego, California.

Z Is for Zamboni

Let's face it: The one star on the ice that everyone loves does not stand upright on two blades. The one star on the ice that is popular from one generation to the next has never been entered in competition, has never won a medal, and has never turned pro. And yet, this star has been seen in practically every ice rink around the world.

Everyone loves the Zamboni Ice Resurfacer. Every skater would love to be adored as much as the public adores the Zamboni. Who among us wouldn't jump at the chance to drive a Zamboni around the rink, preparing the ice surface for the next round of eager skaters? After all, even the best skaters have an occasionally bad performance and don't receive the applause they would hope for after they're done. But the Zamboni . . . well, the Zamboni *always* receives applause when it completes its task.

A miniature Zamboni is even used by Snoopy and Woodstock and their gang of bird friends from the "Peanuts" comic strip, resurfacing the ice of a birdbath in between periods of the troupe's hockey games.

Make no mistake: A Zamboni isn't a glamorous vehicle. It has a top speed of only ten miles per hour. The most popular model weighs 6,580 pounds when empty and 8,780 pounds when full of water. However, glamorous or not, the machines have the distinction of having been featured on their own commemorative ice hockey trading card, right along with all top hockey players in the National Hockey League.

Why the need for Zambonis? Since the time of the first artificially produced ice surfaces in the mid- to late 1800s, ice rink caretakers have attempted to create consistently perfect ice surfaces. "Perfect" ice had to be the right temperature and the right consistency—not too mushy and not too hard. It also had to be smooth and stay smooth. Making ice of the right temperature and consistency was the easy part. The hard part was keeping it smooth after numerous blades cut into the ice, marring the surface and creating etchings in the ice that could catch the skates of later skaters and cause them to fall.

Even when an ice surface is sitting with no skaters, dust and dirt in the air settle on it and have to be removed. Ice rink caretakers always had to make sure their ice surface was not only smooth but also clean. The surface also had to be flat, and a specified ice thickness had to be maintained. And all this sometimes had to be done rather quickly, by hand.

In the days before the Zamboni, resurfacing the ice was a com-

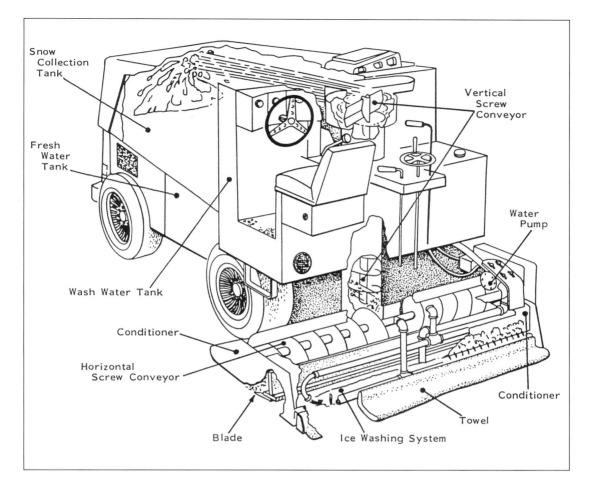

Snow Collection Tank

Fresh Water Tank

Vertical Screw Conveyor

Water Pump

Wash Water Tank

Conditioner

Horizontal Screw Conveyor

Conditioner

Towel

Blade

Ice Washing System

THE INNER WORKINGS OF A ZAMBONI ICE RESURFACER

1. The ice surface is first shaved by the blade.
2. The ice scrapings are picked up by the augerlike horizontal screw conveyor, which transfers the scrapings to the center.
3. The vertical screw conveyor lifts the scrapings to the top and throws them into the snow collection tank.
4. The ice washing system cleans the ice surface, and the water pump sucks up the dirty water into the wash water tank.
5. The towel component of the conditioner spreads the clean water in a thin, even layer.
6. The snow collection tank is emptied after the Zamboni leaves the rink surface. Every several resurfacings, the water in the wash water tank is replaced with clean water.

plex procedure. A group of three to five workers had to scrape down the ice surface with giant hand-pushed scrapers and then get the shavings to the end of the rink for disposal. For a better surface, the rink would occasionally be shaved by a planer towed behind a tractor. After the rink was planed down, the ice surface was washed off with a hose to eliminate dirt. The workers then had to use giant hand-pushed rubber squeegees to push off the dirty water and to smooth the water evenly across the surface so it would form level ice. Then a very thin film of fresh, clean water was flooded over the rink so that the top surface of the ice would cover up any ripples and offer the skaters the best possible skating surface. Needless to say, the act of resurfacing ice was very time-consuming, taking up to two hours.

In 1940, Frank J. Zamboni started down the road to making history. He opened up a rink in Paramount, California, and became increasingly frustrated with the time and labor needed to resurface the ice. Three years later, he began to experiment with a variety of mechanical methods of resurfacing the ice, starting out with a sled towed behind a tractor. The results were less than impressive.

By 1949, Zamboni had developed the Model A Zamboni Ice Resurfacer, a single machine able to pick up a sufficient amount of old ice, spread water across the entire surface, and smooth it out to a glossy sheen, all in one pass.

Essentially, this is how the Zamboni Ice Resurfacer works: A sharp blade shaves the ice down to a depth that is controlled by the operator. The old ice is moved to the center of the blade, where a rotating screw encased in a tube lifts the old ice up and transfers it to a holding tank, where it will stay until disposed of. Clean water is washed across the ice surface, flushing out the dirt left in the exposed grooves of ice. The water, now dirty, is vacuumed up by a pump, passed through a filter, and returned into the water tank. A thin layer of fresh, hot water is spread evenly onto the ice from the very back of the machine. The hot water soaks into the ice, creating a strong bond and a glassy, smooth surface. (The introduction of the hot water onto the frozen ice is why it looks like steam is rising from the surface after the Zamboni passes by.)

No one knows how long it would have taken Frank Zamboni's machine to become world famous if it were not for one little fortunate coincidence. In 1950, Sonja Henie and the cast of her new show, the *Sonja Henie Ice Review*, ended up practicing at Zamboni's Paramount rink. Henie saw the value of the machine and asked Zamboni to build a second one. She took it on tour through the United States, Canada, and Europe, introducing much of the world to the invention. When managers of other ice rinks saw the Zamboni do in minutes—and better—what it took a number of workers hours to do, orders started to arrive in Paramount for more machines. *Ice Capades* soon started to travel with one and gave the machine further exposure.

The Zambonis of today are sleek and stylish compared with the early machines. There is a variety of different models—some are huge, and one very small model is towed behind a garden tractor. Some Zambonis are even made to suck the water off of artificial turf stadium surfaces. There have been more than six thousand shipped in the half century since the first Zamboni Ice Resurfacer was made, and they are now seen throughout the world in about sixty countries. But the machine's main purpose remains as it always has been—to resurface ice surfaces quickly for the benefit of skaters everywhere.

Today's Zambonis are sleek and stylish.

Coaches

THE ONLY TIME THE PUBLIC IS AWARE OF COACHES is when they are seen on televised amateur competitions, sitting next to their students in the "kiss and cry" area as they wait for and finally witness the judges' scores. The coach then often gives the skater either an enthusiastic or sympathetic embrace.

A figure skater not quite competitive on the national level might be able to get by without a lot of support staff. If he is extremely creative himself, he might be able to do his own choreography. He might get by without a costume designer. He might not need an athletic trainer, even though, for his health, one would be recommended. Perhaps he could do without a dance instructor.

But no skater can do without a coach.

Coaches are the unsung heroes of skating. They guide and direct skaters through the first steps on the ice, the first spins, the first jumps, the first competitions, the first successes, and the first failures. Coaches make sure skaters are learning proper technique. Sometimes a skater will think he knows how to do something, and to his way of thinking, how he's doing it is good enough. But coaches look beyond what the skater sees, studying the technique to find and correct basic flaws.

If a skater is learning something not quite right, it may look just fine to most people, but to his coach all sorts of warning signs go up. The coach knows that, without corrections as soon as possible, the skater might be hindered in the future. It's always easier to correct problems in the early stages, before the skater has to unlearn physical muscle memory and mental approaches to executing a specific element.

Coach Frank Carroll shows Michelle Kwan how a proper layback form should feel and look.

The coach, therefore, strives to push the skater as far as possible. Coaches are not paid to be loved. Skaters don't always want to go through the program one more time, or practice a specific jump over and over until they can do it in their sleep, or eat right and get enough rest. Or they might fight the idea of spending time with a choreographer or changing their diet. But with a firm coach directing them and telling them what they *need* to hear and not necessarily what they *want* to hear, they will do what's needed to succeed.

Why is Brian Boitano still coached by Linda Leaver (his only coach since he started skating in group lessons in 1972) whenever he's home? His answer is "Feedback. Something may feel right, but it doesn't look right. Every skater needs someone who knows their skating well enough to say, 'You know, it just doesn't *look* right. The landings are weird, the height isn't good.'"

A good coach knows a skater better than the skater knows himself.

Choreographers

Good coaches also know when they alone cannot take a skater to the next level. The best case in point was after Boitano's 1987 Worlds silver medal finish. Leaver contacted the famous choreographer Sandra Bezic and brought her and Boitano together to work on his style and musical interpretation. In 1987, some felt that Boitano was more interested in nailing a quad jump at Worlds than he was in delivering an artistically balanced program that made an emotional connection with judges and fans.

Bezic has a reputation for reaching into a skater's soul and helping him become one with the music, getting him to put himself into the music, and making him hear the music in a different way from what he thought possible. The progress she made with Boitano in one season was stunning, and as a consequence his 1988 Olympic gold medal performance ranks as one of the most magnificently emotional and creative programs ever delivered on an international stage.

Eight years later, another choreographer accomplished stunning results with a top-level skater. Lori Nichol started working with Michelle Kwan, a student of famed coach Frank Carroll, three years before her 1996 Worlds victory over defending World Champion Lu Chen. She tried to get Michelle to "be herself," to express her inner self rather than imitate others—in other words, to be creative.

When it came time to work on the sophisticated *Salome's Dance* long program of 1996, Nichol played a part of the music and asked Kwan, "Well, what would you do to this music?" Kwan replied, "Well, Brian [Boitano] would do this," proceeding to show Nichol all the things Brian might do with the same music. Then she showed Nichol what Oksana Baiul might do.

Nichol looked at her and asked, "Well, if someone were going to imitate *you*, what would they do?" Kwan thought about that and said, "Well, that's an interesting question." They talked about who *she* was as an artist, exploring how she could find the artist within her. Kwan was learning how to "skate from the heart."

Kwan remembers the experience. "At the beginning I was thinking, What are you talking about? I always wanted to skate like Brian and Oksana, and I finally found out that everyone's original and everyone has their own style. I had to find it from within and not just rely on Lori giving me the movements."

Prior to the experience that changed Kwan's perspective, she simply took the choreographic movements Nichol gave her and did them with no

Choreographer Lori Nichol accomplished stunning results with student Michelle Kwan.

argument. Says Nichol, "I know it sounds strange, but I want the arguments. I want to hear 'I don't like that, I like this,' because then the movements are also coming from her. She's moving how *she* wants to move."

When done right, the process of choreography is one of give-and-take between skater and choreographer. The choreographer may conceive a movement and then show it to the skater, who in turn tries it out and offers another spin on it. They each inspire the other to come up with different ways of interpreting the music.

After a show is put together, a skater may not see the choreographer for quite some time, as he primarily works with his coach during that period to polish the techniques needed to execute the program flawlessly. The skater may run into the choreographer now and then to polish the creative part of the program, to keep it fresh and lively. Coaches and choreographers try hard to work hand in hand, frequently discussing movements with each other. And in Kwan's case, they had her work with a Russian ballet teacher to learn how to convey facial expressions.

In some ways, a choreographer is like an architect who designs a building, while a coach is like a structural engineer who figures out how to build it.

Athletic Trainers

Through the training process, skaters have to take care of their bodies. Their coaches may have them consult with a dietitian to make sure they're eating right, a doctor to make sure they're healthy inside and out, and an athletic trainer to keep them limber and free of pain.

Eric Lang is one of the best-known athletic trainers in the business. Although he works at the Center for Sports Medicine in San Francisco, California, he spends much of the year traveling with *Champions on Ice* and also provides his services at some professional competitions.

Lang discusses some of the problems faced by figure skaters: "Skaters generally experience a lot of lower back problems due to compression from jumps putting a lot of load on the spine. On a blade that's so narrow, there's less area to spread out the compression forces, so more load goes up the spine, causing many lower back problems.

"Skaters on tour for several months—who are on planes and buses more than they're on the ice—experience a lot of problems. Muscles get tight and shortened from being in the sitting position all day, and that can have mechanical consequences for the back. The life of being on tour is more problematic and produces more back injuries than the actual skating."

But preventive maintenance is always preferable to having to fix skaters after they're "broken." Lang teaches skaters "about posture, how to sit, and how to do stretching exercises to stabilize their lower back while they're sitting. I show them how to carry their luggage and other things that seem mundane to most people. Athletes in such great condition don't tend to think about everyday body mechanics."

Lang points out, "It's said that eighty percent of the people in the world are going to have back pain sometime in their lives. Skaters are even more at risk because of all the sitting they do [traveling to performances], and then they go from being totally sedentary to doing explosive, ballistic activity on the ice where the compression forces are so great."

And for the young skaters out there who wonder what sort of advice Lang might give them: "They should do hip flexor flexibility and upper trunk/torso–arm strength exercises to help rotations and jumps. They should work with weights for basic strength and not forget to do lots of stretching."

Managers: Don't Leave Home without One

Skating is more than an art form and an athletic endeavor—it's a business. With all the opportunities open to skaters today, they need someone to help them take care of their business interests so they can concentrate on keeping their skating in top form.

Every top-level skater needs a manager to pull everything together. The manager sometimes is also her agent, and sometimes the manager coordinates other agents on the skater's behalf. There is a difference between a sports manager and an agent, but it's a distinction that is often lost. While the manager coordinates agents and oversees a skater's overall career, agents tend to be specialists in a particular field, such as commercials, book deals, and competitions or exhibitions. Sometimes a single person, a manager/agent, will do it all. For the sake of this explanation, let's assume that the word *manager* also means manager/agent.

Michael Rosenberg, president of Marco Entertainment, is one of the best-known managers in the business. His clients have included numerous Olympic and World Champions and other skaters who are less well known. Marco Entertainment and IMG (International Management Group) are the two best-known management companies for figure skaters.

Rosenberg points out that a star figure skater's basic earning potential goes far beyond the competitive ice rink. The skater will also have many opportunities to earn income from tours, TV shows, specials, commercials, books, and other merchandise. Once she becomes famous, she needs someone to intervene for her, field calls from interested parties, initiate calls to possible interested parties, and establish contacts between those parties and the skater.

Someone like Rosenberg will negotiate the contract and work out details such as how much the skater is going to get paid for her services. A manager also arranges for travel and lodging, makes sure the skater will have a proper dressing room, and finds out where the skater will be in the show order and even in the final bow. Afterward, the manager collects the money being paid to the skater and forwards it to the skater's account.

Periodically, the manager discusses with the skater inquiries that

were received and helps her decide which opportunities are in her best interest. It is important to remember that the manager does not make decisions for the skater. The skater is always in charge of what she will and won't do. The manager just points out the pluses and minuses of each opportunity and makes recommendations when asked.

In short, the skater concerns herself with working with the people who can help her be successful on the ice—her coach, choreographer, costume designer, athletic trainer, and dance instructor. The skater is in charge of concentrating on her technique, musical numbers, total look, and technical proficiency. The manager concerns himself with everything else.

Skating Explodes on TV

Since the 1994 Winter Olympics in Lillehammer, Norway, the media have become extremely interested in figure skating. It seems hardly a week goes by without a skating special on television. During the late fall, winter, and early spring months, one might find oneself having to choose which skating events to watch live and which to tape for later viewing. It wasn't always this way.

According to Michael Rosenberg of Marco Entertainment, skating has always been a popular sport: It combines glamour, sport, and art into one package. It is appealing because of its beauty, strength, suspense, speed, and drama. But it was not a sport that garnered overwhelming interest from the public.

In 1988, the Calgary, Alberta, Winter Olympics offered the public two highly publicized matchups, dubbed by the media the Battle of the Brians (Boitano versus Orser, both doing military programs) and Duel of the Carmens (Katarina Witt versus Debi Thomas, both doing music from the Georges Bizet opera). The public took an interest in the matchups. How could it not? Listening to the media hype, one could be forgiven for mistaking the two impending head-to-head matchups for upcoming professional wrestling bouts.

And in the hype, one simple fact was lost: Skaters don't skate "against" one another. They go out, do their best, and are supposed to be judged by how well or poorly they do, not by how well or poorly someone else skates.

But the public ate up the hype, and for the first time ever figure skating got the highest ratings of any Olympic sport on American television. Figure skating tours and shows started selling out their seating capacity, doing big, big business. The television networks saw that skating was great drama, perfect for TV.

In 1991, American Kristi Yamaguchi won the World Championship, making her the leading contender for the 1992 Winter Olympic crown in Albertville, France. This heightened interest among American viewers, and after she became the first American woman to win the Olympic Ladies' Championship since Dorothy Hamill in 1976, interest in skating tours and skating on TV was further stimulated. Suddenly there were five skating tours crossing the continent instead of two, and more hours of prime time skating could be seen on TV.

In 1994, the dam burst.

First was the clubbing of Nancy Kerrigan's knee at a practice session at the 1994 USFSA Championships, followed by the suspicions that teammate Tonya Harding was somehow involved, the eventual confirmation of those suspicions, and Harding's legal fight to stay on the U.S. Olympic Team. This was better than the most tawdry soap opera. The network evening news followed the story breathlessly as the Olympics approached, and the world watched not only the noose starting to close around Harding but also Kerrigan's rapid recuperation, painful physical rehabilitation, and her triumphant return to training on the ice.

By the time the Olympics began, a few weeks after the clubbing incident, the world was worked up by the suspense and impending on-ice matchup of Harding and Kerrigan. The public knew what restaurants Harding was eating in and what stores Kerrigan was shopping in. They became two of the most watched people on the planet.

Finally, after all the ballyhoo, the night arrived of the Ladies' short programs. TV viewership went through the roof, placing fourth among all American television broadcasts ever. The Ladies' long program was the sixth highest-rated TV broadcast in history, with an estimated one billion people watching worldwide.

Since 1994, televised skating events are said to grab higher ratings than many other big sporting events—higher than the Masters in golf, Wimbledon in tennis, the All-Star Game and World Series in baseball, the National Hockey League All-Star Game, and the National Basketball Association Finals. Figure skating has become the second most popular spectator sport in the United States, behind football.

American interest was high for the 1998 Winter Olympics,

because two Americans—Michelle Kwan and Tara Lipinski, each with a World Championship title to her name—were going for the Ladies' gold. And an American former World Champion—Todd Eldredge—and Canadian World Champion Elvis Stojko were going for the Men's gold. Four of the biggest names in amateur skating, and all were from North America.

But some of the suspense was missing from the Nagano, Japan, festivities. Because of the time zone differences between the United States and Japan, the televised events were broadcast on a tape-delayed basis. Hours before the skating broadcasts, results had been posted on the Internet and announced on radio and TV. Ratings suffered tremendously.

In the long run, however, the TV ratings from the 2002 Winter Olympics in Salt Lake City, Utah, have the potential to be stronger than those from the Lillehammer games. Because of the location—within the United States—the competitions will be shown live, not tape-delayed. Advertisers can expect to pay top dollar to have their names and products tied in to the events.

Media Frenzy

Canadian Gia Guddat has made quite a name for herself as a professional, as a designer of skating clothes, and as a skating teacher. She has also been one of the biggest hits, with sometime partner Gary Beacom, on the extensive tour now known as *Champions on Ice*. She has perfected the art of skating on four skates (two on the feet and two on the hands) at once, an innovation one has to see in person even to begin to comprehend.

Like all skaters, she has witnessed the media frenzy and sometimes the overenthusiasm of some fans. But her perspective is different. Because she was never on TV as an amateur and doesn't compete in televised professional contests, she can walk through a crowd of cameras or fans and not be noticed. This gives her a chance to observe without being observed.

According to Guddat, the media image of a skater is now more important than the skating itself. Nicole Bobek was a victim of media image making, portrayed for some time as a "wild girl out of control." Those who knew Bobek realized that wasn't true, but in the time after the Harding/Kerrigan incident, someone needed to fill in the media vacuum. Says Guddat, "[Bobek] just can't go out and skate anymore. It's a full-time job for her to try to project the right, more accurate image of what she's really like. She has to be careful of how she dresses, how she acts, and what she says. All the skaters are starting to face that. I think the skaters have a more difficult role now in that what they do on the ice may not be the major story once the media gets hold of it."

Indeed, it seems that we are beginning to know almost too much about the thoughts and deeds of our favorite skaters. Guddat feels that "the media blitz over the Tonya/Nancy affair gave people too much access to skaters' personal lives, which opened the door to people wanting to know everything about skaters behind-the-scenes."

Perhaps there has never been a more compelling sports image, outside an actual competition, than the horrific sight of Nancy Kerrigan crying out "Why me?" while sitting on the hallway floor after the unprecedented attack after her 1994 U.S. Nationals practice session. It still would have been a major story, but the presence of a video camera—at the moment when Kerrigan thought her lifelong dreams of Olympic success had just been stolen from her—assured that millions would suddenly pay added attention to the goings-on in figure skating.

And if one skater had some goons turn on one of her competitors, wouldn't it be likely that the entire activity is full of backbiting and ill wishes?

Well, to be truthful, no.

To spend any time with skaters and witness how they talk to one another over meals and in the halls on a tour such as *Champions on Ice* is to realize that the rivalries one has heard about are nothing but fabrications. As Guddat points out, although the skaters are competitive, "they're competitive on the ice. They want to put on their best performance. The competitions are healthy, and the skaters don't carry the competition backstage. Everybody has a good time. Everybody's friendly and everybody's joking."

But a TV commercial extolling the merits of skaters' being best friends wouldn't encourage many non-hard-core skating fans to watch skating on TV. That's why you'll often hear commercials using words that sound more like they're describing armed conflict among warring nations, such as the two slogans mentioned previously, the Battle of the Brians and the Duel of the Carmens.

After the 1994 Winter Olympics, the media, which had put Kerrigan in the limelight every day after the attack, seemed to do an about-face on the type of exposure she got. Everything she did and said was big news—except now the "big" news portrayed her in less than positive terms.

Kerrigan left the Olympics before the closing ceremony and flew to Disney World for a parade in her honor. She had decided that the past was past; now she had an opportunity to get on with her life and enjoy her business opportunities, in which Disney played a large role. On the float she was riding, the microphone picked up Kerrigan commenting, "This is the corniest thing I ever did." She wasn't criticizing Disney or the parade, and yet the comment was broadcast on all the networks. More small "big" news. According to Kerrigan, she never wore any of her medals once a competition's medal ceremony was over, since she had been taught when she was young "that to wear my medals would be showing off, as if saying, 'Everyone look at what I did.'" The comment that got sent around the world was in reference to being told to wear her medal on the float. The simple comment was broadcast on news programs and became the butt of jokes on a variety of talk shows.

Yet, despite their obsession with skaters' personal lives and the willingness to treat small, inconsequential comments and events as major stories, the media are the best friend figure skating has ever had. Through the media's efforts, millions who will never see a live skating competition or exhibition get a chance to enjoy the artistry and athleticism of one of the world's greatest and most remarkable sports.

Skaters as Rock Stars

Top-level figure skaters and rock stars do have a few things in common. Both are at the top of their profession and perform in large arenas in front of thousands of screaming fans. And both have trouble slipping out in public and enjoying some privacy when desired.

One of the problems skaters encounter in this age of media saturation is that, on occasion, fans get carried away with their enthusiasm. Usually this is innocent enough, sometimes involving fans' waiting outside arenas for autographs. Often skaters will pay their respects by going to the area where the fans are and signing a number of autographs before they have to move on to their hotel or next destination. The people who run the shows will sometimes create an area, cordoned off from the skaters, where fans can wait, hoping for their favorite skater to come by. If you've been to one of these post-performance sessions, you've heard all the screaming that happens when skaters walk out to sign autographs or just to say hi.

On rare occasions, skaters have felt threatened by someone who did not know where to draw the line. There was a famous stalking case in which a skater had to go to court to protect herself from a fan. When another skater hired a bodyguard in the early 1990s, supposedly to protect herself from rowdy fans, people scoffed. Today, though, the idea appears to have been ahead of its time.

Guddat has seen some fans display a lack of respect for certain skaters' personal spaces, stating that "some of the skaters have to look over their shoulders all the time." She's seen fans go up to skaters in restaurants to seek autographs, not really caring if the skater is trying to eat in peace or carry on a conversation. Guddat observes, "It's almost too hard for the skaters to go out and sign a few program books because other fans will . . . demand the skater also sign their book. They are really offended if the skaters don't spend an hour or two after the show signing autographs.

"Once they step off the ice, they're still as big a star as they are on the ice and every bit as much still in the spotlight. It's kind of getting to the point where they're being treated like rock stars."

Someday, perhaps, we'll talk about rock stars being treated like figure skaters.

part **Five**

An Armchair Guide

The Mystique of Judging

TO THOSE WHO AREN'T JUDGING SKATING PERFOR-mances, the art and science of judging often seem to make as much sense as the deepest mysteries of the universe. One is often left to ponder, "Why did they put that skater ahead of the other skater?" Or, one might think, "I could have done a better job in picking the right skater."

Yes, judges are human. They do make mistakes. And sometimes, though not as often as they used to be, they are victims of national bias. But, for the most part, they are ordinary people called upon to do a most out-of-the-ordinary thing—separate themselves from the emotions of the fans as they watch skaters going through their routines, intensely analyze every performance down to the smallest detail, and then give it a number.

Judges rate each skater based on the performance delivered at the time—they don't rank a skater order-wise with the other skaters. The scores of all the judges combined ultimately decide what the order will be. Well, sort of. Something called ordinals seems to confuse a majority of fans.

Figure skating is unique to the world of winter sports. In speed skating, downhill skiing, and cross-country skiing, the fastest performance wins the gold. In ski jumping, points for the distance jumped are combined with style points, the score given for how graceful the jump was. The athlete with the most points wins.

In figure skating, higher points are generally better than lower points, but only if they translate to lower ordinals. What ordinals mean is that the score a judge gives each skater is important only when compared with the scores the same judge gave to other skaters. Whoever receives the highest score from a given judge in a particular competition wins that judge's "card" with an ordinal of 1. But actual scores are irrelevant. All that matters on each judge's card is the placement order of each skater.

If two skaters tie score-wise, the lower ordinal would go to the one with the higher Presentation mark. (It used to be that the Technical Merit marks broke a tie, but the ISU decided that too much emphasis was being placed on jumps. This is how the tie between Oksana Baiul and Nancy Kerrigan was broken—in Baiul's favor—at the 1994 Winter Olympics.)

However, that's not all there is to ordinals. The skater with a *majority* of first-place ordinals will win that segment of the competition. The skater with a *majority* of second-place ordinals will be in second, and so on.

Sometimes a skater will see his position drop *two* placements after just *one* other score is announced, a score whose ordinals were not as good as what he had been awarded. It's possible that a single new score can turn everything upside down. It's all in how the ordinals compare, and not just *near* the end of the competition but at the very, very end.

This is why computers are used to figure out the ordinal rankings. In the days before computers and calculators, this was all done by hand. Imagine how time-consuming that must have been, because each new score could juggle the order, and every ordinal from every judge had to be factored in.

One more thing needs to be considered: After each stage of a competition, the placement of each skater is multiplied by a factored value representing the percentage of the total represented by that stage of the competition. For example, in singles skating (and Pairs), the short program is worth one-third (33.3 percent) of the total score and the long program/free skate is worth two-thirds (66.7 percent). Each skater's placement after the short program is multiplied by a factored placement of .5. Their placement after the long program is multiplied by a factored placement of 1.0 (because two-thirds and 1.0 is twice what one-third and .5 is). At the end, the factored placements are added together for every skater. The skater with lowest factored placements wins.

If you still don't understand how the system works, don't worry. You're far from alone. This is why there is increased talk of eliminating the entire ordinal system, so that when one skater beats another skater, their position relative to each other won't change, no matter how the other skaters place.

Sometimes a judge will be suspended by the ISU for making a big mistake or for exhibiting obvious nationalism, purposely putting skaters from his own country above skaters of other countries when it is clearly wrong to do so. At other times, a judge might merely be reprimanded for his error, if the ISU feels he made an honest mistake. The incident mentioned earlier, about a Soviet judge "propping up" Alexandr Fadeev in 1986 by giving him marks of 5.8 and 5.9 while other judges scored him in the 5.4 to 5.6 range, resulted in a suspension for nationalistic bias.

Although they sit right next to the ice, judges don't always have the best seats from which to view a competition. Because they sit in a straight row along the side of the ice, the judge farthest away from where a skater is at the time may have difficulty seeing exactly what is happening. Sometimes a judge will miss a quick fall or bobble in its entirety because she happens to be looking down at her judge's sheet to mark something when the incident happens. And because judges don't have access to instant replay, they can't make up what they miss.

In the past, good but unknown skaters have sometimes skated quite well on the national or world level, but have not received good marks. Sometimes good well-known skaters have skated poorly and gotten very good scores, making it seem as if familiarity were a hidden criteria on the judging sheets.

* * *

What Judges Look For

Each year, the ISU provides all judges with a suggested list of deductions for maneuvers that are executed less than perfectly or are omitted altogether. In a recent competitive season, a jump, jump combination, flying spin, spin, or spin combination that was performed incorrectly would result in a deduction ranging from .1 to .4, the range allowing for the judge to deduct less for small bobbles and more for large ones. Total omission of the above maneuvers, if they were required elements in a singles short program, was a flat .5 deduction. It's rare for skaters to omit a move completely, the sequence of moves being so ingrained in their muscle memory. But when it happens, it's disastrous in the short program. (If skaters omit a move in the long program, they can try it again later on without penalty.)

There are other suggested deductions for other maneuvers, and Pairs have their own list of deductions and omissions. For example, among their list of deductions, a less-than-perfect lift, twist lift, solo jump, solo spin, pair spin combination, or death spiral would earn a deduction in the range of .1 to .4, while a total omission was a deduction of .5.

While fans respond to the drama of jumps and spins for single skaters and lifts and throws for Pairs, the judges have to analyze things the average fan doesn't pay much attention to—the quality of the maneuver, good technique, and the cleanness of the takeoff and landing, among other things. They must also take into consideration the difficulty of the maneuvers. A skater having problems on a simple maneuver is going to be scored lower than a skater having problems on extremely difficult maneuvers. For instance, a missed quad jump won't count off as much as a missed double jump. Falling on an easy jump, especially in the short program of required elements, can sound a death knell to a skater's hopes.

Judges carefully study stroking technique across the ice: Is the skater gliding gracefully or is she attacking the ice in an inappropriate fashion? They look for proper leg position in stroking and spins. Some world-level skaters still have problems with achieving proper leg positions because they weren't taught correctly from the beginning. Judges take into consideration the quality and variety of the skater's footwork: Is she employing several techniques, or does she do everything the same way? Do spins stay in one spot as they should, or does the skater "travel" down the ice while attempting to spin in one spot?

Much of judging is objective, based not on opinion but on fact. The maneuvers are either clean or they aren't. The jumps are hit or they're missed. But some elements of a skating performance can be judged only subjectively. This is where the Presentation marks come in. The judges ask themselves questions such as, How is the music interpreted? Is the music appropriate for the skater? Does the interpretation bring something unique to the music? Does the skater put her soul into the presentation? Does the judge feel a special connection between the skater and the music?

Skaters must be in great physical condition, certainly among the world's top athletes. But they must possess a further quality—one that can't be measured by muscle mass, aerobic conditioning, or flexibility. They must have in their soul the ability to interpret music and give it life on the rink. The goal of every skater, coach, and choreographer is to let the music dictate the action.

To score high, skaters have to make the judges "feel" their performance. Judges won't "feel" the performance if it doesn't have a sense of flow, if it feels chopped up. The entire routine must seem as if it has a beginning of anticipation, a middle of wonder, and an ending of awe. If jumps are just thrown in wherever they land, one after another, and it appears that the elements of the routine could be switched around any which way without affecting the continuity, then the skater has failed to create an appropriate sense of flow. But a good routine with good flow will give the impression that the elements are in the order they are because they couldn't possibly be in any other order. Everything is so right that to put something else in or take something out would be sacrilege.

A fall on a jump, while devastating to the Technical Merit marks, may not affect the Presentation marks at all, especially if the flow of the program isn't affected. However, if the skater interrupts the program or even skates around in a daze for a while after a hard fall, then the Presentation marks would be affected because the flow of the program was damaged.

When a skating performance flows from beginning to end, it turns into something far beyond a mere routine—it turns into a work of art.

Short and Long Programs

In the short program, singles and Pairs skate for no longer than two minutes and forty seconds. The judges' first mark is for Required Elements, and the second mark is for Presentation. The list of Required (technical) Elements each year is dictated by the ISU. For singles skaters, the list dictates which jumps, combination jumps, and footwork sequences (sometimes called "straight line sequence") are to be performed by all skaters, to the music of their choice. For Pairs skaters, the list specifies which jumps, spins, lifts, death spirals, and footwork sequences are to be performed. These elements are to be worked into the music in an artistic fashion.

Technical points are deducted for incorrectly performed elements, and any missed elements cannot be attempted later in the short program without a mandatory penalty, in contrast to the long program, where skaters are allowed to throw in another attempt at an element they missed earlier.

Ice Dancers don't have a short program. Instead, they start their part of the competition with a compulsory dance program, usually requiring them to skate two dances from specific styles that were assigned by the ISU before the season began, such as fox-trot, tango, blues, or flamenco. They receive two sets of marks, for Technique and for Timing/Expression. Then they move into the original dance phase, where they perform to music of their own choice to a specified style of dance. This program is only two minutes in length and is often referred to as the "original set pattern dance," as the skaters perform to a very specific dance pattern that they created themselves. Judges' marks are given for Composition and Presentation. Instead of a long program, Ice Dancers skate a free dance of four minutes in length and are judged on Technical Merit and Presentation, just like singles skaters and Pairs.

Compulsories count for 20 percent of the total score (10 percent for each compulsory dance), the original dance counts for 30 percent, and the free dance counts for the remaining 50 percent.

Curiously, the Men and Pairs have a free skate time limit of four and a half minutes, while the Ladies have to skate only for four minutes. The long program has fewer rules than the short program, with no required elements. Think of it as a blank canvas upon which the skaters are free to do whatever they wish. But if a skater doesn't perform the same feats as the other skaters, then he will receive a lower score. That's why whenever someone perfects a new, more difficult jump, all the other skaters feel obligated to put one in their repertoire as soon as possible.

Often, only a certain number of skaters will move on to the long program. In the long program, skaters are broken into groups of no more than six for singles and four for Pairs and Ice Dancing. The skaters then warm up on the ice with other skaters who are in their group.

Skaters draw for position within each group, with the lower-placing skaters from the short program taking the ice in the earlier groups and the higher-placing skaters taking the ice in the later groups. There has long been speculation on the value of skating last in the final group. Some feel that judges hold out on giving their highest possible score—even for what seems to be a perfect performance—to skaters who aren't on last, just in case the last skater comes out and delivers a performance that is even better. Judges want to have some "head room" to work with, which is gone if they give perfect scores out too early.

By having the skaters draw for position, everyone has an equal chance of skating last. Of course, judges will tell you that it makes no difference where someone skates—they'll get whatever score they deserve no matter what order they skate in. So, maybe the thought that it is better to be on last is a myth.

HOW TO RECOGNIZE SELECTED JUMPS, SPINS, AND PAIRS MOVES

JUMPS

Edge jumps *do not utilize the toe pick of the foot opposite to the takeoff foot to assist the jump.*

axel   an edge jump launched while moving forward, making it easy to identify. Requires an extra half rotation to land backward. (A double axel is really 2 ½ rotations; a triple is 3 ½.) Takeoff: forward outside edge. Landing: back outside edge of opposite foot.

loop   an edge jump launched while moving backward. Takeoff: back outside edge. Landing: back outside edge of same foot.

salchow   an edge jump launched while moving backward. Takeoff: back inside edge. Landing: back outside edge of opposite foot.

Toe jumps *utilize the toe pick of the foot opposite to the takeoff foot to assist the jump.*

flip   a toe jump launched while moving backward. Takeoff: back inside edge. Landing: back outside edge of opposite foot.

lutz   a toe jump launched while moving backward. The rotation is in the opposite direction of the broad curved approach. Takeoff: back outside edge. Landing: back outside edge of opposite foot.

toe loop   a toe jump launched while moving backward. Takeoff: back outside edge. Landing: back outside edge of same foot.

SPINS

camel   a variety of spins where the body and free leg typically remain parallel to the ice

combination   any number of spins combined with no stop in between. Feet and body positions are changed during the continuous spin, ideally with no loss of speed.

layback   a spin in which the back is arched, the head is tilted back, and the free foot is lifted behind the skater. The Biellmann Spin is a type of layback spin.

scratch   a spin in which the body is straight, with arms pulled in tightly for speed. When this is done quickly, the skater becomes a blur.

sit   a variety of spins where the body appears to be sitting while rotating, with the free leg extended in any number of positions

PAIRS MOVES

death spiral   The man spins in one place while holding the hand of the woman. She glides around him on one foot, with her back and head close to the ice.

hand-to-hand loop lift   The woman starts in front, facing the same direction as the man. He lifts her overhead, and she continues to face the same direction in a sitting position, supported by the man from below, with her hands behind her.

hydrant lift   The woman is thrown over the head of the man while he's skating backward. He turns half a rotation and catches the woman, who is now facing him.

lateral twist   The man throws the woman overhead. She rotates in the air and is caught by the man and set back on the ice.

platter lift   The man lifts the woman overhead with his hands on her hips. She remains parallel to the ice, facing his back.

split twist   The man throws the woman into the air. She goes into a split position before rotating vertically to the ice, and is caught by the man and set back on the ice.

star lift   The man lifts the woman overhead by her hips, from his side. Her legs are in a scissors position. One of her hands may touch his shoulder, or she may stay hands-free.

throw jump   The man assists the woman in becoming airborne. Before landing backward, she completes up to three revolutions. Common throw jumps include the throw double axel, throw triple salchow, and triple toe loop.

toe overhead lift The man lifts the woman overhead from his side, with assistance from her toe pick. She enters the overhead split position from behind his head, facing the same direction as he.

twist lift The man lifts the woman overhead while both are skating backward. She's tossed in the air and rotates any number of rotations before being caught by the man and set back on the ice.

The World Figure Skating Museum and Hall of Fame

THE WORLD FIGURE SKATING MUSEUM AND HALL OF FAME IS a not-for-profit facility dedicated to preserving figure skating's past and present, offering fans a glimpse into all aspects of the sport. The museum is located next to the United States Figure Skating Association's National Headquarters in Colorado Springs, Colorado.

Sponsored by the USFSA, the museum is recognized by the International Skating Union as the official repository of the history and records of figure skating. It also contains the World Figure Skating Hall of Fame and the United States Figure Skating Hall of Fame.

The museum contains the world's largest collection of figure skating art and memorabilia, and skating artifacts from the past four centuries. The collection of historical documents and reference materials from skating's earliest days includes insights on the personalities that made skating what it is, as well as films and videos of skating performances. There is also a large collection of skating costumes, skates, medals, trophies, photos, posters, show programs, magazines, and collectors' pins.

The museum is located at 20 First Street, Colorado Springs, CO 80906. For more information, phone 719-635-5200. On the Internet, the museum's Web page can be found at http://www.worldskatingmuseum.org.

USFSA

The United States Figure Skating Association (USFSA) is the national governing body of amateur skating in the United States. It was founded in 1921 with only seven charter member clubs; there are now about five hundred skate club members and about 125,000 individual members, consisting of athletes and supporters. Membership more than doubled in the ten years prior to 1998. The USFSA is a member of both the International Skating Union and the United States Olympic Committee. About 1,250 events are sanctioned by the USFSA each year.

Skating Magazine is the official publication of the USFSA. In-depth articles include a look at various skating personalities as well as articles on health and fitness. Ticket information and schedules for USFSA events are a regular feature, as are extensive results of various regional, national, and world competitions.

Each year, the USFSA distributes several hundred thousand dollars in athlete grants and assistance programs to members of the United States World Team as well as to juvenile-level skaters. The USFSA also processes at least five thousand skill tests per month, administered to skaters throughout the country so that the skaters can move up to the next level of proficiency.

The USFSA maintains the USFSA Memorial Fund, offering financial assistance to skaters in need. The fund was founded in memory of those who perished in the 1961 airplane crash on the way to the World Championships.

Sports science is an increasingly important part of USFSA activity. At the USFSA Sports Science and Medicine Camp, skaters are educated about how to enhance their athletic performance and prevent injuries. They learn about sports medicine, warm-up techniques, psychology, nutrition, biomechanics, exercise physiology, strength training, and conditioning.

The USFSA's National Headquarters is at 20 First Street, Colorado Springs, CO 80906. For more information, phone 719-635-5200 or send e-mail to USFSA1@aol.com. USFSA Online can be accessed through America Online. Keyword: USFSA. On the Internet, look for the USFSA home page at http://www.usfsa.org.

CFSA

Figure skating is one of the oldest sports in Canada and a national pastime. Reflecting this, the Canadian Figure Skating Association (CFSA, known to French-speaking Canadians as Association canadienne de patinage artistique) is the largest figure skating governing body in the world. The national governing body of amateur figure skating in Canada has more than 190,000 members and at least 1,465 member clubs.

The CFSA is a member of the International Skating Union and selects the Canadian World and Olympic figure skating teams, with approval from the Canadian Olympic Association.

Approximately 74 percent of CFSA members are registered in recreational skating programs, and 17 percent actively take CFSA tests to move up to higher levels of competition—these test skaters average fourteen years of age. The CFSA offers a variety of skating programs for skaters from preschool age through adulthood, as well as testing programs on a variety of levels.

The CFSA distributes funding to approximately one thousand athletes each year. Athlete Trust Grants are available to the top eight novice, junior, and senior entrants at the Canadian Championships. In addition, the CFSA provides standards, training, and certification for coaches and judges.

The CFSA's National Office is located at 1600 James Naismith Drive, Gloucester, Ontario K1B 5N4, Canada. A mail order department provides publications, jewelry, music, and other items of interest. For more information, phone 613-748-5635, or access the Internet home page at http://www.cfsa.ca.

American Skating World

The first issue of *American Skating World* was published in 1981, promoting figure skating at a time when the mass media had not yet discovered the sport to any great degree. Since then, this monthly, year-round, independent publication has brought fans closer to the action of figure skating, taking them behind the scenes with articles about all major competitions, exhibitions, and tours.

Reviews are offered of the latest skating books, videos, and skating tours. A number of interviews are presented each month with top skaters, as well as those not yet in the limelight. Regular features look at the inside workings of judging and the latest developments in health and fitness. Other regular features include classified ads, an extensive list of upcoming skating events throughout the world, and a listing of skating events to be televised.

American Skating World also annually presents the World Professional Skater of the Year award.

American Skating World is located at 1816 Brownsville Road, Pittsburgh, PA 15210-3908. For more information, phone 800-245-6280. Outside the United States, call 412-885-7600. For subscription information, you may also send an e-mail to subscription@americansk8world.com. Or, visit its Web page at http://www.americansk8world.com.

Other Web Pages

1. International Skating Union
   http://virtserve.interhop.net/~isu
2. United States Olympic Committee
   http://www.olympic-usa.org
3. Champions on Ice
   http://www.championsonice.com/index.html
4. Stars on Ice
   http://www.starsonice.com

OLYMPIC AND WORLD FIGURE SKATING CHAMPIONS

WORLD FIGURE SKATING CHAMPIONS

Men/Ladies/Pairs/Ice Dancing

1896	Gilbert Fuchs, Germany
1897	Gustav Hugel, Austria
1898	Henning Grenander, Sweden
1899	Gustav Hugel, Austria
1900	Gustav Hugel, Austria
1901	Ulrich Salchow, Sweden
1902	Ulrich Salchow, Sweden
1903	Ulrich Salchow, Sweden
1904	Ulrich Salchow, Sweden
1905	Ulrich Salchow, Sweden
1906	Gilbert Fuchs, Germany
	Madge Syers, Great Britain
1907	Ulrich Salchow, Sweden
	Madge Syers, Great Britain
1908	Ulrich Salchow, Sweden
	Lily Kronberger, Hungary
	Anna Hubler and Heinrich Burger, Germany
1909	Ulrich Salchow, Sweden
	Lily Kronberger, Hungary
	Phyllis Johnson and James Johnson, Great Britain
1910	Ulrich Salchow, Sweden
	Lily Kronberger, Hungary
	Anna Hubler and Heinrich Burger, Germany
1911	Ulrich Salchow, Sweden
	Lily Kronberger, Hungary
	Ludowika Eilers and Walter Jakobsson, Finland
1912	Fritz Kachler, Austria
	Opika von Horvath, Hungary
	Phyllis Johnson and James Johnson, Great Britain
1913	Fritz Kachler, Austria
	Opika von Horvath, Hungary
	Helene Engelmann and Karl Mejstrik, Austria

1914	Gosta Sandahl, Sweden
	Opika von Horvath, Hungary
	Ludowika Jakobsson and Walter Jakobsson, Finland
1915–1921	No championship held (World War I)
1922	Gillis Grafstrom, Sweden
	Herma Plank-Szabo, Austria
	Helene Engelmann and Alfred Berger, Austria
1923	Fritz Kachler, Austria
	Herma Plank-Szabo, Austria
	Ludowika Jakobsson and Walter Jakobsson, Finland
1924	Gillis Grafstrom, Sweden
	Herma Plank-Szabo, Austria
	Helene Engelmann and Alfred Berger, Austria
1925	Willy Boeckl, Austria
	Herma Plank-Szabo, Austria
	Herma Jaross-Szabo and Ludwig Wrede, Austria
1926	Willy Boeckl, Austria
	Herma Jaross-Szabo, Austria
	Andrée Joly and Pierre Brunet, France
1927	Willy Boeckl, Austria
	Sonja Henie, Norway
	Herma Jaross-Szabo and Ludwig Wrede, Austria
1928	Willy Boeckl, Austria
	Sonja Henie, Norway
	Andrée Joly and Pierre Brunet, France
1929	Gillis Grafstrom, Sweden
	Sonja Henie, Norway
	Lilly Scholz and Otto Kaiser, Austria
1930	Karl Schafer, Austria
	Sonja Henie, Norway
	Andrée Joly and Pierre Brunet, France
1931	Karl Schafer, Austria
	Sonja Henie, Norway
	Emilie Rotter and Laszlo Szollas, Hungary

1932   Karl Schafer, Austria
        Sonja Henie, Norway
        Andrée Joly and Pierre Brunet,
            France
1933   Karl Schafer, Austria
        Sonja Henie, Norway
        Emilie Rotter and Laszlo Szollas,
            Hungary
1934   Karl Schafer, Austria
        Sonja Henie, Norway
        Emilie Rotter and Laszlo Szollas,
            Hungary
1935   Karl Schafer, Austria
        Sonja Henie, Norway
        Emilie Rotter and Laszlo Szollas,
            Hungary
1936   Karl Schafer, Austria
        Sonja Henie, Norway
        Maxi Herber and Ernst Baier,
            Germany
1937   Felix Kaspar, Austria
        Cecilia Colledge, Great Britain
        Maxi Herber and Ernst Baier,
            Germany
1938   Felix Kaspar, Austria
        Megan Taylor, Great Britain
        Maxi Herber and Ernst Baier,
            Germany
1939   Graham Sharp, Great Britain
        Megan Taylor, Great Britain
        Maxi Herber and Ernst Baier,
            Germany
1940–1946 No championship held (World War II)

Note: Prior to 1940, the Men's, Ladies', and
Pairs World Championships were often held in
different cities.

1947   **Stockholm, Sweden**
        Hans Gerschwiler, Switzerland
        Barbara Ann Scott, Canada
        Micheline Lannoy and Pierre
            Baugniet, Belgium
1948   **Davos, Switzerland**
        Richard Button, U.S.A.
        Barbara Ann Scott, Canada

        Micheline Lannoy and Pierre
            Baugniet, Belgium
1949   **Paris, France**
        Richard Button, U.S.A.
        Alena Vrzanova, Czechoslovakia
        Andrea Kekesy and Ede Kiraly,
            Hungary
1950   **London, Great Britain**
        Richard Button, U.S.A.
        Alena Vrzanova, Czechoslovakia
        Karol Kennedy and Peter Kennedy,
            U.S.A.
1951   **Milan, Italy**
        Richard Button, U.S.A.
        Jeannette Altwegg, Great Britain
        Ria Falk and Paul Falk, Federal
            Republic of Germany
1952   **Paris, France** (first year for Ice
            Dancing)
        Richard Button, U.S.A.
        Jacqueline du Bief, France
        Ria Falk and Paul Falk, Federal
            Republic of Germany
        Jean Westwood and Lawrence
            Demmy, Great Britain
1953   **Davos, Switzerland**
        Hayes A. Jenkins, U.S.A.
        Tenley Albright, U.S.A.
        Jennifer Nicks and John Nicks,
            Great Britain
        Jean Westwood and Lawrence
            Demmy, Great Britain
1954   **Oslo, Norway**
        Hayes A. Jenkins, U.S.A.
        Gundi Busch, Federal Republic of
            Germany
        Frances Dafoe and Norris Bowden,
            Canada
        Jean Westwood and Lawrence
            Demmy, Great Britain
1955   **Vienna, Austria**
        Hayes A. Jenkins, U.S.A.
        Tenley Albright, U.S.A.
        Frances Dafoe and Norris Bowden,
            Canada

Jean Westwood and Lawrence
Demmy, Great Britain

1956 **Garmisch, Federal Republic of
Germany**
Hayes A. Jenkins, U.S.A.
Carol Heiss, U.S.A.
Elizabeth Schwarz and Kurt Oppelt,
Austria
Pamela Weight and Paul Thomas,
Great Britain

1957 **Colorado Springs, U.S.A.**
David Jenkins, U.S.A.
Carol Heiss, U.S.A.
Barbara Wagner and Robert Paul,
Canada
June Markham and Courtney Jones,
Great Britain

1958 **Paris, France**
David Jenkins, U.S.A.
Carol Heiss, U.S.A.
Barbara Wagner and Robert Paul,
Canada
June Markham and Courtney Jones,
Great Britain

1959 **Colorado Springs, U.S.A.**
David Jenkins, U.S.A.
Carol Heiss, U.S.A.
Barbara Wagner and Robert Paul,
Canada
Doreen Denny and Courtney Jones,
Great Britain

1960 **Vancouver, Canada**
Alain Giletti, France
Carol Heiss, U.S.A.
Barbara Wagner and Robert Paul,
Canada
Doreen Denny and Courtney Jones,
Great Britain

1961 No championship held (U.S.A.
World Team plane crash)

1962 **Prague, Czechoslovakia**
Donald Jackson, Canada
Sjoukje Dijkstra, Holland
Maria Jelinek and Otto Jelinek,
Canada

Eva Romanova and Pavel Roman,
Czechoslovakia

1963 **Cortina, Italy**
Donald McPherson, Canada
Sjoukje Dijkstra, Holland
Marika Kilius and Hans Baumler,
Federal Republic of Germany
Eva Romanova and Pavel Roman,
Czechoslovakia

1964 **Dortmund, Federal Republic of
Germany**
Manfred Schnelldorfer, Federal
Republic of Germany
Sjoukje Dijkstra, Holland
Marika Kilius and Hans Baumler,
Federal Republic of Germany
Eva Romanova and Pavel Roman,
Czechoslovakia

1965 **Colorado Springs, U.S.A.**
Alain Calmat, France
Petra Burka, Canada
Ludmila Belousova and Oleg
Protopopov, U.S.S.R.
Eva Romanova and Pavel Roman,
Czechoslovakia

1966 **Davos, Switzerland**
Emmerich Danzer, Austria
Peggy Fleming, U.S.A.
Ludmila Belousova and Oleg
Protopopov, U.S.S.R.
Diane Towler and Bernard Ford,
Great Britain

1967 **Vienna, Austria**
Emmerich Danzer, Austria
Peggy Fleming, U.S.A.
Ludmila Belousova and Oleg
Protopopov, U.S.S.R.
Diane Towler and Bernard Ford,
Great Britain

1968 **Geneva, Switzerland**
Emmerich Danzer, Austria
Peggy Fleming, U.S.A.
Ludmila Belousova and Oleg
Protopopov, U.S.S.R.
Diane Towler and Bernard Ford,

Great Britain

1969 Colorado Springs, U.S.A.
Tim Wood, U.S.A.
Gabriele Seyfert, German
  Democratic Republic
Irina Rodnina and Alexsei Ulanov,
  U.S.S.R.
Diane Towler and Bernard Ford,
  Great Britain

1970 Ljubljana, Yugoslavia
Tim Wood, U.S.A.
Gabriele Seyfert, German
  Democratic Republic
Irina Rodnina and Alexsei Ulanov,
  U.S.S.R.
Liudmila Pakhomova and Aleksandr
  Gorshkov, U.S.S.R.

1971 Lyons, France
Ondrej Nepela, Czechoslovakia
Beatrix Schuba, Austria
Irina Rodnina and Alexsei Ulanov,
  U.S.S.R.
Liudmila Pakhomova and Aleksandr
  Gorshkov, U.S.S.R.

1972 Calgary, Canada
Ondrej Nepela, Czechoslovakia
Beatrix Schuba, Austria
Irina Rodnina and Alexsei Ulanov,
  U.S.S.R.
Liudmila Pakhomova and Aleksandr
  Gorshkov, U.S.S.R.

1973 Bratislava, Czechoslovakia
Ondrej Nepela, Czechoslovakia
Karen Magnussen, Canada
Irina Rodnina and Alexandr Zaitsev,
  U.S.S.R.
Liudmila Pakhomova and Aleksandr
  Gorshkov, U.S.S.R.

**1974 Munich, Federal Republic of
Germany**
Jan Hoffmann, German Democratic
  Republic
Christine Errath, German
  Democratic Republic
Irina Rodnina and Alexandr Zaitsev,

U.S.S.R.
Liudmila Pakhomova and Aleksandr
  Gorshkov, U.S.S.R.

1975 Colorado Springs, U.S.A.
Sergei Volkov, U.S.S.R.
Dianne de Leeuw, Holland
Irina Rodnina and Alexandr Zaitsev,
  U.S.S.R.
Irina Moiseeva and Andrei
  Minenkov, U.S.S.R.

1976 Gothenberg, Sweden
John Curry, Great Britain
Dorothy Hamill, U.S.A.
Irina Rodnina and Alexandr Zaitsev,
  U.S.S.R.
Liudmila Pakhomova and Aleksandr
  Gorshkov, U.S.S.R.

1977 Tokyo, Japan
Vladimir Kovalev, U.S.S.R.
Linda Fratianne, U.S.A.
Irina Rodnina and Alexandr Zaitsev,
  U.S.S.R.
Irina Moiseeva and Andrei
  Minenkov, U.S.S.R.

1978 Ottawa, Canada
Charles Tickner, U.S.A.
Anett Pötzsch, German Democratic
  Republic
Irina Rodnina and Alexandr Zaitsev,
  U.S.S.R.
Natalia Linichuk and Gennadi
  Karponosov, U.S.S.R.

1979 Vienna, Austria
Vladimir Kovalev, U.S.S.R.
Linda Fratianne, U.S.A.
Tai Babilonia and Randy Gardner,
  U.S.A.
Natalia Linichuk and Gennadi
  Karponosov, U.S.S.R.

**1980 Dortmund, Federal Republic of
Germany**
Jan Hoffmann, German Democratic
  Republic
Anett Pötzsch, German Democratic
  Republic

Marina Cherkasova and Sergei
Shakhrai, U.S.S.R.
Krisztina Regoeczy and Andras
Sallay, Hungary

1981 **Hartford, U.S.A.**
Scott Hamilton, U.S.A.
Denise Biellmann, Switzerland
Irina Vorobieva and Igor Lisovsky,
U.S.S.R.
Jayne Torvill and Christopher Dean,
Great Britain

1982 **Copenhagen, Denmark**
Scott Hamilton, U.S.A.
Elaine Zayak, U.S.A.
Sabine Baess and Tassilo Thierbach,
German Democratic Republic
Jayne Torvill and Christopher Dean,
Great Britain

1983 **Helsinki, Finland**
Scott Hamilton, U.S.A.
Rosalynn Sumners, U.S.A.
Elena Valova and Oleg Vasiliev,
U.S.S.R.
Jayne Torvill and Christopher Dean,
Great Britain

1984 **Ottawa, Canada**
Scott Hamilton, U.S.A.
Katarina Witt, German Democratic
Republic
Barbara Underhill and Paul Martini,
Canada
Jayne Torvill and Christopher Dean,
Great Britain

1985 **Tokyo, Japan**
Alexandr Fadeev, U.S.S.R.
Katarina Witt, German Democratic
Republic
Elena Valova and Oleg Vasiliev,
U.S.S.R.
Natalia Bestemianova and Andrei
Bukin, U.S.S.R.

1986 **Geneva, Switzerland**
Brian Boitano, U.S.A.
Debi Thomas, U.S.A.
Ekaterina Gordeeva and Sergei

Grinkov, U.S.S.R.
Natalia Bestemianova and Andrei
Bukin, U.S.S.R.

1987 **Cincinnati, U.S.A.**
Brian Orser, Canada
Katarina Witt, German Democratic
Republic
Ekaterina Gordeeva and Sergei
Grinkov, U.S.S.R.
Natalia Bestemianova and Andrei
Bukin, U.S.S.R.

1988 **Budapest, Hungary**
Brian Boitano, U.S.A.
Katarina Witt, German Democratic
Republic
Elena Valova and Oleg Vasiliev,
U.S.S.R.
Natalia Bestemianova and Andrei
Bukin, U.S.S.R.

1989 **Paris, France**
Kurt Browning, Canada
Midori Ito, Japan
Ekaterina Gordeeva and Sergei
Grinkov, U.S.S.R.
Marina Klimova and Sergei
Ponomarenko, U.S.S.R.

1990 **Halifax, Canada**
Kurt Browning, Canada
Jill Trenary, U.S.A.
Ekaterina Gordeeva and Sergei
Grinkov, U.S.S.R.
Marina Klimova and Sergei
Ponomarenko, U.S.S.R.

1991 **Munich, Germany**
Kurt Browning, Canada
Kristi Yamaguchi, U.S.A.
Natalia Mishkutenok and Artur
Dmitriev, U.S.S.R.
Isabelle Duchesnay and Paul
Duchesnay, France

1992 **Oakland, U.S.A.**
Viktor Petrenko, Commonwealth of
Independent States
Kristi Yamaguchi, U.S.A.
Natalia Mishkutenok and Artur

Dmitriev, Commonwealth of
Independent States
Marina Klimova and Sergei
Ponomarenko, Commonwealth
of Independent States

1993 **Prague, Czechoslovakia**
Kurt Browning, Canada
Oksana Baiul, Ukraine
Isabelle Brasseur and Lloyd Eisler,
Canada
Maia Usova and Alexandr Zhulin,
Russia

1994 **Chiba, Japan**
Elvis Stojko, Canada
Yuka Sato, Japan
Evgenia Shishkova and Vadim
Naumov, Russia
Oksana Grishuk and Evgeny Platov,
Russia

1995 **Birmingham, Great Britain**
Elvis Stojko, Canada
Lu Chen, China
Radka Kovarikova and Rene
Novotny, Czechoslovakia
Oksana Grishuk and Evgeny Platov,
Russia

1996 **Edmonton, Canada**
Todd Eldredge, U.S.A.
Michelle Kwan, U.S.A.
Evgenia Shishkova and Vadim
Naumov, Russia
Oksana Grishuk and Evgeny Platov,
Russia

1997 **Lausanne, Switzerland**
Elvis Stojko, Canada
Tara Lipinski, U.S.A.
Mandy Wötzel and Ingo Steuer,
Germany
Oksana Grishuk and Evgeny Platov,
Russia

1998 **Minneapolis, U.S.A.**
Alexei Yagudin, Russia
Michelle Kwan, U.S.A.
Elena Berezhnaya and Anton
Sikharulidze, Russia

Anjelika Krylova and Oleg
Ovsyannikov, Russia

**WINTER OLYMPIC FIGURE SKATING
CHAMPIONS**

Men/Ladies/Pairs/Ice Dancing
1908 **London, Great Britain**
Ulrich Salchow, Sweden
Madge Syers, Great Britain
Anna Hubler and Heinrich Burger,
Germany
1912 No skating events held
1916 No Olympic Games held
1920 **Antwerp, Belgium**
Gillis Grafstrom, Sweden
Magda Julin-Mauroy, Sweden
Ludowika Jakobsson and Walter
Jakobsson, Finland
1924 **Chamonix, France**
Gillis Grafstrom, Sweden
Herma Plank-Szabo, Austria
Helene Engelmann and Alfred
Berger, Austria
1928 **St. Moritz, Switzerland**
Gillis Grafstrom, Sweden
Sonja Henie, Norway
Andrée Joly and Pierre Brunet,
France
1932 **Lake Placid, U.S.A.**
Karl Schafer, Austria
Sonja Henie, Norway
Andrée Joly and Pierre Brunet,
France
1936 **Garmisch, Germany**
Karl Schafer, Austria
Sonja Henie, Norway
Maxi Herber and Ernst Baier,
Germany
1940, 1944 No Olympic Games held
1948 **St. Moritz, Switzerland**
Richard Button, U.S.A.
Barbara Ann Scott, Canada
Micheline Lannoy and Pierre
Baugniet, Belgium

1952   **Oslo, Norway**
Richard Button, U.S.A.
Jeannette Altwegg, Great Britain
Ria Falk and Paul Falk, Federal
    Republic of Germany

1956   **Cortina, Italy**
Hayes A. Jenkins, U.S.A.
Tenley Albright, U.S.A.
Elizabeth Schwarz and Kurt Oppelt,
    Austria

1960   **Squaw Valley, U.S.A.**
David Jenkins, U.S.A.
Carol Heiss, U.S.A.
Barbara Wagner and Robert Paul,
    Canada

1964   **Innsbruck, Austria**
Manfred Schnelldorfer, Federal
    Republic of Germany
Sjoukje Dijkstra, Holland
Ludmila Belousova and Oleg
    Protopopov, U.S.S.R.

1968   **Grenoble, France**
Wolfgang Schwarz, Austria
Peggy Fleming, U.S.A.
Ludmila Belousova and Oleg
    Protopopov, U.S.S.R.

1972   **Sapporo, Japan**
Ondrej Nepela, Czechoslovakia
Beatrix Schuba, Austria
Irina Rodnina and Alexsei Ulanov,
    U.S.S.R.

1976   **Innsbruck, Austria** (first year for
    Ice Dancing)
John Curry, Great Britain
Dorothy Hamill, U.S.A.
Irina Rodnina and Alexandr Zaitsev,
    U.S.S.R.
Liudmila Pakhomova and Aleksandr
    Gorshkov, U.S.S.R.

1980   **Lake Placid, U.S.A.**
Robin Cousins, Great Britain
Anett Pötzsch, German Democratic
    Republic
Irina Rodnina and Alexandr Zaitsev,
    U.S.S.R.

Natalia Linichuk and Gennadi
    Karponosov, U.S.S.R.

1984   **Sarajevo, Yugoslavia**
Scott Hamilton, U.S.A.
Katarina Witt, German Democratic
    Republic
Elena Valova and Oleg Vasiliev,
    U.S.S.R.
Jayne Torvill and Christopher Dean,
    Great Britain

1988   **Calgary, Canada**
Brian Boitano, U.S.A.
Katarina Witt, German Democratic
    Republic
Ekaterina Gordeeva and Sergei
    Grinkov, U.S.S.R.
Natalia Bestemianova and Andrei
    Bukin, U.S.S.R.

1992   **Albertville, France**
Viktor Petrenko, Commonwealth of
    Independent States
Kristi Yamaguchi, U.S.A.
Natalia Mishkutenok and Artur
    Dmitriev, Commonwealth of
    Independent States
Marina Klimova and Sergei
    Ponomarenko, Commonwealth
    of Independent States

1994   **Lillehammer, Norway**
Alexei Urmanov, Russia
Oksana Baiul, Ukraine
Ekaterina Gordeeva and Sergei
    Grinkov, Russia
Oksana Grishuk and Evgeny Platov,
    Russia

1998   **Nagano, Japan**
Ilia Kulik, Russia
Tara Lipinski, U.S.A.
Oksana Kazakova and Artur
    Dmitriev, Russia
Pasha Grishuk and Evgeny Platov,
    Russia

INDEX

DATE DUE

MAR 1 4 2001	
FEB 1 3 2002	
OCT 2 7 2002	
FEB 0 1 2003	
FEB 2 7 2006	
MAR 0 6 2006	
APR 0 2 2006	